ENCYCLOPEDIA

OF

SURNAMES

ENCYCLOPEDIA
OF
SURNAMES

JOHN AYTO

A & C Black • London

First published in Great Britain in 2007

A & C Black Publishers Ltd
38 Soho Square, London W1D 3HB

© John Ayto 2007

A CIP record for this book is available from the British Library.

ISBN: 978 0 7136 8144 4

A & C Black uses paper produced with elemental chlorine-free pulp, harvested from managed sustainable forests.

Text processed and typeset by A & C Black
Printed in Great Britain by Caligraving

INTRODUCTION

We may live in Burgess Hill or Ballyjamesduff, Vancouver or Monrovia, and take our holidays in Porthmadog or Robin Hood's Bay, Butlin's or Disneyland, or even the Pitcairn Islands; indulge ourselves with a Mars Bar or one of Mr Kipling's cakes, a graham cracker (conscientiously fletcherized) and a slice of yarg (see GREY), a bowl of Campbell's soup, a cup of Maxwell House, or a glass of Château Palmer; have some oysters in Wheeler's or a hamburger in a Wimpy Bar; down a stiff Johnnie Walker; chew some Wrigley's; smoke a Churchill cigar; live the life of Reilly; try to lose weight with the Atkins diet; shop in Bloomingdale's, Borders or Brooks Brothers, B&Q (see BLOCK) or M&S; wear bloomers or a Barbour jacket, a bowler hat or an Anthony Eden, Alan Whickers or Claire Rayners; carry a Kelly bag; have our hair done in a Tony Curtis; suffer from Parkinson's disease or a Pott's fracture, Addison's disease or Bell's palsy; dose ourselves with Eno's, Rennies, or Carter's Little Liver Pills; improve our posture with the Alexander technique; drive a Buick or a Chrysler, a Mini Cooper or an MG (see MORRIS) (or hire a car from Avis); ride our Moulton bike or burn up the highway on our Harley-Davidson; hoover our carpet; do our best to keep up with the Joneses; read the latest Mills and Boon; take our Jack Russell for a walk; bite into a Granny Smith; be wounded by shrapnel; hammer in a Rawlplug; play with Newton's balls; climb a Corbett or a Munro; exclaim 'Gordon Bennett!'; consult our Fowler's; prune our Ena Harknesses and Dorothy Perkins and chop down our neighbour's Leylandii (probably with a Black and Decker rather than a Stanley knife); dig a hole with a JCB (see BAMFORD); fill in our Littlewoods football pools with a Parker pen; get our emergency water supplies from a bowser; and so on, almost ad infinitum.

The vocabulary of English is saturated with surnames: from proprietary names for products and services, through place-names, names of books, plays, films, etc., names of institutions, plants and diseases, to the furthest reaches of metaphor (*according to Hoyle*, *the real McCoy*, *the Nelson touch*) and slang (*peeler* 'policeman', *Britney Spears* 'beers'), family names have taken the leap from mere nomenclature to meaningfulness, from the phone book to the dictionary. In tribute to their central role in our language, the *Encyclopedia of Surnames* presents profiles of some 7000 of the most notable surnames in the English-speaking world. It explains where they came from. It gives lists of famous (or notorious) people who have borne a particular name (if any), both the real (including those whose names have been assumed for professional and other purposes) and the fictional. And it presents a wide-ranging overview of all the various lexical highways and byways into which the English language has led the name.

The use in England of what we would recognize today as surnames goes back to the late Middle Ages. Certainly it would have been commonplace long before then to use some sort of additional name or description (such as a nickname, or an indication of parentage or place of origin) to distinguish between people with the same Christian or given name (of which there was a limited supply). But it seems not to have been until the 14th century that the convention firmed up of a family name that could be passed down the generations (the earliest record of *surname* in that sense in the OED is from 1375). By the 15th century it had become institutionalized to the extent that an Act of Parliament of Edward IV's reign could stipulate 'Qe chescun irroys home ... preigne a luy surname englois de vne vile come Sutton Chestr..ou color come White Blake' (that every Irishman ... should take to himself an English surname from a town like Sutton or Chester ... or a colour like White or Black).

Like place-names, family names can be slippery customers. Their modern form can be altogether misleading. The origin of many is obvious enough: an ancestor, for instance, of someone called Smith was a skilled craftsman who worked with metal, especially as a blacksmith, and someone by the name of Edwards is likely to have had a forefather called Edward. But at the other end of the spectrum, the chances of guessing that the original Haddocks may have been 'people from Haydock' or the descendants of an Anglo-Saxon called Ædduc are vanishingly small. And what of the double-entendrist's delight, Shufflebottom? Nothing more sensational than a person from Shipperbottom, Lancashire (a place-name which means literally 'valley with a spring where sheep are washed'). Spellings change and merge over the centuries, and in order to disentangle them, it is necessary to go back to the earliest recorded forms, and trace them forwards. Ground-breaking work by onomasticians (those who study proper names) over the past half-century and more has greatly increased our knowledge in this area, culminating particularly in P.H. Reaney and R.M. Wilson's *Oxford Dictionary of English Surnames* (revised 3rd ed., 1997) and Patrick Hanks and Flavia Hodges's *The Oxford Dictionary of Surnames* (1988), on which much of the information about the history of surnames in this encyclopedia is based. Patrick Hanks's *Dictionary of American Family Names* (2003) is also indispensible for information on recently introduced surnames, especially from non-European sources.

Reflecting the English-speaking people's ancestry, the pool of their surnames is a decidedly mixed and murky one. From earliest times, the basically Anglo-Saxon substrate was expanded by names of Scandinavian origin, by Celtic names (mainly Scottish and Irish, but also Welsh, Cornish, Manx and Breton), and by French names (or more accurately, in most cases, names from Anglo-Norman, the form of northern Old French spoken by the Norman conquerors of England and their descendants). These family names were subsequently taken around the world by British explorers, traders, soldiers, etc. and are now firmly entrenched wherever English is spoken as a first language. In more recent centuries the traffic has become heavy in the opposite direction, with whole stocks of new surnames coming into English-speaking societies from central and eastern Europe (most notably as a consequence of Jewish immigration into the United States), from Latin America (as Spanish-speakers have come to live in the US), from East Asia, and (in the case of the United Kingdom) from the Indian subcontinent.

There are essentially five ways in which the surnames used by English-speaking people evolved. First, there are those which specify where a person (the, or an, ancestor of the name) came from. This can be a particular named settlement – a village, town, or city. So someone by the name of Seaton or Seton had an ancestor who came from a place called Seaton, and someone with the surname Greville had an ancestor who came from a place called Gréville in France (many English family names originated in northern France, where the Normans came from). It can also be a much larger area, such as a region or a whole country – hence the names Welsh, Cornish, Western, etc. Surnames of this sort are generally termed 'habitational'.

Within the same general category of 'place of origin' are names which do not specify a named place but rather the type of area or place a person came from, or a particular feature by which it was recognizable. So the ancestor of a person called Bridge – or indeed Bridges or Bridgman – lived by or guarded a bridge; someone called Grove or Grover or Groves is a descendant of someone who lived by a grove of trees; and the original Shapcott was a person who lived by a sheepcote (i.e. an enclosure for sheep). Names of this type are called 'toponymic'.

The second class of surname is one that arises out of a relationship to a parent. Since in English-speaking cultures family descent passes down through the male line, this tends to be a father-son relationship. Not exclusively: English does have some native mother-son (metronymic) surnames (e.g. Leeson), and Jewish nomenclature, where this is much more common, has lent it several more (e.g. Sarson, Susskind, Tilson); but it has not gone in for the sort of parent-daughter surnames found for example in Icelandic (e.g. *Gisladottir* 'daughter of Gisli'). Home-grown English father-son (patronymic) names tend to take the form of either 'name + *son*' (so the original Anderson was the 'son of *Ander* or *Anders*', northern Middle English or Scottish forms of *Andrew*) or 'name + the possessive ending -s' (so the original Richards was the 'son of *Richard*'). In addition, several given names appear on their own as surnames (e.g. John, Rolf); it is not clear whether or not these originated as patronymics. In this last subcategory must also be included informal or 'childish' versions of given names, generally known as 'pet-forms' or, much more technically, as 'hypocoristic' forms: examples include Jack, Gibb (from *Gilbert*), Hodge (from *Roger*) and diminutive forms such as Atkin and Howey.

Patronymic formations of non-English origin flourish as English surnames. From the Celtic languages come names prefixed with *Mac-* 'son of' (mainly Scottish and Manx but also Irish), the Irish *O*' 'descendant of' and (heavily disguised) Welsh *ap* '(son) of', which appears in much eroded form in such names as Bowen, originally 'son of *Owen*', and Parry, originally 'son of *Harry*'. And Anglo-Norman contributed a small but distinguished set of patronymics beginning with *Fitz-*, literally 'son of' (e.g. Fitzwalter). More recent additions include, for instance, Russian (or Russian-Jewish) patronyms ending in -*vich* (e.g. Aronovitch, 'son of *Aron*' – note that in the names of Russian people, the patronym precedes and is distinct from the family name).

The third category of surnames specifies the job the ancestor did or the office he held. A full list of such names would offer a fairly comprehensive overview of the work medieval Englishmen and Englishwomen did, from Arkwright ('maker of chests'), Sawyer ('sawer of wood') and Fuller ('fuller of cloth' – i.e. someone who makes cloth bulkier by dampening and beating it) to Cheeseman ('person who makes or sells cheese'), Fowler ('bird-catcher') and Shacklock ('gaoler'). More exalted-sounding names, such as Abbot, King and Chancellor, are seldom as grand as they seem: they mostly refer to someone who was a servant in the household of such a personage, who played the part so designated in a pageant or other public performance, or who was given the name as a nickname (see below) because of some personal characteristic. The technical term for such occupation-based family names is 'metonymic'.

Fourthly come surnames based on nicknames. The Middle Ages were no less keen on encapsulating an individual in a single epithet – whether affectionate or cruel – than we are, and they made very serviceable family names. They might be based on some aspect of a person's appearance: the ancestor of all Foots, for example, had a deformed foot or some other pedal peculiarity; Browns were originally someone with brown hair or a tanned complexion; Redhead had red hair. Character traits were also deployed: Good and Wisdom speak for themselves (or seem to – they may have been applied ironically), while Moody ('courageous or quick-tempered person') and Girling ('brave man' – literally 'lion-heart') now require elucidation.

All the types of surname discussed so far are ones that evolved by the normal processes of natural selection. But there are some that are artificial creations, deliberately invented. The majority of those in use in English-speaking cultures are of north-central-European Jewish origin. Historically, Ashkenazic Jews (those from Germany and northern Europe) tended not to go in for surnames in the Western Christian sense (the main exceptions to that rule were the priestly names Cohen and Levy). At the end of the 18th century, however, bureaucracy caught up with them. The Holy Roman Emperor Joseph II decreed a census in all his realms in 1780, and Jews who did not possess a surname were forced to acquire one with all speed. Many conjured up habitational or metonymic names, but some were more inventive, deploying (completely arbitrary) combinations of natural objects and locations: hence the presence now in English of such family names as Sternberg (literally 'star-mountain') and Rosenthal (literally 'valley of roses').

Names, not least surnames, are very personal and precious things (one of the sharpest of insults is to forget someone's name or call them by the wrong name). At a time when interest in ancestry and family history has probably never been higher (and probing of DNA enables us to trace them back further and more precisely than ever before), additional pleasure and perhaps insight can be had by plugging into the wider network of that most intimate of our possessions. To reach back towards the founder of our own 'clan', and to see some of the journeys other members of it have made in the past and are making now, may enable us to see our self in a fresh context. The *Encyclopedia of Surnames* offers the opportunity to do just that.

John Ayto
London, 2007

A

Aaron, Aron from the male personal name *Aaron*, from Hebrew *Aharon*, traditionally interpreted as 'mountain of strength'. See also **Arkin**, **Aronoff**, **Aronovitch**

Aarons, Arons 'son of **Aaron**'

Aaronson, Aronson, Aaronsohn, Aronsohn 'son of **Aaron**'

Abbas a Muslim surname, from the Arabic personal name *'Abbās*, literally 'stern, austere'

Abbey, Abby 'person who works in or lives in or by an abbey'. See also **Abdie**

Abbott, Abbot, Abbett 'person employed in the household of an abbot', or from a medieval nickname for someone of abbot-like religiosity or sanctimoniousness [Russ Abbot (original name Russ Roberts), 1947–, British comedian]
— **Abbott and Costello** a US comedy double act consisting of Bud Abbott (original name William Abbott), 1897–1974, and Lou Costello (original name Louis Francis Cristillo), 1906–59. They first performed together in 1935, and their popularity continued into the mid 1950s.

Abbs 'son or servant of **Abel** (i)'

Abdie, Abdey 'person who works in or lives in or by an abbey' (from Latin *abbātia* 'abbey')

Abdullah, Abdulla a Muslim surname, from the Arabic personal name *'Abdullāh*, literally 'servant of Allah'

Abel (i) *also* **Abell** *or* **Able** from the male personal name *Abel*, from Hebrew *Hevel*, apparently based on *hevel* 'breath'. See also **Abbs**, **Ables**, **Ablett**; (ii) from the German male personal name *Abel*, a pet-form of *Albert* [Sir Frederick Augustus Abel, 1827–1902, British chemist]

Abelson (i) *also* **Ableson** 'son of **Abel** (i)'; (ii) 'son of *Abele*', a Yiddish male personal name meaning literally 'little *Abe*' (from Aramaic *aba* 'father')

Abercrombie, Abercromby 'person from Abercrombie', Fife ('confluence of the river called "crooked"') [Sir Patrick Abercrombie, 1879–1957, British town planner and architect; Sir Ralph Abercromby, 1734–1801, British general]

Abernathy, Abernathey different forms of **Abernethy**

Abernethy 'person from Abernethy', Perth and Kinross ('confluence of the (river) Nethy')
— **Abernethy biscuit** a type of hard biscuit flavoured with caraway seeds. It is said to have been named after a British surgeon called John Abernethy, 1764-1831.

Able see **Abel** (i)

Ables 'son or servant of **Abel** (i)'

Ableson see **Abelson** (i)

Ablett, Ablitt 'little **Abel** (i)'

Abner from the male personal name *Abner*, from Hebrew *Avner*, literally 'God is (my) light'

Abraham from the male personal name *Abraham*, from Hebrew *Avraham*, traditionally interpreted as 'father of a multitude of nations'. See also **Aprahamian**, **Brahms**

Abrahams 'son of **Abraham**' [Harold Abrahams, 1899–1978, British athlete]

Abrahamson 'son of **Abraham**'

Abram (i) a reduced form of **Abraham**; (ii) 'person from Abram', Lancashire (formerly *Adburgham*, literally 'Eadburg's homestead')

Abramov 'son of **Abram** (i)'

Abramovich 'son of **Abram** (i)'

Abramovitz a different form of **Abramowitz**

Abramowitz 'son of **Abram** (i)'

Abrams 'son of **Abram** (i)'. See also **Brahms**

Abramski, Abramsky 'son of **Abram** (i)'

Abramson 'son of **Abram** (i)'

Acheson see **Atchison**

Ackerley probably 'person from Ackerley', an unidentified place probably in northwestern England [J.R. Ackerley, 1896–1967, British author and literary journalist]

Ackerman (i) 'person who lives by an area of cultivated land' (from Middle English *acker* 'field' + *man*), or 'person of relatively low status in the medieval feudal system' (from Middle English *ackerman*, from Old English *æcerman*, literally 'field-man'); (ii) 'ploughman' (from Middle English *ackerman* or Dutch *akkerman*). See also **Akers**

Ackland, Acland 'person from Ackland', the name of various places in England ('oak land'), 'person from Acland Barton', Devon ('Acca's lane'), or 'person from Acklam', Yorkshire ('oak woods or clearings') [Joss Ackland, 1928–, British actor; June Ackland, long-serving police officer (played by Trudie Goodwin) in the ITV police soap *The Bill* (1984–); Rodney Ackland, 1908–91, British playwright]

Ackroyd, Akroyd 'person who lives in a clearing in an oak forest' (from northern Middle English *ake* 'oak' + *royd* 'clearing') [Dan Ackroyd, 1952–, Canadian comedian and actor; Peter Ackroyd, 1949–, British author]
— **Akroydon** a district of Halifax, Yorkshire, originally planned in 1849 as a model village for

mill-workers by the local industrialist Edward Akroyd, 1810–87, and named after him

Acland see **Ackland**

Acosta from a mistaken analysis of **Da Costa** as *d'Acosta*

Acres see **Akers**

Acton 'person from Acton', the name of numerous places in England (mostly 'farmstead by the oak tree') [Eliza Acton, 1799–1859, British cookery writer; Sir Harold Acton, 1904–94, British writer and aesthete; Sir John Emerich Edward Dalberg Acton (Lord Acton), 1834–1902, British historian]

Adair from the Scottish male personal name *Adair*, a different form of **Edgar** [Red Adair (original name Paul Neil Adair), 1915–2004, US oil-field firefighter]

Adam from the male personal name *Adam*, from Hebrew, literally 'man'. See also **Adcock, Addis, Ade, Adie, Adkins, Adney** (ii)**, Aitchison, Aitkin, Atchison, Atkin, Aycock, McAdam** [James Adam, 1732–94, British architect, brother of Robert; Robert Adam, 1728–92, British architect and interior designer; William Adam, 1689–1748, British architect, father of James and Robert]
— **Adam** used attributively to denote something designed by James and/or Robert Adam (see above) (as 'an Adam ceiling')

Adams, Addams 'son of **Adam**' [Abigail Adams, 1744–1818, US feminist; Ansel Adams, 1902–84, US photographer; Charles Addams, 1912–88, US cartoonist; Cliff Adams, 1923–2001, British bandleader and choral conductor; Gerry Adams, 1948–, Northern Irish Sinn Fein politician; Sir Grantley Adams, 1898–1971, Barbados politician, prime minister of Barbados 1954–58 and of the West Indies Federation 1958–62; Henry Adams, 1838–1918, US historian; John Adams, 1735–1826, US statesman, president 1797–1801; John Adams, 1947–, US composer; John Couch Adams, 1819–92, British astronomer; John Quincy Adams, 1767–1848, US politician, son of John, president 1825–29; Richard Adams, 1920–, British novelist; Samuel Adams, 1722–1803, US politician]
— **Addams Family** an assemblage of grotesques and eccentrics (e.g. the sepulchrally sultry Morticia Addams) created by Charles Addams (see above) in his *New Yorker* cartoons from the 1930s. They were introduced to the small screen in the mid-1960s in the US sitcom *The Addams Family*, and feature films subsequently appeared.
— **Fanny Adams** originally, in late 19th-century British naval slang, tinned meat. The gruesome metaphor was based on the name of an eight-year-old girl who in August 1867 was murdered and dismembered at Alton, Hampshire. In the early 20th century the phrase came to be used (often in the form *sweet fanny adams*) as a euphemistic substitute for *fuck-all*.

Adamson 'son of **Adam**' [Joy Adamson (*née* Gessner), 1910–80, Silesian-born naturalist and author]

Adcock from the medieval personal name *Ade* (see **Addis**), with the suffix *-cock* (literally 'cockerel',

hence 'jaunty or bumptious young man'), that was often added to create pet-forms of personal names in the Middle Ages [Fleur Adcock, 1934–, New Zealand poet]

Addams see **Adams**

Adderley 'person from Adderley', Staffordshire and Shropshire (respectively 'Ealdred's glade' and perhaps 'Ealdthryth's glade')

Addington 'person from Addington', the name of various places in southern England ('Eadda's (or Æddi's) estate') [Henry Addington (Viscount Sidmouth), 1757–1844, British Tory politician, prime minister 1801–04]

Addis, Ades, Addess 'son of *Ade* or *Addie*', pet-forms of **Adam**
— **Addis** a British manufacturer of brushes, founded in London in 1780 by William Addis

Addison 'son of *Addie*', a pet-form of **Adam** [Joseph Addison, 1672–1719, British essayist, poet and Whig politician]
— **Addison of the North** a nickname bestowed (by Sir Walter Scott) on the Scottish lawyer and author Henry Mackenzie, 1745–1831, whose writings were considered to resemble those of Joseph Addison (see above)
— **Addison's disease** a wasting disease caused by underactivity of the adrenal glands and characterized by bronzing of the skin, low blood pressure and weakness. It is named after the British physician Thomas Addison, 1793–1860, who first described it.

Ade from the male personal name *Ade*, a pet-form of **Adam**, or from the German and Frisian male personal name *Ade*, a pet-form of **Adam** or of any of various Germanic compound names beginning with *adal* 'noble' (e.g. *Adalbrecht* 'noble-bright') [George Ade, 1866–1944, US writer]

Adelman (i) an invented Jewish name formed from German *Adel* 'nobility' + Yiddish *man*; (ii) *also* **Adelmann** from the Old High German male personal name *Adalman*, literally 'noble man'

Ades (i) see **Addis**; (ii) perhaps 'person from *Ades*', the Yiddish name for Odessa; (iii) perhaps an anglicization of the Jewish surname *Eydes*, literally 'son of *Eyde*', a Yiddish female personal name derived from *Eydl*, literally 'noble' [Thomas Adès, 1971–, British composer]

Adie from the medieval Scottish male personal name *Adie*, a pet-form of **Adam** [Kate Adie, 1945–, British television journalist]

Adkins 'son of *Adkin*', literally 'little *Addie*', a medieval male personal name that was a mainly Midlands pet-form of **Adam**

Adler (i) 'person who lives in a house with the sign of an eagle' (from Middle High German *adelar* 'eagle'); (ii) an invented Jewish name based on German *Adler* 'eagle' [Larry Adler, 1914–2001, US harmonica-player]

Adney (i) 'person from Adeney', Shropshire ('Eadwynn's island'); (ii) from a medieval male personal name that was a pet-form of **Adam**

Adrian from the male personal name *Adrian* (from Latin *Adriānus* or *Hadriānus*, literally 'person from the Adriatic coast') [Edgar Douglas Adrian (Lord Adrian), 1889–1977, British physiologist; Max Adrian (original name Max Bor), 1903–73, British actor]

Adshead 'person from Adshead', an unidentified place, probably in Lancashire (probably 'Æddi's headland')

Affleck a different form of **Auchinleck** [Ben Affleck, 1972–, US actor]

Agar from the medieval male personal name *Agar*, a different form of **Edgar**
— **Agar Town** a former district of London, to the north of Kings Cross and St Pancras stations, named after William Agar, a developer who built houses there in the early 1830s

Agate 'person who lives by a gate (i.e. a city gate)' (from Middle English *a gate* 'by (the) gate') [James Agate, 1877–1947, British dramatic critic]

Agee a French Huguenot surname, perhaps a different form of the name *Ajean* (from French *à Jean* 'of John (i.e. John's child)') [James Agee, 1909–55, US poet, novelist, screenwriter and film critic]

Agnew (i) 'person from Agneaux', northern France; (ii) from a medieval nickname for a mild-mannered person (from Old French *agneau* 'lamb'); (iii) from Irish Gaelic *Ó Gnímh* 'descendant of *Gnímh*', a nickname meaning literally 'action' [Jonathan Agnew ('Aggers'), 1960–, English cricketer and journalist; Spiro T. Agnew, 1918–96, US Republican politician, vice-president 1969–73]

Aguilera 'person from Aguilera', Spain ('eagle's nest') [Christina Aguilera, 1980–, US pop singer/songwriter]

Agutter 'person who lives by a (natural or artificial) watercourse' (from Middle English *a gutter* 'by (the) watercourse or channel') [Jenny Agutter, 1952–, British actress]

Ahern, Aherne, Ahearne from Irish Gaelic *Ó hEachthighearna* 'descendant of *Eachthighearna*', a personal name meaning literally 'horse-master'. See also **Hearn** (iv) [Bertie Ahern, 1951–, Irish Fianna Fáil politician, prime minister 1997–; Caroline Aherne, 1963–, British comic writer and actress]

Ahmed, Ahmad a Muslim surname, from the Arabic male personal name *Ahmad*, literally 'the most praised' (an alternative name of the prophet Muhammad)

Aichison see **Aitchison**

Aiello 'person from Aiello', the name of various places in southern Italy ('little field')

Aiken, Aikin, Aken, Akin different forms of **Aitkin** [Conrad Aiken, 1889–1973, US writer and critic; Howard Hathaway Aiken, 1900–73, US mathematician, pioneer of the computer]
— **Aiken's Solution** a strategy for curtailing the Vietnam War, put forward in 1966 by the US Republican Senator George Aiken, 1892–1984. It amounted essentially to 'Claim victory and get out'.

Aikens, Aikins, Akens, Akins 'son of **Aiken**'

Ainley 'person from Ainley Top', Yorkshire [Henry Ainley, 1879–1945, British actor]

Ainscough, Ainscow 'person from Ainscough', an unidentified place in Lancashire (perhaps 'solitary wood')

Ainsley, Ainslie, Aynsley 'person from Ansley', Warwickshire ('glade with a hermitage') or 'person from Annesley', Nottinghamshire ('Ān's glade')

Ainsworth 'person from Ainsworth', Lancashire ('Ægen's enclosure') [William Harrison Ainsworth, 1805–82, British historical novelist]

Aird 'person from Aird', Ayrshire and Dumfries and Galloway ('headland')

Airey, Airy, Arey 'person from Airey', an unidentified place in northwestern England ('gravel-bank stream') [Sir George Biddell Airy, 1801–92, British astronomer]
— **Airey house** a house made from precast concrete sections. Dating from the 1920s, they were originally made by the Leeds firm of William Airey and Son Ltd., founded by Sir Edwin Airey, 1878–1955.

Aitchison, Aichison Scottish variants of **Atchison** [Craigie Aitchison, 1926–, British painter; Jean Aitchison, 1938–, British linguistician]

Aitkin, Aitken from the medieval Scottish male personal name *Aitken*, a pet-form of **Adam** [Jonathan Aitken, 1942–, British Conservative politician, great-nephew of Max; Maria Aitken, 1945–, British actress, sister of Jonathan; Max Aitken (Lord Beaverbrook), 1879–1964, Canadian-born British newspaper proprietor]

Aken, Akin see **Aiken**

Akens, Akins see **Aikens**

Akers, Acres 'person who lives by an area of arable land'

Akhtar a Muslim name, from the Persian personal name *Akhtar*, literally 'star', hence 'good luck'

Akroyd see **Ackroyd**

Alabaster 'crossbowman' (from Anglo-Norman *arblaster*, from Old French *arbalestre* 'crossbow'). See also **Arblaster, Armbruster**

Alam a Muslim surname, from the Arabic male personal name *'Alam*, literally 'banner', or from the Arabic male personal name *'Ālam*, literally 'world'

Alan see **Allen**

Alban from the male personal name *Alban* (from Latin *Albānus*, literally 'person from Alba', the name of several places in Italy). See also **Albon, Alborn, Allbond, Allbone**

Albany 'servant or retainer of the dukes of Albany (a dukedom of the royal house of Stuart)' (from a Gaelic name for Scotland)

Albee, Alby 'person from Ailby or Alby', respectively Lincolnshire and Norfolk ('Áli's farmstead') [Edward Albee, 1928–, US playwright]

Albert from the male personal name *Albert* (of Germanic origin, and meaning literally 'noble-bright'). See also **Alpert** (ii) [Eddie Albert (original name Edward Albert Heimberger), 1906–2005, US actor]

Alberts 'son of **Albert**'

Albertson 'son of **Albert**'

Albery probably a different form of **Aubrey** or **Albury** [Sir Donald Albery, 1914–88, British theatrical impresario; Tim Albery, 1952–, British theatre and opera director]
— **Albery Theatre** a theatre in St Martin's Lane, in the West End of London. Opened in 1903 as the New Theatre, it was renamed in 1973 in honour of its former manager Sir Bronson Albery, 1881–1971, father of Sir Donald (see above). In 2006 its name changed again, to the Noël Coward Theatre.

Albin from the medieval male personal name *Albin* (from Latin *Albīnus*, literally 'white one')

Albon, Allbon differents form of **Alban**

Alborn a different form of **Alban**

Albright (i) an anglicization of *Albrecht*, the German equivalent of English **Albert**; (ii) a medieval variant of **Albert** [Madeleine Albright (original name Marie Jana Korbelová), 1937–, Czech-born US stateswoman and scholar]

Albury 'person from Albury', Hertfordshire and Surrey ('old stronghold')

Albutt, Allbutt from the Germanic male personal name *Albodo* (literally 'noble messenger'), brought into England by the Normans [Sir Thomas Clifford Allbutt, 1836–1925, British physician who introduced the modern clinical thermometer]

Alcock, Allcock 'little Alan', 'little Alexander', etc. (a pet-form produced by adding the suffix -*cock* to the shortened form of any of a range of male personal names, especially *Alan* and *Alexander*) [Sir John Alcock, 1892–1919, British aviator who, with Sir Arthur Brown, was the first to fly the Atlantic Ocean (1919)]
— **Alcock Convention** a commercial treaty (1869) between Britain and China, drawn up by Sir Rutherford Alcock, 1809–1907

Alcott, Allcott (i) 'person who lives in an old cottage' (from Middle English *ald* 'old' + *cott* 'cottage'); (ii) a euphemistic variant of **Alcock** [Amos Bronson Alcott, 1799–1888, US transcendentalist and writer; Louisa May Alcott, 1832–88, US novelist]

Alden (i) from the medieval male personal name *Aldine* (from Old English *Ealdwine*, literally 'former friend'); (ii) a different form of **Haldane** (i). See also **Alwyn, Auden**

Alder (i) 'person who lives by an alder tree or alder copse'. See also **Alderman** (ii); (ii) from the medieval male personal name *Alder* (from either Old English *Ealdhere*, literally 'ancient army', or Old English *Æthelhere*, literally 'noble army'). See also **Alderson**

Alderdice a different form of **Allardyce** [John Alderdice (Lord Alderdice), 1955–, Northern Irish psychotherapist and Alliance Party politician]

Alderman (i) 'person holding the office of alderman (in the Middle Ages, a city or borough magistrate)'; (ii) a different form of **Alder** (i)

Alderson 'son of **Alder** (ii)'

Alderton 'person from Alderton', the name of numerous places in England (variously 'estate associated with Ealdhere' and 'farmstead where alders grow') [John Alderton, 1940–, British actor]

Aldington 'person from Aldington', Kent and Worcestershire ('estate associated with Ealda') [Richard Aldington, 1892–1962, British poet, novelist and biographer]

Aldous, Aldis, Aldiss, Alldis from the medieval female personal name *Aldus*, a pet-form of any of a range of compound personal names beginning with *Ald*-, literally 'old' [Brian Aldiss, 1925–, British science-fiction novelist; John Alldis, 1929–, British choral conductor]
— **Aldis lamp** a signalling device in the form of a portable lamp used to flash messages in Morse code. It was named after its British inventor, A.C.W. Aldis, 1878–1953.

Aldred from the medieval male personal name *Aldred* (from either Old English *Ealdrǣd*, literally 'ancient counsel', or Old English *Æthelrǣd*, literally 'noble counsel'). See also **Allred**

Aldrich from the medieval male personal name *Aldrich* (from a combination of Old English *Ælfrīc*, literally 'elf ruler', and Old English *Æthelrīc*, literally 'noble ruler'). See also **Arledge** [Thomas Bailey Aldrich, 1836–1907, US short-story writer and poet]

Aldridge, Aldredge (i) a different form of **Aldrich**; (ii) 'person from Aldridge', West Midlands ('farm among the alders'). See also **Arledge** [Michael Aldridge, 1920–94, British actor]

Alexander from the male personal name *Alexander* (ultimately from Greek *Alexandros*, literally probably 'repeller of men (i.e. he who drives back the enemy)'). See also **McAllister, Sanders** [Harold Alexander (Earl Alexander of Tunis), 1891–1969, British field marshal; Terence Alexander, 1923–, British actor; Sir William Alexander (1st earl of Stirling), ?1576–1640, Scottish poet and colonist, founder of Nova Scotia]
— **Alexander technique** a method of improving the posture that involves developing awareness of it. It is named after the Australian physiotherapist Frederick Alexander, 1869–1955, who developed it.

Alexis from the French personal name *Alexis* (ultimately from Greek *alexios* 'helping, defending')

Alford, Allford 'person from Alford', the name of several places in England and Scotland (variously 'old ford', 'high ford' and 'Ealdgȳth's ford')

Alfred from the medieval male personal name *Alvred* (from Old English *Ælfrǣd*, literally 'elf counsel')

Alger from the medieval male personal name *Alger* or *Algar* (from a combination of Old English *Æthelgār*, literally 'noble spear', *Ælfgār*, literally 'elf spear', and *Ealdgār*, literally 'old spear', reinforced by their Continental Germanic cognates (*Adalgar, Albgar* and *Aldgar*) that were brought to England by the Normans) [Horatio Alger, 1832–99, US writer and clergyman]

Ali, Aly a Muslim surname, from the Arabic male personal name *'Ālī*, literally 'high, lofty' (one of the 99 names of God in Islam) [Muhammad Ali (original name Cassius Clay), 1942–, US boxer; Tariq Ali, 1943–, Indian-born British writer and political activist]

Alison see **Allison**

Allam see **Allum**

Allan see **Allen**

Allard from the medieval male personal name *Allard* (from Old English *Æthelheard*, literally 'noble-hardy', reinforced by its Continental Germanic cognate *Adelard* that was brought to England by the Normans)

Allardyce, Allardice 'person from Allardice', Aberdeenshire ('alder', with a second element of unknown meaning). The name is traditionally pronounced 'airdis'. See also **Alderdice** [Sam Allardyce, 1954–, British football manager]

Allason see **Allison**

Allbond a different form of **Alban**

Allbone a different form of **Alban**

Allbutt see **Albutt**

Allcock see **Alcock**

Allcott see **Alcott**

Alldis see **Aldous**

Allen, Alan, Allan, Alleyn, Alleyne, Allin, Allyn from the male personal name *Alan*, of Celtic origin but unknown meaning. In England, the surname is most commonly spelled *Allen*, in Scotland, *Allan*. See also **Allinson, Allis** (i), **Allison, FitzAlan, McKellan** [Barbara Allen, eponymous heroine of an old Scottish ballad, who suffers agonies of remorse for her cruelty to the young man who was in love with her; Dave Allen (original name David O'Mahony), 1936–2005, Irish comedian; Edward Alleyn, 1566–1626, English actor; Ethan Allen, 1739–89, American military commander in the War of Independence; Sir George ('Gubby') Allen, 1902–89, English cricketer and administrator; Grant Allen, 1848–99, Canadian-born British philosopher and novelist; Sir Hugh Allen, 1869–1946, British musicologist; Ian Allan, 1922–, British author and publisher of transport books; Keith Allen, 1952–, British actor; Lily Allen, 1985–, British pop singer, daughter of Keith; Patrick Allen, 1927–2006, British actor; Ray Alan, 1930–, British ventriloquist; Roderick Alleyn, Old Etonian police detective in the novels of Ngaio Marsh; Sir Thomas Allen, 1944–, British baritone; William Allen, 1532–94, English Catholic churchman; Woody Allen (original name Allen Stewart Konigsberg), 1935–, US film director and actor]

— **Allen charge** in US law, an instruction by a judge to a hung jury in which he or she instructs dissenting jurors to reconsider their views in the light of the majority opinion. It takes its name from

the case of Allen *v.* United States (1897), in which it was first used.

— **Alleyn's School** an independent co-educational school in East Dulwich, Southeast London. It was founded (as a boys' school) in 1882 as an offshoot of the nearby Dulwich College, which was established on the basis of an endowment by Edward Alleyn (see above), and whose old boys are called **Old Alleynians**.

— **Allentown** a town in Pennsylvania, USA, founded in 1762 by the wealthy shipping merchant William Allen, 1704–80

— **George Allen and Unwin** a British publishing firm founded in 1871 as George Allen and Sons. Its name was revised when Sir Stanley Unwin bought a controlling interest in 1914. It is now (as plain Allen and Unwin) an Australian firm.

Allenby 'person from Allonby', Cumbria ('Alein's farmstead') [Edmund Allenby (Viscount Allenby), 1861–1936, British field marshal]

Allenson see **Allinson**

Allerton 'person from Allerton', the name of numerous places in England (variously 'farmstead where alders grow', 'Ælfhere's farmstead' and 'Ælfweard's farmstead')

Alley from the medieval male personal name *Alli*, of Scandinavian origin

Alleyn, Alleyne see **Allen**

Allford see **Alford**

Allgood from the medieval male personal name *Algod*, probably from an unrecorded Old Norse *Alfgautr*, literally 'elf-Goth', or *Athalgautr*, literally 'noble Goth'

Allin see **Allen**

Allingham 'person from Alvingham', Lincolnshire ('Ælf's people's homestead') [Helen Allingham, 1848–1926, British artist; Margery Allingham, 1904–66, British detective-story writer; William Allingham, 1824–89, Irish-born British poet]

Allington 'person from Allington', the name of numerous places in England (variously 'farmstead associated with Ealda', 'farmstead associated with Ælla or Ælle' and 'farmstead of the princes')

Allinson, Allenson 'son of **Allen**'

Allis, Alliss (i) a different form of the surname *Allins*, literally 'son of **Allen**'; (ii) from the female personal name *Alice*, brought into England by the Normans but ultimately of Germanic origin and meaning literally 'noble beauty'. See also **Allott** [Peter Alliss, 1931–, British golfer and television commentator]

Allison, Alison, Allyson 'son of **Allis** (ii)', 'son of **Allen**', or 'son of **Ellis**' [June Allyson (original name Ella Geisman), 1917–2006, US actress; Malcolm Allison, 1927–, British football manager]

Allman, Alman, Allmon 'German person' (from Anglo-Norman *aleman* 'German' or *alemayne* 'Germany'). See also **Almond** (ii)

Allnutt from the medieval male personal name *Alnoth* (from Old English *Æthelnōth*, literally 'noble daring') [Charlie Allnutt, rough-diamond but warm-hearted river trader in C.S. Forester's novel *The African Queen* (1935) (portrayed in the film (1951) by Humphrey Bogart)]

Allom see **Allum**

Allott, Allot 'little **Allis** (ii)'

Alloway (i) 'person from Alloway, Alloa or Alva', the name of various places in Scotland ('rocky plain'); (ii) from the medieval male personal name *Ailwi* (from Old English *Æthelwīg*, literally 'noble battle')

Allport, Alport 'person from Allport', Derbyshire and Shropshire ('old town')
— **Alport's syndrome** a genetic disease characterized by kidney disease and loss of hearing and sight. It takes its name from the British physician Arthur Alport, 1880–1959, who first identified it in a British family.

Allred (i) from the medieval male personal name *Alvred* (see **Alfred**); (ii) a different form of **Aldred**

Allsop, Allsopp, Allsup see **Alsop**

Allston see **Alston**

Allum, Allom, Allam (i) 'person from Alham', Somerset ('(place by the river) Alham', a Celtic river-name of unknown meaning), 'person from Alnham', Northumberland ('homestead on the (river) Aln', a Celtic river-name of unknown meaning), or 'person from Hallamshire', Sheffield ('(place at) the rocks'); (ii) a shortened form of **McCallum**

Allwood, Alwood different forms of **Ellwood**

Allyn see **Allen**

Allyson see **Allison**

Alman (i) see **Allman**; (ii) 'widower' (from Hebrew *alman* 'widower')

Almeida 'person from Almeida', the name of various places in Portugal ('the city')

Almond (i) from the medieval male personal name *Almund* (from Old English *Æthelmund*, literally 'noble protection'); (ii) a different form of **Allman**

Alpert (i) a different form of **Halpern**; (ii) from a German and Dutch different form of **Albert** [Herb Alpert, 1935–, US trumpeter and bandleader]

Alport see **Allport**

Alsop, Alsopp, Allsop, Allsopp, Allsup 'person from Alsop', Derbyshire ('Ælle's valley') [Joseph Alsop, Jr., 1910–89, US journalist; Madge Allsop, long-suffering companion (played by Emily Perry) of Dame Edna Everage; Marin Alsop, 1956–, US conductor]

Alston, Allston (i) 'person from Alston or Alstone', the name of numerous places in England (variously 'Ælfsīge's farmstead', 'Halfdan's farmstead', 'Ælfrēd's farmstead', etc.); (ii) from the medieval male personal name *Alstan* (from a combination of Old English *Æthelstān*, literally 'noble stone', *Ælfstān*, literally 'elf stone', *Ealdstān*, literally 'old stone' and *Ealhstān*, literally 'altar stone') [Washington Allston, 1779–1843, US painter]

Altman the Jewish form of German *Altmann*, literally 'old man', used mainly to distinguish an older

from a younger person [Robert Altman, 1925–2006, US film director]

Alton 'person from Alton', the name of numerous places in England (variously 'farmstead at the river source', 'Ælfa's farmstead' and 'old farmstead')

Alvarez an anglicization of Spanish *Álvarez*, literally 'son of *Álvaro*', a Spanish male personal name of Visigothic origin but unknown meaning [Al Alvarez, 1929–, British poet and author; Luis W. Alvarez, 1911–88, US physicist]

Alvey from the medieval male personal name *Alfwy* (from Old English *Ælfwīg*, literally 'elf battle')

Alwood see **Allwood**

Alwyn, Allwyn, Alwen, Alwin from the medieval male personal name *Alwin* (from a combination of Old English *Æthelwine*, literally 'noble friend', *Ælfwine*, literally 'elf-friend', and *Ealdwine*, literally 'former friend'). See also **Alden** (i), **Auden**, **Aylwin** [William Alwyn, 1905–85, British composer]

Aly see **Ali**

Amberson probably 'son of **Ambrose**'
— *The Magnificent Ambersons* a film (1942), directed by Orson Welles, about the decline and fall of a wealthy American family

Ambler (i) 'enameller' (from Anglo-Norman *amayler* 'enameller'); (ii) 'walker' (from a derivative of Middle English *amble* 'to walk slowly'). The precise import of the name is uncertain; in the Middle Ages, *amble* was usually used of horses or their riders. [Eric Ambler, 1909–98, British thriller writer]

Ambrose from the male personal name *Ambrose* (from Latin *Ambrosius*, from Greek *ambrosios* 'immortal'). See also **Amberson**, **McCambridge**

Amery, Amory from the male personal name *Emaurri*, brought into England by the Normans but ultimately of Germanic origin and meaning literally 'busy power'. See also **Emery, Hemery, Imray, Imrie** [Julian Amery (Lord Amery), 1919–96, British Conservative politician, son of Leo; Leo Amery, 1873–1955, British Conservative politician]

Ames see **Amis**

Amey, Amy from the Old French personal name *Amé* (from Latin *Amātus*, literally 'beloved')

Amherst 'person from Amhurst Hill', Kent (probably 'wooded hill on the boundary') [Jeffrey Amherst (Lord Amherst), 1717–97, British soldier, governor general of British North America 1760–63]
— **Amherst** a town in western Massachusetts, USA. It was named in honour of Jeffrey Amherst (see above).

Amin a Muslim and Indian surname, from the Arabic personal name *Amīn*, literally 'trustworthy' [Idi Amin, 1925–2003, Ugandan head of state 1971–79]

Amis, Amiss, Amies, Ames from the Old French personal name *Amis* (either from Late Latin *Amīcius* or directly from its source, Latin *amīcus* 'friend'). See also **Amos** (ii) [Dennis Amiss,

1943–, English cricketer; Sir Hardy Amies, 1909–2003, British fashion designer; Sir Kingsley Amis, 1922–95, British novelist and poet; Leslie Ames, 1905–90, English cricketer; Martin Amis, 1949–, British novelist, son of Kingsley]

Ammons a different form of **Hammons**

Amory see **Amery**

Amos (i) from the Hebrew male personal name *Amos*, literally 'borne (i.e. by God)'; (ii) probably a different form of **Amis**

Amundson an anglicization of Danish and Norwegian *Amundsen* or Swedish *Amundsson*, both literally 'son of *Ogmundr*', an Old Norse male personal name meaning literally 'awe-protection' (or perhaps 'sword-point-protection')

Amy see **Amey**

Ancona 'person from Ancona', Italian seaport ('elbow-shaped (cape)') [Ronni Ancona, 1968–, British impressionist and actress]

Ancrum, Ancram 'person from Ancrum', Borders ('bend in the river Ale')

Andersen 'son of *Anders*', the Danish and Norwegian form of *Andreas* (see **Andrew**)

Anderson 'son of *Ander* or *Anders*', northern Middle English or Scottish forms of **Andrew** [Carl David Anderson, 1905–91, US physicist; Clive Anderson, 1953–, British barrister and humorist; Elizabeth Garrett Anderson, 1836–1917, British physician; Gerry Anderson, 1929–, British puppeteer; Gillian Anderson, 1968–, US-born actress; Jean Anderson, 1907–2001, British actress; Sir John Anderson (Viscount Waverley), 1882–1958, British civil servant and National (non-party) MP; Laurie Anderson, 1947–, US composer and performance artist; Leroy Anderson, 1908–75, US composer; Lindsay Anderson, 1923–94, British film director; Marian Anderson, 1897–1993, US contralto; Philip W. Anderson, 1923–, US physicist; Robert Anderson, 1917–, US playwright; Sherwood Anderson, 1876–1941, US author]

— **Anderson shelter** a small arch of corrugated metal designed to act as a shelter during air raids in World War II. It was named after its designer, David A. Anderson, although it came to be popularly associated with Sir John Anderson (see above), home secretary 1939–40.

— **Andersonstown** a district of west Belfast, Northern Ireland, probably named after a 16th- or early 17th-century Scottish settler called Anderson. A working-class Nationalist area, it was a focus of tension and conflict during the Troubles. Its nickname is 'Andytown'.

— **'John Anderson, my jo'** a ballad (1788) by Robert Burns: a wife is addressing her husband, recollecting their youthful love

Anderton 'person from Anderton', Cheshire or Lancashire ('Ēanrēd's farmstead' or 'Eindrithi's farmstead') [Sophie Anderton, 1977–, British model]

Ando from the Hungarian male personal name *Andó*, a pet-form of *András*, the Hungarian form of *Andreas* (see **Andrew**)

Andrade 'person from Andrade', the name of various places in Portugal and northwestern Spain (probably 'Andreas's estate')

Andre, André from the male personal name *André*, the French form of *Andreas* (see **Andrew**) [Carl Andre, 1935–, US sculptor; John André, 1751–80, British soldier shot as a spy during the American Revolution; Peter André (original name Peter Andrea), 1973–, British pop singer]

Andrew from the male personal name *Andrew* (from Greek *Andreas*, a derivative of *andreios* 'manly'). See also **Anderson**, **Drew**, **Kendrew**, **McAndrew**, **Tancock**, **Tandy** [Rob Andrew, 1963–, English rugby player]

Andrews, Andrewes 'son of **Andrew**' [Anthony Andrews, 1948–, British actor; Archie Andrews, ventriloquist's dummy popular in Britain in the 1950s; Eamonn Andrews, 1922–87, Irish sports commentator and television compere; Harry Andrews, 1911–89, British actor; Dame Julie Andrews (original name Julia Elizabeth Wells), 1935–, British actress and singer; Lancelot Andrewes, 1555–1626, Anglican bishop and writer]

— **Andrews Air Force Base** a US air force base near Washington, DC, the home base of Air Force One, the presidential aircraft. Originally called Camp Springs Army Air Base, it was renamed Andrews Field in 1945 in honour of Frank Maxwell Andrews, 1888–1943, a pioneer of military aviation in the US.

— **Andrews Sisters** a US close-harmony singing trio popular especially in the 1940s, consisting of the sisters Laverne Andrews, 1911–67, Maxene Andrews, 1916–95, and Patti Andrews, 1918–

Andrus, Andruss different forms of **Andrews**

Angas see **Angus**

Angel, Angell (i) from a medieval nickname for someone of an angelic disposition or for someone who played the part of an angel in a pageant; (ii) an anglicization of any of various related surnames in other European languages (e.g. **Angelo** or Hungarian *Angyal*) [Sir Norman Angell, 1874–1967, British author, economist and Labour politician]

Angelo from the Italian male personal name *Angelo* (ultimately from Greek *angelos* 'messenger, angel')

Angers 'person from Angers', Anjou, France ('settlement of the Andrecavi (a Gaulish tribe)')

Angle 'person who lives in a nook or corner of land'

Angus, Angas from the Gaelic male personal name *Aonghus*, traditionally interpreted as 'one choice'. See also **Hennessy**, **Innes** (ii), **McGuinness**, **McNeice**, **Neeson**, **Nish**

Annan 'person from Annan', Dumfries and Galloway ('place by the water') [Noel Annan (Lord Annan), 1916–2000, British academic and author]

Annis, Anness from the medieval female personal name *Annes*, an English variant of Late Latin *Agnes* [Francesca Annis, 1945–, British actress]

Ansell from the medieval male personal name *Ansell*, an English variant of Latin *Anselmus* (of Germanic origin and meaning literally 'god helmet, god protection')

Anson perhaps 'son of **Hann**', or alternatively 'son of *Annes*' (see **Annis**) or 'son of **Ansell**' [George Anson (Lord Anson), 1697–1762, British admiral]
— **Avro Anson** a two-engined multi-role military aircraft used by the RAF especially as a trainer. Named after Admiral Anson (see above), it first flew in 1936.

Anstey, Anstee 'person from Anstey or Ansty', the name of numerous places in England (either 'single track' or 'steep track') [F. Anstey, the pen-name of Thomas Anstey Guthrie, 1856–1934, British barrister and author]

Anstice, Anstis, Anstiss from the medieval male personal name *Anastase* or *Anastayse* (from Latin *Anastasius*, ultimately from Greek *anastasis* 'resurrection'), or from its female equivalent *Anastasie* (from Latin *Anastasia*)

Anstruther 'person from Anstruther', Fife ('the little stream')

Anthony, Antony from the male personal name *Anthony* (from Latin *Antōnius*, a Roman family name of unknown origin and meaning). See also **Toney** [Susan B. Anthony, 1820–1906, US social reformer]
— **Anthony dollar** a US dollar coin with a likeness of Susan B. Anthony (see above) on one side. It was issued in 1979.

Antrobus 'person from Antrobus', Cheshire ('Andrithi's thicket')

Anyon, Anyan different forms of **Onion** (i)

Apgar perhaps 'person from Epgert', Germany
— **Apgar score** a score that is given after assessing the condition of a newborn baby in the five areas of heart rate, breathing, skin colour, muscle tone and reflex response. It is named after the US obstetric anaesthetist Virginia Apgar, 1909–74.

Apple (i) 'person who grows or sells apples', or 'person who lives by an apple orchard'; (ii) from a medieval nickname for someone supposed to resemble an apple (e.g. in having rosy cheeks); (iii) an anglicization of the related German and Jewish surnames *Apfel* and *Appel* [Johnny Apple (original name Raymond Walter Apple, Jr.), 1934–2006, US journalist]

Applebaum a partial anglicization of the German and Jewish surnames *Apfelbaum* and *Appelbaum*, literally 'apple tree'

Appleby 'person from Appleby', the name of various places in northern England ('apple farm') [Inspector Appleby (John Appleby), an erudite police detective inspector featuring in a series of novels (from 1936) by Michael Innes (pen-name of J.I.M. Stewart)]

Appleton 'person from Appleton', the name of various places in England ('apple enclosure (i.e. orchard)') [Sir Edward Appleton, 1892–1965, British physicist]
— **Appleton layer** the highest part of the ionosphere, that reflects high-frequency radio waves. It is named after Sir Edward Appleton (see above), who investigated the properties of the ionosphere.

Appleyard 'person who lives by an apple orchard'
— **The Appleyards** a children's drama serial about the life of a suburban middle-class English family. Broadcast by the BBC between 1952 and 1957, it was the first soap opera on British television.

Apps 'person who lives by an aspen tree' (from Middle English *apse* 'aspen')

Aprahamian an Armenian surname, literally 'son of **Abraham**'

Apthorpe, Apthorp 'person from Apethorpe', Northamptonshire ('Api's farmstead') [Captain Apthorpe, eccentric British army officer in Evelyn Waugh's *Men at Arms* (1952) who has an obsessional attachment to his 'thunder box' (chemical closet)]

Arblaster a different form of **Alabaster**

Arbogast from a Germanic compound personal name meaning literally 'inheritance-stranger' [Milton Arbogast, insurance detective in Robert Bloch's *Psycho* (1959) (played in the 1960 Hitchcock film by Martin Balsam)]

Arbuckle 'person from Arbuckle', Lanarkshire ('herdsman's portion (of land)') [Roscoe ('Fatty') Arbuckle, 1887–1933, US silent-film comedian]

Arbus, Arbuss a Jewish name probably based on either Yiddish *arbes* 'pea' or Russian *arbuz* 'watermelon' [Diane Arbus, 1923–71, US photographer]

Arbuthnot, Arbuthnott 'person from Arbuthnott', Aberdeenshire ('confluence of the *Buadhnat*', a Gaelic river-name meaning literally 'little virtuous one, little holy one') [John Arbuthnot, 1667–1735, Scottish writer and physician]

Archbold a different form of **Archibald**

Archer 'bowman' [Frederick Scott Archer, 1813–57, British inventor, photographer and sculptor; Jeffrey Archer (Lord Archer), 1940–, British Conservative politician and author; Robyn Archer, 1948–, Australian singer and actress; Thomas Archer, 1668–1743, English baroque architect; William Archer, 1856–1924, British dramatic critic]
— **The Archers** a BBC radio soap opera revolving about life in the fictional rural village of Ambridge, first broadcast in 1951. At its centre is the farming family of the Archers: its patriarch was Dan Archer, and other notable Archers have included his wife Doris and, from among their numerous progeny, Philip, David and Shula.

Archibald from the male personal name *Archibald*, brought into Scotland by the Normans but ultimately of Germanic origin and meaning literally 'precious-bold'
— **Archibald Prize** an annual prize awarded for portrait painting in Australia. It was first awarded in 1921, under the terms of a bequest by the Australian journalist and publisher J.F. Archibald, 1856–1919.

Archie from the male personal name *Archie*, a pet-form of **Archibald**

Arden 'person from Arden', Yorkshire, or 'person from the Forest of Arden', Warwickshire ('high district') [Elizabeth Arden (original name Florence Nightingale Graham), 1881–1966, US cosmetician; John Arden, 1930–, British playwright; Mary Arden, ?1540–1608, mother of William Shakespeare]
— *Arden of Feversham* a play (1592), attributed by some to William Shakespeare, about a plot by his wife and her lover to murder Mr Arden
— *Enoch Arden* a narrative poem (1864) by Alfred, Lord Tennyson, about a man who goes to sea and is shipwrecked. After some time his wife remarries. Many years later Arden is rescued, returns home and finds his wife married to another; he does not reveal himself to her.

Ardizzone from the medieval Italian personal name *Ardizzone*, ultimately from a compound name of Germanic origin beginning with the element *ard-* 'hard' [Edward Ardizzone, 1900–79, British illustrator and writer]

Ardley, Ardleigh 'person from Ardley, Ardeley or Ardleigh', the name of various places in England (mainly 'Earda's or Eardwulf's glade')

Ardrey 'person from Airdrie', the name of various places in Scotland (in some cases probably 'high slope') [Robert Ardrey, 1908–80, US palaeoanthropologist, playwright and screenwriter]

Arendt from a different form of the German male personal name *Arndt* (literally 'eagle-rule'), perhaps adopted as a Jewish surname because of its resemblance to **Aaron** [Hannah Arendt, 1906–75, German-born US philosopher and political theorist]

Arey (i) see **Airey**; (ii) a different form of **Avery**

Argyle 'person from Argyll', a region of south-western Scotland ('coastland of the Gaels')

Arias from the medieval Spanish male personal name *Arias*, perhaps of Germanic origin

Arkin 'son of *Arke*', a Yiddish pet-form of **Aaron**

Arkle, Arkell from the Old Norse male personal name *Arnkell*, literally 'eagle-helm'

Arkley a different form of **Arkle**

Arkwright 'maker of chests' (from Middle English *arc* 'ark, chest' + *wright* 'craftsman, maker') [Sir Richard Arkwright, 1732–92, British inventor and industrialist, inventor of a water-powered spinning frame]
— *Arkwright Town* a village in Derbyshire, named after descendants of Sir Richard Arkwright (see above), who bought a manor in the area in 1824

Arledge a different form of **Aldrich** or **Aldridge**

Arlen an alteration of the German surname *Erlen* [Harold Arlen (original name Hyman Arluck), 1905–86, US composer of popular music; Michael Arlen (original name Dikran Kuyumjian), 1895–1956, Bulgarian-born British novelist]

Arlott, Arlot from a medieval nickname for a ne'er-do-well (from Middle English *harlot* or *arlot*

'vagabond, base fellow'; 'prostitute' is a 15th-century development) [John Arlott, 1914–91, British journalist, poet and cricket commentator]

Armbruster 'crossbowman' or 'maker of crossbows' (from a derivative of Middle High German *armbrust* 'crossbow', from Old French *arbalestre* (see **Alabaster**))

Armer 'maker of arms and armour; armourer' (from Anglo-Norman *armer* 'armourer'). See also **Armour**

Armetrading, Armatrading 'person from Armetridding', Lancashire ('hermit's clearing') [Joan Armatrading, 1950–, West Indian-born British singer/songwriter]

Armfield probably 'person from Arnfield', Cheshire ('Earnwīg's open land') [Jimmy Armfield, 1935–, English footballer]

Armison 'son of *Armin*', a medieval personal name, from the first element of any of a range of Germanic compound names beginning with *ermin* 'world, great'. See also **Armson, Harmison**

Armistead (i) 'person who lives near a hermit's cell' (from Middle English *ermite* 'hermit' + *stede* 'place'); (ii) an anglicization of the German surname *Darmstädter*, literally 'person from Darmstadt'. See also **Armstead**

Armitage, Armytage 'person who lives by a hermitage' (from Middle English *ermitage* 'hermitage') [Simon Armitage, 1963–, British poet]

Armour, Armor 'maker of arms and armour; armourer' (from Old French *armure* 'arms, weapons'). See also **Armer** [Philip D. Armour, 1832–1901, US meat-packing tycoon]

Armson a different form of **Armison**

Armstead a different form of **Armistead**

Armstrong from a medieval nickname for someone with strong arms [Alun Armstrong, 1946–, British actor; Anthony Armstrong-Jones (Earl of Snowdon), 1930–, British photographer; Jack Armstrong, youthful, sports-loving hero of the US radio serial *Jack Armstrong, the All-American Boy* (1933–51); Lance Armstrong, 1971–, US cyclist; Louis Armstrong, 1900–71, US jazz musician; Neil Armstrong, 1930–, US astronaut, first man to set foot on the moon; Robert Armstrong (Lord Armstrong), 1927–, British civil servant; Warwick Armstrong, 1879–1947, Australian cricketer; William Armstrong (Lord Armstrong), 1810–1900, British engineer and industrialist]
— *Armstrong Siddeley* a British manufacturer of cars, aero engines, etc. formed in 1919 by the merger of Armstrong Whitworth (see below) with the firm Siddeley-Deasy, which had been founded as Siddeley Autocars in 1902 by John Davenport Siddeley, 1866–1953. Its aeronautical side merged with Hawkers in 1936 to become Hawker Siddeley, and it ceased car production in 1960.
— *Armstrong Whitworth* a British manufacturer of ships, armaments, aircraft, etc. (in full, Sir W.G. Armstrong Whitworth & Co. Ltd.), formed in 1897 by a merger of Lord Armstrong's (see above) interests with those of Joseph Whitworth. In 1927 its

defence and engineering components merged with Vickers to become Vickers Armstrong, but it continued to produce aircraft under its own name until the 1950s.

Armytage see **Armitage**

Arnatt a different form of **Arnold** (i)

Arne from the medieval male personal name *Arne*, a pet-form of **Arnold**, or from the Scandinavian male personal name *Arne*, a shortened form of any of various compound names beginning with *arn* 'eagle' (e.g. *Arnsten*) [Thomas Arne, 1710–78, British composer]

Arnold (i) from the male personal name *Arnold*, brought into England by the Normans but ultimately of Germanic origin and meaning literally 'eagle-rule'. See also **Arnatt**, **Arnott** (ii), **Hornet**; (ii) 'person from Arnold', Nottinghamshire and Yorkshire ('corner of land where eagles are seen'); (iii) a Jewish name probably adopted from the German personal name *Arnold* (see i), possibly because of a perceived resemblance to **Aaron** [Benedict Arnold, 1741–1801, American Revolutionary general and traitor; Eve Arnold, 1925–, US photographer; Sir Malcolm Arnold, 1921–2006, British composer; Matthew Arnold, 1822–88, British poet and critic; Thomas Arnold ('Dr Arnold'), 1795–1842, British educator, father of Matthew]
— **Arnoldian** of or characteristic of Matthew or Thomas Arnold (see above)

Arnott, **Arnot** (i) 'person from Arnot', Perth and Kinross (probably 'place where barley grows'); (ii) a different form of **Arnold** (i)

Aron see **Aaron**

Aronoff, **Aronov** 'son of **Aaron**'

Aronovitch, **Aronovich** 'son of **Aaron**'

Arons see **Aarons**

Aronson, **Aronsohn** see **Aaronson**

Arrington (i) a different form of **Harrington** (i); (ii) 'person from Arrington', Cambridgeshire ('farmstead of Earna's people')

Arrowsmith 'maker of arrowheads' [Aaron Arrowsmith, 1750–1823, British cartographer; Pat Arrowsmith, 1930–, British peace activist]

Arroyo 'person from Arroyo', the name of numerous places in Spain ('channel, watercourse')

Arthur from the male personal name *Arthur*, of Celtic origin but uncertain meaning (perhaps 'bear'). See also **McArthur** [Chester A. Arthur, 1830–86, US Republican politician, president 1881–84; Jean Arthur (original name Gladys Georgianna Greene), 1900–91, US actress]
— **Port Arthur** the former name (now Lüshun) of a city and port in northeastern China. It was established as a British naval base in 1857, during the Anglo-French war against China, and named after a Royal Navy lieutenant surnamed Arthur, who reconnoitred the site. (Port Arthur in Texas was named after its founder, the US railway magnate Arthur Edward Stilwell, 1859–1928).

Arthurs 'son of **Arthur**'

Arundel, **Arundell** (i) 'person from Arundel', Sussex ('valley where horehound grows'); (ii) from a medieval nickname for someone thought to resemble a swallow (from Old French *arondel* 'swallow') [Thomas Arundel, 1353–1414, English churchman]

Asbury 'person from Astbury', Cheshire ('eastern stronghold'), or 'person from Ashbury', Devon and Oxfordshire ('stronghold where ash trees grow')

Asch, **Asche** see **Ash**

Ascham, **Askham** 'person from Askham', Cumbria ('place by the ash trees') or Nottinghamshire and Yorkshire ('homestead or enclosure where ash trees grow') [Roger Ascham, 1515–68, English scholar and writer]

Ascher see **Asher** (ii)

Ascot, **Ascott** 'person from Ascot or Ascott', Berkshire and Oxfordshire respectively ('eastern cottage')

Ash, **Asch**, **Asche** (i) *also* **Ashe** 'person who lives by an ash tree'. See also **Asher** (i), **Dash**, **Nash**; (ii) an acronymic Jewish surname derived from the Yiddish names *Altshul*, literally 'old synagogue', or *Ayznshtot* (German *Eisenstadt*), literally 'Iron City' [Arthur Ashe, 1943–93, US tennis player; Leslie Ash, 1960–, British actress; Oscar Asche, 1871–1936, Australian actor; Sholem Asch, 1880–1957, Polish-born US novelist]
— **Oscar Asche** Australian rhyming slang for *cash*, based on the name of the actor (see above). In modern usage it is usually shortened to *oscar*.

Ashbee see **Ashby**

Ashburton 'person from Ashburton', Devon ('farmstead by the stream where ash trees grow')

Ashby, **Ashbee** 'person from Ashby', the name of various places in northern and eastern England (mainly 'farmstead where ash trees grow') [C.R. Ashbee, 1863–1942, British designer and entrepreneur, son of Henry; Henry Ashbee, 1834–1900, British businessman, book collector and pornography aficionado, said to be 'Walter', pseudonymous author of *My Secret Life* (1888)]

Ashcroft 'person from Ashcroft', the name of various places in England ('enclosure with ash trees') [Dame Peggy Ashcroft, 1907–91, British actress]
— **Ashcroft Theatre** a theatre in Croydon, opened in 1962 and named in honour of the Croydon-born Peggy Ashcroft (see above)

Ashdown 'person from Ashdown', Berkshire, or 'person from Ashdown Forest', Sussex ('hill overgrown with ash trees') [Paddy Ashdown (Lord Ashdown), 1941–, British Liberal Democrat politician]

Ashe see **Ash** (i)

Ashenden 'person who lives in a valley overgrown with ash trees' (from Old English *æscen* 'of ash trees' + *denu* 'valley' [William Ashenden, the secret agent in a series of short stories (published in book form as *Ashenden* (1928)) by William Somerset Maugham]

Asher (i) 'person who lives by an ash tree'; (ii) *also* **Ascher** from the Hebrew personal name *Asher*, literally 'blessed' [Jane Asher, 1946–, British actress]

Ashfield 'person from Ashfield', the name of various places in England ('open land where ash trees grow')

Ashford 'person from Ashford', the name of various places in England (mostly 'ford by the ash trees') [Daisy Ashford, 1881–1972, British child-author]

Ashkettle from the Old Norse male personal name *Ásketill*, literally 'god-kettle (i.e. vessel used for sacrificing to the gods)'. See also **Haskell** (i), **Haskin** (i), **McCaskell**

Ashley 'person from Ashley', the name of various places in England ('ash-tree wood or glade') [Anthony Ashley Cooper (7th earl of Shaftesbury), 1801–85, British reformer and philanthropist; Laura Ashley (*née* Mountney), 1925–85, British fashion designer]

Ashman (i) from the medieval male personal name *Asheman* (from Old English *Æscmann*, probably literally 'sailor' or 'pirate' (ash wood was used for building boats) or alternatively 'spearman, soldier' (ash was used for the shaft of spears)); (ii) 'person who lives by an ash tree'

Ashmole perhaps 'person from Ashmole', an unknown location in England (possibly 'Æschelm's hollow place') [Elias Ashmole, 1617–92, English antiquarian and astrologer]
— **Ashmolean Museum** a museum of art and antiquities in Oxford. Its founding seed was a collection of rarities presented to Oxford University in 1682 by Elias Ashmole (see above). The name 'Ashmolean Museum' was not applied to it until 1899.

Ashmore 'person from Ashmore', the name of various places in England ('marsh where ash trees grow' or 'pool where ash trees grow')
— **Ashmore and Cartier Islands** an island group in the Indian Ocean, northwest of Australia, a territory of Australia. It consists of Ashmore Reef (named after Captain Samuel Ashmore, the first European to discover it, in 1811) and Cartier Island (named after a ship).

Ashton 'person from Ashton', the name of various places in England (mainly 'farmstead where ash trees grow') [Sir Frederick Ashton, 1904–88, British ballet dancer and choreographer; Sylvia Ashton-Warner, 1905–84, New Zealand novelist and teacher]

Ashurst 'person from Ashurst', the name of various places in England ('wooded hill where ash trees grow')

Ashwell 'person from Ashwell', the name of various places in England ('spring where ash trees grow')

Ashwood 'person from Ashwood', Staffordshire ('ash-tree wood')

Ashworth 'person from Ashworth', the name of various places in England ('enclosure where ash trees grow')

Askew 'person from Aiskew', Yorkshire ('oak-tree wood'). See also **Ayscough**

Askey (i) from the medieval personal name *Askey*, of Scandinavian origin and related to Old Norse *askr* 'ash tree'; (ii) a different form of **Askew** [Arthur Askey, 1900–82, British comedian]

Askham see **Ascham**

Aspell, Aspel 'person from Aspull or Aspall', Greater Manchester and Suffolk respectively ('hill where aspens grow') [Michael Aspel, 1933–, British television presenter]

Aspinall, Aspinal, Aspinell 'person from Aspinwall (or Asmall)', Lancashire ('stream where aspens grow')

Asquith 'person from Askwith', Yorkshire ('ash-tree wood') [Anthony Asquith, 1902–68, British film director, son of Herbert Henry; Herbert Henry Asquith (1st earl of Oxford and Asquith), 1852–1928, British Liberal politician, prime minister 1908–16]

Astbury 'person from Astbury', Cheshire ('eastern stronghold') [John Astbury, 1688–1743, English potter]
— **Astburyware** a type of high-quality Staffordshire pottery decorated with coloured clays, as produced by John Astbury (see above) and his son Thomas Astbury, 1719–60

Astle (i) 'person from Astle', Cheshire ('east hill'); (ii) a different form of **Astley**

Astley 'person from Astley', Warwickshire ('eastern glade')
— **Astley's Amphitheatre** a large stadium for the presentation of circuses, equestrian events, theatrical productions, etc., opened in Westminster Bridge Road in 1794 by Philip Astley, 1742–1814. It was demolished in 1893.

Aston (i) 'person from Aston', the name of various places in England (either 'eastern farmstead' or 'farmstead where ash trees grow'); (ii) 'person who lives by a (particular noticeable) stone' (from Middle English *atte ston* 'by the stone'); (iii) from the medieval male personal name *Astan* (probably from Old English *Æthelstān*, literally 'noble stone', with perhaps also an admixture of *Ælfstān*, literally 'elf stone', *Ealdstān*, literally 'old stone' and *Ealhstān*, literally 'altar stone') [Francis William Aston, 1877–1945, British chemist]

Astor from a medieval Provençal nickname for someone thought to resemble a bird of prey (from Old Provençal *astur* 'goshawk') [John Jacob Astor, 1763–1848, German-born US fur trader and property millionaire; Nancy Astor (Viscountess Astor; *née* Langhorne), 1879–1964, US-born British Unionist politician (the first woman to sit as an MP in the British House of Commons), wife of Waldorf; Waldorf Astor (2nd Viscount Astor), 1879–1952, US-born British Conservative politician and newspaper proprietor, great-great-grandson of John Jacob (see above)]
— **Astoria** a city in northwestern Oregon, USA, established in 1811 and named in honour of John Jacob Astor (see above)

— **Astoria** a book (1836) by Washington Irving, giving an account of John Jacob Astor's development of the fur trade

— **Waldorf-Astoria** a luxury hotel in New York City. It began life as two separate entities: the Waldorf Hotel, established in 1893 by William Waldorf Astor (1st Viscount Astor), 1848–1919, great-grandson of John Jacob (who was born in Walldorf near Heidelberg, Germany); and the Astoria Hotel, established in 1897 by John Jacob Astor IV, 1864–1912. Within a few years the two, which had been built next to each other, became one. The name *Astoria* was subsequently applied to a cinema opened in London in 1927, and was widely used as a cinema name in the 1930s.

Atallah, Attallah a Muslim surname, from the Arabic male personal name *'Atāllāh*, literally 'gift of God' [Naim Attallah, 1931–, British publisher]

Atchison, Atcheson, Acheson 'son of *Atty*', a pet-form of **Adam**. See also **Aitchison** [Dean Acheson, 1893–1971, US statesman]

— **Atchison** a city in Kansas, USA. It was named in honour of David Rice Atchison, 1807–86, a Democratic senator who supported the admission of Kansas to the Union. It was the original eastern terminus of the Atchison, Topeka and Santa Fe railway.

Atherton 'person from Atherton', Lancashire ('Æthelhere's farmstead') [David Atherton, 1944–, British conductor; Michael Atherton, 1968–, English cricketer]

Athey (i) 'person who lives by an enclosure' (from Middle English *atte hey* 'by the enclosure'); (ii) a different form of **Athy** (i)

Athill, Athell 'person who lives by the hill' (from Middle English *atte hill* 'by the hill')

Athol 'person from Athol', Perth and Kinross ('new Ireland')

Athy (i) 'person from Athy', Kildare, Ireland ('ford of the yew tree'); (ii) a different form of **Athey** (i)

Atkin 'little *Atty*', a pet-form of **Adam**

Atkins 'son of **Atkin**' [Dame Eileen Atkins, 1934–, British actress]

— **Atkins diet** a weight-loss programme that advocates a high-protein, high-fat, low-carbohydrate diet. It was devised by the US physician Robert Atkins, 1932–2003 (who reportedly weighed 160kg (25 stone) at the time of his death).

— **Thomas Atkins** a representative name for a private soldier, as printed on specimen forms issued by the British Army from 1815; hence, in the colloquial form *Tommy Atkins* (standardly shortened to simply *tommy*), a generic term for a private

Atkinson 'son of **Atkin**' [Ron Atkinson, 1939–, British football manager and television commentator; Rowan Atkinson, 1955–, British comic actor]

Atlee, Attlee 'person who lives by the glade or meadow' (from Middle English *atte lee* 'by the glade or meadow') [Clement Attlee (1st Earl Attlee), 1883–1967, British Labour politician, prime minister 1945–51]

Attallah see **Atallah**

Attaway 'person who lives by the roadside' (from Middle English *atte weye* 'by the road')

Attenborough, Attenbrough 'person who lives near or is a servant at the manor house' or 'person who lives in a fortified town' (from Middle English *atten burh* 'at the manor house or fortified town') [Sir David Attenborough, 1926–, British naturalist, broadcaster and television executive, brother of Richard; Richard Attenborough (Lord Attenborough), 1923–, British film actor, director and producer]

Atterberry, Atterbury 'person who lives near or is a servant at the manor house' or 'person who lives in a fortified town' (from Middle English *atter bery* 'at the manor house or fortified town')

Attewell see **Atwell**

Attlee see **Atlee**

Attride, Attryde 'person who lives in a woodland clearing' (from Middle English *atte ryde* 'by the clearing or glade'; see **Read** (ii))

Attwood see **Atwood**

Attwool, Attwooll different forms of **Atwell**

Atwater 'person who lives by a river or lake' (from Middle English *atte water* 'by the water')

Atwell, Attwell 'person who lives by the spring or stream' (from Middle English *atte welle* 'by the spring or stream') [Winifred Atwell, 1914–83, Trinidadian popular pianist]

Atwood, Attwood 'person who lives by the woodland clearing' (from Middle English *atte wood* 'by the wood') [Margaret Atwood, 1939–, Canadian author]

Aubrey from the medieval male personal name *Aubri*, brought into England by the Normans but ultimately of Germanic origin and meaning literally 'elf-power'. See also **Avery**. [John Aubrey, 1626–97, English antiquary]

Auchinleck 'person from Auchinleck', Angus and East Ayrshire ('field of the flat stones'). The name is traditionally pronounced 'aflek', but the form *Auchinleck* is now usually pronounced as it is spelled. See also **Affleck** [Sir Claude Auchinleck, 1884–1981, British field marshal]

Auden a different form of **Alden** [W.H. Auden, 1907–73, British poet]

Audley 'person from Audley', Staffordshire ('Aldgȳth's glade') [Maxine Audley, 1923–92, British actress]

— **Audley End** a Jacobean mansion in Essex, just to the south of Saffron Walden, built on land given by Henry VIII to Sir Thomas Audley, 1488–1544, in the late 1530s. The house has given its name to a nearby village.

— **Lady Audley's Secret** a sensation novel (1862) by Mary Russell Braddon featuring the beautiful but turpitudinous Lady Audley, who deserts her child, (apparently) murders her husband and contemplates murdering her second (bigamous) husband

— **South Audley Street** a street in the West End of London, connecting Grosvenor Square with

Curzon Street. Laid out in the 1720s, it was named after Hugh Audley, a 16th-century lawyer from whose heirs the land on which it stood was acquired (by marriage) by the Grosvenor Estate.

Audrey, Awdrey, Awdry (i) from the medieval female personal name *Audrey*, brought into England by the Normans but ultimately of Germanic origin and meaning literally 'ancient power'; (ii) 'son of *Aldreda*', a medieval female personal name (from Old English *Æthelthrȳth*, literally 'noble strength'). See also **Autry** [Rev. W.V. Awdry, 1911–97, British clergyman and children's author, creator of 'Thomas the Tank Engine']

Auerbach 'person from Auerbach', the name of several places in southern Germany (traditionally interpreted as 'stream frequented by aurochs (a type of wild ox)') [Frank Auerbach, 1931–, German-born British painter]

Auld a Scottish variant of **Old** (ii)

Aumonier from a medieval French nickname for a beggar (from a derivative of Old French *aumone* 'alms')

Austin, Austen from the male personal name *Austin* (via Old French from Latin *Augustīnus*, literally 'little *Augustus*', a male personal name meaning literally 'venerable'). See also **Costain** (i) [Alfred Austin, 1835–1913, British poet; H.W. ('Bunny') Austin, 1906–2000, British tennis player; Herbert Austin (Lord Austin), 1866–1941, British engineer and industrialist; J.L. Austin, 1911–60, British philosopher; Jane Austen, 1775–1817, British novelist; John Austin, 1790–1859, British jurist; Steve Austin, the bionic man played by Lee Majors in the US television science-fiction series *The Six Million Dollar Man* (1974–79)]

— **Austin** the capital city of Texas, in the south of the state. It was named in honour of Stephen F. Austin, 1793–1836, the so-called 'Father of Texas', who inspired the Anglo-American colonization of the area.

— **Austin-Healey** a British marque of sports car, produced between 1952 and 1972 as a cooperative venture between the Austin Motor Company (see below) and the automotive engineer and designer Donald Healey, 1898–1988

— **Austin Motor Company** a British car producer founded by Herbert Austin (see above) in 1906. In 1952 it merged with Morris Motors to form the British Motor Corporation.

Autry (i) 'person from Autrey or Autry', the name of various places in France; (ii) from the medieval French male personal name *Audry*, equivalent to English **Audrey** (i) [Gene Autry, 1907–98, US singing cowboy]

Avedon probably 'person from Avedon', an unidentified place in England (probably 'hill by the (river) Avon') [Richard Avedon, 1923–2004, US photographer]

Averill (i) perhaps 'person associated with April (e.g. by being born in that month)' (from Middle English *Averil* 'April', from Old French *Avrill*); (ii)

perhaps 'person from Haverhill', Suffolk ('hill where oats are grown')

Avery, Avory (i) from the Anglo-Norman male personal name *Auvery*, the Norman form of **Alfred**; (ii) a different form of **Aubrey** [Oswald Avery, 1877–1955, Canadian bacteriologist and geneticist]

Avis from the medieval female personal name *Avice* (via Old French from Latin *Avitia*, perhaps an adaptation of a Celtic or Germanic name)

— **Avis** a vehicle-rental company founded in 1946 in Detroit, Michigan by Warren E. Avis.

Avison 'son of **Avis**' [Charles Avison, 1709–70, British composer and writer on music]

Avory see **Avery**

Awdrey, Awdry see **Audrey**

Axelrod from the Yiddish male personal name *Akslrod*, perhaps ultimately a different form of **Alexander** [George Axelrod, 1922–2003, US screenwriter, producer and director]

Ayckbourn 'person from Ayckbourn', an unidentified place in northern England ('stream by which oak trees grow') [Sir Alan Ayckbourn, 1939–, British playwright]

Aycock 'little *Ade*', 'little *Addie*', 'little *Aitkin*', etc. (a pet-form produced by adding the suffix *-cock* to any of various shortened forms of **Adam**)

Ayer, Ayr, Ayre (i) *also* **Eyre** *or* **Eyer** from a medieval nickname for someone who was an heir (to a title or to great wealth). See also **Heyer**; (ii) 'person from Ayr', southwestern Scotland ('(mouth of the river) Ayr' (a Celtic river-name meaning literally 'river')) [Sir Alfred Ayer (A.J. Ayer), 1910–89, British philosopher]

Ayers, Ayres 'son of **Ayer** (i)' [Gillian Ayres, 1930–, British painter; Pam Ayres, 1947–, British poet and entertainer]

— **Ayers Rock** a massive red rock in southwestern Northern Territory, Australia, the largest monolith in the world. It was named in 1873 in honour of Sir Henry Ayers, 1821–97, premier of South Australia (in the local Pitjantjatjam language its name is 'Uluru', and since 2002 it has been officially designated 'Uluru/Ayers Rock').

Ayliff from the medieval female personal name *Ayleve* (from Old English *Æthelgifu*, literally 'noble gift'), or from the Old Norse nickname *Eilífr*, literally 'ever-life'

Ayling from the medieval male personal name *Ayling* (from Old English *ætheling* 'prince')

Aylmer (i) from the medieval male personal name *Ailmar* (from Old English *Æthelmǣr*, literally 'noble-famous'). See also **Elmer**; (ii) perhaps 'person from Aylmer', an unidentified place in Scotland [Sir Felix Aylmer (original name Felix Edward Aylmer Jones), 1889–1979, British actor]

Aylward from the medieval male personal name *Ailward* (from Old English *Æthelweard*, literally 'noble-guard') [Gladys Aylward, 1903–70, British missionary in China]

Aylwin, Aylwen different forms of **Alwyn**

Aynsley see **Ainsley**

Ayr, Ayre, Ayres see **Ayer, Ayers**

Ayrton 'person from Airton', Yorkshire ('farmstead on the (river) Aire', probably a Celtic or pre-Celtic river-name meaning literally 'strongly flowing') [Michael Ayrton (original name Michael Gould; Ayrton was his mother's maiden name), 1921–75, British artist and writer]

Ayscough a different form of **Askew**

Ayto probably 'person who lives by a … hill' (from Old Norse *haugr* 'mound, cairn') or 'person who lives by a … hill spur' (from Old English *hōh*), with an unexplained first element, possibly Middle English *æit* 'small island' or Scottish or northern English dialect *ait* 'oat'

Ayton, Aytoun 'person from Ayton', Borders and Yorkshire ('estate or farmstead on the river')

Aziz a Muslim name, from the Arabic male personal name *'Abd al-'Azīz* 'servant of the mighty' or 'servant of the beloved'

B

Babb probably from the Old English personal name *Babba*. See also **Bebb**

Babbage a Devon surname of unknown origin [Charles Babbage, 1792–1871, British mathematician and inventor, who devised the forerunner of the modern computer]

Babbitt 'little **Babb**' [Irving Babbitt, 1865–1933, US scholar and critic; Milton Babbitt, 1916–, US composer]
— *Babbitt* a novel (1922) by Sinclair Lewis which tells the story of George Babbitt, a self-satisfied narrow-minded real-estate agent in the mid-western town of Zenith. The name came to be used generically for such a person, and **Babbittism** or **Babbittry** for his typical behaviour.
— **babbitt metal** a soft alloy used especially in the manufacture of antifriction bearings. It is named after its originator, Isaac Babbitt, 1799–1862.

Babcock from the medieval personal name *Babb* (see **Babb**), with the suffix *-cock* (literally 'cockerel', hence 'jaunty or bumptious young man'), that was often added to create pet-forms of personal names in the Middle Ages
— **Babcock and Wilcox Company** a US manufacturer of power-generation systems. It was created in 1867 in Providence, Rhode Island by George Herman Babcock and Stephen Wilcox to produce their newly invented 'Babcock and Wilcox Non-Explosive Boiler'.

Babel (i) from the medieval French personal name *Babel*, apparently adopted from that of St *Babylas*, a 3rd-century Christian patriarch of Antioch, the origins of which are uncertain; (ii) an invented Jewish name based on German or Polish *Babel* 'Babylon'

Babington 'person from Babington or Bavington', Somerset and Northumberland respectively ('settlement associated with Babba') [Anthony Babington, 1561–86, English conspirator who plotted to kill Elizabeth I and put Mary, Queen of Scots on the throne]

Bacchus (i) a different form (inspired by *Bacchus*, the name of the god of wine in classical mythology) of **Backhouse**; (ii) from a medieval French nickname for a heavy drinker of alcohol (from *Bacchus* the wine god – see (i))

Bach (i) *also* **Bache** *or* **Batch** 'person who lives by a stream' (from Middle English *bache* and Middle High German *bach*, both 'stream'). See also **Back** (vi); (ii) from the Polish, Czech and Slovak male personal name *Bach*, a pet-form of the vernacular versions of *Bartolomaeus* (see **Bartholomew**) or **Sebastian**; (iii) an acronymic Jewish surname based on the initial letters of the Hebrew phrase

ben chayim 'son of life' [Barbara Bach (original name Barbara Goldbach), 1947–, US model and actress]
— **Bach flower remedy** a healing method using extracts of 38 flowers, each treating a different emotional disorder, to promote physical health. It is named after the British physician Edward Bach, 1886–1936.

Bacharach 'person from Bacharach', Germany [Burt Bacharach, 1928–, US composer and pianist]

Bache see **Bach** (i)

Bachelor, Bacheler, Batchelor, Batcheler 'young knight (one not yet qualified to display his own banner)' (from Middle English *bacheler*, from Old French). See also **Batchelder**
— **Batchelor's Foods** a British company producing soups and other processed foodstuffs. It was created in 1895 by William Batchelor, originally as a producer of tinned vegetables.

Bacher (i) 'person who lives by a stream' (from a derivative of Middle High German *bach* 'stream'); (ii) *also* **Bachar** 'dealer in spices' (from Turkish *bahar* 'spices, aroma'); (iii) a different form of **Baker** [Aron ('Ali') Bacher, 1942–, South African cricketer and administrator]

Back (i) 'person who lives at the back or rear of a settlement'; (ii) 'person who lives on the ridge of a hill'; (iii) from a medieval nickname for a hunchback or someone with some other deformity or peculiarity of the back or backbone; (iv) from the Old English male personal name *Bacca*. See also **Bax**; (v) from a medieval nickname for someone thought to resemble a bat (the animal) (from Middle English *bakke* 'bat'); (vi) a different form of **Bach** (i)

Backhouse 'person living in or employed in a bakery' (from Old English *bæchūs* 'bakehouse, bakery'). See also **Bacchus**, **Backus** (i)

Backman a different form of **Back** (i–ii)

Backs see **Bax**

Backus (i) a different form of **Backhouse**; (ii) an anglicization of Lithuanian *Bačkus*, literally 'barrel-maker' (from *bačka* 'barrel'), also used as a nickname for a stout person

Bacon (i) 'producer and seller of bacon'; (ii) from *Bacon*, the oblique case of the Norman male personal name *Bacus* (from the Germanic name *Baco* – see **Bagge** (ii)) [Sir Francis Bacon (1st Baron Verulam, Viscount St Albans), 1561–1626, English lawyer, philosopher and statesman; Francis Bacon, 1909–92, Irish-born British painter; John Bacon, 1740–99, British neoclassical sculptor; Kevin Bacon, 1958–, US actor; Roger

Bacon, ?1214–94, English philosopher and scientist]

— **Baconian** typical of or similar to the philosophy of Sir Francis Bacon (see above), particularly his method of inductive reasoning in which the emphasis is placed on collecting instances rather than testing theories. As a noun, the term denotes a follower or disciple of Bacon, and also an adherent of the theory that he was the true author of the plays of Shakespeare.

Badcock from the medieval personal name *Bade* (see **Bade**), with the suffix *-cock* (literally 'cockerel', hence 'jaunty or bumptious young man'), that was often added to create pet-forms of personal names in the Middle Ages

Baddeley 'person from Baddeley Green', Staffordshire ('Badda's glade') [Angela Baddeley (original name Madeline Angela Clinton-Baddeley), 1904–76, British actress]

Bade (i) probably from an unrecorded medieval male personal name descended from Old English *Badda*, perhaps an abbreviated form of any of various compound names beginning with *beadu* 'battle'; (ii) from a medieval North German male personal name that was an abbreviated form of any of various Germanic compound names beginning with *badu* 'battle'

Baden 'son of **Bade** (ii)' [Agnes Baden-Powell, 1858–1945, British founder of the Girl Guides Association, sister of Robert; Robert Baden-Powell (Lord Baden-Powell), 1857–1941, British general and founder of the Scout Movement]

Bader (i) 'attendant at a public bath-house' (from a derivative of Old High German *bad* 'bath'); (ii) 'janitor' (from Old Provençal, from Medieval Latin *baderius*) [Sir Douglas Bader, 1910–82, British fighter pilot]

Badger (i) 'person from Badger', Shropshire ('Bæcg's ridge top'); (ii) 'person who makes bags or who goes around selling things from a bag' (from a derivative of Middle English *bagge* 'bag')

Badgett a different form of **Baggett**

Badham (i) 'person from Badham', an unidentified place probably in the West Midlands ('Bēada's homestead'); (ii) perhaps 'son of Adam' (from Welsh *ap Adam*)

Badman probably 'servant of *Badd* or *Batt*'

Baer, Baehr, Behr (i) anglicizations of German *Bär*, literally 'bear', used as a nickname for someone thought to resemble a bear, or to denote someone who lived in a house with the sign of a bear or a travelling entertainer who kept a dancing bear; (ii) from the Yiddish male personal name *Ber*, literally 'bear' [Max Baer, 1909–59, US boxer]

Baez an anglicization of Spanish *Báez*, a different form of *Peláez*, literally 'son of *Pelayo*', a medieval Spanish male personal name (ultimately from Greek *Pelagios*, a derivative of *pelagos* 'sea') [Joan Baez, 1941–, US singer and activist]

Baffin a different form of **Baughan** [William Baffin, ?1584–1622, English navigator]

— **Baffin Bay** a bay that is part of a strait separating Baffin Island from Greenland

— **Baffin Island** the largest island in the Canadian Arctic, to the north of Hudson Strait. It was discovered by William Baffin (see above).

Bagby (i) 'person from Bagby', Yorkshire ('Baggi's farmstead'); (ii) perhaps a different form of **Begbie**

Bagehot a different form of **Baggett** [Walter Bagehot, 1826–77, British economist, political theorist, literary critic and journalist]

Bagge, Bagg (i) 'maker of bags and similar receptacles'; (ii) from the medieval male personal name *Bagge*, from Germanic *Baco, Bacco* or *Bahho* (ultimately a derivative of the root *bag-* 'fight'). See also **Bacon** (ii)

Baggett, Baggott 'little **Bagge** (ii)'. See also **Badgett, Bagehot**

Bagley 'person from Bagley', the name of various places in England ('Bæcga's glade')

Bagnall, Bagnell 'person from Bagnall', Staffordshire ('Badeca's nook of land')

Bagnold a different form of **Bagnall** [Enid Bagnold (Lady Jones), 1889–1981, British novelist and playwright]

Bagshaw, Bagshawe 'person from Bagshaw', Derbyshire (probably 'Bæcga's copse')

Bagwell (i) perhaps 'person from Backwell', Somerset ('spring by the ridge'); (ii) perhaps a different form of **Bakewell**

Bailey, Baily, Bayley, Bayly, Bailly (i) 'steward or similar (household) official' (from Middle English *baili*, from Old French *bailli*, earlier *baillis* – see **Bayliss**). See also **Baillie**; (ii) 'person who lives by the outer wall of a castle' (from Middle English *baily, baile* 'outer courtyard of a castle', from Old French *baille* 'enclosure'). See also **Bale**; (iii) 'person from Bailey', Lancashire ('woodland glade with many berries') [Bill Bailey (original name Mark Bailey), 1964–, British comedian; David Bailey, 1938–, British photographer; Harry Bailly, host of the Tabard Inn in Chaucer's *Canterbury Tales* (1387); Nathan (or Nathaniel) Bailey, died 1742, British lexicographer; Pearl Bailey, 1918–90, US singer; Robin Bailey, 1919–99, British actor; Trevor Bailey, 1923–, English cricketer]

— **Bailey bridge** a temporary steel bridge made of prefabricated parts and designed for quick construction. It was named after its designer, the British engineer Sir Donald Coleman Bailey, 1901–85.

— **Baily's beads** bright points of sunlight that briefly appear around the Moon immediately before and after a total eclipse of the Sun. They are named after the British amateur astronomer Francis Baily, 1774–1844.

— **Barnum and Bailey Circus** see **Barnum**

— **'Won't you come home, Bill Bailey?'** a popular song (1902) by Hughie Cannon, in which Bill Bailey's lover, who had thrown him out, beseeches him to return

Baillie, Bailie 'chief magistrate in a barony or (later) city' (from Older Scots *baili*, from Middle English – see **Bailey** (i)) [Dame Isobel Baillie, 1895–1983, British soprano]

Bain, Baine, Bayne (i) from a medieval Scottish nickname for someone with fair hair (from Gaelic *bàn* 'white, fair'). See also **Bawn**; (ii) from a medieval nickname in northern England for someone thought to resemble a bone (presumably in being thin) (from northern Middle English *bane* 'bone'). See also **Baines** (i); (iii) from a medieval nickname in northern England for someone welcoming or hospitable (from northern Middle English *bayn* 'welcoming', from Old Norse); (iv) 'attendant at a public bath-house' (from Middle English *baine* 'bath', from Old French) [Alexander Bain, 1818–1903, Scottish psychologist and scholar]

Bainbridge 'person from Bainbridge', Yorkshire ('bridge over the (river) Bain', a river-name of Scandinavian origin meaning literally 'straight') [Dame Beryl Bainbridge, 1934–, British author]

Baines, Bains, Baynes, Banes (i) from a medieval nickname in Scotland and northern England for someone thought to resemble bones or a skeleton (presumably in being thin) (from northern Middle English *banes* 'bones'). See also **Bain** (ii); (ii) from Welsh *ap Einws* 'son of *Einws*', literally 'little *Einion*' (see **Onion**)

Baird 'minstrel, poet' (from Gaelic *bàrd* 'bard'). See also **Bard** (i) [John Logie Baird, 1888–1946, British electrical engineer, who invented an early television system]

Bairnsfather from a medieval nickname in Scotland and northern England for the (alleged) father of an illegitimate child (from northern Middle English *bairnes* 'child's' + *father*) [Bruce Bairnsfather, 1888–1959, British cartoonist and author]

Bairstow 'person from Bairstow', Yorkshire (probably 'place where berries grow'). See also **Barstow** [Sir Edward Bairstow, 1874–1946, British composer and conductor]

Baker 'baker'. See also **Bacher** (iii), **Baxter** [Sir Benjamin Baker, 1840–1907, British civil engineer, co-designer of the first underground railway; George Baker, 1931–, British actor; Hylda Baker, 1908–86, British comedian; James Baker, 1930–, US lawyer and statesman; Dame Janet Baker, 1933–, British mezzosoprano; Josephine Baker (original name Freda Josephine McDonald), 1906–75, US-born French dancer and entertainer; Kenneth Baker (Lord Baker), 1934–, British Conservative politician; Richard Baker, 1925–, British television newsreader; Sir Samuel Baker, 1821–93, British explorer; Tom Baker, 1934–, British actor]

— **Baker day** in Britain in the late 20th century, any of a number of days in the school year set aside for the in-school training of teachers. They were introduced by Kenneth Baker (see above), secretary of state for education 1986–89.

— **Baker Street** a street in the West End of London, running from Regent's Park in the north to Portman Square in the south. It is named after William Baker, a speculative builder who laid it out in the mid-1750s.

Bakewell 'person from Bakewell', Derbyshire ('Badeca's spring') [Joan Bakewell, 1933–, British broadcaster and writer; Robert Bakewell, 1725–95, British agriculturalist]

Balch, Baulch (i) probably from a medieval nickname for a vain or arrogant person (from Middle English *balche* 'swelling'); (ii) perhaps 'person who lives in a house with a beamed roof' (from Middle English *balch* 'balk, beam'); (iii) perhaps from a medieval nickname for a heavily built person (from Middle English *balch* 'balk, beam'). See also **Boakes** [Jamie Baulch, 1973–, British athlete]

Balchin 'little **Balch**' [Nigel Balchin, 1908–70, British novelist]

Balcombe, Balcom 'person from Balcombe', Sussex ('calamity valley' or 'Bealda's valley')

Balderston, Balderstone 'person from Balderstone', Lancashire ('Baldhere's farmstead')

Baldick a different form of **Baldock**

Balding from an unrecorded Old English personal name *Bealding*, probably literally 'son of *Bealda*' [Clare Balding, 1971–, British television sports presenter; Toby Balding, 1936–, British racehorse trainer, uncle of Clare]

Baldock 'person from Baldock', Hertfordshire ('Baghdad': in the Middle Ages the lords of the manor were the Knights Templar, whose headquarters were in Jerusalem, and they named the town *Baldac*, the Old French name for Baghdad). See also **Baldick**

Baldry, Baldrey from the medieval male personal name *Baldri*, brought into England by the Normans but ultimately of Germanic origin and meaning literally 'brave power' [Long John Baldry (original name John William Baldry), 1941–2005, British blues singer]

Baldwin (i) from the medieval male personal name *Baldwin*, brought into England by the Normans but ultimately of Germanic origin and meaning literally 'brave friend'. See also **Bawden, Boyden**; (ii) a 'translation' of the Irish Gaelic surname *Ó Maolagáin* (see **Milligan**), based on the association of *Maolagáin* (literally 'little little bald one') with the *bald* of English *Baldwin* [Alec Baldwin, 1958–, US actor; James Baldwin, 1924–87, US writer; Stanley Baldwin (1st Earl Baldwin), 1867–1947, British Conservative politician, prime minister 1923–24, 1924–29 and 1935–37; William Baldwin, 1963–, US actor]

Bale 'person who lives by the outer wall of a castle' (from Middle English *baile* – see **Bailey** (ii)) [Christian Bale, 1974–, British actor]

Balfe from the Irish Gaelic name *Balbh*, literally 'stammering' (itself probably a translation of a Norman surname with the same literal meaning) [Michael Balfe, 1808–70, Irish-born British composer]

Balfour 'person from Balfour', the name of several places in eastern Scotland ('homestead in the pasture') [Arthur Balfour (1st earl of Balfour),

1848–1930, British Conservative politician, prime minister 1902–05; David Balfour, the protagonist of Robert Louis Stevenson's *Kidnapped* (1886) and its sequel *Catriona* (1893)]

— **Balfour Declaration** a British undertaking to support the establishment of a Jewish homeland in Palestine, made known in a letter of 2 November 1917 from Arthur Balfour (see above), at that time British foreign secretary, to Lord Rothschild

— **Balfour's poodle** a nickname bestowed on the House of Lords for its readiness, at the behest of the Conservative leader Arthur Balfour, to block legislation introduced by the 1906 Liberal government. It originated in a remark made by Lloyd George in 1908.

Baliol see **Balliol**

Ball (i) 'person who lives on a small rounded hill'; (ii) *also* **Balle** from a medieval nickname for a short fat person; (iii) from the Old Norse male personal name *Balle*, a derivative of either *ballr* 'dangerous' or *bollr* 'ball'. See also **Balls** [Alan Ball, 1945–2007, English footballer; John Ball, ?1338–81, English rebel, one of the leaders of the Peasants' Revolt; Lucille Ball, 1911–89, US comic actress; Michael Ball, 1962–, British actor and singer; Zoë Ball, 1970–, British television and radio presenter]

— **Balls Green** a village in Sussex, named after Rychard Balle, a local landowner in the late 16th century

— **Balls Pond Road** a road in North London, leading from Islington to Hackney, named after a former pond in the area owned in the 17th century by a man called John Ball

Ballantyne, Ballantine, Ballentine probably 'person from Bellenden', Borders (perhaps 'farmstead of the dean') [R.M. Ballantyne, 1825–94, British novelist]

Ballard from a hostile medieval nickname for a bald man, equivalent to modern *baldy* (from a derivative of Middle English *balle* 'bald patch') [J.G. Ballard, 1930–, British science-fiction writer]

Ballaster, Ballester, Ballister 'person who makes or is armed with a crossbow' (from a derivative of Middle English *baleste* 'crossbow', from Old French)

Balliol, Baliol 'person from Bailleul', the name of various places in northern France (probably 'fortified settlement') [John Balliol, ?1250–1313, king of Scotland 1292–96]

— **Balliol College** a college of Oxford University, founded in 1263 by John Balliol, died 1269, father of John Balliol, king of Scots (see above)

Balls 'son of **Ball** (iii)'

Balmer (i) 'person who sells spices and perfumes' (from a derivative of Middle English *balme* 'balm, ointment'); (ii) 'person from Balm', the name of various places in Switzerland and southern Germany (probably 'hollow place, cave')

Balmforth a different form of **Bamford**

Balogh, Balog from a Hungarian nickname for a left-handed person (usually with the implication of clumsiness) (from Hungarian *balog* 'left-handed') [Thomas Balogh (Lord Balogh), 1905–85,

Hungarian-born British economist and government advisor]

Balsam (i) 'person from Balsham', Cambridgeshire ('Bælli's homestead'); (ii) an invented Jewish name based on German *Balsam* or Yiddish *balzam* 'balsam, balm'; (iii) 'person who sells spices and perfumes' (from German *Balsam* – see (i)) [Martin Balsam, 1919–96, US actor]

Bamber 'person from Bamber Bridge', Lancashire ('(bridge made of) tree trunks')

Bambrough 'person from Bamburgh', Northumberland ('Bebbe's stronghold')

Bamfield a different form of **Banfield**

Bamford 'person from Bamford', the name of various places in England ('tree-trunk ford (i.e. either one with a wooden bridge or one marked with a wooden post)'). See also **Balmforth**

— **JCB** a proprietary name for an excavating and earth-moving vehicle. It is based on the initials of Joseph Cyril Bamford, 1916–2001, who founded his firm making such vehicles in Uttoxeter in 1945.

Bampton 'person from Bampton', the name of various places in England (mostly 'farmstead made of beams')

Banbury 'person from Banbury', Oxfordshire ('Bana's stronghold')

Bancroft 'person from Bancroft', the name of various places in England ('smallholding where beans are grown') [Anne Bancroft (original name Anna Maria Louisa Italiano), 1931–2005, US actress]

Banerjee a Hindu (Brahman) name, literally 'teacher from (the village of) Bandoghat'

Banes see **Baines**

Banfield (i) 'person from Banfield', the name (variously spelled) of several places in England ('area of land where beans are grown'). See also **Bamfield, Benfield**; (ii) a different form of **Banville**

Bangs a different form of **Banks** (i)

Banham 'person from Banham', Norfolk ('homestead or enclosure where beans are grown')

— **Banhams** a British firm of lockmakers established by William Banham, who invented his automatic bolt lock in 1926

Banister see **Bannister**

Bankhead 'person from Bankhead', the name of various places in Scotland ('top of a hill or end of a bank'), or 'person who lives at the top of a hill or at the end of a bank' [Tallulah Bankhead, 1902–68, US actress]

Banks (i) *also* **Bankes** 'person who lives by a riverbank or on the side of a hill'. See also **Bangs**; (ii) from Irish Gaelic *Ó Bruacháin* 'descendant of *Bruachán*', a nickname for someone with a large paunch, based on the misapprehension that the name is connected with Gaelic *bruach* 'bank' [Gordon Banks, 1937–, English footballer; Iain Banks, 1954–, British author; Jeff Banks, 1943–, British fashion designer; Sir Joseph Banks, 1743–1820, British botanist and explorer; Lynne Reid Banks, 1929–, British author; Tony Banks

(Lord Stratford), 1943–2006, British Labour politician]

— **banksia** a small Australian evergreen tree or shrub (family Proteaceae) with leathery narrow leaves and cylindrical flowers. It was named after Sir Joseph Banks (see above).

— **Banksian pine** a pine tree, *Pinus banksiana*, named after Sir Joseph Banks. It is alternatively known as the Labrador, Grey, or Jack Pine.

— **Banksian rose** a Chinese species of climbing rose, with small white or yellow flowers borne in clusters. It was named in honour of Lady Banks, wife of Sir Joseph.

— **Banks Island** an island in the Arctic Ocean, Northwest Territories, Canada. It was named, in 1820, in honour of Sir Joseph Banks.

— **Banks Peninsula** a peninsula on the eastern coast of South Island, New Zealand. It was named, in 1769, in honour of Sir Joseph Banks.

— **Banksy** the pseudonym of Robert or Robin Banks, 1974–, British street artist

Bannan, Bannen, Bannon from Irish Gaelic *Ó Banáin* 'descendant of *Banán*', a personal name meaning literally 'little white one' [Ian Bannen, 1928–99, British actor]

Bannerman 'standard-bearer' [Helen Bannerman, ?1862–1946, British children's writer, author of *Little Black Sambo* (1899)]

Bannister, Banister 'basket-weaver' (from Anglo-Norman *banastre* 'basket') [Sir Roger Bannister, 1929–, British neurologist and middle-distance runner, first to run a mile in under 4 minutes (1954)]

Banville 'person from Banville', Normandy ('estate belonging to a woman called Bada'). See also **Banfield** (ii), **Bonfield**

Banwell 'person from Banwell', Somerset ('killer spring (perhaps alluding to a contaminated water source)')

Baptiste from the medieval personal name *Baptiste* (via French and Latin from Greek *baptistēs* 'one who washes', an epithet applied to St John the Baptist). See also **Batista**

Barber (i) 'barber (someone who cut hair and also, in the Middle Ages, extracted teeth and performed minor surgical operations)'. See also **Barbour**; (ii) an anglicization of various foreign surnames meaning literally 'barber' (e.g. Spanish *Barbero*) [Anthony Barber (Lord Barber), 1920–2005, British banker and Conservative politician; Chris Barber, 1930–, British jazz bandleader; Samuel Barber, 1910–81, US composer]

Barbera (i) from a southern Italian nickname for a slatternly or dishonest woman or a prostitute (from Italian *barbera* 'barber's wife'); (ii) 'person from Barberà', Spain ('Barbarius's settlement') [Joseph Barbera, 1911–2006, US cartoon artist and animator]

Barbour a Scottish and Northern Irish variant of **Barber** (i) [John Barbour, 1316–95, Scottish poet]

— **Barbour jacket** a waxed jacket for country wear, as developed in the 1890s by the South Shields draper John Barbour, 1849–1918, and manufactured by J. Barbour & Sons Ltd. In the late 20th century it came to be seen as emblematic of the wealthy urban classes masquerading as country gentry.

Barclay, Berkeley, Berkley 'person from Berkeley', Gloucestershire ('birch wood or glade') [Alexander Barclay, ?1475–1552, Scottish poet and scholar; Busby Berkeley (original name William Berkeley Enos), 1895–1976, US choreographer and film director; George Berkeley, 1685–1753, Irish Anglican bishop and idealist philosopher; Sir Lennox Berkeley, 1903–89, British composer; Michael Berkeley, 1948–, British composer, son of Lennox; Sir William Berkeley, 1606–77, English colonist, governor of Virginia 1641–49, 1660–77]

— **Barclay brothers** the name usually applied to Sir David Barclay, 1934–, and his twin brother Sir Frederick Barclay, 1934–, British newspaper proprietors

— **Barclays plc** a British bank. It had its beginnings in a goldsmith's business established in Lombard Street, London in 1690 by John Freame and Thomas Gould. In 1736 Freame's son-in-law James Barclay, 1708–66, became a partner. Its modern incarnation as a leading clearing bank dates from 1896, when it merged with several other banks to become Barclays & Co. In the 1930s *Barclays Bank* came to be used as rhyming slang for 'wank' (often abbreviated to simply *Barclays*).

— **Berkeleian** relating to George Berkeley (see above) or his philosophy, especially his view that the material world is an idea in God's mind and that an object's existence consists in its being perceived

— **Berkeley** a city in western California, on San Francisco Bay. It is the site of the University of California, Berkeley. It was named, in the 1860s, in honour of George Berkeley. It is pronounced 'berkly' (not 'barkly').

Bard (i) a different form of **Baird**; (ii) 'person from Bard', the name of various places in France ('hill'); also perhaps 'person from Bard', an unidentified place in Scotland; (iii) from the medieval French personal name *Bardo*, an abbreviated form of various Germanic compound names beginning with *Bard-* (perhaps from *barta* 'axe'); (iv) 'person whose work involves using a barrow' (from Old French *bard* 'barrow'); (v) 'bricklayer, builder', or alternatively 'person who lives in a muddy place' (in either case from Old French *bart* 'mud, clay'); (vi) 'person with a particularly remarkable or magnificent beard' (from an amalgamation of German *Bart* and Yiddish *bord* 'beard'); (vii) probably a different form of **Bart** [Wilkie Bard, 1874–1944, British music-hall comedian]

Bardell a different form of **Bardwell** [Mrs Bardell, Mr Pickwick's landlady in Charles Dickens's *Pickwick Papers* (1837), who sued him for breach of promise]

Barden 'person from Barden', Yorkshire ('valley where barley is grown')

Bardsley 'person from Bardsley', Lancashire ('Beornrēd's glade') [Warren Bardsley, 1882–1954, Australian cricketer]

Bardwell 'person from Bardwell', Suffolk ('Bearda's spring'). See also **Bardell**

Bareham a different form of **Barham**

Barfield (i) 'person who lives by a place where barley is grown' (from Middle English *berefeld* 'barley field'); (ii) probably 'person from Bardfield', Essex ('open land by a bank')

Barham 'person from Barham', the name of various places in England (mostly 'homestead or enclosure on a hill') [Richard Barham, 1788–1845, British clergyman and humorous writer, author of *The Ingolsby Legends* (1840, 1842, 1847)]

Baring 'son of *Bar*', a medieval German nickname for someone thought to resemble a bear (from Middle Low German *bar* 'bear') [Evelyn Baring (1st earl of Cromer), 1841–1917, British soldier and diplomat; Maurice Baring, 1874–1945, British author; Sabine Baring-Gould, 1834–1924, British hymnist and novelist]
— **Baring Brothers and Co. Ltd.** a British merchant bank, founded in Queen Street, London in 1762 by Francis Baring, 1740–1810. It collapsed in 1995 when one of its traders, Nick Leeson, lost $1.4 billion of its money in futures speculations.

Barker (i) 'tanner of leather' (from a derivative of Middle English *barken* 'to tan', itself based on *bark* – bark was used in the tanning process); (ii) 'shepherd' (from Anglo-Norman *bercher* 'shepherd') [Eric Barker, 1912–90, British comic actor; George Barker, 1913–91, British poet; Pat Barker (*née* Drake), 1943–, British novelist; Ronnie Barker, 1929–2005, British comic actor and writer; Sue Barker, 1956–, British tennis player and television presenter]
— **Barker's** a department store in Kensington High Street, West London, which had its origins in two small drapery shops opened there in 1870 by John Barker, 1840–1914. It closed down in 2005.

Barkis, Barkus 'person who works in a tannery' (from Middle English *barkhous* 'tannery' – bark was used in the tanning process) [Barkis, a carrier in Charles Dickens's *David Copperfield* (1849) who sends a message via David to Clara Peggotty that 'Barkis is willin'' (i.e. to marry her)]

Barkworth 'person from Barkwith', Lincolnshire (perhaps 'pig-farm')

Barley, Barlee (i) 'person who grows or sells barley'; (ii) 'person from Barley', the name of various places in England (mostly either 'glade where boars are seen' or 'woodland clearing where barley is grown')

Barling 'person from Barling', Essex ('settlement of Bærla's people'). See also **Burling**

Barlow, Barlowe 'person from Barlow', the name of various places mainly in northern England (mostly either 'woodland clearing where barley is grown' or 'woodland clearing with a barn') [Charlie Barlow, irascible police detective played by Stratford Johns in *Z Cars* and other BBC television police dramas of the 1960s and 70s; Gary Barlow, 1971–, British pop singer/songwriter; Patrick Barlow, 1947–, British actor and writer]

— **Barlow knife** a penknife with one blade for cutting and another for poking or gouging. It is named after a family of Sheffield cutlers.

Barnaby, Barnabee (i) 'person from Barnaby', Yorkshire ('Beornwald's settlement'); (ii) from the medieval male personal name *Barnaby*, the English form of *Barnabas*, a biblical name ultimately from Aramaic *Barnabia* 'son of Nabia'

Barnard a different form of **Bernard** [Christiaan Barnard, 1922–2000, South African surgeon who performed the first successful heart transplant operation (1967); Edward Emerson Barnard, 1857–1923, US astronomer]
— **Barnard's star** a red dwarf star in the constellation Ophiuchus. It was discovered in 1916 by Edward Barnard (see above).

Barnes (i) *also* **Barns** 'son or servant of a "barne", a member of the medieval aristocracy'; (ii) *also* **Barns** 'person who lives or works in a barn'; (iii) from Irish Gaelic *Ó Bearáin* 'descendant of *Bearán*', a nickname meaning literally 'spear'. See also **Baron** (iii), **Barrington** (ii); (iv) a different form of **Parnes** [Clive Barnes, 1927–, British theatrical critic; Djuna Barnes, 1892–1982, US novelist and playwright; John Barnes, 1963–, Jamaican-born English footballer; Julian Barnes, 1946–, British novelist; Sidney Barnes, 1916–73, Australian cricketer; Sydney Barnes, 1873–1967, English cricketer; William Barnes, 1801–86, British poet]

Barnett, Barnet (i) 'person from Barnet', the name of various places in England ('place cleared by burning'); (ii) from the medieval male personal name *Barnet*, a different form of **Bernard** [Correlli Barnett, 1927–, British historian and writer; Lady Isobel Barnett, 1918–80, British doctor and television game-show panellist; Joel Barnett (Lord Barnett), 1923–, British Labour politician]

Barney (i) from the male personal name *Barney*, a pet-form of **Bernard**; (ii) 'person from Barney', Norfolk ('Bera's island')

Barnfield 'person from Barnfield', the name of various places in England ('area of open land with a barn')

Barnhart from the male personal name *Barnhart*, the Dutch form of **Bernard**

Barnsley 'person from Barnsley', the name of several places in England (variously 'Beorn's glade' and 'Beornmōd's glade')

Barnum (i) 'person who lives or works among barns' (from Old English *bernum* 'at the barns'); (ii) *also* **Barnham** 'person from Barnham', the name of various places in England (mostly 'homestead of the warrior' or 'Beorn's homestead') [Phineas T. Barnum, 1810–91, US showman]
— **Barnum and Bailey Circus** a US circus, formed in 1881 when the circus established by Phineas T. Barnum (see above) in 1871 merged with that of his rival J.A. Bailey, 1847–1906.

Barnwell 'person from Barnwell', Cambridgeshire and Northamptonshire ('spring of the warriors')

Baron (i) *also* **Barron** 'servant in the household of a baron'; (ii) *also* **Barron** from the medieval male personal name *Baron*, from the oblique case of the Old French personal name *Baro*; (iii) from Irish Gaelic *Ó Bearáin* (see **Barnes** (iii)); (iv) an invented Jewish name perhaps based on the word for 'baron' in German, Polish or Russian (but popularly reinterpreted in Israel as being from Hebrew *Bar-On* 'Son of Strength') [John Barron, 1920–2004, British actor; Keith Barron, 1934–, British actor; Sacha Baron Cohen, 1971–, British comic actor, creator of the personas of Ali G, incongruous hip-hopster, and the Kazakhstani television reporter Borat]

Barr (i) 'person who lives by a barrier (e.g. a city gateway)' (from Middle English *barre* 'bar, obstruction'); (ii) 'person from Barr', the name of several places in southwestern Scotland and also in England ('hill'); (iii) *also* **Barre** 'person from Barre-en-Ouche or Barre-de-Semilly', northern France ('barrier, gateway'); (iv) 'person who makes (metal) bars'; (v) from a medieval nickname for a tall thin person (reminiscent of a bar); (vi) from Irish Gaelic *Ó Bairr*, a different form of *Ó Báire* (see **Barry** (vi)) [Roseanne Barr, 1952–, US comedian and comic actress]
— **Barr body** an inactive X chromosome present in the cells of females, used in a test to determine sex. It is named after the Canadian anatomist Murray L. Barr, 1908–95.

Barraclough, Barrowclough 'person from Barrowclough', Yorkshire ('ravine with groves of trees')

Barrett, Barret, Barratt, Barrat, Barritt (i) from the medieval personal name *Baret*, brought into England by the Normans but ultimately of Germanic origin (perhaps from *Bernwald*, literally 'bear-rule'); (ii) perhaps 'maker of caps' (from Old French *barette* 'cap, bonnet'); (iii) from a medieval nickname for a quarrelsome or untrustworthy person (from Middle English *barrette* 'strife, deception') [Elizabeth Barrett Browning (*née* Barrett), see **Browning**; John Barrett, 1931–, British tennis commentator; Ray Barrett, 1926–, Australian actor; Syd Barrett (original name Roger Keith Barrett), 1946–2006, British pop musician, member of Pink Floyd]
— **Barratt Developments plc** a British house-building company, founded in 1956 by Sir Lawrie Barratt, 1927–
— **The Barretts of Wimpole Street** a play (1930) by Rudolf Besier based on Elizabeth Barrett's (see above) plans to marry the poet Robert Browning, against her tyrannical father's wishes. In the 1934 film version, Charles Laughton played Barrett *père*.

Barrie see **Barry** (ii)

Barrington (i) 'person from Barrington', Cambridgeshire, Gloucestershire and Somerset (respectively 'Bāra's farmstead', 'estate associated with Beorn' and 'estate associated with Bāra'); (ii) from Irish Gaelic *Ó Bearáin* (see **Barnes** (iii)) [Jonah Barrington, 1941–, British squash player; Ken Barrington, 1930–81, English cricketer]

Barrow (i) 'person from Barrow', Cumbria ('promontory island'); (ii) 'person who lives by a grove', or 'person from Barrow', the name of various places in England (in either case from Old English *bearo* 'grove, wood'); (iii) 'person who lives by a hill or burial mound', or 'person from Barrow', Leicestershire and Somerset (in either case from Old English *beorge* 'at the hill or burial mound') [Clyde Barrow, 1909–34, US outlaw]

Barrows a different form of **Barrow** (ii–iii)

Barry (i) 'person from Barry', the name of various places in Wales ('hill'); (ii) *also* **Barrie** 'person from Barrie', the name of various places in Scotland ('hill'); (iii) 'person who lives in a suburb' (from Anglo-Norman *barri* '(suburb outside) the ramparts of a town'); (iv) a different form of **Parry**; (v) from Irish Gaelic *Ó Beargha* 'descendant of *Beargh*', a nickname meaning literally 'robber'. See also **Berry** (ii); (vi) from Irish Gaelic *Ó Báire* 'descendant of *Báire*', a shortened form of the personal names *Bairrfhionn* and *Fionnbharr*. See also **Barr** (vi) [Sir Charles Barry, 1795–1860, British architect; Sir James Barrie, 1860–1937, British dramatist and novelist; James Barry, 1741–1806, Irish-born British history painter; John Barry (original name John Barry Prendergast), 1933–, British composer of film scores; Philip Barry, 1896–1949, US dramatist]

Barstow a different form of **Bairstow** [Dame Josephine Barstow, 1940–, British mezzosoprano; Stan Barstow, 1928–, British novelist and dramatist]

Bart (i) from the male personal name *Bart*, a shortened form of **Bartholomew** and its variants; (ii) a different form of **Barth** (i) [Lionel Bart (original name Lionel Begleiter), 1930–99, British composer and playwright (the name *Bart* was based on *G & B Arts*, the name of a silk-screen printing firm begun by Begleiter and John Gorman)]

Barth (i) from a medieval German nickname for a bearded man (from Middle High German *bart* 'beard'); (ii) a different form of **Bart** (i); (iii) 'person from Barth', Pomerania [John Barth, 1930–, US novelist and scholar]

Bartholomew (i) from the male personal name *Bartholomew* (via Latin *Bartholomaeus* or *Bartolomaeus* from Aramaic *bar-Talmay* 'son of Talmay'). See also **Bate** (i); (ii) from Gaelic *Mac Pharthaláin* (see **McFarlane**) [Freddie Bartholomew (original name Frederick Llewellyn March; Bartholomew was his aunt's name), 1924–92, British child actor]

Bartlett from the medieval male personal name *Bartlet*, a pet-form of **Bartholomew**
— **Bartlett pear** the US name for what in Britain is usually called the Williams pear. It commemorates the US merchant Enoch Bartlett, 1779–1860, who marketed it.
— **Bartlett's Familiar Quotations** a US dictionary of quotations, compiled by the publisher John Bartlett, 1820–1905. Its first edition appeared in 1855.

Bartley 'person from Bartley or Bartley Green', Hampshire and West Midlands ('birch glade')

Barton (i) 'person from Barton', the name of numerous places in England ('barley farm'); (ii) an anglicization of Czech *Bartoň*, from the male personal name *Bartoň*, a pet-form of *Bartolomaeus* (see **Bartholomew** (i)) [Clara Barton, 1821–1912, US schoolteacher, founder of the American Red Cross; Sir Edmund Barton, 1849–1920, Australian politician, prime minister 1901–03; Elizabeth Barton, ?1506–34, English nun, known as the 'Maid of Kent'; John Barton, 1928–, British theatrical director]
— *Dick Barton – Special Agent* a BBC radio series (1946–51) featuring the crime-busting adventures of ex-commando Captain Richard Barton
— **Château Léoville-Barton** a wine-producing chateau in the St Julien commune of Bordeaux. It was acquired in 1822 by Hugh Barton, 1766–1854, an Irish wine-shipper based in Bordeaux, who also gave his name to the nearby **Château Langoa-Barton**.
— *Stand Up, Nigel Barton* a class-warfare television drama (1965) by Dennis Potter featuring the miner's son Nigel Barton as a fish out of water at Oxford. In the sequel, *Vote, Vote, Vote for Nigel Barton* (1965), Nigel stands as a Labour candidate in a safe Conservative seat.

Bartram a different form of **Bertram**

Baruch from the Hebrew male personal name *Baruch*, literally 'blessed, fortunate' [Bernard Baruch, 1870–1965, US economist and presidential adviser]

Barwell 'person from Barwell', Leicestershire ('stream where boars come')

Barwick 'person from Barwick', the name of various places in England ('barley farm')

Basham, Bassham perhaps 'person from Barsham', Norfolk and Suffolk ('Bār's homestead')

Bashford 'person from Basford', Cheshire, Nottinghamshire and Staffordshire (respectively 'Barkr's ford', 'Basa's ford' and 'Beorcol's ford')

Bashir a Muslim surname, from the Arabic personal name *Bashīr*, literally 'bringer of good news' [Martin Bashir, 1963–, British television journalist]

Basil from the male personal name *Basil* (ultimately from Greek *Basileios*, literally 'royal'). See also **Bazeley**

Basinger 'person from Bösingen', the name of two places in southern Germany [Kim Basinger, 1953–, US film actress]

Baskerville 'person from Boscherville', northern France ('settlement by a copse') [John Baskerville, 1706–75, British printer]
— **Baskerville** a typeface characterized by serifs. It was designed by John Baskerville (see above).
— *The Hound of the Baskervilles* a novel (1902) by Arthur Conan Doyle in which Sherlock Holmes, assisted by Dr Watson, pits his wits against a supposed homicidal supernatural hound that

haunts Dartmoor and is out to kill off members of the local landed family, the Baskervilles

Baskin 'son of *Baske*', a Yiddish female personal name (a pet-form of the Biblical name *Bath Seba*)
— **Baskin-Robbins** a US chain of ice-cream parlours founded in Glendale, California in 1945 by Burt Baskin, 1913–69, and Irv Robbins, 1918–

Bass (i) 'catcher or seller of fish', or from a medieval nickname for someone thought to resemble a fish (in either case from Middle English *bace* 'bass (the fish)'); (ii) from a medieval nickname for a short person (from Middle English *basse* 'low, short', from Old French); (iii) 'person from Bass', Aberdeenshire (perhaps 'forehead'); (iv) 'maker or player of bass viols' (from Polish, Ukrainian and Yiddish *bas* 'bass viol') [Alfie Bass, 1921–87, British actor]
— **Bass & Co. Brewery** a brewery established in Burton upon Trent in 1777 by William Bass, 1717–87. By the middle of the 19th century its bitter, India Pale Ale, etc. were the most widely consumed proprietary beers in Britain. Its red triangle was Britain's first registered trademark.
— **Bass Strait** the channel between Tasmania and mainland Australia. It was named after George Bass, 1771–after 1803, who was ship's doctor on Matthew Flinders's 1795–1800 voyage of discovery.

Bassett 'little **Bass** (ii)' [Bertie Bassett, a figure assembled out of liquorice allsorts, introduced in Britain in 1929 to market Bassett's Allsorts (see below)]
— **Bassett's Liquorice Allsorts** assorted varieties of liquorice-based sweet, introduced in 1899 by the confectionery firm established in 1842 by George Bassett

Bast from a German shortened form of the personal name **Sebastian** [Leonard Bast, the poor insurance clerk who is enamoured of Helen Schlegel in E.M. Forster's *Howards End* (1910)]

Bastable perhaps 'person from Barnstaple or Barstable Hall', Devon and Essex respectively ('post or pillar of the battleaxe')

Bastard from a medieval nickname for an illegitimate child [Alan B'Stard (a version of the name euphemized for comic effect), the unscupulous Conservative MP played by Rik Mayall in the ITV sitcom *The New Statesman* (1987–92)]

Bastedo perhaps 'person who lives in a fortified village' (from Old French *bastide* or Old Provençal *bastido* 'building, fortified village')

Batch see **Bach** (i)

Batchelder a different form of **Bachelor**

Batchelor, Batcheler see **Bachelor**

Bate (i) from the medieval male personal name *Bate* or *Batte*, a pet-form of **Bartholomew**. See also **Batt** (i), **Beatty**; (ii) 'boatman' (from northern Middle English *bate* 'boat')

Bateman 'servant of **Bate** (i)'
— *Bateman's* the name of the house in Burwash, Sussex, in which Rudyard Kipling lived from 1902. It was built in 1634 for the owner of a local forge called Bateman.

Bates 'son of **Bate** (i)' [Alan Bates, 1934–2003, British actor; H.E. Bates, 1905–74, British author; H.W. Bates, 1825–92, British naturalist; Jeremy Bates, 1962–, British tennis player; Norman Bates, psychotic proprietor of the Bates Motel in Robert Bloch's *Psycho* (1959) (played in the 1960 Hitchcock film by Anthony Perkins)]
— **Batesian mimicry** mimicry in which a harmless species is protected from predators by its resemblance to a species that is harmful or unpalatable to them. The name comes from H.W. Bates (see above).
— **Bates method** a system of eye-strengthening exercises devised in the 1920s by the US ophthalmologist William H. Bates, 1860–1931.

Bateson 'son of **Bate** (i)' [William Bateson, 1861–1926, British biologist]

Batey a different form of **Beatty**

Bath (i) 'person from Bath', Somerset ('place at the (Roman) baths'); (ii) a Scottish variant of **McBeth**

Bathgate 'person from Bathgate', West Lothian (probably 'boar wood')

Bathurst 'person from Bathurst', Sussex ('Bada's wooded hill')
— **Bathurst** a city in eastern central New South Wales, Australia. Founded in 1815, it was named in honour of Henry Bathurst (3rd Earl Bathurst), 1762–1834, at that time British colonial secretary.
— **Bathurst** a resort city in northeastern New Brunswick, Canada. It was named after Henry Bathurst (see above).
— **Bathurst** the former name of the capital of the Gambia, West Africa, so designated in 1816 in honour of Henry Bathurst (see above). The name was changed to Banjul in 1973.
— **Bathurst Island** the name of an island off the coast of Northern Territory, Australia, and also of an island, one of the Queen Elizabeth Islands, off the coast of Nunavut, northwestern Canada. It both cases the dedicatee was Henry Bathurst (see above).

Batista from the male personal name *Batista*, a Spanish, Catalan and Portuguese form of **Baptiste**

Batley 'person from Batley', Yorkshire ('Bata's glade')

Batsford 'person from Batsford', Gloucestershire ('Bæcci's hill slope')

Batson 'son of **Batt** (i–ii)'

Batt (i) a different form of **Bate** (i); (ii) perhaps from the Old English male personal name *Bata*; (iii) 'person who lives by a *batte*', a Middle English topographic term of unknown meaning; (iv) from the medieval German male personal name *Batt* (from Latin *Beatus*, literally 'blessed') [Mike Batt, 1949–, British musician and songwriter]

Batten a pet-form of **Batt** (i–ii) [Jean Batten, 1909–82, New Zealand aviator]

Battersby 'person from Battersby', Yorkshire ('Bothvarr's farmstead')

Battey see **Batty**

Battisford 'person from Battisford', Suffolk ('Bætti's ford')

Battle 'person from Battle', a name given to a number of places in England (and northern France) where a battle had taken place (notably in Sussex, at the site of the battle of Hastings) [Kathleen Battle, 1948–, US opera singer]

Battrick a different form of **Betteridge**

Batty, Battey a pet-form of **Batt** (i–ii) [Nora Batty, redoubtable matron (played by Kathy Staff) in the BBC television sitcom *Last of the Summer Wine* (1973–)]

Bauch from a medieval German nickname for a fat or greedy person (from Middle High German *būch* 'belly')

Bauer, Baur 'peasant', or from a medieval German nickname meaning roughly 'neighbour' (in either case from Middle High German and Middle Low German *būr* 'person who lives in a *būr* (a small dwelling)') [Jack Bauer, US special agent (played by Kiefer Sutherland) who is the main character in the US television series *24* (2001–)]

Baugh from a Welsh nickname for a small or short person (from Welsh *bach* 'small')

Baughan, Baughn 'little **Baugh**'. See also **Baffin**

Baulch see **Balch**

Baum (i) 'person who lives by a (prominent, noticeable or remarkable) tree', or from a medieval German nickname for a tall person (in either case from Middle High German *boum* 'tree'), or an invented Jewish name, based on German *Baum* 'tree'; (ii) from a shortened form of any of a range of invented German-based Jewish compound names with *-baum* 'tree' as their second element (e.g. *Feigenbaum*, literally 'fig tree') [L. Frank Baum, 1856–1919, US novelist, author of *The Wonderful Wizard of Oz* (1900)]

Baumgarten 'person who owns, lives near or works in an orchard' (from Middle High German *boumgarte* 'orchard')

Baumgartner a different form of **Baumgarten**

Baur see **Bauer**

Baverstock 'person from Baverstock', Wiltshire ('Babba's outlying farmstead')

Bawden a different form of **Baldwin** (i) [Edward Bawden, 1903–89, British painter; Nina Bawden, 1925–, British novelist]

Bawn a different form of **Bain** (i)

Bax, Backs 'son of **Back** (iv)' [Sir Arnold Bax, 1883–1953, British composer; Clifford Bax, 1886–1962, British playwright, poet and journalist, brother of Arnold]

Baxendale probably 'person from Baxenden', Lancashire ('bakestone valley'), with a substitution of *-dale* for *-den* 'valley'

Baxter 'baker' (from Old English *bæcestre* '(female) baker') [Anne Baxter, 1923–85, US actress; Glenn Baxter, 1944–, British artist; Raymond Baxter, 1922–2006, British television presenter and commentator; Richard Baxter, 1615–91, English Puritan minister and author; Stanley Baxter, 1926–, British comedian and impersonator]

— **Baxters** a British food production company that had its beginnings in a grocery shop opened by George Baxter in Fochabers, Scotland, in 1868. It is best known for its soups and jams.

Bay (i) from the medieval personal name *Baye* (from Old English *Bēaga* (male) and *Bēage* (female)); (ii) from a medieval nickname for someone with auburn hair (from Middle English *bay* 'reddish brown', from Old French)

Bayes 'son of **Bay** (i)'
— **Bayes' theorem** a theorem of conditional probability that allows estimates of probability to be continually revised based on observations of occurrences of events. It is named after its formulator, the British mathematician Thomas Bayes, 1702–61.

Bayfield 'person from Bayfield', Norfolk ('Bǣga's area of open land')

Bayley, Bayly see **Bailey**

Bayliss, Baylis, Bayless 'court official, bailiff' (from Middle English *bailis*, from Old French *baillis* – see also **Bailey**) [Lilian Baylis, 1874–1937, British theatre manager; Trevor Baylis, 1937–, British inventor; Sir William Bayliss, 1860–1924, British physiologist]

Bayne, Baynes see **Bain**, **Baines**

Bazeley, Bazley from the medieval female personal name *Basillie*, the feminine form of **Basil**

Beach, Beech (i) 'person who lives by a beech tree or beech wood'; (ii) 'person who lives by a stream' (from Middle English *beche* 'stream') [Amy Beach (*née* Cheney), 1867–1944, US composer and pianist]

Beacham see **Beauchamp**
Beacher see **Beecher**
Beadle, Beadel, Beadell, Beedle, Bedell 'beadle (a medieval court official)'. See also **Biddle** [George Wells Beadle, 1903–89, US geneticist; Jeremy Beadle, 1948–, British television presenter]

Beadles 'son of **Beadle**'
Beake perhaps from a medieval nickname for someone with a prominent nose. See also **Beck** (iii)

Beal, Beale, Beall (i) 'person from Beal', Northumberland and Yorkshire (respectively 'hill where bees are kept' and 'nook of land in a river bend'); (ii) from a medieval nickname for a good-looking person (from Old French *bel* 'beautiful') [Dorothea Beale, 1831–1906, British schoolmistress and suffragette, headmistress of Cheltenham Ladies' College; Simon Russell Beale, 1961–, British actor]

Beam (i) 'person who lives by a marker post or by a wooden footbridge' (from Middle English *beme* 'beam, post'); (ii) 'weaver' (from Middle English *beme* 'beam of a loom'); (iii) an anglicization of German **Baum** or **Boehm**
— **Jim Beam** the proprietary name of a make of Kentucky bourbon whiskey, first produced in 1795 by Jacob Beam, 1770–1834. It commemorates Jacob's descendant, Colonel James B. Beam, 1864–1947.

Beaman see **Beeman**
Beamish 'person from Beaumais or Beaumetz', the name of various places in northern France ('beautiful dwelling') [Sally Beamish, 1956–, British composer; Sir Tufton Beamish (Lord Chelwood), 1917–89, British Conservative politician]

Beamon see **Beeman**
Bean, Beane (i) 'grower or seller of beans'; (ii) from a medieval nickname for an agreeable or congenial person (from Middle English *bene* 'friendly'); (iii) from Gaelic *Beathán* (see **McBean**) [Sean Bean (original name Shaun Bean), 1959–, British actor]
— **Mr Bean** the gormless accident-prone protagonist (played by Rowan Atkinson) of the ITV comedy series *Mr Bean* (1990–95) and of subsequent feature films

Bear (i) from a medieval nickname for someone thought to resemble a bear; (ii) *also* **Beare** 'person from Bear or Beare', the name of various places in southwestern England (mostly '(place) by the grove or wood'). See also **Beer** (i)

Bearce see **Bierce**
Beard (i) from a medieval nickname for a bearded man; (ii) 'person from Beard', Derbyshire ('edge, bank')

Beardmore probably 'person from Beardmore', an unidentified place in England, possibly in Staffordshire ('Beard's marsh')
— **Beardmore Glacier** a glacier in Antarctica, at over 160 km/100 miles in length the largest in the world. It was named in honour of the Scottish industrialist Sir William Beardmore, 1856–1936, who sponsored Ernest Shackleton's 1907 Antarctic expedition.

Beardsley probably 'person from Beardsley', an unidentified place in England, probably in Nottinghamshire ('Beard's glade') [Aubrey Beardsley, 1872–98, British illustrator; Peter Beardsley, 1961–, English footballer]

Beare see **Bear** (ii)
Bearse see **Bierce**
Beasley, Beazley, Beesley 'person from Beesley', Lancashire (perhaps 'glade where rough grass grows')
— **Mitchell Beazley** see **Mitchell**

Beaston see **Beeston**
Beaton, Beeton (i) from the medieval personal name *Beton* or *Beaton*, based on a shortened form of the names **Bartholomew** and *Beatrice*; (ii) 'person from Béthune', Picardy (probably 'Betto's settlement') [Sir Cecil Beaton, 1904–80, British photographer and designer; Isabella Beeton ('Mrs Beeton'; *née* Mayson), 1836–65, British cookery writer]

Beatty, Beattie, Beaty (i) from the personal name *Beattie*, a Scottish pet-form of **Bartholomew**; (ii) from Gaelic *Mac Bhiadhtaigh* (see **McVitie**) [David Beatty (1st Earl Beatty), 1871–1936, British admiral; Robert Beatty, 1909–92, Canadian actor; Warren Beatty (original name Henry Warren Beaty), 1937–, US actor, director and producer]

Beauchamp, Beecham, Beacham 'person from Beauchamp', the name of various places in northern France ('beautiful field'). The name is pronounced (as it is often spelled) 'beecham'. [Stephanie Beacham, 1947–, British actress; Sir Thomas Beecham, 1879–1961, British conductor]
— **Beecham** a British pharmaceutical company founded in 1859 by the Wigan chemist Thomas Beecham (grandfather of Sir Thomas; see above), 1820–1907. In 1989 it combined with SmithKline Beckman to become SmithKline Beecham (see **Smith**).
— **Beecham's Pills** a patent laxative tablet containing aloes, ginger and soap, first produced in 1850 by Thomas Beecham (see above), and immensely popular and (commercially) successful in the late 19th and early 20th centuries

Beauclerk from a Norman nickname for either a handsome priest or someone with attractive hand-writing (from Old French *beu clerc* 'fair clerk')

Beaufort 'person from Beaufort', the name of various places in northern France ('beautiful fortress'). See also **Buford** [Beaufort, the name of a powerful English family of the 14th and 15th centuries, descended (originally illegitimately) from John of Gaunt; Sir Francis Beaufort, 1774–1857, Irish-born British admiral and hydrographer; Henry Beaufort, ?1374–1447, English cardinal, son of John of Gaunt and half-brother of Henry IV; Margaret Beaufort, 1443–1509, countess of Richmond, mother of Henry VII]
— **Beaufort scale** an international scale of wind speeds indicated by numbers ranging from 0 for calm to 12 for hurricane. It was devised in 1805 by Sir Francis Beaufort (see above).
— **Beaufort Sea** a section of the Arctic Ocean northwest of Canada and north of Alaska. It was named in honour of Sir Francis Beaufort (see above).
— **Bristol Beaufort** a British torpedo bomber of the Second World War, developed from the Bristol Blenheim. It first flew in 1938.
— **Yale of Beaufort** a mythical animal resembling an antelope with a pair of horns and a pair of tusks, that is part of the armorial bearings of the Beaufort family. It is one of the Queen's Beasts.

Beaulieu 'person from Beaulieu', the name of numerous places in northern France and also of a village (pronounced 'byooly') in Hampshire ('beautiful place'). See also **Bewley**

Beaumont 'person from Beaumont', the name of numerous places in northern France and also of villages in Cumbria, Essex and Lancashire ('beautiful hill'). See also **Beeman, Belmont** [Bill Beaumont, 1952–, English rugby player; Sir Francis Beaumont, 1584–1616, English dramatist; Hugh ('Binkie') Beaumont, 1908–73, British theatre manager; William Beaumont, 1785–1853, US physician]

Beauregard (i) 'person from Beauregard', the name of numerous places in France ('fine view'); (ii) from a medieval nickname for an attractive or handsome person (from Old French *beu regard* 'beautiful aspect')

Beaver, Beever, Beevor, Bever (i) 'person from Beauvoir or Belvoir', the name of numerous places in France and also (*Belvoir*) of a village in Leicestershire ('fine view'); (ii) from a medieval nickname for someone thought to resemble a beaver (perhaps in industriousness) [Anthony Beevor, 1946–, British historian and author]

Beavin, Beavins different forms of **Bevin** (i), **Bevins**

Beavis, Beevis, Bevis (i) 'person from Beauvais', the name of various places in northern France ('fine view'); (ii) 'person from Béthune', Picardy (probably 'Betto's settlement'). See also **Bovis**

Beazley see **Beasley**

Bebb perhaps a different form of **Babb**

Bebbington 'person from Bebington', Cheshire ('estate associated with Bebba or Bebbe')

Beck (i) 'person who lives by a stream' (from northern Middle English *bekke* 'stream'); (ii) 'person from Bec', the name of various places in northern France ('stream'); (iii) a different form of **Beake**. See also **Beckett** (i); (iv) 'person who makes, sells or uses pickaxes' (from Old English *becca* 'pickaxe, mattock'); (v) 'baker' (from German dialect *Beck* and Western Yiddish *beh* 'baker') [Harry Beck, 1903–74, British engineering draughtsman, designer of the London Underground map]
— **Beckton** a district of the East London borough of Newham, named in the 1860s after Simon Adams Beck, a governor of the local Gas, Light and Coke Company

Becker (i) 'baker (of bread or bricks)' (from a derivative of German *backen* 'to bake'); (ii) 'person who makes, sells or uses pickaxes' (from a derivative of Old English *becca* – see **Beck** (iv)) [Roger Becker, 1934–, British tennis player]

Beckett, Becket (i) 'little **Beck** (iii)'; (ii) 'person from Beckett', Berkshire and Devon (respectively 'beehive' and 'Bicca's cottage') [Margaret Beckett (*née* Jackson), 1943–, British Labour politician; Samuel Beckett, 1906–89, Irish playwright, novelist and poet; St Thomas Becket, ?1118–70, English churchman, martyr and saint]

Beckford 'person from Beckford', Gloucestershire ('Becca's ford') [William Beckford, 1760–1844, British writer and art collector]

Beckham 'person from Beckham', Norfolk ('Becca's homestead') [David Beckham, 1975–, English footballer; Victoria Beckham (*née* Adams), 1974–, British pop singer ('Posh Spice' of the Spice Girls), wife of David]

Beckley 'person from Beckley', Kent, Oxfordshire and Sussex ('Becca's glade')

Beckwith 'person from Beckwith', Yorkshire ('beech wood') [Reginald Beckwith, 1908–65, British actor]

Beddoe, Beddow from the Welsh male personal name *Bedo*, a pet-form of **Meredith**

Beddoes, Beddows, Beddowes 'son of **Beddoe**' [Thomas Lovell Beddoes, 1803–49, British poet]

Bedell see **Beadle**

Bedford 'person from Bedford', Bedfordshire and Lancashire ('Bēda's ford') [David Bedford, 1937–, British composer; David Bedford, 1949–, British athlete; Steuart Bedford, 1939–, British conductor; Sybille Bedford (*née* von Schoenbeck), 1911–2006, German-born British writer]

Bedi a Hindu and Sikh surname, literally 'one who knows the Vedas (ancient Hindu hymns)'

Bedser 'person from Bedser', an unidentified place, probably in Sussex [Sir Alec Bedser, 1918–, English cricketer; Eric Bedser, 1918–2006, English cricketer, twin brother of Alec]

Bedwell a different form of **Bidwell**

Bee (i) 'beekeeper'; (ii) from a medieval nickname for someone thought to resemble a bee, especially in industriousness

Beebe probably a different form of **Beeby** [Charles William Beebe, 1877–1962, US explorer and naturalist]

Beeby 'person from Beeby', Leicestershire ('farmstead where bees are kept'). See also **Bybee**

Beech see **Beach**

Beecham see **Beauchamp**

Beecher, Beacher, Becher different forms of **Beach** [Henry Ward Beecher, 1813–87, US Congregational preacher and author, brother of Harriet Beecher Stowe (see **Stow**)]
— **Becher's Brook** a jump on the Grand National course at Aintree, Liverpool (number 6 and number 22 as the race is currently run), notorious for unseating jockeys. It is named after Martin Becher ('Captain Becher'), 1797–1864, who fell at the fence when the race was first run in 1839.

Beeching a different form of **Beach** [Richard Beeching (Lord Beeching; 'Dr Beeching'), 1913–85, British engineer and businessman, chairman of British Railways 1961–65]
— **Beeching Axe** a polemical term for the extensive reductions to the British railway network introduced by Richard Beeching (see above) in the early 1960s
— **Oh Doctor Beeching!** a BBC television sitcom (1996–97) set in a rural English railway station threatened by the Beeching Axe

Beeman, Beaman, Beamon (i) a different form of **Beaumont**; (ii) 'beekeeper' [Bob Beamon, 1946–, US long jumper]

Beer (i) *also* **Beere** *or* **Bere** 'person from Beer, Beere or Bere', the name of various places in southwestern England (mostly '(place) by the grove or wood'). See also **Bear** (ii); (ii) from a medieval German and Dutch nickname for someone thought to resemble a bear (from Middle Low German *bāre* and Middle Dutch *bēre* 'bear') [Patricia Beer, 1924–99, British poet]

Beery perhaps a different form of the surname *O'Berry*, from Irish Gaelic *Ó Béara* 'descendant of *Béara*', a personal name of unknown origin [Wallace Beery, 1885–1949, US actor]

Beesley see **Beasley**

Beeson a different form of **Beeston**

Beeston, Beaston 'person from Beeston', the name of various places in England (mostly 'farmstead where rough grass grows')

Beetham 'person from Beetham', Cumbria ('place by the embankments')

Beeton see **Beaton**

Beever, Beevor see **Beaver**

Beevis see **Beavis**

Begbie 'person from Begbie', East Lothian. See also **Bagby** (ii)

Begg from a medieval Scottish nickname for a diminutive person (from Gaelic *beag* 'small'). See also **Bigg**

Beggs 'son of **Begg**'. See also **Biggs**

Begley from Irish Gaelic *Ó Beaglaoich* 'descendant of *Beaglaoch*', a personal name meaning literally 'small hero' [Ed Begley, 1901–70, US actor; Ed Begley, Jr., 1949–, US actor, son of Ed]

Begum from a Muslim title of honour for a married or widowed woman (ultimately from East Turkic *begum* 'my mistress')

Behan from Irish Gaelic *Ó Beachain* 'descendant of *Beachán*', a personal name meaning literally 'little bee' [Brendan Behan, 1923–64, Irish playwright]

Beharry from the final element of any of a range of Hindu personal names based on Sanskrit *vihārī* 'beautiful'

Behn from the German male personal name *Behn*, a shortened form of **Bernhard** [Aphra Behn, 1640–89, English novelist and dramatist]

Behr see **Baer**

Belasco from the Basque personal name *Belasco*, literally 'little raven' [David Belasco, 1853–1931, US theatre manager and dramatist]

Belcher (i) from a medieval nickname for someone of an attractive appearance or disposition (from Old French *bel chere* 'beautiful face, beautiful disposition'); (ii) from a medieval nickname for someone much given to belching [Muriel Belcher, 1908–78, founder and proprietor of the Colony Room Club, Soho]

Belisha a different form of the Yiddish surname *Belich*, literally 'person from Belitsa', a place in western Belarus [Leslie Hore-Belisha (Lord Hore-Belisha), 1893–1957, British National Liberal politician]
— **Belisha beacon** a sign at each end of a zebra crossing consisting of an amber ball with a flashing light inside it on top of a black-and-white striped pole. It is named after Leslie Hore-Belisha (see above), the British minister of transport who introduced it in 1934.

Bell (i) 'person who lives in a house at the sign of a bell or within the sound of a particular bell'; (ii) 'ringer or maker of bells'; (iii) from the medieval female personal name *Bel*, a shortened form of *Isobel*; (iv) from the medieval male personal name *Bel* (from Old French *bel* 'handsome'); (v) from Scottish Gaelic *Mac Giolla Mhaoil* 'son of the follower of the devotee' [Acton Bell, pen-name of

Anne Brontë; Alexander Graham Bell, 1847–1922, Scottish-born US scientist and inventor, father and patentee (1876) of the telephone; Clive Bell, 1881–1962, British art critic; Colin Bell, 1946–, English footballer; Currer Bell, pen-name of Charlotte Brontë; Ellis Bell, pen-name of Emily Brontë; Gertrude Bell, 1868–1926, British archaeologist and traveller; Joshua Bell, 1967–, US violinist; Martin Bell, 1938–, British journalist and MP; Steve Bell, 1951–, British cartoonist; Tim Bell (Lord Bell), 1941–, British public-relations consultant; Tom Bell, 1932–2006, British actor; Vanessa Bell (née Stephen), 1879–1961, British painter and designer, wife of Clive]

• People with the surname Bell are traditionally given the nickname 'Ding-Dong' or 'Dinger', or sometimes 'Daisy' (from the heroine of a music-hall song)

— **Bell Helicopter** a US company (now Bell Helicopter Textron) manufacturing helicopters and rotors. It was established in 1935 by Larry Bell, 1894–1956.

— **Bell's palsy** the inability to move the muscles on one side of the face, causing a distorted facial expression. It is named after the Scottish anatomist Sir Charles Bell, 1774–1842.

— **Bell Telephone Co.** a US telephone company founded in 1878 by Gardiner Greene Hubbard, father-in-law of Alexander Graham Bell (see above). It became part of American Telephone & Telegraph, Inc. (AT&T), which continued (from 1921) to use the trademark **Bell System**.

— **Ma Bell** a colloquial US name for the Bell Telephone Company (see above)

Bellamy from a medieval nickname for someone considered a good friend or (ironically) a faithless friend (from Old French bel ami 'fine friend') [David Bellamy, 1933–, British botanist and conservationist]

Bellew 'person from Belleu or Belleau', the name of various places in northern France (respectively 'beautiful place' and 'beautiful water'). See also **Bellow** (i)

Bellinger, Bellenger different forms of **Beringer**

Bellingham 'person from Bellingham', Greater London and Northumberland (respectively 'Bera's people's homestead' and 'homestead of the dwellers at the bell hill')

Bellman (i) 'bell-ringer'; (ii) an anglicization of German Bellmann, literally 'person from Bell, Belle or Bellen', the name of various places in Germany

Belloc, Bellock 'person from Belloc', the name of various places in Normandy ('beautiful place') [Hilaire Belloc, 1870–1953, French-born British poet; Marie Adelaide Belloc Lowndes (née Belloc; pen-name Belloc Lowndes), 1868–1947, French-born British novelist, sister of Hilaire]

Bellow (i) a different form of **Bellew** or of **Beloff**; (ii) 'bellows-maker' or 'person who pumps bellows' [Saul Bellow, 1915–2005, Canadian-born US writer]

Bellows a different form of **Bellow**

Belmont a different form of **Beaumont**

Beloff 'son of Bel', from a medieval Jewish nickname based on Russian bely 'white, pale' [Max Beloff (Lord Beloff), 1913–99, British historian; Nora Beloff, 1919–97, British journalist]

Belton 'person from Belton', the name of several places in England (variously 'farmstead in a glade' or 'farmstead on dry ground in a marsh')

Benbow 'archer' (from Middle English benden 'to bend' + bowe 'bow') [John Benbow, 1653–1702, English admiral]

Benchley probably 'person from Benchley', an unidentified place in England (the second syllable means 'glade') [Peter Benchley, 1940–2006, US author; Robert Benchley, 1889–1945, US humorist]

Bendall a different form of **Bentall**

Bender (i) 'maker of barrels, cooper' (from a shortened form of the German name Fassbender, literally 'cooper'); (ii) probably 'archer' (from a specific application of bender 'one who bends (i.e. a bow)')

Bendick a Scottish variant of **Benedict**

Bendix from a reduced German and Jewish form of Latin Benedictus (see **Benedict**) [William Bendix, 1906–64, US actor]

— **Bendix** the proprietary name of a make of washing machines, originally developed by the US inventor and industrialist Vincent Bendix, 1882–1945

Benedict from the male personal name Benedict (from Latin Benedictus, literally 'blessed'). See also **Bennett, Bentinck, Betjeman**

Benfield a different form of **Banfield** (i)

Benham 'person from Benham', Berkshire ('Benna's water meadow'), or 'person from Benholm', Angus (a name of unexplained meaning)

Benjamin from the male personal name Benjamin, from Hebrew Binyamin, literally 'son of the south (i.e. of the right-hand side)' [Floella Benjamin, 1949–, British actress; George Benjamin, 1960–, British composer]

Benn from the medieval male personal name Benne, partly a shortened form of **Benedict** and partly from Old Norse Bjorn, literally 'bearcub', hence 'warrior'. See also **Benney, Benskin, Benson** [Sir Ernest Benn, 1875–1954, British publisher; Hilary Benn, 1953–, British Labour politician, son of Tony; Tony Benn (original name Anthony Wedgwood Benn), 1925–, British Labour politician]

— **Bennite** a supporter of Tony Benn (see above) or his left-wing policies

— **Mr Benn** a BBC television children's entertainment series, 1971–72, created by David McKee and centred on Mr Benn, an escapist businessman who in each episode had an adventure in a guise obtained from his local fancy-dress shop

Bennett, Bennet from the medieval male personal name Bennet (from Beneit, the Old French form of Latin Benedictus – see **Benedict**) [Alan Bennett,

1934–, British playwright and actor; Arnold Bennett, 1867–1931, British novelist; Hywel Bennett, 1944–, British actor; James Gordon Bennett, 1795–1872, Scottish-born US newspaper proprietor and editor, founder (1835) of the *New York Herald*; James Gordon Bennett, 1841–1918, US newspaper proprietor and editor, son of James; Jill Bennett, 1931–90, British actress; Richard Bedford Bennett (1st Viscount Bennett), 1870–1947, Canadian Conservative politician and business executive, prime minister 1930–35; Sir Richard Rodney Bennett, 1936–, British composer; Sir William Sterndale Bennett, 1816–75, British pianist, conductor and composer]

— **Bennettites** the name of a genus of fossil plants with seeds carried on long stalks, honouring the British botanist John Joseph Bennett, 1801–76

— **Gordon Bennett** a colloquial exclamation of astonishment or exasperation, first recorded in 1967 but current well before then. It probably invokes the name of the younger James Gordon Bennett (see above), after whom several motor and aeronautical events were named and whose colourful lifestyle became somewhat notorious.

Benney, Benny from a pet-form of the male personal name *Benne* (see **Benn**) [Jack Benny (original name Benjamin Kubelsky), 1894–1974, US comedian]

Benskin from a pet-form of the male personal name *Benne* (see **Benn**)

Benson (i) 'person from Benson', Oxfordshire ('estate associated with Benesa'); (ii) 'son of *Benne*' (see **Benn**), or 'son of *Bien*', a Jewish pet-form of **Benjamin** [A.C. Benson, 1862–1925, British author; E.F. Benson, 1867–1940, British author, brother of A.C.; Sir Frank Benson, 1858–1939, British actor-manager; Ivy Benson, 1913–93, British bandleader]

— **Benson and Hedges** a British brand of cigarettes, established in 1873 by Richard Benson and William Hedges

Bentall, Benthall 'person from Benthall', Shropshire ('corner of land where rough grass grows'). See also **Bendall**

— **Bentalls** a department store in Kingston upon Thames, Greater London, founded (as a draper's shop) in 1867 by Frank Bentall, 1843–1923

Bentham 'person from Bentham', the name of various places in England ('homestead where rough grass grows') [Jeremy Bentham, 1748–1832, British philosopher, jurist and social reformer]

— **Benthamism** the utilitarian philosophy of Jeremy Bentham, which argues that the highest good is the happiness of the greatest number

— **Benthamite** (an advocate or follower) of Benthamism

Bentinck 'son of *Bent*', a Dutch contracted form of the Latin personal name *Benedictus* (see **Benedict**) [William Henry Cavendish Bentinck (3rd duke of Portland), 1738–1809, British statesman, prime minister 1783, 1807–09; Lord William Bentinck, 1774–1839, British administrator, first governor general of India, 1828–35, son of William Henry]

Bentley 'person from Bentley', the name of numerous places in England ('glade where rough grass grows') [Derek Bentley, 1933–53, British teenager hanged for a murder he did not commit; Dick Bentley (original name Charles Walter Bentley), 1907–95, Australian comedian and actor; Edmund Clerihew Bentley, 1875–1956, British writer, inventor of the humorous verse form known as a 'clerihew'; Richard Bentley, 1662–1742, English scholar]

— **Bentley** a British maker of upmarket luxury cars, established in 1919 by Walter Owen Bentley, 1888–1971. It is now part of the Volkswagen Group.

— **Bentley's Miscellany** a British periodical (1837–69) begun by Richard Bentley, 1794–1871, which included contributions by most of the major fiction writers of the time

Benton 'person from Benton', Northumberland ('farmstead where beans are grown' or 'settlement where rough grass grows') [Thomas Hart Benton, 1889–1975, US painter of rural life]

Berberian 'son of a barber', Armenian, from a derivative of *berber* 'barber', from Turkish [Cathy Berberian, 1925–83, US singer]

Bere see **Beer** (i)

Berenson 'son of *Ber*', a Yiddish male personal name meaning literally 'bear' [Bernard Berenson (original name Bernard Valvrojenski), 1865–1959, Lithuanian-born US art critic]

Beresford, Berisford 'person from Beresford', Staffordshire ('Beofor's ford') [Bruce Beresford, 1940–, Australian film director]

Berg (i) 'person who lives at a farmstead named with Old Norse *bjarg* "hill, mountain"'; (ii) 'person who lives on or near a hill or mountain' (from Middle High German *berc* 'hill, mountain'); (iii) an invented Jewish name based on German *Berg* 'mountain' [Paul Berg, 1926–, US molecular biologist]

Berger (i) a different form of **Berg**; (ii) 'shepherd' (from Old French *bergier*) [John Berger, 1926–, British novelist and art critic]

Bergin from Irish Gaelic *Ó Beirgin* or *Ó Meirgin*, alterations of *Ó hAimheirgin* 'descendant of *Aimheirgin*', a personal name perhaps meaning literally 'wonderful birth'. See also **Berrigan**

Bergman, Bergmann different forms of **Berg** (i–ii) [Ingrid Bergman, 1915–82, Swedish-born US film actress]

Beringer, Berringer from the Old French personal name *Berenger*, of Germanic origin and meaning literally 'bear-spear'. See also **Bellinger**

Berisford see **Beresford**

Berkeley, Berkley see **Barclay**

Berkoff 'son of *Berke*', a pet-form of the Yiddish male personal name *Ber* (see **Berenson**) [Steven Berkoff (father's original surname Berkovitch), 1937–, British actor, director and dramatist]

Berlin 'person from Berlin', Germany [Irving Berlin (original name Israel Baline), 1888–1989, Russian-born US songwriter; Sir Isaiah Berlin, 1909–97, Latvian-born British philosopher and historian]

Berliner a different form of **Berlin**

Berman (i) 'porter' (from Middle English *berman*, literally 'carry-man'); (ii) perhaps from a medieval male personal name *Berman* (from Old English *Beornmund*, literally 'warrior-protection'); (iii) *also* **Bermann** from the Yiddish male personal name *Berman*, literally 'bear man'

Bermingham see **Birmingham**

Bernard (i) from the male personal name *Bernard* (from Germanic **Bernhard**); (ii) an anglicization of **Bernhard**. See also **Barnard**, **Barnett**, **Barney**, **Barnhart**

Berner (i) from the Norman male personal name *Bernier*, of Germanic origin and meaning literally 'bear-army'; (ii) 'lime-burner' or 'charcoal-burner'; (iii) 'keeper of hounds' (from Old Northern French *bernier* or *berner*, a derivative of *bren* 'bran' (which was fed to the hounds)); (iv) 'person who works in or lives by a barn' (from a derivative of Middle English *bern* 'barn'). See also **Brenner** (ii)

Berners 'son of **Berner** (i)' [Sir Tim Berners-Lee, 1955–, British computer scientist and Internet pioneer]

Bernett (i) see **Burnett**; (ii) from a French pet-form of the personal name **Bernard**

Bernhard, **Bernhardt** from the German, Dutch and Scandinavian forms of the Germanic male personal name *Bernhard*, literally 'bear-brave' or 'bear-strong'. See also **Barnhart**, **Bernard**

Bernstein (i) 'person from Bernstein', the name of two places in Germany; (ii) an invented Jewish surname based on German *Bernstein* 'amber' [Leonard Bernstein, 1918–90, US composer, conductor and pianist; Sidney Bernstein (Lord Bernstein), 1899–1993, British film and television executive]

Berridge a different form of **Beveridge**

Berrigan a different form of **Bergin**

Berriman see **Berryman**

Berry (i) see **Bury**; (ii) a different form of **Barry** (v); (iii) 'person from Berry', former province of central France (probably 'Boirius's or Barius's settlement') [Chuck Berry (original name Charles Edward Berry), 1926–, US singer/songwriter; Halle Berry, 1966–, US actress]
— **Berry Bros. and Rudd** a firm of London wine merchants with premises in St James's Street. It was founded in 1698.

Berryman, **Berriman** 'person who lives in a fortified place' (from Old English *byrig* 'at the stronghold' + *man*) [John Berryman (original name John Smith; Berryman was his stepfather's surname), 1914–72, US poet, writer and critic]

Bertram from the male personal name *Bertram*, brought into England by the Normans but ultimately of Germanic origin and meaning literally 'bright raven, illustrious raven'. See also **Bartram**, **Bertrand**

Bertrand a different form of **Bertram**

Besant 'maker of coins', or from a medieval nickname for a wealthy person (in either case from Middle English *besant*, the name of a type of gold coin) [Annie Besant (*née* Wood), 1847–1933, British theosophist and political campaigner; Sir Walter Besant, 1836–1901, British novelist and social reformer]

Bessell perhaps a different form of **Bissell**

Bessemer 'maker of brooms' (from a derivative of Middle English *besem* 'broom') [Sir Henry Bessemer, 1813–98, British metallurgist]
— **Bessemer process** a largely obsolete method for making steel from impure iron by forcing air through the molten metal in a specialized furnace called a **Bessemer converter**. It is named after Sir Henry Bessemer (see above), who invented it in 1855.

Best, Beste (i) 'person who looks after animals, herdsman' (from Middle English *beste* 'animal'); (ii) from a medieval nickname for an uncouth person (from Middle English *beste* 'animal'); (iii) 'person from Besten', the name of various places in Germany (perhaps 'place with poor soil'); (iv) 'person who lives by the Beste', a river in Germany [Charles H. Best, 1899–1978, US physiologist; George Best, 1946–2005, Northern Irish footballer; Margot Beste-Chetwynde (Lady Metroland), a character in several of Evelyn Waugh's novels]

Beswick, **Bestwick** 'person from Beswick', Lancashire and Yorkshire (respectively perhaps 'Bēac's dairy farm' and 'Bøsi's or Bessi's dairy farm'). The standard pronunciation is 'bezzik'.

Bethel, Bethell (i) from the medieval female personal name *Bethell*, a pet-form of *Beth*, itself a shortening of *Elizabeth*; (ii) from Welsh *ap Ithel* 'son of *Ithael*', a male personal name meaning literally 'bounteous lord'. See also **Bissell** (iii)

Bethune 'person from Béthune', northeastern France (probably 'Betto's settlement') [Mary McLeod Bethune, 1875–1955, US civil-rights activist]

Betjeman from Dutch, from *Betje*, a pet-form of *Benedict* + *man* [Sir John Betjeman, 1906–84, British poet]

Bett from the medieval personal name *Bett*, a pet-form of **Bartholomew**, *Beatrice* and *Elizabeth*. See also **Betts**

Bettany perhaps from *betony*, the name of a plant of the mint family, formerly used in medicines

Bettencourt 'person from Bettencourt', the name (variously spelled) of several places in France ('Betto's farm')

Betteridge, **Bettridge** from the Old English male personal name *Beaduric*, literally 'battle-power'. See also **Battrick**

Betterton 'person from Betterton', Berkshire ('settlement associated with Bēthere') [Thomas Betterton, ?1635–1710, English actor]

Betts 'son of **Bett**'

Betty from a pet-form of **Bett** [William Betty, 1791–1874, British child actor]

Bevan from Welsh *ap Iefan* 'son of *Iefan*' (see **Evans**). See also **Bevin** [Aneurin ('Nye') Bevan, 1897–1960, British Labour politician]

Bever see **Beaver**

Beveridge, Beverage apparently from a medieval nickname based on Middle English *beverage* 'drink', perhaps denoting someone who was in the habit of accepting a drink to seal a bargain and then failing to keep it. See also **Berridge** [William Beveridge (Lord Beveridge), 1879–1963, British economist, writer and academic]
— **Beveridge Report** the name usually given to the *Report on Social Insurance and Allied Services* (1942) by William Beveridge (see above), generally regarded as a blueprint for the post-Second World War British welfare state

Beverley, Beverly 'person from Beverley', Yorkshire ('beaver lodge')

Bevin (i) from a medieval nickname for someone who overindulged in wine (from Old French *beivre* 'to drink' + *vin* 'wine'); (ii) a different form of **Bevan**. See also **Beavin** [Ernest Bevin, 1881–1951, British trade-union leader and Labour politician]
— **Bevin boy** a name given during the Second World War to a young man of age for military service but selected under a scheme introduced by Ernest Bevin (see above), minister of labour and national service 1940–45, to work in the coal mines instead

Bevins 'son of **Bevin**'

Bevis see **Beavis**

Bewes (i) from Welsh *ap Hugh* 'son of **Hugh**' (with the tautological addition of the English suffix -*s* denoting 'son of'); (ii) 'person from Bayeux', Normandy ('settlement of the Baiocasses tribe') [Rodney Bewes, 1937–, British actor]

Bewick, Buick 'person from Bewick', Northumberland and Yorkshire ('bee farm' (i.e. where honey is produced)) [Thomas Bewick, 1753–1828, British wood engraver and naturalist]
— **Bewick's swan** a small swan (*Cygnis columbianus*) of northern Europe and Asia. It was named after Thomas Bewick (see above).

Bewley, Bewlay 'person from Bewley Castle or Bewley', Cumbria and Durham respectively ('beautiful place') or 'person from Beaulieu', Hampshire (see **Beaulieu**)

Beynon from Welsh *ap Einion* 'son of *Einion*' (see **Onion**). See also **Binyon**

Bhatia a Hindu and Sikh surname based on the name of the Bhatia merchant community, derived ultimately from Sanskrit *bhaṭia* 'lord, learned one'

Bhattacharya, Bhattacharyya a Hindu surname, from Sanskrit *bhaṭia* (see **Bhatia**) + *ācārya* 'teacher'

Bibb from the medieval female personal name *Bibbe*, a pet-form of *Isabel*

Bibby, Bibbee pet-forms of **Bibb**

Bick (i) perhaps from the Old English male personal name *Bicca*; (ii) 'person who works with a pickaxe or chisel (e.g. a stonemason)' (from Middle Dutch and Middle High German *bicke* 'pickaxe, chisel'); (iii) 'ox, bull' (from eastern Yiddish *bik*, of Slavic origin)

Bickerdike 'person from Bickerdike', an unidentified place, probably in Yorkshire ('disputed ditch')

Bickerstaff, Bickerstaffe 'person from Bickerstaff', Lancashire ('beekeepers' landing-place')

Bickersteth a different form of **Bickerstaff**

Bickerton 'person from Bickerton', the name of various places in England ('beekeepers' farmstead')

Bickford 'person from Bickford', Devon ('Bicca's ford')

Bickley 'person from Bickley or Bickleigh', Cheshire, Devon, Kent and Worcestershire ('glade by a pointed hill')

Bicknell 'person from Bickenhall or Bickenhill', Somerset and Warwickshire ('Bicca's hill'). See also **Bignell** (ii)

Biddle a different form of **Beadle** [John Biddle, 1615–62, English religious leader, founder of Unitarianism]

Biddlecombe 'person from Bittiscombe', Somerset ('Bitel's valley') [Terry Biddlecombe, 1941–, British National Hunt jockey]

Biddulph 'person from Biddulph', Staffordshire ('place by the quarry')

Bidwell, Biddwell 'person from Bidwell', the name of various places in England ('stream or spring in a shallow valley'). See also **Bedwell**

Bierce a different form of **Pierce** [Ambrose Bierce, 1842–?1914, US writer]

Bigelow probably 'person from Big Low', Cheshire ('large hill') [Billy Bigelow, smooth-talking fairground barker in Rodgers and Hammerstein's musical *Carousel* (1945)]

Bigg (i) from a medieval nickname for a large powerful person; (ii) a different form of **Begg**. See also **Biggs**

Biggar, Bigger 'person from Biggar', South Lanarkshire ('barley plot')

Biggins 'person from Biggin', the name of various places in England ('building') [Christopher Biggins, 1948–, British actor and presenter]

Biggs a different form of **Bigg** [Ronnie Biggs, 1929–, British train robber]

Bignell, Bignall (i) 'person from Bignell', Oxfordshire ('Bicga's hill'); (ii) a different form of **Bicknell**

Biles, Byles 'person who lives on a promontory' (from Old English *bil* 'beak, promontory')

Bilko from a Ukrainian nickname for a fair-haired person (literally 'little blond one') [Master Sgt Ernie Bilko, sharp-witted wisecracking scheming protagonist (played by Phil Silvers) of *The Phil Silvers Show* (1957–60)]

Bill (i) from the medieval male person name *Bill* (either from the Old English personal name *Billa* or a shortening of any of various Germanic compound names (e.g. *Bilhard*) beginning with *bil* 'sword'; it is not the same name as *Bill* the short form of *William*). See also **Billings**, **Billson**; (ii) 'maker of bladed agricultural implements (e.g. pruning hooks)' (from Middle English *bill* 'bladed weapon')

Billingham 'person from Billingham', probably an unidentified place in the West Midland (rather than Billingham in Northeast England) ('Billa's people's homestead')

Billings 'son of **Bill** (i)'

Billingsley, **Billingslea**, **Billingsly** 'person from Billingsley', Shropshire ('woodland glade by a sharp ridge')

Billington 'person from Billington', Bedfordshire, Lancashire and Staffordshire (respectively 'Billa's hill', 'hill with a steep ridge' and 'Billa's farmstead') [Rachael Billington (*née* Pakenham), 1942–, British author]

Billson, **Bilson** 'son of **Bill** (i)'

Bilton 'person from Bilton', Northumberland and Yorkshire ('Billa's farmstead')

Binchy an Irish surname perhaps related to **Binks** [Maeve Binchy, 1940–, Irish author]

Binder 'maker of barrels, cooper' (from German *Binder*, a shortened form of *Fassbinder* 'cooper', literally 'binder of barrels')

Bing (i) *also* **Byng** perhaps 'person who lives near a "bing" (in northern English dialect, a heap or receptacle)' (from Old Norse *bingr* 'stall'); (ii) 'person from *Bing*', the Yiddish form of *Bingen*, the name of a town in Germany [George Byng (Viscount Torrington), 1663–1733, English admiral; John Byng, 1704–57, British admiral, son of George, shot for dereliction of duty, 'pour encourager les autres' (Voltaire); Julian Byng (Viscount Byng), 1862–1935, British field marshal; Sir Rudolf Bing, 1902–97, Austrian-born British opera administrator]

— **Bing Boys** a nickname given to Canadian troops during World War I, from the name of their commanding officer, Viscount Byng (see above)

Bingham 'person from Bingham', Nottinghamshire ('Bynna's people's homestead') [Bingham, family name of the earls of Lucan; Judith Bingham, 1952–, British composer]

Binks 'person who lives by a "bink" (in northern English dialect, a bank of earth or a flat stone that can be sat on)'

Binney, **Binnie** (i) 'person who lives on land enclosed by a bend in a river' (from Old English *binnan ēa* 'within the river'); (ii) 'person from Binney or Binniehill', Falkirk ('at the hill'); (iii) 'person from Binny or Binney', both in Kent ('land enclosed by a bend in a river')

Binns 'son of *Binne*', a medieval male personal name (from Old English *Binna*)

Binyon a different form of **Beynon** [Laurence Binyon, 1869–1943, British poet]

Birch, **Burch** 'person who lives in or by a birch wood or by a particular birch tree'

— **John Birch Society** a right-wing political organization founded in the US in 1958 to combat Communism. John Birch was a US Army intelligence officer killed by the Chinese Communists in 1945, and represented by the Society as the first victim of the Cold War.

Birchall, **Birchell**, **Burchall**, **Burchill** 'person from Birchill or Birchills', Derbyshire and Staffordshire respectively ('hill where birch trees grow') [Julie Burchill, 1959–, British journalist]

Birchfield see **Burchfield**

Bird (i) *also* **Burd** *or* **Byrd** 'bird-catcher', or from a medieval nickname for a callow youngster (from Middle English *bird* 'young bird'); (ii) *also* **Burd** *or* **Byrd** from a medieval nickname for an effeminate or weakly youth (from Middle English *burde* 'maiden'); (iii) from Irish Gaelic *Ó hÉanacháin* 'descendant of *Éanachán*', a personal name of uncertain origin and meaning of which the *Éan*-has been identified with Gaelic *éan* 'bird'. See also **Bride** [Harold ('Dickie') Bird, 1933–, English cricket umpire; John Bird, 1936–, British actor and writer; Richard Byrd, 1888–1957, US explorer; William Byrd, 1543–1623, English composer]

● Men with the surname Bird are traditionally given the nickname 'Dicky' or 'Dickie'

— **Bird's Custard** the brand name of a cornflour-based custard sauce invented in 1837 by Alfred Bird, 1811–78 (originally for the sake of his wife, who was allergic to the eggs from which authentic custard is made)

— **Marie Byrd Land**, **Byrd Land** a region of western Antarctica, on the Amundsen Sea, east of the Ross Ice Shelf. It was named by Richard Byrd (see above) in honour of his wife.

Birdsall, **Birdsell** 'person from Birdsall', Yorkshire ('Bridd's nook of land')

Birdseye probably 'person from Birdsey', an unidentified place in England ('island of birds') [Clarence Birdseye, 1886–1956, US inventor and business executive, godfather of the modern frozen-food industry]

— **Birds Eye** an international frozen-food brand, created in the US in 1929 by General Foods after they had bought the patents to the food-freezing process from Clarence Birdseye (see above)

— **Captain Birdseye** an avuncular nautical personage created in 1967 as the marketing mascot of Birds Eye foods in the UK

Birkbeck 'person from Birkbeck', Cumbria ('birch stream') [George Birkbeck, 1776–1841, British educationalist]

— **Birkbeck College** a college of London University, founded as the London Mechanics' Institute in 1824 by George Birkbeck (see above)

Birkenshaw see **Burkinshaw**

Birkett, **Birket** 'person who lives by a grove of birch trees' (from Old English *bircet* 'birch copse'). See also **Burkett** [Myles Birket Foster, 1825–99, British artist; Norman Birkett (Lord Birkett), 1883–1962, British barrister and judge]

Birkin see **Burkin**

Birley 'person from Birley', Derbyshire and Herefordshire ('woodland clearing by or belonging to a fortified place'). See also **Burley** [Mark Birley (original name Marcus Lecky Oswald Hornby Birley), 1933–, British entrepreneur, founder (1963) of 'Annabel's' club in Berkeley Square, London]

Birling see **Burling**

Birmingham, **Bermingham** 'person from Birmingham', West Midlands ('Beorma's people's homestead')

Birnbaum 'person who lives by a pear tree' (from German *Birnbaum* 'pear tree')

Birrell a different form of **Burrell**

Birt see **Burt**

Birtenshaw see **Burtenshaw**

Birtwistle, **Birtwhistle,** **Burtwistle** 'person from Birtwistle', Lancashire ('stream-junction frequented by young birds') [Sir Harrison Birtwistle, 1934–, British composer]

Biscoe probably 'person from Burscough', Lancashire ('wood by the fort') [John Biscoe, 1794–1843, British mariner and Antarctic explorer]

Bishop 'servant in the household of a bishop', or 'person whose demeanour or appearance resembles that of a bishop' [Elizabeth Bishop, 1911–79, US poet; Sir Henry Bishop, 1786–1855, British composer, originator of 'Home, Sweet Home'; Stephen Bishop, former name of Stephen Kovacevich, 1940–, US pianist (Kovacevich was his original name, Bishop that of his step-father)]

Bisley 'person from Bisley', Gloucestershire and Surrey ('Bisa's glade' and 'Byssa's glade' respectively)

Bissell (i) 'corn merchant' (from Middle English *bysshell* 'bushel'). See also **Bushell**, **Bussell**; (ii) 'little *Biss*', a medieval nickname for someone with a wan complexion or drab clothing (from Middle English *bis* 'dingy, grey'); (iii) a different form of **Bethel** (ii)

Bissett, **Bisset** 'little *Biss*' (see **Bissell**) [Jacqueline Bissett, 1944–, British actress]

Biswas a Hindu name, based on Sanskrit *viśvāsa* 'trust'
— *A House for Mr Biswas* a novel (1961) by V.S. Naipaul, set in Trinidad and charting the life of its mild but resilient eponymous hero

Black, **Blacke** (i) 'person with a dark complexion or hair' (from Old English *blac, blæc* 'black'). See also **Blake** (ii); (ii) a different form of **Blake** (i); (iii) an anglicization of the Norman surname *Blanc*, literally 'person with a pale complexion or fair hair' (from Old French *blanc* 'white' – English-speakers tended to denasalize French nasal vowels); (iv) a translation of any of a range of Scottish and Irish names based on Gaelic *dubh* 'black' (e.g. **Duff**); (v) a translation of any of a range of German and Jewish names meaning 'black' (e.g. **Schwarz**) [Cilla Black (original name Priscilla White), 1943–, British pop singer and television presenter; Conrad Black (Lord Black), 1944–, Canadian newspaper proprietor; Dr Black, the murder victim in the game of 'Cluedo'; Sir James Whyte Black, 1924–, British pharmacologist; Joseph Black, 1728–99, Scottish physician and chemist; Shirley Temple Black, see **Temple**; Stanley Black, 1913–2002, British light-music conductor, arranger and pianist]
— **A & C Black** a British publishing firm, established in Edinburgh in 1807 by Adam Black, 1784–1874. He was joined in business later by his nephew Charles Black, 1807–54. The company was acquired by Bloomsbury Publishing plc in 2000.
— **Black & Decker** a manufacturer of power tools. The seed from which it grew was an electric drill invented in Baltimore, Maryland in 1916 by S. Duncan Black and Alonzo G. Decker.

Blackadder 'person from Blackadder', Berwickshire ('place by the (river) Blackadder', a river-name meaning literally 'dark river'). See also **Blacketer** [Dame Elizabeth Blackadder, 1931–, British artist]
— *Blackadder* the collective name of a sequence of BBC sitcom series (starting with *The Black Adder* (1983)) starring Rowan Atkinson as renewed incarnations of Edmund Blackadder from the Middle Ages to the First World War

Blackburn, **Blackburne** 'person from Blackburn', Lancashire ('dark stream') [Tony Blackburn, 1943–, British disc jockey]

Blacker 'person who bleaches textiles' (from a derivative of Middle English *blāken* 'to bleach', from *blāc* – see **Blake** (i)). See also **Blaker**

Blacketer a different form of **Blackadder**

Blackett (i) 'little **Black**'; (ii) 'person who lives on or by a dark headland' (from Middle English *blak heved* 'black head'); (iii) 'person with black hair' (from Middle English *blak heved* 'black head') [Patrick Blackett (Lord Blackett), 1897–1974, British physicist]

Blackford 'person from Blackford', the name of various places in England ('dark ford')

Blackham 'person from Blackham', an unidentified place in England (probably 'dark homestead' or 'Blaca's homestead')

Blackhurst 'person from Blackhurst', an unidentified place probably in northwestern England ('dark wooded hill')

Blackie (i) 'little **Black**'; (ii) from a medieval Scottish nickname for someone with dark eyes or someone thought to be able to put the evil eye on others. See also **Blakey**
— **Blackie and Son Ltd.** a Scottish publishing company founded in 1809 by John Blackie, 1782–1874. It ceased business in 1991.

Blackledge 'person from Blacklache', Lancashire ('dark boggy stream')

Blackley a Scottish variant of **Blakeley**

Blacklock from a medieval nickname for someone with dark hair. See also **Blaylock**

Blackman a different form of **Black** (i–ii) [Honor Blackman, 1925–, British actress]

Blackmon a different form of **Blackman**

Blackmore, Blackmoor 'person from Blackmore or Blackmoor', the name of several places in England (variously 'dark moor or marsh' and 'dark lake'). See also **Blakemore** [R.D. Blackmore, 1825–1900, British historical novelist]

Blackshaw 'person from Blackshaw', Yorkshire ('dark copse')

Blackstock 'person who lives by a blackened tree stump'

Blackstone 'person who lives by a dark (boundary) stone', or 'person from Blackston or Blaxton', the name of various places in England ('dark (boundary) stone'). See also **Blakiston** [Sir William Blackstone, 1723–80, British jurist]

Blackwell 'person from Blackwell', the name of various places in England ('dark spring or stream') [Sir Basil Blackwell, 1889–1984, British publisher and bookseller]
— **Blackwell's** an Oxford firm of booksellers founded in 1879 by Benjamin Henry Blackwell, father of Basil (see above). It subsequently formed a (now separate) publishing business.

Blackwood 'person from Blackwood', the name of various places in England and Scotland ('dark wood') [Algernon Blackwood, 1869–1951, British novelist and short-story writer]
— **Blackwood's Magazine** an influential monthly literary magazine published between 1817 and 1980 by the Edinburgh firm of William Blackwood and Son (founded by William Blackwood, 1776–1834)

Blades, Blaydes (i) 'maker of bladed implements, cutler'; (ii) 'person from Blades', an unidentified place in England

Blaikie see **Blakey**

Blain, Blaine (i) from the Scottish Gaelic personal name *Bláán*, literally 'little yellow one'; (ii) from a medieval Scottish and northern English nickname for someone with boils (from Middle English *blain* 'pustule')

Blair 'person from Blair', the name of various places in Scotland ('plain, (battle)field') [Lionel Blair (original name Henry Lionel Ogus), 1932–, Canadian-born British dancer and television personality; Tony Blair, 1953–, British New Labour politician, prime minister 1997–2007]
— **Blairism** the political policies and style of government of Tony Blair, typified by moderate and gradual social reform, financial prudence and tight control over policy presentation
— **Blairista** a fanatical supporter or apparatchik of Tony Blair
— **Tony Blairs** British rhyming slang of the 1990s for 'flares' (i.e. flared trousers). In the 1970s, an earlier generation had called them **Lionel Blairs**.

Blaisdell 'person from Blaisdell', Cumbria ('Blesi's valley'). See also **Bleasdale**

Blaise, Blaize from the medieval male personal name *Blaise* (from Latin *Blasius*, a derivative of *blaesus* 'stammering' or 'limping') [Modesty Blaise, British strip-cartoon heroine, created in 1963 by Peter O'Donnell as a simplified female version of James Bond]

Blake (i) 'person with a pale complexion or fair hair' (from Old English *blāc* 'pale, fair'). See also **Black** (ii); (ii) a different form of **Black** (i); (iii) from Irish Gaelic *Ó Bláthmhaic* 'descendant of *Bláthmhac*', a personal name meaning literally 'son of fame, son of prosperity' [George Blake (original name Georg Behar), 1922–, Dutch-born British spy, double agent for the Soviet Union; Sir Peter Blake, 1932–, British painter; Quentin Blake, 1932–, British artist and illustrator; Robert Blake, 1599–1657, English admiral; Robert Blake (Lord Blake), 1916–2003, British historian; Sexton Blake, fictional British detective created in 1893 by Harry Blyth; William Blake, 1757–1827, British visionary poet, painter and engraver]
— **Blakeian** of William Blake (see above) or characteristic of his style or subject matter
— **Blake's 7** a BBC television science-fiction series (1978–81) featuring a band of escaped criminals led by Roj Blake in an intergalactic struggle against tyranny
— **Sexton Blake** (see above) British rhyming slang for 'fake', and also for 'cake' and 'snake'

Blakeley, Blakely 'person from Blakeley or Blakely', the name of various places in England and Scotland ('dark glade'). See also **Blackley** [Colin Blakely, 1930–87, Northern Irish actor]

Blakemore a different form of **Blackmore** [Colin Blakemore, 1944–, British physiologist; Michael Blakemore, 1928–, Australian theatre director]

Blakeney 'person from Blakeney', Gloucestershire and Norfolk ('dark island') [Sir Percy Blakeney, the real name of the 'Scarlet Pimpernel' in the novels of Baroness Orczy]

Blaker a different form of **Blacker**

Blakeway 'person from Blakeway Farm', Shropshire ('dark road')

Blakey, Blaikie different forms of **Blackie**
— **blakey** a metal boot protector of a type manufactured in Leeds from the late 1880s by the firm of John Blakey, especially a small curved piece of metal fixed into the heel or sole of a boot or shoe to reduce wear

Blakiston a different form of **Blackstone**

Blamire, Blaymire perhaps 'person from Blamire', an unidentified place in northern England ('dark marsh') (the Yorkshire place-name *Blamires* probably comes from the surname rather than vice versa) [Cyril Blamire, one of the original trio of old codgers in the BBC television sitcom *Last of the Summer Wine* (1973–)]

Blanc (i) from a medieval French and Catalan nickname for a man with a pale complexion or fair hair (from Old French and Catalan *blanc* 'white, pale'); (ii) *also* **Blank** an invented Jewish name based on German *blank* 'bright, shiny' [Mel Blanc, 1908–89, US cartoon voicer]

Blanchard from the medieval French personal name *Blanchard*, of Germanic origin and meaning literally 'shining-brave'

Blanchett 'little white or pale one' (from a derivative of Old French *blanc* – see **Blanc**) [Cate Blanchett, 1969–, Australian actress]

Blanchflower from a medieval nickname applied probably to an effeminate man (from Old French *blanche flour* 'white flower') [Danny Blanchflower, 1926–93, Northern Irish footballer]

Bland 'person from Bland', Yorkshire (perhaps 'stormy place') [Colin Bland, 1938–, South African cricketer]

Blandford 'person from Blandford', Dorset ('ford where gudgeon are seen')

Blaney 'person who lives at the end or top (e.g. at the top of a hill or on the upper reaches of a river)' (from Welsh *blaenau* 'points, tips')

Blatchford 'person from Blatchford', Devon (probably 'Blæcca's ford')

Blatt a shortened form of any of various compound Jewish names based on German *Blatt* 'leaf' (e.g. *Rosenblatt* 'rose leaf')

Blaylock perhaps a different form of **Blacklock**

Blears from a medieval nickname for a bleary-eyed person

Bleasdale a different form of **Blaisdell** [Alan Bleasdale, 1946–, British playwright]

Bledsoe 'person from Bledisloe', Gloucestershire ('Blīth's hill')

Blenkinsopp, Blenkinsop 'person from Blenkinsopp', Northumberland (perhaps 'Blenkyn's valley') [John Blenkinsop, 1783–1831, British engineer, builder of the first practical steam locomotive]

Blennerhasset 'person from Blennerhasset', Cumbria ('summit with a summer pasture where hay is stored')

Blessed from a medieval nickname for a fortunate person. See also **Blissett** [Brian Blessed, 1937–, British actor]

Blethyn from the Welsh male personal name *Bleddyn*, literally 'wolf cub' [Brenda Blethyn, 1946–, British actress]

Blew see **Blue**

Blewett, Blewitt, Bluett, Bluet from a medieval nickname for a blue-eyed person or one who habitually wore blue clothing (from Middle English *bleuet* 'cornflower' or *bluet* 'blue cloth')

Blick (i) perhaps from a medieval nickname for a wan or pale-complexioned person (from Middle English *bleik* 'pallid', from Old Norse *bleikr*); (ii) a Jewish surname, perhaps based on German *Blick* or Yiddish *blik* 'look, glance'

Bligh, Bly, Blye (i) a different form of **Blythe**; (ii) from a medieval Cornish nickname for someone thought to resemble a wolf (from Cornish *blyth* 'wolf'); (iii) from Irish Gaelic *Ó Blighe* 'descendant of *Blighe*', a personal name probably adapted from Old Norse *Blígr* [William Bligh, 1754–1817, British admiral, against whom the crew of HMS *Bounty* mutinied]

Bliss (i) from a medieval nickname for a happy or cheerful person; (ii) 'person from Blay (formerly Bleis)', Normandy; (iii) from Welsh *ap Ellis* 'son of **Ellis**' [Sir Arthur Bliss, 1891–1975, British composer]

Blissett a different form of **Blessed** [Luther Blissett, 1958–, Jamaican-born English footballer ('Luther Blissett' has been used since 1994 as a cover name for activists engaging in anti-cultural establishment polemics and spoofs on the Internet and elsewhere)]

Blitstein an invented Jewish name meaning literally 'blossom-stone'

Blizzard a different form (influenced by *blizzard* 'heavy snowstorm') of **Blissett**

Bloch (i) an East European Jewish name meaning 'person from Italy' (from Polish *włoch* 'foreigner', hence 'Italian'); (ii) a different form of **Block** (i) [Ernest Bloch, 1880–1959, Swiss-born US composer; Felix Bloch, 1905–83, US physicist]

Block (i) from a medieval German and Dutch nickname for a large ungainly person, or possibly for one who was locked up in the stocks on a regular basis (from Middle High German *bloch* and Middle Dutch *blok* 'block (of wood), stocks'); (ii) perhaps 'person who uses a block in their trade (e.g. as a bookbinder or shoemaker)'. See also **Bloggs**; (iii) an anglicization of **Bloch** (i) [Herbert Block ('Herblock'), 1909–2001, US political cartoonist]
— **B&Q** a British retailer of hardware and do-it-yourself supplies, established in Southampton in 1969 by Richard Block and David Quayle

Blofeld 'person from Blofield', Norfolk ('exposed open country') [Ernst Stavro Blofeld, Polish-born evil genius and über-villain in the James Bond novels of Ian Fleming (the name was inspired by that of Henry Blofeld's (see next) father, whom Fleming had known at school); Henry Blofeld, 1939–, British journalist and cricket commentator]

Bloggs perhaps a different form of **Block** (ii)
— **Joe Bloggs** a name used colloquially as representative of the ordinary uncomplicated unsophisticated man, the average man in the street. The equivalent in US, Canadian and Australian English is 'Joe **Blow**'.

Blom (i) a different form of **Blum**; (ii) an invented Swedish name meaning literally 'flower'

Blomberg (i) 'person from Blomberg', the name of places in Denmark and Germany; (ii) an invented Swedish name meaning literally 'flower-hill'

Blomquist an invented Swedish name meaning literally 'flower-twig'

Blond from a medieval Jewish nickname for a fair-haired person (from Yiddish *blond*), or from a medieval French nickname for a fair-haired person or one with a light complexion (from Old French *blond*)

Blondell (i) perhaps a different form of **Blundell**; (ii) an invented Swedish name based on *blond* 'blond' [Joan Blondell, 1906–79, US actress]

Blood (i) from a medieval nickname based on the word *blood*, though with what connotations is not

clear; (ii) from Welsh *ap Llwyd* 'son of **Lloyd**' [Colonel Thomas Blood, ?1618–80, Irish adventurer who tried to steal the English crown jewels]
— *Captain Blood* a novel (1922) by Rafael Sabatini, set in the 17th century and featuring the adventures of medical doctor turned pirate captain Peter Blood. In the 1935 film, Blood was played by Errol Flynn.

Bloodworth, **Bludworth** 'person from Blidworth', Nottinghamshire ('Blītha's enclosure')

Bloom (i) an anglicization of **Blum**; (ii) 'iron worker' (from Middle English *blome* 'iron ingot') [Claire Bloom, 1931–, British actress; Leopold Bloom and his wife Molly Bloom, leading characters in James Joyce's *Ulysses* (1922); Orlando Bloom, 1977–, British actor]
— **Bloomsday** 16 June, the day on which the events of James Joyce's *Ulysses* take place and since 1954 an annual day of celebration in the Republic of Ireland in honour of the author, creator of Leopold and Molly Bloom (see above)

Bloomer a different form of **Bloom** (ii) [Amelia Bloomer (*née* Jenks), 1818–94, US feminist and reformer]
— **bloomers** originally, long loose trousers for women, the use of which was advocated in the 1850s by Amelia Bloomer (see above). The application to underwear was a later development.

Bloomfield (i) an alteration of the surname *Blundeville*, literally 'person from Blonville-sur-Mer', Normandy; (ii) an anglicization of the invented Jewish surname *Blumfeld*, based on Yiddish *blum* 'flower' + *feld* 'field' [Leonard Bloomfield, 1887–1949, US linguistician]
— **Bloomfieldian** (an adherent) of Leonard Bloomfield or his linguistic theories

Bloomingdale an anglicization of German **Blumenthal** or Dutch *Bloemendaal*, invented Jewish surnames meaning literally 'flower-valley'
— **Bloomingdale's** a US chain of department stores founded in New York City in 1861 by Joseph and Lyman Bloomingdale

Blore, **Bloor** 'person from Blore', Staffordshire ('place on the hill')

Blount see **Blunt**

Blow, **Blowe** from a medieval nickname for someone with a pale complexion (from Middle English *blowe* 'pale') [John Blow, 1649–1708, English composer]
— **Joe Blow** the US, Canadian and Australian equivalent of 'Joe **Bloggs**'

Bloxham, **Bloxam**, **Bloxom**, **Bloxsom** 'person from Bloxham or Bloxholm', Oxfordshire and Lincolnshire respectively ('Blocc's homestead')

Bludworth see **Bloodworth**

Blue an anglicization of the German surname *Blau*, literally 'blue' (from a nickname with various applications, e.g. someone with blue eyes) [Lionel Blue, 1930–, British rabbi and broadcaster]

Bluett, **Bluet** see **Blewett**

Blum, **Blume** (i) an invented Jewish name based on Yiddish *blum* 'flower'; (ii) 'flower gardener' or

'florist' (from Middle High German *bluom* 'flower'). See also **Blom** (i), **Bloom** (i)

Blumberg (i) 'person from Blumberg', the name of various places in Germany; (ii) an invented Jewish name based on German *Blume* 'flower' + *Berg* 'hill'

Blumenfeld (i) 'person from Blumenfeld or Blumenfelde', the name of various places in Germany; (ii) an invented Jewish name based on German *Blume* 'flower' + *Feld* 'field'

Blumenthal an invented Jewish name based on German *Blume* 'flower' + *Thal* 'valley'. See also **Bloomingdale** [Heston Blumenthal, 1966–, British chef and restaurateur]

Blundell 'little **Blunt**'
— **Blundellsands** a district of Crosby, Merseyside, named after a local landowner called Blundell who developed the area in the early 19th century
— **Blundell's School** a public school in Tiverton, Devon founded in 1604 under the terms of a bequest from the wealthy merchant Peter Blundell, 1520–1601

Blunden perhaps from a medieval nickname for someone with fair hair (from Middle English *blonden* 'fair-haired') [Edmund Blunden, 1896–1974, British poet and critic]

Blunkett a different form of **Plunkett** [David Blunkett, 1947–, British Labour politician]

Blunt, **Blount** (i) from a medieval nickname for a stupid person (from Middle English *blunt* 'dull, stupid'); (ii) from a medieval nickname for a fair-haired person or one with a light complexion (from Anglo-Norman *blunt* 'blond') [Anthony Blunt, 1907–83, British art historian and Soviet spy; Wilfred Scawen Blunt, 1840–1922, British poet, diplomat, traveller and Arabist]

Bly, **Blye** see **Bligh**

Blythe, **Blyth** (i) 'person from Blyth', Northumberland ('place on the (river) *Blyth*', a river-name meaning literally 'gentle' or 'pleasant'); (ii) from a medieval nickname for a happy or cheerful person [Sir Chay Blyth (original name Charles Blyth), 1940–, British yachtsman; Ronald Blythe, 1922–, British author]

Blyton 'person from Blyton', Lincolnshire ('Blītha's farmstead') [Enid Blyton, 1897–1968, British children's author]

Boakes a different form of **Balch**

Board 'carpenter'; also, 'person who lives in a cottage made of planks' [Lilian Board, 1949–70, British athlete]

Boarder (i) a different form of **Board**; (ii) see **Border**

Boardman a different form of **Board** [Chris Boardman, 1968–, British cyclist]

Boas, **Boase**, **Boaz** from the Hebrew male personal name *Boaz*, of unknown origin and meaning [Franz Boas, 1858–1942, German-born US anthropologist]

Bobbitt, **Bobbett** 'little *Bobb*', a medieval male personal name (from Old English *Bubba*)

— **bobbitt** to amputate the penis of, as a deliberate act of vengeance or vindictiveness. The largely journalistic usage was inspired by an incident in the US in 1993 in which Lorena Bobbitt cut off her husband's penis with a kitchen knife in revenge for alleged acts of abuse and rape.

Bocquet see **Bouquet**

Boddey, Boddie, Boddy see **Body**

Boddington 'person from Boddington', Gloucestershire and Northamptonshire (respectively 'estate associated with Bōta' and 'Bōta's hill')

Bodell perhaps a different form of **Beadle** [Jack Bodell, 1940–, British boxer]

Boden (i) 'son of *Bodo*', a North German male personal name meaning literally 'messenger'; (ii) 'person living in a low-lying area' (from Middle High German *boden* 'bottom, ground'); (iii) perhaps a different form of **Baldwin**

Bodie see **Body**

Bodine a French name, perhaps derived ultimately from Germanic *bald* 'bold'

Bodkin from the medieval male personal name *Bowdekyn*, a pet-form of **Baldwin**

Bodley probably 'person from Buddeley', a former place in Cheshire ('Budda's glade')
— **Bodleian Library** the library of Oxford University, refounded and enlarged from 1598 to 1602 by the English diplomat Sir Thomas Bodley, 1545–1613
— **Bodley Head** a British publishing house founded in London in 1887 by Elkin Mathews and John Lane. They took a head-portrait of Sir Thomas Bodley (see above) as their colophon.

Body, Bodie, Boddey, Boddie, Boddy (i) probably from a medieval nickname for a fat person; (ii) 'messenger' (from Middle English *bode* 'messenger')

Boehm 'person from Bohemia', now part of the Czech Republic (from German *Böhmen* 'Bohemia')

Boeing 'son of *Boio*', a Germanic male personal name of uncertain origin and meaning
— **Boeing Company** a US aerospace manufacturer founded in 1916 by the aviation pioneer William E. Boeing, 1881–1956.

Boettcher, Boetcher 'maker of barrels, cooper' (from Middle High German *botecher*, a derivative of *botech* 'barrel')

Bogard, Bogarde an anglicization of Dutch *van den Bogaard*, literally 'person who lives by an orchard' (from Dutch *boomgaard* 'orchard') [Sir Dirk Bogarde (original name Derek van den Bogaerde), 1921–99, British actor]

Bogart a different form of **Bogard** [Humphrey Bogart, 1899–1957, US actor]
— **bogart** in US slang, to coerce or bully, and also to take someone else's marijuana cigarette greedily or selfishly. The usage was inspired by Humphrey Bogart (see above) in the former sense from his frequent tough-guy roles and in the latter from his enthusiastic on- (and off-) screen smoking.

Boggis from a medieval nickname for a braggart (from Middle English *boggish* 'boastful')

Boggs a different form of **Boggis**

Bogle from a medieval Scottish and Northern Irish nickname for someone of scary appearance (from Middle Scots *bogill* 'hobgoblin')

Bohun see **Boon**

Boice see **Boyce**

Bolam 'person from Bolam', County Durham and Northumberland ('place by the tree trunks') [James Bolam, 1938–, British actor]

Bolan a different form of **Boland** [Marc Bolan (original name Mark Feld), 1947–77, British guitarist and singer/songwriter]

Boland, Bowland (i) 'person from Bowland', the name (variously spelled) of several places in England ('land in the bend of a river'); (ii) from Irish Gaelic *Ó Beólláin* 'descendant of *Beóllán*', a personal name of unknown origin and meaning. See also **Bolland**

Bold, Bould (i) from a medieval nickname for a courageous or intrepid person; (ii) 'person who lives or works at the main house in a particular place' (from Middle English *bolde* 'dwelling'). See also **Boodle**; (iii) 'person from Bold', Lancashire ('dwelling'). See also **Bolt** (iii)

Bolden, Boulden 'son of **Bold**' [Buddy Bolden (original name Charles Bolden), 1868–1931, US jazz cornettist]

Boles perhaps a variant spelling of **Bowles**

Boleyn a different form of **Bullen** (historically pronounced 'bullen', but now almost universally 'bəlin') [Anne Boleyn, ?1507–36, second wife of Henry VIII, mother of Elizabeth I]

Bolger (i) 'leather worker' (from Middle English *boulgier* 'leather worker', from Old French); (ii) from Irish Gaelic *Ó Bolguidhir* 'descendant of *Bolgodhar*', a personal name meaning literally 'yellow belly'. See also **Boulger, Bulger** [Jim Bolger, 1935–, New Zealand National Party politician, prime minister 1990–97; Ray Bolger (original name Raymond Wallace Bulcão), 1904–87, US entertainer who played the Scarecrow in the film *The Wizard of Oz* (1939)]

Bolingbroke 'person from Bolingbroke', Lincolnshire ('brook associated with Bulla') [Bolingbroke, family name used by Henry IV of England before he seized the throne in 1399 (he was born in Bolingbroke, Lincolnshire)]

Bolitho 'person from Bolitho', Cornwall ('dwelling belonging to an unidentified personal name')

Bolland a different form of **Boland**

Bollom 'person from Bolham', Nottinghamshire (probably either 'place by the tree trunks' or 'place by the rounded hills')

Bolt, Boult (i) 'maker of bolts', or from a medieval nickname for a short stocky person (in either case from Middle English *bolt* 'bolt, bar, crossbow arrow'); (ii) 'person who sifts flour' (from Middle English *bolten* 'to sift'); (iii) a different form of **Bold** (iii) [Sir Adrian Boult, 1889–1983, British conductor; Robert Bolt, 1924–95, British playwright]

Bolter, Boulter different forms of **Bolt** (i–ii) [Hugh Boulter, 1672–1742, English churchman]

Bolton, Boulton 'person from Bolton', the name of various places in England (especially the town in Lancashire) ('settlement with buildings') [Matthew Boulton, 1728–1809, British engineer and entrepreneur]

Bolus perhaps from a nickname for a contemptible person (from *bolus* 'large pill')

Bompas a different form of **Bumpus**

Bonar, Bonnar (i) see **Bonner** (i); (ii) a 'translation' of Irish Gaelic *Ó Cnáimhsighe* 'descendant of *Cnáimhseach*', a nickname meaning literally 'midwife' and ostensibly a derivative of Gaelic *cnámh* 'bone' [Andrew Bonar Law, see **Law**]

Bond, Bonde 'peasant farmer' (from Middle English *bonde* 'peasant farmer, husbandman'). See also **Bundy** [Alan Bond, 1938–, British-born Australian businessman; Edward Bond, 1934–, British playwright and director; James Bond, British secret agent created by Ian Fleming (the name was borrowed from that of the US ornithologist James Bond, 1900–89, a neighbour of Fleming's in Jamaica); Jennie Bond, 1950–, British television journalist; Michael Bond, 1926–, British author, creator of Paddington Bear; Ward Bond, 1903–60, US actor]

— **Bond Street** a street in Mayfair, London, linking Oxford Street and Piccadilly. The original, southern section (now known as Old Bond Street) was developed in the 1680s by, among others, Sir Thomas Bond, Comptroller of the Household to Queen Henrietta Maria (widow of Charles I).

Bondfield see **Bonfield**

Bondi (i) from the Italian personal name *Bondí*, literally 'good day', or from a shortened form of the Italian personal name *Abbondio* (from Latin *Abundius*, a derivative of *abundus* 'abundant'); (ii) 'son of **Bond**', a medieval Hungarian personal name [Sir Hermann Bondi, 1919–2005, Austrian-born British mathematician and cosmologist]

Bonds 'son of **Bond**'

Bone (i) from a medieval nickname for a good person (from Old French *bon* 'good'). See also **Boon** (i), **Bunn**; (ii) from a medieval nickname for a very thin person [Sir Muirhead Bone, 1876–1953, Scottish etcher and painter]

Bones (i) a different form of **Bone** (ii); (ii) 'son of **Bone**', a Yiddish female personal name adopted from Italian *Bona*, literally 'good'

Bonetti (i) 'little **Bono**'; (ii) from the Latin male personal name *Bonitus*, a derivative of *bonus* 'good' [Peter Bonetti, 1941–, British footballer]

Bonfield, Bondfield 'person from Bonneville', the name of three places in northern France ('good settlement') [Margaret Bondfield, 1873–1953, British trade-union leader and Labour politician, first female cabinet minister]

Bonham (i) 'person from Bonham', an unidentified place in England (perhaps 'Buna's homestead'); (ii) from a medieval nickname for a good man (from Old French *bon homme* 'good man'); (iii) 'peasant farmer' (from Old French *bonhomme* 'peasant farmer') [Helena Bonham Carter, 1966–, British actress, granddaughter of Lady Violet; Lady Violet Bonham Carter (Baroness Asquith; *née* Asquith), 1887–1969, British Liberal politician, daughter of H.H. Asquith]

— **Bonhams** a British auction house established in London in 1793 by the book specialist Walter Bonham and the antique print dealer Thomas Dodd

— **Bonham's case** a *cause célèbre* of 1610 in which a Henry Bonham was convicted and imprisoned by the Royal College of Physicians for practising medicine without a licence. The conviction was overturned by Sir Edward Coke, chief justice of Common Pleas, whose ruling established the principle that the courts have the power to overrule acts of Parliament.

Bonington see Bonnington

Bonner (i) *also* **Bonar** *or* **Bonnar** from a medieval nickname for a courteous or good-looking person (from Middle English *boner* 'gentle, courteous, handsome'); (ii) from Welsh *ap Ynyr* 'son of *Ynyr*', a medieval Welsh male personal name based on Latin *Honorius*

Bonnet, Bonnett (i) 'milliner', or from a medieval French nickname for someone who wore strange or noticeable hats (from Old French *bonnet* 'hat'); (ii) from a medieval French nickname meaning literally 'little good person', or from the medieval French male personal name *Bonnet* (from Latin *Bonītus*, a derivative of *bonus* 'good')

Bonney, Bonny from a medieval nickname for a handsome and well set-up person (from northern Middle English *bonnie* 'fine, beautiful') [Barbara Bonney, 1956–, US soprano; William Bonney, an alias of the US outlaw Henry McCarty, 1859–81, commonly known as 'Billy the Kid']

Bonnington, Bonington 'person from Bonnington', the name of various places in England and Scotland ('settlement associated with Buna') [Sir Chris Bonington, 1934–, British mountaineer, author and photographer; Richard Bonington, 1801–28, British landscape painter]

Bono (i) from the Italian male personal name *Bono*, literally 'good'. See also **de Bono**; (ii) from a medieval Italian nickname for a good person (from Italian *buono, bono* 'good') [Sonny Bono (original name Salvatore Phillip Bono), 1935–98, US pop singer (as one half of the duo 'Sonny and Cher') and Republican politician]

Bonser, Bonsor from a medieval nickname for a fine gentleman or (with heavy irony) for a despicable man, or for someone who was in the habit of using the French expression *bon sire* 'good sir' as a term of address

Boodle 'person who lives or works at the main house in a particular place', or 'person from Buddle', the name of various places in England (in either case from Old English *bōtl* 'dwelling'). See also **Bold** (ii), **Bootle**, **Boydell**, **Buddle**

— **Boodle's Club** a gentleman's club in St James's Street, London, founded in 1762 by

William Almack and named after its first manager, Edward Boodle

Book (i) perhaps a different form of **Buck**; (ii) from the medieval German male personal name *Bogo*, literally 'bow' (the weapon)

Booker (i) 'bookbinder' or 'scribe who produced books'; (ii) a different form of **Bowker** (ii) [Christopher Booker, 1937–, British journalist and author, original editor of *Private Eye*]
— **Booker Prize** an annual British prize for fiction, launched in 1968 by the food-distribution firm Booker McConnell Ltd (later Booker plc). Since 2002, when the Man Group, a British hedge fund, took over sponsorship, it has been officially the Man Booker Prize.

Bool, Boole different forms of **Bull** [George Boole, 1815–64, British mathematician and logician]
— **Boolean** using a system of symbolic logic, developed by George Boole (see above), that uses combinations of such logical operators as 'AND', 'OR' and 'NOT' to determine relationships between entities
— **Boolean algebra** a form of algebra concerned with the logical functions of variables that are restricted to two values, true or false

Boon, Boone (i) from a medieval nickname for a good person (from Old French *bon* 'good'). See also **Bone** (i); (ii) *also* **Bohun** 'person from Bohon', northern France; (iii) 'grower or seller of beans', or perhaps from a medieval Dutch nickname for a thin person (like a bean pod) (in either case from Middle Dutch *boene* 'bean'). See also **Bown** [Daniel Boone, 1734–1820, American pioneer; David Boon, 1960–, Australian cricketer; Pat Boone, 1934–, US popular singer]
— **Mills & Boon** see **Mills**

Boorman, Borman 'personal servant in a medieval household' (from Middle English *bour* 'inner room' + *man*). See also **Bower** [John Boorman, 1933–, British film director]

Boosey, Boosie (i) 'person from Balhousie', Fife (probably 'farmstead of the wood'); (ii) 'cowherd', or 'person who lives by a cattle shed' (from Middle English *bose* 'cattle stall')
— **Boosey and Hawkes** a British firm of music publishers and instrument manufacturers, founded in 1816 by Thomas Boosey as Boosey & Company. In 1930 it amalgamated with Hawkes & Son (founded in 1865 by William Henry Hawkes) to become Boosey and Hawkes.

Boot (i) *also* **Boote** 'maker or seller of boots'; (ii) 'boatman' (from Dutch *boot* 'boat') [Sir Jesse Boot (Baron Trent), 1850–1931, British pharmaceutical manufacturer; William Boot, hapless writer of nature notes who is dispatched to Africa as a war correspondent in Evelyn Waugh's *Scoop* (1938)]
— **The Boots Company** a chain of shops selling pharmaceutical products and a wide range of other items, founded as a chemist's shop in Nottingham in 1849 by John Boot, 1815–60, and greatly expanded by his son Jesse Boot (see above)

Booth, Boothe 'person (typically a shepherd or cowherd) who lives in a small hut' (from Middle English *both* 'hut, shelter, bothy') [Charles Booth,

1840–1916, British sociologist who developed the idea of the old-age pension; Cherie Booth, 1954–, British barrister, wife of Tony Blair; John Wilkes Booth, 1838–65, US actor and assassin of Abraham Lincoln; Webster Booth, 1902–84, British tenor; William Booth, 1829–1912, British religious leader, founder of the Salvation Army]
— **Booth's Gin** a brand of London dry gin first produced around 1740 by the Booth family
— **Booth's rising** an unsuccessful attempt in 1659 by royalists to overthrow the Commonwealth regime in England, led by Sir George Booth, 1622–84

Boothby 'person from Boothby', Lincolnshire ('farmstead with shelters') [Sir Robert Boothby (Lord Boothby), 1900–86, British Conservative politician]

Boothman a different form of **Booth**

Boothroyd 'person from Boothroyd', Yorkshire ('glade with huts') [Basil Boothroyd, 1910–88, British journalist and humorist; Betty Boothroyd (Baroness Boothroyd), 1929–, British Labour politician, speaker of the House of Commons 1992–2000]

Bootle 'person from Bootle', Cumbria and Lancashire ('dwelling' – from Old English *bōtl* (see also **Boodle**))

Boquet see **Bouquet**

Borden 'person from Borden', Kent [Lizzie Borden, 1860–1927, US woman acquitted of murdering her father and stepmother; Sir Robert Borden, 1854–1937, Canadian Conservative politician, prime minister 1911–20]

Border, Boarder 'person who lives at the edge of a village, or by some particular boundary line' [Allan Border, 1955–, Australian cricketer]

Borders a different form of **Border**
— **Borders** a chain of bookshops founded by Tom and Louis Borders in Ann Arbor, Michigan, US in 1971

Borg (i) 'person who lives by a hill-fort or on a hill', or 'person from Borg', the name of various places in Scandinavia (in either case from Old Norse *borg* 'fortification'); (ii) 'person from Borg', the name of several places in southern Germany ('fortification'); (iii) 'money lender' (from Yiddish *borg* 'credit')

Borland 'person from Borland, Boreland or Bordland', the name of various places in Scotland ('area that provides food for the lord's board (i.e. table)')

Borley 'person from Borley or Boreley', Essex and Worcestershire respectively ('glade frequented by wild boars')

Borman see **Boorman**

Borrow a different form of **Burrows** [George Borrow, 1803–81, British writer and traveller]

Borthwick 'person from Borthwick', Midlothian ('castle farmstead')

Borton a different form of **Burton**

Bosanquet (i) 'person from Bosanketh', Cornwall ('dwelling belonging to an unidentified personal name'); (ii) from a medieval Huguenot

nickname for a short person (from southern French dialect *bouzanquet* 'dwarf') [B.J.T. Bosanquet, 1877–1936, English cricketer, originator of the 'googly'; Reginald Bosanquet, 1932–84, British television newsreader, son of B.J.T.]
— **bosie, bosey** the Australian term for a googly. It is short for *Bosanquet.*

Boscawen 'person from Boscawen', the name of three places in Cornwall ('dwelling by the elder tree') [Edward Boscawen, 1711–61, British admiral]

Bose an anglicization of the Hindu surname *Basu* (from Bengali *bošu*, from Sanskrit *vasu* 'gem, wealth, radiance')

Bossom 'person from Bosham', Sussex ('Bōsa's promontory') [Alfred Bossom (Lord Bossom), 1881–1965, British architect and Conservative politician of whose name, when he was told it, Sir Winston Churchill allegedly remarked that it was neither one thing nor the other]

Bostick (i) a different form of **Bostock**; (ii) probably an anglicization of the Slovenian surname *Bostič*, literally 'son of *Boštjan*', a shortened form of **Sebastian**

Bostock 'person from Bostock', Cheshire ('Bōta's outlying farmstead')

Boston 'person from Boston', Lincolnshire ('Bōtwulf's stone')

Boswell, Boswall 'person from Beuzeville', northern France ('Beuze's settlement') [Eve Boswell (original name Eva Keleti; 'Boswell' was the name of a circus in which she once performed), 1922–98, Hungarian-born British pop singer; James Boswell, 1740–95, Scottish writer, the biographer of Samuel Johnson]

Bosworth 'person from Market Bosworth', Leicestershire ('Bōsa's enclosure')

Botha from the Old Frisian male personal name *Botho*, literally 'messenger'

Botham a different form of **Bottom** [Sir Ian Botham, 1955–, English cricketer]

Bothwell 'person from Bothwell', Lanarkshire ('small hut by a stream')

Bott (i) perhaps from an unrecorded Old English male personal name *Botta*; (ii) perhaps a different form of **Butt** (iv) [Violet Elizabeth Bott, obnoxious little girl in the 'William' stories of Richmal Crompton]

Botting 'son of **Bott**'

Bottom 'person who lives in a broad valley' (from Old English *botm* 'valley bottom'). See also **Botham**

Bottomley 'person from Bottomley', Yorkshire ('glade in a broad valley') [Horatio Bottomley, 1860–1933, British financier, politician and swindler; Virginia Bottomley (Baroness Bottomley; *née* Garnett), 1948–, British Conservative politician]

Bottoms a different form of **Bottom** [Timothy Bottoms, 1951–, US actor]

Bottrell, Botterell, Botterill probably 'person from Les Bottereaux', northern France ('place infested with toads'). See also **Butteriss** (ii)

Boucher 'butcher' (from Middle English *boucher* 'butcher', from Old French)

Bough (i) a different form of **Bow**; (ii) 'herdsman, cowherd', or from a medieval nickname for a large strong man (in either case from Old French *boeuf* 'bull'). Historically, (i) is pronounced 'bow' (rhyming with *show*) and (ii) 'bof', but in modern usage 'bof' predominates irrespective of the name's origin. [Frank Bough, 1933–, British television presenter]

Boughton 'person from Boughton', the name of various places in England (mostly 'Bucca's farmstead') [Rutland Boughton, 1878–1960, British composer]

Boulden see **Bolden**

Boulger a different form of **Bolger**

Boult, Boulter, Boulton see **Bolt, Bolter, Bolton**

Bouquet, Boquet, Bocquet from a medieval nickname for a man thought to resemble a goat, in appearance or lecherousness (from French, literally 'little goat', a derivative of *bouc* 'billy goat'). See also **Bucket**

Bourgeois 'town-dweller, freeman of a town, burgess' (from Old French *burgeis*, a derivative of *bourg* 'fortification, town'). See also **Burgess**

Bourke see **Burke**

Bourne, Bourn 'person who lives by a stream' (from Old English *burna* 'spring, stream'). See also **Burn**
— **Bourne and Hollingsworth** a department store in Oxford Street, London, originally established as a draper's shop in Westbourne Grove in 1894 by Mr Bourne and Mr Hollingsworth. It closed in 1983.
— *The Bourne Identity* a novel (1980) by Robert Ludlum about a CIA assassin, Jason Bourne, who loses his memory. A film version appeared in 2002.

Bousfield 'person from Bousfield', Cumbria (perhaps 'area of open land with bushes')

Boutell, Bouttell different forms of **Bulteel**
— *Boutell's Heraldry* a British standard work of reference on heraldry, compiled by Charles Boutell, 1812–77, originally published in 1863 and continuously updated since

Bouverie 'person who lives or works in a cowshed' (from Old French *boverie* 'cowshed')
— **Bouverie Street** a street in the City of London, leading off Fleet Street. Laid out around 1799, it was named after the Pleydell-Bouverie family, earls of Radnor, who were the ground landlords at the time.

Bouvier 'herdsman' (from Old French *bouvier* 'herdsman') [Jacqueline Bouvier, maiden name of Jacqueline **Kennedy**-Onassis]

Bovey 'person from Bovey', Devon ('settlement by the (river) Bovey', a pre-English river-name of unknown meaning)

Bovis a different form of **Beavis**

Bow, Bowe, Bough (i) 'maker or seller of bows (the weapon)'; (ii) 'person who lives by a bridge, a bend in the river, etc'. (from Middle English *bowe* 'arch, curve'); (iii) from Irish Gaelic *Ó Buadhaigh* 'descendant of *Buadhach*', a personal name meaning literally 'victorious'. See also **Bowes** (ii), **Boyce** (iii) [Clara Bow, 1905–65, US film actress]

Bowater 'person who lives on the bank of a river, lake, etc'. (from Middle English *buven* 'above' + *water*)

Bowden (i) 'person from Bowden or Bowdon', the name of numerous places in England and Scotland (mostly 'hill shaped like a bow'); (ii) 'person who lives at the top of a hill', or 'person from Bovingdon', Hertfordshire (in either case from Old English *būfan dūne* 'at the top of the hill'); (iii) from Irish Gaelic *Ó Buadáin* 'descendant of *Buadán*'

Bowditch probably 'person from Bowditch', Devon ('above the ditch')

Bowdler perhaps 'miner' (from a derivative of English dialect *buddle* 'to wash ore')
— **bowdlerize** to excise parts of a work of literature that are considered indecent. The verb was inspired by Thomas Bowdler, 1754–1825, who published an edition of Shakespeare omitting scenes that he considered unsuitable.

Bowe see **Bow**

Bowen (i) from Welsh *ap Owain* 'son of **Owen**'; (ii) from Irish Gaelic *Ó Buadhacháin* 'descendant of *Buadhachán*', a personal name meaning literally 'little victorious one' [Elizabeth Bowen, 1899–1973, Anglo-Irish novelist; Jim Bowen (original name James Whittaker), 1937–, British comedian; Norman Levi Bowen, 1887–1956, Canadian experimental petrologist; York Bowen, 1884–1961, British composer and pianist]
— **Bowen therapy** a therapeutic technique that initiates healing and encourages emotional stability using manipulation of muscles and connective tissue. It was developed by the Australian therapist Tom Bowen, 1916–82.

Bower (i) 'person from Bower or Bowers', Essex and Somerset ('small cottage(s)'); (ii) 'person who lives in a small cottage' (from Middle English *bour* 'cottage'); (iii) 'personal servant in a medieval household' (from Middle English *bour* 'inner room'). See also **Boorman**; (iv) a Scottish variant of **Bowyer**. See also **Bowra** [Frederick Orpen Bower, 1855–1948, British botanist]

Bowering see **Bowring**

Bowers a different form of **Bower** (i–iii) [Henry Robertson ('Birdie') Bowers, 1883–1912, British Antarctic explorer]

Bowes (i) 'person from Bowes', County Durham ('bends (in the river)'); (ii) a different form of **Bow** (ii) [Bill Bowes, 1908–87, English cricketer and journalist; Lady Elizabeth Bowes Lyon, maiden name of Queen Elizabeth, wife and consort of George VI (later Queen Elizabeth the Queen Mother), 1900–2002]

Bowie from a Scottish and Irish nickname for a fair-haired person (from Gaelic *buidhe* 'yellow, blond') [David Bowie (original name David Jones), 1947–, British pop singer; Jim Bowie, ?1796–1836, US pioneer]

— **bowie knife** a single-edged hunting knife, about 35 cm/15 in long and curved near the point, with a short hilt and a guard for the hand. It is named after Jim Bowie (see above), who popularized it.

Bowker (i) a northern English variant of **Butcher**; (ii) 'person who cleans cotton or linen in a strongly alkaline liquid' (from a derivative of Middle English *bouken* 'to wash'). See also **Booker** (ii)

Bowler 'person who makes or sells bowls (the vessels)', or from a medieval nickname for a heavy drinker of alcohol
— **bowler hat** a hard felt hat with a round crown and narrow upturned brim. It appears to have been named after the Bowlers, a family of 19th-century London hatters who specialized in its manufacture.

Bowles (i) a different form of **Bowler**; (ii) 'person from Bouelles', northern France ('enclosures, dwellings') [Camilla Parker Bowles, see **Parker**; Chester Bowles, 1901–86, US economist and diplomat; Paul Bowles, 1910–99, US writer and composer; Peter Bowles, 1936–, British actor; Sally Bowles, American cabaret singer in 1930s Berlin, created by Christopher Isherwood and first appearing in print in 1937 (her exploits were dramatized in John Van Druten's *I am a Camera* (1951) and turned into a stage musical as *Cabaret* (1966, filmed 1972)); Stan Bowles, 1948–, English footballer]

Bowley, Bowlly 'person from Bowley', Devon and Herefordshire (respectively 'glade by a river bend' and 'Bola's glade') [Al Bowlly, ?1890–1941, Mozambique-born British popular singer]

Bowling from a medieval nickname for someone with a large head or hair cut very short (from Middle English *bolling* 'pollard'), or for a heavy drinker of alcohol (from Middle English *bolling* 'boozing', a derivative of *bolle* 'bowl (the vessel)')
— **'Tom Bowling'** a sea song by Charles Dibdin. It is said to have been inspired by Dibdin's brother Tom, a naval captain who died at Cape Town in 1780.

Bowman (i) 'archer'; (ii) an anglicization of the German name *Baumann* or Dutch *Bouman*, in both cases either literally 'peasant' or from a medieval nickname meaning 'neighbour' [James Bowman, 1941–, British countertenor]
— **Bowman's capsule** a cup-shaped part of the kidney that extracts waste and water from the blood and produces urine. Its name commemorates the British surgeon Sir William Bowman, 1816–92.

Bown, Bowne different forms of **Boon** [Jane Bown, 1925–, British photographer]

Bowra, Bowrah different forms of **Bower** (i–ii). See also **Burra** [Sir Maurice Bowra, 1898–1971, British scholar and critic]

Bowring, Bowering 'person who lives in a small cottage' (probably from an unrecorded Old English *būring* 'small cottage')
— **Bowring Bowl** a trophy presented annually to the winners of the Oxford v. Cambridge Varsity rugby match. It was donated in 1976 by C.T. Bowring & Co., a shipping line founded in Newfoundland in 1820 by Benjamin Bowring. The

firm was taken over in 1980 by Marsh and McClennan Companies, and the trophy subsequently became known as the MMC Trophy.

Bowser from a medieval nickname for a fine gentleman or (with heavy irony) for a despicable man, or for someone who was in the habit of using the Norman French expression *beu sire* 'fine sir' as a term of address
— **bowser** a mobile container for a large quantity of liquid (e.g. water or aviation fuel). In Australian and New Zealand the term is used for a petrol pump. It originated in a tradename established for oil and petrol pumps in the early 1920s by S.F. Bowser & Co. Inc. of Indiana, US.

Bowyer 'maker or sellers of bows (the weapon)'
— **Bowyer's Ltd.** a manufacturer of sausages and other pork products, based in Trowbridge, Wiltshire

Box 'person from Box', Gloucestershire, Hertfordshire and Wiltshire ('place by a box tree'), 'person who lives by a box tree', or perhaps 'person who makes articles out of box wood' [Betty Box, 1915–99, British film producer]
— **Box and Cox** a farce (1847) by J.M. Morton in which John Box, a journeyman printer, and James Cox, a journeyman hatter, occupy the same room in a lodging house at different times of day. By the 1880s the expression *Box and Cox* was being used to allude to a situation in which two people share the use of something in rotation.

Boxall, Boxell 'person from Boxholte', a no longer existent place in Sussex ('wood made up of box trees')

Boyce (i) 'person who lives by a wood' (from Old French *bois* 'wood'); (ii) 'son of *Boy*', either a nickname for a young lad or young male servant or from an unrecorded Old English male personal name *Boia*. See also **Boyson**; (iii) from Irish Gaelic *Ó Buadhaigh* (see **Bow** (iii)). See also **Boyse** [Max Boyce, 1945–, Welsh singer and comedian; William Boyce, ?1710–79, British composer]

Boycott 'person from Boycott', Buckinghamshire, Shropshire and Worcestershire ('Boia's cottage') [Geoffrey Boycott, 1940–, English cricketer; Rosie Boycott, 1951–, British journalist]
— **boycott** to refuse to deal with something, such as an organization, company or process, as a protest against it or in an effort to force it to become more acceptable. The verb was inspired by Captain Charles Boycott, 1832–97, a British estate manager in Ireland who clashed with the Land League over its request for rent reduction.

Boyd perhaps 'person from Bute', island in the Firth of Clyde ('island of fire') [William Boyd, 1895–1972, US actor, notably as 'Hopalong Cassidy'; William Boyd, 1952–, British author]

Boydell probably 'person from Bodle Street', Sussex ('dwelling' – from Old English *bōtl* (see also **Boodle**))

Boyden from the Old French male personal name *Bodin*, a different form of *Baudin* '**Baldwin**'

Boyes see **Boyse**

Boyle (i) from Irish Gaelic *Ó Baoithghill* 'descendant of *Baoithgheall*', a personal name perhaps meaning literally 'rash pledge'. See also **O'Boyle**; (ii) 'person from Boyville', northern France ('Boio's settlement') [Katie Boyle (*née* Imperiali di Francabilla), 1926–, Italian-born British model and television personality; Robert Boyle, 1627–91, Irish-born British physicist and chemist]
— **Boyle's law** the principle that the volume of a confined gas at constant temperature varies inversely with its pressure. It was enunciated by Robert Boyle (see above).

Boyles a different form of **Boyle**

Boynton probably 'person from Boynton', Yorkshire ('settlement associated with Bōfa')

Boyse, Boys, Boyes different forms of **Boyce**

Boysen 'son of Boje or Böhe', Scandinavian and North German male personal names related to Old English *Boia* (see **Boyce** (ii))
— **boysenberry** a plant that is a hybrid of the loganberry, the blackberry and the raspberry, and that produces large purplish-black fruit similar to the loganberry. It was produced in the 1930s by the US botanist and plant breeder Rudolf Boysen, 1895–1950.

Boyson a different form of **Boyce** (ii) [Sir Rhodes Boyson, 1925–, British teacher and Conservative politician]

Brabazon (i) 'person from Brabant', in what is now central Belgium (from Anglo-Norman *Brabançon* 'of Brabant'); (ii) 'mercenary soldier, brigand' (originally from Brabant) [John Moore-Brabazon (Lord Brabazon), see **Moore**]
— **Brabazon Trophy** a trophy awarded to the winner of the British open amateur golf championships. It was presented in 1947 by Lord Brabazon (see above).
— **Bristol Brabazon** an extremely large four-engined propeller-driven airliner produced by the Bristol Aircraft Company. Only one was ever made, in 1949, and it was scrapped in 1953. It was named after Lord Brabazon, who chaired the committee set up to make recommendations for the development of the British aircraft industry after World War II.

Brabham an alteration (influenced by surnames based on place-names ending in *-ham*) of *Brabant*, literally 'person from Brabant' (see **Brabazon** (i)) [Sir Jack Brabham, 1926–, Australian racing driver]

Brace 'maker or seller of armour' (from Middle English *brace* 'armour protecting the arms', from Old French *brace* 'arms'). See also **Brass** (i)

Bracegirdle 'maker of belts for holding up breeches' (from Old English *brēc, bræc* 'breeches' + *gyrdel* 'belt') [Anne Bracegirdle, ?1673–1748, British actress]

Bracewell 'person from Bracewell', Lancashire ('Breithr's spring')

Bracken (i) from Irish Gaelic *Ó Breacáin* 'descendant of *Breacán*', a personal name meaning literally 'little speckled or spotted one'; (ii) 'person who lives in an area much overgrown with bracken', or 'person from Bracken', Yorkshire ('area growing with bracken') [Brendan Bracken (1st Viscount Bracken), 1901–58, Irish-born British Conservative politician]

Brackenbury 'person from Brackenber', the name, variously spelled, of several places in England ('hill growing with bracken')

Brackenridge a different form of **Breckenridge**

Brackley 'person from Brackley', Northamptonshire ('Bracca's glade')

Bracknell 'person from Bracknell', Berkshire ('Bracca's nook of land')

Bradbrook 'person from Bradbrook', an unidentified place in England ('broad brook')

Bradbury 'person from Bradbury', the name of various places in England (mostly 'broad fortification') [Sir Malcolm Bradbury, 1932–2000, British novelist, critic and scholar; Ray Bradbury, 1920–, US science-fiction writer]
— *Bradbury* in Britain in the early part of the 20th century, a colloquial term for a £1 note. It was inspired by John Swanwick Bradbury (Lord Bradbury), 1872–1950, joint permanent secretary to the Treasury 1913-19.

Braddock 'person who lives by a particular large oak tree', or 'person from Braddock', an unidentified place in England (in either case from Old English *brād* 'broad' + *āc* 'oak') [Bessie Braddock, 1899–1970, British Labour politician; James Braddock, 1905–74, US boxer]

Braddon 'person from the Braddons', a range of hills in Devon ('broad hills') [Mary Elizabeth Braddon, 1837–1915, British novelist; Russell Braddon, 1921–95, Australian writer]

Braden from Irish Gaelic *Ó Bradáin* 'descendant of *Bradán*', a personal name meaning literally 'salmon' [Bernard Braden, 1916–93, Canadian actor and television presenter]

Bradey see **Brady**

Bradfield 'person from Bradfield', the name of various places in England ('broad area of open country')

Bradford 'person from Bradford', the name of various places in England, notably the city in Yorkshire ('broad ford') [Barbara Taylor Bradford (*née* Taylor), 1933–, British author]

Bradlaugh a different form of **Bradley** (i) [Charles Bradlaugh, 1833–91, British social reformer and freethinker]

Bradley (i) 'person from Bradley', the name of various places in England and Scotland ('broad glade'); (ii) from Irish Gaelic *Ó Brolcháin* 'descendant of *Brolchán*', a personal name meaning literally 'little beast' [A.C. Bradley, 1851–1935, British literary critic, brother of F.H.; F.H. Bradley, 1846–1924, British philosopher; Henry Bradley, 1845–1923, British philologist and lexicographer; James Bradley, 1693–1762, British astronomer; Omar Bradley, 1893–1981, US general]

Bradman from a medieval nickname for a large muscular fellow (from Old English *brād* 'broad' + *mann* 'man') [Sir Donald Bradman, 1908–2001, Australian cricketer]

Bradshaw 'person from Bradshaw', the name of various places in England ('broad thicket'). See also **Brayshaw**
— *Bradshaw* a colloquial shortening, common in the 19th and early 20th centuries, of the name of *Bradshaw's Railway Guide*, a timetable of all trains running in Britain, the earliest form of which was first produced in Manchester in 1839 by the printer and engraver George Bradshaw, 1801–53. During World War II, RAF pilots used *Bradshaw* as a verb, meaning 'to follow a railway in flying'.

Bradstreet 'person who lives by a Roman road or similar major highway' (from Old English *brād* 'broad' + *strǣt* 'paved way') [Anne Bradstreet (*née* Dudley), 1612–72, English-born American poet]

Bradwell 'person from Bradwell', the name of various places in England ('broad stream')

Brady, Bradey, Bradie (i) from Irish Gaelic *Ó Brádaigh* 'descendant of *Brádach*', a personal name of unknown origin and meaning. See also **O'Brady**; (ii) 'person from Brady', an unidentified place in England ('broad island'); (iii) 'person who lives in a broad enclosure' (from Old English *brād* 'broad' + *hæg* 'enclosure'); (iv) from a medieval nickname for someone with eyes that are large or wide apart (from Old English *brād* 'broad' + *eage* 'eye') [Ian Brady (original name Ian Duncan Stewart; Brady was his stepfather's name), 1938–, British child-murderer; Terence Brady, 1939–, British playwright and novelist]
— *The Brady Bunch* a US television sitcom (1969–74) featuring widowed architect Mike Brady and his family containing the combined offspring of previous marriages

Bragg, Bragge from a medieval nickname for a cheerful or lively person (from Middle English *bragge* 'spirited, brisk, lively, cheerful') [Billy Bragg, 1957–, British singer/songwriter; Sir Lawrence Bragg, 1890–1971, Australian-born British physicist, son of Sir William; Melvyn Bragg (Lord Bragg), 1939–, British writer and radio and television presenter; Sir William Bragg, 1862–1942, British physicist]
— *Bragg's law* a law stating the directions in which X-rays reflected from a crystal are most intense. It is named after Sir William and Sir Lawrence Bragg (see above).

Braham, Brayham different forms of **Bream** (i)

Brahms 'son of *Brahm*', a German shortened form of **Abraham** [Caryl Brahms (original name Doris Caroline Abrahams), 1901–82, British writer]

Brain, Braine from Scottish Gaelic *Mac an Bhreitheamhan*, literally 'son of the judge' [Dennis Brain, 1921–57, British horn player; John Braine, 1922–86, British novelist]

Brainin 'son of *Brayne*', a shortened form of the Yiddish female personal name *Brayndl*, literally 'little brown one'

Braithwaite, Brathwaite 'person from Braithwaite', the name of various places in Cumbria and Yorkshire ('broad clearing') [Edward Kamau Brathwaite, 1930–, Barbadian poet]

Brake 'person who lives by a thicket or bushy area' (from Middle English *brake* 'thicket'), or 'person who lives by an area overgrown with bracken' (from southern Middle English *brake* 'bracken')

Bramah, Bramma different forms of **Bramall** [Joseph Bramah, 1748–1814, British engineer and inventor who in 1784 designed a pick-proof lock]

Bramall, Brammall, Bramhall 'person from Bramall or Bramhall', Yorkshire and Cheshire respectively ('corner of land where broom grows'). See also **Brummell**

Bramble, Brambell (i) 'person who lives where brambles grow thickly'; (ii) perhaps from a medieval nickname for a 'prickly' short-tempered person; (iii) a different form of **Bramall** [Wilfred Brambell, 1912–85, British actor]

Bramley 'person from Bramley', the name of various places in England ('glade where broom grows'). See also **Bromley**
— **Bramley's seedling** a type of cooking apple. It is named after Matthew Bramley, an English butcher, in whose garden at Southwell, Nottinghamshire, it is said to have been first grown around 1850.

Bramma see **Bramah**

Bramwell 'person from Bramwell', an unidentified place in England ('spring or stream where broom grows')

Branagan see **Brannigan**

Branagh, Brannagh from Irish Gaelic *Breathnach* 'British person, Briton' [Kenneth Branagh, 1960–, British actor and director]

Branch (i) from a medieval nickname for someone thought to resemble a branch, although the reasons for the comparison are not clear; (ii) an anglicization of any of a range of Swedish surnames (e.g. **Lundgren**) ending in *gren* 'branch'

Brand (i) from the Germanic male personal name *Brando*, a derivative of any of a range of Germanic compound personal names (e.g. *Hildebrand*) containing the element *brand* 'sword'. See also **Braund, Brawn**; (ii) 'person who lives in an area where burning has taken place (e.g. to clear ground for crops)' (from Middle English *brand* 'burning'). See also **Brent** (ii); (iii) a different form of **Brandt** [Jo Brand (original name Joanne Brand), 1957–, British comedian; Russell Brand, 1975–, British comedian and radio DJ]

Brandeis 'person from Brandýs (German *Brandeis*)', Czech Republic [Louis Brandeis, 1856–1941, US supreme court justice (the first Jew to hold such a post)]
— **Brandeis University** a non-sectarian Jewish-sponsored university in Waltham, Massachusetts, US, founded in 1948. It was named in honour of Louis Brandeis (see above).

Brando from the Italian form of the Germanic male personal name *Brando* (see **Brand** (i)) [Marlon Brando, 1924–2004, US actor]

Brandon (i) 'person from Brandon', the name of numerous places in England (mostly 'hill where broom grows'); (ii) from *Brandon*, the oblique case of the French form of the Germanic male personal name *Brando* (see **Brand** (i))

Brandt 'person who lives in an area where burning has taken place (e.g. to clear ground for crops)' (from Middle High German *brant* 'burning'). See also **Brand** (ii–iii) [Bill Brandt, 1904–83, German-born British photographer]

Brangwyn, Brangwin perhaps from the Welsh female personal name *Branwen*, literally 'fair or holy raven' [Sir Frank Brangwyn, 1867–1956, Belgian-born British artist]

Braniff from Irish Gaelic *Ó Brandhuibh* 'descendant of *Brandubh*', a personal name meaning literally 'black raven'
— **Braniff International Airways** a US airline founded in 1928 by Thomas E. Braniff, 1883–1954, and his brother Paul Revere Braniff, 1897–1954. It ceased operations in 1982.

Brannagh see **Branagh**

Brannigan, Branigan, Branagan from Irish Gaelic *Ó Branagáin* 'descendant of *Branagán*', a personal name meaning literally 'little raven' [Owen Brannigan, 1908–73, British bass-baritone]

Branson (i) 'son of **Brand** (i)'; (ii) 'person from Briençun', northern France [Sir Richard Branson, 1950–, British businessman and entrepreneur]

Branston (i) a different form of **Branson**; (ii) 'person from Branston', the name (variously spelled) of numerous places in England ('Brant's or Brandr's farmstead')

Brant a different form of **Brand** [Joseph Brant (original name Thayendanegea; birth surname perhaps Tehonwaghkwangearahkwa), 1742–1807, Mohawk Indian chief who fought on the British side in the American Revolution]

Brasher (i) 'brewer' (from a derivative of Old French *brasser* 'to brew'); (ii) a different form of **Brazier** [Chris Brasher, 1928–2003, British athlete and sports journalist, co-founder of the London Marathon]

Brass, Brasse (i) a different form of **Brace**; (ii) from a medieval North German nickname for a noisy person (from Middle Low German *brās* 'noise'); (iii) 'person who lives where broom grows' (from German *Brass* 'broom, gorse')

Bratby 'person from Bretby', Derbyshire ('farm of the Britons') [John Bratby, 1928–92, British painter]

Brathwaite see **Braithwaite**

Bratten, Brattain from Scottish Gaelic *Mac an Bhreatnaich*, literally 'son of the Briton' (originally referring to Welsh-speakers in Strathclyde) [Walter H. Brattain, 1902–87, Chinese-born US physicist]

Braun from a medieval German nickname for a brown-haired person, or one with a tanned complexion, or one who habitually wore brown clothes (from Middle High German *brūn* 'brown'), or from the German male personal name *Bruno*, literally 'brown'

Braund a different form of **Brand** (i)

Braunstein an invented Jewish name, from German *braun* 'brown' + *stein* 'stone'. See also **Bronstein**

Bravo from a Spanish and Portuguese nickname for a fierce or violent man (from Spanish and Portuguese *bravo* 'fierce, violent') [Charles Bravo, 1845–76, British lawyer and possible murder victim]

Brawley from Irish Gaelic *Ó Brólaigh* 'descendant of *Brólach*', a personal name perhaps based on *brollach* 'breast'

Brawn, Brawne perhaps different forms of **Brand** (i) [Fanny Brawne, 1800–65, fiancée of the poet John Keats]

Braxton 'person from Braxton', an unidentified place in England ('Bracca's farmstead')

Bray 'person from Bray', Berkshire and Devon (respectively 'marshy place' and 'hill')

Brayham see **Braham**

Brayshaw a different form of **Bradshaw**

Brazier 'worker in brass' (from a derivative of Old English *bræsian* 'to cast in brass'). See also **Brasher** (ii)

Brazil, Brazill, Brazel, Brazell, Brazzell, Brazzle from Irish Gaelic *Ó Breasail* 'descendant of *Breasal*', a nickname meaning literally 'strife'. The name is traditionally stressed on the first syllable. [Angela Brazil, 1868–1947, British writer of girls' school stories]

Breakspear from a medieval nickname for someone who had achieved notable success in jousts or in battle [Nicholas Breakspear, ?1100–59, the original name of Pope Hadrian IV, the only English pope]

Breakwell 'person from Breakwell', an unidentified place probably in the West Midlands

Bream (i) 'person from Braham', Yorkshire ('homestead or enclosure where broom grows'). See also **Braham**; (ii) 'person from Bramham', Yorkshire ('homestead or enclosure where broom grows'); (iii) 'person from Brantham', Suffolk ('Brant's homestead'); (iv) from a medieval nickname for an energetic or ferocious person (from Middle English *breme* 'fierce, vigorous') [Julian Bream, 1933–, British guitarist and lutenist]

Brearley see **Brierley**

Breckenridge 'person from Brackenrig', Lanarkshire ('ridge growing with bracken'). See also **Brackenridge**
— *Myra Breckenridge* a novel (1968) by Gore Vidal in which the transsexual (formerly male) Myra Breckenridge advances the cause of feminism via sexual predation. A film version appeared in 1970.

Bredin from Irish Gaelic *Mac Giolla Bhrídín*, a diminutive form of *Mac Giolla Bhrighde* (see **Kilbride** (ii))

Breed 'person from Breed', the name of several places (variously spelled) in England ('broad stretch of land')

Breedlove probably from a medieval nickname for a likable or popular person (from Middle English *breden* 'to produce' + *love*) [Craig Breedlove, 1937–, US land-speed record holder]

Breedon, Breeden, Bredon 'person from Breedon or Bredon', Leicestershire and Worcestershire respectively ('place by *Bre* Hill', from a Celtic word meaning 'hill')

Breeze, Breese (i) from a medieval nickname for an annoying person (from Middle English *breeze* 'gadfly'); (ii) from Welsh *ap Rhys* 'son of **Rhys**'. See also **Brice** (ii)

Bremner 'person from Brabant', in what is now central Belgium (from medieval Scots *Brabanare, Brebner* 'person from Brabant') [Billy Bremner, 1942–97, Scottish footballer; Rory Bremner, 1961–, British impressionist]

Brenchley 'person from Brenchley', Kent ('Brænci's glade')

Brennan, Brenan from Irish Gaelic *Ó Braonáin* 'descendant of *Braonán*', a personal name meaning literally 'little drop of moisture' [Christopher Brennan, 1870–1932, Australian poet; Gerald Brenan, 1894–1987, Maltese-born British author; Walter Brennan, 1894–1974, US actor; William J. Brennan, Jr., 1906–97, US associate justice of the US Supreme Court]

Brenner (i) 'burner' (e.g. one who distils spirits or makes charcoal by burning, or one who clears land by burning) (from a derivative of Middle High German *brennen* 'to burn'); (ii) a different form of **Berner** (ii–iii) [Sydney Brenner, 1927–, South African molecular biologist]

Brent (i) 'person from Brent', the name of various places in Devon and Somerset ('high place'); (ii) 'person who lives by an area of land cleared by burning' (from Middle English *brent* 'burnt'). See also **Brand** (ii); (iii) from a medieval nickname for a criminal who had been branded [David Brent, office manager from hell (played by Ricky Gervais) in the BBC television sitcom *The Office* (2001–03)]

Brenton 'person from Brenton', Devon ('farmstead associated with Brȳni') [Howard Brenton, 1942–, British playwright]

Brereton 'person from Brereton', Cheshire and Staffordshire (respectively 'farmstead among the briars' and 'hill where briars grow')

Breslau, Bresslaw 'person from Breslau', the German name of the Polish city of Wrocław [Bernard Bresslaw, 1934–93, British comic actor]

Bresnahan from Irish Gaelic *Ó Brosnacháin* 'descendant of *Brosnachán*', a personal name meaning literally 'person from Brosna' (a town in County Kerry). See also **Brosnan**

Bretherton 'person from Bretherton', Lancashire ('farmstead of the brothers')

Brett 'person from Brittany, Breton' (from Old French *bret* 'Breton') [Jeremy Brett (original name

Jeremy Huggins), 1935–95, British actor; Simon Brett, 1945–, British author]

Bretton (i) 'person from Bretton', Derbyshire and Yorkshire ('farmstead of the (ancient) Britons'); (ii) *also* **Breton** a different form of **Brett** (from Old French *breton*, the oblique case of *bret*). See also **Brittain**

Brew (i) from Irish Gaelic *Ó Brughadha* 'descendant of *Brughaidh*', a nickname meaning literally 'strong or prosperous farmer'; (ii) 'judge' (from Manx Gaelic *breitheamh* 'judge')

Brewbaker see **Brubaker**

Brewer (i) 'brewer of beer or ale'. See also **Brewster**; (ii) 'person from Bruyère', Normandy ('place where heather grows') [Ebenezer Cobham Brewer, 1810–97, British author and reference-book editor; Sir Herbert Brewer, 1865–1928, British organist and composer]
— *Brewer's Dictionary of Phrase and Fable* a dictionary of folklore, mythology, etymology and assorted curiosities, originally compiled by Ebenezer Cobham Brewer (see above) and first published in 1870

Brewis (i) 'person who works in a brewery' (from Middle English *brewhus* 'brewery'); (ii) 'person from Briouse', northern France (probably 'muddy place')

Brewster a different form of **Brewer** (i) (originally literally 'female brewer', but the gender distinction had died out by the early Middle Ages) [Sir David Brewster, 1781–1868, British physicist]
— *Brewster's law* a law relating a material's index of refraction to the tangent of the material's angle of polarization. It was formulated by Sir David Brewster (see above).
— *Brewster's Millions* a novel (1902) by George McCutcheon in which a man called Montgomery Brewster stands to gain seven million dollars under the terms of his uncle's will if he can succeed in spending one million within a year. It has been filmed several times, most recently (1985) with Brewster (Richard Pryor) transformed into a baseball player.

Brian, Briant see **Bryan, Bryant**

Brice, Bryce (i) from a Celtic personal name which survives only in the Latinized form *Britius* or *Brixius*. See also **Bryson**; (ii) a different form of **Breeze** (ii); (iii) an anglicization of the Jewish surname *Briess*, of unknown origin and meaning [Fanny Brice (original name Fania Borach), 1891–1951, US comedian, singer and entertainer; Martin Bryce, obsessive loser (played by Richard Briers) in the BBC television sitcom *Ever Decreasing Circles* (1984–89)]

Bride a different form of **Bird**

Bridge (i) 'person who lives by or guards a bridge'; (ii) 'person from Bridge', the name of various places in England. See also **Burge** [Frank Bridge, 1879–1941, British composer]

Bridgeman, Bridgman different forms of **Bridge** (i) [Percy Williams Bridgman, 1882–1961, US physicist]

— **Bridgeman Art Library** an international archive of reproductions of works of art, established in 1972 by Harriet Bridgeman (Viscountess Bridgeman; *née* Turton), 1942–, British editor and author

Bridges (i) a different form of **Bridge** (i). See also **Briggs**; (ii) 'person from Bruges', Flanders ('bridges') [Kate Bridges (Mrs Bridges), testy cook (played by Angela Baddeley) in the ITV drama series *Upstairs, Downstairs* (1971–75); Robert Bridges, 1844–1930, British poet]

Bridgewater, Bridgwater 'person from Bridgwater', Somerset ('Walter's bridge')

Brien see **Bryan**

Brierley, Brierly, Brearley 'person from Brierley or Brierly', the name of various places in England ('glade where briars grow') [Michael Brearley, 1942–, English cricketer, psychoanalyst and writer]

Briers, Bryers, Bryars 'person who lives by a briar patch' [Gavin Bryars, 1943–, British composer; Richard Briers, 1934–, British actor]

Brigden probably 'person from Brigden', an unidentified place in northern England (perhaps 'valley with a bridge')

Brigginshaw a different form of **Burkinshaw**

Briggs a northern English and Scottish variant of **Bridges** (i) [Asa Briggs (Lord Briggs), 1921–, British historian; Henry Briggs, 1561–1630, English mathematician; Raymond Briggs, 1934–, British author and illustrator]

Brigham 'person from Brigham', Cumbria and Yorkshire ('homestead or enclosure by a bridge')

Bright (i) from a medieval nickname or personal name meaning literally 'bright, attractive, pretty'; (ii) from a shortened form of any of a range of Old English compound personal names beginning with *Beorht-* or *Byrht-*, literally 'bright, shining' (e.g. *Byrhtnoth*); (iii) an anglicization of the German surname *Brecht*, from a shortened form of any of a range of Germanic compound personal names based *berht* 'bright, famous' (e.g. *Albrecht*) [John Bright, 1811–89, British radical politician; Richard Bright, 1789–1858, British physician]
— **Bright's disease** an inflammatory disease of the kidneys, such as glomerulonephritis. The symptoms were first described by Richard Bright (see above).

Brightman (i) a different form of **Bright**; (ii) 'servant of a man called "Bright"' [Sarah Brightman, 1960–, British singer and actress]

Brightwell 'person from Brightwell', the name of various places in England ('clear spring or stream') [Robbie Brightwell, 1939–, British athlete]

Brignell, Brignall 'person from Brignall', County Durham ('Brȳni's people's nook of land')

Brigstocke 'person from Brigstock', Northamptonshire ('outlying farm by a bridge')

Brill (i) 'person from Brill', the name of various places in northwestern Germany and the Netherlands ('wet lowlands'); (ii) 'person from Brill', Buckinghamshire ('*Bre* hill', from a Celtic word meaning 'hill' – hence, 'hill hill'); (iii) 'spectacle-maker', or from a medieval German nickname for someone who wore glasses (in either case from Middle Low German *brill* 'spectacles, glasses'); (iv) an acronymic Jewish surname based on Hebrew *bar* 'son of' and a two-part male personal name beginning with *Y* and *L*

Brindley 'person from Brindley', Cheshire ('woodland clearing created by burning') [James Brindley, 1716–72, British canal builder]

Brink 'person who lives by a pasture' (from Middle Low German *brinc* 'meadow, pasture') [André Brink, 1935–, South African novelist and playwright]

Brinkley 'person from Brinkley', Cambridgeshire and Nottinghamshire ('Brynca's glade')

Brinton 'person from Brinton', Norfolk ('estate associated with Brȳni')

Brisbane perhaps from a medieval nickname for a hot-tempered and belligerent person (from Old French *briser* 'to break' + Middle English *ban* 'bone')
— **Brisbane** the capital and chief port of Queensland, Australia, on the Brisbane River. It was named in honour of Sir Thomas Brisbane, 1773–1860, governor of New South Wales 1821–25, who was instrumental in establishing the place as a penal colony in the 1820s.

Briscoe, Brisco 'person from Briscoe or Brisco', the name of various places in northern England ('wood of the Britons')

Bristow, Bristowe 'person from Bristol (originally Bristow)' ('assembly place by the bridge') [Bristow, lowly clerk with lofty ideas drawn (from 1962) by the British cartoonist Frank Dickens; Eric Bristow, 1957–, British darts player]

Brittain, Brittan, Britten, Britton (i) 'person from Britain or Brittany; Briton, Breton'; (ii) 'British person' (as adopted patriotically by new immigrants to Britain) [Benjamin Britten (Lord Britten), 1913–76, British composer; Fern Britton, 1958–, British television presenter, daughter of Tony; Leon Brittan (Lord Brittan), 1939–, British Conservative politician, brother of Samuel; Ronald Brittain, 1899–1981, British regimental sergeant-major renowned for his extremely loud voice; Sir Samuel Brittan, 1933–, British journalist; Tony Britton, 1924–, British actor; Vera Brittain, 1893–1970, British writer, pacifist and feminist]

Broad from a medieval nickname for a well-built or fat person, or from the Old English male personal name *Brāda* (a derivative of *brād* 'broad') [Chris Broad, 1957–, English cricketer]

Broadbent 'person from Broadbent', Lancashire ('place where broad-leaved grass grows') [Jim Broadbent, 1949–, British actor; Michael Broadbent, 1927–, British wine auctioneer and writer]

Broadhead from a medieval nickname for someone with a large head or a wide forehead

Broadhurst 'person who lives by a broad wooded hill' (from Old English *brād* 'broad' + *hyrst* 'wooded hill')

Broadway 'person who lives by a broad road', or 'person from Broadway', Somerset and Worcestershire (in either case from Old English *brād* 'broad' + *weg* 'way')

Broadwood person who lives by a broad wood' (from Old English *brād* 'broad' + *wudu* 'wood') [John Broadwood, 1732–1812, British maker of pianos and harpsichords]

Brock (i) a different form of **Brook**. See also **Brockman** (i); (ii) from a medieval nickname for someone thought to resemble a badger (from Old English *broc* 'badger', a borrowing from Celtic); (iii) from a medieval nickname for someone thought to resemble a young stag (from Middle English *brock*, a shortened form of *brocket* – see **Brockett** (ii)); (iv) probably an acronymic Jewish surname based on Hebrew *bar* 'son of' and a two-part male personal name [C.T. Brock, 1843–81, British firework manufacturer]
— **Brock's benefit** originally (from the spectacular firework displays held annually at the Crystal Palace from 1865 to 1936, organized by C.T. Brock & Co. (see above)), a breathtaking illumination of the night sky. The expression gained currency during the First World War, to describe the night-time scene of shellbursts, searchlights, etc. over the Flanders trenches. It subsequently came to be used metaphorically for any spectacular outburst.

Brockett (i) 'person from Brocket', Ayrshire; (ii) from a medieval nickname for someone thought to resemble a young stag (from Middle English *brocket* 'young stag', from Old French *brocart*). See also **Brock** (iii)

Brocklebank 'person from Brocklebank', Cumbria ('bank containing badger sets')

Brocklehurst 'person from Brocklehurst', Lancashire ('wooded hill frequented by badgers')

Brocklesby 'person from Brocklesby', Lancashire ('Bróklauss's farmstead')

Brockman (i) a different form of **Brock** (i); (ii) an anglicization of German *Brockmann*, literally 'person who lives by a marsh' (from Middle Low German *brook* 'marsh, swamp' + *man*)

Brockway 'person who lives by a path beside a brook' (from Middle English *broke* 'brook' + *way*) [Fenner Brockway (Lord Brockway), 1888–1988, British Labour politician and peace activist]

Brockwell probably 'person from Brockwell', Derbyshire or other unidentified locations ('badger stream' or 'badger hole')

Broderick (i) from Irish Gaelic *Ó Bruadair* 'descendant of *Bruadar*', a personal name of Old Norse origin; (ii) from Welsh *ap Rhydderch* 'son of *Rhydderch*' (see **Roderick** (ii)) [Matthew Broderick, 1962–, US actor]

Brodie (i) 'person from Brodie Castle', Moray (*Brodie* probably 'muddy place'); (ii) *also* **Brody** *or* **Brodi** different forms of **Brodski** (i)
— *The Prime of Miss Jean Brodie* a novel (1961) by Muriel Spark about a sharp-minded Edinburgh schoolmistress and her coterie of favoured pupils,

the 'crème de la crème'. In the film version (1969), Miss Brodie was played by Maggie Smith.

Brodski, Brodsky (i) '(Jewish) person from Brod or Brody', Moravia and the Ukraine respectively ('place by a ford'). See also **Brodie** (ii); (ii) from a medieval Polish nickname for a bearded man (from *boroda* 'beard') [Joseph Brodsky, 1940–96, Soviet-born US poet and essayist]

Brogan from Irish Gaelic *Ó Brógáin* 'descendant of *Brógán*', a personal name perhaps meaning literally 'little shoe'

Brogden 'person from Brogden', Yorkshire ('valley with a brook')

Bromage, Brommage, Bromwich, Bromidge 'person from Bromwich', the name of various places in the West Midlands ('farm where broom grows')

Brome see **Broom**

Bromfield 'person from Bromfield', Cumbria and Shropshire ('open land where broom or gorse grows'). See also **Broomfield**

Bromley 'person from Bromley', the name of numerous places in England ('glade where broom grows'). See also **Bramley** [Peter Bromley, 1929–2003, British horse-racing commentator]

Bronowski probably '(Jewish) person from Bronów or Bronowo', an unidentified place in Poland or a contiguous Slavic country [Jacob Bronowski, 1908–74, Polish-born British mathematician, science writer and broadcaster]

Bronson 'son of **Brown**'. See also **Brunson** [Charles Bronson (original name Charles Buchinsky), 1921–2003, US actor]

Bronstein a different form of **Braunstein**

Brontë an alteration of the Irish surname *Prunty*, itself from Irish Gaelic *Ó Proinntigh* 'descendant of *Proinnteach*', a personal name perhaps meaning literally 'bestower'. The impulse for the change appears to have come from the popularity in the early 19th century of Lord Nelson, who in 1799 was created duke of Bronte by King Ferdinand of the Two Sicilies (Bronte is a place in Sicily). [Anne Brontë, 1820–49, British novelist and poet; Charlotte Brontë, 1816–55, British novelist, sister of Anne; Emily Brontë, 1818–48, British novelist and poet, sister of Anne; Patrick Branwell Brontë, 1817–48, British artist, brother of Anne]

Brook, Brooke, Broke 'person who lives by a brook'. See also **Brock** (i), **Brooking**, **Brooks** [Alan Brooke (1st Viscount Alanbrooke), 1883–1963, British field marshal; Sir Basil Stanlake Brooke (1st Viscount Brookeborough), 1883–1973, Northern Irish Unionist politician, prime minister of Northern Ireland 1943–63; Clive Brook, 1887–1974, British actor; Sir James Brooke (Raja Brooke), 1803–68, British explorer, the 'White Raja of Sarawak'; Peter Brook, 1925–, British theatre director; Rupert Brooke, 1887–1915, British poet; Tim Brooke-Taylor, 1940–, British comic actor and writer]
— **Brooke Bond & Co.** a tea producer established in Manchester in 1869 by Arthur Brooke, 1845–1918. (There never was a Mr Bond).

— **Brookeborough** a village in Fermanagh, Northern Ireland, named after the local Brooke family (of which Alan Brooke (see above) and Sir Basil Brooke (see above) were members)
— **brookite** a translucent or reddish-brown to black crystalline mineral composed of titanium oxide. It was named after the British mineralogist Henry Brook, 1771–1857.
— **Raja Brooke butterfly** a large black and green birdwing butterfly (*Trogonoptera brookiana*) of Borneo and Malaysia. It was named after Sir James Brooke (see above).

Brookfield 'person from Brookfield', an unidentified place probably in Lancashire ('area of open land with a brook')

Brooking a different form of **Brook** [Sir Trevor Brooking, 1948–, English footballer and administrator]

Brookner an anglicization of the German surname *Bruckner*, literally 'someone who lives by or guards a bridge' [Anita Brookner, 1928–, British novelist]

Brooks, Brookes different forms of **Brook** [Elkie Brooks, 1945–, British jazz singer; Mel Brooks (original name Melvin Kaminsky), 1926–, US film actor and director]
— **Brooks Brothers** a US men's clothier, founded in New York City in 1818 by Henry Sands Brooks. Its name dates from the 1850s, when his grandsons Daniel, John and Elisha Brooks inherited the business.
— **Brooks's** a British gentleman's club in St James's Street, London, founded in 1764 by William Almack. It took its name from William Brooks, a wine merchant and moneylender who was its manager when it moved to its present premises in 1778.
— **Oxford Brookes University** a university in Oxford, created in 1992 from the former Oxford Polytechnic and named in honour of J.H. Brookes, principal of the (as it then was) Schools of Technology, Art and Commerce from 1934

Broom, Broome, Brome 'person from Broom, Broome or Brome', the name of numerous places in England ('place where broom or gorse grows') [David Broome, 1940–, British show jumper]

Broomfield 'person from Broomfield', Essex, Kent and Somerset ('open land where broom or gorse grows'). See also **Bromfield**

Brophy from Irish Gaelic *Ó Bróithe* 'descendant of *Bróth*', a personal name of unknown origin and meaning [Brigid Brophy, 1929–95, British novelist]

Brosnan from Irish Gaelic *Ó Brosnacháin* 'descendant of *Brosnachán*', a personal name based on *Brosne*, the name of a town and river in County Kerry [Pierce Brosnan, 1953–, Irish actor]

Brother (i) from a medieval nickname for a younger son (seen from the point of view of his status in relation to his older or oldest 'brother'); (ii) 'fellow member of a guild or similar fraternal association'; (iii) from the Old Norse male personal name *Bróthir*, originally used for a younger son

Brothers from Irish Gaelic *Ó Bruadhair*, a clan name from Donegal, of uncertain meaning

Brotherstone, Brotherston 'person from Brotherstone', Berwickshire and Midlothian ('Bróthir's stones' or 'twin stones')

Brotherton 'person from Brotherton', Suffolk and Yorkshire ('brother's farmstead' or 'Bróthir's farmstead')

Brough 'person from Brough', the name of several places in England ('stronghold') [Peter Brough, 1916–99, British ventriloquist]

Brougham 'person from Brougham', Cumbria ('homestead by the stronghold'). The name is pronounced 'broom'.
— **brougham** a one-horse carriage with an open seat at the front for the driver and a closed compartment at the back for passengers, used in the 19th century. It was named after its designer Henry Brougham (Lord Brougham and Vaux), 1778–1868.

Broughton 'person from Broughton', the name of several places in England (variously 'farmstead by a brook', 'fortified farmstead' and 'farmstead by a hill') [Rhoda Broughton, 1840–1920, British novelist]

Brown, Browne (i) from a medieval nickname for someone with brown hair or a tanned complexion; (ii) from the Old English male personal name *Brūn*, either an adoption of the nickname (as in (i)) or a shortened form of any of a range of compound personal names (e.g. *Brūnwine*) beginning with *brūn* 'brown' [Sir Arthur Whitten Brown, 1886–1948, British aviator (see also **Alcock**); 'Capability' Brown (original name Lancelot Brown), 1716–83, British landscape gardener; Casey Brown, a mythical early 20th-century who fought for African-American rights and against racism; Charlie Brown, boy who is one of the main characters of the 'Peanuts' cartoon strip (1950–99) by Charles M. Schulz; Craig Brown, 1957–, British journalist and humorist; Father Brown, Roman Catholic priest and detective in stories by G.K. Chesterton; Ford Madox Brown, 1821–93, British painter; George Brown (Lord George-Brown), 1914–85, British Labour politician; George Mackay Brown, 1921–96, British poet and novelist; Gordon Brown, 1951–, British Labour politician, prime minister 2007–; Hablot Knight Browne ('Phiz'), 1815–82, British artist and illustrator; James Brown, 1933–2006, US soul singer; Janet Brown, 1924–, British comedian and impressionist; Jerry Brown, 1938–, US Democratic politician; Joe Brown, 1930–, British mountaineer; Joe Brown, 1941–, British pop singer and entertainer; Joe E. Brown, 1892–1973, US actor and comedian; John Brown, 1800–59, US campaigner for the abolition of slavery; John Brown, 1826–83, Scottish gillie, servant to Queen Victoria; Robert Brown, 1773–1858, Scottish botanist; Robert Browne, ?1550–1633, English Puritan separatist; Roy 'Chubby' Brown (original name Royston Vasey), 1945–, British comedian; Sir Thomas Browne, 1605–82, English physician and writer; Tina Brown, 1953–, British journalist; William Brown, middle-class urchin in the 'William' books (1922–70) of Richmal Crompton]

☆ The second commonest surname in Canada; third commonest in New Zealand; 4th commonest in Britain, the US and Australia

— **Brown Brothers** an Australian wine-producer established in Milawa, Victoria in 1885 by John Francis Brown, 1867–1943, in collaboration with his father (although he had several brothers, they never actually joined him in the firm)

— **Brownian motion** the random movement of microscopic particles suspended in a liquid or gas that occurs as a result of collisions with molecules of the surrounding medium. It was named after Robert Brown (see above), who first observed it.

— **Brownist** a follower of Robert Browne (see above). Brownists were the spiritual ancestors of Congregationalists.

— *Brown on Resolution* a novel (1929) by C.S. Forester which tells how Seaman Brown, a British sailor in World War I, is captured by the Germans and escapes on to the fictional island of Resolution

— **Brown's Hotel** a hotel in Dover Street, in the West End of London, opened in 1837 by James Brown, a former manservant

— **Brown University** a university in Providence, Rhode Island, USA, founded in 1764 as Rhode Island College. It changed its name in 1804 in honour of Nicholas Brown, Jr., 1769–1841, a graduate and generous benefactor of the college whose father Nicholas and uncle John had been signatories of its original charter.

— **John Brown & Company** originally, a British steel manufacturer, established in Sheffield in 1840 by Sir John Brown, 1816–96. In 1899 it took over J. & G. Thomson's shipyard on Clydeside (founded 1851), and thereafter was best known as a shipbuilder.

— **'John Brown's Body'** an American popular song in praise of the abolitionist John Brown (see above), sung to the tune of a 19th-century camp-meeting and revival hymn

— **Mrs Brown** a sarcastic nickname bestowed on Queen Victoria by those who felt that she had become too attached to her gillie John Brown (see above) after the death of the Prince Consort. A 1997 film *Mrs Brown* portrayed their relationship.

— **'Mrs Brown you've got a lovely daughter'** a pop song by Trevor Peacock, with which Herman's Hermits had a hit in 1965

— **Sam Browne belt** a belt worn by British army officers consisting of a wide leather belt round the waist supported by a diagonal strap that passes from the left-hand side over the right shoulder. It is named after its inventor, the British general Sir Samuel Browne, 1824–1901. It was also adopted by other military and police forces.

— **'Shallow Brown'** a West Indian shanty telling the story of Shallow Brown, a former slave who signs on to a whaling ship to earn money to buy the freedom of his girlfriend. By the time he returns, however, she is gone, sold to a new master. The best-known setting is by Percy Grainger.

Browning 'son of **Brown** (ii)' [Elizabeth Barrett Browning (*née* Barrett), 1806–61, British poet, wife of Robert; Robert Browning, 1812–89, British poet]

— **Browing automatic rifle** an air-cooled gas-operated magazine-fed rifle with a .30 in calibre barrel, which was the main US infantry weapon of the first half of the 20th century. It was designed in 1917 by James Moses Browning, 1855–1926. From the same stable came the **Browning machine gun**, an air- or water-cooled belt-fed automatic machine gun with either a .30 or .50 in calibre barrel.

— *The Browning Version* a play (1948) by Terence Rattigan in which the emotionally consti- pated schoolmaster Andrew Crocker-Harris is touched to be presented by one of his pupils with a copy of Robert Browning's (see above) translation of Aeschylus's *Agamemnon*

Brownjohn from a medieval nickname for a man called John with brown hair or a tanned complexion [Alan Brownjohn, 1931–, British poet]

Brownlee, Brownley, Brownlie 'person from Brownlee or Brownley', Lanarkshire and Warwickshire respectively ('brown glade')

Brownlow 'person from Brownlow', Cheshire, Greater Manchester and Staffordshire ('brown hill') [Kevin Brownlow, 1938–, British author and film director]

Brownrigg 'person from Brownrigg', Cumbria ('brown ridge')

Brubaker, Brewbaker anglicizations of the German and Swiss German surname *Brubacher*, literally 'person from Braubach', the name of various places in Germany and Switzerland

Brubeck (i) an anglicization of the German surname *Brubach*, literally 'person from Brau- bach' (see **Brubaker**) or 'person from Bruebach', Alsace; (ii) an anglicization of the Norwegian surname *Brubekk*, literally 'person from Brubekk', Norway [Dave Brubeck, 1920–, US jazz pianist and composer]

Bruce perhaps 'person from Brix', or alternatively 'person from Briouze or Le Brus', all places in northern France [Christopher Bruce, 1945–, British dancer and choreographer; James Bruce, 1730–94, British explorer; Robert the Bruce (Robert I), 1274–1329, king of Scotland 1306–29; Stanley Melbourne Bruce (1st Viscount Bruce), 1883–1967, Australian National party politician, prime minister 1923–29]

— *The Bruce* a lengthy verse chronicle of the deeds of Robert the Bruce (see above), written by John Barbour in 1376

— **brucellosis** a chronic infectious disease of some domestic animals that can be transmitted to human beings through contaminated milk. The causative bacteria are of the genus *Brucella*, which was named after the Scottish physician Sir David Bruce, 1855–1931.

— **brucite** a magnesium hydroxide mineral found in hydrothermal deposits and metamorphosed limestone. It was named after the US mineralogist Archibald Bruce, 1777–1818.

Brudenell 'person from Brittany', or from a deri- sive medieval nickname for a Breton (in either case

from Old Northern French *Bretonnel*, literally 'little Breton')

Brummell a different form of **Bramall** [George Bryan Brummell ('Beau' Brummell), 1778–1840, British dandy]

Brummitt, Brummett perhaps 'person from Broomhead', Yorkshire ('headland where broom grows')

Brunel, Brunell from a medieval French nickname for someone with brown hair or a tanned complexion (from Old French *brunel* 'little brown one') [Isambard Kingdom Brunel, 1806–59, British engineer; Sir Marc Isambard Brunel, 1769–1849, French-born British engineer, father of Isambard]

— **Brunel University** a university in Uxbridge, West London, founded in 1966. It was named in honour of Isambard Kingdom Brunel (see above), whose Great Western Railway passes nearby.

Brunner 'person who lives by a spring or well', or 'person from Brunn', the name of various places in Germany (in either case from Middle High German *brunne* 'spring')

Bruno (i) from an Italian nickname for someone with brown hair or a tanned complexion (from Italian *bruno* 'brown'); (ii) from an Italian and Portuguese surname based on the Germanic personal name *Bruno* (see **Braun**) [Frank Bruno, 1961–, British boxer]

Brunson a different form of **Bronson**

Brunton 'person from Brunton', Northumberland ('farmstead by a stream')

Brush (i) perhaps 'maker of brushes'; also perhaps from a medieval nickname for someone thought to resemble a brush; (ii) perhaps 'forester, wood- cutter' (from Middle English *brusche* 'brush- wood')

Bruton 'person from Bruton', Somerset ('farm- stead on the (river) Brue')

Bryan, Brian, Brien (i) from the male personal name *Brian*, of Celtic origin and perhaps meaning literally 'high' or 'noble'; (ii) 'person from Brionne', northern France [Dora Bryan (original name Dora Broadbent), 1924–, British comic actress; Havergal Brian, 1876–1972, British composer]

Bryant, Briant different forms of **Bryan** [Sir Arthur Bryant, 1899–1985, British historian; David Bryant, 1931–, British bowler]

— **Bryant and May** a British firm of match manu- facturers established in London in 1852 by the Quakers William Bryant and Francis May

Bryce see **Brice**

Bryden, Brydon (i) probably 'person from Brydon', an unidentified place probably in south- western Scotland; (ii) perhaps 'bridle maker' (from Old French *bridon* 'bridle') [Bill Bryden, 1942–, British theatre director]

Bryers, Bryars see **Briers**

Bryson (i) 'son of **Brice** (i)'; (ii) from Irish Gaelic *Ó Briosáin*, an alteration of *Ó Muirgheasáin* (see **Morrissey**) [Bill Bryson, 1951–, US author]

Buchan 'person from Buchan', a region of Aberdeenshire ('place of cows') [John Buchan (1st Baron Tweedsmuir), 1875–1940, British writer and statesman]

Buchanan 'person from Buchanan', Highlands (perhaps 'house of the canon') [George Buchanan, 1506–82, Scottish scholar and humanist; Jack Buchanan, 1891–1957, British actor and singer; James Buchanan, 1791–1868, US Democratic politician, president 1857–61]

Buchholz, Buchholtz 'person who lives by a beech wood', or 'person from Buchholz', the name of various places in Germany (in either case from Middle High German *buoch* 'beech' + *holz* 'wood'), or an invented Jewish name based on German *Buchholz* 'beech wood'

Buchman an anglicization of the German surname *Buchmann*, literally 'someone who lives by a beech tree' (from Middle High German *buoch* 'beech' + *man*) [Frank Buchman, 1878–1961, US moralist and evangelist who founded the Moral Rearmament movement]
— **Buchmanism** an alternative name for Moral Rearmament, founded by Frank Buchman (see above)

Buchwald (i) 'person who lives by a beech forest', or 'person from Buchwald', the name of various places in Germany (in either case from Middle High German *buoch* 'beech' + *walt* 'forest'); (ii) an invented Jewish name based on German *Buchwald* 'beech forest' [Art Buchwald, 1925–2007, US journalist]

Buck (i) from a medieval nickname for someone thought to resemble a male goat; (ii) 'person who lives near a notable or prominent beech tree' (from Middle English *buk* 'beech'); (iii) from a medieval Dutch and North German nickname for a fat person (from Middle Low German *būk* 'belly'); (iv) from a German male personal name that is a shortened form of *Burkhardt* (see **Burkett**) [Pearl Buck (*née* Sydenstricker), 1892–1973, US novelist; Sir Peter Buck (Maori name Te Rangi Hiroa), 1879–1951, New Zealand anthropologist and politician, Maori on his mother's side]

Buckel (i) from a pet-form of the German male personal name *Burkhardt* (see **Burkett**); (ii) from a medieval German nickname for a hunchback; (iii) *also* **Buckell** see **Buckle**

Buckeridge see **Buckridge**

Bucket, Buckett a different form of **Bouquet** [Hyacinth Bucket, snobbish heroine (played by Patricia Routledge) of the BBC television sitcom *Keeping Up Appearances* (1990–95), who resolutely pronounces the name 'boukay']

Buckingham 'person from Buckingham', Buckinghamshire ('Bucca's people's river bend')

Buckland 'person from Buckland', the name of numerous places in southern England ('charter land' (referring to an estate that has certain rights and privileges created by written royal decree)) [William Buckland, 1784–1856, British geologist and cleric]

Buckle, Buckel, Buckell (i) 'maker of buckles'; (ii) an anglicization of **Buckel**

Buckler a different form of **Buckle** (i)
— **Bucklers Hard** a village in Hampshire, near the mouth of the Beaulieu River, named after a local family (Richard Buckler is recorded as living there in 1664). *Hard* means 'firm landing-place'.

Buckley (i) *also* **Buckleigh** 'person from Buckley or Buckleigh', the name of various places in England (mostly 'glade frequented by male deer or male goats'); (ii) from Irish Gaelic *Ó Buachalla* 'descendant of *Buachaill*', a nickname meaning literally 'boy', 'servant' or 'cowherd' [William F. Buckley, Jr., 1925–, US writer and editor]
— **Buckley's chance** in Australian and New Zealand slang, the slimmest of chances. The expression has been tentatively derived from the name of William Buckley, 1780–1856, an escaped convict who lived for over 30 years with the Aborigines in southern Victoria in the early 19th century, and also from that of the Melbourne business house Buckley and Nunn (hence, punningly, 'two chances: Buckley's and none').

Buckman (i) 'goatherd' (from Middle English *bukke* 'male goat' + *man*); (ii) 'scholar, scribe' (from northern Middle English *buke* 'book' + *man*)

Buckmaster 'person from Buckminster', Leicestershire ('Bucca's large church') (later altered folk-etymologically, as if 'master of goats') [Herbert Buckmaster, British cavalry officer, founder (1919) of Buck's Club, a London gentlemen's club; Maurice Buckmaster, 1910–92, British spymaster]

Bucknell, Bucknall 'person from Bucknell', Oxfordshire and Shropshire ('Bucca's hill'), or 'person from Bucknall', Lincolnshire and Somerset ('Bucca's nook of land') [Barry Bucknell, 1912–2003, British television do-it-yourself expert]

Buckner, Bucknor an anglicization of the German surname *Buchner*, literally either 'person who lives by a beech wood or beech tree' or 'person from Buchen', the name of various places in Germany

Buckridge, Buckeridge 'person from Buckridge', Worcestershire ('ridge where beech trees grow') [Anthony Buckeridge, 1912–2004, British author of the 'Jennings' school stories]

Budd from the medieval personal name *Budde*, itself descended from a nickname for a fat person, perhaps based on Old English *budda* 'beetle' [Zola Budd, 1966–, South African athlete]
— **Billy Budd** an opera (1951) by Benjamin Britten, based on an unfinished novella, *Billy Budd, Foretopman* (1891), by Herman Melville, telling of a young sailor who is hanged for killing a brutal master-at-arms

Buddle a different form of **Boodle**

Budge from a medieval nickname for someone with a large or deformed mouth or for someone who talked or ate too much (from Anglo-Norman *buge* 'mouth') [Donald Budge, 1916–2000, US tennis player]

Budgen from a medieval nickname based on the Anglo-Norman phrase *bon Jean* 'good John'
— **Budgens** a British chain of convenience food stores founded in Maidstone, Kent in 1872 by John Budgen

Buerk see **Burke**

Buffington perhaps 'person from Bovington', Dorset ('estate associated with Bōfa')

Buford probably a different form of **Beaufort** [Bill Buford, 1954–, US journalist and writer]

Bugg from the Old Norse nickname *Buggi*, literally 'fat man', or from a medieval nickname for an eccentric or strangely behaved person (from Middle English *bugge* 'bogeyman, scarecrow')

Buggins from a medieval nickname for an eccentric or strangely behaved person (from a diminutive form of Middle English *bugge* – see **Bugg**)
— **Buggins's turn** the principle of awarding promotion by rotation (especially on the grounds of seniority) rather than on merit. The expression, first recorded in 1901, probably exploits a hint of comical drudgery about the name (there very likely was never an actual Buggins to inspire it).

Buick (i) see **Bewick**; (ii) from a medieval Dutch nickname for a fat person (from Middle Dutch *buuc* 'belly')
— **Buick** a US make of motor vehicles, part of General Motors. It was founded in Detroit, Michigan in 1903 by the Scottish-American inventor David Dunbar Buick, 1854–1929.

Bulger a different form of **Bolger**

Bull, Bool, Boole from a medieval nickname for a man who resembles a bull in size, aggression, etc. [Deborah Bull, 1963–, British ballet dancer; John Bull, ?1562–1628, English composer and organist; Peter Bull, 1912–84, British actor]
— **John Bull** the personification of England and the English; also, an individual Englishman, especially one regarded as embodying Englishness. The name comes from that of a character in John Arbuthnot's *Law is a Bottomless Pit* (1712).

Bullard (i) probably 'person who looks after bulls' (from early Modern English *bulward* 'bull-keeper'); (ii) perhaps from a medieval nickname for a fraudster (from a derivative of Middle English *bole* 'deceit', from Old French); (iii) perhaps from a medieval French nickname for a fat person (from a derivative of Old French *boule* 'round thing')

Bullen, Bulleyn 'person from Boulogne', port in northern France. See also **Boleyn**

Buller (i) 'scribe, copyist' (from a derivative of Middle English *bulle* 'document', from Old French); (ii) 'person from Buller', an unidentified place in northern France; (iii) from a medieval German nickname for a loud talker (from a derivative of Middle High German *bullen* 'to roar') [Sir Redvers Buller, 1839–1906, British general; Syd Buller, 1909–70, English cricket umpire]

Bulley, Bully (i) 'person from Bully or Bouillé', northern France; (ii) 'person from Bulleigh or Bulley', Devon and Gloucestershire respectively ('glade where bulls graze')

Bullivant from a medieval nickname for a 'good chap' or amiable companion (from Old French *bon enfant*, literally 'good child')

Bullock 'keeper of bullocks', or from a medieval nickname for an obstreperous or exuberant young man [Alan Bullock (Lord Bullock), 1914–2004, British historian; Sandra Bullock, 1964–, US actress]

Bulman, Bullman 'keeper of bulls'

Bulmer 'person from Bulmer', Essex and Yorkshire ('pool where bulls come')
— **Bulmers** a firm of cider manufacturers established in Hereford in 1887 by Percy Bulmer, 1867–1919

Bulstrode 'person from Bulstrode', Buckinghamshire and Hertfordshire (respectively 'area of brushwood by the stronghold' and 'area of brushwood where bulls come')

Bulteel 'person who sifts flour' (from Middle English *boultel* 'cloth for sifting flour', from Old French). See also **Boutell**

Bumpus (i) from a medieval nickname for a vigorous walker (from Old French *bon* 'good' + *pas* 'pace'); (ii) perhaps 'person who lives by a place through which travel is easy' (from Old French *bon* 'good' + *pas* 'passage')

Bunbury 'person from Bunbury', Cheshire ('Buna's stronghold') [Bunbury, an imaginary sickly country-dwelling relative of Algernon Moncrieff in Oscar Wilde's *The Importance of Being Earnest* (1895), invoked by him whenever he wished to avoid a social engagement]
— **Bunburying** the offering of the need to visit an (imaginary) sick relative as the reason for breaking or avoiding a social engagement, as practised by Algernon Moncrieff (see above)

Bunch, Bunche from a medieval nickname for a hunchback (from Middle English *bunche* 'hump') [Ralph Bunche, 1904–71, US political scientist and UN official]
— **Mother Bunch** a noted English alewife of the late Elizabethan period, of legendary proportions and appetites. The name subsequently came to be used generically for any fat and frowsty old woman.

Buncombe 'person from Buncombe', an unidentified place in England ('valley where reeds grow')

Bundy, Bundey different forms of **Bond** [McGeorge Bundy, 1919–96, US national security advisor]

Bunker from a medieval nickname for a well-disposed or reliable person (from Old French *bon* 'good' + *cuer* 'heart') [Archie Bunker, loud-mouthed bigot who is the central character in the US television sitcom *All in the Family* (1971–83) (the US equivalent of Alf Garnett in the BBC's *Till Death Us Do Part*)]
— **Bunker Hill** a hill in Boston, Massachusetts, near the site of the first battle of the American Revolution of 1775. It is on land owned in the early 17th century by Paul Bunker, an immigrant from Bedfordshire, England.

Bunn a different form of **Bone** (i) [Douglas Bunn, 1928–, British showjumping impresario]

Bunney (i) perhaps 'person who lives by a ravine' (from southwestern English dialect *bunny* 'ravine'); (ii) perhaps from a medieval nickname for someone with a lump or swelling (from Middle English *buny* 'swelling')

Bunter 'person who sifts flour' (from a derivative of Middle English *bunten* 'to sift') [Billy Bunter, fat greedy pusillanimous bespectacled schoolboy in the school stories (1908–61) of Frank Richards; Mervyn Bunter, manservant of Lord Peter Wimsey in the crime novels of Dorothy Sayers]

Bunting from a medieval nickname for someone thought to resemble a bunting (the small bird) [Basil Bunting, 1900–85, British poet]

Bunton a different form of **Bunting** [Emma Bunton, 1976–, British pop singer, 'Baby Spice']

Bunyan, Bunyon from a medieval nickname for someone with a lump or swelling (from Old French *bugnon* 'little swelling') [John Bunyan, 1628–88, English preacher and writer; Paul Bunyan, giant lumberjack whose exploits are the stuff of legend in the northwestern US]

Burbage, Burbidge 'person from Burbage', Derbyshire, Leicestershire and Wiltshire (either 'ridge by a fortified place' or 'stream by a fortified place') [Richard Burbage, ?1567–1619, English actor]

Burbank perhaps 'person from Burbank House', Cumbria ('bank by a fortified place') [Luther Burbank, 1849–1926, US plant breeder]

Burch see **Birch**

Burchall, Burchill see **Birchall**

Burchfield, Birchfield 'person from Birchfield', the name of various places in England ('area of open country where birch trees grow') [Robert Burchfield, 1923–2004, New Zealand-born lexicographer]

Burd see **Bird** (i–ii)

Burden, Burdon (i) 'person from Burdon', County Durham and Yorkshire ('hill by a fortified place'); (ii) from the male personal name *Burdo*, brought into England by the Normans but ultimately probably of Germanic origin; (iii) from a medieval nickname for a pilgrim or someone who carried the staff of a pilgrim (from Middle English *bourdon* 'pilgrim's staff', from Old French) [Eric Burdon, 1941–, British pop musician, lead singer of 'The Animals']

Burdett from the male personal name *Burdett*, a pet-form of *Burdo* (see **Burden** (ii)) [Angela Burdett-Coutts (1st Baroness Burdett-Coutts; *née* Burdett), 1814–1906, British philanthropist, daughter of Sir Francis; Sir Francis Burdett, 1770–1844, British Tory-radical politician]

Burell see **Burrell**

Burford 'person from Burford', Oxfordshire and Shropshire ('ford by a fortified place')

Burge (i) a different form of **Bridge** (with the *r* swapped round with the vowel); (ii) a different form of **Burke**

Burger (i) 'freeman of a borough, burgess' (from a derivative of Middle English *burg* 'town'); (ii) 'person from Burg', the name of various places in Germany

Burgess, Burges 'freeman of a borough, burgess' (from Middle English *burgeis*, from Old French) [Anthony Burgess (original name John Anthony Burgess Wilson), 1917–93, British writer and critic; Guy Burgess, 1911–63, British Soviet spy; William Burges, 1827–81, British architect and designer]

— **Burgess Hill** a commuter town in Sussex. Its name comes from the Burgess family, which owned land in the area in the 16th century.

— **Burgess Shale** a bed of black shale in the Rocky Mountains, near the town of Field in British Columbia, Canada. It was named after the nearby Mount Burgess and Burgess Pass, which in turn were named in honour of the Canadian politician Alexander MacKinnon Burgess, 1850–1908. It is famous for the rich deposits of fossils from the Middle Cambrian period that have been unearthed there.

Burgon a different form of **Burgoyne** [Geoffrey Burgon, 1941–, British composer]

Burgoyne 'person from Burgundy' (from Old French *Bourgogne* 'Burgundy') [John Burgoyne, 1722–92, British general and dramatist]

Burke, Burk, Bourke, Buerk 'person who lives in a fortress' (from Middle English *burk* 'fortress'). See also **de Burgh, Burge** (ii) [Edmund Burke, 1729–97, British political philosopher and Whig politician; James Burke, 1936–, British presenter of television science programmes; Kathy Burke, 1964–, British actress; Martha Jane Burke ('Calamity Jane'; *née* Canary), ?1852–1903, US frontierswoman; Michael Buerk, 1946–, British television journalist and newsreader; Robert O'Hara Burke, 1820–61, Irish explorer of Australia; William Burke, 1792–1829, Irish murderer and body-snatcher (see below)]

— **burke** to murder someone surreptitiously, without leaving a mark or trace, especially by suffocation, as William Burke (see above) did; also, metaphorically (and now by far the commoner meaning), to cover up or suppress an issue or question

— **Burke and Hare** William Burke and his accomplice William Hare, who murdered at least 15 people and sold their bodies to the Edinburgh surgeon Robert Knox for dissection

— **Burke's Law** a US television detective drama (1963–66) starring Gene Barry as Captain Amos Burke, a millionaire policeman

— **Burke's Peerage** an annually published register of the titled classes of the United Kingdom, with an account of their pedigrees. It was founded by the Irish genealogist John Burke, 1787–1848, and first appeared in 1826.

Burkett, Burkitt (i) from the Old English male personal name *Burgheard*, literally 'fortress-hard'; (ii) a different form of **Birkett**

— **Burkitt's lymphoma** a rare malignant tumour attacking white blood cells, associated with a virus spread by insects. It is named after the British surgeon Denis Burkitt, 1911–93.

Burkin, Birkin 'person from Birkin', Yorkshire ('birch grove') [Jane Birkin, 1946–, British singer and actress]
— **Birkin bag** a type of handbag co-designed by Jane Birkin (see above), who found the Kelly bag (see **Kelly**) too small

Burkinshaw, Birkenshaw 'person from Birkenshaw', Yorkshire ('birch copse'). See also **Brigginshaw, Burtenshaw**

Burland 'person from Burland', Cheshire and Yorkshire (respectively 'peasants' land' and 'piece of land with a cowshed')

Burley, Burleigh 'person from Burley', the name of various places in England ('woodland clearing by or belonging to a fortified place'). See also **Birley**

Burling, Birling probably 'person from Birling', Kent ('Bærla's people's settlement'). See also **Barling**

Burman (i) 'inhabitant of a (fortified) town' (from Middle English *burghman*); (ii) an anglicization of the German surname *Buhrmann*, literally 'farmer'

Burn, Burne different forms of **Bourne** [Sir Edward Burne-Jones (original name Edward Coley Jones), 1833–98, British Pre-Raphaelite painter and designer]

Burnett, Burnet from a medieval nickname for someone with brown hair or a tanned complexion (from Old French *burnete*, literally 'little brown one') [Sir Alastair Burnet (original name James Burnet), 1928–, British journalist and television presenter; Carol Burnett, 1933–, US comedian; Frances Hodgson Burnett (*née* Hodgson), 1849–1924, British novelist and children's author; Sir Frank Mcfarlane Burnet, 1899–1985, Australian biologist; Gilbert Burnet, 1643–1715, English bishop and historian]

Burney (i) 'person from Bernay', Normandy ('Brenno's settlement'); (ii) from Irish Gaelic *Mac Biorna* 'son of *Biorna*' (see **McBurney**) [Charles Burney, 1726–1814, British musicologist, organist and composer; Fanny Burney (Mrs Frances D'Arblay), 1752–1840, British novelist, daughter of Charles]

Burnham 'person from Burnham', the name of various places in England (mostly 'village by a stream')

Burnley 'person from Burnley', Lancashire ('glade by the (river) *Brun*', a river-name meaning literally either 'brown' or simply 'stream')

Burns, Burnes (i) 'person who lives by a stream or streams'; (ii) 'person who lives in a house by a stream' (from a shortened form of the name *Burnhouse*); (iii) from Irish Gaelic *Ó Broin* (see **Byrne**); (iv) a radical anglicization of **Bernstein** [George Burns (original name Nathan Birnbaum), 1896–1996, US comedian; John Elliot Burns, 1858–1943, British socialist and trade-union leader; Robert Burns, 1759–96, Scottish poet]
— **Burns and Oates** a British Roman Catholic publishing company, established in 1835 by James Burns, 1808–71. He was later joined in business by William Wilfred Oates.
— **Burns Night** 25 January, the anniversary of the birth of Robert Burns (see above), which is traditionally celebrated in Scotland with a Burns Supper
— **Burns Supper** a celebratory meal marking Burns Night

Burnside 'person who lives beside a stream', or 'person from Burnside', the name of various places in Scotland
— **burnsides** heavy side whiskers and a moustache worn with a clean-shaven chin. The term commemorates the US general Ambrose Burnside, 1824–81, who sported such facial adornments.

Burr perhaps from a medieval nickname for a tiresomely persistent person (as difficult to 'shake off' as a burr) [Aaron Burr, 1756–1836, US Republican politician, vice-president 1801–05; Raymond Burr, 1917–93, Canadian actor]

Burra a different form of **Bowra** [Edward Burra, 1905–76, British painter]

Burrell, Burrill probably 'maker or seller of coarse woollen cloth' (from Middle English *burel*, a term for such cloth). See also **Birrell**
— **Burrell Collection** an art collection in Glasgow that contains paintings, textiles, glass, ceramics and many other artefacts that once belonged to the Scottish shipping magnate Sir William Burrell, 1861–1958

Burridge, Burrage (i) from the medieval personal name *Burrich* (from Old English *Burgrīc*, literally 'fortress-power'); (ii) 'person from Burridge', Devon ('ridge with a fortification')

Burrows, Burrowes, Burroughs 'person who lives by a hill or (burial) mound' (from Middle English *borowes* 'of the hillock, heap or mound') [Edgar Rice Burroughs, 1875–1950, US novelist, creator of Tarzan; Stuart Burrows, 1933–, Welsh tenor; William Burroughs, 1914–97, US novelist]

Burstin an invented Jewish name based on Yiddish *burshtin* 'amber'

Burt, Burtt, Birt from the Old English male personal name *Byrht*, literally 'bright' [John Birt (Lord Birt), 1944–, British television executive]

Burtenshaw, Birtenshaw different forms of **Burkinshaw**

Burton 'person from Burton', the name of numerous places in England (mostly 'fortified farmstead') [Amanda Burton, 1956–, Northern Irish actress; Humphrey Burton, 1931–, British television producer and presenter; Sir Montague Burton (original name Meshe Osinsky), 1885–1952, Russian (Lithuanian)-born British tailor and businessman; Sir Richard Burton, 1821–90, British explorer, diplomat and translator; Richard Burton (original name Richard Jenkins), 1925–84, British actor; Robert Burton, 1577–1640, English scholar; Tim Burton, 1958–, US film director and producer]
— **Burton** a British clothing retailer established in Mansfield in 1906 by Montague Burton (see above)

Burtwistle see **Birtwistle**

Bury, Berry 'person who lives in a fortified place', or 'person from Bury', Lancashire (in either case from Old English *byrig* 'at the stronghold'). See also **Berryman**

Busby, Busbee 'person from Busby', Yorkshire ('homestead in a thicket of bushes'). See also **Bushby** (ii) [James Busby, 1800–71, British government official, a founding father of New Zealand; Sir Matt Busby, 1909–94, British football manager]
— **Busby Babes** a journalistic collective name given to the young players brought to Manchester United football club in the late 1940s and 1950s by its manager, Matt Busby (see above). Eight of them were killed in the Munich air crash of 1958.

Bush (i) 'person who lives in an area growing thickly with bushes'. See also **Bysh**; (ii) an anglicization of the German surname *Busch*, literally 'bush', adopted by some Jews with reference to the story of the burning bush in the Old Testament [Alan Bush, 1900–95, British composer; George Bush, 1924–, US Republican politician, president 1989–93; George W. Bush, 1946–, US Republican politician, president 2001–, son of George; Kate Bush, 1958–, British popular singer/songwriter]
— **Bush House** a building in Aldwych, central London, headquarters of the BBC external services. Planned in 1919 and finished in 1935, it was intended by its instigator, the American Irving T. Bush, as a trade centre.

Bushby (i) 'person from Bushby', Leicestershire ('Butr's homestead'); (ii) a different form of **Busby**

Bushell a different form of **Bissell** (i) [Garry Bushell, 1955–, British newspaper columnist and television presenter]

Buss 'maker of barrels, cooper' (from Middle English *busse* 'cask'), or from a medieval nickname for a rotund, barrel-like man [Frances Mary Buss, 1827–94, British schoolmistress, headmistress of the North London Collegiate School]

Bussell a different form of **Bissell** (i) [Darcey Bussell, 1969–, British ballet dancer]

Bussey 'person from Bucy', the name of several places, variously spelled, in northern France ('Buccius's settlement')

Bustamante 'person from Bustamante', Spain ('Amantius's pasture') [Sir Alexander Bustamante (original name William Alexander Clarke; he claimed he got the name Bustamante from a Spanish sea captain who befriended him in his youth), 1884–1977, Jamaican trade-union leader and politician, prime minister 1962–67]

Butcher 'butcher, slaughterer' [Basil Butcher, 1933–, West Indian cricketer; Mark Butcher, 1972–, English cricketer]

Butler 'wine steward' (from Anglo-Norman *butuiller*, ultimately a derivative of Latin *buticula* 'bottle') [Alban Butler, 1710–73, British Roman Catholic priest and hagiographer; David Butler, 1924–, British political scientist; Daws Butler, 1916–88, US cartoon voicer, the voice of (among others) Yogi Bear; Joseph Butler ('Bishop Butler'),

1692–1752, English theologian; R.A. ('Rab') Butler (Lord Butler), 1902–82, British Conservative politician; Reg Butler, 1913–81, British sculptor; Rhett Butler, Scarlett O'Hara's handsome dashing lost love in Margaret Mitchell's *Gone with the Wind* (1936), played in the 1939 film by Clark Gable; Robin Butler (Lord Butler), 1938–, British civil servant; Samuel Butler, 1612–80, British satirical poet; Samuel Butler, 1835–1902, British novelist]
— **Butler's *Lives*** the shorthand name commonly used for *The Lives of the Fathers, Martyrs and Other Principal Saints* (1756–59) by Alban Butler (see above), an English rendition of the Latin *Acta Sanctorum*
— **Butskellism** the perceived consensus in British politics, and especially in economic policy, between the Labour and Conservative parties in the 1950s, when the right-wing Labour Hugh Gaitskell and the left-wing Conservative R.A. Butler (see above) were chancellor of the exchequer
— **Newtownbutler** a village in County Fermanagh, Northern Ireland, named after a 17th-century English settler called Butler

Butlin (i) perhaps 'Butt the peasant' (from the medieval personal name *Butt* (see **Butt** (i)) + Anglo-Norman *vilain* 'peasant'); (ii) perhaps from a medieval nickname meaning literally 'hit the peasant' (from Anglo-Norman *buter* 'to hit' + *vilain* (as in (i))) [Sir Billy Butlin, 1899–1980, British holiday-camp pioneer]

Butt (i) from the medieval male personal name *Butt*, perhaps originally a nickname for a short stocky person (from Middle English *butt* 'stump'). See also **Butts**; (ii) 'person who lives by archery butts (a range where archery is practised)'; (iii) 'person who lives by a strip of land abutting another'; (iv) 'maker of barrels, cooper', or from a medieval nickname for a stout, barrel-like person (in either case from Middle English *butte* 'cask'). See also **Bott** (ii) [Dame Clara Butt, 1873–1936, British contralto]

Butter (i) 'maker or seller of butter'; (ii) from a medieval nickname for someone thought to resemble a bittern (probably in having a loud booming voice) (from Middle English *butor* 'bittern'). See also **Butters** (i)

Butterfield 'person who lives by pasturage in which dairy cattle are kept', or 'person from Butterfield', the name of various places in England (in either case from Old English *butere* 'butter' + *feld* 'pasture') [William Butterfield, 1814–1900, British architect]

Butteriss, Buttriss, Buttress (i) 'servant who works in a wine cellar, cellarman' (from Anglo-Norman *boteries* 'of the wine cellar'); (ii) perhaps a different form of **Bottrell**

Butters (i) 'son of **Butter** (ii)'; (ii) a different form of **Butteriss**

Butterworth 'person from Butterworth', Lancashire and Yorkshire ('enclosure where butter is made') [Peter Butterworth, 1919–79, British actor]

Button 'maker or seller of buttons' [Jenson Button, 1980–, British racing driver]

— **Button Boys** a name given to a group of young British professional golfers (e.g. Tommy Horton and Ian Clarke) sponsored in the 1960s by Ernest Button

Butts 'son of **Butt** (i)'

Buxton 'person from Buxton', Derbyshire and Norfolk (respectively 'rocking stones' and 'Bucc's farmstead')

Buzzard from a medieval nickname for someone thought to resemble a buzzard (perhaps from its lowly status as a bird of prey, not used by falconers)

Byam probably 'person from Bytham', Lincolnshire ('homestead in a valley bottom') [Glen Byam Shaw, 1904–86, British theatre director]

Byas 'person who lives in a house at a bend' (from Middle English *bye* 'bend' + *hous* 'house')

Byatt 'person who lives by a gate' (from Middle English *by* 'by, beside' + *yate* 'gate') [Dame Antonia Byatt (*née* Drabble), 1936–, British novelist and critic]

Bybee perhaps a different form of **Beeby**

Bye 'person who lives by a bend in a river' (from Middle English *bye* 'bend')

Byers 'person who lives by cowsheds', or 'person from Byers', the name of various places in northern England and Scotland (in either case from Middle English *byres* 'cowsheds')

Byfield 'person who lives by open country', or 'person from Byfield', the name of various places in England (in either case from Middle English *by* 'by, beside' + *felde* 'open land')

Byford (i) 'person from Byford', Herefordshire ('ford by the river bend'); (ii) 'person who lives by a ford'

Bygrave 'person who lives by a ditch or dyke', or 'person from Bygrave', Hertfordshire (in either case from Middle English *by* 'by, beside' + *grave* 'ditch')

Bygraves a different form of **Bygrave** [Max Bygraves (original name Walter Bygraves), 1922–, British singer and entertainer]

Byles see **Biles**

Byng see **Bing** (i)

Byrd see **Bird** (i–ii)

Byrne from Irish Gaelic *Ó Broin* 'descendant of *Bran*', a personal name based on *bran* 'raven'. See also **Burns** (iii), **O'Byrne**

Byrnes a different form of **Byrne**

Byron 'person who lives by cowsheds', or 'person from Byrom or Byram', Lancashire and Yorkshire respectively (in either case from Old English *bȳrum* 'at the cowsheds') [George Gordon Byron (Lord Byron), 1788–1824, British poet; Kathleen Byron, 1923–, British actress; Robert Byron, 1905–41, British travel writer]

— **Byron Bay** a coastal resort town in northeastern New South Wales, Australia. It and the nearby **Cape Byron**, the most easterly point on the Australian mainland, were named by Captain Cook in honour of Vice-Admiral John Byron, 1723–86, who had circumnavigated the globe and led expeditions to the South Pacific. (He was the grandfather of the poet Lord Byron – see above).

— **Byronic** of or typical of Lord Byron or his poetry, especially in evoking a brooding and solitary man who seems capable of great passion and suffering

Bysh, Bysshe different forms of **Bush** (i)

Bywater (i) 'person who lives by a lake or river'; (ii) from Irish Gaelic *Ó Srutháin* 'descendant of *Sruthán*', a personal name meaning literally perhaps 'little stream' (but in fact more likely 'little wise one')

C

Cable 'maker of ship's ropes'

Cabot (i) 'fisherman' (from Old French *cabot* 'miller's thumb (a type of small freshwater fish)', etymologically 'big head'); (ii) from a medieval French nickname for someone with a large head (from Old French *cabot*, as in (i)) [Sebastian Cabot, ?1476–1557, Italian-born English navigator and cartographer]

Cabrera 'person from Cabrera', the name of various places in Spain ('place of goats')

Cadbury 'person from Cadbury', Devon and Somerset ('Cada's fort')
— **Cadbury's** a British chocolate manufacturer. It had its beginnings in a small chocolate business established in Birmingham by the Quaker John Cadbury, 1801–89. It was taken over in 1861 by his sons George Cadbury, 1839–1922, and Richard Cadbury, 1835–99, who expanded it greatly. In 1969 it merged with Schweppes to become Cadbury Schweppes. It reverted to plain Cadbury in 2007.

Caddick from the Welsh male personal name *Cadog*, a pet-form of *Cadfael* (a derivative of Welsh *cad* 'battle')

Cade (i) 'maker of barrels, cooper' (from Middle English *cade* 'cask', from Old French); (ii) from the medieval male personal name *Cade*, from Old English *Cada*, probably originally a nickname for a fat person. See also **Cadman**; (iii) from a medieval nickname from a mild-mannered agreeable person (from Middle English *cade* 'pet') [Jack Cade, died 1450, Irish-born English rebel leader]

Cadell, Caddell, Caddel from the Old Welsh male personal name *Cadell*, literally 'little battle'

Cadman 'servant of **Cade** (ii)'

Cadogan from the Welsh male personal name *Cadwgan*, literally probably 'battle-scowler'
— **Cadogan Estate** an area of Chelsea and Belgravia, including Cadogan Square, Sloane Street and Sloane Square, owned by the earls Cadogan, descended from Charles Sloane Cadogan, 1728–1807, 1st Earl Cadogan

Cadwallader, Cadwalader from the Welsh male personal name *Cadwallader*, literally 'battle-leader'

Caesar from the name of the Roman emperor Gaius Julius Caesar, 100–44 BC, probably as adopted either as an English personal name or as a nickname for someone who had played the part of Julius Caesar in a medieval pageant

Cafferty a reduced form of **McCafferty**

Caffrey, Caffery reduced forms of **McCaffrey**

Caffyn 'person from Cyffin or Gyffin', the name of various places in Wales ('place by a boundary')

Cage 'person who makes or sells cages for pet animals'; also 'keeper of a cage in which prisoners are kept' [John Cage, 1912–92, US composer; Nicolas Cage (original name Nicholas Coppola), 1964–, US actor]

Cagney from Irish Gaelic *Ó Caingnigh* 'descendant of *Caingneach*', either a personal name meaning literally 'pleader' or from a nickname for an argumentative person [James Cagney, 1899–1986, US actor]
— **Cagney and Lacey** a US television police drama (1982–88) featuring Tyne Daly as Detective Mary Beth Lacey and Meg Foster (later Sharon Gless) as Detective Christine Cagney

Cahill from Irish Gaelic *Ó Cathail* 'descendant of *Cathal*', a personal name meaning literally 'powerful in battle'

Cain, Caine, Cane, Kain, Kane (i) 'person who gathers reeds (e.g. for strewing on floors)' (from Middle English *cane* 'reed'); (ii) from Scottish Gaelic *Mac Iain* (see **McKane**); (iii) 'person from Caen', Normandy ('field of battle'); (iv) a Manx variant of **Coyne** (ii) [Hall Caine, 1853–1931, British novelist; James M. Cain, 1892–1977, US journalist and novelist; Marti Caine (original name Lynne Shepherd), 1945–95, British comedian and singer; Sir Michael Caine (original name Maurice Micklewhite), 1933–, British actor]
— **Citizen Kane** see **Kane**

Caines see **Keynes**

Caird 'tinker' (from Scottish Gaelic *ceard* 'tinker')

Cairns, Cairnes 'person who lives by a cairn (i.e. a pile of stones set as a marker or a memorial)'. See also **Carne, Carnes**
— **Cairns** a coastal city in northeastern Queensland, Australia. It was settled in 1876, and named in honour of Sir William Wellington Cairns, ?1828–88, at that time governor of Queensland.

Cake 'baker of high-quality bread' (from Middle English *cake* 'flat loaf made from extra-fine flour')

Cakebread 'baker of high-quality bread' (from Middle English *cake* (see **Cake**) + *bread*)

Calcutt, Calcut, Calcote, Calcot, Calcott different forms of **Caldicott**

Calder 'person from Calder, Caldor or Cawdor', the name of various places in Scotland (of uncertain but probably etymologically distinct origins), or 'person from Calder', Cumbria ('place by the (river) *Calder*', a river-name meaning 'rapid stream') [Alexander Calder, 1898–1976, US painter and sculptor, inventor of the mobile; Peter

Ritchie Calder (Lord Ritchie-Calder), 1906–82, British author, journalist and academic]

Calderwood 'person from Calderwood', Lanarkshire ('wood by the (river) Calder'). See also **Catherwood**

Caldicott, Caldicot, Caldecott, Caldecot 'person from Caldecote', the name (variously spelled) of several places in England ('cold shelter'). See also **Calcutt**
— **Charters and Caldicott** see **Charteris**

Caldwell 'person from Caldwell', the name (variously spelled) of several places in England, Scotland and Northern Ireland ('cold spring, cold stream'). See also **Cardwell, Coldwell, Cowdell** [Erskine Caldwell, 1903–87, US novelist; Taylor Caldwell, 1900–85, British-born US author]

Caley, Cayley (i) 'person from Cailly', the name of various places in northern France ('Callius's settlement'), or 'person from Cayley', Lancashire ('glade frequented by jackdaws'); (ii) a different form of **MacAulay**; (iii) a Manx variant of **Callow** (iii) [Arthur Cayley, 1821–95, British mathematician, inventor of matrices; Sir George Cayley, 1773–1857, British engineer and pioneer of flying machines]

Calf from the Old Norse personal name *Kalfr*, originally a nickname meaning literally 'calf (i.e. young cow or bull)'

Calhoun, Calhoon different forms of **Colquhoun** [Rory Calhoun (original name Francis Timothy McCown Durgin), 1922–99, US actor]

Callaghan, Callahan from Irish Gaelic *Ó Ceallacháin* 'descendant of *Ceallachán*', a personal name meaning literally 'little contentious one'. See also **O'Callaghan** [James Callaghan (Lord Callaghan), 1912–2005, British Labour politician, prime minister 1976–79]

Callan (i) from Irish Gaelic *Ó Cathaláin* 'descendant of *Cathalán*', a personal name meaning literally 'little *Cathal*' (see **Cahill**); (ii) from Scottish Gaelic *Mac Ailin* 'son of *Ailin*', a personal name derived from *ail* 'rock'. See also **McCallan**
— **Callan** an ITV drama series (1967–72) about a secret agent called David Callan (played by Edward Woodward)

Callander, Callender, Callendar (i) 'person from Callendar or Callender', Falkirk and Stirling respectively ('place by the turbulent stream'); (ii) 'person who treats newly woven cloth in a calender (a machine with rollers which press it smooth)'

Callard (i) from the French surname *Calard*, literally 'one who wears a *cale* (a type of close-fitting woman's hat)'; (ii) a Devon surname of unknown origin
— **Callard and Bowser** a British manufacturer of toffee and other confectionery, established in Finchley in 1837 by Daniel Callard and his brother-in-law J. Bowser.

Callaway, Calloway 'person from Caillouet', northern France ('place of pebbles'). See also **Kellaway** [Cabel ('Cab') Calloway, 1907–94, US jazz musician]

Callender, Callendar see **Callander**

Callow (i) 'person from Callow or Calow', the name of several places in England (variously 'bare hill' and 'bare corner of land'); (ii) probably from a medieval nickname for a bald man (from Middle English *calewe* 'bald'); (iii) from Manx Gaelic *Mac Caolaidhe* 'son of *Coaladhe*', a personal name meaning literally 'slender one, beautiful one'. See also **Caley** (iii) [Simon Callow, 1949–, British actor]

Calloway see **Callaway**

Calman see **Kalman**

Calverley 'person from Calverley', Yorkshire ('glade where calves are pastured')

Calvert 'person who looks after young cattle' (from Middle English *calfhirde* 'calf-herdsman') [Cecilius Calvert (2nd Baron Baltimore), 1605–75, English-born American colonial administrator, son of George; Charles Calvert (3rd Baron Baltimore), 1637–1715, English-born American colonial administrator, son of Cecilius; Eddie Calvert, 1922–78, British trumpeter; George Calvert (1st Baron Baltimore), ?1580–1632, English-born American absentee colonial administrator (the city of Baltimore, Maryland took its name from his barony, which in turn was derived from Baltimore Manor in County Longford, Ireland); Phyllis Calvert (original name Phyllis Bickle), 1915–2002, British actress]

Calvin from a medieval French nickname for a bald man (from Old Provençal *calvin* 'little bald one') [Melvin Calvin, 1911–97, US biochemist]
— **Calvin cycle** a series of reactions that take place in photosynthesis by which carbon dioxide is converted to glucose. It is named after Melvin Calvin (see above).

Camden perhaps 'person from Broad Campden or Chipping Campden', Gloucestershire ('valley with enclosures') [William Camden, 1551–1623, English historian and antiquarian]
— **Camden Society** an association formed in 1838 for the purpose of publishing documents relating to the early history and literature of the British Empire. It was named in honour of William Camden (see above). It was taken over by the Royal Historical Society in 1897.

Camel see **Cammell**

Cameron (i) 'person from Cameron', the name of various places in the Scottish Lowlands (probably 'bent hill'); (ii) from a medieval nickname in the Scottish Highlands for someone with a crooked or broken nose (from Scottish Gaelic *cam sròn* 'bent nose') [David Cameron, 1966–, British Conservative politician; James Cameron, 1911–85, British journalist; James Cameron, 1954–, Canadian film director; Julia Margaret Cameron (*née* Pattle), 1815–79, British photographer; Richard Cameron, 1648–80, Scottish Covenanter and field preacher]
— **Cameron Highlanders** a Scottish infantry regiment, the 79th Foot, raised in 1793 by Alan Cameron of Erracht. In 1961 it amalgamated with the Seaforth Highlanders to become the Queen's Own Highlanders, which in turn in 1994 merged with the Gordon Highlanders.

— **Cameronian** a follower of Richard Cameron (see above), who opposed the union of church and state under Charles II and preached the cause of Presbyterianism (the Cameronians were also known as Reformed Presbyterians)

— **Cameronian Regiment** a Scottish infantry regiment, the 26th Foot, formed originally of Cameronians and other Presbyterians who supported the cause of William III and fought at the Battle of Killiecrankie (1689). It was disbanded in 1969.

Cammell, Camel (i) from a medieval nickname for someone thought to resemble a camel, perhaps in being ungainly or ill-tempered; (ii) perhaps 'person who lives in a house at the sign of a camel'; (iii) perhaps 'person from Queen Camel or West Camel', Somerset (perhaps 'bare hill on the border'); (iv) a different form of **Campbell**

— **Cammell Laird** a Merseyside firm of ship-builders, established at the beginning of the 20th century by the merger of Johnson Cammell & Co., a Sheffield iron-founder established in 1837 by Charles Cammell and Henry and Thomas Johnson, with the Birkenhead shipbuilders Laird, Son & Co., founded in 1824 by William Laird. It completed its last ship in 1993, and shortly afterwards ceased to exist.

Camoys from a medieval nickname for someone with a snub nose (from Old French *camus* 'snub nose')

Campbell from a medieval Scottish nickname for someone with a wry expression (from Scottish Gaelic *cam beul* 'crooked mouth') (the original recipient of the nickname, in the early 13th century, was Gillespie Ó Duibhne, founder of the clan Campbell) [Campbell, family name of the dukes of Argyll; Alastair Campbell, 1957–, British journalist and spin doctor; Colin Campbell (Lord Clyde; original surname Macliver), 1792–1863, British field marshal; Donald Campbell, 1921–67, British world land- and water-speed record-holder, son of Sir Malcolm; Glen Campbell, 1936–, US pop-country singer and guitarist; Sir Henry Campbell-Bannerman, 1836–1908, British Liberal politician, prime minister 1905–08; Ken Campbell, 1941–, British actor and director; Kim Campbell (original name Avril Phaedra Campbell), 1947–, Canadian Progressive Conservative politician, prime minister 1993; Sir Malcolm Campbell, 1885–1949, British world land- and water-speed record-holder; Sir Menzies Campbell, 1941–, British Liberal Democrat politician; Mrs Patrick Campbell (Beatrice Stella Tanner), 1865–1940, British actress; Roy Campbell, 1901–57, South African-born British poet; Thomas Campbell, 1777–1844, British poet]

— **Campbell College** a public school in Belfast, Northern Ireland, established in 1894 under the terms of the will of Henry James Campbell

— **Campbell Island** an uninhabited island in the southwestern Pacific Ocean, south of New Zealand. It was discovered in 1810 by Captain Frederick Hasselburg in the sealing brig *Perseverance*, which was owned by the Sydney firm of Campbell & Co. – whence the name.

— **Campbellite** in Scotland, a follower of John McLeod Campbell, 1800–72, who preached the universality of atonement and was ejected from the Church of Scotland for his pains. In the US, a member of the Disciples of Christ, a sect founded in 1809 by Alexander Campbell, 1788–1866.

— **Campbell Soup Company** a US firm (commonly known simply as **Campbell's**) that produces tinned soup and related food products. It was founded in 1869 by the fruit merchant Joseph A. Campbell.

— **'The Campbells are Coming'** a stirring Scottish song, said to have been composed in 1715 when the forces of John Campbell, duke of Argyll, defeated the Jacobites under the Earl of Mar

— **Campbeltown** a town and port in Argyll and Bute. Its name dates from 1667, when it was awarded as a free burgh of barony to Archibald Campbell, earl of Argyll (it was formerly Kinlochkerran).

Campion (i) '(professional) champion (i.e. someone who fought on behalf of another, especially in a trial by combat)'. See also **Champion**; (ii) 'person from Compiègne', northern France ('shortcut') [Albert Campion, fictional detective created by Margery Allingham (he first appeared in print in 1929); St Edmund Campion, 1540–81, English Jesuit martyr; Gerald Campion, 1921–2002, British actor; Jane Campion, 1954–, New Zealand film director; Thomas Campion, 1567–1620, English composer and poet]

— **Campion Hall** a Roman Catholic college attached to Oxford University, founded (as Clarke's Hall) in 1895 and named Campion Hall (after Edmund Campion – see above) in 1918

Camps 'person who lives in fields or open country' (from Old Northern French, southern French or Catalan *camps* 'fields')

Canavan, Cannavan from Irish Gaelic *Ó Ceanndubháin* 'descendant of *Ceanndubhán*', a nickname meaning literally 'little black-headed one'

Cane see **Cain**

Canfield 'person from Great or Little Canfield', Essex ('Cana's area of open land')

Cann (i) 'person from Cann', Dorset ('deep valley'); (ii) a reduced form of **McCann**

Canning (i) 'person from Cannings', Wiltshire ('settlement of Cana's people'); (ii) a different form of **Cannon** (ii) [George Canning, 1770–1827, British Tory politician, prime minister 1827]

— **Canning Town** a district in the borough of Newham, East London. It probably got its name from Sir Samuel Canning, chairman of the India Rubber, Gutta Percha and Telegraph Works Company there in the 19th century, or alternatively from George Canning, an engineer connected with the building of local docks and railways.

Cannon (i) *also* **Canon** *or* **Cannan** from a medieval nickname for someone thought to resemble a canon (e.g. in piety or solemnity of bearing). See also **Channon**; (ii) from Irish Gaelic *Ó Canáin* 'descendant of *Canán*', a personal name derived from *cana* 'wolf cub'. See also **Canning** (ii); (iii) from Irish and Manx Gaelic *Mac Canannáin* 'son of *Canannán*', a personal name perhaps meaning literally 'little little wolf cub' [Walter Bradford Cannon, 1871–1945, US physiologist]

— **Cannon** a US television detective drama (1972–78) starring William Conrad as the rotund private detective Frank Cannon

— **Cannon and Ball** a British comedy double act consisting of Tommy Cannon (original name Thomas Derbyshire), 1938–, and Bobby Ball (original name Robert Harper), 1944–

Cant 'singer in a chantry chapel' (from Old Northern French *cant* 'song'), or from a medieval nickname for someone who was continually singing (from Old Northern French *cant* 'song')

Cantellow, Cantello 'person from Canteleu, Canteloup, etc'., the name of various places in northern France ('song of the wolf')

Canter, Cantor (i) different forms of **Cant**; (ii) see **Kantor**

Canterbury, Canterberry 'person from Canterbury', Kent ('stronghold of the people of Kent')

Cantrell (i) 'person from Cantrell', Devon (a name of unexplained meaning); (ii) 'maker or ringer of bells' (from Old French *chanterelle* 'little bell'); (iii) 'little **Canter** (i)'

Cantwell probably 'person from Cantwell', an unidentified place in England ('Canta's spring or stream')

Cape 'maker of capes and cloaks', or from a medieval nickname for someone who habitually wore a cape or cloak. See also **Capes**

— **Jonathan Cape** a British publishing firm, founded in 1919 as Jonathan Page and Company. It changed its name to Cape in 1921.

Capel (i) 'person living by or employed in a chapel' (from Old Northern French *capel*, a different form of standard Old French *chapel* (see **Chappell**)); (ii) 'person from Capel', the name of various places in southern England ('place with a chapel')

Capes 'son of **Cape** or **Capp**' [Geoff Capes, 1949–, British shot putter]

Caplan (i) see **Kaplan**; (ii) a different form of **Caplin**

Caplin 'singer in a chantry chapel' (from Old Northern French *capelain*, a variant of standard Old French *chapelain* (see **Chaplin**))

Capone (i) from a medieval Italian nickname for a conceited person (from Italian *capone* 'big head'); (ii) 'keeper of poultry', or from a medieval Italian nickname for a cuckold (from Italian *capone* 'castrated cock', hence 'cuckold') [Al Capone, 1899–1947, Italian-born US gangster]

Capote 'maker of capes and cloaks' (from Spanish *capote* 'hooded cloak, cape') [Truman Capote, 1924–84, US novelist]

Capp 'maker of caps and hats', or from a medieval nickname for someone who habitually wore a cap or hat. See also **Capes** [Al Capp (original name Alfred Caplin), 1909–79, US cartoonist, creator of Li'l Abner; Andy Capp, lazy cloth-capped anti-hero of a British newspaper comic strip created by Reg Smythe in 1957]

Capper a different form of **Capp**

Capra 'goatherd', or from a medieval Italian nickname for someone thought to resemble a goat (in either case from Italian *capra* 'female goat') [Frank Capra, 1897–1991, Italian-born US film director]

Capron 'maker of special hoods for the nobility', or from a medieval nickname for someone who wore such headgear (from Old Northern French *caprun* 'such a hood')

Capstick a different form of **Copestake**

Caraway probably 'spice merchant' (from Middle English *carewei* 'caraway')

Carberry (i) 'person from Carberry', Lothian ('tree-hedge'); (ii) *also* **Carbery** from Irish Gaelic *Ó Cairbre* and *Mac Cairbre* 'descendant *or* son of *Cairbre*', a nickname perhaps meaning literally 'charioteer'

Carbonell from a medieval nickname for a dark-haired or swarthy person, from Anglo-Norman *carbonel*, literally 'little charcoal'. See also **Shrapnel**

Card 'person who cards (i.e. disentangles) wool for spinning into yarn'. See also **Carder**

Carden a different form of **Carwardine**

Cardenas 'person from Cárdenas', Almería and Logroño, Spain ('lands growing with thistles or other bluish-purple flowers')

Carder (i) a different form of **Card**; (ii) 'maker of carders (i.e. implements for carding – see **Card**)'

Cardew 'person from Cardew', Cornwall and Cumbria ('black fort'). See also **Carthew**

Cardiff 'person from Cardiff', Wales ('fort on the (river) Taf', a river-name meaning literally 'water, stream') [Jack Cardiff, 1914–, British cinematographer and film director]

Cardinal from a medieval nickname for someone who habitually wore red clothes, like a cardinal's, or for someone who behaved haughtily, in the manner of a cardinal; also, 'servant in a cardinal's household'

Cardona 'person from Cardona', Spain

Cardus a different form of **Carruthers** [Sir Neville Cardus, 1888–1975, British writer on cricket and music]

Cardwell a different form of **Caldwell** [Edward Cardwell (Viscount Cardwell), 1813–86, British politician and army reformer]

Carew 'person from Carew', the name of various places in Wales ('castle-hill'). The name is pronounced either as spelled or as 'Carey' (see also **Carey** (i)). [Mad Carew, the tragic hero of the dramatic ballad 'The Green Eye of the Yellow God' (1911) by J. Milton Hayes; Thomas Carew, ?1595–1640, English poet, diplomat and author]

Carey, Cary (i) different forms of **Carew**; (ii) 'person from Cary', the name of various places in Devon and Somerset ('place by the (river) Cary', a Celtic river-name probably meaning literally 'pleasant stream'); (iii) 'person from Carrey', Normandy; (iv) from Irish Gaelic *Ó Ciardha* 'descendant of *Ciardha*', a personal name meaning literally 'dark one' [George Carey (Lord Carey), 1935–, British churchman, archbishop of Canterbury 1991–2002; Joyce Cary, 1888–1957, British novelist; Peter Carey, 1943–, Australian writer; William Carey, 1761–1834, British Baptist missionary in India]

— **Carey Street** a street in central London, to the north of the Strand. It is named after one Nicholas Carey, who had a house in the area in the 17th century. It was once the home of the Bankruptcy Division of the Supreme Court, whence the colloquial expression 'in Carey Street' applied to someone with no money.

— **Mother Carey's chicken** a name given by sailors to the stormy petrel (*Procellaria pelagica*). *Mother Carey* has been variously interpreted as an alteration of *Mother Mary* or of *mater cara* 'dear mother'. A former alternative, now defunct, was *Mother Carey's goose*.

Cargill 'person from Cargill', Perth and Kinross (probably 'fort of the pledge') [Patrick Cargill, 1918–96, British actor]

Carless from a medieval nickname for a carefree person (from Old English *carlēas* 'carefree'). See also **Corless**

Carleton see **Carlton**

Carlile see **Carlisle**

Carlin (i) from Irish and Scottish Gaelic *Ó Cearbhalláin* 'descendant of *Cearbhallán*', literally 'little *Cearbhall*' (see **Carroll**); (ii) see **Karlin**; (iii) from a French surname meaning literally 'little Charles'

Carling 'son of *Karl*', a Swedish male personal name equivalent to **Charles** [Will Carling, 1965–, English rugby player]

— **Carling** a brand of lager, developed in Ontario around 1840 by the Canadian brewer Thomas Carling

Carlisle, **Carlile**, **Carlyle** 'person from Carlisle', Cumbria ('fortified town of Luguvalos', a Celtic personal name meaning literally 'strong as Lugus', the name of a Celtic god) [Robert Carlyle, 1961–, British actor; Thomas Carlyle, 1795–1881, Scottish historian and essayist]

Carlson an anglicization of Danish and Norwegian *Carlsen* and Swedish *Carlsson*, both literally 'son of *Karl*', a Scandinavian male personal name equivalent to **Charles**

Carlton, **Carleton** 'person from Carlton or Carleton', the name of various places in northern and eastern England ('farmstead of the freemen'). See also **Charlton**

— **Carlton-Browne of the FO** a film comedy (1958) about an ineffectual Foreign Office official (played by Terry-Thomas) sent to restore order in a forgotten British colony

— **Carlton Club** a gentlemen's club in St James's Street, London, with strong connections with the Conservative party. Its initial premises were in Carlton House Terrace, on the site of the former Carlton House, a mansion built at the beginning of the 18th century for Henry Boyle, 1669–1725, Lord Carleton (he took his title from the village of Carleton in Yorkshire).

Carlyle see **Carlisle**

Carman (i) 'carter' (from Anglo-Norman *car* 'cart' + Middle English *man*); (ii) from the Old Norse male personal name *Karlmathr* or *Karmathr*, literally 'male person'

Carmichael 'person from Carmichael', South Lanarkshire ('Michael's fort') [Hoagy Carmichael, 1899–1981, US songwriter and singer; Ian Carmichael, 1920–, British actor]

Carmody from Irish Gaelic *Ó Cearmada* 'descendant of *Cearmaid*', a personal name of unknown origin and meaning

— **Carmody field** a mainly Australian term for an 'umbrella' field in cricket, with up to eight or nine close fielders set for a fast bowler. It is named after the Australian cricketer Keith Carmody, 1919–77, who as a captain and coach pioneered the use of such a field.

Carne 'person who lives by a cairn', or 'person from Carne', the name of various places in Cornwall (in either case from Cornish *carn* 'cairn')

Carnegie, **Carnegey**, **Carnegy** 'person from Carnegie', Angus ('fort at the gap') [Carnegie, family name of the dukes of Fife; Andrew Carnegie, 1835–1919, Scottish-born US industrialist and philanthropist; Dale Carnegie (original name Dale Carnegey), 1888–1955, US writer, author of *How to Win Friends and Influence People* (1936)]

— **Carnegie College** a college of physical education established in Leeds in 1933 with the help of funds from the Carnegie Trust, founded by Andrew Carnegie (see above). In 1976 it merged with Leeds Polytechnic, which in 1992 became Leeds Metropolitan University.

— **Carnegie Hall** a concert hall in Midtown Manhattan, New York City, founded in 1890 by Andrew Carnegie

Carnes a Scottish variant of **Cairns**

Carney from Irish Gaelic *Ó Catharnaigh* 'descendant of *Catharnach*', a nickname meaning 'warlike'

Caro from a medieval Italian and Spanish nickname for a beloved person (from Italian and Spanish *caro* 'dear') [Sir Anthony Caro, 1924–, British sculptor]

Caron (i) from the medieval French personal name *Caron*, probably a derivative of Celtic *car-* 'love'; (ii) 'person from Cairon', Normandy; (iii) *also* **Carron** 'carter' (from Old Northern French *carron* 'cart')

Carpenter 'worker in wood, carpenter' [Harry Carpenter, 1925–, British television sports presenter and boxing commentator]

— **The Carpenters** a US vocal and instrumental duo consisting of the siblings Karen Carpenter, 1950–83, and Richard Carpenter, 1946–

Carr (i) a northern English and Scottish variant of **Kerr**; (ii) from Irish Gaelic *Ó Carra* 'descendant of *Carra*', a nickname meaning 'spear', or from Irish Gaelic *Mac Giolla Chathair* 'son of the follower of *Cathar*', a personal name based on *cath* 'battle' [Robert Carr (Lord Carr), 1916–, British Conservative politician]

Carrell (i) 'pillow-maker' (from Old French *carrel* 'pillow, bolster'); (ii) see **Carroll**

Carreras 'person who lives at a crossroads' (from Spanish *carreras* 'thoroughfares') [Michael Carreras, 1927–94, British film director and producer]
— **Carreras** a British make of cigarette, established by José Joaquim Carreras, a Spanish nobleman's son who opened a shop in London in 1843

Carrick 'person from Carrick', district of Ayrshire ('rock')

Carrier (i) 'person who transports goods'; (ii) 'quarryman, stonemason' (from Old French *carrier*) [Robert Carrier (original name Robert Carrier MacMahon), 1923–2006, US-born British chef, restaurateur and cookery writer]

Carrigan a different form of **Corrigan**

Carrington 'person from Carrington', Cheshire, Lincolnshire and Lothian ('estate associated with Cāra' or (Lincolnshire) 'Cora's people's estate') [Dora Carrington, 1893–1932, British painter; Peter Carrington (Lord Carrington), 1919–, British Conservative politician]
— **Carrington VC** a film (1954) about a British army major (played by David Niven) who is court-martialled for embezzling mess funds

Carrodus a different form of **Carruthers**

Carroll, Carol, Carrell from Irish Gaelic *Ó Cearbhaill* or *Mac Cearbhaill* 'descendant or son of *Cearbhall*', a personal name perhaps derived from *cearbh* 'hack' and hence meaning literally perhaps 'butcher' or 'ferocious warrior'. See also **Carvell** (ii) [Leo G. Carroll, 1892–1972, British actor; Lewis Carroll, pen-name of Charles Lutwidge Dodgson, 1832–98, British mathematician and children's author]

Carron see **Caron** (iii)

Carruthers, Carrothers 'person from Carruthers', Dumfries and Galloway ('Ruther's fort'). See also **Cardus, Carrodus, Crothers**

Carse 'person who lives in an area of low-lying wet land' (from Scottish English *carse* 'such an area')

Carslake 'person from Carslake', an unidentified place in England (perhaps 'stream where watercress grows'). See also **Kerslake**

Carson perhaps a different form of **Curzon** [Sir Edward Carson (Lord Carson), 1854–1935, Irish-born British Unionist politician and lawyer; Frank Carson, 1926–, Northern Irish comedian; Johnny Carson, 1925–2005, US television chat-show host; Kit Carson (original name Christopher Carson), 1809–68, US frontiersman; Rachel Carson, 1907–64, US ecologist and author; Violet Carson, 1898–1983, British actress, portrayer of Ena Sharples on the Granada television soap opera *Coronation Street* (1960–); Willie Carson, 1942–, British jockey]
— **Carson City** the capital city of Nevada, USA. It was named after Kit Carson (see above).

Carstairs 'person from Carstairs', South Lanarkshire ('Tarra's castle') [John Paddy Carstairs (orig-inal surname Keys; Carstairs was his mother's maiden name), 1910–70, British writer and director]

Carswell (i) 'person from Carswell', Oxfordshire ('stream where watercress grows'); (ii) a different form of **Creswell**

Cart, Carte (i) 'person who makes or drives carts'; (ii) perhaps 'tax collector' (from Old Provençal *cart* 'quart (i.e. a tax levied on wine)'); (iii) a shortened form of **McCart** [Richard D'Oyley Carte, see **Doyley**]

Carter (i) 'person who transports goods in a cart, carter'; (ii) a Manx variant of **MacArthur** [Angela Carter, 1940–92, British author; Elliott Carter, 1908–, US composer; Graydon Carter, 1949–, Canadian-born US journalist and author; Howard Carter, 1874–1939, British archaeologist; Jimmy Carter, 1924–, US Democratic politician, president 1977–81]
— **Carter's Little Liver Pills** a proprietary cascara-based laxative introduced in the early 19th century by Dr John Samuel Carter of Erie, Pennsylvania. US trading-standards legislation compelled a change of name in 1959 to plain 'Carter's Little Pills' (they have no effect on the liver).
— **Carterton** a town in Oxfordshire founded in 1910 by William Carter, with the (unrealized) intention of establishing a self-sufficient colony of smallholders there
— **Get Carter** a film (1971) starring Michael Caine as Jack Carter, a London racketeer who goes north to avenge his brother's death at the hands of gangsters. A pale US-set remake appeared in 2000.

Carteret 'little **Carter**' [John Carteret (1st Earl Granville), 1690–1763, British Whig politician, prime minister 1742–44]

Carthew 'person from Carthew', Cornwall ('black fort'). See also **Cardew**

Cartland 'person from Cartland', Devon [Dame Barbara Cartland, 1901–2000, British romantic novelist]

Cartledge, Cartlidge 'person from Cartledge', Derbyshire ('boggy stream flowing through rough stony ground')

Carton (i) 'person who transports goods in a cart, carter' (from Old Northern French *carreton* 'carter'); (ii) 'grain merchant' (from Old French *carton*, a term for a measure of cereals); (iii) a reduced form of **McCartney** [Sydney Carton, lawyer who sacrifices his life on the scaffold to save Charles Darnay in Charles Dickens's *A Tale of Two Cities* (1859)]

Cartwright 'maker of carts' [Edmund Cartwright, 1743–1823, British inventor and industrialist]

Carty from Irish Gaelic *Ó Cárthaigh* 'descendant of *Cárthach*', a nickname meaning literally 'loving'. See also **McCarthy** [Todd Carty, 1963–, Irish-born British actor]

Carvell, Carvel (i) 'person from Carville', the name of two places in northern France ('Kári's settlement'); (ii) a different form of **Carroll**

Carver (i) 'wood-carver' or 'sculptor'; (ii) 'ploughman' (from Anglo-Norman *caruier* 'ploughman')

Carwardine 'person from Carden (earlier Cawardyn)', Cheshire (probably 'rocky enclosure')

Cary see **Carey**

Casaubon, Cazaubon from a medieval French nickname for someone who lives in a fine house (from Old Provençal *casal* 'cottage' + *bon* 'good')

Case (i) 'maker of boxes or chests' (from Anglo-Norman *casse* 'case'). See also **Cash**; (ii) from a medieval French nickname for someone who lives in a (fine) house (from Old Provençal *case* 'house')

Casement from Manx Gaelic *Mac Asmuint* 'son of *Ásmundr*' (see **Osmond**) [Sir Roger Casement, 1864–1916, Irish-born British consular official and rebel]

Casey from Irish Gaelic *Ó Cathasaigh* 'descendant of *Cathasach*', a nickname meaning literally 'vigilant' or 'noisy'. See also **O'Casey**

Cash a different form of **Case** (i) [Johnny Cash, 1932–2003, US country and rock-and-roll singer/songwriter; Pat Cash, 1965–, Australian tennis player]

Cashman (i) a different form of **Cash**; (ii) from Irish Gaelic *Ó Ciosáin* 'descendant of *Ciosán*', a personal name perhaps derived from *ceas* 'coracle'

Cashmore 'person from Cashmoor', Dorset (probably 'marsh where cress grows')

Casper, Caspar see **Kaspar**

Cass from the female personal name *Cass*, a shortened form of *Cassandra*. See also **Casson**

Cassell, Cassel (i) 'person from Cassel', northern France, or 'person from Kassel', Germany ('fort'); (ii) a different form of **Castle**
— **Cassell & Company** a British publishing company, established in 1848 by John Cassell, 1817–65

Cassidy from Irish Gaelic *Ó Caiside* 'descendant of *Caiside*', a nickname meaning literally 'curly-headed one' [David Cassidy, 1950–, US actor and singer; Hopalong Cassidy, US cowboy hero, created in 1904 by Clarence E. Mulford and portrayed on screen from 1936 by William Boyd]
— **Butch Cassidy and the Sundance Kid** a film (1969) starring Paul Newman and Robert Redford as a pair of Western train robbers on the run

Casson 'son of **Cass**' [Sir Hugh Casson, 1910–99, British architect; Sir Lewis Casson, 1875–1969, British actor]

Castle 'person who lives by or lives or works in a castle'. See also **Cassell** (ii) [Barbara Castle (Baroness Castle; *née* Betts), 1910–2002, British Labour politician; Roy Castle, 1933–94, British entertainer]

Castro 'person who lives by or in a castle or walled town', or 'person from Castro', the name of various places in Italy, Portugal and Spain (in either case from Italian, Portuguese or Spanish *castro* 'castle, walled town')

Catchpole 'bailiff, especially (originally) one who could seize domestic animals in lieu of tax or debt' (from Anglo-Norman *cachepol*, from *cacher* 'to chase' + *pol* 'chicken')

Cater 'person whose job is to buy provisions for a household' (from Anglo-Norman *acatour* 'buyer'). See also **Chater**

Cates 'son of *Káti*', an Old Norse personal name based on *káti* 'boy'

Catesby 'person from Catesby', Northamptonshire ('Káti's settlement') [Robert Catesby, 1573–1605, English leader of the 'Gunpowder Plot' conspiracy]

Cathcart 'person from Cathcart', Glasgow (perhaps 'fort by the (river) Cart')

Cather (i) 'person from Cather or Catter', Dumbartonshire; (ii) an anglicization of Austrian German *Köther*, literally 'person who lives in a cottage or hovel' [Willa Cather, 1873–1947, US writer]

Catherwood a different form of **Calderwood**

Catlin from the medieval female personal name *Catlin*, an Anglo-Norman variant of *Catherine*. See also **Caton** (ii), **Catt** (ii), **Cotton** (ii) [George Catlin, 1796–1872, US artist and author]

Cato (i) a different form of **Catto**; (ii) an anglicization of Spanish *Cató*, from a personal name perhaps inspired by the Roman statesman Cato, 234–149 BC

Caton (i) 'person from Caton', Derbyshire and Lancashire (respectively probably 'Cada's farmstead' and 'Káti's farmstead'); (ii) 'little **Catlin**'

Catt (i) from a medieval nickname for someone thought to resemble a cat; (ii) 'little **Catlin**'

Catterall, Catterell, Cattrall, Cattrell 'person from Catterall', Lancashire (perhaps 'cat's tail' (referring to the shape of some local topographic feature)) [Kim Cattrall, 1956–, British actress]

Cattermole an English surname of unknown origin

Cattley 'person from Catley', Herefordshire and Lincolnshire ('glade frequented by cats')
— **cattleya** a tropical American orchid (genus *Cattleya*) with purple, pink or white flowers that is a popular greenhouse plant. It was named after the British botanical patron William Cattley, 1788–1835.

Catto a different form of *Cattoch*, a Scottish surname of unknown origin and meaning. See also **Cato** (i)

Catton (i) 'person from Catton', the name of various places in England (mostly 'Catta's or Káti's farmstead'); (ii) 'little **Catlin**'

Caughey from Irish Gaelic *Mac Eachaidh* 'son of *Eachaidh*', a nickname meaning literally 'horseman', or *Ó Maolchathaigh* (see **Mulcahy**)

Caulfield, Cauldfield 'person from Cauldfield', Dumfries and Galloway ('cold open country') [Holden Caulfield, mixed-up teenage hero of J.D. Salinger's *The Catcher in the Rye* (1951); Patrick Caulfield, 1936–2005, British artist]

Causey, Cawsey 'person who lives by a causeway'

Causley perhaps 'person from Corsley', Wiltshire ('wood or glade by a marsh') [Charles Causley, 1917–2003, British poet]

Cauthen, Cauthon probably different forms of **Cawthorne** [Steve Cauthen, 1960–, US jockey]

Cavalcanti from a medieval Italian nickname for a horseman or knight (from a derivative of Italian *cavalcare* 'to ride')

Cavanagh see **Kavanagh**

Cave (i) 'person from Cave', Yorkshire ('place by the (river) Cave', a river-name meaning 'swift one'); (ii) from a medieval nickname for a bald man (from Anglo-Norman *cauf* 'bald'); (iii) 'person employed in or in charge of wine cellars' (from Old French *cave* 'cellar'), or 'person who lives in or near a cave' (from Old French *cave* 'cave')

Cavell from a medieval nickname for a bald man (from Anglo-Norman *cauvel* 'little bald one') [Edith Cavell, 1865–1915, British nurse executed by the Germans for helping Allied soldiers escape from Belgium]

Cavendish 'person from Cavendish', Suffolk ('Cāfna's enclosure') [Cavendish, family name of the dukes of Devonshire; 'Cavendish', pen-name of Henry Jones, 1831–99, British authority on card games; Lord Frederick Cavendish, 1836–82, British Liberal politician killed in the Phoenix Park Murders; Henry Cavendish, 1731–1810, British chemist and physicist; Thomas Cavendish, 1560–92, English seaman and pirate]
— **Cavendish Laboratories** the premises of the Department of Physics at Cambridge University. Opened in 1874, they were named in honour of Henry Cavendish (see above).
— **Lucy Cavendish College** a women's college of Cambridge University, founded in 1965 and named in honour of Lucy Cavendish, 1841–1925, a campaigner for the reform of women's education

Cawley a reduced form of **MacAulay** [Evonne Cawley (*née* Goolagong), 1951–, Australian tennis player]

Cawston 'person from Cawston', Norfolk and Warwickshire ('Kalfr's farmstead')

Cawthon a different form of **Cawthorne**

Cawthorne, Cawthorn 'person from Cawthorn or Cawthorne', both in Yorkshire ('cold thorn bush'). See also **Cauthen**

Caxton 'person from Caxton', Cambridgeshire ('Kakkr's farmstead') [William Caxton, ?1422–91, English printer]
— **Caxton Hall** a public meeting and concert hall (formerly also a registry office) in Westminster, built in 1878. It is situated in Caxton Street, which was named after William Caxton (see above), who had his printing press nearby.

Cayley see **Caley**

Cazalet 'person who lives in a small house' (from Old Provençal *cazalet* 'small house, cottage')

Cazaubon see **Casaubon**

Cecil from the Old Welsh male personal name *Seisyllt*, probably ultimately from Latin *Sextilius*, a derivative of *Sextus*, literally 'sixth(-born)' [Lord David Cecil, 1902–86, British literary critic; Henry Cecil, pen-name of Henry Cecil Leon, 1902–76, British lawyer and comic writer; Henry Cecil, 1943–, British racehorse trainer; Sir Robert Cecil, 1563–1612, English statesman, son of William; William Cecil (Lord Burghley), 1520–98, English statesman; Gascoyne-Cecil, see **Gascoigne**]

Chadwick 'person from Chadwick', the name of several places in England (variously 'Ceadda's dairy farm' and 'Ceadel's dairy farm'). See also **Shaddock, Shattock** [Sir Edwin Chadwick, 1800–90, British social reformer; Sir James Chadwick, 1891–1974, British physicist; Lynn Chadwick, 1914–2003, British sculptor and designer]

Chaffey, Chaffee from a medieval nickname for a bald man (from Old French *chauf* 'bald')

Chakrabarti a Hindu name meaning literally 'wheels rolling', hence 'all-powerful ruler' [Shami Chakrabarti, 1969–, British barrister and human-rights campaigner]

Chalk, Chalke 'person who lives on chalky land', or 'person from Chalk or Chalke', the name of various places in southern England ('chalky place')

Chalker (i) a different form of **Chalk**; (ii) 'person who paints things with whitewash'

Challenger probably from a medieval nickname for a touchy or quarrelsome person (from a derivative of Middle English *chalangen* 'to challenge') [Professor George Challenger, irascible scientist and explorer, leader of the expedition to Amazonia in Arthur Conan Doyle's *The Lost World* (1912)]

Challenor, Challener, Challinor, Challoner 'maker or seller of blankets' (from a derivative of Middle English *chaloun* 'blanket', ultimately from *Châlons*-sur-Marne, the name of a French cloth-making town) [Richard Challoner, 1691–1781, English Roman Catholic churchman and writer]

Challis, Challiss 'person from Eschalles', northern France ('ladders')

Chalmers a Scottish variant of **Chambers** [Judith Chalmers, 1935–, British television presenter; Thomas Chalmers, 1780–1847, Scottish preacher and theologian]

Chamberlain, Chamberlaine, Chamberlin 'official in charge of a high-ranking person's private chambers' [Sir Austen Chamberlain, 1863–1937, British Conservative politician, son of Joseph; Joseph Chamberlain, 1836–1914, British Liberal and Conservative politician; Neville Chamberlain, 1869–1940, British Conservative politician, prime minister 1937–40, son of Joseph; Owen Chamberlain, 1920–2006, US physicist; Richard Chamberlain, 1935–, US actor]

Chambers 'person employed in a high-ranking person's private chambers' [Ephraim Chambers, ?1680–1740, British encyclopaedist, man of letters and free thinker; Sir William Chambers, 1723–96, British architect and interior designer]

— **W. and R. Chambers** a publishing firm established in Edinburgh in 1819 by William Chambers, 1800–83, and his brother Robert Chambers, 1802–71. It specializes in dictionaries and other reference books. It is now (as Chambers Harrap) part of the Hachette Livre UK group.

Champion a different form of **Campion** (i) [Harry Champion (original name William Crump), 1866–1942, British music-hall entertainer]

Champney a different form of **Champneys**

Champneys 'person from Champagne', region of northeastern France (from Anglo-Norman *champeneis* 'of Champagne') [Basil Champneys, 1842–1935, British architect]

Chan (i) a different form of **Chen**; (ii) 'person from Chan or Zhan', territorial area of China [Charlie Chan, fictional Chinese-American detective created in the mid-1920s by the US writer Earl D. Biggers; Jackie Chan (original name Chan Kong-Sang), 1954–, Hong Kong-born Chinese martial artist, actor, director and pop singer]

Chance from a medieval nickname for a lucky person or one who relied on luck (e.g. a gambler)

Chancellor 'secretary to a high-ranking person, administrative official' [Richard Chancellor, died 1556, English explorer]

Chancey 'person from Chancé', the name of various places in France. See also **Chauncey**

Chandler 'person who makes or sells candles' (from Middle English *chandeler* 'candle-maker', from Old French) [Jeff Chandler (original name Ira Grossel), 1918–61, US actor; Raymond Chandler, 1888–1959, US writer]

Chandos 'person from Candos', northern France [Sir John Chandos, died 1370, English military leader]

Chandrasekhar a Hindu name meaning literally 'holder of the moon' (an epithet of the god Shiva) [Subrahmanyan Chandrasekhar, 1910–95, Indian-born US physicist]
— **Chandrasekhar limit** the upper limit for the mass of a white dwarf star beyond which the star collapses to a neutron star or a black hole. It is named after Subrahmanyan Chandrasekhar (see above).

Chaney (i) *also* **Cheney** different forms of **Chesney**; (ii) 'person from Chanet', the name of various places in France ('settlement among the reeds') [Lon Chaney (original name Alonso Chaney), 1883–1930, US silent-film actor]

Chang (i) 'bow-stretcher', from an honorary surname given to Hui, in Chinese legend the inventor of bows and arrows; (ii) 'person from Zhang', an area in the Shandong province of China; (iii) from two advisers to the Chinese emperor Huang Di (2697–2595 BC) who had a character 'chang' in their surnames

Channell, Channel 'person who lives by a channel, canal, drain, estuary, etc'.

Channing perhaps a different form of **Channon** [Carol Channing, 1921–, US actress]

Channon a different form of **Cannon** (i) (from central Old French *chanun* 'cannon', rather than Old Northern French *canun*, the source of the English vocabulary word *cannon* and of the name **Cannon**) [Sir Henry ('Chips') Channon, 1897–1958, US-born British Conservative politician and diarist]

Chantry, Chantrey 'singer in a chantry chapel' or 'person who lives by a chantry chapel' (a chantry chapel was one endowed for the singing of masses for the soul of the founder) [Sir Francis Chantrey, 1781–1841, British sculptor]
— **Chantrey Bequest** a fund bequeathed to the Royal Academy by Sir Francis Chantrey (see above) for the purchase of British works of art. The purchases are housed in Tate Britain.

Chapel, Chapell see **Chappell**

Chaplin (i) 'clergyman' or 'servant of a clergyman' (from Old French *chapelain* 'singer in a chantry chapel (see **Chantry**)'). See also **Caplin**; (ii) 'son of *Chaplya*', from a Belorussian and Ukrainian nickname for someone with long thin legs (from Belorussian and Ukrainian *chaplya* 'stork, heron') [Charlie Chaplin (Sir Charles Chaplin), 1889–1977, British-born US film actor, director and producer]
— **Chaplinesque** characteristic of the comedy or style of Charlie Chaplin (see above), especially in his pathos-filled persona as the 'Little Tramp'

Chapman 'merchant, trader' (from Middle English *chapman* 'merchant') [Colin Chapman, 1928–82, British car designer; George Chapman, ?1559–1634, English dramatist and translator; Graham Chapman, 1941–89, British comedian and comic writer]
— **Chapman and Hall** a British publishing company founded in London in 1830 by Edward Chapman and William Hall. It was bought up by Methuen in 1938.
— **Chapman brothers** Dinos Chapman, 1962–, and his brother Jake Chapman, 1966–, British conceptual artists

Chappell, Chappel, Chapel, Chapell, Chapple 'person who lives by or works in a chapel' [Greg Chappell, 1948–, Australian cricketer, brother of Ian; Ian Chappell, 1943–, Australian cricketer]
— **Chappell** a British firm of music publishers and concert agents, established in 1810 by J.B. Cramer, F.T. Latour and Samuel Chappell

Charles from the male personal name *Charles* (via French from Germanic *Carl*, literally 'man') [Bob Charles, 1936–, New Zealand golfer; John Charles, 1931–2004, Welsh footballer; Ray Charles (original name Ray Charles Robinson), 1932–2004, US singer and pianist]

Charleson 'son of **Charles**'

Charleston a different form of **Charleson**

Charlesworth 'person from Charlesworth', Derbyshire ('Ceafl's enclosure')

Charlton, Charleton 'person from Charlton or Charleton', the name of various places in southern and western England ('farmstead of the freemen'). See also **Carlton** [Sir Bobby Charlton, 1937–,

English footballer, brother of Jack; Jack Charlton, 1935–, English footballer and manager]

Charnley 'person from Charnley', an unidentified place perhaps in Lancashire (probably 'glade with a cairn') [Sir John Charnley, 1911–82, British orthopaedic surgeon]

Charrington a different form of **Cherrington**

Charteris (i) *also* **Charters** 'person from Chartres', northern France ('settlement of the Carnutes (a Gaulish tribe)'). The name is traditionally pronounced 'charters', but in modern usage more usually as spelled.; (ii) a different form of **Chatteris** [Leslie Charteris (original name Leslie Charles Bowyer Yin), 1907–93, Singapore-born British and later US crime novelist]
— **Charters and Caldicott** two bumbling but brave cricket-mad buffers (played respectively by Basil Radford and Naunton Wayne) who provide the comic relief in the Alfred Hitchcock film *The Lady Vanishes* (1938). The characters were revived in a BBC television drama *Charters and Caldicott* (1985).

Chase (i) from a medieval nickname for a skilled hunter; (ii) 'person who lives in a (particular important or impressive) house' (from southern French *chase* 'house', from Latin *casa*) [Chevy Chase (original name Cornelius Crane Chase), 1943–, US comedian and actor (he renamed himself after Chevy Chase, a suburb of Washington, DC, that in turn got its name from the 15th-century 'Ballad of Chevy Chase', which has as its subject the rivalry between the Percy and Douglas families, who met at the Battle of Chevy Chase near Otterburn, Northumberland in 1388); James Hadley Chase, pen-name of Rene Brabazon Raymond, 1906–85, British author]
— **Chase Manhattan Bank** a US-based bank formed in 1955 by the merger of the Bank of Manhattan (founded in 1799) and the Chase National Bank of the City of New York (founded in 1877 and named in honour of the US politician and jurist Samuel Portland Chase, 1808–73, Secretary to the Treasury 1861–64)

Chater 'person whose job is to buy provisions for a household' (from Old French *achateur* 'buyer'). See also **Cater**

Chatfield 'person from Chatfields', Sussex ('Ceatta's open land')

Chatham 'person from Chatham', Kent ('settlement by a wood')

Chattaway, Chataway 'person from Chattaway', an unidentified place probably in the West Midlands ('Ceatta's path') [Sir Christopher Chattaway, 1931–, British athlete and Conservative politician]

Chatteris 'person from Chatteris', Cambridgeshire ('Ceatta's raised strip of land'). See also **Charteris** (ii)

Chatterjee a Hindu name meaning literally 'teacher from Chatta', a village in Bengal

Chatterley 'person from Chatterley', Staffordshire (probably 'wood by Cadeir', a Celtic hill-name meaning literally 'chair')

— *Lady Chatterley's Lover* a novel (1928) by D.H. Lawrence about the love affair between Lady Chatterley and her husband's gamekeeper Mellors. Its steamy sex scenes saw it banned in the UK until 1960.

Chatterton 'person from Chadderton', Lancashire ('farmstead by Cadeir (see **Chatterley**)') [Thomas Chatterton, 1752–70, British poet]

Chatto 'person from Chatto', Scottish Borders [Beth Chatto, 1923–, British garden designer]
— **Chatto and Windus** a British publishing company founded in 1874 by Andrew Chatto, 1841–1913. He was joined soon afterwards by William Windus.

Chatwin a different form of **Chetwynd** [Bruce Chatwin, 1940–89, British writer]

Chaucer 'maker of leggings' (from a derivative of Middle English *chauces* 'leggings', from Old French) [Geoffrey Chaucer, ?1343–1400, English poet]
— **Chaucerian** of or characteristic of Geoffrey Chaucer (see above)
— **Scottish Chaucerians** a diverse group of 15th- and 16th-century Scottish writers (including William Dunbar and Robert Henryson) once thought to have been significantly influenced by the work of Geoffrey Chaucer

Chaudhry, Chaudry, Chaudhary see **Chowdhury**

Chauhan a Hindu and Sikh surname of uncertain origin and meaning

Chauncey a different form of **Chancey**

Chavez 'person from Chaves or Chavez', the name of various places in Spain and Portugal (mainly 'keys')

Cheadle 'person from Cheadle', Cheshire and Staffordshire ('place by the wood'). See also **Chettle**

Cheatham see **Cheetham**

Checkley 'person from Checkley', Cheshire, Herefordshire and Staffordshire ('Ceacca's glade' or (Cheshire) 'Ceadicca's glade')

Cheek, Cheeke, Cheke from a medieval nickname for someone with a peculiarity in the cheek area (e.g. a scar or deformity). See also **Chick** (ii)

Cheeseman, Cheesman 'person who makes or sells cheese'

Cheetham, Cheatham, Chetham 'person from Cheetham', Lancashire ('homestead by a wood')
— **Chetham's School** a school of music founded in Manchester in 1969 on the site of Chetham's Hospital, an orphanage founded in 1653 by the local merchant Humphrey Chetham, 1580–1653

Cheever 'goatherd', or from a medieval nickname for someone thought to resemble a goat (e.g. in capriciousness) (in either case from Anglo-Norman *chivere* 'goat') [John Cheever, 1912–82, US author]

Cheevers a different form of **Chivers**

Chegwin, Chegwyn 'person who lives in or by a white house' (from Cornish *chy* 'house' + *gwyn*

'white') [Keith Chegwin, 1957–, British comic actor and television presenter]

Cheke see **Cheek**

Chen 'person from Chen', Hunan province, China. See also **Chan** (i)

Cheney (i) see **Chaney** (i); (ii) 'person from Cheney', northern France ('Canius's estate') [Richard Cheney, 1941–, US Republican politician, vice-president 2001–]

Cheng 'person from Zheng or Cheng', ancient states or areas of China

Cherrington 'person from Cherrington or Cherington', the name of several places in England (mostly 'village with a church'). See also **Charrington**

Cherry 'person who lives by a cherry tree', or 'grower or seller of cherries'

Cheshire, Chesshire, Chesshyre 'person from Cheshire', county in northwestern England ('district of Chester') [Leonard Cheshire (Lord Cheshire), 1917–92, British bomber pilot and philanthropist]

Chesney 'person who lives in or by an oak wood' (from Old French *chesnai* 'oak wood'). See also **Chaney** (i)

Chesnut see **Chestnut**

Chester 'person from Chester', Cheshire ('Roman city') [Charlie Chester (original name Cecil Victor Manser), 1914–97, British comedian; Frank Chester, 1895–1957, English cricket umpire]

Chesterton 'person from Chesterton', the name of several places in England ('village by a Roman fort') [G.K. Chesterton, 1874–1936, British essayist, novelist, poet and critic]

— **Chesterbelloc** a portmanteau term (coined by G.B. Shaw) combining the personae of G.K. Chesterton (see above) and the poet Hilaire Belloc, both right-of-centre Roman Catholic nostalgiacs

Chestnut, Chesnut 'person who lives by a chestnut tree'; also perhaps from a medieval nickname for someone with chestnut-coloured hair

Chetham see **Cheetham**

Chettle a different form of **Cheadle**

Chetwode, Chetwood 'person from Chetwode', Buckinghamshire ('place by the wood')

Chetwynd 'person from Chetwynd', Shropshire ('Ceatta's winding ascent'). See also **Chatwin**

Chevalier 'knight', or 'knight's servant', or from a medieval nickname for someone who behaved in a knightly or chivalric manner (from Old French *chevalier* 'horseman, knight') [Albert Chevalier, 1861–1923, British music-hall comedian and singer]

Chew (i) 'person from Chew', Somerset ('place on the (river) Chew', a Celtic river-name of unknown meaning), or 'person from Chew', Lancashire and Yorkshire ('ravine'); (ii) from a medieval nickname for someone thought to resemble a chough (a bird of the crow family), e.g. in being talkative or light-fingered (from Old English *cēo* 'chough')

Cheyne 'person who lives by or in an oak wood or by a particular (notable) oak tree' (from Old French *chesne* 'oak'). The name is pronounced 'chain' or 'chainy'.

— **Cheyne-Stokes respiration** a breathing pattern marked by shallow breathing alternating with periods of rapid heavy breathing. The names are those of the Scottish physician John Cheyne, 1777–1836, and the Irish physician William Stokes, 1804–78.

— **Cheyne Walk** a road in Chelsea, London, on the north bank of the River Thames. It was named after the Cheyne family, late 17th-century lords of the manor of Chelsea.

Chichester 'person from Chichester', Sussex ('Cissa's Roman town') [Sir Francis Chichester, 1901–72, British yachtsman]

Chick (i) 'poultry-breeder'; (ii) a different form of **Cheek** [Dame Harriette Chick, 1875–1977, British protein scientist and nutritionist]

Chilcote, Chilcoat (i) 'person from Chilcote', Leicestershire and Northamptonshire ('cottage of the young men'); (ii) different forms of **Chilcott**

Chilcott (i) 'person from Chilcott', Somerset ('Cēola's cottage'); (ii) a different form of **Chilcote**

Child, Childe (i) from a medieval nickname for a young man. See also **Childs**; (ii) 'person who lives by a spring' (from Old English *cielde* 'spring water, spring') [Francis Child, 1825–96, US philologist and ballad editor; Gordon Childe, 1892–1957, Australian archaeologist]

Childers 'person from Childerhouse', an unidentified place in England (perhaps 'orphanage') [Erskine Childers, 1870–1922, British-born Irish nationalist and writer]

Childress a different form of **Childers**

Childs 'son of **Child** (i)'

Chiles a different form of **Childs**

Chilton 'person from Chilton', the name of numerous places in England (mostly 'farm of the young men') [John Chilton, 1932–, British jazz musician]

Chilver probably from the Old English male personal name *Cēolfrith*, literally 'ship-peace'

Chilvers 'son of **Chilver**'

Chinn from a medieval nickname for someone with a prominent chin, or for a man without a beard

Chinnery, Chinery probably 'person from Chenevray', northern France

Chippendale 'person from Chippingdale', Lancashire ('valley with a market') [Thomas Chippendale, 1718–79, British cabinetmaker]

— **Chippendale** denoting furniture in an 18th-century English style developed by Thomas Chippendale (see above), characterized by graceful flowing lines, cabriole legs and elaborate ornamentation

— **The Chippendales** a US troupe of scantily clad male dancers. Their name comes from a Los Angeles night club called 'Chippendales', founded in the early 1980s by Steve Banerjee, where they originally performed.

Chipperfield 'person from Chipperfield', Hertfordshire ('open land where merchants meet')
— **Chipperfield's Circus** a leading British touring circus. The Chipperfield family connection with the circus goes back several centuries, but it was in the mid-20th century, under Dick Chipperfield, 1904–88, and Jimmy Chipperfield, 1912–90, that their circus rose to pre-eminence in Britain.

Chisholm, Chisholme, Chisolm, Chisum 'person from Chisholme', Scottish Borders ('meadow with good pasture (conducive to the production of cheese)') [Caroline Chisholm, 1808–77, British philanthropist; Melanie Chisholm ('Mel C'), 1974–, British pop singer ('Sporty Spice' of the Spice Girls)]
— **Chisholm Trail** a route for cattle drives in the American West, established in the 1860s and running from southern Texas to Kansas. It was named after the Indian trader and guide Jesse Chisholm, ?1805–68, who established several trading posts in the Oklahoma territory (but never actually drove cattle along the trail).

Chisnall, Chisnell 'person from Chisnall Hall', Lancashire (probably 'gravelly nook of land')

Chiswell 'person from Chiswell', an unidentified place probably in Devon (probably either 'gravelly stream' or 'Cissa's stream')

Chittenden 'person from Chittenden', Kent (probably 'pig pasture associated with Citta')

Chitty (i) 'person from Chitty', Kent ('Citta's island'); (ii) from a medieval nickname for someone thought to resemble a young animal (from Middle English *chitte* 'cub, puppy or other young animal')

Chivers 'son of **Cheever**'. See also **Cheevers** [Martin Chivers, 1945–, English footballer]
— **Chivers** a British manufacturer of jams, jellies, etc., established in Cambridgeshire in 1873 by John Chivers

Choate, Choat an English surname of unknown origin and meaning

Choice, Choyce probably different forms of **Joyce**

Cholmondeley, Cholmeley, Chumley 'person from Cholmondeley', Cheshire ('Ceolmund's glade'). The name is standardly pronounced 'chumly'.

Chomsky 'person from Chomsk', Poland [Noam Chomsky, 1928–, US linguistician and polemicist]
— **Chomskyan, Chomskian** relating to the linguistic theories of Noam Chomsky (see above)

Chopin (i) from a medieval nickname for a heavy consumer of alcohol (from Old French *chopine*, a term for a large liquid measure), or for a truculent person (from Old French *chopin* 'violent blow'); (ii) a reduced (French) form of Polish *Szopinski*, literally 'person from Szopa, Szopinek or Szopy', the name of various places in Poland [Kate Chopin, 1850–1904, US novelist, short-story writer and poet]

Chowdhury, Choudhury, Choudhry, Chaudhry, Chaudry, Chaudhary a Hindu and Muslim surname meaning literally 'leader of a community or caste'

Choyce see **Choice**

Christensen 'son of *Christen*', a Scandinavian and North German male personal name meaning literally 'Christian'

Christian from the medieval male (and female) personal name *Christian* (from Latin *Christianus*, literally 'follower of Christ') [Fletcher Christian, 1764–93, British sailor who led the mutiny on HMS *Bounty* (1789)]

Christie, Christy from the Scottish male personal name *Christie*, a pet-form of **Christian** [Dame Agatha Christie (*née* Miller), 1890–1976, British author of detective fiction; John Christie, 1882–1962, British landowner, founder (1934) of Glyndebourne Festival Opera; John Reginald Halliday Christie, 1898–1953, British serial killer; Julie Christie, 1941–, British actress; Linford Christie, 1960–, Jamaican-born British athlete; Tony Christie, 1943–, British popular singer]
— **Christie's** a British auction house, founded in London in 1766 by James Christie, 1730–1803
— **Christy Minstrels** a group of blackface singers performing traditional African-American plantation songs to the accompaniment of banjo and bones (two pieces of bone or ivory rattled together), especially (and originally) one organized in New York in the 1840s by Edwin P. Christy, 1815–62.

Christmas from a medieval nickname for someone born on (or otherwise associated with) Christmas Day
— **Christmas disease** a form of haemophilia caused by lack of a protein needed for blood clotting. It was named (in the early 1950s) after Stephen Christmas, who had the disease.
— **Christmas Pie** a hamlet in Surrey, probably named after a family called Christmas who once lived there

Christopher from the male personal name *Christopher*, literally 'bearer of Christ' (via Latin from Greek *Khristophoros*, from *Khristos* 'Christ' + the element *-phor-* 'carry'). See also **Crystal, Kidd** (iii), **Kitt** (i)

Christophers 'son of **Christopher**' [Harry Christophers, 1953–, British conductor]

Christopherson 'son of **Christopher**'

Christy see **Christie**

Chrysler an anglicization of the German and Jewish surname *Kreisler*, from a medieval nickname for either a hyperactive person or a curly-haired person (in both cases from a derivative of Middle High German *kriusel* or Yiddish *krayzl* 'spiral, curl, spinning top')
— **Chrysler Corporation** a US car manufacturer founded in Michigan in 1925 by Walter P. Chrysler, 1875–1940. In 1998 it merged with Daimler-Benz to become DaimlerChrysler AG.

Chrystal see **Crystal**

Chubb from a medieval nickname for someone thought to resemble a chubb (a type of small freshwater fish), especially in being lazy or slow-witted
— **Chubb Locks Ltd.** a British lock manufacturer founded in Wolverhampton in 1830 by Jeremiah Chubb (inventor of an unpickable lock) and his brother Charles

Chudley, Chudleigh 'person from Chudleigh', Devon ('Ciedda's glade')

Chumley see **Cholmondeley**

Church 'person who lives by a church' [Charlotte Church (original name Charlotte Reed; Church was her stepfather's surname), 1986–, British pop singer; Frederic Church, 1826–1900, US painter; Richard Church, 1893–1972, British poet, novelist and essayist]

Churchill 'person from Churchill', the name of various places in southern England (mostly 'hill with a church') [Caryl Churchill, 1938–, British playwright; Charles Churchill, 1731–64, British poet; John Churchill (1st duke of Marlborough), 1650–1722, English general; Lord Randolph Churchill, 1849–95, British Conservative politician, father of Sir Winston; Randolph Churchill, 1911–68, British Conservative politician, journalist and author, son of Sir Winston; Sir Winston Churchill, 1874–1965, British Conservative and Liberal politician and author, prime minister 1940–45, 1951–55; Winston Churchill, 1940–, British Conservative politician, grandson of Sir Winston; Spencer-Churchill, see **Spencer**]
— **Churchill** a port in northeastern Manitoba, Canada. It was named in honour of John Churchill (see above), who was a governor of the Hudson's Bay Company in the late 17th century.
— **Churchill cigar** a type of cigar 7 inches (178 mm) in length and of ring gauge 47. It was named in honour of Sir Winston Churchill (see above), who in later years was seldom photographed without a large cigar in his mouth or hand.
— **Churchill College** a college of Cambridge University, founded in 1958 and named in honour of Sir Winston Churchill
— **Churchillian** of or typical of Sir Winston Churchill, especially in defiant resistance or in orotundity
— **Churchilliana** items in a collection concerned with Sir Winston Churchill
— **Churchill River** a river in south-central Labrador, Newfoundland, Canada, named (in 1965) in honour of Sir Winston Churchill (it was previously the Hamilton River); also, a river that flows through numerous lakes in Saskatchewan and Manitoba, Canada, into Hudson Bay at Churchill (see above)
— **Churchill tank** a British heavy infantry tank (Mark IV, A22) of the Second World War period, named after Sir Winston Churchill. It first saw action in 1942.

Churchman 'person who lives by a church'

Cimino 'dealer in spices' (from Italian *cimino* 'cumin')

Cipriano from the Italian male personal name *Cipriano*, literally 'Cypriot'

Citrine an invented Jewish name based on Yiddish *tsitrin* 'lemon tree'

Clack from the medieval male personal name *Clac* (from Old English *Clacc* or the related Old Norse *Klakkr*, both originally probably nicknames for someone thought to resemble a lump in large size and ungainliness)

Claffey, Claffy from Irish Gaelic *Mac Fhlaithimh* 'son of *Flaitheamh*', a personal name meaning literally 'prince'

Claggett, Clagett probably 'person from Claygate', Surrey ('gate or gap in the clayey district')

Claiborne probably 'person from Claiborne', an unidentified place probably in southern England (probably 'stream in the clay') [Liz Claiborne, 1929–2007, US fashion designer]

Claire see **Clare**

Clairmont see **Clermont**

Clampitt, Clampett 'person from Clampit or Clampitt', Cornwall and Devon ('clay pit') [Jed Clampett, oil-rich country bumpkin (played by Buddy Ebsen) in the US television sitcom *The Beverly Hillbillies* (1963–71)]

Clancey, Clancy from Irish Gaelic *Mac Fhlannchaidh* 'son of *Flannchadh*', a personal name derived from *flann* 'red' [Tom Clancy, 1947–, US writer]

Clanton probably 'person from Clandon', Dorset and Surrey ('hill not overgrown with weeds')

Clapham 'person from Clapham', the name of several places in England (mostly 'homestead near a hill')

Clapp from a medieval nickname for someone thought to resemble a lump in large size and ungainliness (from Middle English *cloppe* 'lump')

Clapton 'person from Clapton', the name of numerous places in England (mostly 'farmstead by a hill') [Eric Clapton, 1945–, British guitarist and singer/songwriter]

Clare, Claire (i) 'person from Clare', Suffolk ('place on the (river) Clare', a Celtic river-name probably meaning literally 'bright stream'), or 'person from Clare', Oxfordshire ('clayey slope'); (ii) from the medieval female personal name *Clare* or *Claire* (via Old French from Latin *Clāra*, literally 'renowned one'); (iii) 'person who works with clay' (from Middle English *clayere*, a derivative of *clay*). See also **Clear** (i) [Anthony Clare, 1942–, Irish psychologist and psychiatrist; John Clare, 1793–1864, British poet]
— **Clare College** a college of Cambridge University, founded in 1338 (as Clare Hall) and named in honour of Elizabeth de Clare, 1295–1360, a granddaughter of Edward I

Clarey see **Clary**

Clarges 'servant of a clergyman' (from Middle English *clargies* 'of a clergyman')

Claridge (i) from the medieval personal name *Clarice* (via Old French from Latin *Clāritia*, literally 'brightness, renown'); (ii) 'person from Clearhedge Wood', Sussex (probably 'clover ridge')

— **Claridge's** a luxury hotel in the West End of London, founded in the 1850s by William Claridge, a former butler in a royal household

Clark, Clarke, Clerk, Clerke 'scribe or secretary' (originally a member of a minor religious order, capable of reading and writing, but later also a layman). *Clark* is much the commoner spelling in Scotland, *Clarke* in England. [Alan Clark, 1927–99, British Conservative politician and author, son of Sir Kenneth; Alan Clarke, 1946–, English footballer; Sir Arthur C. Clarke, 1917–, British science-fiction writer and scientist; Austin Clarke, 1896–1974, Irish poet and playwright; Charles Clarke, 1950–, British Labour politician; Don Clarke, 1933–2002, New Zealand rugby player; Helen Clark, 1950–, New Zealand Labour politician, prime minister 1999–; James Clerk Maxwell, see **Maxwell**; Jeremiah Clarke, ?1673–1707, English composer; Jim Clark, 1937–68, British racing driver; Joseph Clark, 1939–, Canadian Progressive Conservative politician, prime minister 1979–80; Sir Kenneth Clark (Lord Clark), 1903–83, British art historian; Kenneth Clarke, 1940–, British Conservative politician; Marcus Clarke, 1846–81, British-born Australian writer; Mark Clark, 1896–1984, US general; Mary Higgins Clark (*née* Higgins), 1927–, US author; Nicky Clarke, 1958–, British hair stylist; Petula Clark, 1932–, British popular singer; Ron Clarke, 1937–, Australian athlete; Warren Clarke (original name Alan Clarke), 1947–, British actor]

☆ The 7th commonest name in Britain

• Men with the surname Clark or Clarke are traditionally given the nickname 'Nobby'. This probably came from British slang *nobby* 'of the nobility, upper-crust', the literacy of clerks being associated with the upper echelons of society

— **Clark cell** a standard battery cell with a mercury anode surrounded by a paste of mercury sulphate, and a zinc cathode immersed in saturated zinc sulphate solution. It is named after the British engineer Josiah Latimer Clark, 1822–98.

— **clarkia** any of a genus of plants of the willow-herb family, many of which are cultivated as garden flowering plants. They were named after the American explorer William Clark, 1770–1838.

— **Clarks** a British shoe manufacturer (in full C. & J. Clark Ltd.) founded in Street, Somerset, in 1825 by Cyrus Clark and his brother James (originally to make sheepskin rugs and slippers)

— **Dave Clark Five** a British rock-and-roll group of the 1960s, led by the drummer Dave Clark, 1942–

Clarkson 'son of **Clark**' [Jeremy Clarkson, 1960–, British journalist and broadcaster; Thomas Clarkson, 1760–1846, British campaigner for the abolition of slavery]

Clary, Clarey (i) a different form of **Cleary**; (ii) perhaps 'person who lives where clary (a plant of the mint family) grows' or 'person who gathers or sells clary as a medicinal herb' [Julian Clary, 1959–, British comedian]

Clatworthy 'person from Clatworthy', Somerset ('enclosure where burdock grows')

Claughton 'person from Claughton', Cheshire and Lancashire ('village by a hill')

Clausen 'son of *Claus*', a German and Dutch male personal name that is a shortened form of *Nikolaus* 'Nicholas'

Claxton 'person from Claxton', the name of various places in England ('Clacc's or Klakkr's farmstead' or 'farmstead on a hill')

Clay 'person who lives in a clayey area', or 'person who works in a claypit' [Cassius Clay, original name of Muhammad **Ali**; Henry Clay, 1777–1852, US statesman; Lucius Clay, 1897–1978, US general]

— **Clay Cross** a town in Derbyshire. The name comes from a local family called Clay.

Claydon, Clayden 'person from Claydon', the name of various places in England ('clayey hill')

Claypool, Claypoole, Claypole 'person from Claypole', Lincolnshire ('clayey pool')

Clayton 'person from Clayton', the name of numerous places in England ('farmstead on clayey soil')

— **Clayton's** a colloquial Australian expression for something much spoken of but actually nonexistent. It was inspired (in the early 1980s) by an advertising slogan for a soft drink called Clayton's Tonic: 'It's the drink I have when I'm not having a drink'.

Clear, Cleare (i) a different form of **Clare**; (ii) probably 'person from a place named with the element *clere* (as in, e.g., Kingsclere in Hampshire)' (probably from a Celtic river-name meaning literally 'bright one')

Cleary from Irish Gaelic *Ó Cléirigh* 'descendant of the clerk'. See also **Clary** (i)

Cleave see **Cleeve**

Cleaver (i) 'person who splits timber into planks'; (ii) perhaps 'butcher'; (iii) a different form of **Clive**. See also **Clover** [Eldridge Cleaver, 1935–98, US author and civil-rights activist]

Cleeve, Cleave 'person who lives by a slope or cliff', or 'person from Cleave', Gloucestershire, Somerset and Worcestershire (see **Clive**)

Clegg (i) 'person from Clegg', Lancashire ('haystack' – originally a hill-name); (ii) from Manx Gaelic *Mac Liaigh*, literally 'son of the doctor'

Cleghorn 'person from Cleghorn', Lanarkshire

Cleland, Clelland (i) 'person from Clelland', North Lanarkshire (probably 'clayey land'); (ii) a reduced form of **McClelland** [John Cleland, 1709–89, British novelist, author of *Fanny Hill* (1749)]

Clemence see **Clements**

Clemens (i) a different form of **Clements**; (ii) from the German, Dutch and Danish male personal name *Clemens* '**Clement**' [Samuel Langhorne Clemens, the real name of Mark **Twain**]

Clement (i) from the male personal name *Clement* (via Old French from Latin *Clēmēns*, literally 'merciful'); (ii) 'person from St Clement', Cornwall

Clements, Clemence 'son of **Clement** (i)'. See also **Clemens** (i), **Clemons** [Sir John Clements, 1910–88, British actor; Ray Clemence, 1948–, English footballer]

Clemons, Clemmons different forms of **Clements**

Clench a different form of **Clinch**

Cleobury 'person from Cleobury', Shropshire ('fortified place by Clee (Hill)', a hill-name meaning literally 'rounded hill') [Stephen Cleobury, 1948–, British organist and conductor]

Clerihew a Scottish surname of unknown origin and meaning

— **clerihew** a humorous or satirical verse consisting of two rhyming couplets in lines of irregular metre about someone who is named in the poem. It was invented by the British author Edmund Clerihew Bentley, 1875–1956 (Clerihew was his mother's maiden name). The following example was written by his son Nicholas Clerihew Bentley:

Cecil B. De Mille
Rather against his will
Was persuaded to leave Moses
Out of 'The Wars of the Roses'.

Clerk, Clerke see **Clark**

Clermont 'person from Clermont', the name of several places in France ('clear (i.e. easily visible) hill')

Cleveland 'person from Cleveland', area around Middlesbrough ('hilly district') [Grover Cleveland, 1837–1908, US Democratic politician, president 1885–89, 1893–97; John Cleveland, 1613–58, English poet]

Cleverley, Cleverly probably 'person from Cleveley', Lancashire ('woodland clearing by a cliff')

Cliburn 'person from Cliburn', Cumbria ('stream by a cliff') [Van Cliburn (original name Harvey Lavan Cliburn), 1934–, US pianist]

Cliff, Cliffe 'person who lives by a slope, riverbank or cliff', or 'person from Cliffe', Medway and Yorkshire (in either case from Old English *clif* 'slope, bank, cliff')

Clifford 'person from Clifford', the name of various places in England ('ford by a bank') [Max Clifford, 1943–, British public-relations consultant]

Clift (i) 'person who lives near a rock crevice' (from Middle English *clift* 'cleft'); (ii) probably a different form of **Cliff**

Clifton 'person from Clifton', the name of various places in England ('farmstead on a bank or by a cliff')

Clinch (i) 'person who makes or inserts bolts and rivets' (from Middle English *clinch* 'nail or bolt secured by having its free end turned over or beaten down'); (ii) 'person from Clench', Wiltshire ('place by a hill'). See also **Clench**

Cline see **Klein**

Clinton 'person from Glinton or Glympton', Northamptonshire and Oxfordshire (respectively 'fenced farmstead' and 'farmstead by the (river) Glyme') [Bill Clinton (William Jefferson Clinton), 1946–, US Democratic politician, president 1993–2001; De Witt Clinton, 1769–1828, US statesman, governor of New York 1817–23, 1825–28; Hillary Rodham Clinton (*née* Rodham), 1947–, US lawyer, first lady and Democratic politician, wife of Bill]

— **clintonia** a broad-leaved perennial plant (genus *Clintonia*) of the lily family with blue or purple berries. It was named after De Witt Clinton (see above).

— **Clinton's Ditch** a contemporary colloquial nickname for the Erie Canal, linking the Hudson River with the Great Lakes, which was planned and put into effect by De Witt Clinton

Clitheroe, Clitherow 'person from Clitheroe', Lancashire ('hill with looses stones') [Jimmy Clitheroe, 1921–73, diminutive British comedian; St Margaret Clitherow, 1556–86, English Catholic martyr]

Clive 'person who lives by a slope, riverbank or cliff' (from Old English *clife* 'at the slope, bank or cliff'). See also **Cleeve** [Kitty Clive, 1711–85, British comic actress; Robert Clive (Lord Clive of Plassey; 'Clive of India'), 1725–74, British soldier and colonial administrator]

Clohessy from Irish Gaelic *Ó Clochasaigh* 'descendant of *Clochasach*', a personal name perhaps based on *cloch* 'stone'

Clooney from Irish Gaelic *Ó Cluanaigh* 'descendant of *Cluanach*', a personal name meaning literally 'deceitful one, rogue' [George Clooney, 1961–, US actor, nephew of Rosemary; Rosemary Clooney, 1928–2002, US popular singer]

Close (i) 'person who lives by or in an enclosure (e.g. a courtyard or farmyard)'; (ii) from a medieval nickname for a secretive person (from Middle English *close* 'secret'). See also **Clowes²** [Brian Close, 1931–, English cricketer; Glenn Close, 1947–, US actress]

— **Dean Close School** a public school in Cheltenham, Gloucestershire, founded in 1886 and named in honour of Dr Francis Close, 1797–1882, dean of Carlisle

Cloud (i) 'person who lives near a rocky hill or outcrop of rocks' (from Old English *clūd* 'rock'); (ii) from the medieval French male personal name *Cloud* (from Germanic *Hlodald*, literally 'fame-rule')

Clough, Cluff 'person who lives near a steep slope' (from Old English *clōh* 'ravine'). See also **Clowes¹** [Arthur Hugh Clough, 1819–61, British poet; Brian Clough, 1935–2004, English footballer and football manager]

Clover a different form of **Cleaver** (i–ii)

Clowes¹ a different form of **Clough**. It rhymes with *browse*.

Clowes² a different form of **Close**. It rhymes with *nose*.

Clucas from Scottish and Irish Gaelic *Mac Lucais* 'son of **Lucas**'

Cluff see **Clough**

Clyde 'person who lives on the banks of the river Clyde', Scotland ('cleansing one')

Coad, Coade, Code probably 'cobbler's assistant' (from Middle English *cōde* 'cobbler's wax')
— **Coade stone** a type of artificial weatherproof stone manufactured by members of the Coade family from 1769, when they took over the factory in Lambeth, south London, where it was made, until about 1837. It was used for statues, monuments and other outdoor decorative work.

Coady see **Cody**

Coakley from Irish Gaelic *Mac Caochlaoich* 'son of *Caochlaoch*', a personal name meaning literally 'blind warrior'

Coales see **Coles**

Coates, Coats, Cotes (i) 'person who lives in a small unpretentious dwelling' (from Middle English *cotes* 'cottages' or 'of the cottage'); (ii) 'person from Coates or Cotes', the name of various places in England ('cottages'); (iii) a different form of **Coutts** [Albert Coates, 1882–1953, British conductor; Eric Coates, 1886–1957, British composer; Joseph Gordon Coates, 1878–1943, New Zealand Reform Party politician, prime minister 1925–28]

Cobb, Cobbe (i) from the medieval male personal name *Cobbe* (or the related Old Norse *Kobbi*), probably originally a nickname for a large ungainly man (literally 'lump'); (ii) a shortened form of **Jacob** [John Cobb, 1899–1952, British racing driver and record holder; Ty Cobb (original name Tyrus Raymond Cobb), 1886–1961, US baseball player]

Cobbett (i) 'little **Cobb**'; (ii) 'little **Cobbold**' [William Cobbett, 1763–1835, British radical journalist and author]

Cobbold from the medieval male personal name *Cubald* (from Old English *Cūthbeald*, literally 'famous-brave')

Cobden 'person from Cobden', Derbyshire and Devon ('Cobba's hill') [Richard Cobden, 1804–65, British politician and economist]

Cobham 'person from Cobham', the name of various places in England (mostly 'Cobba's enclosure or homestead') [Sir Alan Cobham, 1894–1973, British aviation pioneer]

Cobley, Cobleigh, Cobbleigh 'person from Cobley', Devon ('Cobba's glade')
— **Uncle Tom Cobbleigh** the seventh and last-named of the Devonshire villagers who borrowed Tom Pearce's grey mare to ride to Widecombe Fair in the eponymous ballad
Wi' Bill Brewer, Jan Stewer, Peter Gurney,
Peter Davy, Dan'l Whidden, Harry Hawk,
Old Uncle Tom Cobbleigh and all,
Old Uncle Tom Cobbleigh and all

Coburn see **Cockburn**

Cochran, Cochrane 'person from Cochran', area near Paisley, Scotland (perhaps 'red place (i.e. with reddish soil)') [C.B. Cochran, 1872–1951, British impresario; Eddie Cochran, 1938–60, US rockabilly musician; Jacqueline Cochran, 1910–80, US aviator; Thomas Cochrane (10th earl of Dundonald), 1775–1860, British admiral]

Cockburn, Coburn 'person from Cockburn', Scottish Borders ('stream frequented by cocks'). The name is traditionally pronounced 'coburn' (originally probably to avoid the perceived indelicacy of 'cock'). See also **Cogburn** [Claud Cockburn, 1904–81, British journalist and author]
— **Cockburn** a British port producer, founded in Vila Nova de Gaia in 1815 by Robert Cockburn

Cockcroft, Cockroft 'person from Cockcroft', Lancashire and Yorkshire ('poultry enclosure') [Sir John Cockcroft, 1897–1967, British physicist]

Cockell, Cockle (i) perhaps 'person who has been on a pilgrimage to Santiago, Spain' (from the custom in the Middle Ages for such a person to wear a cockleshell badge); (ii) perhaps 'person who gathers and sells shellfish' [Don Cockell, 1928–83, British boxer]

Cocker (i) 'builder of haystacks' (from a derivative of Middle English *cock* 'pile of hay'); (ii) from a medieval nickname for an aggressive or truculent person (from a derivative of Middle English *cocken* 'to fight (as a cock does)') [Joe Cocker, 1944–, British rock/blues singer]
— **according to Cocker** in accordance with strict calculation; exactly. A British expression, now somewhat dated, evoking the name of the mathematician Edward Cocker, 1631–75. For the US equivalent, see **Gunter**.

Cockeram see **Cockerham**

Cockerell, Cockerill, Cockrell from a medieval nickname for a (young) man who struts, swaggers or behaves aggressively like a cockerel [Charles Cockerell, 1788–1863, British architect; Sir Christopher Cockerell, 1910–99, British engineer, inventor of the hovercraft]

Cockerham, Cockeram 'person from Cockerham', Lancashire ('homestead or enclosure on the (river) Cocker', a Celtic river-name meaning literally 'crooked')

Cockerill see **Cockerell**

Cockett 'baker' (from Middle English *cocket-bread*, a term denoting a grade of high-quality leavened bread)

Cockfield (i) 'person from Cockfield', County Durham and Suffolk (respectively 'Cocca's and Cohha's area of open land'); (ii) 'person from Cuckfield', Sussex ('Cuca's area of open land')

Cockrell see **Cockerell**

Cockroft see **Cockcroft**

Cocks see **Cox**

Code see **Coad**

Codrington 'person from Codrington', Gloucestershire ('estate associated with Cūthhere') [Christopher Codrington, 1668–1710, British soldier and colonial administrator]
— **Codrington College** an Anglican theological college in Barbados, founded under the terms of a

bequest from Christopher Codrington (see above) and opened in 1745

Cody, Coady (i) from Irish Gaelic *Mac Óda* 'son of *Oda*', a personal name of unknown origin and meaning; (ii) from Irish Gaelic *Ó Cuidighthigh* 'descendant of *Cuidightheach*', a nickname meaning literally 'helpful person' [William ('Buffalo Bill') Cody, 1846–1917, US soldier, buffalo hunter and showman]

Coe from a medieval nickname for someone thought to resemble a jackdaw (from Middle English *co* 'jackdaw'). See also **Kay** (iv) [Jonathan Coe, 1961–, British author; Sebastian Coe (Lord Coe), 1956–, British athlete and Conservative politician]

Coen see **Cohen**

Coffey, Coffee, Coffie from Irish Gaelic *Ó Cobhthaigh* 'descendant of *Cobhthach*', a nickname meaning literally 'victorious'
— **Coffey still** an alcohol still using steam heat and running continuously that produces very pure spirit. It was patented (in 1830) by the Irish exciseman and inventor Aeneas Coffey, 1780–1852.

Coffin 'basket-maker' (from Old French *coffin* 'basket')

Cogan (i) 'person from Cogan', an area near Cardiff (perhaps 'bowl, depression'); (ii) a different form of **Coogan**; (iii) from a Ukrainian variant of **Cohen** [Alma Cogan (original name Alma Cohen), 1932–66, British popular singer]

Cogburn probably a different form of **Cockburn**
— **Rooster Cogburn** a film (1975) starring John Wayne as the eponymous Cogburn, an aging marshal in pursuit of a gang of outlaws

Coggan (i) a different form of **Coogan**; (ii) a different form of **Cogan** (i) [Donald Coggan, 1909–2000, British churchman, archbishop of Canterbury 1974–80]

Coggins a different form of **Coogan**

Coghill (i) 'person from Cogill', Yorkshire ('spring by a cottage'); (ii) perhaps a different form of **Cowgill**; (iii) perhaps an anglicization of the Danish surname *Køgel* (perhaps originally a nickname for a round fat person) [Nevill Coghill, 1899–1980, British literary scholar]

Coghlan see **Coughlan**

Cohan (i) from Irish Gaelic *Ó Cadhain* (see **Coyne** (ii)); (ii) a different form of **Cohen** [George M. Cohan, 1878–1942, US actor and producer]

Cohen, Coen 'priest' (from Hebrew *kohen* 'priest'). See also **Cogan** (iii), **Cohan** (i), **Cohn**, **Coon** (iii), **Kagan**, **Kahn** (i), **Kain** (iii) [Sir John ('Jack') Cohen (original name Jacob Edward Kohen), 1898–1979, British retailer; Leonard Cohen, 1934–, Canadian singer/songwriter; Sacha Baron Cohen, see **Baron**]
— **Tesco** a British supermarket chain founded by Sir Jack Cohen (see above). He coined its name in 1924, as a brand name for his wholesale business, from the first three letters of 'T.E. Stockwell', his original tea supplier, and the first two letters of his

own surname. The first Tesco shops opened in 1931.

Cohn a different form of **Cohen** [Harry Cohn, 1891–1958, US film magnate, founder of Columbia Pictures]
— **Cona** the proprietary name of a type of coffee-brewing equipment, developed in Britain around 1910 by Alfred Cohn (of whose surname it is a fanciful elaboration)

Coke see **Cook**

Coker 'person from Coker', Somerset ('(place by the river) Coker', a Celtic river-name meaning literally 'crooked')

Colbourne, Colborn, Coulbourne, Coulbourn 'person from Colbourne or Colburn', the name of various places in England ('cool stream')

Colby 'person from Colby', Cumbria and Norfolk ('Koli's farmstead')
— **The Colbys** a US television soap opera (1986–87) about the Colbys, a wealthy Los Angeles family, spun off from the earlier *Dynasty*. It starred Charlton Heston as the patriarch Jason Colby.

Colclough, Coleclough 'person from Cowclough (earlier Colleclogh)', Lancashire (probably 'Cola's ravine')

Coldham 'person from Coldham', Cambridgeshire ('cold homestead')

Coldstream 'person from Coldstream', Scottish Borders [Sir William Coldstream, 1908–87, British painter]

Coldwell a different form of **Caldwell**

Cole (i) from a medieval pet-form of **Nicholas**. See also **Coles**, **Coulson** (i); (ii) from the medieval male personal name *Cole* (from Old English *Cola* or the related Old Norse *Koli*, both originally nicknames for a dark-haired or dark-complexioned person); (iii) from Irish Gaelic *Mac Giolla Chomhghaill* and Scottish Gaelic *Mac Gille Chomhghaill* 'son of the followers of (Saint) *Chomhghall*', a personal name of unknown origin and meaning. See also **Coull** (i) [G.D.H. Cole, 1889–1959, British economist; George Cole, 1925–, British actor; Sir Henry Cole, 1808–82, British art historian and administrator; John Cole, 1927–, Northern Irish political journalist; Thomas Cole, 1801–48, British-born US painter]
— **Coleville** an informal name given in the latter part of the 19th century to the conglomeration of museums, concert halls, colleges, etc. that arose in South Kensington, London, at the behest of Prince Albert in the wake of the Great Exhibition of 1851. His plans were largely put into execution by Sir Henry Cole (see above).

Colegate see **Colgate**

Coleman, Colman (i) from Irish Gaelic *Ó Colmáin* 'descendant of *Colmán*', a personal name derived ultimately from Latin *Columba*, literally 'dove'. See also **Cullum** (ii); (ii) from Irish Gaelic *Ó Clumháin* 'descendant of *Clumhán*', a personal name of unknown origin and meaning; (iii) 'charcoal-burner' or 'gatherer of coal' (from Middle English *coleman*, from *cole* 'charcoal, coal' +

man); (iv) 'servant of **Cole**'; (v) an anglicization of **Kalman** [David Coleman, 1926–, British television sports commentator and presenter; George Colman, 1732–94, British dramatist and theatre manager; Ornette Coleman, 1930–, US jazz saxophonist; Ronald Colman, 1891–1958, British actor]

— **Colemanballs** the title of a regular feature in the British satirical magazine *Private Eye* in which broadcasters' solecisms, *double entendres*, mixed metaphors etc. are featured (David Colemen (see above) was allegedly a not infrequent perpetrator)

— **Coleman Country** a name applied to an area of southern County Sligo, Ireland, famous for its traditional musicians. It was the birthplace of the noted Irish fiddler Michael Coleman, 1891–1946.

— **Colman's of Norwich** a British manufacturer of mustard, established in Norwich in 1814 by Jeremiah Colman, 1771–1851, a miller. In 1823 he went into partnership with his nephew James Colman, 1801–54, to form the J. & J. Colman Company. The brand is now owned by Unilever.

— **Reckitt and Colman** see **Reckitt**

Colenso 'person from Colenso', Cornwall (origin unknown)

Coleridge 'person from Coleridge', Devon ('charcoal ridge') [Samuel Taylor Coleridge, 1772–1834, British poet; Samuel Coleridge-Taylor, 1875–1912, British composer]

Coles 'son of **Cole** (i)'. See also **Cowles**

Colet see **Collet**

Coley (i) from a medieval nickname for a dark-haired or dark-complexioned person (from Old English *colig* 'dark'); (ii) perhaps 'person from Coaley', Gloucestershire ('glade with a hut')

Colgan a reduced form of **McColgan**, or from Irish Gaelic *Ó Colgáin* 'descendant of *Colga*', a personal name based on *colg* 'thorn, sword'

Colgate, **Colegate** 'person from Colgate or Colgates', Sussex and Kent respectively ('gate(s) leading to a wood where charcoal is burned')

— **Colgate & Co.** a US manufacturer of toothpaste, soap and related products, founded in New York City in 1806 by the British-born William Colgate, 1783–1857. In 1928 it merged with the Palmolive company, and in 1953 the combined entity became known as Colgate-Palmolive.

Colin (i) *also* **Collin** from the male personal name *Colin*, literally 'little *Coll*', itself a reduced form of **Nicholas**; (ii) from the French male personal name *Colin*, a pet-form of *Nicolas* '**Nicholas**'. See also **Colling** (ii), **Collins** (i), **Collinson**, **Collis**, **Colson**

— **Colindale** a district of northwest London. Originally (in the mid 16th century) *Collyndene*, literally 'Collin's valley', it was named after a local family called Collin.

Colles see **Collis**

Collet, **Colet**, **Collett** (i) 'little *Coll* (see **Colin** (i))'; (ii) 'little *Colle*', a pet-form of *Nicolas* (see **Colin** (ii)) [John Colet, ?1466–1519, English theologian and humanist]

Collier, **Collyer**, **Colyer** 'charcoal-burner' or 'gatherer of coal' (from a derivative of Middle

English *cole* 'charcoal, coal') [Lesley Collier, 1947–, British ballet dancer]

Collin see **Colin** (i)

Colling (i) from the medieval male personal name *Colling* (from either Old English *Colling* or the related Old Norse *Kollungr*); (ii) 'little *Coll* (see **Colin** (i))'

Collinge a different form of **Colling**

Collings 'son of **Colling**'

Collingwood probably 'person from Collingwood', Staffordshire ('disputed wood') [Cuthbert Collingwood (Lord Collingwood), 1750–1810, British admiral; Paul Collingwood, 1976–, English cricketer; R.G. Collingwood, 1889–1943, British philosopher and archaeologist]

— **Collingwood College** a college of Durham University, founded in 1972 and named in honour of the British mathematician Sir Edward Collingwood, 1900–70, former chairman of the University Council

Collins (i) 'son of **Colin**'; (ii) from Irish Gaelic *Ó Coileáin* and *Mac Coileáin* (see **Cullen** (ii)) [Anthony Collins, 1893–1963, British conductor; Jackie Collins, 1939–, British novelist, sister of Joan; Joan Collins, 1933–, British actress; Michael Collins, 1890–1922, Irish nationalist; Michael Collins, 1930–, US astronaut; Pauline Collins, 1940–, British actress; Phil Collins, 1951–, British singer/songwriter and actor; Wilkie Collins, 1824–89, British novelist; William Collins, 1721–59, British poet; William Collins, pompous and obsequious clergyman in Jane Austen's *Pride and Prejudice* (1813)]

— **Collins** a thank-you letter sent to one's hosts after a visit. The term, current in British English especially in the first half of the 20th century, was inspired by the clergyman William Collins (see above), who sent a fulsome letter of this sort to Mr Bennet after a stay with his family.

— **Collins' Music Hall** a music hall in Islington, North London, opened in 1863 by Sam Collins

— **Tom Collins** a tall iced drink consisting of gin with lemon or lime juice, soda water and sugar. It is said to have been named after the barman who invented it (perhaps around the middle of the 19th century), but his precise identity has never been established. The surname half of the term has been used for a range of other similar drinks with different spirit bases (e.g. *Rum Collins*).

— **William Collins Sons & Co.** a British publishing firm, founded in Glasgow in 1819 by William Collins, 1789–1853. In 1991, having previously joined forces with the publishers Harper & Row, it became HarperCollins (of which 'Collins' is an imprint).

Collinson 'son of **Colin**'

Collis, **Colles** 'son of *Coll* (see **Colin** (i))'. See also **Cullis**

— **Colles' fracture** a fracture of the radius bone in which a piece broken off at the end is displaced towards the back of the wrist. It is named after the Irish surgeon Abraham Colles, 1773–1843.

— **J. Collis Browne's Mixture** a proprietary medicine, concocted in the middle of the 19th century by an Indian Army doctor called J. Collis Browne. The original version, also called 'Chlorodyne', contained laudanum (a solution of opium), chloroform and tincture of cannabis; the modern mixture, used to treat diarrhoea and stomach upsets, is mainly morphine and peppermint oil.

Collison 'son of *Coll* (see **Colin** (i))'

Collyer see **Collier**

Collymore 'person from Collymore', an unidentified place in England [Stan Collymore, 1971–, English footballer]

Colman see **Coleman**

Colombo, Columbo from the Italian male personal name *Colombo* (from Latin *Colombus*, literally 'dove')
— *Columbo* a US television detective drama (1972–79, 1991–94) starring Peter Falk as the scruffy and laconic cop Lt. Columbo.

Colquhoun 'person from Colquhoun', a barony in the former county of Dumbartonshire (probably either 'narrow corner of land' or 'narrow wood'). The name is standardly pronounced 'kəhoon'. See also **Calhoun**

Colson 'son of *Coll* (see **Colin** (i))'

Colston, Coulston (i) 'person from Colston', Nottinghamshire ('Kolr's farmstead'), or 'person from Coulston', Wiltshire ('Cufel's farmstead'); (ii) from the medieval male personal name *Colstan* (probably from Old Norse *Kolsteinn*, literally 'charcoal-stone')

Colt 'person who looks after (young) horses and asses'; also, from a medieval nickname for someone thought to resemble a (young) horse or ass (e.g. in skittishness or obstinacy)
— **Colt revolver, Colt 45** a .45-calibre revolver with a five-shot cylinder invented in 1835 by the US engineer Samuel Colt, 1814–62.

Colton 'person from Colton', the name of several places in England (variously 'Cola's or Koli's farmstead', 'Cūla's farmstead' and 'farmstead by the (river) Cole')

Coltrane from Irish Gaelic *Ó Coltaráin* 'descendant of *Coltarán*' [John Coltrane, 1926–67, US jazz saxophonist and composer; Robbie Coltrane (original name Anthony McMillan), 1950–, British actor]

Columbo see **Colombo**

Colville, Colvill 'person from Colleville', northern France ('Koli's settlement')

Colvin apparently a different form of **Colville** [Sir Sidney Colvin, 1845–1927, British art historian and literary critic]

Colwell 'person from Colwell', Devon and Northumberland (respectively 'stream named Coly', a Celtic river-name probably meaning literally 'narrow', and 'cool stream')

Colyer see **Collier**

Combes see **Coombes**

Comer 'person who makes or sells combs', or perhaps 'person who prepares wool or flax for spinning by combing it' (from Middle English *combere*, a derivative of *comb*)

Comerford (i) 'person from Comberford', Staffordshire (either 'Cumbra's ford' or 'ford of the Britons'); (ii) from Irish Gaelic *Mac Cumascaigh* 'son of *Cumascach*', a nickname meaning literally 'confuser'. See also **Comiskey**

Comfort (i) perhaps from a medieval nickname for someone who is a comforting presence; (ii) perhaps 'person from Comports', Kent ('place associated with the de Cumpeworth family') [Alex Comfort, 1920–2000, British sexologist]

Comings, Comins see **Cummings, Cummins**

Comiskey from Irish Gaelic *Mac Cumascaigh* (see **Comerford** (ii))

Commings, Commins see **Cummings, Cummins**

Como (i) from the Italian male personal name *Como*, a shortened form of *Giacomo* (the Italian equivalent of **James**); (ii) 'person from Como', northern Italy [Perry Como (original name Pierino Como), 1913–2001, US popular singer]

Compton 'person from Compton', the name of numerous places in England ('farmstead in a valley') [Arthur Compton, 1892–1962, US physicist; Denis Compton, 1918–97, English cricketer; Dame Ivy Compton-Burnett, 1884–1969, British novelist]
— **Compton effect** the decrease in energy and increase in wavelength experienced by a photon after colliding or interacting with an electron. It is named after Arthur Compton (see above).

Comrie 'person from Comrie', the name of various places in Scotland ('place by the fork in the river')

Comstock probably 'person from Comstock', an unidentified place, perhaps in Devon
— **comstockery** in US English, prudishness in matters of art and literature, or draconian censorship resulting from it. The term was inspired by Anthony Comstock, 1844–1915, a member of the New York Society for the Suppression of Vice.
— **Comstock lode** a very rich lode of silver and gold discovered in Nevada, USA in 1859. It was named after the US prospector H.T.P. Comstock, 1820–70, who was one of the first to work a claim on the site. The term later came to be used allusively of any find promising great riches.

Comyns see **Cummins**

Conan (i) 'person from Conan', Aberdeenshire (perhaps 'hound stream'); (ii) from the medieval male personal name *Conan*, of Old Breton origin and meaning literally 'high, mighty' [Sir Arthur Conan Doyle, see **Doyle**]

Conaty from Irish Gaelic *Ó Connachtáigh* 'descendant of *Connachtach*', a nickname for someone from the Irish province of Connaught

Conaway probably a different form of **Conway**

Conboy from Irish Gaelic *Ó Conbhuidhe* (see **Conway**)

Concannon from Irish Gaelic *Ó Con Cheanainn* 'descendant of *Cúcheanann*', a personal name meaning literally 'hound with a white head'

Condamine 'person from Condamine', France ('place or area owned jointly')

Conder a different form of **Connor** [Charles Conder, 1868–1909, British painter]

Condon from Irish Gaelic *Condún*, a gaelicization of Anglo-Norman *de Caunteton*, perhaps 'person from Caunton', Nottinghamshire ('Calunōth's farmstead'). See also **Congdon** [Sir Paul Condon (Lord Condon), 1947–, British police officer, Metropolitan Police Commissioner 1993–2000]

Cone (i) from Irish Gaelic *Mac Comhdhain* 'son of *Comhdhan*', a personal name of unknown origin and meaning; (ii) an anglicization of the German surname *Kohn*, from the Middle Low German male personal name *Kohn*, a shortened form of *Konrad* '**Conrad**'

Coney 'seller of rabbits', or from a medieval nickname for someone thought to resemble a rabbit (in either case from Middle English *cony* 'rabbit')

Congdon (i) 'person from Congdon', an unidentified place probably in Devon or Cornwall; (ii) a different form of **Condon**

Congreve, Congreave 'person from Congreve', Staffordshire ('small wood in a valley') [William Congreve, 1670–1729, British dramatist; Sir William Congreve, 1772–1828, British soldier, scientist and inventor]
— **Congreve** an early type of friction match said to have been invented by Sir William Congreve (see above) (the actual inventor is more likely to have been John Walker)
— **Congreve rocket** a type of military rocket invented in 1808 by Sir William Congreve

Conlan see **Conlon**

Conley, Conly different forms of **Connolly** [Rosemary Conley (*née* Weston), 1946–, British diet and fitness adviser]

Conlon, Conlan different forms of **Quinlan**

Conly see **Conley**

Conn from a shortened form of any of the Irish Gaelic personal names that were the source of **Connell, Connolly, Connor** and **Conroy**

Connally see **Connolly**

Connell from Irish Gaelic *Mac Conaill* 'son of *Conall*' or *Ó Conail* 'descendant of *Conal*', a personal name perhaps meaning literally 'hound-valour'. See also **McConnell** (ii), **O'Connell**

Connelly see **Connolly**

Conner (i) 'inspector of weights and measures' (from Middle English *connere* 'inspector'); (ii) see **Connor**

Conners see **Connors**

Connery a different form of **Conroy** [Sir Sean Connery, 1930–, British actor]

Conniff (i) a different form of **Cunniff**; (ii) perhaps an anglicization of the German surname *Koneff*, literally 'little boy' [Ray Conniff, 1916–2002, US musician and bandleader]

Connolly, Connolley, Connally, Connelly, Conolly from Irish Gaelic *Ó Conghalaigh* 'descendant of *Conghalach*', a nickname meaning literally 'valiant'. See also **Conley** [Billy Connolly, 1942–, British comedian; Cyril Connolly,

1903–74, British author and critic; Maureen Connolly, 1934–69, US tennis player]
— **Connolly Station** a main railway station in Dublin, Ireland, named in honour of the socialist revolutionary James Connolly, 1870–1916

Connor, Conner from Irish Gaelic *Ó Conchobhair* 'descendant of *Conchobhar*', a personal name perhaps meaning literally 'hound-desiring'. See also **O'Connor** [Kenneth Connor, 1916–93, British comic actor; Sir William Connor ('Cassandra'), 1909–67, British journalist]

Connors, Conners 'son of **Connor**' [Jimmy Connors, 1952–, US tennis player]

Conolly see **Connolly**

Conover an anglicization of the Dutch surname *Couwenhoven*, probably 'person from Couwenhoven', an unidentified place

Conquest probably from a medieval nickname, perhaps applied to a domineering person [Robert Conquest, 1917–, British poet, historian and critic]

Conrad an anglicization of the German name *Konrad*, literally 'daring counsel' [Joseph Conrad (original name Teodor Josef Konrad Korzeniowski), 1857–1924, Polish-born British novelist; William Conrad, 1920–94, US actor]

Conran from Irish Gaelic *Ó Conaráin* 'descendant of *Conarán*', a personal name that was a pet-form of *Conaire* (see **Conroy** (ii)) [Jasper Conran, 1959–, British designer, son of Terence; Shirley Conran (*née* Pearce), 1932–, British writer, former wife of Terence; Sir Terence Conran, 1931–, British designer and businessman]

Conroy (i) from Irish Gaelic *Ó Conraoi* 'descendant of *Cú Raoi*', a personal name meaning literally 'hound of the plain'; (ii) from Irish Gaelic *Ó Conaire* 'descendant of *Conaire*', a nickname meaning literally 'keeper of the hound'. See also **Connery, Conran**

Considine (i) from Irish Gaelic *Mac Consaidín* 'son of *Consaidín*', a Gaelic form of **Constantine**; (ii) a different form of **Constantine**

Constable 'official who enforces the law within a parish' [John Constable, 1776–1837, British painter]
— **Constable & Co.** a British publishing firm, founded in Edinburgh in 1795 by the stationer and bookseller Archibald Constable, 1774–1827
— **Constable Country** the area on the Suffolk-Essex border, in the eastern part of Dedham Vale, where John Constable (see above) lived and painted

Constance (i) from the female personal name *Constance*. See also **Cust**; (ii) 'person from Coutances', northern France (named in honour of the Roman emperor Constantius Chlorus)

Constant from the medieval French personal name *Constant* (from Latin *Constans*, literally 'steadfast, faithful')

Constantine (i) from the male personal name *Constantine*; (ii) 'person from Cotentin', an area of northern France (named in honour of the Roman emperor Constantius Chlorus). See also **Considine, Costain** [Eddie Constantine (original name

Edward Constantinowsky), 1917–93, US-born French actor; Learie Constantine (Lord Constantine), 1901–71, West Indian cricketer and British parliamentarian]

Conte (i) 'servant of a count', or from a medieval Italian nickname for someone who gave himself the airs and graces of a count (in either case from Italian *conte* 'count'); (ii) from the medieval Italian male personal name *Conte*, literally 'companion' [Richard Conte (original name Nicholas Conte), 1910–75, US actor]

Conti 'son of **Conte**' [Tom Conti, 1941–, British actor]

Conway (i) 'person from Conwy', North Wales ('place by the (river) Conwy', a Celtic river-name meaning literally 'reedy one'); (ii) 'person from Conway', Highland (probably 'place where troops are billeted'); (iii) from a range of Irish Gaelic surnames, including *Mac Conmidhe* (see **McNamee**), *Mac Connmhaigh* 'son of *Connmhach*', a personal name meaning literally 'head-smasher' and *Ó Conbhuide* 'descendant of *Cú Bhuidhe*', a personal name meaning literally 'yellow hound'. See also **Conboy** [Russ Conway (original name Trevor Stanford), 1925–2000, British popular pianist]

Conwell from Irish Gaelic *Mac Conmhaoil* 'son of *Conmhaol*', a personal name apparently meaning literally 'bald hound'

Conyers 'person from Coignières or Cogners', northern France

Coogan from Irish Gaelic *Mac Cogadháin* 'son of *Cogadhán*', a personal name meaning literally 'little hound of war'. See also **Cogan** (ii) [Jackie Coogan, 1914–84, US actor (originally a child actor); Steve Coogan, 1965–, British comedian and actor]
— **Coogan's Bluff** a high promontory in upper Manhattan, New York City, named after James J. Coogan, 1845–1915, one-time president of the borough of Manhattan.
— *Coogan's Bluff* a film (1968) in which Clint Eastwood plays a quiet but tough lawman named Coogan

Cook, Cooke, Coke (i) 'person who cooks' or 'proprietor of an eating house'; (ii) an anglicization of **Koch** or of the Jewish surname *Kuk*, of unknown origin and meaning [Alistair Cooke (original name Alfred Cooke), 1908–2004, British-born US journalist; Beryl Cook (*née* Lansley), 1926–, British artist; Deryck Cooke, 1919–76, British musicologist; Sir Edward Coke, 1552–1634, English lawyer and politician; Captain James Cook, 1728–79, British explorer and cartographer; Sir Joseph Cook, 1860–1947, British-born Australian Liberal politician, prime minister 1913–14; Peter Cook, 1937–95, British comedian and writer; Robin Cook, pen-name of Robert Cook, 1931–94, British novelist; Robin Cook, 1946–2005, British Labour politician; Thomas Coke (earl of Leicester), 1752–1842, British agriculturalist; Thomas Cook, 1808–92, British travel agent]

— **Captain Cooker** a colloquial name for the wild boar of New Zealand, descended from those introduced by Captain James Cook (see above)
— **Coke's clippings** a colloquial designation given to the sheepshearing gatherings held by Thomas Coke (see above) at Holkham, Norfolk from 1778
— **Cook Islands** a self-governing island group in free association with New Zealand, in the South Pacific Ocean. It was named after James Cook.
— **Cooksbridge** a village in Sussex, named after a family called Coke, who lived in the area in the 16th century
— **Cook's tour** a quick tour or survey, with attention only to the main feature. The metaphor was inspired by the conducted tours provided by Thomas Cook (see above) and the travel agency he founded, Thomas Cook and Son.
— **Cookstown** a town and local-government area in central Northern Ireland. It is named after Alan Cook, who founded it as a plantation settlement in 1609.
— **Cook Strait** an area of ocean separating the North Island and the South Island of New Zealand, named after James Cook
— **Cooktown** a coastal town in northern Queensland, Australia, named after James Cook
— **Mount Cook** the highest mountain in New Zealand (3754 m/12,316 ft), in the Southern Alps on the South Island. It was named in honour of James Cook.

Cooksey 'person from Cooksey', Worcestershire ('Cucu's island')

Cookson 'son of **Cook**' [Dame Catherine Cookson, 1906–98, British novelist]

Cooley (i) from Irish Gaelic *Mac Giolla Chúille* 'son of the followers of (Saint) *Mochúille*'; (ii) a reduced form of *McCooley*, a different form of **MacAulay**; (iii) a different form of the German surname *Kuhle* or *Kühle*, literally 'person who lives in a hollow place or depression'

Coolidge probably 'person associated with a college' (e.g. a servant in a college or someone who farmed land owned by a college) [John Calvin Coolidge, 1872–1933, US Republican politician, president 1923–29]

Coombes, Coombs, Coomes 'person from Coombes or Coombs', the name of various places in England ('short straight valleys')

Coomer (i) 'person who lives in a short straight valley' (from a derivative of Middle English *combe* 'short straight valley'); (ii) an anglicization of the German surname *Kummer*, literally either 'person who lives by a rubbish heap' or from a medieval nickname for someone who had suffered some loss or other misfortune; (iii) an anglicization of **Kumar**

Coon (i) perhaps from Irish Gaelic *Ó Cuana* (see **Cooney**); (ii) an anglicization of **Kuhn**; (iii) an anglicization *Coen* or *Koen*, Dutch forms of **Cohen**. See also **Coons** (i)

Coonan from Irish Gaelic *Ó Cuanáin* 'descendant of *Cuanán*', literally 'little *Cuana*' (see **Cooney**)

Cooney from Irish Gaelic *Ó Cuana* 'descendant of *Cuana*', a personal name probably derived from *cuanna* 'elegant'

Coons (i) an anglicization of Dutch *Couns, Cuens* or *Cuyns*, literally 'son of *Coen*' (see **Coon** (iii)); (ii) an anglicization of **Kuntz**

Coop, Coope (i) 'maker of barrels, cooper' (from Middle English *coupe* 'barrel, tub'); (ii) 'merchant', or from a medieval Dutch nickname for one who haggles (in either case from Dutch *koop* 'purchase, bargain')

Cooper (i) *also* **Coupar** *or* **Couper** *or* **Cowper** 'maker of barrels' (from a derivative of Middle English *coupe* (see **Coop** (i))). See also **Copper** (i); (ii) an anglicization of the Jewish surname *Kuper*, literally either 'coppersmith' or an invented name meaning 'copper' (from Yiddish *kuper* 'copper') [Lady Diana Cooper (Viscountess Norwich; *née* Manners), 1892–1986, British actress and socialite, wife of Duff; Duff Cooper (Viscount Norwich), 1890–1954, British Conservative politician, diplomat and author; Gary Cooper (original name Frank James Cooper), 1901–61, US actor; Dame Gladys Cooper, 1888–1971, British actress; Sir Henry Cooper, 1934–, British boxer; James Fenimore Cooper, 1789–1851, US novelist; Jilly Cooper (*née* Sallitt), 1937–, British author and journalist; Samuel Cooper, 1609–72, English miniaturist; Tommy Cooper, 1922–84, British comedian; William Cooper, pen-name of Harry Summerfield Hoff, 1910–2002, British novelist]
— **Cooper pair** two electrons that are loosely bound together and act dynamically as a pair in a superconducting material. It is named after the US physicist L.N. Cooper, 1930–.
— **Mini Cooper** a more powerful version of the Austin Mini, first produced in 1961. It was the brainchild of John Cooper, 1923–2000, of the Cooper Car Company, designers and builders of racing and rally cars.

Coopland a different form of **Copeland**

Coopman (i) a different form of **Copeman**; (ii) 'merchant' (Dutch, from *koopman* 'merchant')

Coote, Coot from a medieval nickname for a foolish person or for a bald man (the coot has a reputation as a foolish bird, and the white patch on its head has made it an emblem of baldness)

Cootes, Coots 'son of **Coote**'

Cope 'maker of cloaks or capes', or from a medieval nickname for someone who habitually wore such a garment (in either case from Middle English *cope* 'cape, cloak') [Wendy Cope, 1945–, British poet]
— **'Hey, Johnnie Cope'** a Scottish song celebrating Bonnie Prince Charlie's victory at Prestonpans in 1745 over the forces of the king, led by Sir John Cope, died 1760
Hey, Johnnie Cope, are ye wauking yet?
Or are ye sleeping, I would wit?

Copeland, Copland, Coupland 'person from Copeland or Coupland', Cumbria and Northumberland respectively ('purchased land'). See also **Coopland** [Aaron Copland, 1900–90, US composer; Douglas Coupland, 1961–, Canadian novelist]

Copeman 'merchant, trader' (from Middle English *copman* 'merchant, trader', from Old Norse *kaupmathr*). See also **Coopman** (i)

Copestake probably 'woodcutter' (from Old French *couper* 'to cut' + Middle English *stake* 'pin, stake'). See also **Capstick**

Copland see **Copeland**

Copley 'person from Copley', the name of various places in England ('Coppa's glade')

Copp (i) 'person who lives on top of a hill' (from Middle English *coppe* 'hilltop'). See also **Copping** (ii); (ii) from a medieval nickname for someone with a large or misshapen head (from Middle English *copp* 'head')

Coppard a different form of **Copp** (ii) [A.E. Coppard, 1878–1957, British author]

Copper (i) 'worker in copper, coppersmith'; (ii) a different form of **Cooper** (i) [Bob Copper, 1915–2004, English traditional folk singer; Lord Copper, overbearing newspaper proprietor in Evelyn Waugh's *Scoop* (1938)]

Coppin (i) a different form of **Copping** (i); (ii) from a medieval French nickname for a pleasant companion or good neighbour (from Old French *compain* 'companion')

Copping (i) 'little **Jacob**'. See also **Coppin** (i); (ii) a different form of **Copp** (i)

Coppola 'maker of berets', or from a medieval Italian nickname for someone who wore such headgear (in either case from Neapolitan dialect *coppola*, denoting a type of beret worn in that area) [Francis Ford Coppola, 1939–, US film director]

Coram 'person from Curham', Devon [Thomas Coram, 1668–1751, British seafarer and philanthropist]
— **Coram Fields** a children's playground in central London, on the site of the Foundling Hospital established in 1742 by Thomas Coram (see above)

Corbett, Corbet, Corbitt from a medieval nickname meaning literally 'little crow' (from Anglo-Norman *corbet* 'little crow') [Harry Corbett, 1918–89, British puppeteer; Harry H. Corbett, 1925–82, British actor; James John ('Gentleman Jim') Corbett, 1866–1933, US boxer; Ronnie Corbett, 1930–, British comedian]
— **Corbett** any Scottish mountain between 762 m/2500 ft and 914.4 m/3000 ft in height. The name commemorates John Rooke Corbett, an active member of the Scottish Mountaineering Club between the two World Wars.

Corbin, Corbyn from a medieval French nickname meaning literally 'little crow' (from Old French *corbin* 'little crow')

Corby (i) 'person from Corby', the name of various places in England (mostly 'Kori's village'); (ii) from a medieval French nickname meaning literally 'little crow' (from Old French *corbi* 'little crow')

Corcoran from Irish Gaelic *Ó Corcráin* 'descendant of *Corcrán*', literally 'little *Corcra*' (see **Corkery**)

Cordell (i) 'maker of string', or from a medieval nickname for a habitual wearer of decorative bows and ribbons (in either case from Old French *cordel* 'small rope, string'); (ii) an anglicization of the German surname *Kardel*, literally 'carder of wool'

Corder 'maker of string', or from a medieval nickname for a habitual wearer of decorative bows and ribbons (in either case from a derivative of Old French *corde* 'rope, string')

Corderoy a different form of **Cordray**

Cordingley, Cordingly probably 'person from Cordingley', an unidentified place probably in Yorkshire

Cordray, Cordrey, Cordry from a medieval nickname for a proud man (from Old French *cuer de roi* 'heart of a king')

Coren an anglicization of the Jewish surname *Koren*, literally '(dealer in) corn', or of the Dutch, North German and Norwegian surname *Koren*, a shortened form of **Cornelius** [Alan Coren, 1938–, British writer and broadcaster]

Corey, Cory (i) from the Old Norse male personal name *Kori*, of unknown origin and meaning; (ii) a different form of **Curry** (ii) [Wendell Corey, 1914–68, US actor]
— **Coryton** an industrial village in Essex, on the north bank of the Thames estuary. It grew up around the oil refinery established there in 1922 by Cory & Co., of which the chairman at the time was Sir Clifford Cory. Also, a suburb of Cardiff, named after James Herbert Cory, who built himself a house called Coryton there around 1900.

Cork, Corke 'person who supplies or uses a red or purple dye' (from Middle English *corke* 'red or purple dye', from Gaelic *corcur* 'purple') [Dominic Cork, 1971–, English cricketer]

Corkery from Irish Gaelic *Ó Corcra* 'descendant of *Corcra*', a personal name based on *corcur* (see **Cork**)

Corless, Corliss different forms of **Carless**

Corlett from Manx Gaelic *Mac Thorliot* 'son of *Thorliot*', a male personal name derived from Old Norse *Thórrljótr*, literally 'Thor-bright'

Corley (i) 'person from Coreley or Corley', Shropshire and Warwickshire respectively ('glade frequented by cranes'); (ii) a different form of **Curley**

Corliss see **Corless**

Cormack a reduced form of **McCormack**

Corn, Corne (i) from a medieval nickname for a tall, thin, long-legged person (from Old English *corn*, a variant of *cran* 'crane'); (ii) 'grower or seller of corn (i.e. grain)'; (iii) 'maker or user of querns (i.e. hand-mills)'. See also **Corner** (iii); (iv) an anglicization of the German surname *Korn*, literally 'grower or seller of corn (i.e. grain)', or of a shortened form of any of a range of German and Jewish surnames beginning with *Korn-* (e.g. *Kornfeld*, literally 'cornfield')

Cornelius from the male personal name *Cornelius* (from Latin, probably a derivative of *cornu* 'horn')

Cornell (i) an anglicization of any of a range European surnames based on **Cornelius** (e.g. French *Corneille*); (ii) a different form of **Cornhill**; (iii) a different form of **Cornwell**
— **Cornell University** a university in Ithaca, New York State, USA, founded in 1865 by Ezra Cornell, 1807–74

Corner (i) 'person who blows a horn', or 'person who makes things out of horn' (in either case a derivative of Old French *corn* or *corne* 'horn'); (ii) 'person who lives on a corner'; (iii) a different form of **Corn** (iii)

Corney 'person from Corney', Cumbria and Hertfordshire ('island where cranes are seen')

Cornford 'person from Cornford', the name of various places in southeastern England ('ford where corn is transported') [Frances Cornford (*née* Darwin), 1886–1960, British poet]

Cornforth 'person from Cornforth', County Durham ('ford frequented by cranes')

Cornhill (i) 'person from Cornhill', Northumberland ('nook of land frequented by cranes'); (ii) 'person from Cornhill', a street in the City of London which was the site of a medieval corn exchange. See also **Cornell** (ii)

Cornish 'person from Cornwall'

Cornwall 'person from Cornwall'. See also **Cornwell** (i)

Cornwallis 'person from Cornwall' (from an unrecorded Middle English *Cornwallish* 'of Cornwall') [Charles Cornwallis (1st Marquess Cornwallis), 1738–1805, British general and colonial administrator]
— **Cornwallis Code** a legal code promulgated in 1793 for the government of India, of which at that time Lord Cornwallis (see above) was governor general. It lasted until 1833.

Cornwell (i) a different form of **Cornwall**; (ii) 'person from Cornwell', Oxfordshire ('stream frequented by cranes') [Bernard Cornwell, 1944–, British novelist; Patricia Cornwell, 1956–, US crime novelist]

Corr from Irish Gaelic *Ó Corra* 'descendant of *Corra*', a personal name based on *corr* 'spear'. See also **Curry** (iv)
— **The Corrs** an Irish Celtic folk-rock/pop-rock group consisting of the siblings Sharon, Caroline, Andrea and Jim Corr. It was founded in 1990.

Corral 'person who lives by a livestock enclosure' (from Spanish *corral*)

Corran a different form of **Curran**

Correa perhaps 'maker of straps, belts, and similar fastenings' (from Spanish *correa,* denoting such a fastening)

Corrie, Corry 'person from Corrie', the name of various places in Scotland ('steep-walled hollow on a mountainside'). See also **Curry** (iii) [Martin Corry, 1973–, English rugby footballer]

Corrigan from Irish Gaelic *Ó Corragáin* 'descendant of *Corragán*', a personal name meaning literally 'little little spear'

Corrin (i) a shortened form of *Mac Oran*, from Manx Gaelic *Mac Odhráin* 'son of *Odhran*', a personal name meaning literally 'little dun-coloured one'; (ii) a different form of **Curran**

Corry see **Corrie**

Corteney see **Courtney**

Cory see **Corey**

Coryate 'person from Coryates', Dorset [Thomas Coryate, ?1577–1617, English travel writer]

Cosby 'person from Cosby', Leicestershire ('Cossa's farmstead') [Bill Cosby, 1937–, US comedian and actor]

Cosens see **Cousins**

Cosgrave a different form of **Cosgrove** [Liam Cosgrave, 1920–, Irish Fine Gael politician, prime minister 1973–77, son of William; William T. Cosgrave, 1880–1965, Irish Fine Gael politician, first president of the Irish Free State, 1922–32]

Cosgrove (i) 'person from Cosgrove', Northamptonshire ('Cōf's grove'); (ii) from Irish Gaelic *Ó Coscraigh* 'descendant of *Coscrach*', a nickname meaning literally 'victorious'

Cosin see **Cousin**

Cossens see **Cousins**

Costa (i) 'person who lives on a slope or riverbank or by the coast', or 'person from Costa' (in either case from Italian, Spanish or Portuguese *costa* 'slope, bank, coast'); (ii) a different form of **Costas** (i) [Sam Costa, 1910–81, British bandleader and radio disc jockey]
— **Costa Book Awards** the name post-2005 of what had previously been the Whitbread Awards (see **Whitbread**)
— **Costa Coffee** a British coffee-house company founded in 1971 by the brothers Sergio and Bruno Costa. It is now owned by Whitbread plc.

Costain (i) from Scottish and Irish Gaelic *Mac Austain* 'son of **Austin**'; (ii) a different form of **Constantine**
— **Costain Group plc** a British construction firm (formerly Richard Costain Ltd.), established in Liverpool in 1865 by Richard Costain, a builder from the Isle of Man

Costas (i) from the Greek male personal name *Kostas*, a shortened form of *Konstantinos* '**Constantine**'. See also **Costa** (ii); (ii) a plural variant of **Costa** (i)

Costello from Irish Gaelic *Mac Oisdealbhaigh* 'son of *Oisdealbhach*', a personal name meaning literally 'one who resembles a deer or fawn' [Elvis Costello (original name Declan Patrick MacManus), 1954–, British rock and pop singer/songwriter; John Costello, 1891–1976, Irish Fine Gael politician, prime minister 1948–51, 1954–57]
— **Abbott and Costello** see **Abbott**

Costigan from Irish Gaelic *Mac Oistgín* 'son of *Oistgín*', perhaps a gaelicized version of **Hodgkin**

Costner an anglicization of the German surname *Köstner*, literally either 'treasurer' or 'person from Kösten or Köstenberg', Germany [Kevin Costner, 1955–, US actor]

Cotman 'serf in the medieval feudal system who held a cottage by service rather than by paying rent' (from Middle English *cot* 'cottage' + *man*) [John Sell Cotman, 1782–1842, British landscape watercolourist and etcher]

Cottam a different form of **Cotton** (i)

Cotten (i) see **Cotton**; (ii) perhaps an anglicization of the German surname *Kotten* 'person from Kotten', the name of various places in Germany

Cotter (i) 'serf in the medieval feudal system who held a cottage by service rather than by paying rent' (from a derivative of Middle English *cot* 'cottage'); (ii) from Irish Gaelic *Mac Oitir* 'son of *Oitir*', a personal name adapted from Old Norse *Óttarr*, literally 'fear-army'

Cotterell, Cotterill different forms of **Cottrell**

Cottingham 'person from Cottingham', Northamptonshire and Yorkshire ('homestead of Cott's or Cotta's people')

Cottle (i) 'maker of chain-mail' (from Anglo-Norman *cotel* 'little coat (of mail)'); (ii) 'maker of knives and similar implements; cutler' (from Old French *coutel* 'knife'). See also **Cutler**

Cotton, Cotten (i) 'person from Coton', the name (variously spelled) of several places in England ('(place) at the cottages'). See also **Cottam**; (ii) 'maker of chain-mail' (from Old French *coten* 'little coat (of mail)') [Billy Cotton, 1899–1969, British bandleader; Dot Cotton, gossipy hypochondriac (played by June Brown) in the BBC television soap opera *EastEnders* (1985–); Fran Cotton, 1947–, English rugby player; Sir Henry Cotton, 1907–87, British golfer; Joseph Cotton, 1905–94, US actor; Sir Robert Cotton, 1571–1631, English antiquary and manuscript collector]

Cottrell, Cottrill 'cottager' (from Old French *coterel* 'little cottager', from *cotier* 'cottager'). See also **Cotterell** [Leonard Cottrell, 1913–, British archaeologist]

Coughlan, Coughlin, Coghlan from Irish Gaelic *Ó Cochláin* 'descendant of *Cochlán*', a nickname based on *cochal* 'hood'

Coulbourne, Coulbourn see **Colbourne**

Coull (i) a Scottish variant of **Cole**; (ii) 'person from Coull', Aberdeenshire

Coulson (i) 'son of **Cole** (i)'; (ii) an anglicization of **McCool**

Coulston see **Colston**

Coulter 'person from Coulter', Aberdeenshire and Lanarkshire ('back land')

Coulthard 'person who looks after asses or horses' (from Middle English *coltehird*, literally 'colt-herdsman') [David Coulthard, 1971–, British racing driver]

Coulton 'person from Coulton', Yorkshire ('farmstead where charcoal is made')

Coupar, Couper, Cowper (i) 'person from Coupar', Fife (perhaps 'community'); (ii) see

Cooper (i). The variant *Cowper* is traditionally pronounced as 'cooper' (as are *Coupar* and *Couper*), but in modern usage it is widely pronounced as spelled. [William Cowper, 1731–1800, British poet]
— **Cowper's gland** either of two small glands, just below the prostate, that secrete into the urethra a lubricant fluid that is released just prior to the ejaculation of semen. It is named after the English anatomist William Cowper, 1666–1709.

Coupland see **Copeland**

Courage (i) from a medieval nickname for a fat person (from Middle English *corage* 'stoutness'); (ii) perhaps 'person from Cowridge End', Bedfordshire; (iii) a different form of **Kendrick** (i)
— **Courage Ltd.** a British brewery, founded in Bermondsey, London in 1787 by John Courage, died 1793

Court (i) 'person employed at a manorial court'; (ii) from a medieval nickname for a small or short person (from Middle English *curt* 'short') [Margaret Court (*née* Smith), 1942–, Australian tennis player]

Courtauld from a Huguenot nickname for a small or short person (from Old French, literally 'little short one') [Samuel Courtauld, 1876–1947, British textile manufacturer and art collector]
— **Courthold Institute of Art** an institute within the University of London for the study of art history, founded in 1931 with the financial help of Samuel Courthold (see above) (who also gave his own art collection to the Institute)

Courtney, Courtenay, Corteney (i) 'person from Courtenay', northern France ('Curtenus's settlement'); (ii) from a medieval nickname for a snub-nosed person (from Old French *curt* 'short' + *nes* 'nose'); (iii) from Irish Gaelic *Ó Curnáin* 'descendant of *Curnán*', a personal name meaning literally 'little horn' [Sir Tom Courtenay, 1937–, British actor]

Cousin, Cousen, Cosin from a medieval nickname for someone related to a notable local personage (from Middle English *cosin* 'relative'). See also **Cushing, Cusson**

Cousins, Cousens, Couzens, Cosens, Cozens, Cossens, Cozzens, Cuzons 'son of **Cousin**' [Frank Cousins, 1904–86, British trade-union leader and Labour politician]

Coutts 'person from Cults', Aberdeenshire ('nooks') [Angela Burdett-Coutts, see **Burdett**]
— **Coutts & Co.** a British private bank, founded in 1692 as Campbells Bank by John Campbell, died 1712. James Coutts, 1733–78, became a partner in 1755, and he was joined five years later by his brother Thomas Coutts, 1735–1822. Around 1775 the firm became known as Thomas Coutts & Co.

Covell, Covel 'maker of cloaks', or from a medieval nickname for someone who habitually wore a cloak (in either case from Old English *cufle* 'cloak')

Coveney 'person from Coveney', Cambridgeshire ('Cofa's island' or 'island in the bay')

Coverdale 'person from Coverdale', Lancashire and Yorkshire ('valley of the (river) Cover', a Celtic river-name meaning simply 'stream') [Miles Coverdale, 1488–1568, English Protestant reformer and translator of the Bible]

Covington 'person from Covinton', Lanarkshire ('Colban's farmstead'), or 'person from Covington', Cambridgeshire ('farmstead associated with Cofa')

Cowan, Cowen reduced forms of **McCowan** [Sir Frederic Cowen, 1852–1935, British composer; Sir Zelman Cowen, 1919–, Australian lawyer and statesman]

Cowans, Cowens 'son of **Cowan**'

Coward 'keeper of cattle' (from Middle English *cowherde* 'cow herdsman') [Sir Noël Coward, 1899–1973, British dramatist, actor and songwriter]

Cowart probably a different form of **Coward**

Cowdell a different form of **Caldwell**

Cowden 'person from Cowden', the name of several places in England and Scotland (variously 'valley where charcoal is burned' and 'hill where charcoal is burned')

Cowdrey 'person from Coudrai or Coudray', northern France ('hazel copse'), or 'person from Cowdray or Cowdry', Sussex (probably adoptions of the French place-names) [Colin Cowdrey (Lord Cowdrey), 1932–2000, English cricketer]

Cowell 'person from Cowhill', Gloucestershire and Lancashire ('hill frequented by cows') [Henry Cowell, 1897–1965, US composer; Simon Cowell, 1959–, British music executive and TV talent-show judge]

Cowen, Cowens see **Cowan, Cowans**

Cowgill 'person from Cowgill', the name of several places in northern England (variously 'narrow valley frequented by cows' and 'narrow valley where coal is obtained')

Cowie 'person from Cowie', the name of various places in Scotland (probably 'place where hazel grows')

Cowles a different form of **Coles**

Cowley (i) 'person from Cowley', the name of numerous places in England (variously 'Cofa's or Cufa's galde' or 'glade where cows are pastured'); (ii) a reduced form of **MacAulay** [Abraham Cowley, 1618–67, English poet]

Cowper see **Coupar**

Cox, Coxe, Cocks (i) 'son of *Cocke*', from a medieval nickname for a bumptious, swaggering, self-confident young man, a 'jack-the-lad' (from Middle English *cok* 'male fowl'); (ii) 'son of *Cocke*', a medieval male personal name (from Old English *Cocca*, probably originally a nickname based on either *cocc* 'male fowl' (as in (i)) or on *cocc* 'lump, small hill', hence applied to a large ungainly person); (iii) 'son of a cook' (from Flemish *cok* 'cook') [Brian Cox, 1946–, British actor; David Cox, 1783–1859, British artist; Mark Cox, 1943–, British tennis player]

— **Cox's Orange Pippin** a small variety of eating apple with a yellowish-green skin flecked or patched with red, developed by the British amateur fruit-grower Richard Cox, ?1776–1845

Coxon, Coxson 'son of *Cocke*' (see **Cox** (i–ii))

Coyle a reduced form of **McCool** (i–ii)

Coyne (i) 'person who makes coins at a mint', or from a medieval nickname for a miser (in either case from Middle English *coin*); (ii) from Irish Gaelic *Ó Cúain* 'descendant of *Cúan*', a nickname meaning literally 'little dog', or *Ó Cadhain* 'descendant of *Cadhan*', a nickname meaning literally 'barnacle goose'; (iii) an Irish variant of **Quinn**

Cozens see **Cousins**

Cozier 'tailor' (from Old French *cousere* 'tailor')

Cozzens see **Cousins**

Crabb, Crabbe (i) from a medieval nickname for someone who walks in a crablike way; (ii) 'person who lives by a crab-apple tree'; (iii) perhaps from a medieval nickname for a curmudgeonly person (a metaphor originally based on the sourness of the crab apple, but subsequently also associated with the perceived perversity and truculence of the crustacean) [Buster Crabbe (original name Clarence Linden Crabbe, Jr.), 1908–83, US swimmer and actor; George Crabbe, 1754–1832, British poet and clergyman; Lionel ('Buster') Crabb, 1909–?56, British Royal Navy frogman and spy]

Crabtree 'person who lives by a crab-apple tree'

Crace from a medieval nickname for a fat person (from Middle English *cras* 'fat')

Cracknell, Cracknall 'person from Crakehall or Crakehill', Yorkshire ('nook of land frequented by crows') [James Cracknell, 1972–, British oarsman]

Craddock, Cradock from the Welsh male personal name *Caradog*, literally 'amiable' [Fanny Cradock (*née* Pechey), 1909–94, British cookery writer and television cook; Johnnie Cradock, 1904–87, British cook, writer and broadcaster, husband of Fanny]

Craft (i) a different form of **Croft**; (ii) an anglicization of **Kraft** [Robert Craft, 1923–, US conductor and musicologist]

Cragg a different form of **Craig**

Craig 'person who lives by a steep or precipitous rock' (from Gaelic *creag* 'steep or precipitous rock') [Daniel Craig, 1968–, British actor; Sir Edward Gordon Craig, 1872–1966, British actor, director and stage designer (his father's surname was Godwin; he chose the name Craig himself, from the island Ailsa Craig); James Craig (1st Viscount Craigavon), 1871–1940, Northern Irish Unionist politician, first prime minister of Northern Ireland, 1921–40; Michael Craig (original name Michael Gregson), 1929–, British actor; Wendy Craig, 1934–, British actress]

— **Craigavon** a town in Antrim, Northern Ireland, built as a new town in the mid 1960s and named after James Craig, Lord Craigavon (see above)

Craigie 'person who lives by a rocky place' (from Gaelic *creagach* 'rocky place') [Sir William

Craigie, 1867–1957, British lexicographer and philologist]

Craik 'person from Craik', Aberdeenshire ('steep or precipitous rock') [Dinah Craik (*née* Mulock), 1826–87, British novelist]

Cram (i) perhaps a shortened form of the Scottish surname *Crambie*, literally 'person from Crombie', Fife; (ii) an anglicization of the German surname *Kram*, literally 'shopkeeper' [Steve Cram, 1960–, British athlete]

Cramer (i) an anglicization of **Kramer**; (ii) a different form of **Creamer** (ii)

Cramp (i) a different form of **Crump**; (ii) an anglicization of the German surname *Kramp*, either literally 'locksmith' or from a medieval nickname for a hunchback or someone with a hooked nose (from Middle Low German *krampe* 'hook, staple')

Crampton a different form of **Crompton**

Crandall, Crandell, Crandle from Scottish Gaelic *Mac Raonuill* 'son of *Raonull*' (**Ronald**)

Crane from a medieval nickname for a tall, thin, long-legged person, like a crane (the bird) [Hart Crane, 1899–1932, US poet; Stephen Crane, 1871–1900, US novelist; Walter Crane, 1845–1915, British illustrator, painter and designer of textiles and wallpaper]

Cranfield 'person from Cranfield', Bedfordshire ('area of open land frequented by cranes')

Cranford 'person from Cranford', the name of various places in England ('ford frequented by cranes')

Cranham 'person from Cranham', Gloucestershire ('enclosure frequented by cranes')

Crankshaw 'person from Cranshaw', Lancashire ('thicket frequented by cranes'). See also **Cranshaw, Crenshaw**

Cranmer probably 'person from Cranmore', Somerset ('pool frequented by cranes') [Thomas Cranmer, 1489–1556, English churchman and martyr, archbishop of Canterbury 1532–56]

Cranshaw a different form of **Crankshaw**

Cranston 'person from Cranston', Midlothian ('Cran's settlement')

Crapper a different form of **Cropper** [Thomas Crapper, 1837–1910, British sanitary engineer and manufacturer of water closets]

Crashaw see **Crawshaw**

Crathorne, Craythorne probably 'person from Crathorne', Yorkshire ('thorn bush in a nook of land')

Craven (i) 'person from Craven', a district of West Yorkshire (probably 'garlic place'); (ii) from Irish Gaelic *Ó Crabháin* 'descendant of *Crabhán*' [John Craven, 1940–, British television journalist and presenter; Wes Craven, 1939–, US film director and writer]

Cravens a different form of **Craven**

Crawford, Crawfurd 'person from Crawford', the name of numerous places in England and Scotland ('ford frequented by crows') [Broderick Crawford, 1911–86, US actor; Francis Marion Crawford,

1854–1909, US novelist; Howard Marion-Crawford, see **Marion**; Joan Crawford (original name Lucille Le Sueur), 1908–77, US actress; Marian Crawford ('Crawfie'), 1909–88, British royal nanny; Michael Crawford (original name Michael Dumble Smith), 1942–, British actor]

— William Crawford & Sons a British biscuit manufacturer, established in Leith, Edinburgh in 1813 by William Crawford

Crawley 'person from Crawley', the name of various places in England ('glade frequented by crows'). See also **Crowley** (i) [Sir Pitt Crawley, odious baronet in William Thackeray's *Vanity Fair* (1848), whose son Rawdon Crawley marries the heroine, Becky Sharp]

Crawshaw, Crashaw 'person from Crawshaw Booth', Lancashire ('thicket frequented by crows') [Richard Crashaw, ?1613–49, British poet]

Crawshay a different form of **Crawshaw**

Cray from Irish Gaelic *Ó Craoibhe* 'descendant of *Craobhach*', a nickname meaning literally either 'curly-headed one' or 'prolific one'. See also **Creevy**

Creagan see **Creegan**

Creamer (i) 'seller of cream and other dairy products'; (ii) 'pedlar' (from obsolete Scottish English *cremer* 'pedlar'). See also **Cramer** (ii); (iii) an anglicization of **Kramer**

Crease, Crees, Creese from a medieval nickname for someone of elegant dress or appearance (from Middle English *crease* 'fine, elegant')

Creasy, Creasey different forms of **Crease** [John Creasey, 1908–73, British crime novelist]

Creech (i) 'person from Creich', Fife ('(place by the) hill'); (ii) probably 'person from East Creech or Creech St Michael', Dorset and Somerset respectively ('(place by the) hill')

Creed (i) 'person from Creed Farm', Sussex ('(place of) plants or weeds'); (ii) from the Old English male personal name *Creoda*; (iii) a different form of **Creedon** (i) [Frederick Creed, 1871–1957, Canadian inventor]

— Creed printer an automatic tape-printing machine invented around 1911 by Frederick Creed (see above), the precursor of the teleprinter

Creedon (i) from Irish Gaelic *Ó Críodáin* 'descendant of *Críodán*' or *Mac Críodáin* 'son of *Críodán*', a personal name of unknown origin and meaning; (ii) 'person from Creeton', Lincolnshire ('Cræta's farmstead')

Creegan, Creagan from Irish Gaelic *Ó Croidheagáin* 'descendant of *Croidheagán*', a personal name meaning literally 'little heart'. See also **Creggan**

Crees, Creese see **Crease**

Creevy, Creevey different forms of **Cray**

Creggan a different form of **Creegan**

Creighton, Crichton, Crighton 'person from Crichton', Midlothian (probably 'farmstead by a rock'), or 'person from Creaton or Creighton', Northamptonshire and Staffordshire respectively ('farmstead by a rock') [James Crichton, 1560–82,

Scottish adventurer, scholar, linguist and poet ('The Admirable Crichton'); Michael Crichton, 1942–, US author and film director; Lady Penelope Creighton-Ward, aristocratic London agent of International Rescue in the British television puppet adventure series *Thunderbirds* (1965–66)]

— The Admirable Crichton a play (1902) by J.M. Barrie about a polymath manservant cast away with his employers on a desert island. The title was inspired by the sobriquet applied to James Crichton (see above). It is also the title of a novel (1837) by Harrison Ainsworth.

Crenshaw a different form of **Crankshaw** [Ben Crenshaw, 1952–, US golfer]

Creswell, Cresswell 'person from Creswell', the name of various places in England ('stream where watercress grows'). See also **Carswell** [Madam Cresswell, a notorious London prostitute and madam of the Restoration period]

Crew, Crewe 'person from Crewe', Cheshire ('(place by the) fish trap')

Cribbins from Irish Gaelic *Mac Roibín* 'son of *Robin*', an Anglo-Norman male personal name, literally 'little **Robert**' [Bernard Cribbins, 1928–, British actor]

Crichton see **Creighton**

Crick 'person from Crick', Northamptonshire ('(place by the) hill') [Francis Crick, 1916–2004, British biophysicist]

Crippen, Crippin different forms of **Crispin** [Hawley Harvey Crippen, 1861–1910, US-born British dentist and murderer]

Cripps (i) 'maker of pouches' (from Middle English *crippes* 'pouch'); (ii) a different form of **Crisp** [Sir Stafford Cripps, 1889–1952, British Labour politician]

Crisp, Crispe (i) from a medieval nickname for someone with curly hair (from Middle English *crisp* 'curly'); (ii) a shortened form of **Crispin**. See also **Cripps** (ii) [Donald Crisp (original name George William Crisp), 1882–1974, British actor; Quentin Crisp (original name Denis Charles Pratt), 1908–99, British writer, artist's model, actor and raconteur]

Crispin (i) from the male personal name *Crispin* (via Old French from Latin *Crispīnus*, literally 'little curly-haired one'); (ii) 'little **Crisp** (i)'. See also **Crippen**

Cristal see **Crystal**

Critchley probably 'person from Critchley', an unidentified place in England ('glade with a cross' or 'glade by a hill')

Critchlow 'person from Critchlow', Lancashire ('hill mound')

Croaker 'person from Crèvecoeur', the name of various places in northern France ('heartbreak', an allusion to the poverty of the local soil). See also **Crocker** (ii)

Crocker (i) 'potter' (from a derivative of Middle English *crock* 'pot'); (ii) a different form of **Croaker** [Andrew Crocker-Harris, emotionally constipated schoolmaster in Terence Rattigan's

The Browning Version (1948); Betty Crocker, a fictitious woman, invented by the US marketing industry in the early 1920s, who embodies all the traditional feminine domestic virtues]

Crockett (i) from a medieval nickname for someone who had a hairstyle involving a large curl (from Middle English *croket* 'large curl'); (ii) from Scottish Gaelic *Mac Riocaird* 'son of **Richard**' [Davy Crockett, 1786–1836, US frontiersman]
— **Davy Crockett hat** a coonskin cap (a hat made of a raccoon's pelt, complete with tail), or a fur hat of similar design, as worn by Davy Crockett (see above)

Crockford 'person from Crockford Bridge', Surrey (perhaps 'pot-ford')
— **Crockford's** a gambling club opened in St James's Street, London, in 1827 by William Crockford, 1775-1844, the son of a fishmonger
— ***Crockford's Clerical Directory*** a reference book of all the clergy of the Church of England, originally compiled (1860) by John Crockford, 1823–65

Croft 'person who lives by an enclosure', or 'person from Croft', the name of various places in England (in either case from Old English *croft* 'enclosure'). See also **Craft** (i), **Cruft** [Lara Croft, heroine of the *Tomb Raider* computer-game series and of films based on it]
— **Croft** a British firm of port and sherry shippers, founded (as Phayre and Bradley) in Portugal in 1678. The Croft connection did not begin until 1736, when John Croft, died 1762, joined the firm. It was sold to Gilbeys in 1911.
— **Croft Original** a pale sweet sherry produced by Croft (see above)

Crofton 'person from Crofton', the name of several places in England ('farmstead with an enclosure')
— **Crofton formula** a formula in integral geometry relating the length of a curve to the expected number of times a random line intersects it. It was named after the Irish mathematician Morgan Crofton, 1826–1915.

Crofts a different form of **Croft**

Crohn an anglicization of the German surname *Krohn*, from a medieval German nickname for a tall thin person with long legs, like a crane
— **Crohn's disease** a chronic inflammatory disease, usually of the lower intestinal tract, marked by scarring and thickening of the intestinal wall and obstruction. It is named after the US pathologist B.B. Crohn, 1884–1983.

Croke (i) from Irish Gaelic *Cróc*, from the Old Norse name *Krókr* (see **Crook** (i)); (ii) perhaps from a medieval nickname for someone with an unmelodious voice
— **Croke Park** the national stadium, in Dublin, of Ireland's Gaelic Athletic Association, where Gaelic football and hurling matches are played. It was named in honour of Dr Thomas Croke, archbishop of Cashel and a founder-patron of the GAA in 1884. (The nearby Glasnevin Cemetery is punningly known as Croak Park).

Crombie 'person from Crombie', Aberdeenshire ('crooked place')

Crome see **Croom**

Cromer (i) 'person from Cromer', Norfolk ('lake frequented by crows'); (ii) from the medieval French male personal name *Cromer* (from the Germanic compound name *Hrodmar*, literally 'renown-famous')

Crompton 'person from Crompton', Lancashire ('farmstead in a bend'). See also **Crumpton** [Richmal Crompton, pen-name of Richmal Lamburn (Crompton was her mother's maiden name), 1890–1969, British children's author; Samuel Crompton, 1753–1827, British inventor]
— **Crompton's spinning mule** a piece of machinery for spinning high-quality yarn at high speed, invented in 1779 by Samuel Crompton (see above)

Cromwell 'person from Cromwell', Nottinghamshire and Yorkshire ('crooked stream') [Oliver Cromwell, 1599–1658, English soldier and statesman, lord protector of England 1653–58; Richard Cromwell, 1626–1712, son of Oliver, lord protector of England 1658–59; Thomas Cromwell, ?1485–1540, English statesman]
— **Cromwellian** relating to or typical of Oliver Cromwell (see above). As a noun, it formerly denoted in particular any of those who settled in Ireland at the instigation of Oliver Cromwell, or their descendants.
— **Cromwellian chair** a type of chair of plain 17th-century-style design with a padded leather seat and back
— **Cromwell Road** a road in West London, between Kensington and Earls Court, laid out in the 1850s. It was named after Cromwell House, a former house on its course said to have been lived in by Oliver Cromwell.
— **Cromwell shoe** a shoe of the type supposedly worn by Oliver Cromwell, typically with a large buckle or bow

Cronin from Irish Gaelic *Ó Cróinín* 'descendant of *Cróinín*', a nickname meaning literally 'little swarthy one' [A.J. Cronin, 1896–1981, British novelist; Hume Cronin, 1911–2003, Canadian actor]

Cronkite an anglicization of Dutch *Krankheid* (probably from a medieval nickname (literally 'weakness') for a weak or sickly person) [Walter Cronkite, 1916–, US broadcast journalist]

Crook, Crooke (i) from the medieval personal name *Crook* (from Old Norse *Krókr*, originally a nickname (literally 'crooked') for a cripple or hunchback or for a devious person). See also **Croke** (i); (ii) person who lives by a bend in a road or river' (from Middle English *crook* 'hook, bend', from Old Norse *krókr*); (iii) 'maker of hooks' (from Middle English *crook*, as (ii)); (iv) perhaps 'person from Crook', Cumbria and County Durham ('land in a bend')

Crookes, Crooks 'son of **Crook** (i)'

Crookshank see **Cruikshank**

Croom, Croome, Crome (i) 'person from Croom', Yorkshire ('(place) in the narrow valleys'), or 'person from Croome', Worcestershire ('bendy stream'); (ii) 'person who makes, sells or uses hooks' (from Middle English *crome* 'hook'); (iii) from a medieval nickname for a cripple or hunchback (from Middle English *crom* 'bent'). See also **Crump** [John Crome, 1768–1821, British landscape painter]

Cropper 'person who harvests a crop'. See also **Crapper**

Crosby, Crosbie (i) 'person from Crosby', the name of various places in Scotland and northern England (mostly 'village or farmstead with crosses'); (ii) from Irish Gaelic *Mac an Chrosáin*, literally 'son of the satirist'. See also **Cross** (ii) [Annette Crosbie, 1934–, British actress; Bing Crosby (original name Harry Lillis Crosby), ?1904–77, US singer and actor]

Crosier see **Crozier**

Crosland see **Crossland**

Crosley see **Crossley**

Cross, Crosse (i) 'person who lives by a roadside or market cross or by a crossroads'; (ii) a different form of **Crosby** (ii) [Ben Cross, 1947–, British actor; Gordon Crosse, 1937–, British composer]
— **Crosse and Blackwell** a British manufacturer of soups, pickles and similar foodstuffs. It originated in 1706, as West and Wyatt, and was bought up in 1830 by Edmund Crosse and Thomas Blackwell.

Crossland, Crosland 'person from Crossland', Yorkshire ('land with crosses') [Anthony Crosland, 1918–77, British Labour politician]

Crossley, Crosley 'person from Crossley', Yorkshire ('glade with a cross')

Crossman a different form of **Cross** (i) [Richard Crossman, 1907–74, British Labour politician]

Crothers a different form of **Carruthers**

Crouch 'person who lives by a roadside or market cross or by a crossroads' (from Middle English *crouch* 'cross')

Crow, Crowe (i) from a medieval nickname for someone thought to resemble a crow (e.g. in having black hair); (ii) from Irish Gaelic *Mac Conchradha* (see **McEnroe** (i)); (iii) a translation of any of a range of Irish Gaelic names based on *fiach* 'crow' [Russell Crowe, 1964–, Australian actor; Sheryl Crow, 1962–, US blues-rock singer]
— **Jim Crow** originally, in 19th-century America, a derisive name or nickname for an African American. The term subsequently came to be used in the abstract for the practice of discriminating against black people, especially by operating systems of public segregation. The name came from a popular minstrel song introduced in Louisville, Kentucky in 1828 by Thomas Dartmouth ('Daddy') Rice:
Jim Crow is courting a white gall,
And yaller folks call her Sue.

Crowden 'person from Crowden', Derbyshire and Devon (respectively 'valley frequented by crows' and 'hill frequented by crows')

Crowder a different form of **Crowther**

Crowell 'person from Crowell', Oxfordshire ('stream frequented by crows')

Crowhurst 'person from Crowhurst', Surrey and Sussex (respectively 'wooded hill frequented by crows' and 'wooded hill near the corner of land')

Crowl, Crowle 'person from Crowle', Lincolnshire and Worcestershire (respectively 'place by the (river) Crowle' (a river-name meaning literally 'winding one') and 'glade by the corner')

Crowley (i) 'person from Crowley', the name of various places in England ('glade frequented by crows'). See also **Crawley**; (ii) from Irish Gaelic *Ó Cruadhlaoich* 'descendant of *Cruadhlaoch*', a personal name meaning literally 'hardy hero' [Aleister Crowley (original name Edward Alexander Crowley), 1875–1947, British diabolist]

Crown, Crowne (i) 'person who lives in a house at the sign of a crown'; (ii) 'person from Craon', northern France; (iii) an anglicization of the German or Swedish surname *Kron*, literally 'crown'
— *The Thomas Crown Affair* a film (1968) in which Thomas Crown, a bored property millionaire (played by Steve McQueen), sets up a bank robbery and is pursued by a glamorous female insurance investigator. It was remade in 1999.

Crowner 'coroner' (from Anglo-Norman *corouner* 'coroner', a derivative of Old French *coroune* 'crown')

Crowther 'person who plays the crowd (an ancient Celtic stringed instrument)'. See also **Crowder** [Leslie Crowther, 1933–96, British entertainer]

Croxford 'person from Croxford', an unidentified place in England (probably 'Krókr's ford')

Croxton 'person from Croxton', the name of various places in England ('Krókr's farmstead')

Croy (i) 'person from Croy', the name of various places in Scotland; (ii) a shortened form of the surname *McRoy*, from Irish Gaelic *Mac Rúaidh* 'son of *Rúadh*', literally 'the red one'

Crozier, Crosier 'person who carries a cross or a bishop's crook in a church procession' (from Middle English *croisier*, from Old French, a derivative of *crois* 'cross')

Cruden 'person from Cruden', Aberdeenshire [Alexander Cruden, 1701–70, British scholar and bookseller, compiler of a noted biblical concordance (1737)]

Cruft a different form of **Croft**
— **Cruft's** the premier British dog show, established in 1888 by the dog breeder Charles Cruft, 1852–1938

Cruikshank, Crookshank from a medieval Scottish nickname for someone with a crooked leg (from Scots *cruik* 'bent' + *shank* 'leg') [Andrew Cruikshank, 1907–88, British actor; George Cruikshank, 1792–1872, British caricaturist]

Cruise see **Cruse**

Crum, Crumm shortened forms of **McCrum**

Crump from a medieval nickname for a cripple or hunchback (from Middle English *crump* 'bent'). See also **Cramp**, **Croom** (iii)

Crumpton a different form of **Crompton**

Cruse, Cruise (i) from a medieval nickname for a fearsome or dashing person (from Middle English *crouse* 'bold, fierce'); (ii) perhaps 'person from Cruys-Staëte', a place in northern France ('hard place') [Tom Cruise (original name Thomas Cruise Mapother IV), 1962–, US actor]

Cruttendon 'person from Cruttendon', a lost place in Kent

Cruz from the Spanish and Portuguese personal name *Cruz*, or 'person from (La) Cruz', the name of numerous places in Spain and Portugal (in either case from Spanish or Portuguese *cruz* 'cross')

Cryer 'town crier' [Barry Cryer, 1935–, British comedian and comedy writer]

Crystal, Cristal, Chrystal (i) from a Scottish pet-form of the male personal name **Christopher**; (ii) a shortened anglicization of any of various Jewish surnames beginning with German *Kristall* 'crystal' [Billy Crystal (original name Israel William Krisstalsterne), 1948–, US actor and comedian; David Crystal, 1941–, British linguistician]

Cubitt, Cubit (i) from a medieval nickname for someone with remarkable (probably remarkably strong) forearms (from Middle English *cubit* 'forearm'); (ii) perhaps 'builder' (from Middle English *cubit*, the name of a measure of length, roughly equivalent to that of an adult forearm) [Thomas Cubitt, 1788–1855, British builder and property developer]
— **Cubitt Town** a district in the southeastern corner of the Isle of Dogs, East London. It was named after Sir William Cubitt, 1791–1863, bother of Thomas Cubitt (see above), who developed the area in the 1840s and 1850s.

Cudlip, Cudlipp 'person from Cudlipptown', Devon [Hugh Cudlipp (Lord Cudlipp), 1913–98, British journalist and newspaper editor]

Cudworth 'person from Cudworth', Somerset and Yorkshire (respectively 'Cuda's enclosure' and 'Cūtha's enclosure') [Ralph Cudworth, 1617–88, English theologian]

Cuff, Cuffe (i) 'glove-maker', or from a medieval nickname for someone who habitually wore elegant or showy gloves (in either case from Middle English *cuffe* 'glove'); (ii) from Irish Gaelic *Mac Dhuibh*, a different form of *Mac Duibh* (see **McDuff**); (iii) a rough translation of Irish Gaelic *Ó Doirnín* 'descendant of *Doirnín*', a nickname meaning literally 'little fist'; (iv) from a medieval Cornish nickname for a dearly loved person (from Cornish *cuf* 'dear')

Culbertson 'son of *Culbert*', a different form of the male personal name *Colbert*, brought into England by the Normans but ultimately of Germanic origin and meaning literally 'helm-bright' [Ely Culbertson, 1891–1955, Romanian-born US authority on bridge]

Culkin from Irish Gaelic *Mac Uilcín* 'son of *Uilcín*', a personal name meaning literally 'little little **William**' [Macaulay Culkin, 1980–, US actor]

Cullen (i) 'person from Cullen', Moray ('little nook'); (ii) from Irish Gaelic *Ó Coileáin* 'descendant of *Coileán*', a nickname meaning literally 'puppy' (see also **Collins** (ii)), or *Ó Cuilinn* 'descendant of *Cuileann*', a nickname meaning literally 'holly'; (iii) 'person from Cologne', Germany

Cullinan from Irish Gaelic *Ó Cuileannáin* 'descendant of *Cuileannán*', a personal name meaning literally 'little *Cuileann*' (see **Cullen** (ii))
— **Cullinan diamond** a diamond of 3106 metric carats (about 621 grams) discovered in South Africa in 1905. It was named after Sir Thomas Cullinan, who owned the mine where it was found.

Cullis a different form of **Collis**

Cullum (i) 'person from Culham', Berkshire and Oxfordshire (respectively 'homestead with a kiln' and 'Cūla's river meadow'); (ii) a different form of **Coleman** (i)

Culpepper, Culpeper 'person who collects, prepares and/or sells herbs and spices' (from Middle English *cullen* 'to pick' + *pepper*) [Nicholas Culpeper, 1616–64, English herbalist, physician and astrologer; Thomas Culpeper (2nd Baron Culpeper), 1635–89, English colonial administrator, governor of Virginia 1680–83]
— **Culpeper's Rebellion** an American colonial uprising (1677–79) in North Carolina, led by John Culpeper

Culshaw 'person from Cowlishaw', Lancashire (probably 'dark copse')

Culver 'person who keeps or looks after doves', or from a medieval nickname for someone thought to resemble a dove (e.g. in mild disposition) (in either case from Middle English *culver* 'dove') [Roland Culver, 1900–84, British actor]

Cumberbatch 'person from Comberbach', Cheshire ('stream of the Britons')

Cumberland 'person from Cumberland', former county in northwestern England [Richard Cumberland, 1631–1718, English churchman and moral philosopher]

Cumming (i) from Irish Gaelic *Ó Cuimín* or *Mac Cuimín* 'descendant or son of *Cuimín*', a personal name meaning literally 'little crooked one'; (ii) probably from a Breton personal name derived from *cam* 'bent, crooked'

Cummings, Commings, Comings 'son of **Cumming**' [Bruce Cummings, real name of the British writer W.N.P. Barbellion, 1889–1919; Constance Cummings (*née* Halverstadt; Cummings was her mother's maiden name), 1910–2005, US actress; e.e. cummings (Edward Estlin Cummings), 1894–1962, US poet]

Cummins, Commins, Comins, Comyns different forms of **Cummings** [Peggy Cummins, 1925–, British actress]

Cunard from the Old English male personal name *Cyneheard*, literally 'royal-brave' [Lady Emerald

Cunard (*née* Burke; original forenames Maud Alice), 1872–1948, US-born London society hostess; Nancy Cunard, 1896–1965, British writer and publisher, daughter of Emerald; Sir Samuel Cunard, 1787–1865, Canadian-born British shipping magnate]

— **Cunarder** a ship of the Cunard Line, especially any of its large passenger liners on the North Atlantic route. The term is first recorded in 1850.

— **Cunard Line** a British cruise line, founded in 1838 by Sir Samuel Cunard (see above) as the British and North American Royal Mail Steam Packet Company

Cundall 'person from Cundall', Yorkshire (perhaps 'place in a valley', or alternatively 'hollow of the cows')

Cunliffe 'person from Cunliffe', Lancashire ('slope with a crevice' (literally 'cunt-cliff'))

Cunniff from Irish Gaelic *Mac Conduibh* 'son of *Condubh*', a personal name meaning literally 'black dog'. See also **Conniff**

Cunningham, Cuninghame (i) 'person from Cunningham', Ayrshire (originally *Cunegan*, a Celtic place-name of unknown origin and meaning); (ii) from Irish Gaelic *Ó Cuinneagáin* 'descendant of *Cuinneagán*', a personal name meaning literally 'little little leader' [Alan Cunningham, 1784–1842, Scottish poet; Andrew Cunningham (1st Viscount Cunningham), 1883–1963, British admiral; John ('Cat's Eyes') Cunningham, 1917–2002, British fighter pilot and test pilot; Merce Cunningham, 1919–, US dancer and choreographer]

Cuomo probably from a shortened form of *Cuosëmo*, a Neapolitan variant of the Italian male personal name *Cosimo*

Cupit, Cupitt perhaps a different form of **Cubitt**

Curl, Curle from a medieval nickname for someone with curly hair [Robert Floyd Curl, 1933–, US chemist]

Curley (i) a different form of **Turley**; (ii) 'person from Corlay', the name of various places in northern France [Carlo Curley, 1952–, US organist]

Curran, Curren from Irish Gaelic *Ó Corráin* or *Ó Corraidhín* 'descendant of *Corraidhín*', a personal name meaning literally 'little spear'. See also **Corran, Corrin** (ii)

Currie see **Curry**

Currier 'person who dresses and finishes leather after it has been tanned' (from Middle English *curreyour*, ultimately from Latin *coreum* 'leather')

Curry, Currie (i) 'person from Curry Rivel, Curry Mallet or North Curry', Somerset ('estate on the (river) Curry', a pre-English river-name of unknown origin and meaning), 'person from Curry', Cornwall ('corner place'), or 'person from Currie', Edinburgh ('(place) in the marshland'); (ii) from Irish Gaelic *Ó Comhraidhe* 'descendant of *Comhraidhe*', a personal name of unknown origin and meaning. See also **Corey** (ii); (iii) a different form of **Corrie**; (iv) a different form of **Corr** [Edwina Currie (*née* Cohen), 1946–, British

Conservative politician and broadcaster; Finlay Currie, 1878–1968, British actor; John Curry, 1949–94, British skater]

— **Currys** a British chain of electrical retailers, founded in 1884 (as a bicycle manufacturer) by Henry Curry, 1850–1916. It is now owned by DSG International plc.

Curtin (i) from a medieval French nickname for a short person (from Old French *curtin* 'little short one'). See also **Curzon** (ii); (ii) *also* **Curtain** from Gaelic *Mac Cruitín* 'son of *Cruitín*', a nickname for a hunchback [John Joseph Curtin, 1885–1945, Australian Labor politician, prime minister 1941–45]

Curtis, Curtiss, Curteis from a medieval nickname for someone of great refinement or politeness or, ironically, for a boorish person (from Middle English *curteis* 'refined, courteous'), or for a short person or for someone who wore short stockings (from Middle English *curt* 'short' + *hose* 'stockings') [Glenn Curtiss, 1878–1930, US aviator and aircraft manufacturer; Ian Curteis, 1935–, British dramatist; Richard Curtis, 1956–, British screenwriter; Tony Curtis (original name Bernard Schwarz), 1925–, US actor]

— **Curtis Cup** a biennial competition between amateur women golfers of Britain and Ireland and the US, inaugurated in 1932 at the instigation of the US golfing sisters Harriot Curtis, 1881–1974, and Margaret Curtis, 1883–1965

— **Tony Curtis** a style of men's haircut in which the hair at the sides of the head is combed back and that on the forehead is combed forward, in the manner of Tony Curtis (see above). It was popular in the 1950s and '60s.

Curwen (i) 'person from Colvend', Dumfries and Galloway (perhaps '(place) at the back of the hill'); (ii) *also* **Curwin** from Manx Gaelic *Mac Eireamhóin* (see **Irvine** (iii)) [John Curwen, 1816–80, British Nonconformist minister and teacher, founder of the music publishers J. Curwen and Sons Ltd.]

Curzon (i) 'person from Notre-Dame-de-Courson', Normandy ('Curtius's settlement'); (ii) from a medieval French nickname for a short person (from Old French *curson* 'little short one'). See also **Curtin** (i) [Sir Clifford Curzon, 1907–82, British pianist; George Nathaniel Curzon (1st Marquess Curzon), 1859–1925, British Conservative politician and colonial administrator, viceroy of India 1898–1905]

— **Curzon line** a line separating Poland and the former Soviet Union, suggested in 1919 by Lord Curzon (see above), when he was British foreign secretary, and accepted as a border in 1945

— **Curzon Street** a street in Mayfair, London, leading off Park Lane. It was laid out in the 1720s on land owned by Sir Nathaniel Curzon, an ancestor of Lord Curzon.

Cusack 'person from Cussac', northern France ('Cūcius's or Cussius's settlement') [Cyril Cusack, 1910–93, South African-born Irish actor; Sinéad Cusack, 1948–, Irish actress, daughter of Cyril; Sorcha Cusack, 1949–, Irish actress, sister of Sinéad]

Cushing a different form of **Cousin** [Peter Cushing, 1913–94, British actor]
— **Cushing's disease** a condition caused by excessive production of the hormone ACTH by the pituitary gland and marked by obesity, muscular weakness, hypertension and fatigue. It was named after the US surgeon Harvey Cushing, 1869–1939.

Cushman an anglicization of the Jewish surname *Kushman*, of unknown origin and meaning

Cusson, Cussen different forms of **Cousin**
— **Cussons Sons & Co.** a British manufacturer of soap (notably 'Imperial Leather') and cosmetics, founded in the 1880s (as a pharmaceutical firm) by Thomas Tomlinson Cussons, 1838–1905

Cust a shortened form of *Custance*, a different form of **Constance** (i)

Custer an anglicization of the German surname *Köster* or *Küster*, literally 'sexton' [George Custer, 1839–76, US cavalry general]
— **Custer's Last Stand** a colloquial name given to the battle of Little Bighorn (1876), in which General Custer (see above) and his army were defeated and killed by Sioux and Cheyenne forces under Sitting Bull

Cuthbert from the male personal name *Cuthbert* (from Old English *Cuthbeorht*, literally 'famous-bright'). See also **Cutt**

Cuthbertson 'son of **Cuthbert**' [Allan Cuthbertson, 1920–88, Australian-born British actor; Iain Cuthbertson, 1930–, British actor]

Cutler (i) 'maker of knives' (from a derivative of Middle English *coutel* 'knife'); (ii) an anglicization of the German surname *Kottler* or *Kattler*, of unknown origin and meaning [Ivor Cutler, 1923–, British humorist, poet and composer]

Cutress a different form of **Gutteridge**

Cutt from the medieval male personal name *Cutt*, a pet-form of **Cuthbert**

Cutter (i) perhaps 'tailor' or 'barber'; (ii) an anglicization of the German surnames *Kotter*, literally 'person from Kotten', and *Kötter*, literally 'person who lives in a hovel'

Cutts (i) 'son of **Cutt**'; (ii) an anglicization of the German surname *Kotz*, literally 'person who lives in a hovel' or 'maker or wearer of coarse cloth', or of **Katz**

D

Da Costa 'person who lives by a river bank or on a sea coast' (Spanish or Portuguese, 'from the slope or coast'). See also **Acosta**

Dacre 'person from Dacre', Cumbria and Yorkshire (from the name of a local stream that means literally 'trickling one') [Paul Dacre, 1948–, British newspaper executive]

Dadd a Kentish variant of **Dodd** [Richard Dadd, 1817–86, British painter]

Dade a different form of **Deed**

Daft from a medieval nickname for a meek or gentle person (the adjective's modern connotations of weak-mindedness did not develop until the 15th century)

Dahl 'person who lives in a valley' (ultimately from Old Norse *dalr* 'valley') [Roald Dahl, 1916–90, British writer; Sophie Dahl, 1979–, British fashion model, granddaughter of Roald]

Daintith, Dainteth from a medieval nickname (roughly equivalent to 'precious') applied to a dearly loved person (from Middle English *deinteth* 'pleasure, titbit', from Old French *deintiet*)

Daintry, Daintrey 'person from Daventry', Northamptonshire ('Dafa's tree'). The place-name is traditionally pronounced 'daintry'.

Dainty from a medieval nickname meaning 'handsome, pleasant' (from Middle English *deinte*, from Old French *deint(i)é*) [Billy Dainty, 1927–86, British comedian]

Dalby 'person from Dalby', the name of various places in northern and eastern England ('farmstead in a valley'). See also **Dolby** [W. Barrington Dalby (original name William Henry Dalby), 1894–1975, British boxing referee and commentator]

Dale 'person who lives in a valley' (from Middle English *dale* 'valley', either by direct descent from Old English *dæl* or (in northern and eastern England) reinforced by Old Norse *dalr*) [Sir Henry Hallett Dale, 1875–1968, British physiologist; Jim Dale, 1935–, British actor and singer; Mrs Dale (Mary Dale), central character of the BBC radio soap opera *Mrs Dale's Diary* (later *The Dales*), 1948–69]

Daley see **Daly**

Dalgetty 'person from Dalgetty', near Dunfermline (perhaps derived from Gaelic *dealg* 'prickle')

Dalgleish, Dalglish 'person from Dalgleish', near Selkirk ('green field') [Kenny Dalglish, 1951–, Scottish footballer]

Dalhousie 'person from Dalhousie', near Edinburgh (perhaps 'field of slander')

Dallas (i) 'person from Dallas', near Forres, Moray ('homestead by a meadow'); (ii) 'person living in a valley' or 'person from Dalehouse', the name of various places in England (in either case literally 'house in a valley')
— **Dallas** a city in northeastern Texas, laid out in 1846 and named in honour of George M. Dallas, 1792–1864, vice-president of the US 1845–49.

Dallaway, Dalloway 'person from Dallaway', West Midlands (perhaps from a Norman personal name, 'person from (*de*) Alluyes', northern France) [Mrs Dalloway, central figure of the eponymous novel (1925) by Virginia Woolf]

Dallimore a different form of **Delamare** (based on the mistaken belief that the final syllable represents Middle English *more* 'moor'). See also **Dolamore**

Dalrymple 'person from Dalrymple', Strathclyde (perhaps 'field of the crooked stream') [William Dalrymple, 1965–, British writer]

Dalton (i) 'person from Dalton', the name of various places in northern England ('farmstead in a valley'); (ii) 'person from (*de*) Autun', northern France ('Augustus's hill or fort') [John Dalton, 1766–1844, British chemist]
— **Dalton's law** the principle that mixed gases in a given volume exert a pressure equal to the sum of the pressures they would exert individually in the same volume. It was formulated by John Dalton (see above).

Daltry, Daltrey 'person from (*de*) Hauterive', northern France ('high bank'). See also **Hawtry** [Roger Daltrey, 1944–, lead singer of the pop group *The Who*]

Daly, Daley from Irish Gaelic *Ó Dálaigh* 'descendant of *Dálach*', a personal name based on *dál* 'meeting, assembly' [Arthur Daley, fictional small-time crook, central character of the ITV comedy-drama series *Minder*, 1979–94; Cardinal Cahal Daly, 1917–, Roman Catholic archbishop; Richard Daley, 1902–76, US Democrat politician, mayor of Chicago 1955–76]

Dalziel, Dalzell, Dalyell 'person from Dalyell', in the Clyde valley (probably 'white field'). The name is standardly pronounced 'dee-el'. [Detective Superintendent Andrew Dalziel, one half of the detective team of 'Dalziel and Pascoe' in the novels (1970–) of Reginald Hill; Tam Dalyell, 1932–, British Labour politician]

Dampier 'person from Dampierre', the name of various places in Normandy, in honour of St Peter (Old French title of respect *Don* or *Dam-* (from Latin *dominus* 'lord') + *Pierre* 'Peter') [William Dampier, ?1652–1715, English explorer]

Danby 'person from Danby', Yorkshire ('settlement of the Danes') [Francis Danby, 1793–1861, Irish painter]

Dance 'professional dancer or acrobat' (or a nickname for an enthusiastic amateur) [Charles Dance, 1946–, British actor; George Dance, ?1700–68, British architect]

Dando 'person from (*de*) Aunou', Orne ('alder grove'). See also **Delaney** (i) [Jill Dando, 1961–99, British television presenter]

Danford perhaps 'person from Darnford', Suffolk, or other similarly named places in England ('hidden ford')

Danforth a different form of **Danford** [Thomas Danforth, presiding judge at the witch trials in Arthur Miller's *The Crucible* (1953)]

Dangerfield 'person from (*de*) Angerville', Normandy ('Ásgeirr's town', from the Old Norse personal name *Ásgeirr*, literally 'god's spear')

Daniel, Daniell from the Hebrew male personal name *Daniel*, literally 'God is my judge' [Paul Daniel, 1958–, British conductor; Samuel Daniel, 1562–1619, English poet]
— **Jack Daniel's** a Tennessee whiskey distillery founded in 1866 by Jasper Newton ('Jack') Daniel, 1848–1911

Daniels 'son of **Daniel**' [Bebe Daniels (original name Phyllis Daniels), 1901–71, US actress and singer; Paul Daniels (original name Newton Edward Daniels), 1938–, British conjurer]

Danvers 'person from (*de*) Anvers (the French name of Antwerp)', Belgium ('at the wharf') [Mrs Danvers, the sinister housekeeper in Daphne Du Maurier's *Rebecca* (1938); Bob Danvers Walker, 1906–90, British radio, television and film announcer]

Darby, Darbey, Derby (i) 'person from Derby', Derbyshire, or 'person from West Derby', Lancashire ('farmstead where deer are kept'); (ii) from Irish Gaelic *Ó Diarmada* (see **McDermott**) [Abraham Darby I, 1678–1717, British industrialist who pioneered new methods of iron production; Abraham Darby III, 1750–91, grandson of Abraham Darby I, who manufactured the world's first cold-cast iron bridge, at Ironbridge in Shropshire]
— **Father Darby's** (or **Derby's**) **bands** a 16th-century term for a particularly stringent type of bond which held a debtor in thrall to a creditor. It may have been based on the name of a noted 16th-century usurer. It may also have given rise to the slightly later slang use of **darbies** for 'handcuffs'.

Darbyshire, Darbishire, Derbyshire (i) 'person from Derbyshire'; (ii) 'person from the hundred (an ancient administrative district) of West Derby', Lancashire, which in medieval times was often known as 'Derbyshire'

Darcy, Darcey, D'Arcy (i) 'person from (*de*) Arcy', northern France (based on a Gaulish personal name that may ultimately have meant 'bear'); (ii) from Irish Gaelic *Ó Dorchaidhe* 'descendant of the dark person' (from *dorcha* 'dark, gloomy') [Fitzwilliam Darcy ('Mr Darcy'), eventual hero of Jane Austen's *Pride and Prejudice* (1813)]

Dark, Darke 'person with dark hair or a dark complexion'

Darley 'person from Darley', Derbyshire ('glade frequented by deer')
— **Darley Arabian** one of the three Arab stallions that were the foundation of English thoroughbred bloodstock. He was bought in Aleppo, Syria, in 1714 by Thomas Darley, born 1664.

Darling from a medieval personal name and nickname meaning 'beloved one' [Alistair Darling, 1953–, British Labour politician; Sir Frank Fraser Darling, 1903–79, British ecologist; Grace Darling, 1815–42, British heroine, who rescued five shipwrecked sailors near the lighthouse kept by her father; Joe Darling, 1870–1946, Australian cricketer]
— **River Darling** a major river of eastern Australia. It was named in 1829 in honour of Sir Ralph Darling, 1775–1858, governor of New South Wales. He also gave his name to the **Darling Downs**, a hilly farming region in Queensland.

Darlington 'person from Darlington', County Durham ('settlement associated with Deornoth')

Darrow 'person from Darroch', Stirlingshire (perhaps 'oak tree') [Clarence Darrow, 1857–1938, US lawyer who was counsel for the defence in the Tennessee 'monkey' trial of 1925, in which a science teacher was tried for teaching the Darwinian theory of evolution]

Dart (i) 'maker of arrows'; (ii) 'person living by the River Dart', Devon ('river where oak trees grow') [Thurston Dart, 1921–71, British musician]

Darwin (i) *also* **Darwen** 'person from Darwen', Lancashire (from the river name *Derwent* ('river where oak trees grow')); (ii) from the Old English personal name *Dēorwine* ('dear friend') [Bernard Darwin, 1876–1961, British golfer and writer, grandson of Charles; Charles Darwin, 1809–82, British naturalist, co-originator (with Alfred Russel Wallace) of the concept of evolution by natural selection; Erasmus Darwin, 1731–1802, British physician and biologist, grandfather of Charles]
— **Darwin** the capital of Northern Territory, Australia. It was named in honour of Charles Darwin (see above).
— **Darwin College** a college of Cambridge University, founded in 1965 and named after the Darwin family (that of Charles Darwin), which owned some of the land on which the college was built
— **Darwinian** (a supporter) of Charles Darwin or Darwinian theory
— **Darwinian theory** the theory, first developed by Charles Darwin, that species of living things originate, evolve and survive through natural selection in response to environmental forces
— **Darwinism** (support for or advocacy of) Darwinian theory
— **Darwin's finches** a subfamily (Geospizinae) of finches of the Galapagos Islands on which Charles Darwin based his theory of evolution through

observation of their feeding habits and corresponding differences in beak structure

Das 'servant, votary' (Bengali *daš*)

Dash 'person living near an ash tree, or in a place with a name derived from Old English *æsc* "ash tree"'. The initial *d* is from the Anglo-Norman preposition *de* 'of, from'. [Jack Dash, 1906–89, British trade-union activist]

Dashwood 'person living in or near a wood made up of ash trees, or in a place named *Ashwood*'. The initial *d* is from the Anglo-Norman preposition *de* 'of, from'.

Da Silva 'person living in or near a wood' (Portuguese, 'of the wood')

Datta 'gift' (Hindi)

Daunay see **Dawney**

Davenport (i) 'person from Davenport', Cheshire (a place-name based on that of the River *Dane*, literally 'trickling one'); (ii) from Irish Gaelic *Ó Donndubhartaigh* 'descendant of *Donndubhartach*', literally 'brown-black nobleman' [Nigel Davenport, 1928–, British actor]

Davey see **Davy**

David from the Hebrew male personal name *David*, literally 'beloved'. See also **Daw**, **Day** [Elizabeth David, 1913–92, British food researcher and writer]

Davidson 'son of **David**' [Alan Davidson, 1924–2003, British diplomat, writer and food historian; Alan Davidson, 1929–, Australian cricketer; Jim Davidson, 1953–, British comedian; Randall Davidson (Lord Davidson), 1848–1930, British churchman, archbishop of Canterbury 1903–28]

Davie, **Davy** a Scottish pet-form of the male personal name *David* (see **David**) [Donald Davie, 1922–95, British poet and critic]

Davies 'son of *Davy*', a pet-form (common especially in Wales) of the male personal name *David* (see **David**) [Barry Davies, 1940–, British sports commentator; Freddie Davies, 1937–, British comedian; Sir Henry Walford Davies, 1869–1941, British composer; Jonathan Davies, 1962–, British rugby player; Laura Davies, 1963–, British golfer; Sir Peter Maxwell Davies, 1934–, British composer; Robertson Davies, 1913–95, Canadian novelist; Rupert Davies, 1916–76, British actor; W.H. Davies, 1871–1940, British poet; Windsor Davies, 1930–, British actor]

☆ The 6th commonest surname in Britain

D'Avigdor 'son of *Avigdor*', a Jewish personal name (from Hebrew *avi-Gedor* 'father of Gedor')

Davis 'son of **David**' [Sir Andrew Davis, 1944–, British conductor; Angela Davis, 1944–, US radical activist and academic; Bette Davis, 1908–89, US film actress; Carl Davis, 1936–, US composer; Sir Colin Davis, 1927–, British conductor; David Davis (real name William Eric Davis), 1908–96, BBC radio 'Children's Hour' presenter; David Davis, 1948–, British Conservative politician; Jefferson Davis, 1808–89, US statesman; Joe Davis, 1901–78, British snooker

player; John Davis, ?1550–1605, English navigator; Miles Davis, 1926–91, US jazz trumpeter; Skeeter Davis (original name Mary Frances Penick), 1931–, US country singer; Steve Davis, 1957–, British snooker player]

☆ The 7th commonest surname in the US (56th commonest in Britain)

— **Davis** a city in California, to the west of Sacramento. It was originally called Davisville, in honour of a prominent local farmer by the name of Jerome C. Davis. The name was changed to Davis in 1907. It is home to the University of California, Davis.

— **Davis Cup** an international men's tennis competition instituted in 1900 and named after the US tennis player and politician Dwight Filley Davis, 1879–1945, who donated the trophy

— **Davis Strait** a body of water separating Baffin Island, Canada, from Greenland, and forming the entrance to Baffin Bay. It was discovered in 1585 by the English navigator John Davis (see above).

Davison 'son of **David**' [Emily Davison, 1872–1913, British suffragette]

Davy, **Davey** (i) from the male personal name *Davy*, originally a medieval French variant of **David**; (ii) see **Davie** [Sir Humphry Davy, 1778–1829, British chemist and inventor of the Davy lamp, a safety lamp for miners]

Daw, **Dawe** (i) a pet-form of **David**; (ii) a nickname inspired by the jackdaw; (iii) from Irish Gaelic *Ó Deághaidh* 'descendant of *Deághadh*', perhaps literally 'good luck'. See also **Dow**, **O'Dea** [Margery Daw, who sets off the nursery rhyme 'See-saw, Margery Daw']

Dawes, **Daws** 'son of **Daw** (i)' [Charles G. Dawes, 1865–1951, US financier]

— **Dawes plan** a plan (1924) to reconstruct the German economy after World War I. It was named after Charles G. Dawes (see above), who helped to devise it.

Dawkins 'son of *Dawkin*', literally 'little **Daw** (i)' [Richard Dawkins, 1941–, British evolutionary biologist]

Dawney, **Dawnay**, **Daunay** 'person from (*de*) Aunou or Auney', northern France ('alder-grove'). See also **Delaney** (i)

Dawson 'son of **Daw** (i)' [Bertrand Dawson (Viscount Dawson of Penn), 1864–1945, physician to George V; Les Dawson, 1933–93, British comedian; Matt Dawson, 1972–, English rugby footballer; Peter Dawson, 1882–1961, Australian singer]

— **Castle Dawson** a village in Derry, Northern Ireland, named after the local landed family

— **Dawson** a town in the Yukon, in northwestern Canada. Founded in 1896, it was named in honour of the Canadian explorer George M. Dawson, 1849–1901.

Day, **Daye** (i) from the medieval personal name *Day(e)* or *Dey(e)*, which may go back ultimately to Old English *dæg* 'day', perhaps as a shortening of such names as *Dægberht* and *Dægmund*; (ii) a pet-form of **David**; (iii) from Irish Gaelic *Ó Deághaidh* (see **Daw**). See also **Diamond** [Cecil

Day-Lewis, 1904–72, British poet; Daniel Day-Lewis, 1957–, British actor, son of Cecil; Doris Day (original name Doris von Kappelhoff), 1924–, US film actress and singer; Robin Day, 1915–, British designer; Sir Robin Day, 1923–2000, British political interviewer]

— **Daytona Beach** a coastal city in northeastern Florida, USA, founded in 1870 by Mathias Day

— **Doris Day** (see above) rhyming slang for *gay* 'homosexual'

Dayton probably a different form of **Deighton**

— **Dayton** a city in southwestern Ohio, USA, established in 1796 and named after one of its founders, Jonathan Dayton, 1760–1824

Deadman, Dedman different forms of **Debenham**

Deakin, Deacon 'deacon' (an ordained member of the clergy, below priest in rank) [Alfred Deakin 1856–1919, Australian politician, prime minister 1903–04, 1905–08, 1909–10]

Deakins 'son of **Deakin**'

Dean, Deane (i) 'person living in a valley', or 'person from Dean or Deane' (e.g. East or West Dean, Sussex, or Deane, Hampshire) (in either case from Old English *denu* 'valley'); (ii) 'dean' (a senior member of the clergy) [Basil Dean, 1887–1978, British film producer; Christopher Dean 1958–, British skater; 'Dixie' Dean (William Ralph Dean) 1907–80, English footballer; James Dean 1931–55, US film actor]

Deans, Deanes 'son of **Dean**'

Dear, Deare, Deer (i) from a medieval nickname based either on the noun *dere* 'wild animal' or the adjective *dere* 'wild, fierce'; (ii) from the medieval personal name *Dere* (ultimately from Old English *deore* 'beloved')

Dearden 'person from Dearden', Lancashire ('valley frequented by wild animals'). See also **Durden** [Basil Dearden (original name Basil Dear), 1911–71, British film director]

Deares 'son of **Dear**'

Dearth from a medieval nickname apparently based on Middle English *derth* 'famine'

Death (i) 'death' (perhaps from the figure of Death as personified in medieval pageants); (ii) 'person who gathers or sells wood for fuel' (from Middle English *dethe* 'fuel, tinder'). See also **Deeth**

De Ath probably a deliberate respelling of **Death** (i), intended to distance the name from its original signification

Deaton, Deayton probably different forms of **Deighton** [Angus Deayton, 1956–, British comic actor and television quiz-show host]

Debenham 'person from Debenham', Suffolk ('homestead by the River Deben'). See also **Deadman**

— **Debenhams** a British department store, founded (as Debenham, Son and Freebody) in London in 1851 by William Debenham, 1824–96, his sons William and Frank and his son-in-law Clement Freebody

de Bono Italian, 'of the family of Bono' (see **Bono** (i)) [Edward de Bono, 1933–, British writer]

de Burgh, de Bourgh different forms of **Burke** [Lady Catherine de Bourgh, haughty aunt of Mr Darcy in Jane Austen's *Pride and Prejudice* (1813); Chris de Burgh (original name Christopher Davison; de Burgh was his mother's maiden name), 1948–, Irish singer/songwriter; Hubert de Burgh (earl of Kent), ?1175–1243, justiciar of England 1215–32]

Decourcy, de Courcy, de Courcey 'person from (*de*) Courcy', Normandy ('Curtius's settlement')

Dee (i) 'person who lives by the Dee', a river in Scotland and also in Cheshire (from the name of a Celtic river-goddess); (ii) from a Welsh nickname for someone with black hair or a dark complexion (from Welsh *dhu* 'black') [Jack Dee, 1961–, British comedian; John Dee, 1527–1608, English mathematician and astrologer; Kiki Dee (original name Pauline Matthews), 1947–, British singer/songwriter; Simon Dee (original name Nicholas Henty Dodd), 1935–, British television personality]

Deed probably from a medieval nickname for someone known for their brave deeds. See also **Dade**

Deeds, Deedes a different form of **Deed** [William Deedes (Lord Deedes), 1913–, British journalist and politician]

— *Mr Deeds Goes to Town* a film (1936), directed by Frank Capra, in which a poet (Gary Cooper) from small-town America inherits a fortune, goes to New York and bemuses the big city folks with his honesty. A dismal 2002 remake was called simply *Mr Deeds*.

Deeks, Deekes, Deakes probably different forms of **Dyke**

Deemer, Deamer, Demer 'one who pronounces the verdict, judge' (from Old English *demere* 'judge')

Deeping 'person from Deeping or Deeping Gate', Lincolnshire and Peterborough respectively ('deep place (in the Fens)') [Warwick Deeping, 1877–1950, British popular novelist]

Deeth a different form of **Death**

de Ferranti Italian, 'of the family of *Ferranti*', a different form of *Ferrando*, from a nickname for a grey-haired or grey-clad person (from Old French *ferrand* 'iron grey')

Defoe [Daniel Defoe, 1660–1731, English writer; his family name was *Foe* (a different form of **Vaux**), which he embellished with the 'French' prefix *de*]

de Freitas 'person who lives on a patch of stony ground' (Portuguese (*pedras*) *freitas* 'broken stones') [Phillip DeFreitas, 1966–, English cricketer]

de Havilland 'person from Haveland', Devon [Geoffrey De Havilland, 1882–1965, English aeronautical pioneer and aircraft designer; Olivia de Havilland, 1916–, British-born US film actress]

Deighton 'person from Deighton', Yorkshire ('farmstead surrounded by a ditch'). See also

Dayton, Deaton [Len Deighton, 1929–, British writer of espionage novels]

Dekker 'person who makes or repairs roofs' (from Middle Dutch *deckere*, from *decken* 'to cover') [Desmond Dekker (original name Desmond Dacres), 1941–2006, Jamaican ska and reggae singer/songwriter; Thomas Dekker, ?1570–1632, English dramatist]

Delamare, Delamar, de la Mare 'person from (*de*) La Mare', Normandy ('the pool'). See also **Dallimore, Dolamore** [Walter de la Mare, 1873–1956, British poet]

Delaney, Delany (i) 'person from (*de*) l'Aunou or l'Auney', northern France ('the alder-grove'). See also **Dawney, Dando**; (ii) from Irish Gaelic *Ó Dubhshláine* 'descendant of *Dubhshláine*', literally 'black challenge' [Frank Delaney, 1942–, Irish writer and broadcaster; Shelagh Delaney, 1939–, British playwright]

Delano an anglicization of the French surname *De la Noye*, literally 'person from La Noue or La Noë', the name of various places in France ('swampy place')

Delarue 'person who lives by a road or path' (French, from *de la rue* 'of the path')

de Launay a different form of **Delaney**

De La Warr from a medieval French nickname for a soldier or for a truculent person (from Old French *de la werre* 'of the war') [Thomas West, 3rd Baron De La Warr, 1577–1616 (the US state of Delaware was named after him)]

Delf, Delph 'person who lives by a quarry' (from Old English (*ge*)*delf* 'excavation'). See also **Delve**

de Lisle a different form of **Lisle**

Delius a Latinized form of the Low German name *Diel* or *Diehl*, a diminutive form derived from *Diederick, Theoderic*, source of English **Derrick** [Frederick Delius, 1862–1934, British composer]

Dell 'person who lives in a dell' [Edmund Dell, 1921–99, British Labour politician; Ethel M(ay) Dell, 1881–1939, British romantic novelist]
— **Dell Inc.** a US computer company founded in Austin, Texas in 1984 by Michael Dell, 1965–

Deller, Dellar 'person who lives in a dell' [Alfred Deller, 1912–79, British countertenor]

Delve a different form of **Delf**

Delves a different form of **Delve** [Sir John Henry ('Jock') Delves Broughton, 1888–1942, British settler in Kenya, tried for and acquitted of the murder of the Earl of Errol in 1941]

De Marney 'person from (*de*) Marigni', northern France ('Marinius's settlement')

Dempsey, Dempsy from Irish Gaelic *Ó Díomasaigh* and *Mac Díomasaigh*, respectively 'descendant and son of *Díomasach*', literally 'proud' [Jack Dempsey, 1895–1983, US boxer]

Dempster 'judge' (a feminine form of **Deemer**, but applied to men) [Nigel Dempster, 1941–2007, British gossip columnist]

Denaghy see **Dennehy**

Denby 'person from Denby', Derbyshire or Yorkshire ('farmstead of the Danes')

Dench 'Danish person' (Old English *denisc*). See also **Dennis** (ii) [Dame Judi Dench, 1934–, British actress]
— **Judi Dench** (see above) rhyming slang for *stench*

Denham 'person from Denham', the name of various places in England (mostly 'farm in the valley' [John Denham, 1615–59, English poet; John Denham, 1953–, British Labour politician; Maurice Denham, 1909–2002, British actor]

Denholm, Denholme 'person from Denholm', Borders ('area of dry land in a fen in a valley'), or 'person from Denholme', Yorkshire ('water meadow in a valley')

De Niro 'of the family of *Niro*', from southern Italian *niro, niru* 'black' [Robert De Niro, 1943–, US film actor]

Denis see **Dennis**

Denley probably 'person from Denley', an unidentified place in England ('woodland clearing in a valley')

Denman 'person who lives in a valley' (from Middle English *dene* 'valley' + *man*)

Dennehy, Denaghy different forms of **Donohue**

Dennet, Dennett 'little *Den*', a pet-form of *Denis* (see **Dennis** (i))

Denney, Denny (i) 'person from Denny', Cambridgeshire or Falkirk ('island valley'); (ii) a pet-form of *Denis* (see **Dennis** (i)) [Reginald Denny, 1891–1967, British film actor; Sandy Denny, 1947–78, British folk-rock singer]

Denning (i) 'person who lives in a valley' (from a derivative of Old English *denu* 'valley'); (ii) 'son of *Dynna*' (an Old English personal name); (iii) a different form of **Dineen** [Alfred Denning (Lord Denning), 1899–1999, British judge]

Dennis, Denis, Denness (i) from the male personal name *Denis* (via Old French and Latin from Greek *Dionysios*, literally 'follower of Dionysos', the Greek god of wine); (ii) a different form of **Dench**. See also **Neeson** (ii) [Mike Denness, 1940–, Scottish cricketer; C.J. Dennis, 1876–1938, Australian writer; Les Dennis (original name Leslie Heseltine), 1954–, British comedian; Nigel Dennis, 1912–, British writer]

Dennison, Denison (i) 'son of **Dennis**'; (ii) 'denizen' (a foreigner with rights of residence) (from Anglo-Norman *deinzein*) [Michael Denison, 1915–98, British actor]

Dent 'person from Dent', Yorkshire (from a local river-name of unknown origin) [J.M. Dent (Joseph Malaby Dent), 1849–1926, British publisher, originator of the 'Everyman's Library']

Denton 'person from Denton', the name of numerous places in England ('farmstead in a valley')

Denver 'person from Denver', Norfolk ('passage of the Danes') [John Denver (original name Henry John Deutschendorf, Jr.), 1943–97, US folk singer/songwriter; Karl Denver (original name

Angus Murdo McKenzie), 1931–98, British pop singer]

— **Denver** the capital city of Colorado, USA, in the north-central part of the state. It was founded in 1858, and named in honour of General James W. Denver, 1817–92, at that time governor of the territory.

Denzil, Denzill 'little *Denis*' (see **Dennis** (i))

De Quincey 'person from (*de*) Cuinchy (or from Quincy-sous-Sénart or Quincy-Voisins)', northern France [Thomas De Quincey, 1785–1859, British writer]

Derbyshire see **Darbyshire**

Derham, Dereham 'person from (East or West) Dereham', Norfolk ('deer enclosure') [Katie Derham, 1970–, British television journalist]

Derrick, Derek from the Old German personal name *Theodoric*, introduced into England via the Low Countries (a late 16th-century London hangman called Derick is the origin of the use of *derrick* for a hoisting apparatus) [Bo Derek (original name Mary Cathleen Collins), 1956–, US actress]

Derwent 'person who lives by the (river) Derwent', the name of various rivers in Cumbria, Derbyshire, Yorkshire and northeastern England ('river copiously lined with oak trees')

Desborough, Desbrow (i) 'person from Desborough', Buckinghamshire ('hill on which pennyroyal (a medicinal herb) grows'); (ii) 'person from Desborough', Northamptonshire ('Dēor's stronghold')

Desmond, Desmonde from Irish Gaelic *Ó Deasmhumhnaigh*, literally 'descendant of the man from southern Munster'

de Souza, d'Souza 'person from (*de*) Sousa', the name of various places in Portugal (see **Sousa**)

Despencer, Despenser 'dispenser (of provisions), butler, steward' (from Old French; see **Spencer**)

De Valera 'person from (*de*) Valera', the name of various places in Spain ('homestead of Valerius') [Eamon De Valera, 1882–1975, Irish statesman, prime minister 1932–48, 1951–54, 1957–59, president 1959–73]

Devane a different form of **Devine** (ii)

Devenish, Devonish 'person from Devon' (Old English *defenisc*)

de Vere 'person from (*de*) Ver', Normandy [Aubrey de Vere, 1814–1902, Irish poet]

Devereux, Devereaux 'person from (*de*) Evreux', Normandy (from the Celtic tribal name *Eburovices* 'dwellers on the River Eure'). See also **Everest** [Robert Devereux (2nd earl of Essex) 1566–1601, English soldier and courtier]

Devin a different form of **Devine** (ii)

Devine, Divine (i) from a medieval nickname for a person of great (or, ironically, little) excellence (from Middle English *devin* 'fine'); (ii) from Irish Gaelic *Ó Daimhín* 'descendant of *Daimhín*', literally 'little stag', or of *Ó Duibhín* 'descendant of

Duibhín', literally 'little black one'. See also **Devane, Devin** [George Devine, 1910–66, English stage director; Magenta Devine (original name Kim Taylor), ?1959–, British television presenter and journalist]

Devlin from Irish and Scottish Gaelic *Ó Dobhailéin* 'descendant of *Dobhailéan*', probably 'little unfortunate one' [Bernadette Devlin (married name McAliskey), 1947–, Northern Irish republican political activist]

Devonshire 'person from Devonshire'

Dew, Dewe (i) 'person from (*de*) Eu', northern France; (ii) 'person who lives by damp ground' (from Old English *deaw* 'dew'); (iii) from a medieval Welsh nickname for a fat person (from Welsh *tew* 'fat'). See also **Dewes**

Dewar (i) 'person from Dewar', Midlothian; (ii) 'official charged with the care of holy relics' (from Gaelic *deoradh* 'pilgrim, sojourner') [Donald Dewar, 1937–2000, British Labour politician, first minister of Scotland 1999–2000; Sir James Dewar, 1842–1923, British physicist]

— **Dewar flask** a double-walled silvered glass or metal flask with a vacuum between the walls, providing thermal insulation. It is named after its inventor James Dewar (see above).

— **John Dewar & Sons** a Scotch whisky blender, established in Perth by John Dewar, 1806–80, and much expanded in the 1880s by his sons John Dewar (Lord Forteviot), 1856–1929, and Sir Thomas Dewar, 1864–1930

Dewdney, Dudeney from the Old French personal name *Dieudonné*, literally 'gift of God'

Dewes, Dews different forms of **Dew**

Dewey, Dewy (i) from the Welsh male personal name *Dewi*, the Welsh form of **David**; (ii) perhaps 'person from Douai', northern France ('Dous's settlement') [John Dewey, 1859–1952, US philosopher; Melvil Dewey, 1851–1931, US librarian]

— **Dewey Decimal System** a system of classifying library books that divides them into two main classes, divided in turn into categories with three-digit numbers and subcategories with numbers after a decimal point. It was named after its deviser, Melvil Dewey (see above).

Dewhirst, Dewhurst 'person from Dewhurst', Lancashire (probably 'dewy wooded hill')

Dewsbury 'person from Dewsbury', Yorkshire ('Dewi's stronghold' (see **Dewey** (i)))

Dexter 'female dyer' (Old English *degestre*; see **Dyer**) [Colin Dexter, 1930–, English crime novelist; John Dexter, 1925–90, English stage director; Ted Dexter, 1935–, English cricketer]

Diamond (i) a different form (influenced by the name of the precious stone) of *Dayman*, literally 'servant of someone called **Day**'; (ii) 'diamond', an Anglicized form of a range of invented Jewish names derived (via German or Yiddish) from Middle High German *diemant* 'diamond' [Anne Diamond, 1954–, British journalist and broadcaster; Neil Diamond, 1941–, US singer/songwriter]

Diaz 'son of *Diego* or *Diago*', a Spanish personal name of uncertain origin [Cameron Diaz, 1972–, US actress]

Dibble a different form of **Theobald** [Officer Dibble, the fraught neighbourhood cop in the Hanna-Barbera animated cartoon series *Top Cat* (1962–63)]

Dibden 'person from Dibden', Hampshire ('deep valley')

Dick, Dicke a pet-form of the personal name **Richard**, common particularly in Scotland. See also **Dix, Dixon**

Dickens, Dickins 'son of *Dicken*', literally 'little **Dick**' [Charles Dickens, 1812–70, British novelist; Monica Dickens, 1915–92, British writer, great-granddaughter of Charles]

— **Dickens and Jones Ltd.** a British department store, founded in Oxford Street, London in 1790 by Thomas Dickens, died 1856, and William Smith. It moved to its Regent Street site in 1835, and in the 1890s, after Sir John Prichard Jones, 1841–1917, joined as a partner, it became known as Dickens and Jones. It closed down in 2006.

— **Dickensian** suggestive of the novels of Charles Dickens, especially in being either jolly and jovial or reminiscent of poverty-stricken Victorian Britain

— **what the dickens?** In this and similar phrases (e.g. 'the dickens of a row'), *dickens* is a euphemistic substitute for *devil*. The usage dates back at least to the end of the 16th century.

Dickenson, Dickinson 'son of *Dicken*' (see **Dickens**) [Emily Dickinson, 1830–86, US poet]

Dicks see **Dix**

Dickson see **Dixon**

Diefenbaker 'person from Diefenbach', the name of various places in the Rhineland and Württemberg, Germany [John Diefenbaker, 1895–1979, Canadian Progressive Conservative politician, prime minister 1957–63]

Digby 'person from Digby', Lincolnshire ('settlement by a dyke') [Sir Kenelm Digby, 1603–65, English author and diplomat]

Dill (i) 'grower or seller of the herb dill'; (ii) from a medieval nickname for a fool (from Middle English *dill, dull* 'foolish'); (iii) 'sawyer' (from Middle High German *dill* or *dille* '(floor)board')

Diller (i) 'person from Dill, Dille or Till', the name of various places in Germany; (ii) 'grower or seller of the herb dill'; (iii) 'sawyer' (from a derivative of Middle High German *dill* or *dille* '(floor)board') [Phyllis Diller (original name Phyllis Ada Driver), 1917–, US comedian]

Dilley perhaps a pet-form of an unrecorded Old English personal name *Dylla* [Graham Dilley, 1959–, English cricketer]

Dillinger (i) 'person from Drellingore', Kent ('hill-slope of Dylla's people'); (ii) 'person from Dillingen', Germany [John Dillinger, 1903–34, US bank robber]

Dillon (i) 'person from Dilwyn', Herefordshire ('shady or secret place'); (ii) from the Germanic personal name *Dillo*, brought into Britain by the Normans. Its ultimate source may have been the Germanic root *dīl* 'destroy'.; (iii) an Irish variant of the Anglo-Norman surname *de Leon*, literally 'person from Lyons' (see **Lyon** (iii)); (iv) from Irish Gaelic *Ó Duilleáin* 'descendant of *Duilleáin*', a personal name that was probably a different form of the nickname *Dallán* 'little blind man'; (v) a Jewish surname either from the Biblical place-name *Dilon* or from the Sephardic Jewish surname *de León*, literally 'person from León', Spain [Matt Dillon, 1964–, US film actor; Matt Dillon, fictional marshal of Dodge City, Kansas in the US television series *Gunsmoke* (1956–)]

— **Dillons** a former British chain of bookshops, founded in 1936 as a small bookshop near London University by Una Dillon

Dilnot perhaps from Middle English *dilnut* 'earth nut' (the tuber of the plant *Bunium flexuosum*)

Di Maggio 'of the family of (*di*) *Maggio*', Italian, literally 'May' (the name of the month; see **May**) [Joe Di Maggio, 1914–99, US baseball player]

Dimbleby 'person from Dembleby', Lincolnshire ('settlement near a ravine with a watercourse in it') [David Dimbleby, 1938–, broadcaster, and Jonathan Dimbleby, 1944–, broadcaster and journalist, both sons of Richard Dimbleby, 1913–65, British broadcaster]

Dimmock see **Dymock**

Din a shortened form from any of a range of Arabic names based on *dīn* 'religion' (e.g. *Salahuddin* 'righteousness of religion')

Dineen from Irish Gaelic *Ó Duinnín* 'descendant of *Duinnín*', a nickname derived from *donn* 'brown, dark'. See also **Denning** (iii), **Dunning** [Molly Dineen, 1959–, British documentary film-maker]

Dinsdale 'person from Dinsdale', Durham or Yorkshire ('corner of land belonging to **Deighton**')

Dinwoodie, Dinwiddie different forms of **Dunwoodie**

Dion, Dionne 'person from Dion or Dionne', the name of various places in France (probably 'sacred spring') [Céline Dion, 1968–, Canadian pop singer]

— **Dionne Quins** the five daughters (Annette, Cécile, Émilie, Marie and Yvonne) born on 28 May 1934 to Oliva and Elzire Dionne of Callander, Ontario, Canada

Disley 'person from Disley', Cheshire (a place-name of uncertain origin and meaning)

Disney 'person from (*de*) Isigny', Normany ('place associated with *Isina*', a Gaulish personal name) [Walter Elias ('Walt') Disney, 1901–66, US film producer and animator]

— **Disneyland** any of a range of theme parks created by the Walt Disney Company, based on characters and stories from the films produced by Walt Disney (see above). The first (1955) was in Anaheim, California.

Disraeli 'descendant of (*de*) *Israel*', from Italian, from the Hebrew male personal name *Yisrael* 'Fighter of God', bestowed in the Bible on Jacob [Benjamin Disraeli ('Dizzy'; 1st earl of Beaconsfield), 1804–81, British Conservative politician, prime minister 1868, 1874–80]

Divine see **Devine**

Dix, Dicks 'son of **Dick**' [Dorothy Dix (original name Elizabeth Meriwether Gilmer), 1870–1951, US journalist and pioneering agony aunt. In Australian rhyming slang, *Dorothy Dix* (or *Dorothy* for short) is a six (of the sort hit in cricket)]

Dixie, Dixey a pet-form of **Dick** [Phyllis Dixie, 19??, British striptease dancer]

Dixon, Dickson 'son of **Dick**' [Clarissa Dickson Wright, 1947–, British cook and television presenter; George Dixon, the sturdy and dependable British 'bobby' played by Jack Warner, initially in the film *The Blue Lamp* (1949) and subsequently (brought back to life) in the BBC television series *Dixon of Dock Green* (1955–76); Jim Dixon, the subversive university lecturer who is the eponymous hero of Kingsley Amis's novel *Lucky Jim* (1954)]

— **Dixons** a British chain of electrical retailers, founded by Charles Kalms in Southend in 1937 as a photographic studio. Its name was reputedly chosen from the telephone directory as being of a suitable length to fit on the shopfront. It ceased high street trading in 2006.

— **Mason-Dixon line** see **Mason**

Dobbs 'son of *Dobb*' (see **Dobson**) [Michael Dobbs, 1948–, British writer and broadcaster]

Dobie, Dobey, Dobbie 'little *Dobb*' (see **Dobson**)

Dobson 'son of *Dobb*', a pet-form of **Robert** [Anita Dobson, 1949–, British actress; Frank Dobson, 1888–1963, British sculptor; Frank Dobson, 1940–, British Labour politician]

— *Zuleika Dobson* a novel (1911) by Max Beerbohm, whose eponymous heroine, the beautiful niece of an Oxford don, cuts a romantic swathe through the male undergraduates of that university

Docherty a Scottish spelling of **Doherty** [Tommy Docherty, 1928–, Scottish football manager]

Docker 'person from Docker', Cumbria and Lancashire ('herdsman's hut in the valley') [Sir Bernard Docker, 1896–1978, British businessman, whose wife, Norah, Lady Docker, 1906–83, was noted in the 1950s for her extravagant lifestyle]

Dodd from the Old English male personal name *Dodda* or *Dudda*. It was probably originally a nickname, perhaps meaning 'short round person'. See also **Dadd**, **Dodson**, **Dutton** [Ken Dodd, 1927–, British comedian]

— **Ken Dodd** (see above) rhyming slang for *wad* ¦money' and (in the plural) *cods* 'testicles'

— **Tommy Dodd** originally, in the mid-19th century, rhyming slang for *odd*, referring to the 'odd' man in a coin-tossing game called 'odd man out', and also to the game itself. Subsequently the rhyme has been redeployed for *God, rod* 'gun' and *sod*, and also, in the plural, for *odds* (in the betting sense). The original choice of name seems to have been arbitrary.

Dodds 'son of **Dodd**'

Dodge (i) from the medieval male personal name *Dogge*, a pet-form of **Robert**; (ii) from a medieval nickname based on Middle English *dogge* 'dog'

— **Dodge** a marque of cars and trucks founded in the USA around the turn of the 20th century by the brothers John Francis Dodge and Horace Elgin Dodge. It was bought up in 1928 by the Chrysler Corporation.

— **Dodge City** a city in southern Kansas, USA, founded in 1864 by the US soldier Richard I. Dodge, 1827–95.

Dodgson 'son of **Dodge**' [Charles Lutwidge Dodgson, 1832–98, British mathematician who wrote children's stories under the name Lewis **Carroll**]

Dodson 'son of **Dodd**'

— **Dodson and Fogg** the attorneys acting on behalf of the plaintiff in the case of Bardell v. Pickwick, in Charles Dickens's *Pickwick Papers* (1837).

Dodsworth 'person from Dodworth', Yorkshire ('enclosure belonging to Dodda'; see **Dodd**)

Doggett from a medieval nickname meaning literally 'little dog', based on Middle English *dogge* 'dog', or meaning literally 'dog-head', from Middle English *dogge* 'dog' + *heved* 'head'

— **Doggett's coat and badge** the prize (a red coat with a large silver badge on one sleeve) for the winner of an annual rowing race on the River Thames in London. The race was founded in 1715 by the Irish actor Thomas Doggett, ?1670–1721, and was originally rowed by young, recently qualified Thames watermen. Since the mid-20th century it has been open to all amateur rowers.

Doherty from Irish Gaelic *Ó Dochartaigh* 'descendant of *Dochartaigh*', a nickname meaning 'unlucky' or 'hurtful'. The usual Scottish spelling is *Docherty*. [Pete Doherty, 1979–, British pop singer]

Dolamore, Dollamore different forms of **Dallimore**

Dolby a different form of **Dalby** [Ray Dolby, 1933–, US electrical engineer, originator of the Dolby system for reducing the hiss in sound reproduction]

Dolin (i) 'carpenter' (from a derivative of French *doler* 'to shave, plane'); (ii) 'person from Dolina', the name of various places in Belarus and the Ukraine [Anton Dolin (original name Sydney Francis Patrick Healey-Kay), 1904–83, British ballet dancer]

Dolittle, Doolittle from a medieval nickname applied to a lazy man [Eliza Doolittle, the flower seller in Bernard Shaw's *Pygmalion* (1913); Hilda Doolittle, 1886–1961, US poet; Dr Dolittle, the physician who had the ability to talk to animals, in the series of books written by Hugh Lofting from 1920]

D'Oliveira 'person who lives by an olive grove', from Portuguese *oliveira* 'olive grove'. See also **Oliveira** [Basil D'Oliveira, 1931–, South African-born English cricketer]

Doll from a medieval nickname applied to a foolish person (from Middle English *dolle* 'dull, foolish') [Sir Richard Doll, 1912–2005, British physiologist]

Dominguez 'son of *Domingo*', a Spanish male personal name, from Late Latin *Dominicus* 'of the Lord'

Don, Donn different forms of **Dunn**

Donachie a Scottish variant of **Donohue**

Donaghie, Donaghey, Donaghy different forms of **Donohue**

Donaghue, Donahue see **Donohue**

Donald from the Gaelic male personal name *Domhnall*, literally 'world-mighty'. See also **McConnell**, **McDonald**, **O'Donnell**

Donaldson 'son of **Donald**' [William Donaldson, 1935–2005, British author and rake]

Donat from the medieval male personal name *Donat* (from Latin *Donatus*, from the past participle of *donare* 'to give'; it declared the baptized infant to be a gift from (or to) God) [Robert Donat (original name Friedrich Robert Donath), 1905–58, British actor]

Donegan from Irish Gaelic *Ó Donnagáin* 'descendant of *Donnagáin*', literally 'little brown-haired man'. See also **Doonican, Duncan** [Lonnie Donegan, 1931–2002, British skiffle musician]

Donlevy, Donleavy see **Dunleavy**

Donne see **Dunn**

Donnelly, Donnelley from Irish Gaelic *Ó Donnghaile* 'descendant of *Donnghal*', literally 'brown(-haired)-valour' [Declan Donnelly, 1975–, British television presenter, the second half (with Anthony McPartlin) of 'Ant and Dec']

Donner (i) from a medieval German nickname for loud or bad-tempered individual (from Middle High German *doner* 'thunder'); (ii) an invented Jewish surname, from German *Donner* 'thunder' [Clive Donner, 1926–, British film director]

Donohoe a different form of **Donohue**

Donohue, Donoghue, Donoughue, Donahue, Donaghue from Irish Gaelic *Ó Donnchadha* 'descendant of *Donnchadh*', literally 'brown(-haired) warrior'. See also **Dennehy**, **Donachie, Donaghie, Duncan, McDonough, O'Donohue** [Bernard Donoughue (Lord Donoughue), 1934–, British writer and politician; Steve Donoghue, 1884–1945, British jockey]

Donovan, Donavan from Irish Gaelic *Ó Donndubháin* 'descendant of *Donndubhán*', literally 'dark brown one'. See also **O'Donovan** [Jason Donovan, 1968–, Australian actor and singer; Terence Donovan, 1936–96, British photographer]

Doolan, Doolin from Irish Gaelic *Ó Dubhlain* 'descendant of *Dubhfhlann*', literally 'dark red one'
— **Mick/Mickey Doolan** a different form of **Mick/Mickey Dooley**

Dooley, Dooly from Irish Gaelic *Ó Dubhlaoich* 'descendant of *Dubhlaoch*', literally 'black hero'

— **Mick/Mickey Dooley** in New Zealand slang, a Catholic, especially an Irish one; from its perception as a typically Irish name. It is also shortened to *Mickey Doo*.
— **'Tom Dooley'** a traditional ballad, beginning:
Hang down your head, Tom Dooley,
Hang down your head and cry,
You killed poor Laurie Foster
And you know you're bound to die

Doolittle see **Dolittle**

Doonican a different form of **Donegan** [Val Doonican, 1929–, Irish singer]

Doran (i) from Irish Gaelic *Ó Deoradháin* 'descendant of *Deoradhán*', literally 'little pilgrim' or 'little stranger'; (ii) a different form of **Durant**

Dorfman from a medieval German nickname for a villager or countryman (from Middle High German *dorfman* 'village man')

Dorgan from Irish Gaelic *Ó Dorcháin* 'descendant of *Dorchán*', literally 'little dark or gloomy person', or *Ó Deargáin* 'descendant of *Deargán*', literally 'little red(-haired) person'

Dorsey 'person from (*de*) Orsay', northern France ('Orcius's settlement') [Jimmy Dorsey, 1904–57, US jazz musician and bandleader; Tommy Dorsey, 1905–56, US bandleader, brother of Jimmy]

Doshi 'hawker selling cloth', Hindi, from Persian *dush* 'shoulder' (because the hawker would have carried the cloth over his shoulder)

Dos Santos from a Spanish and Portuguese name applied originally to a child born or baptized on All Saints' Day (from Spanish and Portuguese, literally 'of the saints')

Doubleday perhaps a combination of either a nickname *Doubel* 'twin' or the medieval personal name *Dobbel* (a pet-form of **Robert**) with Middle English *day* 'servant'

Dougall, Dougal, Dugall, Dugald from Gaelic *Dubhgall* 'dark stranger', used as a nickname for Scandinavians (especially dark-haired Danes, as opposed to fair-haired Norwegians). See also **Doyle, McDougall**

Dougan a different form of **Duggan** (i) [Derek Dougan, 1938–2007, Irish footballer]

Doughty from a medieval nickname for a brave or strong man. The name was applied in the Middle Ages particularly to a champion jouster. [C.M. Doughty, 1843–1926, British travel writer and poet]

Douglas, Douglass 'person from Douglas', the name of various places in Scotland and Ireland, but in this context specifically a locality to the south of Glasgow which is the traditional home of the Douglas clan ('dark stream') [Sir Alec Douglas-Home (Lord Home of the Hirsel), 1903–95, British Conservative politician, prime minister 1963–64; Lord Alfred Douglas, 1870–1945, British poet and friend of Oscar Wilde; Gavin Douglas, ?1471–1522, Scottish poet; Keith Douglas, 1920–44, British poet; Kirk Douglas (original name Issur Danielovitch, then

Isidore Demsky), 1916–, US actor; Michael Douglas, 1944–, US actor, son of Kirk; Norman Douglas, 1868–1952, British writer]

— **the Black Douglas** a nickname applied to Sir James Douglas, ?1286–1330, a Scottish grandee-cum-bandit who made a career of raiding and plundering the towns and villages of northern England in the early 14th century, and also subsequently to Sir William Douglas, died ?1392, illegitimate son of Archibald, third earl of Douglas

— **Castle Douglas** a town in Dumfries and Galloway, renamed in 1792 in honour of Sir William Douglas, a merchant who had bought the place (then a village) in 1789. Its previous name was Carlingwark.

— **Douglas fir** a North American species of large hemlock tree (*Pseudotsuga menziesii*), named after the Scottish naturalist-explorer David Douglas, 1798-1834, who first brought it to Europe

— **swing Douglas** in Australian slang, to swing an axe. The expression comes from the name of the Douglas Axe Manufacturing Co., East Douglas, Massachusetts, USA.

Dove (i) 'keeper of doves', or from a medieval nickname for a mild gentle person; (ii) a different form of **Duff**; (iii) a translation of Irish *Colmán* (see **Coleman**) [Jonathan Dove, 1959–, British composer]

Dow, Dowe (i) a different form of **Daw**; (ii) a different form of **Duff**

— **Dow's** a British port shipper in Portugal, founded in 1798 by Bruno da Silva. It took its name from James Ramsay Dow, who joined the firm in 1877.

— **Dow Jones Averages** a trademark for an index of the prices of selected industrial, transportation and utilities shares on the New York Stock Exchange that is based on a formula developed and periodically revised by Dow Jones & Company, Inc. This was founded in 1882 by two US journalists, Charles Dow and Edward Jones, and produced its first index in 1897.

Dowd from Irish Gaelic *Ó Dubhda* 'descendant of *Dubhda*', literally 'dark(-haired) person'. See also **O'Dowd**

Dowding 'son of *Dogod*', an Old English personal name probably derived from *dugan* 'to be of use' [Sir Hugh Dowding (Lord Dowding), 1882–1970, commander-in-chief of RAF Fighter Command during the Battle of Britain]

Dowland 'person from Dowland', Devon ('estate consisting of open land frequented by doves') [John Dowland, 1563–1626, English composer]

Down, Downe (i) 'person who lives on or among the downs' (from Old English *dūn* 'low hill'); (ii) a different form of **Dunn**

— **Down's syndrome** a term coined in the early 1960s for the genetic condition hitherto known as 'mongolism'. It commemorates the English physician J.L.H. Down, 1828–96, who studied the condition.

Downes 'son of **Dunn** (ii)' [Sir Edward Downes, 1924–, British conductor]

Downing 'son of **Dunn** (ii)'

— **Downing College** a college of Cambridge University, founded in 1800 under the terms of the will of Sir George Downing, 1684–1749, grandson of the Sir George after whom Downing Street was named (see below)

— **Downing Street** a street (a turning off Whitehall) in Westminster, named after the English statesman Sir George Downing, 1623–84. The British prime minister lives at Number 10, the chancellor of the exchequer at Number 11.

Downton 'person from Downton', the name of various places in Herefordshire, Shropshire and Wiltshire ('settlement on a hill'). See also **Dunton**

Dowson (i) 'son of Dow (i)'; (ii) 'son of *Dowce*', a medieval female personal name, literally 'sweet, pleasant' (from Old French *dolz, dous*) [Ernest Dowson, 1867–1900, British poet]

Doyle an Irish variant of **Dougall** [Sir Arthur Conan Doyle, 1859–1930, British writer, creator of the fictional detective Sherlock Holmes (see **Sherlock**); Roddy Doyle, 1958–, Irish novelist and playwright]

Doyley 'person from (*de*) Ouilly', the name of various places in Normandy ('Ollius's settlement') [Richard D'Oyley Carte, 1844–1901, British theatre impresario and manager]

— **doily** a sort of ornamental table napkin, said to have got its name from a type of light fabric sold by a certain Mr Doily at his draper's shop in the Strand, London in the late 17th century

Drabble perhaps from a diminutive form of the Old English personal name *Drabba*, of uncertain origin (possibly related to *drab* 'slatternly woman') [Margaret Drabble, 1939–, British novelist]

Drake (i) from the Old English name *Draca*, originally a nickname meaning literally 'snake' or 'dragon' (from Latin *draco* 'snake, monster'); (ii) from a medieval nickname for someone thought to resemble a duck (from Middle English *drake* 'male duck') [Charlie Drake (original name Charles Springall), 1925–2006, British comic actor and performer; Sir Francis Drake, ?1540–96, English navigator and admiral]

— **Drake Passage** a stretch of water between South America and the Antarctic Peninsula that separates the South Atlantic and South Pacific oceans. It is named after Sir Francis Drake (see above), although he did not actually pass through it in 1578 in his circumnavigation of the world (he used the Strait of Magellan, between the mainland and Tierra del Fuego).

— **Drake's Drum** a drum that once belonged to Sir Francis Drake and is now housed in Buckland Abbey (Drake's home) near Plymouth, Devon. According to legend it sounds when England is in peril.

— **Drake's Island** an island in Plymouth Sound, named (around 1590) in honour of Sir Francis Drake, who as a child had taken refuge there from Catholic persecution, and who anchored there in 1580 after his circumnavigation in *Golden Hind*

Draper 'draper' (i.e., originally, someone who made and sold woollen cloth)

Draycott 'person from Draycott', the name of numerous places in England ('building where drays (i.e. sledges for transporting loads over marshy ground) are kept')

Drayton 'person from Drayton', the name of numerous places in England ('estate where drays (see **Draycott**) are used') [Michael Drayton, 1563–1631, English poet]

Drennan from Irish Gaelic *Ó Draighneáin* 'descendant of *Draighneán*', literally 'little black-thorn'

Drew, Drewe (i) 'person from Dreux', the name of various places in France (from the Gaulish tribal name *Durocasses*), or 'person from (*de*) Rieux', the name of various places in France ('place by streams'); (ii) a shortened form of **Andrew**; (iii) from the Germanic personal name *Drogo* (perhaps related to Old Saxon (*gi*)*drog* 'ghost' or to Old High German *tragan* 'to carry'), which was brought into England by the Normans; (iv) from a medieval nickname meaning 'favourite, lover' (from Old French *dru*); (v) from Gaelic *Mac an Druaidh* 'son of the druid' and *Ó Druaidh* 'descendant of the druid'. See also **Drewett, Druce**

Drewett, Drewit, Druett, Druit 'little **Drew** (iii)'

Dreyfuss, Dreyfus 'person from *Trevis*', an old form of the name of the German city of Trier, altered by association with German *Dreifuss* 'tripod' [Richard Dreyfuss, 1947–, US actor]

Driburg, Driberg 'person from Driburg', North Rhineland-Westphalia, Germany (a place-name of uncertain origin) [Tom Driberg (Lord Bradwell), 1905–79, British Labour politician]

Dring 'young man' (from Old Norse *drengr*)

Drinkwater from a medieval nickname applied perhaps to someone too poor to afford beer or too miserly to spend money on it or, ironically, to someone overfond of beer or other strong drink [John Drinkwater, 1882–1937, British poet and dramatist]

Driscoll from Irish Gaelic *Ó hEidirsceóil* 'descendant of the messenger'. See also **O'Driscoll**

Driver 'person who drives horses or oxen pulling a cart or plough, or drives cattle along a path' [Minnie Driver (real name Amelia Driver), 1970–, British actress]

Dromgoole 'person from Dromgoole (present-day Dromgoolestown)', County Lough, Ireland (from the Gaelic place-name *Dromgabhail*)

Druce (i) 'son of **Drew** (ii–iii)'; (ii) a different form of **Drew** (i)

Drummond 'person from Drummond', a Scottish place-name derived from Gaelic *dromainn*, from *druim* 'ridge' [Hugh 'Bulldog' Drummond, fictional hero of mid-20th-century popular thrillers by 'Sapper' (H.C. McNeile); Sir Jack Drummond, 1891–52, British nutritional biochemist; Sir John Drummond, 1934–, British writer and broadcaster]

— **drummond** early 20th-century British slang for *knife*. Although modelled on the surname, it is in fact an alteration of *drum and*, a shortening of rhyming slang *drum and fife*.

— **Drummond light** an early alternative name for limelight (light produced by the burning of quick-lime), which was invented around 1825 by Captain T. Drummond of the Royal Engineers.

— **Phlox drummondii** a species of common garden plant with brightly coloured flowers, native to North America. It was named in honour of the Scottish botanist Thomas Drummond, 1780–1836.

Drury (i) via French from a Germanic male personal name meaning literally 'truth-power' or 'trust-power'; (ii) from a medieval French nick-name meaning 'love token' or 'sweetheart' (from Old French *druerie* 'love, friendship')

— **Drury Lane** a street in the West End of London, famous for its theatres, so named from Drury House, London home of the Drury family (a house on the site was occupied by Sir Robert Drury, ?1456–1535, and a 'Drury House' is recorded from the time of Sir William Drury, 1550–90)

Dryden 'person from Dryden', an unidentified place probably in Cumbria or Northumberland ('dry valley') [John Dryden, 1631–1700, British poet and dramatist]

Drysdale 'person from Dryfesdale', Dumfries and Galloway ('valley of the River Dryfe') [Cliff Drysdale, 1941–, South African tennis player]

d'Souza see **de Souza**

Dubois 'person who lives in a wood', French ('from the wood') [Blanche Dubois, a character in Tennessee Williams's play *A Streetcar named Desire* (1947)]

Duckenfield 'person from Duckenfield', Greater Manchester (probably 'ducks' pasture')

Duckett (i) from a medieval nickname meaning literally 'little duck', or one meaning literally 'duck-head'; (ii) from a medieval French nickname for someone thought to resemble an owl (from Old French *ducquet* 'owl'); (iii) 'little **Duke**'; (iv) 'little *Ducca*', an Old English personal name of unknown origin

Duckworth 'person from Duckworth Fold', in Bury, Lancashire (probably 'Ducca's enclosure')

— **Duckworth** a British publishing firm founded in 1898 by Gerald de l'Etang Duckworth, 1870–1937

— **Duckworth-Lewis** the shorthand name for a method of calculating the result of a rain-affected limited-overs cricket match, devised in the 1990s by the statistician Frank Duckworth and the math-ematician Tony Lewis

Duddleston 'person from Dudleston', Shrop-shire ('Duddel's or Doddel's settlement')

Dudeney see **Dewdney**

Dudley 'person from Dudley', West Midlands ('Dudda's glade') [Robert Dudley, earl of Leicester, ?1532–88, English courtier and favourite of Elizabeth I]

Duff from Gaelic *dubh* 'dark, black', used as a personal name and nickname meaning 'dark-haired or dark-complexioned man' or (meta-phorically) 'man with a dark temperament'. See also **Duggan, McDuff**

— **Ballyjamesduff** a village in Cavan, Ireland, created in 1831 and named in honour of General Sir James Duff, who commanded the Limerick district in the disturbances of 1798 (*Bally* means 'settlement, village')

— **Dufftown** a town in Moray, noted for whisky distilling. It was founded in 1817 by James Duff, 4th earl of Fife, 1776–1857, and named in his honour.

Duffy (i) from Irish Gaelic *Ó Dubhthaigh* 'descendant of *Dubhthach*', a nickname based on *dubh* 'dark, black'; (ii) from Gaelic *Mac Duibhshíthe* 'son of *Dubhshíth*', literally 'black peace'. See also **MacAfee**, **McDuffie**, **McPhee** [Maureen Duffy, 1933–, British writer]

Dugdale 'person from Dugdale (now Dagdale)', Staffordshire ('Ducca's valley')

Duggan (i) from Irish Gaelic *Ó Dubhagáin* 'descendant of *Dubhagán*', literally 'little little dark-haired or dark-complexioned person'. See also **Dougan**; (ii) from the Welsh name *Cadwgan* (see **Cadogan**)

Duguid probably 'do good', from a Scottish nickname for a well-intentioned person or (ironically) a do-gooder

Duke (i) 'person who works in a duke's household'; also, 'person who puts on airs, like a duke'; (ii) from the male personal name *Duke*, a shortened form of *Marmaduke*, perhaps from Irish Gaelic *mael Maedoc* 'devotee of *Maedoc*', a personal name meaning 'my little *Aodh*' (another personal name) [Neville Duke, 1922–2007, British fighter pilot and test pilot]

Dumont 'person who lives on or by a mountain', French ('from the mountain')

Dunant 'person who lives by a stream', French ('from the stream')

Dunbar 'person from Dunbar', near Edinburgh ('fort on the summit') [William Dunbar, ?1460–?1530, Scottish poet]

Duncan (i) from Gaelic *Duinnchinn*, a nickname meaning 'brown head'; (ii) a different form of **Donegan** [Iain Duncan Smith, 1954–, British Conservative politician; Isadora Duncan (original name Dora Angela Duncan), 1878–1927, US dancer]

Duncombe (i) 'person from Duncombe', the name of numerous places throughout England (probably 'hill valley'); (ii) a different form of **Duncan**

Dundas 'person from Dundas', near Edinburgh ('southern hill')

Dunham 'person from Dunham', the name of numerous places throughout England ('homestead on a hill')

Dunhill 'person from Dun Hill', Derbyshire, Dumfries and Galloway and Northumberland ('fortress hill')

— **Alfred Dunhill Ltd.** a British purveyor of luxury goods. Originally a saddlery business, Alfred Dunhill, 1872–1959, raised its profile in the 1890s by going into motoring accessories, and in 1907

moved into the area of tobacco, pipes, etc., for which the firm was best known in the 20th century.

Dunkley perhaps 'person from Dinckley', Lancashire ('fort in a woodland clearing')

Dunleavy, Dunlevy, Donleavy, Donlevy from Gaelic *Ó Duinnshléibhe* 'descendant of *Duinnsliabh*' and *Mac Duinnshléibhe* 'son of *Duinnsliabh*', a personal name meaning literally 'brown mountain'. See also **Dunlop**, **Livingston**, **McLay** [J.P. Donleavy, 1926–, US writer]

Dunlop (i) 'person from Dunlop', near Kilmarnock ('muddy fort'); (ii) from Irish Gaelic *Ó Lapáin* 'descendant of *Lapán*', a nickname meaning literally 'dirt, mud', applied to a poor man; (iii) a further anglicization of **Dunleavy** [John Boyd Dunlop, 1840–1921, Scottish inventor credited with inventing (1888) the pneumatic tyre ('Dunlop' tyres were first produced commercially in 1896 by a company that adopted his name)]

Dunn, Dunne, Donne (i) 'person from Dun', Tayside ('fort'); (ii) 'dark-haired or dark-complexioned person', from Gaelic *donn* 'dark, brown' or from Middle English *dunn* 'dark-coloured'. See also **Don**, **Down**, **Downes**, **Downing**, **Dunnett**, **Dunning**, **Gunn** (iii) [John Donne, 1572–1631, English poet; Clive Dunn, 1922–, British actor; Nell Dunn, 1936–, British playwright]

— **Dick Dunn** late 19th-century British rhyming slang for *sun*, based on the name of the bookmaker and well-known race-course personality Richard ('Dick') Dunn, died 1905

— **Dunn & Co.** a British menswear chain, founded in London in 1887 by George Arthur Dunn, 1865–1939

Dunnett (i) 'little **Dunn**'; (ii) 'person from Downhead or Donhead', in Somerset and Wiltshire respectively ('place at the end of the down') [Dorothy Dunnett (*née* Halliday), 1923–2001, British historical novelist]

Dunning (i) 'son of **Dunn**'; (ii) 'person from Dunning', Perthsire ('small fort'); (iii) an Irish variant of **Dineen**

Dunstable 'person from Dunstable', Bedfordshire ('Dunna's post') [John Dunstable, ?1390–1453, English composer]

Dunstan (i) from the English male personal name *Dunstan*, literally 'dark stone'; (ii) 'person from Dunstone', Devon ('Dunstan's settlement')

Dunton 'person from Dunton', the name of numerous places throughout England ('farmstead on a hill') [Theodore Watts-Dunton (born Watts), 1832–1914, British writer]

Dunwoodie, Dunwoody 'person from Dinwoodie', near Dumfries (perhaps 'forest of bushes'). See also **Dinwoodie** [Gwyneth Dunwoody, 1930–, British Labour politician; Richard Dunwoody, 1964–, British jockey]

Dupont 'person who lives by a bridge', French ('from the bridge')

Dupré, Dupree 'person who lives in a meadow', French ('from the meadow') [Jacqueline du Pré, 1945–87, British cellist]

Durant, Durrant from an Anglo-Norman nickname meaning 'steadfast' or 'obstinate' (ultimately from the present participle of Old French *durer* 'to endure')

Durbin, Durban 'son of (*de*) *Urbain*', a French personal name descended from Latin *Urbanus* (literally 'city-dweller') [Deanna Durbin (real name Edna Mae Durbin), 1921–, Canadian actress and singer]
— **Durban** a port and city in eastern South Africa, named in honour of Sir Benjamin D'Urban, 1777–1849, governor of Cape Colony from 1824

Durden a different form of **Dearden**

Durham 'person from Durham', County Durham ('island with a hill')

Durie 'person from Durie', Fife ('(place) by the stream') [Jo Durie, 1960–, British tennis player]

Durrell from an Anglo-Norman nickname meaning 'little hardy person' (ultimately from Old French *dur* 'hard') [Gerald Durrell, 1925–95, British naturalist and writer; Lawrence Durrell, 1912–90, British writer, brother of Gerald]

Dursley 'person from Dursley', Gloucestershire ('Deorsige's glade') [Vernon and Petunia Dursley, the 'muggle' uncle and aunt with whom the young magician stays in the 'Harry Potter' stories of J.K. Rowling]

Durward 'guardian of the door, door-keeper' [Quentin Durward, eponymous hero of the novel (1823) by Sir Walter Scott]

Dury (i) 'person from Dury', the name of a place in Devon and of several places in France ('(place) by the stream'); (ii) 'person who lives by a stream', French ('from the stream') [Ian Dury, 1942–2000, British rock singer and songwriter]

Dutton 'person from Dutton', the name of various places in England ('Dudda's settlement')

Duval, Duvall 'person who lives in a valley', French ('from the valley') [David Duval, 1971–, US golfer; Robert Duvall, 1931–, US actor]

Dwight from *Diot*, a pet-form of the female personal name **Dye** [Reginald Dwight, the real name of Elton **John**]

Dworkin from a pet-form of the Yiddish female personal name *Dvoyre*, from Hebrew *Devorah* (source of English *Deborah*), literally 'bee' [Andrea Dworkin, 1946–2005, US feminist]

Dwyer from Irish Gaelic Ó *Du(i)bhuidhir* 'descendant of *Du(i)bhuidhir*', a personal name meaning 'dark and sallow or tawny'. See also **Dyer, O'Dwyer**

Dyal, Dyall perhaps a different form of **Doyle** [Valentine Dyall, 1908–85, British actor]

Dye from a pet-form of the personal name **Dennis**, which in the Middle Ages was given to women. See also **Dyson, Tyson**

Dyer (i) 'a dyer of cloth'. See also **Dexter**; (ii) an Irish variant of **Dwyer** [Reginald Dyer, 1864–1927, general who commanded British forces at the so-called 'Amritsar Massacre' of 1919]

Dyke 'someone who lives by a ditch or dyke' or 'someone who digs or repairs ditches or dykes'. See also **Deeks** [Greg Dyke, 1947–, British television executive]

Dykes a different form of **Dyke**

Dylan from the Welsh male personal name *Dylan*, of uncertain origin [Bob Dylan (original name Robert Allen Zimmerman), 1941–, US singer and songwriter]

Dymock, Dymoke, Dimmock 'person from Dymock', Gloucestershire ('fort of pigs') [Charlotte ('Charlie') Dimmock, 1966–, British television gardener; Peter Dimmock, 1920–, British television executive]

Dyson 'son of **Dye**'. See also **Tyson** (ii) [Sir George Dyson, 1883–1964, British composer; James Dyson, 1947–, British inventor and entrepreneur]

E

Eade, Ede from the medieval female personal name *Eda*, a shortened form of *Edith* (literally 'prosperity battle'), or from the medieval male personal name *Ede*, a shortened form of **Adam**. See also **Edison, McKay** [James Chuter Ede, 1882–1965, British Labour politician]

Eagan see **Egan**

Eagar, Eager different forms of **Edgar**

Eagle (i) 'eagle', a nickname given to a man of lordly bearing or exceptionally sharp eyesight; (ii) 'person from Eagle', Lincolnshire ('oak wood'); (iii) 'person from Laigle', Normandy (probably 'the eagle') [Angela Eagle, 1961–, British Labour politician]

Eaglen 'little **Eagle**' [Jane Eaglen, 1960–, British opera singer]

Eagling a different form of **Eaglen** [Wayne Eagling, 1950–, Canadian-born ballet dancer]

Eakin a different form of **Higgins** (ii)

Earhart an anglicization of German *Ehrhardt* (literally 'honour brave') [Amelia Earhart, 1898–1937, US aviator]

Earl, Earle from a medieval nickname given to someone employed in a nobleman's household. See also **Harle** (ii)

Early, Earley (i) 'person from Earley (Arely, Earnley, etc.)', the name of various places in England ('wood or glade where eagles are seen'); (ii) from a medieval nickname meaning 'manly, noble'; (iii) a translation of Irish Gaelic *Ó Mocháin* 'descendant of *Mochán*' and other similar names, all derived ultimately from *moch* 'early'

Earnshaw 'person from Earnshaw', Lancashire ('Earn's nook of land' – *Earn* from an Old English personal name meaning literally 'eagle') [Catherine Earnshaw, her brother Hindley and her nephew Hareton, characters in Emily Brontë's *Wuthering Heights* (1847)]

East 'person living in the eastern part of a place, or to the east of a place, or coming from the east'

Easter (i) 'person from Easter', any of a group of villages in Essex whose name derives from Old English *eowestre* 'sheepfold'; (ii) 'person living to the east of a place'; (iii) from a medieval nickname for someone with some sort of personal connection with Easter (e.g. being born or baptized at that time)

Easterbrook 'person living by a brook to the east of a place'

Eastham 'person from Eastham', the name of various places in England ('eastern homestead' or 'eastern water-meadow') [George Eastham 1936–, British footballer]

Eastman (i) 'person living in the eastern part of a place, or to the east of a place, or coming from the east'; (ii) from the Old English male personal name *Ēastmond* (literally either 'grace protection' or 'east protection'). See also **Esmond** [George Eastman, 1854–1932, US inventor of the Kodak camera (1888)]

Easton 'person from Easton', the name of numerous places in England (mainly 'eastern farmstead')

Eastwood 'person from Eastwood', the name of numerous places in England (mainly 'eastern wood') [Clint Eastwood, 1930–, US actor]

Eaton, Eyton 'person from Eaton', the name of numerous places in England (either 'farmstead by a river' or 'farmstead on an island')

Eatwell 'person from Etwall', Derbyshire ('place by Ēata's stream')

Ebdon, Ebden 'person from Ebdon', North East Somerset (origin unknown)

Ebsen 'son of *Ebbe*', a Frisian diminutive variant of the Germanic personal name *Eggebrecht*, literally 'edge-bright' [Buddy Ebsen (original name Christian Rudolf Ebsen), 1908–2003, US actor]

Eccles, Ecles 'person from Eccles', the name of numerous places in England and Scotland ('church' – the name is a Celtic one, and refers to an ancient (Romano-British) church) [Eccles, a goofy teenager played by Spike Milligan in the 1950s BBC radio comedy series *The Goon Show*; Sir David Eccles, 1904–99, British Conservative politician; Sir John Eccles, 1903–97, Australian physiologist]

Eccleston, Ecclestone 'person from Eccleston', the name of numerous places in England ('farmstead by a church' – see **Eccles**) [Bernie Ecclestone, 1930–, British motor racing administrator; Christopher Eccleston, 1964–, British actor]

Eckersley 'person from Eckersley', Lancashire ('Ecgheard's glade' or 'Ecghere's glade')

Eckstein, Eckstine, Ekstein from a medieval German or Jewish nickname probably given to a trustworthy or reliable person, based on German *Eckstein* or Yiddish *ekshteyn* 'cornerstone' [Billy Eckstine, 1914–93, US singer]

Ecles see **Eccles**

Eddington, Edington 'person from Eddington', Berkshire ('Ēadgifu's settlement'), or 'person from Edington', the name of numerous places in northern England and Scotland ('settlement associated with Ida') [Sir Arthur Eddington, 1882–1944, British theoretical astronomer; Paul Eddington, 1927–95, British actor]

Eddison see **Edison**

Eddy, Eddie from the Middle English male personal name *Edwy*, from Old English *Ēadwīg*, literally 'wealth-war' [Mary Baker Eddy (*née* Baker), 1821–1910, US religious leader, founder of Christian Science; Nelson Eddy, 1901–67, US singer and actor]

Ede see **Eade**

Eden (i) 'person from Castle Eden or Eden Burn', County Durham (*Eden* from a local Celtic river-name meaning literally 'water'); (ii) from the Middle English male personal name *Edun*, from Old English *Ēadhūn*, literally 'wealth-bearcub'; (iii) from a Frisian name meaning 'son of *Ede*', literally 'prosperity, wealth'; (iv) from a Jewish name referring to the garden of Eden [Sir Anthony Eden (Earl of Avon), 1897–1977, British Conservative politician, prime minister 1955–57]
— **Anthony Eden** a black Homburg hat of a type regularly worn in the 1940s by Sir Anthony Eden (see above), who had a reputation as a stylish dresser

Edgar from the Old English male personal name *Ēdgār*, literally 'wealth-spear'. See also **Adair, Eagar** [David Edgar, 1948–, British author and playwright]

Edgerton see **Egerton**

Edgeworth 'person from Edgeworth', Gloucestershire and Lancashire ('enclosure on a hillside') [Maria Edgeworth, 1767–1849, Anglo-Irish writer]
— **Edgeworthstown** a village in County Longford, Ireland, named after the local Anglo-Irish landed family (of which Maria Edgeworth (see above) was a member)

Edington see **Eddington**

Edison, Eddison 'son of **Eade**' [Thomas Alva Edison, 1847–1931, US inventor of the light bulb and the gramophone]

Edmeades, Edmeads 'son of *Edmede*', from a medieval nickname for a self-effacing person (literally 'humble', from Old English *ēadmēde* 'easy mind')

Edmonds, Edmunds 'son of *Edmund*', a male personal name (from Old English *Ēadmund*, literally 'wealth protection') [Noel Edmonds, 1948–, British television presenter]

Edmondson, Edmundson 'son of *Edmund*' (see **Edmonds**)

Edrich from the medieval male personal name *Edrich* (from Old English *Ēadrīc*, literally 'wealth power'). See also **Etheridge** [Bill Edrich, 1916–86, English cricketer; John Edrich, 1937–, English cricketer, cousin of Bill]

Edwards, Edwardes 'son of *Edward*', a male personal name (from Old English *Ēadweard*, literally 'wealth guard') [Jimmy Edwards, 1920–88, British comedian; Jonathan Edwards, 1966–, British athlete; Percy Edwards, 1908–96, British animal imitator]

Egan, Eagan different forms of **Higgins** (ii) [Pierce Egan, 1772–1849, British writer]

Egerton, Edgerton 'person from Egerton', Kent and Cheshire (respectively 'settlement associated with Ecgheard' and (probably) 'Ecghere's settlement') [Egerton, the family name of the dukes of Sutherland]

Eggleston, Egglestone 'person from Eggleston(e)', County Durham and Yorkshire ('Ecgwulf's settlement')

Ehrlich, Erlich from a medieval German or Jewish nickname applied to a well respected person, based on German *ehrlich* or Yiddish *erlekh* 'honest'

Ehrmann an invented Jewish name, from German (literally 'honour man')

Eisenhower a partial anglicization of German *Eisenhauer* 'worker in iron, blacksmith' [Dwight D. Eisenhower, 1890–1969, US military commander and Republican politician, president 1953–61]

Ekstein see **Eckstein**

Elborough, Elbro, Elbrow 'person from Elborough', probably in Somerset ('Ella's grove')

Elder from a medieval nickname given to the older of two people with the same personal name [Mark Elder, 1947–, British conductor]

Elgar from the medieval male personal name *Alger*, which has a multiple Old English, Old Norse and Norman ancestry. The second syllable meant 'spear'; in most ancestor forms the first meant 'elf', but in some cases it meant 'noble' or 'old'. [Sir Edward Elgar, 1857–1934, British composer]
— **Elgarian** in the style of Edward Elgar's music, typically connoting ceremonial pomp or noble sadness

Elgin 'person from Elgin', Moray ('little Ireland')

Elias a different form of **Ellis**

Eliot, Eliott see **Elliot**

Elkin (i) 'little Elias' (see **Ellis**); (ii) 'son of *Elke*', a Yiddish female personal name

Elkington 'person from Elkington', Lincolnshire (perhaps 'Ēanlāc's or Ēalāc's farmstead') [Steve Elkington, 1962–, Australian golfer]

Elkins 'son of **Elkin** (i)'

Ellerman a different form of **Elman**

Ellice see **Ellis**

Ellington 'person from Ellington', the name of various places in England (mainly 'farmstead where eels are found' or 'farmstead associated with Ella or Eli') [Duke Ellington (original name Edward Kennedy Ellington), 1899–1974, US jazz pianist, composer and band leader]

Elliot, Elliott, Eliot, Eliott, Elyot (i) from the medieval personal name *Elyat* or *Elyt*, which was an amalgamation of two Old English personal names: the male name *Athelgēat* (literally 'noble Geat', a tribal name) and the female name *Athelgȳth* (literally 'noble battle'); (ii) 'little **Ellis**'; (iii) from the Gaelic surname *Elloch* or *Eloth* (literally 'person living by a bank', from Gaelic *eileach* 'dam, mound, bank') [Denholm Elliott, 1922–92, British

actor; George Eliot, pen-name of Mary Ann Evans, 1819–80, British novelist; Herb Elliott, 1938–, Australian athlete; T.S. Eliot, 1888–1965, Anglo-American poet and critic; Sir Thomas Elyot, ?1490–1546, English author and diplomat]
— **Billy Elliot** a film (2000) about an 11-year-old boy from Northeast England whose ambition is to be a ballet dancer

Ellis, Elliss, Ellice from the medieval personal name *Elis*, the English form of the biblical name *Elijah* (from Hebrew *Eliyahu* 'Jehovah is God'). The Greek form of the name was *Elias*, which also became an English surname. See also **Bliss** (iii), **Elkin, Elliot, Els, Elson** [Henry Havelock Ellis, 1859–1939, British psychologist; William Webb Ellis, see **Webb**]
— **Ellis Island** an island in upper New York Bay, near Manhattan, which from 1892 to 1954 served as a chief entry point for immigrants to the US It was named after a certain Samuel Ellis, who owned the island in the late 18th century
— **Ellis Park** a rugby ground in Johannesburg, South Africa, opened in 1928 and named after J.D. Ellis, who made land available for the site
— **Ellistown** a coal-mining village in Leicestershire, named in the 1870s after a local colliery owned by Joseph Joel Ellis
— **Gilbert and Ellice Islands** see **Gilbert**

Ellison, Ellisson 'son of **Ellis**'

Ellwood, Elwood (i) 'person from Ellwood', Gloucestershire (probably 'wood consisting of elder trees'); (ii) from the Old English personal name *Ælfweald*, literally 'elf-rule'. See also **Allwood**

Elman (i) 'seller of oil'. See also **Ellerman, Ulman**; (ii) a different form of **Hellman**

Elmer, Elmar different forms of **Aylmer** (i)

Elmore 'person from Elmore', Gloucestershire ('elm ridge')

Elphinston, Elphinstone 'person from Elphinston', Midlothian (probably based on an unknown Gaelic personal name (rather than 'elfin stone'))

Els from a Dutch and Low German form of the biblical name *Elijah* (see **Ellis**) [Ernie Els, 1969–, South African golfer]

Elson, Ellson (i) 'person from Elson', Hampshire and Shropshire ('Æthelswith's settlement' and 'Elli's settlement or hill' respectively); (ii) 'son of **Ellis**'; (iii) 'son of Elye', a Yiddish male personal name, from Hebrew *Eliyahu* (see **Ellis**)

Elston 'person from Elston', the name of various places in England, denoting a farmstead belonging to various named individuals (e.g. 'Eiláfr's farmstead' in Nottinghamshire)

Elsworth 'person from Elsworth', Cambridgeshire ('Elli's enclosure')

Elton 'person from Elton', the name of various places in England (mainly 'Elli's or Ella's farmstead') [Ben Elton, 1959–, British comedian and author; Charles Elton, 1900–91, British zoologist; Sir Geoffrey Elton (original name Gottfried Rudolf Ehrenberg), 1921–94, German-born British historian, uncle of Ben]

Elwell 'person from Elwell', Dorset (probably 'spring from which omens can be read')

Elwes from the Old French female personal name *Eloïse*, which was of Germanic origin, meaning literally 'healthy-wide' [Gervase Elwes, 1866–1921, British tenor]

Ely 'person from Ely', Cambridgeshire ('district where eels are found')

Emerson, Emmerson 'son of **Emery**' [Ralph Waldo Emerson, 1803–82, US essayist and poet; Roy Emerson, 1936–, Australian tennis player]
— **Emerson, Lake and Palmer** a British art-rock band popular in the 1970s. Its members were Keith Emerson, 1944–, Greg Lake, 1948–, and Carl Palmer, 1951–.

Emery a different form of **Amery** [Dick Emery, 1917–83, British comedian]

Emmanuel, Emanuel from the Hebrew personal name *Imanuel*, literally 'God is with us'. See also **Manilow** [David Emanuel, 1952–, and his wife Elizabeth Emanuel, 1953–, British fashion designers]

Emmett, Emmet, Emmitt, Emmott 'little *Emma*', a female personal name ultimately of Germanic origin (a shortened form of various compound names beginning with *ermin* 'entire, whole'), brought into England by the Normans

Empson, Emson 'son of **Emmett**' [Sir William Empson, 1906–84, British poet and critic]

Endecott, Endicott, Endacott 'person who lives at the end of the cottages'

Enderby, Endersby 'person from Enderby', Leicestershire and Lincolnshire ('Eindrithi's farmstead')

Engel (i) from a shortened form of various Germanic compound personal names (e.g. *Engelbert* and *Engelhard*) that begin with *Engel-*. The two main sources of that were *Angel* 'Angle' (the name of the Germanic people) and *Ingal*, an extended form of *Ing* (the name of a Germanic god).; (ii) from a German nickname applied to a very good or kind person (from German *Engel* 'angel'); (iii) an invented Jewish name based on German *Engel*

England 'English person'

English 'English person'. See also **Inglis** [Arthur English, 1919–95, British comedian; Sir David English, 1931–98, British newspaper editor]

Eno a name of uncertain origin (perhaps in some cases from French *Énos*, from the male personal name *Énos*, the French form of *Enoch*, a Biblical name ultimately from Hebrew *Chanoch*, literally 'experienced' or 'dedicated') [Brian Eno, 1948–, British musician and artist]
— **Eno's** a British proprietary formulation of aperient and antacid salts (in full *Eno's Fruit Salts*), based on sodium bicarbonate, introduced in the late 19th century by the Newcastle pharmacist J.C. Eno, ?1828–1915

Enright from Irish Gaelic *Indreachtach*, literally 'attacker' [D.J. Enright, 1920–2002, British poet]

Ensor 'person from Edensor', Derbyshire ('Éadin's sloping bank') [James Ensor, 1860–1949, Belgian painter of British parentage]

Entwistle, Entwhistle 'person from Entwisle', Lancashire ('fork of a river frequented by water hens or ducks')

Epstein, Eppstein 'person from Epstein or Eppstein', perhaps in Bavaria ('wild-boar stone') [Brian Epstein, 1934–67, manager of The Beatles; Sir Jacob Epstein, 1880–1959, US-born British sculptor]
— **Epstein-Barr virus** a virus believed to cause glandular fever and associated with Burkitt's lymphoma and some carcinomas. It is named after the British virologists M.A. Epstein, 1921–, and Y.M. Barr, 1932–.

Erickson 'son of *Erik*', a Scandinavian male personal name descended from Old Norse *Eiríkr*, literally 'always power'. *Erickson* is a partially anglicized spelling, but original Danish, Norwegian and Swedish forms, such as *Ericsson* and *Eriksen*, also occur as English surnames.

Erskine, Erskin 'person from Erskin', on the outskirts of Glasgow (perhaps 'green hill') [Ralph Erskine, 1914–2005, British architect; Thomas Erskine, 1750–1823, British advocate and politician]

Ervin, Ervine, Erving see **Irvine, Irving**

Erwin see **Irwin**

Esmond, Esmonde different forms of **Eastman** [Henry Esmond, the hero of W.M. Thackeray's novel *The History of Henry Esmond* (1852)]

Essex 'person from Essex' [David Essex (original name David Albert Cook), 1947–, British singer, songwriter and actor]

Etchells 'person from Etchells', the name of various places in northern England ('piece of land added to an estate')

Etheridge, Etherege, Ethridge different forms of **Edrich** [Sir George Etherege, ?1635–91, English dramatist]

Etherington a different form of **Hetherington**

Eubank, Eubanks, Ewbank 'person who lives by a bank of yew trees' [Chris Eubank, 1966–, British boxer]

Eustace from the male personal name *Eustace*, a descendant of Greek *Eustakhyos*, literally 'fruitful'. See also **Stacey** [Lizzie Eustace, the heroine of Anthony Trollope's novel *The Eustace Diamonds* (1873)]

Evangelista Italian, 'evangelist'

Evans, Evens 'son of *Iefan*', a Welsh male personal name equivalent to **John**. See also **Bevan, Ifens, Jeavon** [Sir Arthur Evans, 1851–1941, British archaeologist; Chris Evans, 1966–, British radio and television presenter; Petty Officer Edgar ('Taff') Evans RN, 1876–1912, British Antarctic explorer; Sir Edward Evan Evans-Pritchard, 1902–73, British anthropologist; Dame Edith Evans, 1888–1976, British actress; Sir Geraint Evans, 1922–92, Welsh baritone; Gil Evans (original name Ian Ernest Gilmore Green), 1912–88, Canadian-born US jazz musician; Godfrey Evans, 1920–99, English cricketer; Mary Ann Evans, the real name of George **Eliot**; Moss Evans, 1925–2002, British trade-union leader; Oliver Evans, 1755–1819, US engineer, inventor of the production line]

☆ The 9th commonest surname in Britain

— **Cape Evans** a rocky cape on the west side of Ross Island, Antarctica, named after Lieutenant (later Admiral) Edward Evans RN (see below), second-in-command of Captain Scott's second Antarctic expedition, which had its base camp there
— **Evans of the Broke** the sobriquet of Admiral Edward Evans RN (Lord Mountevans), 1881–1957, bestowed in recognition of his defeat of six German destroyers when in command of HMS *Broke* during the First World War (the ship was named after Rear-Admiral Sir Philip Broke, 1776–1841, who commanded the frigate *Shannon* in its celebrated duel with the US frigate *Chesapeake* in 1813)
— **Evansville** a city in southwestern Indiana, USA. Established in 1817, it was named in honour of Robert Morgan Evans, 1783–1844, one of its founders.
— **Mount Evans** a mountain in the Rockies, in north-central Colorado. It was so named in 1895 in honour of John Evans, 1814–97, governor of Colorado Territory 1862–65.
— *Why Didn't They Ask Evans?* a murder mystery novel (1934) by Agatha Christie. The title is the dying words of a man discovered at the foot of a cliff in the opening scene of the book.

Evelyn from the medieval female personal name *Aveline*, brought into English from French but ultimately of Germanic origin, from *Avo*, perhaps meaning literally 'wished for' [John Evelyn, 1620–1706, English diarist]

Evens see **Evans**

Everard a different form of **Everett**

Everest 'person from Evreux', Normandy (from the Celtic tribal name *Eburovices* 'dwellers on the River Eure'). See also **Devereux**
— **Mount Everest** the highest mountain in the world (8,848 m/29,028 ft), in the Himalayas, on the Nepal-China frontier. It was named in 1865 in honour of Sir George Everest, 1790–1866, Surveyor-General of India 1830–43.

Everett, Everitt, Everatt from a Germanic personal name meaning literally 'wild boar brave' [Kenny Everett (original name Maurice Cole), 1944–95, British comedian and disc jockey; Rupert Everett, 1959–, British actor]

Everley, Everly 'person from Everleigh', Wiltshire and Yorkshire ('glade frequented by wild boars')
— **Everly Brothers** a US close-harmony pop duo popular in the 1950s and early 1960s, consisting of Don Everly, 1937–, and his brother Phil, 1939–

Ewan, Ewen from the Gaelic male personal name *Eògann*, a Gaelic form of the Latin name *Eugenius* (from Greek *Eugenios*, literally 'well-born, noble'), source of the English name *Eugene*. See also **Cowan**, **Ewing**, **Keown**, **McEwan**, **Youens**

Ewart (i) 'person from Ewart', Northumberland ('place enclosed by rivers'); (ii) 'shepherd', from Middle English *eweherde* 'herder of ewes'. See also **Howard**; (iii) from the Norman form of the male personal name *Edward* (see **Edwards**) [Gavin Ewart, 1916–95, British poet]

Ewbank see **Eubank**

Ewens, **Ewings** 'son of **Ewan**'

Ewing a different form of **Ewan** [Ewing, Texan oil family (including J.R. Ewing, played by Larry Hagman) portrayed in the US television drama *Dallas* (1978–91); Winifred Ewing, 1929–, Scottish National Party politician]

Eyles see **Isles**

Eyre, **Eyer** see **Ayer** (i)

— **Eyre and Spottiswoode** a British publishing firm founded by George Edward Eyre and William Spottiswoode

— **Eyre Highway** a road in Australia, 1675 km/1041 miles long, linking South Australia and Western Australia. It was named after Edward John Eyre (see below).

— *Jane Eyre* a novel (1847) by Charlotte Brontë, following the romantic and other fortunes of the eponymous heroine, a penniless orphan

— **Lake Eyre** a large shallow salt lake in South Australia. It is named in honour of the British explorer and colonial administrator Edward John Eyre, 1815–1901, as is the **Eyre Peninsula** in South Australia.

F

Faber 'ironworker, blacksmith' (from Latin *faber* 'craftsman'). The name originated in the late Middle Ages as a deliberate translation of German *Schmidt* and Dutch *Smit*, both literally 'smith'. See also **Fèvre**, **Lefevre**

— **Faber and Faber** a British publishing firm founded in 1929 by Sir Geoffrey Faber, 1889–1961 (there was never a second Faber)

Fabian from the Latin personal name *Fabianus*, a derivative of the Roman family name *Fabius* that may have been based on Latin *fava* 'bean' [Robert Fabian, 1901–78, British detective on whose career the BBC television police drama *Fabian of the Yard* (1954–56) was based]

Fagan from Irish Gaelic *Ó Faodhagáin*, of uncertain origin and meaning [Michael Fagan, 1950–, intruder who broke into Buckingham Palace in 1982 and penetrated as far as the Queen's bedroom]

Faherty from Irish Gaelic *Ó Fathartaigh* 'descendant of *Fathartach*', a personal name of unknown origin and meaning

Fahy, Fay, Faye from Irish Gaelic *Ó Fathaigh* 'descendant of *Fathach*', a personal name probably based on Gaelic *fothadh* 'foundation'. See also **Foy**

Fair, Faire, Fayre, Fayer from a medieval nickname meaning 'beautiful'

Fairbairn probably from a northern and Scottish Middle English nickname meaning 'beautiful child' [Sir Nicholas Fairbairn, 1933–95, British Conservative politician]

Fairbank, Fairbanks 'person from Fairbank or Fairbanks', the name of various places (mostly 'beautiful bank or hill', but in some cases perhaps 'ferny bank') [Douglas Fairbanks (original name Douglas Elton Ullman), 1883–1939, and his son Douglas Fairbanks, Jr., 1909–2000, US film actors]

— **Fairbanks** a town in eastern Alaska, USA, founded in 1902 and named in honour of Charles W. Fairbanks, 1852–1918, a US senator who led a commission to settle a dispute about the Alaska boundary.

Fairbrother, Farebrother from a medieval nickname probably meaning either 'better-looking of two brothers' or 'brother of a good-looking person', or perhaps in some cases 'father's brother'

Fairburn, Fairburne 'person from Fairburn or Fairbourne', in Cleveland and Kent respectively ('stream where ferns grow'), or 'person from Fairburn', Highland region ('over the wet place', from Gaelic *far braoin*, but anglicized as if 'beautiful stream')

Fairchild from a medieval nickname meaning 'beautiful child'

Faircliff a different form of **Fairclough**

Faircloth a different form of **Fairclough**

Fairclough 'person living near a beautiful ravine' (see **Clough**) [Len Fairclough, a long-running (1960–83) character in the ITV soap opera *Coronation Street*]

Fairey (i) 'person from Fairy Farm or Fairyhall', both in Essex (*Fairy* perhaps 'pigsty'); (ii) from a medieval nickname meaning 'beautiful eye'

— **Fairey Aviation** a British aircraft company, producer of the biplane fighter-bomber Fairey Swordfish. It was founded in 1915 by the aircraft designer Sir Richard Fairey, 1887–1956.

Fairfax from a medieval nickname for someone with beautiful hair (Old English *feax* 'hair') [Thomas Fairfax (3rd Baron Fairfax of Cameron), 1612–71, English general, commander of the Parliamentary army during the Civil War]

Fairhurst 'person from Fairhurst', Lancashire ('beautiful wooded hill')

Fairlamb, Fairlem perhaps 'person from Farlam', Cumbria ('ferny glade'), later altered by folk etymology, as if 'beautiful lamb'; alternatively, perhaps genuinely 'beautiful lamb', as a term of affection and hence a nickname. See also **Farlam**

Fairley (i) see **Fairlie**; (ii) a different form of **Farley**

Fairlie, Fairley 'person from Fairlie', North Ayrshire ('beautiful glade') [Henry Fairlie, 1924–90, British journalist]

Faith from a medieval nickname for a loyal or trustworthy person [Adam Faith (original name Terence Nelhams-Wright), 1940–2003, British pop singer and actor]

Faithful, Faithfull from a medieval nickname for a loyal or trustworthy person [Marianne Faithfull, 1946–, British singer and actress]

Falcon 'falconer' (see also **Faulkner**); also, from a medieval nickname for someone thought to resemble a falcon

Falconer see **Faulkner**

Falkner see **Faulkner**

Fallon (i) a different form of **Fuller**; (ii) from Irish Gaelic *Ó Fallamhain* 'descendant of *Fallamhan*', a name meaning literally 'leader'

Fane, Fayne from a medieval nickname for a well-disposed person (from Old English *fægen* 'glad, willing'), or from a medieval Welsh nickname for a slim person (Welsh *fain*). See also **Vane** [Fane, family name of the earls of Westmorland]

Fanshaw, Fanshawe see **Featherstonehaugh**

Faraday from Irish Gaelic *Ó Fearadaigh* 'descendant of *Fearadach*', a personal name perhaps meaning literally 'man of the wood'. See also **Ferry** [Michael Faraday, 1791–1867, British chemist and physicist]
— **farad** the SI unit of electrical capacitance, named after Michael Faraday

Farebrother see **Fairbrother**

Fargo a different form of *Varga, Vargo*, from Hungarian, literally 'shoemaker'
— **Wells Fargo** see **Wells**

Farlam 'person from Farlam' (see **Fairlamb**)

Farley (i) *also* **Farleigh** 'person from Farley', the name of various places in England ('glade where ferns grow'). See also **Fairley, Fearnley**; (ii) from Irish Gaelic *Ó Fearghaile* (see **Farrell**)

Farman (i) from an Old Norse personal name denoting literally a seafarer or travelling trader, brought into English via French; (ii) 'itinerant trader, pedlar', from Middle English *fareman* 'traveller'

Farmer, Farmar 'farmer' (the term originally, in the Middle Ages, denoted a tax-collector; its modern agricultural meaning did not become established until the 17th century). See also **Fermor**

Farnes a different form of **Fern**

Farooq from the Muslim male personal name *Farooq*, derived from Arabic *fārūq* 'distinguisher' (that is, someone who can tell truth from falsehood)

Farquhar, Farquar from the Gaelic male personal name *Fearchar*, literally 'beloved man' [George Farquhar, 1678–1707, Irish dramatist]

Farquharson, Farquarson 'son of **Farquhar**'

Farr 'bull-keeper', or from a medieval nickname applied to someone considered as fierce as a bull (from Middle English *farre* 'bull') [Derek Farr, 1912–86, British actor; Tommy Farr, 1914–86, Welsh boxer]
— **Tommy Farr** (see above) rhyming slang for *bar* (of the drinking sort)

Farran a different form of **Farrant**

Farrand a different form of **Farrant**

Farrant (i) from the medieval personal name *Ferant* or *Ferrant*, which may have originated as an Old French variant of **Ferdinand**; (ii) from a medieval nickname meaning literally 'grey person' (from Old French *ferrant* 'grey', a derivative of *fer* 'iron'), applied to someone with grey hair or who dressed in grey. See also **Farren** (ii)

Farrar, Farrer, Farra 'ironworker, blacksmith' (from Old French *ferreor* or *ferour*, a derivative of *fer* 'iron'). See also **Farrier, Farrow, Ferrer, Ferrier, Varah** [Sir Anthony Farrar-Hockley, 1924–, British general; David Farrar, 1908–95, British actor; F.W. Farrar ('Dean Farrar'), 1831–1903, British churchman, philosopher and author]

Farrell, Farrel from Irish Gaelic *Ó Fearghail* 'descendant of *Fearghal*', a male personal name meaning literally 'man of valour'. See also **Ferrell, Frawley, Friel, O'Farrell** [J.G. Farrell, 1935–79, British novelist; J.T. Farrell, 1904–79, US novelist; M.J. Farrell, a pen-name of Mary Nesta Skrine, 1904–96, Irish author (see also Molly **Keane**)]

Farren, Farrin (i) apparently from the Middle English name *Farhyne*, which may mean literally 'oxherd', or alternatively could be a nickname meaning 'handsome servant'; (ii) a different form of **Farrant**; (iii) from Irish Gaelic *Ó Faracháin* 'descendant of *Farachán*', a personal name perhaps meaning literally 'lightning bolt'

Farrier a northern English variant of **Farrar**

Farrimond from *Faramund*, a Norman personal name of Germanic origin, probably meaning literally 'family protection'

Farrington 'person from Farrington', Somerset ('farmstead where ferns grow')

Farrow a different form of **Farrar** [Mia Farrow, 1945–, US actress]

Farson from a medieval nickname meaning literally 'beautiful son' [Daniel Farson, 1927–97, British journalist]

Farthing (i) 'someone who lives on a "farthing" of land' (i.e. a quarter of a larger area); (ii) from a medieval nickname based on *farthing* '1/4 penny', perhaps applied to someone who paid a farthing in rent; (iii) from the Old Norse male personal name *Farthegn*, literally 'voyaging warrior'

Fasey see **Phasey**

Fastolf from the Old Norse male personal name *Fastúlfr*, literally 'strong wolf' [Sir John Fastolf, 1380–1459, English soldier whose name was adapted by Shakespeare as 'Falstaff']

Faulds see **Folds**

Faulkes, Faulks, Fawlks, Fawkes, Faux from the Norman personal name *Faulques* or *Fauques*, which was derived from a Germanic nickname meaning literally 'falcon' [Guy Fawkes, 1570–1606, English Catholic conspirator; Sebastian Faulks, 1953–, British author; Wally Fawkes, 1924–, British cartoonist, creator of 'Flook']

Faulkner, Falconer, Falkner 'falconer' (i.e. someone who looked after, trained and flew a medieval noble's hunting falcons) [Charles Falconer (Lord Falconer), 1951–, British Labour politician; J. Meade Falkner, 1858–1932, British novelist; William Faulkner (originally Falkner), 1897–1962, US novelist]

Faux see **Faulkes**

Fawcett, Fawcitt 'person from Fawcett', Cumbria ('coloured slope, flowery slope') [Farrah Fawcett, 1946–, US actress; Dame Millicent Garret Fawcett, 1847–1929, British suffragette; Colonel Percy Fawcett, 1867–?1925, British archaeologist and explorer]

Fawkes, Fawlkes see **Faulkes**

Fay, Faye (i) 'person who lives near a beech wood', or 'person from Fay', the name of numerous places (variously spelled) in France with a name derived from Old French *faie* 'beech'; (ii) from a medieval nickname for someone believed to have supernatural associations or qualities (Middle English, from Old French *faie* 'fairy'), or for a faithful or loyal person (Middle English, from Old French *fei* 'loyalty, trust'); (iii) see **Fahy** [Alice Faye (original name Alice Jeane Leppert), 1915–98, US actress and singer]

Fayer, Fayre see **Fair**

Fazakerley, Fazackerly 'person from Fazakerley', Liverpool ('glade by the borderland')

Fearn a different form of **Fern**

Fearnley, Fernley 'person from Farnley', Yorkshire ('glade where ferns grow'). See also **Farley** [Duncan Fearnley, 1940–, British bat-maker; Hugh Fearnley-Whittingstall, 1965–, British writer and cook]

Fearon 'ironworker, blacksmith' (from Old French *ferron* 'blacksmith')

Feasey, Feazy, Feesey different forms of **Phasey**

Feather (i) 'trader in feathers', 'maker of down-filled quilts' or 'maker of quill pens'; (ii) from a medieval nickname for a 'lightweight' or 'feather-brained' person [Victor Feather (Lord Feather), 1908–76, British trade-union leader]

Featherstone, Featherston, Fetherston 'person from Featherstone', in Staffordshire, Northumberland and Yorkshire ('four-stones' – a prehistoric stone structure known technically as a 'tetralith')

Featherstonehaugh, Featherstonhaugh, Fetherstonhaugh, Fanshawe, Fanshaw 'person from Featherstonehaugh', Northumberland (now known simply as 'Featherstone') ('nook of land by the four-stones' – see **Featherstone**). *Featherstonehaugh* is traditionally pronounced as 'Fanshaw'.

Febvre see **Fèvre**

Feeney from Irish Gaelic *Ó Fiannaidhe* 'descendant of *Fiannaidhe*', a name meaning literally 'warrior' or 'champion', or *Ó Fidhne* 'descendant of *Fidhne*', a personal name probably derived from *fidh* 'tree, wood'

Feesey see **Feasey**

Fein, Feine from a medieval German nickname for a splendid or excellent person (Middle High German *fîn* 'fine'), or from a Jewish name for an excellent person (from German *fein* and Yiddish *fayn*)

Feinberg a Jewish name, from German, literally 'fine hill'

Feinman, Feynman a Jewish name (literally 'fine man') equivalent in meaning to **Fein** [Richard Feynman, 1918–88, US physicist]

Feinstein a Jewish name, from German, literally 'fine stone' [Elaine Feinstein, 1930–, British writer]

Feldman a Jewish name, from German, literally 'man who lives in open country' (i.e., cleared of forest, but not given over to agriculture) [Marty Feldman, 1933–82, British comedian; Morton Feldman, 1926–87, US composer]

Felix from a medieval personal name based on Latin *Fēlix* (literally 'lucky')

Fell (i) 'someone who lives in high country or on a bare rocky hillside' (from Middle English *fell*, from Old Norse *fjall* 'hill'). See also **Fells**; (ii) 'dealer in furs' (from Old English *fell* or (as a Jewish name) from German *Fell* or Yiddish *fel*, all meaning 'animal hide') [Dr John Fell, 1625–86, English scholar and churchman, subject of the well-known epigram beginning 'I do not love thee, Dr Fell. The reason why I cannot tell' by Thomas Brown, 1663–1704]

Fellow probably 'fellow member of a trade guild'

Fellows, Fellowes (i) 'son of **Fellow**'; (ii) a possible variant of **Fieldhouse** [Julian Fellowes (full name Julian Kitchener-Fellowes), 1949–, British actor and writer]

Fells a different form of **Fell** (i)

Felsted 'person from Felsted', Essex ('place in open land')

Felton 'person from Felton', the name of various places in England (mostly 'farmstead in open land')

Fenby 'person from Fenby', Lincolnshire ('farmstead in a fen or marsh') [Eric Fenby, 1906–97, British musician, amanuensis of Frederick Delius]

Fender (i) from a medieval nickname meaning 'defender'; (ii) 'flag-bearer', from a German name based on the term for the standard-bearer of a town guild [Percy Fender, 1892–1985, English cricketer]

Fenemore, Fennemore, Fenimore, Fennimore from a medieval nickname meaning literally 'fine love' (from Old French *fin amour*)

Feng 'person from Feng', the name of various places in China in former times

Fenn, Fenner 'person who lives in a fen or marsh'. See also **Vance, Vann, Venn**

Fennell, Fennel (i) 'fennel-grower' or 'fennel-seller'. See also **Funnell**; (ii) from Irish Gaelic *Ó Fionnghail* 'descendant of *Fionnghal*', a personal name meaning literally 'fair valour' [Frederick Fennell, 1914–2004, US conductor]

Fentiman 'household servant or retainer of **Fenton**'

Fenton (i) 'person from Fenton', the name of various places in England ('farmstead in marshland'); (ii) from Irish Gaelic *Ó Fionnachta* 'descendant of *Fionnachta*', a personal name meaning literally 'white snow'; (iii) an anglicization of various Jewish names (e.g. **Finkelstein**) that sound not dissimilar to *Fenton* [Fenton, a character in Shakespeare's *The Merry Wives of Windsor* (1597), suitor of Anne Page; James Fenton, 1949–, British writer and poet]

Fenwick, Fennick 'person from Fenwick', Northumberland, Strathclyde and Yorkshire ('dairy farm in fenland'). The name is pronounced as 'Fennick'. See also **Phenix** (ii)

— **Fenwick** a chain of department stores, founded in Newcastle in 1882 by John Fenwick, 1846–1905

Ferber from a different form of the German name *Färber*, literally 'dyer' [Edna Ferber, 1885–1968, US novelist and playwright]

Ferdinand from a Spanish personal name of Germanic origin probably meaning literally 'brave journey'. See also **Farrant**, **Fernandez**, **Hernandez** [Les Ferdinand, 1966–, English footballer; Rio Ferdinand, 1978–, English footballer, cousin of Les]

Fergus from the Gaelic personal name *Fearghus*, literally 'man of vigour'. See also **Ferris**

Ferguson, Fergusson 'son of **Fergus**' [Sir Alex Ferguson, 1941–, British football manager; Sarah Ferguson, 1959–, maiden name of Sarah, Duchess of York]

Fermor a different form of **Farmer** [Sir Patrick Leigh Fermor, 1915–, British author]

Fern, Fearn 'person who lives where there are many ferns'. See also **Farnes**, **Ferns**

Fernandez from a Spanish surname meaning 'son of **Ferdinand**'

Ferneyhough 'person from Ferneyhowe', Grampian ('hill-spur covered with ferns or with alders') [Brian Ferneyhough, 1943–, British composer]

Fernley see **Fearnley**

Ferns a different form of **Fern**

Ferranti see **de Ferranti**

Ferreira 'person who lives by a forge', a Portuguese surname derived ultimately from Latin *ferraria* 'forge'

Ferrell a different form of **Farrell**

Ferrer, Ferrar different forms of **Farrar**

Ferrers 'person from Ferrières', the name of various places in Normandy ('iron workings')

Ferrie see **Ferry** (i)

Ferrier a different form of **Farrar** [Kathleen Ferrier, 1912–53, British contralto]

Ferriman, Ferryman different forms of **Ferry** (i)

Ferris a different form of **Fergus**
— **Ferris wheel** a mainly American term for a giant revolving fairground wheel, commemorating its inventor, the US engineer G.W.G. Ferris, 1859–96

Ferry (i) *also* **Ferrey** *or* **Ferrie** 'ferryman', or 'someone who lives by a ferry crossing on a river'. See also **Ferrier, Ferriman**; (ii) from Irish Gaelic *Ó Fearadhaigh* 'descendant of *Fearadach*', a personal name probably based on *fear* 'man' [Bryan Ferry, 1945–, British musician]

Fetherston see **Featherstone**

Fetherstonhaugh see **Featherstonehaugh**

Feverel from a Middle English form of *February*, probably used as a nickname either for someone born in that month or for someone with a suitably frosty demeanour [Richard Feverel, the central character of George Meredith's novel *The Ordeal of Richard Feverel* (1859)]

Fèvre, Febvre 'ironworker, blacksmith', from Old French *fevre* (from Latin *faber* (see **Faber**); the (silent) *b* in *Febvre* was imported from the Latin word). See also **Lefevre**

Feynman see **Feinman**

Fiedler 'violinist, fiddle player', from German, or from Yiddish *fidler*. See also **Vidler** (ii) [Arthur Fiedler, 1894–1979, US conductor]

Field (i) 'person who lives in open country' (i.e., cleared of forest, but not given over to agriculture); (ii) an anglicization of the first element of various Jewish names beginning with *Feld-* (e.g. **Feldman**, *Feldstein* 'fieldstone') [Frank Field, 1942–, British Labour politician; John Field, 1782–1837, Irish pianist and composer; Sid Field, 1904–50, British comedian]
— **Marshall Field's** a department store in Chicago, Illinois. It had its origins in 1852 as P. Palmer & Co. Marshall Field, 1834–1906, joined the firm in 1856, and oversaw its rise to prominence. It closed down in 2006.

Fielder 'person who lives in open country' (see **Field** (i))

Fieldhouse 'person who lives in a house in open country' (see **Field** (i)). See also **Fellows**

Fielding 'person who lives in open country' (see **Field** (i)) [Fenella Fielding, 1934–, British actress; Henry Fielding, 1707–54, British novelist and dramatist]

Fields 'person who lives in open country' (see **Field** (i)) [Gracie Fields (original name Grace Stansfield), 1898–1979, British popular entertainer; W.C. Fields (original name William Claude Dukenfield), 1880–1946, US film actor]

Fiennes, Fienes 'person from Fiennes', in northern France. The name is standardly pronounced as 'Fines'. [Celia Fiennes, 1662–1741, English diarist; Ralph Fiennes, 1962–, British actor; Sir Ranulph Twisleton-Wykeham-Fiennes, 1944–, British explorer]

Fife see **Fyfe**

Figgis from a medieval nickname for a trustworthy person (from the Anglo-Norman form of Old French *fichais* 'loyal')

Figueiredo 'person from Figueiredo', the name of various places in Portugal and northwestern Spain ('fig-tree grove')

Figueroa 'person from Figueroa', the name of various places in northwestern Spain ('fig tree')

Filby, Filbey, Philby, Philbey 'person from Filby', Norfolk ('Fili's farmstead') [H. St John Philby, 1885–1960, British explorer and Arabist, father of Kim; Kim Philby (original name Harold Adrian Russell Philby), 1912–88, British intelligence officer and Soviet secret agent]

Filkins (i) 'person from Filkins', Oxfordshire ('settlement of Filica's people'); (ii) 'son of *Filkin*', a medieval personal name meaning literally 'little *Phil*', from **Philip**

Fillery from a medieval nickname derived from Anglo-Norman *fitz le rei* 'son of the king' (see also **Fitzroy**), probably applied mainly (and ironically) to an illegitimate person or to someone who put on quasi-royal airs

Fillmore a different form of **Phillimore**

Finch 'finch', the bird-name: probably either 'catcher or seller of finches' or, more likely, from a nickname applied to a stupid person (in medieval times, the finch was thought of as a foolish bird). See also **Fink** [Peter Finch, 1916–77, British actor]

Fincham 'person from Fincham', Norfolk ('homestead or enclosure frequented by finches')

Findlater, Finlater, Finlator 'person from Findlater', Grampian ('white hillside')
— **Findlater Wine** a firm of British wine merchants. The name is that of Alexander Findlater, 1797–1873, who founded the original business.

Findlay, Findley see **Finlay**

Finegan see **Finnegan**

Finger probably from a medieval nickname applied to someone with a peculiarity of the fingers (e.g. more or less than the usual number)

Fingerhut an invented Jewish name applied to a tailor (from the German and Yiddish word for a thimble, literally 'finger-hat')

Fink 'finch' (see **Finch**). As a native English name it represents a northern Middle English variant of *finch*, but it was also introduced into English from German and Yiddish.

Finkelstein an invented Jewish name (from Yiddish) meaning literally 'sparkle-stone' (see **Funke**)

Finlay, Finley, Findlay, Findley from the Gaelic personal name *Fionnlagh* (literally 'fair warrior'). See also **McKinley** [Dr Alan Finlay, fictional Scottish GP created by A.J. Cronin, central character of the BBC television medical drama *Dr Finlay's Casebook* (1962–71); Frank Finlay, 1926–, British actor; Gerald Finley, 1960–, Canadian baritone; Ian Finlay, 1925–, British artist and writer]

Finlayson 'son of **Finlay**'

Finnegan, Finegan, Finnigan, Finigan from Irish Gaelic *Ó Fionnagáin* 'descendant of *Fionnagán*', a personal name meaning 'little *Fionn*' (literally 'white' or 'fair-haired'). See also **McGinn** [Chris Finnegan, 1944–, British boxer; Judy Finnigan, 1948–, British television presenter]
— **Finnegans Wake** a prose work (1939) by James Joyce charting the night-time dream narrative of Humphrey Chimpden Earwicker. The character called Finnegan serves merely as its starting point. The original 'Finnegan's Wake' was a mid-19th-century street ballad.

Finney, Finnie 'person from Finney', Cheshire (probably 'place by the heap (of wood)') [Albert Finney, 1936–, British actor; Sir Tom Finney, 1922–, English footballer]

Finucane from Irish Gaelic *Ó Fionnmhacáin* 'descendant of *Fionnmhacán*', a personal name meaning literally 'little fair-haired son'

Firbank, Furbank 'person from Firbank', Cumbria ('wooded slope') [Ronald Firbank, 1886–1926, British novelist]

Firestone a literal translation of the German and Jewish surname *Feuerstein* (from German *Feuerstein* 'flint')
— **Firestone Tire and Rubber Co.** a US manufacturer of rubber tyres, established in Akron, Ohio in 1900 by Harvey Samuel Firestone, 1868–1938

Firkin either 'barrel-maker', or from a medieval nickname for a short stout man (from Middle English *ferdekyn, ferkyn* 'small barrel')

Firmin, Firman from the medieval personal name *Firmin*, literally 'firm of purpose, resolute' (via Old French from Latin *Firmīnus*)

First see **Furst**

Firth (i) 'person who lives in sparse woodland' (Old English *firhthe*); (ii) 'person who lives on barren land or mountain pasture' (Welsh *ffrith, ffridd*, a borrowing of Old English *firhthe*). See also **Frith** [Colin Firth, 1960–, British actor; J.R. Firth, 1890–1960, British linguistician]

Fischbein (i) 'seller of whalebone' (from Middle High German *(wal)vischbein* 'whalebone'); (ii) an invented Jewish name, apparently mainly from modern German *Fischbein*, literally 'fish-leg', one of a range of deliberately outlandish names imposed on Jews by non-Jewish officials when it became a legal requirement in central Europe to have a surname

Fischer the German form of **Fisher** [Bobby Fischer, 1943–, US chess player]

Fish, Fishe, Fysh 'fisherman', 'fishmonger' or from a medieval nickname applied to someone thought to resemble a fish. The native English version is from English *fish*; as a Jewish name, it comes from German *Fisch* or Yiddish *fish*. See also **Fisk** [Michael Fish, 1944–, British weather forecaster]

Fisher (i) 'fisherman'; (ii) 'person who lives near a fish-weir (an enclosure on a river where fish can be kept or easily caught; Middle English *fischgere*) on a river' [Andrew Fisher, 1862–1928, Scottish-born Australian statesman, prime minister 1908–09, 1910–13, 1914–15; John Fisher (Lord Fisher), 1841–1920, British admiral; Geoffrey Fisher (Lord Fisher), 1887–1972, British churchman, archbishop of Canterbury 1945–61; St John Fisher, ?1469–1535, English prelate, executed by Henry VIII]
— **Fisher-Price** a US firm of toy manufacturers, founded in 1930 by Herman Fisher and Irving Price. It is now a subsidiary of Mattel.

Fishlock 'someone living by a "fishlock" or fish-weir (see **Fisher** (ii))'

Fishman 'fisherman'

Fishwick 'person from Fishwick', Lancashire ('place where fish is traded')

Fisk, Fiske 'fisherman', 'fishmonger' or from a medieval nickname applied to someone thought to resemble a fish (from Old Norse *fiskr* 'fish')

Fitch origin uncertain: perhaps from Old French *fiche* 'stake', denoting someone whose job involved digging with a pointed implement, or (the traditional explanation) from a nickname based on English *fitch* 'polecat'

Fitchet, Fitchett 'little **Fitch**'

Fitt from a medieval nickname for a well-mannered person

Fitter (i) probably 'person who gets things ready for use'; (ii) 'furrier' (from Yiddish *futer* 'fur, fur coat')

Fitton (i) perhaps 'person from Fitton Hall', Cambridgeshire (*Fitton* 'settlement on a grassy riverbank'); (ii) from a medieval nickname based on Middle English *fitten* 'deceit'

Fitz- from the Anglo-Norman prefix *fiz-* or *fitz-* meaning 'son of', ultimately from Latin *filius* 'son'. Added to a personal name (e.g. *William*) it forms a surname (*Fitzwilliam*). It occurs in surnames of both English and Irish origin.

FitzAlan, Fitzalan 'son of **Allen**' [Fitzalan-Howard, family name of the dukes of Norfolk]

FitzGerald, Fitzgerald 'son of Gerald (see **Garrett**)' [Eddie ('Fitz') Fitzgerald, fictional criminal psychologist palyed by Robbie Coltrane in the Granada television drama series *Cracker* (1993–96); Edward Fitzgerald, 1809–83, British poet; Ella Fitzgerald, 1917–96, US jazz singer; F. Scott Fitzgerald, 1896–1940, US novelist; Garrett Fitzgerald, 1926–, Irish statesman, prime minister of Ireland 1981–82, 1982–87; G. F. Fitzgerald, 1851–1901, Irish physicist]

Fitzgibbon 'son of *Gibbon*', a medieval personal name meaning 'little *Gibb*', itself a shortened pet-form of **Gilbert** [Constantine Fitzgibbon, 1919–83, US-born biographer; Theodora Fitzgibbon, 1916–91, British food writer]

FitzHerbert, Fitzherbert 'son of **Herbert**' [Maria Anne Fitzherbert ('Mrs Fitzherbert'; *née* Smythe), 1756–1837, mistress of George IV]

Fitzpatrick 'son of **Patrick**', either from Gaelic *Mac Giolla Pádraig* (see **Kilpatrick**) or as an original Anglo-Norman formation (see **Fitz-**) [Sean Fitzpatrick, 1963–, New Zealand rugby player]

Fitzpayn 'son of **Paine**'

Fitzroy, FitzRoy 'son of the king' (from Anglo-Norman *fitz roy*, see also **Fillery**). The usual implication of the name is that its original bearer was illegitimate. [Henry Fitzroy (Duke of Grafton), 1663–90, illegitimate son of Charles II; Robert FitzRoy, 1805–65, British vice admiral and meteorologist, captain of HMS *Beagle* on the expedition in which Charles Darwin took part, descendant of Henry Fitzroy]
— **FitzRoy** a sea area in the eastern Atlantic, off the west coast of France. It was so named in 2002, in honour of Robert FitzRoy (see above), replacing the previous name *Finisterre*.

Fitzsimmons, Fitzsimons, Fitzsymons, Fitzsymonds 'son of **Simon**' [Bob Fitzsimmons, 1862–1917, British-born New Zealand boxer]

Fitzwalter, Fitzwater 'son of **Walter**'

Fitzwilliam 'son of **William**'
— **Fitzwilliam** a village in West Yorkshire, near Wakefield. It was founded at the beginning of the 20th century by the Fitzwilliam Hemsworth Colliery Company, on land formerly owned by Earl Fitzwilliam. It is the birthplace of the England cricketer Geoffrey Boycott, 1940–.

Flack, Flacke (i) perhaps 'turf-cutter' (from Middle English *flak* 'turf, sod'); (ii) probably 'person living near a stagnant pool' (from an unknown Middle Low German word) [Roberta Flack, 1939–, US popular singer]
— **Roberta Flack** (see above) Australian rhyming slang for *sack*, meaning both 'bed' (so, e.g., *hit the Roberta* 'go to bed') and 'dismissal'

Flagg 'person from Flagg', Derbyshire, or from any of various similarly named places in England, such as Flags, Nottinghamshire (all from either Old English *flage* or Old Norse *flaga* 'slab' or Old Norse *flag* 'turf, sod')

Flaherty, Flagherty from Irish Gaelic *Ó Flaithbheartaigh* (see **O'Flaherty**) [Robert Flaherty, 1884–1951, US documentary film-maker]

Flamstead, Flamstede, Flamsteed 'person from Flamstead', Hertfordshire ('place of refuge') [John Flamsteed, 1646–1719, English astronomer]

Flanagan, Flannagan, Flannigan from Irish Gaelic *Ó Flannagáin* 'descendant of *Flannagán*', a personal name meaning literally 'little red one' [Bud Flanagan (original name Chaim Reuven Weintrop), 1896–1968, British popular entertainer, member of the Crazy Gang, paired in a double act with Chesney Allen (Flanagan and Allen)]

Flanders 'person from Flanders'. See also **Fleming, Flinders** [Michael Flanders, 1922–75, British writer and performer of popular songs, paired in a double act with Donald Swann (Flanders and Swann); Moll Flanders, eponymous heroine of *The Fortunes and Misfortunes of the famous Moll Flanders* (1722) by Daniel Defoe]

Flannery from Irish Gaelic *Ó Flannghaile* 'descendant of *Flannghal*', a personal name meaning literally 'red valour'

Flash 'person who lives near a pool' (Middle English *flasshe* 'pool, marsh')

Flashman 'person who lives near a pool' (see **Flash**) [Flashman, the school bully in *Tom Brown's Schooldays* (1857) by Thomas Hughes, revived as the central character of a series of novels (1969–) by George Macdonald Fraser (who invented his first name, Harry)]

Flatt 'person who lives on an area of flat or low-lying land' [Lester Flatt, 1914–79, US singer-guitarist, pioneer of bluegrass music]

Flavell 'person from Flyford Flavell', Worcestershire (the village's original name, *Flyford*, is of uncertain origin (its first syllable may be from a personal name); *Flavell* is a Normanized version of *Flyford*)

Flax 'grower, seller or processer of flax' (the name is both a native English one and a Jewish one (from German *Flachs* 'flax'))

Flaxman 'grower, seller or processer of flax' [John Henry Flaxman, 1755–1826, British sculptor and illustrator]

Flecker (i) 'person who applies patches (to clothes, utensils, etc.)' (from a derivative of Middle High German *vleck(e)* 'patch'); (ii) 'person living in a place with a name containing the Middle High German element *vleck(e)* "place, spot"', often applied to a settlement in open land surrounded by woods [James Elroy Flecker, 1884–1915, British poet]

Fleet (i) 'person from Fleet', the name of various places in England, or 'person living near a pool, stream or estuary' (the ultimate source, in either case, is Old English *flēot* 'pool, stream, estuary, creek'); (ii) from a medieval nickname applied to a quick runner (from Middle English *flete* 'quick')

Fleetwood 'person from Fleetwood', an unidentified place ('wood by a pool or stream') [Leslie Fleetwood-Smith, 1908–71, Australian cricketer]
— **Fleetwood** a town and port in Lancashire, named after its founder, Sir Peter Hesketh Fleetwood, 1801–66, MP for Preston (his original surname was Hesketh; Fleetwood was his mother's maiden name, which he adopted in 1831)
— **Fleetwood Mac** a British-American blues/rock band founded in 1967. It is named after two of its original members, the drummer Mick Fleetwood, 1942–, and the bass guitarist John McVie, 1945–.

Fleming, Flemming, Flemyng 'Flemish person, person from Flanders'. See also **Flanders**, **Flinders** [Sir Alexander Fleming, 1881–1955, British microbiologist, discoverer of penicillin; Ian Fleming, 1908–64, British thriller writer, creator of James Bond; Peter Fleming, 1907–71, British journalist and travel writer, brother of Ian; Peter Fleming, 1955–, US tennis player; Renée Fleming, 1959–, US soprano]
— **Fleming's rules** a set of memory aids in which the fingers are used to recall the relative direction of the magnetic field, current and motion in an electric generator or motor. They were invented by the British physicist John Fleming, 1849–1945.

Fletcher 'arrowmaker' (Middle English, from Old French *flech(i)er*, from *fleche* 'arrow') [Cyril Fletcher, 1913–2005, British comedian and entertainer; Duncan Fletcher, 1948–, Zimbabwean cricket coach; Horace Fletcher, 1849-1919, US author and food faddist ('the Great Masticator'); John Fletcher, 1579–1625, English dramatist; Keith Fletcher, 1944–, English cricketer; Ken Fletcher, 1940–2006, Australian tennis player; Norman Stanley Fletcher ('Fletch'), the convict (played by Ronnie Barker) who was the central character in the BBC television sitcom *Porridge* (1974–77)]
— **Fletch** a comedy mystery film (1985), based on a novel (1974) by Gregory McDonald, 1937–, centring on the investigations of newspaper columnist Irwin Maurice Fletcher ('Fletch', played by Chevy Chase). It was followed by *Fletch Lives* (1989).
— **Fletcherism** the masticatory theories espoused by Horace Fletcher (see above), which involved chewing each mouthful of food 32 times
— **fletcherize** to chew (food) thoroughly, following the tenets of Fletcherism

Flett probably 'person from Flett', Orkneys ('strip of arable land')

Flinders a different form of **Flanders** [Matthew Flinders, 1774–1814, British explorer; Sir William

Matthew Flinders Petrie, 1853–1942, British Egyptologist, grandson of Matthew]
— **Flinders Range** a mountain chain in eastern South Australia. Like **Flinders Island**, an island off Tasmania, and the **Flinders** river in Queensland, it was named in honour of Matthew Flinders (see above), who surveyed the Australian coast.
— **'Little Polly Flinders'** an English nursery rhyme, first recorded in *c*.1805. It begins:
Little Polly Flinders
Sat among the cinders,
Warming her pretty little toes.
The name *Polly Flinders* has been used as rhyming slang for *cinders* and, singularized to *Polly Flinder*, for *window*.

Flinn see **Flynn**

Flint (i) either 'someone who lives in an area where there is much flint' or from a medieval nickname applied to a hard-hearted person; (ii) 'person from Flint', Clwyd ('place of hard rock'); (iii) an invented Jewish name derived from German *Flinte* 'shotgun' [Captain Flint, originator of the treasure map which drives the plot of Robert Louis Stevenson's *Treasure Island* (1883); Derek Flint, the James Bond-like spy (played by James Coburn) in the films *Our Man Flint* (1966) and *In Like Flint* (1967); F.S. Flint, 1885–1960, British poet; Rachel Heyhoe-Flint, 1939–, English cricketer; Sir William Russell Flint, 1880–1969, British painter]

Flintoff probably an alteration of *Flintcroft*, literally 'someone who lives by an enclosure containing many flints, or walled with flints' [Andrew Flintoff, 1977–, English cricketer]

Flockhart perhaps a different form of **Folkard** [Calista Flockhart, 1964–, US actress]

Flockton 'person from Flockton', Yorkshire ('Flóki's farmstead')

Flood, Floud, Fludd, Flude (i) 'person who lives by a small stream' (Old English *flōd(e)*); (ii) a different form of **Lloyd**; (iii) an English translation of various Irish names taken (correctly or otherwise) to be derived from Gaelic *tuile* 'flood' (see **Toole**) [Henry Flood, 1732–91, Irish politician; Robert Fludd, 1574–1637, English physician and follower of Paracelsus]

Florence (i) from the personal name (in the Middle Ages, male as well as female) *Florence*, brought into English from French and ultimately derived from Latin *flōrens* 'flowering'; (ii) 'person from Florence', Italy

Flores, Florez 'son of *Floro*', a medieval Spanish personal name meaning literally 'flower'

Florey, Flory (i) 'person from Fleury', the name of various places in northern France (based on the Gallo-Roman personal name *Florus*, ultimately from Latin *flōs* 'flower'); (ii) from the medieval personal name *Fleuri*, brought into English from French and ultimately derived from Latin *flōs* 'flower'; (iii) from a medieval nickname meaning 'blotchy' (from Old French *fluri*), perhaps alluding to the complexion [Sir Howard Florey (Lord Florey), 1898–1968, Australian pathologist who, with Ernst Chain, developed penicillin as an antibiotic; Paul Flory, 1910–85, US chemist]

Florio from the medieval Italian personal name *Florio*, ultimately from Latin *flōs* 'flower' [John Florio, 1553–1625, English lexicographer and translator]

Flower (i) from a medieval nickname commonly applied to a woman; (ii) 'miller' or 'flour merchant', or perhaps from a medieval nickname applied to a pale-faced person (etymologically, *flower* and *flour* are the same word); (iii) 'maker of arrows' (from Middle English *floere*, a derivative of *flo* 'arrow'); (iv) from Welsh *Llywarch*, a name of unknown origin and meaning

Flowers 'son of **Flower**'

Floyd an anglicization (approximating roughly to its Welsh pronunciation) of **Lloyd** [Keith Floyd, 1943–, British television cook; Ray Floyd, 1942–, US golfer]

Fluck from the Old Norse personal name *Flóki*, which itself was based on a nickname meaning 'outspoken' or 'enterprising' [Diana Fluck, the real name of Diana Dors, 1931–84, British actress; Peter Fluck, 1941–, British puppeteer, creator (with Roger Law) of the satirical television puppet show *Spitting Image* (1984–96)]

Fludd, Flude see **Flood**

Flynn, Flinn from Irish Gaelic *Ó Floinn* 'descendant of *Flann*', a personal name meaning literally 'red' or 'ruddy'. See also **Lynn, O'Flynn** [Errol Flynn, 1909–59, Australian-born US actor]
— **Errol Flynn** (see above) rhyming slang for *chin* and (in the plural) *bins* 'spectacles'
— **in like Flynn** quickly and decisively 'in', especially in the sense of sexual conquest. The phrase is commonly associated with Errol Flynn (see above), no slouch in that area, but chronological considerations favour a link with the US Democratic party 'boss' Edward J. Flynn, 1891–1953.

Foakes see **Foulkes**

Fogarty, Fogerty, Foggarty from the Irish Gaelic personal name *Fógartach*, a derivative of *fógartha* 'banished, outlawed'. See also **Gogarty, Howard**

Fogg from Middle English *fogge*, denoting grass left to grow long in the winter or grass that grows after the hay crop has been taken. The name refers to someone who lived by a patch of such grass or who grazed cattle on it. [Phileas Fogg, the circumnavigator in Jules Verne's *Around the World in Eighty Days* (1873)]
— **Dodson and Fogg** see **Dodson**

Fokes see **Foulkes**

Folds, Foldes, Foulds, Fouldes, Fowlds, Faulds 'person who lives near an animal enclosure or fold' or 'person who works in an animal enclosure' [Andrew Faulds, 1923–2000, British actor and Labour politician; Derek Fowlds, 1937–, British actor; John Foulds, 1880–1939, British composer]

Foley (i) from Irish Gaelic *Ó Foghladha* 'descendant of *Foghlaidh*', a nickname meaning literally 'pirate'; (ii) a 'translation' of Gaelic *Mac Searraigh*, which means literally 'son of foal' (see

McSharry) [John Henry Foley, 1818–74, Irish-born British sculptor]
— **Foley** a jargon term used in the film industry for an artificially created sound effect. It commemorates the US expert Jack Foley, 1891–1967, who established many of the modern techniques for producing these.

Folger a different form of **Fulcher**

Folkard from the medieval male personal name Folchard, brought into England by the Normans but ultimately of Germanic origin, meaning literally 'people-brave'. See also **Flockhart**

Folkes, Folks see **Foulkes**

Follett, Follitt from a medieval nickname for an idiotic or weak-minded person, literally 'little fool' [Barbara Follett (*née* Hubbard), 1942–, British Labour politician, wife of Ken; Ken Follett, 1949–, British author]

Fonda (i) perhaps 'person who lives by an inn' (Spanish *fonda*); (ii) 'person who lives near a mine' (Dutch *fonda*) [Henry Fonda, 1905–82, US actor; Jane Fonda, 1937–, US actress and political activist, daughter of Henry; Peter Fonda, 1939–, US actor and director, son of Henry]

Fontaine, Fonteyn, Fonteyne 'person who lives near a spring or well' (Old French *fontane*) [Joan Fontaine (original name Joan de Beauvoir de Havilland; sister of Olivia de Havilland), 1917–, Japan-born (of British parents) US film actress; Dame Margot Fonteyn (original name Margaret Hookham), 1919–91, British ballet dancer]

Fookes, Fooks different forms of **Foulkes**

Foord see **Ford**

Foot, Foote from a medieval nickname for someone with a deformed foot or other pedal peculiarity [Sir Hugh Foot (Lord Caradon), 1907–90, British diplomat, brother of Michael; Michael Foot, 1913–, British Labour politician and writer; Paul Foot, 1937–2004, British journalist, son of Hugh]

Forbes (i) 'person from Forbes', near Aberdeen ('place by the field'); (ii) from Gaelic *Mac Fearbhisigh* 'son of *Firbhsigh*', a personal name meaning literally 'man of prosperity' [Bryan Forbes, 1926–, British film director and author; Malcolm Forbes, 1907–90, US millionaire, publisher of *Forbes Magazine*, a magazine founded in 1917 and featuring the lives of the very wealthy]

Ford, Forde, Foord (i) 'person who lives near a ford'; (ii) a 'translation' of various Gaelic surnames of which the last syllable was erroneously interpreted as *áth* 'ford' [Anna Ford, 1943–, British television newsreader; Ford Madox Ford (original name Ford Hermann Hueffer), 1873–1939, British novelist; Gerald R. Ford (original name Leslie King), 1913–2006, US Republican politician, president 1974–77; Glenn Ford (original name Gwyllyn Samuel Newton Ford), 1916–2006, Canadian-born US film actor; Harrison Ford, 1942–, US film actor; Henry Ford, 1863–1947, US industrialist; John Ford, 1586–?1640, English dramatist; John Ford (orig-

inal name John Martin Feeney), 1895–1983, US film director]
— **Betty Ford Center** a drug and alcohol rehabilitation centre in Rancho Mirage, California founded in 1982 by Betty Ford (*née* Bloomer), 1918–, wife of Gerald Ford (see above)
— **Ford Foundation** a US-based charitable foundation established in 1936 by Edsel Ford, 1893–1943, son of Henry Ford (see above)
— **Ford Motor Company** a US-based car manufacturer, founded in 1903 by Henry Ford

Fordham 'person from Fordham', the name of various places in England ('homestead by a ford')

Fordyce 'person from Fordyce', near Banff ('southern field') [Keith Fordyce, 1928–, British disc jockey]

Foreman see **Forman**

Forest, Forester see **Forrest, Forrester**

Forgan (i) 'person from Forgan', Fife (perhaps 'ground where pigs are kept'); (ii) from Irish Gaelic *Ó Mhurcháin* (see **Morgan**)

Forman, Foreman (i) 'leader of a group'; (ii) 'swineherd' (Middle English *foreman*, based ultimately on Old English *fōr* 'pig'); (iii) 'driver of a cart' (Czech *forman*) [George Foreman, 1949–, US boxer]

Formby 'person from Formby', Merseyside ('Forni's farmstead', or possibly 'old farmstead') [George Formby (original name George Hoy Booth), 1904–61, British popular entertainer]

Forrest, Forest 'person who lives in or near a royal forest' or 'person who is employed in a royal forest'. See also **Forster, Foster** [Tom Forrest, long-running gamekeeper character in the BBC radio soap opera *The Archers*]

Forrester, Forester different forms of **Forrest** [C.S. Forester (original name Cecil Lewis Troughton Smith), 1899–1966, British author]

Forsdyke, Forsdike different forms of **Fosdyke**

Forshaw 'person from Forshaw', a place (no longer existent) in Lancashire ('four-oak wood')

Forster (i) 'person who lives in or near a royal forest' or 'person who is employed in a royal forest'. See also **Forrest, Foster**; (ii) 'scissor-maker' (Old French *forcetier*); (iii) 'woodworker' (Old French *fust(r)ier*); (iv) a Jewish name derived from German *Forst* 'forest' [E.M. Forster, 1879–1970, British novelist; Margaret Forster, 1938–, British novelist; W.E. Forster, 1818–86, British Liberal politician, architect of the 1870 Education Act (often known as the Forster Education Act)]

Forsyth, Forsythe from Gaelic *Fearsithe*, a personal name meaning literally 'man of peace' [Bruce Forsyth (original name Bruce Forsyth-Johnson), 1928–, British popular entertainer; Frederick Forsyth, 1938–, British author]
— **forsythia** any of a genus of shrubs that produce yellow flowers in spring. They were named in honour of the British botanist William Forsyth, 1737-1804.

Fort (i) from a medieval nickname for a strong or brave person (from Old French); (ii) 'person who lives by or in a fortress' or 'person employed in a fortress' [Charles H. Fort, 1874–1932, US student of the paranormal]
— *Fortean Times* a journal devoted to the paranormal, founded in 1973 by Robert Rickard. Its name commemorates Charles H. Fort (see above).

Forte (i) from the Italian personal name *Forte*, meaning literally 'strong'; (ii) a different form of **Fort** [Charles Forte (Lord Forte), 1908–2007, British businessman]

Fortescue from a medieval nickname applied to a brave warrior (from Old French, literally 'strong shield')

Fortnum, Fortnam from a medieval nickname applied to a strong man of limited brain power (from Old French, literally 'strong little donkey')
— **Fortnum and Mason** an exclusive grocer's shop in Piccadilly, London. It was founded in 1707 by William Fortnum, a footman in the household of Queen Anne, and his grocer friend Hugh Mason.

Fortune (i) from a medieval nickname applied to a gambler; (ii) 'person from Fortune', Lothian ('enclosure where pigs are kept') [John Fortune, 1939–, British scriptwriter and actor]

Forward, Forwood 'swineherd' (based ultimately on Old English *fōr* 'pig')

Fosbury perhaps an anglicization of Norwegian *Fosberg* 'person living at a farm called *Fossberg*' ('waterfall mountain')
— **Fosbury flop** a high-jump technique that involves first clearing the bar with the back of the shoulders, which are then followed by the rest of the arched body. It is named after the US athlete Richard ('Dick') Fosbury, 1947–, who introduced it.

Fosdyke 'person from Fosdyke', Lincolnshire ('Fōt's ditch'). See also **Forsdyke**

Foskett 'person from any of a number of English places (e.g. Foxcott in Hampshire) with a name that means literally "fox's burrow"'

Fosse, Foss 'person from a place taking its name from either Old English *foss* or Old French *fosse*, both meaning "ditch" and both ultimately from Latin *fossa*'. Among other possibilities, the name could refer to the Fosse Way, a Roman road in England. See also **Voss** [Bob Fosse, 1927–87, US dancer, choreographer and director]

Foster (i) a different form of **Forster**; (ii) perhaps an anglicization of the Jewish name **Forster** (iv) or another similar-sounding Jewish name; (iii) from a medieval nickname applied to a foster-child [Barry Foster, 1931–, British actor; Brendan Foster, 1948–, British athlete; Jodie Foster (original name Alicia Christian Foster), 1962–, US actress; Norman Foster (Lord Foster), 1935–, British architect; R.E. ('Tip') Foster, 1878–1914, English cricketer; Stephen Foster, 1826–64, US songwriter]
— **Fostershire** a jocular early 20th-century cricketing nickname for Worcestershire, for which county seven Foster brothers (including R.E. – see above) played at that time
— **Foster's Lager** a brand of lager, originally produced in Collingwood, near Melbourne,

Australia in 1888 by two Irish-Americans, W.M. Foster and (the unrelated) R.R. Foster

Fothergill 'person from Fothergill', Cumbria, Yorkshire, etc. ('steep valley that affords pasture') [John Fothergill, 1712–80, British physician]

Fotheringham 'person from Fothringham' near Forfar (the Scottish place-name was apparently a deliberate medieval adaptation of *Fotheringhay*, Northamptonshire)

Fouldes, Foulds see **Folds**

Foulger a different form of **Fulcher**

Foulkes, Foulks, Folkes, Folks, Foakes, Fokes, Fowkes from a Norman personal name that originated as an abbreviation of various Germanic names beginning with *folk* 'people'. See also **Fookes** [George Foulkes, 1942–, British Labour politician]

Fowlds see **Folds**

Fowle, Fowell from a medieval nickname applied to someone bearing some sort of resemblance to a bird. See also **Vowell**

Fowler 'bird-catcher'. See also **Fullerton** [Harry Fowler, 1926–, British actor; Henry Watson Fowler, 1858–1933, British lexicographer and usage writer; Norman Fowler (Lord Fowler), 1938–, British Conservative politician]
— '**Fowler', 'Fowler's**' a shorthand title sometimes applied to *A Dictionary of Modern English Usage* (1926 and subsequent editions) by H.W. Fowler (see above), which has become for many the standard work of reference on English usage.
— '**Fowler's match**' the name given to a celebrated cricket match between Eton and Harrow at Lord's in 1910 in which, completely against the run of the game, R.St.L. Fowler, 1891–1925, bowled Eton to victory with eight wickets for 23 in Harrow's second innings.
— **Fowler's solution** a patent medicinal solution of potassium arsenite with a little lavender water, widely taken as a cure-all in the 19th century and responsible for many deaths. It was developed by the chemist Thomas Fowler, 1735–1801.

Fowles, Fowls, Fowells 'son of **Fowle**' [John Fowles, 1926–2005, British novelist]

Fox, Foxe (i) from a medieval nickname applied to someone considered to resemble a fox in some way (e.g. in cunning, or in having red hair); (ii) a translated adaptation of Gaelic *Mac an tSionnaigh*, literally 'son of the fox'; (iii) a euphemizing translation of **Fuchs**, especially in avoidance of the spellings *Fucks* and *Fuks* [Charles James Fox, 1749–1806, British Whig politician, first British foreign secretary (1782); Edward Fox, 1937–, British actor; George Fox, 1624–91, English religious leader, founder of the Quakers; James Fox (original name William Fox), 1939–, British actor, brother of Edward; Jamie Foxx (original name Eric Morlon Bishop, Jr.), 1967–, US actor; John Foxe, 1516–87, English religious writer, author of *The Book of Martyrs* (1563); Liam Fox, 1961–, British Conservative politician; Michael J. Fox (original name Michael Andrew Fox), 1961–, Canadian-born film actor; Sir Paul Fox, 1925–, British television executive; Samantha Fox, 1966–, British

photographic model; Uffa Fox, 1898–1972, British boat designer and yachtsman; William Henry Fox Talbot, see **Talbot**]
— **Fox's Glacier Mints** a British proprietary brand of mint sweet, developed around 1918 by Eric Fox, son of one of the founders of Fox's Confectionery, William Richard Fox of Leicester
— **20th Century Fox** a US film production company, now a subsidiary of Rupert Murdoch's News Corporation. It was established in 1935 with the merger of the Fox Film Corporation, founded in 1914 by William Fox, and Twentieth Century Pictures, founded in 1932.

Foxley 'person from Foxley', name of various places in England ('glade frequented by foxes')

Foxton 'person from Foxton', name of various places in England (either 'farmstead where foxes are seen' or 'valley frequented by foxes')

Foy (i) from a medieval nickname based on Old French *foi* 'faith', applied either to a notably pious person or to one who frequently used the word as an oath; also, from the medieval French female personal name *Foy*, from Old French *foi* 'faith'; (ii) a different form of **Fahy**

Foyle 'person who lives near a pit or excavation' (Old French *fouille* 'pit') [Christina Foyle, 1911–99, British bookshop proprietor, the most formidable figure in the history of Foyles bookshop (see below), daughter of William Foyle]
— **Foyles** a bookshop situated in the Charing Cross Road, London. It was founded in 1903 by the brothers William and Gilbert Foyle.
— *Foyle's War* a British television police detection series set in the World War II period and featuring Detective Chief Superintendant Christopher Foyle as its central character. First broadcast in 2002, it is written by Anthony Horowitz.

Fraine, Frain, Frayne, Frayn 'person who lives near an ash tree or ash wood' (Old French *fraisne, fresne* 'ash'). See also **Frean** [Michael Frayn, 1933–, British writer]

Frame (i) a Scottish name of unknown origin and meaning; (ii) a Jewish name, possibly an anglicization of the personal name and surname *Ephraim* (probably from a Hebrew word meaning 'fruitful') [Janet Frame (original name Janet Paterson Frame Clutha), 1924–2004, New Zealand writer; Ronald Frame, 1953–, British writer]

Frampton 'person from Frampton', the name of various places in England (mainly 'farmstead on the river Frome') [Sir George Frampton, 1860–1928, British sculptor, creator of the *Peter Pan* sculpture in Kensington Gardens]

France 'French person' (in the Middle Ages, when the name originated, the term would have referred only to the northern part of what is now France)

Francis, Frances, Francies from the personal name *Francis*, brought into English from Old French *François* and ultimately from Latin *Franciscus*, literally 'Frenchman' [Clare Francis, 1946–, British yachtswoman and author; Connie Francis (original name Concetta Rosa Maria Franconero), 1938–, US pop singer; Dick Francis, 1920–, British jockey and author]

Francombe, Frankcombe, Francome 'free man' (i.e. not a serf), from the Anglo-Norman feudal term *franchomme* [John Francome, 1953–, British jockey]

Frank, Franke, Franck, Francke (i) from the Norman male personal name *Franc*, literally 'member of the Frankish people', a Germanic tribe which lived along the Rhine valley and spread westwards during the decline of the Roman Empire in the 4th century ad; (ii) 'person from Franconia', an area of southwestern Germany (German *Franken*)

Frankel a German and Jewish name (German *Fränkel*) meaning literally 'little **Frank**'. See also **Frenkel** [Benjamin Frankel, 1906–73, British composer]

Franklin, Francklin, Franklyn, Francklyn 'franklin' (in the feudal system of the Middle Ages, a landowner of free but not noble birth, ranking below the gentry) [Aretha Franklin, 1942–, US soul singer; Benjamin Franklin, 1706–90, American diplomat, scientist and author; Sir John Franklin, 1786–1847, British naval officer and explorer; Rosalind Franklin, 1920–58, British physical chemist and crystallographer who contributed to the discovery of the structure of DNA; William Franklyn, 1926–2006, British actor]

— **Franklin** a river in southwestern Tasmania. It is named in honour of Sir John Franklin (see above), who at one time was Governor of Tasmania.

— **Franklin** a former (until 1999) regional administrative district of the Northwest Territories of Canada, consisting of Canada's Arctic archipelago. Its name commemorates that of Sir John Franklin, who died there (on King William Island) in the course of his ill-fated expedition to gather magnetic data.

Franks 'son of **Frank** (i)' [Oliver Franks (Lord Franks), 1905–92, British philosopher and diplomat]

Fraser, Frazer a Scottish name of uncertain origin and meaning. See also **Frazier, Frizzell** [Angus Fraser, 1965–, English cricketer; Lady Antonia Fraser (*née* Pakenham), 1932–, British writer; Bill Fraser, 1908–87, British actor; Dawn Fraser, 1937–, Australian swimmer; 'Mad' Frankie Fraser, 1923–, British gangster; George MacDonald Fraser, 1925–, British writer; Gordon Fraser, 1911–81, British greetings-card producer; Sir James Frazer, 1854–1941, British anthropologist and mythologist; Liz Fraser, 1930–, British actress; Malcolm Fraser, 1930–, Australian statesman, prime minister 1975–83; Neale Fraser, 1933–, Australian tennis player; Peter Fraser, 1884–1950, British-born New Zealand statesman, prime minister 1940–49]

— **Dawn Fraser** (see above) Australian rhyming slang in the 1960s for *razor*

— **Fraser** a river in British Columbia, Canada. It is named in honour of the Canadian explorer Simon Fraser, 1776–1862, who in 1808 followed the course of the river to its mouth.

— **Fraserburgh** a town and fishing port in Aberdeenshire, renamed at the end of the 16th century in honour of Sir Alexander Fraser, ?1537–1623, who built the harbour there. Its previous name was Faithlie.

— **Fraser Island** an island off the coast of southern Queensland, Australia, the largest sand island in the world (1662 sq. km./642 sq. mi.). It is named in honour of Eliza Fraser, who became an involuntary resident of the island after a ship captained by her husband, James Fraser, was shipwrecked there in 1836.

— **Frazer Nash** a British car-manufacturing company, founded in 1922 by Archibald Frazer-Nash, 1889–1965. It ceased production in 1960. The name has been used as rhyming slang for *slash* 'act of urinating'.

— **House of Fraser** a British department-store group. It had its beginnings in a small drapery shop set up in Glasgow in 1849 by Hugh Fraser, 1815–73, and James Arthur. Under the direction of Lord Hugh Fraser, 1903–66, it expanded and moved to London in 1959.

Frawley from Irish Gaelic *Ó Freaghaile*, an alteration of *Ó Fearghail*, source of the name **Farrell** [William Frawley, 1887–1966, US actor]

Frayne, Frayn see **Fraine**

Frazer see **Fraser**

Frazier a different form of **Fraser** [Joe Frazier, 1944–, US boxer]

Frean, Freen different forms of **Fraine**

Frederick from the male personal name *Frederick*, of Germanic origin and meaning literally 'peace-power'. It was brought into England by the Normans. See also **Freer, Vick** [Lynn Frederick, 1954–, British actress]

Fredericks 'son of **Frederick**' [Roy Fredericks, 1942–2000, West Indian cricketer]

Frederickson an anglicization of various Scandinavian surnames (e.g. Danish and Norwegian *Frederiksen*, Swedish *Fredriksson*) that mean literally 'son of **Frederick**' and that have themselves in many cases become English surnames

Freebody (in the feudal system of the Middle Ages) 'free man' (i.e. not a serf)

Freedman (i) (in the feudal system of the Middle Ages) 'serf who has been freed'; (ii) an anglicization of **Friedman**

Freeland (in the feudal system of the Middle Ages) 'person who lives on land which entails no feudal obligations'

Freeman (in the feudal system of the Middle Ages) 'free man' (i.e., not a serf) [Alan Freeman, 1927–2006, Australian-born disc jockey; A.P. ('Tich') Freeman, 1888–1965, English cricketer; Cathy Freeman, 1973–, Australian sprinter; John Freeman, 1915–, British journalist, politician and diplomat; Morgan Freeman, 1937–, US actor; 'Mrs Freeman', the name under which Sarah Churchill, Duchess of Marlborough corresponded with Queen Anne ('Mrs **Morley**')]

— **Freeman, Hardy and Willis** a British chain of shoe shops. It was established in 1875, and named after three of its original employees, William

Freeman, Arthur Hardy and Frederick Willis. It closed down in 1996.

Freen see **Frean**

Freer (i) *also* **Freear** or **Frear** or **Frere** from a nickname applied in the Middle Ages to someone of great piety, or who worked in a monastery (Middle English *frere* 'friar, monk'). See also **Frier**; (ii) a Flemish variant of **Frederick**

Freers, Frears 'son of **Freer** (i)' [Stephen Frears, 1941–, British film director]

Freitas see **de Freitas**

Fremantle, Freemantle 'person from Fromentel', the name of various places in France (literally 'cold cloak', perhaps an ironic reference to a patch of forest that afforded scant shelter to those forced to live there)
— **Fremantle** a major seaport in Western Australia, at the mouth of the Swan river. It was named in honour of Admiral Sir Charles Howe Fremantle, 1800–69, who established a colony on the Swan river in 1829.

French 'person from France' (or in some cases perhaps from a nickname applied to someone who put on affected airs, like a stereotypical Frenchman) [Dawn French, 1957–, British comic actress; Sir John French, 1852–1925, British field marshal; Philip French, 1933–, British film critic]

Frend see **Friend**

Frenkel, Frenkiel different forms of **Frankel**

Freud from a medieval German nickname applied to a cheerful person (German *Freude* 'joy') [Sir Clement Freud, 1924–, British writer, broadcaster and Liberal politician, grandson of the Austrian psychoanalyst Sigmund Freud, 1856–1939; Emma Freud, 1961–, British journalist, daughter of Clement; Lucien Freud, 1922–, British painter, brother of Clement]
— **Emma Freuds** (see above) rhyming slang for *haemorrhoids*

Frewin, Frewen from the Middle English personal name *Frewine*, literally 'noble or generous friend'

Freyse see **Fries**

Friar see **Frier**

Frick from a Low German shortened form of the German male personal name *Friedrich* (see **Fried** (ii))
— **Frick Collection** a New York art gallery based on the collection of the US industrialist Henry Clay Frick, 1849–1919

Fried (i) from a Jewish name meaning literally 'peace' (Yiddish *frid*); (ii) from a German male personal name, a shortening of *Friedrich* (equivalent to English **Frederick**)

Friedman, Friedmann an elaborated form of **Fried** (i) [Milton Friedman, 1912–2006, US economist]

Friel from Irish Gaelic *Ó Frighil*, probably an alteration of *Ó Fearghail* (see **Farrell**) [Anna Friel, 1975–, British actress; Brian Friel, 1929–, Irish author]

Friend, Frend (i) from a nickname applied in the Middle Ages to a friendly or sociable person; (ii) a

translation of the German and Jewish name *Freund* [Charles Frend, 1909–71, British film director]

Frier, Friar, Fryer different forms of **Freer**

Fries, Friese, Freyse (i) 'person from Friesland', a province in the northern Netherlands; (ii) 'builder of dams or dykes' (probably originally a transferred use of the ethnic term, dyke-building being a frequent occupation in the Low Countries); (iii) 'little *Friedrich*' (equivalent to English **Frederick**) [William Friese-Greene (original name William Edward Green; Friese was his wife's maiden name), 1855–1921, British photographer and inventor, credited by some with the invention of cinematography]

Frisby, Frisbie 'person from Frisby', Leicestershire ('farmstead of the Frisians')
— **Frisbee** a plastic disc thrown from person to person as a game. The trademarked name was registered in 1959 by Fred Morrison. It was inspired by the Frisbie bakery of Bridgeport, Connecticut, whose pie tins were the original models for the plastic discs.

Frith a different form of **Firth** [William Frith, 1819–1909, British painter]

Frizzell (i) from *Friseal*, the Scottish Gaelic form of **Fraser**; (ii) from a medieval nickname applied to someone who dressed in a showy or gaudy style (from Old French *frisel* 'decoration, ribbon')

Frobisher 'metal-polisher' (applied in the Middle Ages particularly to someone whose job was to buff up armour) (from Old French *fourbisseor*, from *fourbir* 'to burnish, polish') [Sir Martin Frobisher, ?1535–94, English navigator]
— **Frobisher Bay** a bay on Baffin Island, Canada. It is named in honour of Sir Martin Frobisher (see above), who attempted to find the Northwest Passage around the top of Canada.

Froggett, Froggat, Froggitt 'person from Froggett', Derbyshire ('cottage where frogs are seen') [Selwyn Froggitt, a character (created by Alan Plater) who figured in the Yorkshire Television sitcom *Oh No It's Selwyn Froggitt* (1976–77)]

Frost from a medieval nickname applied to someone with white hair or beard or with a frosty demeanour or temperament [Sir David Frost, 1939–, British television interviewer, presenter and producer; 'Jack' Frost (full name William Edward Frost), detective inspector created by R.D. Wingfield and appearing (played by David Jason) in the ITV drama series *A Touch of Frost* (1992–); Robert Frost, 1874–1963, US poet]

Froud, Froude, Frood from the Old English personal name *Frōda* or Old Norse *Frōthi*, both meaning literally 'wise' or 'prudent' [James Anthony Froude, 1818–94, British historian]

Fry, Frye (i) from a medieval nickname applied to a small person (Middle English *fry* 'offspring, children'); (ii) (in the feudal system of the Middle Ages) 'free man' (i.e. not a serf) (from Old English *frīg*, a variant of *frēo* 'free, freeborn') [C.B. Fry, 1872–1965, English cricketer; Christopher Fry (original name Christopher Harris), 1907–2005, British dramatist; Elizabeth Fry (*née* Gurney), 1780–1845, British prison reformer; Northrop

Frye, 1912–91, Canadian literary critic; Roger Fry, 1866–1934, British painter and art critic; Stephen Fry, 1957–, British actor, comedian and writer]

— **Fry's** the British confectionery firm J.S. Fry and Sons, Ltd., a pioneer in the commercial production of chocolate bars. It was formed in 1822 by Joseph Fry, 1769–1835, but traced its origins in the Quaker Fry family back to the mid-18th century. In 1919 it merged with Cadbury's, but confectionery continued to be produced under its brand name.

Fryer see **Frier**

Fuchs from a medieval German nickname applied to someone considered to resemble a fox in some way (e.g. in cunning, or in having red hair) (German *Fuchs* 'fox'). See also **Fox** [Sir Vivian Fuchs, 1908–99, British geologist and explorer]

Fulbright, Fullbright an anglicization of *Vollbrecht*, a German name meaning literally 'famous among the people' [J. William Fulbright, 1905–95, US educator and statesman]

— **Fulbright scholarship** an educational grant awarded under the auspices of the **Fulbright program** for graduate studies, advanced research, etc. in countries around the world. The programme was set up in 1946 largely thanks to the efforts of Senator William Fulbright (see above).

Fulcher from a Germanic personal name meaning literally 'people's army', brought into England by the Normans. See also **Folger, Foulger, Fulger**

Fulford 'person from Fulford', the name of various places in England ('muddy ford')

Fulger a different form of **Fulcher**

Fullbrook 'person from Fullbrook', the name of various places in England ('muddy stream')

Fuller 'fuller of cloth' (i.e. someone who makes cloth bulkier by dampening and beating it) [Buckminster Fuller, 1895–1983, US engineer, designer, architect and writer; Roy Fuller, 1912–92, British poet and novelist; Thomas Fuller, 1608–61, British historian]

— **buckminsterfullerene** a stable form of carbon containing 60 atoms. The term was inspired by the molecule's resemblance to the geodesic dome structure invented by Buckminster Fuller (see above).

— **fullerene** a form of carbon made up of up to 500 carbon atoms arranged in a sphere or tube. The term is a shortening of *buckminsterfullerene*.

— **Fuller's Ltd** a British firm of cake makers established at the turn of the 20th century by William Bruce Fuller

Fullerton, Fullarton 'person from Fullerton', the name of various places in Scotland and England

('bird-catcher's farmstead') [Fiona Fullerton, 1956–, British actress]

Fulton (i) 'person from Fulton', Borders ('farmstead frequented by birds'); (ii) a different form of **Fullerton** [Robert Fulton, 1765–1815, American inventor]

Funke, Funk from a medieval German nickname applied to a lively person (German *Funke* 'spark'); also a Jewish name, from Yiddish *funk* 'spark'. See also **Finkelstein**

— **Funk and Wagnalls** a New York publishing firm best known for its dictionaries and encyclopedias. It was founded in 1876 by Isaac Kaufmann Funk, 1839–1912, as I.K. Funk and Company.

Funnell a different form of **Fennell** (i)

Furbank see **Firbank**

Furey, Fury, Furie from Irish Gaelic *Ó Fiúra*, an alteration of earlier *Ó Furreidh* 'descendant of him with bushy eyebrows' [Billy Fury (original name Ronald Wycherley), 1940–83, British pop singer; Sidney J. Furie, 1933–, Canadian film director]

Furlong probably 'person who lives near a furlong' in a now obsolete sense of that term (e.g. 'an indefinite division of an unenclosed field' or 'the headland of a common field')

Furneaux 'person from Furneaux', the name of various places in northern France ('little oven')

Furness, Furniss 'person from Furness', a district on the southern Cumbrian coast ('headland opposite buttock island', so called from its cloven shape)

Furnival, Furnivall 'person from Fournival or Fourneville', places in northern France (both originally 'Furnus's settlement' or 'settlement with an oven or kiln') [Frederick Furnivall, 1825–1910, British philologist and lexicographer]

Fursdon 'person from Fursdon', Devon ('hill growing with gorse')

Furst, First a Jewish name adopted from German *Fürst* 'prince' [Ruth First, 1925–82, South African anti-apartheid campaigner]

Fyfe, Fyffe, Fife 'person from the former kingdom of Fife', eastern Scotland (traditionally the 'land of *Fib*', one of the seven sons of Cruithe, legendary father of the Picts, but the chronology of the evidence makes that unlikely) [Will Fyffe, 1885–1947, Scottish music-hall entertainer]

— **Fyffe's** a British firm of banana importers, founded, as E.W. Fyffe Son and Company, by the tea merchant Edward Wathen Fyffe, 1853–1935. It introduced its first bananas into the UK in 1888. It is now Fyffe's plc.

G

Gable perhaps 'person from a place named Gable'. The place-name usually alluded to a gable-shaped (i.e. triangular) hill (e.g. Great Gable, a Cumbrian mountain). [Clark Gable, 1901–60, US film actor]

Gabriel from the Hebrew personal name *Gavriel*, literally 'God has given me strength' [Walter Gabriel, archetypal rustic elder in the BBC radio soap opera *The Archers* (he 'died' in 1988 at the age of 92)]

Gadd 'cattle-driver', or from a medieval nickname applied to an incorrigibly troublesome person (in either case from Middle English *gad* 'goad, sting') [Paul Gadd, 1944–, real name of the glam-rock singer Gary Glitter]

Gaddesden, Gadsden, Gadsdon 'person from Gaddesden', Hertfordshire ('Gǣte's valley')

— **Gadsden Purchase** an area of southern Arizona and New Mexico bought by the USA from Mexico in 1853. The sale was negotiated by James Gadsden, 1788–1858, US Minister to Mexico.

Gadsby 'person from Gaddesby', Leicestershire ('Gaddr's farmstead'). See also **Gatsby**

Gaffney from Irish Gaelic *Ó Gamhna* 'descendant of *Gamhain*', from a personal name meaning literally 'calf'

Gagan a different form of **Gahan** and **Geoghegan**

Gage, Gauge (i) 'moneylender' (ultimately from Old French *gage* 'pledge, security'); (ii) 'assayer' (i.e. an official who determines and verifies measurements) (ultimately from Old French *gage, gauge* 'measure') [Alexander Gauge, 1914–60, British actor; Thomas Gage, 1721–87, British soldier, commander-in-chief of British forces in North America, 1763–74; Sir William Gage, 1657–1727, English botanist who gave his name to the greengage]

Gahan from Gaelic *Mac Eacháin* 'son of *Eachán*', literally 'little horse', or *Ó Gaoithín* 'descendant of *Gaoithín*', literally 'little wise person'. See also **Gagan, Keogh**

Gail see **Gale**

Gaines, Gains from a medieval nickname applied to a tricky, sly or ingenious person (ultimately from Old French *engaine* 'craftiness, ingenuity')

Gainsborough 'person from Gainsborough', Lincolnshire ('Gegn's stronghold') [Thomas Gainsborough, 1727–88, British painter]

Gait see **Gate**

Gaitskell, Gaitskill different forms of **Gaskell** [Hugh Gaitskell, 1906–63, British Labour politician]

Galbraith, Galbreath 'British foreigner', a Gaelic ethnic name applied to a descendant of a Celtic tribe that once lived in Scotland (possibly Britons who lived there before the Gaels moved into Scotland from Ireland in the 5th century AD) [John Kenneth Galbraith, 1908–2006, Canadian-born US economist and diplomat]

Gale, Gail, Gayle (i) from the medieval personal name *Gal* or *Galon*, of Germanic origin but brought into England by the Normans; (ii) from a medieval nickname applied to someone who enjoyed having a noisy good time (from Middle English *gale, gaile* 'jovial, rowdy'); (iii) 'jailer', 'person who lives near a jail' or from a nickname applied to an (ex-)convict (in all cases from Old Northern French *gaiole* 'jail') [Cathy Gale, leather-clad sidekick (played by Honor Blackman) of John Steed in the ABC television drama series *The Avengers* (1961–69); George Gale, 1927–90, British journalist]

Gall, Gaul (i) 'stranger, foreigner' (principally a medieval Gaelic nickname (*Ghoill*) applied in Scotland to English-speakers and Scandinavians and in Ireland to English and Welsh settlers); (ii) from a widespread medieval European personal name descended from Latin *Gallus*. See also **Galley, Gallo, Galt, Gill, McGill** [Sandy Gall, 1927–, British television journalist and newsreader]

Gallagher, Gallacher, Gallaher from Irish Gaelic *Ó Gallchobhair* 'descendant of *Gallchobhar*', a personal name meaning literally 'foreign help' [Bernard Gallacher, 1949–, British golfer; Liam Gallagher (original name William John Paul Gallagher), 1972–, British pop singer; Noel Gallagher, 1967–, British pop singer, brother of Liam]

— **Gallaher Group plc** a British tobacco and cigarette producer, founded in Londonderry, Northern Ireland in 1863 by Thomas Gallaher (the 'Tobacco King'), 1840–1927

Gallatly a different form of **Golightly**

Gallaway see **Galloway**

Galley, Gallie, Gally (i) 'seaman, seafarer' (from Middle English *galye* 'ship'); (ii) 'person who has been on a pilgrimage to the Holy Land' (from *Galilee*); (iii) a Scottish variant of **Gall** (i)

Gallo (i) from the medieval Italian and Spanish personal name *Gallo* (from Latin *Gallus* – see **Gall** (ii)); (ii) from a medieval Italian and Spanish nickname applied to a man thought to resemble a cockerel (*gallo*), e.g. in raucousness or alleged sexual prowess

— **Ernest and Julio Gallo** a US wine-producing firm (now the world's largest), set up in 1933 by Ernest Gallo, 1909–2007, and his brother Julio Gallo, 1910–93

Gallop, Gallup probably either 'messenger' or from a medieval nickname for a hasty or impetuous person [George Gallup, 1901–84, US public-opinion pollster]

— **Gallup poll** a survey in which a sample of people taken as a representative cross-section of society are asked their opinions on a given subject. It is named after George Gallup (see above), who pioneered such surveys.

Galloway, Gallaway 'person from Galloway', a region in southwestern Scotland ('territory of the foreign Gaels', a reference to the people of mixed Irish and Scandinavian birth who settled in the area in the 9th century AD). See also **Galway** [George Galloway, 1954–, British Respect politician]

Galsworthy, Golsworthy 'person from Galsworthy', Devon (formerly *Galeshore* 'slope where bog myrtle grows') [John Galsworthy, 1867–1933, British novelist and dramatist]

Galt (i) *also* **Gault** from a medieval nickname applied to someone thought to resemble a wild boar (Middle English *galte* 'wild boar', from Old Norse); (ii) a Scottish variant of **Gall** (i) [John Galt, 1779–1839, Scottish novelist]

Galton 'person from Galton', Dorset ('estate held by payment of rent') [Sir Francis Galton, 1822–1911, British scientist, proponent of eugenics; Ray Galton, 1930–, British comedy scriptwriter]

Galvin (i) from a medieval French nickname applied to a merry drunkard (from Old French *galer* 'to entertain, gratify, waste' + *vin* 'wine'); (ii) from Irish Gaelic *Ó Gealbháin* 'descendant of *Gealbhán*', a personal name meaning literally 'bright white'

Galway probably an Irish variant of **Galloway** (rather than 'person from Galway', in the Irish province of Connacht) [Sir James Galway, 1939–, Northern Irish flautist]

Gamage, Gammage, Gammidge 'person from Gamaches', the name of various places in northern France (perhaps 'winding water')

— **Gamage's** a former London department store, situated in Holborn. It was founded in 1878 by Arthur Gamage, 1857–1930, and closed down in 1972.

Gamble, Gambell from the medieval personal name *Gamall*, of Old Norse origin and meaning literally 'old'. See also **Gemmell**

— **Procter & Gamble** see **Proctor**

Gambon a different form of **Gammon** [Sir Michael Gambon, 1940–, British actor]

Gammell, Gammil different forms of **Gamble**

Gammon, Gammond from a medieval nickname applied to a merry or sportive person (from Middle English *gamen* 'game'), or to someone who walked in a strange way or had some peculiarity of the legs (from Anglo-Norman *gambon* 'ham')

Gander (i) 'gooseherd', or from a medieval nickname for someone thought to resemble a gander (male goose) in some way; (ii) 'glover' (see **Gaunt** (iii))

Gandy, Gandey perhaps 'glover' (from Old French *gantier*), or from a medieval nickname applied to someone who habitually wore gloves (from Old French *ganté* 'gloved'). See also **Gaunt** (iii)

Gannon from Irish Gaelic *Mag Fhionnán* 'son of *Fionnán*', a personal name meaning literally 'little white or fair person'

Gant a different form of **Gaunt** (iii)

Garabedian 'son of *Garabed*', an Armenian personal name meaning literally 'leader, precursor' and traditionally used as an epithet of John the Baptist in the Armenian church

Garapedian a different form of **Garabedian**

Garbett from the Norman personal name *Gerberht*, of Germanic origin and meaning literally 'bright spear'. The form of the name has been influenced by the similar but unrelated **Garbutt**.

Garbo (i) from the *via del Garbo*, the name of a street in Florence that in former times was the place of work of spinners, weavers, etc. of *lana del Garbo* 'wool from the Algarve' in Portugal; (ii) probably from a medieval Italian nickname for an urbane or well-mannered person (from Italian *garbo* 'polite, kind') [Greta Garbo (original name Greta Gustaffson), 1905–90, Swedish-born US film actress]

Garbutt from the Norman personal names *Geribodo*, of Germanic origin and meaning literally 'spear-messenger', and *Geribald*, of Germanic origin and meaning literally 'spear-brave'

Garcia from a medieval Spanish and Portuguese personal name of uncertain origin and meaning (possibly related to Basque *hartz, artz* 'bear') [Jerry Garcia (original name Jerome John Garcia), 1942–95, US rock musician]

Gard see **Guard**

Garden 'gardener' (see **Gardener**) [Graeme Garden, 1943–, British comedy performer]

— **gardenia** an evergreen bush or tree, genus *Gardenia*, with shiny leaves and fragrant white flowers. The name honours the Scottish-American naturalist Alexander Garden, 1730–91.

— **Gardenstown** a village in Aberdeenshire, founded in 1720 by Alexander Garden, 1685–1756, a local laird

Gardener, Gardiner, Gardner 'person who tends a garden' (the original reference would have been to a kitchen garden or other such source of produce, rather than a flower garden or other ornamental garden). See also **Garner, Jardine** [Ava Gardner, 1922–90, US film actress; Erle Stanley Gardner, 1889–1970, US writer, creator of Perry Mason; Dame Helen Gardner, 1908–86, British scholar and critic; Henry Balfour Gardiner, 1877–1950, British composer; Sir John Eliot Gardiner, 1943–, British conductor, great nephew of Balfour; Stephen Gardiner, ?1490–1555, English churchman]

Garfield probably 'person from Garfield', the name of a place now lost, originally a field-name ('triangular field') [James Garfield, 1831–81, US Republican politician, president 1881]

Garfinkel, Garfinkle a Jewish name derived from Yiddish *gorfinkl* or German *Karfunkel*, both 'carbuncle'. If it is a consciously invented surname, it presumably carries the word's original literal meaning, 'large red gemstone', but it could also be from a nickname, applied to someone with a carbuncle (i.e. a large boil) on their skin.

Garforth 'person from Garforth', Yorkshire ('Gǣra's ford')

Garfunkel a different form of **Garfinkel** [Art Garfunkel (full name Arthur Ira Garfunkel), 1941–, half of the US folk-rock duo Simon and Garfunkel (see **Simon**)]

Garland (i) 'maker of garlands'; (ii) 'person from Garland', Devon ('triangular area of land') [Judy Garland (original name Frances Gumm), 1922–69, US film actress and singer; Nicholas Garland, 1935–, British political cartoonist; Patrick Garland, 1935–, British writer, director and producer]

Garlick, Garlicke (i) 'grower or seller of garlic'; (ii) perhaps from a medieval personal name descended from Old English *Gārlāc*, literally 'spear-play'; (iii) an anglicization of the Belorussian Jewish name *Garelick*, literally 'distiller'

Garner (i) 'person who lives near a barn or granary' or 'person who works in or is in charge of a barn or granary' (Anglo-Norman *gerner* 'granary', from Old French *grenier*); (ii) a different form of **Gardener**; (iii) a different form of **Warner** (i) [Alan Garner, 1934–, British author; Erroll Garner, 1921–77, US jazz pianist and composer; James Garner (original name James Baumgarner), 1928–, US actor; Joel Garner, 1952–, West Indian cricketer]

Garnett, Garnet (i) 'maker or fitter of hinges' (from a diminutive form of Old French *carne* 'hinge'); (ii) 'grower or seller of pomegranates' (Old French *(pome) grenate* 'pomegranate'); (iii) 'little **Garner** (i; iii)' [Alf Garnett, the irascible and bigoted central character (played by Warren Mitchell) of the BBC television sitcom *Till Death Us Do Part* (1966–68, 1972–75), written by Johnny Speight; David Garnett, 1892–1981, British novelist and critic; Tony Garnett, 1936–, British television producer]

Garnham 'person from Garnham', the name of an unidentified place in England (probably 'Gāra's homestead')

Garnier a different form of **Garner** (i)

Garrard, Garard different forms of **Garrett** (i)
— **Garrard and Co. Ltd.** a firm of jewellers (the Crown Jewellers) in Albemarle Street (until 1998 in Regent Street), London. It was founded in the 1730s by George Wickes, and takes its name from Robert Garrard, who joined the company in 1780 and by 1792 had gained a controlling interest.

Garretson, Garrettson 'son of **Garrett**'

Garrett, Garratt, Garrit, Garred (i) from the male personal name *Gerard*, brought into England by the Normans but ultimately of Germanic origin, meaning literally 'spear-brave' or 'spear-strong'; (ii) from the male personal name *Gerald*, brought into England by the Normans but ultimately of Germanic origin, meaning literally 'spear-rule'. See also **FitzGerald, Garrard, Garrison, Garrod, Gerard, Jarrell, Jarrett, Jerrold** [Pat Garrett, 1850–1908, US lawman who shot Billy the Kid]

Garrick (i) an anglicization of the French (Huguenot) surname *Garrigue* 'person living near a grove of holm oaks' (from Old Provençal *garrique* 'grove of holm oaks'); (ii) 'person from Garioch', a district in Aberdeenshire, or 'person from Garwick', Lincolnshire ('Gǣra's dairy farm') [David Garrick, 1717–79, British actor-manager]
— **Garrick Club** a members' club in Garrick Street, London, founded by the Duke of Sussex in 1831. Named after David Garrick (see above), its membership has always contained a high proportion of actors and others connected with the theatre and similar modes of entertainment.

Garrison a different form of **Garretson**

Garrod a different form of **Garrett** (ii)

Garside, Gartside 'person from Gartside or Garside', Lancashire (perhaps 'enclosure on a hill slope')

Garstang 'person from Garstang', Lancashire ('spear-post')

Garston 'person from Garston', the name of numerous places in England (mainly 'grass enclosure')

Garth 'person who lives near an enclosure (e.g. a paddock or orchard)' (Middle English *garth* 'enclosure, yard', from Old Norse *garthr*)

Garton 'person from Garton', Yorkshire ('farmstead on a triangular piece of ground')

Garvey, Garvie from Irish Gaelic *Ó Gairbhshíth* 'descendant of *Gairbhshíth*', a personal name meaning literally 'cruel peace' [Marcus Garvey, 1887–1940, Jamaican-born US civil-rights advocate]

Garvin from Irish Gaelic *Ó Gairbhín* 'descendant of *Gairbhín*', a personal name meaning literally 'little rough or cruel one' [J. L. Garvin, 1868–1947, British journalist, editor of the *Observer* 1908–42]

Garwood 'person from Garwood', the name of an unidentified place in England (probably 'triangular wood')

Gary (i) a different form of **Geary**; (ii) a shortened form of **McGary**
— **Gary** a city in northwestern Indiana, USA, on Lake Michigan. It was established in 1906 by the US Steel Corporation, and named in honour of its chairman, Judge Elbert H. Gary, 1846–1927.

Gascoigne, Gascoyne 'person from *Gascogne*', the French province of Gascony. See also **Gaskin** [Gascoyne-Cecil, family name of the marquesses of Salisbury; Bamber Gascoigne, 1935–, British author and quizmaster; George Gascoigne,

?1534–77, English soldier and poet; Paul Gascoigne, 1967–, English footballer]

Gash a different form of **Wass** (i)

Gaskell, Gaskill 'person from Gatesgill', Cumbria ('goat's shelter'). See also **Gaitskell** [Elizabeth Gaskell, 1810–65, British novelist]

Gaskin a different form of **Gascoigne**

Gass (i) also **Gas** 'person who lives in a narrow lane or alley', from German *Gasse* or Yiddish *gas*, both 'street'; (ii) a different form of **Wass** (i)

Gate, Gait (i) 'person who lives on a main road' (Middle English *gate* 'street', from Old Norse *gata*), or 'person who lives by a gate' (Middle English *gate*, from Old English *geat*). See also **Gates**; (ii) 'goatherd', or from a medieval nickname applied to someone who resembled a goat (e.g. in smell); (iii) 'watchman' (Middle English *gate*, from Old French *gaite*, a derivative of *gaiter* 'to watch')

Gatehouse 'person who lives in a gatehouse (i.e. in lodgings above or beside a city gate)'

Gately from Irish Gaelic *Mag Athlaoich* 'son of *Athlaoch*', a personal name meaning literally 'former warrior'

Gatenby 'person from Gatenby', Yorkshire ('Gaithan's farmstead')

Gates 'person who lives by the town or city gates' [Bill Gates (full name William Henry Gates III), 1955–, US business executive; Horatio Gates, ?1728–1806, British-born American general]

Gatlin, Gatling perhaps from a medieval nickname applied to a disreputable person (Middle English *gadling* 'companion, ne'er-do-well')

— **Gatling gun** an early form of machine gun, developed in the mid-19th century by the US inventor R.J. Gatling, 1818–1903

Gatsby a different form of **Gadsby** [Jay Gatsby, the central character of F. Scott Fitzgerald's novel *The Great Gatsby* (1925)]

Gauge see **Gage**

Gault see **Galt** (i)

Gaunt (i) 'person from Ghent', in Flanders (there was a large influx of textile workers from Ghent and the surrounding areas into England in the early Middle Ages); (ii) from a medieval nickname applied to a thin or scraggy person; (iii) 'glover' (from Old French *gant* 'glove'). See also **Gant**

Gavin from the male personal name, in the Middle Ages mainly from Old French *Gauvin* but also in the Middle English form *Gawayne*, ultimately probably from an Old Welsh name meaning literally 'white hawk'. It was popularized by Sir Gawain's role in the Arthurian legends. See also **Walwyn** (ii)

— **Gavinton** a village in the Scottish Borders, so renamed around 1760 by its owner, David Gavin (its previous name was Langton)

Gawkrodger, Gawkroger from a medieval nickname meaning 'clumsy Roger'

Gay, Gaye (i) 'person from Gaye', the name of various places in Normandy; (ii) from a nickname applied to a cheerful person; (iii) from the medieval Catalan personal name *Gai*, from Latin *Gaius* [John Gay, 1685–1732, British poet and dramatist; Marvin Gaye (original name Marvin Pentz Gay, Jr.), 1939–84, US soul and R&B singer and songwriter]

Gayle see **Gale**

Gaylord an anglicization of the surname *Gaillard*, which is associated particularly with Huguenot immigrants from France. This came either from the personal name *Gailhard*, of Germanic origin and meaning literally 'happy-brave', or from a nickname for a cheerful or forceful person, based on the Old French adjective *gaile* 'cheerful'.

Gaynor (i) from Irish Gaelic *Mag Fhionnbhairr* 'son of *Fhionnbharr*', a personal name meaning literally 'white head'; (ii) from the Welsh female personal name *Gaenor*, a different form of *Gwenhwyfar* (see **Juniper** (ii)) [Gloria Gaynor (original name Gloria Fowles), 1949–, US disco-music singer; Janet Gaynor (original name Laura Gainor), 1906–84, US actress; Mitzi Gaynor (original name Francesca Marlene de Czanyi von Gerber), 1931–, US actress and singer]

Gear, Geare see **Geer**

Geary (i) from Irish Gaelic *Ó Gadhra* 'descendant of *Gadhra*', a male personal name derived from *gadhar* 'hound'. See also **O'Gara**; (ii) from a medieval male personal name based on the first element of various Germanic compound names beginning with *gari* or *geri* 'spear' (e.g. *Gerard* or *Gerald* – see **Garrett**); (iii) from a medieval nickname for a capricious or moody person (Middle English *geary, gery* 'changeable in opinion or mood'). See also **Gary** (i), **Geer**

Gebhardt, Gebhard, Gebhart from a Germanic male personal name meaning literally 'strong gift'. See also **Gibbard**

Geddes, Geddis 'person from Geddes', Highland region (perhaps 'mountain ridge') [Barbara Bel Geddes, 1922–2005, US actress]

Gee as an English name, of uncertain origin; perhaps an English use of the Scottish and Irish name *Gee*, which is a shortened form of **McGee**. See also **Geeson**

Geer, Geere, Gear, Geare, Gere different forms of **Geary** [Richard Gere, 1949–, US film actor]

Geeson 'son of **Gee**' [Judy Geeson, 1948–, British actress]

Geeves a different form of **Jeeves**

Geffrye see **Jeffrey**

Gehrig a different form of *Gehring*, a name of German and Swiss German origin, literally 'son of *Gerhard* (or some other personal name beginning with *Ger-*)'

— **Lou Gehrig's disease** an alternative name for amyotrophic lateral sclerosis, a fatal degenerative disease of the nervous system. It commemorates the US baseball player Henry Louis ('Lou') Gehrig, 1903–41, who died from the disease.

Gelatly a different form of **Golightly** (ii)

Gell (i) from a medieval Jewish nickname for someone with red hair (Yiddish *gel* 'red-headed', from Middle High German *gel* 'yellow'); (ii) from a shortened form of **Julian**

— **Via Gellia** a road between Cromford and Grangemill in Derbyshire, so named (in mock-Latin) by Philip Gell, a local man who had it constructed in the late 18th century. The fabric tradenamed 'Viyella' was originally produced in a textile works on the road, and took its name from it.

Geller (i) 'person from Geldern', a town in northern Germany, or 'person from Gelderland', a province of the Netherlands: both probably derived ultimately from a word meaning 'marsh'; (ii) 'town crier' (German *Geller*, cognate with English *yeller*); (iii) from a medieval Jewish nickname for someone with red hair (Yiddish *gel* 'red-headed' – see **Gell** (i)). See also **Gelman**; (iv) a different form of **Heller** (iii) (the substitution of /g/ for /h/ is due to Russian influence)

Gelling a different form of **Lewin** (ii)

Gelman, **Gellman**, **Gellmann** different forms of **Geller** (iii) [Murray Gell-Mann, 1929–, US physicist (the hyphen was added by his father)]

Gemmell, **Gemmill** Scottish variants of **Gamble**

Genn (i) a different form of **Jane**; (ii) a Cornish variant of **Juniper** (ii) [Leo Genn, 1905–78, British actor]

Gent a different form of **Gentle**

Gentle from a medieval nickname applied to a well-born or polite person or (with heavy irony) to an ill-bred, vulgar or rude person (Middle English *gentil* 'well born, courteous')

Gentleman a different form of **Gentle**, or a translation of an equivalent name in another language (e.g. Italian *Gentiluomo*) [David Gentleman, 1930–, British artist and designer]

Gentry from a medieval nickname applied to a well-born or polite person or (with heavy irony) to an ill-bred, vulgar or rude person (Middle English *genterie* 'noble birth or status') [Bobbie Gentry (original name Roberta Lee Streeter), 1944–, US singer-songwriter]

Geoffrey, **Geoffreys** see **Jeffrey**, **Jeffries**

Geoghegan from Irish Gaelic *Mag Eochagáin* 'son of *Eochagán*', a personal name probably meaning literally 'little little horseman'. It is standardly pronounced as 'gaygen'. See also **Gagan**, **McGuigan**

George from the male personal name *George*, ultimately from Greek *Geōrgios*, literally 'farmer' [Bobby George, 1945–, British darts player; Charlie George, 1950–, English footballer; Susan George, 1950–, British actress]

Georgeson 'son of **George**'

Geraghty from Irish Gaelic *Mag Oireachtaigh* (see **McGeraghty**)

Gerald, **Gerold** different forms of **Garrett** (ii)

— **Jim Gerald** an old Australian rhyming nickname for any newspaper with *Herald* as part of its name. It does not commemorate any particular Jim Gerald.

Gerard, **Gerrard** different forms of **Garrett** (i) [John Gerard, 1545–1612, English herbalist]

— **Brigadier Gerard** the hero (first name Etienne) of a series of comic short stories by Arthur Conan Doyle, first published between 1894 and 1903 in the *Strand* magazine and in book form as *The Exploits of Brigadier Gerard* (1896) and *The Adventures of Gerard* (1903). He was a hussar in Napoleon's army. Brigadier Gerard was also the name given to a highly successful British Thoroughbred racehorse, 1968–89, which won 17 of its 18 races.

— **Gerrards Cross** a residential town in Buckinghamshire, named, probably in the 17th century, after a local family called Gerrard or Jarrard

Gere see **Geer**

German, **Germann**, **Jerman**, **Jermine**, **Jermyn** (i) from the male personal name *Germain*, brought into English from Old French and descended partly from the name of the people and partly from etymologically unrelated Old French *germain* 'brother, cousin'; (ii) 'person from Germany' or 'person who has commercial or other dealings with Germany'. See also **Jarman** [Sir Edward German (original name Edward German Jones), 1862–1936, British composer]

— **Jermyn Street** a street in the West End of London. It was named after Henry Jermyn, earl of St Albans, on whose land it was built.

Gervais, **Gervase** from the Norman male personal name *Gervase* (see **Jarvis** (i)) [Ricky Gervais, 1961–, British comedy writer and performer]

Gething, **Gethin** different forms of **Gittings**

Getty from Irish Gaelic *Mag Eitigh* 'son of *Eiteach*', a personal name derived from *eiteach* 'winged' [J. Paul Getty, 1892–1976, US businessman; Sir John Paul Getty (original name Eugene Paul Getty), 1932–2003, US-born British philanthropist, son of J. Paul]

Gettys a different form of **Getty**

— **Gettysburg** a borough in southern Pennsylvania, USA, site of a decisive Northern victory in 1863 during the American Civil War. Founded in the 1780s, it was named after James Gettys (son of the Scots-Irish settler Samuel Gettys), who laid it out.

Ghosh 'cowherd' (Sanskrit *ghos.a*)

Gibb from the medieval male personal name *Gib*, a pet-form of **Gilbert**. See also **Gibbon**, **Gibbs**, **Gibson** [Maurice Gibb, 1949–2003, British pop musician, member of the Bee Gees group]

— **Gibbs SR** a brand of toothpaste, produced by a firm that can probably be traced back to Alexander Gibb, a London candlemaker in the mid-18th century. The first advertisement to appear on British commercial television, on 22 September 1955, was for Gibbs SR (*SR* stands for 'sodium ricinoleate').

Gibbard, **Gibberd** from a Germanic male personal name meaning literally 'strong gift'. See also **Gebhardt** [Sir Frederick Gibberd, 1908–84, British architect]

Gibbon, **Gibben** (i) 'little **Gibb**'. See also **Fitzgibbon**, **McGibbon**; (ii) from the Germanic male personal name *Gebwine*, literally 'gift-friend' [Edward Gibbon, 1737–94, British historian;

Lewis Grassic Gibbon, pen-name of James Leslie Mitchell, 1901–35, British novelist]

Gibbons, Gibbens 'son of **Gibbon** (i)' [Carroll Gibbons (full name Richard Carroll Gibbons), 1903–54, US-born British bandleader; Grinling Gibbons, 1648–1721, English wood carver and sculptor; Orlando Gibbons, 1583–1625, English composer; Stella Gibbons, 1902–89, British author]

— **Stanley Gibbons Ltd** a British firm of stamp dealers, founded in London in 1856 by the philatelist Edward Stanley Gibbons, 1840–1913

Gibbs 'son of **Gibb**' [Cecil Armstrong Gibbs, 1889–1960, British composer; James Gibbs, 1682–1754, British architect; J. Willard Gibbs, 1839–1903, US physical chemist; Lance Gibbs, 1934–, West Indian cricketer]

— **Gibbs free energy** a measure of the capacity of a system to do work, or of the likelihood of a particular chemical reaction to form products. The term commemorates J. Willard Gibbs (see above).

— **gibbsite** a grey-white mineral consisting of hydrated aluminium oxide. It was named after the US mineralogist George Gibbs, 1776–1833.

Gibson 'son of **Gibb**' [Sir Alexander Gibson, 1926–95, British conductor; Charles Dana Gibson, 1867–1944, US artist and illustrator; Mel Gibson (original name Columcille Gerard Gibson), 1956–, US-born Australian actor]

— **Gibson** a cocktail, similar to a martini, consisting of gin and vermouth embellished with a cocktail onion. It came on the scene around 1930, and may have been named in honour of Charles Dana Gibson (see above).

— **Gibson Desert** a desert in central Western Australia, 156,000 sq. km./60,200 sq. mi. in area. Its name commemorates the Australian explorer Alfred Gibson, who died while crossing it in 1874.

— **Gibson girl** a fashionable American girl of the late 1890s and early 1900s, of the sort illustrated by Charles Dana Gibson (see above)

— **Gibson guitar** a guitar made by the Gibson Guitar Corporation, formed in the US in 1902 to make and market guitars designed by Orville Gibson, 1856–1918 (who had begun by making mandolins in 1894). The term refers particularly to those made to the design of the US guitarist Les Paul, which were the required instrument for rock 'n' roll musicians from the late 1960s.

Giddings, Giddens 'person from Gidding', any of a group of Cambridgeshire villages ('settlement of Gydda's people')

Gideon from the Biblical name *Gideon*, literally 'one who cuts down' in Hebrew [Commander George Gideon, Scotland Yard detective created by the writer John Creasey and featuring in the television drama series *Gideon's Way* (1965–66)]

Giffard (i) from a medieval nickname applied to a fat person, especially one with fat cheeks (from Old French *giffard* 'chubby-cheeked'); (ii) from the Old German personal name *Gifard*, a different form of **Gebhardt**. See also **Jefford**

Giffin, Giffen from Irish Gaelic *Mag Dhuibhfinn* 'son of *Duibhfionn*', a personal name meaning literally 'black-fair'

Gifford (i) 'person from Giffords Hall', Suffolk ('Gydda's ford'); (ii) a different form of **Giffard** (i)

Gilberd a different form of **Gilbert**

Gilbert, Gilburt (i) from the Norman male personal name *Giselbert*, of Germanic origin and meaning literally 'pledge-bright, hostage-bright'. See also **Gibb**, **Gibbon**, **Gilby**; (ii) an anglicization of **Kilbride** [Sir Humphrey Gilbert, ?1539–83, English navigator; Sir Martin Gilbert, 1936–, British historian; William Gilbert, 1544–1603, English physician and scientist; Sir William Schwenck Gilbert (W.S. Gilbert), 1836–1911, British librettist and dramatist, collaborator with Sir Arthur Sullivan]

— **gilbert** a unit of magnetomotive force in the centimetre-gram-second system, equal to 0.7958 ampere-turns in the SI system. It is named after William Gilbert (see above).

— **Gilbert and Ellice Islands** a former British colony in the western Pacific Ocean, comprising present-day Tuvalu and Kiribati. The Gilbert Islands (Kiribati) were discovered by Captain Thomas Gilbert in 1788; the Ellice Islands (Tuvalu) were named after the British merchant and MP Edward Ellice, who owned the cargo on the British brigantine *Rebecca*, whose American skipper Arent de Peyster discovered the islands in 1819.

Gilburd, Gilbird different forms of **Gilbert**

Gilby, Gilbey (i) 'person from Gilby', Lincolnshire ('Gilli's farm'); (ii) 'little **Gilbert**'

Gilchrist from the Scottish Gaelic personal name *Gille Crìosd*, literally 'servant of Christ'

Giles, Gyles (i) from the male personal name *Giles*, a descendant of Latin *Ægidius* (from Greek *aigidion* 'young goat'). See also **Gill** (iv), **Gillard**, **Gillett**; (ii) from Irish Gaelic *Ó Glasáin* (see **Gleeson**) [Ashley Giles, 1973–, English cricketer; Bill Giles, 1939–, British weather forecaster; Carl Giles ('Giles'), 1916–95, British cartoonist; Johnny Giles, 1940–, Irish footballer]

— **Farmer Giles** a generic name, since at least the late 18th century, for a farmer. It has also been used as rhyming slang for *piles* 'haemorrhoids'. J.R.R. Tolkien's tale *Farmer Giles of Ham* was published in 1949.

— **Wade-Giles** see **Wade**

Gilfedder a different form of **Kilfedder**

Gilfoil, Gilfoyle, Guilfoyle from Irish Gaelic *Mac Giolla Phóil* 'son of *Giolla Phóil*', a personal name meaning literally 'servant of (St) Paul'. See also **Kilfoyle**

Gilford see **Guilford**

Gilhooley, Gilhooly from Irish Gaelic *Mac Giolla Chomhghaill* (see **Cole**)

Gill (i) 'person who lives by a ravine' (Middle English *gill* 'ravine', from Old Norse *gil*); (ii) from a pet-form of the male personal names **Giles**, **Julian** and **William**; (iii) from Irish Gaelic *Mac Giolla* and Scottish Gaelic *Mac Gille* 'son of

Giolla or *Gille*', literally 'servant' (see also **McGill**); and *Mac An Ghoill* 'son of the stranger' (see **Gall** (i)); (iv) from the Dutch form of **Giles** (i) [Eric Gill, 1882–1940, British sculptor, engraver and typographer]
— **Gill Sans** a sans-serif typeface designed by Eric Gill (see above) in the 1920s

Gillard (i) from *Gislehard*, a personal name of Germanic origin meaning literally 'pledge-hardy, hostage-hardy'; (ii) from an insulting nickname for someone called **Giles** (i)

Gillespie from Irish Gaelic *Mac Giolla Easbuig* and Scottish Gaelic *Mac Gille Easbuig* 'son of the servant of the bishop'. See also **Archibald** [Dizzy Gillespie (original name John Birks Gillespie), 1917–93, US jazz musician]

Gillett (i) *also* **Gillatt** *or* **Gillet** 'little **Gill** (ii)'. See also **Gillette**, **Gilliatt**; (ii) 'someone living at the top of a ravine' (Middle English *gilheved*, literally 'ravine-head')

Gillette (i) a feminine form of **Gillett** (i); (ii) from a French pet-form of the personal name **Giles** (i)
— **Gillette Cup** the trophy presented to the winners of a limited-overs inter-county cricket competition, the first of its type in England, which ran from 1963 to 1980 (it was succeeded by the NatWest Trophy). It was sponsored by the Gillette Company (see below), as subsequently were other cricket competitions of the same name in other countries.
— **Gillette safety razor** a safety razor with disposable blades, the brainchild of the US inventor King Camp Gillette, 1855–1932, who founded the Gillette Safety Razor Company in 1902 to make and market it

Gilliam a different form of **William** [Terry Gilliam, 1940–, US animator and film director]

Gilliatt, **Gillyatt** different forms of **Gillett** (i)

Gillibrand, **Gillebrand** from the Norman personal name *Gillebrand*, of Germanic origin and meaning literally 'hostage-sword'

Gillick a different form of **Gullick**

Gillies, **Gillis** from the Scottish Gaelic personal name *Gilla Iosa*, literally 'servant of Jesus'. See also **Lees**, **McLeish** [Sir Harold Gillies, 1882–1960, New Zealand surgeon]

Gilliland from Scottish Gaelic *Mac Gille Fhaoláin* or Irish Gaelic *Mac Giolla Fhaoláin*, literally 'son of the servant of (St) Faolán'

Gillingham 'person from Gillingham', the name of various places in England ('homestead of Gylla's people')

Gillman, **Gilman** from the Old French male personal name *Guillemin*, a pet-form of *Guillaume* 'William'

Gillow 'person from Gillow', Herefordshire ('retreat by a pool')

Gilmartin from Irish Gaelic *Mac Giolla Mhartain*, literally 'son of the servant of (St) Martin'. See also **Kilmartin**

Gilmore, **Gilmour**, **Gillmor**, **Gillmore** (i) from Irish Gaelic *Mac Giolla Mhuire* and Scottish

Gaelic *Mac Gille Mhoire*, literally 'son of the servant of (the Virgin) Mary'. See also **Kilmuir**, **Murray**; (ii) 'person from Gillamoor', Yorkshire ('marshy land near the town of Gilling') [Gary Gilmore, 1940–77, US serial killer; Gary Gilmour, 1951–, Australian cricketer]

Gilpin from Irish Gaelic *Mac Giolla Fionn*, literally 'son of the fair-haired boy' [John Gilpin, the eponymous hero of William Cowper's ballad (1782), a Cheapside linen-draper whose horse runs away with him]

Gilroy from Irish Gaelic *Mac Giolla Ruaidh*, literally 'son of the red-haired boy'. See also **Kilroy**, **McIlroy**, **Milroy**

Gimpel, **Gimbel** (i) from the Yiddish male personal name *Gimpl*, an alteration of German *Gumprecht*, literally 'famous in battle'; (ii) a Jewish name based on German *Gimpel* 'bullfinch', either deliberately invented and invoking the word's literal sense, or from a nickname alluding to its metaphorical sense 'stupid or gullible person'

Gimson a different form of **Jameson** [A.C. Gimson, 1917–85, British phonetician]

Gingell, **Gingle**, **Gyngell** (i) from a shortened form of the Germanic male personal name *Gangulf*, literally 'walking wolf'; (ii) a different form of **Gingold** [Bruce Gyngell, 1929–2000, Australian television executive]

Gingold an invented Jewish name, from Yiddish, literally 'fine gold' [Hermione Gingold, 1897–1987, British actress]

Gingrich, **Gingerich** from the Germanic male personal name *Gundric*, literally 'powerful in battle' [Newton ('Newt') Gingrich, 1943–, US Republican politician]

Ginn (i) either 'trapper' or from a nickname applied to a sly person (in either case from Middle English *gin* 'trap, trick'); (ii) from Irish Gaelic *Mag Fhinn*, literally 'son of White'

Ginsberg, **Ginsburg**, **Ginzberg**, **Ginzburg** (i) 'person from Gunzberg', Bavaria ('hill where gorse grows'); (ii) 'person from Günzburg', Swabia ('fortress on the river Günz'); (iii) perhaps 'person from *Gintsshprik*', the Yiddish name of Königsberg ('king's hill'), now Kaliningrad in Russia [Allen Ginsberg, 1926–97, US poet]

Girling from a medieval nickname applied to a brave man (or, with heavy irony, to a cowardly one), from Old French *cuer de lion* 'lion heart'

Girtin, **Girton** different forms of **Gurton** [Thomas Girtin, 1775–1802, British landscape painter]

Gish from a shortened form of the Germanic personal name *Gisulf*, literally 'hostage wolf' [Lillian Gish (original name Lillian de Guiche), ?1893–1993, US actress]

Gissing 'person from Gissing', Norfolk ('settlement of Gyssa's or Gyssi's people') [George Gissing, 1857–1903, British novelist]

Githens a different form of **Gittings**

Gittings, **Gittins**, **Gittens** (i) from the Welsh male personal name *Gutyn*, a pet-form of *Gruffydd* (see **Griffith**), with the English ending -*s*, signifying 'son of', tacked on to it; (ii) perhaps from a medieval nickname based on Welsh *cethin* 'swarthy'

Glad (i) from a shortened form of any of a range of Old English personal names (e.g. *Glæding* and *Glædwine* – see **Gladwin**) that began with *glæd* 'shining, happy'; (ii) from a medieval nickname applied to a cheerful person

Gladstone 'person from Gladstone', near Biggar, Strathclyde region (perhaps 'kite-stone' (referring to the bird)) [William Ewart Gladstone, 1808–98, British Liberal politician, prime minister 1868–74, 1880–85, 1886, 1892–94]
— **Gladstone** a small four-wheeled horse-drawn carriage with a collapsible roof, of a sort in use in the second half of the 19th century. It appears to have been named after William Gladstone (see above).
— **Gladstone bag** a small suitcase or portmanteau consisting of a rigid frame on which two compartments of the same size are hinged together. The name was inspired by the amount of travelling William Gladstone undertook in his public life.
— **Gladstone claret** a facetious name given in the second half of the 19th century to cheap imported French red wine, suggested by William Gladstone's reduction of excise duty on such wine when he was chancellor of the exchequer in 1860

Gladwin, Gladwyn from the Old English personal name *Glædwine*, literally 'joyful friend'

Glaister a Scottish surname of uncertain origin: perhaps 'person from Glaister', an unidentified place (possibly 'green hillside')

Glanville, Glanvill (i) 'person from Clanville' in Hampshire and Somerset or any of a range of similarly named places elsewhere in England, all meaning literally 'clean field' – i.e. open country that has been cleared of scrub and undergrowth; (ii) 'person from Glanville', Normandy (formed from the Old French suffix *-ville* 'settlement' and an unknown Germanic personal name) [Brian Glanville, 1931–, British author and journalist]

Glascott, Glasscote (i) 'person from Glascote', Warwickshire ('hut where glass is made'); (ii) 'person from Glascoed', Gwent ('grey-green wood'). See also **Glasscock**

Glaser, Glazer 'glass-blower' or 'glazier', either from Middle High German or, as a Jewish name, from modern German. See also **Glasser** [Paul Michael Glaser, 1943–, US actor]

Glasgow (i) 'person from Glasgow', Scotland (perhaps 'grey-green hollow'); (ii) a different form of **McCluskey** [Alex Glasgow, 1935–2001, British folk singer; Ellen Glasgow, 1873–1945, US novelist; R.C. Robertson-Glasgow, see **Robertson**]

Glass, Glasse (i) 'glass-blower' or 'glazier'. See also **Glaze, Glazier**; (ii) from Gaelic *glas* 'grey-green', appearing as the first element in several Irish and Scottish names (e.g. **McGlashan**); (iii) *also* **Glas** as a Jewish name, either 'glass-blower' or 'glazier' or, as an invented name, simply 'glass' (in both cases from German *Glass* 'glass') [Hannah Glasse, 1708–70, British cookery writer; Philip Glass, 1937–, US composer]

Glasscock, Glascock different forms of **Glascott**

Glasscote see **Glascott**

Glasser a different form of **Glaser**

Glaze a different form of **Glass** (i) [Peter Glaze, 1924–83, British comedian and entertainer]

Glazebrook 'person from Glazebrook', Lancashire (from the *Glaze Brook*, literally 'grey-green brook')

Glazer see **Glaser**

Glazier, Glazyer different forms of **Glass** (i)

Gleave either 'sword-maker' or 'sword-seller', or from a nickname applied to a skilled swordsman (in either case from Middle English *gleyve* 'sword')

Gleaves a different form of **Gleave**

Gledhill 'person from Gledhill', Yorkshire ('kite-hill' (referring to the bird))

Gleeson, Gleason from Irish Gaelic *Ó Glasáin* 'descendant of *Glasán*', a personal name meaning literally 'little grey-green one' [Jackie Gleason, 1916–87, US comedian and actor]

Glen, Glenn (i) 'person who lives in a glen' (Gaelic *gleann*) or 'person from Glen', the name of various places in Scotland. See also **Glynn** (ii); (ii) 'person from Glen', Leicestershire ('valley') [John Glenn, 1921–, US astronaut and politician]

Glendenning, Glendening, Glendinning 'person from Glendenning', Dumfries and Galloway (probably 'valley of the white fort') [Raymond Glendenning, 1907–74, British radio sports commentator; Victoria Glendinning, 1937–, British author]

Glenny, Glennie 'person who lives in a valley' (Gaelic *an ghleanna* 'of the glen') [Evelyn Glennie, 1965–, British percussionist]

Glock 'person who lives by a church bell-tower or in a house with the sign of a bell', 'bell-ringer' or 'town crier' (German *Glocke* 'bell') [Sir William Glock, 1908–2000, British music administrator]

Glossop 'person from Glossop', Derbyshire ('Glott's valley') [Sir Roderick Glossop, a fearsome psychiatrist who makes frequent appearances in the comic novels of P.G. Wodehouse]

Gloster 'person from Gloucester', Gloucestershire ('Roman town of Glaevum' (a name of Celtic origin); *Gloster* was a common alternative spelling)

Glover 'maker or seller of gloves' [Brian Glover, 1934–97, British actor; Jane Glover, 1949–, British conductor]

Gluck (i) from a medieval German nickname applied to someone considered lucky (German *Glück* 'luck'); (ii) a Jewish invented name based on German *Glück*

Glynn, Glyn (i) 'person who lives in a valley' (Welsh *glyn*, Cornish *glin*); (ii) a different form of **Glen** (i) [Elinor Glyn (*née* Sutherland), 1864–1943, British romantic novelist]
— **Williams and Glyn's Bank Ltd** see **Williams**

Godber from the medieval male personal name *Godbert*, of Germanic origin and meaning literally 'god-bright'

Goddard, Godard, Godart from the medieval male personal name *Godhard*, of Germanic origin and brought into England by the Normans, and meaning literally 'god-hardy' [Paulette Goddard (original name perhaps Pauline Marion Levy), 1910–90, US actress; Robert Goddard, 1882–1945, US physicist, pioneer of rocket technology; Trevor Goddard, 1931–, South African cricketer]

Godfrey from the medieval male personal name *Godefrei, Godefroi*, of Germanic origin and brought into England by the Normans, and meaning literally 'god-peace' [Private Charles Godfrey, elderly platoon member in the BBC television sitcom *Dad's Army* (1968–77); Sir Dan Godfrey, 1868–1939, British conductor]

Godley, Godly 'person from Godley or Goodleigh', in Cheshire and Hampshire respectively (both 'Gōda's glade'). See also **Goodley**

Godman a different form of **Goodman**

Godwin a different form of **Goodwin** [William Godwin, 1756–1836, British political philosopher and novelist]
— **Mount Godwin Austen** a mountain in the Karakoram Range of northern Pakistan, the second highest in the world at 8611 m./28,250 ft. It was named after the British topographer and geologist Henry Godwin-Austen, 1834–1923, who was the first to survey it. It is more generally known as K2 (designating the second Karakoram peak to be measured).

Goff see **Gough**

Gogarty, Gogerty 'son of **Fogarty**' [Oliver St John Gogarty, 1878–1957, Irish poet and surgeon]

Golby 'person from Golby', an unidentified place (perhaps 'settlement where marigolds grow')

Gold (i) 'person who works with gold (e.g. refines gold or makes jewellery with it)'; (ii) 'person with golden yellow hair'. See also **Golden** (i); (iii) from the Old English male personal name *Golda* or female personal name *Golde*, both derived from *gold* 'gold'; (iv) an invented Jewish name based on German *Gold* and Yiddish *gold* 'gold'. See also **Golding, Goldman, Gould** [Jack Gold, 1930–, British film director; Jimmy Gold (original name James McGonigal), 1886–1967, British comedian and member of the Crazy Gang]

Goldberg (i) 'person from Goldberg', the name of various places in Germany ('golden hill'); (ii) an invented Jewish name, from German *Goldberg* 'golden hill' [Reuben ('Rube') Goldberg, 1883-1970, US humorous artist; Whoopi Goldberg (original name Caryn Elaine Johnson), 1955–, US comedian and actress]
— **Rube Goldberg** ingenious in conception but overelaborate and mechanically implausible, like the contraptions and devices illustrated by Rube Goldberg (see above). The term is the US equivalent of *Heath Robinson*.

Goldblum, Goldbloom an invented Jewish name, literally 'golden flower' [Jeff Goldblum, 1952–, US actor]

Golden (i) a different form of **Gold** (ii). See also **Goulden**; (ii) from Irish Gaelic *Mag Ualghairg* (see **McGoldrick**)

Goldie (i) 'little **Gold**'; (ii) from a medieval Scottish nickname for someone with abnormal golden pigmentation in one of their eyes. See also **Goudie**

Golding (i) 'person from *Golding*', the German and Yiddish name of the Latvian city of Kuldīga; (ii) 'son of *Golda*' (see **Gold** (iii)) [Sir William Golding, 1911–93, British novelist]

Goldman, Goldmann (i) different forms of **Gold** (i–ii; iv); (ii) 'son of Golde', a Yiddish female personal name
— **Goldman Sachs** an international investment bank, founded in New York in 1869 by Marcus Goldman (died 1904). In 1882 the firm was joined by his son-in-law Samuel Sachs.

Goldring (i) from a medieval English or German nickname applied to someone who wore a gold ring, or an invented Jewish name meaning literally 'gold ring'; (ii) 'person from Goldring', Ayr

Goldsmith 'maker of gold objects' (mainly a translation of the equivalent German and Jewish surname *Goldschmidt*) [Sir James Goldsmith, 1933–97, French-born British businessman; Oliver Goldsmith, 1730–74, Irish-born British writer]

Goldstein (i) an invented Jewish name meaning literally 'gold stone'; (ii) from a medieval German name or nickname meaning 'precious stone' (referring in many cases to a stone used in alchemical experiments)

Goldstone (i) 'person from Goldstone', Kent and Shropshire ('Goldstān's settlement'); (ii) from the Old English personal name *Goldstān*, literally 'gold stone'; (iii) an anglicization of **Goldstein** (i)

Goldthorpe 'person from Goldthorpe', Yorkshire ('Golda's village' (see **Gold** (iii)))

Goldwater an anglicization of the German and Jewish surnames *Goldwasser*, the former 'person who lives by a stream where gold is found', the second an invented name meaning 'golden water' [Barry Goldwater, 1901–90, US Republican politician]

Goldwyn, Goldwin (i) from the Old English personal name *Goldwine*, literally 'gold friend'; (ii) an anglicization of the Jewish surname *Goldwein*, literally 'golden wine' [Samuel Goldwyn (original name Schmuel Gelbfisz, subsequently anglicized to Samuel Goldfish; the '-wyn' came from his business associates Edgar and Archibald Selwyn – see below), 1882–1974, Russian-born US film producer]
— **Goldwynism** a humorously mixed metaphor or other linguistic incongruity of the sort (allegedly) often uttered by Sam Goldwyn (e.g. 'A verbal contract isn't worth the paper it's written on')
— **Metro-Goldwyn-Mayer** a US-based media company (commonly known as **MGM**), founded in 1924 as a film production company by the merger of Metro Pictures Corporation, Goldwyn

Pictures Corporation (founded in 1916 by Samuel Goldfish (see above) in partnership with the Broadway producers Edgar and Archibald Selwyn) and Louis B. Mayer Pictures (see **Meyer**).

Golightly (i) from a medieval English nickname applied to someone who moves swiftly (e.g. as a messenger); (ii) a Scottish surname of unknown origin and meaning. See also **Gelatly**; (iii) from Irish Gaelic *Mac an Ghallóglaigh* 'son of the galloglass' (a mercenary soldier or armed servant of a Celtic chieftain). See also **Ingoldsby** [Holly Golightly, the playgirl who is the heroine of Truman Capote's *Breakfast at Tiffany's* (1958)]

Gomer from Middle English *Godmer*, a personal name of Germanic origin meaning literally 'good-famous'. See also **Gummer**

Gomersall 'person from Gomersal', Yorkshire ('Gūthmǣr's nook of land')

Gomes the Portuguese form of **Gomez** [Hilary Angelo ('Larry') Gomes, 1953–, West Indian cricketer]

Gomez from a medieval Spanish personal name, probably of Germanic origin and meaning literally 'man' [Jill Gomez, 1942–, Guyanese-born British soprano]

Gomme, Gomm perhaps from a medieval nickname based on Middle English *gome* 'man'. See also **Gumm**

Gonzalez 'son of **Gonzalo**' [Pancho Gonzalez (original name Ricardo Alonso González), 1928–95, US tennis player]
— **Gonzalez, Byass** a firm of sherry producers, established in Jerez, Spain in 1835 by Manuel María González. Robert Blake Byass became a partner in 1855.
— **Speedy Gonzalez** a cartoon Mexican mouse in the Warner Brothers *Looney Tunes* cartoon series. Created in 1953, his name has come to be applied metaphorically to someone who moves very fast or (ironically) very slowly.

Gonzalo from the Spanish personal name *Gonzalo*, of Germanic origin and based on *gunth* 'battle'

Gooch a different form of **Gough** (ii) [Graham Gooch, 1953–, English cricketer]

Good, Goode from a medieval nickname applied to a good person; also, from the Old English male personal name *Gōda* (ultimately from *gōd* 'good') [Tom and Barbara Good, self-sufficiency enthusiasts in the BBC television sitcom *The Good Life* (1975–78)]

Goodall (i) *also* **Goodhall** 'person from Gowdall', Yorkshire ('nook of land growing with marigolds'); (ii) *also* **Goodale** 'brewer' or 'innkeeper' [Dame Jane Goodall, 1934–, British conservationist; Sir Reginald Goodall, 1901–90, British conductor]

Goodbody from a medieval nickname applied to a good person

Goodchild (i) from the Old English personal name *Gōdcild*, literally 'good child'; (ii) from a medieval nickname applied to the godchild of a local notable

Goode see **Good**

Gooden perhaps from a medieval nickname meaning literally 'good servant'

Goodenough from a medieval nickname probably applied either to someone of average abilities or to an easily satisfied person; also, perhaps from a medieval nickname meaning 'good servant'

Goodey, Goodee, Goody (i) from the Old English female personal name *Gōdgifu* 'good gift' or 'god gift'; (ii) from a medieval nickname applied to a widow or the female head of a household (Middle English *goodwife*). See also **Goodison** [Jade Goody, 1981–, British celebrity]

Goodfellow from a medieval nickname applied to an agreeable companion

Goodhart from a medieval nickname applied to a kindly person

Goodhew (i) from a medieval nickname applied to a good servant; (ii) from an Old Norse personal name meaning literally 'battle spirit' [Duncan Goodhew, 1957–, British swimmer]

Gooding, Goodinge 'son of *Gōda*' (see **Good**)

Goodison 'son of **Goodey**'

Goodlad from a medieval Scottish nickname applied to a good servant

Goodley, Goodly different forms of **Godley**

Goodman (i) 'master of the household'; (ii) from the Old English personal names *Gōdmann*, literally 'good man' or 'god man', and *Gūthmund*, literally 'battle protection'; (iii) an anglicization of German *Gutmann* or Jewish *Gutman*, both literally 'good man' [Arnold Goodman (Lord Goodman), 1913–95, British lawyer and political advisor; Benny Goodman, 1909–86, US jazz musician]

Goodrich a different form of **Gutteridge**

Goodson (i) from the Old English personal name *Gōdsonu*, literally 'good son'; (ii) from a medieval nickname applied to an obedient or well-behaved son

Goodwin from the Old English personal name *Gōdwine*, literally 'good friend'. See also **Godwin**

Goodwright a different form of **Gutteridge** [Peter Goodwright, 1936–, British impressionist]

Goody see **Goodey**

Goodyear, Goodyer perhaps from a medieval nickname applied to someone who characteristically used the greeting 'good year!' (e.g. as a New Year salutation) [Charles Goodyear, 1800–60, US inventor of the vulcanization of rubber (the US tyre-producing company that bears his name was founded in 1898)]

Goold see **Gould**

Goolden see **Goulden**

Goosens, Goossens a surname of Flemish and Dutch origin meaning literally 'son of *Gozzo*', a Germanic personal name that was a pet-form of a range of personal names beginning *Got-* or *God-* (from *gōd* 'good' or *god, got* 'god') [Sir Eugene Goossens, 1893–1962, British conductor and composer; Leon Goossens, 1896–1988, British oboist, brother of Eugene]

Gordon (i) 'person from Gordon', Borders region ('large fort'); (ii) 'person from Gourdon', Saône-et-Loire (a place-name based on the Gallo-Roman personal name *Gordus*); (iii) from Irish Gaelic *Mag Mhuirneacháin* 'son of *Muirneachán*', a personal name meaning literally 'little beloved one'; (iv) from a medieval French nickname applied to a fat person (Old French *gort, gord* 'fat') [Adam Lindsay Gordon, 1833–70, Azores-born Australian poet; Charles George Gordon ('Chinese Gordon', 'Gordon of Khartoum'), 1833–85, British general; Colin Gordon, 1911–72, British actor; Richard Gordon, pen-name of Gordon Ostlere, 1921–, British doctor and author; Noele Gordon, 1923–85, British actress]

— **Flash Gordon** a fictional spaceman who pursued a course of derring-do around the galaxies, notably on the planet Mongo. He was created by US strip-cartoonist Alex Raymond in 1934.

— **Gay Gordons** originally, a nickname for the Gordon Highlanders (see below), dating from the days when *gay* did not mean 'homosexual'. It subsequently came to be applied to a type of lively old-time Scottish dance, apparently popular in the regiment.

— **Gordon and Gotch** rhyming slang for *watch* (the timepiece). The name is that of a firm of book and magazine importers in Plaistow, East London.

— **Gordon Highlanders** a Scottish infantry regiment. It was originally raised in 1794 as the 100th Highlanders by the 5th duke of Gordon, 1770–1836 (whose family name was Gordon). In 1798 it became the 92nd Highlanders, and in 1881 they amalgamated with the 75th Stirlingshire Regiment to become the Gordon Highlanders. They were disbanded in 1994.

— **Gordon Riots** anti-Roman Catholic riots in London in 1780, fomented by Lord George Gordon, 1751–93

— **Gordon setter** a Scottish breed of gun-dog with a long black-and-tan coat. It is named after Alexander Gordon, 1743–1827, 4th duke of Gordon.

— **Gordon's gin** a British brand of gin, developed in London in the 1760s by the Scotsman Alexander Gordon

— **Gordonstoun** a public school in Moray, Scotland, founded in 1934 at a location named after himself in 1638 by Sir Robert Gordon, a local landowner

— **Invergordon** a town and port on the shores of the Cromarty Firth, Highland. It was developed in the 18th century by Sir William Gordon, in whose honour its name was changed from the earlier Inverbreckie.

Gore (i) 'person from Gore', the name of various places in England ('triangular piece of land'); (ii) from a medieval French nickname for a greedy lazy person (Old French *gore* 'sow') [Albert ('Al') Gore, 1948–, US Democratic politician, vice-president 1993–2001; Ormsby Gore, see **Ormsby**]

Goreham, Gorham 'person from Goreham', Norfolk ('homestead on a triangular piece of land')

Goring (i) 'person from Goring', Oxfordshire and Sussex ('settlement of Gāra's people'); (ii) a

Jewish surname of unknown origin and meaning [Marius Goring, 1912–98, British actor]

Gorman (i) from the Old English personal name *Gārmund*, literally 'spear protection'; (ii) 'person who lives on or near a triangular piece of land' (Old English *gāra* 'spearhead-shaped piece of land'); (iii) from Irish Gaelic *Mac Gormáin* 'son of *Gormán*' and *Ó Gormáin* 'descendant of *Gormán*', a personal name meaning literally 'little blue one'. See also **O'Gorman**; (iv) a Jewish surname of unknown origin and meaning [Teresa Gorman, 1931–, British Conservative politician]

Gormley, Gormly from Irish Gaelic *Ó Gormghaile* 'descendant of *Gormghal*', a personal name meaning literally 'noble valour'. See also **Grimley** (ii) [Antony Gormley, 1950–, British sculptor; Joe Gormley (Lord Gormley), 1921–93, British trade-union leader]

Gorse (i) 'person who lives in an area overgrown with gorse bushes'; (ii) 'person from Gorse', the name of various places in northern France ('place by or surrounded with a hawthorn hedge') [Ralph Gorse, confidence trickster who is the antihero of a trilogy of novels by Patrick Hamilton (the first was *The West Pier* (1952))]

Gorst a different form of **Gorse** (i)

Gorton 'person from Gorton', Lancashire ('dirty farmstead')

Gosling (i) from a medieval nickname applied to someone thought to resemble a gosling (i.e. a young goose); (ii) a different form of **Jocelyn**

Goss see **Gosse**

Gossage 'person from Gorsuch', Lancashire ('stream on which there is a ford for geese')

Gossart, Gossard (i) 'goose-keeper' (literally 'goose-herd'); (ii) from an insulting French variant of **Gosse**

Gosse, Goss from the Old French personal name *Gosse*, from Germanic *Gozzo* (see **Goosens**) [Sir Edmund Gosse, 1849–1928, British writer]

Gostellow 'person from Gorstella', Cheshire ('mound on a hill growing with gorse')

Gott (i) from the medieval personal name *Gott*, an abbreviated form of various Germanic names beginning with *gōd* 'good' or *got, god* 'god', brought into England by the Normans; (ii) *also* **Got** an invented Jewish name, based on German *Gott* or Yiddish *got* 'god'

Gottlieb, Gotlieb (i) from the German personal name *Gottlieb*, literally 'god-love' (i.e. 'one who loves God'; the name was often a direct translation of Greek *Theophilos*); (ii) a Jewish name, either from the Yiddish person name *Gotlib* (from German *Gottlieb*), or a newly invented one formed from the Yiddish elements *Got* 'god' and *lib* 'love'

Goudie, Gowdie different forms of **Goldie**

— *The Confession of Isobel Gowdie* an orchestral work (1990) by James MacMillan based on the story of Isobel Gowdie, a young Scottish housewife who was tried for witchcraft in 1662

Gough (i) *also* **Goff** 'metal worker, smith' (from Gaelic *gobha* and Cornish and Breton *goff*). See also **Gove**, **Gow**, **McGowan**; (ii) from a Welsh nickname for a red-haired person (from Welsh *coch* 'red'). See also **Gooch** [Darren Gough, 1970–, English cricketer]

Gould, Goold different forms of **Gold** [Bryan Gould, 1939–, New Zealand-born British Labour politician; Shane Gould, 1956–, Australian swimmer; Stephen Jay Gould, 1941–2002, US palaeontologist, evolutionary biologist and writer]

Goulden, Goolden different forms of **Golden** (i) [Jilly Goolden, 1956–, British wine journalist; Richard Goolden, 1895–1981, British actor]

Gourlay, Gourley a Scottish name of uncertain origin and meaning – perhaps from the name of an unidentified place in Normandy. See also **Gurley** (ii)

Govan (i) 'person from Govan', Glasgow ('dear rock'); (ii) 'metal worker, smith' (from Gaelic *gobhan* 'little smith')

Gove a Scottish variant of **Gough** (i) [Philip Gove, 1902–72, US lexicographer]

Gover (i) an English name of uncertain origin and meaning – perhaps from a medieval nickname based on *go fair*, denoting someone who proceeds in an elegant fashion; (ii) a Jewish name of unknown origin and meaning. See also **Gower** (iv) [Alf Gover, 1908–2001, English cricketer]

Gow a Scottish variant of **Gough** (i) [Ian Gow, 1937–90, British Conservative politician]

Gowans a different form of **McGowan** (i). See also **Gowing** (ii)

Gowdie see **Goudie**

Gower (i) 'person who lives in the Gower peninsula', southwestern Wales (Welsh *Gŵyr*, literally 'curved', from the peninsula's hook-like shape); (ii) 'person from *Gohiere*', the Old French name of a region of northeastern France, or 'person from Gouy', the name of various places in northern France (derived from the Gallo-Roman personal name *Gaudius*); (iii) from the Norman personal name *Gohier* or *Goier*, of Germanic origin and meaning literally 'good army'; (iv) a different form of **Gover** (ii) [David Gower, 1957–, English cricketer; John Gower, ?1330–1408, English poet; Leveson Gower, see **Levison**]

— **Gower Street** a street in Bloomsbury, central London, built in the late 18th century and today dominated by the institutions of London University. It was named in honour of Lady Gertrude Leveson-Gower, wife of the 4th duke of Bedford, who supervised its development.

Gowers 'son of **Gower** (iii)' [Sir Ernest Gowers, 1880–1966, British civil servant and writer on English usage]

Gowing, Gowin (i) from the Middle English personal name *Gowin*, from Old French *Gouin*, *Godin*, a pet-form of various Germanic personal names beginning with *God-*, *Got-* 'god'; (ii) a different form of **Gowans**

Grable 'digger of ditches or graves' (from a derivative of Middle High German *graben* 'ditch') [Betty Grable, 1916–73, US actress, dancer and singer]

Grace (i) from the female personal name *Grace*; (ii) from a medieval nickname for someone of a pleasant disposition [W.G. Grace, 1848–1915, English cricketer]

— **Grace Gates** gates at the main entrance to Lord's cricket ground (see **Lord**), installed in 1923 in honour of W.G. Grace (see above)

Grade (i) from a medieval German nickname based on either Middle High German *grātac* 'greedy' or *gerāde* 'swift'; (ii) an invented Jewish name based on German *gerade* 'upright' [Lew Grade (Lord Grade; original name Louis Winogradsky), 1906–98, Ukrainian-born British film and television producer; Michael Grade, 1943–, British television executive, nephew of Lew]

Grady a different form of **O'Grady**

Graf from Middle High German *grāve*, *grābe*, a term of rank ranging from middling aristocracy to municipal officialdom. As a surname it may denote literally a person of that title, or a servant of such a person, or (as a nickname) someone who put on aristocratic airs; also, an invented Jewish name based on Middle High German *grāve*, *grābe*.

Grafton 'person from Grafton', the name of various places in England ('farmstead by a grove')

Graham, Grahame, Graeme 'person from Grantham' (see **Grantham**) [Billy Graham, 1918–, US evangelist; Claude Graham-White, 1879–1959, British aviator; Katherine Graham, 1917–2001, US newspaper executive; Kenneth Grahame, 1859–1932, British children's author; Martha Graham, 1893–1991, US dancer and choreographer; Thomas Graham, 1805–69, British physicist]

— **graham cracker** (in the US) a flat dry biscuit made with **graham flour**, an unbolted whole-wheat flour named after the American dietary reformer Dr Sylvester Graham, 1794–1851

— **Graham Land** the northern section of the Antarctic Peninsula, part of the British Antarctic Territory. It was named in honour of Sir James Graham, 1792–1861, First Lord of the Admiralty when the area was first explored in 1832.

— **Graham's law** a law in chemistry relating the diffusion rate of a gas to the inverse square root of its density. It is named after Thomas Graham (see above).

— **Grahamstown** a city in southern South Africa. Its name commemorates Lieutenant-Colonel John Graham, who established it in 1812.

— **W. & J. Graham & Co.** a firm of port shippers, founded in the 1820s by the brothers William and John Graham. Since 1970 it has been part of the Symington Group.

Grainger see **Granger**

Grand a different form of **Grant** (i). See also **Legrand**

Grandison 'person from Granson', on Lake Neuchâtel, Switzerland

— *Sir Charles Grandison* a novel (1754) by Samuel Richardson. Its eponymous hero is a paragon of virtue beset by amorous complications.

Granger, Grainger 'farm bailiff' (Anglo-Norman *grainger*, ultimately from Latin *grānica* 'granary') [Percy Grainger, 1882–1961, Australian composer and pianist; Stewart Granger (original name James Lablache Stewart), 1913–93, British film actor]

— **grangerize** to cut pictures out of a book and use them to illustrate another. The verb commemorates James Granger, 1723–76, whose *Biographical History of England* (1769) had blank pages for illustrations.

Grant (i) a medieval nickname applied to a large person, or a distinguishing name for the senior, more important, etc. of two or more people with the same name (in both cases from Anglo-Norman *graund, graunt* 'large, tall', from Old French *grand, grant*). See also **Grand**; (ii) from the Old English personal name *Granta* (see **Grantham**) [Cary Grant (original name Alexander Archibald Leach), 1904–86, British-born US film actor; Duncan Grant, 1885–1978, British painter; Hugh Grant, 1960–, British actor; Richard E. Grant, 1957–, Swaziland-born British actor; Russell Grant, 1952–, British astrologist; Ulysses S. Grant, 1822–85, US general and politician, president 1869–77]

— **Glen Grant** a whisky distillery established at Rothes, Scotland in 1840 by James and John Grant

— **Grantown-on-Spey** a small resort town on the River Spey, in Highland. It was founded in 1766 as a model village by the local laird, Sir James Grant, 1738–1811.

— **Jimmy Grant** 19th-century Australian and New Zealand rhyming slang for *immigrant*

— **William Grant & Sons Ltd.** a Scottish whisky producer, established in Glenfiddich in 1886 by William Grant, 1839–1923

Grantham 'person from Grantham', Lincolnshire ('village built on gravel', or possibly 'Granta's homestead', from an Old English personal name probably meaning literally 'snarler'). See also **Graham** [Leslie Grantham, 1947–, British actor]

Granville 'person from Grainville', the name of various places in Normandy ('Guarin's settlement', from a Germanic personal name meaning literally 'guard' (see **Waring**)). See also **Greenfield**, **Grenfell**, **Grenville** [Harley Granville-Barker, 1877–1946, British actor, producer and dramatist]

Grass (i) 'person who lives on an area of grassland'; (ii) 'shoemaker' (Gaelic *greusaiche*); (iii) from a medieval nickname for a fat person (Anglo-Norman *gras* 'fat')

Gratton, Gratten, Grattan 'person from Gratton', the name of several places in England (variously 'large settlement' and 'large hill') [Henry Grattan, 1746–1820, Irish politician]

Grave (i) 'steward' (Middle English *greyve*, from Old Norse *greifi*); (ii) 'person who lives in an area of gravelly soil' (Old French *grave* 'gravel'); (iii) a different form of **Grove** (i)

Graves 'son of **Grave** (i)' [Peter Graves (original name Peter Aurness), 1925–, US actor; Robert Graves, 1895–1985, British poet]

— **Graves' disease** an inflammatory disorder of the thyroid gland commonly associated with protrusion of the eyes. It is named after the Irish physician Robert J. Graves, 1796–1853.

Graveson 'son of **Grave** (i)'

Gray (i) *also* **Grey** from a medieval nickname for someone with grey hair or a grey beard; (ii) 'person from Graye', Normandy ('place associated with *Grātus*', a Gallo-Roman personal name meaning literally 'pleasing') [Dame Beryl Grey, 1927–, British ballet dancer; Charles Grey (2nd Earl Grey), 1764–1845, British Whig politician, prime minister 1830–34; Cornelia Gray, a female detective created by the mystery novelist P.D. James; Dolly Gray, the heroine of the song 'Goodbye Dolly, I must leave you', popular amongst soldiers of the First World War; 'Monsewer' Eddie Gray, 1898–1969, British comic performer, member of the 'Crazy Gang'; Sir Edward Grey (Viscount Grey of Falloden), 1862–1933, British Liberal politician, foreign secretary 1905–16; Sir George Edward Grey, 1812–98, Portuguese-born British explorer and colonial administrator; Lady Jane Grey, 1537–54, queen of England for nine days (1553); John Gray, 1951–, US family therapist; Simon Gray, 1921–, British playwright; Thomas Gray, 1716–71, British poet; Zane Grey, 1872–1939, US writer of Westerns]

— **Alma Gray, Dolly Gray** see above, **Dora Gray** Australian rhyming slang for *trey*, an Australian slang term for a threepenny coin

— **Earl Grey** a tea made by flavouring China tea with bergamot oil. The recipe for it was supposedly given to the 2nd Earl Grey (see above) in the 1830s by a grateful Chinese mandarin whose life had been saved by a British diplomat.

— **gray** the derived SI unit (symbol **Gy**) for the absorbed dose of ionizing radiation, equal to an absorption of 1 joule per kilogram. It takes its name from the British radiobiologist L.H. Gray, 1906–65.

— **Grey College** a college of Durham University, founded in 1959 and named in honour of the 2nd Earl Grey. Grey College is also a school in Bloemfontein, South Africa, founded in 1855 by Sir George Grey (see above), then governor of Cape Colony.

— **Gray's Anatomy** an anatomical textbook, written by Henry Gray, 1821–65, and first published in 1858 under the title *Gray's Anatomy: Descriptive and Surgical*

— **'Gray's Elegy'** the name commonly given to Thomas Gray's *Elegy Written in a Country Churchyard* (1751), a meditation on mortality

— **Gray's Inn** one of the four London Inns of Court, formerly the residence of the de Grey family

— **Grey's Monument** a monument commemorating the 2nd Earl Grey. Situated in the centre of Newcastle upon Tyne, it consists of a 41 m/135 ft column with a statue of Grey on top.

— **yarg** a mild white moist cheese made in Cornwall. Its name is that of its makers, Allan and Jennifer Gray, spelled backwards.

— **Zane Grey** (see above) Australian rhyming slang for *pay* (in the sense 'wages')

Grayshon a different form of **Graveson**

Grayson a different form of **Graveson** [Larry Grayson (original name William White), 1923–95, British popular entertainer]

Grayston a different form of **Graveson**

Grealey from a medieval nickname for someone with a pock-marked face (from Old Northern French *greslé* 'pitted'). See also **Gresley**, **Gridley**

Greathead from a medieval nickname for someone with a large head

Greatrex, **Greatorex** 'person from Greterakes', Derbyshire (literally 'large paths', but used by Derbyshire lead-miners as a term for a vertical vein of ore)

Greave, **Greve** 'person who lives in an area of brushwood' (Old English *græfe* 'brushwood, thicket') or 'person from a place so named'

Greaves, **Greves**, **Greeves** different forms of **Greave** [Jimmy Greaves, 1940–, English footballer]

Greco 'Greek person' (Italian) [Buddy Greco, 1926–, US singer and pianist]

Green, **Greene** (i) from a medieval nickname applied to someone who characteristically wore green clothing or to someone who played the part of the 'Green Man' in May Day festivities, or 'person who lives by a village green'. See also **Greening**; (ii) an anglicization of the German name *Grün* or the Yiddish name *Grin*, both literally 'green'; (iii) a translation of any of a range of Irish Gaelic surnames based on *glas* 'grey-green' or *uaithne* 'green' [Graham Greene, 1904–91, British novelist; Henry Green, pen-name of Henry Vincent Yorke, 1905–73, British novelist; Sir Hugh Greene, 1910–87, British journalist and television executive, brother of Graham; Hughie Green, 1920–97, Canadian-born British television quiz and talent-show compere; Lorne Greene, 1915–87, US actor; Lucinda Green (*née* Prior-Palmer), 1953–, British three-day-event rider; Nathaneal Greene, 1742–86, American general; Philip Green, 1952–, British businessman; Richard Greene, 1918–85, British actor; Robert Greene, 1558–92, English pamphleteer and dramatist; Robson Green, 1964–, British actor]

— **Green College** a college of Oxford University, founded in 1979 from funds provided by Dr and Mrs Cecil Green of Dallas, Texas (the Lancashire-born Dr Green was founder and chairman of Texas Instruments, Inc.)

— **Greeneland** a facetious name given to the imaginative world inhabited by the characters in the novels of Graham Greene (see above). It puns on *Greenland*.

— **Jimmy/Jamie Green** a name given in the 19th century to a type of sail found on tea-clippers. It is not known who the original Jimmy or Jamie Green may have been.

Greenall a different form of **Greenhalgh**

Greenaway (i) 'person who lives by a grassy path'; (ii) an alteration of the Welsh personal name *Geronwy* (perhaps literally 'heron'). See also **Greenway** [Kate Greenaway, 1846–1901, British

artist and book illustrator; Peter Greenaway, 1942–, British film director]

Greenberg a partial anglicization of the German surname *Grünberg* 'person who lives in *Grünberg*' (literally 'green hill') or of the invented Jewish surname *Grinberg* (Yiddish, with the same literal meaning). See also **Greenhill** (ii)

Greene see **Green**

Greener (i) 'person from Greenhaugh', Northumberland ('green nook of land'); (ii) an anglicization of the Jewish surname *Griner*, a different form of *Grin* (see **Green** (ii))

Greenfield (i) 'person from Greenfield', the name of numerous places in England ('green open country'); (ii) a different form of **Granville**; (iii) an anglicization of the German name *Grünfeld* or the Yiddish name *Grinfeld*, both literally 'green field'

Greengrass 'person who lives in a place where the grass is notably green'

Greenhalgh, **Greenhall** 'person from Greenhalgh', Lancashire ('green hollow'). See also **Greenall**, **Greenhough** (ii)

Greenhill (i) 'person from Greenhill', the name of various places in England ('green hill'); (ii) an anglicization of the German surname *Grünberg* 'person who lives in *Grünberg*' (literally 'green hill') or of the invented Jewish surname *Grinberg* (Yiddish, with the same literal meaning). See also **Greenberg**

Greenhough, **Greenhow**, **Greenough** (i) 'person from Greenhow or Gerna', Yorkshire and Lancashire respectively (both literally 'green mound'); (ii) a different form of **Greenhalgh** [Horatio Greenough, 1805–52, US sculptor]

Greenidge 'person from Greenhedge Farm', Nottinghamshire ('green hedge') [Gordon Greenidge, 1951–, West Indian cricketer]

Greening a different form of **Green** (i)

Greenough see **Greenhough**

Greenslade 'someone who lives in a fertile valley'

Greensmith 'coppersmith' (with reference to verdigris, the greenish patina on oxidized copper)

Greenspan an anglicization of the invented Jewish surname *Grünspan*, from German *Grünspan* 'verdigris' (see **Greensmith**) (ultimately a partial loan translation of medieval Latin *viride hispanicum* 'Spanish green') [Alan Greenspan, 1926–, US businessman and economist]

Greenstreet 'person who lives by a grassy road' [Sydney Greenstreet, 1879–1954, British-born US actor]

Greenway a different form of **Greenaway**

Greenwell 'person who lives by a stream amongst fertile pastureland' or 'person from Greenwell', the name of various places in England

Greenwood (i) 'person who lives in a leafy forest' or 'person from Greenwood', the name of various places in England; (ii) an anglicization of the invented Jewish surnames *Grünholz* and *Grünwald*, from German *Grünholz*, *Grünwald* 'green forest' [Ron Greenwood, 1921–2006, English football manager; Walter Greenwood, 1903–74, British novelist]

Greer see **Grier**

Greerson see **Grierson**

Gregg, Greg reduced forms of **Gregory** [Hubert Gregg, 1914–2004, British broadcaster and songwriter]

Gregor, Greggor reduced forms of **McGregor**

Gregory from the male personal name *Gregory*, ultimately from Greek *Grēgorios*, a derivative of *grēgorein* 'to be awake or alert' but popularly associated in the Middle Ages with Latin *greg-* 'assembly, flock' and the metaphor of Christ as the 'good shepherd'. See also **Gregg, Greig, Grier, Grigg, McGregor** [Lady Augusta Gregory, 1852–1932, Irish theatre patron and dramatist; Maundy Gregory, 1877–1941, British spy and seller of honours; Richard Gregory, 1923–, British psychologist]

Gregson 'son of **Gregory**' [Edward Gregson, 1945–, British composer; John Gregson, 1919–75, British actor]

Greig a reduced form of **Gregory**. It is standardly pronounced 'greg'. [Tony Greig, 1946–, South African-born English cricketer]

Grenfell a different form of **Grenville** [Joyce Grenfell (*née* Phipps), 1910–79, British actress and comedienne; Julian Grenfell, 1888–1915, British poet]
— **Grenfell cloth** the proprietary name (registered in 1926) for a type of tough windproof cotton fabric. It was taken from that of Sir Wilfred Thomason Grenfell, 1865–1940, a British medical missionary who in 1893 founded the Labrador Medical Mission.

Grenville a different form of **Granville** [Sir Richard Grenville, ?1541–91, English naval warrior; William Grenville (Lord Grenville), 1759–1834, British statesman, prime minister 1806–07]

Gresham 'person from Gresham', Norfolk ('grassy homestead or enclosure'). See also **Grisham** [Sir Thomas Gresham, ?1519–79, English financier and philanthropist, founder of the Royal Exchange]
— **Gresham College** an institution founded in 1579 by Sir Thomas Gresham (see above) for the delivery of public lectures on a range of academic subjects. The Royal Society evolved from it in the mid-17th century.
— **Gresham's law** the theory that bad money drives good money out of circulation because a currency of lower intrinsic value will be used while one of higher intrinsic value will be hoarded. It was attributed in the 19th century to Sir Thomas Gresham.

Gresley (i) 'person from Gresley', Derbyshire ('gravelly glade'); (ii) a different form of **Grealey** [Sir Nigel Gresley, 1876–1941, British engineer and locomotive designer]

Gretton a different form of **Gritton**

Greville 'person from Gréville', northern France ('Creiz's settlement', from a personal name of Germanic origin) [Sir Fulke Greville, 1554–1628, English poet and biographer]
— **grevillea** an ornamental Australian evergreen tree or shrub. It was named in honour of the Scottish horticulturist Charles Francis Greville, 1749–1809.

Grewcock a different form of **Grocott**

Grey see **Gray** (i)

Grice (i) 'swineherd', or from a medieval nickname for someone felt to resemble a pig (in either case from Middle English *grice* 'pig', from Old Norse *griss*); (ii) from a medieval nickname for a man with grey hair or a grey beard (from Old French *gris* 'grey')

Gridley a different form of **Grealey**

Grier, Greer reduced forms of **Gregory** [Germaine Greer, 1939–, Australian writer and feminist]
— **Germaine Greer** (see above) rhyming slang for *beer*

Grierson, Greerson 'son of **Grier**' [John Grierson, 1898–1972, British documentary film-maker]

Grieve 'steward, manager' (Middle English *greve*)

Grieves 'son of **Grieve**'

Griffin (i) from a medieval nickname for a fierce person (from Middle English *griffin* 'gryphon'); (ii) a different form of **Griffith**; (iii) from Irish Gaelic *Ó Gríobhtha* 'descendant of *Gríobhtha*', a personal name meaning literally 'gryphon'

Griffith from the Old Welsh male personal name *Gruffydd* (the second syllable represents *udd* 'lord', but the origin and meaning of the first is not known) [Arthur Griffith, 1872–1922, Irish journalist and nationalist; Charlie Griffith, 1938–, West Indian cricketer; D.W. Griffith, 1875–1948, US film director; Florence Griffith Joyner (*née* Griffith), 1959–98, US athlete; Hugh Griffith, 1912–80, British actor; Kenneth Griffith, 1921–2006, British actor and documentary film-maker]

Griffiths 'son of **Griffith**' [Richard Griffiths, 1947–, British actor; Terry Griffiths, 1947–, Welsh snooker player]

Grigg a reduced form of **Gregory** [John Grigg (Lord Altrincham 1955–63), 1924–2001, British historian and politician]

Griggs 'son of **Grigg**'

Grigson 'son of **Grigg**' [Geoffrey Grigson, 1905–85, British poet and critic; Jane Grigson (*née* McIntire), 1928–90, British food writer, wife of Geoffrey]

Grimaldi 'son of *Grimaldo*', an Italian and Spanish personal name of Germanic origin, meaning literally 'helmet-rule' [Joseph Grimaldi, 1779–1837, British clown]

Grimes 'son of *Grim*', a medieval male personal name, from Old Norse *Grímr*, literally 'mask' [Captain Grimes, the egregious bigamous schoolmaster in Evelyn Waugh's novel *Decline and Fall* (1928); Peter Grimes, the misanthropic Suffolk fisherman who is the subject of one of the tales in George Crabbe's *The Borough* (1810), the basis of Benjamin Britten's opera *Peter Grimes* (1945)]

Grimley (i) 'person from Grimley', Worcestershire ('Grima's glade'); (ii) a different form of **Gormley**

Grimshaw 'person from Grimshaw', Lancashire (either 'Grim's wood' or 'wood haunted by ghosts') [John Atkinson Grimshaw, 1836–93, British artist; Sir Nicholas Grimshaw, 1939–, British architect]

Grimston, Grimstone 'person from Grimston', the name of various places in England ('Grim's settlement')

Grindrod 'person from Grindrod', Lancashire ('green glade')

Grisham a different form of **Gresham** [John Grisham, 1955–, US author]

Griswold 'person from Griswolds Farm', Warwickshire (probably 'gravelly wood')

Gritton 'person from Gretton', the name of various places in England (mostly 'settlement on gravelly ground'). See also **Gretton**

Grobelaer, Grobelaar, Grobbelaar, Grobler probably from a medieval Dutch nickname for an untidy person, from Middle Dutch *grobellen* 'to rummage' [Bruce Grobbelaar, 1957–, South African football goalkeeper playing in England]

Grocock a different form of **Grocott**

Grocott, Growcott from a medieval nickname for a lanky person (from Old French *gruot* 'little crane'). See also **Grewcock**, **Grocock**

Grogan from Irish Gaelic Ó *Grúgáin* 'descendant of *Grúgán*', a personal name meaning literally 'little angry one', or Ó *Gruagáin* 'descendant of *Gruagán*', a personal name meaning literally 'little hairy one'

Groom, Groome 'servant' (Middle English *grome* 'boy, servant')

Gross from a medieval nickname for a large man. The name evolved in Middle English, from Old French *gros* 'big', and was also introduced independently as a German and Jewish name, from Middle High German *grōz* 'big' (the French and German adjectives are ultimately related).

Grossmann, Grosmann, Grosman different forms of the German and Jewish name **Gross**

Grosvenor 'chief huntsman' (i.e. the man in charge of hunting on a great feudal estate) (from Anglo-Norman *gros veneour* 'great hunter'). The name is pronounced as 'grove-ner'. [Grosvenor, the family name of the earls of Wilton and of the dukes of Westminster]
— **Grosvenor Square** a square in the West End of London, in Mayfair, home to the US Embassy. It was laid out in the 1720s on land owned by the Grosvenor family (now dukes of Westminster).

Grout 'dealer in coarse meal' (Old English *grūt* 'coarse meal, porridge') [Wally Grout, 1927–68, Australian cricketer]

Grove (i) 'someone who lives by a grove' (Old English *grāf* 'grove, thicket'); (ii) an anglicization of the French surname *Le Groux* or *Le Greux*,

brought into England by the Huguenots and of uncertain origin and meaning
— ***Grove's Dictionary*** an encyclopedic musical reference work, in full *Grove's Dictionary of Music and Musicians*, first published 1879–89. Its founder and first editor was the British musicologist Sir George Grove, 1820–1900. A new edition (the *New Grove*) was published in 1980.
— ***The Grove Family*** a soap opera, the first for an adult audience on British television, broadcast by the BBC between 1954 and 1957. The eponymous lower-middle-class family lived in Hendon.

Grover a different form of **Grove**

Groves a different form of **Grove** [Sir Charles Groves, 1915–92, British conductor]

Grubb, Grubbe from a medieval nickname applied to an undersized person (Middle English *grub* 'midget')

Gruber from a German and Jewish name meaning literally 'someone who lives in a hollow in the ground' (from German *Grube* 'pit')

Grundy probably from a different form of the personal name *Gondri*, brought into England by the Normans and ultimately of Germanic origin, meaning literally 'battle-power' [Eddie Grundy, good-natured rustic wide boy in the BBC radio soap opera *The Archers* (he was 'born' in 1951)]
— **Eddie Grundies** (see above) rhyming slang for *undies* 'underwear'
— **Mrs Grundy** someone who has a prudish narrow-minded attitude towards others. The name is that of such a character in Thomas Morton's play *Speed the Plough* (1798), who has also given English the term **Grundyism** to encapsulate the attitude.
— **Reg Grundies** Australian rhyming slang for *undies* 'underwear'. Reg Grundy, 1924–, was the television producer responsible for the Australian soap opera *Neighbours*.

Guard, Gard 'protector, guard' or 'watchman'

Guerrero from a Spanish, Portuguese and Italian nickname for a soldier or for a truculent person (from *guerrero* 'warrior')

Guest from a medieval nickname for someone who is new to an area or a stranger
— **Guest, Keen and Nettlefold** a British engineering company (its name latterly abbreviated to **GKN**). It grew from an ironworks set up in Wales in 1767 by John Guest. A merger in 1900 with the Patent Nut and Bolt Co. (founded by Arthur Keen, 1835–1915) produced Guest, Keen and Co. In 1902 it was joined by Nettlefolds Ltd., founded by John Sutton Nettlefold, 1792–1866, and established as a limited company in 1880 by his son John Henry Nettlefold, 1827–81.

Guggenheim, Gugenheim a Jewish name probably meaning 'person from Guggenheim', Alsace (a place-name of unknown origin and meaning) [Peggy Guggenheim, 1898–1979, US art collector and philanthropist]

Guilford, Gilford 'person from Guildford', Surrey ('ford by the golden one')
— **Hutchinson-Gilford syndrome** see **Hutchinson**

Guinness, **Guiness** reduced forms of **McGuinness** [Sir Alec Guinness (original name allegedly Alec Guinness de Cuffe), 1914–2000, British actor; Arthur Guinness, 1725–1803, Irish brewer; Bryan Guinness (Lord Moyne), 1905–92, British socialite, businessman and writer, heir to the Guinness brewing fortune]
— **Guinness** a brand of stout produced by the brewery founded in 1759 by Arthur Guinness (see above)
— *Guinness Book of Records* an annual reference book detailing world records in a wide range of natural and human fields. Commissioned by Guinness brewery, it was first published in 1955, its records having been assembled by the brothers Norris and Ross McWhirter. Since 2000 it has been called *Guinness World Records*.

Gullick, **Gulick** from the Middle English personal name *Gullake*, a descendant of Old English *Gūthlāc*, literally 'battle-sport'. See also **Gillick**

Gulliver from a medieval nickname for a greedy person (from Old French *goulafre* 'glutton')
— *Gulliver's Travels* a satire (1726) by Jonathan Swift. The adventures of the shipwrecked ship's surgeon Lemuel Gulliver offer opportunities for a wide-ranging and often savage lampooning of human stupidity and vice.

Gumm, **Gumme** different forms of **Gomme** [Frances Gumm, original name of Judy **Garland**]

Gummer a different form of **Gomer** [John Selwyn Gummer, 1939–, British Conservative politician]

Gunn (i) 'someone who operates a cannon or other large gun'; (ii) *also* **Gun** from the Old Norse male personal name *Gunnr* or the female personal name *Gunne*, both from a shortened form of any of a range of compound names beginning with *gunne* 'battle'. See also **Gunson**; (iii) from Scottish Gaelic *Mac Ghille Dhuin* 'son of the brown one's servant' (see **Dunn** (ii)) [George Gunn, 1879–1958, English cricketer; Thom Gunn, 1929–2004, British poet]
— **Gunn effect** in a semiconductor, the microwave oscillation produced by a steady electric field that is larger than the normal threshold value. It was named after the Egyptian-born British physicist J.B. Gunn, 1928–.

Gunnell from the Middle English female personal name *Gunnild*, from Old Norse *Gunnhildr*, literally 'battle-strife' [Sally Gunnell, 1966–, British athlete]

Gunson 'son of **Gunn** (ii)'

Gunter, **Gunther** from the Norman personal name *Gunter*, of Germanic origin and meaning literally 'battle-army' [Edmund Gunter, 1581–1626, English mathematician; Ray Gunter, 1909–77, British Labour politician]
— **according to Gunter** in accordance with strict calculation; exactly. The expression, which evokes the mathematical precision of Edmund Gunter (see above), is the American equivalent of 'according to Cocker' (see **Cocker**).
— **Gunter's chain** a chain 66 ft. long (consisting of 100 links) that is used as a measuring device in surveying. It is named after Edmund Gunter.

Gunton 'person from Gunton', Suffolk and Norfolk ('Gunni's settlement')

Guppy, **Guppey**, **Guppie** 'person from Guppy', Dorset ('Guppa's enclosure') [Darius Guppy, 1964–, British confidence trickster]
— **guppy** a small freshwater fish (*Poecilia reticulata*) of the Caribbean and South America that has a brightly coloured tail, produces live young and is popular in aquariums. It was named after the Reverend R.J. Lechmere Guppy, 1836–1916, who sent the first specimen from Trinidad to the British Museum.

Gupta 'secret, protected' (Sanskrit)

Gurley (i) an anglicization of the French name *Gourlé*, from Old French *gourle* 'money-belt' (perhaps as a nickname for a mean person); (ii) a different form of **Gourlay** [Helen Gurley Brown, 1922–, US author, publisher and businesswoman, editor of *Cosmopolitan* magazine]

Gurney 'person from Gournay-en-Brai', northern France ('settlement of *Gordīnus*', a Gallo-Roman personal name) [Ivor Gurney, 1890–1937, British composer and poet]

Gurton 'person from Girton', Cambridgeshire and Nottinghamshire ('farmstead on gravelly ground'). See also **Girtin**
— *Gammer Gurton's Needle* an English verse comedy (1566) of uncertain authorship. The plot, such as it is, concerns the loss and rediscovery of a needle used to mend the clothes of Hodge, the servant of Gammer Gurton (*gammer* was a title of respect for an old woman).

Gustavsson, **Gustafsson** 'son of *Gustaf*', a Swedish male personal name meaning literally 'cudgel of the Gaut people'

Guthrie (i) 'person from Guthrie', Forfar ('windy place'); (ii) from Scottish Gaelic *Mac Uchtre* 'son of *Uchtre*', a personal name perhaps related to *uchtlach* 'child'; (iii) a substitution for Irish Gaelic *Ó Flaithimh* 'descendant of *Flaitheamh*', a personal name meaning literally 'prince' (the *F* was silent, so the name seems to have been misidentified with Gaelic *laithigh* 'mud'; 'mud' goes with 'gutters', and 'gutter' apparently suggested the name *Guthrie*) [Sir Tyrone Guthrie, 1900–71, British stage director; Woody Guthrie, 1912–67, US folk singer and composer]

Gutierrez 'son of *Gutierre*', a medieval Spanish male personal name of Germanic origin, perhaps meaning literally 'battle-sword'

Gutteridge, **Guttridge**, **Gutridge** from the Old English male personal names *Gōdrīc*, literally 'good power' (see also **Goodrich** and **Goodwright**), and *Cūthrīc*, literally 'famous power'. See also **Cutress** [Reg Gutteridge, 1924–, British boxing journalist and commentator]

Guy, **Guye** (i) from the male personal name *Guy*, a French alteration of the Germanic personal name *Wido*, of uncertain origin and meaning (perhaps related to English *wood* or *wide*); (ii) 'guide' (from Old French *gui*)

— **Guy's Hospital** a hospital in London, on the south bank of the River Thames by London Bridge. It was established in 1721 by the bookseller Thomas Guy, 1644–1724.

Guyler from a medieval nickname for a deceitful person (a derivative of Middle English *guylen* 'to deceive') [Derek Guyler, 1914–99, British comedy actor]

Guyton 'person from Gayton', Norfolk ('farmstead where goats are kept')

Gwyn, Gwynn, Gwynne, Gwinn from a medieval Welsh nickname for someone with fair hair or pale skin (Welsh *gwyn* 'light, fair') [Nell Gwyn *or* Gwynn, 1650–87, English actress, mistress of Charles II]

— **Nell Gwyn** (see above) rhyming slang for *gin*

H

Hacker (i) 'woodcutter' (from a derivative of Middle English *hacken* 'to hack'); (ii) from a German, Dutch and Jewish name meaning literally 'butcher', or possibly in some cases 'woodcutter' (ultimately from the same Germanic source as the native English name) [James Hacker, politician (played by Paul Eddington) at the mercy of civil servants in the BBC television sitcoms *Yes, Minister* (1980–82) and *Yes, Prime Minister* (1986–88)]

Hackett (i) 'little *Hake*', a medieval male personal name, from Old Norse *Haki*, originally a nickname for a hunchback or someone with a hooked nose (literally 'hook'); (ii) 'person from Halkhead', Strathclyde region ('hawkwood'). See also **Halkett** — **Hackett** a British firm of men's outfitters, established in 1983 by Jeremy Hackett and Ashley Lloyd-Jennings

Hacking 'person from Hacking', Lancashire (perhaps 'fish weir')

Hackmann, Hackman different forms of **Hacker** (ii) [Gene Hackman, 1930–, US film actor]

Hackney (i) 'person from Hackney', Greater London ('Haca's island'); (ii) perhaps 'stable-hand' (from Middle English *hakenei* 'medium-sized riding horse')

Hadaway a different form of **Hathaway**

Haddock (i) perhaps 'fishmonger', or from a medieval nickname for someone thought to resemble a fish (from Middle English *hadduc* 'haddock'); (ii) perhaps 'person from Haydock', near Liverpool ('barley place'); (iii) perhaps from the Old English personal name *Ædduc* 'little *Æddi*', a name formed from the first syllable (from *ēad* 'prosperity') of a range of compound personal names

Haddon (i) 'person from Haddon', the name of various places in England ('heather-hill'); (ii) *also* **Hadden** a different form of **Howden** (i)

Haddow 'person from Haddo', Grampian region ('half a *dabhach*', a Gaelic term of land measurement)

Haden (i) 'person from Haden Hill', Worcestershire (perhaps 'heather-hill'); (ii) a different form of **Hayden** (i)

Hadfield a different form of **Hatfield**

Hadley, Hadlee, Hadleigh 'person from Hadley or Hadleigh', the name of various places in England (mainly 'glade where heather grows') [Patrick Hadley, 1899–1973, British composer; Sir Richard Hadlee, 1951–, New Zealand cricketer]

Hadlow 'person from Hadlow', Kent ('mound where heather grows')

Haendel see **Handel**

Hafner, Haffner 'potter', a German and Jewish surname based ultimately on German dialect *Hafen* 'pot'. See also **Heffner**

Hagan from Irish Gaelic *Ó hÁgáin* 'descendant of *Ógán*', a personal name meaning literally 'little young one'. See also **O'Hagan**

Hagen a different form of **Hain** (iv–v) [Walter Hagen, 1892–1969, US golfer]

Hagerty, Haggerty, Haggarty different forms of **Hegarty**

Haggard, Hagard from a medieval nickname applied to a wild or unruly person (from Old French *hagard* 'wild') [Sir Henry Rider Haggard, 1856–1925, British adventure novelist]

Haggart a different form of **Haggard**

Hagler 'person who lives by a hedge or enclosure' (from a derivative of Middle High German *hac* 'hedge, enclosure') [Marvin Hagler, 1954–, US boxer]

Hague see **Haig**

Hahn (i) from a medieval German nickname for a swaggering or conceited man (from Middle High German *hane* 'cockerel'); (ii) an invented Jewish name based on German *Hahn* 'cockerel'; (iii) a different form of **Hain** (iv–v)

Haifetz see **Heifetz**

Haig, Haigh, Hague (i) 'person who lives by an enclosure surrounded by a hedge or fence' (from Old English *haga*) or 'person from Haigh or Haig', the name of various places in northern England ('hedge, enclosure', from Old English *haga or* Old Norse *hagi*); (ii) 'person from Hague', the name (variously spelled) of numerous places in northern France ('hedge, enclosure', from Old Norse *hagi*) [Alexander Haig, 1924–, US general and politician; Douglas Haig (Earl Haig), 1861–1928, British field marshal; Kenneth Haigh, 1931–, British actor; William Hague, 1961–, British Conservative politician]

— **Haig Fund** a British charity (more fully the 'Earl Haig Fund') founded in 1921 by Douglas Haig (see above) to help ex-servicemen. It is responsible for the manufacture and distribution of Remembrance Day poppies.

— **Haigspeak** language use characterized by tortured syntax, extravagant and often impenetrable metaphor, and enthusiasm for converting nouns into verbs. It became a trademark of Alex-

ander Haig (see above), particularly during his time as US secretary of state, 1981–82.
— **Haig whisky** any of a range of Scotch whiskies produced by John Haig & Company Ltd. (now part of Diageo). The firm was founded in 1824 by John Haig, 1802–78. Probably its best-known product is **Haig Dimple**, in a distinctive bottle with three concave sides. Its most successful advertising slogan was 'Don't be vague, ask for Haig!'.

Haile see **Hale** (i)

Hailes, Hails (i) 'person from Hailes', Lothian ('place by a manor or other large house'), or 'person from Hailes', Gloucestershire ('dirty stream'); (ii) *also* **Hales** 'person who lives in a nook or hollow of land' (Old English *halh*). See also **Hallows**

Hailey see **Haley**

Hailwood 'person from Halewood', Lancashire ('wood in a nook of land') [Mike Hailwood, 1940–81, British racing motorcyclist]

Hain, Haine (i) 'person from Hayne', the name (variously spelled) of numerous places in England ('hedge, enclosure'); (ii) from the medieval personal name *Hain*, popularized in England by the Normans but ultimately from a Germanic name meaning literally 'hawthorn'. See also **Haines**; (iii) from a medieval nickname for a pathetic or despicable person (from Old English *hēan* 'wretch'); (iv) 'person who lives by an enclosure surrounded by a hedge or fence' (from Middle High German *hagen* 'hedge, enclosure'); (v) from the medieval German personal name *Hagin* (from the same ultimate source as English *Hain* (see (ii))). See also **Hagen, Hahn** [Peter Hain, 1950–, British Labour politician]

Haines, Haynes, Hayns (i) 'person from Haynes', Bedfordshire, a name of uncertain origin and meaning; (ii) 'son of **Hain** (ii)'; (iii) from the Welsh personal name *Einws*, literally 'little *Einion*', a name of uncertain origin and meaning [Arthur Haynes, 1915–66, British comedian; Joe Haines, 1928–, British journalist, press secretary to Harold Wilson 1969–76]

Hainsworth (i) 'person from Hainsworth', Yorkshire ('Hagena's enclosure'); (ii) a different form of **Ainsworth**

Hair, Haire see **Hare** (ii)

Haldane, Halden, Haldin, Hallding (i) from the late Old English personal name *Healfdene*, literally 'half-Dane' (i.e. someone of mixed English and Danish parentage). See also **Alden** (ii); (ii) a different form of **Howden** (i) [J.B.S. Haldane, 1892–1964, British geneticist and philosopher; Richard Haldane (Viscount Haldane), 1856–1928, British Liberal politician and (as secretary of state for war, 1905–12) army reformer, uncle of J.B.S.]

Hale (i) *also* **Haile** 'person who lives in a nook or hollow of land' (Old English *halh*). See also **Hailes** (ii), **Hayler** (ii), **Heal**; (ii) from either of two Old English personal names, *Hæle* (literally 'hero') and *Hægel* (probably literally 'hawthorn') [Binnie Hale, 1899–1984, British musical-comedy and revue actress]

— **Binnie Hale** (see above) rhyming slang for *tale* (usually in the sense of a story told by conmen to fleece their victim)
— **Comet Hale-Bopp** a comet discovered on 23 July 1995 by the US astronomers Alan Hale, 1958–, and Thomas Bopp, 1949–. Its original designation was C/1995 01.
— **Hale and Pace** a British comedy double act consisting of Gareth Hale, 1953–, and Norman Pace, 1953–
— **Hale Observatories** a group of observatories in California and Chile, sponsored by the Californian Institute of Technology and the Carnegie Institution, Washington. They are named after the US astronomer G.E. Hale, 1868–1938, who helped to develop the Mount Wilson and Palomar observatories.

Hales see **Hailes** (ii)

Halevy a different form of **Levi** (with the Hebrew definite article *ha*)

Haley, Haly, Hayley, Hailey 'person from Haley', the name (variously spelled) of numerous places in England ('clearing where hay is made') [Alex Haley, 1921–92, US writer; Bill Haley, 1927–81, US musician; Sir William Haley, 1901–87, British press and broadcasting executive, editor of the *Times* 1952–66]

Halford 'person from Halford', the name of various places in England ('ford by a nook of land')

Halfpenny from a medieval nickname for someone of small stature, of limited financial resources, or who was a tenant paying rent of a halfpenny

Halkett, Halket different forms of **Hackett** (ii)

Hall 'someone who lives near a large or important house' or 'person employed in a manor house or other large house'. See also **Halley** [Henry Hall, 1898–1989, British bandleader; Sir Peter Hall, 1930–, British theatre director; Radclyffe Hall, 1883–1943, British (female) novelist; Wesley Hall, 1937–, West Indian cricketer]
— **Annie Hall** a film comedy (1977) by Woody Allen exploring the neuroses of New York life and featuring Diane Keaton as the eponymous Annie, object of Allen's desires
— **Hallmark** the brand name (registered in the USA in 1923) of a range of greetings cards developed by Joyce Clyde Hall, 1891–1982
— **Henry Halls** (see above) rhyming slang for *balls* 'testicles'
— **Nobby Halls** rhyming slang for *balls* 'testicles'. Nobby Hall was the monotesticular hero of an old music-hall song.

Hallam, Hallum 'person from Hallam', a district in South Yorkshire ('place at the rocks') or a town in Derbyshire ('place at the corners of land') [Arthur Henry Hallam, 1811–33, close friend of Alfred Tennyson and subject of his elegiac poem *In Memoriam A.H.H.* (1850)]

Halley, Hally 'person from Halley', an unidentified place, possibly in Scotland, of which the name is of uncertain origin and meaning (perhaps 'large house within an enclosure'); also perhaps 'person from Hawley', Hampshire ('large house in a glade') [Edmund Halley, 1656–1742, British astronomer, describer of the periodicity of Halley's comet]

Halliday, Haliday, Halladay, Halleday perhaps from a medieval nickname for someone born at Christmas or Easter (from Old English *hāligdæg* 'holy day'). See also **Holiday**

Halliwell, Hallawell, Hallewell, Hallowell 'person from Halliwell', the name (variously spelled) of numerous places in England ('holy well'). See also **Helliwell** [Geri Halliwell, 1972–, British pop singer ('Ginger Spice' of the Spice Girls)]
— *Halliwell's Film Guide* a descriptive catalogue of all the main feature films, originally compiled by Leslie Halliwell, 1929–89. It first appeared in 1977.

Halloran from Irish Gaelic *Ó hAllmhuráin* 'descendant of *Allmhurán*', a personal name meaning literally 'little foreigner'. See also **O'Halloran**

Hallows, Hallowes different forms of **Hailes**

Halpern a different form of **Heilbronn**. See also **Alpert** (i)

Halsey 'person from Halsey', the name of an unidentified place in or near London ('island on a neck of land, peninsula') [William F. Halsey, 1882–1959, US admiral]

Halstead, Halsted 'person from Halstead', the name of numerous places in England (variously 'site of a temporary shelter' and 'site of a hall')

Ham (i) 'person from Ham', Highland region ('homestead'); (ii) *also* **Hamm** 'person living on low-lying land by a stream' or 'person from Ham', the name of various places in southern England (both from Old English *hamm*)

Hamblin, Hamblyn, Hambling, Hamblen from the Anglo-Norman personal name *Hamblin* or *Hamlin*, literally 'little little *Hamo*' (see **Hammond** (i)). See also **Hamley, Hamlin** [Maggi Hambling, 1945–, British artist]

Hambro 'person from Hambro', an unidentified place in northern Germany or Denmark (probably 'water-meadow marsh')
— **Hambros Bank** a British merchant bank established in London in 1839 by the Danish merchant and banker Carl Joachim Hambro

Hambury see **Hanbury**

Hamer (i) 'person from Hamer', Lancashire ('rock, crag'); (ii) 'maker or user of hammers' (from Dutch *hamer* 'hammer'); (iii) a different form of **Hammer** (ii) [Robert Hamer, 1911–63, British film director]

Hamersley see **Hammersley**

Hamill, Hammill (i) 'person from Haineville or Henneville', northern France ('Hagano's settlement'); (ii) from a medieval nickname for someone with scars or other mutilations (from Old English *hamel* 'scarred, crooked') [Mark Hamill, 1951–, US actor]

Hamilton 'person from Hamilton', Leicestershire ('crooked hill') [Alexander Hamilton, ?1755–1804, US statesman, first US secretary of state; Charles Hamilton, 1876–1961, British writer (under many pen-names, notably 'Frank Richards') of boys' stories; David Hamilton (original name David Pilditch), 1939–, British radio presenter; Emma Hamilton (Lady Hamilton; *née* Lyon), 1765–1815, wife of Sir William (the diplomat) and mistress of Horatio Nelson; Lewis Hamilton, 1985–, British racing driver; Neil Hamilton, 1949–, British Conservative politician and entertainer; Patrick Hamilton, 1904–62, British novelist and playwright; Richard Hamilton, 1922–, British painter; Sir William Hamilton, 1730–1803, British diplomat and archaeologist; Sir William Hamilton, 1788–1856, British philosopher; Sir William Rowan Hamilton, 1805–65, Irish mathematician; William Hamilton, 1936–2000, British evolutionary biologist; Willie Hamilton, 1917–2000, British anti-royalist Labour politician]
— **Hamilton** a town near Glasgow. It is said to have been founded in the 13th century by members of the Hamilton family, originally from Leicestershire. Their descendant, the duke of Hamilton, is the premier peer of Scotland. Also, a city in southeastern Ontario, Canada, named after George Hamilton, 1787–1835, a local landowner. Also, a town in Ohio, USA, named in honour of the US statesman Alexander Hamilton (see above). Also, a city in the western North Island, New Zealand, named after the British naval captain John Hamilton, killed in battle with the Maoris in 1864.
— **Hamilton** in US slang, a ten-dollar bill – from the portrait of Alexander Hamilton (see above) on the note
— **Hamiltonian function** a mathematical function (symbol *H*) used to describe the dynamics of a system, e.g. particles in motion, that uses momentum and spatial coordinates. It is named after Sir William Rowan Hamilton (see above).
— **Hamish Hamilton** a British publishing company, founded in London in 1931 by the Scottish-American Hamish Hamilton, 1900–88

Hamley, Hamly different forms of **Hamblin**
— **Hamleys** a large toy store in Regent Street, London. It traces its origins back to 'Noah's Ark', a toyshop opened in London in 1760 by William Hamley. It established its Regent Street site in 1881.

Hamlin, Hamlyn different forms of **Hamblin** [Paul Hamlyn (Lord Hamlyn), 1926–2001, German-born British publisher]

Hammer (i) 'person living on low-lying land by a stream' (from both Old English *hamm* and Old High German *ham* 'low-lying land by a stream'); (ii) 'maker or user of hammers', or from a medieval German nickname for a belligerent person (from Middle High German and Yiddish *hamer* 'hammer') [Armand Hammer, 1898–1990, US industrialist, art collector and philanthropist; M.C. Hammer (original name Stanley Kirk Burrell), 1962–, US rapper; Mike Hammer, a fictional hard-bitten US detective created by the writer Mickey Spillane]

— **Hammer Films** a British film-production company founded in 1934 by the comedian and businessman 'Will Hammer', 1887–1957, and Sir James Carreras. It made its reputation in the 1950s with a series of highly successful horror movies. Will Hammer's real name was William Hinds: 'Hammer' was a stage name that arose out of a short-lived vaudeville double act called 'Hammer and Smith'.

Hammersley, Hamersley probably 'person from Hammersley', an unidentified place with a name of unknown origin and meaning

— **Hamersley Range** a mountain range in northern Western Australia. It was named in honour of Edward Hamersley, 1810–74, an early Australian settler who promoted the expedition led by F.T. Gregory in 1861 that explored the area.

Hammerstein (i) 'person from Hammerstein', the name of various places in Germany and central Europe ('crag stone'); (ii) an invented Jewish name, from German, literally 'hammer-stone' [Oscar Hammerstein II, 1895–1960, German-born US lyricist and librettist]

Hammett, Hammitt from a pet-form of the Anglo-Norman personal name *Hamo* (see **Hammond** (i)) [Dashiell Hammett, 1894–1961, US writer]

Hammond (i) from the Anglo-Norman personal name *Hamo* or *Hamon*, itself of Germanic origin, a shortened form of various compound personal names beginning with *haim* 'home'. See also **Hampson, Haymes**; (ii) from the Old Norse personal names *Hámundr*, literally 'high protection', and *Amundr*, literally 'ancestor protection'. See also **Oman** (i) [Dame Joan Hammond, 1912–96, New Zealand-born British soprano; Walter Hammond, 1903–65, English cricketer]

— **Hammond organ** the proprietary name of a type of electric organ produced from the mid-1930s by the Hammond Instrument Company of Chicago. It was invented in 1929 by the US engineer Laurens Hammond, 1895–1973.

Hammonds 'son of **Hammond**'

Hammons probably a different form of **Hammonds**. See also **Ammons**

Hampden 'person from Hampden', Buckinghamshire ('valley with an enclosure') [John Hampden, 1594–1643, English parliamentarian, opponent of Charles I]

— **Hampden Park** a football stadium in Glasgow, home of Queens Park FC and also venue of Scotland's home international matches. It was named after the nearby Hampden Terrace, which in turn was named after John Hampden (see above).

Hampshire 'person from Hampshire', county of southern England ('Hampton (i.e. Southampton)-shire'), or 'person from Hallamshire', South Yorkshire (see **Hallam**) [Susan Hampshire, 1937–, British actress]

Hampson, Hamson 'son of *Hamo*' (see **Hammond** (i)) [Thomas Hampson, 1955–, US baritone]

Hampton 'person from Hampton', the name of numerous places in England (variously 'high farm-

stead' and 'farmstead in a river-bend') [Christopher Hampton, 1946–, British playwright; Lionel Hampton, 1913–2002, US jazz bandleader]

— **Lionel Hampton** a slang euphemism (inspired by the name of the jazz musician – see above) for *penis*, based on *hampton*, short for *Hampton Wick*, rhyming slang for *prick*

Han (i) a Chinese name, from *Han*, the name of a state that existed about 3000 years ago, in what is now Shaanxi province; (ii) a Korean name

Hanbury, Handbury, Hambury 'person from Hanbury', Staffordshire or Worcestershire ('high fortress') [Robin Hanbury-Tenison, 1936–, British explorer]

Hancock from the medieval personal name *Han* (see **Hann**), with the suffix -*cock* (literally 'cockerel', hence 'jaunty or bumptious young man'), that was often added to create pet-forms of personal names in the Middle Ages [Herbie Hancock, 1940–, US jazz pianist and composer; Sheila Hancock, 1933–, British actress; Tony Hancock, 1924–68, British comic actor, star of the BBC radio and television comedy series *Hancock's Half Hour* (1954–61)]

— **John Hancock** an American colloquialism for a person's signature. It invokes the real John Hancock, 1737–93, the first person to sign the US Declaration of Independence.

Hand from a medieval nickname for someone with a deformed hand or with only one hand. See also **Hands**

Handel, Handl (i) *also* **Haendel** 'little *Hans*', a German personal name that is a shortened form of *Johannes* 'John'; (ii) 'merchant', a Jewish name, from German *Handel* 'trade' [George Frederick Handel, 1685–1759, German-born British composer; Ida Haendel, 1928–, Polish-born British violinist; Irene Handl, 1901–87, British actress]

Handley (i) 'person from Handley or Hanley', the name of various places in England ('high glade'); (ii) from Irish Gaelic *Ó hÁinle* 'descendant of *Áinle*', a personal name meaning literally 'champion'. See also **Hanley** [Vernon Handley, 1930–, British conductor]

— **Handley Page Ltd** the first British aircraft manufacturing company, founded in 1909 by the aircraft designer Sir Frederick Handley Page, 1885–1962. It specialized in bombers, including the World War II Halifax and the Victor V-bomber.

Hands a different form of **Hand** [Israel Hands, an early 18th-century pirate, second-in-command to Blackbeard, whose name was used for one of Long John Silver's piratical henchmen in Robert Louis Stevenson's *Treasure Island* (1883); Terry Hands, 1941–, British theatre director]

Handy perhaps from a medieval nickname for a dextrous person, or alternatively a different form of **Hendy** [W.C. Handy, 1873–1958, US jazz musician]

Handyside, Handasyde 'person from Handyside', Borders region (probably 'hanging slope')

Hanham 'person from Hanham', Gloucestershire ('place by the rocks')

Hankin (i) from the medieval personal name *Hankin*, literally 'little **Hann**'; (ii) 'son of *Khanke*', a Yiddish female personal name, a pet-form of *Khane* (see **Hanna**)

Hankins 'son of **Hankin** (i)'

Hanks 'son of *Hank*', a male personal name that is a shortened form of **Hankin** [Tom Hanks, 1956–, US film actor]

Hanley a different form of **Handley** [Jimmy Hanley, 1918–70, British actor]

Hanlon, Hanlan from Irish Gaelic *Ó hAnluain* 'descendant of *Anluan*', a personal name meaning literally 'great light' or 'great warrior'

Hanmer 'person from Hanmer', Clwyd ('Hagena's lake')

Hann from the medieval male personal name *Han* or *Hann*, a shortened form of *Johan* '**John**'. See also **Anson, Hancock, Hankin, Hansom, Hanson**

Hanna, Hannah (i) from the medieval female personal name *Hannah* or *Anna* (from Hebrew *Chana*, literally 'he (i.e. God) has favoured me (i.e. by allowing me to become pregnant)'); (ii) 'person from Hannethe', an unidentified Scottish place with a name of unknown origin and meaning. See also **Hannay**; (iii) from Irish Gaelic *Ó hAnnaigh* 'descendant of *Annach*', a personal name meaning literally 'inquiry' [Vincent Hanna, 1939–97, British television journalist]

Hannay a different form of **Hanna** (ii) [Richard Hannay, the hero of a number of adventure novels (including *The Thirty-nine Steps* (1915)) by John Buchan]

Hanrahan from Irish Gaelic *Ó hAnradháin* 'descendant of *Anradhán*', a personal name meaning literally 'little hero, little champion'. See also **Horan, Horgan** [Brian Hanrahan, 1949–, British television journalist]

Hanratty from Irish Gaelic *Ó hInreachtaig* 'descendant of the lawyer'. See also **Enright** [James Hanratty, 1936–62, British petty criminal, hanged for the murder of Michael Gregsten in 1961]

Hansard 'maker of knives and other bladed weapons' (from Old French *hansard* 'cutlass, dagger')
— *Hansard* the official published reports of proceedings in the British or Canadian parliaments or similar legislative bodies in the Commonwealth. The name, which was officially adopted in 1943, commemorates the family that originally printed the reports: from 1774, Luke Hansard, 1752–1828, and from 1807 his son, Thomas Curson Hansard, 1776–1833.

Hansen see **Hanson**

Hansford perhaps 'person from Ansford', Somerset ('Ealhmund's ford') [Pamela Hansford Johnson, see **Johnson**]

Hansom a different form of **Hanson**
— hansom cab a covered two-wheeled vehicle drawn by one horse and carrying two passengers inside while the driver sits outside on a raised seat at the rear. It is named after the British architect

Joseph Aloysius Hansom, 1803–82, who invented it.

Hanson, Hansen 'son of **Hann**'. See also **Anson** [Alan Hansen, 1955–, British football pundit; James Hanson (Lord Hanson), 1922–2004, British businessman; John Hanson, 1920–98, Canadian singer and actor]

Harald see **Harrald**

Harber 'keeper of an inn or other lodging place' (from late Old English *herebeorg* 'shelter, lodging' (modern English *harbour*))

Harborne 'person from Harborne', Birmingham ('dirty stream')

Harbottle 'person from Harbottle', Northumberland ('hireling's dwelling')

Harcourt (i) 'person from Harcourt', the name of two places in Shropshire (one 'hawker's cottage', the other 'harper's cottage'); (ii) 'person from Harcourt', the name of two places in northern France, both based on Old French *court* 'court' but with an unknown first element
— **Harcourt Brace and Company** a US publishing firm, now 'Harcourt Trade Publishers'. It was founded in 1919 by Alfred Harcourt and Donald Brace.
— **Port Harcourt** a port in southern Nigeria, founded in 1912 and named after Lewis Harcourt (1st Viscount Harcourt), 1863–1922, British colonial secretary of the day

Hardaker, Hardacre from a medieval nickname for someone who lives on a piece of stony land that is hard to cultivate

Hardcastle 'person from Hardcastle', Yorkshire ('impregnable castle', or possibly 'grim, cheerless castle') [William Hardcastle, 1918–75, British journalist]

Harden 'person from Harden', Yorkshire ('hare valley')

Hardie see **Hardy**

Hardiman (i) from a medieval nickname for a brave man or a foolhardy man; (ii) from Irish Gaelic *Ó hArgadáin* 'descendant of *Argadán*', a personal name meaning literally 'little silver one'

Harding, Hardinge from the Old English male personal name *Hearding* 'son of *Heard*', a personal name meaning literally 'brave, strong' [Gilbert Harding, 1907–60, British panel-game host and guest; Warren Harding, 1865–1923, US Republican politician, president 1921–23]

Hardisty 'person from Hardisty', Yorkshire ('Heardwulf's path')

Hardman (i) from the Old English male personal name *Heardmann*, literally 'brave or strong man'; (ii) 'herdsman'

Hardstaff perhaps from a medieval nickname for a man with legendary erectile powers, or alternatively 'person from Hardstoft', Derbyshire ('Heorot's plot') [Joe Hardstaff Jr.,1911–90, English cricketer]

Hardwick, Hardwicke 'person from Hardwick', the name of various places in England ('herd farm') [Sir Cedric Hardwicke, 1893–1964, British actor]

Hardy, Hardie from a medieval nickname for a brave or foolhardy man [G.H. Hardy, 1877–1947, British mathematician; Keir Hardie, 1856–1915, British Labour politician; Oliver Hardy, 1892–1957, US comic actor (see Laurel and Hardy at **Laurel**); Robert Hardy, 1925–, British actor; Sir Thomas Hardy ('Captain Hardy'), 1769–1839, British naval officer, Lord Nelson's flag captain at the Battle of Trafalgar; Thomas Hardy, 1840–1928, British novelist and poet]

— **Hardy Boys** two teenage brothers, Frank and Joe Hardy, who were the heroes of a series of US adventure books for boys written between 1927 and 1979 by Franklin W. Dixon.

— **Hardy Island** an island off the Sunshine Coast of British Columbia, Canada. It is named after Sir Thomas Hardy (see above).

— **Hardy-Weinberg law** a principle of genetics stating that gene frequencies remain constant from one generation to the next if mating is random and there are no outside influences such as mutation and immigration. It is named after G.H. Hardy (see above) and the German physician Wilhelm Weinberg.

Hare (i) from a medieval nickname for someone thought to resemble a hare, especially in being a fast runner or being timid; (ii) *also* **Hair** or **Haire** from Irish Gaelic *Ó hAichir* 'descendant of *Aichear*', a personal name perhaps meaning literally 'fierce one'. See also **O'Hare** [Darrell Hair, 1952–, Australian cricket umpire; Sir David Hare, 1947–, British playwright; William Hare, 1792 *or* 1804–59, Irish murderer and body-snatcher, accomplice of William **Burke**]

Harewood see **Harwood**

Hargreave a different form of **Hargreaves**

Hargreaves, Hargreves 'person from Hargreave or Hargrave', the name of various places in England ('boundary wood') [James Hargreaves, 1720–78, British inventor, developer of the 'spinning jenny']

Harington see **Harrington** (i)

Harker (i) 'person from Harker', Cumbria ('marshland frequented by male deer') or Lancashire ('grey marshland' or 'marshland frequented by hares'); (ii) from a medieval nickname for an eavesdropper (someone who 'harks' or listens) [Kay Harker, an orphan boy who is the hero of John Masefield's *The Midnight Folk* (1927) and *The Box of Delights* (1935)]

Harkness 'person from Harkness', an unidentified Scottish place (probably 'Hereca's headland')

— **Ena Harkness** a red hybrid-tea rose developed in 1946 by the British amateur grower Albert Norman and marketed by R. Harkness and Company Ltd. In the 1950s it was the most popular rose of its type in the world. It was named after Robert Harkness's great aunt.

— **Harkness Ballet** a US ballet company founded in 1964 by the composer and philanthropist Rebekah Harkness, 1915–82

Harlan a different form of **Harland** [John Marshall Harlan, 1833–1911, US jurist]

Harland 'person from Harland', the name of various places in England (either 'grey area of land' or 'area of land frequented by hares')

— **Harland and Wolff** a British heavy-industrial company based in Belfast. It was founded as a shipbuilder in 1861 by Edward James Harland, 1831–95, and the German-born Gustav Wilhelm Wolff, 1834–1913. Its most famous product was the *Titanic*.

Harle (i) 'person from Harle', Northumberland (perhaps 'Herela's glade'); (ii) a different form of **Earl**

Harley 'person from Harley', Shropshire and Yorkshire (either 'rocky glade' or 'glade frequented by hares') [Robert Harley (1st Earl of Oxford), 1661–1724, English Tory statesman]

— **Harleian Manuscripts** a collection of ancient and medieval manuscripts made by Robert Harley (see above). It is now in the British Library.

— **Harley-Davidson** a make of US motorcycle, first produced in 1903 and named after its designers, William Harley and the brothers Arthur, Walter and William Davidson

— **Harley Lyrics** a set of 32 Middle English lyric poems contained in Harley Manuscript 2253

— **Harley Street** a street in Marylebone, in the City of Westminster, laid out in the mid-18th century on land owned by Edward Harley, 2nd Earl of Oxford. Its association with the medical profession dates from the 19th century.

Harlow, Harlowe 'person from Harlow', the name of various places in England (either 'mound associated with an army' or 'rocky hill') [Clarissa Harlowe, the central character of Samuel Richardson's novel *Clarissa* (1749); Jean Harlow (original name Harlean Carpenter), 1911–37, US film actress]

Harman from the medieval male personal name *Harman*, brought into England by the Normans but ultimately of Germanic origin (see **Hermann**) [Harriet Harman, 1950–, British Labour politician]

Harmison a different form of **Armison** [Steve Harmison, 1978–, English cricketer]

Harmsworth 'person from Harmondsworth', Greater London ('Heremund's enclosure') [Alfred Harmsworth (Viscount Northcliffe), 1865–1922, Irish-born British newspaper proprietor; Harold Harmsworth (Viscount Rothermere), 1868–1940, British newspaper proprietor, brother of Alfred]

Harper, Harpur 'harp-player' [Heather Harper, 1930–, Northern Irish soprano]

— **Harper and Row** a US publishing firm, formed in 1962 by the merger of Harper and Brothers (established in New York City in 1817 by James Harper, 1795–1869, and his brother John Harper, 1797–1875) with Row, Paterson and Company. In 1991 it joined with William Collins to form **HarperCollins**.

— **Harper's and Queen** a British fashion magazine introduced in 1970, as a coming-together of *Harper's Bazaar UK* (first published in 1929) with

Queen magazine (1862). In 2006 it reverted to the title *Harper's Bazaar*.

— ***Harper's Bazaar*** a US fashion magazine, originally published by Harper and Brothers (see above) in 1867

Harrald, Harald different forms of **Harrod** (i–ii)

Harrap see **Harrop**

Harrell, Harrel, Harral different forms of **Harrod** (i–ii)

Harriman 'Harry's servant' [Averell Harriman, 1891–1986, US diplomat]

Harrington (i) *also* **Harington** 'person from Harrington', Cumbria ('estate associated with Hæfer'), Lincolnshire ('Hæring's farmstead') and Northamptonshire ('estate associated with Heath-uhere'). See also **Arrington** (i); (ii) from Irish Gaelic *Ó hArrachtáin* 'descendant of *Arrachtán*', a personal name meaning literally 'little powerful one' [James Harrington, 1611–77, English republican; Sir John Harington, ?1561–1612, English writer and translator, proponent of the water closet]

— **Harrington** in early 17th-century slang, a farthing. The term came from the name of Sir John Harington (see above), who obtained a patent from James I to mint farthings.

Harriott, Harriot different forms of **Herriot** (ii) [Ainsley Harriott, 1957–, British television chef]

Harris, Harries 'son of **Harry**' [Sir Arthur Harris ('Bomber' Harris), 1892–1984, British air marshal, commander-in-chief of RAF Bomber Command in World War II; Frank Harris (original name James Thomas Harris), 1856–1931, Irish-born British journalist and writer; Jet Harris (original name Terence Harris), 1939–, British bass guitarist, member of The Shadows pop group; Joel Chandler Harris, 1848–1908, US novelist and short-story writer, creator of 'Uncle Remus'; Robert Harris, 1957–, British journalist and writer; Rolf Harris, 1930–, Australian artist and entertainer; Roy Harris, 1898–1979, US composer]

— **Harrisburg** the capital city of Pennsylvania, USA, in the south of the state. It was founded in 1785 and named after John Harris, 1727–91, son of an English settler of the same name.

— **Treharris** a village in Mid Glamorgan, Wales, named after Frederick William Harris, a local colliery owner who died in 1917. The name means literally 'village of Harris'.

Harrison 'son of **Harry**' [Audley Harrison, 1971–, British boxer; Beatrice Harrison, 1893–1965, British cellist; Benjamin Harrison, 1833–1901, US Republican politician, president 1889–93; George Harrison, 1943–2001, British pop musician, member of The Beatles; John Harrison, 1693–1776, English clockmaker, inventor of the chronometer that enabled longitude to be calculated; Kathleen Harrison, 1892–1995, British actress; Sir Rex Harrison, 1908–90, British actor; Tony Harrison, 1937–, British poet; William Henry Harrison, 1773–1841, US soldier and statesman, president 1841, grandfather of Benjamin]

— **Harrison and Harrison** a British firm of organ-builders, based in Meadowfield, County

Durham. It was founded in 1861 by Thomas Harrison, and he was joined in 1872 by his brother James.

Harrod (i) from the Old English male personal name *Hereweald*, or the related Old Norse *Haraldr* or Anglo-Norman *Herold*, all ultimately from a Germanic compound name meaning literally 'army-power'; (ii) 'herald' (from Old French *herault, heraut*, ultimately from the same Germanic source as (i)); (iii) a different form of **Harwood**. See also **Harrald**, **Harrell**, **Harrold** [Sir Roy Harrod, 1900–78, British economist]

— **Harrods** a renowned department store in Brompton Road, Knightsbridge, London. It was founded in 1849 by Henry Charles Harrod, 1799–1885, a wholesale tea merchant.

Harrold a different form of **Harrod** (i–ii)

Harrop, Harrap, Harrup 'person from Harrop', the name of various places in northern England ('hare valley')

— **Harraps** a British publishing firm, founded in 1901 by George Harrap, 1867–1938. It is now part of Chambers Harrap Publishers Ltd.

Harrow 'person from Harrow', the district of northwest Greater London, or various places of the same name in Scotland ('heathen shrine')

Harry from the male personal name *Harry*, a different form of **Henry**. See also **Harris**, **Harrison**, **Herriot** (ii) [Debbie Harry, 1945–, US rock-and-roll musician]

Hart (i) *also* **Heart** from a medieval nickname for someone thought to resemble a stag (Middle English *hert*), for instance in swiftness. See also **Hurt**; (ii) *also* **Harte** from Irish Gaelic *Ó hAirt* 'descendant of *Art*', a personal name meaning literally 'bear' or 'hero'; (iii) an invented Jewish name, or nickname, based on German and Yiddish *hart* 'hard'. See also **Hartmann** (iii) [Francis Bret Harte, 1836–1902, US short-story writer; Dame Judith Hart (*née* Ridehalgh), 1924–91, British Labour politician; Lorenz Hart, 1895–1943, US lyricist; Moss Hart, 1904–61, US dramatist; Sir Rupert Hart-Davis, 1907–99, British publisher; Tony Hart, 1925–, British artist on children's television]

— ***Hart's Rules*** a reference book (in full, *Hart's Rules for Compositors and Readers at the University Press, Oxford*) giving recommendations on typesetting style, punctuation and usage, compiled by Horace Hart, 1840–1916, Controller of Oxford University Press, and first published in 1893

— ***Hart to Hart*** a US television drama series (1980–85) featuring the husband-and-wife detective team Jonathan and Jennifer Hart

— **Lemon Hart** the proprietary name of a brand of rum, as originally sold by a Penzance wine and spirit merchant called Lemon Hart [sic], died 1845

Hartigan 'little **Hart** (ii)'

Hartley, Hartly 'person from Hartley', the name of various places in England (mostly 'glade frequented by stags') [J.R. Hartley, fictitious author of a book called *Fly Fishing* who appeared in British television advertisements for Yellow

Pages in the 1980s; L.P. Hartley, 1895–1972, British novelist]

— **Hartley's** a British brand of jam and related foodstuffs. The firm was founded in 1871 by Sir William Pickles Hartley, 1846–1922.

— **Hartley's Village** a district of Liverpool, Merseyside, originating in 1888 as an estate of cottages built by Sir William Hartley (see above) for workers in his local jam factory

— **Taft-Hartley Act** see **Taft**

Hartmann (i) from a medieval German nickname for someone thought to resemble a stag (Middle Low German *harte*); (ii) from a German personal name meaning literally 'strong man'; (iii) an expanded form of **Hart** (iii)

Hartnell perhaps 'person from Hartnell', an unidentified place in England (perhaps 'Heorta's hill') [Sir Norman Hartnell, 1901–79, British couturier; William Hartnell, 1908–75, British actor]

Harty, Hearty from Irish Gaelic *Ó hA(th)rtaigh* 'descendant of *Faghartach*', a name applied to a noisy person [Sir Hamilton Harty, 1879–1941, Irish composer; Russell Harty, 1934–88, British television chat-show host]

— **Russell Harty** (see above) rhyming slang for *party*

Harvard from the Old English male personal name *Hereweard*, literally 'army-guard'

— **Harvard University** a university in Cambridge, Massachusetts, founded in 1636 and named in honour of John Harvard, 1607–38, son of a London butcher who emigrated to America and bequeathed his books to the newly founded college

Harvey (i) *also* **Harvie** *or* **Hervey** from the Breton male personal name *Aeruiu* or *Haerviu*, literally 'battle-worthy', brought into England after the Norman Conquest; (ii) from Irish Gaelic *Ó hAirmheadhaigh* 'descendant of *Airmheadhach*', a personal name of uncertain origin and meaning [Sir John Harvey-Jones, 1924–, British businessman; Laurence Harvey (original name Zvi Mosheh (Hirsh) Skikne), 19128–73, Lithuanian-born British actor; Neil Harvey, 1928–, Australian cricketer; William Harvey, 1578–1657, English physician and anatomist, discoverer of the circulation of the blood]

— **Harvey Nichols** an upmarket clothing store in Knightsbridge, London (with other branches now in other cities). It began with a draper's shop opened around 1813 by Benjamin Harvey. As the business expanded in the mid-19th century, Colonel Nichols joined as a partner.

— **Harvey's sauce** a British proprietary bottled savoury sauce originally concocted in the mid-18th century by Peter Harvey, owner of the Black Dog inn in Bedfont, Middlesex and produced commercially by the Elizabeth Lazenby company (she was Harvey's sister)

— **John Harvey & Sons** a British firm of sherry-shippers and wine merchants, founded in Bristol in 1796. The name comes from John Harvey, 1806–79, who joined the company in 1822.

Harwood, Harewood 'person from Harwood', the name of numerous places in England and Scotland (variously 'grey wood' and 'wood frequented by hares'). See also **Harrod** (iii) [Ronald Harwood (original name Horwitz), 1934–, South African-born British novelist and playwright]

Hasan, Hassan from the Arabic personal name *Ḥasān*, literally 'good, handsome'

Hasel see **Hazel**

Haselden see **Hazelden**

Haselhurst see **Hazelhurst**

Haselton see **Hazelton**

Haselwood see **Hazelwood**

Haskell, Haskel (i) a different form of **Ashkettle**; (ii) from *Kheskl* or *Khatskl*, Yiddish forms of the Hebrew male personal name *Yechezkel*, literally 'God will strengthen' (English *Ezekiel*)

Haskin (i) from the Anglo-Norman male personal name *Asketin*, a pet-form based on Old Norse *Ásketill* (see **Ashkettle**); (ii) from Irish Gaelic *Ó hUiscín* 'descendant of *Uiscín*', a personal name probably meaning literally 'little waters'

Haskins (i) 'son of **Haskin** (i)'; (ii) a different form of **Haskin** (ii)

Haslam, Haslem 'person who lives by a stand of hazel trees' or 'person from Haslam', Lancashire (in either case from Old English *hæslum* 'by the hazels') [Nicky Haslam, 1939–, British interior designer and socialite]

Haslett see **Hazlett**

Hassall, Hassell 'person from Hassall', Cheshire ('witch's corner of land')

Hassan (i) from a Muslim personal name derived from Arabic *hassan* 'beautifier'; (ii) see **Hasan**

Hassett (i) from Irish Gaelic *Ó hAiseadha* 'descendant of *Aisidh*', a personal name meaning literally 'strife'; (ii) a shortened form of **Blennerhasset** [Lindsay Hassett, 1913–93, Australian cricketer]

Hastings (i) 'person from Hastings', Sussex ('settlement of Hæsta's people'); (ii) 'son of *Hastenc*', an Anglo-Norman personal name of Old Norse origin, literally 'high stone' [Captain Arthur Hastings, frequent adjutant of Hercule Poirot in the detective stories of Agatha Christie; Sir Max Hastings, 1945–, British journalist and author; Sir Patrick Hastings, 1880–1952, British barrister; Selina Hastings (*née* Shirley; Countess of Huntingdon), 1707–91, British Methodist leader; Selina Hastings, 1945–, British writer; Warren Hastings, 1732–1818, British colonial administrator]

Hastleton a different form of **Hazelton**

Hasty, Hastie from a medieval nickname for an impetuous person

Hatch 'person who lives by a gate' or 'person from Hatch', the name of various places in England (in either case from Middle English *hacche* 'gate') [Tony Hatch, 1939–, British composer and songwriter]

Hatchard from the Anglo-Norman personal name *Aschard*, of Germanic origin and meaning literally 'edge-brave'
— **Hatchard's** a bookseller's in Piccadilly, London, founded in 1797 by John Hatchard, 1768–1849

Hatcher a different form of **Hatch**

Hateley a different form of **Hatley**

Hatfield 'person from Hatfield', the name of various places in England ('open land where heather grows')

Hathaway (i) from the Old English female personal name *Heathuwīg*, literally 'strife-war'; (ii) 'person who lives by a path across a heath' (Middle English *hath* 'heath'). See also **Hadaway** [Anne Hathaway, 1556–1623, wife of William Shakespeare]

Hatley 'person from Hatley', Bedfordshire and Cambridgeshire ('woodland clearing on the (hat-shaped) hill')

Hatt 'maker or seller of hats' or from a nickname applied to a noted hat-wearer

Hatter 'maker or seller of hats'

Hattersley 'person from Hattersley', Cheshire (perhaps 'glade frequented by deer') [Roy Hattersley (Lord Hattersley), 1932–, British Labour politician]

Hatton (i) 'person from Hatton', the name of various places in England ('farmstead on a heath'); (ii) from *Hatton-*, the stem form of the Old French personal name *Hatto*, of Germanic origin and probably a shortened form of various compound names beginning with *Hadu-*, literally 'strife' [Derek Hatton, 1948–, British Labour politician]
— **Hatton Garden** a street in Central London, latterly associated particularly with the jewellery trade. It was named after Hatton House, the mansion built there in the late 16th century by Elizabeth I's chancellor, Sir Christopher Hatton, 1540–91.

Haughey from Irish Gaelic *Ó hEachaidh* 'descendant of *Eachaidh*', a personal name meaning literally 'horseman'. See also **Howey** (ii) [Charles Haughey, 1925–2006, Irish Fianna Fáil politician, prime minister 1979–81, 1982, 1987–92]

Haughton 'person from Haughton', the name of various places in England (mainly 'farmstead by a corner of land')

Havelock from the Middle English male personal name *Havelok* (from Old Norse *Hafleikr*, literally 'sea sport') [Sir Henry Havelock, 1795–1857, British general]

Haversham, Havisham 'maker of chain-mail coats' (Middle English *haubergeon* 'small coat of mail', from Old French) [Miss Havisham, the jilted bride grown old and half crazed who is a main driver of the plot of Charles Dickens's *Great Expectations* (1861)]

Haw, Hawe (i) from the Middle English male personal name *Haw*, a reduced form of *Hawkin* (see **Hawkins** (i)); (ii) 'person who lives by an enclosure' or 'person from Haw', the name of various places in England (in either case from Old English *haga*)

Haward a different form of **Hayward** and **Howard**

Hawdon 'person from Hawdon', the name of an unidentified place in England, probably in Northumberland (perhaps 'enclosure on a hill')

Hawes (i) from the Anglo-Norman female personal name *Haueis*, ultimately of Germanic origin and meaning literally 'battle-wide'; (ii) 'son of **Haw** (i)'

Hawk, Hawke (i) 'breeder and trainer of hawks' or from a nickname for someone held to resemble a hawk (e.g. in ferocity, or in having a beaklike nose); (ii) 'person who lives in a nook of land' (Middle English *halke*) [Bob Hawke, 1929–, Australian Labor politician, prime minister 1983–91; Edward Hawke (Lord Hawke), 1705–81, British admiral; Martin Hawke (Lord Hawke), 1860–1938, English cricketer and cricket administrator]
— **Hawke's Bay** a region in the North Island of New Zealand. It takes its name from **Hawke Bay** in the region, itself named (1769) by its discoverer, Captain Cook, in honour of Edward Hawke (see above), at that time First Lord of the Admiralty.

Hawker 'breeder and trainer of hawks' [Harry George Hawker, 1889–1921, Australian aviation pioneer]
— **Hawker Aircraft Ltd** a British aircraft manufacturer founded in 1920 by Harry Hawker (see above) and others. In 1935 it merged with Armstrong Siddeley to become **Hawker-Siddeley**, and in 1977 it disappeared into British Aerospace. Its most famous aircraft were the Hawker Hurricane, the World War II fighter, and the Hawker Hunter, a jet fighter.

Hawkes, Hawks 'son of **Hawk** (i)' [Howard Hawks, 1896–1977, US film director; Jacquetta Hawkes (*née* Hopkins), 1910–96, British archeologist and writer]

Hawking (i) from the Middle English male personal name *Hawkin* (see **Hawkins** (i)); (ii) a different form of **Hawkinge** [Stephen Hawking, 1942–, British physicist and mathematician]

Hawkinge 'person from Hawkinge', Kent ('place frequented by hawks')

Hawkins (i) 'son of *Hawkin*', a Middle English male personal name, literally 'little **Hawk** (i)'; (ii) a different form of **Hawkinge** [Sir Anthony Hope Hawkins, real name of the writer Anthony Hope (see **Hope**); Coleman Hawkins, 1904–69, US jazz musician; Jack Hawkins, 1910–73, British actor; Jim Hawkins, narrator and central character of Robert Louis Stevenson's *Treasure Island* (1883); Sir John Hawkins, 1532–95, English navigator; Sir Richard Hawkins, ?1562–1622, English navigator, son of Sir John]
— **Sadie Hawkins Day** 9 November, on which day in the US by 'tradition' (going back no further than 1938 and inspired by the 'L'il Abner' cartoon series, in which Sadie Hawkins is a character) women can propose marriage to men

Hawks see **Hawkes**

Hawksworth 'person from Hawksworth', Yorkshire ('Hafoc's enclosure')

Hawley 'person from Hawley', the name of numerous places in England (variously 'holy glade', 'clearing with a large house in it' and 'clearing with a mound')

Haworth (i) 'person from Haworth', Yorkshire ('enclosure with a hedge'); (ii) a different form of **Howarth** [Sir Norman Haworth, 1883–1950, British biochemist]
— **haworthia** a southern African succulent herb with densely overlapping, often warty leaves, clustered in rosettes. It is named after the British entomologist and botanist Adrian Hardy Haworth, 1768–1833.

Hawthorn, Hawthorne 'person who lives by a hawthorn hedge or bush' or 'person from Hawthorn', Durham [Mike Hawthorn, 1929–58, British motor-racing driver; Nathaniel Hawthorne, 1804–64, US novelist and short-story writer; Sir Nigel Hawthorne, 1929–2001, British actor]

Hawtry, Hawtree, Hawtrey 'person from Hauterive', Orne, Normandy ('high bank'). See also **Daltry** [Sir Charles Hawtrey, 1858–1923, British actor; Charles Hawtrey (original name George Frederick Joffre Hartree; he is said to have chosen his stage-name under the mistaken impression that Sir Charles Hawtrey was his father), 1914–88, British comedy actor]

Hay, Haye (i) 'person who lives by an enclosure' (Middle English *haye*); (ii) from the medieval personal name *Hay*, which came partly directly from the Old English nickname *Hēah*, literally 'tall', and partly from various compound personal names beginning with *hēah*; (iii) 'person from *Les Hays* or *La Haye*', Normandy ('the hedge(s)'); (iv) from a medieval nickname for a tall man (Middle English *hey, hay* 'high, tall') [Ian Hay, pen-name of John Hay Beith, 1876–1952, British teacher and light novelist; Will Hay, 1888–1949, British comedian]
— **Hay diet** a diet in which protein and carbohydrates are not eaten at the same time, claimed to be helpful for digestive complaints and weight loss. It is named after the US doctor and author William Howard Hay, 1866–1940, who devised it.

Haycock, Heycock from the medieval personal name *Haycock*, from **Hay** (ii) with the suffix *-cock* (literally 'cockerel', hence 'jaunty or bumptious young man') that was often added to create pet-forms of personal names in the Middle Ages. See also **Heacock, Hickock**

Hayden, Haydon, Heydon (i) 'person from Hayden or Haydon', the name of numerous places in England (variously 'valley where hay is made' and 'hill where hay is made'); (ii) from Irish Gaelic *Ó hÉideáin* or *Ó hÉidín* 'descendant of *Éideán* or *Éidín*', personal names meaning literally 'little armour' [Benjamin Robert Haydon, 1786–1846, British painter; Bill Hayden, 1933–, Australian Labor politician]

Hayem see **Hyam**

Hayes, Hays, Heyes, Heys (i) 'person from Hayes', the name of numerous places in England

(variously 'enclosures' and 'brushwood'); (ii) 'son of **Hay** (ii)'; (iii) from Irish Gaelic *Ó hAodha* 'descendant of *Aodh*', a personal name meaning literally 'fire' [Patricia Hayes, 1909–98, British actress; Rutherford B. Hayes, 1822–93, US Republican politician, president 1877–81]
— **Hays Code** a set of moral guidelines imposed on the US film industry in the middle years of the 20th century, stipulating what was permitted to be shown and said on screen. Adopted in 1930, it was named after Will H. Hays, 1879–1954, head of the Motion Pictures Producers and Distributors Association. It was abandoned in 1967.

Hayhoe, Heyhoe 'person who lives on a high spur of land' (Old English *hēah hōh*) [Rachel Heyhoe-Flint, see **Flint**]

Hayhurst 'person from Hay Hurst', Lancashire (probably 'wooded hill with an enclosure')

Hayler, Hayller, Haylor (i) 'haulier' (from a derivative of Middle English *halien* 'to transport'); (ii) 'person who lives in a nook or hollow of land' (Old English *halh*). See also **Hale** (i)

Hayley see **Haley**

Hayling (i) 'person from Hayling', Hampshire ('settlement of Hægel's people'); (ii) from the Old Welsh personal name *Heilyn*, literally 'cup-bearer'. See also **Palin**

Haym, Hayem see **Hyam**

Hayman (i) 'person who lives by an enclosure' (see **Hay** (i)); (ii) 'servant of **Hay** (ii)'; (iii) from a medieval nickname for a tall man (see **Hay** (iv))

Haymes 'son of *Hamo*' (see **Hammond** (i))

Haynes see **Haines**

Hayter, Haytor different forms of **Height** [James Hayter, 1907–83, British actor]

Hayward, Heyward 'official in charge of the fences and enclosures in a particular area' (Middle English, literally 'enclosure guardian') [Sir Jack Hayward, 1923–, British businessman and philanthropist; Susan Hayward (original name Edythe Marrenner), 1917–75, US film actress]
— **Hayward Gallery** an art gallery in London, opened in 1968 as part of the South Bank arts complex. It was named in honour of Sir Isaac James Hayward, 1884–1976, who was responsible for the planning of the area.

Haywood 'person from Haywood', the name of various places in England ('enclosed wood')

Hayworth 'person from Haywards Heath', Sussex ('enclosure with a hedge') [Rita Hayworth (original name Margarita Carmen Cansino), 1918–87, US film actress]

Hazel, Hazell, Hasel 'person who lives by a hazel tree or grove'. See also **Haslam, Hazlett, Heslop**
— **Hazell** a British television detective drama (1978–80) featuring a private investigator called James Hazell

Hazelden, Hazeldon, Haselden, Hasleden 'person from Hazelden', the name of various places in England ('valley growing with hazel trees'). See also **Heseltine**

Hazelhurst, Haselhurst 'person from Hazelhurst', Lancashire, Surrey and Sussex ('wooded hill growing with hazel trees')

Hazelrigg 'person from Hazelrigg', the name of various places in northern England ('ridge growing with hazel trees')

Hazelton, Haselton 'person from Hazelton', the name of various places in England ('valley growing with hazel trees'). See also **Hastleton**

Hazelwood, Hazlewood, Haselwood, Haslewood 'person from Hazelwood', the name of various places in England ('wood growing with hazel trees')

Hazlett, Hazlitt, Haslett, Haslitt 'person who lives by a hazel copse' (Old English *hæslett* 'hazel copse') [William Hazlitt, 1778–1830, British essayist]

Heacock a different form of **Haycock**

Head (i) 'person who lives on the top of a hill or at the head of a valley'; (ii) from a nickname for someone with a strangely shaped or sized head

Headley, Hedley 'person from Headley', the name of various places in England ('glade where heather grows'). See also **Heatley** [George Headley, 1909–83, West Indian cricketer]

Heal, Heale different forms of **Hale** (i) [Sir Ambrose Heal, 1872–1959, British furniture designer]

Heald 'person who lives on a hillside' (Old English *hielde* 'slope')

Healey, Healy, Heeley, Heely (i) 'person from Healey', near Manchester ('high woodland clearing'); (ii) from Irish Gaelic *Ó hÉilidhe* 'descendant of the claimant', from *éilidhe* 'claimant', or *Ó hÉalaighthe* 'descendant of *Éalathach*', a personal name perhaps meaning literally 'ingenious one' [Austin Healey, 1973–, English rugby player; Denis Healey (Lord Healey), 1917–, British Labour politician]
— **Austin-Healey** see **Austin**

Heaney, Heany, Heney, Heeney from Irish Gaelic *Ó hÉanna* 'descendant of *Éanna*', a personal name of uncertain meaning [Seamus Heaney, 1939–, Irish poet]

Heap, Heape, Heep 'person who lives by a mound or hill' or 'person from Heap Bridge', Lancashire [Uriah Heep, the oleaginously humble lawyer's clerk in Charles Dickens's *David Copperfield* (1850)]

Heard, Herd, Hird, Hurd 'shepherd, cowherd or other herdsman' [Douglas Hurd (Lord Hurd), 1930–, British Conservative politician; Dame Thora Hird, 1913–2003, British actress]
— **Douglas Hurd** (see above) rhyming slang for *third* 'third-class degree' and *turd*

Heardman, Herdman, Hurdman different forms of **Heard**

Hearn, Hearne, Hern, Herne, Hurn, Hurne (i) 'person who lives by a bend in a river or in a hollow of a hill' or 'person from Herne', the name of various places (variously spelled) in England (in either case from Old English *hyrne* 'corner, angle, nook'); (ii) 'person from Herne', Bedfordshire ('place of stones'); (iii) different forms of **Heron** (i); (iv) a different form of **Ahern**. See also **Horniman** [Lafcadio Hearn, 1850–1904, Greek-born Irish orientalist, author and translator (from 1890 he lived in Japan, and took the name Yakumo Koizumi); Richard Hearne, 1909–79, British comic actor and clown, 'Mr Pastry']
— *The Lonely Passion of Judith Hearne* a novel (1955) by Brian Moore about a disappointed middle-aged Belfast Catholic spinster

Hearst see **Hurst**

Heart see **Hart** (i)

Hearty see **Harty**

Heath 'person who lives on a heath' or 'person from Heath', the name of various places in England [Sir Edward Heath, 1916–2005, British Conservative politician, prime minister 1970–74; Michael Heath, 1935–, British cartoonist; Neville Heath, 1917–46, British murderer; Ted Heath, 1902–69, British bandleader]
— **Edward/Ted Heath** rhyming slang for *teeth* and *thief*
— **Heath Robinson** see **Robinson**

Heathcote, Heathcoat, Heathcott 'person from Heathcote', the name of various places in England ('cottage on a heath') [Derick Heathcoat Amory (Viscount Amory), 1899–1981, British Conservative politician]

Heatherington see **Hetherington**

Heatley, Heatlie 'person from Heatley', the name of various places in northern England, Scotland and Northern Ireland ('glade where heather grows')

Heaton 'person from Heaton', the name of various places in northern England ('high farmstead')

Hebblethwaite 'person from Hebblethwaite', Yorkshire ('meadow with a plank-bridge'). See also **Hepplewhite**

Hebborn, Hebburn different forms of **Hepburn**

Hebden, Hebdon 'person from Hebden', Yorkshire ('valley where rosehips grow'). See also **Hepton**

Hecht (i) from a medieval German nickname for a fierce or greedy person, from German *Hecht* 'pike' (the fish); (ii) an invented Jewish name, based on German *Hecht* or Yiddish *hekht* 'pike' [Ben Hecht, 1894–1964, US novelist and screenwriter]

Hector an anglicization (influenced by the name of the Trojan prince) of the Gaelic personal name *Eachdonn*, literally 'brown horse'

Hedge 'person who lives by a hedge'

Hedgecock a different form of **Hitchcock**

Hedges a different form of **Hedge**
— **Benson and Hedges** see **Benson**

Hedley see **Headley**

Heeley see **Healey**

Heeney see **Heaney**

Heffer 'cowherd', or possibly from a medieval nickname for someone thought to resemble a cow

(Middle English *heffre* 'young cow') [Simon Heffer, 1960–, British journalist]

Heffernan, Heffernon from Irish Gaelic *Ó hIfearnáin* 'descendant of *Ifearnán*', a personal name meaning literally 'little demon'

Heffner, Hefner different forms of **Hafner** [Hugh Hefner, 1926–, US publisher]

Hegarty, Hegerty from Irish Gaelic *Ó hEigceartaigh* 'descendant of *Eigceartach*', a nickname meaning literally 'unjust'. See also **Hagerty**

Heifetz, Haifetz an invented Jewish name based on Hebrew *chefets* 'pleasure' [Jascha Heifetz, 1901–87, Lithuanian-born US violinist]

Height, Hight, Hite 'person who lives on an area of high ground or on top of a hill'. See also **Hayter** [Shere Hite, 1942–, US sexologist]

Heilbronn, Heilbron, Heilbrunn 'person from Heilbronn', Württemberg, Germany ('holy well'). See also **Halpern**

Heimlich from a medieval German nickname for a secretive person, from Middle High German *heimelich* 'secret'
— **Heimlich manoeuvre** an emergency technique for removing an obstruction from a choking person's throat, consisting of grasping the person round the chest from behind and pressing sharply upwards. It was named after its deviser, the US surgeon Henry J. Heimlich, 1920–.

Heinlein from a pet-form of the German male personal name *Heinrich* '**Henry**' [Robert Heinlein, 1907–88, US author]

Heinz from a pet-form of the German male personal name *Heinrich* '**Henry**'
— **H.J. Heinz Company** a US food processing company, founded in Sharpsburg, Pennsylvania in 1869 by Henry J. Heinz, 1844–1919.

Heller (i) from a medieval German nickname for a small person, from *heller*, the name of a coin of small value; (ii) from a medieval Jewish nickname for a fair-haired person, from German *hell* or Yiddish *hel* 'light'; (iii) a different form of **Hill** (i) [Joseph Heller, 1923–99, US author]

Helliwell, Hellawell different forms of **Halliwell**

Hellman, Hellmann different forms of **Heller** (ii–iii)
— **Hellmann's Mayonnaise** a commercial brand of mayonnaise first produced by the German-born immigrant Richard Hellmann at his New York City delicatessen in the first decade of the 20th century

Helmsley a different form of **Hemsley**

Hemery a different form of **Amery** [David Hemery, 1944–, British athlete]

Hemingway, Hemmingway probably 'person from Hemingway', an unidentified place in Yorkshire ('Hemming's path'; see **Hemming**) [Ernest Hemingway, 1899–1961, US novelist; Margaux Hemingway, 1955–96, US film actress and model, granddaughter of Ernest; Mariel Hemingway, 1961–, US film actress, sister of Margaux]

Hemming from the Old Norse personal name *Hemmingr*, of uncertain origin and meaning

Hemmings 'son of **Hemming**' [David Hemmings, 1941–2003, British actor]

Hemphill, Hempill 'person from Hemphill', Strathclyde region (probably 'hill growing with hemp')

Hemsley, Hemesley 'person from Hemsley', the name of two places in Yorkshire (respectively 'Helm's wood' and 'Hemele's island'). See also **Helmsley**

Hemsworth 'person from Hemsworth', Yorkshire ('Hymel's enclosure')

Henderson 'son of **Hendry**' [Arthur Henderson, 1863–1935, British Labour politician; Dickie Henderson, 1922–85, British entertainer]
— **Henderson the Rain King** a novel (1959) by Saul Bellow in which the disillusioned millionaire Eugene Henderson finds a new meaning to life when he travels to Africa and finds he has a talent as a rainmaker

Hendricks, Hendriks, Hendrix 'son of *Hendrick*', the Dutch, Flemish and Low German form of **Henry** [Barbara Hendricks, 1948–, US soprano; Jimi Hendrix, 1942–70, US rock singer and guitarist]

Hendricksen 'son of *Hendrick*', the Dutch, Flemish and Low German form of **Henry**

Hendry, Hendrie different forms (especially Scottish) of **Henry** [Ian Hendry, 1931–84, British actor; Stephen Hendry, 1969–, Scottish snooker player]

Hendy from a medieval nickname for a kind or courteous man (from Middle English *hende* 'kind, courteous'). See also **Handy**

Heneghan, Henegan from Irish Gaelic *Ó hEidhneacháin* 'descendant of *Eidhneachán*', a personal name of uncertain origin and meaning

Henley, Henly 'person from Henley', the name of numerous places in England (variously 'high wood' and 'glade frequented by hens') [W.E. Henley, 1849–1903, British poet]

Henman probably 'person who looks after poultry' [Tim Henman, 1974–, British tennis player]

Hennessy, Hennessey, Henessy from Irish Gaelic *Ó hAonghusa* 'descendant of **Angus**'
— **Hennessy** a brand of cognac, as produced in the distillery founded in Cognac in 1765 by the Irishman Richard Hennessy. It is now part of the Moët-Hennessy-Louis Vuitton group.

Henri from the French form of **Henry** [Adrian Henri, 1932–2000, British poet]

Henriquez, Henriques 'son of, respectively, *Enrique* and *Henrique*', the Spanish and Portuguese forms of **Henry**

Henry (i) from the male personal name *Henry*, brought into England by the Normans but ultimately of Germanic origin and meaning literally 'home-rule'. See also **Harris, Henderson, Hendry, Henson**; (ii) from Irish Gaelic *Ó hInnéirghe* 'descendant of *Innéirghe*', a personal name meaning literally 'abandonment' or 'elopement' [Joseph Henry, 1797–1878, US physicist;

Lenny Henry (original name Lenworth Henry), 1958–, British comedian; O. Henry, pen-name of William Sidney Porter, 1862–1910, US short-story writer]

— **henry** the SI unit of electrical inductance (symbol H). It was named after Joseph Henry (see above).

— **Henry's law** the principle that the amount of gas dissolved under equilibrium in a volume of liquid is in direct proportion to the pressure of the gas that contacts the liquid surface. Its name commemorates the British chemist William Henry, 1774–1836.

Henryson 'son of **Henry**' [Robert Henryson, ?1424–?1506, Scottish poet]

Henshall, Henshell different forms of **Henshaw**

Henshaw 'person from Henshaw', Northumberland ('Hethinn's nook of land'), or 'person from Henshaw', Cheshire ('wood frequented by hens')

Hensher a different form of **Henshaw**

Hensley 'person from Hensley', the name of two places in Devon (respectively 'Hēahmund's glade' and 'glade frequented by stallions')

Henson 'son of **Henn**', a medieval male personal name that was a shortened form of **Henry** [Jim Henson, 1936–90, US puppeteer, creator of the Muppets; Leslie Henson, 1891–1957, British actor and comedian]

Henty 'person from Antye Farm', Sussex ('high enclosure') [G.A. Henty, 1832–1902, British writer of adventure stories]

Henwood 'person from Henwood', Cornwall ('wood frequented by hens')

Hepburn 'person from Hepburn', Northumberland ('high burial place'). See also **Hebborn** [Audrey Hepburn (original name Edda van Heemstra Hepburn-Ruston), 1929–93, Belgian-born US film actress; Katharine Hepburn, 1907–2003, US film actress]

Heppenstall a different form of **Heptinstall**

Hepplewhite a different form of **Hebblethwaite** [George Hepplewhite, died 1786, British furniture designer]

Heptinstall, Heptonstall 'person from Heptonstall', Yorkshire ('cattle-stall belonging to **Hebden**')

Hepton a different form of **Hebden** [Bernard Hepton, 1925–, British actor]

Hepworth 'person from Hepworth', Suffolk and Yorkshire ('Heppa's enclosure') [Dame Barbara Hepworth, 1903–75, British sculptor]

Herbert from the Old English male personal name *Herebeorht* and the Anglo-Norman *Herbert*, both ultimately from a Germanic name meaning literally 'army-bright'. See also **FitzHerbert** [Sir Alan Herbert (A.P. Herbert), 1890–1971, British humorous writer; George Herbert, 1593–1633, English poet; James Herbert, 1943–, British author; Sir Wally Herbert, 1934–, British Polar explorer]

Herd see **Heard**

Herdman see **Heardman**

Herlihy from Irish Gaelic *Ó hIarfhlatha* 'descendant of *Iarfhlaith*', a personal name meaning literally 'lord of the west'. See also **Hurley**

Hermann, Herrmann (i) from the German male personal name *Hermann*, literally 'army man'; (ii) usually **Herman** a Jewish surname based on *Hermann* [Bernard Herrmann, 1911–75, US composer of film music]

Hern see **Hearn**

Hernandez 'son of *Hernando*', a different form of the Spanish male personal name *Fernando* (English **Ferdinand**)

Herne see **Hearn**

Heron (i) *also* **Herron** from a medieval nickname for someone who resembled a heron, especially in being tall and thin; (ii) *also* **Herron** from Irish Gaelic *Ó hEaráin* 'descendant of *Earán*', a personal name derived from *earadh* 'fear'; (iii) from Irish Gaelic *Ó hUidhrín* 'descendant of *Uithrín*', a personal name probably meaning literally 'little swarthy man', or *Mac Giolla Chiaráin* 'son of the servant of (St) Ciarán' [Patrick Heron, 1920–99, British artist]

Herrick from the Old Norse male personal name *Eiríkr* (English *Eric*), literally 'mercy-power' [Robert Herrick, 1591–1674, English poet]

Herring 'herring-seller' [Albert Herring, the shy young shop assistant who is the central character of the eponymous opera (1947) by Benjamin Britten]

Herrington 'person from Herrington', Durham ('estate associated with Here')

Herriot (i) *also* **Heriot** 'person from Heriot', Edinburgh ('piece of land restored to its feudal owner after the death of its tenant'); (ii) 'little **Harry**'. See also **Harriott** [James Herriot, pen-name James Alfred Wight, 1916–95, British author]

— **George Heriot's School** a large public school in Edinburgh, founded in 1624 by the goldsmith and philanthropist George Heriot, 1563–1624

— **Heriot-Watt University** a university in Edinburgh, founded in 1821 as the School of Arts of Edinburgh for the Education of Mechanics. In the 1870s, having absorbed George Heriot's Hospital (founded by George Heriot (see above) and opened in 1659), it became Heriot-Watt College ('Watt' in honour of James Watt; see **Watt**). It became a university in 1966.

Herschel, Herschell from a pet-form of the Yiddish male personal name *Hirsh*, literally 'deer' (from German *Hirsch* 'male deer, hart') [Caroline Herschel, 1750–1848, German-born British astronomer, sister of Sir William; Sir John Herschel, 1792–1871, British astronomer, son of Sir William; Sir William Herschel, 1738–1822, German-born British astronomer, discoverer of Uranus]

Hershey (i) 'person from Hercé or Hercy', France; (ii) a US anglicization of any of a range of similar sounding Jewish names (e.g. *Hershberger, Hershkowitz*)

— **Hershey bar** a US brand of chocolate bar, manufactured by the Hershey Chocolate Corporation, founded in 1903 by Milton S. Hershey, 1857–1945. In US slang, the term also refers to a gold-coloured bar awarded to service personnel who have done six months' overseas duty: it puns on the chocolate bar and the name of General Lewis B. Hershey, director of the US Selective Service Scheme from 1941 to 1970.

— **Hershey Highway** a US slang term for the rectum, based on the similarity in colour between chocolate (as in the Hershey bar – see above) and faeces

Hervey see **Harvey**

Herzog, Hertzog (i) 'servant of a duke', or from a German nickname for someone who calls to mind a duke, e.g. in putting on airs (German *Herzog* 'duke'); (ii) an invented Jewish name adopted from German *Herzog* 'duke' [J.B.M. Hertzog, 1866–1942, South African statesman, prime minister 1924–39]

— *Herzog* a novel (1964) by Saul Bellow, laying bare the inner life of a Jewish intellectual, Moses Herzog, though a succession of his unsent letters

Heseltine a different form of **Hazelden** [Michael Heseltine (Lord Heseltine), 1933–, British Conservative politician; Philip Heseltine, the real name of the composer Peter **Warlock**]

Hesketh 'person from Hesketh', Cumbria, Lancashire and Yorkshire ('racecourse')

Heslop 'person from Heslop', an unidentified place in northern England ('enclosed valley growing with hazel trees'). See also **Hislop**

Hess (i) 'person from the German state of Hesse'; (ii) from the Germanic personal name *Hesso* [Dame Myra Hess, 1890–1965, British pianist; Victor Francis Hess, 1883–1964, Austrian-born US physicist]

Heston 'person from Heston', western Greater London ('farmstead in the brushwood') [Charlton Heston (original name John Charlton Carter), 1924–, US actor]

Hetherington, Heatherington 'person from Hetherington', Northumberland (probably 'estate associated with Heathuhere'). See also **Etherington**

Heward a different form of **Howard** (i)

Hewison 'son of **Hewitt**'

Hewitson, Hewetson 'son of **Hewitt**'

Hewitt, Hewit, Hewett, Hewet, Hewat (i) 'person who lives in a newly cleared area of woodland' (Middle English *hewett*, from *hewen* 'to cut'); (ii) from the medieval male personal name *Huet*, literally 'little **Hugh**'. See also **Howat** [Angela Hewitt, 1958–, British pianist; James Hewitt, 1958–, British former cavalry officer and paramour of Princess Diana; Lleyton Hewitt, 1981–, Australian tennis player; Patricia Hewitt, 1948–, Australian-born British Labour politician]

Hewlett, Hewlitt 'little little **Hugh**'. See also **Howlett**

— **Hewlett-Packard** a US manufacturer of electronic equipment, founded in 1939 by William R. Hewlett, 1913–2001, and David Packard, 1912–96.

Hewson (i) *also* **Hughson** 'son of **Hugh**'. See also **Hooson**; (ii) from Gaelic *Mac Aodha* (see **McKay**)

Heycock see **Haycock**

Heydon see **Hayden**

Heyer, Hayer different forms of **Ayer** (i)

Heyes, Heys see **Hayes**

Heyhoe see **Hayhoe**

Heyward see **Hayward**

Heywood 'person from Heywood', Manchester ('high wood') [Thomas Heywood, ?1574–1641, English dramatist]

Heyworth 'person from Heyworth', Lancashire ('high enclosure')

Hibbert, Hibberd, Hibbard from the Norman male personal name *Hilbert, Hildebert*, of Germanic origin and meaning literally 'battle-bright'

Hibbs (i) 'son of *Hibb*', a reduced form of **Hibbert**; (ii) 'son of *Ibb*', a medieval female personal name that was a pet-form of *Isabel*. See also **Ibbotson**

Hichens, Hichins see **Hitchins**

Hick from the medieval male personal name *Hicke*, a pet-form of **Richard**. See also **Higgins, Higgs, Hitch, Hitchins, Icke** [Graeme Hick, 1966–, Zimbabwean-born English cricketer]

Hickenbotham, Hickinbottom different forms of **Higginbottom**

Hickes see **Hicks**

Hickey, Hickie, Hicky from Irish Gaelic *Ó hÍcidhe* 'descendant of *Ícidhe*', a nickname meaning literally 'healer' [William Hickey, ?1749–1830, British memoirist (his name was adopted in 1933 as the pen-name of the *Daily Express* gossip columnist; the first 'William Hickey' was Tom Driberg)]

Hickling (i) 'person from Hickling', Norfolk and Nottinghamshire ('settlement of Hicel's people'); (ii) 'little **Hick**'

Hickman 'servant of **Hick**'

Hickmott 'relative of **Hick**'

Hickock, Hickok (i) from the medieval personal name *Hickock*, from **Hick** with the suffix -*cock* (literally 'cockerel', hence 'jaunty or bumptious young man') that was often added to create pet-forms of personal names in the Middle Ages; (ii) a different form of **Haycock**. See also **Hiscock, Hitchcock** [James Butler ('Wild Bill') Hickok, 1837–76, US lawman, gunfighter and scout]

Hickox 'son of **Hickock**' [Richard Hickox, 1948–, British conductor]

Hicks, Hickes 'son of **Hick**'. See also **Higgs** [David Hicks, 1929–98, British interior designer]

— **Jimmy Hicks** US crap and poker players' rhyming slang for *six*. The name is probably just an arbitrary choice, rather than based on a real person.

Hickson, Hixon 'son of **Hick**'. See also **Higson** [Joan Hickson, 1906–98, British actress]

Hidalgo 'servant of a nobleman' (Spanish *hidalgo* 'nobleman')

Hide see **Hyde**

Higginbottom, Higginbotham, Higginbottam, Higgenbottom 'person from Higginbottom (now Oakenbottom)', Lancashire (probably 'broad valley growing with oak trees'). See also **Hickenbotham**

Higgins, Higgens (i) 'son of *Higgen*', a medieval male personal name, literally 'little **Hick**'; (ii) from Irish Gaelic *Ó hUiginn* 'descendant of *Uiginn*', a nickname meaning literally 'Viking', or *Ó hAodhagáin* 'descendant of *Aodhagán*', a nickname meaning literally 'little little fire'. See also **Eakin, Egan, O'Higgins** [Alex Higgins, 1949–, Northern Irish snooker player; Professor Henry Higgins, the phonetician who attempts to transform Eliza Doolittle in Bernard Shaw's *Pygmalion* (1913); Jack Higgins (original name Henry Patterson), 1929–, British writer]
— **Terrence Higgins Trust** a British Aids charity founded in 1982 in memory of Terrence Higgins, 1945–82, one of the first British gay men to die of the disease

Higginson 'son of **Higgins** (i)'

Higgs 'son of **Hick**'
— **Higgs boson** a theoretical subatomic particle that enables all other types of particle to have mass. It is named after Peter Higgs, 1929–, the British physicist who postulated its existence.

High, Highe (i) 'person who lives on a high place (e.g. a hilltop)'; (ii) from a medieval nickname for a tall man

Higham, Hyam 'person from Higham', the name of various places in England (variously 'high homestead' and 'high enclosure')

Highet 'person from Highgate', Strathclyde region ('high gate'). See also **Hyatt**

Highfield 'person from Highfield', the name of various places in England ('high open country')

Highland see **Hyland**

Highsmith probably 'smith working at a forge in a relatively high location' [Patricia Highsmith, 1921–95, US author of crime fiction]

Hight see **Height**

Highton 'person from Hightown', Lancashire ('high settlement')

Hignett from the medieval personal name *Hignett*, probably literally 'little little **Hick**'

Higson 'son of **Hick**' [Charlie Higson, 1958–, British actor and writer]

Hilary, Hillary, Hillery (i) from the medieval male personal name *Hilary* (from Latin *Hilarius*, a derivative of *hilaris* 'cheerful'). See also **McKellar**; (ii) from the medieval female personal name *Eulalie* (from Latin *Eulalia*, based on Greek *eulalos* 'eloquent') [Sir Edmund Hillary, 1919–, New Zealand mountaineer and explorer; Patrick Hillery, 1923–, Irish statesman, president 1976–90]

Hildebrand, Hildebrandt from the personal name *Hildebrand*, brought into England by the Normans but ultimately of Germanic origin and meaning literally 'flaming sword of battle'

Hill (i) 'person who lives on or near a hill'. See also **Hull** (i); (ii) from the medieval personal name *Hill*, a shortened form of **Hilary, Hildebrand** or **Hilliard**; (iii) from a Low German shortened form of **Hildebrand** [Archibald Hill, 1886–1977, British physiologist; Benny Hill (original name Alfred Hawthorne Hill), 1925–92, British comedian; Charles Hill (Lord Hill), 1904–89, British general practitioner and Conservative politician; Damon Hill, 1960–, British motor-racing driver, son of Graham; David Hill, 1802–70, British photographer and painter; Graham Hill, 1929–75, British motor-racing driver; Harry Hill (original name Matthew Hall), 1964–, British comedian; Jimmy Hill, 1928–, British footballer and football pundit; Octavia Hill, 1838–1912, British philanthropist and social reformer, moving spirit behind the National Trust; Sir Rowland Hill, 1795–1879, British postal expert, introducer of the penny post]
— ***Fanny Hill*** the alternative, and more commonly used, title of John Cleland's *Memoirs of a Woman of Pleasure* (1749), in which 'Fanny' recounts her sexual exploits in some detail. Someone who is **on the Fanny Hill** is on the (contraceptive) pill.
— **Hillsborough** a small town in County Down, Northern Ireland, founded around 1650 by the planter Colonel Sir Arthur Hill, ?1601–63. In the 18th century his descendants built **Hillsborough Castle**, seat of Northern Ireland governance since 1925.
— **Jimmy Hills** (see above) rhyming slang for *pills*
— **William Hill plc** a British firm of bookmakers, founded in 1934 by William Hill, 1903–71, the leading bookmaker of the day

Hiller a different form of **Hill** (i) [Dame Wendy Hiller, 1912–2003, British actress]

Hilliard, Hilleard, Hillyard from the Norman female personal name *Hildiarde* or *Hildegard*, of Germanic origin and meaning literally 'battle fortress' [Nicholas Hilliard, 1547–1619, English portrait miniaturist]

Hillier, Hillyar, Hillyer (i) 'person who makes or repairs roofs' (from a derivative of Middle English *helen* 'to cover'); (ii) from the French personal name *Hillier* '**Hilary**' [Bevis Hillier, 1940–, British author and journalist]

Hillman a different form of **Hill** (i)
— **Hillman Cars** a British car marque, from the late 1920s under the umbrella of the Rootes Group (see **Rootes**). The firm was founded in the 1880s in Coventry as a cycle manufacturer by William Hillman, and produced its first car in 1907.

Hills (i) a different form of **Hill** (i); (ii) 'son of **Hill** (ii)'

Hilton, Hylton 'person from Hilton', the name of various places in England (mainly 'farmstead by a hill' or 'farmstead on a slope') [Conrad Hilton, 1887–1979, US hotelier, founder of the Hilton Hotels chain (of which the first was the Dallas Hilton (1925)); Jack Hylton, 1892–1965, British bandleader; James Hilton, 1900–54, British novelist; Paris Hilton, 1981–, US heiress and socialite, great-granddaughter of Conrad; Walter Hilton, died 1396, English religious author]

Hinchcliffe, Hinchcliff 'person from Hinchcliffe', Yorkshire ('steep cliff')

Hinckley, Hinkley 'person from Hinckley', Leicestershire ('Hȳnca's glade')

Hind, Hinde (i) from a medieval nickname for someone thought to resemble a hind (a female deer), especially in being gentle or timorous; (ii) a different form of **Hine**

Hindes see **Hinds**

Hindley, Hindeley 'person from Hindley', near Manchester ('glade frequented by female deer') [Myra Hindley, 1942–2002, British murderer]

Hindmarsh, Hindmarch 'person from Hindmarsh', an unidentified place in England (probably 'wet land frequented by female deer')

Hinds, Hindes 'son of **Hind**' [Alfred ('Alfie') Hinds, 1917–91, British criminal noted for his prison escapes]

Hine, Hyne 'servant' (Middle English *hīne* 'lad, servant')
— **Hine** a brand of cognac, as produced in the distillery founded in Cognac in the late 1790s by the Englishman Thomas Hine, 1775–1822. Thomas Hine and Co. is now part of the Moët-Hennessy-Louis Vuitton group.

Hines see **Hynes**

Hinkley see **Hinckley**

Hinton 'person from Hinton', the name of numerous places in southern England and the Midlands (variously 'high farmstead' and 'farmstead belonging to a religious community')

Hird see **Heard**

Hirst see **Hurst**

Hiscock, Hiscoke different forms of **Hickock**

Hislop, Hyslop different forms of **Heslop** [Ian Hislop, 1960–, British journalist and broadcaster, editor of *Private Eye* 1986–]

Hitch a different form of **Hick**

Hitchcock a different form of **Hickock** [Sir Alfred Hitchcock, 1899–1980, British film director]

Hitchins, Hitchens, Hichins, Hichens, Hitchings 'son of *Hitchen*', literally 'little **Hick**' [Christopher Hitchens, 1949–, British journalist and polemicist]

Hite see **Height**

Hixon see **Hickson**

Hoad 'person who lives on a heath' (Middle English *hōth* 'heath') [Lew Hoad, 1934–94, Australian tennis player]

Hoadley 'person from East or West Hoathley', Sussex ('glade where heather grows')

Hoare, Hoar, Hore (i) 'person who lives by a slope or shore' (Old English *ōra*); (ii) from a medieval nickname for an old or grey-haired person (Middle English *hore* 'grey'). See also **Orr** [Leslie Hore-Belisha, see **Belisha**]
— **C. Hoare & Co.** a banking firm (commonly known as **Hoares Bank**) founded in London in 1672 by Sir Richard Hoare, 1648–1718. It is the UK's oldest privately owned bank.

Hoban from Irish Gaelic *Ó hÚbáin* 'descendant of *Úbán*', a personal name of unknown origin [Russell Hoban, 1925–, US writer]

Hobart a different form of **Hubert**
— **Hobart** the capital city of Tasmania. It was named in honour of Robert Hobart (4th earl of Buckinghamshire), 1760–1816, who was British colonial secretary at the time of its establishment at the beginning of the 19th century.

Hobbs, Hobbes 'son of *Hobb*', a medieval male personal name that was a pet-form of **Robert**. See also **Hopkins** [Sir Jack Hobbs, 1882–1963, English cricketer; Thomas Hobbes, 1588–1679, English political philosopher]
— **Russell Hobbs** see **Russell**

Hobday, Hobdey 'servant of *Hobb*' (see **Hobbs**) or '*Hobb* the servant'

Hobson 'son of *Hobb*' (see **Hobbs**) [Sir Harold Hobson, 1904–92, British theatre critic]
— **Hobson's choice** a choice between what is offered and nothing at all. The phrase commemorates the English liveryman Thomas Hobson, 1554–1631, who would only let his customers take the horse nearest the door.
— *Hobson's Choice* a play (1916) by Harold Brighouse which portrays the humbling of a tyrannical shoe-shop owner

Hockley 'person from Hockley', the name of numerous places in England (variously 'Hocca's glade', 'glade where mallows grow' and 'Hucca's hill')

Hockney 'person from Hokeney', near Tirley, Gloucestershire (now only a field-name) [David Hockney, 1937–, British painter]

Hodd a different form of **Hood** (i)

Hodder 'maker or seller of hoods'
— **Hodder and Stoughton** a British publishing firm, established in 1868 when a previously existing company founded by Matthew Hodder, 1830–1911, was joined by Thomas Wilberforce Stoughton, 1840–1917. It is now an imprint of **Hodder Headline**.

Hoddinott, Hodinott 'person from Hoddnant', the name of various places in Wales, or 'person from Hodnet', Shropshire (in both cases 'pleasant valley' or 'pleasant stream') [Alun Hoddinott, 1929–, British composer]

Hodge (i) from the medieval male personal name *Hodge*, a pet-form of **Roger**; (ii) from a medieval nickname for someone thought to resemble a pig (Middle English *hogge, hodge* 'hog') [Patricia Hodge, 1946–, British actress]

Hodges 'son of **Hodge**' [William Hodges, the bad-tempered greengrocer and ARP warden (played by Bill Pertwee) in the BBC television sitcom *Dad's Army* (1968–77)]

Hodgkin 'little **Hodge**'. See also **Costigan** [Alan Hodgkin, 1914–98, British physiologist; Dorothy Hodgkin, 1910–94, Egyptian-born British chemist; Sir Howard Hodgkin, 1932–, British painter, cousin of Dorothy and great-great-grandnephew of Thomas; Thomas Hodgkin, 1798–1866, British pathologist]

— **Hodgkin's disease** a malignant form of lymphoma marked by progressive enlargement of the lymph nodes and the spleen. It is named after Thomas Hodgkin (see above), who first described it.

Hodgkins 'son of **Hodgkin**'. See also **Hotchkins**

Hodgkinson 'son of **Hodgkins**'

Hodgkiss a different form of **Hodgkins**

Hodgson 'son of **Hodge**' [Frances Hodgson Burnett, see **Burnett**; Ralph Hodgson, 1871–1962, British poet]

Hoe 'person who lives on or by a hill-spur' or 'person from Hoe', the name of various places in England (in either case from Old English *hōh* 'hill-spur'). See also **Hough**

Hoey see **Howey** (ii)

Hofer, Hoffer 'person who lives or works on or manages a farm or estate' (Middle High German *hof* (see **Hoffmann**))

Hoffa a different form of **Hofer** [Jimmy Hoffa, 1913–75, US trade-union leader who disappeared in mysterious circumstances]

Hoffmann, Hofmann (i) 'manager of a farm or estate' (Middle High German *hof* 'settlement, farm, court'); (ii) *also* **Hoffman** *or* **Hofman** a Jewish name, mainly an adoption of *Hoffmann* (i) but also possibly influenced by German *hoffen* or Yiddish *hofn* 'to hope' [Abbie Hoffman (original name Abbott Howard Hoffman), 1936–89, US political activist, founder of the Youth International Party (Yippies); Dustin Hoffman, 1937–, US film actor]

Hoffnung an invented Jewish name based on German *Hoffnung* 'hope' [Gerard Hoffnung, 1925–59, German-born British musician, artist and entertainer]

Hogan from Irish Gaelic *Ó hÓgáin* 'descendant of *Ógán*', a personal name meaning literally 'little young one' [Ben Hogan, 1912–97, US golfer; Paul Hogan, 1940–, Australian actor]

Hogarth, Hoggarth probably different forms of **Hoggard** [William Hogarth, 1697–1764, British painter and engraver]

— **Hogarth Press** a publishing firm founded by Leonard and Virginia Woolf in 1917 in Hogarth House, their home in Richmond, southwest London

Hogben, Hogbin from a medieval nickname for someone with a crippled or deformed hip (Middle English *huckbone* 'hip bone') [Lancelot Hogben, 1895–1975, British zoologist and popular-science writer]

Hogg, Hogge (i) 'person employed to look after pigs; swineherd', or from a medieval nickname for someone though to resemble a pig in appearance; (ii) a translation of Gaelic *Mac an Bhanbh*, literally 'son of the pig' [James Hogg, 1770–1835, Scottish poet and writer; Quintin Hogg, 1845–1903, British philanthropist; Quintin Hogg (Lord Hailsham), 1907–2001, British Conservative politician, lord chancellor 1970–74, 1979–87, grandson of Quintin]

Hoggard 'person employed to look after pigs; swineherd' (Middle English *hogherd*). See also **Hogarth** [Matthew Hoggard, 1976–, English cricketer]

Hoggart a different form of **Hoggard** [Richard Hoggart, 1918–, British scholar and author; Simon Hoggart, 1946–, British journalist, son of Richard]

Hogwood probably 'person from Hogwood or Hog Wood', the name of an unidentified place in England (probably 'wood where pigs live or are kept') [Christopher Hogwood, 1941–, British musician]

Holander see **Hollander**

Holbrook, Holbrooke, Holdbrook, Holebrook 'person from Holbrook', the name of various places in England ('stream in a hollow')

Holcombe, Holcomb, Holcom 'person from Holcombe', the name of various places in England ('deep valley')

Holdcroft, Holcroft, Houldcroft 'person from Holcroft', Lancashire ('smallholding in a hollow')

Holden, Houlden 'person from Holden', Lancashire and Yorkshire ('deep valley'). See also **Holding**

Holder (i) 'person employed to look after animals' (from a derivative of Middle English *holden* 'to guard, keep'); (ii) 'person who lives by an elder tree' (Middle High German *holder* 'elder'); (iii) an invented Jewish name based on German *Holder* 'elder tree'

Holderness 'person from Holderness', coastal region of Yorkshire ('headland governed by a hold (a high-ranking official in the Danelaw)'). See also **Holness**

Holding a different form of **Holden** [Michael Holding, 1954–, West Indian cricketer]

Holdroyd a different form of **Holroyd**

Holdsworth, Holsworth, Holesworth, Houldsworth 'person from Holdsworth', Yorkshire ('Halda's enclosure')

Hole 'person who lives by or in a depression in the ground or a low-lying area'. See also **Holman, Hoyle**

Holford 'person from Holford', the name of various places in England ('ford in a hollow')

Holgate 'person from Holgate', the name of various places in England ('road in a hollow')

Holiday, Holliday different forms of **Halliday** [Billie Holiday (original name Eleanora Gough McKay, *née* Fagan), 1915–59, US jazz singer]

Holinshed see **Hollinshead**

Holland (i) 'person from Holland', the name of various places in England ('land of hill-spurs'). See also **Howland, Hoyland**; (ii) 'person from Holland (i.e. the Netherlands)'; (iii) from Irish Gaelic *Ó hÓileáin* 'descendant of *Faolán*', a personal name probably meaning literally 'little wolf'. See also **Whelan** [Henry Holland, 1745–1806, British architect; Jools Holland (original name Julian Holland), 1958–, British keyboards player and television presenter; Philemon Holland, 1552–1637, English translator;

Sir Sidney Holland, 1893–1961, New Zealand National Party politician, prime minister 1949–57]

Hollander, Holander different forms of **Holland** (ii)

Hollaway see **Holloway**

Holles see **Hollis**

Holley, Holly 'person who lives by a holly tree' [Buddy Holly (original name Charles Hardin Holley), 1938–59, US musician]
— **The Hollies** a British pop group, founded in Manchester in 1962. Their name was inspired by Buddy Holly (see above).

Holliday see **Holiday**

Hollies a different form of **Hollis**

Hollingsworth, Hollingworth 'person from Hollingworth', Cheshire and Lancashire ('enclosure where holly grows')

Hollins a different form of **Hollis**

Hollinshead, Hollingshead, Hollinshed, Holinshed 'person from Hollingside or Holmside', a place, now lost, in County Durham ('hillside growing with holly') [Raphael Holinshed, died 1580, English chronicler (much of the material in Shakespeare's history plays comes from his work)]

Hollis, Holliss, Holles 'person who lives by a group of holly trees'

Holloway, Hollaway 'person from Holloway', the name of various places in England ('road in a hollow') [James Henry Holloway, 1897–1975, real name of the British comedian and Crazy Gang member Jimmy Nervo; Robin Holloway, 1943–, British composer; Stanley Holloway, 1890–1982, British actor and singer; Thomas Holloway, 1800–83, British philanthropist]
— **Royal Holloway** a college of London University, founded as Royal Holloway College at Egham, Surrey by Thomas Holloway (see above) in 1879. In 1985 it merged with Bedford College to become Royal Holloway and Bedford New College, and in 1992 simplified its name to Royal Holloway.

Holly see **Holley**

Hollyhock a different form of **Holyoak**

Hollyoak, Hollyoake different forms of **Holyoak**

Holman, Hollman (i) 'person who lives by a holly tree or on an island' (see **Holme**); (ii) 'person who lives by or in a depression in the ground or a low-lying area'

Holme, Holm (i) 'person who lives by a holly tree' (Middle English holm 'holly', from Old English); (ii) 'person who lives on an island (in this context, usually an area of dry land in the middle of a fen)' (Middle English holm 'island', from Old Norse). See also **Homer, Hulme, Hume** [Sir Ian Holm (original name Ian Holm Cuthbert), 1932–, British actor]

Holmes a different form of **Holme** [Eamonn Holmes, 1959–, British television presenter; Dame Kelly Holmes, 1970–, British athlete; Oliver Wendell Holmes, 1809–94, US physician and writer; Oliver Wendell Holmes, Jr., 1841–1935, US jurist, son of Oliver Wendell; Robert Holmes à

Court, 1937–90, South African-born Australian businessman; Sherlock Holmes, consulting detective invented by Sir Arthur Conan Doyle]

Holness a different form of **Holderness**

Holroyd 'person from Holroyd', the name of various places in northern England ('clearing in a hollow'). See also **Holdroyd** [Michael Holroyd, 1935–, British biographer]

Holst, Holste 'occupier of a patch of woodland' (Middle Low German holtsäte, literally 'wood-tenant') [Gustav Holst, 1874–1934, British composer]

Holsworth see **Holdsworth**

Holt 'person who lives in or near a wood' (Middle English holt 'wood, copse'). See also **Hoult** [Harold Holt, 1908–67, Australian Liberal politician, prime minister 1966–67]

Holtby 'person from Holtby', Yorkshire ('Holt's farmstead' or 'farmstead by a wood') [Winifred Holtby, 1898–1935, British writer]

Holton 'person from Holton', the name of numerous places in England (variously 'farmstead on a spur of land', 'farmstead in a corner of land' and 'farmstead in a hollow')

Holyoak, Holyoake (i) 'person who lives near a sacred oak tree'; (ii) 'person from Holy Oakes', Leicestershire. See also **Hollyhock, Hollyoak** [Sir Keith Holyoake, 1904–83, New Zealand National Party politician, prime minister 1957, 1960–72]

Home see **Hume**

Homer (i) 'helmet-maker' (Old French heaumier); (ii) a different form of **Holme** [Winslow Homer, 1836–1910, US painter]

Homewood 'person from Homewood', the name of various places in southeastern England ('wood with a homestead')

Hone 'person who lives by a rock' (Middle English hōn 'stone, rock'). The rock would have been either a prominent natural feature of the landscape or an artificially placed one (e.g. a boundary stone).

Honey 'person who harvests or sells honey'

Honeyball, Hunneyball from the medieval person name Honeyball, of uncertain origin: perhaps an alteration of Anabel, or alternatively from a Germanic compound name meaning literally 'bear-cub brave'. See also **Honneyball, Hunnable, Hunnibal**

Honeycombe (i) 'person from Honeycomb', Cornwall ('honey valley'); (ii) from the Middle English term of endearment honeycomb, used as a nickname [Gordon Honeycombe, 1936–, British television newsreader]

Honeycutt, Hunnicutt 'person from Hunnacott', Devon (either 'Huna's cottage' or 'honey cottage') [Gayle Hunnicutt, 1943–, US actress]

Hong 'water, flood' (Chinese)

Honneyball a different form of **Honeyball**

Hood (i) 'person who makes hoods', or from a medieval nickname for someone who characteristically wears a hood. See also **Hodd**; (ii) from Irish Gaelic Mac hUid 'son of Ud', a personal name of

unknown origin and meaning [Robin Hood, legendary English outlaw; Samuel Hood (Viscount Hood), 1724–1816, British admiral; Thomas Hood, 1799–1845, British poet]
— **HMS *Hood*** a British battlecruiser, launched in 1918 and sunk by the German warships *Bismarck* and *Prinz Eugen* in 1941. It was named after Admiral Hood (see above).

Hook, Hooke (i) 'person who makes or sells hooks' or 'person who uses a hook' (mainly referring to a curved agricultural implement for reaping); also, 'person who lives by a curved topographical feature' (e.g. a bend in a river); (ii) from a medieval nickname for a hunchback or someone with a hooked nose [Robert Hooke, 1635–1703, British physicist and instrument maker]

Hooker a different form of **Hook** (i) [Richard Hooker, ?1554–1600, English churchman and theologian; John Lee Hooker, 1917–2001, US blues singer, guitarist and songwriter; Joseph Hooker, 1814–79, US general; Sir Joseph Hooker, 1817–1911, British botanist, son of William; Sir William Hooker, 1785–1865, British botanist, first director of Kew Gardens]

Hookes, Hooks different forms of **Hook** (i)

Hooley 'person from Hoole', Cheshire and Lancashire (respectively 'place by a hollow' and 'place by a hut')

Hooney from Irish Gaelic *Ó hUaithnigh* 'descendant of *Uaithneach*', a personal name derived from *uaithne* 'green'

Hooper 'person who puts hoops on barrels'

Hooson a different form of **Hewson** (i)

Hoover a different form of **Huber** [Herbert Hoover, 1874–1964, US Republican politician, president 1929–33; J. Edgar Hoover, 1895–1972, US lawyer, director of the Federal Bureau of Investigation 1924–72; William H. Hoover, 1849–1932, US industrialist]
— **Hoover** originally, a proprietary name (registered in 1927) for a type of vacuum cleaner manufactured by the US Hoover company, named after its founder W.H. Hoover (see above). In British English it became a generic term for any vacuum cleaner. The use of *hoover* as a verb is first recorded in 1926.
— **Hoover Dam** a dam on the Colorado River, on the Arizona-Nevada border. It was completed in 1936 and named after Herbert Hoover (see above) who, as US secretary of commerce, chaired the commission that initiated its construction.
— **Hoover hog** a US slang euphemism for a wild rabbit or an armadillo used for food during the Depression years of the early 1930s, when Herbert Hoover was president. In similar vein, newspapers used as bedding were **Hoover blankets**.
— **Hooverize** to be economical, especially in one's use of food. The usage was inspired by the exhortations of Herbert Hoover, as US food commissioner in the late 1910s, to frugality in conditions of wartime scarcity.
— **Hooverville** in the US, a shanty town. The original reference was to the temporary accommodation provided for unemployed workers in the US in the early 1930s, the years of the Depression, when Herbert Hoover was president.

Hopcraft 'person from Hopcraft', the name of an unidentified place in England (probably 'smallholding in a valley among the hills')

Hope 'person who lives in an enclosed valley' or 'person from Hope', the name of various places in England and Scotland (in either case from Middle English *hop* 'enclosed valley') [Anthony Hope, pen-name of Sir Anthony Hope Hawkins, 1863–1933, British novelist; Bob Hope (original name Leslie Townes Hope), 1903–2003, British-born US comedian]
— **Bob Hope** (see above) rhyming slang for *dope* (in the sense 'cannabis', or more broadly 'drugs') and *soap*
— **Hope diamond** a large, deep blue diamond, now in the Smithsonian Natural History Museum, Washington. It gets its name from its 19th-century owners, the Hope family: it was acquired, some time before 1824, by Henry Philip Hope, died 1839, heir to the banking firm of Hope & Co.

Hopkin from the medieval personal name *Hopkin*, literally 'little *Hobb*' (see **Hobbs**) [Mary Hopkin, 1950–, British singer]

Hopkins 'son of **Hopkin**' [Sir Anthony Hopkins, 1937–, British actor; Sir Frederick Hopkins, 1861–1947, British biochemist; Gerard Manley Hopkins, 1844–89, British poet]
— **Johns Hopkins University** a leading US university, founded in Baltimore in 1876 under the terms of a bequest from the US businessman and philanthropist Johns Hopkins, 1795–1873

Hopkinson 'son of **Hopkin**' [Harry Hopkinson, 1890–1946, US administrator; John Hopkinson, 1849–98, British physicist and electrical engineer]

Hopkirk 'person from Hopekirk', near Hawick, Scotland ('church in the valley among the hills') [Paddy Hopkirk, 1933–, Northern Irish rally driver]

Hopper (i) 'acrobat, tumbler', or from a medieval nickname for a fidgety or overactive person; (ii) 'hop-grower' or 'hop-seller' (from a derivative of Middle Dutch *hoppe* 'hops'); (iii) from a medieval German nickname for a lame person (from a derivative of Middle High German *hoppen* 'to limp') [Dennis Hopper, 1936–, US actor; Edward Hopper, 1882–1967, US artist; Hedda Hopper (original name Elda Furry), 1885–1966, US show-business gossip columnist]

Hopwood 'person from Hopwood', Lancashire ('wood in a valley among hills')

Horan (i) from Irish Gaelic *Ó hUghróin* 'descendant of *Ughrón*', a personal name meaning literally 'warlike one'; (ii) from Irish Gaelic *Ó hOdhráin* 'descendant of *Odhrán*', a personal name meaning literally 'dun-coloured one'; (iii) a different form of **Hanrahan**

Hore see **Hoare**

Horgan (i) a different form of **Hanrahan**; (ii) a different form of **Morgan**

Horlick a different form (perhaps influenced by *cowlick* 'lock of hair which looks as if it had been licked by a cow') of the name *Horlock*, from a medieval nickname for someone with (a lock of) grey hair (from Middle English *hore* 'grey(-haired)' + *loke* 'lock of hair')

— **Horlicks** a malted-milk-powder drink, manufactured by a firm established in Chicago, Illinois in 1873 by the British immigrant William A. Horlick, 1846–1936, and his brother James.

Horn, Horne (i) 'person who plays a horn'; (ii) 'person who lives by a horn-shaped topographical feature (e.g. a tongue of land between rivers)', or 'person from Horn', the name of various places in England, derived from such a feature; (iii) 'maker of articles (e.g. mugs) out of horn'; (iv) from a medieval nickname perhaps alluding to some aspect of a person's appearance, or perhaps denoting a cuckold (men thus deceived were stereotyped as wearing horns) [Kenneth Horne, 1907–69, British comedian and businessman, presenter of the BBC radio comedy programme *Round the Horne* (1965–69); Lena Horne, 1917–, US popular singer; Marilyn Horne, 1917–, US mezzosoprano]

Hornby 'person from Hornby', the name of various places in northern England ('farmstead on a horn-shaped piece of land') [Lesley Hornby, the original name of Twiggy, 1949–, British fashion model; Nick Hornby, 1957–, British novelist]

— **Hornby Railways** model railways as originally manufactured by the Meccano Company, founded by the British inventor and businessman Frank Hornby, 1863–1936. The first Hornby train set was marketed in 1920; the '00' gauge model, tradenamed **Hornby Dublo**, appeared in 1938.

Horner a different form of **Horn**

— **Johnny Horner** British rhyming slang, since the late 19th century, for *corner*

— **'Little Jack Horner'** a traditional English nursery rhyme, first published in 1725:

Little Jack Horner
Sat in the corner,
Eating a Christmas pie;
He put in his thumb,
And pulled out a plumb,
And said, What a good boy am I!

It has been claimed that 'Jack Horner' is identical with Thomas Horner, steward to the last Abbot of Glastonbury at the time of the Dissolution of the Monasteries, who was supposedly dispatched to London with a pie containing the title deeds of twelve manors as a gift for Henry VIII

Hornet, Hornett different forms of **Arnold** (i)

Horniman a different form of **Hearn** (i) [Annie Horniman, 1860–1937, British theatrical promoter]

— **Horniman Museum** a museum of anthropology and natural history in Forest Hill, South London, founded by the tea trader Frederick John Horniman, 1835–1906, and opened in 1901

Hornsby 'person from Hornsby', Cumbria ('Ormr's settlement')

Horowitz, Horovitz 'person from Hořovice', Bohemia (a derivative of Slavic *gora* 'hill'). A

Jewish name. See also **Horwitz, Hurwitz** [Vladimir Horowitz, 1904–89, Russian-born US pianist]

Horrocks 'person from Horrocks', Greater Manchester ('piles of stones or rubbish') [Sir Brian Horrocks, 1895–1985, British general; Jane Horrocks, 1964–, British actress]

Horsburgh 'person from Horsburgh', Borders region (originally 'horses' brook')

Horsefall 'person from Horsefall', Yorkshire ('clearing where horses are pastured')

Horsley 'person from Horsley', the name of numerous places in England ('clearing where horses are pastured')

Horton 'person from Horton', the name of various places in England (mostly 'muddy farmstead')

Horwell 'person from Horwell', Devon ('muddy stream')

Horwitz a different form of **Horowitz**

Horwood 'person from Horwood', Buckinghamshire and Devon (respectively 'muddy wood' and probably 'grey wood' or 'wood frequented by hares' (see **Harwood**))

Hoseason 'son of *Hosea*', a personal name that was originally probably *Osie*, a pet-form of *Oswald*, but came to be associated with the biblical personal name *Hosea*

Hosie, Hosey different forms of **Hussey**

Hoskin, Hoskyn, Hosken from the medieval personal name *Osekin*, literally 'little *Os*', a shortened form of various Old English personal names beginning with *ōs* 'god' (e.g. *Osmund, Oswald*). See also **Huskisson**

Hosking a different form of **Hoskin** [Eric Hosking, 1909–91, British natural-history photographer]

Hoskins, Hoskyns 'son of **Hoskin**' [Bob Hoskins, 1942–, British actor]

Hossain a different form of **Husain**

Hotchkins a different form of **Hodgkins**

Hough, Huff 'person who lives by a hill-spur' or 'person from Hough', the name of various places in England (in either case from Old English *hōh* 'hill-spur, ridge') [Stephen Hough, 1961–, British pianist]

Houghton 'person from Houghton', the name of numerous places in England (mainly 'farmstead on a hill-spur')

Houldsworth see **Holdsworth**

Houlihan from Irish Gaelic *Ó hUallacháin* 'descendant of *Uallachán*', a personal name meaning literally 'little proud one'

— **Kathleen ni Houlihan** a personification of Ireland as a woman (as Britannia is of Great Britain). She originated among the Jacobite poets of the 18th century. In W.B. Yeats's play *Cathleen ni Houlihan* (1902) she appears as a mysterious wandering old woman who inspired the uprising of the United Irishmen in 1798.

Hoult a different form of **Holt**

House (i) 'person who lives in a (large or important) house' or 'person who lives in his own house'; (ii) a different form of **Howes**

Household a different form of **House** (i) [Geoffrey Household, 1900–88, British novelist]

Householder a different form of **House** (i)

Houseman, Housman a different form of **House** (i) [A.E. Housman, 1859–1936, British poet and scholar; Laurence Housman, 1865–1959, British writer and dramatist, brother of A.E.]

Houston (i) *also* **Houstoun** *or* **Huston** 'person from Houston', near Glasgow ('Hugo's village'); (ii) from Gaelic *Mac Uisdein* (see **McCutcheon**) [Anjelica Huston, 1951–, US actress, daughter of John; John Huston, 1906–87, US film director and actor; Walter Huston, 1884–1950, Canadian-born film actor, father of John; Whitney Houston, 1963–, US pop and R&B singer]

— **Houston** a city in Texas, founded in 1836 and named in honour of the US soldier and statesman Sam Houston, 1793–1836

How see **Howe**

Howard, Howerd (i) from the Norman male personal name *Huard* or *Heward*, of Germanic origin and meaning literally 'heart-brave'. See also **Heward**; (ii) from the Anglo-Scandinavian male personal name *Hāward*, meaning literally 'high guardian'. See also **Haward**; (iii) a different form of **Ewart** (ii); (iv) an anglicization of **Fogarty** [Howard, family name (now Fitzalan-Howard) of the dukes of Norfolk; Alan Howard, 1937–, British actor; Anthony Howard, 1934–, British journalist and broadcaster; Catherine Howard, ?1520–42, fifth wife of Henry VIII; Charles Howard (Lord Howard of Effingham), 1536–1624, English Lord High Admiral who led the English victory over the Spanish Armada; Sir Ebenezer Howard, 1850–1928, British theorist of town planning; Elizabeth Jane Howard, 1923–, British novelist; Frankie Howerd, 1917–92, British comedian; Henry Howard, Earl of Surrey, 1517–47, English poet; John Howard, ?1726–90, British prison reformer; John Howard, 1939–, Australian Liberal politician, prime minister 1996–; Leslie Howard (original name Leslie Howard Steiner), 1893–1943, British actor; Michael Howard, 1941–, British Conservative politician; Trevor Howard, 1916–88, British actor]

— **Castle Howard** a large country house in North Yorkshire, designed by Sir John Vanbrugh for Charles Howard, 1674–1738, 3rd earl of Carlisle, and built between 1701 and 1712

— **Charlie Howards, Frankie Howerds** (see above) rhyming slang for *cowards*

— **Howard de Walden** an English barony created in 1597 for Admiral Lord Thomas Howard, 1561–1626. A 19th-century marriage with an heiress of the dukes of Portland brought the family much wealth and property, and the Howard de Walden Estates are now one of the largest landowners in London.

— **Howardian Hills** a range of hills in the Vale of Pickering, Yorkshire, named after Castle Howard (see above), which is at their eastern end

— **Howard League for Penal Reform** a British organization devoted to the enlightened treatment of prison inmates. It was founded in 1866 as the Howard Association and named after John Howard (see above).

— *Howards End* a novel (1910) by E.M. Forster about human relationships and misunderstandings. The title is the name of a house belonging to one of the protagonists.

— *Howards' Way* a BBC television drama series (1985–90), an up-market soap opera centred on the boat-builder Tom Howard

Howarth, Howorth, Haworth 'person from Howarth', Lancashire (probably 'enclosure on a mound') [Elgar Howarth, 1935–, British conductor and composer]

Howat a different form of **Hewitt**

Howcroft 'person from Howcroft', Lancashire and Yorkshire ('smallholding on a hill-spur')

Howden (i) 'person from Howden', Borders region (probably 'valley in a corner of land'). See also **Haddon**; (ii) 'person from Howden', Yorkshire ('valley by the headland')

Howe, How (i) 'person who lives by a mound or small hill' or 'person from Howe', the name of various places in England (in either case from Middle English *how* 'small hill', from Old Norse *haugr*); (ii) a different form of **Hugh**. See also **Howes** [Elias Howe, 1819–67, US inventor of the lockstitch sewing machine; Sir Geoffrey Howe (Lord Howe), 1926–, British Conservative politician; Richard Howe (1st Earl Howe), 1726–99, British admiral; William Howe (Viscount Howe), 1729–1814, British military commander, brother of Richard]

— **Jacky Howe** in Australian English, a sleeveless flannel shirt. The inspiration was the Australian sheep-shearer Jacky Howe, 1855–1922, who in 1892 created a world record by hand-shearing 321 merino sheep in 8 hours 40 minutes. The garment is sometimes also called a **Jimmy Howe**.

— **Lord Howe Island** an island in the South Pacific Ocean, off the east coast of New South Wales. It was named after the 1st Earl Howe (see above), First Lord of the Admiralty at the time of its discovery in 1788.

Howell, Howel (i) 'person from Howell', Lincolnshire (probably 'Huna's spring'); (ii) from the Welsh male personal name *Hywel*, literally 'eminent'. See also **Powell** (i) [David Howell (Lord Howell), 1936–, British Conservative politician; Denis Howell (Lord Howell), 1923–98, British Labour politician]

Howells, Howels 'son of **Howell** (ii)' [Herbert Howells, 1892–1983, British composer]

Howes, Howse (i) 'person who lives by a group of mounds or barrows' (see **Howe** (i)); (ii) 'son of **Hugh**' [Sally Ann Howes, 1930–, British actress]

Howey (i) *also* **Howie** from the medieval male personal name *Howey*, literally 'little **Hugh**'; (ii) *also* **Hoey** from Irish Gaelic *Ó hEochaidh* 'descendant of *Eochaidh*', a different form of *Eachaidh* (see **Haughey**). See also **Huey** [Kate Hoey, 1946–, British Labour politician]

Howland a different form of **Holland** (i)

Howlett a different form of **Hewlett**

Hoyland a different form of **Holland** (i) [John Hoyland, 1934–, British painter]

Hoyle a northern English variant of **Hole** [Sir Fred Hoyle, 1915–2001, British astronomer and writer]
— **according to Hoyle** strictly according to the rules. The allusion is to Edmond Hoyle, 1672–1769, a British authority on card games whose *Short Treatise on the Game of Whist* (1742) became the standard work on the rules of the game.

Hu (i) from the Chinese personal name *Hu*; (ii) 'person from *Youhu*', the name of a Chinese state during the Xia dynasty (2205–1766 BC)

Huang 'person from Huang', an ancient Chinese territory. See also **Wong** (ii)

Hubbard a different form of **Hubert**
— **'Old Mother Hubbard'** a traditional English nursery rhyme, first printed (in a version much enlarged and elaborated by Sarah Martin) in 1805. The first verse runs:
Old Mother Hubbard
Went to the cupboard
To fetch her poor dog a bone;
But when she came there
The cupboard was bare
And so the poor dog had none.
According to Miss Martin, the original Mother Hubbard was a housekeeper in Kitley, Devon.

Hubble, Hubbell, Hubball from the Norman male personal name *Hubald*, of Germanic origin and meaning literally 'mind-bold' [Edwin Hubble, 1889–1953, US astronomer]
— **Hubble constant, Hubble's constant** the ratio that expresses the rate of the universe's expansion, equal to the speed at which the galaxies appear to be moving away from the Earth divided by their distance. It is named after Edwin Hubble (see above).
— **Hubble's law** the law holding that the speed at which distant galaxies are moving away from the Earth is proportional to their distance from the observer. It was formulated by Edwin Hubble in 1929.
— **Hubble Space Telescope** a telescope mounted on a satellite that orbits the Earth, used to observe distant parts of the universe and photograph them. Launched in 1990, it was named in honour of Edwin Hubble.

Huber (i) 'holder or owner of a large area of land designated in Middle High German as a *huobe*'; (ii) an invented Jewish name, from a southern Yiddish pronunciation of Yiddish *hober* 'oats'. See also **Hoover**

Hubert from the Germanic male personal name *Hubert*, literally 'mind-bright'. See also **Hobart**, **Hubbard**

Huck from the medieval male personal name *Hucke*, which was probably descended from the Old English personal name *Ucca* or *Hucca*, perhaps a shortened form of *Ūhtrǣd*, literally 'dawn-power'

Huckaby, Huckabee, Huckeby 'person from Huccaby', Devon (perhaps 'crooked river-bend'), or 'person from Uckerby', Yorkshire ('Úkyrri's or Útkári's farmstead')

Huckfield probably 'person from Huckfield', an unidentified place probably in Somerset (perhaps 'Hucca's open land' (see **Huck**))

Hucknall 'person from Hucknall', Nottinghamshire ('Hucca's corner of land' (see **Huck**)) [Mick Hucknall, 1960–, British pop singer]

Hudd from the medieval male personal name *Hudde*, a descendant of the Old English personal name *Hūda*, later influenced by **Hugh**. See also **Hudson, Hutt** [Roy Hudd, 1936–, British comedian]
— **Roy Hudd** (see above) rhyming slang for *blood* or (in the plural) *spuds* 'potatoes'

Huddleston, Huddlestone 'person from Huddleston', Yorkshire ('Hūdel's settlement') [Trevor Huddleston, 1913–98, British missionary and bishop]

Hudson 'son of **Hudd**' [Henry Hudson, ?1565–?1611, English navigator; Hugh Hudson, 1936–, British film director; Mrs Hudson, Sherlock Holmes's landlady at 221B Baker Street; Rock Hudson (original name Roy Harold Scherer, Jr), 1925–85, US film actor; W.H. Hudson, 1841–1922, British naturalist and writer]
— **Hudson Bay** an almost landlocked inland sea of east-central Canada, 730,000 sq. km/280,000 sq. mi. in area. It was named in honour of Henry Hudson (see above), who discovered it and probably died there.
— **Hudson River** a river in eastern New York State, emptying into Upper New York Bay at New York City. It is 492 km/306 mi. long, and was named in honour of Henry Hudson, the first European to sail down it.

Huey a different form of **Howey** (ii)

Huff see **Hough**

Huffington 'person from Uffington', the name of various places in England ('estate of or associated with Uffa') [Arianna Huffington (*née* Stassinopoulos), 1950–, Greek-born US author and journalist]

Huggett (i) 'person from Huggate', Yorkshire (perhaps 'road by a mound'); (ii) from a pet-form of **Hugh**
— **Meet the Huggetts** a BBC radio series (1953–61) featuring the doings of the fictional working-class Joe and Ethel Huggett and their family

Huggins 'son of little **Hugh**' [Sir William Huggins, 1824–1910, British astronomer]

Hugh from the Old French male personal name *Hughe* or *Hue*, brought to England by the Normans but ultimately of Germanic origin, from a shortened form of various compound personal names beginning with *hug* 'heart, spirit'. See also **Hewitt**, **Hewlett, Hewson, Howe, Huggett, Huggins**, **Hugo, Hull** (ii), **Hutchins, McCutcheon, Pugh**

Hughes, Hughs 'son of **Hugh**' [Emlyn Hughes, 1947–2004, British footballer; Howard Hughes,

1905–76, US industrialist; Langston Hughes, 1902–67, US writer; Owain Arwel Hughes, 1942–, British conductor; Richard Hughes, 1900–76, British writer; Robert Hughes, 1938–, Australian art critic and writer; Simon Hughes, 1951–, British Liberal politician; Ted Hughes, 1930–98, British poet; Thomas Hughes, 1822–96, British writer, author of *Tom Brown's Schooldays* (1857); William M. Hughes, 1864–1952, British-born Australian Labor and Nationalist politician, prime minister 1915–23]
— **Hughes Hall** a graduate college of Cambridge University, founded (as Cambridge Training College) in 1885 by Elizabeth Phillips Hughes, 1851–1925

Hughson see **Hewson** (i)

Hugo a Latinized variant of **Hugh**

Huish 'person from Huish', the name of various places in English ('area of land sufficient to support a household')

Hulbert from the medieval male personal name *Hulbert*, probably descended from an unrecorded Old English personal name *Holdbeorht*, literally 'gracious-bright' [Jack Hulbert, 1892–1978, British actor]

Hull (i) a different form of **Hill** (i); (ii) from a pet-form of **Hugh** [Cordell Hull, 1871–1955, US Democratic politician; Rod Hull, 1935–99, British puppeteer, partner of 'Emu']

Hulme a different form of **Holme** [Denny Hulme, 1936–94, New Zealand motor-racing driver; Keri Hulme, 1947–, New Zealand writer; T.E. Hulme, 1883–1917, British poet, critic and philosopher]

Hulse (i) 'person from Hulse', Cheshire (probably 'low-lying places'); (ii) *also* **Hulce** 'person who lives where holly grows' (Middle Low German *huls* 'holly') [Tom Hulce, 1953–, US actor]

Hulton 'person from Hulton', Lancashire and Staffordshire ('farmstead by a hill') [Edward Hulton, 1906–88, British magazine proprietor, owner of *Picture Post*]

Human (i) from the late Old English male personal name *Hygemann*, literally 'heart-man, spirit-man'; (ii) perhaps 'servant of **Hugh**'

Humber 'person from Humber', the name of various places in England so called from their proximity to a River *Humber* (a pre-English river-name of uncertain meaning)
— **Humber** a British car marque that had its beginnings in a bicycle-manufacturing business started in Sheffield in 1868 by Thomas Humber. It produced its first car in 1899. In 1931 it became part of the Rootes Group.

Humberstone, **Humberston** 'person from Humberstone', Leicestershire and Lincolnshire (perhaps respectively 'Humbert's stone' and 'stone by the River Humber')

Humbert from a Germanic male personal name meaning literally 'bear-cub famous' [Humbert Humbert, the main character in Vladimir Nabokov's *Lolita* (1955), who is in love with the 12-year-old Lolita]

Hume, **Home** different forms of **Holme** [Sir Alec Douglas-Home, see **Douglas**; Basil Hume, 1923–99, British cardinal, archbishop of Westminster 1976–99; Daniel Douglas Home, 1836–88, British spiritualist and medium; David Hume, 1711–76, Scottish philosopher and historian; Hamilton Hume, 1797–1873, Australian explorer; John Hume, 1937–, Northern Irish politician; Joseph Hume, 1777–1855, British radical politician]
— **Hume Highway** the main road from Melbourne to Sydney, Australia. It is named in honour of Hamilton Hume (see above).

Humphrey, **Humphry**, **Humphery**, **Humfrey** from the Old French male personal name *Humfrey*, brought into England by the Normans but ultimately of Germanic origin, meaning literally 'bear-cub peace' [Hubert Humphrey, 1911–78, US Democratic politician, vice-president 1965–69]

Humphries, **Humphreys**, **Humphrys** 'son of **Humphrey**'. See also **Humphriss** [Barry Humphries, 1934–, Australian writer and performer, alter ego of Dame Edna Everage; John Humphrys, 1943–, British radio and television journalist and presenter; Wilberforce Humphries ('Mr Humphries'), the camp shop assistant (played by John Inman) in the BBC television sitcom *Are You Being Served?* (1973–85)]

Humphriss, **Humphris**, **Humphress** different forms of **Humphries**

Hunnable a different form of **Honeyball**

Hunnibal, **Hunniball** different forms of **Honeyball**

Hunnicutt see **Honeycutt**

Hunt, **Hunte** 'hunter' [Sir Conrad Hunte, 1932–99, West Indian cricketer; Geoff Hunt, 1947–, Australian squash player; Henry Hunt ('Orator Hunt'), 1773–1835, British radical; Holman Hunt, 1827–1910, British painter; James Hunt, 1947–93, British motor-racing driver; Sir John Hunt (Lord Hunt), 1910–98, British army officer and mountaineer, leader of the 1953 Everest expedition; Laura Hunt, the mysterious femme fatale wrongly assumed murdered in Vera Caspary's novel *Laura* (1943); Leigh Hunt, 1784–1859, British poet; Roger Hunt, 1938–, English footballer]
— **Charlie Hunt**, **Joe Hunt** rhyming slang for *cunt*, usually in the sense 'despicable person' or 'fool'. The former may have been the origin of *charlie* 'fool'. Neither seems to have been based on a real person.

Hunter a different form of **Hunt** [John Hunter, 1728–93, Scottish anatomist and surgeon, brother of William; Norman Hunter, 1943–, English footballer; William Hunter, 1718–83, Scottish obstetrician]
— **Hunterian Museum** a museum in Glasgow, established to house the art collection and the collection of anatomical specimens bequeathed by William Hunter (see above). Opened in 1807, it is the oldest museum in Scotland.
— **Hunter River** a river in New South Wales, Australia. It is 467 km./290 mi. long, and enters the Pacific Ocean at Newcastle. Discovered by Euro-

peans in the 1790s, it was named in honour of Captain John Hunter, 1737–1821, the second governor of the British colony in New South Wales. The **Hunter Valley** is one of Australia's oldest and best-known wine-producing areas.

Huntington, Huntingdon 'person from Huntington', the name of various places in England ('hunters' settlement' or 'hunters' hill'), or 'person from Huntingdon', Cambridgeshire ('hunter's hill' or 'Hunta's hill')

— **Huntington Library** an educational and research institute in San Marino, California, founded in 1919 by the US railway pioneer and art collector Henry Huntington, 1850–1927

— **Huntington's chorea** a hereditary disorder of the nervous system that manifests as jerky involuntary movements in early middle age, with behavioural changes and progressive dementia. It is named after the US neurologist George Huntington, 1851–1916.

Huntley, Huntly 'person from Huntley', Gloucestershire ('hunter's glade'), or 'person from Huntlie', a former place in what is now Borders region ('hunter's glade') [Raymond Huntley, 1904–90, British actor]

— **Huntley & Palmers** a British biscuit-manufacturing firm, founded in 1822 by Joseph Huntley, 1775–1857. It was joined in 1841 by George Palmer, 1818–97. In 1969 it merged with other companies to form Associated Biscuits, and its Reading factory closed in 1972, but it survives as a brand name.

Hurd see **Heard**

Hurford 'person from Hurford', an unidentified place in England (probably 'ford at a bend in the river')

Hurley, Hurly (i) 'person from Hurley', Berkshire and Warwickshire ('woodland clearing in a recess'); (ii) a different form of **Herlihy** [Elizabeth Hurley, 1965–, British actress and model]

Hurst, Hearst, Herst, Hirst 'person who lives on a wooded hill' or 'person from Hurst or Hirst', the name of numerous places in England (in either case from Old English *hyrst* 'wooded hill') [Damien Hirst, 1965–, British artist; Sir Geoff Hurst, 1941–, English footballer; George Hirst, 1871–1954, English cricketer; George Hurst, 1926–, British conductor; Patricia ('Patty') Hearst, 1954–, US newspaper heiress, kidnap victim and bank robber, granddaughter of William Randolph; William Randolph Hearst, 1863–1951, US newspaper proprietor, model for Orson Welles's *Citizen Kane* (1941)]

— **Patty Hearst** (see above) rhyming slang for *first* 'first-class degree'

Hurt (i) a different form of **Hart** (i); (ii) 'person who lived by a plaited fence' (from Middle High German *hurt* 'fence of intertwined branches, hurdle'); (iii) from a medieval Dutch nickname for a belligerent person, from Middle Dutch *hort, hurt* 'attack' [John Hurt, 1940–, British actor; William Hurt, 1950–, US actor]

Hurwitz a different form of **Horowitz**

Husain, Hussain, Hussein from the Arabic male personal name *H.usayn*, literally 'little *Ḥasān*', a personal name meaning literally 'good, handsome'. See also **Hossain** [Nasser Hussain, 1968–, Indian-born English cricketer]

Husband 'peasant farmer, husbandman'

Huskisson 'son of **Hoskin**' [William Huskisson, 1770–1830, British politician and financier, the first man in the world to be killed in a railway accident (by Stephenson's *Rocket*)]

Hussey, Hussy (i) 'person from Houssaye', northern France ('stand of holly trees'); (ii) from a medieval nickname for a female householder (Middle English *husewif*), or one equivalent to modern 'Bootsie', applied to someone who wore unusual boots or was unusual in even possessing a pair (from Old French *husé* 'booted'); (iii) from Irish Gaelic *Ó hEodhusa* 'descendant of *Eodhus*', the name of a bardic family. See also **Hosie** [Marmaduke Hussey (Lord Hussey), 1923–2006, British media executive]

Huston see **Houston**

Hutchins, Hutchings 'son of *Hutchin*', literally 'little **Hugh**'

Hutchinson, Hutchingson 'son of *Hutchin*' (see **Hutchins**) [Maxwell Hutchinson, 1948–, British architect and writer]

— **Hutchinson** a British publishing firm, founded in London in 1887 by George Thompson Hutchinson, 1857–1931. It is now an imprint of Random House.

— **Hutchinson-Gilford syndrome** an alternative name for progeria, a condition characterized by rapidly accelerated ageing. It commemorates the British physicians Sir Jonathan Hutchinson, 1828–1913, and Hastings Gilford, 1861–1941.

Hutchison, Hutcheson different forms of **Hutchinson** [Francis Hutcheson, 1694–1746, Scottish philosopher]

Huth (i) 'hat-maker', or from a medieval German nickname for someone who wore a remarkable hat (from Middle High German *huot* 'hat'); (ii) 'herdsman' (Middle High German *huote*)

Hutt a different form of **Hudd**

Hutton 'person from Hutton', the name of various places in England ('farmstead by a hill-spur') [Barbara Hutton, 1912–79, US Woolworth heiress and socialite, dubbed by the press the 'Poor Little Rich Girl'; James Hutton, 1726–97, Scottish geologist; Sir Leonard Hutton, 1916–90, English cricketer; Will Hutton, 1950–, British journalist and writer]

— **Hutton Inquiry** a judicial inquiry into the death of the British government weapons expert Dr David Kelly, led by Lord Hutton (Brian Hutton), 1931–, a former Law Lord. It reported in 2004.

Huxley 'person from Huxley', Cheshire ('Hucc's glade') [Aldous Huxley, 1894–1963, British novelist and essayist, bother of Julian; Sir Andrew Huxley, 1913–, British physiologist, half-brother of Julian; Sir Julian Huxley, 1887–1975, British biologist, grandson of T.H.; T.H. Huxley, 1825–95, British biologist]

Hyam (i) *also* **Haym** *or* **Hayem** from the Yiddish male personal name *Khayim* (from Hebrew *chayim* 'life'); (ii) see **Higham**

Hyams 'son of **Hyam**'

Hyatt, Hyett (i) different forms of **Highet**; (ii) 'tailor' (from Yiddish *khayet*)

Hyde, Hide 'person who lives on and farms a hide of land (a medieval measure equal to up to 49 ha./120 acres)' [Douglas Hyde, 1860–1949, Irish scholar; Edward Hyde (1st earl of Clarendon), 1609–74, English historian; Herbie Hide, 1971–, British boxer; Mr Hyde, the incarnation of the evil side of Dr Jekyll's nature in Robert Louis Stevenson's *The Strange Case of Dr Jekyll and Mr Hyde* (see **Jekyll**)]

— **Herbie Hides** (see above) rhyming slang for *strides* 'trousers'

— **Hyde Park** a town in New York State, US, the birthplace and home of Franklin D. Roosevelt. Its name comes ultimately from Edward Hyde, 3rd earl of Clarendon, 1661–1723, governor of New York. (Hyde Park in London gets its name from a former manor in the area, which itself was named after the medieval measure of land – see above).

Hyland (i) *also* **Highland** 'person who lives in an upland area'; (ii) a different form of **Wheelan**

Hylton see **Hilton**

Hyman a different form of **Hyam** (i)

Hyne see **Hine**

Hynes, Hines (i) from Irish Gaelic *Ó hEidhin* 'descendant of *Eidhin*', a personal name perhaps derived from *eidhean* 'ivy'; (ii) 'son of **Hine**' [Earl Hines, 1905–83, US jazz pianist and songwriter]

I

Ibbotson, Ibbetson 'son of **Hibbs**' [Derek Ibbotson, 1932–, British athlete]

Ibrahim from the Muslim personal name *Ibrāhīm*, the Arabic form of **Abraham**

Icke a different form of **Hick** (pronounced to rhyme with *bike*) [David Icke, 1952–, British former television sports presenter and self-styled religious prophet and guru]

Iddon from the Old Norse female personal name *Idunn*, literally probably 'perform love'

Idle, Idel (i) 'person from Idle', Yorkshire ('idle place' (probably a reference to unprofitable land)); (ii) from a medieval nickname for a lazy person; (iii) from the Old Welsh personal name *Ithel*; (iv) a different form of **Isles** [Eric Idle, 1943–, British actor and writer, member of the *Monty Python* team]

Ifens a different form of **Evans**

Iglesias 'person from Iglesias', Spain ('churches')

Ikin 'little *Ida* or *Ide*', a medieval personal name brought into England by the Normans but ultimately of Germanic origin. Its derivation and meaning are uncertain.

Iles see **Isles**

Illingworth 'person from Illingworth', Yorkshire ('enclosure associated with Illa') [Raymond Illingworth, 1932–, English cricketer]

Ilsley 'person from Ilsley', Berkshire ('Hild's glade')

Imber (i) 'person from Imber', Surrey and Wiltshire (respectively 'Imma's enclosure' and 'Imma's pond'); (ii) 'seller of spices', from Yiddish *imber* 'ginger'

Imbert from the medieval French personal name *Imbert*, of Germanic origin and meaning literally 'vast-bright'

Impey, Impy 'person from Impey', the name of various places in England ('enclosure of young trees'). See also **Wimpey**

Imray a different form of **Amery**

Imrie a different form of **Amery**

Ince 'person from Ince', Greater Manchester and Merseyside ('strip of land between two rivers')

Inch a different form of **Innes**

Inchbald from the medieval male personal name *Ingebald*, brought into England by the Normans but ultimately of Germanic origin and meaning literally 'brave Ingel' (*Ingel* was a different form of *Engel*; see **Engel** (i))

Ing, Inge (i) from the Old English male personal name *Ing* or *Inga*, a shortened form of various personal names beginning with *Ing-* (e.g. **Ingram**), from the name of a Germanic fertility god; (ii) 'person from Ing', Essex ('(place of) Giga's people') [William Inge, 1860–1954, British Anglican churchman, nicknamed the 'Gloomy Dean']

Ingersoll 'person from Inkersall', Derbyshire (perhaps 'Ingvarr's hill' or 'Hynkere's hill') [Robert Green Ingersoll, 1833–99, US agnostic who established something of a following for his brand of secularism]
— **Ingersoll** the proprietary name of a make of wristwatch, the first widely available mass-produced watch, introduced in 1892 by the US mail-order and chain-store entrepreneur Robert Hawley Ingersoll, 1859–1928

Ingham (i) 'person from Ingham', the name of various places in England ('Inga's homestead'); (ii) from a medieval nickname for a clever or crafty person (from Old French *engaine* 'ingenuity') [Sir Bernard Ingham, 1932–, British journalist and civil servant, press secretary to Margaret Thatcher 1979–90]

Ingle (i) 'person from Ingol', Lancashire ('Inga's hollow'); (ii) from the Old Norse male personal name *Ingjaldr*, literally 'Ing tribute' (see **Ing** (i))

Ingleby 'person from Ingleby', the name of various places in England ('settlement of the English')

Inglis a different form of **English**

Ingoldsby (i) 'person from Ingoldsby', Lincolnshire ('Ingjaldr's settlement'); (ii) a different form of **Golightly** (iii)
— *The Ingoldsby Legends* a collection (1840) of myths, legends, ghost stories and poems by R.H. Barham, written in the persona of Thomas Ingoldsby Esquire of Tappington Manor

Ingram from the medieval personal name *Ingram*, brought into England by the Normans but ultimately of Germanic origin and meaning literally 'Ing's raven' (see **Ing** (i))

Ingrams 'son of **Ingram**' [Richard Ingrams, 1937–, British journalist and author, editor of *Private Eye* 1963–86]

Inman 'innkeeper' [John Inman, 1935–2007, British actor]

Innes, Inness, Innis, Inniss (i) 'person from Innes', Grampian region ('land between two rivers, island'); (ii) a different form of **Angus**
— **John Innes Compost** any of a range of commercial loam-based composts as originally developed at the John Innes Centre, a horticultural institute founded in Merton, Southwest London,

with funds provided by the local property developer John Innes, 1829–1904

Inns a different form of **Innes**

Inskip, Inskipp, Inskeep 'person from Inskip', Lancashire (perhaps 'island by the osier basket')

Insley 'person from Insley', an unidentified place (perhaps 'Inga's glade')

Inverarity 'person from Inverarity', Angus ('mouth of the *Arity*', perhaps a Celtic river-name meaning literally 'slow')

Iqbal from a Muslim male personal name derived from Arabic *'iqbāl* 'prosperity, success'

Iredale, Iredell 'person from Iredale', a former place in Cumbria ('valley of the Irish')

Ireland 'person from Ireland' [Innes Ireland, 1930–93, British motor-racing driver; John Ireland, 1879–1962, British composer]

Iremonger a different form of **Ironmonger**

Ireton 'person from Ireton or Irton', Derbyshire and Yorkshire respectively ('settlement of the Irishmen'), or 'person from Irton', Cumbria ('settlement by the *Irt*', a river-name of unknown origin and meaning) [Henry Ireton, 1611–51, English Parliamentarian soldier in the Civil War]

Ironmonger 'dealer in iron goods'. See also **Iremonger**

Irons 'person from Airennes', northern France ('sands') [Jeremy Irons, 1948–, British actor]

Ironside (i) from a medieval nickname for a soldier clad in iron armour (of which a notable recipient was King Edmund II of England, ?981–1016); (ii) 'person from Ironside', Aberdeenshire (probably 'eagle-hillside') [Robert T. Ironside, a fictional wheelchair-bound US detective played on television (1967–76) by Raymond Burr; W.E. Ironside (Lord Ironside), 1880–1959, British field marshal]

Irvine, Irvin, Ervine, Ervin (i) 'person from Irvine or Irving', Strathclyde and Dumfries and Galloway respectively ('place on the *Irvine*', a Celtic river-name probably meaning 'green river'); (ii) a different form of **Irwin**; (iii) from Irish Gaelic *Ó hEireamhóin* 'descendant of *Eireamhón*', a personal name of unknown origin and meaning. See also **Curwen** (ii) [Alexander Andrew ('Derry') Irvine (Lord Irvine), 1940–, British lawyer, lord chancellor 1997–2003; St John Ervine, 1883–1971, British playwright and novelist]

Irving, Erving different forms of **Irvine** [Sir Henry Irving (original name John Henry Brodribb), 1838–1905, British actor and manager; John Irving, 1942–, US novelist; Julius Erving ('Dr J'), 1950–, US basketball player; Washington Irving, 1783–1859, US short-story writer and historian]

Irwin, Erwin, Urwin from the medieval male personal name *Irwyn* (from Old English *Eoforwine*, literally 'wild-boar friend')

Isaac, Isaak from the Hebrew male personal name *Yitschak*, literally 'he laughs' (probably with the underlying sense 'may God smile on him')

Isaacs 'son of **Isaac**' [Sir Jeremy Isaacs, 1932–, British television producer and executive; Sir Rufus Isaacs (1st marquess of Reading), 1860–1935, British lawyer and Liberal politician]

Isaacson 'son of **Isaac**'

Isard see **Izard** (i)

Isherwood 'person from Isherwood', a former place in Lancashire, of unknown origin and meaning [Christopher Isherwood, 1904–86, British writer]

Islam from a Muslim personal name derived from Arabic *islām* 'peace'

Isles, Iles, Eyles 'person who lives on an island' (Anglo-Norman *isle*, from Old French *isel*). See also **Idle** (iv)

Ismail, Ismael from the Arabic male personal name *'Ismā'īl*, the name of a Prophet, the son of Ibrahim

Israel, Izrael from the Hebrew male personal name *Yisrael*, literally 'fighter of God'. See also **Seiler** (iii)

Issett, Issitt different forms of **Izard** (i)

Iverson 'son of *Ívarr*', an Old Norse male personal name meaning literally either 'yew-bow warrior' or 'Ing's spear' (see **Ing** (i)). See also **McIver, Ure**

Ivery see **Ivory**

Ives 'son of *Ive*', a medieval male personal name, brought into England by the Normans but ultimately of Germanic origin, a shortened form of any of a range of compound names beginning with *īv* 'yew' [Charles Ives, 1874–1954, US composer]

Ivey, Ivy, Ivie (i) a different form of *Ive* (see **Ives**); (ii) 'person from Ivoy', northern France ('stand of yew trees')

Ivory, Ivery 'person from Ivry-la-Bataille', northern France ('place of *Eburius*', a Gallo-Roman personal name based on Latin *ebur* 'ivory') [James Ivory, 1928–, US film director]

Ivy see **Ivey**

Izard (i) *also* **Izzard** *or* **Isard** *or* **Issard** from the medieval female personal name *Iseult* or *Isolde*, brought into England by the Normans but ultimately of Germanic origin and meaning literally 'ice-battle'. See also **Issett**; (ii) from *Ishard*, a medieval French male personal name of Germanic origin, meaning literally 'ice-brave'; (iii) from a Provençal nickname for a skilful and agile climber (from Old Provençal *izar* 'mountain goat') [Eddie Izzard, 1962–, British comedian]

J

Jablonski 'person from Jablonka, Jablonna or Jablonica', Poland (in all cases 'place of apple trees')

Jack (i) from a pet-form of the male personal name **John**, probably based on Low German and Dutch *Jankin* and *Jackin*, themselves pet-forms of *Jan*; (ii) from the Old French male personal name *Jacques*, from Latin *Jacōbus* (see **Jacob**)

Jacklin 'little **Jack**' [Tony Jacklin, 1944–, British golfer]

Jackman (i) 'servant of **Jack**'; (ii) an anglicization of French *Jacquème* (see **James**). See also **Jakeman** [Hugh Jackman, 1968–, Australian actor]

Jackson 'son of **Jack**' [Andrew Jackson, 1767–1845, US military leader and Democratic politician, president 1829–37; Sir Barry Jackson, 1879–1961, British theatrical manager and producer; Colin Jackson, 1967–, British athlete; Glenda Jackson, 1936–, British actress and Labour politician; Gordon Jackson, 1923–90, British actor; Jack Jackson, 1906–78, British bandleader and disc jockey; Janet Jackson, 1966–, US singer-songwriter, sister of Michael; Jesse Jackson, 1941–, US civil-rights leader, clergyman and Democratic politician; Mahalia Jackson, 1911–72, US gospel singer; Michael Jackson, 1958–, US entertainer; Samuel Leroy Jackson, 1948–, US actor; Thomas ('Stonewall') Jackson, 1824–63, US Confederate general in the Civil War]
— **Jackson** the capital city of Mississippi, USA. Founded in 1821, it was named after Andrew Jackson (see above).
— **Jackson** in US slang, a twenty-dollar bill – from the portrait of Andrew Jackson on the note
— **Jackson 5, Jackson Five** a US popular singing group consisting of members of the Jackson family of Gary, Indiana. It was active from to 1962 to 1990, latterly as the **Jacksons**. Its membership has varied over the years, including non-family members, but at its peak around 1970 it included the brothers Jackie, Jermaine, Marlon, Michael (see above) and Tito.
— **Jackson's of Piccadilly** a British tea merchant and grocer. It had its beginnings in the first decade of the 17th century, with the chandler and oil man John Jackson. Its connections with Piccadilly date from the 1680s. Its shop there closed in 1980, but it still produces its own-brand tea.
— **Jacksonville** the largest city of Florida, USA. It was named in honour of Andrew Jackson, who was Florida's first territorial governor.
— **Spear & Jackson** see **Spear**

Jacob from the male personal name *Jacob*, which came via Latin *Jacōbus* from Hebrew *Yaakov*. That was the name given to the younger twin brother of Esau in the Bible, and is said to have been derived from Hebrew *akev* 'heel', alluding to the tradition that Jacob was born holding on to Esau's heel. See also **Cobb** (ii), **Copping** (i), **Jacques**, **James**, **Jekel** [Gordon Jacob, 1895–1984, British composer]
— **W. & R. Jacob & Co.** a British firm of biscuit manufacturers, founded in Dublin in 1883 by William Beale Jacob, born 1825, and his brother Robert, and noted especially for their 'cream crackers' (introduced in 1885)

Jacobi 'son of **Jacob**' [Sir Derek Jacobi, 1938–, British actor]

Jacobs 'son of **Jacob**' [David Jacobs, 1926–, British radio and television presenter; W.W. Jacobs, 1863–1943, British short-story writer]

Jacobson 'son of **Jacob**' [Howard Jacobson, 1942–, British novelist and critic]

Jacques, Jaques from the Old French male personal name *Ja(c)ques* (see **Jack** (ii)) [Hattie Jacques (original name Josephina Edwina Jacques), 1924–80, British actress and comedienne]

Jaeger 'hunter' (German *Jäger*). See also **Yeager**
— **Jaeger** the brand-name of a range of British clothing. It was introduced in the mid-1880s incorporating the principles of the German naturalist and hygienist Gustav Jäger, 1832–1917, who held that clothes should be made only from animal fibres.

Jaffe, Jaffee an invented Jewish name meaning 'beautiful, pleasant' (Hebrew *yafe*) [Sam Jaffe, 1893–1984, US actor]

Jagger 'pedlar', from a Yorkshire dialect word descended from Middle English *jag* 'load' [Charles Jagger, 1885–1934, British sculptor; Sir Mick Jagger, 1943–, British pop musician]

Jaggers 'son of **Jagger**' [Mr Jaggers, the shrewd Old Bailey lawyer in Dickens's *Great Expectations* (1861)]

Jain (i) *also* **Jaine** see **Jane**; (ii) 'follower of *Jina*', the name of a saint in the Jain religion, literally (in Sanskrit) 'triumphant'

Jakeman a different form of **Jackman**

James from the male personal name *James*, from Late Latin *Jacomus* or *Jacmus,* an alteration of Latin *Jacōbus* (see **Jacob**) [C.L.R. James, 1901–89, Trinidadian writer; Clive James, 1939–, Australian journalist and author; Edward James, 1907–84, British poet and patron of Surrealism;

Harry James, 1916–83, US bandleader; Henry James, 1843–1916, US-born British novelist; Jesse James, 1847–82, US outlaw; M.R. James, 1862–1936, British scholar and ghost-story writer; P.D. James (Baroness James), 1920–, British thriller-writer; Sidney James, 1913–76, South African-born British comic actor; William James, 1842–1910, US philosopher and psychologist, brother of Henry]

— **Jamesian** relating to or characteristic of Henry James (see above) or his literary style, e.g. in containing long complex sentences, or describing emotional states and relationships in minute detail

— **James's powder** a fever-reducing preparation devised by Dr Robert James, 1703–76, popular in the late 18th and early 19th centuries

Jameson 'son of **James**'. See also **Gimson**, **Jimson** [Derek Jameson, 1929–, British journalist and radio presenter; Storm Jameson, 1891–1986, British novelist]

— **Jameson** the proprietary name (registered in 1877) of a brand of Irish whiskey produced by William Jameson & Co. of Dublin.

— **Jameson Raid** an ill-advised raid led (with the probable connivance of the British and Cape authorities) by Dr Leander Starr Jameson (1853–1917; later Sir Leander) from Cape Colony into the Transvaal in an attempt to overthrow the independent Boer government of Paul Kruger

Jamieson, Jamison mainly Scottish variants of **Jameson**

Jane, Jain, Jaine, Jayne from the medieval personal name *Jan*, a different form of **John** (later, in the form *Jane*, specialized as a female name). See also **Genn**, **Janson**, **Jenkin**

— *Jane's Fighting Ships* a British reference book giving details of the ships of the world's navies. It was first published, as *All the World's Fighting Ships*, in 1898 by Fred T. Jane, 1865–1916. It spawned several companion volumes, under the 'Jane's' name, dealing with various other aspects of military hardware, all now under the Jane's Information Group umbrella.

Janes, Jaynes 'son of **Jane**'. See also **Jeans**

Janeway 'person from Genoa', Italy (a folk-etymological alteration of Italian *Genova* 'Genoa')

Jankowski 'person from Janków, Jankowo or Jankowice', Poland (place-names based on the Polish male personal name *Janek*, a pet-form of *Jan*, from Latin *Johannes* (see **John**))

Jannings a different form of **Jennings**

Janson 'son of Jan' (see **Jane**). See also **Jenson** (ii)

Janus from the Polish male personal name *Janus*, a derivative of *Jan* (see **Jankowski**) [Samantha Janus, 1972–, British actress]

Jaques see **Jacques**

Jardine a different form of **Gardener** [Douglas Jardine, 1900–58, English cricketer]

Jarman a different form of **German**

Jarrell a different form of **Garrett** (ii) [Randall Jarrell, 1914–65, US poet and critic]

Jarrett a different form of **Garrett**

Jarvie a Scottish variant of **Jarvis** (i)

Jarvis (i) from the Norman male personal name *Gervase*, of Germanic origin. Its first syllable meant literally 'spear', but the meaning of its second element is unknown. See also **Gervais**; (ii) 'person from Jervaulx', monastic site in North Yorkshire ('valley of the river Ure'). See also **Jervis** [Martin Jarvis, 1941–, British actor]

Jason (i) an anglicization of Greek *Iassonides* 'son of Jason' (a Greek personal name meaning 'healer'); (ii) probably 'son of **James**' [Sir David Jason (original name David White), 1940–, British actor]

Jaworski 'person who lives near a maple or syca-more tree' (from Polish *jawor* 'maple, sycamore')

Jay, Jaye from a medieval nickname for a garrulous or ostentatious person, from the name of the bird [Sir Anthony Jay, 1930–, British television journalist and scriptwriter; John Jay, 1745–1829, US Revolutionary patriot; Margaret Jay (Baroness Jay; *née* Callaghan), 1939–, British Labour politician, formerly wife of Peter; Peter Jay, 1937–, British journalist and diplomat]

Jayes, Jeyes 'son of **Jay**'

— **Jeyes Fluid** a British brand of disinfectant, patented in 1877 by its inventor John Jeyes, 1817–92, a Nottingham pharmacist's son

Jayne, Jaynes different forms of **Jane, Janes** [Jennifer Jayne (original name Jennifer Jones), 1932–, British actress]

Jeans, Jeanes, Jeens different forms of **Janes** [Sir James Jeans, 1877–1946, British mathematician, astronomer and science writer]

Jeavon, Jevon (i) from an epithet distinguishing the younger of two people with the same name (e.g. a son) (from Anglo-Norman *jovene* 'young'); (ii) from the Welsh male personal name *Iefan* (see **Evans**)

Jeavons, Jevons 'son of **Jeavon**' [W.S. Jevons, 1835–82, British economist, logician and statistician]

Jebb from a different form of the male personal name *Jeff* (see **Jeffes**)

Jeckell a different form of **Jekyll**

Jeens see **Jeans**

Jeeves, Jeves 'son of *Geva*', a medieval female person name that was a pet-form of *Genevieve*, a name of uncertain ultimate origin that was brought into England by the Normans. See also **Geeves** [Jeeves (first name Reginald), the omniscient valet in P.G. Wodehouse's Bertie Wooster stories (his surname was borrowed from the Warwickshire cricketer Percy Jeeves, 1888–1916)]

— **Ask Jeeves** an Internet search engine founded in 1996 by Garrett Gruener and David Warthen in Berkeley, California. Its name was inspired by the imperturbable omniscience of P.G. Wodehouse's Jeeves (see above); in 2006, however, it became plain 'Ask.com'.

Jeffcock, Jefcock from the male personal name *Jeff* (see **Jeffes**), with the suffix *-cock* (literally 'cockerel', hence 'jaunty or bumptious young man'), that was often added to create pet-forms of personal names in the Middle Ages

Jeffcott, Jefcott, Jeffcote, Jefcote, Jeffcoat, Jefcoat, Jephcott, Jephcote different forms of **Jeffcock**

Jefferson 'son of **Jeffrey**' [Thomas Jefferson, 1743–1826, US statesman, president 1801–09]
— **Jefferson airplane** in US drugs slang of the 1960s, a split paper match used as a holder for a marijuana cigarette that has burned down to a barely holdable end. The identity of Jefferson has never been established. Also, as *Jefferson Airplane*, the name of one of the most successful US rock groups of the 60s, formed in San Francisco in 1965. It has been claimed that the group got their name from the spliff-holder, but never proved; indeed, one of the group maintained it was an invented name, intended as a parody of the type of blues performers' name typified by 'Blind Lemon' Jefferson, 1897–1929.
— **Jefferson City** the capital city of Missouri, USA, founded in 1821. It was named in honour of Thomas Jefferson (see above).

Jeffery, Jefferies, Jeffereys see **Jeffrey**, **Jeffries**

Jeffes, Jeffs 'son of *Jeff*', a shortened form of **Jeffrey**

Jefford, Jefferd different forms of **Giffard**

Jeffrey, Jeffry, Jeffery, Jeffree, Geoffrey, Geffrye from the medieval male personal name *Geffrey*, which was brought into England by the Normans. Its original Old French form was *Jefroi* or *Jeufroi*, which may simply have been a different form of **Godfrey**, but could also have been a distinct name with a first element derived from Germanic *gala* 'sing' or *gawi* 'region'. [Francis Jeffrey (Lord Jeffrey), 1773–1850, British critic and jurist]
— **Geffrye Museum** a museum in London, just to the north of the City, specializing in the history of domestic artefacts and interiors. It was founded in 1715 under the terms of a bequest by Sir Robert Geffrye, 1613–1703, sometime Lord Mayor of London.

Jeffries, Jefferies, Jeffreys, Jeffereys, Jeffrys, Jeffris, Geoffreys 'son of **Jeffrey**' [Sir Alec Jeffreys, 1950–, British geneticist; George Jeffreys (Lord Jeffreys; 'Judge Jeffreys'), 1648–89, English judge noted for the harsh sentences he passed during the 'Bloody Assizes' following Monmouth's rebellion (1685); Lionel Jeffries, 1926–, British actor and director; Richard Jefferies, 1848–87, British novelist and naturalist]

Jekel from the Yiddish male personal name *Yekl*, a pet-form of **Jacob**

Jekyll from a Celtic male personal name meaning literally 'generous lord'. The name is traditionally pronounced 'jeekəl', but 'jeckəl' is also common. See also **Jeckell**, **Jewell**, **Joelson**, **Juggins** [Dr Jekyll, the protagonist of Robert Louis Stevenson's *The Strange Case of Dr Jekyll and Mr Hyde* (1886), a physician who discovers a drug that separates off the evil side of his character into a distinct persona, Mr Hyde; Gertrude Jekyll, 1843–1932, British garden designer and writer]

Jencks see **Jenks**

Jenkin, Jenken from the medieval male personal name *Jenkin*, literally 'little **John**'. See also **Junkin**

Jenkins 'son of **Jenkin**' [Florence Foster Jenkins (*née* Foster), 1868–1944, vocally challenged US soprano; Katherine Jenkins, 1980–, Welsh mezzo-soprano; Roy Jenkins (Lord Jenkins), 1920–2003, British Labour and SDP politician; Simon Jenkins, 1943–, British journalist]
— **War of Jenkins' Ear** a mid-18th-century war between Britain and Spain, the pretext for which was the claim by Captain Robert Jenkins that he had had his ear cut off by Spanish coastguards in the West Indies. It began in 1738, and by 1742 had merged into the War of the Spanish Succession.

Jenkinson 'son of **Jenkin**'

Jenks, Jencks 'son of *Jenk*', a medieval male personal name that was a shortened form of **Jenkin**

Jennens a different form of **Jennings** [Charles Jennens, 1701–73, British patron of the arts, librettist of Handel's *Messiah* and *Saul*]

Jenner (i) 'engineer', from a reduced form of Old French *engineor* (in the Middle Ages, the term denoted mainly someone who designed large pieces of military equipment, such as siege engines); (ii) from the medieval German personal name *Januārius*, literally 'January', probably originally denoting someone born or baptized in that month [Edward Jenner, 1749–1823, British physician, pioneer of vaccination]

Jennings 'son of *Jenyn*', a medieval male personal name, literally 'little **John**' [Jennings (first names John Christopher Timothy), the English preparatory schoolboy who is the central character in a series of books (1950–94) by Anthony Buckeridge (said to have been based on a schoolfriend of Buckeridge called Diarmid Jennings); Elizabeth Jennings, 1926–2001, British poet; Humphrey Jennings, 1907–50, British documentary film-maker]

Jennins, Jenyns different forms of **Jennings**

Jensen 'son of *Jens*', a Danish, Norwegian and Low German male personal name, a shortened form of *Johannes* (see **John**)
— **Jensen Cars** a British car manufacturer, founded in West Bromwich in 1934 by the brothers Richard and Alan Jensen and specializing in luxurious and expensive sports cars. It closed down in 1984, although there have been attempts at revival since.

Jenson (i) an anglicization of **Jensen**; (ii) a different form of **Janson**

Jephcott, Jephcote see **Jeffcott**

Jephson a different form of **Jepson**

Jepson, Jeppeson 'son of *Jeff*' (see **Jeffes**)

Jeremy from the male personal name, of biblical origin, from Hebrew *Yirmeyahu*, literally 'may God exalt him'

Jerman, Jermine, Jermyn see **German**

Jerome, Jerrome from the male personal name *Jerome*, ultimately from Greek *Hieronymos*, literally 'sacred name' [Jerome K. Jerome, 1859–1927, British humorous writer]

Jerrold a different form of **Garrett** (ii)

Jervis a different form of **Jarvis**

Jessel from a pet-form of **Jessop** [Miss Jessel, the governess who has charge of the two troubled and enigmatic children in Henry James's ghost story *The Turn of the Screw* (1898)]

Jessop, Jessup from the medieval male personal name *Jessop*, a different form of **Joseph** [Gilbert Jessop, 1874–1955, English cricketer]

Jeves see **Jeeves**

Jevon, Jevons see **Jeavon, Jeavons**

Jewell, Jewel different forms of **Jekyll**. See also **Joel, Joule, Jowell** [Jimmy Jewel (original name James Marsh), 1909–95, British comedian and comic actor; John Jewel, 1522–71, Anglican churchman and Protestant reformer]

Jewry see **Jury**

Jeyes see **Jayes**

Jiang 'person from the Jiang Hills, or from the state of Jiang, or living by the Jiang Creek', all locations in China

Jimenez from Spanish *Jiménez*, literally 'son of *Jimeno*', a medieval Spanish male personal name, perhaps related to **Simon**

Jimson, Jimpson different forms of **Jameson** [Gulley Jimson, the artist whose life is chronicled in Joyce Cary's novels *Herself Surprised* (1941), *To Be a Pilgrim* (1942) and *The Horse's Mouth* (1944)]

Jin (i) from the honorary surname (literally 'gold' or 'metal') applied to a son of the legendary Chinese emperor Huang Di of the 26th century BC, or from the name of Jin Shang, a state official during the Zhou dynasty; (ii) 'person living by the River Jin', China

Job, Jobe (i) from the biblical male personal name *Job* (Hebrew *Iyov*, perhaps meaning literally 'Where is the father?' or 'Persecuted one'), probably as used in the Middle Ages as a nickname for a person who suffered many tribulations, like Job in the Bible; (ii) from a medieval nickname for a foolish person (from Old French *job* or *joppe* 'fool'); (iii) perhaps 'barrel-maker', or from a medieval nickname for a heavy drinker or a fat person (from Middle English *jobbe* 'four-gallon vessel'); (iv) 'person who makes or sells *jupes*', a Middle English term for a type of long woollen garment. See also **Jobson, Joplin, Jupp**

Jobson 'son of **Job**'

Jocelyn, Joscelyn, Joslin from the Old French personal name *Joscelin*, popularized in England by the Normans but ultimately of Germanic origin, based on the Germanic tribal name *Gaut* (it latterly came to be interpreted as 'little *Josse*' – see **Joyce**). See also **Gosling**

Joel (i) from the male personal name *Joel*, an anglicization of the Hebrew name *Yoel* (borne by an Old

Testamant prophet); (ii) a different form of **Jewell** [Billy Joel, 1949–, US pop singer and songwriter]

Joelson, Jolson 'son of **Joel** (i)' [Al Jolson (original name Asa Yoelson), 1886–1950, Lithuanian-born US entertainer]

Johansen, Johanson 'son of *Johann*', a German and Scandinavian form of *Johannes* (see **John**)

John, Jon from the male personal name *John*, which came into English via Latin *Johannēs* and Greek *Iōannēs* from Hebrew *Yochanan*. That meant literally either 'Jehovah has favoured' (i.e. favoured me with a child) or 'May Jehovah favour' (i.e. favour this child). See also **Evans, Jack, Jane, Jankowski, Jenkin, Jennings, Johncock, Johns, Johnson, Johnston, Joinson, Jones** [Augustus John, 1878–1961, British painter; Barry John, 1945–, Welsh rugby footballer; Sir Elton John (original name Reginald Dwight), 1947–, British pop singer and pianist; Gwen John, 1876–1939, British painter, sister of Augustus]

Johncock, Joncock from the male personal name **John**, with the suffix *-cock* (literally 'cockerel', hence 'jaunty or bumptious young man'), that was often added to create pet-forms of personal names in the Middle Ages

Johns 'son of **John**' [Glynis Johns, 1923–, British actress, daughter of Mervyn; Jasper Johns, 1930–, US painter; Mervyn Johns, 1899–1992, British actor; Stratford Johns (original name Alan Stratford John), 1925–2002, South African-born British actor; 'Captain' W.E. Johns, 1893–1968, British writer, author of the 'Biggles' adventure stories for boys, published between 1932 and 1970]

Johnson, Jonson 'son of **John**' [Amy Johnson, 1903–41, British flyer; Andrew Johnson, 1808–75, US Democratic politician, president 1865–69; Ben Jonson, 1572–1637, English playwright and poet; Boris Johnson, 1964–, British journalist and Conservative politician; B.S. Johnson, 1933–73, British novelist; Graham Johnson, 1950–, British concert accompanist; Hugh Johnson, 1939–, British wine writer; Jack Johnson (original name Arthur John Johnson), 1878–1946, US boxer; Linton Kwesi Johnson, 1952–, British-based Jamaican Dub poet; Lyndon Baines Johnson, 1908–73, US Democratic politician, president 1963–69; Magic Johnson (real name Earvin Johnson, Jr.), 1959–, US basketball player; Martin Johnson, 1970–, English rugby footballer; Michael Johnson, 1967–, US athlete; Nunnally Johnson, 1897–1977, US screenwriter, director and producer; Pamela Hansford Johnson, 1912–81, British critic and novelist; Paul Johnson, 1928–, British journalist; Philip Johnson, 1906–2005, US architect; Richard Johnson, 1927–, British actor; Samuel Johnson, 1709–84, British critic, poet and lexicographer; Van Johnson, 1916–, US film actor; William E. ('Pussyfoot') Johnson, 1862–1945, US temperance advocate]

☆ The second commonest surname in the US; 7th commonest in Canada and Australia; 12th commonest in Britain

— **Howard Johnson's** a US chain of restaurants and motels, founded in 1925 by Howard Deering Johnson, 1897–1972

— **Jim Johnson** a slang term for the penis. It is commonly abbreviated to simply **Johnson**.

— **Johnson & Johnson** a US pharmaceutical company, founded in 1885 in New Brunswick, New Jersey by Robert Wood Johnson, 1845–1910, and his brothers James Wood Johnson and Edward Mead Johnson, originally to manufacture antiseptic surgical dressings

— **Johnson bar** a US term for a long heavy lever used to reverse the motion of a steam locomotive. It is not known who the original Johnson was.

— **Johnson City** a city in Texas, USA, the home town of Lyndon Baines Johnson (see above), and founded by James Polk Johnson, nephew of LBJ's grandfather. Also, a city in Tennessee, USA, founded in 1856 by Henry Johnson.

— **Johnson grass** a coarse perennial variety of sorghum (*Sorghum halepense*) of the Mediterranean region. It was named after William Johnson, an Alabama planter.

— **Johnsonian** characteristic of Samuel Johnson (see above) or his literary style, especially in the abundant use of polysyllabic Latinate words

— **Johnson noise** electrical noise caused by the random thermal motion of conduction electrons. The phenomenon was named after the Swedish-born US physicist J.B. Johnson, 1887–1970.

— *Johnson over Jordan* a play (1939) by J.B. Priestley chronicling the afterlife experiences of Robert Johnson

— **Masters and Johnson** see **Masters**

— *Mister Johnson* a novel (1939) by Joyce Cary about a native clerk in a British colony in West Africa who attempts, unsuccessfully, to be more English than the English

Johnston, Johnstone (i) 'person from Johnstone', the name of various places in Scotland, especially one in Dumfries and Galloway ('John's farm'); (ii) a different form of **Johnson** [Brian Johnston, 1912–94, British broadcaster; Jennifer Johnston, 1930–, Irish author; Sue Johnston, 1943–, British actress]

Joice see **Joyce**

Joiner, Joyner 'maker of wooden furniture'

Joinson, Joynson 'son of **John**' [Sir William Joynson-Hicks (1st Viscount Brentford; original name William Hicks; nickname 'Jix'), 1865–1932, British Conservative politician]

Jolliff, Jolliffe different forms of **Jolly**

Jolly, Jolley, Jollie, Jollye from a medieval nickname for a cheerful person [Elizabeth Jolley, 1923–, British-born Australian writer]

Jolson see **Joelson**

Jonas from the biblical male personal name *Jonas* (Hebrew *Yona*, literally 'dove')

Joncock see **Johncock**

Jones 'son of **John**'. The name is particularly associated with Wales. [Alan Jones, 1947–, Australian motor-racing driver; Allen Jones, 1937–, British artist; Ann Jones (*née* Haydon),

1938–, British tennis player; Bobby Jones, 1902–71, US golfer; Brian Jones, 1942–69, British rock musician, Rolling Stones guitarist; Bridget Jones, fictional British thirty-something whose 'diary' (by Helen Fielding) laid bare the neuroses of late 20th-century womanhood; Buck Jones (original name Charles Frederick Gebhart), ?1889–1942, US star of Western movies; Casey Jones (original name John Luther Jones), 1864–1900, US train driver who became a folk hero following the fatal crash of the train he was driving between New Orleans and Chicago; Catherine Zeta-Jones (original name Catherine Jones), 1969–, British actress; Courtney Jones, 1933–, British ice skater; Daniel Jones, 1881–1967, British phonetician, describer of 'Received Pronunciation'; Daniel Jones, 1912–85, British composer; Ernest Jones, 1879–1958, British psychoanalyst, disciple of Freud; Gemma Jones (original name Jennifer Jones), 1942–, British actress; Grace Jones (original name Grace Mendoza), 1948–, Jamaican-born US model, singer and actress; Griff Rhys Jones, 1953–, British actor and comedian; Dame Gwyneth Jones, 1936–, British soprano; Lieutenant-Colonel H. (Herbert) Jones VC, 1940–82, British soldier; Indiana Jones, fictional US archaeologist and adventurer; Inigo Jones, 1573–1652, English architect and stage designer; Jack Jones, 1913–, British trade-union leader; Jack Jones, 1938–, US jazz and pop singer; Lance Corporal Jack Jones, elderly butcher and Home Guardsman (played by Clive Dunn) in the BBC sitcom *Dad's Army* (1968–77); Jennifer Jones (original name Phylis Isley), 1919–, US film actress; Jim Jones, 1931–78, US cult leader (see 'Jonestown' below); John Paul Jones, 1747–92, Scottish-born US naval commander; LeRoi Jones, 1934–, US dramatist and poet; Peter Jones, 1920–2000, British comic actor; Ruth Jones ('Miss Jones'), long-suffering spinster (played by Frances de la Tour) in the ITV sitcom *Rising Damp* (1974–78); Spike Jones (original name Lindley Armstrong Jones), 1911–65, US popular musician and comedian; Terry Jones, 1942–, British writer and film director, member of the *Monty Python* team; Sir Tom Jones (original name Thomas Jones Woodward), 1940–, British pop singer; Vinnie Jones, 1965–, English footballer and actor; Sir William Jones, 1746–94, British jurist, linguist and orientalist, father of historical linguistics]

☆ The second commonest surname in Britain and Australia; 5th commonest in the US; 6th commonest in New Zealand

— *Carmen Jones* a musical based on Bizet's opera *Carmen*, with lyrics by Oscar Hammerstein II. It was filmed in 1954.

— **Davy Jones's locker** the bottom of the sea, especially considered as the final resting place of drowned sailors. 'Davy Jones' was the sailors' name for the often malevolent spirit of the sea.

— **Dickens and Jones** see **Dickens**

— *The Emperor Jones* a play (1920) by Eugene O'Neill about an African-American prison escapee who sets himself up as an emperor on a Caribbean island

— **Ernest Jones** a British chain of jewellery shops, the original of which was established in London in 1949

— **'Have you met Miss Jones?'** a song (1937) by Richard Rodgers and Lorenz Hart about a romantic encounter

— **keep up with the Joneses** to maintain the visible level of one's standard of living (as expressed through consumer goods) on a par with that of one's neighbours. The phrase was invented around 1913 by the US comic-strip artist Arthur R. Momand ('Pop').

— **jones** in US slang, a drug addiction, and particularly a heroin addiction, and more broadly any all-consuming craving or desire for something; also, drug withdrawal symptoms, especially from heroin. The term, which dates from the 1960s and originated in Black English, is evidently a use of the surname, but any original allusion has been lost.

— **Jonestown** a 'town' created in Guyana for the Peoples Temple cult by its founder and leader Jim Jones (see above). Over 900 members of the cult committed mass suicide there in 1978.

— **on one's Jack Jones** on one's own. A piece of (more or less) rhyming slang that originated in the early 20th century. It is often shortened to *on one's Jack*.

— **Paul Jones** a dance, popular in the 1920s, in which partners are exchanged in a prearranged pattern. It was probably named after John Paul Jones (see above).

— **Peter Jones** a department store in Sloane Square, London, founded in 1877 by the Welsh draper Peter Jones, 1843–1905

— **Tom Jones** a novel (1749) by Henry Fielding, recording the amorous and other adventures of its eponymous hero

Joplin 'son of **Job**' [Janis Joplin, 1943–70, US rock singer; Scott Joplin, 1868–1917, US composer]

Jopling a different form of **Joplin**

Jordan from the personal name *Jordan*, which itself was an adaptation of the name of the River Jordan, the river in which Christ was baptized by John the Baptist. See also **Judd**, **Jude**, **Judson** [Michael Jordan, 1963–, US basketball player]

Joseph from the male personal name *Joseph* (from Hebrew *Yosef*, literally 'may he add' (i.e. may God send another son)). See also **Jessel**, **Jessop** [Sir Keith Joseph (Lord Joseph), 1918–94, British Conservative politician]

Josephs 'son of **Joseph**'

Josephson 'son of **Joseph**' [B.D. Josephson, 1940–, British physicist]

— **Josephson effect** the passage of an electric current through a thin insulating layer between two superconducting metals. It was named after B.D. Josephson (see above).

— **Josephson junction** in electrical or electronic circuits, a junction that utilizes the Josephson effect, consisting of two superconducting materials separated by a thin insulating layer

Joule a different form of **Jewell** [James Joule, 1818–89, British physicist]

— **joule** the SI unit of energy or work (symbol J), equal to the work done when the application point of one newton force moves one metre in the direction of application. It was named after James Joule (see above).

— **Joule effect** an increase in heat resulting from the passage of a current through a conductor

Jowell a different form of **Jewell** [Tessa Jowell, 1947–, British Labour politician]

Jowett, Jowitt from the medieval male personal name *Jowet* or the female personal name *Jowette*, both literally 'little *Jowe*', a pet-form of **Julian** [Benjamin Jowett, 1817–93, British theologian and classical scholar]

Joyce from the Breton personal name *Iodoc*, literally 'little lord'. See also **Choice** [James Joyce, 1882–1941, Irish novelist and poet; William Joyce (nickname 'Lord Haw-Haw'), 1906–46, British traitor]

Juarez from Spanish *Juárez*, a different form of *Suárez*, from Latin *Suerius*, literally 'swineherd'

Judd a pet-form of **Jordan**

Jude (i) from the male personal name *Jude*, from Hebrew *Yehuda* 'Judah', the name of Jacob's eldest son in the Bible; (ii) 'Jew' (Old French *jude* 'Jew', ultimately from Hebrew *Yehudi* 'member of the tribe of *Yehuda*'); (iii) a pet-form of **Jordan**

Judge (i) 'judicial official', or from a nickname for someone thought to have the demeanour of a judge; (ii) from Irish Gaelic *Mac an Bhreitheamhain*, literally 'son of the judge'

Judson 'son of **Judd**'

Juggins 'son of little **Jekyll**'

— **juggins** an old-fashioned colloquial term (first recorded in 1882) for a simpleton or fool. It may have been partially a fanciful alteration of *muggins*, but the surname no doubt inspired it (Disraeli had given the name to a Lancashire miner in his novel *Sybil* (1845)).

Julian, Julien from the personal name *Julian*, from Latin *Iuliānus*, a derivative of *Iulius*, which itself may have been based on *Iuppiter* 'Jupiter'. See also **Gill** (ii)

Juniper (i) 'person who lives in a place where juniper grows'; (ii) from the medieval female personal name Junifer (modern Jennifer), from Welsh *Gwenhwyfar* (literally 'fair-smooth-large'). See also **Gaynor** (ii), **Genn** (ii)

Junkin a different form of **Jenkin**

Jupp a different form of **Job**

Jury, Jewry 'person (especially a non-Jew) living in the Jewish quarter of a town' (from Middle English *jurie* 'Jewish quarter')

Just (i) from the medieval personal name *Just*, from Latin *Justus*, literally 'fair, honourable'; (ii) 'well-off person', a Jewish name based on a German or Polish spelling of Yiddish *yust* 'well-to-do'

Justice (i) from a medieval nickname applied to someone considered fair or just; (ii) 'judge' [James Robertson Justice, 1907–75, British actor]

K

Kagan a different form of **Cohen**

Kahn (i) a different form of **Cohen**; (ii) 'bargeman', from Low German *kane* 'boat'; (iii) from a shortened form of the Germanic personal name *Cagano*, derived ultimately from *gegen* 'against' [Herman Kahn, 1922–83, US scientist and futurologist; Louis I. Kahn, 1901–74, US architect]

Kain (i) see **Cain**; (ii) see **Kane**; (iii) a different form of **Cohen**

Kaiser (i) 'servant at the court of an emperor', or from a medieval German nickname applied to someone who behaved in an imperious manner (from German *Kaiser* 'emperor'); (ii) a Jewish surname based on German *Kaiser*

Kalman, Kallman, Calman (i) from the Yiddish male personal name *Kalmen*, ultimately from the Hebrew name *Kalonimos*, based on a Greek phrase meaning 'beautiful name'; (ii) from the Hungarian male personal name *Kálmán*, literally 'remainder'. See also **Coleman** [Mel Calman, 1931–94, British cartoonist]

Kane, Kain (i) a different form of **Keane** (i). See also **O'Kane**; (ii) see **Cain**
— *Citizen Kane* a film (1941), directed by and starring Orson Welles, that centres on the career of the US newspaper magnate Charles Foster Kane (a fictional figure based on William Randolph Hearst)

Kantor, Kanter, Cantor, Canter (i) 'choirmaster' or 'village schoolmaster' (from German *Kantor*, from Latin *cantor* 'singer'); (ii) 'Jewish cantor' (from German *Kantor*) [Eddie Cantor (original name Israel Iskowitz), 1892–1964, US singer]

Kaplan, Caplan (i) 'curate', or from a medieval German or Czech nickname for someone resembling a clergyman in demeanour (from German *Kaplan* 'chaplain'); (ii) used as a Jewish surname translating **Cohen** [Hyman Kaplan, the night-school prodigy in a series of stories by the US Jewish author Leo Rosten, originally appearing in *The New Yorker* in the 1930s]

Kapoor, Kapur from a Sanskrit personal name meaning literally 'camphor'

Karlin, Carlin '(Jewish) person from Karlin', Belorussia [Miriam Karlin (original name Miriam Samuels), 1925–, British actress]

Kaspar, Kasper, Casper, Caspar from the German and Polish male personal name *Kaspar*, ultimately of Persian origin and meaning literally 'treasurer' [Billy Casper, 1931–, US golfer]

Katz an acronymic Jewish name based on Hebrew *kohen tsedek* 'priest of righteousness'. See also **Cutts** (ii)

Kaufer, Kauffer 'trader, shopkeeper' (from German *Kaufer* 'trader') [E. McKnight Kauffer, 1890–1954, US-born British artist and illustrator]

Kaufman, Kauffman, Kaufmann (i) 'merchant' (from German *Kaufmann* 'merchant'); (ii) from the Jewish personal name *Kaufman* (from Yiddish *koyfman* 'merchant') [George S. Kaufman, 1889–1961, US playwright and director; Sir Gerald Kaufman, 1930–, British Labour politician]

Kaur a Hindu and Sikh name meaning literally 'daughter' (ultimately from Sanskrit *kumārī* 'girl, daughter'). It is traditionally used as a naming element by Sikh women, suffixed to a male name.

Kavanagh, Cavanagh from the Irish Gaelic personal name *Caomhánach*, literally '(follower) of (St) *Caomhán*', a personal name itself meaning literally 'little gentle one' [P.J. Kavanagh, 1931–, British writer; Patrick Kavanagh, 1905–67, Irish poet; Trevor Kavanagh, 1943–, British journalist]
— *Kavanagh QC* an ITV drama series, first broadcast in 1995, featuring a barrister called James Kavanagh (played by John Thaw)

Kay, Kaye (i) from the medieval male personal name *Kay*, immediately of Celtic origin but perhaps ultimately from Latin *Gaius*; (ii) 'key-maker' or '(ceremonial) key-bearer' (from Old English *cǣg* 'key'); (iii) 'person who lives by or works on a wharf' (from Middle English *kay* 'quay'); (iv) from a medieval nickname for someone thought to resemble a jackdaw (from northern Middle English *kay* 'jackdaw'). See also **Coe**; (v) from a medieval nickname for a left-handed person (from Danish dialect *kei* 'left'); (vi) an improvised surname adopted by non-English-speaking immigrants with an unwieldy surname beginning with K-. See also **Key** [Danny Kaye (original name David Daniel Kaminsky), 1913–87, US actor and entertainer; John Kay, 1704–64, British inventor; M.M. Kaye (full name Mary Margaret ('Mollie') Kaye), 1908–2004, Indian-born British novelist; Peter Kay, 1973–, British comedian, writer and producer; Sheila Kaye-Smith, 1887–1956, British novelist]

Keach see **Keech**

Keane, Kean (i) from Irish Gaelic *Ó Catháin* 'descendant of *Cathán*', a personal name meaning literally 'little battle'. See also **Kane** (i); (ii) see **Keen** [Edmund Kean, 1787–1833, British actor; Molly Keane, a pen-name of Mary Nesta Skrine,

1904–96, Irish author (see also M.J. **Farrell**); Roy Keane, 1971–, Irish footballer]

Kearney from Irish Gaelic *Ó Ceithearnaigh* 'descendant of *Ceithearnach*', a nickname meaning literally 'soldier'

Keat, Keate different forms of **Kite**

Keating (i) 'son of **Keat**'; (ii) from Irish Gaelic *Céitinn*, itself a gaelicization of the Anglo-Norman surname *de Ketyng*, probably denoting habitation in an unidentified place [Paul Keating, 1944–, Australian Labor politician, prime minister 1991–96; Tom Keating, 1918–84, British artist and faker of old masters]
— **Keating's powder** the proprietary name of an insecticide powder originally manufactured in the mid-19th century by the chemist Thomas Keating, ?1799–1861

Keatley see **Keetley**

Keaton see **Keeton**

Keats, Keates 'son of **Keat**' [John Keats, 1795–1821, British poet]

Keay, Keays see **Key, Keyes**

Keble, Keable, Keeble from a medieval nickname for a thickset stocky man or for a belligerent man (from Middle English *kibble* 'cudgel') [John Keble, 1792–1866, British churchman and poet]
— **Keble College** a college of Oxford University, founded in 1870 in memory of John Keble (see above)

Keech, Keach from a derisive medieval nickname for a fat person (from Middle English *keech* 'lump of fat') [Stacy Keach, 1941–, US film actor]

Keefe, Keeffe from Irish Gaelic *Ó Caoimh* 'descendant of *Caomh*', a nickname meaning literally 'gentle, kind'. See also **Cavendish**, **O'Keefe**

Keegan (i) from Irish Gaelic *Mac Aodhagáin* 'son of *Aodhagán*', a personal name meaning literally 'little little fire'; (ii) *also* **Kegan** from Irish Gaelic *Mac Thadhgáin* 'son of *Tadgán*', a personal name meaning literally 'little poet' [Kevin Keegan, 1951–, English footballer]

Keeler 'boatman' or 'boatbuilder' (from a derivative of Middle English *kele* 'ship') [Christine Keeler, 1942–, British model and showgirl]

Keeley (i) *also* **Keely** or **Kealey** or **Kealy** or **Kiely** from Irish Gaelic *Ó Caollaidhe* 'descendant of *Caollaidhe*', a personal name meaning literally 'graceful one'; (ii) a different form of **Keighley**

Keen, Keene (i) from the medieval personal name *Kene*, a shortened form of various names of Old English origin that began with either *cēne* 'brave, fierce' or *cyne-* 'royal'. See also **Kenning**; (ii) from a medieval nickname for a brave or fierce person; (iii) a different form of **Keane** [Geoffrey Keen, 1916–2005, British actor]
— **Guest, Keen and Nettlefold** see **Guest**

Keenlyside 'person from Keenlyside', an unidentified place in northern England (probably 'Cēna's glade on a hillside') [Simon Keenlyside, 1959–, British baritone]

Keetley, Keatley different forms of **Keighley**

Keeton, Keaton 'person from Ketton', County Durham or Rutland ('Catta's farmstead' and 'place on the river Ketton' respectively) or 'person from Keaton', Devon (perhaps 'settlement by a bank') [Buster Keaton (original name Joseph Francis Keaton), 1895–1966, US silent-film comedian; Diane Keaton (original name Diane Hall; Keaton was her mother's maiden name), 1946–, US actress; Michael Keaton (original name Michael Douglas), 1951–, US actor]

Kegan see **Keegan** (ii)

Kehoe see **Keogh**

Keighley, Keighly 'person from Keighley', Yorkshire ('Cyhha's glade'). See also **Keetley**

Keir 'person from Keir', Stirlingshire

Keith 'person from Keith', Moray ('place by the wood') [Penelope Keith (*née* Hatfield; Keith is her mother's surname), 1939–, British actress]
— **Keith Prowse** a British firm of ticket agents founded in 1780 by Robert Keith and William Prowse

Kellaway a different form of **Callaway**

Kelleher, Kelliher from Irish Gaelic *Ó Céileachair* 'descendant of *Céileachar*', a nickname meaning literally 'wife-loving'

Keller a different form of **Kellner** [Helen Keller, 1880–1968, US social worker and writer, blind since babyhood]
— **Keller plan** a method of instruction in US colleges that involves study units taken at each individual student's own pace. It was devised in the mid-1960s by the US psychologist Fred S. Keller, 1899–1996.

Kellermann a different form of **Kellner** (i)

Kellett, Kellet, Kellitt 'person from Kellet', Lancashire ('spring on a hillside')

Kellner, Kelner (i) 'person in charge of a wine cellar' (from Middle High German *kelnære* 'cellarer'). See also **Kellermann**; (ii) 'person from Keln', the Yiddish name of Cologne (German *Köln*)

Kellogg, Kellog (i) 'person from Keiloch or Killoch', Aberdeenshire and Ayrshire respectively; (ii) 'pork butcher' (literally 'kill hog'); (iii) a Welsh name of uncertain origin, linked in the popular imagination with Welsh *ceiliog* 'cock'; (iv) from the Old Norse personal name *Kjallákr* (from Celtic *Ceallach* – see **Kelly**)
— **Kellogg-Briand Pact** an international agreement of 1928 intended to outlaw war as a means of settling international disputes. It was negotiated by the US secretary of state Frank B. Kellogg, 1856–1937, and the French foreign minister Aristide Briand.
— **Kellogg College** a college of Oxford University, founded in 1990 with the financial assistance of the **Kellogg Foundation**, which was established in 1930 by W.K. Kellogg (see below)
— **Kellogg Company** a US-based multinational breakfast-food producer, founded in 1906 as the Battle Creek Toasted Corn Flake Company by William Keith Kellogg, 1860–1951. He was business manager of the Battle Creek Sanatarium,

Michigan, where his brother, Dr John Harvey Kellogg, was chief surgeon. They invented cornflakes around 1894.

Kelly (i) *also* **Kelley** from Irish Gaelic *Ó Ceallaigh* 'descendant of *Ceallach*', a nickname meaning literally 'bright-headed'. See also **O'Kelly**; (ii) 'person from Kelly', Angus, or various other places in Scotland similarly named (all ultimately from Gaelic *coille* 'wood, grove'), or 'person from Kelly', Devon ('place by the grove') [Barbara Kelly, 1924–2007, Canadian-born actress; Dr David Kelly, 1944–2003, British weapons expert; Gene Kelly, 1912–96, US film actor, dancer and director; Grace Kelly, 1929–82, US film actress; Henry Kelly, 1946–, Irish journalist and broadcaster; Ned Kelly, 1855–80, Australian bushranger and folk hero]

☆ The second commonest surname in Ireland

— **Derby/Darby Kelly** old rhyming slang for *belly*. It was often reduced to *Derby kel*, and *Kelly* could be used on its own in the same sense. It is not known if there was a gentleman of that name.

— **'Grace Kelly'** a song (2006) by the Lebanese-born pop singer Mika (Mica Penniman), satirizing musicians who self-servingly reinvent themselves. The eponymous lines (invoking the US actress – see above) run:

I try to be like Grace Kelly

But all her looks were too sad.

— **HMS** *Kelly* a Royal Navy K-class destroyer launched in 1938, commanded by Captain (later Lord) Mountbatten, sunk off Crete in 1941 and immortalized (in the guise of HMS *Torrin*) in the film *In Which We Serve* (1942). It was named after the British admiral Sir John Kelly, 1871–1936.

— **kelly** in Australian slang, an axe (from the name of a company that made axes); in US slang, a man's hat (probably suggested by *Derby Kelly* (see below) and *derby*, a type of hat)

— **Kelly bag** a type of relatively small handbag produced by the Hermès company. It got its name through its close association with Grace Kelly (see above), particularly after she was pictured carrying one on the cover of *Life* magazine in 1956.

— **Kelly College** a coeducational independent school in Tavistock, Devon, founded in 1877 by Admiral Benedictus Marwood Kelly

— **Kelly pool** pool played with fifteen numbered balls, in which each player draws a number by lot and tries to pot the ball of that number. The identity of the Kelly who presumably first thought it up is not known.

— **Kelly's Directory** a commercial directory to British cities and towns, established in 1799 as the Post Office London Directory. In 1835 Frederick Festus Kelly took over responsibility for it, and in due course it became known as 'Kelly's Directory'. Versions for provincial towns began to appear in 1845.

— **Kelly's eye** bingo caller's slang for the number 'one'

— **Ned Kelly** (see above) or **Nellie Kelly** Australian rhyming slang for *belly* or (in the case of Ned) *telly*

— **'On Mother Kelly's Doorstep'** a popular sentimental song (1925) by George A. Stevens. **Mother Kelly** has been used as rhyming slang for both *jelly* and *telly*.

Kelner see **Kellner**

Kelsey 'person from Kelsey', Lincolnshire ('Cēnel's low-lying land')

— **Kelsey's nuts** a phrase used in various US slang similes, especially 'as dead as Kelsey's nuts', meaning 'completely dead'. The allusion may be (with a pun on *nuts* 'testicles') to the nuts and bolts on wheels made by the Kelsey Wheel Co., a leading US automotive component manufacturer in the 1920s.

Kemble (i) 'person from Kemble', Gloucestershire ('place at the border'); (ii) from the medieval personal name *Kimbel*, from Old English *Cynebeald*, literally 'royal-bold'; (iii) from the Old Welsh personal name *Cynbel*, literally 'war-chief' [Charles Kemble, 1775–1854, British actor, son of Roger; Frances Ann ('Fanny') Kemble, 1809–93, British actress, daughter of Charles; John Philip Kemble, 1757–1823, British actor, son of Roger; Roger Kemble, 1722–1802, British travelling actor]

Kemp, Kempe 'champion in jousting or wrestling' (Middle English *kempe* 'champion') [Margery Kempe, ?1373–?1440, English mystic; Ross Kemp, 1964–, British actor]

— **Kemp Town** a district of Brighton, Sussex, named after the local MP Thomas Read Kemp, ?1781–1844, who designed and built it in the 1820s

Kempson 'son of **Kemp**' [Rachel Kempson, 1910–2003, British actress]

Kempton 'person from Kempton', Shropshire ('Cempa's farmstead') or 'person from Kempton Park', Surrey ('Cēna's farmstead')

Kendall, Kendal, Kendell 'person from Kendal', Cumbria ('valley of the river Kent') or 'person from Kendale', Yorkshire ('valley with a spring') [Edward Calvin Kendall, 1886–1972, US biochemist; Felicity Kendal, 1946–, British actress; Henry Kendall, 1841–82, Australian poet; Kaye Kendall (original name Justine Kendall McCarthy), 1927–59, British actress; Kenneth Kendall, 1924–, British television newsreader]

Kendrew a reduced form of **McAndrew** [Sir John Kendrew, 1917–97, British molecular biologist]

Kendrick (i) from the medieval personal name *Cenric*, from Old English *Cynerīc*, literally 'royal power'. See also **Courage** (iii), **Kerridge**; (ii) from the Welsh personal name *Cynrig*, of uncertain origin; (iii) a reduced form of **McKendrick**

Kennard from the medieval personal name *Keneward*, from Old English *Cyneweard*, literally either 'royal-brave' or 'royal guard'. See also **Kenward**

Kennaway from the medieval personal name *Kenewi*, from Old English *Cynewīg*, literally 'royal war', or *Cēnwīg*, literally 'bold war'. See also **Kenway**

Kenneally, **Kennelly, Keneally, Kinneally** from Irish Gaelic *Ó Cionnfhaolaidh* 'descendant of *Cionnfhaoladh*', a personal name meaning literally 'wolf-head' [Thomas Keneally, 1935–, Australian novelist]

Kennedy from Irish Gaelic *Ó Cinnéidigh* 'descendant of *Cinnéidigh*', a personal name meaning literally 'armoured head', used also as a nickname for someone with an ugly or deformed head [Charles Kennedy, 1959–, British Liberal Democrat politician; Edmund Kennedy, 1818–48, Australian explorer; Edward ('Ted') Kennedy, 1932–, US Democratic politician, brother of John; Jacqueline Kennedy-Onassis (*née* Bouvier), 1929–94, US first lady 1961–63, wife of John; John F. ('Jack') Kennedy, 1917–63, US Democratic politician, president 1961–63; Joseph P. Kennedy, 1888–1969, US businessman and diplomat, father of Edward, John and Robert; Sir Ludovic Kennedy, 1919–, British writer and broadcaster; Nigel Kennedy, 1956–, British violinist; Robert ('Bobby') Kennedy, 1925–68, US Democratic politician]
— **Cape Kennedy** the name between 1963 and 1973 of Cape Canaveral, the US launching site in Florida of crewed space flights. It was named in honour of John F. Kennedy (see above).
— **Kennedy Space Center** the headquarters of the US crewed space-flight programme, at Cape Canaveral (see above)
— **Mount Kennedy** a mountain in the St Elias Range in the Yukon Territory, Canada. At 4238 m./13,905 ft., it was the highest unclimbed peak in North America at the time of President Kennedy's death, and was named in his honour.

Kennett 'person from Kennet', Wiltshire ('place by the river Kennet')

Kenning 'son of **Keen** (i)'

Kenny, **Kenney** from Gaelic *Cionaodha*, a personal name of unknown origin and meaning, and Irish Gaelic *Ó Coinnigh* 'descendant of *Coinneach*', a personal name meaning literally 'handsome'. See also **Kinney, McElhinney, McKenna**

Kent 'person from Kent' [Bruce Kent, 1929–, British campaigner for nuclear disarmament; Clark Kent, the human persona inhabited by Superman when not in active mode; William Kent, ?1686–1748, English architect and landscape designer]

Kentish a different form of **Kent**

Kenton 'person from Kenton', the name of several places in England (in many cases 'Cēna's farmstead')

Kenward a different form of **Kennard**

Kenway a different form of **Kennaway**

Kenwood a different form of **Kenward**

Kenworthy 'person from Kenworthy', Cheshire (either 'Cyna's enclosure' or 'Cēna's enclosure')

Kenyon 'person from Kenyon', Lancashire (perhaps a shortened form of Old Welsh *Cruc Einion* 'Einion's mound') [Dame Kathleen Kenyon, 1906–78, British archaeologist]

— **KP** the tradename of Kenyon Products, peanuts, crisps and similar comestibles produced by Kenyon, Son and Craven of Rotherham, Yorkshire

Keogh, **Keoghoe, Kehoe** from Irish Gaelic *Mac Eochaidh* 'son of *Eochaidh*', a personal name derived from *each* 'horse'. See also **McGuigan**

Keown from Irish Gaelic *Mac Eoghain* (see **McEwan**)

Ker see **Kerr**

Kerk see **Kirk**

Kermode from Irish Gaelic *Mac Dhiarmada* (see **McDermott**)

Kern (i) 'farmer', or from a medieval German nickname for a small person (from Middle High German *kerne* 'seed, pip'); (ii) an invented Jewish name, based on German *Kern* or Yiddish *kern* 'grain' [Jerome Kern, 1885–1945, US composer of musical comedies]

Kerr, **Ker** 'person who lives by an area of wet boggy ground' (from northern Middle English *kerr*, from Old Norse *kjarr*). The name is pronounced either 'kar' or 'ker'. See also **Carr** [Bill Kerr, 1922–, South African-born Australian actor; Deborah Kerr, 1921–, British actress; Sir John Kerr, 1914–90, Australian statesman; W.P. Ker, 1855–1923, British literary scholar]
— **Kerr effect** the property of some transparent substances that makes them refract doubly when placed in an electric field. It is named after the Scottish physicist John Kerr, 1824–1907.

Kerridge a different form of **Kendrick** (i)

Kerrigan, **Kerigan** from Irish Gaelic *Ó Ciaragáin* 'descendant of *Ciaragán*', a nickname meaning literally 'little little dark one'

Kersey 'person from Kersey', Suffolk ('high ground where cress grows')

Kershaw 'person from Kershaw', Lancashire ('church grove')

Kerslake a different form of **Carslake**

Ketch from a medieval nickname for a lively person (from Middle English *kedge* 'brisk, lively') [Jack Ketch, died 1686, English hangman, notorious for his cruelty]

Ketley 'person from Ketley', Shropshire ('glade frequented by cats')

Key, **Keye** different forms of **Kay**

Keyes, **Keys, Keays** (i) different forms of **Kay**; (ii) 'person from Guise', Picardy; (iii) from Irish Gaelic *Mac Aodha* (see **McKay**) [Sidney Keyes, 1922–43, British poet]

Keynes, **Caines** 'person from Cahaignes or Cahaynes', northern France (in both cases probably 'place where juniper grows') [John Maynard Keynes (Lord Keynes), 1883–1946, British economist]
— **Keynsianism** the theory, associated with J.M. Keynes (see above), that government spending must compensate for insufficient business investment in times of recession

Keyte a different form of **Kite**

Khan from a Muslim personal name meaning literally 'ruler' or 'nobleman' (ultimately from Turkic *khān* 'lord, ruler') [Amir Khan, 1986–, British boxer]

Kidd, Kid, Kidde, Kydd, Kyd (i) 'goatherd', or from a medieval nickname for a frisky person (from Middle English *kid* 'young goat'); (ii) 'seller of faggots (i.e. bundles of sticks)' (from Middle English *kidde* 'faggot'); (iii) from the medieval Scottish personal name *Kid*, a different form of *Kit*, itself a pet-form of **Christopher** [Thomas Kyd, 1558–94, English dramatist; Sam Kydd, 1915–82, British character actor; William Kidd ('Captain Kidd'), ?1645–1701, Scottish pirate]

Kidman a different form of **Kidd** (i–ii) [Nicole Kidman, 1967–, Hawaiian-born Australian actress] — **Kidman's delight** a colloquial Australian term for golden syrup. It was inspired by Sir Sidney Kidman, 1857–1935, an Australian cattleman.

Kidson 'son of **Kidd** (iii)'

Kiefer (i) 'person who lives in a pine forest or by a pine tree' (from German *Kiefer* 'pine'); (ii) 'barrel-maker' (from a derivative of German dialect *Kiefe* 'barrel'); (iii) from a medieval German nickname for a greedy person (from a derivative of Middle High German *kīfen* 'to chew'), or for a truculent person (from a derivative of Middle High German *kiffen* 'to quarrel')

Kiely (i) from Irish Gaelic *Ó Cadhla* 'descendant of *Cadhla*', a personal name meaning literally 'beautiful'; (ii) see **Keeley** (i)

Kieran from the Irish Gaelic personal name *Ciarán*, literally 'little dark one'

Kiernan a different form of (**McKiernan**)

Kilbride (i) 'person from Kilbride', the name of various places in Scotland ('church of (St) Brigit'); (ii) from Irish Gaelic *Mac Giolla Brighde* or Scottish Gaelic *Mac Gille Brighde* 'son of the servant of (St) Brigit'. See also **Bredin, McBride**

Kilburn 'person from Kilburn', Derbyshire or Yorkshire ('place by Cylla's stream')

Kilby, Kilbey, Killby 'person from Kilby', Leicestershire ('farmstead of the young men')

Kildare, Kildaire from Irish Gaelic *Mac Giolla Dhorcha* 'son of the dark-haired lad' — **Dr Kildare** a television medical drama series (1962–66) featuring Richard Chamberlain as Dr James Kildare. The character was created in the 1930s by the US pulp-magazine writer Max Brand.

Kilfeather from Irish Gaelic *Mac Giolla Pheadair* 'son of the servant of (St) Peter'

Kilfedder a different form of **Kilfeather**. See also **Gilfedder**

Kilfoyle a different form of **Gilfoil**

Kilgour, Kilgore 'person from Kilgour', Fife ('wood frequented by goats') — **Kilgour French Stanbury** a firm of Savile Row tailors, founded in 1882. It is usually known simply as 'Kilgour'.

Killeen from the Irish Gaelic personal name *Cillín*, literally 'little *Ceallach*' (see **Kelly**)

Killigrew 'person from Killigrew', Cornwall (probably 'hazel grove')

Killingbeck 'person from Killingbeck', Yorkshire (probably 'Killing's stream')

Kilmartin a different form of **Gilmartin**

Kilmuir a different form of **Gilmore** (i)

Kilner 'potter' or 'lime burner' (from a derivative of Old English *cylene* 'kiln') — **Kilner jar** the proprietary name (registered in 1930 by Kilner Brothers Ltd. of London) of a type of glass preserving jar with an airtight lid, used for bottling fruit or vegetables

Kilpatrick (i) 'person from Kilpatrick', the name of various places in Scotland ('church of (St) Patrick'); (ii) from Irish Gaelic *Mac Giolle Phádraig* 'son of the servant of (St) Patrick'

Kilroy a different form of **Gilroy** [Robert Kilroy-Silk, 1942–, British Labour and Veritas politician and television broadcaster] — **Kilroy was here** a phrase widely written up on walls by American service personnel in the UK during World War II. The identity of the probably mythical Kilroy has been much debated (one theory is that he was a shipyard inspector of Quincy, Massachusetts, who chalked the phrase on material he had checked).

Kilvert probably from an Old Norse personal name *Ketilfrith*, literally 'cauldron peace' [Francis Kilvert, 1840–79, British clergyman and diarist]

Kim 'gold', Korean

Kimball, Kimble (i) 'person from Great or Little Kimble', Buckinghamshire ('royal bell' – referring to the shape of a hill in the vicinity); (ii) from the medieval male personal name *Kimbel* (from Old English *Cynebeald*, literally 'royal brave'). See also **O'Hara**

Kimber from the Old English female personal name *Cyneburh*, literally 'royal fortress'

Kimberley, Kimberly 'person from Kimberley', the name of several places in England (variously 'Cyneburg's glade', 'Cynemǣr's glade', etc.)

Kimble see **Kimball**

Kincaid, Kincade, Kinkade, Kinkead 'person from Kincaid', former place to the north of Glasgow (perhaps 'head of the pass') [Thomas Kinkade, 1958–, US painter, known especially for his mass-produced prints]

King 'king', probably mainly as a medieval nickname for someone with a regal demeanour, but also denoting a servant in a royal household, someone who played the part of a king in a pageant, etc. [B.B. King (original name Riley B. King), 1925–, US blues singer; Billie Jean King (*née* Moffitt), 1943–, US tennis player; Carole King (original name Carole Klein), 1942–, US singer and songwriter; Cecil King, 1901–87, British newspaper executive; Dave King (original name David Kingshott), 1929–2002, British actor and entertainer; Don King, 1931–, US boxing promoter; Hetty King (original name Winifred Emms), 1883–1972, British music-hall male impersonator; J.B. King, 1873–1965, US cricketer; Larry King (original name Lawrence Zeiger), 1933–, US television interviewer; Mackenzie King, 1874–1950, Canadian Liberal politician, prime minister 1921–26,

1926–30, 1935–48; Martin Luther King, Jr, 1929–68, US civil-rights leader; Nosmo King, stage-name (based on 'No Smoking') of H. Vernon Watson, 1886–1949, British black-face music-hall entertainer; Stephen King, 1947–, US author]

Kingdon 'person from Kingdon or Kendon', Devon (both 'king's hill')

Kingman 'servant of **King**'

Kingsbury 'person from Kingsbury', the name of various places in England (mainly 'king's stronghold')

Kingsford 'person from Kingsford', the name of various places in England (mainly 'king's ford') [Sir Charles Kingsford Smith, 1897–1935, Australian aviator]
— **Kingsford Smith International Airport** the airport of Sydney, Australia. Opened in 1920, it was renamed after Charles Kingsford Smith (see above) in 1953.

Kingsley 'person from Kingsley', the name of various places in England ('king's glade') [Sir Ben Kingsley (original surname Bhanji), 1943–, British actor; Charles Kingsley, 1819–79, British clergyman and writer]

Kingston 'person from Kingston', the name of various places in England (mainly 'king's settlement')

Kington 'person from Kington', the name of various places in England ('royal settlement')

Kinloch, Kinlock 'person from Kinloch', the name of various places in Scotland ('head of the loch')

Kinnaird 'person from Kinnaird', Tayside ('summit')

Kinneally see **Kenneally**

Kinnear, Kinneir 'person from Kinneir', Fife (perhaps 'western headland') [Roy Kinnear, 1934–88, British actor and comedian]

Kinney a different form of **Kenny**

Kinsella from Irish Gaelic *Ó Cinnsealaigh* 'descendant of *Cinnsealach*', a nickname meaning literally 'haughty'

Kinsey from the medieval personal name *Kynsey*, from Old English *Cynesige*, literally 'royal victory' [Alfred Kinsey, 1894–1956, US biologist and surveyor of human sexual behaviour]

Kipling 'person from Kiplin', Yorkshire ('Cyppel's people's settlement'), or 'person from Kipling Cotes', Yorkshire (perhaps 'cottages associated with Cybbel') [Rudyard Kipling, 1865–1936, British writer and poet]
— **Mr Kipling** a British brand of cakes, introduced (1967) and owned by Rank Hovis McDougall. The persona of the (fictitious) Kipling is of a traditional English baker, quite possibly rotund, apple-cheeked and twinkly-eyed (although no image of him has ever been promulgated).

Kirby, Kirkby 'person from Kirby or Kirkby', the name of various places in northern England ('village with a church') [Dame Emma Kirkby, 1949–, British soprano; Kathy Kirby, 1940–, British popular singer]

— **Kirbigrip** the proprietary name (registered in 1926) of a type of sprung hair-grip produced in Birmingham by Messrs Kirby, Beard & Co. (founded 1743).

Kirk, Kirke 'person who lives near a church' or 'person employed in a church' (from northern Middle English *kirk* 'church') [Captain James T. Kirk, commander of the USS *Enterprise* in the television science-fiction series *Star Trek* (1969–71); Norman Kirk, 1923–74, New Zealand Labour politician, prime minister 1972–74]
— **Captain Kirk** (see above) rhyming slang for *work*

Kirkbride 'person from Kirkbride', the name of various places in northern England ('church dedicated to (St) Bridgit')

Kirkby see **Kirby**

Kirkham 'person from Kirkham', Lancashire and Yorkshire ('village with a church')

Kirkland 'person living on land belonging to the Church'

Kirkman 'person who looks after a church'

Kirkpatrick 'person from Kirkpatrick', the name of numerous places in Scotland and Northern Ireland ('church dedicated to (St) Patrick')

Kirkup 'person from Kirkup', an unidentified place in Northumberland (probably 'valley with a church') [James Kirkup, 1918–, British writer and poet]

Kirkwood 'person from Kirkwood', the name of various places in Scotland ('wood belonging to the Church or with a church nearby')

Kirton 'person from Kirton', the name of various places in northern England ('village with a church')

Kirwan, Kirwen, Kirwin from Irish Gaelic *Ó Ciardhubháin* 'descendant of *Ciardhubhán*', a personal name meaning literally 'little dark black one'

Kiss (i) *also* **Kis** from a medieval Hungarian (and Jewish-Hungarian) nickname for a small person, or designating the younger of two people with the same name (from Hungarian *kis* 'small'); (ii) 'maker of (leather) leg armour' (from Anglo-Norman *cuisse* 'thigh')

Kissinger 'person from Kissingen', Franconia, or 'person from Kissing', Bavaria [Henry Kissinger, 1923–, German-born US diplomat and political scientist]

Kitchen, Kitchin 'person who works in a kitchen, cook' [Michael Kitchen, 1948–, British actor]

Kitchener a different form of **Kitchen** [Horatio Herbert Kitchener (Earl Kitchener), 1850–1916, British field marshal]
— **Kitchener** a city in southwestern Ontario, Canada. Until 1916 it was called Berlin. Anti-German sentiment necessitated a new name, which was chosen to honour Lord Kitchener (see above).

Kite, Kyte from a medieval nickname for a fierce person (from Middle English *kete* 'kite (the bird of prey)'). See also **Keat**, **Keyte** [Fred Kite, the archetypal British trade-union shop steward played by Peter Sellers in the film *I'm All Right, Jack* (1959)]

Kitson 'son of *Kit*' (see **Kitt** (i))

Kitt (i) from the medieval personal name *Kit*, a pet-form of **Christopher**; (ii) 'maker or seller of hooped wooden tubs or buckets' (Middle English *kitte*) [Eartha Kitt, 1928–, US cabaret singer]
— **Eartha Kitt** (see above) rhyming slang for *shit*. In the plural it denotes diarrhoea, and *Eartha Kitts* also means 'tits'.

Klein, Cline from a medieval nickname for a small man (from German and Dutch *klein* and Yiddish *kleyn* 'small') [Calvin Klein, 1942–, US fashion designer; Joe Klein, 1946–, US journalist and author; Patsy Cline, 1932–63, US pop/country singer]
— **Calvin Klein** (see above) rhyming slang for *wine*

Knapp (i) 'person from Knapp or Knepp', the name of various places in southern England and the West Country ('place on a hilltop'); (ii) *also* **Knappe** 'servant' or 'squire' (from German *Knappe* 'boy, male servant')

Knatchbull 'slaughterer and butcher' (from Middle English *knatchen* 'to fell' and *bull* 'bull')

Kneale see **Neil**

Kneebone perhaps from a medieval nickname for someone with knobbly knees

Kneller (i) from a medieval German nickname for a noisy or disruptive person (from a derivative of Middle High German *knellen* 'to make a noise'); (ii) 'teacher in a Jewish elementary school' (from Yiddish *kneler*) [Sir Godfrey Kneller, 1646–1723, German-born English portrait painter]

Knickerbocker 'marble baker (i.e. someone who made children's clay marbles)' (from Dutch *knickerbacker*) [Diedrich Knickerbocker, the fictional 'author' of Washington Irving's *History of New York* (1809) (illustrations of him in the book showed him wearing knee breeches which came to be known as 'knickerbockers' – whence, ultimately, *knickers* for women's underpants)]
— **Knickerbocker glory** a dessert consisting of layers of different layers of ice cream, fruit, jelly and cream, served in a tall conical glass. The reason for its name is unknown.

Knight 'knight' (the precise connotations of the name may well reflect any of the changing meanings of the word as it evolved from Old English *cniht* 'boy, young man, young male servant' through early Middle English 'tenant with a feudal obligation to serve as a mounted soldier' to later Middle English 'military nobleman'. In the last context it could also connote a servant in a knight's household) [Gladys Knight, 1944–, US R&B/soul singer; Dame Laura Knight (*née* Johnson), 1877–1970, British painter]
— **Knight's Castile** a British brand of toilet soap, introduced in 1919 by John Knight & Co. (later part of Lever Brothers).

Knightley, Knightly 'person from Knightly', the name of various places in England ('young men's glade') [Keira Knightley, 1985–, British actress;

Mr Knightley (George Knightley), undertaker of Emma's *éducation sentimentale* in Jane Austen's *Emma* (1816)]

Knighton 'person from Knighton', the name of various places in England ('young men's farmstead')

Knobloch 'grower or seller of garlic' (from Middle High German *knobelouch* 'garlic')

Knoll (i) 'person who lives at the top of a hill' or 'person from Knole, Knowle etc'., the name of various places in England (in either case from Old English *cnoll* 'hilltop'); (ii) from a medieval nickname for a short fat person. See also **Knowles**

Knopf 'button-maker' (from German *Knopf* 'button')

Knopfler a different form of **Knopf** [Mark Knopfler, 1949–, British guitarist, singer and songwriter]

Knott (i) 'person who lives by a hillock' (from Middle English *knot*); (ii) from the medieval male personal name *Knut* (from Old Norse *Knútr*); (iii) from a medieval nickname for a thickset stocky person (from Old English *cnotta* 'knot, lump'). See also **Nott** [Alan Knott, 1946–, English cricketer]

Knowles, Knollys (i) 'person who lives at the top of a hill' (from the plural or genitive singular of Old English *cnoll* 'hilltop'); (ii) 'son of **Knoll** (ii)' [Beyoncé Knowles, 1981–, US R&B singer/songwriter]

Knox 'person who lives at the top of a hill' (from the plural or genitive singular of Old English *cnocc* 'round-topped hill') or 'person from Knock', the name of various places in Scotland or northern England (from *cnocc*) [Alexander Knox, 1907–95, Canadian actor; John Knox, ?1513–72, Scottish religious reformer; Sir Robin Knox-Johnston, 1939–, British yachtsman; Ronald Knox, 1888–1957, British Roman Catholic priest and author]
— **Collie Knox** rhyming slang for *pox* The identity of the man is unknown
— **Fort Knox** a military post and reservation in central Kentucky, USA, the site of the US Gold Depository since 1936. It was named in honour of Henry Knox, 1750–1806, George Washington's Secretary for War.
— **Knoxville** a city in Tennessee, USA. It was named after Henry Knox (see above).
— **Nervo and Knox** one of the comedy pairings within the British variety combo 'The Crazy Gang', consisting of Jimmy Nervo, 1890–1975, and Teddy Knox, 1896–1974. The combination has also been used as rhyming slang for *box* (as in *the box* 'television'), *pox* and *socks*.

Knudsen 'son of *Knud*', the Danish variant of *Knut* (see **Knott** (i))

Koch (i) 'cook' (from German *Koch* 'cook'); (ii) from a pet-form of any of a range of medieval Czech personal names beginning with *Ko-* (e.g. *Kocián*)

Koenig (i) from the German equivalent of English **King** (German *König* 'king'); (ii) an invented Jewish name based on German *König*

Kovacs 'blacksmith' (Hungarian, from *kovács* 'blacksmith') [Ernie Kovacs, 1919–62, US television comedian]

Kowalski 'blacksmith' (Polish, from *kowal* 'blacksmith')

Kraft, Krafft from a medieval German, Danish and Jewish nickname for a strong man (from German *Kraft*, Danish *kraft* 'strength'). See also **Craft** (ii)
— **Kraft Foods Inc.** a US-based food and beverage manufacturing company, founded in 1903 by the Canadian-born entrepreneur and inventor James L. Kraft, 1874–1953.

Kramer, Kraemer 'shopkeeper' (from German *Krämer* 'shopkeeper'). See also **Cramer** (i), **Creamer** (iii) [Billy J. Kramer (original name William Ashton), 1943–, British pop singer; Jack Kramer, 1921–, US tennis player; Stanley Kramer, 1913–2001, US film director]
— *Kramer versus Kramer* a US film (1979) centring on the relationship between a divorced couple (Dustin Hoffman and Meryl Streep) and their seven-year-old son

Kranz, Krantz (i) 'wreath-maker' or 'person who lives in a house bearing the sign of a wreath or garland' (from German *Kranz* 'wreath, garland'); (ii) an invented Jewish name based on German *Kranz* [Judith Krantz, 1928–, US novelist]

Kraus, Krauss from a medieval German and Jewish nickname for a curly-haired person (from German *kraus* 'curly')

Kravitz, Kravetz, Kravets 'tailor' (from Ukrainian and Belorussian *kravets* 'tailor') [Lenny Kravitz, 1964–, US singer/songwriter]

Kray (i) 'person from Kray', near Essen, Germany; (ii) from a medieval German nickname for someone thought to resemble a crow (from Middle High German *krā* 'crow') [Reggie Kray, 1933–2000, and Ronnie Kray, 1933–95, British gangsters. They were identical twins]

Krebs (i) 'catcher or seller of crabs or other crustaceans', or from a medieval German or Swiss German nickname for someone thought to resemble a crab (from Middle High German *krebez* or Middle Low German *crevet* 'crab, shrimp'); (ii) an invented Jewish name based on German *Krebs* 'crab' [Sir Hans Krebs, 1900–81, German-born British biochemist]
— **Krebs cycle** a sequence of biochemical reactions occurring in cells that is part of the metabolism of carbohydrates to produce energy. It was named after its discoverer, Sir Hans Krebs (see above).

Kretschmar, Kretschmer 'inn-keeper' (from a derivative of Middle High German *kretscham* 'inn')

Kroger a different form of **Kruger**

Kruger (i) 'maker or seller of jugs' (from German *Krüger*, from *Krug* 'jug'); (ii) 'inn-keeper' (from German *Krüger*, from *Krug* 'inn') [Paul Kruger, 1825–1904, South African statesman, president of Transvaal 1883–1902]
— **Kruger National Park** a national park in northeastern South Africa. Established in 1926, it was named in honour of Paul Kruger (see above).
— **Krugerrand** a South African gold coin weighing one ounce. It is so named from the portrait of Paul Kruger on the obverse.
— **Krugersdorp** a city in northeastern South Africa. It was named in honour of Paul Kruger.

Kuhn (i) from the medieval German male personal name *Kuno*, a pet-form of *Kunrat* '**Conrad**' (probably also influenced by German *kühn* 'brave'); (ii) an invented Jewish name based on German *kühn* 'brave'. See also **Coon** (ii)

Kumar, Kumer 'child, son, prince' (from Sanskrit *kumāra*). See also **Coomer** (iii)

Kuntz, Kunz from the medieval German male personal name *Chunizo*, derived from either Old High German *kuoni* 'brave' or *chunni* 'people, race'. See also **Coons** (ii)

Kyd, Kydd see **Kidd**

Kyle 'person from Kyle', district of Ayrshire (from its 5th-century British ruler, the *Coel Hen*), or 'person from Kyle', the name of various places in Scotland ('strait')

Kynaston 'person from Kynaston', Herefordshire and Shropshire ('Cyneweard's farmstead')

L

Lacey, Lacy 'person from Lassy', Normandy ('Lascius's settlement')

Lachlan a different form of **Laughlan**

Lack a different form of **Lake**

Ladbrooke, Ladbroke 'person from Ladbroke', Warwickshire ('place by the brook used for predicting the future') (Ladbrokes, the British firm of bookmakers, got its name from Ladbroke Hall, Warwickshire, home in the late 19th century to one of the firm's founders, the racehorse trainer Harry Schwind)
— **Ladbroke Estate** an area of residential streets (including **Ladbroke Grove**) in North Kensington, London, developed in the 1840s by the local landowner James Weller Ladbroke, 1772–1847

Ladd 'servant' (Middle English *ladde*) [Alan Ladd, 1913–64, US film actor; Cheryl Ladd (*née* Stoppelmoor), 1951–, US actress, daughter-in-law of Alan; Diane Ladd (original name Rose Diane Ladner), 1932–, US actress]

Lafferty a different form of **Laverty**

Laidlaw a Scottish name of uncertain origin

Laidler a different form of **Laidlaw**

Lain, Laine (i) see **Lane** (i); (ii) a reduced form of **McLean** [Dame Cleo Laine, 1927–, British jazz vocalist; Frankie Laine (original name Frank Paul LoVecchio), 1913–2007, US popular singer]

Laing a Scottish variant of **Lang** [R.D. Laing, 1927–89, British psychiatrist]

Laird 'landlord, landowner (in Scotland, Northern Ireland and northern England)' [Macgregor Laird, 1808–61, Scottish explorer]

Laithwaite 'person from Laithwaite', Lancashire and Merseyside ('meadow with a barn' and probably 'Leikr's meadow' respectively)

Lake 'person who lives near a stream' or 'person from Lake', the name of various places in southwestern England (in either case from Old English *lacu* 'stream'). See also **Lack, Laker** [Meg Lake, 1942–, real name of the British newspaper and television astrologist 'Mystic Meg'; Veronica Lake (original name Constance Frances Marie Ockleman), 1919–73, US actress]
— *Bunny Lake Is Missing* a film (1965), based on a novel by Evelyn Piper, centring on the search for the missing 4-year-old daughter of an American woman in London
— **Emerson, Lake and Palmer** see **Emerson**

Laker (i) 'actor, player' (from northern Middle English *leyker*, a derivative of *leyken* 'to play'); (ii) a different form of **Lake** [Sir Freddie Laker,

1922–2006, British airline entrepreneur; Jim Laker, 1922–86, English cricketer]

Lamb (i) *also* **Lamm** 'keeper of lambs, shepherd', or from a medieval nickname for a mild-mannered person; (ii) *also* **Lamm** a reduced form of **Lambert**; (iii) from Irish Gaelic *Ó Luain* (see **Lane** (ii)) [Alan Lamb, 1954–, South African-born English cricketer; Lady Caroline Lamb, 1785–1828, British novelist notorious for her infatuation with Lord Byron; Charles Lamb, 1775–1834, British essayist and critic; Mary Lamb, 1764–1847, British writer, sister of Charles, with whom she collaborated]
— **Lambs' *Tales from Shakespeare*** a retelling (1807) of Shakespeare's plays for young readers by Charles and Mary Lamb (see above)

Lambert (i) from the personal name *Lambert*, popularized in England by the Normans but of Germanic origin, meaning literally 'land-bright'; (ii) 'shepherd' (from Old English *lambhierd*, literally 'lamb-herd'). See also **Lampard** [Constant Lambert, 1905–51, British composer and conductor; Verity Lambert, 1935–, British film and television producer]

Lamm see **Lamb** (i–ii)

Lamont from the medieval Scottish personal name *Lagman*, from Old Norse *Logmathr*, literally 'law-man'. See also **Lawman, Lemon** [Norman Lamont (Lord Lamont), 1942–, British Conservative politician]

Lampard a different form of **Lambert** [Frank Lampard, 1978–, English footballer]

Lamplugh 'person from Lamplugh', Cumbria ('bare valley')

Lampton 'person from Lampton', Greater London, or 'person from Lambton', County Durham ('farmstead where lambs are bred') [Joe Lampton, upwardly-mobile working-class hero of John Braine's novel *Room at the Top* (1957)]

Lancaster, Lankester 'person from Lancaster', Lancashire ('Roman fort on the river Lune') [Burt Lancaster, 1913–94, US actor; Sir Edwin Ray Lankester, 1847–1929, British zoologist; Sir Osbert Lancaster, 1908–86, British writer and cartoonist]
— **Charley Lancaster** mid-19th-century rhyming slang for *handkerchief* (roughly approximating to the contemporary colloquial pronunciation 'ankercher')

Lance from the medieval personal name *Lanzo*, brought into England by the Normans but ultimately of Germanic origin, a shortened form of any of a range of compound names that began with *land* (latterly also influenced by *lance* 'cavalry spear')

Land (i) 'person who lives in the countryside'; (ii) 'person who lives in a woodland glade' or 'person from Launde', Leicestershire (in either case from Middle English *lande* or *launde* 'glade', from Old French) [Edwin Herbert Land, 1909–91, US inventor of Polaroid and of the Polaroid Land Camera]

Landau 'person from Landau', the name of places in Alsace and Rhineland-Palatinate ('territory in a damp valley') [Martin Landau, 1931–, US actor]

Lander (i) 'indigenous inhabitant' or 'person who lives in the countryside' (from German *Lander* 'person of the land'); (ii) a different form of **Landau**; (iii) a different form of **Lavender**

Landon (i) from the medieval French personal name *Landon*, from Germanic *Lando*; (ii) perhaps a different form of **Langdon** [Michael Landon (original name Eugene Orowitz), 1936–91, US actor and producer]

Landor (i) from the Hungarian personal name *Lándor*; (ii) perhaps a different form of **Lander** [Walter Savage Landor, 1775–1864, British poet and prose writer]

Landry from the medieval personal name *Landry*, brought into England by the Normans but ultimately of Germanic origin, literally 'land-powerful'

Landseer 'person who lives near a border' (from Middle English *landschare* 'land-boundary') [Sir Edwin Landseer, 1802–73, British artist]

Landy 'person from Landy', the name of various places in France [John Landy, 1930–, Australian athlete]

Lane (i) *also* **Lain** *or* **Laine** *or* **Layne** 'person who lives by a lane'; (ii) from Irish Gaelic *Ó Laighin* 'descendant of *Laighean*', a nickname meaning literally 'spear' (see also **Lean**, **Lyon** (iv)), *Ó Luain* 'descendant of *Luan*', a nickname meaning literally 'warrior', and *Ó Liatháin* (see **Lehane**); (iii) 'wool-worker' (from Old French *lane, laine* 'wool'). See also **Lyne** [Sir Allen Lane, 1902–70, British publisher, founder of Penguin Books; Carla Lane (original name Romana Barrack), 1937–, British writer of television comedies; Lupino Lane (original name Henry Lane George Lupino), 1892–1959, British comic actor]

• Men with the surname Lane are traditionally given the nickname 'Shady'

— **Harriet Lane** in late 19th- and early 20th-century nautical slang, preserved meat, especially Australian tinned meat. The name was originally that of the wife and victim of Henry Wainwright, who was hanged for her murder in 1875.

— **Lanesborough** a town in County Longford, Ireland. It was named in the late 17th century after a local land-owner, Sir George Lane (1st Viscount Lanesborough).

Lang a different form of **Long** (i). See also **Laing** [Andrew Lang, 1844–1912, British writer; k.d.

lang (full name Kathryn Dawn Lang), 1961–, Canadian singer and songwriter]

Langan from Irish Gaelic *Ó Longáin* 'descendant of *Longán*', a personal name perhaps derived from the adjective *long* 'tall' or the noun *long* 'ship'. See also **Long** [Peter Langan, 1940–88, Irish restaurateur]

Langdon 'person from Langdon', the name of various places in southern England and the Midlands ('long hill'). See also **Longdon** [David Langdon, 1914–, British cartoonist]

Langford 'person from Langford', the name of various places in England ('long ford'). See also **Longford** [Bonnie Langford, 1958–, British singer, dancer and actress]

Langham 'person from Langham', the name of various places in England (mostly 'long homestead or enclosure') [Chris Langham, 1949–, British comedy actor]

— **Langham Place** a street in the West End of London, named after the owner of the land on which it was built in the early 19th century, Sir James Langham. BBC Broadcasting House is situated there.

Langland 'person who lives on a long piece of land' [William Langland, ?1330–?1400, English poet, author of *Piers Plowman*]

Langley (i) 'person from Langley', the name of numerous places in England ('long glade'); (ii) from the Old Norse female personal name *Langlif*, literally 'long life'. See also **Longley**

— **langley** a unit of solar radiation equal to one calorie per square centimetre. It was named after the US astronomer Samuel P. Langley, 1834–1906.

Langridge 'person who lives on or by a long ridge of land' or 'person from Langridge', the name of various places in England ('long ridge') [Philip Langridge, 1939–, British tenor]

Langston 'person from Langston or Langstone', the name of various places in England ('tall stone' (perhaps a marker stone))

Langton 'person from Langton', the name of various places in England (mainly 'long farmstead') [Stephen Langton, ?1150–1228, English theologian, archbishop of Canterbury 1207–28]

Langtry 'person from Langtree', Devon, Oxfordshire and Lancashire ('tall tree') [Lillie Langtry (*née* le Breton), 1853–1929, British actress and intimate friend of the Prince of Wales (later Edward VII)]

Lanier (i) 'pack-driver' (from Old French *l'asnier* 'the pack-driver', from *asne* 'donkey'); (ii) 'worker in wool' (from a derivative of Old French *lane, laine* 'wool') [Sidney Lanier, 1842–81, US poet]

Lanigan from Irish Gaelic *Ó Lonagáin* 'descendant of *Lonagán*', a personal name probably meaning literally 'little little blackbird'

Lankester see **Lancaster**

Lansbury, Lansberry 'person from Lansbury', an unidentified English place [Angela Lansbury, 1925–, British-born US actress, granddaughter of

George; George Lansbury, 1859–1940, British Labour politician]

Lansdown, Lansdowne 'person from Lansdown', Dorset and Somerset (probably 'hill with a long ridge')

Lara 'person from Lara de los Infantes', in Burgos province, Spain [Brian Lara, 1969–, West Indian cricketer]

Lardner 'servant in charge of a larder or provisions store' (Middle English *lardiner*, from Anglo-Norman, an alteration of *larder*, ultimately from Late Latin *lardum* 'bacon fat') [Ring Lardner, 1885–1933, US short-story writer]

Large from a medieval nickname for a generous or (ironically) mean person (from Middle English *large* 'generous')

Larimer a different form of **Lorimer**

Larkin (i) from the medieval personal name *Larkin*, literally 'little **Lawrence**'; (ii) from Irish Gaelic *Ó Lorcáin* 'descendant of *Lorcán*', a personal name meaning literally 'little cruel one' [Philip Larkin, 1922–85, British poet; 'Pop' Larkin, chirpy paterfamilias of the Larkin family, which features in five novels by H.E. Bates, beginning with *The Darling Buds of May* (1958)]

Larkins 'son of **Larkin**'
— **The Larkins** an ITV situation comedy series (1958–64) featuring the Larkins family

Larner (i) 'scholar' or 'schoolmaster' (from Middle English *lerner*, which meant both 'learner' and 'teacher'). See also **Lerner**; (ii) a different form of **Delaney**

Larson an anglicization of Swedish *Larsson* and Danish and Norwegian *Larsen*, both 'son of *Lars*' (the Scandinavian form of **Lawrence**) [Gary Larson, 1950–, US cartoonist]

Larue, La Rue 'person who lives by a road or pathway' (from Old French *la rue* 'the road') [Danny La Rue (original name Daniel Patrick Carroll), 1927–, Irish female impersonator]

Lascelles 'person from Lacelle', Normandy ('the (hermit's) cell')

Lasenby see **Lazenby**

Laski 'person who lives in a forest clearing' (Polish *Łaski*, from *las* 'clearing') [Harold Laski, 1893–1950, British political scientist; Marghanita Laski, 1915–88, British novelist and critic, niece of Harold]

Lasseter, Lassiter different forms of **Leicester**
— **Lasseter's Lost Reef** a huge gold-bearing reef claimed in 1929 to have been discovered in central Australia by the Australian writer and explorer Lewis Hubert Lasseter, 1880–1931. He led an expedition to refind it, but died in the attempt.

Last (i) 'cobbler' (from Middle English *last*, the wooden form on which cobblers make or repair shoes); (ii) 'porter' (from German *Last* 'burden')

Latchford 'person from Latchford', the name of various places in England ('ford at a boggy place')

Latham, Laytham, Lathom, Lathem 'person from Latham', the name of various places in

northern England ('place by the barns'). See also **Leatham**

Latimer, Latymer, Lattimer, Latimore 'writer or keeper of Latin documents' (from Anglo-Norman *latinier* 'Latinist') [Hugh Latimer, ?1485–1555, Anglican reformer and martyr]
— **Latymer Upper School** a coeducational independent school, founded in 1624 by Edward Latymer, 1557–1626, an English crown official. It moved to its present site, in Hammersmith, West London, in 1890.

Lauder, Lawder 'person from Lauder', Borders ('place on the *Leader* Water', a river-name perhaps meaning literally 'wash') [Afferbeck Lauder, the ostensible author of *Let's Talk Strine* (1965) by Alistair Morrison (the name is in fact an 'australianized' version of 'alphabetical order'); Estée Lauder (*née* Mentzer), 1908–2004, US cosmetics entrepreneur; Sir Harry Lauder (original name Hugh MacLennan), 1870–1950, British music-hall comedian and singer]

Lauderdale 'person from Lauderdale', Borders ('Lauder valley' – see **Lauder**)
— **Fort Lauderdale** a city in southeastern Florida, USA, on the Atlantic Ocean. Founded in 1895, it was named after Major William Lauderdale, who led an expedition against the local Seminole Indians in 1838.

Laughlan, Laughlin, Loughlan, Loughlin from the Irish Gaelic personal name *Lochlann*, literally 'stranger', originally applied as a nickname to Viking settlers. See also **Lachlan**, **Loftus**, **McLaughlin**, **O'Loughlin**

Laughton 'person from Laughton', the name of various places in England (mostly 'enclosure where leeks are grown') [Charles Laughton, 1899–1962, British actor]

Launder a different form of **Lavender** [Frank Launder, 1907–97, British screenwriter and film director and producer]

Laurel 'little *Laur*', a French personal name and surname meaning literally 'someone who lives by a laurel tree' (Old French *laur*) [Stan Laurel (original name Arthur Stanley Jefferson), 1890–1965, British film comedian]
— **Laurel and Hardy** Stan Laurel (see above) and Oliver Hardy (see **Hardy**), a duo of comic actors who made a series of memorable (initially silent, latterly talking) pictures in the 1920s and 1930s. They first joined forces in 1926. The duo's name has been used as rhyming slang for *Bacardi*, the name of a brand of white rum.

Laurence see **Lawrence**

Laurie, Lawrie, Lawry 'little **Lawrence**' [Bill Lawry, 1937–, Australian cricketer; Hugh Laurie, 1959–, British actor; John Laurie, 1897–1980, British actor; Marie McDonald McLaughlin Lawrie, original name of Lulu, 1948–, British popular singer]
— **'Annie Laurie'** a Scottish song concerning a certain Annie Laurie, 1682–1764, daughter of Sir Robert Laurie of Maxwelton, Dumfriesshire. The words were written by her rejected lover William Douglas:

Maxwelton's braes are bonnie,
Where early fa's the dew,
'Twas there that Annie Laurie
Gi'ed me her promise true.

Lavender 'launderer, washerwoman' (from Anglo-Norman *lavendier, lavender*, ultimately from Latin *lavare* 'to wash'). See also **Lander**, **Launder** [Ian Lavender, 1946–, British actor]

Laver (i) 'launderer, washerman' (from Anglo-Norman *laver*, ultimately from Latin *lavare* 'to wash'); (ii) from a medieval French nickname for a rich man (from Old Provençal *l'aver* 'the possessions') [Rod Laver, 1938–, Australian tennis player]

Laverty from Irish Gaelic *Ó Fhlaithbheartaigh* and *Mac Fhlaithbheartaigh*, respectively 'descendant' and 'son of *Fhlaithbheartach*', a personal name meaning literally 'princely doer of valiant deeds'. See also **Lafferty**

Lavery from Irish Gaelic *Ó Labhradha* 'descendant of *Labraidh*', a nickname meaning literally 'spokesman'. See also **Lowry** [Sir John Lavery, 1856–1941, Irish painter]

Law (i) 'person who lives near a hill' (from Middle English *law* 'hill'); (ii) from a medieval pet-form of **Lawrence**. See also **Lawson** [Andrew Bonar Law, 1858–1923, Canadian-born British Conservative politician, prime minister 1922–23; Denis Law, 1940–, Scottish footballer; Jude Law, 1972–, British actor; William Law, 1686–1761, Anglican divine]
— **Denis Law** (see above) rhyming slang for *saw* (the tool)

Lawes, Laws 'son of **Law** (ii)' [Henry Lawes, 1596–1662, English composer; Sir John Bennet Lawes, 1814–1900, British agriculturalist; William Lawes, 1602–45, English composer, brother of Henry]

Lawford 'person from Lawford', Essex and Warwickshire ('Lealla's ford') [Peter Lawford, 1923–84, US actor]

Lawler, Lawlor from Irish Gaelic *Ó Leathlobhair* 'descendant of *Leathlobar*', a personal name meaning literally 'rather ill' [Ray Lawler, 1921–, Australian playwright]

Lawless from a medieval nickname for a man of uncontrolled appetites

Lawley 'person from Lawley', Shropshire ('Lāfa's glade') [Sue Lawley, 1946–, British broadcaster]

Lawlor see **Lawler**

Lawman a different form of **Lamont**

Lawrence, Lawrance, Laurence, Laurance from the male personal name *Laurence*, ultimately from Latin *Laurentius*, literally 'person from *Laurentum*', a town in Italy ('place of laurels or bay trees'). See also **Larkin**, **Laurie**, **Law**, **Lowry**, **McLauren** [D.H. Lawrence, 1885–1930, British novelist; Gertrude Lawrence (original name Gertrud Alexandra Dagmar Lawrence Klasen), 1898–1952, British actress; T.E. Lawrence ('Lawrence of Arabia'), 1888–1935, British

soldier and writer; Sir Thomas Lawrence, 1769–1830, British painter]
— **lawrencium** a short-lived radioactive metallic element (symbol *Lr*). It was named in honour of the US physicist Ernest O. Lawrence, 1901–58.

Lawrenson 'son of **Lawrence**'

Lawrie, Lawry see **Laurie**

Laws see **Lawes**

Lawson 'son of **Law** (ii)' [Nigel Lawson (Lord Lawson), 1932–, British Conservative politician; Nigella Lawson, 1960–, British journalist and broadcaster, daughter of Nigel; Wilfrid Lawson (original name Wilfred Worsnop), 1900–66, British actor]
— **lawsoniana** an alternative name for Lawson's cypress (see below)
— **Lawson's cypress** a conifer (*Chamæcyparis lawsoniana*) from southwest Oregon and northwest California first introduced to cultivation by Lawson and Son, a firm of Edinburgh nurserymen, after seeds had been collected in 1854 by the Scottish botanist Andrew Murray, 1812–78, who named the tree after the Lawsons (Peter Lawson, died 1820, and his son Charles, 1794–1873)

Lawton 'person from Lawton', Cheshire and Herefordshire ('settlement on or near a hill') [Tommy Lawton, 1919–96, English footballer]

Laxton 'person from Laxton', Northamptonshire, Nottinghamshire and Yorkshire ('Leaxa's settlement') [William Laxton, 1830–90, British horticulturist]
— **Laxton's Superb** a variety of late-ripening eating apple introduced in 1921 by Messrs Laxton of Bedford, a firm founded by the sons of William Laxton (see above)

Lay see **Ley**

Layborn, Laybourn see **Leyburn**

Laycock 'person from Laycock', Wiltshire and Yorkshire ('small stream'). See also **Leacock**

Layland see **Leyland**

Laytham see **Latham**

Layton, Leyton 'person from Layton', the name of numerous places in England (variously 'settlement by a water-course' and 'enclosure where leeks are grown')

Lazenby, Lasenby 'person from Lazenby or Lazonby', Yorkshire and Cumbria respectively ('farmstead of the freedmen') [George Lazenby, 1939–, Australian actor]

Lea see **Lee**

Leach (i) 'person who lives by a boggy stream' (from Old English *læcc* 'boggy stream'); (ii) *also* **Leech** 'doctor, physician' (from the therapeutic application of leeches) [Bernard Leach, 1887–1979, British potter; Johnny Leach, 1922–, British table-tennis player]

Leacock a different form of **Laycock** [Stephen Leacock, 1869–1944, British-born Canadian humorist]

Leadbeater a different form of **Leadbetter**

Leadbetter, Ledbetter 'worker in lead' (literally 'beater of lead') [Huddie Ledbetter ('Leadbelly'), 1888–1949, US folksinger and songwriter]

Leadbitter a different form of **Leadbetter**

Leader (i) 'person who leads a horse and cart'; (ii) 'worker in lead (the metal)'

Leaf, Leafe (i) from the Old English male personal name *Lēofa* and the female personal name *Lēofe*, both literally 'beloved'. See also **Leavis**; (ii) 'person who lives in an area of abundant foliage'; (iii) a translation of the Jewish name *Blatt* (from German *Blatt* or Yiddish *blat* 'leaf'); (iv) a translation of the Swedish name *Löf* or *Löv*, literally 'leaf', or of the first element of any of the various compound names that begin with it (e.g. *Löfgren*, literally 'leaf-branch')

Leahy, Leahey from Irish Gaelic *Ó Laochdha* 'descendant of *Laochdh*', a personal name based on *laoch* 'hero'

Leake, Leak, Leek (i) 'grower or seller of leeks'; (ii) 'person who lives by a brook' or 'person from Leak(e) or Leek', the name of various places in northern England (in either case from Old Norse *lœkr* 'brook')

Leakey a Somerset surname of unknown origin [Louis Leakey, 1903–72, British palaeontologist; Mary Leakey (*née* Nicol), 1913–96, British palaeontologist, wife of Louis; Richard Leakey, 1944–, Kenyan-born British palaeontologist, son of Louis]

Leal from a Spanish and Portuguese nickname for a loyal person (from Spanish and Portuguese *leal* 'loyal')

Leaman a different form of **Lemon**

Lean, Leane (i) from a medieval nickname for a thin person (from Middle English *lene* 'lean'); (ii) a shortened form of **McLean**; (iii) from Irish Gaelic *Ó Laighin* (see **Lane** (ii)), or *Ó Liatháin* (see **Lehane**) [Sir David Lean, 1908–91, British film director]

Leaper, Leeper different forms of **Leapman**

Leapman 'basket-maker' (from Old English *lēap-mann* 'basket-man')

Lear (i) 'person from Leire', Leicestershire ('place on the river *Leire*', a river-name that may also be the ancestor of *Leicester*); (ii) 'person from Lear', any of several variously spelled places in northern France with a name based on Germanic *lār* 'clearing' [Edward Lear, 1812–88, British artist and poet]

Learmonth, Learmont 'person from Learmonth', Borders, a place-name of uncertain origin

Leary from Irish Gaelic *Ó Laoghaire* 'descendant of *Laoghaire*', a nickname meaning literally 'keeper of the calves'. See also **O'Leary** [Timothy Leary, 1920–96, US psychologist and advocate of psychedelic drug use]

Leason see **Leeson**

Leatham a different form of **Latham**

Leathead see **Leithead**

Leather 'leatherworker' or 'seller of leather goods'

Leaver see **Lever**

Leavett, Leavitt see **Levett**

Leavey, Leavy see **Levy**

Leavis 'son of **Leaf** (i)' [F.R. Leavis, 1895–1978, British literary critic]
— **Leavisite** a follower or advocate of the literary theories of F.R. Leavis, especially in stressing the importance of a close reading of texts over a study of their authors' biographical and social backgrounds

Lebon, Le Bon from a medieval French nickname for a good person or (with heavy irony) a bad person (from Old French *le bon* 'the good') [Simon Le Bon, 1958–, British pop singer]

Le Carré from a medieval French nickname for a squat, thickset man (from Old French *le carré* 'the square'). See also **Quarry** (ii) [John Le Carré, pen-name of David Cornwell, 1931–, British novelist]

Leckie, Leckey 'person from Leckie', Aberdeenshire ('place of flagstones')

Leclerc 'scribe, secretary' (from French *le clerc* 'the clerk')

Ledbetter see **Leadbetter**

Lederer 'leatherworker, tanner' (from Middle High German *lēderære*)

Ledger (i) *also* **Leger** from the male personal name *Legier*, brought into England by the Normans but ultimately of Germanic origin and meaning literally 'tribe-spear'; (ii) a euphemistic alteration of the surname *Letcher* (a different form of **Leach** (i))

Lee (i) *also* **Lea** or **Leigh** 'person who lives by a meadow or area of arable land' (from Middle English *lee, lea*); (ii) *also* **Lea** or **Leigh** 'person from Lee, Lea or Leigh', the name of numerous places in England ('place by the wood or by the glade'); (iii) from Irish Gaelic *Ó Laoidhigh* 'descendant of *Laoidheach*', a personal name meaning literally 'poet'; (iv) *also* **Li** from the Chinese character *li* 'minister', as from the Chinese character *li* 'plum'. See also **Atlee, Lees** (i–ii), **Ley, Lye** [Adele Leigh, 1928–2004, British soprano; Brett Lee, 1976–, Australian cricketer; Bruce Lee (original name Lee Yuen Kam), 1940–73, US film actor and kung fu expert; Christopher Lee, 1922–, British actor; Gypsy Rose Lee (original name Rose Louise Hovick), 1914–70, US striptease dancer; Jennie Lee, 1904–88, British Labour politician; Laurie Lee, 1914–97, British writer; Lorelei Lee, the gold-digging heroine of Anita Loos's novel *Gentlemen Prefer Blondes* (played in the film version (1953) by Marilyn Monroe); Mike Leigh, 1943–, British film writer and director; Peggy Lee (original name Norma Deloris Egstrom), 1920–2002, US singer; Robert E. Lee, 1807–70, US Confederate commander in the Civil War; Spike Lee (original name Shelton Jackson Lee), 1957–, US film writer and director; Terry Lee, the young blond hero of the US comic strip *Terry and the Pirates*, created in 1934 by Milton Caniff;

Vivien Leigh (original name Vivien Hartley), 1913–67, British actress]

— **Gertie Lee** in bingo callers' rhyming slang, thirty-three. The rhyme is not known to have been based on any real person of that name.

— **Lea and Perrins** a British food producer. The Worcester pharmacists John Wheeley Lea, 1791–1874, and William Henry Perrins, 1793–1867, went into partnership in 1823, and first produced their renowned Worcestershire sauce in 1838. The firm is now owned by Heinz.

— **Lee Cooper** a brand of jeans, originally produced in 1946 and named by their manufacturer, Harold Cooper, after himself and his wife, whose maiden name was Daphne Leigh. The company had been founded in 1908 by Cooper's father, Morris Cooper, as M. Cooper Overalls Ltd.

— **Lee-Enfield** a type of rifle widely used by the British Army in the first half of the 20th century. It takes its name from James Lee, 1831–1904, the Scottish-Canadian inventor who designed its bolt action, and Enfield, the North London borough where the British Royal Small Arms Factory, designers of the rifling, was situated.

— **Peterlee** a town in County Durham, designated as a new town in 1948 and named in honour of the locally born mining trade-union leader Peter Lee, 1864–1935

— **Peters and Lee** see **Peters**

— **Robert E. Lees** (see above) rhyming slang for *knees*

— **Rosie Lee, Rosy Lee** rhyming slang for *tea*. The identity of the real Rosie Lee, if she ever existed, is not known. Other 'Lee' rhymes for *tea* are **Jenny Lee, Nancy Lee** and (from Australia) **Dicky Lee** and **Jimmy Lee**.

Leech see **Leach** (ii)

Leeds 'person from Leeds', Yorkshire ('place of the people who live by the (river) Lat')

Leek, Leeke see **Leake**

Leeman a different form of **Lemon**

Leeming (i) 'person from Leeming', Yorkshire ('place on the *Leeming* Beck', a river-name perhaps meaning 'bright stream'); (ii) a different form of **Lemon** [Jan Leeming, 1942–, British television presenter]

Leeper see **Leaper**

Lees, Leese, Leece (i) 'person who lives by meadows' (see **Lee** (i)); (ii) 'person from Lees', the name, variously spelled, of several places in England ('place by the woods' (see **Lee** (ii)); (iii) from the medieval female personal name *Lece*, a contracted form of *Lettice* (see **Lett**); (iv) a shortened form of **Gillies**

Leeson, Leason 'son of **Lees** (iii)' [Nick Leeson, 1967–, British fraudster]

Lefevre, Lefebvre, Lefever 'the ironworker, the blacksmith' (from Old French *le fevre* (from Latin *faber* (see **Faber**); the (silent) *b* in *-febvre* was imported from the Latin word)). See also **Fèvre**

Legard from the medieval female personal name *Legard*, brought into England by the Normans but descended from Germanic *Liutgard*, literally 'tribe enclosure'

Leger see **Ledger** (i)

Legg, Legge (i) 'person with remarkable legs (e.g. unusually long ones, or deformed ones)'; (ii) a different form of **Leigh** [Walter Legge, 1906–79, British record producer]

Leggatt, Leggat, Leggett, Legget, Leggitt, Leggate 'ambassador, representative' (Middle English, from Old French *legat*)

Legh see **Leigh**

Legrand a medieval nickname applied to a large person, or a distinguishing name for the senior, more important, etc. of two or more people with the same name (in both cases from Old French *le grand* 'the large one'). See also **Grand**

Lehane from Irish Gaelic *Ó Liatháin* 'descendant of *Liathán*', a personal name meaning literally 'little grey one'. See also **Lane** (ii), **Lean** (iii)

Lehmann (i) 'feudal tenant' (from Middle High German *lēheman*, literally 'loan-man'); (ii) *also* **Lehman** from the Jewish personal name *Lehman*, of uncertain origin [Beatrix Lehmann, 1903–79, British actress; Rosamond Lehmann, 1901–90, British novelist, sister of Beatrix]

Lehrer (i) 'teacher in a Jewish elementary school' (from German *Lehrer* and Yiddish *lerer* 'teacher'); (ii) 'person from Lehr', the name of various places in Germany ('marshy place') [Tom Lehrer, 1928–, US teacher and songwriter]

Leibowitz, Leibovitz 'son of *Leyb*', a Jewish male personal name meaning literally 'lion' [Annie Leibovitz, 1949–, US photographer]

Leicester, Lester 'person from Leicester', Leicestershire ('Roman town of the Ligore tribe'). See also **Lasseter** [Mark Lester, 1958–, British actor; Richard Lester, 1932–, US film director]

Leigh, Legh see **Lee** (i–ii). See also **Legg** (ii)

Leighton, Leyton 'person from Leighton', the name of various places in England (mostly 'enclosure where leeks are grown') [Frederic Leighton (Lord Leighton), 1830–96, British painter and sculptor; Kenneth Leighton, 1929–88, British composer; Margaret Leighton, 1922–76, British actress]

Leishman 'servant of *Leish*' (see **McLeish**)

— **leishmaniasis** an infection such as kala-azar and some other skin diseases that are caused by a protozoan that is a parasite in the tissue of vertebrates. It is named after the Scottish pathologist Sir William Boog Leishman, 1865–1926.

Leith 'person from Leith', near Edinburgh ('damp place') [Prue Leith, 1940–, British restaurateur and writer]

Leithead, Leithhead, Leathead 'person from the area at the head of the Water of Leith', a river which flows through Edinburgh

Lejeune 'the young', used originally to denote the younger of two people with the same name (from French)

Leland a reduced form of *McClelland* (see **McClellan**) [John Leland, ?1506–52, English antiquary]

Lely see **Lilly**

Lemon, Lemmon (i) from the medieval male personal name *Lefman*, from Old English *lēofman*, literally 'beloved man'; (ii) from a medieval nickname for a sweetheart or lover, from the same ultimate origin as (i); (iii) a different form of **Lamont**. See also **Leaman, Leeman, Leeming** [Jack Lemmon, 1925–2001, US actor]

Lenahan, Lenehan, Lenihan, Lenaghan from Irish Gaelic *Ó Leanacháin* 'descendant of *Leanachán*', a personal name possibly derived from *leann* 'cloak'

Lennon, Lennan from Irish Gaelic *Ó Leannáin* 'descendant of *Leannán*', a nickname meaning literally 'lover', or *Ó Lonáin* 'descendant of *Lonán*', a personal name meaning literally 'little blackbird'. See also **Lanigan, Leonard** [John Lennon, 1940–80, British pop musician and founding member of the Beatles]
— **Liverpool John Lennon Airport** Liverpool's airport. Originally Speke Airport, it was renamed in 2002 in honour of the Liverpudlian John Lennon.

Lennox, Lenox 'person from Lennox', ancient territory near Dumbarton ('place of many elms') [Annie Lennox, 1954–, British singer and songwriter]
— **Lennoxtown** a small town in East Dumbartonshire, established in the 1780s and taking its name from the local Lennox family (earls and dukes of Lennox)

Leonard, Lennard (i) from the male personal name *Leonard*, brought into England by the Normans but ultimately of Germanic origin, meaning literally 'lion-brave'; (ii) a different form of **Lennon** [Sugar Ray Leonard (original name Ray Charles Leonard), 1956–, US boxer]

Leopold from the male personal name *Leopold*, of Germanic origin and meaning literally 'people-brave'

Lepage 'the young male servant' (Old French, from *le page*)

Leppard, Lepperd, Leopard probably from a nickname for someone thought to resemble a leopard in some way, or possibly 'person who lives in a house with the sign of a leopard' [Raymond Leppard, 1927–, British conductor]

Lerner (i) 'pupil, apprentice' (from German *Lerner* 'learner'); (ii) 'student of the Talmud' (from Yiddish *lerner*); (iii) a different form of **Larner** (i) [Alan Jay Lerner, 1918–86, US playwright and lyricist]

Leroux from a medieval French nickname for someone with red hair (from Old French *le rous* 'the red-haired one')

Leroy 'servant of the king', or perhaps from a medieval French nickname for someone with regal airs (from Old French *le roy* 'the king')

Leslie, Lesley 'person from Leslie', in the former county of Aberdeenshire ('court of hollies') [Sir Shane Leslie (original name John Randolph Leslie), 1885–1971, Irish diplomat and writer]

Lester see **Leicester**

Lestrange, L'Estrange from a medieval French nickname for someone new to an area (from Old French *l'estrange* 'the foreign one'). See also **Strange**

Lethaby 'person from Lethaby', an unidentified place probably in northern England

Lethbridge 'person from Lethbridge', an unidentified place probably in southwestern England

Lett, Lette (i) from the medieval female personal name *Lett*, a shortened form of *Lettice* (from Latin *Laetitia*, literally 'happiness'); (ii) 'person who farms on clay' (from Middle High German *lette*) [Kathy Lette, 1958–, Australian author]

Letterman (i) *also* **Lettermann** 'person from Letter', near Hanover, Germany; (ii) from a medieval Dutch nickname for a short person (from Middle Dutch *lettel man*); (iii) *also* **Lettermann** a different form of **Lett** (ii) [David Letterman, 1947–, US comedian and talk-show host]

Letts 'son of **Lett** (i)'
— **Letts Diaries** a British brand of diary established by the stationer and printer John Letts, 1772–1851. He founded his business in 1796, and in 1812 produced the first example of the modern printed diary.

Letwin a different form of **Litwin** (ii) [Oliver Letwin, 1956–, British Conservative politician]

Leven, Levene, Levenson see **Levin, Levine, Levinson**

Lever, Leaver (i) 'person living in a place growing with rushes' (from Old English *lǣfer* 'rush, reed'); (ii) from a medieval Norman nickname for a swift-running or timorous person (from Old French *levre* 'hare'); (iii) perhaps from the Old English personal name *Lēofhere*, literally 'beloved army' [Harold Lever (Lord Lever), 1914–95, British lawyer and Labour politician; William Hesketh Lever (Viscount Leverhulme), 1851–1925, British soap manufacturer]
— **Lever Brothers** a soap-manufacturing company founded in 1885 by William Hesketh Lever (see above) and his brother James Lever. In 1930 it merged with the Dutch firm Margarine Unie to form **Unilever**, the world's first modern multinational company.
— **Leverburgh** a village and port on Harris, in the Western Isles, renamed after the islands of Lewis and Harris were bought by William Hesketh Lever (see above) in 1918. Its previous name was Obbe, and the local people themselves suggested the new name when it was learnt that Lord Leverhulme did not like *Obbe*.

Leveson see **Levison**

Levett, Levitt, Leavett, Leavitt (i) 'person from Livet', the name of various places in Normandy, of unknown origin; (ii) from the medieval personal name *Lefget* (from Old English *Lēofgēat*, literally 'beloved Geat' (a tribal name)); (iii) from a medieval Norman nickname based on Anglo-Norman *leuet* 'wolf cub'
— **Levittown** a post-Second World War US housing development area of a type pioneered by the building firm William Levitt and Sons. The

first was built in New York State between 1947 and 1951.

Levi, Levy from the Hebrew male personal name *Levi*, literally 'joining' [Peter Levi, 1931–2000, British poet and classical scholar]
— **Levy and Frank** rhyming slang for *wank*. The expression comes from the name of an old firm of London pub and restaurant proprietors, Levy and Franks.

Levin, Leven (i) from the German and Jewish personal name *Levin*, variously interpreted as a different form of German *Liebwin*, literally 'dear friend', and as a pet-form of the Jewish name *Löwe*, literally 'lion'; (ii) a Slavicized form of **Levi**; (iii) 'son of *Lëva*', a pet-form of the Russian personal name *Lev* [Bernard Levin, 1928–2004, British journalist]

Levine, Levene different forms of **Levin** [Harry Levene, 1898–1988, British boxing promoter; James Levine, 1943–, US conductor]

Levinson, Levenson 'son of **Levin** or of **Levi**'

Levis (i) 'person from Levis', in northern France; (ii) an anglicization of such Jewish surnames as **Levi** and **Levinson** [Carroll Levis, 1910–68, Canadian talent-show host]

Levison, Leveson 'son of **Levi**' [Leveson Gower, family name of Earl Granville; H.D.G. Leveson Gower, 1873–1954, English cricketer]

Levy (i) *also* **Leavy** from the medieval personal name *Lefwi* (from Old English *Lēofwīg*, literally 'beloved war'); (ii) see **Levi**

Lewin (i) from the medieval personal name *Lefwine* (from Old English *Lēofwīne*, literally 'dear friend'); (ii) from Irish Gaelic *Mac Giolla Guillin*, literally 'son of the servant of William'; (iii) from a German and Polish spelling of **Levin**

Lewins, Lewens 'son of **Lewin** (i)'

Lewinski, Lewinsky (i) 'person from Lewin, Lewino or Lewiny', various places in Poland; (ii) 'son of **Levin**' [Monica Lewinsky, 1973–, US political interne notorious for a sexual liaison with President Bill Clinton]

Lewis, Lewes (i) from the medieval personal name *Lowis*, brought into England by the Normans but ultimately of Germanic origin, and meaning literally 'fame-war' (its Latinized forms were *Lodovicus* and *Chlodovechus*, which evolved respectively into German *Ludwig* and French *Louis*); (ii) from Welsh **Llewellyn**; (iii) from Scottish and Irish Gaelic *Mac Lughaidh* 'son of *Lughaidh*', a personal name derived from *lugh* 'brightness'; (iv) 'person from Lewis', island in the Hebrides ('boggy place'); (v) an anglicization of various similar-sounding Jewish names [Carl Lewis, 1961–, US athlete; C.S. Lewis, 1898–1963, Irish-born British critic, scholar and novelist; G.H. Lewes, 1817–78, British author and literary critic; Gilbert Newton Lewis, 1875–1946, US chemist; Jerry Lee Lewis, 1935–, US rock-and-roll and country singer/songwriter and pianist; Jerry Lewis (original name Joseph Levitch), 1926–, US actor, screenwriter, film director and film producer; Lennox Lewis, 1965–, British boxer; Martyn

Lewis, 1945–, British television newsreader and presenter; Matthew Lewis ('Monk' Lewis), 1775–1818, British Gothic novelist; Richard Lewis (original name Thomas Thomas), 1914–90, British tenor; DS Robbie Lewis, Inspector Morse's long-suffering assistant in the police novels of Colin Dexter; Sinclair Lewis, 1885–1951, US novelist; Wyndham Lewis, 1882–1957, British painter, novelist and critic]
— **John Lewis Partnership** a British retail chain consisting of department stores and supermarkets (Waitrose – see **Waite**). It had its beginnings in a draper's shop set up in Oxford Street, London in 1864 by John Lewis, 1836–1928. Its corporate structure, in which its employees are all 'partners' in the business, was established in 1920 by Lewis's son John Spedan Lewis, 1885–1963.
— *Lewis* an ITV police drama series (2006–) based on the character Robbie Lewis (see above; played by Kevin Whateley), promoted to Detective Inspector after the 'death' of his boss Morse
— **Lewis acid** a substance that can accept a pair of electrons from a base to form a covalent bond. The name comes from Gilbert Newton Lewis (see above).
— **Lewis and Clark expedition** a notable journey of exploration across the American continent in 1804–06 by Meriwether Lewis, 1774–1809, and William Clark, 1770–1838
— **Lewis and Short** the name by which Charlton T. Lewis and Charles Short's Latin-English dictionary, first published in 1879, is commonly known.
— **Lewis and Witties** Australian rhyming slang for *titties*, based on the name of a well-known Melbourne department store, Lewis and Witty
— **Lewis base** a substance that can donate a pair of electrons to an acid to form a covalent bond; also, a substance that donates an electron pair to an acid during the formation of a covalent bond. The name comes from Gilbert Newton Lewis.
— **Lewis gun** a gas-powered machine gun with a circular magazine, first used during the First World War. It was named after its inventor, Colonel Isaac Newton Lewis, 1858–1931, of the US army.
— **lewisite** a colourless or brownish oily poisonous liquid ($C_2H_2AsCl_3$) that was used in gaseous form in chemical warfare during the First World War. It was named after the US chemist Winford Lee Lewis, 1878–1943, who developed procedures for producing it.
— **Lewis rule of eight** the observation that chemical elements react together by losing, gaining or sharing electrons so that they attain eight electrons in their outer shells. The name comes from Gilbert Newton Lewis.

Lewison 'son of **Lewis** (i–ii)'

Ley, Lay different forms of **Lee** (i–ii)

Leyburn, Leyborne, Leybourn 'person from Leyburn or Leybourne', Yorkshire and Kent ('stream with a shelter' and 'Lylla's stream' respectively)

Leyden, Leydon, Lydon from Irish Gaelic *Ó Loideáin* 'descendant of *Loideán*', a personal name of unknown origin and meaning [John Lydon

('Johnny Rotten'), 1956–, British (or possibly Irish) punk-rock singer]

Leyland, Layland 'person from Leyland', Lancashire, or 'person who lives on uncultivated land' (in either case ultimately from Old English *lǣgeland* 'land left uncultivated') [Maurice Leyland, 1900–67, English cricketer]

— **Leylandii** the common name for a rapidly growing hybrid conifer, *Cupressocyparis leylandii*, that is widely cultivated in gardens as a hedging plant and has become notorious for causing disputes between neighbours. In the vernacular it is the **Leyland cypress**. The name comes from the British sailor and horticulturist Christopher Leyland, 1849–1926, who first grew it from seedlings he discovered at Leighton Hall, Welshpool in 1888.

Leyton (i) 'person from Leyton', Essex ('farmstead on the (river) Lea'); (ii) see **Layton**; (iii) see **Leighton**

Li see **Lee** (iv)

Libby from the medieval female personal name *Libby*, a pet-form of *Elizabeth* or *Isabel*

— **Libbys** the brand name of tinned foodstuffs (fruit juices, corned beef, etc.) produced by the firm founded in 1868 by the brothers Arthur and Charles Libby, Chicago meat-packers

Liberman see **Liebermann** (ii)

Lichfield, Litchfield 'person from Lichfield', Staffordshire ('open land near Letocetum (a Roman station)'), or 'person from Litchfield', Hampshire (probably 'shelter ledge')

Lichtenstein, Liechtenstein (i) 'person from Lichtenstein or Liechtenstein', the name of various places in German-speaking territory ('bright stone'); (ii) an invented Jewish name based on German *Licht* 'light' and *Stein* 'stone' [Roy Lichtenstein, 1923–97, US painter, graphic artist and sculptor]

Liddell, Liddel, Lidell, Liddle, Liddall 'person from Liddell', the name of various places in northern England and the Scottish Borders ('valley of the loud stream') [Alice Liddell, 1852–1934, the model for Lewis Carroll's Alice; Sir Basil Liddell Hart, 1895–1970, British journalist and military strategist; Eric Liddell, 1902–45, British athlete and missionary, whose running exploits were recounted in the film *Chariots of Fire*]

— **Liddell and Scott** the name by which the Greek lexicon compiled by Henry Liddell, 1811–98 (father of Alice Liddell – see above), and Robert Scott, 1811–87, is commonly known. It was first published in 1843.

Liddiard 'person from Lydiard or Lydeard', Wiltshire and Somerset respectively ('grey ridge')

Liddiatt 'person from Liddiatt', the name of some variously spelled places in England, or 'person who lives by a gate leading from a ploughed field to a meadow' (in either case from Old English *hlid-geat*, literally 'swing-gate'). See also **Lidgett, Liggatt, Lydgate**

Liddy from Irish Gaelic *Ó Lideadha* 'descendant of *Lideadh*', a personal name of uncertain origin and meaning

Lidgett a different form of **Liddiatt**

Liebermann (i) from a medieval German and Jewish nickname for an agreeable person (German, literally 'dear man'); (ii) *also* **Lieberman** *or* **Liberman** from the Yiddish male personal name *Liberman*, literally 'dear man' (as (i))

Liechtenstein see **Lichtenstein**

Liggatt, Liggett different forms of **Liddiatt**

Light, Lyte from a medieval nickname for a cheerful person (from Middle English *lyght* 'bright, cheerful'), for a busy, bustling person (from Middle English *lyght* 'not heavy, nimble'), or for a small person (from Middle English *lite* 'small'). See also **Lightbody, Lightman**

Lightbody a Scottish and northern English variant of **Light**

Lightfoot from a medieval nickname for a fast runner [Terry Lightfoot, 1935–, British jazz clarinettist and bandleader]

Lightman, Lyteman different forms of **Light**. See also **Littman** (ii)

Lightoller 'person from Lightollers', Cheshire ('bright alders') [Herbert Lightoller, 1874–1952, Second Officer on *RMS Titanic*]

Lilburn, Lilburne 'person from Lilburn', Northumberland ('Lilla's stream') [Douglas Lilburn, 1915–2001, New Zealand composer; John Lilburne, ?1614–57, English political agitator and pamphleteer]

Lillicrap from a medieval nickname for someone with very fair hair (literally 'lily-head')

Lilly, Lilley, Lillie, Lillee, Lely (i) from the female personal name *Lilly* 'little Elizabeth'; (ii) 'person from Lilley', Berkshire and Hertfordshire (respectively 'wood associated with Lilla' and 'woodland clearing where flax is grown'); (iii) from a medieval nickname for someone with very fair hair or complexion (from Middle English *lilie* 'lily') [Beatrice Lillie (Lady Peel; original name Constance Sylvia Munston), 1898–1989, Canadian-born British actress; Dennis Lillee, 1949–, Australian cricketer; Colonel Eli Lilly, 1839–98, US soldier, chemist and industrialist, founder (1876) of the giant US pharmaceutical corporation that bears his name; Sir Peter Lely (original name Pieter van der Faes), 1618–80, German-born British portrait painter; Peter Lilley, 1943–, British Conservative politician]

— **Lilley and Skinner** a chain of British shoe shops that grew from a shop established in Southwark, London in 1835 by Thomas Lilley. The name has been used as rhyming slang for *dinner*.

Lillywhite from a medieval nickname for someone with very fair hair or complexion [James Lillywhite, 1842–1929, English cricketer, first captain of England; William Lillywhite, 1792–1854, English cricketer, pioneer of overarm bowling, uncle of James]

— **Lillywhite's** a sports goods shop at Piccadilly Circus, London. It was founded in 1863 by James

Lillywhite, 1825–82, son of William (see above), and moved to its present site in 1925.

Lime 'lime-burner' or 'whitewasher' (from Old English *līm* 'lime') [Harry Lime, the drug-racketeering villain (played by Orson Welles) in the film *The Third Man* (1949), scripted by Graham Greene]

Linacre, Linaker, Lineker, Liniker 'person who lives by a field in which flax is grown' or 'person from Linacre', Cambridgeshire and Lancashire (in either case from Old English *līn æcer* 'flax field') [Gary Lineker, 1960–, English footballer; Thomas Linacre, ?1460–1524, English physician and humanist]
— **Linacre College** a college of Oxford University, founded in 1962 and named after Thomas Linacre (see above)

Lincoln 'person from Lincoln', Lincolnshire ('Roman colony by the pool') [Abraham Lincoln, 1809–65, US Republican politician, president 1861–65]
— **Lincoln** in US slang, a five-dollar bill – from the portrait of Abraham Lincoln (see above) on the note

Lindberg, Lindbergh an invented Swedish name meaning literally 'lime-tree hill' [Charles Lindbergh, 1902–74, US aviator]

Lindemann, Lindeman 'person who lives by a lime tree' (from Middle High German *linde* 'lime tree')

Linden (i) *also* **Lindon** 'person from Linden or Lindon', the name of various places in England (either 'lime-tree hill' or 'flax hill'); (ii) 'person who lives by a group of lime trees' (from Middle High German and Dutch *linden* 'lime trees'). See also **McAlinden**

Lindgren an invented Swedish name meaning literally 'lime-tree branch'

Lindley, Linley 'person from Lindley or Linley', Shropshire, Wiltshire and Yorkshire ('woodland clearing where flax is grown'), or 'person from Lindley', Leicestershire and Yorkshire ('lime-tree wood')

Lindop 'person from Lindop', an unidentified place probably in Yorkshire ('enclosed valley growing with lime trees')

Lindsay, Lindsey, Linsey (i) 'person from Lindsay', Lincolnshire ('island of the Lindes (the people of Lincoln)'), or 'person from Lindsay', Suffolk ('Lelli's island'); (ii) an anglicization of a range of Irish Gaelic surnames, including *Ó Loingsigh* (see **Lynch**) and *Ó Floinn* (see **Flynn**) [Sir David Lindsay, ?1486–1555, Scottish poet; Norman Lindsay, 1879–1969, Australian painter, critic and novelist; Robert Lindsay, 1949–, British actor; Vachel Lindsay, 1879–1931, US poet]
— **Lindsay Quartet** a British string quartet formed in 1967 and latterly known simply as 'The Lindsays'. The name is in honour of Alexander Dunlop Lindsay (Lord Lindsay), 1879–1952, first principal of the University College of North Staffordshire, later Keele University, where it was the quartet in residence 1967–72. It disbanded in 2005.

Lindstrom an invented Swedish name meaning literally 'lime-tree river'

Lindwall an invented Swedish name meaning literally 'lime-tree bank' [Ray Lindwall, 1921–96, Australian cricketer]

Line, Lyne (i) from the medieval female personal name *Line*, a shortened form of various names (including *Adeline, Cateline* and *Emmeline*) ending in *-line*; (ii) 'person who lives by a lime tree' (from Middle English *line* 'lime tree')

Lineham see **Lyneham**

Lineker see **Linacre**

Linford 'person from Linford or Lynford', Buckinghamshire and Norfolk (perhaps 'maple ford' and 'flax ford' respectively)

Ling (i) 'person from Lyng', Norfolk ('hillside'); (ii) 'ice' (Chinese)

Link from a medieval German, Dutch and Jewish nickname for a left-handed person (Middle High German *linc*, Dutch *linker*, Yiddish *link* 'left')
— **Link trainer** a type of flight simulator invented in 1929 by the US pilot Edward A. Link, 1904–81.

Linklater 'person from Linklater', Orkneys ('rock growing with heather') [Eric Linklater, 1899–1974, British novelist]

Linsey see **Lindsay**

Linton 'person from Linton', the name of numerous places in England and the Scottish Borders (mostly 'farmstead where flax is grown')

Lipman, Lipmann, Lippmann from the Yiddish male personal name *Lipman*, literally 'dear man'. See also **Littman** [Maureen Lipman, 1946–, British actress; Walter Lippmann, 1889–1974, US journalist and political commentator]

Lippiatt, Lippiett 'person from Lypiatt or Lipiate', Gloucestershire and Somerset ('leap-gate' (i.e. a type of gate low enough to be jumped by horses but presenting an insurmountable obstacle to sheep and cattle))

Lipton 'person from Lipton', Devon (a name of uncertain origin and meaning) [Sir Thomas Johnstone Lipton, 1850–1931, British tea merchant and yachtsman, founder of the Lipton's tea brand and of the Lipton's chain of grocery shops]

Lisle, Lyle (i) 'person who lives on an island' (from Old French *l'isle* 'the island'); (ii) 'person from Lille', France ('the island'). See also **de Lisle**

Lister (i) 'dyer' (Middle English *lister* '(female) dyer', from *litten* 'to dye'); (ii) from Scottish Gaelic *Mac an Fleideir*, literally 'son of the arrow-maker' [Joseph Lister (Lord Lister), 1827–1912, British surgeon and pioneer of antisepsis]
— **Listerine** an antiseptic fluid developed around 1879 by the US pharmacist Jordan W. Lambert. Its proprietary name was based on that of Joseph Lister (see above), who was none too pleased by the appropriation.

Liston 'person from Liston', Essex ('Lissa's settlement'), or 'person from Liston', Midlothian and West Lothian (probably 'Lissa's settlement')

[Sonny Liston (original name Charles Liston), ?1917–70, US boxer]

Litchfield see **Lichfield**

Litherland 'person from Litherland', near Liverpool ('cultivated land on a slope')

Lithgow, Lithgoe 'person from Linlithgow', West Lothian ('lake in the damp hollow')

Little, Littell (i) from a medieval nickname for a small person, or a distinguishing name for the smaller of two people with the same name; (ii) a translation of the Scottish and Irish name **Begg**; (iii) a translation of names meaning literally 'small' in various European languages, including French **Petit** [Alastair Little, 1950–, British chef; Malcolm Little, the original name of the US black activist Malcolm X, 1925–65; Richard 'Bingo' Little, perennially love-sick character who makes frequent appearances in the Bertie Wooster stories of P.G. Wodehouse; Stuart Little, an anthropomorphized mouse, the eponymous hero of a children's novel (1945) by E.B. White, later (1999) filmed; Tasmin Little, 1965–, British violinist]
— **Vernon God Little** a novel (2003) by D.B.C. Pierre about the tribulations of an American teenager, Vernon Little, caught up in the aftermath of a school shooting

Littlejohn, Litteljohn a distinguishing name for the smaller of two people called 'John' [Richard Littlejohn, 1954–, British journalist]

Littler a distinguishing name for the smaller of two people with the same name [Prince Littler, 1901–73, British theatrical impresario]

Littleton, Lyttleton, Lyttelton 'person from Littleton', the name of numerous places, variously spelled, in England ('small farmstead') [Lyttelton, the family name of Viscount Chandos and of Viscount Cobham; Humphrey Lyttelton, 1921–, British jazz musician, journalist and broadcaster]
— **Lyttelton Theatre** the second largest auditorium of the Royal National Theatre, on the South Bank, London. Opened in 1976, it was named in honour of Oliver Lyttelton (Lord Chandos), 1893–1972, first chairman of the National Theatre board.

Littlewood 'person from Littlewood', Yorkshire ('small wood') [Joan Littlewood, 1914–2002, British theatre director]
— **Littlewoods** a British football-pools and retail (including mail-order) company. It was founded in Liverpool in 1923 by John (later Sir John) Moores (soon joined by his brother Cecil), Colin Askam (whose original name was Colin Henry Littlewood) and Bill Hughes. The retail side ceased trading in 2004.

Littleworth 'person from Littleworth', the name of various places in England ('small enclosure')

Littman, Littmann (i) from the Yiddish male personal name *Litman*, a different form of *Lipman* (see **Lipman**); (ii) a different form of **Lightman**

Litton, Litten, Lytton 'person from Litton', the name of various places in England ('farmstead by a noisy stream', 'farmstead on a slope' and 'farmstead by a gate') [Andrew Litton, 1959–, US conductor]

Litvin a different form of **Litwin** (ii)

Litwin, Littwin (i) from the Old English personal name *Lēohtwine*, literally 'bright friend'; (ii) 'person from Lithuania', country on the Baltic Sea (from Polish *Litwa* 'Lithuania'). See also **Letwin**

Liu 'person from the Chinese state of Liu'

Lively from a nickname for a lively person [Penelope Lively, 1933–, British author]

Livermore probably 'person from Livermere', Suffolk ('lake growing with rushes', or possibly 'liver-shaped lake')

Liversidge, Liversedge 'person from Liversedge', Yorkshire ('Lēofhere's ridge')

Livesey, Livsey, Livesay (i) 'person from Livesey', Lancashire ('shelter island'); (ii) perhaps from an Old English personal name *Lēofsige*, literally 'beloved victory' [Roger Livesey, 1906–76, British actor]

Livingston, Livingstone (i) 'person from Livingston', West Lothian ('Leving's farmstead'); (ii) from Gaelic *Ó Duinnshléibhe* and *Mac Duinnshléibhe* (see **Dunleavy**); (iii) an anglicization of **Lowenstein** [David Livingstone, 1813–73, British missionary and explorer; Ken Livingstone, 1945–, British Labour politician, mayor of London 2000–]

Llewellyn, Llewelyn, Llywelyn from the Old Welsh personal name *Llywelin* (probably a derivative of *llyw* 'leader') [Harry Llewellyn, 1911–99, British show jumper and equestrian; Laurence Llewelyn-Bowen, 1965–, British interior designer and television personality; Richard Llewellyn (original name Richard Llewellyn Lloyd), 1906–83, British novelist; Roddy Llewellyn, 1947–, British landscape gardener and sometime paramour of Princess Margaret]

Lloyd, Loyd from a medieval Welsh nickname for a grey-haired person, or for someone who usually wears grey clothes (from Welsh *llwyd* 'grey'). See also **Blood** (ii), **Flood**, **Floyd** [Andrew Lloyd Webber (Lord Lloyd Webber), 1948–, British composer of musicals; Clive Lloyd, 1944–, West Indian cricketer; David Lloyd, 1948–, British tennis player; David Lloyd George, 1863–1945, British Liberal politician, prime minister 1914–22; Harold Lloyd, 1893–1971, US film comedian; John Lloyd, 1954–, British tennis player, brother of David; Julian Lloyd Webber, 1951–, British cellist, brother of Andrew; Marie Lloyd (original name Matilda Wood), 1870–1922, British music-hall entertainer]
— **Lloyd's** a British association of insurance underwriters, incorporated by Act of Parliament in 1871. It is named after the 17th-century London coffee house, owned by Edward Lloyd, where underwriters used to meet.
— **Lloyd's Bank** a British clearing bank founded (as Taylor and Lloyd's Bank) in Birmingham in 1677 by Charles Lloyd (born 1637) and John Taylor. In 1995 it merged with TSB to become **Lloyds TSB**.
— **Lloyd's Register of Shipping** an annual publication issued by Lloyd's (see above) that reports on

the condition (for insurance purposes) of all ocean-going vessels over 100 tonnes. Ships in first-class condition are rated '**A1 at Lloyd's**'.

Lo from the name of the ancient states of Lu and Luo in China

Loach from a medieval nickname for someone thought to resemble a loach (a type of freshwater fish) [Kenneth Loach, 1936–, British film director]

Loader, Loder 'person who lives by a road or waterway' (from a derivative of Middle English *lode* 'path, road, waterway'); also, 'person who transports things, carter' (from a derivative of Middle English *loden* 'to carry')

Lobb, Lobbe 'person from Lobb', Devon (perhaps 'lump, hill')

Lock, Locke (i) 'lockmaker'. See also **Lockyer**; (ii) 'person who lives by a lockable enclosure'; (iii) 'lock-keeper'; (iv) from a medieval nickname for someone with a fine head of curly hair; (v) a Scottish and northern English variant of **Lucas** [John Locke, 1632–1704, English philosopher; Josef Locke, 1917–99, Irish tenor; Matthew Locke, born ?1622, English composer; Tony Lock, 1929–95, English cricketer]

Locket, Lockett from a northern English pet-form of **Lucas**

Lockhart, Lockart (i) 'herdsman in charge of an animals' enclosure' (from Old English *loc* 'animals' enclosure, fold' and *hierde* 'herdsman'). The account of the exploits of Sir Simon Locard of Lee, who in the early 14th century supposedly carried the heart of Robert the Bruce back from Spain to Scotland, had it interred in Melrose Abbey and subsequently changed his surname to Lockheart and adopted the family motto *Corda serrata pando* ('I open locked hearts'), owes more to myth than to reality.; (ii) perhaps from a Germanic personal name meaning literally 'lock-brave' [Sir Bruce Lockhart, 1887–1970, British diplomat and writer; Gilderoy Lockhart, flamboyant teacher of Defence against the Dark Arts at Hogwarts in the Harry Potter novels of J.K. Rowling; Chief Supt. Tom Lockhart, Scotland Yard detective (played by Raymond Francis) in several ITV series in the 1950s and 1960s (beginning with *Murder Bag* (1957–59))]

Locklear probably a different form of **Lockyer**

Lockwood 'person from Lockwood', Yorkshire (probably 'wood within an enclosure') [Margaret Lockwood (original name Margaret Lockwood Day), 1916–90, British actress]

Lockyer, Lockyear different forms of **Lock** (i). See also **Locklear** [Sir Joseph Lockyer, 1836–1920, British astronomer]

Loder see **Loader**

Lodge 'person who lives in a lodge' (Middle English *logge* generally denoted a temporary structure, especially one lived in by masons during a construction project) [David Lodge, 1935–, British novelist, critic and scholar; Henry Cabot Lodge, 1850–1924, US Republican politician; Sir Oliver Lodge, 1851–1940, British physicist; Thomas

Lodge, 1558–1625, English poet, dramatist and writer]

Loeb from a medieval German or Jewish nickname for a strong man, or 'person who lives in a house with the sign of a lion' (in either case from Middle High German *lebe* 'lion') [Jacques Loeb, 1859–1924, German-born US zoologist]

Loewe (i) from a medieval German nickname for a strong man, or 'person who lives in a house with the sign of a lion' (in either case from Middle High German *lewe* 'lion'); (ii) an invented Jewish name based on German *Löwe* 'lion' [Frederick Loewe, 1904–88, Austrian-born US composer of musicals]

Loewenstein see **Lowenstein**

Loewenthal see **Lowenthal**

Lofthouse a different form of **Loftus** (i) [Nat Lofthouse, 1925–, English footballer]

Lofts a different form of **Loftus** (i)

Loftus (i) 'person from Loftus or Lofthouse', Yorkshire ('house with an upper storey'); (ii) from Irish Gaelic *Lachlann* (see **Laughlan**) or *Ó Lachtnáin* (see **Lough**)

Logan (i) 'person from Logan', the name of various places in Scotland ('small hollow'); (ii) from Irish Gaelic *Ó Leocháin* 'descendant of *Leochán*', a personal name of unknown origin [Jimmy Logan, 1928–2001, Scottish entertainer; Kenny Logan, 1972–, Scottish rugby footballer]

— **loganberry** the large edible berry of a bramble-like shrub that is a cross between a raspberry and a blackberry. It is named after the US horticulturist James H. Logan, 1841–1928, who developed it.

— **Logan International Airport** the main airport of Boston, Massachusetts, USA, opened in 1923 (as Boston Airport) and renamed in 1956 after General Edward Lawrence Logan, 1875–1939, Boston-born hero of the Spanish-American War

— **Logan's Run** a novel (1967) by William F. Nolan and George Clayton Johnson, set in a post-nuclear Earth in the year 2319. The hero Logan seeks to escape the now mandatory termination of life at the age of 30. It was made into a film (1976) starring Michael York.

— **Mount Logan** the highest peak in Canada (5959 m/19,551 ft), in the St Elias Range in southwestern Yukon Territory. It was named in honour of the Canadian geologist Sir William Logan, 1798–1875.

Logie 'person from Logie', the name of various places in Scotland ('hollow place')

— **Jimmy Logie** rhyming slang for *bogie* (in the nasal sense). The name is that of the Arsenal footballer Jimmy Logie, 1919–84.

Lomas a different form of **Lomax**

Lomax 'person from Lomax', a place, now lost, in Lancashire (probably 'nook of land with a pool'). See also **Loomis** [Alan Lomax, 1915–2002, US ethnomusicologist; John Lomax, 1867–1948, US ethnomusicologist, father of Alan]

Lombard (i) 'person from Lombardy', Italy; (ii) 'banker, money-lender' (the occupation of many Italian immigrants in England in the Middle Ages)

[Carole Lombard (original name Jane Alice Peters), 1908–42, US film actress]

London (i) 'person from London', UK; (ii) an invented Jewish name, possibly based on Hebrew *lamdon* 'Talmudic scholar' [Brian London (original name Brian Harper), 1934–, British boxer; Jack London, 1876–1916, US novelist; Julie London (original name Gayle Peck), 1926–2000, US singer and actress]

Loney a different form of **Looney**

Long (i) from a medieval nickname for a tall person. See also **Lang**, **Longman**; (ii) from Irish Gaelic *Ó Longáin* (see **Langan**); (iii) from the name of an official treasurer called Long, who lived in the reign of the Chinese emperor Shun (2257–05 BC) [Huey Long ('Kingfish'), 1893–1935, populist US politician]

● Men with the surname Long are traditionally nicknamed 'Shorty'

Longbottom, Longbotham 'person who lives in a long valley' (from Middle English *long bodme* 'long valley')

Longden 'person from Longden', the name of various places in England ('long valley')

Longdon a different form of **Langdon**

Longfellow from a medieval nickname for a tall and convivial man [Henry Wadsworth Longfellow, 1807–82, US poet]

Longfield 'person who lives by or in a large area of open country or pastureland'

Longford a different form of **Langford**

Longhurst 'person from Longhurst', the name of various places in England ('long wooded hill') [Henry Longhurst, 1909–78, British golf writer and commentator]

Longley a different form of **Langley**

Longman a different form of **Long** (i)
— **Longman** a British publishing firm, founded in 1724 by Thomas Longman, 1699–1755. It is now part of Pearson Education Ltd.

Longmire 'person who lives in a large area of marshland'

Longmuir a Scottish variant of **Longmire**

Longstaff (i) 'person who carries a long staff as a symbol of office'; (ii) from a medieval nickname for a tall thin man, or possibly for a man with a large penis

Longworth 'person from Longworth', the name of various places in England ('long enclosure')

Lonsdale 'person from Lonsdale', Cumbria and Lancashire ('valley of the (river) Lune') [Gordon Lonsdale (real name Konon Trofimovich Molody), 1924–70, Soviet secret agent in the UK, 1954–61; Dame Kathleen Lonsdale, 1903–71, Irish physicist]

Loomis a different form of **Lomax** [R.S. Loomis, 1887–1966, US literary scholar]

Looney from Irish Gaelic *Ó Luanaigh* 'descendant of *Luanach*', a personal name derived from *luan* 'warrior'. See also **Loney**

Lopez 'son of *Lope*', a medieval Spanish personal name perhaps descended ultimately from Latin *lupus* 'wolf' [Jennifer Lopez, 1969–, US actress and singer]

Lord (i) 'landlord' or 'lord of the manor'; (ii) 'servant in a lord's household'; (iii) 'person who plays the part of a lord (e.g. as the "Lord of Misrule")'; (iv) from a medieval nickname for someone who gave himself aristocratic airs; (v) a translation of Irish Gaelic *Ó Tighearnaigh* (see **Tierney**) and *Mac Thighearnáin* (see (**McKiernan**)) [Cyril Lord, 1911–84, British carpet manufacturer; Jack Lord (original name John Joseph Patrick Ryan), 1920–98, US actor]
— **Cyril Lord** (see above) British rhyming slang for *bald* (reflecting an *l*-less Cockney pronunciation)
— **Lord's** a cricket ground in St John's Wood, London, widely regarded as the headquarters of the game. It was founded in White Conduit Fields, Islington by the cricketer and entrepreneur Thomas Lord, 1755–1832. It subsequently transferred to Dorset Square, and moved to its present site in 1814.

Lorimer, Lorrimer 'maker or seller of metal items of a horse's harness and associated equipment (e.g. bits and spurs)' (from Anglo-Norman *loremier*, a derivative of Old French *lorain* 'harness')

Lorrie, Lorie different forms of **Lowry**

Loss (i) 'person who lives in an area of marshland' (from Middle High German *los* 'marsh'); (ii) from the German male personal name *Loss*, a pet-form of *Ludwig* (see **Lewis** (i)) [Joe Loss, 1909–90, British bandleader]

Lothian 'person from Lothian', a region in southeastern Central Scotland. The origin of its name is unknown. See also **Lowden** (ii)

Lott, Lotte (i) from the medieval person name *Lott*, brought into England by the Normans but of uncertain ultimate origin (perhaps from Hebrew *Lot*, literally 'covering'); (ii) 'person who owns a plot of land' (from Middle English *lotte* 'share, portion') [Dame Felicity Lott, 1947–, British soprano]

Loud, Lowde (i) 'person from Louth', Lincolnshire ('(place by the river) Lud', literally 'loud stream'); (ii) 'person who lives by a loud stream' (from Old English *hlȳde* 'loud one'); (iii) from a medieval nickname for a noisy person

Louden see **Lowden**

Lough from Irish Gaelic *Ó Lachtnáin* 'descendant of *Lachtnán*', a personal name derived from *lachtna* 'grey' [Ernest Lough, 1911–2000, British boy soprano]

Loughlan, Loughlin see **Laughlan**

Loughran from Irish Gaelic *Ó Luchaireáin* 'descendant of *Luchaireán*', a personal name derived from *luchair* 'radiance' [James Loughran, 1931–, British conductor]

Louis from the French male personal name *Louis* (see **Lewis** (i)) [Joe Louis, 1914–81, US boxer]

Lovatt, Lovat, Lovett (i) 'person from Lovat', Highland region ('place of putrefaction'); (ii) from a medieval nickname for a rapacious or cunning person (from Anglo-Norman *louvet* 'young wolf') [William Lovett, 1800–77, British Chartist leader]

Love (i) from the Old English male personal name *Lufa* and the female personal name *Lufu*, both literally 'beloved'; (ii) from a medieval nickname based on Anglo-Norman *louve* 'female wolf', often applied (approvingly) to men. See also **Luff** [Courtney Love (original name Courtney Michelle Harrison), 1964–, US rock musician and actress; Geoff Love, 1917–91, British band leader]

Loveday (i) 'person particularly associated with a "loveday"' (a day when, by custom, old differences were settled and reconciliations were made); (ii) from the medieval female personal name *Loveday*, a descendant of Old English *Lēofdæg*, literally 'beloved day'
— **'Mr Loveday's Little Outing'** a short story (1936) by Evelyn Waugh that culminates in the brief but calamitous release of a homicidal maniac from his asylum

Lovegrove 'person from Lovegrove', the name of an unidentified place ('Lufa's grove')

Lovejoy from a medieval nickname for someone addicted to pleasure
— *Lovejoy* a BBC television comedy drama (1986–94) starring Ian McShane as Lovejoy, a slightly dodgy antiques dealer cum amateur detective. The character originally appeared in a series of comic mystery novels (the first in 1977) by Jonathan Cash.

Lovelace, Loveless from a medieval nickname for a woman-chaser or lothario (from Old English *lufuléas*, literally 'without love', hence 'fancy-free') [Richard Lovelace, 1618–57, English poet]

Lovell, Lovel from a medieval nickname for a rapacious or cunning person (literally 'little wolf', from Anglo-Norman *louel*). See also **Lowell** [Sir Bernard Lovell, 1913–, British astronomer]

Lovelock from a medieval nickname for a dandy or a man conceited about his appearance (from *lovelock*, a term for an elaborately curled lock of hair) [James Lovelock, 1919–, British scientist, formulator of the 'Gaia' concept]

Lovett see **Lovatt**

Low, Lowe (i) 'person who lives near a hill' (from Old English *hlāw* 'hill'); (ii) from a medieval nickname for a short man (from Middle English *lāh* 'low'), or for a rapacious or cunning person (from Anglo-Norman *lou* 'wolf'). See also **Lovatt** (ii), **Love** (ii), **Lovell**; (iii) from a Scottish pet-form of **Lawrence**. See also **Lowson**; (iv) an anglicization of **Loewe** (ii) [Arthur Lowe, 1915–82, British actor; Sir David Low, 1871–1963, New Zealand-born British cartoonist; John Lowe, 1945–, British darts player; Rob Lowe, 1964–, US actor]
— **Jimmy Low** a colloquial Australian name for the red mahogany tree, *Eucalyptus resinifera*. It appears to have been based on that of a 19th-century Queenslander called James Low.

Lowden, Lowdon, Louden, Loudon (i) 'person from Loudoun', Ayrshire (probably 'beacon hill'); (ii) a different form of **Lothian**

Lowell a different form of **Lovell** [Amy Lawrence Lowell, 1874–1925, US poet and critic; James Russell Lowell, 1819–91, US poet, critic and diplomat; Percival Lowell, 1855–1916, US astronomer; Robert Lowell, 1917–77, US poet]
— **Lowell** a city in Massachusetts, historically one of the most important textile centres in the USA. It was named in honour of the textile manufacturer Francis Cabot Lowell, 1775–1817.

Lowenstein, Loewenstein an invented Jewish name meaning literally 'lion-stone'. See also **Livingston** (iii)

Lowenthal, Loewenthal an invented Jewish name meaning literally 'lion-valley'

Lownes, Lowns, Lowndes 'son of *Lovin*', a medieval personal name descended from Old English *Lēofhūn*, literally 'beloved bear cub' [Belloc Lowndes, see **Belloc**]
— **Lowndes Estate** an area of land to the south of Hyde Park, London, originally purchased the early 1720s by William Lowndes, 1652–1724, Secretary to the Treasury, and developed by his grandson (also William) in the 1820s. It includes **Lowndes Square**.

Lowry, Lowery, Lowrey (i) 'little **Lawrence**'; (ii) from Irish Gaelic *Ó Labhradha* (see **Lavery**). See also **Lorrie** [L.S. Lowry, 1887–1976, British painter; Malcolm Lowry, 1909–57, British novelist]

Lowson 'son of **Low** (iii)'

Lowther 'person from Lowther', Cumbria ('place on the (river) Lowther', perhaps from a Scandinavian river-name meaning 'foaming river')

Lu 'person from Lu', an ancient Chinese state in present-day Henan province, and also an area in present-day Shandong province

Lubbock 'person from Lübeck', a port in north-western Germany, or from a medieval nickname for a merchant who had regular business connections with Lübeck [Eric Lubbock (Lord Avebury), 1928–, British Liberal politician]

Lucas from the personal name *Lucas*, a latinization of Greek *Loucas*, literally 'man from Lucania' (a region of southern Italy). See also **Clucas, Lock** (v), **Lugg, Luke** [E.V. Lucas, 1868–1938, British journalist and essayist; George Lucas, 1944–, US film director and producer; Matt Lucas, 1974–, British comic actor]
— **Lucas** a British producer of lamps, batteries, etc. founded by Joseph Lucas, 1834–1902, who set up a shop selling household goods in Birmingham in 1860

Luce a different form of **Lucey** (i) [Clare Boothe Luce (*née* Boothe), 1903–87, US playwright, Republican politician and diplomat, wife of Henry; Henry F. Luce, 1898–1967, US publisher, co-founder of *Time* magazine]

Lucey, Lucy, Lucie (i) from the medieval female personal name *Lucie* (ultimately from Latin *Lūcia*, the feminine form of *Lūcius*, probably a derivative of *lux* 'light'); (ii) 'person from Lucey', the name of various places in northern France ('place associated with Lucius' (see ii)); (iii) from Irish Gaelic *Ó Luchaireáin*, itself an alteration of *Mac Clusaigh* 'son of *Clusach*', a nickname derived from *cluas* 'ear' and denoting someone with large ears [Edward Lucie-Smith, 1935–, Jamaican-born British poet and art critic]

Luff a different form of **Love**

Lugg a southwestern English variant of **Lucas**

Luke a different form of **Lucas**

Luker (i) 'person whose job is keeping a look-out' (from Middle English *lukere* 'looker'); (ii) 'person from Lucker', Northumberland ('marsh with a pool')

Lumb, Lum 'person from Lumb', Lancashire and Yorkshire ('place by a pool')

Lumley, Lumbley 'person from Lumley', County Durham ('glade with a pool') [Joanna Lumley, 1946–, British actress]

Lumsden, Lumsdaine 'person from Lumsden', Berwickshire (probably 'Lum's valley')

Lund 'person who lives in a grove' (from Old Norse *lundr* 'grove'). See also **Lunn**, **Lunt**

Lundgren from an invented Swedish name meaning literally 'grove branch'

Lundquist from an invented Swedish name meaning literally 'grove twig'

Lundy, Lundie (i) 'person from Lundie', the name of various places in Scotland ('place by a marsh'); (ii) a different form of **McAlinden**

Lunn a different form of **Lund** [Sir Arnold Lunn, 1888–1974, British skier, mountaineer and writer, son of Henry; Sir Henry Lunn, 1859–1939, British humanitarian and Methodist leader, pioneer of winter-sports holidays]
— **Lunn Poly** a British travel company formed in the 1960s by the combination of Sir Henry Lunn Travel (founded by Henry Lunn – see above) with the Polytechnic Touring Association. In 1972 it was taken over by the Thomson Travel Group, and in 2004 its name finally disappeared.
— **Sally Lunn** a large bun or teacake made with yeast dough including cream, eggs and spice. The name reputedly comes from that of a late 18th-century Bath baker called Sally Lunn.

Lunsford 'person from Lundsford', Sussex ('Lundræd's ford')

Lunt a northern English variant of **Lund** [Alfred Lunt, 1892–1977, US actor]

Lupton 'person from Lupton', Cumbria ('Hluppa's enclosure')

Lurie (i) a Scottish variant of **Lowry**; (ii) a Jewish name perhaps meaning 'person from Loria or Luria', the name of two places in Italy [Alison Lurie, 1926–, US novelist and scholar]

Luscombe 'person from Luscombe', Devon ('pigsty valley')

Lush perhaps 'the gate-keeper' (from Old French *l'ussier* – see **Usher**)

Lustgarten an invented Jewish name based on German *Lustgarten* 'pleasure garden' (perhaps alluding to the Garden of Eden) [Edgar Lustgarten, 1907–78, British barrister, writer and broadcaster, presenter of television crime reconstructions]

Lustig from a medieval German nickname for a cheerful person (from Middle High German *lustig* 'cheerful')

Luton 'person from Luton', Bedfordshire ('farmstead on the (river) Lea')

Lutton 'person from Lutton', the name of numerous places in England (variously 'estate associated with Luda' and 'pool settlement')

Luttrell 'person who hunts otters', or from a medieval nickname for someone thought to resemble an otter (from Old French *loutrel* 'little otter')
— **Luttrell Psalter** a richly illuminated manuscript psalter (now British Library Additional MS 42130) commissioned by the Lincolnshire landowner Sir Geoffrey Luttrell, 1276–1345, and produced between about 1325 and 1335. Its illustrations document rural life of the period.

Lutwyche, Lutwidge 'person from Lutwyche', Shropshire (perhaps 'outlying village in which drainage shovels are much in use')

Lutyens from a pet-form of a compound Germanic personal name with either *liut*- 'people' or *hlod*- 'famous' as its first element [Sir Edwin Lutyens, 1869–1944, British architect; Elisabeth Lutyens, 1906–83, British composer, daughter of Edwin]

Luxford 'person from Luxford', the name of an unidentified place in England (probably 'Luke's ford')

Luxmoore, Luxmore 'person from Luxmoore', the name of an unidentified place, probably in Devon (probably 'Luke's marsh')

Luxon perhaps a different form of **Luxton** [Benjamin Luxon, 1937–, British baritone]

Luxton 'person from Luxton', Devon ('Luke's settlement')

Lyall, Lyal, Lyell, Lyel, Lyle probably from the Old Norse personal name *Liulfr*, of which the second element (-*ulfr*) meant 'wolf' [Sir Charles Lyell, 1797–1875, British geologist; Sandy Lyle, 1958–, British golfer]

Lydgate, Lidgate different forms of **Liddiatt** [John Lydgate, ?1370–?1450, English poet]

Lydon see **Leyden**

Lye a different form of **Lee** (i–ii) [Len Lye, 1901–80, New Zealand artist]

Lyell, Lyel see **Lyall**

Lyle (i) see **Lisle**; (ii) see **Lyall**
— **Tate and Lyle** see **Tate**

Lynam see **Lyneham**

Lynch (i) from Irish Gaelic *Ó Loingsigh* 'descendant of *Loingseach*', a personal name meaning literally 'mariner'; (ii) from Irish Gaelic *Linseach*, a gaelicization of the Anglo-Norman surname *de Lench*, which was probably based on an unidentified Norman place-name; (iii) 'person who lives on a slope or hillside', or 'person from Lynch or Linch', Somerset and Sussex respectively (in either case ultimately from Old English *hlinc* 'slope, hillside') [Bet Lynch, buxom barmaid at the Rovers Return in the Granada Television soap opera *Coronation Street* (1960–); David Lynch, 1946–, US film director; Jack Lynch, 1917–99, Irish Fianna Fáil politician, prime minister 1966–73, 1977–79; Kenny Lynch, 1939–, British entertainer, singer and actor]

— **lynch law** the condemnation and punishment of someone by a mob or self-appointed group without a legal trial. The term commemorates Captain William Lynch, 1742–1820, a planter and justice of the peace of Pittsylvania, Virginia, USA, who took it upon himself to set up unofficial tribunals to try suspects. The verb *lynch* itself (based on *lynch law*) dates from the 1830s.

Lyndon 'person from Lyndon', Rutland ('hill growing with lime trees')

— *Barry Lyndon* a novel (1844) by W.M. Thackeray, recounting the career of an Irish adventurer (his original name was Redmond Barry; he acquired the surname Lyndon when he married the countess of Lyndon, a wealthy foolish widow)

Lyne (i) see **Line**; (ii) an Irish variant of **Lane**; (iii) 'person from Lyne', Borders ('place by a pool or stream'). See also **Lynn** (iii) [Adrian Lyne, 1941–, British filmmaker and producer]

Lyneham, Lynham, Lynam, Lineham (i) 'person from Lyneham', the name of various places in southern England ('homestead or enclosure where flax is grown'); (ii) from Irish Gaelic *Ó Laidhgh-neáin* 'descendant of *Laidhghneán*', a personal name perhaps meaning literally 'snowflake' [Desmond Lynam, 1942–, British radio and television presenter]

Lynn, Lynne (i) 'person from King's Lynn', Norfolk ('district by the pool'); (ii) from Irish Gaelic *Mac Fhloinn* and *Ó Fhloinn* (see **Flynn**); (iii) a Scottish variant of **Lyne** (iii); (iv) an anglici-

zation of the Jewish surname *Linn* or *Lin*, which is of unknown origin [Jonathan Lynn, 1943–, British actor, writer and director; Ralph Lynn, 1882–1964, British actor and farceur; Dame Vera Lynn (*née* Welch), 1917–, British singer]

— **Ralph/Vera Lynn** (see above) rhyming slang for *gin*

Lyon (i) from a medieval nickname for someone known for their lion-like bravery or ferocity; (ii) from the medieval English and French male personal name *Leon*, literally 'lion'; (iii) 'person from Lyon or Lyons', France (see also **Dillon** (iii)); (iv) from Irish Gaelic *Ó Laighin* (see **Lane** (ii)) [Ben Lyon, 1901–79, US actor and film executive; Bowes Lyon, see **Bowes**]

— *Life with the Lyons* a British radio and television sitcom of the 1950s and early 1960s featuring the doings of Ben Lyon (see above), his wife Bebe Daniels and their family

Lyons a different form of **Lyon** (iii) [Sir John Lyons, 1932–, British theoretical linguist; Joseph Aloysius Lyons, 1879–1939, Australian politician, prime minister 1931–39; Sir Joseph Nathaniel Lyons, 1848–1917, British business executive]

— **J. Lyons and Co.** a British food production and catering company, founded in 1878 by Joseph Lyons (see above) and others. In the first part of the 20th century it was the largest such company in Europe. It was particularly famous for its chain of modest restaurants, known as **Lyons Corner-houses**, the first of which opened in Piccadilly, London in 1894. In 1978 it merged with Allied Breweries to become **Allied Lyons**. The name (often affectionately colloquialized to 'Joe Lyons') finally disappeared in 1998.

Lyte, Lyteman see **Light, Lightman**

Lyttelton, Lyttleton see **Littleton**

M

Ma from an element in the honorific title awarded to a prince in the Chinese state of Zhao in the period 403–221 BC

Mabbett, Mabbitt, Mabbutt from a pet-form of the medieval female personal name *Mabbe*, a shortened form of *Amabel* (ultimately from Latin *amābilis* 'lovable'). See also **Mapp**

Mabey (i) from the French female personal name *Amable* (ultimately from Latin *amābilis*; see **Mabbett**); (ii) perhaps from a pet-form of *Mabbe* (see **Mabbett**) [Richard Mabey, 1941–, British writer and broadcaster]

Mabon, Maben from the medieval Scottish male personal name *Maban* or *Mabon*, literally perhaps 'great son'

Mac-, Mc- from Goidelic (northern) Celtic *mac* 'son'. Prefixed to a personal name or nickname (e.g. *Diarmaid*) it forms a surname (*McDiarmid* – i.e. 'son of Diarmaid'). It is particularly characteristic of Scottish and Manx Gaelic, but it also occurs in Irish Gaelic names. Its spelling is sometimes reduced to simply *M'* (e.g. *M'Naughton* for *McNaughton*).
— **Mac** since at least the early 17th century, a colloquial term for a Scottish person or an Irish person. Its US slang use as a term of address to a man, especially one whose name is unknown, emerged in the early 20th century. See also **McDonald, McIntosh**
— **Mac Fisheries** a chain of British fishmongers shops established by Lord Leverhulme in 1919. The 'Mac' was intended to suggest the Scottish source of the fish (Lord Leverhulme had recently bought the islands of Lewis and Harris, in the Outer Hebrides, and wished to encourage local fisheries). The shops disappeared from the high street in the 1980s.

McAdam, MacAdam from Gaelic, 'son of **Adam**' [John Loudon McAdam, 1756–1836, British civil engineer, inventor of the macadam road surface (see below)]
— **macadam** a smooth hard road surface made from small pieces of stone in compressed layers. It is named after John Loudon McAdam (see above), who developed it in the early 19th century. Towards the end of the century, by which time tar or bitumen was standardly being used to keep the top layer of gravel in place, it came to be called **tarmacadam**. The tradename **Tarmac**, for a kind of tarmacadam consisting of iron slag impregnated with tar and creosote, was registered in 1903.
— **macadamia** an evergreen tree (genus *Macadamia*) of Australia and Southeast Asia cultivated for its waxy edible nuts. Its name commemorates the Scottish-born Australian chemist John Macadam, 1827–65.

MacAfee, McAfee 'son of **Duffy** (ii)'

McAlinden from Irish Gaelic *Mac Giolla Fhiontáin* 'son of the servant of (St) *Fiontán*', a personal name derived from *fionn* 'white'

McAllister, MacAllister, McAlister, McAllaster, McCallister from Gaelic, 'son of *Alasdair*', a Scottish variant of **Alexander**

McAlpine, MacAlpine from Scottish and Irish Gaelic, 'son of *Ailpean*', a personal name perhaps derived from *alp* 'lump' [Kenneth I McAlpine, died *c*. 858, king of the Scots; Sir Robert McAlpine, 1847–1934, British engineer, founder of the UK construction company that bears his name]

McAnally a different form of **McNally**

McAndrew from Scottish and Irish Gaelic, 'son of **Andrew**'

McAndrews a different form of **McAndrew**

McArdle, McCardle from Irish Gaelic, 'son of *Ardghal*', a personal name meaning literally 'height-valour'

McArthur, MacArthur from Scottish Gaelic, 'son of **Arthur**'. See also **Carter** (ii) [Douglas MacArthur, 1880–1964, US general; Dame Ellen Macarthur, 1976–, British yachtswoman; John Macarthur, 1767–1834, British-born Australian pioneer and wool merchant]

Macartney see **McCartney**

McAteer a Northern Irish variant of **McIntyre**. See also **McTeer**

MacAulay, MacAuley, McCauley, McCaulley, McCawley (i) from Gaelic *Mac Amhalghaidh* 'son of *Amhalghadh*', a personal name of unknown origin and meaning; (ii) from Gaelic *Mac Amhlaoibh* 'son of Olaf'. See also **Caley** (ii), **Cawley, Cowley** (ii), **McAuliffe** [Dame Rose Macaulay, 1881–1958, British novelist; Thomas Babington Macaulay (Lord Macaulay), 1800–59, British historian and essayist]

McAuliffe an Irish variant of **MacAulay** (ii)

McBain, MacBain (i) from Gaelic *Mac a' Ghille Bháin* 'son of the pale or white-haired boy'; (ii) a different form of **McBean** [Ed McBain, pen-name (as a crime-writer) of Evan Hunter (original name Salvatore Albert Lombino), 1926–2005, US author and screenwriter]

McBean from Gaelic, 'son of *Beathán*', a personal name derived from *beatha* 'life'. See also **Bean** (iii) [Angus McBean, 1904–90, British photographer]

McBeth, MacBeth from Scottish Gaelic *Mac Beatha* 'son of life' (implying 'religious man'). See also **Bath** (ii), **McVeagh** [George MacBeth, 1932–92, British poet]

McBride, MacBride from Gaelic *Mac Brighde*, a reduction of earlier Irish Gaelic *Mac Giolla Brighde* or Scottish Gaelic *Mac Gille Brighde* (see **Kilbride** (ii)) [Seán MacBride, 1904–88, Irish diplomat; Willie John MacBride, 1939–, Irish rugby footballer]

McBurney from Gaelic, 'son of *Biorna*', a personal name adopted from Old Norse *Bjarni* (a derivative of *björn* 'bearcub', hence 'warrior'). See also **Burney** (ii)
— **McBurney's point** a point on the lower abdomen which is immediately above the appendix, and is the location of maximum tenderness in cases of appendicitis. It was named after the US surgeon Charles McBurney, 1845–1913, who described it in 1889.

McCabe from Gaelic, 'son of *Cába*', a nickname meaning literally 'cape' [Eamonn McCabe, 1948–, British photographer; John McCabe, 1939–, British composer and pianist; Stan McCabe, 1910–68, Australian cricketer]

McCafferty from Irish Gaelic *Mac Eachmharcaigh* 'son of *Eachmharcach*', a personal name meaning literally 'horse-knight'. See also **Cafferty**, **McCaverty**

McCaffrey, McCaffery, McCaffray, McCaffrae from Gaelic, 'son of *Gafradh*', a Gaelic variant of the Old Norse personal name *Guthfróthr*, literally 'god-wise'. See also **Caffrey**

McCaig, MacCaig, McKaig from Gaelic *Mac Thaidhg* 'son of *Tadhg*', a nickname meaning literally 'poet, philosopher'. See also **Montagu** [Norman MacCaig, 1910–96, British poet]

McCain see **McKane**

McCall (i) from Irish Gaelic, 'son of *Cathmhaol*', a personal name meaning literally 'battle-chief'; (ii) a different form of (**McKail**) [Alexander McCall Smith, 1948–, Rhodesian-born British academic and author; Davina McCall, 1967–, British television presenter]
— **McCall's** a US women's magazine, founded in 1897 as *McCall's Magazine*. It ceased publication in 2001.

McCallan a different form of **Callan** (ii)

McCallister see **McAllister**

McCallum, MacCallum from Scottish Gaelic *Mac Coluim* 'son of *Colum*', a personal name derived from Latin *columba* 'dove'. See also **Allum**, **Coleman** (i), **McCollum** [David McCallum, 1933–, British actor]

McCambridge from Gaelic *Mac Ambróis* 'son of Ambrose' [Mercedes McCambridge, 1916–2004, US actress]

McCann, McCan from Irish Gaelic, 'son of *Cana*', a nickname meaning literally 'wolfcub'. See also **Cann** (ii), **McGann** (ii) [Terry McCann, the 'minder' (played by Dennis Waterman) of Arthur Daley in the ITV comedy-drama series of that name, 1979–94]

McCart from Irish Gaelic *Mac Airt* 'son of *Art*', a nickname meaning literally 'bear', hence 'hero'. See also **Cart** (iii), **McCartney**

McCarthy, MacCarthy from Irish Gaelic, 'son of *Cárthach*', a nickname meaning literally 'loving'. See also **Carty** [Charlie McCarthy, a dummy used by the US ventriloquist Edgar Bergen, 1903–78, highly popular on US radio in the mid-20th century; Sir Desmond McCarthy, 1877–1952, British critic; Joseph McCarthy, 1908–57, US Republican politician; Mary McCarthy, 1912–89, US novelist and critic]
— **McCarthyism** the name given to the anticommunist witchhunt in US public life instigated by Senator Joseph McCarthy (see above) in the early 1950s

McCartney, MacCartney, MacArtney from Scottish Gaelic *Mac Artaine* and Irish Gaelic *Mac Artnaigh* 'son of little *Art*' (see **McCart**). See also **Carton** (iii) [Charles Macartney, 1886–1958, Australian cricketer; Sir Paul McCartney, 1942–, British rock musician and former member of The Beatles]

McCarty an Irish variant of **McCarthy**

McCary a different form of **McGary**

McCaskell, McCaskill from Gaelic *Mac Asgaill* 'son of little *Asgall*', a Gaelic form of the Old Norse personal name *Ásketill* (see **Ashkettle**) [Ian McCaskill, 1938–, British weather forecaster]

McCauley, McCaulley see **MacAulay**

McCaverty a different form of **McCafferty** [McCavity, the criminal cat in T.S. Eliot's *Old Possum's Book of Practical Cats* (1939)]

McCawley see **MacAulay**

McClain see **McLean**

McClaren see **McLaren**

McClatchie, McClatchey, McLatchie from Gaelic *Mac Gille Eidich*, perhaps 'son of the ugly young man' (from *éidigh* 'ugly')

McClay see **McLay**

McClean see **McLean**

McClellan, McLellan from Scottish Gaelic *Mac Gille Fhaolain* and Irish Gaelic *Mac Giolla Fhaoláin* 'son of the servant of (St) *Faolán*' (see **Whelan**) [George B. McClellan, 1826–85, Federal general in the US Civil War]

McClelland a different form of **McClellan**. See also **Cleland**

McClennan, McLennan from Scottish Gaelic *Mac Gille Fhinneain* 'son of the servant of (St) *Fionnán*', a personal name meaning literally 'little white(-haired) one' [Robert Maclennan (Lord Maclennan), 1936–, British Liberal Democrat politician]

McClintock from Scottish Gaelic *Mac Gille Fhionndaig* and Irish Gaelic *Mac Giolla Fhiontóg* 'son of the servant of (St) *Finndag*', a personal name meaning literally 'little white(-haired) one'

McCloud see **McLeod**
— **McCloud** a US television police drama (1972–76) featuring Dennis Weaver as Deputy Marshal Sam McCloud

McClure from Scottish Gaelic *Mac Gille Uidhir* 'son of the servant of (St) *Odhar*', a personal name meaning literally 'sallow', and *Mac Gille Dheòradha* 'son of the servant of the pilgrim' [Doug McClure, 1935–95, US actor; Sir Robert McClure, 1807–73, Irish naval officer and explorer]

McCluskey, McClusky, McCluskie from Gaelic *Mac Bhloscaidhe* 'son of *Bloscadh*', a personal name probably based on *blosc* 'loud noise'

McColgan from Gaelic, 'son *Colga*', a personal name based on *colg* 'thorn, sword'. See also **Colgan** [Liz McColgan (*née* Lynch), 1964–, British athlete]

McColl, MacColl from Scottish Gaelic, 'son of *Coll*', a personal name based on *coll* 'hazel tree'. See also **Quill** [Ewan MacColl (original name James Miller), 1915–89, British folk singer and songwriter; Kirsty MacColl, 1959–2000, British pop singer and songwriter, daughter of Ewan]

McCollum, McCollam Irish variants of **McCallum**

McComb, McCombe from Gaelic *Mac Thóm* 'son of *Thóm*', a pet-form of **Thomas**

McConnell, McConnel, McConnal (i) from Scottish Gaelic *Mac Dhomhnuill* 'son of *Domhnall*' (see **Donald**); (ii) from Irish Gaelic, 'son of *Conall*' (see **Connell**)

McCool (i) from Gaelic *Mac Dhubhghaill* (see **McDougall**); (ii) from Scottish Gaelic *Mac Gille Chomghaill* or of Irish Gaelic *Mac Giolla Comhghaill* 'son of the servant of (St) *Comhghall*', a personal name perhaps based on *gall* 'stranger'; (iii) perhaps from Irish Gaelic *Mac Cumhaill* 'son of *Cumhall*', a nickname meaning literally 'champion'. See also **Coulson** (ii), **Coyle**

McCord from Gaelic *Mac Cuairt* and *Mac Cuarta*, perhaps 'son of a journey'. See also **McCourt**

McCormack, McCormick from Gaelic, 'son of *Cormac*', a personal name meaning literally 'raven's son' [John McCormack, 1884–1945, Irish-born US tenor]

McCorquodale from Gaelic *Mac Thorcadail* 'son of *Torcodal*', a personal name of Old Norse origin meaning literally 'Thor's kettle'. See also **Thirkell**

McCosker a different form of **McCusker**

McCourt a different form of **McCord**

McCowan, McCowen from Gaelic *Mac Eoghain* (see **McEwen**), and *Mac Gille Comhghain* 'son of the servant of (St) *Comhghan*', a personal name meaning literally 'born together', used as a nickname for a twin. See also **Cowan** [Alec McCowen, 1925–, British actor]

McCoy, McKoy from Gaelic *Mac Aodha* (see **McKay**) [Leonard ('Bones') McCoy, ship's doctor (played by DeForest Kelley) on the USS *Enterprise* in the US television science-fiction series *Star Trek* (1969–71)]

— **the real McCoy** someone or something that is genuine. The origin of the metaphor was probably a publicity slogan used by the US boxer Norman

Selby, 1873–1940, who fought under the name 'Kid McCoy' and employed the phrase to distinguish him from other boxers called McCoy.

McCracken, McCrackan, McCrackin from Gaelic *Mac Reachtain*, a Northern Irish variant of *Mac Neachtain* (see **McNaughton**)

McCrae, McCray, McRae from Scottish Gaelic *Mag Raith* 'son of *Rath*', a personal name meaning literally 'grace, prosperity'. See also **McCree, McGrath, McGraw, Reith**[1] [Colin McRae, 1968–, British rally driver; Duncan Macrae, 1905–67, British actor; Joel McCrea, 1905–90, US actor]

McCready, McCreadie, McCreedy, McReady, McReadie from Gaelic *Mac Riada* 'son of *Riada*', a personal name meaning literally 'trained, expert' [William Charles Macready, 1793–1873, British actor and theatre manager]

McCreary, McCreery from Gaelic *Mac Ruidhrí*, a different form of *Mac Ruaidhrí* (see **McCrory**)

McCree, Machree different forms of **McCrae**

— '**Mother Machree**' a sentimental ballad (1910) by Rida Johnson Young. In Australia, *Mother Machree* has been used as rhyming slang for *tea*.

McCrory, McCrorey from Gaelic *Mac Ruaidhrí* 'son of *Ruaidhrí*' (see **Rory**)

McCrum, McCrumb, McCrumm from Gaelic *Mac Chruim*, literally 'son of the cripple' (from *crom* 'bent'). See also **Crum**

McCue from Gaelic *Mac Aodha* (see **McKay**)

McCullers, McCullars different forms of **McKellar** [Carson McCullers, 1917–67, US novelist and playwright]

McCulloch, McCullach, McCullough, McCullagh from Gaelic *Mac Cú Uladh*, literally 'son of the hound of Ulster' [Colleen McCullough, 1937–, Australian novelist; Derek McCulloch ('Uncle Mac'), 1897–1967, British radio presenter and producer; Warren McCulloch, 1898–1972, US neurophysiologist]

McCusker from Gaelic *Mac Oscair* 'son of *Oscar*', a personal name of Old Norse origin meaning literally 'god-spear'. See also **McCosker**

McCutcheon, McCutchen from Gaelic *Mac Uisdein* 'son of *Uisdean*', a gaelicization of the Old French personal name *Huchon*, a pet-form of **Hugh**. See also **Houston** [Martine McCutcheon, 1976–, British actress and singer]

McDade, McDaid from Gaelic *Mac Daibháid* 'son of **David**'. See also **McDevitt**.

McDermott, McDermitt from Gaelic, 'son of *Diarmaid*', a personal name perhaps meaning literally 'free from envy'. See also **McDiarmid**

McDevitt from Gaelic *Mac Daibháid* (see **McDade**)

McDiarmid, MacDiarmid Scottish variants of **McDermott** [Hugh MacDiarmid, pen-name Christopher Murray Grieve, 1892–1978, Scottish poet; Ian McDiarmid, 1944–, British actor]

McDonagh a different form of **McDonough**

McDonald, MacDonald from Scottish Gaelic, 'son of *Domhnall*' (see **Donald**) [Flora MacDonald, 1722–90, Scottish Jacobite who smuggled Bonnie Prince Charlie to safety; Sir John Macdonald, 1815–91, Canadian politician, prime minister 1857–58, 1864, 1867–73, 1878–91; Ramsay MacDonald, 1866–1937, British Labour politician, prime minister 1924, 1929–35; Ronald McDonald, a clown character created in 1963 as an advertising mascot for the McDonald's (see below) chain; Sir Trevor McDonald, 1939–, Trinidad-born British newscaster]

— **McDonald's** a US-based worldwide chain of fast-food outlets founded in 1955 by Ray A. Kroc, a milk-shake machine manufacturer. It originated in a hamburger restaurant opened in San Bernardino, California in 1940 by Richard ('Dick') McDonald, 1909–98, and his brother Maurice ('Mac'), died 1971. Its iconic product is the **Big Mac**, the largest hamburger in its range. The chain's ubiquity and a widespread public identification of it with 'junk-food' culture have led to the appropriation of its prefix *Mc-* in a number of derogatory coinages, notably *McJob* for a low-paid or menial job (invented by Douglas Coupland in 1991) and *McMansion* for a large and lavish but tasteless modern house.

— **mac out** to overeat, especially on Big Mac (see above) hamburgers. A US teenage slang coinage of the 1980s.

McDonnell, **McDonell** Irish variants of **McDonald** [A.G. Macdonell, 1895–1941, British writer]

— **Macdonnell Ranges** a system of mountain ranges in northern Australia. They were named in honour of Sir Richard MacDonnell, 1814–81, governor of South Australia.

McDonough from Scottish and Irish Gaelic, 'son of *Donnchadh*' (see **Donohue**). See also **McDonagh**

McDougall, **McDougal** from Gaelic, 'son of *Dubhghall*' (see **Dougall**). See also **McCool** (i)

— **McDougall** a British flour-milling company, founded in the 1860s by two Manchester brothers called McDougall. It merged with Hovis in 1957, and in 1962 it joined forces with Joseph Rank Ltd (see **Rank**) to become Rank Hovis McDougall.

McDowell, **McDowall** different forms of **McDougall** [Edward MacDowell, 1861–1908, US composer; Malcolm McDowell (original name Malcolm Taylor), 1943–, British actor; Roddy McDowall, 1928–98, British actor]

McDuff, **MacDuff** from Gaelic, 'son of *Dubh*', a personal name derived from *dubh* 'black'. See also **Cuff** (ii)

— **lead on, McDuff** an injunction to someone to take the lead vigorously in some enterprise, especially one that they have suggested

— **Macduff** a fishing port in Aberdeenshire, originally called Doune but renamed in 1783 in honour of his father by James Duff, the earl of Fife

McDuffie, **McDuffy**, **McDuffee** from Gaelic, 'son of *Duibhshíth*' (see **Duffy**). See also **McPhee**

McElhinney, **McElhinny** from Irish Gaelic *Mac Giolla Choinnigh* 'son of the servant of (St) Coinneach' (see **Kenny**)

McElroy see **McIlroy**

McElwaine see **McIlwaine**

McElwee from Gaelic *Mac Giolla Bhuidhe*, literally 'son of the yellow-haired boy'

McEnerney see **McInerney**

McEnery, **McEnerie** from Irish Gaelic, 'son of *Innéirghe*', a personal name probably derived from *éirghe* 'to arise'

McEnroe (i) from Irish Gaelic, 'son of *Conchradh*', a personal name meaning literally 'hound of torment'. See also **Crow** (ii); (ii) from Irish Gaelic *Mac Con Rubha* 'son of *Cú Rubha*', a name meaning 'hound of the promontory' [John McEnroe, 1959–, US tennis player]

McEntyre see **McIntyre**

McEvoy, **McAvoy** from Gaelic *Mac Giolla Bhuidhe* 'son of the yellow-haired boy', and from Irish Gaelic *Mac Fhíodhbhuidhe* 'son of the woodman'

McEwan, **McEwen** from Gaelic, 'son of *Eògann*' (see **Ewan**; see also **Owens** (ii)), and 'son of *Eathan*', a Scottish Gaelic form of Latin *Johannes* (see **John**). See also **McKeown** [Geraldine McEwan (original name Geraldine McKeown), 1932–, British actress; Ian McEwan, 1948–, British author; Sir John McEwen, 1900–80, Australian statesman; William McEwan, 1827–1913, Scottish brewer and philanthropist, founder of the brewery that produces, among other beers, McEwan's Export]

Macey, **Macy** different forms of **Massey**

— **Macy's** a US chain of department stores, founded in 1851 in Haverhill, Massachusetts by Rowland Hussey Macy, 1822–77. Its flagship store, in Herald Square, New York City, is reputedly the world's largest department store building.

McFadden, **McFaddin** from Gaelic *Mac Phaidin*, literally 'son of little **Patrick**'

McFadyen, **McFadyean**, **McFadyon** different forms of **McFadden**

McFail, **McPhail** different forms of **McFall**

McFall, **McFaul** from Scottish Gaelic *Mac Phàil* and Irish Gaelic *Mac Phóil*, literally 'son of **Paul**'. See also **Quail** (iii)

McFarland a different form of **McFarlane**

McFarlane, **MacFarlane**, **McFarlan**, **McFarlin** from Gaelic *Mac Pharthaláin*, literally 'son of **Bartholomew**'

— **Macfarlane** a type of overcoat, originating in the mid-19th century, with a shoulder cape and slits at the side to allow access to pockets in the clothing beneath. It is not known whether the original MacFarlane was its designer, manufacturer or wearer.

— **Macfarlane Lang & Co.** a British firm of biscuit manufacturers, originating in a bakery established in Glasgow in 1817 by James Lang. Later in the century it grew and prospered under John Macfarlane and his sons, and in 1885 it became Macfarlane Lang.

McFaul see **McFall**

McFee see **McPhee**

McGann (i) from Gaelic *Mag Annaidh* 'son of *Annadh*', a personal name of unknown origin and meaning; (ii) a different form of **McCann** [Paul McGann, 1959–, British actor]

McGary (i) *also* **McGarry** from Gaelic *Mac Fhearadhaig* 'son of *Fhearadhach*', a personal name meaning literally 'manly'; (ii) from Irish Gaelic *Mac Fhiachra* 'son of *Fiachra*', a personal name perhaps meaning literally 'battle-king'. See also **Gary** (ii), **McCary**

McGee, McGhee, Magee from Gaelic *Mac Aodha* (see **McKay**) [Bryan Magee, 1930–, British writer, academic and Labour/SDP politician; Fibber McGee, a fictional compulsive liar who originally appeared in the US radio comedy series *Fibber McGee and Molly* (1935–37) and subsequently in films and television series; Henry McGee, 1929–2006, British actor and comedian's straight man]

McGeorge from Gaelic *Mac An Deoraidh*, literally 'son of the pilgrim' (see **Dewar**). There is no etymological connection with the personal name **George**.

McGeraghty from Irish Gaelic *Mag Oireachtaig* 'son of *Oireachtach*', a nickname meaning literally 'member of the assembly'

McGibbon from Gaelic *Mac Giobúin* 'son of **Gibbon** (i)'. See also **McKibben** (ii)

McGill, Magill (i) from Gaelic *Mac An Ghoill*, literally 'son of the stranger' (see **Gall** (i)); (ii) a shortened form of various Irish Gaelic names beginning with *Mac Giolla* 'son of the servant of …'; (iii) from Scottish Gaelic *Mac Ghill Mhaoil* (see **McMillan**) [Donald McGill, 1875–1962, British illustrator of picture postcards]
— **McGill University** an English-language university based in Montreal, Canada. It was founded in 1821 under the terms of a bequest by James McGill, 1744–1813, a Montreal merchant.

McGillicuddy, McGillacuddy from Irish Gaelic *Mac Giolla Chuda* 'son of the servant of (St) *Chuda*', a personal name of unknown origin and meaning
— **Macgillicuddy's Reeks** a mountain range in County Kerry, Ireland. Mention of the somewhat outlandish name (from the Irish Clan McGillicuddy, landowners in Kerry, who used the mountains as a refuge, and Irish English *reek* 'mountain' (essentially the same word as 'hay *rick*')) was banned on BBC comedy programmes in the 1950s for fear that some risqué double entendre might lurk there.

McGillis from Scottish Gaelic *Mac Gille Iosa* 'son of the servant of Jesus' [Kelly McGillis, 1957–, US actress]

McGillivray from Scottish Gaelic *Mac Gille Bhràdha*, literally 'son of the servant of judgment'

McGilvray a different form of **McGillivray**

McGinley from Irish Gaelic *Mag Fhionnghaile* 'son of *Fionnghal*', a personal name meaning literally 'fair valour'

McGinn from Irish Gaelic *Mag Finn* 'son of *Fionn*' (see **Finnegan**)

— **Andy McGinn** rhyming slang for *chin*

McGinnis see **McGuinness**

McGinty from Irish Gaelic *Mag Fhionnachtaigh* 'son of *Fionnshneachtach*', a personal name meaning literally 'snow-white'
— **'Paddy McGinty's Goat'** an 'Irish' comical song (1917) by R.P. Weston and Bert Lee recounting the astounding exploits of a goat acquired by Paddy McGinty (they included attacking and seeing off a German U-boat)

McGivern a different form of **McGovern**

McGlashan, McGlashen from Gaelic, 'son of *Glasan*', a personal name meaning literally 'little grey-green one'

McGoldrick from Irish Gaelic *Mag Ualghairg* 'son of Ualgharg', a male personal name probably meaning literally 'proud-fierce'. See also **Golden**

McGonigle, McGonigal, McGonagle, McGonagall from Gaelic, 'son of *Conghal*', a personal name meaning literally 'hound-valour' [James McGonigal, the real name of the Crazy Gang's Jimmy **Gold**; William McGonagall, 1830–1902, bad Scottish poet]

McGough from Irish Gaelic *Mag Eochadha* 'son of *Eochaidh*', a personal name meaning literally 'horseman' [Roger McGough, 1937–, British poet]

McGovern from Irish Gaelic *Mag Shamhradháin* or *Shamhráin* 'son of *Samhradháin*', a personal name meaning literally 'little summer'. See also **McGivern, McGowran** [George McGovern, 1922–, US diplomat and Democratic politician; Jimmy McGovern, 1949–, British dramatist]

McGowan (i) *also* **McGowen** *or* **McGown** from Scottish Gaelic *Mac Gobhann* and Irish Gaelic *Mac Gabhann*, literally 'son of the smith'; (ii) from Scottish Gaelic *Mac Owein* 'son of **Owen**' [Alistair McGowan, 1964–, British impressionist and actor; Cathy McGowan, 1944–, British presenter of television pop-music programmes; Shane MacGowan, 1957–, Irish musician]

McGowran, MacGowran a different form of **McGovern** [Jack MacGowran, 1918–73, Irish actor]

McGrath from Irish Gaelic *Mac Raith* 'son of *Rath*', a personal name meaning literally 'grace, prosperity'. See also **McRae, McGraw, Reith**[1] [Glenn McGrath, 1970–, Australian cricketer; John McGrath, 1935–2002, British playwright; Rory McGrath, 1956–, British comedian and writer]

McGraw, MacGraw a different form of **McGrath** [Ali MacGraw (full name Alice MacGraw), 1938–, US actress; John Joseph McGraw, 1873–1934, US baseball manager]
— **McGraw-Hill** a US publishing company formed in 1909 by the uniting of two existing publishing firms founded by James H. McGraw, 1860–1948, and John A. Hill, died 1916.

McGregor, MacGregor from Scottish Gaelic *Mac Griogair* 'son of **Gregory**' [Bobby McGregor, 1944–, British swimmer; Ewan McGregor, 1971–, British actor; Ian MacGregor, 1912–98, British-born US-based industrialist, chairman of British Coal during the 1984–85 miners' strike;

Joanna MacGregor, 1959–, British pianist; John MacGregor (Lord MacGregor), 1937–, British Conservative politician; Rob Roy MacGregor (original name Robert MacGregor), 1671–1734, Scottish brigand, celebrated in Walter Scott's novel *Rob Roy* (1817); Sue MacGregor, 1941–, South African-born British radio presenter]
— **MacGregor's Leap** the point near the foot of Glen Lyon, Perth and Kinross, at which in 1565 Gregor MacGregor of Glenstrae supposedly made a stupendous jump over the rocky rapids of the River Lyon to avoid pursuing Campbell bloodhounds

McGruder from Scottish Gaelic *Mac Grudaire*, literally 'son of the brewer'

McGuffin from Irish Gaelic *Mag Dhuibhfinn* 'son of *Duibhfionn*', a personal name meaning literally 'dark-fair'
— **McGuffin** a term invented by the film director Alfred Hitchcock, 1899–1980, for something that sets the plot of a story going but has no essential relevance to the action. He purportedly got it from the name of a Scotsman who appeared in a story about two men on a train.

McGuigan, **McGuiggan** from Irish Gaelic *Mac Guagáin*, an alteration of *Mag Eochagáin* (see **Geoghegan**) [Barry McGuigan (original name Finbar Patrick McGuigan), 1961–, British boxer]

McGuinness, **McGinnis**, **Maginnis** from Irish Gaelic *Mag Aonghuis* 'son of **Angus**'. See also **Guinness**, **McInnes** [Frank McGuinness, 1953–, Irish playwright; Martin McGuinness, 1950–, Northern Ireland Sinn Féin politician; Niall MacGinnis, 1913–78, Irish actor]
— **maginnis** in Australian slang of the first half of the 20th century, a wrestling hold that is very difficult to get out of, and by extension, any sort of pressure exerted on someone; hence, to 'put or clap the maginnis on' someone was to coerce them. It has been speculated that the term came from a wrestler named McGinnis.

McGuire, **Maguire** from Irish Gaelic *Mag Uidhir* 'son of *Odhar*', a nickname meaning literally 'sallow'
— **Andy Maguire**, **Barney Maguire**, **Mollie Maguire** Australian rhyming slang for *fire* (in the context especially of the domestic hearth)
— **Molly Maguires** a mid-19th-century Irish secret society whose young male members dressed up as women to ambush rent collectors

McGurk from Scottish Gaelic *Mac Coirc* 'son of *Corc*', a personal name meaning literally 'heart', and Irish Gaelic *Mag Oirc* 'son of *Orc*', a personal name apparently derived from *orc* 'pig'

McHaigh a different form of **McCaig**

McHale from Irish Gaelic, 'son of *Céile*', a nickname meaning literally 'companion', and 'son of *Haol*', itself a gaelicization of **Howell**

McHenry from Scottish Gaelic *Mac Eanruig* and Irish Gaelic *Mac Éinrí* 'son of **Henry**'. See also **McKendrick**

Machin, **Machen** 'stonemason' (from Anglo-Norman *machun*, a variant of Old French *masson* (see **Mason**)). See also **Meacham** [Arthur

Machen, 1863–1947, Welsh novelist; Edward Henry ('Denry') Machin, upwardly mobile hero of Arnold Bennett's *The Card* (1911)]

McHugh from Gaelic *Mac Aodha* (see **McKay**)

McIlroy, **McElroy** from Irish Gaelic *Mac Giolla Ruaidh* 'son of the red-haired boy'. See also **Gilroy**, **Kilroy**, **Milroy**

McIlvenny a different form of **McIlwaine**

McIlwaine, **McElwaine** from Scottish Gaelic *Mac Gille Bheathain* 'son of the servant of (St) *Beathan*', a personal name meaning literally 'little life'. See also **Melvin** (i)

McIndoe perhaps from Scottish Gaelic *Mac Iain Duibh* 'son of black-haired Ian' [Sir Archibald McIndoe, 1900–60, New Zealand plastic surgeon]

McInerney, **McEnerney** from Irish Gaelic *Mac An Airchinnigh* 'son of the overseer' [Jay McInerney (original name John Barrett McInerney), 1955–, US author]

McInnes, **MacInnes** from Scottish Gaelic *Mac Aonghuis* 'son of **Angus**'. See also **McGuinness** [Colin MacInnes, 1914–76, British novelist]

McIntosh, **MacIntosh**, **Mackintosh** from Scottish Gaelic *Mac An Toisich* 'son of the leader'. See also **Tosh**, **Toshack** [Sir Cameron Mackintosh, 1946–, British theatrical producer; Charles Rennie Mackintosh, 1868–1928, Scottish architect and interior designer]
— **Apple Macintosh** a make of personal computer introduced in 1984 by the US company Apple Computers. The latter (founded in 1976) took its name from that of the fruit, and *Macintosh* comes from the name of a North American variety of apple introduced around 1870 by the Ontario farmer John McIntosh.
— **John Mackintosh and Sons Ltd** a sweet-manufacturing firm established in Halifax, Yorkshire in 1890 by John Mackintosh, 1868–1920. It was famous in particular for its toffee. After a 1969 merger it became **Rowntree-Mackintosh**, and it was subsequently taken over by Nestle.
— **mackintosh**, **macintosh** a waterproof coat worn for protection against the rain. It takes its name from the Scottish inventor Charles Macintosh, 1766–1843, who devised the method of rubberizing cloth that made it possible. The abbreviated form **mac** dates from the early 20th century.

McIntyre, **MacIntyre**, **McEntire** from Scottish Gaelic *Mac An tSaoir* 'son of the carpenter or mason'. See also **McAteer**

McIver, **McIvor** from Gaelic, 'son of *Íomhar*', a personal name derived from Old Norse *Ivarr*

McKaig see **McCaig**

McKane, **McKain**, **McCain** from Scottish Gaelic *Mac Iain* 'son of Ian'. See also **Cain** (ii)

McKay, **MacKay**, **Mackay** from Gaelic *Mac Aodha* 'son of *Aodh*', a personal name (originally that of a god) meaning literally 'fire'. See also **Hughes**, **McCoy**, **McCue**, **McGee**, **McHugh**, **Mackie** [Fulton Mackay, 1922–87, British actor, portrayer of the martinet prison officer Mr Mackay in the

BBC television sitcom *Porridge* (1974–77); Heather McKay, 1941–, Australian squash player]

McKean a different form of **McKane**

McKechnie from Scottish Gaelic *Mac Eacharna* 'son of *Eacharn*', a personal name derived from *each* 'horse'

McKellan, McKellen from Gaelic *Mac Ailín* or *Mac Aileáin* 'son of **Allen**' [Sir Ian McKellen, 1939–, British actor]

McKellar, McKeller from Scottish Gaelic *Mac Ealair* 'son of **Hilary** (i)' [Kenneth McKellar, 1927–, Scottish singer]

McKendrick from Scottish Gaelic *Mac Eanruig* and Irish Gaelic *Mac Éinraic* 'son of **Henry**'. See also **McHenry** [Alexander Mackendrick, 1912–93, US-born film director]

McKenna from Gaelic, 'son of *Cionaodh*', a personal name probably meaning literally 'beloved of Aodh' (see **McKay**) [Siobhán McKenna, 1923–86, Irish actress; Virginia McKenna, 1931–, British actress]

McKenzie, MacKenzie, Mackenzie from Scottish Gaelic, 'son of *Coinneach*', a personal name meaning literally 'attractive'. See also **Menzies** [Sir Alexander Mackenzie, 1847–1935, British composer; Sir Compton Mackenzie, 1883–1972, British novelist; Julia McKenzie, 1941–, British actress and singer; Kelvin MacKenzie, 1946–, British newspaper editor; Precious McKenzie, 1936–, South African-born British and New Zealand weightlifter; Robert McKenzie, 1917–81, Canadian political scientist]

— **Mackenzie** a former administrative district of northern Canada. It was named in honour of the Scottish-Canadian explorer Sir Alexander Mackenzie, 1764–1820.

— **McKenzie friend** someone who attends a court case as a helper to one of the parties (e.g. by taking notes, giving advice, etc.). The term comes from the case of McKenzie v. McKenzie (1970), in which the English Court of Appeal ruled that such a helper was permissible.

— **Mackenzie River** a river in northern Canada, the second longest in North America after the Mississippi-Missouri. Like Mackenzie district (see above) it was named after Sir Alexander Mackenzie, who discovered it in 1789.

McKeown a different form of **McEwan**

McKern from Irish Gaelic, 'son of *Cearán*', a personal name meaning literally 'little dark one', and 'son of *Corrghamhain*', a personal name meaning literally 'sharp calf' [Leo McKern (full name Reginald Leo McKern), 1920–2002, Australian actor]

Mackey (i) from Irish Gaelic *Ó Macdha* 'son of *Macdha*', a personal name meaning literally 'manly'; (ii) see **Mackie**

McKibben, McKibbin, McKibbon (i) from Irish Gaelic, 'son of *Fibín*', a pet-form of **Philip**; (ii) a different form of **McGibbon**

Mackie, Mackey from Gaelic *Mac Aodha* (see **McKay**)

McKillop from Gaelic, 'son of **Philip**'

McKim, McKimm from Scottish Gaelic, 'son of *Shim*', a pet-form of **Simon**

McKinley, McKinlay from Scottish Gaelic *Mac Fionnlaigh* 'son of *Fionnlaoch*' (see **Finlay**) [Chuck McKinley (full name Charles Robert McKinley), 1941–86, US tennis player; William McKinley, 1843–1901, US Republican politician, president 1897–1901]

— **Mackinlays** a brand of Scotch whisky, produced by the firm established in 1847 by the Leith whisky merchant Charles Mackinlay, 1795–1867

— **Mount McKinley** a mountain in Alaska, the highest (6194 m./20,320 ft.) in North America. It was named in 1897 by the prospector William A. Dickey in honour of President McKinley (see above).

McKinnon, MacKinnon from Gaelic *Mac Fhionghuin* 'son of *Fhionghuin*', a personal name meaning literally 'fair born' or 'fair son'

— **Mackinnon's Cave** a sea cave on the west coast of the Hebridean island of Mull. According to legend a man called Mackinnon entered it in an attempt to outdo the fairies at the playing of the pipes, and was never heard of again.

McKinstry from Gaelic *Mac An Aistrigh*, a reduced form of *Mac An Aistrighthigh* 'son of the traveller'

McKittrick, McKitrick from Gaelic, 'son of *Shitrig*', a personal name adapted from Old Norse *Sigtryggr*, literally 'victory-true'

McKnight (i) a Northern Irish anglicization of Scottish Gaelic *Mac Neachtain* (see **McNaughton**); (ii) a partial translation of Gaelic *Mac An Ridire* 'son of the horseman' [Edward McKnight Kauffer, 1890–1954, US-born British artist and illustrator]

McKoy see **McCoy**

McLachlan a Scottish variant of **McLaughlin**

McLain, McLaine see **McLean**

McLane see **McLean**

McLaren, McLaran, McClaren, MacLaren from Gaelic *Mac Labhruinn* 'son of **Lawrence**'. See also **McLauren** [Archie MacLaren, 1871–1944, English cricketer; Bill McLaren, 1923–, British television rugby commentator; Bruce McLaren, 1937–70, New Zealand racing driver; Malcolm McLaren, 1946–, British punk impresario; Steve McClaren, 1961–, English football manager]

— **McLaren** a Formula 1 motor-racing team, founded in 1966 by Bruce McLaren (see above)

McLatchie see **McClatchie**

McLaughlin, McLaughlan, McLauchlin, McLoughlin from Gaelic, 'son of *Lochlann*' (see **Laughlan**). See also **McLachlan**

McLauren, McLaurin different forms of **McLaren** [Ian MacLaurin (Lord MacLaurin), 1937–, British businessman]

McLay, McLea, McClay from Scottish Gaelic *Mac An Léigh* and Irish Gaelic *Mac An Leagha* 'son of the physician'

McLean, MacLean, McLane, McLain, McLaine, McClean, McClain from Scottish Gaelic *Mac Gille Eáin* and Irish Gaelic *Mac Giolla Eóin* 'son of the servant of (St) **John**' [Alistair Maclean, 1922–87, British novelist; Donald Maclean, 1913–83, British spy for the former Soviet Union; Sir Fitzroy Maclean, 1911–96, British diplomat, adventurer and writer; Shirley MacLaine (original name Shirley MacLean Beaty), 1934–, US actress]
— **Macleans** the brand name of toothpaste produced by a company started in Britain in 1919 by the New Zealand-born corset salesman Alex C. Maclean to make own-brand chemists' products. It introduced its own 'Macleans' dentifrice in 1930. The name is pronounced, appropriately enough, 'm@kleenz' rather than the standard 'm@klaynz'.
— **Maclean's** a Canadian current-affairs magazine, founded in 1905 by the Toronto journalist and entrepreneur Lt.-Col. John Bayne Maclean, 1862–1950, as *The Business Magazine*. It became *Maclean's* in 1911.
— **Maclean's Nose** a headland on the south side of the Ardnamurchan peninsula, Highland, named (presumably) after a certain Maclean

McLees, McLeese, McLise different forms of **McLeish** [Daniel Maclise, 1806–70, Irish portrait and history painter]

McLeish from Gaelic *Mac Gille Íosa* 'son of the servant of Jesus' [Archibald Macleish, 1892–1982, US poet; Henry McLeish, 1948–, British Labour politician, First Minister of Scotland 2000–01]

McLellan see **McClellan**

McLennan see **McClennan**

McLeod, MacLeod, McCloud from Scottish Gaelic, 'son of *Leòd*', a personal name descended from the Old Norse nickname *Ljótr* 'ugly' [Iain Macleod, 1913–70, British Conservative politician; John James Rickard Macleod, 1876–1935, British physiologist]
— **McLeod gauge** a manometer for measuring the pressure in a near vacuum. It was named after its inventor, the British scientist Herbert McLeod, 1841–1923.
— **McLeod's Tables** two flat-topped hills on the island of Skye. It is said that, having been generously entertained in Edinburgh by James V, the chieftain of the clan McLeod returned the compliment by inviting the king to a great banquet laid out on the summit of the higher one – whence the name.

McLise see **McLees**

McLoughlin see **McLaughlin**

McMahon from Irish Gaelic, 'son of *Mathghamhain*', a nickname meaning literally 'good calf' [Marie Edme Patrice Maurice, Comte de MacMahon, 1808–93, French marshal and statesman, president 1873–79; Robert Carrier MacMahon, original name of Robert **Carrier**; Sir William McMahon, 1908–88, Australian Liberal politician, prime minister 1971–72]

McManaman a different form of **McMenemy**

McManus, McMannas, McMannes from Irish Gaelic *Mac Maghnuis* 'son of **Magnus**' [Mark McManus, 1935–94, British actor; Mick McManus, 1928–, British wrestler]

McMaster from Scottish Gaelic *Mac Maighstir* or *Mac A'Mhaighstir* 'son of (the) master'

McMenemy, McMenamy, McMenamie from Gaelic, 'son of *Meanma*', a personal name meaning literally 'spirited'. See also **McManaman** [Lawrie McMenemy, 1936–, British football manager]

McMillan, MacMillan, McMillen from Scottish Gaelic, 'son of *Maolán*', a nickname meaning literally 'little bald one' (usually referring to a person in a religious order, with a tonsure). See also **McMullen, Milligan** [Edwin Mattison McMillan, 1907–91, US physicist; Harold Macmillan (Earl of Stockton), 1894–1986, British Conservative politician, prime minister 1957–63; James MacMillan, 1959–, British composer; Sir Kenneth MacMillan, 1929–92, British choreographer; Kirkpatrick Macmillan, died 1878, Scottish blacksmith, maker of the first bicycle]
— **Macmillan and Company** a British publishing firm founded in 1843 by the Scottish bookseller Daniel Macmillan (grandfather of Harold Macmillan – see above), 1813–57, and his brother Alexander, 1818–96
— **McMillan and Wife** a US television police drama series (1972–79) starring Rock Hudson as Commissioner Stewart McMillan
— **Macmillan Cancer Relief** a British charity founded (as the Society for the Prevention and Relief of Cancer) in 1911 by Douglas Macmillan, whose father had died from the disease. Nurses funded by it are known as **Macmillan nurses**.

McMordie from Scottish Gaelic, 'son of *Muircheartach*' (see **Moriarty**). See also **McMurdo**

McMorris from Gaelic *Mac Muiris* or *Mhuiris* 'son of **Morris**' [Captain Macmorris, an Irish soldier in Shakespeare's *Henry V* (1599)]

McMullen, McMullan, McMullin different forms of **McMillan**

McMurdo a different form of **McMordie**
— **McMurdo Sound** an arm of the Ross Sea in eastern Antarctica, east of Victoria Land. It was named after Lieutenant Archibald McMurdo RN, born 1812, an officer on HMS *Terror* on its exploratory voyages in the Antarctic in the early 1840s.

McMurray, McMurry from Gaelic, 'son of *Muireadhach*', a personal name meaning literally 'seafarer' [Fred MacMurray, 1908–91, US actor]

McNabb, McNab from Gaelic *Mac An Aba* or *Abadh* 'son of the abbot' [Andy McNab, 1959–, British former SAS soldier turned novelist]
— **John Macnab** a novel (1925) by John Buchan, revolving round a plan to poach undetected on three separate Scottish estates
— **Sandy McNab** rhyming slang for *cab*, (in the plural) *crabs* 'body lice' and (in Australia) *scab* 'strike-breaker'. The name is merely that of a generalized Scotsman.

McNair from Scottish Gaelic *Mac Iain Uidhir* 'son of sallow John' and *Mac An Oighre* 'son of the heir', and Irish Gaelic *Mac An Mhaoir* 'son of the steward'. See also **Weir** (ii)

McNally from Irish Gaelic *Mac An Fhailghigh* 'son of the poor man'. See also **McAnally**

McNamara, McNamarra from Irish Gaelic *Mac Conmara* 'son of *Cú Mhara*', a personal name meaning literally 'hound of the sea' [Peter McNamara, 1955–, Australian tennis player, doubles partner of Paul McNamee; Robert McNamara, 1916–, US academic and politician, secretary of defense 1961–68]

McNamee from Irish Gaelic *Mac Conmidhe* 'son of *Cú Mhidhe*', a personal name meaning literally 'hound of Meath'. See also **Conway** (iii), **Mee** (i) [Paul McNamee, 1954–, Australian tennis player, doubles partner of Peter McNamara]

McNaughton, McNaughten, McNaghten from Gaelic, 'son of *Neachtan*', a name (related to Latin *Neptunus*) of the ancient Irish god of water. See also **McNutt** (ii), **Naughton**
— **McNaughten rules** in English law, a legal ruling establishing that a defence of insanity depends on proving that the defendant was unaware or unable to understand that wrong was being done. The name commemorates Daniel M'Naghten, who was tried for murder in 1843 and acquitted on a plea of insanity.

McNeal see **McNeil**

McNee from Gaelic, 'son of *Nia*', a nickname meaning 'champion'. See also **Neville** (ii) [Patrick Macnee, 1922–, British actor]

McNeely from Scottish Gaelic *Mac an Fhilidh* 'son of the poet', and Irish Gaelic *Mac Conghaile* 'son of *Conghal*' (see **Connolly**). See also **Neely**

McNeice, McNeese from Irish Gaelic *Mac Naois*, a shortened form of *Mac Aonghuis* 'son of **Angus**'. See also **Neeson**, **Nish** [Louis MacNeice, 1907–63, Irish-born British poet and playwright]

McNeil, MacNeil, McNeill, McNeile, McNeal from Gaelic, 'son of *Niall*', a personal name probably meaning literally 'champion'. See also **Neil** [Herman Cyril McNeile, 1888–1937, the real name of 'Sapper', creator of 'Bulldog' Drummond; James McNeill Whistler, see **Whistler**]

McNulty from Irish Gaelic *Mac An Ultaigh* 'son of the Ulsterman'

McNutt (i) from Irish Gaelic *Mac Nuadhat* 'son of *Nuadha*', the name of an ancient Celtic god; (ii) a different form of **McNaughton**

McPhail see **McFail**

McPhee, McFee from Gaelic, 'son of *Duibhshíth*' (see **Duffy**)

McPherson, MacPherson from Scottish Gaelic *Mac An Phearsain* 'son of the parson' [Aimee Semple McPherson (*née* Kennedy), 1890–1944, US evangelist; Elle Macpherson (original name Eleanor Gow), 1963–, Australian model and actress; James Macpherson, 1736–96, Scottish poet, fabricator of the allegedly ancient verses of Ossian; Sandy MacPherson (original name Roderick Hallowell MacPherson), 1897–1975, Canadian organist]

McQuaid, McQuaide from Irish Gaelic *Mac Uaid* 'son of *Uad*', a gaelicization of the English personal name *Wat*, a pet-form of **Walter**. See also **Quaid**

McQuarrie, McQuarie, Macquarie from Scottish Gaelic, 'son of *Guaire*', a personal name meaning literally 'proud, noble'. See also **Quarry** (iii) [Lachlan Macquarie, 1762–1824, Australian colonial administrator]
— **Lake Macquarie** a coastal lake in New South Wales, Australia, named after Lachlan Macquarie (see above)
— **Macquarie Island** an uninhabited Australian island in the Southern Ocean, southeast of Tasmania. It was named in honour of Lachlan Macquarie.
— **Macquarie University** a university in Sydney, Australia, founded in 1964. It was named after Lachlan Macquarie.

McQueen from Scottish Gaelic, 'son of *Suibhne*', a personal name meaning literally 'pleasant'. See also **Sweeney** [Alexander McQueen (original name Lee McQueen), 1969–, British fashion designer; Steve McQueen, 1930–80, US actor]

McRae, MacRae see **McCrae**. See also **Rae**

McRea probably a different form of **McCrae**. See also **Rea** (ii)

McReady, McReadie see **McCready**

McRoberts from Scottish Gaelic *Mac Roibeirt* 'son of Robert' (see **Roberts**)

McShane from Gaelic, 'son of *Seán*', the Irish form of **John**. See also **Shane** (ii) [Ian McShane, 1942–, British actor]

McSharry from Irish Gaelic, 'son of *Searrach*', a nickname meaning literally 'foal'

McSherry (i) from Irish Gaelic, 'son of *Séartha*', a Gaelic equivalent of English **Geoffrey**. See also **Sherry**; (ii) a different form of **McSharry**

McTaggart from Gaelic *Mac An tSagairt* 'son of the priest'. See also **Taggart**

McTavish from Scottish Gaelic *Mac Tamhais* 'son of **Thomas**'

McTeague, McTigue from Irish Gaelic, 'son of *Tadhg*', a nickname meaning 'poet, philosopher'. See also **Montagu** (ii)
— *McTeague* a novel (1899) by Frank Norris, set in San Francisco, which shows how McTeague, a slow-witted unlicensed dentist, becomes a thief and a murderer

McTeer, McTear a different form of **McAteer**

McTigue see **McTeague**

McTurk from Scottish Gaelic, 'son of *Torc*', a nickname meaning literally 'boar'. See also **Turk** (iii)

McVeagh, McVeigh, McVey, McVea different forms of **McBeth**

McVicar, McVicker from Scottish Gaelic *Mac áBhiocair* or Irish Gaelic *Mac An Bhiocaire* 'son of the vicar' [John McVicar, 1941–, British journalist and former armed robber]

McVitie, McVittie, McVitty from Gaelic *Mac Bhiadhtaigh* 'son of the victualler' (see **Beatty**)
— **McVitie's** a biscuit producer, originating in an Edinburgh bakery founded in 1809 by Robert McVitie. In 1839 it produced the world's first

digestive biscuit. In 1888 it became **McVitie and Price**, and in 1948 it became part of United Biscuits.

McWhinney, McWhinnie from Gaelic, 'son of *Coinneach*' (see **McKenzie**). See also **Mawhinney**

McWhirter, McWhorter from Gaelic *Mac An Chruiteir* 'son of the harpist or fiddler' [Norris McWhirter, 1925–2004, British writer, right-wing political activist and, with his twin brother Ross McWhirter, 1925–75, founder of the *Guinness Book of Records*]

McWilliam from Scottish Gaelic *Mac Uilleim* 'son of **William**'

McWilliams a different form of **McWilliam**

Macy see **Macey**

Madden from Irish Gaelic *Ó Madáin* 'descendant of *Madán*', a different form of *Madadhán*, a name based on *madadh* 'dog'

Maddison, Madison 'son of *Madde*', a medieval female personal name, a different form of **Maud** or of *Magdalen* (see **Maudling**) [James Madison, 1751–1836, US statesman, president 1809–17]
— *The Bridges of Madison County* a novel (1992) by Robert James Waller, telling of a love affair between an Italian war bride and a visiting photographer who is taking pictures of the covered bridges of Madison County, Iowa. A film version appeared in 1995.
— **Madison** the capital of Wisconsin, USA, founded in 1836. It was named after James Madison (see above).
— **Madison Avenue** a street in Manhattan, New York City. It is the hub of the US advertising and public-relations industries, and its name is often used metonymically for them. It was inherited from the adjacent Madison Square, which in turn was named in honour of James Madison.
— **Madison Square Garden** a sports and entertainment arena in New York City, so named because the original building was on the corner of Madison Square

Maddocks, Maddox 'son of **Madoc**'

Madeley 'person from Madeley', the name of various places in England ('Māda's glade'). See also **Medley** (iii) [Richard Madeley, 1956–, British television presenter]

Madoc, Maddock from the Welsh personal name *Madog*, perhaps a derivative of *mad* 'fortunate, good'
— **Porthmadog, Portmadoc** a resort town in Gwynedd, Wales, named after William Alexander Maddocks, 1772–1828, an MP who built a harbour there in the early 19th century
— **Tremadog, Tremadoc** a village in Gwynedd, Wales, developed around 1805 by William Alexander Maddocks (see above) (the name means literally 'village of Maddocks')

Madsen 'son of *Mathias*', a Danish and Norwegian form of **Matthew**

Magee see **McGee**

Mager see **Major** (i)

Maggs 'son of *Magge*', a pet-form of *Margaret*, a female personal name which came into English via

French from Late Latin *Margarita*, literally 'pearl'. See also **Margeson, Megson, Mogg, Moxon**

Magill see **McGill**

Maginnis see **McGuinness**

Magnus from the Scandinavian male personal name *Magnus*, from Latin *magnus* 'great' (the use of the word as a personal name originated with the Norwegian king Magnus the Good (died 1047), whose parents adopted it from the sobriquet of the Emperor Charlemagne, in Latin *Carolus Magnus*, literally 'Charles the Great'). See also **Manson** (ii)

Magnusson, Magnuson 'son of **Magnus**' (Swedish) [Magnus Magnusson (original name Magnus Sigursteinnson), 1929–2007, Icelandic television presenter active in Britain]

Maguire see **McGuire**

Maher from Irish Gaelic *Ó Meachair* 'descendant of *Meachar*', a personal name meaning literally 'hospitable'. See also **Meacher**

Mahew see **Mayhew**

Mahmood, Mahmoud, Mahmud from the Arabic personal name *Maḥmūd*, literally 'praiseworthy' [Sajid Mahmood, 1981–, English cricketer]

Mahon (i) from Irish Gaelic *Ó Mathghamhna* (see **Mahoney**); (ii) a different form of **Mohan** [Christy Mahon, the personable fugitive from justice who is the hero of J.M. Synge's *The Playboy of the Western World* (1907)]

Mahoney from Irish Gaelic *Ó Mathghamhna* 'descendant of *Mathghamhain*', a nickname meaning 'good calf'

Maiden, Mayden from a medieval nickname for an effeminate man

Maidment 'servant employed by young women or nuns' (Middle English *maidman*)

Maier see **Mayer**

Mailer (i) 'enameller' (from Middle English *ameillur* 'enameller'), or 'maker of chain mail' (Middle English *mailler*, from *maille* 'mail'); (ii) 'person from Mailer', Perth and Kinross (perhaps 'bare height'); (iii) 'person from Maelor', Clwyd ('Mael's territory'); (iv) from the Old Welsh personal name *Meilyr*, literally 'chief ruler'; (v) a Jewish name perhaps denoting a charcoal burner (from German *Meiler* 'charcoal kiln') [Norman Mailer, 1923–, US writer]

Mailey 'person from Mailly', the name of various places in northern France [Arthur Mailey, 1886–1967, Australian cricketer]

Main see **Mayne**

Mains, Maines (i) 'person who lives on the main farm on an estate' (Scottish English *mains* 'main farm, home farm', a derivative of *domain*); (ii) a different form of **Main**

Mainwaring, Manwaring, Mannering 'person from Mainwaring', a place of unknown location ('Warin's domain'). The name is standardly pronounced 'mannering'. [Captain George Mainwaring, the pompous bank manager and Home Guard commander (played by Arthur Lowe) in the BBC television sitcom *Dad's Army* (1968–77)]

Mair (i) 'Scottish court official dealing with petty offenders' (Scottish English *mair*, from Old French – see **Mayer** (i)); (ii) a different form of **Meyer** (ii)

Maitland perhaps from a medieval nickname for a boorish person (from Anglo-Norman *maltalent* 'ill disposition, bad temper'), or alternatively possibly 'person from Mautalent', Pontorson, Normandy ('ill-disposed place', referring to its infertile soil) [F.W. Maitland, 1850–1906, British historian]

Maitlis, Maitles, Meitlis 'son of *Meytl*', a Yiddish female personal name, literally 'little *Meyte*', a Yiddish female personal name derived from Middle High German *maget* 'maid'

Major (i) *also* **Mager** *or* **Mauger** from the Norman male personal name *Malgier* or *Maugier*, of Germanic origin and meaning literally 'council-spear'; (ii) a different form of **Meyer** (ii) [Ivan Mauger, 1939–, New Zealand speedway rider; Sir John Major, 1943–, British Conservative politician, prime minister 1990–97]

Majors 'son of **Major** (i)' [Lee Majors (original name Harvey Lee Yeary), 1939–, US actor]

Makepeace, Makepiece from a medieval nickname for a skilled conciliator [Harry Makepeace, 1881–1952, English cricketer]

Makin, Maykin (i) 'little **May** (ii)'; (ii) from a medieval nickname for an effeminate man (from Middle English *maidkin*, literally 'little maid'). See also **Meakin**

Makins 'son of **Makin** (i)'

Malcolm, Malcom from the Scottish Gaelic personal name *Mael-Colum* 'follower of (St) Columba' [Derek Malcolm, 1932–, British film critic; Devon Malcolm, 1963–, Jamaican-born English cricketer; George Malcolm, 1917–97, British harpsichordist; Mary Malcolm, 1918–, British radio announcer]

Malden 'person from (New) Malden', Greater London [Karl Malden (original name Karl Mladen Sekulovich), 1914–, US actor]

Maley see **Malley**

Malik 'ruler, chief' (from Arabic *malik* 'king')

Malinowski 'person from Malinow', the name (with variations) of numerous places in Poland and the Ukraine, derived from Slavic *malina* 'raspberry'

Mallard (i) from the Old French male personal name *Malhard*, brought into England by the Normans but ultimately of Germanic origin and meaning literally 'council-brave'; (ii) from a medieval nickname for someone thought to resemble a male wild duck

Mallett, Mallet (i) 'blacksmith', or from a medieval nickname for an aggressive hammer-wielder (in either case from *mallet* 'hammer'); (ii) from the medieval female personal name *Malet*, literally 'little *Mal*', a pet-form of *Mary*; (iii) a different form of **Mallard** (i); (iv) from a medieval nickname for an unlucky person (from Old French *maleit* 'accursed'); (v) from a pet-form of the French female personal name *Malo*, of Celtic origin

Malley, Maley shortened forms of **O'Malley**. See also **Melia** (i), **Melly**

Mallinson 'son of *Malin*', a medieval female personal name, literally 'little *Mal*', a pet-form of *Mary*

Mallison, Malleson different forms of **Mallinson** [Miles Malleson, 1888–1969, British actor and dramatist]

Mallon a different form of **Malone**

Mallory, Malory from a medieval nickname for an unlucky person (from Old French *malheure* 'unfortunate, unhappy') [George Mallory, 1886–1924, British mountaineer; Sir Thomas Malory, ?1400–71, English writer and translator]

Malloy see **Molloy**

Malone from Irish Gaelic *Ó Maoil Eoin* 'descendant of the follower of (St) John'. See also **Mallon**
— **Mike/Molly Malone** (see below) rhyming slang for *telephone*
— **'Molly Malone'** a song, reputedly written in the early 1880s by James Yorkston, about an itinerant female fish-seller in 17th-century Dublin, who announced her wares with a cry of 'Cockles and mussels, alive, alive-o!' She is not known to have a basis in any actual historical character
— **on your Pat Malone** on your own. A rhyming expression first recorded (in Australian English) in 1908. There seems to have been no particular Pat Malone.

Maloney see **Moloney**

Malpas, Malpass 'person from Malpas', the name of various places in England and Wales ('difficult passage', denoting e.g. a muddy road or an unpleasant river crossing)

Maltravers probably 'person from Maltravers', an unidentified place ('difficult crossing'). See also **Matravers**

Mancini 'son of *Mancino*', from a medieval Italian nickname for a left-handed person [Henry Mancini (original name Enrico Nicola Mancini), 1924–94, US composer and arranger]

Mandeville 'person from Mannville or Manneville', the name of various places in France (either 'Manno's settlement' or 'great settlement'). See also **Manville** [Sir John Mandeville, supposed author (probably fictional) of the highly popular *Travels* (1356–57)]

Mangan from Irish Gaelic *Ó Mongáin* 'descendant of *Mongán*', from a nickname for someone with an abundant head of hair (from *mong* 'hair')

Mangold (i) perhaps 'operator of a mangonel (a medieval seige catapult)'; (ii) from the Germanic personal name *Managwald*, literally 'much rule'

Manilow from the Jewish male personal name *Manele*, a pet-form of **Emmanuel** [Barry Manilow (original name Barry Alan Pincus), 1943–, US popular singer]

Manley, Manly, Manleigh (i) 'person from Manley', Cheshire and Devon ('woodland glade held in common'); (ii) from a medieval nickname for a manly or virile man [Michael Manley,

1923–97, Jamaican politician, prime minister 1972–80, 1989–92]

Mann (i) from a medieval nickname for one regarded as quintessentially a man, either for qualities of virility or ferocity, or as explicitly contrasted with a boy; (ii) 'male servant'; (iii) from the Old English male personal name *Manna*, which may have originated in a nickname (as in (i)) or as a shortened form of any of the many Germanic personal names ending in -*man*; (iv) a Jewish name perhaps from Hebrew and Yiddish *man* 'manna'. See also **Manning, Manson** [Anthony Mann (original name Emil Anton Bundmann), 1906–67, US film director; Michael Mann, 1943–, US screenwriter and film director]

— **Manfred Mann** a British R&B and pop band founded in 1962 by the South African-born Manfred Mann (original name Manfred Liebowitz), 1940–. He was the group's keyboards player.

— **Mann Act** the unofficial name of the US White-Slave Traffic Act of 1910, which outlawed 'white slavery' and the transportation of prostitutes across interstate boundaries. It commemorates the act's author, the Republican politician James Robert Mann, 1856–1922.

Mannering see **Mainwaring**

Manners 'person from Mesnières', northern France ('residence, settlement'). See also **Menzies**

Manning 'son of **Mann** (i–iii)' [Bernard Manning, 1930–2007, British comedian; Frederic Manning, 1892–1935, Australian-born British writer; Cardinal Henry Manning, 1808–92, British cleric; Olivia Manning, 1908–80, British novelist; Robert Mannyng, flourished 1288–1338, English chronicler and religious writer]

Mansell, Mansel (i) 'feudal tenant occupying a manse (an area of land large enough to support one family)'; (ii) 'person from Le Mans', northwestern France (from Old French *mansel* 'inhabitant of Le Mans', literally '(town of the) Ceromanni', a Gaulish tribe) [Nigel Mansell, 1953–, British racing driver]

Manser (i) 'maker of handles' (from a derivative of Anglo-Norman *mance* 'handle'); (ii) from the Jewish male personal name *Manasseh* (from Hebrew *Menashe*, literally 'one who causes forgetfulness'; originally bestowed on Joseph's elder son in the hope that he might enable his grandfather Jacob to forget the sorrows of the past)

Mansfield 'person from Mansfield', Nottinghamshire ('open land by the (river) Maun') [Jayne Mansfield (original name Vera Jayne Palmer), 1933–67, US film actress; Katherine Mansfield (original name Katherine Mansfield Beauchamp), 1888–1923, New Zealand-born British writer; Sir Peter Mansfield, 1933–, British physicist, co-inventor of the MRI body-scanner]

— **Mansfield College** a college of Oxford University, established in 1886 as a college for students from the Free Churches. It was essentially a relocation of Spring Hill College, which had been founded in Birmingham in 1838 by the Mansfield family – whence the name.

Manson (i) 'son of **Mann** (i–iii)'; (ii) 'son of **Magnus**' [Charles Manson, 1934–, US cult leader and murderer; Marilyn Manson, stage-name of Brian Hugh Warner, 1969–, androgynous US heavy-metal singer/songwriter, lead singer of the eponymous band 'Marilyn Manson']

Mantell, Mantel (i) *also* **Mantle** 'maker of cloaks, coats, etc'., or from a medieval nickname for someone who conspicuously wore such a garment (from Anglo-Norman *mantel* 'cloak, coat'); (ii) a Jewish surname derived from German *Mantel* or Yiddish *mantl* 'coat' [Gideon Mantell, 1790–1852, British obstetrician, geologist and palaeontologist, discoverer of the first known dinosaur fossils]

Manton 'person from Manton', the name of various places in England (mainly either 'Manna's farmstead' or 'farmstead held in common')

Manville, Manvell different forms of **Mandeville**

Maple 'person who lives by a maple tree'

— **Maples** a British firm of furniture manufacturers, founded in 1842 by John Maple, died 1900, and developed by his son Sir John Blundell Maple, 1845–1903

Mapp, Map from a variant of the medieval female personal name *Mabbe* (see **Mabbett**) [Elizabeth Mapp, busybodyish spinster in the 'Mapp and Lucia' novels of E.F. Benson; Walter Map, ?1140–1210, English cleric and author]

Mappin a different form of **Maupin**

— **Mappin and Webb** a firm of goldsmiths, silversmiths and jewellers established in London in 1860 by John Newton Mappin, 1836–1913, son of a Sheffield cutler. He was later joined by a Mr Webb.

— **Mappin Terraces** a series of mountain-like reinforced-concrete terraces for bears, goats, etc. in London Zoo, built in 1913 to the designs of the architectural firm of Belcher and Joass and named after John Newton Mappin (see above), who sponsored them

March (i) 'person from March', Cambridgeshire ('place at the boundary'); (ii) 'person born in March, or with some other sort of connection with that month'; (iii) 'person who lives in a border area, especially the English-Welsh borders (the Welsh *Marches*) or the English-Scottish borders' [Fredric March (original name Ernest Frederick McIntyre Bickell), 1897–1975, US actor; Jo March and her sisters Meg, Beth and Amy, the 'little women' of Louisa May Alcott's novel (1868) of that name]

Marchant 'buyer and seller of goods' (Middle English *marchant* 'merchant', from Old French). See also **Merchant**

Marchbanks see **Marjoribanks**

Marciano (i) 'person from Marciano', the name of various places in southern Italy; (ii) from the Italian male personal name *Marciano*, from Latin *Marcianus*, ultimately from *Marcus* (see **Mark** (i)) [Rocky Marciano (original name Rocco Franco Marchegiano), 1923–69, US boxer]

Marcus from the Latin male personal name *Marcus* (see **Mark** (i))

Marden, Mardon 'person from Marden', the name of numerous places in England (variously 'enclosed settlement in Maund (a district)', 'place in the boundary valley' and 'woodland pasture where mares are kept')

Margeson, Margesson 'son of *Marge*', a pet-form of the female personal names *Margery* and *Margaret* (see **Maggs**; *Margery* was the usual medieval form of *Margaret*)

Margolis, Margolies, Margolyes from the Jewish female personal name *Margolis*, literally (in Hebrew) 'pearls' [Miriam Margolyes, 1941–, British actress]

Marin (i) from the French personal name *Marin*, from Latin *Marīnus*, a derivative of the Roman family name *Marius*; (ii) 'sailor' (French)

Mariner, Marriner 'sailor' [Sir Neville Marriner, 1924–, British conductor]

Marion from the female personal name *Marion* (from Old French, literally 'little Mary') [Howard Marion-Crawford, 1914–69, British actor]

Marjoribanks, Marchbanks reputedly from the name of a Scottish estate (*Ratho-Marjoribankis*) bestowed on Robert the Bruce's daughter Marjorie on her marriage in 1316. The standard pronunciation is 'marchbanks'.

Mark (i) from the Latin male personal name *Marcus*, which may have some connection with *Mars*, the Roman god of war; (ii) *also* **Marke** 'person who lives in a border area' (from Old English *mearc* 'boundary'); (iii) an anglicization of various similar-sounding Jewish names (e.g. *Markowitz*) [Sir Robert Mark, 1917–, British police commissioner]

Marker (i) 'person who lives in a border area' (from a derivative of Old English *mearc* 'boundary'); (ii) 'person whose job is to mark or put marks on things'; (iii) a different form of **Mercer** [Frank Marker, the down-at-heel private detective played by Alfred Burke in the ITV drama series *Public Eye* (1965–75)]

Markes see **Marks**

Markey, Markie from Irish Gaelic *Ó Marcaigh* 'descendant of *Marcach*', a nickname meaning literally 'horseman, knight'

Markham (i) 'person from Markham', Nottinghamshire ('homestead by a boundary'); (ii) from Irish Gaelic *Ó Marcacháin* 'descendant of *Marcachán*', literally 'little *Marcach*' (see **Markey**) [Gervase Markham, 1568–1637, English author]

Marks, Markes (i) 'son of **Mark** (i)'; (ii) a different form of **Mark** (ii); (iii) *also* **Marx** a contracted form of German *Markus* '**Mark** (i)' [Alfred Marks, 1921–96, British comedian and comic actor; Lilian Alicia Marks, the original name of the British ballerina Dame Alicia Markova, 1910–2004; Harrison Marks, 1926–97, British glamour photographer]

— **Marks and Spencer** a British chain of retail stores founded in 1887 by Michael Marks, died 1907, and Thomas Spencer, died 1905, and devel-oped by Marks's son Simon Marks (Lord Marks), 1888–1964

— **Marx Brothers** an early 20th-century fraternal US band of screen and stage comedians, led by Groucho Marx (original name Julius Marx), 1895–1977. The other brothers were Chico (Leonard Marx), 1891–1961, Gummo (Milton Marx), 1901–77, the dumb harp-playing Harpo (Adolph Marx), 1893–1964, and Zeppo (Herbert Marx), 1900–79.

Marler, Marlar 'person who lives in an area of clayey soil' (Middle English *marl*)

Marley 'person from Marley', the name of numerous places in England (variously 'glade at a boundary', 'pleasant glade' and 'glade frequented by martens') [Bob Marley, 1945–81, Jamaican musician; Jacob Marley, the deceased former business partner of Ebenezer Scrooge who appears to him as a ghost in Dickens's *A Christmas Carol* (1843)]

Marlow, Marlowe (i) 'person from Marlow', Buckinghamshire ('place by the remnants of a lake'); (ii) a different form of **Marley** [Christopher Marlowe, 1564–93, English playwright and poet; Philip Marlowe, a hard-bitten US private detective created by Raymond Chandler, most memorably portrayed on screen by Humphrey Bogart]

Marple 'person from Marple', Cheshire ('pool by the boundary') [Jane Marple ('Miss Marple'), the self-effacing spinster-detective created (in 1930) by Agatha Christie]

Marples a different form of **Marple** [Ernest Marples (Lord Marples), 1907–78, British Conservative politician]

Marquis (i) 'servant in the household of a marquess', or from a nickname applied to someone who behaved with the hauteur of a marquess; (ii) a shortening of *McMarquis*, from Scottish Gaelic *Mac Marcuis* 'son of **Mark** (i)'

Marr, Marre 'person from Mar', Aberdeenshire (perhaps 'place by the marsh'), or 'person from Marr', Yorkshire ('place by the marsh') [Andrew Marr, 1959–, British journalist]

Marriner see **Mariner**

Marriott from the medieval English female personal name *Mariot*, literally 'little Mary'. See also **Merritt**

— **Marriott Hotels** a US-based international chain of hotels founded in 1929 by the entrepreneur and businessman J. Willard Marriott, 1900–85.

Marryat (i) from the medieval personal name *Meryet*, literally 'border Geat' (*Gēat* was a Germanic tribal name); (ii) a different form of **Marriott** [Frederick Marryat ('Captain Marryat'), 1792–1848, British novelist]

Mars (i) a different form of **Marsh**; (ii) from the French male personal name *Mard* or *Mart*, a colloquial form of *Médard*, a saint's name; (iii) 'person from Mars', the name of various places in France ('Marcius's settlement'); (iv) 'grower of crops' (from French *mars* 'March', the month of seed-sowing) [Eddie Mars, gangster who figures in Raymond Chandler's *The Big Sleep* (1939)]

— **Eyes of Laura Mars** a film (1978) about a fashion photographer, Laura Mars (played by Faye Dunaway), who has violent premonitions about a series of murders

— **Mars Bar** the proprietary name of a chocolate-covered bar with a toffee-like filling, first produced in 1933 by Mars Confections Ltd. The business was started in Slough by the US confectioner Forrest Mars, 1904–99, who left the American candy firm owned by his father, Frank C. Mars, after the two fell out.

Marsalis probably from a Dutch variant of French *Marchal*, literally 'marshal' (see **Marshall**) [Wynton Marsalis, 1961–, US musician and bandleader]

Marsden 'person from Marsden', Lancashire and Yorkshire ('valley forming a boundary') [Betty Marsden, 1919–98, British comedy actress; Roy Marsden (original name Roy Mould), 1941–, British actor]

— **Royal Marsden Hospital** a cancer hospital in Southwest London, founded in 1851 by Dr William Marsden, 1796–1867. It was originally called simply the Cancer Hospital, and changed to its present name in 1954.

Marsh 'person who lives by or in the middle of a marsh or fen'. See also **Mars** (i) [Graham Marsh, 1944–, Australian golfer; Jean Marsh, 1934–, British actress; Dame Ngaio Marsh, 1899–1981, New Zealand detective-story writer; Richard Marsh (Lord Marsh), 1928–, British Labour politician; Rodney Marsh, 1944–, English footballer; Rodney Marsh, 1947–, Australian cricketer, brother of Graham]

Marshall 'high-ranking servant in a great household' or 'farrier, blacksmith', both occupations covered in the Middle Ages by the term *marshal* (from Old French *mareschal*, but ultimately of Germanic origin and meaning literally 'horse-servant'). See also **Maskall** [Arthur Marshall, 1910–89, British writer and broadcaster; E.G. Marshall, 1914–98, US actor; Sir Edward Marshall Hall, 1858–1929, British barrister; George C. Marshall, 1880–1959, US general and statesman; Malcolm Marshall, 1958–99, West Indian cricketer]

— **Marshall and Snelgrove** a former British department store, in Oxford Street. It originated in a shop opened in nearby Vere Street in 1837 by James Marshall and a certain Mr Wilson. John Snelgrove joined them in 1848.

— **Marshall Cavendish** a British publishing company, founded in 1968 by Norman Marshall and Patrick Cavendish. In 1980 it became part of the Times Publishing Group.

— **Marshall Islands** an island republic in the central northern Pacific Ocean. It is named after the British sea captain John Marshall, 1748–1819, who visited in 1788.

— **Marshall Plan** a programme of loans and other economic assistance provided by the US government between 1947 and 1952 to help western European nations rebuild after the Second World War. It was devised and promoted by George C. Marshall (see above).

Marsland 'person from Marsland', an unidentified place probably in northern England (probably 'marshy land')

Marston 'person from Marston', the name of numerous places in England ('farmstead by a marsh') [John Marston, ?1575–1634, English playwright and satirist]

Martin, Marten, Martyn from the male personal name *Martin*, from Latin *Martīnus*, a derivative of *Mars*, the name of the Roman god of war. See also **Mortensen** [Archer Martin, 1910–2002, British biochemist; Christopher Martin-Jenkins, 1945–, British journalist and cricket commentator; Sir George Martin, 1926–, British musician and record producer; John Martin, 1789–1854, British painter; Millicent Martin, 1934–, British singer; Paul Martin, 1938–, Canadian Liberal politician, prime minister 2003–; Richard Martin, 1754–1834, Irish politician, co-founder of the RSPCA]

— **Aston Martin** a British marque of luxury sports car, founded in 1914 by Lionel Martin, 1878–1945, and Robert Bamford. The 'Aston' comes from the Aston Hill Climb, held near Aston Clinton, Buckinghamshire.

— **Pincher Martin** a novel (1956) by William Golding about a man, Christopher 'Pincher' Martin, shipwrecked alone on a bare rock in the North Atlantic

Martindale 'person from Martindale', Cumbria

Martineau (i) 'little **Martin**', French; (ii) 'person from Martineau', France [Harriet Martineau, 1802–76, British writer]

Martinez from Spanish *Martínez* 'son of **Martin**'

Martins, Martens, Martyns 'son of **Martin**'

Marvel, Marvell (i) from a medieval nickname (often ironic) for someone regarded as a prodigy; (ii) 'person from Merville', the name of two places in northern France ('smaller settlement' and 'settlement belonging to a man with a Germanic name beginning with *Meri*-, literally "famous"') [Andrew Marvell, 1621–78, English poet]

Marvin a different form of **Mervyn** [Hank Marvin (original name Brian Robson Rankin), 1941–, British guitarist; Lee Marvin, 1924–87, US actor]

— **Hank/Lee Marvin** rhyming slang for *starving* 'very hungry'

Marwick 'person from Marwick', Orkneys ('sea bay')

Marx see **Marks** (iii)

Masefield 'person from Masefield', an unidentified place possibly in the West Midlands (probably 'Mæssa's area of open land') [John Masefield, 1878–1967, British poet]

Maskall, Maskell, Maskill different forms of **Marshall** [Dan Maskell, 1908–92, British tennis commentator; Virginia Maskell, 1936–68, British actress]

Maslin, Maslen (i) from the medieval male personal name *Masselin*, brought into English from Old French, where it was a pet-form of various names of Germanic origin beginning with *Mathal*-, literally 'speech, advice'. It later came to be regarded as a pet-form of **Matthew.**; (ii) perhaps 'maker of wooden bowls' (from Middle English *maselin* 'maple-wood vessel', from Old French)

Mason 'stonemason' (Middle English *masson, mason*, from Old French). See also **Machin, Masson** [A.E.W. Mason, 1865–1948, British novelist; James Mason, 1909–84, British actor; Perry Mason, US investigating lawyer in a series of 89 crime novels (beginning in 1933) by Erle Stanley Gardner; Roy Mason (Lord Mason), 1924–, British Labour politician]

— **Charley Mason, Jimmy Mason** rhyming slang for *basin* (usually in the metaphorical sense of *basinful*, 'more than enough')

— **Fortnum and Mason** see **Fortnum**

— **Mason-Dixon Line** the boundary that separates Pennsylvania from Maryland and West Virginia, regarded as the dividing line between free and slave states before the American Civil War. It is named after the two English surveyors who drew it in 1767, Charles Mason, 1730–87, and Jeremiah Dixon, 1733–79.

Masseter perhaps 'brewery worker' (from Middle English *mash* 'fermentable mixture of hot water and grain' + *rudder* 'rudder-shaped stirrer'). See also **Messiter**

Massey, Massie 'person from Massey', northern France ('Maccius's settlement'). See also **Macey** [Anna Massey, 1937–, British actress, daughter of Raymond; Daniel Massey, 1933–98, British actor, son of Raymond; Raymond Massey, 1896–1983, Canadian actor; William Ferguson Massey, 1856–1925, Irish-born New Zealand Conservative politician, prime minister 1912–25]

— **Massey-Ferguson** a manufacturer of agricultural machinery. It had its origins in a company founded in 1847 by the Canadian blacksmith Daniel Massey (great-grandfather of Raymond – see above), 1798–1856, to make agricultural implements. In 1891 it joined forces with A. Harris Sons & Co. to become **Massey-Harris**, and another merger in the 1950s transformed it into Massey-Ferguson.

Massingberd, Massingbird perhaps from a medieval nickname for someone with an auburn or reddish beard (from Middle English *massing* 'brass' + *berd* 'beard')

Massingham 'person from Massingham', Norfolk ('homestead associated with Mæssa')

Masson (i) 'stonemason', French, from Old French *masson* (see **Mason**); (ii) a Scottish variant of **Mason**; (iii) from a French pet-form of **Thomas**

Master (i) 'schoolmaster'; (ii) 'master craftsman'; (iii) from a medieval nickname for someone with masterful ways. See also **McMaster**

Masterman 'servant of a master craftsman, or of someone called **Master**' [J.C. Masterman, 1891–1977, British academic, spymaster and author]

Masters 'son of **Master**' [Edgar Lee Masters, 1869–1950, US poet; John Masters, 1914–83, Indian-born British soldier and novelist]

— **Masters and Johnson** the US team of physician William Howell Masters, 1915–2001, and psychologist Virginia Eshelman Johnson, 1925–, who published the pioneering and controversial work *Human Sexual Responses* (1966)

Masterson 'son of **Master**'

Masterton 'person from Masterton', Fife ('master's settlement' – the land was once held by the Master of Dunfermline Abbey)

Mather 'mower of grass or hay' (from Old English *mæthere*)

Matheson, Mathieson 'son of **Matthew**' [Muir Mathieson, 1911–75, British conductor and musical director]

Mathew, Mathews see **Matthew, Matthews**

Mathias see **Matthias**

Matravers a different form of **Maltravers**

Matthew, Mathew from the male personal name *Matthew*, popularized as a biblical name and ultimately from Hebrew *Matityahu*, literally 'gift of god'. See also **Matthias, Mayhew**

Matthews, Mathews 'son of **Matthew**' [A.E. Matthews, 1869–1960, British actor; Bernard Matthews, 1930–, British turkey-rearer and businessman; Colin Matthews, 1946–, British composer; Jessie Matthews, 1907–81, British actress and singer; Sir Stanley Matthews, 1915–2000, English footballer]

Matthias, Mathias a mainly Welsh variant of **Matthew**, based on the New Testamant Greek form of the name [William Mathias, 1934–92, British composer]

Mattingley, Mattingly 'person from Mattingley', Hampshire ('glade associated with Matta')

Maturin from the French male personal name *Maturin*, from Latin *Mātūrīnus*, a derivative of *Mātūrus*, literally 'timely' [Charles Maturin, 1782–1824, Irish 'Gothic' novelist]

Maud, Maude different forms of **Moult** [Angus Maude (Lord Maude), 1912–93, British Conservative politician; John Maud (Lord Redcliffe-Maud), see **Redcliffe**]

Maudling from the medieval female personal name *Maudeleyn*, the English form of Greek *Magdalēnē*, the sobriquet in the New Testament of the woman Mary who was cured of evil spirits by Jesus. It means literally 'woman from Magdala', the name of a village on the Sea of Galilee. [Reginald Maudling, 1917–79, British Conservative politician]

Maudslay, Maudsley see **Mawdesley**

Mauger see **Major** (i)

Maugham a different form of **Maughan** [William Somerset Maugham, 1874–1965, British author]

Maughan (i) 'person from Machan', Strathclyde ('small (river) plain'); (ii) 'person from (St) Maughan', Monmouthshire ('(church of St) Mochán' – see **Moon** (iv)); (iii) 'person from Machen', Caerphilly ('place of Cain'); (iv) from Irish Gaelic *Ó Macháin* 'descendant of *Machán*', perhaps a different form of *Mochán* (see **Moon** (iv))

Mauleverer from a medieval nickname of uncertain relevance based on Old French *mal leverier* 'bad harrier (i.e. hunter of hares)'

Maupin 'person who lives by a bad pine tree' (from French, literally 'bad pine'). See also **Mappin** [Armistead Maupin, 1944–, US author]

Maurice see **Morris**

Maw, Mawe (i) from the Old English personal name *Mawa*, perhaps originally a nickname based on *mǣw* 'seagull'; (ii) 'person who lives in or by a meadow' (from Middle English *mawe* 'meadow'); (iii) from a medieval nickname for some who was a relative of a notable person (from Middle English *maw* 'relative, especially by marriage; brother-in-law') [Nicholas Maw, 1935–, British composer]

Mawdesley, Mawdsley, Maudslay, Maudsley 'person from Mawdesley', Lancashire (probably 'Maud's glade')

Mawhinney a different form of **McWhinney** [Brian Mawhinney (Lord Mawhinney), 1940–, British Conservative politician]

Maxey 'person from Maxey', Northamptonshire ('Maccus's island')

Maxim from the French personal name *Maxim* (from Latin *Maximus*, literally 'greatest')
— **Maxim gun** an early type of water-cooled single-barrel machine gun invented by the US-born British engineer Sir Hiram Maxim, 1840–1916

Maxwell (i) 'person from Maxwell', Borders ('Mack's spring'); (ii) an anglicization of any of various similar-sounding Jewish names [James Clerk Maxwell, 1831–79, Scottish physicist; Sir Peter Maxwell Davies, see **Davies**; Robert Maxwell (original name Ján Ludvik Hoch), 1923–91, Slovakian-born British media proprietor, Labour politician and fraudster]
— **maxwell** the centimetre-gram-second unit of magnetic flux (symbol *Mx*), equal to the flux over one square centimetre perpendicular to a magnetic field of one gauss. It is named after James Clerk Maxwell (see above).
— **Maxwell House** a brand of instant coffee, now owned by Kraft Foods Inc. Its name comes from the Maxwell House hotel in Nashville, Tennessee, owned by its original formulator (1883), Joel Owsley Cheek, 1852–1935.
— **Maxwell's demon** a hypothetical creature devised in 1871 by James Clerk Maxwell as a way of testing the second law of thermodynamics, which says that heat cannot of its own accord flow from a cold to a hot body. The demon supposedly would be able to separate a gas into a cold region and a hot one by opening and closing a shutter to allow only fast-moving molecules to enter the hot region. No such phenomenon has ever been demonstrated.
— **Maxwelltown** a district of Dumfries, in Dumfries and Galloway. It was renamed in 1810 after its proprietor, Marmaduke Constable Maxwell, having previously been called Bridgend.

May, Maye, Mey, Meye (i) from a medieval nickname or personal name based on the name of the month *May* (e.g. indicating someone born in May, or with a sunny or youthful disposition that might be considered typical of the month); (ii) from the medieval personal name *May*, a pet-form of **Matthew**; (iii) from a medieval nickname based on Middle English *may* 'young person'; (iv) an invented Jewish name based on Yiddish *may* 'lilac'. See also **Makin** (i), **Mayes** [Billy May, 1916–2004, US composer and arranger; Peter May, 1929–94, English cricketer; Phil May, 1864–1903, British political and social caricaturist]
— **Bryant and May** see **Bryant**

Mayall, Mayell, Mayle from a medieval nickname for a notably virile man (from Middle English *male* 'masculine') [Peter Mayle, 1939–, British author; Rik Mayall, 1958–, British comic actor and writer]

Mayberry, Maybury probably different forms of **Mowbray**

Mayden see **Maiden**

Maye see **May**

Mayer (i) *also* **Mayor** 'mayor (of a borough)' (Middle English *mair*, from Old French). See also **Mair** (i); (ii) see **Meyer**

Mayers see **Meyers**

Mayes, Mays 'son of **May** (ii)'

Mayfield 'person from Mayfield', Staffordshire and Sussex (respectively 'open land where madder (a plant used for making red dye) grows' and 'open land where mayweed grows')

Mayhew, Mahew from the Anglo-Norman male personal name *Mahieu*, a different form of *Mathieu* '**Matthew**'. See also **Mayo** [Christopher Mayhew (Lord Mayhew), 1915–97, British Labour and Liberal politician; Henry Mayhew, 1812–87, British journalist, author of *London Labour and the London Poor* (1851–62)]

Maykin see **Makin**

Maynall see **Meynell**

Maynard from the medieval male personal name *Mainard*, brought into England by the Normans but ultimately of Germanic origin and meaning literally 'strength-strong' [Bill Maynard (original name Walter Williams), 1928–, British comic actor]

Mayne (i) 'person from Maine', former province of northwestern France; (ii) from the medieval male personal name *Maino* or *Meino*, brought into England by the Normans but ultimately of Germanic origin, from the first element (literally 'strength') of any of a range of Germanic compound names (e.g. **Maynard**). See also **Mencken**; (iii) from a medieval nickname for a large man (from Anglo-Norman *magne* 'large'); (iv) from a medieval nickname for someone with some manual peculiarity (e.g. a deformed or extra-large hand) (from Old French *main* 'hand') [Ferdie Mayne, 1916–98, German-born British actor]

Mayo a different form of **Mayhew** [Simon Mayo, 1958–, British radio presenter]
— **Mayo Clinic** a clinic in Rochester, Minnesota, established and developed by members of the Mayo medical family, including its founder William Worrall Mayo, 1819–1911, his sons

William James Mayo, 1861–1939, and Charles Horace Mayo, 1865–1939, and Charles's son Charles William Mayo, 1898–1968. It pioneered the concept of group practice.

Mayor (i) see **Mayer** (i); (ii) from a Spanish distinguishing name for the elder of two people with the same personal name (from Spanish *mayor* 'elder'); (iii) see **Meyer** (ii)

Meacham a different form of **Machin**

Meacher a different form of **Maher** [Michael Meacher, 1939–, British Labour politician]

Mead, Meade (i) 'person who lives by a meadow' (from Old English *mǣd* 'meadow'). See also **Meads**; (ii) 'maker or seller of mead (an alcoholic drink made from honey)' [George Gordon Meade, 1815–72, US Union general; James Meade, 1907–95, British economist; Margaret Mead, 1901–78, US anthropologist; Richard Meade, 1938–, British three-day-event rider]

Meadow 'person who lives by a meadow'

Meadows a different form of **Meadow**

Meads, Meades different forms of **Mead** (i) [Colin Meads, 1936–, New Zealand rugby player; Jonathan Meades, 1947–, British writer and journalist]

Meakin a different form of **Makin**

Meaney, Meany, Meeny from Irish Gaelic *Ó Maonaigh* 'descendant of *Maonach*', a personal name based on *maoineach* 'rich'. See also **Money, Mooney** [George Meany, 1894–1980, US labour leader]

Meares, Mears 'person who lives in a border area or by a boundary line' (from Old English *gemǣre* or *mǣre* 'boundary'), or 'person who lives by a pond' (from Old English *mere* 'pond') [Ray Mears, 1964–, British survivalist and television presenter]

Medcalf a different form of **Metcalf**

Medhurst a different form of **Midhurst**

Medina 'person from Medina', the name of various places in Spain (from Arabic *medina* 'city')

Medley (i) 'person from Medley', Oxfordshire ('middle island'); (ii) from a medieval nickname for an aggressive person (from Middle English *medlee* 'conflict'); (iii) a different form of **Madeley**

Mee (i) from Irish Gaelic *Mac Conmidhe* (see **McNamee**); (ii) from Irish Gaelic *Ó Miadhaigh* 'descendant of *Miadhach*', a nickname meaning literally 'honourable'. See also **Meehan, Meeson** [Arthur Mee, 1875–1943, British writer, journalist and educator; Bertie Mee, 1918–2001, English football manager]

Meece, Meese 'person from Meece', Staffordshire ('moss')

Meehan from Irish Gaelic *Ó Miadhacháin* 'descendant of *Miadhachan*', literally 'little *Miadhach*' (see **Mee** (ii)), or *Ó Maotháin* 'descendant of *Maothán*', a personal name meaning literally 'little tearful one' [Tony Meehan, 1943–2005, British drummer, member of The Shadows pop group]

Meek, Meeke from a medieval nickname for a humble or submissive person

Meeker (i) 'craftsman, manufacturer' (from Middle Dutch dialect *meker* 'maker'); (ii) from the Germanic personal name *Magherus*

Meeny see **Meaney**

Meese (i) see **Meece**; (ii) 'birdcatcher', from Middle Dutch *mees* 'titmouse'

Meeson 'son of **Mee**'

Megson 'son of *Magge*' (see **Maggs**)

Mehta a Hindu name meaning literally 'chief'

Meier see **Meyer** (ii)

Meiklejohn a Scottish distinguishing name for identifying the larger (Older Scots *meikle* 'large') or elder of two men called 'John'

Meitlis see **Maitlis**

Meldrum 'person from Meldrum', Aberdeenshire ('noble ridge')

Melhuish, Mellish 'person from Melhuish', Devon ('brightly coloured (i.e. flowery) area of land'). The standard pronunciation is 'mellish'.

Melia (i) 'person from Melia', the name of various places in southern Italy and Sicily; (ii) perhaps from a shortened form of the Italian female personal name *Amelia*; (iii) a different form of **Malley**

Mellanby 'person from Melmerby', Cumbria and Yorkshire (respectively 'Melmor's farm' and 'farm in the sandy field')

Melling 'person from Melling', Lancashire ('settlement of Mealla's people')

Mellish see **Melhuish**

Mellon, Mellan from Irish Gaelic *Ó Mealláin* 'descendant of *Meallán*', a personal name meaning literally 'little pleasant one' [Andrew William Mellon, 1855–1937, US businessman, philanthropist and art collector; Paul Mellon, 1907–99, US philanthropist and art collector, son of Andrew]

Mellor 'person from Mellor', Derbyshire, Lancashire and Yorkshire ('bare hill') [David Mellor, 1930–, British silversmith and designer; David Mellor, 1949–, British Conservative politician and broadcaster]
— **David Mellor** (the politician; see above) rhyming slang for *Stella* (*Artois*), a brand of lager

Mellors a different form of **Mellor** [Oliver Mellors, gamekeeper and Lady Chatterley's lover in D.H. Lawrence's *Lady Chatterley's Lover* (1928)]

Melly a different form of **Malley** [George Melly, 1926–2007, British author, journalist and jazz singer]

Melrose 'person from Melrose', Scottish Borders ('bare moor')

Melson a different form of **Milson**

Melton 'person from Melton', the name of various places in England ('middle farmstead')

Melville, Melvil (i) 'person from Malleville', the name of various places in Normandy ('bad settlement'); (ii) from Irish Gaelic *Ó Maoil Mhichil*

'descendant of the follower of (St) Michael' [Alan Melville, 1910–83, British playwright and actor; Alan Melville, 1910–83, South African cricketer; Herman Melville, 1819–91, US novelist]

Melvin (i) from Scottish Gaelic *Mac Gille Bheathain* (see **McIlwaine**), or Irish Gaelic *Ó Maoil Mhín* 'descendant of the follower of (St) Min'; (ii) a different form of **Melville**

Mencken 'son of little *Maino* or *Meino*' (see **Mayne**) [H.L. Mencken, 1880–1956, US journalist and critic]

Mendes from the Portuguese form of Spanish *Méndez* (see **Mendez**) [Sam Mendes, 1965–, British theatre and film director]

Mendez from Spanish *Méndez* 'son of *Mendo*', a reduced form of *Menendo* (see **Menendez**)

Mendoza 'person from Mendoza', Spain ('the cold mountain') [Daniel Mendoza, 1764–1836, British prizefighter]

Menendez from Spanish *Menéndez* 'son of *Menendo*', a medieval personal name derived from Visigothic *Hermenegild*, literally 'entire tribute'

Menuhin 'son of *Menukhe*', a Yiddish female personal name derived from Hebrew *menucha* 'tranquillity' [Yehudi Menuhin (Lord Menuhin), 1916–99, US-born British violinist]

Menzies a Scottish variant of **Manners**, in which the medieval letter ʒ (called 'yogh'), which sounded like *y*, has been replaced by the similar-looking but very different-sounding *z*. In Scotland it is commonly pronounced 'mingiz' or 'ming-giz'. [Sir Robert Menzies, 1894–1978, Australian Liberal politician, prime minister 1939–41, 1949–66]
— **John Menzies plc** a Scottish-based firm formerly occupying much the same niche as newsagents and stationers in Scotland as W.H. Smith does in England. It was founded in Edinburgh in 1833 by John Menzies, 1808–79. It is now a newspaper and magazine distributor.

Mercer 'trader, dealer in textiles' (Middle English, from Old French *mercier*) [David Mercer, 1928–80, British dramatist; Joe Mercer, 1914–90, English football manager]

Merchant (i) 'buyer and seller of goods, trader' (late Middle English *merchant*, from Middle English *marchant* – see **Marchant**); (ii) 'trader', a Muslim and Parsi name adopted in India from the English word *merchant* [Ismail Merchant, 1936–2005, Indian film producer; Vijay Merchant, 1911–87, Indian cricketer; Vivien Merchant (original name Ada Thompson), 1929–83, British actress]

Meredith from the Welsh male personal name *Meredydd*, perhaps literally 'lord of splendour'. See also **Beddoe**, **Merridew**, **Priddy** [George Meredith, 1828–1909, British novelist and poet]

Merrett see **Merritt**

Merriam 'person from Merriams', Kent

Merrick (i) 'person from Merrick', Dumfries and Galloway ('fork of a road or river'); (ii) from the personal name *Merric*, brought into England by the Normans but ultimately of Germanic origin and

meaning literally 'fame-power'; (iii) *also* **Meyrick** from the personal name *Meurig*, the Welsh form of *Maurice* (see **Morris**) [Joseph Merrick, 1862–90, whose gross physical deformities earned him the sobriquet 'The Elephant Man'; Ronald Merrick, the superintendent in the Indian Police Service and later British army officer who is the main unsympathetic character in Paul Scott's *Raj Quartet* (1965–75)]

Merridew a different form of **Meredith**

Merrifield, Merryfield 'person from Merryfield or Mirfield', the name of various places in England ('pleasant area of open land') [Buster Merryfield, 1920–99, British actor]

Merrill, Merrall (i) from the female personal name *Muriel*, literally 'sea-bright'; (ii) 'person from Merrill', the name of various places in England ('pleasant hill'). See also **Murrell**

Merriman, Merryman different forms of **Merry** (i)

Merriott a different form of **Merritt**

Merritt, Merrett (i) 'person from Merriott', Somerset ('boundary gate' or 'mare gate'); (ii) a different form of **Marriott** or **Marryat**

Merriweather, Merryweather from a medieval nickname for someone of a cheerful disposition

Merry (i) from a medieval nickname for someone of a cheerful disposition. See also **Merriman**; (ii) from Irish Gaelic *Ó Mearadhaigh* 'descendant of *Mearadhach*' or *Ó Meardha* 'descendant of *Meardha*', personal names meaning literally 'wild or lively one'

Merryfield see **Merrifield**

Merryman see **Merriman**

Merryweather see **Merriweather**

Merson (i) 'trader' (from Old French, a derivative of *mers* 'merchandise'); (ii) 'son of Mary'; (iii) 'son of **Meyer** (ii)'

Merton 'person from Merton', the name of various places in England ('farmstead by the pool') [Mrs Merton, an unexpectedly sharp-tongued old lady invented by Caroline Aherne, who made her main impact ambushing unwary chat-show guests on BBC television's *The Mrs Merton Show* (1995–98); Paul Merton (original name Paul Martin; he changed it to Merton after the Southwest London borough in which he grew up), 1957–, British comedian]
— **Merton College** a college of Oxford University, founded in 1264 by Walter de Merton, died 1277, chancellor of England

Mervyn, Mervin (i) from the medieval personal name *Merewine*, literally 'fame-friend'; (ii) from the Old English personal names *Mǣrwynn*, literally 'famous joy', and *Merefinn*, from Old Norse *Mora-Finnr*; (iii) from the Welsh personal name *Merfyn*, literally probably 'marrow-eminent' [William Mervyn (original name William Mervyn Pickwoad), 1912–76, British actor]

Messenger, Messinger 'carrier of messages'

Messer (i) 'person who guards harvested crops' (Middle English *messer, messier*, from Old French *messier* 'harvest-master'); (ii) 'knife-maker, cutler' (from German *Messer* or Yiddish *meser* 'knife'); (iii) 'official in charge of measuring payments made in kind by feudal tenants' (Middle High German, from *mezzen* 'to measure')

Messina 'person from Messina', Sicily

Messinger (i) see **Messenger**; (ii) 'worker in brass' (from a derivative of German *Messing* 'brass')

Messiter a different form of **Masseter**

Metcalf, Metcalfe perhaps 'herdsman' or 'slaughterer', or from a medieval nickname for a healthily plump person, from an unrecorded Middle English *metecalf* 'calf being fattened up for slaughter'. See also **Medcalf** [Adrian Metcalfe, 1942–, British athlete; Jean Metcalfe, 1923–2000, British radio presenter]

Methuen a different form of **Methven**
— **Methuen Publishing Ltd** a firm of publishers, founded in London in 1889 by Algernon Methuen Marshall Stedman, 1856–1924. In 1899 he changed his name to Algernon Methuen.
— **Methuen Treaty** a military and commercial treaty concluded in 1703 between England and Portugal, negotiated on the English side by the diplomat John Methuen, *c.*1650–1706. Among its longest-lasting effects was the popularity of port in Britain.

Methven 'person from Methven', Perth and Kinross (probably 'mead-stone')

Mey, Meye see **May**

Meyer, Mayer (i) 'steward, bailiff or overseer' (from Middle High German *meier*); (ii) *also* **Mayor** or **Meier** from the Yiddish male personal name *Meyer* (from Hebrew *Meir*, literally 'enlightenment'). See also **Mair** (ii), **Major** (ii), **Merson** (iii) [Louis B. Mayer, 1885–1957, Russian-born US film producer]
— **Metro-Goldwyn-Mayer** see **Goldwyn**

Meyers, Mayers 'son of **Meyer**'. See also **Myers**

Meynell, Maynall (i) from a Norman female personal name of Germanic origin, meaning literally 'strength-battle'; (ii) 'person who lives in an isolated house or in a fortified manorhouse' or 'servant in the household of a fortified manorhouse' (Middle English *meinil*, from Old French *mesnil*, from Late Latin *mansiōnillum* 'small house') [Alice Meynell (*née* Thompson), 1847–1922, British poet and essayist]

Meyrick see **Merrick** (iii)

Miah a Bangladeshi name, based on a title of respect for a man (from Urdu *mian* 'sir')

Michael from the male personal name *Michael*, ultimately from Hebrew, literally 'who is like God?' [Alun Michael, 1943–, British Labour politician; George Michael (original name Georgios Kyriacos Panayiotou), 1963–, British singer and songwriter]

Michaels 'son of **Michael**'

Michaelson 'son of **Michael**'

Michell a different form of **Mitchell** [Keith Michell, 1926–, Australian actor]

Michelmore see **Mitchelmore**

Michelson (i) 'son of *Michel*' (see **Mitchell**); (ii) 'son of *Mikhl*', the Yiddish form of **Michael**; (iii) 'son of *Michel*', the Dutch form of **Michael**
— **Michelson-Morley experiment** an experiment performed in 1881 by the German-born US physicist Albert Abraham Michelson, 1852–1931, and the US physicist Edward Morley, 1838–1923, in an attempt to measure the difference in speed between light beams travelling in different directions by using interference effects

Michener see **Mitchener**

Michie from the former Scottish personal name *Michie*, a pet-form of **Michael**

Michieson, Micheson, Mitchieson, Mitcheson, Mitchison 'son of **Michie**' [Naomi Mitchison (*née* Haldane), 1897–1999, British novelist and poet]

Middlemass, Middlemas 'person from Middlemess', district near Kelso, Borders ('middlemost') [Frank Middlemass, 1919–2006, British actor]

Middlemiss a different form of **Middlemass**

Middleton, Myddleton 'person from Middleton', the name of numerous places in England and Scotland (mainly 'middle farmstead') [Guy Middleton, 1907–73, British actor; John Middleton Murry, see **Murray**; Thomas Middleton, 1580–1627, English dramatist]

Midgley 'person from Midgley', the name of various places in northern England ('glade frequented by midges')

Midhurst 'person from Midhurst', Sussex ('place amid wooded hills'). See also **Medhurst**

Miers see **Myers**

Milburn 'person from Milburn', Cumbria ('millstream') [Alan Milburn, 1958–, British Labour politician; Colin Milburn, 1941–90, English cricketer; Jackie Milburn, 1924–88, English footballer]

Mildmay from a medieval nickname for an inoffensive person (literally 'mild maiden')

Miles, Myles (i) from the Anglo-Norman male personal name *Miles*, from Germanic *Milo* (of unknown origin). See also **Milson**; (ii) 'servant' (from Latin *miles* 'soldier'); (iii) 'son of *Mihel*', an Old French contracted form of **Michael** [Bernard Miles (Lord Miles), 1907–91, British theatre director and actor; Michael Miles, 1919–71, New Zealand-born television quizmaster; Sarah Miles, 1941–, British actress]

Milford 'person from Milford', the name of various places in England ('ford by a mill')

Milhous, Milhouse see **Millhouse**

Mill, Mille 'person who lives near a mill' (in practice, usually 'miller' or 'mill-worker'). See also **Mills, Milne, Molyneux, Mullen** [James Mill, 1773–1836, British philosopher and economist; John Stuart Mill, 1806–73, British philosopher and economist, son of James]

Millais, Millay 'person from Miliez', northern France [Edna St Vincent Millay, 1892–1950, US poet; Sir John Everett Millais, 1829–96, British painter]

Millar a Scottish and Northern Irish variant of **Miller**

Millard (i) from French, from a Germanic personal name meaning literally 'good-brave'; (ii) 'person living by a millet field' (from a variant of Old Provençal *milhar* 'millet field'); (iii) a different form of **Millward**

Millen a different form of **Mullen**

Miller 'owner or operator of a (flour) mill'. See also **Millar**, **Milner** [Arthur Miller, 1915–2005, US playwright; George Miller, 1945–, Australian film director; Glenn Miller, 1904–44, US bandleader and composer; Henry Miller, 1891–1980, US writer; Sir Jonathan Miller, 1934–, British writer, director and broadcaster; Keith Miller, 1919–2004, Australian cricketer; Max Miller (original name Thomas Henry Sargent), 1894–63, British comedian; Sienna Miller, 1981–, US actress]

● Men with the surname Miller are traditionally given the nickname 'Dusty'

— **Joe Miller** in 19th-century slang, a stale joke. The term was inspired ultimately by *Joe Miller's Jests* (1739), a collection of the witticisms of the British actor and comedian Joseph Miller, 1684–1738, compiled by John Mottley.

— **Max Miller** (see above) rhyming slang for *pillow*

— **Miller's Antiques Price Guide** an annual British listing of current prices realized by antiques, first published in 1979 by Martin Miller, 1946–, and his then wife Judith Miller, 1951–

— **Miller effect** the effect by which capacitance in the output of a valve or transistor increases its input impedance. It is named after the US physicist John Milton Miller, 1882–1962.

— **Miller index** a series of numbers for specifying the positions of planes in crystals, as developed by the British scientist W.H. Miller, 1801–80

— **Millerite** a believer in the doctrines of William Miller, died 1849, a US preacher who interpreted the Scriptures as foretelling the early coming of Christ and the end of the world

— **millerite** sulphide of nickel, usually occurring in bronze crystals. It was named (originally in German) in 1845 in honour of W.H. Miller (see above), who was professor of mineralogy at Cambridge 1832–70.

— **Miller Lite** a low-alcohol lager launched in 1975 by the Miller Brewing Company of Milwaukee, Wisconsin (founded in 1855 by the German-born Frederick Miller, 1824–88)

Millet (i) *also* **Millett** 'grower or seller of millet'; (ii) 'someone living by a millet field' (from Catalan *millet* 'millet field'); (iii) 'little **Miles** (i)' (French) [Kate Millett, 1934–, US feminist]

— **Millets** a British chain of outdoor leisure equipment and clothing shops, founded in 1893 by J.M. Millet

Millhouse, Milhous, Milhouse 'person who lives at the mill (house) (i.e. the miller)' [Richard Milhous Nixon, see **Nixon**]

Millican a different form of **Milligan**

Milligan, Milligen from Irish Gaelic *Ó Maolagáin* 'descendant of *Maolagán*', a nickname meaning literally 'little little bald one' (usually referring to a person in a religious order, with a tonsure). See also **McMillan, Mulgan, Mullen, Mulligan** [Spike Milligan (original name Terence Milligan), 1918–2002, Indian-born Irish comedian and writer]

Milliken, Millikin, Millikan different forms of **Milligan** [Robert Andrews Millikan, 1868–1953, US physicist]

Millington 'person from Millington', Cheshire and Yorkshire ('farmstead with a mill')

Mills a different form of **Mill**. See also **Milnes** [Freddie Mills, 1919–65, British boxer; Gladys Mills ('Mrs Mills'), 1918–78, British popular pianist; Hayley Mills, 1946–, British actress, daughter of John; Sir John Mills, 1908–2005, British actor]

— **Bertram Mills** a British circus company set up in 1920 by Bertram Mills, 1873–1938, son of a coach proprietor. For many decades the most famous circus in Britain, it finally closed down in 1967.

— **Mills & Boon** a publishing firm founded in London in 1908 by Gerald Mills, 1877–1928, and Charles Boon, 1877–1943, and strongly associated since the 1930s with romantic fiction aimed chiefly at a female readership

— **Mills bomb** a type of oval hand grenade designed by the British engineer Sir William Mills, 1856–1932

Millstein, Milstein 'miller' (from Yiddish *milshteyn* 'millstone') [Nathan Milstein, 1903–92, Russian-born US violinist]

Millward, Milward 'person in charge of a (flour) mill; miller'. See also **Millard** (iii)

Milne, Miln different forms of **Mill** (from Old English *mylen* 'mill') [A.A. Milne, 1882–1956, British novelist and dramatist, creator of Winnie-the-Pooh; Alasdair Milne, 1930–, British television executive]

Milner a different form of **Miller** (from Middle English *mylnere* 'miller') [Sir Alfred Milner (Viscount Milner), 1854–1925, British colonial administrator]

— **Milner's Kindergarten** the nickname given to the enthusiastic group of young men who associated themselves with Sir Alfred Milner (see above) and his aspirations for British colonial expansion in Africa in the period after the Boer War

Milnes a different form of **Mills** [Richard Monckton Milnes, 1809–85, British poet and critic]

Milroy (i) a different form of **McIlroy**; (ii) a different form of **Mulroy**

Milson, Milsom 'son of **Miles** (i)'. See also **Melson**

Milstein see **Millstein**

Milton 'person from Milton', the name of numerous places in England (either 'middle farmstead' or 'farmstead with a mill') [John Milton, 1608–74, English poet]

— **Miltonic** relating to John Milton or his poetry or style

Milward see **Millward**

Minogue from Irish Gaelic *Ó Muineog* 'descendant of *Muineog*', a personal name meaning literally 'little monk' [Kylie Minogue, 1968–, Australian actress and singer]

Minter, Mintor 'maker of coins, moneyer' [Alan Minter, 1951–, British boxer]

Minto 'person from Minto', Borders ('place by the mountain')

Minton 'person from Minton', Shropshire ('farmstead by the mountain') [John Minton, 1917–57, British artist]
— **Minton ware** porcelain produced at the pottery founded in Stoke-on-Trent in 1796 by Thomas Minton, 1765–1836

Miranda 'person from Miranda', the name of various places in Spain and Portugal (perhaps 'look-out post')

Mirren an anglicization of Russian *Mironov* 'son of *Miron*', a personal name adopted from Greek *Myron* [Dame Helen Mirren (original name Ilynea Lydia Mironoff), 1945–, British actress]

Mishkin (i) 'son of *Mishka*', a Russian personal name meaning literally 'little Michael'; (ii) 'son of *Mishke*', a Yiddish personal name meaning literally both 'little Michael' and 'little Moses'

Miskin (i) from a condescending medieval nickname for a young man (from Anglo-Norman *meschin*); (ii) a different form of **Mishkin** (ii)

Mistry a Hindu and Parsi surname meaning literally 'skilled worker' (ultimately from Portuguese *mestre* 'master, expert')

Mitcham see **Mitchem**

Mitchell, Mitchel from the medieval personal name *Michel*, the usual medieval English form of **Michael**. See also **Michell** [Adrian Mitchell, 1932–, British poet; Grant Mitchell, Cockney hard man (played by Ross Kemp) in the BBC television soap opera *EastEnders* (1985–); Joni Mitchell (original name Roberta Joan Anderson), 1943–, Canadian singer and songwriter; Julian Mitchell, 1935–, British novelist and playwright; Leslie Mitchell, 1905–85, British television announcer; Margaret Mitchell, 1900–49, US novelist, author of *Gone with the Wind* (1936); R.J. Mitchell, 1895–1937, British aeronautical engineer, designer of the Spitfire; Warren Mitchell (original name Warren Misell), 1926–, British actor]
— **mitchella** (any of) a genus of trailing evergreen plants, named by Linnaeus in 1753 after the botanist John Mitchell, died 1768
— **Mitchell Beazley** a British publishing company, founded in 1969 by James Mitchell and John Beazley
— **Mitchell grass** a type of Australian grass (genus *Astrebla*), used for feeding livestock. It is named after Sir Thomas Livingstone Mitchell, 1792–1855, a Scottish-born Australian explorer and surveyor.
— **North American B-25 Mitchell** a US bomber aircraft of the World War II period. It was named in honour of General Billy Mitchell, 1879–1936, a notable US pioneer of air power.

Mitchelmore, Michelmore 'the great *Michel*', from *Michel* (see **Mitchell**) + Gaelic *mór* 'large', used to distinguish the largest or oldest of several people called Michel [Cliff Michelmore, 1919–, British television presenter]

Mitchem, Mitchum, Mitcham 'person from Mitcham', Greater London ('large homestead') [Robert Mitchum, 1917–97, US film actor]

Mitchener, Michener perhaps 'person from Michen Hall', Surrey [James A. Michener, ?1907–97, US novelist]

Mitchieson, Mitcheson see **Michieson**

Mitford 'person from Mitford', Northumberland ('ford at a confluence') [Mary Russell Mitford, 1787–1855, British writer; the Mitford sisters (daughters of David Bertram Ogilvy Freeman-Mitford, 1878–1958, second Baron Redesdale): Deborah Mitford (Dowager Duchess of Devonshire), 1920–; Diana Mitford (Lady Mosley), 1910–2003; Jessica Mitford, 1917–97, British-born US writer; Nancy Mitford, 1904–73, British writer; Pamela Mitford, 1907–94; Unity Valkyrie Mitford, 1914–48]

Mix perhaps an anglicization of the German name *Micksch*, from the personal name *Mikusch*, a pet-form of *Mikolaj*, itself a Slavic form of **Nicholas**. The name may also have had independent English origins, but it is not clear what these were. [Tom Mix, 1880–1940, US star of silent cowboy films]
— **Tom Mix** (see above) rhyming slang for *fix* 'an injection of heroin' and *six* (usually in the sense '£6')

Mo (i) *also* **Moe** 'person from Mo or Moe', the name of numerous farmsteads in Norway ('moor, heath'); (ii) *also* **Moe** 'person who lives on a sandy heath' (Swedish *mo*); (iii) 'person from Mo', a legendary Chinese city [Timothy Mo, 1950–, Hong Kong-born British novelist]

Moat, Moate 'person from Moat', Dumfries and Galloway ('moat, ditch')

Moats, Moates different forms of **Moat**

Moeran see **Moran** (i)

Moffatt, Moffat, Moffett, Moffitt 'person from Moffatt', Dumfries and Galloway ('long plain'). See also **Muffatt**

Mogg from the medieval female personal name *Magge* (see **Maggs**) [William Rees-Mogg, see **Rees**]

Mohammed, Mohamed, Mohammad see **Muhammad**

Mohan from Irish Gaelic *Ó Mocháin* 'descendant of *Mochán*' (see **Moon** (iv))

Moir a different form of **Muir**

Mold, Molde see **Mould**

Mole from a medieval nickname for someone thought to resemble a mole (the animal) (e.g. in being very short-sighted), or for someone with a prominent mole or similar skin blemish [Adrian Mole, intellectually ambitious but nerdish schoolboy in Sue Townsend's humorous novel in *The Secret Diary of Adrian Mole Aged 13 3/4*

(1982), whose growing pains are further chronicled in later novels]

Molesworth 'person from Molesworth', Cambridgeshire ('Mul's enclosure') [Mary Louisa Molesworth, 1839–1921, British writer; Nigel Molesworth, anarchic schoolboy character invented by Geoffrey Willans and Ronald Searle and appearing in such classics as *Down with Skool!* (1953) and *How to be Topp* (1954)]

Molina 'person from Molina', the name of various places in Spain [Alfred Molina, 1953–, British actor]

Molineux see **Molyneux**

Moll (i) from the medieval female personal name *Moll*, a pet-form of *Mary*; (ii) from a medieval Spanish nickname for a weak or ineffectual person (from Catalan *moll* 'soft, weak'); (iii) from a medieval southern German nickname for a plump person

Molloy, Malloy, Mulloy from Irish Gaelic *Ó Maolmhuaidh* 'descendant of *Maolmhuaidh*', a personal name meaning literally 'proud chieftain', *Ó Maol Aodha* 'descendant of the followers of (St) *Aodh*' (see **McKay**), or *Ó Maol Mhaodhóg* 'descendant of the followers of (St) *Maodhóg*', a different form of **Madoc**

Moloney, Molony, Maloney from Irish Gaelic *Ó Maol Dhomhnaigh* 'descendant of a devotee of the church' or of *Mac Giolla Dhomhnaigh* 'son of the servant of the church' (often used as a name for the illegitimate children of priests). See also **Muldowney**

Molyneux, Molyneaux, Molineux 'person from Moulineaux', northern France ('little mills') [Captain Edward Molyneux, 1891–1974, British fashion designer]
— **Molineux** the home ground of Wolverhampton Wanderers Football Club. It was named after the nearby Molineux Hotel, formerly the home of the local Molineux family.

Monaghan from Irish Gaelic *Ó Manacháin* 'descendant of *Manachan*', a personal name meaning literally 'little monk'

Monash from the Yiddish male personal name *Monish*, a pet-form of *Menakhem*, from Hebrew *Menachem*, literally 'consoler'
— **Monash University** an Australian university, founded in Melbourne in 1958. It was named in honour of the Australian military commander, engineer and administrator Sir John Monash, 1865–1931.

Monck see **Monk**

Monckton 'person from Monkton', the name of various places in England ('farmstead of the monks') [Lionel Monckton, 1862–1924, British composer of musical comedies; Walter Monckton (Viscount Monckton), 1891–1965, British lawyer and Conservative politician]

Moncrieff, Moncrief 'person from Moncrieff', near Perth ('hill of the tree') [Algernon Moncrieff, young man-about-town who is one of the leading characters in Oscar Wilde's *The Importance of Being Earnest* (1895)]

Moncur 'person from Moncur', an unidentified place, possibly on Tayside

Mondale an anglicization of Norwegian *Mundahl* 'person from Mundal', the name of two places in Norway ('valley of the river Mun') [Walter Mondale, 1928–, US diplomat and Democratic politician, vice-president 1977–81]

Monday, Mondy, Munday, Munday (i) from a medieval nickname for someone with a particular association with Mondays (usually feudal service owed on that day); (ii) from the Old Norse personal name *Mundi*, a shortened form of various compound names beginning with *mundr* 'protection'; (iii) an anglicization (facilitated by a confusion with Irish Gaelic *Luain* 'Monday') of Irish *Mac Giolla Eoin* 'son of the servant of *Eoin*'

Money (i) 'maker of coins, moneyer', or from a medieval nickname for a rich person; (ii) from Irish Gaelic *Ó Maonaigh* (see **Meaney**)

Moneypenny, Monypenny probably from a medieval nickname for a rich person or a miser [Miss Moneypenny, secretary to M (the head of MI6) in the James Bond novels of Ian Fleming and in the films based on them]

Monk, Monck, Munk, Munke (i) 'servant employed at a monastery', or from a medieval nickname for someone with monklike characteristics; (ii) a literal translation of the names **Minogue** and **Monaghan**; (iii) a Jewish surname of unknown origin [George Monck (Duke of Albemarle), 1608–70, English Civil War general; Meredith Monk, 1942–, US performer, choreographer, dancer and musician; Thelonius Monk, 1920–82, US jazz pianist and composer]
— **Maria Monk** 19th-century rhyming slang for *spunk* 'semen'. The name comes from the title of the anonymous anti-Catholic pornographic novel *Awful disclosures of Maria Monk, a narrative of her sufferings in the Hotel Dieu nunnery at Montreal* (1836).
— **Victoria Monk** rhyming slang for *spunk* 'semen'. It appears to be a variation on the name of the British music-hall entertainer Victoria Monks, 1884–1972.

Monkhouse 'person who lives in a house close to or owned by a monastery', or 'servant employed at a monastery' [Bob Monkhouse, 1928–2003, British comedian]

Monroe, Monro, Munroe, Munro, Munrow 'person from the mouth of the river Roe', Derry, Northern Ireland (from Gaelic *mun*, a variant of *bun* 'river-mouth' + the Gaelic river-name *Ratha*). The name is Scottish in origin, and refers to Irish immigrants to Scotland. [David Munrow, 1942–76, British early musician; H.H. Munro ('Saki'), 1870–1916, British short-story writer; James Monroe, 1758–1831, US statesman, president 1817–25; Marilyn Monroe (original name Norma Jean Mortenson), 1926–62, US film actress; Matt Monro (original name Terence Parsons), 1930–85, British ballad singer]
— **Monroe doctrine** the political principle, as stated by President James Monroe (see above) in

1823, that Europe should no longer involve itself in the American continent by exerting influence

— **Monrovia** the capital of Liberia, West Africa. It was named after James Monroe.

— **Munro** a Scottish mountain over 3000 feet (914 m) in height. The name comes from Hugh T. Munro, 1856–1919, who published a list of them (there are 277 in all) in 1891.

Montagu, Montague (i) 'person from Montagu', northern France ('pointed hill'); (ii) from Irish Gaelic *Mac Taidhg* (see **McTeague**) [Douglas-Scott-Montagu, family name of Lord Montagu of Beaulieu; Lady Mary Wortley Montagu (*née* Pierrepont), 1689–1762, English writer]

— **Montague curl** any of a series of flat curls forming a fringe along the top of the forehead, a women's style fashionable in the 1880s. The identity of Montague and his or her hand in the curl are not known.

— **Montague grammar** a grammatical theory, postulated by the US logician Richard Montague, 1930–71, which states that a grammar is built up from individual syntactic units, each of which has a corresponding semantic unit

— **Montagu's blenny** a small fish (*Coryphoblennius galerita*) of the Mediterranean and Northeast Atlantic. It was named in honour of the British naturalist George Montagu, 1751–1815.

— **Montagu's harrier** a small European bird of prey (*Circus pygargus*). Its name commemorates George Montagu (see above).

— **Montagu whaler** a small sailing boat of a type formerly used by the Royal Navy, with an arrangement of sails and masts based on suggestions made by Rear Admiral Victor Montagu, 1841–1915

Montefiore 'person from Montefiore', an unidentified Italian place ('flowery hill') [Sir Moses Montefiore, 1784–1885, Italian-born British philanthropist]

Monteith, Monteath 'person from Monteith', Perth and Kinross ('hill pasture above the (river) Teith')

— **monteith** a silver or pewter basin with notches round the edge, made to hold punch, or to cool punch glasses by resting their bases over the scalloped edge. Its name supposedly commemorates a certain Scotsman called Monteith, noted for his capes with scalloped hems.

— **Monteith** a type of coloured cotton handkerchief with a pattern of white dots. It is said to be named after a Scotsman called Henry Monteith, who manufactured them.

Montez 'mountain-dweller' (from Spanish *montés* and Portuguese *montês* 'of the mountain') [Lola Montez (original name Elizabeth Rosanna Gilbert), 1818–61, Irish 'Spanish' dancer and mistress of King Ludwig I of Bavaria]

Montgomery, Montgomerie 'person from Montgomery', Normandy ('hill of *Gomery*', a personal name of Germanic origin, meaning literally 'man-power') [Bernard Montgomery (Viscount Montgomery), 1887–1976, British field marshal; Colin Montgomerie, 1963–, British golfer; David

Montgomery, 1948–, British media executive; Elizabeth Montgomery, 1933–95, US actress, daughter of Robert; Robert Montgomery (original name Henry Montgomery, Jnr.), 1904–81, US actor]

— **Montgomery** a small market town in Powys (formerly Montgomeryshire), Wales, close to the border with England. It was named in the late 11th century by Roger de Montgomery, 1st earl of Shrewsbury, who came from Montgomery in Normandy (see above) and built a castle there.

— **Montgomery** the state capital of Alabama, USA. It was named in honour of the Irish-American soldier Richard Montgomery, 1736–75, who was a general in the American War of Independence.

Montmorency 'person from Montmorency', northern France ('hill of *Maurentius*', a Gallo-Roman personal name, apparently a blende of *Maurus* and *Laurentius*)

Moody, Moodey, Moodie, Mudie from a medieval nickname for a courageous or quick-tempered person (from Middle English *modie* 'bold, impetuous, angry') [Helen Wills Moody (*née* Wills), 1905–98, US tennis player; Ron Moody (original name Ronald Moodnick), 1924–, British actor]

— **Moody and Sankey** two US evangelists, Dwight Lyman Moody, 1837–99, and Ira David Sankey, 1840–1908, who conducted revivalist campaigns in America and Britain and produced the *Sankey and Moody Hymn Book* (1873) (largely the work of Sankey)

— **Mudie's Lending Library** a commercial circulating library founded in London in the mid-19th century by Charles Edward Mudie, 1818–90. It became renowned for its policy of refusing to stock any book with the least hint of immorality.

Moog (i) from a medieval German nickname for someone related to a person of influence or consequence (from Middle High German *māc, māge* 'relative'); (ii) a shortened variant of the Dutch name *van Mook* 'person from Mook', Dutch Limberg

— **Moog synthesizer** a type of keyboard-operated musical instrument that generates and modifies sounds electronically. It was invented in 1965 by Roger Moog, 1934–2005.

Moon, Moone (i) from a medieval nickname derived from Anglo-Norman *moun* 'monk'; (ii) from a Cornish nickname for a thin person (from Cornish *mon* 'thin'); (iii) 'person from Moyon', northern France ('Modius's settlement'); (iv) from Irish Gaelic *Ó Mocháin* 'descendant of *Mochán*', a personal name meaning literally 'little early one'. See also **Mohan**; (v) an ancient Korean clan name derived from the Chinese character *Mun*, literally 'writing, literature' [Keith Moon, 1946–78, British pop musician, drummer in 'The Who'; William Moon, 1818–94, British inventor]

— **Shine On Harvey Moon** a British television comedy drama (1982–85) about post-World War II family life, centring on the recently demobbed Harvey Moon. The title was a pun on the popular song title 'Shine on, harvest moon'.

Mooney from Irish Gaelic *Ó Maonaigh* (see **Meaney**) [Bel Mooney, 1946–, British writer and broadcaster]

Moorcock from a medieval nickname for someone thought to resemble a moorcock (the male of the red grouse) [Michael Moorcock, 1939–, British author]

Moorcraft a different form of **Moorcroft**

Moorcroft 'person from Moorcroft', the name of various places in Lancashire and Yorkshire ('marshland smallholding') [David Moorcroft, 1953–, British athlete]

Moore, Moor (i) 'person from Moore or More', the name of various places in England ('settlement on a moor or by a fen'), or 'person who lives on a moor or by a fen' (from Middle English *more* 'moor, fen'). See also **Muir**; (ii) from the medieval personal name *More* (ultimately from Latin *Maurus* – see (ii)). See also **Morrell, Morris, Seymour**; (iii) from a medieval nickname for someone with a dark complexion (from Old French *more* 'Moor, black person', from Latin *maurus*); (iv) *also* **More** from a medieval Scottish and Welsh nickname for a large man (from Gaelic *mór*, Welsh *mawr* 'large'); (v) from Irish Gaelic *Ó Mórdha* 'descendant of *Mórdha*', a nickname meaning literally 'great', 'proud' or 'stately' [Dr Barbara Moore, 1904–77, British vegetarian long-distance walker; Bobby Moore, 1941–93, English footballer; Brian Moore, 1921–99, Irish novelist; Brian Moore, 1932–2001, British football commentator; Brian Moore, 1962–, English rugby player; Dudley Moore, 1935–2002, British actor, comedian and pianist; G.E. Moore, 1873–1958, British philosopher; Gerald Moore, 1899–1987, British pianist; Henry Moore, 1898–1986, British sculptor; Henry More, 1614–87, English philosopher; Sir John Moore, 1761–1809, British general; John Moore-Brabazon (Lord Brabazon of Tara), 1884–1964, British aircraft pioneer and Conservative politician; Kenneth More, 1914–82, British actor; Marianne Moore, 1887–1972, US poet; Mary Tyler Moore, 1936–, US actress and television executive; Michael Moore, 1954–, US polemical writer and director; Mrs Moore, the sympathetic elderly lady in E.M. Forster's *A Passage to India* (1924); Sir Patrick Moore, 1923–, British astronomer; Sir Roger Moore, 1927–, British actor; Thomas Moore, 1779–1852, Irish poet; Sir Thomas More (St Thomas More), 1478–1535, English statesman and scholar]
— **'Don't Have Any More, Mrs Moore'** a humorous song (1926) by Harry Castling and James Walsh, pleading for reproductive restraint. *Mrs Moore* has been used as rhyming slang for *floor*.
— **George Moore** Australian rhyming slang for *four*, in the cricketing sense. George Moore, 1923–, was an Australian jockey.
— **Maria Moores** Australian rhyming slang for *drawers* 'women's underpants'. It is not known who Maria Moore was.
— **Old Moore's Almanac** an almanac originated by the English physician, astrologist and almanac-maker Francis Moore, 1657–1714. First

published in 1700, under the title *Vox Stellarum*, it featured astrological predictions, and its name came to be synonymous with the (spurious) foretelling of the future. Since 1930 it has been published as *Foulsham's Old Moore's Almanack*.
— **2602 Moore** a small asteroid in the asteroid belt between Mars and Jupiter. Discovered in 1982, it was named in honour of Patrick Moore (see above).

Moorehead, Moorhead different forms of **Muirhead** [Agnes Moorehead, 1900–74, US actress; Alan Moorehead, 1910–83, Australian journalist and author]

Moores, Moors, Mores different forms of **Moore** [Sir John Moores, 1896–1993, British businessman and philanthropist, founder of Littlewoods football pools]
— **Liverpool John Moores University** a university founded in 1992 from the former Liverpool Polytechnic, and named in honour of Sir John Moores (see above)

Moorhouse, Morehouse 'person from Moorhouse', the name of various places in England, mainly Yorkshire

Moraes from the Portuguese form of Spanish *Morales* (see **Morales**)

Morahan from Irish Gaelic *Ó Murcháin* 'descendant of *Murchán*', a personal name meaning literally 'little sea-warrior'

Morales 'person who lives among mulberry trees', from Spanish, from *morales* 'mulberry trees'

Moran (i) *also* **Moeran** (accented on the first syllable) from Irish Gaelic *Ó Móráin* 'descendant of *Móran*', a personal name meaning literally 'large'; (ii) (accented on the second syllable) a different form of **Morant** [Diana Moran, 1940–, British television fitness demonstrator ('the Green Goddess'); E.J. Moeran, 1894–1950, British composer of Irish descent; Gertrude ('Gussie') Moran, 1923–, US tennis player]

Morant from the Old French personal name *Morant*, perhaps from a nickname meaning 'steadfast', or alternatively of Germanic origin and meaning literally 'courage-raven' [Breaker Morant (original name Edwin Henry Murrant), ?1864–1902, British-born Australian soldier and poet]

More see **Moore** (iv)

Morehouse see **Moorhouse**

Moreland, Morland 'person from Moreland', the name of various places in northern England and southern Scotland ('marshy land') [Catherine Morland, the gullible young heroine of Jane Austen's *Northanger Abbey* (1818); George Morland, 1763–1804, British painter]

Moreno from a medieval Spanish and Portuguese nickname for someone with dark hair and complexion (from *moreno* 'dark-haired')

Moresby 'person from Moresby', Cumbria ('Maurice's farmstead')
— **Port Moresby** the capital of Papua New Guinea. The first Europeans to explore the area were an expedition led by Captain John Moresby

RN, 1830–1922, and he named the settlement in 1873 in honour of his father, Admiral Sir Fairfax Moresby, 1786–1877.

Morgan from an Old Celtic personal name probably meaning literally 'sea-bright' [Charles Morgan, 1894–1958, British novelist and dramatist; Cliff Morgan, 1930–, Wesh rugby player and television executive; Sir Henry Morgan ('Captain Morgan'), ?1635–88, Welsh buccaneer; John Pierpont Morgan, 1837–1913, US financier; Organ Morgan, the church organ player in Dylan Thomas's *Under Milk Wood* (1954); Piers Morgan, 1965–, British journalist; Thomas Hunt Morgan, 1866–1945, US geneticist and biologist]

— **Captain Morgan** (see Henry Morgan above) rhyming slang for *organ* (in the musical sense)

— **morgan** a unit of chromosome length, named after Thomas Hunt Morgan (see above)

— **Morgan** a black, bay, brown or chestnut horse with a full mane and tail, short deep body and slender legs, of a breed descended from a stallion born in 1790 and named after its owner, the US teacher Justin Morgan, 1747–98

— **morganite** a pink gemstone that is a variety of beryl. It was named after J. Pierpont Morgan (see above).

— **Morgan – A Suitable Case for Treatment** a play and (1966) film by David Mercer starring David Warner as a loopily obsessed artist

— **Morgan Car Company** a British car manufacturer, specializing in sports cars, founded in 1910 by H.F.S. Morgan, 1881–1959

— **Morgan Grenfell** a London-based overseas securities house founded in 1854 as Peabody, Morgan and Company (the Morgan was Junius Spencer Morgan, 1813–90, father of J. Pierpont Morgan – see above). Edward Grenfell, 1870–1941, joined as a partner in 1904, and in 1909 the firm became Morgan Grenfell.

— **Morgan Stanley** a New York-based investment bank founded in 1935 by Henry S. Morgan, 1900–82, grandson of J. Pierpont Morgan, and Harold Stanley, 1885–1963, of J.P. Morgan & Co.

Morgenstern an invented Jewish name based on German *Morgenstern* and Yiddish *morgn-shtern* 'morning star'

Moriarty from the Irish Gaelic personal name *Muircheartach*, literally 'skilled navigator' [Professor James Moriarty, arch-criminal and deadly foe of Sherlock Holmes; Count Jim Moriarty, a character played by Spike Milligan in the 1950s' BBC radio comedy *The Goon Show*]

Morison see **Morrison**

Morland see **Moreland**

Morley, Morely 'person from Morley', the name of various places in England ('woodland clearing by a moor') [John Morley (Viscount Morley), 1838–1923, British journalist and biographer; 'Mrs Morley', the name under which Queen Anne corresponded with Sarah Churchill, Duchess of Marlborough ('Mrs **Freeman**'); Robert Morley, 1908–92, British actor; Thomas Morley, 1557–1603, English composer]

— **Michelson-Morley experiment** see **Michelson**

— **Morley College** an adult-education college on London's South Bank, founded in the 1880s under the terms of an endowment bequeathed by the British industrialist, MP and philanthropist Samuel Morley, 1809–86

Moroney from Irish Gaelic *Ó Maol Ruanaidh* 'descendant of the follower of (St) *Ruanaidh*' (see **Rooney**). See also **Mulrooney**

Morphy a different form of **Murphy** [Paul Charles Morphy, 1837–84, US chess player]

— **Morphy Richards** a British firm of electrical domestic appliance manufacturers, founded in 1936 by the electrical engineers Donal Morphy, 1901–75, and Charles Frederick Richards, 1900–64

Morpurgo an Italian-Jewish name meaning 'person from Maribor', Slovenia, or 'person from Marburg', Germany

Morrell, Morell, Morel, Morrel, Morrall, Morrill from the medieval personal name *Morel*, literally 'little **Moore** (ii)'. See also **Murrill** [Lady Ottoline Morrell (*née* Bentinck), 1873–1938, British literary and political hostess; Paul Morel, D.H. Lawrence's alter ego in his autobiographical novel *Sons and Lovers* (1913)]

Morris, Morriss, Morrice, Maurice from the medieval personal name *Maurice* (from Old French, from Latin *Mauritius*, a derivative of *Maurus* – see **Moore** (ii–iii)). See also **McMorris, Morse** [Arthur Morris, 1922–, Australian cricketer; Chris Morris, 1962–, British comedy writer and satirist; Desmond Morris, 1928–, British zoologist and anthropologist; Jan Morris, 1926–, British writer; Johnny Morris, 1916–99, British radio and television broadcaster; Mark Morris, 1956–, US dancer and choreographer; William Morris, 1834–96, British artist, craftsman, poet and social activist; William Morris (Viscount Nuffield), 1877–1963, British car manufacturer and philanthropist; Sir William Morris (Bill Morris), 1938–, Jamaican-born British trade-union leader]

— **Margaret Morris Movement** (**MMM**) a form of co-ordinated exercise and dance developed by the physiotherapist and dancer Margaret Morris, 1891–1980

— **MG** a British car marque, short for 'Morris Garages'. It had its beginnings in 1924 when Morris Garages, a Morris dealer in Oxford, began to produce customized versions of Morris cars to the designs of Cecil Kimber. The firm became established in Abingdon, Berkshire (now Oxfordshire) in 1930. Since 2007 the brand has been owned by Nanjing Automobile Group.

— **Morris chair** a light carved wooden armchair with removable cushions and a reclining back that can be set at varying angles, of a type designed by the poet-craftsman William Morris (see above)

— **Morris Motor Company** a car-manufacturing firm founded in Oxford in 1910 by William Morris (later Lord Nuffield – see above). In 1952 it merged with its great rival Austin to form the British Motor Corporation. The Morris marque finally disappeared in 1983. Its most famous product was probably the **Morris Minor** (1948–71).

— **Morriston** a district of Swansea, named after Sir John Morris, who built it in the late 18th century to house the employees at his copper works

— **Philip Morris** the world's largest tobacco company. Now US-based, it traces its origins back to a tobacconist's shop opened in Bond Street, London in 1847 by Philip Morris, died 1873.

Morrison, Morison 'son of **Morris**' [Arthur Morrison, 1863–1945, British novelist; Herbert Morrison (Lord Morrison), 1888–1965, British Labour politician; Jim Morrison, 1943–71, US rock singer and songwriter; Toni Morrison (original name Chloe Anthony Wofford), 1931–, US writer; Van Morrison (original name George Ivan Morrison), 1945–, British singer and songwriter]

— **Morrisons** a British supermarket chain, founded (as an egg and butter merchants) in Bradford in 1899 by William Morrison

— **Morrison shelter** a transportable indoor steel table-shaped air-raid shelter, of a type introduced by Herbert Morrison (see above) as home secretary during the Second World War

Morrissey, Morrisey from Irish Gaelic *Ó Muirgheas* 'descendant of *Muirgheasa*', a personal name perhaps meaning literally 'sea-taboo'. See also **Bryson** (ii) [Neil Morrissey, 1962–, British actor; Stephen Patrick Morrissey (usually known simply as 'Morrissey'), 1959–, British pop singer and songwriter]

Morrow from the Gaelic personal name *Murchadh* (see **Murphy**). See also **Murrow**

Morse a different form of **Morris** [Inspector Morse (Endeavour Morse), the grumpy police detective in a series of (much televised) crime novels by Colin Dexter; Samuel Morse, 1791–1872, US inventor and artist]

— **Morse code** a system for representing letters and numbers by signs consisting of one or more short or long signals of sound or light that are printed out as dots or dashes. It was invented by Samuel Morse (see above).

Mort perhaps from a Norman nickname based on Old French *mort* 'dead', possibly referring to someone with a deathly pallor or otherwise sepulchral appearance

Mortensen, Mortenson 'son of *Morten*', a Scandinavian form of **Martin** [Norma Jean Mortenson, the original name of Marilyn **Monroe**; Stan Mortensen, 1921–91, English footballer]

Mortiboys 'person from Mortiboys', an unidentified place with a name apparently of Norman origin ('dead wood')

Mortimer, Mortimor, Mortimore 'person from Mortemer' northern France ('dead sea') [Angela Mortimer, 1932–, British tennis player; Bob Mortimer, 1959–, British comedian; Sir John Mortimer, 1923–, British novelist, playwright and barrister; Penelope Mortimer (*née* Fletcher), 1918–99, British novelist, sometime wife of John; Roger de Mortimer (Earl of March), ?1287–1330, English courtier]

Mortlock probably 'person from Mortlake', Surrey ('Morta's stream')

Morton, Moreton 'person from Morton or Moreton', the name of various places in England and Scotland ('marshland farmstead') [H.V. Morton, 1892–1979, British travel writer; J.B. Morton ('Beachcomber'), 1893–1975, British journalist and humorous writer; Jelly Roll Morton (original name Ferdinand Joseph La Menthe), 1885–1941, US jazz pianist and composer; Samantha Morton, 1977–, British actress]

— **Morton's fork** a paradoxical situation similar to Catch-22, in which one is trapped by either of two alternatives, one or other of which might have seemed to offer a way out. The term originally denoted a justification for enforcing contributions to royal funds from everyone, advanced by Henry VII's chancellor, Archbishop John Morton, ?1420–1500: the rich can obviously afford it, and those who live frugally must have some money tucked away somewhere.

Moseley, Mosley 'person from Moseley or Mosley', the name of numerous places in England (variously 'glade frequented by mice', 'glade by a marsh' and 'Moll's glade') [Henry Gwyn-Jeffreys Moseley, 1887–1915, British physicist; Sir Oswald Mosley, 1896–1980, British fascist politician]

Moses from the biblical name of the Hebrew prophet who led the Children of Israel out of captivity, from Hebrew *Moshe*, probably of Egyptian origin. See also **Moss, Moyes** [Edwin Moses, 1955–, US athlete; Grandma Moses (full name Anna Mary Robertson Moses), 1860–1961, US artist]

Moss (i) *also* **Mosse** 'person who lives by a peat bog' (Middle English *mos*); (ii) from the medieval personal name *Moss*, an anglicized form of **Moses**; (iii) an anglicization of **Moses** or another similar-sounding Jewish surname [Kate Moss, 1974–, British model; Kate Mosse, 1961–, British author; Sir Stirling Moss, 1929–, British racing driver]

— **Moss Bros.** a British firm of tailors and outfitters, best known for the hire of formal clothing. It had its origins in a shop set up in Covent Garden in 1860 by Moses Moses, 1820–94. The 'Bros'. (brothers) were two of his sons, George Moses, 1855–1905, and Alfred Moses, 1862–37, who inherited the business in 1894 and anglicized their name to *Moss*.

— **Moss Empires** a British chain of variety theatres (including the London Palladium) formed from the 1880s by the impresario Sir Edward Moss, 1852–1912. In the 1950s it combined with the Stoll Group (founded by the Australian-born Sir Oswald Stoll, 1867–1942) to form **Stoll-Moss Theatres**. That company was bought in 2000 by Lord Lloyd Webber.

Mossman a different form of **Moss** (i)

Most (i) 'person who lives by a peat bog' (Dutch and Flemish *most*); (ii) 'maker or seller of must (unfermented grape juice)' (German *Most*); (iii) a Jewish name derived from Polish and Russian *most* 'bridge'

Mostyn 'person from Mostyn', Wales

Motherwell 'person from Motherwell', North Lanarkshire ('Our Lady's well') [Robert Motherwell, 1915–91, US artist]

Motion a Scottish name of uncertain origin [Andrew Motion, 1952–, British poet]

Motte, Mott 'person who lives by a fortified stronghold' (Middle English *motte*, from Old French)

Mottram 'person from Mottram', Cheshire ('place where assemblies are held') [Christopher ('Buster') Mottram, 1955–, British tennis player; Tony Mottram, 1920–, British tennis player]

Mould, Mold, Molde different forms of **Moult** (i)

Moult (i) from the medieval female personal name *Mahalt* (variously *Mauld, Malt, Maud*), vernacular versions of Anglo-Norman *Matilda*, ultimately of Germanic origin and meaning literally 'strength-battle'. See also **Mowatt** (ii), **Mudd** (ii); (ii) from a medieval nickname for a bald person or one with some sort of cranial peculiarity (from Middle English *mould* 'top of the head') [Ted Moult, 1926–86, British farmer and radio and television personality]

Moulton 'person from Moulton', the name of various places in England (mainly 'Mūla's farmstead')
— **Moulton bike** a type of bicycle with small wheels and a crossbar-less frame. It was designed by the British engineer and inventor Alex Moulton, 1920–, and was introduced in 1962.

Mount 'person who lives on or near a hill' (Middle English *mount* 'hill') [Ferdinand Mount, 1939–, British author and journalist; Peggy Mount, 1916–2001, British actress]

Mountbatten a partial translation of German *Battenberg*, a town on the river Eder to the east of Cologne (perhaps 'hill by a water-meadow'). The name change was instigated by the Austrian-born British admiral Prince Louis of Battenberg (Marquess of Milford Haven), 1854–1921, in 1917, when all things German were under a cloud in Britain. [Louis Mountbatten (Earl Mountbatten of Burma), 1900–79, British naval commander and diplomat, son of Prince Louis of Battenberg (see above)]

Mountford (i) an anglicization of Norman *Montfort* 'person from Montfort', the name of various places in northern France ('impregnable hill'); (ii) perhaps 'person from Mundford', Norfolk ('Munda's ford'). See also **Mumford**

Mowatt, Mowat (i) 'official in charge of communal pasturage' (from Middle English *moward*, literally 'meadow guardian'); (ii) from the medieval female personal name *Mohaut*, a variant of *Mahalt* (see **Moult** (i)); (iii) 'person from Monthaut or Monhaut', the name of various places in northern France ('high hill')

Mowbray 'person from Montbrai', northern France ('muddy hill')

Mower 'person who mows pasture lands'

Moxon 'son of *Magge*' (see **Maggs**)

Moyes from the medieval personal name *Moise*, a vernacular variant of **Moses**

Moyle from a medieval Cornish and Welsh nickname for a bald man (from Cornish *moyl* and Welsh *moel* 'bald')

Moynihan from Irish Gaelic *Ó Muimhneacháin* 'descendant of *Muimhneachán*', literally 'little Munsterman' [Daniel Patrick Moynihan, 1927–2003, US Democratic politician]

Mudd (i) 'person who lives in a muddy area'; (ii) from the medieval female personal name *Mudd*, a variant of *Maud* (see **Moult** (i)); (iii) from the Old English personal name *Mōd* or *Mōda*, a shortened form of various compound names beginning with *mōd* 'courage'

Mudie see **Moody**

Muffatt, Muffett different forms of **Moffatt**
— **'Little Miss Muffet'** a traditional nursery rhyme:
Little Miss Muffett
Sat on a tuffet,
Eating her curds and whey;
There came a big spider,
Who sat down beside her
And frightened Miss Muffet away.
It has been speculated that 'Miss Muffett' is Patience Muffet, the daughter of the physician and entomologist Dr. Thomas Muffet, 1553–1604.

Muggeridge, Muggridge 'person from Mogridge', Devon (probably 'Mogga's ridge') [Edward James Muggeridge, the original name of the British-born US photographer Eadweard Muybridge, 1830–1904; Malcolm Muggeridge, 1903–90, British journalist and pundit]

Muhammad, Muhammed, Mohammed, Mohamed, Mohammad from the Muslim male personal name *Muhammad* (the name of the Prophet Muhammad, 570–632, the founder of Islam), based on Arabic *muhammad* 'praiseworthy'

Muir 'person who lives on a moor' (from a Scottish variant of Middle English *more* – see **Moore** (i)). See also **Moir** [Edwin Muir, 1887–1959, British poet, translator and critic; Frank Muir, 1920–98, British writer and humorist; Jean Muir, 1928–95, British fashion designer]

Muirhead 'person from Muirhead', the name of various places in southern Scotland ('end of the moor'). See also **Moorehead**

Mukherjee a Hindu name meaning literally 'teacher from Mukhati'

Mulcahy from Irish Gaelic *Ó Maolchathaigh* 'descendant of a follower of *(St) Cathach*', a nickname meaning literally 'warlike'. See also **Caughey**

Mulcaster a different form of **Muncaster**

Mulcreevy from Irish Gaelic *Ó Maolchraoibhe* 'descendant of a follower of (St) *Craobh*.' See also **Mulgrew**

Mulder (i) 'miller' (Dutch *mulder*); (ii) 'maker of wooden bowls' (from a derivative of Middle High German *mulde* 'bowl, tub')

Muldoon from Irish Gaelic *Ó Maoldúin* 'descendant of *Maoldún*', a personal name meaning literally 'chief fortress'

Muldowney a different form of **Moloney**

Mulgan a different form of **Milligan**

Mulgrew a different form of **Mulcreevy**

Mulhall from Irish Gaelic *Ó Maolchathail* 'descendant of the follower of (St) *Cathal*' (see **Cahill**)

Mulhern from Irish Gaelic *Ó Maoilchiaráin* 'descendant of the follower of *(St) Ciarán*', a nickname meaning literally 'little black one'

Mulholland from Irish Gaelic *Ó Maolchalann* 'descendant of the follower of *(St) Calann*' (see **Callan**)

Mullally, Mullaley from Irish Gaelic *Ó Maolalaidh* 'descendant of *Maolaladh*', a personal name meaning literally 'speckled chieftain'

Mullard from a medieval nickname for a stubborn person (from Old French *mulard*, a pejorative variant of *mule* 'mule') [Arthur Mullard (original name Arthur Mullord), 1913–95, British comic actor]
— **MFI** the abbreviated trade-name of Mullard Furniture Industries, a British manufacturer of low-cost furniture founded in 1964 by Noel Lister and Donald Searle. Mullard was the maiden name of Searle's wife.
— **Mullard Ltd.** a British manufacturer of electronic components, founded in 1920 by Captain Stanley R. Mullard. It merged with Philips in 1926 and disappeared as a brand in 1988. It sponsored the **Mullard Radio Astronomy Observatory** (1957) at Cambridge University and the **Mullard Space Science Laboratories** (1966), part of London University.

Mullarkey from Irish Gaelic *Ó Maoilearca* 'descendant of the follower of (St) *Earc*', a personal name meaning literally either 'speckled one' or 'salmon'

Mullen, Mullin (i) 'miller' or 'person who lives by a mill' (from Anglo-Norman *moulin, mulin* 'mill'); (ii) *also* **Mullan** from Irish Gaelic *Ó Maoláin* 'descendant of *Maolán*', a nickname meaning literally 'bald one, tonsured one', hence 'religious follower, disciple'. See also **McMillan, Milligan** [Barbara Mullen, 1914–79, US-born British actress; Chris Mullin, 1947–, British journalist and Labour politician]

Mullens, Mullins different forms of **Mullen, Mullin**

Muller 'miller' (German *Müller*) [Hermann Joseph Muller, 1890–1967, US geneticist]

Mullery from Irish Gaelic *Ó Maolmhuire* 'descendant of *Maolmhuire*', a personal name meaning literally 'servant of (the Virgin) Mary'

Mullet, Mullett (i) 'catcher or seller of mullets (the fish)'; (ii) from a medieval nickname for a stubborn person, literally 'little mule'

Mulligan a different form of **Milligan** [Mick Mulligan, 1928–2006, British jazz trumpeter and bandleader]
— **Mulligan** a derisive US slang term for an Irish person
— **mulligan** in US slang, a term for both a stew made from leftover scraps of vegetables and meat,

and a second chance to play a golf shot after making a mess of the first attempt. Both usages presumably came from the surname, but it is not known who the Mulligans in question were.

Mulloy see **Molloy**

Mulrooney, Mulroney different forms of **Moroney** [Brian Mulroney, 1939–, Canadian lawyer and Progressive Conservative politician, prime minister 1984–93]

Mulroy from Irish Gaelic *Ó Maolruaidh* 'descendant of *Maolruadh*', a personal name meaning literally 'red-haired chieftain'. See also **Milroy**

Mulvaney, Mulvany from Irish Gaelic *Ó Maoilmheana* 'descendant of the follower of (St) *Meana*', a personal name probably derived from *mion* 'tiny thing'

Mulvey from Irish Gaelic *Ó Maoilmhiadhaigh* 'descendant the follower of (St) *Miadhach*', a nickname meaning literally 'honourable'

Mumby 'person from Mumby', Lincolnshire ('Mundi's settlement')

Mumford a different form of **Mountford** [Lewis Mumford, 1895–1990, US social philosopher]

Muncaster 'person from Muncaster', formerly Mulcaster, Cumbria ('Mūla's Roman fort'). See also **Mulcaster**

Munday, Mundy see **Monday**

Munden 'person from Munden', Hertfordshire ('Munda's valley')

Munk, Munke see **Monk**

Munroe, Munro, Munrow see **Monroe**

Murchison from Gaelic *Mac Mhurchaidh* 'son of *Mhurchadh*', a personal name meaning literally 'sea-warrior' [Sir Robert Murchison, 1792–1871, British geologist]

Murdoch, Murdock from Gaelic *Murchadh* (see **Murchison**) and *Muireadhach* or *Muireach*, a personal name meaning literally 'seafarer' [Dame Iris Murdoch, 1919–99, Irish-born British novelist and philosopher; Sir Keith Murdoch, 1885–1952, Australian journalist and newspaper proprietor, father of Rupert; Richard ('Stinker') Murdoch, 1907–90, British actor and comic performer; Rupert Murdoch, 1931–, Australian-born US media proprietor; William Murdock, 1754–1839, British inventor]

Murgatroyd 'person from Murgatroyd', former place near Halifax, Yorkshire (probably 'Margaret's glade')
— **'Heavens to Murgatroyd!'** the catchphrase of Snagglepuss, a pink lion animated-cartoon character introduced in the US in 1959

Murnahan, Murnaghan from Irish Gaelic *Ó Muirneacháin* 'descendant of *Muirneachán*', a nickname derived from *muirneach* 'lovable'

Murphy from Irish Gaelic *Ó Murchadha* 'descendant of *Murchadh*', a personal name meaning literally 'sea-warrior'. See also **Morphy** [Cardinal Cormac Murphy-O'Connor, 1932–, Roman Catholic priest, archbishop of Westminster

2000–; Dervla Murphy, 1931–, Irish writer; Eddie Murphy, 1961–, US comedian and actor]

☆ The commonest surname in Ireland

● Men with the surname Murphy are traditionally given the nickname 'Spud' (see next)

— **murphy** in 19th-century slang, a potato (from the commonness of *Murphy* as an Irish name and the prevalence of potatoes in the Irish diet)

— **Murphy bed** a bed that can be folded or swung into a cupboard or wall recess when not in use. It was designed by the US inventor William Murphy, 1876–1959.

— **Murphy game, Murphy swindle** in US underworld slang, any of a range of stratagems by which gullible people are conned by criminals. The term is said to commemorate a New York (or Boston) madam by the name of Murphy, whose accomplices lured punters to a brothel and then robbed them. Hence, to 'murphy' someone is to swindle them, especially by means of the Murphy game.

— **Murphy's Law** a mainly US name for Sod's Law, the informal principle that if anything can go wrong, it will. It is said to have been inspired by a remark made in 1949 by Captain E. Murphy of Wright Field Aircraft Laboratory, but there is no evidence to support the claim.

Murray, Murry (i) 'person from Moray', region of northeastern Scotland (probably 'sea settlement'); (ii) from Irish Gaelic *Mac Muireadhaigh* (see **McMurray**), or *Mac Giolla Mhuire* (see **Gilmore** (i)) [Andrew Murray, 1987–, British tennis player; Bill Murray, 1950–, US actor; Gilbert Murray, 1866–1957, British scholar; Sir James Murray, 1837–1915, British philologist and lexicographer; Jenni Murray (*née* Bailey), 1950–, British radio broadcaster; John Middleton Murry, see **Middleton**; Les Murray, 1938–, Australian poet and critic; Lionel Murray (Lord Murray), 1922–2004, British trade-union leader; Ruby Murray, 1935–96, Irish popular singer]

— **John Murray** a British publishing firm, founded in 1768 by John Murray, 1745–93, and brought to prominence in the early 19th century by his son John Murray, 1778–1843. From the 1820s it produced a well-known series of guide books and railway timetables which came to be known colloquially as 'Murrays'.

— **Murrayfield** a residential area of western Edinburgh, which also gives its name to the Scottish national rugby stadium, situated there. It was named after Archibald Murray (Lord Henderson), a local landowner in the 18th century.

— **Murray Mints** a minty sweet introduced in the UK in 1944. The time of their highest profile was the late 1950s, thanks to the television advertising jingle 'Murray Mints, Murray Mints, Too-good-to-hurry mints!' The identity of their originator, 'Murray', remains clouded in obscurity.

— **Murray River** a river in southeastern Australia, 2,520 km/1,566 miles in length. It was originally 'discovered' in 1824 by the explorers W.H. Hovell and Andrew Hume, and was named the 'Hume'. It was 'rediscovered' in 1830 by Charles Sturt, and renamed by him in honour of Sir George Murray, 1772–1846, British secretary of state for war and the colonies.

— **Ruby Murray** (see above), rhyming slang for *curry*

Murrell, Murril different forms of **Merrill**

Murrill a different form of **Morrell**

Murrow a different form of **Morrow** [Edward R. Murrow, 1908–65, US radio and television journalist]

Murry see **Murray**

Musgrave 'person from Musgrave', Cumbria ('glade frequented by mice') [Thea Musgrave, 1928–, British composer]

— **'Little Musgrave and Lady Barnard'** an ancient balled that tells how an amorous assignation between Little Musgrave and Lady Barnard ends in the death of both of them at the hands of her jealous husband

— **'The Musgrave Ritual'** a 'Sherlock Holmes' story (1894) by Arthur Conan Doyle, centring on the recovery of the ancient crown jewels of England, the location of which was revealed by the performance of a cryptic ritual

— ***Serjeant Musgrave's Dance*** a play (1959) by John Arden about a group of deserting soldiers, led by Serjeant Musgrave, who descend on a northern mining town

Musgrove a different form of **Musgrave**

Musto, Mustoe 'person who lives near an area of land used as a meeting place' (from Middle English *motestowe* 'meeting place')

Myatt from the medieval personal name *Myat*, literally 'little *Mihel*', an Anglo-Norman variant of **Michael**

Myddleton see **Middleton**

Myers a different form of **Meyers**

Myerscough 'person from Myerscough', Lancashire ('copse by a marsh')

N

Nabarro a different form of **Navarro** [Sir Gerald Nabarro, 1913–73, British Conservative politician]

Nabokov 'son of *Nabok*', a nickname of uncertain import apparently based on Russian *na bok* 'on one's side' [Vladimir Nabokov, 1899–1977, Russian-born US writer]

Nadel, Nadell 'needle-maker' or 'tailor' (from Middle High German *nādel* 'needle')

Nader (i) 'embroiderer, tailor' (from a derivative of Middle High German *næjen* 'to embroider' and 'to sew'); (ii) from an Arabic personal name based on *nādir* 'extraordinary, exceptional' [Ralph Nader, 1934–, US attorney and consumer-protection advocate]
— **Nader's Raiders** a group of young activists in the 1960s and 1970s who worked in the US under the aegis of Ralph Nader (see above) in the field of consumer protection

Nadler 'needle-maker' (from a derivative of Middle English *nadle* 'needle')

Nagle (i) *also* **Nagel** 'nail-maker' (from Middle High German and Middle Dutch *nagel* 'nail'); (ii) a different form of the Irish-Norman surname *Nangle*, itself from a Pembrokeshire place-name meaning literally '(place) at the angle'. See also **Neagle**

Nahum from the Hebrew male personal name *Nachum*, literally 'consoled'

Nail (i) 'nail-maker'; (ii) from a medieval nickname for a tall thin person [Jimmy Nail (original name James Bradford), 1954–, British actor and singer]

Nairn, Nairne 'person from Nairn', Highland region ('(place at the mouth of the river) *Nairn*', a Celtic river-name perhaps meaning 'penetrating one') [Ian Nairn, 1930–83, British architectural critic; Nick Nairn 1959–, British chef]

Naish see **Nash**

Naismith, Naysmith, Nasmith (i) 'nail-maker' (from Old English *nægelsmith*); (ii) 'knife-maker' (from Old English *cnīfsmith*)

Nakamura 'village in the middle' (Japanese)

Nancarrow 'person from Nancarrow', Cornwall (either 'valley frequented by deer' or 'rough valley') [Conlon Nancarrow, 1912–97, US composer]

Napier 'seller of table linen' or 'servant in charge of table linen in a household' (Middle English, from Old French *nappier*, a derivative of *nappe* 'table cloth') [Sir Charles Napier, 1782–1853, British general and colonial administrator; John Napier, 1550–1617, Scottish mathematician;

Robert Cornelis Napier (Lord Napier), 1810–90, British field marshal]
— **Napier** a city in the eastern part of North Island, New Zealand. It was named in honour of Sir Charles Napier (see above).
— **Napierian** relating to the mathematician John Napier (see above). 'Napierian logarithm' is an alternative term for a natural logarithm.
— **Napier's bones** an elementary calculating machine produced by John Napier, consisting of a set of graduated rods
— **Napier University** a university in Edinburgh, Scotland, founded in 1964 as Napier Technical College. It became a university in 1992. It was named in honour of John Napier.

Nash, Nashe, Naish 'person who lives by an ash tree' (the initial *n* comes from the misdivision of Middle English *atten ashe* 'at the ash') [Heddle Nash, 1896–1961, British tenor; J. Carrol Naish, 1897–1973, US actor; John Nash, 1752–1835, British architect; Ogden Nash, 1902–71, US writer and lyricist; Paul Nash, 1889–1946, British painter; Richard Nash ('Beau Nash'), 1674–1762, British dandy; Thomas Nashe, 1567–?1601, English pamphleteer and dramatist; Sir Walter Nash, 1882–1968, British-born New Zealand Labour politician, prime minister 1957–60]
— **Frazer Nash** see **Fraser**
— **Nash Ensemble** a British chamber-music ensemble, founded in 1964. Its name was inspired by the elegant London terraces designed by John Nash (see above).
— **Nashville** the capital of the US state of Tennessee. It was founded in 1779 and named in honour of Francis Nash, ?1742–77, an American general in the War of Independence.

Nasmith see **Naismith**

Nathan from the Hebrew male personal name *Natan*, literally 'given (i.e. by God)'

Nathanson 'son of **Nathan**'

Nation a folk-etymological anglicization of **Nathan** [Terry Nation, 1930–97, British television scriptwriter, inventor of the Daleks]

Naughton, Naughten, Naghten (i) 'person from Naughton', Suffolk ('Nagli's farmstead'); (ii) a reduced form of **McNaughton**. See also **Norton** (ii) [Bill Naughton, 1910–92, Irish-born British playwright and author]
— **Naughton and Gold** one of the comedy pairings within the British variety combo 'The Crazy Gang', consisting of Charlie Naughton, 1887–1976, and Jimmy Gold, 1887–1967. The combination has also been used as rhyming slang for a *cold*.

Navarro 'person from Navarre', former Basque kingdom in northern Spain (Spanish *Navarra*, from Basque *Nafarroa*, a derivative of *naba* 'plain next to the mountains'). See also **Nabarro**

Naylor, Nayler 'nail-maker'

Naysmith see **Naismith**

Neagle a different form of **Nagle** (ii) [Dame Anna Neagle (original name Florence Marjorie Robertson), 1904–86, British actress]

Neal, Neale, Neall see **Neil**

Neame (i) 'uncle' (Middle English, arising from a misdivision of *mine eame* 'my uncle', a common form of address in the Middle Ages); (ii) from a medieval nickname for a person of restricted growth (from Old French *nain* 'dwarf') [Ronald Neame, 1911–, British film director]

Neary from Irish Gaelic *Ó Náraigh* 'descendant of *Nárach*', a nickname meaning literally 'modest'

Neason see **Neeson**

Neave, Neve, Neeve 'nephew' (from Old English *nefa* 'nephew') [Airey Neave, 1916–79, British Conservative politician]

Needham 'person from Needham', Derbyshire, Norfolk and Suffolk ('poor homestead')

Neely, Neilly, Neily shortened forms of **McNeely**

Neeson, Neason (i) from Irish Gaelic *Mac Naois* (see **McNeice**); (ii) from Dutch *Niesen* 'son of *Nijs*' (a shortened form of *Denijs* '**Dennis**') or German *Niesen* 'son of *Agnes*' [Liam Neeson (original name William John Neeson), 1952–, Northern Irish actor]

Neeve see **Neave**

Negus (i) perhaps 'person living in a house near a main settlement' (from a possible Old English *nēahhūs*, literally 'near house'); (ii) 'merchant' (Romanian, from Late Latin *negotiator*) [Arthur Negus, 1903–85, British antiques expert]

Neighbour 'neighbour' (probably from the use of the word as a term of address)

Neil, Neill, Neal, Neale, Neall, Niall, Niel, Kneale shortened forms of **McNeil** and **O'Neil** (*Neil*, etc. is the main spelling in Scotland, Ireland and northern England, *Neal*, etc. in southern and central England). See also **Nell, Niles, Nilon** [A.S. Neill, 1883–1973, British educationalist, child psychologist and writer; Andrew Neil, 1949–, British journalist; Nigel Kneale, 1922–2006, British writer, creator of 'Quatermass'; Sam Neill (original name Nigel Neill), 1948–, New Zealand actor]

Neilly, Neily see **Neely**

Neilson, Nielson, Nilson 'son of **Neil**'

Nell (i) from the medieval personal name *Nel*, a different form of **Neil**; (ii) from the Dutch and German personal name *Nel*, a shortened form of *Cornelius*

Nelligan from Irish Gaelic *Ó Niallagáin* 'descendant of *Niallagán*', literally 'little little Neil'

Nellis, Nelis (i) from Irish Gaelic *Mac Niallghuis* 'son of *Niallghus*', a personal name meaning literally 'champion choice' or 'champion vigour'; (ii) from a shortened form of the Dutch names *Cornelius* and *Daniels*

Nelmes, Nelms 'person who lives in or near a grove of elm trees' (from a misdivision of Middle English *atten elmes* 'at the elm trees')

Nelson 'son of **Neal**' [Baby Face Nelson (original name Lester Joseph Gillis), 1908–34, diminutive US gangster; Horatio Nelson (Viscount Nelson), 1758–1805, British admiral; Prince Rogers Nelson, 1958–, the original name of the US pop singer latterly known as 'Prince'; Ricky Nelson (original name Eric Hilliard Nelson), 1940–85, US pop singer; Willie Nelson, 1933–, US country singer/songwriter]

— **nelson** a wrestling hold in which one arm (**half nelson**) or both arms (**full nelson**) are passed through the opponent's arms from behind and pulled back, levering against the opponent's back. It is presumably named after someone called Nelson, but his or her identity is unknown.

— **Nelson** the name of various places in the English-speaking world named directly or indirectly after Lord Nelson (see above), including a town in Lancashire (which grew up around an inn called the 'Lord Nelson'), a city in New Zealand and a village (**Nelson Village**) in Northumberland

— **Nelsonian** relating to or characteristic of Lord Nelson

— **Nelson Mass** (in German *Nelsonmesse*) the Mass no. 11 in D major (1798) by Josef Haydn. The composer himself called it 'Missa in angustiis' (that is, 'mass composed in great tribulation'), and it is also known as the 'Coronation Mass'. There are two (unsubstantiated) accounts of the Horatio Nelson connection: that it was written to celebrate his victory in the Battle of the Nile in 1798; and that he attended a performance in Eisenstadt in 1800.

— **Nelson's Column** a monument (officially 'the Nelson Column') to Lord Nelson, erected in Trafalgar Square, London, in 1843. It consists of a 44-m (145-foot) column with a statue of Nelson on top.

— **Nelson's Pillar** a former monument to Lord Nelson in O'Connell Street, Dublin. It was blown up by the IRA in 1966.

— **the Nelson touch** an action or manner thought of as characteristic of Lord Nelson

Nemo a different form of **Nimmo**

Nesbitt, Nesbit 'person from Nesbitt or Nisbit', the name of various places in the Border region of Scotland (either 'nose-shaped piece of land' or 'nose-shaped bend in a river'). See also **Nisbit** [Edith Nesbit, 1858–1924, British children's writer; James Nesbitt, 1965–, Northern Irish actor]

Ness 'person who lives on a promontory or headland' (from Old Norse *nes*) [Eliot Ness, 1903–57, US Treasury agent responsible (at the head of a team known as 'The Untouchables') for enforcing Prohibition laws]

Netherton 'person from Netherton', Devon ('lower farmstead')

Nettlefold 'person from Nettlefold', lost place in Surrey ('enclosure or open country growing with nettles')
— **Guest, Keen and Nettlefold** see **Guest**

Nettles 'person who lives in a place growing with nettles' [John Nettles, 1948–, British actor]

Nettleton 'person from Nettleton', Lincolnshire or Wiltshire ('enclosure growing with nettles')

Neumann, Neuman from a medieval German and Jewish nickname for a newcomer to a place (literally 'new man')

Neve see **Neave**

Neville, Nevil, Nevill (i) 'person from Neuville or Néville', places in northern France (both 'new settlement'); (ii) from Irish Gaelic *Ó Niadh* 'descendant of *Nia*' (see **McNee**). See also **Newell** [John Neville, 1925–, British actor; Richard Neville, 1428–71, 1st earl of Warwick ('Warwick the Kingmaker')]

Nevin from Scottish and Irish Gaelic *Mac Naoimhín* 'son of *Naomhín*', a personal name meaning literally 'little saint', or from Irish Gaelic *Mac Cnáimhín* 'son of *Cnámh*' and *Ó Cnáimhín* 'descendant of *Cnámh*', literally 'little bone', apparently a nickname applied to a very thin man. See also **Niven**

Nevins a different form of **Nevin**

Nevinson 'son of **Nevin**'

New (i) from a medieval nickname for someone new to a place; (ii) 'person who lives by a yew tree' (from a misdivision of Middle English *atten ew* 'at the yew')

Newall 'person who lives or works in the "new hall"'

Newberry, Newbery, Newbury 'person from Newbury', the name of various places in England ('new borough')

Newbold, Newbould 'person who lives in a new building', or 'person from Newbold', the name of various places in England (both ultimately from Old English *nēowe bold* 'new building')

Newbolt, Newboult different forms of **Newbold** [Sir Henry Newbolt, 1862–1938, British barrister, poet and man of letters]

Newby 'person from Newby', the name of various places in northern England ('new farmstead') [Eric Newby, 1919–, British travel writer]

Newcombe, Newcomb, Newcome from a medieval nickname for a newly arrived person [John Newcombe, 1944–, Australian tennis player]
— **The Newcomes** a novel (1855) by W.M. Thackeray, following the lives of the descendants of Thomas Newcome

Newcomen a different form of **Newcombe** [Thomas Newcomen, 1663–1729, English blacksmith, inventor of an early steam engine]

Newdigate 'person from Newdigate', Surrey ('gate by the new wood')
— **Newdigate Prize** an annual prize for poetry presented at Oxford University, instituted in 1806 by Sir Roger Newdigate, 1719–1806, a politician and collector of antiquities

Newell a different form of **Neville**

Newey 'person who lives in a new enclosure', or 'person from Newhey or Newhay', the name of various places in Cheshire (both ultimately from Old English *nēowe haga* 'new enclosure')

Newham 'person from Newham', the name of various places in England ('new homestead'). See also **Newnham**

Newhouse (i) 'person who lives in a new house', or 'person from Newhouse', the name of various places in England (both ultimately from Old English *nēowe hūs*); (ii) a translation of various synonymous surnames in other languages (e.g. German *Neuhaus*, Swedish *Nyhus*, Hungarian *Újházi*) [Samuel Irving ('SI') Newhouse, Jr., 1927–, US publisher]

Newland 'person who lives on new land (e.g. a newly cultivated area, or land recently added to a settlement)', or 'person from Newland', the name of various places in England

Newman (i) from a medieval nickname for someone new to a place; (ii) an anglicization or translation of various synonymous surnames in other languages (e.g. German *Neumann*, Czech *Novák*) [Barnett Newman, 1905–70, US painter; Ernest Newman, pen-name of William Roberts, 1868–1959, British music critic; John Henry Newman (Cardinal Newman), 1801–90, British churchman; Nanette Newman, 1934–, British actress and writer; Paul Newman, 1925–, US actor; Randy Newman (original name Randall Stuart Newman), 1943–, US songwriter, singer and pianist]

Newmark an anglicization of German *Neumark* 'person from Neumark' and Swedish *Nymark* 'person from Nymark', place-names meaning literally 'new field'

Newnes an anglicized spelling of **Nunes** [Sir George Newnes, 1851–1910, British publisher and magazine proprietor]

Newnham, Nuneham different forms of **Newham**

Newport 'person from Newport', the name of various places in England ('new market town')

Newsome, Newsom, Newsam, Newsum 'person from Newsome', the name of various places in northern England ('new houses')

Newson (i) 'son of someone called **New** (i)'; (ii) a different form of **Newsome**

Newton 'person from Newton', the name of numerous places in England ('new farmstead') [Sir Isaac Newton, 1642–1727, English physicist and mathematician; Olivia Newton-John, 1948–, Australian singer and actress; Robert Newton, 1905–56, British actor]
— **newton** an SI unit (symbol **N**) of force equivalent to the force that produces an acceleration of one metre per second on a mass of one kilogram. It is named in honour of Isaac Newton (see above).
— **Newtonian** relating to or following the scientific principles established by Isaac Newton
— **Newton's cradle** an executive toy consisting of five metal balls hanging side by side in a frame, in

which swinging the ball at one end transmits force along the line so the other end ball swings away, illustrating principles of conservation of momentum and energy that can be derived from Newton's second and third laws of motion. It was invented and named in 1967 by the British actor Simon Prebble. It is commonly known colloquially as **Newton's balls**.

— **Newton's rings** a pattern of light interference created by the contact of a convex lens with a glass plate, appearing as a series of alternating bright and dark rings. It is named after Isaac Newton.

Ney a different form of **Nye**

Nguyen from a Vietnamese surname of unknown origin

Niall see **Neil**

Niblett perhaps from a medieval nickname for someone with a long or large nose (from a derivative of Middle English *nibbe* 'beak')

Nice from a medieval nickname for a foolish or simple-minded person (from Middle English *nice* 'foolish, simple')

Nichol, Nicholl, Nicoll, Nickol, Nickel, Nickell, Nickle different forms of **Nicholas**

— **Nicol prism** a device for producing light polarized in a plane, consisting of two specially shaped calcite prisms cemented together with Canada balsam. It is named after the Scottish physicist and geologist William Nicol, 1768–1851.

Nicholas from the male personal name *Nicholas*, ultimately from Greek *Nikolaos*, literally 'victory-people'. See also **Cole** (i), **Colin**

Nichols, Nicholls, Nicolls, Nickols, Nickoles 'son of **Nichol**' [Dandy Nichols (original name Daisy Nichols), 1907–86, British actress; Peter Nichols, 1927–, British playwright]

— **Harvey Nichols** see **Harvey**

Nicholson, Nicolson, Nickleson 'son of **Nichol**' [Ben Nicholson, 1894–1982, British painter and sculptor; Sir Harold Nicolson, 1886–1968, British diplomat and diarist; Jack Nicholson, 1937–, US actor; William Nicholson, 1753–1815, British chemist]

— **Weidenfeld & Nicolson** see **Weidenfeld**

Nickel (i) from the German and Dutch personal name *Nickel*, a pet-form of *Nick*, a shortened form of *Nikolaus* 'Nicholas'; (ii) *also* **Nickell** see **Nichol**

Nickerson 'son of *Nicker*', a medieval pet-form of **Nicholas**

Nicklaus from German, from a variant of the personal name *Nickolaus* 'Nicholas'. See also **Clausen** [Jack Nicklaus, 1940–, US golfer]

Nickless a different form of **Nicholas**

Nicklin 'little **Nicholas**'

Nickol, Nickols see **Nichol, Nichols**

Nickson see **Nixon**

Nicoll, Nicolls, Nicolson see **Nichol, Nichols, Nicholson**

Niel see **Neil**

Nielsen, Nilsen 'son of *Niels*', a German, Danish and Norwegian personal name that is a reduced form of *Nickolaus* '**Nicholas**' [Dennis Nilsen,

1945–, British serial killer; Leslie Nielsen, 1926–, Canadian actor]

— **Nielsen ratings** a US popularity rating (generally known simply as **the Nielsens**) for television programmes developed in the early 1950s by Arthur Clarke Nielsen, using a device called an Audiometer

Niemeyer from a medieval German nickname for a newly arrived steward or tenant farmer (from Middle Low German *nie* 'new' + *meier* (see **Meyer** (i)))

Nightingale from a medieval nickname for someone with a mellifluous singing voice [Annie Nightingale, 1942–, British radio broadcaster; Florence Nightingale, 1820–1910, British hospital reformer and founder of the nursing profession; Mary Nightingale, 1963–, British television newsreader]

Nighy see **Nye**

Niles 'son of **Neil**'

Nilon 'descendant of little **Neil**'

Nilsen see **Nielsen**

Nimmo a Scottish name of unknown origin. See also **Nemo** [Derek Nimmo, 1932–99, British actor]

Nisbit a different form of **Nesbitt**

Nish an abbreviated different form of **McNeice**

Nissen (i) 'son of *Nis*', a variant of the Scandinavian personal name *Niels* (see **Nielsen**); (ii) from the Yiddish male personal name *Nisn*, from Hebrew *nisan*, the name of a Jewish month

— **Nissen hut** a temporary shelter made of corrugated steel in the shape of a half cylinder that was first used by the British during World War I. It is named after its inventor, Lt-Col. Peter Norman Nissen, 1871–1930.

Niven a different form of **Nevin** [David Niven, 1909–83, British film actor]

Nixon, Nickson, Nixson 'son of *Nik*', a shortened form of **Nicholas** [David Nixon, 1919–78, British conjurer; Richard Milhous Nixon, 1913–94, US Republican politician, president 1969–74]

— **Nixonian** relating to or characteristic of Richard M. Nixon (see above).

— **Nixonomics** the economic policies of Richard M. Nixon.

Noakes 'person who lives by a stand of oak trees' (from a misdivision of Middle English *atten okes* 'at the oaks')

Nobbs 'son of *Nobb*', a medieval pet-form of the personal name **Robert**

Noble (i) from a medieval nickname for someone of high birth or noble character or, ironically, for a mean-spirited low-born person; (ii) an anglicization of the Jewish surnames *Knöbel*, literally 'servant', and *Knobel*, literally 'garlic' [Adrian Noble, 1950–, British theatre director; Sir Andrew Noble, 1831–1915, British physicist]

Noblett (i) *also* **Noblet** 'little **Noble** (i)'; (ii) 'little little *Nobb*' (see **Nobbs**)

Noel, Nowell from a medieval nickname for someone with a particular connection with Christmas (e.g. being born at that time, or presenting the lord of the manor with a yule-log) (Middle English, from Old French *noel* 'Christmas')

Nolan from Irish Gaelic *Ó Nualláin* 'descendant of *Nuallán*', a personal name meaning literally 'little famous one' [Sir Sidney Nolan, 1917–92, Australian painter]
— **The Nolans** a singing group of Irish-born sisters (known originally as the **Nolan Sisters**). Popular particularly in the late 1970s and early 1980s, their sororal composition has changed over the years, but has always included two or more (usually five) out of Anne, Denise, Maureen, Linda, Bernardette and Coleen Nolan.

Noon (i) from a medieval nickname for someone of a sunny disposition (noon being the sunniest part of the day); (ii) see **Noone**

Noonan, Nunan from Irish Gaelic *Ó hIon-mhaineáin* 'descendant of *Ionmhaineán*', a personal name meaning literally 'beloved'

Noone, Noon from Irish Gaelic *Ó Nuadháin* 'descendant of *Nuadhán*', a personal name based on *Nuadha*, the name of various Celtic gods

Norbury 'person from Norbury', the name of various places in England ('northern fortress' or 'northern manor')

Norcross 'person from Norcross', Lancashire ('northern cross')

Norden 'person from Norden', Devon ('northern woodland pasture'), or 'person from Norden', northern Germany ('northern', perhaps referring to a north-facing field) [Denis Norden, 1922–, British comedy writer]

Nordqvist from an invented Swedish name, literally 'north twig'

Nordstrom from *Nordström*, an invented Swedish name, literally 'north river'

Norman (i) 'person from Normandy'; (ii) 'man from the north' (Swedish, from *norr* 'north' + *man* 'man'); (iii) an anglicization of the Ukrainian Jewish name *Novominsky* [Barry Norman, 1933–, British film critic; Greg Norman, 1955–, Australian golfer; Jessye Norman, 1945–, US soprano; Montagu Norman (Lord Norman), 1871–1950, British banker, governor of the Bank of England 1920–44]

Normand a different form of **Norman** (i)

Norrington, Norington (i) 'person who lives to the north of a main settlement', or 'person from Norrington', the name of various places in England (in either case literally 'north in the settlement'); (ii) 'person from Northampton', Northamptonshire ('northern home farm'). See also **Norton** (ii) [Sir Roger Norrington, 1934–, British conductor]

Norris (i) 'person who lives in a house in the northern part of a settlement' (from Old English, *north* + *hūs* 'house'); (ii) 'nurse' (i.e. wet-nurse, who suckles a child) (from Old French *norrice* 'nurse'). See also **Nurse**; (iii) 'immigrant from the north' (from Old French *norreis* 'northerner') [Frank Norris, 1870–1902, US novelist; Steven Norris, 1945–, British Conservative politician]

— *Mr Norris Changes Trains* a largely autobiographical novel (1935) by Christopher Isherwood in which the central character is the con-man and double agent Arthur Norris

North (i) 'person who lives to the north of a settlement or in the northern part of it'; (ii) 'immigrant from the north'; (iii) 'person from Ulster' (as opposed to southern Ireland) [Frederick North (Lord North), 1732–92, British statesman, prime minister 1770–82; Sir Thomas North, ?1535–?1601, English translator (notably of Plutarch)]

Northam 'person from Northam', Devon ('northern enclosure') [Jeremy Northam, 1961–, British actor]

Northcott, Northcote 'person from Northcott', the name of various places in England ('northern cottage') [C. Northcote Parkinson, see **Parkinson**]

Northern a different form of **North**

Northey 'person from Northey', the name of various places in England ('northern enclosure')

Northrop 'person from Northorpe', Yorkshire ('northern outlying farmstead') [John Howard Northrop, 1891–1987, US biochemist]
— **Northrop Corporation** a US aircraft manufacturing company, founded in 1932 by John Knudsen ('Jack') Northrop, 1895–1981

Norton (i) 'person from Norton', the name of various places in England ('northern farmstead'); (ii) a different form of **Naughton** (ii) and **Norrington** [Graham Norton (original name Graham Walker), 1963–, Irish comedian and television presenter]
— **Norton** a British make of motorcycle, founded in Birmingham in 1898 by James Norton, 1869–1925. The company ceased production in the early 1990s.

Norwood 'person from Norwood', the name of various places in England ('northern wood')

Nott from a medieval nickname for a bald or very short-haired person (from Middle English *not* 'bald') [Sir John Nott, 1932–, British Conservative politician]

Nourse a different form of **Nurse**

Novak from Czech *Novák*, from a nickname for a newcomer, a derivative of Czech *nový* 'new' [Kim Novak (original name Marilyn Pauline Novak), 1933–, US actress]

Novello from Italian, from the personal name *Novello*, literally 'little new one' (probably applied to the youngest child), also a nickname for a newcomer [Ivor Novello (original name David Ivor Davies), 1893–1951, British composer, playwright and actor]
— **Novello and Co.** a British firm of music publishers founded in 1811 by Vincent Novello, 1781–1861

Nowell see **Noel**

Noy, Noye (i) from the medieval male personal name *Noye*, the English form of the Hebrew name *Noach* 'Noah'; (ii) an invented Jewish name based on Hebrew *noy* 'decoration, adornment' [Kenneth Noye, 1947–, British criminal]

Noyes 'son of **Noy** (i)' [Alfred Noyes, 1880–1959, British poet, playwright and novelist]

Nugent 'person from Nogent', northern France (from a Latinized form of a Gaulish place-name meaning 'new settlement')

Nulty a reduced form of **McNulty**

Nuneham see **Newnham**

Nunes 'son of *Nuno*', a Portuguese male personal name, from Latin *Nunnus*, of unknown origin and meaning. See also **Newnes**

Nunn 'person who works in a convent', or from a medieval nickname for a man of demure piety (from Middle English *nunn* 'nun') [Sir Trevor Nunn, 1940–, British theatre director]

Nurse a different form of **Norris** (ii). See also **Nourse** [Seymour Nurse, 1933–, West Indian cricketer]

Nutt 'gatherer and seller of nuts'; also, from a medieval nickname for someone thought to resemble a nut (e.g. in having a nut-brown complexion)

Nuttall 'person from Nuttall or Nuthall', the name of various places in England (mainly 'nook of land where nut-trees grow')

Nutter (i) 'scribe, clerk' (from Middle English *notere*, ultimately from Latin *notārius*); (ii) 'person who keeps or tends oxen' (from a derivative of Middle English *nowt* 'ox') [Tommy Nutter, 1943–92, British tailor]

Nutting 'son of **Nutt**'

Nye, Nighy 'person who lives by a river or on an island' (from a misdivision of Middle English *atten eye* 'at the river' and 'at the island') [Bill Nighy, 1949–, British actor]

Nyman (i) from a Scandinavian nickname for someone new to a place (from *ny* 'new' + *man* 'man'); (ii) an anglicization of the Yiddish surname *Naiman*, literally 'new man, newcomer' [Michael Nyman, 1944–, British composer]

O

O'- from Irish Gaelic *ó* or *ua* 'descendant' (from Old Irish *au*). Prefixed to a personal name or nickname (e.g. *Donovan*) it forms a surname (*O'Donovan* – i.e. 'descendant of Donovan' or 'grandson of Donovan').

Oak, Oake, Oke 'person who lives by an oak tree or in an oak wood' [Gabriel Oak, the young shepherd and constant suitor of Bathsheba Everdene in Thomas Hardy's *Far from the Madding Crowd* (1874)]

Oakden a different form of **Ogden**

Oakland 'person who lives on an area of land with an oak tree or oak trees growing on it'

Oakley, Oakeley, Okeley 'person from Oakley', the name of various places in England ('glade where oak trees grow'). See also **Oatley** (ii) [Annie Oakley (original name Phoebe Anne Oakley Moses), 1860–1926, US sharpshooter]

Oakman from the Old English personal name *Ācmann*, literally 'oak-man'

Oaks, Oakes different forms of **Oak**

Oaten from *Odon*, a form of the Old French personal name *Odo* (see **Ott**)

Oates 'son of *Ode*' (see **Ott**). See also **Otis** [Joyce Carol Oates, 1938–, US writer; Captain Lawrence Edward Grace Oates, 1880–1912, British Polar explorer; Titus Oates, 1649–1705, English conspirator]

Oatley (i) 'person from Oteley', Shropshire ('glade where oats grow'); (ii) a different form of **Oakley**

O'Boyle a different form of **Boyle** (i)

O'Brady a different form of **Brady** (i)

O'Brien, O'Brian 'descendant of **Bryan**' [Conor Cruise O'Brien, 1917–, Irish diplomat; Edna O'Brien, 1936–, Irish author; Flann O'Brien, pen-name of Brian O'Nolan or O'Nuallain, 1911–66, Irish novelist and journalist; Vincent O'Brien, 1917–, Irish racehorse trainer; William O'Brien, 1852–1928, Irish nationalist politician and journalist; William Smith O'Brien, 1803–64, Irish politician]

O'Byrne 'descendant of **Byrne**'

O'Callaghan 'descendant of **Callaghan**'

O'Casey 'descendant of **Casey**' [Sean O'Casey, 1880–1964, Irish playwright and nationalist]

Ockenden 'person from Ockenden', Essex ('Wocca's hill')

O'Connell 'descendant of **Connell**' [Daniel O'Connell, 1775–1847, Irish politician]
— **O'Connell Street** the principal street in Dublin on the north side of the River Liffey. Previously

Sackville Street, it was renamed in 1924 in honour of Daniel O'Connell (see above), 'the Liberator', who campaigned successfully for Catholic Emancipation in Ireland.

O'Connor, O'Conner 'descendant of **Connor**' [Des O'Connor, 1932–, British entertainer; Feargus O'Connor, 1794–1855, Irish politician; Flannery O'Connor, 1925–64, US novelist and short story writer; Frank O'Connor, pen-name of Michael O'Donovan, 1903–66, Irish short-story writer; Tom O'Connor, 1939–, British comedian]
— **O'Connorville** a village in Hertfordshire, now more usually known as Heronsgate. It was named after the Irish Chartist leader Feargus O'Connor (see above), who bought land in the area to be let to members of the Chartist Cooperative Land Company.

Oddie, Oddy 'little *Ode*' (see **Ott**) [Bill Oddie, 1941–, British actor and broadcaster]

O'Dea from Irish Gaelic, 'descendant of *Deaghadh*', a personal name perhaps meaning literally 'good luck'

Odell 'person from Odell or Woodhill', Bedfordshire ('hill where the woad plant grows'). See also **Waddell**

O'Dell an alteration of **Odell**, as if it were a name of Irish origin

Odham from a medieval nickname for someone who had climbed the social ladder by marrying the daughter of a local notable (from Middle English *odam* 'son-in-law')

O'Doherty 'descendant of **Doherty**'

O'Donnell, O'Donnel from Irish Gaelic, 'descendant of *Domhnall*' (see **Donald**) [Sir Augustine ('Gus') O'Donnell, 1952–, British civil servant]

O'Donohue, O'Donoghue 'descendant of **Donohue**'

O'Donovan 'descendant of **Donovan**'

O'Dowd 'descendant of **Dowd**'

O'Driscoll 'descendant of **Driscoll**'

O'Dwyer 'descendant of **Dwyer**'

O'Farrell 'descendant of **Farrell**'

Offord 'person from Offord', Cambridgeshire ('upstream ford')

O'Flaherty, O'Flagherty 'descendant of **Flaherty**' [Liam O'Flaherty, 1896–1984, Irish novelist; Oscar Fingal O'Flahertie Wills Wilde, see **Wild**]

O'Flynn 'descendant of **Flynn**'

O'Gara 'descendant of *Gadhra*' (see **Geary** (i))

Ogden, Ogdon 'person from Ogden', Yorkshire ('oak valley') [C.K. Ogden, 1889–1957, British writer and scholar, deviser of 'Basic English'; John Ogdon, 1937–89, British pianist; Stan and Hilda Ogden, husband-and-wife pairing of work-shy boozer and gossip in the Granada soap-opera *Coronation Street*]

Ogg from a medieval Scottish nickname (based on Gaelic *óg* 'young') applied to the younger of two people with the same name

Ogilvy, Ogilvie 'person from Ogilvy', Angus (probably 'high place' or 'high hill') [Sir Angus Ogilvy, 1928–2004, husband of Princess Alexandra]

Ogle 'person from Ogle', Northumberland ('Ocga's hill')

Oglesby perhaps 'person from Ugglebarnby', Yorkshire ('Uglubárthr's settlement')

Oglethorpe 'person from Oglethorpe', Yorkshire ('Oddketill's settlement') [James Edward Oglethorpe, 1696–1785, English general and colonizer in North America]

O'Gorman 'descendant of **Gorman** (iii)'

O'Grady from Irish Gaelic, 'descendant of *Gráda*', a nickname meaning literally 'noble'. See also **Grady** [Paul O'Grady, 1955–, British chat-show host and (as Lily Savage) drag comedian]
— **Judy O'Grady** Rudyard Kipling's embodiment of the lower-order female of the species in his *Seven Seas* (1896):
For the Colonel's lady an' Judy O'Grady
Are sisters under their skins!

O'Hagan 'descendant of **Hagan**'

O'Halloran 'descendant of **Halloran**'

O'Hara from Irish Gaelic, 'descendant of *Eaghra*', a personal name of unknown origin and meaning. See also **O'Hora** [John O'Hara, 1905–70, US novelist; Kimball O'Hara, orphaned son of an Irish soldier in India who is the central character of Rudyard Kipling's *Kim* (1901); Maureen O'Hara (original name Maureen FitzSimons), 1920–, Irish-born US actress; Scarlett O'Hara, the headstrong heroine of Margaret Mitchell's *Gone with the Wind* (1936), played in the 1939 film by Vivien Leigh]

O'Hare, O'Hair 'descendant of **Hare** (ii)'
— **O'Hare International Airport** the main airport of Chicago, Illinois, USA, constructed in 1942/43 and named in 1949 after Lt. Comdr. Edward ('Butch') O'Hare, 1914–43, US World War II flying ace.

O'Hearn a different form of **Ahern**

O'Higgins 'descendant of **Higgins** (ii)' [Bernardo O'Higgins, 1778–1842, Chilean national hero (son of an Irishman) who fought against Spanish colonial rule and was the first effective head of state of an independent Chile, 1817–23]
— **O'Higgins** a department (Spanish *Departamento de O'Higgins*) of the northern Argentine province of Chaco, named in honour of Bernardo O'Higgins (see above)

O'Hora a different form of **O'Hara**

O'Kane 'descendant of **Kane** (i)'

O'Keefe, O'Keeffe 'descendant of **Keefe**' [Georgia O'Keefe, 1887–1986, US artist]

O'Kelly, O'Kelley 'descendant of **Kelly** (i)'

Old (i) 'old person'; (ii) from a distinguishing name used to denote the older of two people with the same personal name. See also **Auld**, **Oldman**, **Olds**

Oldenburg 'person from Oldenburg', Germany ('old fortress') [Claes Oldenburg, 1929–, Swedish-born US sculptor]

Oldfield 'person from Oldfield', the name of various places in England ('old area of open land') [Bert Oldfield, 1894–1976, Australian cricketer; Bruce Oldfield, 1950–, British fashion designer; Mike Oldfield, 1953–, British musician and composer]

Oldham 'person from Oldham', Lancashire ('old island' (referring to a high moorland ridge))

Oldman a different form of **Old** [Gary Oldman, 1958–, British actor]

Oldroyd 'person from Oldroyd', the name of various places in northern England ('old clearing')

Olds 'son of **Old**'
— **Oldsmobile** a US motor-car marque, founded in 1897 by Ransom Eli Olds, 1864–1950. It was bought up by General Motors in 1908, and became defunct in 2004.

O'Leary 'descendant of **Leary**' [Dermot O'Leary, 1973–, British television presenter]

Oliphant 'elephant' (from Middle English, Old French and Middle High German *olifant* 'elephant'), perhaps used as a nickname for a large cumbersome person, or denoting someone who lived in a building distinguished by the sign of an elephant [Margaret Oliphant, 1828–97, Scottish writer; Sir Mark Oliphant, 1901–2000, Australian physicist]

Oliva (i) 'person who lives by an olive grove', 'grower or seller of olives' or 'maker or seller of olive oil' (from Italian *oliva* 'olive'); (ii) 'person from (Santa) Oliva', the name of various places in Spain ('olive')

Oliveira 'person who lives by an olive grove', or 'person from Oliveira', the name of various places in Portugal (in either case from Portuguese *oliveira* 'olive grove'). See also **D'Oliveira**

Oliver from the male personal name *Oliver*, from Old French *Olivier*. That name is probably ultimately of Germanic origin (perhaps related to *Álvaro* – see **Alvarez**), but its form became altered by association with Latin *olīva* 'olive'. [Isaac Oliver, ?1556–1617, French-born English portrait miniaturist; Jamie Oliver, 1975–, British celebrity chef]
— **Bath Oliver** a thin dry unsweetened biscuit, usually eaten with cheese. It is named after its creator, Dr William Oliver, 1695–1764, of Bath.

Olivier from the French male personal name *Olivier* (see **Oliver**) [Laurence Olivier (Lord Olivier), 1907–89, British actor and director]

— **Laurence Olivier Awards** an annual set of awards for excellence on the London stage, instituted in 1976 and named in honour of Laurence Olivier (see above)

— **Olivier Theatre** the largest auditorium of the Royal National Theatre, on the South Bank, London. Opened in 1976, it was named in honour of Laurence Olivier.

Ollerenshaw 'person from Ollerenshaw', Derbyshire ('alder copse')

Ollerton 'person from Ollerton', Cheshire and Nottinghamshire ('farmstead where alders grow') and Shropshire ('Ælfhere's farmstead')

Olney 'person from Olney', Buckinghamshire and Northamptonshire (respectively 'Olla's island' and 'solitary glade')

O'Loughlin 'descendant of *Lochlann*' (see **Laughlan**)

Olsen 'son of *Olaf* or *Olav*', a Danish and Norwegian male personal name meaning literally 'ancestor heir'

Olson an anglicization of Danish and Norwegian *Olsen* (see **Olsen**) or of the related Swedish *Olsson*

O'Malley from Irish Gaelic *Ó Máille* 'descendant of the nobleman'. See also **Malley**

Oman (i) a different form of **Hammond**; (ii) an anglicization of Swedish *Öman*, an invented name meaning literally 'island-man'

Omar from an Arabic male personal name perhaps related to Arabic *'āmir* 'substantial, prosperous'

O'Mara from Irish Gaelic *Ó Meadhra* 'descendant of *Meadhra*', a personal name based on *meadhair* 'mirth'

O'Neil, O'Neill from Irish Gaelic, 'descendant of *Niall*', a personal name probably meaning literally 'champion'. See also **Neil** [Eugene O'Neill, 1888–1953, US playwright; Jonjo O'Neill, 1952–, Irish jockey and racehorse trainer; Martin O'Neill, 1952–, Northern Irish football manager; Norman O'Neill, 1875–1934, British composer and conductor; Norman O'Neill, 1937–, Australian cricketer; Terence O'Neill (Lord O'Neill), 1914–90, Northern Irish Unionist politician, prime minister 1963–69]

Onion (i) from the Welsh male personal name *Einion*, probably from Latin *Anniānus*. See also **Anyon**; (ii) 'grower or seller of onions'. The perceived indignity of association with the vegetable has led to it being euphemistically pronounced, and sometimes even written, as the quasi-Irish *O'Nion*.

Onions 'son of **Onion** (i)'. For the spelling *O'Nions*, see **Onion**. See also **Baines** (ii), **Beynon** [C.T. Onions, 1873–1965, British philologist and lexicographer]

Ono 'small field', Japanese [Yoko Ono, 1933–, Japanese-born US artist]

Onslow 'person from Onslow', Shropshire ('Andhere's hill or burial-mound')

Openshaw 'person from Openshaw', Greater Manchester ('open wood' (i.e. one not bounded by a hedge))

Opie from the medieval personal name *Oppy* or *Obby*, pet-forms of such names as *Osbert* and *Osbold* [John Opie, 1761–1807, British portrait and history painter; Peter Opie, 1918–82, and his wife Iona Opie (*née* Archibald), 1923–, British authors and folklorists]

Oppenheim 'person from Oppenheim', Rhineland (perhaps 'homestead in a marsh')

Oppenheimer a different form of **Oppenheim** [J. Robert Oppenheimer, 1904–67, US nuclear physicist, leader of the team that developed the atomic bomb]

Orbach (i) 'person from Orbach', North Rhine-Westphalia; (ii) a different form of **Auerbach** [Susie Orbach, 1946–, British psychotherapist and author]

Orchard 'fruit grower' or 'person who lives by an orchard'

Ord, Orde (i) 'person from Ord', Northumberland ('point'), or 'person from Ord', the name of various places in Scotland ('rounded hill'); (ii) from the Germanic personal name *Ort*, a shortened form of various compound names beginning with *ord* 'point' [Boris Ord (original name Bernhard Ord), 1897–1961, British organist and composer]

O'Reilly 'descendant of **Reilly**' [Bill O'Reilly, 1905–92, Australian cricketer; Tony O'Reilly (Sir Anthony O'Reilly), 1936–, Irish rugby player and businessman]

Orford 'person from Orford', the name of numerous places in England (variously 'ford near the shore' (Suffolk), 'upstream ford' and 'ford of the Irish')

Organ (i) 'player of a musical instrument'; (ii) from the rare medieval personal name *Organ*, of unknown origin and meaning [Brian Organ, 1935–, British painter]

O'Riordan from Irish Gaelic, 'descendant of *Ríoghbhárdán*', a nickname meaning 'little royal bard'. See also **Riordan**

Ormiston 'person from Ormiston', Borders and Lothian ('Ormr's settlement')

Ormond, Ormonde from Irish Gaelic *Ó Ruaidh* 'descendant of *Ruadh*', a nickname meaning literally 'red'. In the process of anglicization it has been accommodated to *Ormond* (Gaelic *Ur Mhumhain*), the name of an area in the ancient region of East Munster.

Ormrod, Ormerod 'person from Ormerod', Lancashire ('Ormr's or Ormarr's glade')

Ormsby 'person from Ormsby or Ormesby', Lincolnshire, Norfolk and Yorkshire ('Ormr's settlement') [Ormsby Gore, the family name of Baron Harlech]

O'Rourke, O'Rorke 'descendant of **Rourke**' [Patrick O'Rourke, 1947–, US journalist and author]

Orpin, Orpen 'herbalist' (from Middle English *orpin* 'yellow stonecrop', a plant prescribed by medieval herbalists for healing wounds) [Sir William Orpen, 1878–1931, British painter]

Orr (i) from a medieval Scottish nickname for someone with a pale, unhealthy complexion (from Gaelic *odhar* 'pale'); (ii) 'person who lives by the sea shore or on the edge of a hill', or 'person from Ore or Oare', the name of various places in southern England (in either case from Old English *ōra* 'edge'); (iii) from the Old Norse nickname *Orri*, literally 'blackcock'; (iv) an invented Jewish name, based on Hebrew *or* 'light' [Robin Orr, 1909–, British composer]

Ortega 'person from Ortega', the name of various places in Spain

Ortiz 'son of *Orti*', a Basque personal name derived from Latin *Fortunius*

Orton 'person from Orton', the name of numerous places in England and Scotland (variously 'farmstead by or on a hill', 'higher farmstead', 'farmstead by a riverbank' and 'edge of the fortress') [Joe Orton, 1933–67, British playwright]

Orwell (i) 'person from Orwell', Cambridgeshire ('spring by a pointed hill'), or 'person from Orwell', Perth and Kinross (probably 'new village'); (ii) an invented name derived from *Orwell*, the name of an estuarine river in Suffolk ('Or stream' – *Or* being a pre-Celtic river-name of unknown meaning) [George Orwell, the pen-name (from iii above) of Eric Blair, 1903–50, British writer]
— **Orwellian** characteristic of George Orwell (see above) or his work, especially in portraying a future of totalitarian tyranny, as in his novel *1984* (1949)

Osborn, Osborne, Osbourn, Osbourne from the Old Norse male personal name *Ásbjorn*, literally 'god-bear'. See also **Usborne** [Dorothy Osborne, 1627–95, English letter writer; John Osborne, 1929–94, British playwright and screenwriter; Ozzy Osbourne (original name John Michael Osbourne), 1948–, British rock musician and television personality; Sharon Osbourne (*née* Levy), 1952–, British television personality, wife of Ozzy]

Oscar from the male personal name *Oscar*, of Gaelic origin, literally 'deer-friend' [Henry Oscar, 1891–1969, British actor]

Osgood from the Old Norse male personal name *Ásgautr*, literally 'god-Gaut' (a tribal name) [Peter Osgood, 1947–2006, English footballer]

O'Shaughnessy 'descendant of **Shaughnessy**' [Arthur O'Shaughnessy, 1844–81, British poet]

O'Shea 'descendant of **Shea**' [Tessie O'Shea, 1913–95, British singer and entertainer]

Osler see **Ostler**

Osmond, Osmon, Osman, Osmund from the Old Norse male personal name *Ásmundr*, literally 'god-protection'. See also **Casement** [Donny Osmond, 1957–, US pop singer, a member of The Osmonds (see below)]
— **The Osmonds** a US singing family, popular particularly in the 1970s. Its membership, apart from Donny Osmond (see above), consisted of Alan, Jay, Jimmy, Marie, Merrill and Wayne Osmond.

Ostler, Osler 'innkeeper' (from Middle English *hosteler, osteler* 'innkeeper') [Sir William Osler, 1849–1919, Canadian physician]

O'Sullivan, O'Sullevan 'descendant of **Sullivan**' [Sir Peter O'Sullevan, 1918–, British horse-racing commentator; Ronnie O'Sullivan, 1975–, British snooker player]

Oswald from the Old English male personal name *Oswald*, literally 'god-power' [Lee Harvey Oswald, 1939–63, US alleged assassin of President John F. Kennedy]

Otis a different form of **Oates** [Elisha Graves Otis, 1811–61, US inventor of the elevator]
— **'Miss Otis regrets'** a song (1934) by Cole Porter, beginning 'Miss Otis regrets she's unable to lunch today, Madam'. Porter is said to have been inspired by an overheard message delivered by a waiter to a restaurant customer.

O'Toole 'descendant of **Toole** (i)' [Peter O'Toole, 1932–, Irish-born British actor]

Ott from the medieval personal name *Ode*. The immediate source of this was Old English *Oda* or *Odda*, a shortened form of a name beginning with *ord* 'point of a weapon'. That was reinforced by Old Norse *Oda*, *Odda* (from a similar source) and Continental Germanic *Odo* or *Otto*, a shortened form of a name beginning with *od* 'wealth'. All were Latinized as *Odo* (whence also Old French *Odo*, *Odon* – see **Oaten**).

Ottaway see **Ottoway**

Otter (i) 'otter hunter', or from a medieval nickname for someone though to resemble an otter; (ii) from the Old English male personal name *Ohthere*, literally 'fear-army'

Ottoway, Ottaway, Otterway from the Norman male personal names *Otoïs*, of Germanic origin and meaning literally 'wealth-wide' or 'wealth-wood', and *Otewi*, of Germanic origin and meaning literally 'wealth-war'

Ottway, Otway different forms of **Ottoway** [Thomas Otway, 1652–85, British dramatist]

Ousley, Ouseley, Owsley 'person from Ousley', an unidentified place (perhaps 'woodland glade by the river Ouse')
— **Owsley acid** high-quality LSD. The slang expression was inspired by Augustus Owsley Stanley III, 1935–, who manufactured the drug illegally.

Ovenden 'person from Ovenden', Yorkshire ('Ōfa's valley')

Overall, Overal 'person who lives in the upper hall' (from Middle English *overe hall* 'upper hall') [Mrs Overall, the bizarre charlady played by Julie Walters in Victoria Wood's television soap spoof *Acorn Antiques*]

Overton 'person from Overton', the name of several places in England (variously 'higher farmstead' and 'farmstead by a river bank')

Overy 'person from Overy', the name of various places in England (mainly 'place across the river')

Owen from the Welsh male personal name *Owain*, probably from Latin *Eugenius*. See also **Bowen**

[Alun Owen, 1925–94, British dramatist; Bill Owen (original name Bill Rowbotham), 1914–99, British actor; Clive Owen, 1966–, British actor; David Owen (Lord Owen), 1938–, British Labour and SDP politician; Michael Owen, 1979–, English footballer; Nick Owen, 1947–, British journalist and television presenter; Robert Owen, 1771–1858, British philanthropist and manufacturer; Wilfred Owen, 1893–1918, British poet]

Owens (i) 'son of **Owen**'; (ii) from Gaelic *Mac Eògain* (see **McEwan**) [Jesse Owens (original name James Cleveland Owens), 1913–80, US athlete]

Owsley see **Ousley**

Oxenham 'person from Oxenham', Devon ('water meadow where oxen are grazed')

Oxford 'person from Oxford', Oxfordshire ('ford where oxen cross')

Oxley 'person from Oxley', the name of various places in England ('glade where oxen are grazed')

P

Pace, Paice (i) from a medieval nickname for a mild-mannered unaggressive person (from Middle English *pace* 'peace'). See also **Paz** (i), **Peace**; (ii) from a medieval English shortened form of the Latin personal name *Paschālis* (see **Pascall**)
— **Hale and Pace** see **Hale**

Pacey, Pacy 'person from Pacy-sur-Eure', northern France ('Paccius's settlement')

Pack from the medieval personal name *Pack*, probably derived from the Latin name *Paschālis* (see **Pascall**). See also **Patch**

Packard (i) an insulting form of the medieval personal name *Pack* (see **Pack**), formed with the derogatory Anglo-Norman suffix *-ard*; (ii) from the Norman personal name *Pachard* or *Baghard*, ultimately of Germanic origin and meaning literally 'fight-brave'; (iii) from an insulting medieval term for a pedlar, based on *pack* with the derogatory Anglo-Norman suffix *-ard* [Vance Packard, 1914–96, US social critic]
— **Hewlett-Packard** see **Hewlett**
— **Packard Motor Car Company** a US automobile manufacturer, founded in 1899 by James Ward Packard, 1863–1928

Packer (i) 'wool-packer'; (ii) 'wholesale trader' (from a derivative of German *Pack* 'package') [Ann Packer, 1942–, British athlete; Kerry Packer, 1937–2005, Australian media proprietor]

Packham (i) 'person from Pagham', Sussex ('Pæcga's homestead'); (ii) a different form of **Pakenham**

Packman (i) '**Pack**'s servant'; (ii) 'pedlar, hawker'

Paddock (i) 'person who lives in or by a paddock or enclosed meadow'; (ii) from a medieval nickname for someone felt to resemble a toad or frog (from Middle English *paddock* 'toad, frog')

Padfield 'person from Padfield', Derbyshire ('Padda's area of open land')

Padgett, Paget, Pagett 'little **Page**' [Nicola Pagett (original name Nicola Scott), 1945–, British actress]
— **Paget's disease** an alternative name for brittle-bone disease or osteoporosis. It commemorates the British surgeon Sir James Paget, 1814–99, who described the condition.

Padilla 'person from Padilla', the name of various places in Spain ('frying pan', denoting a settlement within a shallow depression)

Padmore (i) 'person from Padmore', Shropshire ('marsh frequented by toads'); (ii) a different form of **Patmore**

Page, Paige 'young male servant'. See also **Padgett** [Sir Earle Page, 1880–1961, Australian Country Party politician, prime minister 1939; Elaine Paige, 1948–, British actress and singer; Sir Frederick Handley Page, see **Handley**; Mrs Page and her daughter Anne Page, characters in Shakespeare's *The Merry Wives of Windsor* (1597); Patti Page (original name Clara Ann Fowler), 1927–, US popular singer]

Paget, Pagett see **Padgett**

Paglia perhaps 'gatherer of straw' or 'maker of articles (e.g. hats) out of straw' (from Italian *paglia* 'straw') [Camille Paglia, 1947–, US writer]

Paice see **Pace**

Paige see **Page**

Paine, Pain, Payne, Payn from the medieval personal name *Paine* or *Payne*, which came via Old French from Latin *Pāgānus*, literally 'country-dweller', then 'civilian' and finally 'heathen'. See also **Fitzpayn** [Anthony Payne, 1936–, British composer; Jack Payne, 1899–1969, British bandleader; Thomas Paine, 1737–1809, British writer and political theorist, author of *The Rights of Man* (1791–2)]

Painter, Paynter 'painter' (typically, in the Middle Ages, a painter of stained glass) [Eddie Paynter, 1901–79, English cricketer]

Paish a different form of **Pask**

Paisley 'person from Paisley', Renfrewshire ('place with a church') [Rev. Ian Paisley, 1926–, Northern Irish Democratic Unionist politician, first minister 2007–]

Pak a Korean clan name, from the name of its mythical founder, Pak Hyokkose (probably derived from the Korean noun *pak* 'gourd' or the verb *pak* 'shine brightly': Pak was discovered as a youth in a gourd-shaped egg, and light radiated from his head). See also **Park** (iii)

Pakenham 'person from Pakenham', Suffolk ('Pacca's homestead'). See also **Packham** (ii) [Pakenham, family name of the earls of Longford]

Pal, Pall (i) from the Hungarian personal name *Pál* '**Paul**'; (ii) from the Hindu personal name *Pal*, from Sanskrit *pāla* 'guard, protector, herdsman'. It is an epithet of the god Krishna.

Paley probably 'person from Paley', an unidentified place in Yorkshire [William Paley, 1743–1805, British churchman and Anglican theologian]

Palfrey 'servant who looks after riding-horses (as opposed to war-horses)' (from Middle English *palfrey* 'riding-horse, saddle-horse')

Palfreyman a different form of **Palfrey**

Palgrave 'person from Palgrave', Suffolk ('grove where poles are obtained') [Francis Palgrave, 1824–97, British poet and anthologist, compiler of *The Golden Treasury* (1861)]

Palin (i) 'person from Palling', Norfolk ('settlement of Pælli's people') or 'person from Poling', Sussex ('settlement of Pāl's people'); (ii) from the Welsh name *ap Heilyn* 'son of *Heilyn*', a personal name perhaps meaning 'one who serves at table' [Michael Palin, 1943–, British actor, writer and traveller]

Pall see **Pal**

Palliser 'maker of palings and fences' (from a derivative of Old French *palis* 'palisade')
— **Palliser Novels** a series of six political novels by Anthony Trollope, beginning with *Can You Forgive Her?* (1864) and ending with *The Duke's Children* (1880), in which the Palliser family plays a central role

Pallister, Palister different forms of **Palliser**

Palmer from a medieval nickname for someone who had been on a pilgrimage to the Holy Land (from Old French *palmer*, from *palme* 'palm', referring to the palm branch brought back by such pilgrims to prove they had been) [Arnold Palmer, 1929–, US golfer; Felicity Palmer, 1944–, British mezzo-soprano; Geoffrey Palmer, 1927–, British actor; Harry Palmer, the low-key laid-back British agent in the espionage novels of Len Deighton; Lilli Palmer (original name Lillie Marie Peiser), 1914–86, German-born US actress; Samuel Palmer, 1805–81, British landscape painter and etcher; Tony Palmer, 1937–, British writer and director; William Palmer, 1824–56, British murderer]
— **Château Palmer** a French wine-producing chateau in the Margaux commune of Bordeaux. It was owned between 1814 and 1843 by Major-General Charles Palmer, 1777–1851.
— **Emerson, Lake and Palmer** see **Emerson**
— **Palmer Land** a mountainous area of Antarctica, named after the US sea captain Nathaniel Palmer, 1799–1877, who led an expedition to Antarctica in 1820
— **Palmer's Green** an area of North London, in the borough of Enfield. It takes its name (first recorded in the early 17th century) from a local family called Palmer, the details of which are unknown.

Palumbo from the medieval southern Italian personal name *Palumbo*, literally 'dove' [Peter Palumbo (Lord Palumbo), 1935–, British patron of the arts]

Pankhurst perhaps 'person from Pinkhurst', Surrey and Sussex [Emmeline Pankhurst, 1858–1928, and her daughters Dame Christabel Pankhurst, 1880–1958, and Sylvia Pankhurst, 1882–1960, British suffragettes]

Panton 'person from Panton', Lincolnshire (perhaps 'settlement on a hill')

Pardew a different form of **Pardoe** [Alan Pardew, 1961–, British football manager]

Pardoe from a medieval nickname based on the Old French oath *par Dieu* 'by God'. See also **Pardew, Perdue, Purdy**

Pardon 'pardoner' (in the Middle Ages, someone licensed to sell papal pardons)

Parent from a medieval nickname for someone related to an important figure in the local community (from Middle English *parent* 'parent, relative'), or for someone of striking appearance (from Middle English *parent* 'notable')

Parfitt probably from a medieval nickname for an apprentice who had just completed his training (from Middle English *parfit* 'fully trained, completed, perfect')

Pargetter, Pargeter 'craftsman who applies decorative plasterwork (pargetting)' (from a derivative of Old French *pargeter* or *parjeter* 'to apply plaster') [Edith Pargeter, 1913–95, British author; Nigel Pargetter, eccentric rural entrepreneur in the BBC radio soap opera *The Archers*]

Parham 'person from Parham', Suffolk and Sussex ('homestead where pears are grown')

Paris, Parris (i) 'person from Paris', France, or from a medieval nickname for someone associated in some way with that city; (ii) from the medieval personal name *Paris*, a different form of *Patrice*, the Old French form of **Patrick**; (iii) from a shortened form of *Aparici*, a Catalan personal name given to children born in 6 January, the Feast of the Epiphany (from Spanish *aparición* 'appearance') [Matthew Paris, died 1259, English monk and historian; Matthew Parris, 1949–, British author, journalist and Conservative politician]

Parish, Parrish (i) a surname given in the 17th and 18th centuries to orphans brought up at the expense of the parish; (ii) different forms of **Paris** [Maxfield Parrish, 1870–1966, US artist]

Park, Parke (i) 'person employed in or living in a park (a large enclosed hunting ground)'; (ii) from a medieval pet-form of the personal name **Peter**. See also **Parkin**; (iii) a different form of **Pak** [Sir Keith Park, 1892–1975, New Zealand air marshal; Mungo Park, 1771–1806, Scottish explorer; Nick Park, 1958–, British animator]

Parker 'gamekeeper employed in a park (a large enclosed hunting ground)' [Parker, Cockney butler and chauffeur of Lady Penelope in the British television puppet adventure series *Thunderbirds* (1965–66); Sir Alan Parker, 1944–, British film director; Bonnie Parker, 1910–34, small-time US gangster, one half of 'Bonnie and Clyde' (see also **Barrow**); Camilla Parker Bowles (HRH Duchess of Cornwall; *née* Shand), 1947–, wife of the Prince of Wales; Cecil Parker, 1897–1971, British actor; Charlie 'Bird' Parker, 1920–55, US jazz saxophonist and composer; Dorothy Parker, 1893–1967, US writer, critic and humorist; Eleanor Parker, 1922–, US actress; Fess Parker, 1925–, US actor; Matthew Parker, 1504–75, Anglican churchman; Robert Parker, 1947–, US wine critic; Theodore Parker, 1810–60, US clergyman and reformer; 'Colonel' Tom Parker (original name Andreas Cornelius van Kuijk), 1909–97, Dutch-born US business manager of Elvis Presley]

— **Nosey Parker** a nickname for an over-inquisitive person. It is sometimes said to have been originally applied to Matthew Parker (see above), who as archbishop of Canterbury was noted for the rigour of his enquiries into ecclesiastical affairs, but the expression is not recorded until the early 20th century, so this seems unlikely.

— **Parker** the proprietary name (registered in 1906) of a pen manufactured by the Parker Pen Company, established in Janesville, Wisconsin, US in 1888 by George Safford Parker, 1863–1937

— **Parkerizing** a rust-proofing process that involves coating iron or steel in a metal phosphate. It was introduced by the Parker Rust-Proof Company of the US, which was established in 1915.

— **Parker Knoll** a British furniture brand established in 1930 when Tom Parker, of Frederick Parker & Sons, joined forces with the German furniture manufacturer Willi Knoll

— **Parker's Piece** a large tree-lined common near the centre of Cambridge. It is named after Edward Parker, who farmed it as a tenant of Trinity College before it became common land in 1613.

Parkes see **Parks**

Parkhouse 'person who lives in a warden's lodge in a park'

Parkin from the medieval personal name *Parkin*, a different form of *Perkin* (see **Perkins**) [Molly Parkin, 1932–, British journalist and writer]

Parkinson 'son of **Parkin**' [Cecil Parkinson (Lord Parkinson), 1931–, British Conservative politician; Cyril Northcote Parkinson, 1909–93, British author, historian and journalist; Michael Parkinson, 1935–, British journalist and television chat-show host; Norman Parkinson, 1913–90, British photographer]

— **Parkinsonism** a nervous disorder (e.g. Parkinson's disease) marked by symptoms of trembling limbs and muscular rigidity

— **Parkinson's disease** a progressive nervous disorder marked by symptoms of trembling limbs, lifeless face, monotonous voice and a slow, shuffling walk. It was named after the British physician James Parkinson, 1755–1824, who first described it in 1817.

— **Parkinson's law** the observation, made by C. Northcote Parkinson (see above), that work always expands to fill the time set aside for it.

Parkman (i) 'servant of **Park** (ii)'; (ii) 'game-keeper employed in a park (a large enclosed hunting ground)' [Francis Parkman, 1823–93, US historian]

Parks, Parkes 'son of **Park** (ii)'. See also **Perks** [Sir Henry Parkes, 1815–96, Australian statesman; Jim Parks, 1931–, English cricketer; Rosa Parks, 1913–2005, US civil-rights leader]

— **Parkes** a market town in New South Wales, Australia. It was named in 1873 in honour of Sir Henry Parkes (see above), several times prime minister of that state.

Parley, Parly, Parlie 'person from Parley', the name of various places in England and Scotland ('glade with pear trees growing in it')

Parmenter, Parminter 'maker of facings and trimmings' (from Old French *parmentier*, a derivative of *parement* 'decoration')

Parnell, Parnall from the medieval female personal name *Parnell*, an anglicized form of Latin *Petrōnilla* (literally 'little *Petrōnia*', the feminine form of *Petrōnius*, a Roman family name probably of Etruscan origin). See also **Pennell, Purnell** [Charles Stewart Parnell, 1846–91, Irish politician; Val Parnell, 1892–1972, British theatre manager and impresario]

Parnes 'president of a Jewish community' (from Yiddish *parnes*) [Larry Parnes, 1930–, British pop-group manager and impresario]

Parnham 'person from Parnham', Dorset ('homestead with pear trees')

Parr (i) 'person from Parr', Lancashire ('enclosure'); (ii) perhaps from a medieval German nickname for a foundling (from Middle Low German *parre* 'parish') [Catherine Parr, 1512–48, sixth wife of Henry VIII; George Parr, 1826–91, English cricketer]

— **Old Parr** the sobriquet of the Shropshire husbandman Thomas Parr, who was reputedly born in 1483 and died in 1635. He was buried in Westminster Abbey.

Parris, Parrish see **Paris, Parish**

Parrott, Parrot, Parrett, Parret, Parratt (i) 'person from (North or South) Perrott', Somerset ('place by the river *Parrett*', a pre-English river-name of unknown meaning); (ii) from the medieval personal name *Parot* (with numerous alternative forms, such as *Perot* and *Paret*), a pet-form of **Peter**. See also **Perot** [Andrew Parrott, 1947–, British conductor; John Parrott, 1964–, British snooker player]

Parry from Welsh *ap Harry* 'son of Harry'. See also **Barry** (iv) [Sir Hubert Parry, 1848–1918, British composer; Sir William Parry, 1790–1855, British Arctic explorer]

Parsley a different form of **Parslow**

Parslow, Parsloe from a medieval nickname for someone who passed over water (e.g. a crusader or merchant voyager, or a ferryman), from Old French *passer l'ewe* 'cross the water'. See also **Pashley**

Parsons 'servant or child of a parish priest or parson' [Sir Charles Algernon Parsons, 1854–1931, British engineer, inventor of the steam turbine; Geoffrey Parsons, 1930–95, Australian pianist; Nicholas Parsons, 1928–, British actor and quizmaster; Talcott Parsons, 1902–78, US sociologist]

Partington 'person from Partington', Greater Manchester ('settlement associated with Pearta')

— **Dame Partington** a lady who, according to legend, attempted to push back the Atlantic with a mop during a great storm at Sidmouth in 1824

Parton 'person from Parton', the name of various places in England (mainly 'pear orchard') [Dolly Parton, 1946–, US singer, songwriter and actress]

Partridge (i) 'hunter of partridges', 'person who lives in a house designated by the sign of a partridge' or from a medieval nickname for someone felt to resemble a partridge; (ii) a different form of **Patrick** [Eric Partridge, 1894–1979, New Zealand-born British lexicographer; Frances Partridge (*née* Marshall), 1900–2004, British painter, critic and diarist; Ian Partridge, 1938–, British tenor]

Pascall, Pascal from the medieval personal name *Pascal*, from Latin *Paschālis*, a derivative of *pascha* 'Easter'. See also **Pace** (ii), **Pack**, **Pascoe**, **Pask**

Pascoe, Pasco Cornish variants of **Pascall** [Alan Pascoe, 1947–, British athlete; Richard Pasco, 1926–, British actor]

Pashley (i) 'person from Pashley', Sussex ('Pæcca's glade'); (ii) perhaps a different form of **Parslow**

Pask, Paske from a medieval nickname for someone with a special personal association with Easter, particularly being born at that time of year (from Middle English *paske* 'Easter', ultimately from Latin *pascha* – see also **Pascall**). See also **Paish**, **Paxman**

Passmore, Pasmore (i) from a medieval nickname for someone who crossed marshy moorland (e.g. who lived on the opposite side of a moor, or who knew the safe paths across it); (ii) perhaps from an alteration of *Passemer*, literally 'cross-sea', an Anglo-Norman nickname for a seafarer [John Passmore, 1904–84, Australian artist; Victor Pasmore, 1908–98, British artist]

Paston 'person from Paston', the name of various places in England (mainly 'Pæcci's farmstead')
— **Paston Letters** a collection of correspondence written between 1422 and 1509 and preserved by the well-to-do Paston family of Norfolk. They provide important material relating to the social and political history of the times.

Patch a different form of **Pack**

Pate (i) *also* **Patt** from the male personal name *Pat*, *Pate* or *Patt*, shortened forms of **Patrick**. See also **McFadden**, **Patey**, **Paton**, **Patten**, **Patterson**, **Pattinson**, **Pattison**; (ii) from a medieval nickname for a bald man

Patel a Hindu and Parsi name meaning literally 'village headman'

Pater from a medieval Dutch nickname for a solemn or sanctimonious man (from Middle Dutch *pater* 'father superior in a monastery') [Walter Pater, 1839–94, British essayist and philosopher]

Paterson see **Patterson**

Patey 'little **Pate** (i)'

Patillo see **Pattillo**

Patison see **Pattison**

Patmore 'person from Patmore', Hertfordshire ('Peatta's lake'). See also **Padmore** [Coventry Patmore, 1823–96, British poet]

Paton 'little **Pate** (i)' [Alan Paton, 1903–88, South African novelist]

Patrick, Pattrick from the male personal name *Patrick*, from Latin *Patricius*, literally 'member of the patrician class'. See also **Fitzpatrick**,

Kilpatrick, **Kirkpatrick**, **Partridge** (ii), **Pate**, **Petrie** (i) [Nigel Patrick (original name Nigel Wemyss), 1913–81, British actor]

Patt see **Pate** (i)

Patten (i) 'maker, seller or wearer of clogs' (from Middle English *paten* 'clog'); (ii) *also* **Patton** 'little **Pate** (i)' [Brian Patten, 1946–, British poet; Chris Patten (Lord Patten), 1944–, British Conservative politician and diplomat; George Patton, 1885–1945, US general; Marguerite Patten (*née* Brown), 1915–, British cookery writer and presenter]

Patterson, Paterson 'son of little **Pate** (i)' [Banjo Paterson (original name Andrew Barton Paterson), 1864–1941, Australian poet; Sir Les Patterson, boozily gross Australian cultural attaché character created by Barry Humphries; Paul Patterson, 1947–, British composer; William Paterson, 1658–1719, Scottish merchant and banker, founder of the Bank of England]
— **Paterson's curse** a colloquial Australian name for the plant *Echium plantagineum*, which is said to have been introduced by the Paterson family as a garden plant in New South Wales around 1880 and thereafter spread like a weed

Pattillo, Patillo 'person from Pittilloch', Fife and Perth and Kinross ('portion of the hill'). See also **Pattullo**

Pattinson 'son of little **Pate** (i)'

Pattison, Patison 'son of little **Pate** (i)'

Pattullo, Patullo different forms of **Pattillo**

Paul, Paule, Paull, Pawle from the male personal name *Paul*, from Latin *Paulus*, literally 'small'. See also **Pollard**, **Pool**, **Poulson**, **Powell**

Pauley, Pauly, Pawley 'little **Paul**'

Pauli 'son of *Paulus*' (see **Paul**), a humanistic name utilizing the possessive form of the Latin name, originating in Germany and Sweden [Wolfgang Pauli, 1900–58, Austrian-born US physicist]
— **Pauli exclusion principle** a law of quantum physics, formulated by Wolfgang Pauli (see above), stating that no two identical particles of a particular type (fermions) may occupy the same quantum state at the same time

Paulin, Pawlyn 'little **Paul**' [Tom Paulin, 1949–, British poet and critic]

Pauling, Paulling, Pawling different forms of **Paulin** [Linus Pauling, 1901–94, US chemist and peace activist]

Paulson (i) 'son of **Paul**'; (ii) an anglicization of *Paulsen*, the equivalent name in various Scandinavian languages. See also **Pawson**

Paveley, Pavley different forms of **Pawley** (i)

Pavey, Pavy, Pavie (i) from the medieval female personal name *Pavia*, perhaps from Old French *pavie* 'peach'; (ii) 'person from Pavia', Italy

Pawley (i) 'person from Pavilly', northern France ('Pavilius's settlement'). See also **Paveley**; (ii) see **Pauley**

Pawling, Pawlyn see **Pauling**, **Paulin**

Pawson 'son of *Paw*', a different form of **Paul**

Paxman (i) 'servant of **Pask**'; (ii) an anglicization of German *Paxmann*, perhaps from a Germanic personal name based on *bag* 'fight' [Jeremy Paxman, 1950–, British journalist, author and broadcaster]

Paxton 'person from Paxton', Cambridgeshire and Borders ('Pæcc's settlement') [Sir Joseph Paxton, 1801–65, British architect, designer of the Crystal Palace; Tom Paxton, 1937–, US singer and songwriter]

Payne, Payn see **Paine**

Paynter see **Painter**

Payton, Peyton 'person from Peyton', Sussex ('Pæga's settlement')

Paz (i) from the Spanish and Portuguese epithet (meaning 'peace') associated with the Virgin Mary (e.g. Spanish *María de la Paz*); (ii) an invented Jewish name based on Hebrew *paz* 'pure gold'

Peabody probably from a medieval nickname for a flamboyantly dressed person, from Middle English *pe* 'peacock' + *body* 'body, person' [George Peabody, 1795–1869, US businessman and philanthropist]
— **Peabody** a city in Massachusetts, US, so named in 1868 in honour of George Peabody (see above), who was born there
— **Peabody bird** a name in the US for the white-throated sparrow, *Zonotrichia albicollis*, whose call is said to resemble 'Sam Peabody, Peabody, Peabody'
— **Peabody Trust** a London charitable housing trust, established in 1862 by George Peabody

Peace a different form of **Pace** (i) [Charles Peace, 1832–79, British murderer]

Peach, Peache, Peech different forms of **Peachey**

Peachey from a good-natured medieval nickname for a ne'er-do-well (from Old French *pechie* or *peche* 'sin'). See also **Petchey**

Peacock, Peacocke, Pecock from a medieval nickname for a vain or flamboyantly dressed person. See also **Pocock, Poe** [Mrs Peacock, the 41-year-old socialite who is one of the six suspects in the murder of Dr Black in the board game Cluedo; Captain Stephen Peacock, the pompous floor-walker (played by Frank Thornton) in the BBC television sitcom *Are You Being Served?* (1973–85); Thomas Love Peacock, 1785–1866, British satirical novelist]

Peagram a different form of **Pilgrim**

Peak, Peake 'person who lives on or by a pointed hill' (from Old English *pēac* 'peak, pointed hill'); also, 'person from the Peak District', Derbyshire ('area of pointed hills'). See also **Peck** (ii) [Mervyn Peake, 1911–68, British novelist and artist]

Peal, Peale see **Peel**

Pearce, Pearse, Peirce, Pierce from the male personal name *Piers*, the standard Anglo-Norman form of **Peter**. See also **Pears, Pearson** [Charles Sanders Peirce, 1839–1914, US philosopher and logician; Patrick Henry Pearse, 1879–1916, Irish nationalist, Gaelic enthusiast and teacher; Philippa Pearce, 1920–, British children's author; Stuart Pearce, 1962–, English footballer; Tom Pearce, owner of the grey mare on which Uncle Tom Cobbleigh and his friends rode to Widecombe Fair]

Pearcey, Pearcy different forms of **Percy**

Pearl (i) 'trader in pearls'; (ii) an anglicization of **Perl**

Pearman 'grower or seller of pears', or 'person who lives by a pear orchard'

Pears, Peers, Piers different forms of **Pearce**. The name is pronounced 'peerz' or (in the case of *Pears*) alternatively as 'pairz'. [Sir Peter Pears, 1910–86, British tenor]
— **Pears Cyclopedia** a concise encyclopedia first published in 1879 by A. & F. Pears Ltd (see below). It was the brainchild of the company's marketing wizard Thomas J. Barrett.
— **Pears Soap** an amber-coloured transparent soap, introduced on to the market in 1807. It was developed by Andrew Pears, 1768–1845, and produced by his company, A. & F. Pears.

Pearson, Pierson 'son of *Piers*' (see **Pearce**) [Hesketh Pearson, 1887–1964, British actor and biographer; Lester Pearson, 1897–1972, Canadian Liberal politician, prime minister 1963–68]
— **Pearson plc** a British-based media conglomerate, founded by Samuel Pearson in 1844 as a building and engineering company (S. Pearson & Co.). It went into newspaper ownership in 1920 and book publishing in 1968.

Peart perhaps 'person from Pert', Angus ('wood, copse')

Peary see **Peery**

Pease 'grower or seller of peas', or from a medieval nickname for an undersized or insignificant person

Peat, Peate see **Peet**

Peck (i) 'person with an occupation (e.g. corn seller) that involves weighting and measuring' (from Middle English *pekke* 'peck' (an old measure of capacity for dry goods)); (ii) a different form of **Peak** [Bob Peck, 1945–99, British actor; Gregory Peck, 1916–2003, US actor]
— **Peck's bad boy** an unruly or mischievous child. The expression comes from the name of a fictional character created by the US author George Wilbur Peck, 1840-1916.

Peckenpaugh, Peckinpaugh, Peckinpah anglicizations of German *Bickenbach*, 'person from Bickenbach', the name of various places in Germany [Sam Peckinpah, 1926–84, US film director]

Peckham 'person from Peckham', Greater London and Kent ('homestead by a peak')

Pedder, Peddar 'pedlar' (from Middle English *pedder*, a derivative of *pedde* 'pannier'). See also **Pedler**

Pedersen 'son of *Peder*', a Danish and Norwegian form of **Peter**

Pedler, Pedlar 'pedlar' (from Middle English *pedler*, probably a different form of *pedder* – see **Pedder**). See also **Pegler**

Pedley from an Anglo-Norman nickname for a stealthy person, from Old French *pie de leu* 'wolf's foot'. See also **Pellew**

Peebles 'person from Peebles', Borders ('place with shelters') [Ian Peebles, 1908–80, English cricketer and journalist]

Peech see **Peach**

Peel, Peele, Peal, Peale from a medieval nickname for a tall thin person (from Anglo-Norman *pel* 'pole, stake') [Emma Peel, leather-clad karate-chopping sidekick (played by Diana Rigg) of John Steed in the ABC television drama series *The Avengers* (1961–69) (the name supposedly represented 'M-appeal' – i.e. 'man-appeal'); George Peele, 1556–96, English dramatist; John Peel, 1776–1854, English huntsman who is the hero of the hunting song 'D'ye ken John Peel?'; John Peel (original name John Ravenscroft), 1939–2004, British disc jockey; Sir Robert Peel, 1788–1850, British Conservative politician, prime minister 1834–35, 1841–46]

— **peeler** a colloquial term applied initially to a member of the Irish Constabulary, and subsequently to any policeman. It was based on the name of Sir Robert Peel (see above), who founded both the Irish Constabulary and the Metropolitan Police.

Peery, Peary different forms of **Perry** (i) [Robert Peary, 1856–1920, US Arctic explorer]

Peet, Peete, Peat, Peate from a pet-form of the personal name **Peter**

Pegg (i) 'maker or seller of wooden pegs'; also perhaps from a medieval nickname for someone with a wooden leg; (ii) perhaps from the female personal name *Peg*, a pet-form of *Margaret*

Pegler (i) a different form of **Pedler**; (ii) from an Anglo-Norman nickname for a fast runner, from Old French *pie de lievre* 'hare's foot'

Pei (i) from *Pei*, the name of a Chinese village; (ii) from *Beiqiu*, the name of a place in China [I.M. Pei (full name Ieoh Ming Pei), 1917–, Chinese-born US architect]

Peirce see **Pearce**

Pelham 'person from Pelham', Hertfordshire ('Pēotla's homestead') [Pelham, family name of the earls of Chichester and Yarborough]

— **pelham** a bit for a horse's bridle that is midway between the simple snaffle bit and the harsher curb bit. The term is presumed to come from the surname, but the story behind it is not known.

— *Pelham: or The Adventures of a Gentleman* a novel (1828) by Edward Bulwer-Lytton, telling the story of the young dandy and aspiring politician Henry Pelham

Pelissier an anglicization of French *Pélissier*, literally 'maker of fur garments', from a derivative of Old French *pellice* 'fur cloak'

Pell (i) 'fur dealer' (from Middle English *pel* 'skin', from Old French); (ii) from the medieval male personal name *Pell*, a pet-form of **Peter**; (iii) 'person who lives by a creek or sea inlet' (from Old English *pyll*). See also **Pill** (ii)

Pelletier 'furrier' (from Old French *pelletier*)

Pellew a different form of **Pedley**

Pellman, Pelman 'servant of **Pell** (ii)'

— **Pelmanism** a game in which a pack of cards is laid face down on a table and players try to select matching pairs by remembering their positions from previous attempts. The name commemorates the British psychologist Christopher Louis Pelman, who developed the system of memory training on which the game is based.

Pellow (i) a different form of **Pellew**; (ii) 'little **Pell** (ii)'

Pemberton 'person from Pemberton', Greater Manchester ('barley farm on the hill')

Pender 'official responsible for rounding up and impounding stray animals' (from a derivative of Middle English *pinden* 'to shut up, enclose'). See also **Pinder**

Pendlebury 'person from Pendlebury', Greater Manchester ('manor by Pendle' (the name of a hill, literally 'hill hill')) [John Pendlebury, 1904–41, British archaeologist]

Pendleton, Pendelton 'person from Pendleton', Greater Manchester and Lancashire (respectively 'manor by Pendle' and 'farmstead by Pendle' – see **Pendlebury**)

Pendry from Welsh *ap Hendry* 'son of **Hendry**' (Henry)

Penfold 'person who lives by or is in charge of a pound for stray animals' (from Middle English *punfold* 'pound'). See also **Pinfold**

Pengelly, Pengelley 'person from Pengelly', Cornwall ('top end of the copse')

Penhaligon 'person from Penhaligon', Cornwall ('willow-tree hill') [Susan Penhaligon, 1950–, British actress]

Penn (i) 'person from Penn', the name of various places in England ('hill'); (ii) 'shepherd' or 'person in charge of an animal pound' (from Middle English *penn* 'pen for sheep or other animals'); (iii) a pet-form of **Parnell** [Sean Penn, 1960–, US actor and director; William Penn, 1644–1718, English-born American Quaker reformer and colonist]

— **Pennsylvania** a state ('Penn's wooded land') in the northeastern USA. In 1681 the area was given by Charles II to William Penn (see above) as a haven for Quakers. It became a state in 1787.

Pennell, Pennall different forms of **Parnell**

Pennington 'person from Pennington', Cumbria and Hampshire ('farmstead paying a penny rent') and Lancashire ('settlement associated with Pinna')

Penny, Penney probably from a medieval nickname of uncertain import based on *penny* (perhaps denoting someone who paid a rent of one penny, or (a penny being formerly a coin of some value) a wealthy person) [William Penney (Lord Penney), 1909–91, British physicist]

Pennycuik, Penneycuik, Pennecuik, Penny-cook 'person from Penycuik', near Edinburgh (probably 'hill frequented by cuckoos')

Pennypacker an anglicization of Low German *Pannebacker*, literally 'tile-baker'

Penrose 'person from Penrose', Cornwall, Herefordshire and Wales ('highest part of the heath or moorland') [Sir Roger Penrose, 1931–, British mathematician]

Penton 'person from Penton Mewsey', Hampshire ('farmstead paying a penny rent')

— **Pentonville** a district of North London, in the borough of Islington. It was named after Henry Penton, MP for Winchester, who owned the land on which it was developed in the 1770s.

Peplow, Peploe 'person from Peplow', Shropshire (perhaps 'pebble hill')

Pepper (i) 'dealer in spices'; also perhaps from a medieval nickname for someone with a hot temper, or for a small person (no bigger than a peppercorn); (ii) an anglicization of the invented Jewish names *Pfeffer* and *Feffer*, based respectively on German *Pfeffer* and Yiddish *fefer*, both literally 'pepper'. See also **Peverel**

— **Dr Pepper** the brand name of a US carbonated soft drink, first made in 1885. The original 'Dr Pepper' is said to have been Charles T. Pepper, whose daughter was a friend of the owner of the drug store where the drink was originally made.

— *Sergeant Pepper's Lonely Hearts Club Band* the title track of perhaps the best-known Beatles album (1967). The 'Band' (the name of which was probably inspired by the vaudeville-influenced names of contemporary US West Coast groups) formed a sort of mythical counterpart to the Beatles themselves.

Peppiatt, Peppiett 'little *Pepis*' (see **Pepys**)

Pepys from the medieval personal name *Pepis*, a form of Old French *Pepin*, brought into England by the Normans. It may have been based on an earlier nickname meaning 'awesome'. It is standardly pronounced 'peeps'. See also **Peppiatt** [Samuel Pepys, 1633–1703, English diarist]

Percival, Perceval from the male personal name *Perceval*, apparently originally the name of the hero of Arthurian legend who first appeared in Chrétien de Troyes's 12th-century *Conte du Graal*. It may have evolved from or been based on the Gaulish personal name *Pritorīx* or the Celtic personal name *Peredur* (perhaps literally 'hard spears'), possibly remodelled on the basis of Old French *perce val*, literally 'pierce valley'. [Spencer Perceval, 1762–1812, British politician, prime minister 1809–12]

Percy 'person from Percy', the name of various places in northern France ('Persius's settlement'). See also **Pearcey, Piercy** [Percy, family name of the dukes of Northumberland; Sir Henry Percy ('Harry Hotspur'), 1364–1403, English rebel; Thomas Percy (original name Piercy), 1729–1811, British antiquary and poet, publisher of *Reliques of Ancient English Poetry* (*Percy's Reliques*) (1765), a collection of medieval ballads]

Perdue a different form of **Pardoe**

Pereira, Perera 'person who lives by a pear tree' (from Portuguese *pereira* 'pear tree')

Perelman (i) a different form of **Perl** (iii); (ii) 'husband of *Perl*' (see **Perl** (iv)). See also **Perlman** [S.J. Perelman, 1904–79, US humorist]

Perez, Peres (i) 'son of *Pedro*', the Spanish form of **Peter**; (ii) a different form of the Jewish surname *Peretz*, from a Biblical name meaning literally 'burst forth'

Perham 'person from Perham', the name of various places in England ('homestead where pears are grown')

Perkins, Purkins 'son of *Perkin*', a medieval male personal name, literally 'little **Peter**'. See also **Parkin** [Carl Perkins, 1932–98, US rockabilly singer/songwriter]

— **Dorothy Perkins** a variety of rambling rose with double pink flowers. It gets its name from the granddaughter of Charles H. Perkins, of the Jackson and Perkins Company of Newark, New Jersey, who developed it in the first decade of the 20th century.

— **Dorothy Perkins** a British chain of women's wear shops. It was founded in 1909 as H.P. Newman, and adopted the trade name *Dorothy Perkins* (from the rose – see above) in 1919.

Perks a different form of **Parks**

Perl, Perle (i) 'person from Perl, Berel or Berl', the name of various places in Germany; (ii) 'jeweller', from Middle High German *perle* 'pearl'; (iii) an invented Jewish name based on Yiddish *perl* 'pearl'. See also **Perelman** (i); (iv) from a Jewish female personal name that is a translation of Hebrew *Margalit*, literally 'pearl'. See also **Perelman** (ii); (v) from an Austrian pet-form of the German male personal name *Bernhard* (see **Bernard**) [Richard Perle, 1941–, US political advisor]

Perlman a different form of **Perelman** [Itzhak Perlman, 1945–, Israeli-born US violinist]

Perot an anglicization of French *Pérot*, from the male personal name *Perrot*, a pet-form of *Perre*, the Old French form of **Peter**. See also **Parrott** (ii) [Ross Perot, 1930–, US businessman and philanthropist, independent presidential candidate 1992 and 1996]

Perrin from the medieval male personal name *Perrin*, from Old French, literally 'little *Perre*' (see **Perot**)

Perrins 'son of **Perrin**'

Perron a different form of **Perrowne** [Guy Perron, wry observer of events in Paul Scott's 'Raj Quartet' (1966–75)]

Perrowne, Perowne from the southern French male personal name *Perron*, literally 'little *Perre*' (see **Perot**). The name was brought to England by the Huguenots.

Perry (i) 'person who lives by a pear tree' (from Middle English *perrie* 'pear tree'). See also **Peery, Pirie**; (ii) from Welsh *ap Herry* 'son of *Herry*', a Welsh form of **Henry**; (iii) an invented Jewish name based on Hebrew *peri* 'fruit, reward' [Fred Perry, 1909–95, British tennis player; Grayson Perry, 1960–, British ceramic artist; Matthew C. Perry, 1794–1858, US naval officer]

Perryman a different form of **Perry** (i)

Persaud a different form of **Prasad**

Pershing an anglicization of the German surname *Pfersching*, literally 'grower or seller of peaches' [John J. Pershing, 1860–1948, US general, commander of US forces in World War I]
— **Pershing missile** a two-stage US Army ballistic missile capable of delivering a nuclear warhead. It was named after Gen. J.J. Pershing (see above).

Pertwee 'person from Perthuis, Pertuis or Pertuy', the name of various places in northern France ('place in a ravine') [Bill Pertwee, 1926–, British actor; Jon Pertwee, 1919–96, British actor]

Petchey a different form of **Peachey**

Peter, Petre from the male personal name *Peter*, from Greek *Petros*, literally 'rock' (translating Aramaic *kefa* 'rock' as the name given by Jesus to his chief disciple, symbolizing the foundation on which he would build his Church). See also **Parkin, Parrott** (ii), **Pearce, Peet, Pell** (ii), **Perez, Perkins, Perot, Perrin, Perrowne, Pethick, Petrie** (ii)
— **Peter Principle** the theory that all members of an organization will eventually be promoted to a level at which they are no longer competent to do their job. It was first enunciated by the Canadian-born US educationalist Laurence Johnston Peter, 1919–90.

Peters 'son of **Peter**' [Jim Peters, 1918–99, English marathon runner; Martin Peters, 1943–, English footballer; Dame Mary Peters, 1939–, Northern Irish athlete]
— **Peters and Lee** a British folk/pop singing duo popular in the 1970s, consisting of Lennie Peters, 1933–92, and Dianne Lee, 1950–

Petersen from the Scandinavian and North German form of **Peterson**

Peterson 'son of **Peter**' [Oscar Peterson, 1925–, Canadian jazz pianist]

Pethick from the male personal name *Petroc* or *Pedrec*, Cornish forms of **Peter**

Petit see **Pettit**

Peto 'person from Poitou', France

Petre see **Peter**

Petrie (i) 'little **Patrick**' (Scottish); (ii) 'little **Peter**' (Scottish) [Sir William Matthew Flinders Petrie, see **Flinders**]

Pettifer from an Anglo-Norman nickname for someone with an artificial foot, or perhaps for a walker of great stamina, from Old French *pie de fer* 'iron foot' [Julian Pettifer, 1935–, British writer and broadcaster]

Pettigrew probably from an Anglo-Norman nickname for a small person, from Old French *petit cru* 'small growth'

Pettingell 'person from Portugal or with Portuguese connections' (from Late Latin *Portucale* 'Portugal')

Pettit, Pettitt, Petit (i) from a distinguishing name for the younger of two people with the same name,

from Anglo-Norman *petit* 'small'; (ii) from a medieval nickname for a small person

Petty, Pettie different forms of **Pettit**

Peverel, Peverell, Peveril, Peverill, Peverall 'little **Pepper**'
— *Peveril of the Peak* a novel (1823) by Sir Walter Scott, set in the Peak District and centring on the love affair between Julian Peveril and Alice Bridgenorth

Pevsner, Pevzner 'person from the city or province of Poznan', Poland (from Yiddish *Poyzner*, a derivative of *Poyzn* 'Poznan') [Sir Nikolaus Pevsner, 1902–83, German-born British art historian]

Pew see **Pugh** [Blind Pew, the blind pirate in Robert Louis Stevenson's *Treasure Island* (1883)]

Pewsey 'person from Pewsey', Wiltshire ('Pefe's island')

Peyton see **Payton**

Pfeiffer, Pfeifer 'piper, pipe player' (from a derivative of Middle High German *pfife* 'pipe') [Michelle Pfeiffer, 1958–, US actress]

Phasey, Phaisey, Phazey, Fasey, Pheasey, Pheasy, Feasey, Feazy, Feesey different forms of **Vaisey**

Phelan a different form of **Whelan**

Phelps 'son of **Philip**'

Phenix, Phoenix (i) an anglicization of French Canadian *Phénix*, literally 'phoenix', probably originally a nickname of now lost import; (ii) different forms of **Fenwick** [Patricia Phoenix (original name Patricia Pilkington), 1923–86, British actress; River Phoenix (original name River Jude Bottom), 1970–93, US actor]

Philbert from the medieval French male personal name *Filibert*, of Germanic origin and meaning literally 'very bright, very famous'

Philibert a different form of **Philbert**

Philip, Philipp, Phillip from the male personal name *Philip*, ultimately from Greek *Philippos*, literally 'lover of horses'. See also **Phelps, Philpott** [Arthur Phillip, 1738–1814, British admiral, founder of New South Wales]

Philips, Philipps, Phillips 'son of **Philip**'. See also **Phillis, Phipps** [Ambrose Philips, 1674–1749, English poet; Leslie Phillips, 1924–, British actor; Captain Mark Phillips, 1948–, British horseman; Siân Phillips, 1934–, British actress; Zara Phillips, 1981–, British horsewoman, daughter of Mark]
— **Philips** a manufacturer of electrical equipment, founded in Eindhoven, Holland in 1891 by the Dutch engineer Gerard Philips
— **Phillips** a British firm of fine art auctioneers and valuers, founded in 1796 by Harry Phillips
— **Phillips curve** a statistical curve representing a supposed inverse relationship between the level of unemployment and the rate of inflation. It was named after its begetter, the New Zealand economist A.W.H. Phillips, 1914–75.
— **Phillips screw** the proprietary name for a type of screw with a cross-shaped slot on its head. It was

invented and patented in the 1930s by Henry F. Phillips of Portland, Oregon.

— **phillipsite** a hydrous silicate of aluminium, calcium, and potassium, found in cruciform twin crystals of a white colour. It was named (in 1825) after the English mineralogist J.W. Phillips.

Philipson, Phillipson 'son of **Philip**'

Phillimore from the Norman personal name *Filimor*, of Germanic origin and meaning literally 'very famous'. The *Ph* spelling comes from **Philip**. See also **Fillmore**

Phillis a different form of **Philips**

Philpott, Phillpott, Philpot from the medieval personal name *Philpot*, a pet-form of **Philip**. See also **Pott** (ii) [Trevor Philpott, 1924–98, British television journalist and documentary-maker]

Philpotts, Phillpotts 'son of **Philpott**' [Eden Phillpotts, 1862–1960, British novelist, playwright and poet]

Phipps a different form of **Philips**

Phoenix see **Phenix**

Phythian a different form of **Vivian**

Pick (i) 'pickaxe-maker' or 'someone who works with a pickaxe'; (ii) a Jewish name of unknown origin

Pickard (i) 'person from Picardy', a region of northern France; (ii) perhaps from a Germanic personal name meaning literally 'pointed-weapon-brave'. See also **Pitcher** (ii)

Picken, Pickin 'little **Pick**'

Pickens a different form of **Picken** [Slim Pickens (original name Louis Bert Lindley), 1919–83, US cowboy and actor]

Pickering 'person from Pickering', Yorkshire ('settlement of Pīcer's people') [Ron Pickering, 1930–91, British athletics coach and television commentator]

Pickersgill, Pickersgil 'person from Pickersgill', Yorkshire ('robber's ravine')

Pickett a different form of **Piggott** [Wilson Pickett, 1941–2006, US R&B and soul singer]

Pickford 'person from Pickforde', Sussex ('pig ford') [Mary Pickford (original name Gladys Marie Smith), 1893–1979, Canadian-born US actress and producer]

— **Pickfords** a British removals and storage company, which had its beginnings in a carriage business developed in the 17th century by the Pickford family in Adlington, south of Manchester

Pickles 'person who lives by a small field or paddock' (from Middle English *pighel* 'small field') [Wilfred Pickles, 1904–78, British actor and radio presenter]

Pickup 'person from Pickup', Lancashire ('hill with a pointed top') [Ronald Pickup, 1940–, British actor]

— **Harpic** the proprietary name of a lavatory cleaning fluid, invented in the 1920s by Harry Pickup

Picton, Pickton 'person from Picton', the name of various places in England ('Pīca's farmstead')

Pidgeon, Pigeon (i) from a medieval nickname for a gullible person (pigeons being regarded as easy prey); (ii) 'hunter of (wood) pigeons'; (iii) from the medieval nickname *Petyjon* or *Petjon*, literally 'little John', applied to a small man or (with heavy irony) to a large man [Walter Pidgeon, 1897–1984, Canadian actor]

Pierce see **Pearce**

Piercy a different form of **Percy**

Pierrepoint, Pierpoint different forms of **Pierrepont** [Albert Pierrepoint, 1905–92, British hangman]

Pierrepont, Pierpont 'person from Pierrepont', the name of various places in northern France ('stone bridge')

Pigg (i) from a medieval nickname for someone thought to resemble a pig; (ii) 'swineherd'

Piggott, Piggot, Pigott from the medieval personal name *Pigot* or *Picot* (from Old French, 'little *Pic*' – see **Pike** (v)). See also **Pickett** [Lester Piggott, 1935–, British jockey; Tim Pigott-Smith, 1946–, British actor]

Pike, Pyke (i) 'person who lives near or on a pointed hill' (from Old English *pīc* 'pointed hill'); (ii) 'person who uses or works with a pickaxe'; (iii) 'soldier armed with a pike'; (iv) 'person who fishes for pike', or from a medieval nickname for someone thought to resemble a pike (the fish) (e.g. in rapacity or predatoriness); (v) from the medieval personal name *Pic*, from Old French, ultimately of Germanic origin and meaning literally 'pointed'; (vi) from a medieval nickname for a tall thin person; (vii) from a medieval nickname for someone thought to resemble a woodpecker (from Old French *pic* 'woodpecker'). See also **Peak**, **Pick** [Frank Pike, the callow young private in the BBC television sitcom *Dad's Army* (1968–77); Magnus Pyke, 1908–92, British scientist and television personality]

— **Pikes Peak** a mountain in the central Colorado section of the Rocky Mountains, USA. It was named after the US soldier and explorer Zebulon Pike, 1779–1813, who led an expedition in the area in 1806.

Pilcher 'person who makes or sells garments made of leather with the fur still on it, or who wears such a garment' (from Old English *pylece* 'such a garment', ultimately from Latin *pellis* 'skin, hide'). See also **Pilger** [Rosamunde Pilcher, 1924–, British author]

Pile (i) *also* **Pyle** 'person who lives by a landmark stake' (from Middle English *pile* 'pointed stake'); (ii) 'person who lives in an area of low-lying land' (from Old French *pile* 'trough')

Pilger a different form of **Pilcher** [John Pilger, 1939–, Australian journalist]

Pilgrim 'person who has been on a pilgrimage to a holy place'

Pilkington 'person from Pilkington', Lancashire ('settlement associated with Pīleca')

— **Pilkington plc** a British glass-manufacturing firm, founded in 1826 as the St Helens Crown Glass Company. William Pilkington, 1800–72, was one of its first shareholders, and he was soon joined by his brother Richard Pilkington, 1795–1869. In 1849 the firm became Pilkington Brothers.

Pill (i) from a medieval nickname for a short fat person (from Middle English *pille* 'ball'); (ii) a different form of **Pell** (iii). See also **Pilling**, **Puller**, **Pullman**

Pilling a different form of **Pill** (ii)

Pillsbury, Pilsbury 'person from Pillsbury', Derbyshire ('Pīl's fortified place')
— **Pillsbury Bakery** a US flour-milling and bakery firm founded in Minneapolis, Minnesota in 1872 by Charles Alfred Pillsbury, 1842–99, and his uncle John Sargent Pillsbury, 1828–1901

Pimlett, Pimlet 'little **Pimm**'

Pimlott a different form of **Pimlett**

Pimm, Pim, Pymm, Pym from the medieval female personal name *Pymme*, a pet-form of *Euphemia* (of Greek origin and meaning literally 'well speaking') [Barbara Pym, 1913–80, British novelist; Francis Pym (Lord Pym), 1922–, British Conservative politician; John Pym, ?1583–1643, English Parliamentary leader]
— **Pimm's** a proprietary spirit-based drink designed to be diluted with a mixer (e.g. lemonade or soda water), especially the gin-based **Pimm's No.1**. It was named after its supposed late 19th-century inventor, the barman at Pimm's Restaurant, in the City of London.

Pinchbeck 'person from Pinchbeck', Lincolnshire ('stream of minnows')
— **pinchbeck** an alloy of copper and zinc used as imitation gold in inexpensive jewellery. It was named after the English watchmaker Christopher Pinchbeck, died 1732, who invented it.

Pincher from a medieval nickname probably applied to a carping or ungenerous person (from a derivative of Middle English *pinchen* 'to pinch, carp, be sparing or mean') [Chapman Pincher, 1914–, British journalist]

Pinck see **Pink**

Pinckney see **Pinkney**

Pinder a different form of **Pender**

Pine, Pyne 'person who lives by a pine tree or in or by a pine wood', or from a medieval nickname for a tall thin person [Courtney Pine, 1964–, British jazz saxophonist]

Pinero an anglicization of Spanish *Piñero* or Portuguese *Pinheiro* 'person from Piñero or Pinheiro', the name of various places in Spain and Portugal ('pine-tree') [Sir Arthur Wing Pinero, 1855–1934, British dramatist]

Pinfold a different form of **Penfold**
— *The Ordeal of Gilbert Pinfold* a semi-autobiographical novel (1957) by Evelyn Waugh about a famous novelist who is driven to the point of madness by persecutive hallucinations while on a cruise to Ceylon

Pink, Pinck from a medieval nickname for a cheerful jaunty person (from Middle English *pink* 'finch')

Pinkerton 'person from Pinkerton', East Lothian (a place-name of uncertain origin and meaning) [Allan Pinkerton, 1819–84, Scots-born US detective, founder (1850) of the Pinkerton National Detective Agency; Lieutenant B.F. Pinkerton, faithless American husband of Cho Cho San in Puccini's opera *Madam Butterfly* (1904)]

Pinkney, Pinckney 'person from Picquigny', northern France ('Pincino's settlement')
— **Pinckney's Treaty** a treaty (1795) between the US and Spain, fixing the boundary between their American territories at 31°N latitude. It was negotiated on the US side by Thomas Pinckney, 1750–1828.

Pinner (i) 'person from Pinner', Greater London ('place by the pointed bank'); (ii) 'maker of pins or pegs'; (iii) 'maker of combs' (from Anglo-Norman *peigner*, from *peigne* 'comb')

Pinnock from a medieval nickname for someone thought to resemble a sparrow (from Middle English *pinnock* 'hedge sparrow')

Pinsent a different form of **Pinson** (i–ii) [Sir Matthew Pinsent, 1970–, British oarsman]

Pinson (i) 'person who works with pincers or forceps' (from Old French *pinson* 'pincers'); (ii) from a medieval nickname for a cheerful jaunty person (from Old French *pinson* 'finch'); (iii) 'son of *Pine*', a pet-form of the Yiddish male personal name *Pinkhes*, from Hebrew *Pinechas*, of Egyptian origin

Pinter (i) an anglicization of the Jewish surname *Pinta*, perhaps from a medieval nickname for a bold or outrageous person, from Spanish *pinta* 'imprudent, outrageous, shameless'; (ii) from Bavarian German *Pinter*, a variant of standard German *Binder*, literally 'barrel-maker, cooper' [Harold Pinter, 1930–, British playwright and actor]
— **Pinteresque** characteristic of the plays of Harold Pinter (see above), especially in their elusive pause-filled dialogue and atmosphere of menace

Pipe a different form of **Piper**

Piper 'player of the pipes' [Billie Piper (original name Leanne Paul Piper), 1982–, British actress; John Piper, 1903–92, British artist]

Pirie a different form of **Perry** (i) [Gordon Pirie, 1931–, British athlete]

Pitcairn 'person from Pitcairn', Fife [Robert Pitcairn, ?1747–70, Royal Navy officer]
— **Pitcairn Islands** a group of islands in the central South Pacific Ocean that is a British dependency. They are named after Robert Pitcairn (see above), who was the first to sight them, in 1767.

Pitcher (i) 'person with the job of caulking a ship's seams with pitch'; (ii) a different form of **Pickard** (ii)

Pitchford 'person from Pitchford', Shropshire ('ford where pitch is found')

Pitman see **Pittman**

Pitney 'person from Pitney', Somerset ('Pytta's or Pēotta's island') [Gene Pitney, 1940–2006, US popular singer]

Pitt 'person who lives by a pit or hollow in the ground', or 'person from Pitt', Hampshire ('place by a pit') [Augustus Henry Lane-Fox Pitt-Rivers, 1827–1900, British anthropologist and archaeologist; Brad Pitt (original name William Bradley Pitt), 1963–, US actor; William Pitt (Pitt the Elder; 1st earl of Chatham), 1708–78, British Whig politician, prime minister 1766–68; William Pitt (Pitt the Younger), 1759–1806, British Tory politician, prime minister 1783–1801, 1804–06]

— **Pitt diamond** a diamond of Indian origin weighing about 137 carats that was bought in 1702 by Thomas Pitt, 1653–1726, grandfather of William Pitt the Elder (see above). He was subsequently known as 'Diamond Pitt'.

— **Pittsburgh** a city in southwestern Pennsylvania, USA. It was founded in 1764 on the site of Fort Pitt, completed by the British in 1761 and named in honour of William Pitt the Elder.

— **Pittville** a district of Cheltenham, Gloucestershire, named after its developer, Joseph Pitt, 1759–1842, a local attorney

Pittman, Pitman different forms of **Pitt** [Sir Isaac Pitman, 1813–97, British pioneer of shorthand; Jennifer Pitman, 1946–, British racehorse trainer]

Pitts a different form of **Pitt** [Walter Pitts, 1923–69, US mathematician; ZaSu Pitts, ?1894–1963, US actress]

Pizey, Pizzey different forms of **Pusey** (i)

Place, Plaice (i) 'person who lives in or by the market place'; (ii) 'person who lives by a fence made from interlaced growing plants' (from Middle English *pleis* 'such a fence or hedge'); (iii) 'fishmonger', or possibly from a medieval nickname for a thin person (from Middle English *plaise* 'plaice') [Francis Place, 1771–1854, British radical]

Plant 'gardener'

Plater (i) 'maker of armour plate'; (ii) 'advocate, attorney' (from a derivative of Old French *plaitier* 'to plead') [Alan Plater, 1935–, British playwright and screenwriter]

Plath (i) 'person from Plath', Germany; (ii) 'person who lives by a fence made from interlaced growing plants' (from Sorbian *płot* 'such a fence or hedge') [Sylvia Plath, 1932–63, US poet and novelist]

Platt (i) 'person from Platt or Platt Bridge', Lancashire ('plank bridge'); (ii) from a medieval nickname for a thin person (from Old French *plat* 'flat'); (iii) from a medieval Jewish nickname based on German *platt* 'flat'

Player (i) 'actor' or 'musician'; (ii) from a medieval nickname for a good or successful athlete [Gary Player, 1935–, South African golfer]

— **Player's** the proprietary name (registered in 1885) of a cigarette made by John Player & Sons of Nottingham, founded in the mid-19th-century by John Player, 1839–84. In 1901 the company became part of the Imperial Tobacco Group.

Playfair (i) from a medieval nickname for an enthusiastic competitor in sports and games (from Middle English *pleyfere* 'companion in play, playmate'); (ii) a different form of **Playford**

— **Playfair cipher** a type of code in which successive pairs of letters are replaced by pairs chosen in a prescribed manner from a matrix of 25 letters, usually arranged in accordance with a key-word. It is named after its deviser, the British chemist and administrator Lyon Playfair (Lord Playfair), 1818-98.

Playford 'person from Playford', Suffolk ('ford where sports are held')

Pleasance, Pleasence (i) from the medieval female personal name *Plaisance*, literally 'pleasantness'; (ii) 'person from Piacenza', Italy (from Latin *Placentia*, literally 'pleasing things') [Donald Pleasence, 1919–95, British actor]

Plenderleith, Plenderleath 'person from Plenderleith', Borders (perhaps 'timber farm by the broad river')

Plimpton 'person from Plympton', Devon ('plum-tree farmstead')

Plimsoll a Huguenot name of uncertain origin

— **Plimsoll line** a mark on the side of a merchant ship indicating the limit to which it can legally be submerged when loaded. It is named after the British politician and reformer Samuel Plimsoll, 1824–98, who campaigned for its introduction. (The light canvas shoes called 'plimsolls' appear to have been so named (around 1900) because the line of their rubber sole resembled a Plimsoll line).

Plomer a different form of **Plummer**. It is standardly pronounced 'ploomer'. [William Plomer, 1903–73, South African poet and novelist]

Plomley see **Plumley**

Plowden 'person from Plowden', Shropshire ('valley where games are played') [Bridget Plowden (Lady Plowden), 1910–2000, British educational reformer, responsible for the 'Plowden Report' (1967) on primary education in England]

— **'The case is altered', quoth Plowden** an old saying, signifying much the same as 'Circumstances alter cases'. It was used by Ben Jonson as the title of one of his comedies (*c*.1597). The 'Plowden' is assumed to be the celebrated lawyer Edmund Plowden, 1518–85, but the occasion on which he made his pronouncement is disputed.

Plowman 'maker of ploughs' or 'ploughman'

Plowright 'maker of ploughs' [Dame Joan Plowright, 1929–, British actress]

Plucknett a different form of **Plunkett** (ii)

Plum, Plumb 'person who lives by a plum tree' [Professor Plum, the 38-year-old archaeologist who is one of the six suspects in the murder of Dr Black in the board game Cluedo; Sir John ('Jack') Plumb, 1911–2001, British historian]

Plumley, Plomley 'person from Plumley', the name of various places in England ('wood or glade where plum trees grow') [Roy Plomley, 1914–85, British broadcaster, originator of the BBC radio programme *Desert Island Discs*]

Plummer (i) 'person who lives by a plum tree'; (ii) 'plumber'; (iii) 'dealer in feathers' (from a derivative of Middle English *plume* 'feather'). See also **Plomer** [Christopher Plummer, 1929–, Canadian actor]

Plumtree, Plumptre, Plumptree 'person who lives by a plum tree'

Plunkett, Plunket (i) 'maker of blankets' (from Middle English *blaunket* 'blanket'). See also **Blunkett**; (ii) 'person from Plouquenet', Brittany ('parish of Guenec'). See also **Plucknett** [St Oliver Plunket, 1629–81, Irish churchman and martyr, the last Roman Catholic martyr in England]

Pocock a different form of **Peacock**

Podmore 'person from Podmore or Podimore' Somerset and Staffordshire respectively (perhaps 'marsh frequented by frogs')

Poe from a medieval nickname for a vain or flamboyantly dressed person (from Old Norse *pá* 'peacock') [Edgar Allan Poe, 1809–49, US poet, short-story writer and critic]

Poggs 'son of *Pogg*', a medieval female personal name, a different form of *Mogg*, a pet-form of *Margaret*

Pogson a different form of **Poggs**. See also **Poxon**

Pogue a Northern Irish variant of **Pollock**

Pohlmann, Pohlman 'person who lives by a muddy pool' (from German)

Poindexter a Huguenot name, from a medieval nickname based on Old French *poing destre* 'right fist'
— **poindexter** in US slang, an over-industrious student, especially a socially inept one; a swot or nerd. The term comes from a character so named in the US television animated-cartoon series *Felix the Cat* (1959), who was a genius but spoke impenetrable jargon; he in turn is said to have been based on Emmett Poindexter, attorney for the creator of the series.

Poinsett, Poinset 'maker of pointed instruments' (from a derivative of Old French *poinson* 'pointed instrument')
— **poinsettia** a shrub with bright red bracts resembling petals, popular as a houseplant. It is named after the US diplomat and amateur botanist Joel Poinsett, 1775–1851.

Pointer, Poynter 'maker of points (laces for fastening doublet and hose)'

Pointon, Poynton 'person from Pointon', Lincolnshire ('estate associated with Pohha') or 'person from Poynton', Cheshire and Shropshire ('estate associated respectively with Pofa and Pēofa')

Poitier probably a different form of French *Pothier*, literally 'maker of drinking vessels', from a derivative of Old French *pot* 'drinking vessel' [Sidney Poitier, 1927–, US actor]

Polanski (i) an anglicization of Polish *Polański*, literally 'Pole'; (ii) 'person who lives in a woodland glade' (from a derivative of Polish *polana* 'glade, clearing')

Poliakov, Poliakoff 'son of *Polák*' (see **Pollack**) [Stephen Poliakoff, 1952–, British playwright and director]

Polk (i) a contracted form of **Pollock**; (ii) *also* **Polke** from a German form of the Slavic personal name *Boleslav*, literally 'great glory' [James Polk, 1795–1849, US Democratic politician, president 1845–49]

Pollack '(Jewish) person from Poland (or other Slavic-speaking area)', from Polish *Polák* 'Pole'. See also **Pollock** (ii) [Sydney Pollack, 1934–, US film director and producer]

Pollard (i) from a medieval nickname for someone with a large or misshapen head (from Middle English *poll* 'head' with the derogatory suffix *-ard*); (ii) from a derogatory name for someone called **Paul** [Eve Pollard, 1945–, British journalist; Su Pollard, 1949–, British actress and comedian; Vicky Pollard, the chavette with attitude in the BBC television comedy series *Little Britain* (2003–)]

Pollitt from the medieval male personal name *Pollit*, an anglicization of Greek *Hippolytos*, literally 'freer of horses' [Harry Pollitt, 1890–1960, British Communist politician]

Pollock, Pollok (i) 'person from Pollock', Strathclyde (probably 'little pool' or 'little pit'); (ii) a different form of **Pollack**. See also **Polk** (i) [Graeme Pollock, 1944–, South African cricketer; Jackson Pollock, 1912–56, US artist]

Pomeroy 'person from Pomeroy', the name of various places in northeastern France ('apple orchard')

Pomfret, Pomfrett 'person from Pontefract', Yorkshire ('broken bridge'). The spelling of the surname represents the evolved pronunciation of the original form of the place-name, from Old French *pont freit*; the modern spelling of the place-name is a Latinized form.

Pond 'person who lives beside a pond or lake'
— **Pond's Cream** the brand name of a type of medicinal cream invented in the US in 1846 by Theron T. Pond. The company he formed later moved into cosmetic creams, such as 'Pond's Vanishing Cream' and 'Pond's Cold Cream'.

Ponder a different form of **Pond**
— **Ponders End** a district in the London borough of Enfield. It gets its name from the Ponder family, which owned land in the area in the 14th century (*End* in this context means 'district').

Ponsford (i) 'person from Ponsford', Devon (probably 'ford of the river Pont'); (ii) an alteration of the surname *Pauncefoot*, from a medieval nickname for someone with a fat belly (from Anglo-Norman *paunce vout* 'rounded stomach')

Ponsonby 'person from Ponsonby', Cumbria ('Puncun's settlement')

Pont 'person who lives near a bridge' (from Anglo-Norman *pont* 'bridge')

Pontin 'little **Pont**'
— **Pontins** a British holiday company, founded in 1946 by Sir Fred Pontin, 1906–2000

Ponting a different form of **Pontin** [Ricky Ponting, 1974–, Australian cricketer]

Pool (i) *also* **Poole** 'person who lives by a pool'; (ii) a different form of **Paul**; (iii) from Dutch, literally '(Jewish) person from Poland (or other Slavic-speaking area)'

Pooley 'person from Pooley', Warwickshire (a name of uncertain origin and meaning), or 'person from Pooley Bridge', Cumbria ('mound by a pool')

Poor, Poore different forms of **Power** (i)

Pope from a medieval nickname for a pompous man, who behaved as if he were the pope, or for a man who played the part of the pope in a pageant or play [Alexander Pope, 1688–1744, British poet]

Popham 'person from Popham', Hampshire (a name of uncertain origin and meaning)
— **Popham's Eau** an artificial waterway in Cambridgeshire and Norfolk, joining the River Nene with Well Creek. *Popham* is presumably the name of the man who had the waterway constructed and the surrounding fen drained, though it is not known who he was. *Eau* means 'drainage canal'.

Popplewell 'person from Popplewell', the name of various places in Yorkshire (probably 'bubbling spring' or 'pebbly spring')

Port (i) *also* **Porte** 'person who lives in a market town or by a harbour' (from Middle English *port* 'market town, harbour'); (ii) *also* **Porte** 'person who lives by (and is in charge of) the gates of a town' (from Middle English *port* 'gateway'); (iii) from a Jewish name of unknown origin and meaning. See also **Portman**

Portal 'person who lives by (and is in charge of) the gates of a town' (from Old French *portal* 'gateway') [Charles Portal (Viscount Portal), 1893–1971, British Chief of the Air Staff during World War II]

Porteous probably 'person who lives in the entrance lodge of a manor house' (from Middle English *port hous* 'gateway house')
— **Porteous Riots** riots which occurred in Edinburgh in 1736 after an unruly crowd at a public execution was fired on, on the orders of Lieutenant Porteous. He was subsequently lynched and hanged.

Porter (i) 'person in charge of the gates of a town or of a large house' (from Middle English *porter* 'gatekeeper'); (ii) 'person who carries loads' (from Old French *porteor* 'carrier') [Cole Porter, 1891–1964, US composer and lyricist; Eric Porter, 1928–95, British actor; Janet Street-Porter, see **Street**; Jimmy Porter, the angry young man who is the antihero of John Osborne's *Look Back in Anger* (1956); Katherine Anne Porter, 1890–1980, US short-story writer and novelist; Nyree Dawn Porter, 1940–2001, New Zealand-born British actress; Peter Porter, 1929–, Australian poet and critic; Rodney Porter, 1917–85, British biochemist; Dame Shirley Porter (Lady Porter; *née* Cohen), 1930–, British Conservative politician]

Porterfield 'person who lives on land owned by a porter (**Porter** (i))'

Portillo 'person from Portillo', the name of various places in Spain ('little mountain pass') [Michael Portillo, 1953–, British Conservative politician, broadcaster and journalist]

Portman a different form of **Port** (i–ii) [Eric Portman, 1903–69, British actor; Natalie Portman (original name Natalie Hershlag), 1981–, Israeli-US actress]
— **Portman Estate** an area of land and buildings in the West End of London owned and administered by Portman Settled Estates Ltd. The land was originally purchased in 1553 by Sir William Portman, and developed from the mid-18th century by his descendant, Henry William Portman.

Portnoy 'tailor' (a Jewish name, from Russian *portnoj*, a derivative of *port* 'uncut cloth')
— **Portnoy's Complaint** a novel (1969) by Philip Roth, recording the intimate confessions of Alexander Portnoy to his psychoanalyst

Poskett, Poskitt different forms of **Postgate**

Posner 'person from Poznan', Poland

Post (i) 'person who lives by a (landmark) post or pole' (from Middle Low German *post*); (ii) from a Jewish name of unknown origin and meaning [Emily Post, 1873–1960, US writer on etiquette; Wiley Post, 1898–1935, US airman, the first to fly solo round the world]
— **Post Toasties** a US breakfast cereal similar to cornflakes, created in the first decade of the 20th century by the food manufacturer Charles William Post, 1854–1914

Postgate 'person from Postgate', Yorkshire ('road marked by posts') [Raymond Postgate, 1896–1971, British writer and gourmet, founder of the *Good Food Guide*]

Postlethwaite, Postlethwait 'person from Postlethwaite', Cumbria ('Possel's glade' or 'apostle's glade') [Pete Postlethwaite, 1945–, British actor]

Pott (i) 'person who lives in a pot-shaped hole in the ground'; (ii) from the medieval personal name *Pott*, a shortened form of *Philpot* (see **Philpott**)
— **Pott's disease** a tubercular disease of the spine, marked by the destruction of the bone and discs and curvature of the spine. It is named after the British surgeon Sir Percivall Pott, 1713–88.
— **Pott's fracture** a fracture of the fibula close to the ankle, of a type first described by Sir Percivall Pott (see above)

Potter 'maker of vessels for drinking and storage (from clay, but also other materials, such as metal)' [Beatrix Potter, 1866–1943, British children's author and illustrator; Dennis Potter, 1935–94, British playwright; Harry Potter, the boy-wizard who is the hero of a series of children's novels by J.K. Rowling; Stephen Potter, 1900–69, British humorist and critic]
— **Potter's Bar** a town in Hertfordshire, to the north of London. *Bar* in this context is a gate providing admittance to Enfield Chase, and it is thought that in the early 16th century it was owned by a man called Potter.

Potterton 'person from Potterton', Yorkshire

Potts 'son of **Pott** (ii)'

Poulson 'son of *Pole* or *Poul*', Middle English variants of **Paul** [John Poulson, 1910–93, British architect and fraudster]

Poultney a different form of **Pountney**

Poulton 'person from Poulton', the name of various places in England ('farmstead by a pool')

Pound 'person who lives by an animal pound'; also, 'official responsible for rounding up and impounding stray animals' [Ezra Pound, 1885–1972, US poet and critic]

Pounds a different form of **Pound**

Pountney 'person from Poultney', Leicestershire ('Pulta's island'). The substitution of *n* for the original *l* is due to Norman influence. See also **Poultney, Pulteney**

Povey from Welsh *ap Hwfa* 'son of *Hwfa*', a Welsh personal name of unknown origin and meaning

Powell (i) from Welsh *ap Hywel* 'son of *Hywel*' (see **Howell** (ii)); (ii) a different form of **Paul**. The first syllable of the name is now generally pronounced to rhyme with 'now', though some Powells still insist on the traditional rhyme with 'know'. [Sir Anthony Powell, 1906–2000, British novelist; Cecil Frank Powell, 1903–69, British physicist; Colin Powell, 1937–, US general and politician; Enoch Powell, 1912–98, British Conservative and Unionist politician; Michael Powell, 1905–90, British film director; Robert Powell, 1944–, British actor; Sandy Powell (original name Albert Arthur Powell), 1900–82, British comedian; William Powell, 1892–1984, US actor]
— **Powellism** the political and economic policies advocated by Enoch Powell (see above), in particular the restriction of coloured immigration into Britain
— **Powellite** a supporter of Enoch Powell or advocate of Powellism
— **Powellize** to preserve and harden wood by boiling it in a sugar solution. The process was developed at the end of the 19th century by the British inventor William Powell.

Power (i) from a medieval nickname for a poor person or (ironically) for a miser (from Middle English *povre* 'poor', from Old French). See also **Poor**; (ii) an anglicization of Old French *Pohier* 'person from Pois', a town in northern France [E. Power Biggs, 1906–77, British-born US organist]

Powers a different form of **Power** [Austin Powers, spoof British spy portrayed by Mike Myers in *Austin Powers: International Man of Mystery* (1997) and subsequent films; Gary Powers, 1929–77, pilot of the US spy plane shot down over the Soviet Union in 1960; Stefanie Powers (original name Stefania Federkiewicz), 1942–, US actress]

Pownall 'person from Pownall', Cheshire ('Pohha's nook of land')

Powney a different form of **Pownall**

Poxon a different form of **Pogson**

Poynter see **Pointer**

Poynton see **Pointon**

Prager (i) *also* **Praeger** an anglicization of German *Präger*, literally 'maker of coins'; (ii) 'person from Prague', Czech Republic

Prasad a Hindu name, from Sanskrit *prasāda* 'favour, gift'

Pratt from a medieval nickname for a confidence trickster (from Old English *prætt* 'tricky, cunning')
— **Pratt's Bottom** a village on the southeastern edge of Greater London (formerly in Kent). It gets its name from a family called Pratt who lived in the area from the 14th century (*bottom* in this context is a valley).
— **Pratt's Club** a gentleman's club in the West End of London, established in 1841 by William Nathaniel Pratt, steward to the 7th duke of Beaufort
— **Prattware** a type of lightweight, typically highly coloured earthenware produced by the Staffordshire pottery-manufacturer Felix Pratt, 1780-1859

Prebble perhaps 'person from Préville', an unidentified place in northern France ('meadow-town')

Preece a different form of **Price** (i)

Prejean 'John's meadow' (from French *pré de Jean*)

Prendergast reputedly 'person from Prendergast (Brontegeest)', Flanders

Prentice (i) *also* **Prentis** *or* **Prentiss** from a medieval nickname for a new and inexperienced person (from a reduced form of Middle English *aprentis* 'apprentice'); (ii) from Irish Gaelic *Ó Pronntaigh* 'descendant of *Pronnteach*', a personal name meaning literally 'bestower'. See also **Brontë** [Paula Prentiss (original name Paula Ragusa), 1939–, US actress; Reg Prentice (Lord Prentice), 1923–2001, British Labour and Conservative politician]

Prescott, Prescot 'person from Prescott', the name of various places in England ('priests' cottage') [John Prescott, 1938–, British Labour politician; William Prescott, 1796–1859, US historian]

Presley (i) a different form of **Priestley**; (ii) an anglicization of German *Pressler* 'person from Breslau', Silesia [Elvis Presley, 1935–77, US popular singer]

Preston 'person from Preston', the name of numerous places in England and Scotland ('priests' farmstead') [Robert Preston, 1918–87, US actor; Simon Preston, 1935–, British conductor and organist]

Pretty, Pritty from a medieval nickname for an admirable or gallant man (from Middle English *prety, prity* 'fine, excellent')

Prettyman a different form of **Pretty**

Prevost 'person in charge, official' (from Old French *prevost* 'provost')

Price, Pryce (i) from Welsh *ap Rhys* 'son of *Rhys*' (see **Reece**); (ii) perhaps 'fixer of prices' (from Middle English *pris* 'price'); (iii) an anglicization of the Jewish surnames *Preuss* and *Preis* 'person from Prussia' [Alan Price, 1942–, British musician and songwriter; Dennis Price, 1915–73, British actor; Jonathan Pryce, 1947–, British actor; Leontyne Price, 1927–, US soprano; Dame Margaret Price, 1941–, British soprano; Vincent Price, 1911–93, US actor]

— **Price Waterhouse** a British accountancy firm, founded in London in 1849 by Samuel Price. It was joined in 1865 by Edwin Waterhouse, 1841–1917, and in 1874 it became Price, Waterhouse & Co. In 1998 it merged with Coopers & Lybrand and became Pricewaterhouse Coopers.

Prichard see **Pritchard**

Prickett 'little **Pryke**'

Priddy, Priddey (i) from Welsh *ap Rhiddid* 'son of *Rhiddid*', a personal name of unknown origin and meaning, or *ap Redith* 'son of *Redith*', a shortened form of **Meredith** 'bard' (from Welsh *prydudd*); (ii) from the Welsh personal name *Predyr*, perhaps literally 'steel spears'

Pride, Pryde (i) from a medieval nickname for a vain person, or for someone who had played the part of Pride in a play or pageant; (ii) from a Welsh nickname for a much beloved person (from Welsh *prid* 'precious, dear')

— **Pride's Purge** the expulsion of over a hundred Presbyterian members from Parliament in 1648 by the Parliamentary soldier Thomas Pride, died 1658

Prideaux 'person from Prideaux, earlier Pridias', Cornwall (perhaps based on Cornish *prÿ* 'clay'). The modern Frenchified spelling is based on the idea that the name comes from French *près d'eaux* 'near waters' or *pré d'eaux* 'meadow of waters'.

Pridgen, Pridgeon perhaps from Old French *preux Jean* 'wise John, brave John'

Pridham from a medieval nickname based on Old French *prud'homme* 'wise man, sensible man'. See also **Purdom**

Priest (i) 'minister of the church, priest'; (ii) 'son of a priest'; (iii) from a medieval nickname for a sanctimonious person, or for someone who played the part of a priest in a play or pageant

Priestland 'person who farmed land held by the Church'

Priestley, Priestly 'person from Priestley', the name of various places in England ('wood or woodland clearing belonging to the Church'). See also **Presley** [J.B. Priestley, 1894–1984, British novelist and dramatist; Joseph Priestley, 1733–1804, British chemist and one of the discoverers of oxygen]

Priestman 'servant of the priest'

Prime (i) from a medieval nickname for an admirable person (from Middle English *prime* 'fine, excellent'); (ii) from the medieval personal name *Prime* (from Old English *prim* 'early morning'). See also **Prinne**

Primrose 'person from Primrose', Fife (originally *Prenrhos*, literally 'tree-moor') [Primrose, family name of the earls of Rosebery; William Primrose, 1904–82, British viola player]

Prince (i) from a medieval nickname for someone who behaved in a princely way; (ii) an anglicization of the invented Jewish name *Prinz* (from German *Prinz* 'prince') [Harold Prince, 1928–, US theatre director and producer]

Pringle 'person from Pringle', Borders (formerly *Hopringle*, literally 'Prjónngil's enclosed valley')

— **Pringles** the brand name of a type of potato crisp manufactured by Procter & Gamble, and originally sold in North America in 1968. It came from Pringle Avenue, the name of a street in Finneytown, Ohio, which itself may have been inspired by someone called Pringle.

Prinne, Prynn, Prynne different forms of **Prime** [William Prynne, 1600–69, English Puritan pamphleteer]

Prior, Pryor, Pryer 'servant of the prior' [James Prior (Lord Prior), 1927–, British Conservative politician; Matthew Prior, 1664–1721, English poet]

Pritchard, Prichard from Welsh *ap Richard* 'son of **Richard**' [Sir John Pritchard, 1921–89, British conductor]

Pritchett, Pritchet 'little **Pryke**' [V.S. Pritchett (Sir Victor Pritchett), 1900–97, British short-story writer and critic]

Pritty see **Pretty**

Privett 'person from Privett', Hampshire (probably 'privet copse')

Probert from Welsh *ap Roppert* 'son of **Robert**'

Proctor, Procter, Procktor, Prockter 'one who manages affairs on behalf of another; a steward, agent or attorney' [Adelaide Anne Proctor, 1825–64, British poet, author of 'A Lost Chord'; Harvey Proctor, 1947–, British Conservative politician; Mike Procter, 1946–, South African cricketer; Patrick Procktor, 1936–2003, British artist]

— **Procter & Gamble** a US-based producer of consumer goods, founded in Cincinnati, Ohio in 1837 by the candlemaker William Procter and the soapmaker James Gamble, 1803–91

Proffitt, Profitt 'person with an ability to foretell the future' (from Middle English *profit* 'prophet')

Profumo 'maker or seller of perfumes and aromatic oils' (from Italian, from *profumo* 'perfume') [John Profumo, 1915–2006, British Conservative politician and social worker]

Prosser from Welsh *ap Rhosier* 'son of **Roger**'

Prothero, Protheroe from Welsh *ap Rhydderch* 'son of **Roderick**'

Proud, Proude from a medieval nickname for a vain person. See also **Prout**

Proudfoot from a medieval nickname for someone who walks in a proud or haughty way

Proulx from a medieval French nickname for a prudent or brave person (from *proulx*, a southern and western variant of standard French *preux* 'wise, brave'). It is pronounced 'proo'. [E. Annie Proulx, 1935–, US journalist and author]

Prout a mainly Cornish variant of **Proud** [Ebenezer Prout, 1835–1909, British musicologist; William Prout, 1785–1850, British chemist and physiologist]

Prowse, Prouse from a medieval nickname for a brave warrior (from Middle English *prous* 'brave') — **Keith Prowse** see **Keith**

Pryce see **Price**

Pryde see **Pride**

Pryke 'maker or user of pointed implements' (from Middle English *prike* 'point, prick'), or from a medieval nickname for a tall thin person. See also **Prickett**, **Pritchett** [Paula Pryke, 1960–, British florist]

Prynn, Prynne see **Prinne**

Pryor, Pryer see **Prior**

Psmith see **Smith**

Puddephat, Pudephat from a medieval nickname for someone with a roly-poly physique (from Middle English *puddy fat* 'round-bellied vat')

Pugh from Welsh *ap Hugh* or *ap Hew* 'son of Hugh'. See also **Pye** (iii)

Pulham, Pullam, Pullum 'person from Pulham', Dorset and Norfolk ('homestead or enclosure by the pools')

Pullen, Pullein, Pulleyn, Pullin 'horsebreeder' (from Old French *poulain* 'colt'), or from a medieval nickname for a coltish, frisky person

Puller, Pullar different forms of **Pill** (ii)

Pullman, Pulman (i) a different form of **Pill** (ii); (ii) an anglicization of German *Pullmann*, a different form of *Puhlmann*, itself a different form of **Pohlmann**; (iii) 'blower of glass bottles', a Jewish name, based on German *Pulle* 'bottle' [George Mortimer Pullman, 1831–97, US inventor and manufacturer] — **Pullman car, Pullman** a luxury-standard railway carriage for sitting, eating or sleeping in, of a type devised by George M. Pullman (see above) and originally introduced in 1865.

Pulteney a different form of **Pountney**

Purcell 'person who looks after pigs, swineherd' (from Old French *pourcel* 'piglet'), or from a (possibly affectionate) medieval nickname for someone thought to resemble a little pig [Henry Purcell, 1659–95, English composer]

Purchase, Purchas, Purchés 'person in charge of buying supplies for a large household' (from Anglo-Norman *purchacer* 'to buy'). See also **Purkiss** [Samuel Purchas, 1577–1626, English clergyman and compiler of travel books]

Purdom a different form of **Pridham** [Edmund Purdom, 1924–, British actor]

Purdy, Purdey, Purdie different forms of **Pardoe** [Purdey, the elegant sidekick (played by Joanna Lumley) of John Steed in the ITV adventure series *The New Avengers* (1976–77)] — **James Purdey & Sons Ltd.** a firm of gunsmiths founded in London in 1814 by James Purdey, 1784–1863

Purkins see **Perkins**

Purkiss, Purkis different forms of **Purchase**

Purnell a different form of **Parnell**

Purser (i) 'maker or seller of bags'; (ii) 'official in charge of expenditure'; (iii) from Scots Gaelic *Mac an Sparain* 'son of the sporran' (a name traditionally borne by purse-bearers to the Lords of the Isles)

Purvis, Purves, Purvess probably 'person in charge of buying supplies for a large household' (from Middle English *purveys* 'provisions') [Libby Purves, 1950–, British journalist and broadcaster; Peter Purves, 1939–, British television presenter]

Pusey (i) 'person from Pusey', Oxfordshire ('island where peas grow'). See also **Pizey**; (ii) 'person from Pusey', northern France ('Pusius's settlement') [Edward Pusey, 1800–82, British clergyman and theologian] — **Puseyism** the teachings of Edward Pusey (see above), leader of the Oxford Movement, who advocated a renewal of Catholic practices in the Church of England — **Puseyite** a follower of Edward Pusey or advocate of Puseyism

Putnam, Puttnam, Puttenham 'person from Puttenham', Hertfordshire and Surrey ('Putta's homestead') [David Puttnam (Lord Puttnam), 1941–, British film producer; George Puttenham, ?1529–91, English author and critic]

Pye (i) 'baker or seller of pies'; (ii) from a medieval nickname for someone thought to resemble a magpie (e.g. in talkativeness or light-fingeredness) (from Middle English *pye* 'magpie'); (iii) a different form of **Pugh** — **Mr Pye** a novel (1953) by Mervyn Peake in which the enigmatic Mr Pye disrupts the moral universe of the inhabitants of Sark

Pyke see **Pike**

Pyle see **Pile**

Pymm, Pym see **Pimm**

Q

Quaid, Quade a shortened form of **McQuaid** [Dennis Quaid, 1954–, US actor]

Quail (i) see **Quayle**; (ii) a different form of **Quill**; (iii) from Irish Gaelic *Mac Phóil* (see **McFall**); (iv) an anglicization of the Jewish invented name *Kvalvaser*, in Yiddish literally 'spring water'

Quaine a Manx variant of **Coyne** (ii)

Quant from a medieval nickname for a crafty, knowledgeable or elegant person (from Middle English *quointe* 'known, knowledgeable, crafty, elegant') [Mary Quant, 1934–, British fashion designer]

Quantrell, Quantrill from a medieval nickname for an elegantly or flamboyantly dressed person (from Middle English *quointerel* 'dandy, fop', from *quointe* – see **Quant**)

Quarles 'person from Quarles', Norfolk ('circles' – perhaps a reference to prehistoric stone circles) [Francis Quarles, 1592–1644, English poet]

Quarmby a different form of **Wharmby**

Quarry, Quarrie (i) 'person who lives by or works in a quarry'; (ii) from a medieval nickname for a well-built or somewhat portly man (from Anglo-Norman *quaré* 'square' – see also **Le Carré**); (iii) a Manx reduced form of **McQuarrie** [Don Quarrie, 1951–, Jamaican athlete]

Quartermain, Quartermaine from a medieval nickname for a very dextrous person, or for someone who habitually wore gloves (from Old French *quatremains*, literally 'four hands') [Allan Quartermain, the hero of *King Solomon's Mines* (1886) and other adventure novels by H. Rider Haggard; Leon Quartermaine, 1876–1967, British actor]

Quatermass 'person from Quatremares', Normandy [Professor Bernard Quatermass, central character in a series of television and cinema fantasy-horror stories by Nigel Kneale, beginning with *The Quatermass Experiment* (1953)]

Quayle, Quail from a medieval nickname for someone thought to resemble a quail (e.g. in plumpness, timorousness or lecherousness) [Sir Anthony Quayle, 1913–89, British actor; Dan Quayle, 1947–, US lawyer and Republican politician, vice-president 1989–93]

Quennell, Quenell from the medieval female personal name *Quenilla*, from Old English *Cwēnhild*, literally 'woman-battle'. See also **Quinell** [Peter Quennell, 1905–93, British poet, critic and historian]

Quentin a different form of **Quinton** (iii)

Quested perhaps 'person from Questers', a lost village in Essex ('quern-site') [Adela Quested, the earnest young Englishwoman in E.M. Forster's *A Passage to India* (1924)]

Quick, Quicke (i) 'person who lives in an area overgrown with couch grass' (from Old English *cwice* 'couch grass'); (ii) 'person who lives at an outlying dairy farm' (from Old English *cūwīc*, literally 'outlying cow settlement'); (iii) 'person who lives in or by a wood', or 'person from Gweek', Cornwall (in either case from Cornish *gwyk* 'wood'); (iv) from a medieval nickname for a lively person (from Middle English *quik* 'alive, lively'). See also **Quickley** (i)

Quickley, Quickly (i) a different form of **Quick** (iv); (ii) a different form of **Quigley** [Mistress Quickly, hostess of the Boar's Head Tavern in Shakespeare's *Henry IV 1* and *2*]

Quigley from Irish Gaelic *Ó Coigligh* 'descendant of *Coigleach*', a nickname probably meaning 'untidy person'. See also **Quickley** (ii)

Quill from Irish Gaelic *Ó Cuill* 'descendant of *Coll*', a personal name derived from *coll* 'hazel' (see also **Colgan**), or from Scottish Gaelic *Mac Cuill* 'son of *Coll*' (see **McColl**). See also **Woods** (ii)

Quiller 'spoon-maker' (from Old French *cuiller* 'spoon') [Sir Arthur Quiller-Couch, 1863–1944, British critic, novelist and anthologist]
— ***The Quiller Memorandum*** an espionage film (1966) in which Quiller (played by George Segal) investigates the death of two British agents in Berlin. The screenplay was written by Harold Pinter.

Quilly, Quilley from Irish Gaelic *Mac Conchoille* 'son of *Cú Choille*', a personal name meaning literally 'dog of the woods', or *Mac an Choiligh*, literally 'son of the cock' [Denis Quilley, 1927–2003, British actor]

Quilter 'maker of quilts and quilted garments' [Roger Quilter, 1877–1953, British composer]

Quin see **Quinn**

Quincey, Quincy 'person from Quincy', the name of various places in northern France ('Quintus's settlement')
— **Quincy** a city (pronounced 'kwinzi') in eastern Massachusetts, USA. It was founded in 1792 and named after Colonel John Quincy, a prominent local citizen. The future president John Quincy Adams, a descendant of John Quincy, was born there.

— *Quincy* a US television detective drama series (1977–85) starring Jack Klugman as the eponymous medical examiner (first name unknown)

Quine (i) a different form of **Quinn**; (ii) from the French personal name *Jacquine*, a female pet-form of *Jacques* (see **Jack** (ii)) [Willard Quine, 1908–2000, US philosopher]

Quinell a different form of **Quennell**

Quinlan from Irish Gaelic *Ó Caoindealbháin* 'descendant of *Caoildealbhán*', a personal name meaning literally 'little beautiful form', or *Ó Conailláin* 'descendant of *Conall*' (see **Connell**). See also **Conlon**

Quinlivan a different form of **Quinlan**

Quinn, Quin from Irish Gaelic *Ó Cuinn* 'descendant of *Conn*', a nickname meaning 'leader, chief'. See also **Coyne** (iii), **Quine** (i) [Anthony Quinn (original name Antonio Quinn), 1915–2001, Mexican-American actor]
— **'The Mighty Quinn'** a folk-rock song (1967) by Bob Dylan, originally entitled 'Quinn the Eskimo (The Mighty Quinn)'. Quinn is an enigmatic godlike character who brings joy and peace. Dylan reportedly took his name from the actor Anthony Quinn (see above). *The Mighty Quinn* is also the name of a 1989 film starring Denzel Washington as police officer Xavier Quinn.

Quint (i) from the Catalan personal name *Quint* (from Latin *Quintus* – see **Quinton** (iii)); (ii) from the German personal name *Quint* (from Latin *Quintīnus* – see **Quinton** (iii)); (iii) from a medieval nickname for a lively person (from Middle English *quik* 'alive, lively'). See also **Quick** (iv) [Peter Quint, the evil servant who appears as a ghost in Henry James's *The Turn of the Screw* (1898)]

Quinton (i) 'person from Quinton', the name of various places in England ('queen's manor'); (ii) 'person from Saint-Quentin', the name of various places in northern France, honouring St Quentin of Amiens; (iii) from the Old French personal name *Quentin* (from Latin *Quentīnus*, a derivative of *Quintus*, literally 'fifth-born')

Quirk, Quirke from Irish and Manx Gaelic *Ó Cuirc* 'descendant of *Corc*', a personal name based on either *corc* 'heart' or *curc* 'tuft of hair' [John Shirley-Quirk, see **Shirley**; Pauline Quirke, 1959–, British actress; Randolph Quirk (Lord Quirk), 1920–, British linguistician and grammarian]

Quist from the invented Swedish surname *Qvist*, literally 'twig'
— **Adrian Quist** in Australian rhyming slang, 'pissed' (i.e. 'drunk'). Adrian Quist, 1913–91, was a noted Australian tennis player.

Qureshi 'descendant of the Quraish', a leading tribe in Mecca at the time of the birth of the Prophet Muhammad

R

Rabbitt (i) *also* **Rabet** 'little *Rabb*', a pet-form of **Robert**; (ii) from the Norman personal name *Rabbode*, of Germanic origin and meaning literally 'advice-message'; (iii) a mistranslation of Irish Gaelic *Ó Coinín* 'descendant of *Coinín*', a personal name probably meaning literally 'little hound', as if it were derived from *coinín* 'rabbit'

Raben, Raban (i) from a shortened form of a Germanic personal name based on *hraban* 'raven'; (ii) different forms of **Rabin**

Rabin 'rabbi' (from Polish *rabin* 'rabbi', from Hebrew *rav*). See also **Robin** (ii)

Rabinovich, Rabinovitch 'son of **Rabin**'

Rabinowitz a Germanized variant of **Rabinovich**

Race perhaps from a medieval nickname for a clean-shaven man (from Old French *ras* 'shaven') [Steve Race, 1921–, British musician and broadcaster]

Rackham 'person from Rackham', Sussex ('homestead or enclosure with ricks') [Arthur Rackham, 1867–1939, British watercolourist and book illustrator]

Rackley 'person from Rackley', an unidentified place perhaps in Berkshire ('glade with a mound' or 'glade with a gulley')

Radcliff, Radcliffe different forms of **Ratcliff** [Ann Radcliffe (*née* Ward), 1764–1823, British Gothic novelist; Paula Radcliffe, 1973–, British athlete]
— **Radcliffe Camera** a circular library in Oxford, built between 1737 and 1748 to the designs of James Gibbs under the terms of a bequest from the physician John Radcliffe, 1652–1714
— **Radcliffe College** a US women's college associated with Harvard University. It was founded in 1879 and named after Lady Ann Mowlson (*née* Radcliffe), died 1661, who established the first Harvard scholarship in 1643. It was absorbed into Harvard University in 1999.
— **Radcliffe Infirmary** a hospital in Oxford, built in the 1760s under the terms of a bequest from the physician John Radcliffe (see above)

Radford 'person from Radford', the name of various places in England (mainly 'red ford'). See also **Redford** [Basil Radford, 1897–1952, British actor]

Radley, Radleigh 'person from Radley', Devon and Oxfordshire ('red glade' or 'red wood'). See also **Raleigh**

Rae a shortened form of **McRae**

Raeburn, Rayburn 'person from Raeburn', Borders ('stream frequented by roebuck') [Sir Henry Raeburn, 1756–1823, Scottish portraitist]
— **Rayburn** the proprietary name of a type of oven. It was adopted from a Mr Rayburn, an American friend of W.T. Wren, managing director of the manufacturers, Allied Ironfounders (who no doubt found the notions of 'rays' and 'burning' singularly appropriate to an oven).

Rafael see **Raphael**

Rafferty from Irish Gaelic *Ó Rabhartaigh* or *Ó Robhartaigh* 'descendant of *Robhartach*', a personal name meaning literally 'possessor of prosperity' [Chips Rafferty (original name John William Pilbean Goffage), 1909–71, Australian actor]
— **Rafferty's rules** in Australian and New Zealand slang, no rules at all, especially in boxing; mayhem. In spite of the implied connection with an Irishman, *Rafferty* is more likely to be from *reffatory*, a British dialectal different form of *refractory*.

Raffles (i) 'person from Raffles', Dumfries and Galloway; (ii) 'son of **Raphael**' [A.J. Raffles, fictional gentleman burglar created by E.W. Hornung; Sir Thomas Stamford Raffles, 1781–1926, British colonial administrator and oriental scholar, founder of Singapore]
— **rafflesia** a leafless tropical plant (genus *Rafflesia*) with large foul-smelling flowers that is a parasite of other plants. It was named after Sir Stamford Raffles (see above).

Rafter a different form of **Raftery** [Patrick Rafter, 1972–, Australian tennis player]

Raftery from Irish Gaelic *Ó Reachtabhra* 'descendant of *Reachtabhra*', a personal name based on *reacht* 'decree'

Rahman from a Muslim personal name based on Arabic *rahmān* 'most gracious'

Raikes, Rakes 'person who lives in a narrow valley or pass' (from Old English *hraca* 'throat, narrow valley') [Robert Raikes, 1735–1811, British journalist and philanthropist]

Rainbird from the Old French male personal name *Rainbert*, of Germanic origin and meaning literally 'counsel-bright'. The modern form of the name has been influenced by English *rainbird* 'plover'. See also **Rambert**

Rainbow (i) from the Old French male personal name *Rainbaut*, of Germanic origin and meaning literally 'counsel-brave'. The modern form of the name has been influenced by English *rainbow*. See also **Rambo** (i), **Rammell**, **Raybould**; (ii) a translation of the German and Jewish name *Regen-bogen*, literally 'rainbow'

Raine, Rayne (i) 'person from Rayne', Aberdeen-shire ('strip of land'); (ii) from the medieval female personal name *Rayne* (from Old French *reine* 'queen'); (iii) from a shortened form of any of a range of personal names of Germanic origin begin-ning with the element *regin* 'counsel' (e.g. **Raymond**); (iv) from a medieval nickname for someone thought to resemble a frog (from Old French *raine* 'frog') [Craig Raine, 1944–, British poet; Kathleen Raine, 1908–2003, British poet]
— **Raynes Park** a southwestern suburb of London, dating from the late 19th century. It was named after Edward Rayne, 1778–1847, who owned farmland on which it was developed.

Rainer see **Rayner**

Raines (i) *also* **Rains** 'person from Rayne', Essex (perhaps 'shelter'); also, 'person from Rennes', Brittany; (ii) 'son of **Raine** (iii)'; (iii) 'son of *Rayne*', a Jewish female personal name related to **Raine** (ii) and meaning literally 'queen' [Claude Rains, 1889–1967, British actor]

Rainey from Gaelic *Ó Raighne, Ó Ráighne* 'descendant of *Raighne*', a personal name derived from Old Norse *Rögnvaldr* (see **Ronald**). See also **Reaney**, **Renison**, **Rennie** [Ma Rainey (original name Gertrude Malissa Nix Rainey, *née* Pridgett), 1886–1939, US blues singer]

Rainford 'person from Rainford', Lancashire ('Regna's ford')

Rains see **Raines** (i)

Rainsford probably a different form of **Rainford**

Rainwater an anglicization of German *Rein-wasser*, literally 'pure water'

Raison from a medieval nickname for an intelli-gent person (from Old French *raison* 'reason, intel-ligence'). See also **Reason**

Raistrick 'person from Raistrick', Yorkshire (perhaps 'resting-place ridge'). See also **Rastrick**

Raj a Hindu name, from Sanskrit *rājā* 'king'

Rajgopal a Hindu name, from Sanskrit *rājag-opāla* 'king of cowherds'

Rakes see **Raikes**

Raleigh, Ralegh 'person from Raleigh', Devon ('red wood' or 'red glade'). The name is tradition-ally pronounced 'rawly', but in modern usage more commonly 'rahly'. See also **Rally**, **Rawley**, **Rayleigh** [Sir Walter Raleigh, 1554–1618, English navigator and writer]
— **Raleigh** the state capital of North Carolina, USA. It was named after Sir Walter Raleigh (see above).
— **Raleigh** a British make of bicycle, produced by the Raleigh Cycle Company. It was established in 1887 in Raleigh Street, Nottingham, which was named after Sir Walter. The name is pronounced 'rally' (no doubt at least in part to reinforce an association with bicycle 'rallying').

Raley a different form of **Raleigh**

Ralls see **Rawls**

Rally a different form of **Raleigh**

Ralph from the male personal name *Ralph*, origi-nally brought into England in the form of Old Norse *Ráthulfr*, literally 'advice-wolf', and later reinforced by the related Norman *Radulf* or *Raulf*. See also **Rawle**, **Rawls**

Ralston 'person from Ralston', Renfrewshire

Ram (i) *also* **Ramm** from a medieval nickname for a forceful person. See also **Rampling**; (ii) 'person who lives in an area of thick woodland' (from Old French *raim, ram* 'branch'). See also **Ramey**; (iii) 'person who lives near a border or boundary' (from Swedish *ram* 'border'); (iv) *also* **Ramm** an invented Jewish name based on Hebrew *ram* 'lofty'; (v) a Hindu name, from Sanskrit *rāma* 'pleasing'

Ramachandran a Hindu name, from Sanskrit *rāma* 'pleasing' and *chandra* 'shining, moon'

Ramage from a medieval Scottish nickname for a hot-tempered or unpredictable person (from Old French *ramage* 'wild, uncontrollable' (applied to birds of prey))

Ramakrishnan a Hindu name, from Sanskrit *rāma* 'pleasing' and *kŕṣṇa* 'black', the name of Krishna, an incarnation of the god Vishnu

Ramaswamy a Hindu name, from Sanskrit *rāma* 'pleasing' and *svāmī* 'lord'

Rambert from the Old French male personal name *Rainbert* (see **Rainbird**) [Dame Marie Rambert (original name Cyvia Rabbam, later Miriam Rambach), 1888–1982, Polish-born British ballet dancer and choreographer]

Rambo (i) from a different form of the southern French surname *Rambeau*, from the Old French male personal name *Rainbaut* (see **Rainbow** (i)); (ii) from a different form of the German surname *Rambow* 'person from Rambow', the name of various places in eastern Germany [John Rambo, the aggressive protagonist (played by Sylvester Stallone) in the film *First Blood* (1982) and various sequels]
— **Ramboesque** displaying gung-ho aggression in the style of John Rambo (see above)

Ramey a different form of **Ram** (ii) [Samuel Ramey, 1942–, US bass-baritone]

Ramirez from Spanish *Ramírez* 'son of *Ramiro*', a male personal name of Germanic origin meaning literally 'counsel-fame'

Ramm see **Ram** (i), (iv)

Rammell a different form of **Rainbow** (i)

Ramnarine from a Trinidadian and Guyanese different form of the Indian personal name *Ramnarayan*, from Sanskrit *rāma* 'pleasing' and *nārāyaṅa*, an epithet of the god Vishnu

Ramos 'person who lives in a heavily wooded area', or 'person from Ramos', the name of various places in Spain and Portugal (in either case from Spanish and Portuguese *ramos* 'branches')

Rampling 'little **Ram** (i)' [Charlotte Rampling, 1946–, British actress]

Ramsay see **Ramsey**

Ramsbottom, Ramsbotham 'person from Ramsbottom', Lancashire ('valley where wild garlic grows')

Ramsden 'person from Ramsden', the name of various places in England ('valley where wild garlic grows')
— **Harry Ramsden's** a chain of British fish-and-chip restaurants, which grew out of an establishment opened by Harry Ramsden in Guiseley, Yorkshire in 1928

Ramsey, Ramsay 'person from Ramsey', Cambridgeshire and Essex ('island where wild garlic grows'), or 'person from Ramsey', Dumfries and Galloway ('Ramm's island') [Sir Alf Ramsey, 1922–99, English football manager; Allan Ramsay, ?1685–1758, Scottish poet and editor; Allan Ramsay, 1713–84, British portrait painter, son of Allan; Gordon Ramsay, 1966–, British chef; Michael Ramsey (Lord Ramsey), 1904–88, British churchman, 100th archbishop of Canterbury, 1961–74; Sir William Ramsay, 1852–1916, British chemist]

Rana a Hindu and Parsi name meaning literally 'king'

Rance 'son of **Rand** (ii)'

Rand (i) 'person who lives on the edge of a settlement or by the banks of a river', or 'person from Rand', the name of various places in England (in either case from Old English *rand* 'rim, edge'); (ii) from a shortened form of any of a range of personal names of Germanic origin beginning with the element *rand* 'shield rim' (e.g. **Randolph**). See also **Rance, Randall, Rankin, Ransome** [Mary Rand (*née* Bignal), 1940–, British athlete]
— **Rand McNally & Co.** a US publisher of maps, atlases, travel guides, etc., founded in Chicago in 1856 by William Rand. He was joined two years later by Andrew McNally.

Randall, Randal, Randell, Randle from the medieval personal name *Randel*, literally 'little **Rand** (ii)'. See also **Rendall**
— **Randall and Hopkirk (Deceased)** an ITV detective drama series (1969–70) featuring two dead private investigators, Jeff Randall and Marty Hopkirk, who pursued their work in ghostly form

Randolph from the male personal name *Randolph*, originally brought into England in the form of Old Norse *Rannúlfr*, literally 'shield-wolf', and later reinforced by the related Norman *Randolf*
— **Randolph Hotel** a hotel in Oxford, opened in 1866. It was named after the Randolph Gallery, then opposite on Beaumont Street, which in turn was named after the Rev. Dr Francis Randolph, an 18th-century benefactor of the Ashmolean Museum.

Rank (i) from the medieval personal name *Rank*, a shortened form of **Rankin**; (ii) from a medieval nickname for a powerfully built or headstrong person (from Old English *ranc* 'proud, rebellious') [J. Arthur Rank (Lord Rank), 1888–1972, British industrialist and film executive]

— **J. Arthur Rank** British rhyming slang (usually shortened to *J. Arthur* or plain *Arthur*) for *bank* and *wank*
— **Rank Hovis McDougall Ltd.** a British producer of flour, bread and other foodstuffs, formed in 1962 by the merger of Joseph Rank Ltd. (the creation of Joseph Rank, 1854–1943, flour miller, philanthropist and father of J. Arthur – see above) with McDougall, owners of the Hovis brand. It ceased to exist in 2007.
— **Rank Organization** a British film production, distribution and exhibition company founded in 1946 by J. Arthur Rank.

Rankin, Rankine from the medieval personal name *Rankin*, literally 'little **Rand** (ii)' [Rankin (full name John Rankin Waddell), 1966–, British photographer; Ian Rankin, 1960–, British novelist]
— **Rankine scale** an absolute temperature scale in which each degree equals one degree on the Fahrenheit scale, with the freezing point of water being 491.67° and its boiling point 671.67°. It is named after the British physicist and engineer W.J.M. Rankine, 1820–72.

Ransome, Ransom 'son of **Rand** (ii)' [Arthur Ransome, 1884–1967, British journalist and children's author; John Crowe Ransom, 1888–1974, US poet and critic]

Rao a Hindu name, derived from Sanskrit *rājā* 'king'

Raphael, Rafael from the Hebrew male personal name *Refael*, literally 'heal-God'. See also **Raffles** (ii) [Frederic Raphael, 1931–, British author]

Rappaport, Rapaport, Rappoport a Jewish name of uncertain origin, perhaps derived from German *Rappe* 'raven'

Rashid from the Muslim male personal name *Rashid*, derived from Arabic *rashīd* 'wise, judicious'

Rasmussen 'son of *Rasmus*', a reduced Scandinavian, North German and Dutch form of the male personal name *Erasmus*

Rastrick a different form of **Raistrick**

Ratcliff, Ratcliffe 'person from Ratcliff or Radcliff', the name of various places in England ('red cliff'). See also **Radcliff, Redcliffe**

Rathbone probably 'person from Radbourn or Radbourne', Warwickshire and Derbyshire respectively ('reedy stream') [Basil Rathbone, 1892–1967, South African-born British actor]

Rather (i) 'counsellor', or from a medieval German nickname for a wise person (in either case from Middle High German *rāter* 'adviser'); (ii) from a variant of the Germanic personal name *Rathert*, literally 'counsel-brave'; (iii) an anglicization of German *Räther* 'person from Rath', Germany [Dan Rather, 1931–, US television journalist]

Ratner, Rattner (i) 'person from Ratno', Ukraine, or 'person from Rathenau', Germany; (ii) 'councillor' (from Yiddish *ratner*) [Gerald Ratner, 1949–, British business executive]

Rattenbury 'person from Rattenbury', Cornwall

Rattigan, Ratigan from Irish Gaelic Ó *Reachtagáin* 'descendant of *Reachtagán*', a personal name meaning literally 'little steward' [Sir Terence Rattigan, 1911–77, British playwright]

Rattray 'person from Rattray', feudal barony in Perth and Kinross ('fortress settlement')

Rauschenberg 'person from Rauschenberg', the name of various places in Germany [Robert Rauschenberg, 1925–, US artist]

Raven from a medieval nickname for someone thought to resemble a raven (e.g. in having black hair or a predisposition to steal) [Simon Raven, 1927–2001, British novelist and screenwriter]

Ravenscroft 'person from Ravenscroft', Cheshire ('Hrafn's smallholding')

Rawdon 'person from Rawdon', Yorkshire ('red hill')

Rawle a different form of **Ralph**

Rawley a different form of **Raleigh**

Rawlings a different form of **Rawlins** [Jerry Rawlings, 1947–, president of Ghana 1992–2001]
— **Rawlplug** the proprietary name (registered in 1912) for a type of hollow cylindrical plug inserted into a wall to hold a screw firmly. It was based on the name of its inventor, the British electrical engineer John Rawlings.

Rawlins 'son of *Rawlin*', a medieval male personal name, from Old French *Raulin*, literally 'little little **Ralph**'

Rawlinson 'son of *Rawlin*' (see **Rawlins**) [Sir Henry Rawlinson, 1810–95, British orientalist]

Rawls 'son of **Ralph**' [Lou Rawls, 1933–2006, US soul, jazz and blues singer]

Rawnsley 'person from Rawnsley', Yorkshire ('Hrafn's hill') [Andrew Rawnsley, 1962–, British journalist]

Rawson 'son of *Raw*', a different form of **Ralph**

Rawsthorne, Rawsthorn 'person from Rostherne', Cheshire ('Rauthr's thorn bush') [Alan Rawsthorne, 1905–71, British composer]

Ray, Raye, Rey (i) from a medieval nickname for someone who behaved in a regal manner, or who played the king in a pageant or festivity (from Old French *rey, roy* 'king'). See also **Fitzroy**, **Roy**; (ii) from a medieval nickname for a shy or retiring person (from Middle English *ray* 'female roe deer'). See also **Roe** (i); (iii) a different form of **Rye** (ii–iii). See also **Rea** (i); (iv) a different form of **Wray** [John Ray, 1627–1705, English naturalist; Johnnie Ray, 1927–90, US pop singer; Man Ray (original name Emanuel Rudnitsky), 1890–1976, US artist and photographer; Robin Ray (original name Robin Olden), 1935–98, British actor and broadcaster, son of Ted; Ted Ray (original name Charles Olden), 1905–77, British comedian]
— **Ray's bream** a European sea fish, *Brama brama*, so named in 1797 in honour of John Ray (see above)

Raybould a different form of **Rainbow** (i)

Rayleigh (i) 'person from Rayleigh', Essex ('glade where deer are seen'); (ii) a different form of **Raleigh**

Rayment a different form of **Raymond**

Raymond from the Norman male personal name *Raimund*, of Germanic origin and meaning literally 'counsel-protection'. See also **Redmond** [Paul Raymond (original name Geoffrey Anthony Quinn), 1925–, Irish pornographer, striptease impresario and property developer]

Rayne see **Raine**

Rayner (i) *also* Raynor from the Norman male personal name *Rainer*, of Germanic origin and meaning literally 'counsel-army'; (ii) an invented Jewish name based on German *rein* or Yiddish *reyn* 'pure' [Claire Rayner, 1931–, British journalist and agony aunt]
— **Claire Rayners** British rhyming slang for *trainers* (i.e. training shoes)
— **Rayners Lane** a district of northwest London, in the borough of Harrow. According to local tradition it takes its name from an old shepherd called Rayner who lived by a lane there in the 19th century.

Rea, Reay (i) a different form of **Rye** (ii–iii); (ii) a shortened form of **McRea** [Chris Rea, 1951–, British singer-songwriter; Stephen Rea, 1949–, Northern Irish actor]

Read, Reade, Reed, Reid (i) from a medieval nickname for a person with red hair or a red face (from Middle English *read* 'red'). See also **Redman** (i); (ii) 'person who lives in a woodland clearing' (from Old English *rīed, rȳd* 'clearing, glade'). See also **Attride**; (iii) 'person from Read', Lancashire ('headland frequented by female roe deer'), 'person from Reed', Hertfordshire ('place thickly growing with brushwood'), or 'person from Rede', Suffolk ('reedy place') [Beryl Reid, 1920–96, British actress and comedian; Sir Carol Reed, 1906–76, British film director; Charles Reade, 1814–84, British novelist; Sir George Reid, 1845–1918, Scottish-born Australian politician, prime minister 1904–05; Henry Reed, 1914–86, British poet; Sir Herbert Read, 1893–1968, British poet and critic; John Reed, 1887–1920, US journalist and advocate of Communism; John Reid, 1928–, New Zealand cricketer; John Reid, 1947–, British Labour politician; Leonard Ernest ('Nipper') Read, 1925–, British detective; Lou Reed, 1942–, US rock singer/songwriter and guitarist; Miss Read, the pen-name of Dora Jesse Saint, 1913–, British author; Oliver Reed, 1938–99, British actor; Thomas Reid, 1710–96, Scottish philosopher; Walter Reed, 1851–1902, US army physician]
— **Austin Reed** a British firm of men's outfitters, founded in London in 1900 by Austin Reed, 1873–1954
— **Reed International** a British firm of paper manufacturers, founded in 1894 by Albert Edwin Reed, 1846–1920
— **Walter Reed National Army Medical Center** the main US Army medical facility, established in Washington DC in 1909 and named in honour of

Walter Reed (see above), who ascertained the role of mosquitoes in spreading yellow fever

Reader, Reeder 'person who thatches cottages with reeds'

Reading, Redding (i) 'person from Reading', Berkshire ('settlement of Reada's people'). See also **Reddington**; (ii) 'person who lives in a woodland clearing' (from Old English *ryding* 'glade, clearing'). See also **Riding** [Cyrus Redding, 1785–1870, British journalist and wine connoisseur; Otis Redding, 1941–67, US soul singer]

Ready[1], Readey, Reddy, Reddie (i) from a medieval nickname for someone who makes prudent provision for the future (from Middle English *readie* 'prepared, prompt'); (ii) from Irish Gaelic *Ó Rodaigh* 'descendant of *Rodach*', a personal name probably based on *rod* 'spirited, angry'

Ready[2], Reedie, Reedy, Reidy 'person from Reedie', Angus

Reagan see **Regan**

Reaney a different form of **Rainey**

Rearden, Reardon see **Riordan**

Reason a different form of **Raison**

Reaves see **Reeves**

Reay see **Rea**

Rebuck from a different form of the German surname *Rehbock*, probably from a medieval nickname for a hunter, from Middle High German *rēchboc* 'roebuck'

Reckitt a different form of **Rickett**
— **Reckitt and Colman** a British manufacturer of domestic products, formed in 1938 by the merger of Isaac Reckitt & Sons (see below) with Colman's of Norwich. In 1999 it merged with the Dutch firm Benckiser NV to become Reckitt Benckiser.
— **Reckitt's blue** the proprietary name (registered in 1877) of a type of blue substance used in laundering to prevent white materials turning yellow, produced by the Yorkshire firm of starch manufacturers Isaac Reckitt & Sons

Redcliffe a different form of **Ratcliff**
— **Redcliffe-Maud Report** a report of a commission (1966–69) on British local government and county boundary changes, chaired by John Maud (Lord Redcliffe-Maud), 1906–82

Reddick 'person from Rerwick or Rerrick', Dumfries and Galloway (perhaps 'robbers' outlying settlement') (see also **Riddick, Roddick**), or 'person from Redwick', Gloucestershire ('dairy farm among the reeds')

Redding see **Reading**

Reddington probably 'person from Reading' (see **Reading**)

Reddish 'person from Reddish', Lancashire ('reed ditch'), or 'person from Redditch', Worcestershire ('red ditch')

Reddy (i) a Hindu name, from Telugu *reḍi* 'village headman'; (ii) *also* **Reddie** see **Ready[1]**

Redfern, Redfearn 'person from Redfern', Greater Manchester ('place growing with red bracken')

Redford a different form of **Radford** [Robert Redford, 1937–, US actor, producer and director]

Redgrave 'person from Redgrave', Suffolk (either 'reedy ditch' or 'red grove') [Corin Redgrave, 1939–, British actor, son of Michael; Jemma Redgrave (original name Jemima Redgrave), 1965–, British actress, daughter of Corin; Lynn Redgrave, 1944–, British actress, daughter of Michael; Sir Michael Redgrave, 1908–85, British actor; Sir Steven Redgrave, 1962–, British oarsman; Vanessa Redgrave, 1937–, British actress, daughter of Michael]

Redhead from a medieval nickname for someone with red hair [Brian Redhead, 1929–94, British author, journalist and broadcaster]

Redman (i) a different form of **Read** (i); (ii) a translation of **Rothmann**

Redmayne 'person from Redmain', Cumbria (perhaps 'red cairn')

Redmond from Irish Gaelic *Ó Réamoinn* 'descendant of *Réamonn*', an Irish form of **Raymond** [John Redmond, 1856–1918, Irish politician; Phil Redmond, 1949–, British writer and television producer]

Redpath 'person from Redpath', Borders ('red path'). See also **Ridpath**

Redwood 'person from Redwood', the name of an unidentified place probably in southern England ('red wood') [John Redwood, 1951–, British Conservative politician]

Reece see **Rhys**

Reed see **Read**

Reeder see **Reader**

Reedie, Reedy see **Ready[2]**

Reekie perhaps 'person from Reikie', Aberdeenshire, or from a different form of the Scottish male personal name *Rikie*, literally 'little **Richard**'

Rees, Reese see **Rhys**

Reeve 'steward, bailiff' (from Middle English *reeve*) [Christopher Reeve, 1952–2004, US actor, noted for his portrayal of 'Superman']

Reeves (i) 'son of **Reeve**'; (ii) 'person who lives at the edge of a wood' (the initial *r* comes from the misdivision of Middle English *atter eaves* 'at the edge') [George Reeves (original name George Brewer), 1914–59, US actor, the original television 'Superman'; Jim Reeves, 1923–64, US country singer; Keanu Reeves, 1964–, Lebanon-born Canadian actor; Kynaston Reeves, 1893–1971, British actor; Vic Reeves (original name Jim Moir), 1959–, British comedian; William Pember Reeves, 1857–1932, New Zealand politician and writer]
— **Reeves** a British manufacturer of artist's paints, founded in London in 1766 by William Reeves

Regan, Reagan from Irish Gaelic *Ó Riagáin* 'descendant of *Riagán*', a personal name of uncertain origin and meaning. *Regan* is standardly pronounced 'reegən', *Reagan* as 'raygən' or 'reegən'. See also **Ryan** [Jack Regan, the jack-the-laddish detective inspector (played by John Thaw) in the ITV police drama series *The*

Sweeney (1975–78); Ronald Reagan, 1911–2004, US actor and Republican politician, president 1981–89]

— **Reaganomics** the free-market economic policies espoused by US President Ronald Reagan (see above), involving cuts in taxes and social spending together with deregulation of domestic markets

Rego 'person who lives by a ditch or drainage channel' (from Portuguese *rego* 'ditch') [Paula Rego, 1935–, Portuguese-born British artist]

Reich (i) from a shortened form of a Germanic compound personal name containing the element *rīhhi* 'power, might'; (ii) from a medieval German and Jewish nickname for a rich or powerful man (from Middle High German *rīch* 'powerful, rich') [Steve Reich, 1936–, US composer; Wilhelm Reich, 1897–1957, Austrian-born US psychiatrist]

Reid see **Read**

Reidy see **Ready**[2]

Reilly, Riley from the Irish Gaelic personal name *Raghailleach*, of unknown origin and meaning. See also **O'Reilly** [Bridget Riley, 1931–, British painter; Sidney Reilly (original name Salomon Rosenblum), ?1873–1925, Russian-born British spy]

— **the life of Riley/Reilly** a life of luxury. The identity of the original Riley (or Reilly) is unknown. Late 19th-century music-hall songs contain references to a character of that name, but the earliest recorded instance of the phrase is in Harry Pease's 'My Name is Kelly' (1919):

Faith and my name is Kelly, Michael Kelly,
But I'm living the life of Reilly just the same.

— **Old Mother Riley** the stage persona (a garrulous old washerwoman) of the music-hall comedian Arthur Lucan (original name Arthur Towle), 1887–1954. The act's heyday was the 1930s.

— **Riley Motors** a British car manufacturer which originated in Coventry as the Riley Cycle Co., established in 1890 by William Riley, Jr., died 1944. It produced its first cars in 1905. The marque disappeared in 1969.

Reinhardt, Reinhard, Reinhart from a Germanic male personal name meaning literally 'counsel-brave' [Max Reinhardt (original name Max Goldmann), 1873–1943, Austrian-born US film director]

Reith[1] perhaps a shortened form of *McCreath*, a different form of **McCrae** [Sir John Reith (Lord Reith), 1889–1971, British broadcasting executive, first director-general of the BBC]

— **Reith Lectures** an annual series of radio lectures given by an expert in a particular field and broadcast on the BBC. Established in 1947, they were named in honour of Lord Reith (see above).

Reith[2] a different form of **Reuter** (i)

Relph, Relf from the Old French male personal name *Riulf*, of Germanic origin and meaning literally 'power-wolf'

Remick, Remmick (i) from a different form of the German surname *Remig*, from a personal name derived from Latin *Remigius*; (ii) an anglicization of the Slovenian surname *Remic*, from a nickname

derived from *remec*, the name of a type of small bird [Lee Remick, 1935–91, US actress]

Remington a different form of **Rimmington** [Eliphalet Remington, 1793–1863, US inventor and gun manufacturer]

— **Remington Rand** a US manufacturer of typewriters, computers, firearms and electric shavers. It had its beginnings in E. Remington & Sons, founded in New York in 1816 by Eliphalet Remington (see above) to make the rifle he invented. It went into typewriters in 1873. It ceased to exist in 1986, although a successor firm still makes Remington shavers.

Renaud, Renault from the Old French male personal name *Renault*, of Germanic origin and meaning literally 'counsel-rule' (the equivalent of English **Reynold**). See also **Reno** [Mary Renault, the pen-name of Mary Challans, 1905–83, British historical novelist]

Rendall, Rendell, Rendle different forms of **Randall** [Ruth Rendell (Baroness Rendell; *née* Grasemann), 1930–, British crime novelist]

Renison 'son of **Rainey**'

Rennie a Scottish variant of **Rainey** [John Rennie, 1761–1812, British civil engineer; Michael Rennie (original name Eric Alexander Rennie), 1909–71, British actor]

— **Rennies** the proprietary name of a type of indigestion tablet, developed by the Yorkshireman John Rennie

Reno an alteration of **Renaud**

— **Reno** a city in western Nevada, USA, founded around 1860 and named in honour of the Union general Jesse Lee Reno, 1823–62

Renshaw 'person from Renishaw', Derbyshire ('Reynold's copse')

Renton 'person from Renton', Borders ('Regna's settlement')

— **Renton** a town in West Dunbartonshire, Scotland, founded in 1782 by the local Smollett family, of which the novelist Tobias Smollett was a member, and named by his sister, Jean Telfer, after her daughter-in-law Cecilia Renton

Rentoul a different form of **Rintoul**

Renwick 'person from Renwick', Cumbria ('Hrafn's dwelling'). The name is standardly pronounced 'rennik'.

Repton 'person from Repton', Derbyshire ('hill of the Hreope', a tribe of which nothing is known) [Humphry Repton, 1752–1818, British landscape gardener]

Restorick 'person from Restowrack', farm in Cornwall ('watery hill-spur')

Reuben, Ruben, Rubin from the Hebrew male personal name *Reuven*, traditionally interpreted as 'behold the son'. The variants *Ruben* and particularly *Rubin* were probably influenced by *rubin*, the word for 'ruby' in German, Yiddish and many Slavic languages. See also **Rubinstein** [Jerry Rubin, 1938–94, US social activist]

— **Reuben sandwich** a hot sandwich containing corned beef, Swiss cheese and sauerkraut, said to have been named after Arnold Reuben, 1883–1970, a US restaurant owner

Reuter, Reuther (i) 'person who lives in or by a woodland clearing' (from Middle High German *riute* 'clearing'); (ii) from a medieval German nickname for a mugger or highwayman (from Middle High German *riutære* 'mugger, highwayman'); (iii) a Jewish name perhaps derived from one or both of the German names [Paul Julius Reuter (Baron von Reuter; original name Israel Beer Josephat), 1816–99, German-born British journalist]

— **Reuters** a London-based news agency providing international news reports. It grew from a telegraph office opened in London in 1851 by P.J. Reuter (see above).

Revell, Revel, Revill, Reville from a medieval nickname for someone who is full of noisy enthusiasm and energy (from Middle English *revel* 'festivity, tumult')

Revere (i) from a medieval nickname for a robber (from Middle English *revere* 'robber'); (ii) 'person who lives on the brow of a hill', or 'person from River or Rivar', the name of various places in England (in both cases the initial *r* comes from the misdivision of Middle English *atter evere* 'at the edge'); (iii) an anglicization of French *Rivière* or *Rivoire*, 'person who lives by the banks of a river' (from French *rivier* 'bank') [Paul Revere, 1735–1818, American silversmith and patriot]

Rey (i) see **Ray**; (ii) 'servant of the king', or from a medieval Spanish nickname for someone who behaved in a regal manner, or who played the king in a pageant or festivity (from Spanish *rey* 'king')

Reyes (i) a plural variant of **Rey** (ii); (ii) a Castilian Spanish form of the Portuguese and Galician surname *Reis*, a shortening of *dos Reis* 'of the (Three) Kings'

Reynold from the male personal name *Reynold*, originally brought into England in the form of Old Norse *Rögnvaldr* (see **Ronald**), and later reinforced by the related Norman *Reinald* or *Reynaud*

Reynolds 'son of **Reynold**' [Albert Reynolds, 1932–, Irish Fianna Fáil politician, taoiseach 1992–94; Burt Reynolds, 1936–, US actor; Debbie Reynolds (original name Mary Frances Reynolds), 1932–, US actress; Sir Joshua Reynolds, 1723–92, British painter]

— **Reynolds number** a number (symbol *Re*) used to indicate the flow of fluid through a pipe or round an obstruction. It is named after the Irish physicist Osborne Reynolds, 1842–1912.

Rhodes, Rhoades, Roads, Roades 'person who lives in or by a woodland clearing' (from Old English *rod* 'clearing, glade'). The spelling *Rhodes* has been influenced by that of the Greek island *Rhodes*. See also **Rodd** [Cecil Rhodes, 1853–1902, British-born South African financier and statesman; Gary Rhodes, 1960–, British chef; Wilfred Rhodes, 1877–1973, English cricketer; Zandra Rhodes, 1940–, British fashion designer]

● Men with the surname Rhodes are traditionally given the nickname 'Dusty' (punning on *roads*)

— **Rhodesia** the name, commemorating Cecil Rhodes (see above), of former British territories in East Africa: Northern Rhodesia (now Zambia) and Southern Rhodesia (now Zimbabwe)

— **Rhodes scholarship** a sum of money awarded annually to students from the United States, South Africa and several Commonwealth countries to help pay for studies at Oxford University. The fund was endowed by Cecil Rhodes.

Rhys, Reece, Rees, Reese from the Old Welsh male personal name *Rīs*, literally 'fieriness, ardour'. See also **Breeze** (ii), **Rice** [Dai Rees, 1913–83, British golfer; Jean Rhys, pen-name of Ellen Gwendolen Rees Williams, 1894–1979, Caribbean-born British writer; Sir Martin Rees (Lord Rees), 1942–, British astronomer; Merlyn Rees (Lord Merlyn-Rees), 1920–2006, British Labour politician; Roger Rees, 1944–, British actor; Sir William Rees-Mogg (Lord Rees-Mogg), 1928–, British journalist]

— **Reese's Pieces** the brand name of a type of peanut-butter-flavoured sugar-coated sweet resembling a Smartie that is manufactured by the US Hershey company. Their name commemorates H.B. Reese, 1879–1956, who around 1928 created their forerunner 'Reese's Peanut Butter Cups' and whose company later merged with Hershey's.

Rice a different form of **Rhys** [Anne Rice (original name Howard Allen O'Brien [sic]), 1941–, US horror/fantasy writer; Anneka Rice (original name Annie Rice), 1958–, British television presenter; Archie Rice, the faded music-hall comedian in John Osborne's *The Entertainer* (1957); Condoleeza Rice, 1954–, US national security adviser and secretary of state, 2005–; Elmer Rice (original name Elmer Reizenstein), 1892–1967, US playwright; Mandy Rice-Davies, 1944–, British courtesan; Sir Tim Rice, 1944–, British librettist]

Rich (i) from a medieval nickname for a wealthy person (or, ironically, for a poor one); (ii) from the medieval personal name *Rich*, a shortened form of **Richard**. See also **Rickett, Ritchie, Ritson, Rix, Rixon**; (iii) 'person from Riche', a lost village in Lincolnshire ('drainage channel') [John Rich, ?1692–1761, English theatrical producer; Richard Rich, ?1496–1567, English lawyer, lord chancellor 1547–51]

Richard from the male personal name *Richard*, of Germanic origin and meaning literally 'power-brave'. See also **Rickard** [Sir Cliff Richard (original name Harry Webb), 1940–, British pop singer and entertainer; Ivor Richard (Lord Richard), 1932–, British lawyer and Labour politician; Wendy Richard, 1946–, British actress]

Richards 'son of **Richard**' [Barry Richards, 1945–, South African cricketer; Frank Richards, pen-name of Charles Hamilton, 1876–1961, British children's writer; Sir Gordon Richards, 1904–88, British jockey; I.A. Richards, 1893–1979, British critic, poet and teacher; Keith Richards, 1943–, British rock musician, Rolling Stones guitarist; Mark Richards, 1957–, Australian surfer; Sir Vivian Richards, 1952–, West Indian cricketer]

Richardson 'son of **Richard**' [Charlie Richardson, 1934–, British gangster; Henry Handel Richardson, pen-name of Ethel Florence Lindesay Richardson, 1870–1946, Australian novelist; Henry Hobson Richardson, 1838–86, US architect; Ian Richardson, 1934–2007, British actor; Miranda Richardson, 1958–, British actress; Sir Ralph Richardson, 1902–83, British actor; Samuel Richardson, 1689–1761, British novelist; Tony Richardson, 1928–91, British film director]
— **Richardsonian** of or in the style of the novelist Samuel Richardson (see above)
— **Richardson's equation** an equation that gives the maximum current density of electrons emitted by a hot metal surface in terms of its temperature and work function. Its name is that of the British physicist Sir Owen Richardson, 1879-1959.
— **Richardson's ground squirrel** a North American ground squirrel (*Citellus richardsoni*) that can be a pest of grain crops. It was named after the Scottish naturalist and explorer Sir John Richardson, 1787–1865.
— **Richardson's number** a dimensionless number given by the ratio of the fluid density gradient to the square of the velocity gradient. It is named after the British physicist Lewis Fry Richardson, 1881-1953.
— **Richardson's owl** an alternative name for the Arctic owl (*Ægolius funerea richardsoni*). It commemorates Sir John Richardson (see above).

Richie see **Ritchie**

Richman (i) a different form of **Rich** (i) or of **Richmond**; (ii) 'servant of a wealthy man'; (iii) an anglicization of German *Richmann*, from a Germanic personal name meaning literally 'powerful man'. See also **Rickman**

Richmond 'person from Richmond', the name of various places in England and northern France ('strong hill') [Fiona Richmond, 1945–, British glamour model and actress]

Richter (i) 'judge, arbiter, village headman' (from Middle High German *rihtære* 'judge'); (ii) 'rabbinic judge' (from German *Richter* 'judge')
— **Richter scale** a scale from 1 to 10 used to measure the severity of earthquakes according to the amount of energy released. It is named after the US seismologist Charles Francis Richter, 1900–85.

Rickard a different form of **Richard**

Rickards 'son of **Rickard**'

Rickett 'little *Rick*', a different form of **Rich** (ii). See also **Reckitt**

Ricketts 'son of **Rickett**' [Charles Ricketts, 1866–1931, British illustrator, designer and painter]
— **rickettsia** a parasitic bacterium (order Rickettsiales) that typically lives inside ticks and can be transmitted to humans, causing Rocky Mountain spotted fever, certain forms of typhus and other diseases. It is named after the US pathologist H.T. Ricketts, 1871–1910, who died of typhus while investigating the cause of the disease.

Rickman (i) from the Old English male personal name *Rīcmund*, literally 'rich protection'; (ii) a

different form of **Richman** [Alan Rickman, 1946–, British actor]

Ricks, **Rickson** see **Rix**, **Rixon**

Riddell, **Riddel**, **Riddle**, **Riddall** (i) from the Norman personal name *Ridel*, probably of Germanic origin and based on *rīd* 'ride'; (ii) 'person from Ryedale', Yorkshire ('valley of the River Rye') [Nelson Riddle, 1921–85, US bandleader and arranger]

Riddick a different form of **Reddick**

Rideout, **Ridout** 'outrider (a municiple or monastic official in the Middle Ages whose job was to ride around the country collecting dues and supervising manors)'

Rider, **Ryder** (i) 'mounted warrior or messenger'; (ii) 'person who lives in a woodland clearing' (from a derivative of Old English *rīed*, *rȳd* 'clearing, glade') [Alex Rider, teenage secret agent in the books of Anthony Horowitz; Charles Ryder, narrator and central character of Evelyn Waugh's *Brideshead Revisited* (1945); Steve Rider, 1950–, British television presenter; Sue Ryder (Baroness Ryder), 1923–2000, British philanthropist]
— **Ryder Cup** a biennial contest for a golfing trophy presented in 1927 by the British seed merchant Samuel Ryder, 1856–1936. The original participants were Britain and the US; Ireland joined Britain in 1973, and Europe took over from them in 1979.

Ridge 'person who lives on or by a ridge', or 'person from Ridge', the name of various places in England (in either case from Middle English *rigge* 'ridge'). See also **Rigby**, **Rigg**, **Riggs**, **Rigsby**, **Rudge**

Ridgeway, **Ridgway** 'person who lives on or by a ridgeway (a track running along the top of a line of hills)', or 'person from Ridgeway', the name of various places in England
— **Ridgways** a brand of tea established by Thomas Ridgway, who opened a tea shop in London in 1836

Riding a different form of **Reading** (ii) [Laura Riding (original name Laura Reichenthal), 1901–91, US poet]

Ridley 'person from Ridley', the name of numerous places in England (variously 'woodland glade with a water channel' or 'glade growing with reeds') [Arnold Ridley, 1896–1984, British actor and playwright; Nicholas Ridley, ?1500–55, Anglican reformer and martyr; Nicholas Ridley, 1929–93, British Conservative politician]

Ridout see **Rideout**

Ridpath a different form of **Redpath**

Ridsdale 'person from Ridsdale or Redesdale', Northumberland ('valley of the river Rede')

Rifkin 'son of *Rifke*', a Yiddish female personal name, from Hebrew *Rivka* (literally 'heifer'; anglicized as *Rebecca*) [Joshua Rifkin, 1944–, US conductor]

Rifkind a different form of **Rifkin**, influenced by German *Kind* 'child' [Sir Malcolm Rifkind, 1946–, British Conservative politician]

Rigby 'person from Rigby', Lancashire ('settlement on a ridge')
— **'Eleanor Rigby'** a song by John Lennon and Paul McCartney which appeared on the Beatles' 1966 album *Revolver*. 'Eleanor Rigby' is a lonely spinster who dies alone. Her surname may have been borrowed from the name of a Bristol clothes shop, or alternatively the inspiration may have been a real-life Eleanor Rigby, 1895–1939, who lived in Liverpool.

Rigg a northern variant of **Ridge** [Dame Diana Rigg, 1938–, British actress]

Riggs a different form of **Rigg** [Bobby Riggs, 1918–95, US tennis player]

Rigley see **Wrigley**

Rigsby 'person from Rigsby', Lincolnshire [Rupert Rigsby, the egregious landlord (played by Leonard Rossiter) in the ITV sitcom *Rising Damp* (1974–78)]

Riley (i) see **Reilly**; (ii) *also* **Ryley** 'person from Ryley', Lancashire ('woodland clearing growing with rye')

Rimmer 'composer or reciter of rhymes (verses)' (from a derivative of Middle English *rimen* 'to versify')

Rimmington, **Rimington** 'person from Rimmington', Yorkshire ('settlement on the boundary stream'). See also **Remington** [Dame Stella Rimington, 1935–, British spymaster and author]

Ring 'maker of rings, especially finger-rings'

Rintoul 'person from Rintoul', a lost village in Perth and Kinross. See also **Rentoul**

Riordan, Rearden, Reardon a shortened form of **O'Riordan** [Ray Reardon, 1932–, Welsh snooker player]

Ripley 'person from Ripley', the name of various places in England ('woodland clearing in the form of a strip') [Tom Ripley, the charming psychopath created by Patricia Highsmith, originally in *The Talented Mr Ripley* (1956)]

Ripper 'maker, seller or carrier of baskets' (from a derivative of Middle English *rip* 'basket')

Rippon 'person from Ripon', Yorkshire ('place in the territory of the Hrype (a tribal name)') [Angela Rippon, 1944–, British television presenter and newsreader]

Ritchie, Richie 'little **Rich** (ii)' [Guy Ritchie, 1968–, British film director; Lionel Richie, 1949–, US rhythm-and-blues singer-songwriter]

Ritson 'son of **Rich** (ii)'

Rivera 'person from Rivera', the name of numerous places in Spain ('place on the banks of a river')

Rivers 'person from Rivières', the name of various places in northern France ('place on the banks of a river') [Augustus Henry Lane-Fox Pitt-Rivers, see **Pitt**; Joan Rivers (original name Joan Sandra Molinsky), 1933–, US comedian]

Rivett 'metalworker' (from Middle English *rivet* 'small nail')

Rix, Ricks (i) 'son of *Rick*', a different form of **Rich** (ii); (ii) 'person who lives on land where rushes grow' (from Old English *rixe* 'rush') [Brian Rix (Lord Rix), 1924–, British actor and charity executive]

Rixon, Rickson 'son of *Rick*', a different form of **Rich** (ii)

Roach, Roache, Roche 'person who lives in a rocky place' (from Old French *roche* 'rock') [Hal Roach, 1892–1992, US film producer; Tony Roche, 1945–, Australian tennis player; William Roache, 1932–, British actor]

Roads, Roades see **Rhodes**

Roan (i) 'person from Rouen', France; (ii) a different form of **Ruane**

Robards a different form of **Roberts** [Jason Robards, 1922–2000, US actor]

Robarts a different form of **Roberts**

Robb from the male personal name *Rob*, a shortened form of **Robert**. See also **Robson, Roby** (ii)

Robbie see **Roby** (ii)

Robbins, Robins 'son of **Robin** (i)' [Frederick Chapman Robbins, 1916–2003, US paediatrician and virologist; Jerome Robbins, 1918–98, US ballet dancer and choreographer; Lionel Robbins (Lord Robbins), 1898–1984, British economist]

Roberson a different form of **Robertson**

Robert from the male personal name *Robert*, of Germanic origin and meaning literally 'renown-bright'. See also **Rupert**

Roberts 'son of **Robert**' [Frederick Sleigh Roberts (Earl Roberts), 1832–1914, British field marshal; Julia Roberts, 1967–, US actress; Tom Roberts, 1856–1931, British-born Australian painter]

Robertson 'son of **Robert**'. See also **Roberson** [Fyfe Robertson, 1902–87, British television journalist; George Robertson (Lord Robertson), 1946–, British Labour politician; R.C. Robertson-Glasgow, 1901–65, British cricketer and writer]
— **James Robertson & Sons** a British firm of marmalade and jam manufacturers, founded in Paisley, Scotland by the grocer James Robertson in 1864. It became famous for its 'golliwog' mascot.
— **Robertson's law** a law stating that the number of chromosome arms of a population or species tends to remain constant, although the number of chromosomes may vary. It is named after the US biologist William R. B. Robertson, 1881–1941.

Robeson a different form of **Robson** [Paul Robeson, 1898–1976, US singer and actor]

Robey from a pet-form of **Robert** [Sir George Robey (original name George Edward Wade), 1869–1954, British music-hall comedian and actor]

Robin, Robbin (i) from the male personal name *Robin*, a pet-form of **Robert**; (ii) a different form of **Rabin**

Robins see **Robbins**

Robinson 'son of **Robin** (i)' [Anne Robinson, 1944–, British journalist and television presenter;

Edward Arlington Robinson, 1869–1935, US poet; Edward G. Robinson (original name Emmanuel Goldenberg), 1893–1973, US actor; Henry Crabb Robinson, 1775–1867, British lawyer, diarist and correspondent; Jackie Robinson, 1919–72, US baseball player and civil-rights activist; Jancis Robinson, 1950–, British wine writer; John Robinson, 1919–83, British churchman and theologian; Mary Robinson (*née* Bourke), 1944–, Irish lawyer and stateswoman, president of Ireland 1990–97; Sir Robert Robinson, 1886–1975, British chemist; Robert Robinson, 1927–, British journalist and radio and television presenter; Sugar Ray Robinson (original name Walker Smith), 1921–89, US boxer; Tony Robinson, 1946–, British actor and television presenter; William Heath Robinson, 1872–1944, British cartoonist]

— **before you can say Jack Robinson** very quickly; in no time. The expression is first recorded in 1778. An actual man of that name who might have given rise to it has never been securely identified; attempts to do so (e.g. by Francis Grose, who in his *Dictionary of the Vulgar Tongue* (1811) cites 'a very volatile gentleman of that appellation, who would call on his neighbours, and be gone before his name could be announced') smack of desperate invention.

— **Heath Robinson** constructed or improvised in a way that looks ramshackle and wildly implausible, especially through being overelaborate or overingenious, as in the humorous drawings of bizarre or surreal machinery by W. Heath Robinson (see above).

— **Jackie Robinson** in mid-20th-century US slang, a black person who is the first to enter his or her profession. The expression was inspired by Jackie Robinson (see above), who in 1947 became the first black man to play in major-league baseball.

— **Peter Robinson** a clothing store opened in Oxford Street, central London in 1833 by a Yorkshire draper called Peter Robinson

— **Robinson College** a college of Cambridge University, founded in 1977. It was named in honour of its endower, the British entrepreneur Sir David Robinson, 1904–87.

— **Robinson's Barley Water** a brand of sweet cordial made from water, barley extract and sugar, introduced in 1823 by the firm of Keen, Robinson, Bellville Ltd. It began to be marketed under the name 'Robinson's' at the beginning of the 20th century.

Robledo 'person from Robledo', the name of various places in Spain ('oak wood')

Robles 'person who lives by a group of oak trees', or 'person from Los Robles', Spain (in either case from Spanish *robles* 'oaks')

Robotham see **Rowbottom**

Robson 'son of *Rob*' (see **Robb**). See also **Robeson** [Sir Bobby Robson, 1933–, English football manager; Bryan Robson, 1957–, English footballer; Dame Flora Robson, 1902–84, British actress]

Roby (i) 'person from Roby', Lancashire ('settlement by a boundary marker'); (ii) *also* **Robie** *or* **Robbie** 'little *Rob*' (see **Robb**)

Roche see **Roach**

Rochester 'person from Rochester', Kent (probably 'Roman town or fort called Rovi'). See also **Rossiter** [Mr Rochester, the Byronic hero of Charlotte Brontë's *Jane Eyre* (1847)]

Rochford 'person from Rochford', Essex and Worcestershire ('ford of the hunting dog')

Rock, Rocke (i) 'person who lives in a rocky place', or 'person from Rock', the name of various places in England ('place by the rock'); (ii) 'person who lives by an oak tree' (the initial *r* comes from the misdivision of Middle English *atter oke* 'at the oak'); (iii) 'spinner of wool' or 'maker of distaffs (rods on which wool is wound)' (from Middle English *rok* 'distaff'). See also **Rooker**

Rockefeller 'person from Rockenfeld', Rhineland ('open country growing with rye') [John D. Rockefeller, 1839–1937, US millionaire industrialist and philanthropist, founder of Standard Oil; Nelson Rockefeller, 1908–79, US Republican politician, vice-president 1974–77, grandson of John]

— **Rockefeller Center** a complex of 19 commercial buildings in Midtown Manhattan, New York City, developed between 1929 and 1940 by John D. Rockefeller, Jr, 1874–1960, son of John D. Rockefeller (see above).

— **Rockefeller University** a university in New York City, founded (as the Rockefeller Institute for Medical Research) in 1901 by John D. Rockefeller and his son, John D. Rockefeller, Jr (see above).

Rockley 'person from Rockley', Nottinghamshire ('glade frequented by rooks')

Rockwell 'person from Rockwell', Buckinghamshire and Somerset (respectively 'wood frequented by rooks' and 'well frequented by rooks') [Norman Rockwell, 1894–1978, US illustrator]

Rodd a different form of **Rhodes**

Roddam 'person from Roddam Hall', Northumberland ('place by woodland clearings'). See also **Roden**

Roddick probably a different form of **Reddick** [Andrew Roddick, 1982–, US tennis player; Dame Anita Roddick (*née* Perilli), 1942–, British businesswoman]

Roden (i) from Irish Gaelic *Ó Rodáin* 'descendant of *Rodán*', a personal name meaning literally 'little lively or high-spirited one'; (ii) a different form of **Roddam**

Roderick (i) from the Norman male personal name *Rodric*, of Germanic origin and meaning literally 'fame-power'. See also **Rodriguez**; (ii) from the Welsh male personal name *Rhydderch*, literally either 'reddish-brown' or 'very famous'. See also **Broderick** (ii), **Prothero**

Rodger, Rodgers see **Roger, Rogers**

Rodney 'person from Rodney', Somerset ('Hroda's island') [George Brydges Rodney (Lord Rodney), 1719–92, British admiral]

Rodriguez an anglicization of Spanish *Rodríguez*, literally 'son of *Rodrigo*', the Spanish equivalent of **Roderick**. See also **Ruiz**

Rodway 'person from Rodway', Somerset ('riding path')

Rodwell 'person from Rodwell', an unidentified place in England (perhaps 'Hroda's stream')

Roe (i) a different form of **Ray** (ii); (ii) 'person from Roe or Røe', the name of various Norwegian farmsteads ('clearing') [Erica Roe, 1958–, British streaker]
— **Avro** a British aircraft manufacturer, founded in 1910 by the aircraft designer A.V. Roe (Alliott Verdon Roe), 1877–1958
— **Richard Roe** in US law, a name given to an unidentified defendant in criminal proceedings

Roebuck from a medieval nickname applied to someone thought to resemble a male roe deer
— **Sears, Roebuck and Company** see **Sears**

Roger, Rodger (i) from the Norman male personal name *Roger* or *Rogier*, of Germanic origin and meaning literally 'fame-spear'. See also **Hodge, Rosser** (i), **Rudge** (ii), **Rutgers**; (ii) from Irish Gaelic *Mac Ruaidhrí* (see **Rory**)

Rogers, Rodgers 'son of **Roger**' [Anton Rodgers, 1933–, British actor; Buddy Rogers (original name Charles Rogers), 1904–99, US actor and matinée idol; Ginger Rogers (original name Virginia McMath), 1911–95, US dancer and actress; John Rogers, ?1500–55, English Protestant martyr; Paul Rogers, 1917–, British actor; Peter Rogers, 1914–, British film director, notable for the *Carry On* films; Richard Rodgers, 1902–79, US composer; Sir Richard Rogers (Lord Rogers), 1933–, British architect; Roy Rogers (original name Leonard Slye), 1911–98, US cowboy actor; Will Rogers (original name William Penn Adair), 1879–1935, US actor and humorist; William Rodgers (Lord Rodgers), 1928–, British Labour, SDP and Liberal Democrat politician]

Rogerson 'son of **Roger**'

Roland see **Rowland**

Rolf, Rolfe, Rolph from the male personal name *Rolf*, originally brought into England in the form of Old Norse *Hrólfr*, literally 'fame-wolf', and later reinforced by the related Norman *Roul* (see **Rollo**). See also **Rudolph** [Anthony Rolfe Johnson, 1940–, British tenor; Frederick Rolfe, 1860–1913, British novelist, also known by the pen-name 'Baron Corvo']
— **Rolfing** a proprietary name for a type of therapy involving vigorous massage to alleviate physical or psychological tension, as developed by the US physiotherapist Ida P. Rolf, 1897–1979.

Roll, Rolle different forms of **Rollo** [Richard Rolle, ?1300–49, English mystical writer]

Rollason 'son of little **Rollo**'

Rollins 'son of little **Rollo**' [Sonny Rollins (original name Theodore Walter Rollins), 1930–, US jazz saxophonist]

Rollison 'son of little **Rollo**'

Rollo from a medieval Latinized form of the Norman male personal name *Roul* (see **Rolf**). See also **Rowe** (ii), **Rowling, Rule** (i)

Rolls 'son of **Rollo**' [Charles Stewart Rolls, 1877–1910, British car manufacturer and aviator]
— **Rolls-Royce** a British manufacturer of high-quality cars and of aero engines, founded in 1906 by Charles Rolls (see above) and Sir Henry Royce (see **Royce**)

Rolph see **Rolf**

Rolston 'person from Rowlston or Rolleston', the name of various places (variously spelled) in England (mainly 'Hrólfr's farmstead' or 'Hrōthwulf's farmstead')

Romain, Romaine, Romayn, Romayne different forms of **Roman**

Roman (i) 'person from Rome, or who had been on a pilgrimage to Rome'; (ii) from the Latin male personal name *Rōmānus*, literally 'person from Rome'. See also **Room**

Romero from a medieval Spanish nickname for a pilgrim (from Spanish *romero* 'pilgrim (to Rome)') [Cesar Romero, 1907–94, Cuban-American actor]

Romilly 'person from Romilly or Remilly', the name of various places in northern France ('Romilius's settlement'), or 'person from Romiley', Greater Manchester ('spacious woodland clearing')

Romney, Rumney 'person from Romney', Kent ('district of the broad river') [George Romney, 1734–1802, British portrait painter]

Ronald from the Gaelic male personal name *Raonull*, from Old Norse *Rögnvaldr*, literally 'counsel-rule'. See also **Reynold** [Sir Landon Ronald (original name Landon Ronald Russell), 1873–1938, British conductor and composer]

Ronan from Irish Gaelic *Ó Rónáin* 'descendant of *Rónán*', a personal name perhaps meaning literally 'little seal'

Ronane, Ronayne different forms of **Ronan**

Ronson a different form of **Rowlandson**
— **The Ronson Corporation** a US manufacturer of cigarette lighters, founded in New York City in 1886 by Louis V. Aronson.

Rook, Rooke from a medieval nickname for someone thought to resemble a rook (e.g. in having black hair or a harsh voice). See also **Ruck**

Rooker a different form of **Rock** (iii) [Jeff Rooker (Lord Rooker), 1941–, British Labour politician]

Room a different form of **Roman** (i)

Rooney from Irish Gaelic *Ó Ruanaidh* 'descendant of *Ruanaidh*', a nickname meaning literally 'champion'. See also **Rowney** (ii) [Mickey Rooney (original name Joseph Yule, Jr.), 1920–, US actor; Wayne Rooney, 1985–, English footballer]

Roope, Roop 'maker or seller of rope'

Roose a different form of **Ross** (i)

Roosevelt 'person who lives in an area of land overgrown with roses' (from Dutch *roose* 'rose' + *velt* 'open country') [Eleanor Roosevelt (original name Anna Eleanor Roosevelt), 1884–1962, US first lady, social activist and writer, wife of Franklin and niece of Theodore; Franklin Delano Roosevelt, 1882–1945, US Democratic politician, president 1933–45; Theodore Roosevelt, 1858–1919, US Republican politician, president 1901–09]

Root (i) from a medieval nickname for a cheerful person (from Middle English *rote* 'glad'); (ii) 'player of the rote (a medieval stringed instrument played by plucking)'. See also **Rutter** (i); (iii) 'person who lives by a place where flax is retted (soaked in water to release its fibres)' (from Dutch *root*, a derivative of *rooten* 'to ret') [Elihu Root, 1845–1937, US lawyer and statesman; Henry Root, the pen-name of William Donaldson as the author of a series of spoof letters to well-known people, originally collected in *The Henry Root Letters* (1980)]

Rootes, Roots 'son of **Root** (i)'
— **Rootes Group** a British motor manufacturer, essentially an umbrella company for other marques (e.g. Hillman and Humber), founded in 1919 as a car-sales company by William Rootes (Lord Rootes), 1894–1964. It was taken over by Chrysler in 1967.

Roper (i) 'maker or seller of rope'; (ii) from a northeastern French variant of **Robert**

Rorke see **Rourke**

Rory, Rorie from the Gaelic personal name *Ruaidhrí*, literally 'powerful rule'. See also **McCreary, McCrory**

Roscoe 'person from Roscoe', Lancashire ('copse frequented by roe deer')

Rose (i) 'person who lives in a place where roses grow abundantly', or 'person who lives in a house with the sign of a rose'; (ii) from a medieval nickname for someone with a rosy complexion; (iii) an invented Jewish name based on German *Rose* 'rose'; (iv) a different form of **Royce** (i). See also **Ruskin** (i); (v) 'son of *Royze*', a Yiddish female personal name meaning literally 'rose'. See also **Ross** (v)
— **Rose's Lime Juice** a brand of lime-juice based cordial formulated by Lauchlin Rose, 1829–85, and produced by his firm, L. Rose & Co. of Leith, Edinburgh, from 1865.

Roseman (i) from the Norman female personal name *Rosemunde*, of Germanic origin and meaning literally probably 'horse-protection', but popularly associated in the Middle Ages with Latin *rosa munda* 'pure rose' (an epithet of the Virgin Mary); (ii) 'husband of *Royze*' (see **Rose** (v))

Rosemond a different form of **Roseman** (i)

Rosen, Rozen (i) 'person from Rosen', Germany ('place where roses grow'); (ii) an invented Jewish name based on German *Rosen* 'roses' [Charles Rosen, 1927–, US pianist]

Rosenberg, Rozenberg (i) 'person from Rosenberg', the name of various places in Germany ('rose mountain'); (ii) an invented Jewish name based on German *Rose* 'rose' + *Berg* 'mountain' [Julius Rosenberg, 1918–53, US Soviet spy]

Rosenblatt (i) from a medieval German nickname based on Middle High German *rösenblat* 'rose leaf'; (ii) an invented Jewish name based on German *Rosenblatt* 'rose leaf'

Rosenblum, Rosenbloom an invented Jewish name based on German *Rose* 'rose' and *Blume* 'flower'

Rosenfeld, Rozenfeld (i) 'person from Rosenfeld', Germany ('field of roses'); (ii) an invented Jewish name based on German *Rosenfeld* 'field of roses'

Rosenthal (i) 'person from Rosenthal or Rosendahl', Germany ('valley of roses'); (ii) an invented Jewish name based on German *Rosental* 'valley of roses' [Jack Rosenthal, 1931–2004, British screenwriter; Jim Rosenthal, 1947–, British television sports presenter; Norman Rosenthal, 1944–, British art expert]

Rosewall 'person from Rosewall', Cornwall (perhaps 'rampart by the ford') [Ken Rosewall, 1934–, Australian tennis player]

Ross, Ros (i) 'person from Ross or Roos', the name of various places in England and Scotland (probably 'upland, moorland'). See also **Roose**; (ii) 'person from Rots', Normandy (perhaps 'woodland clearing'); (iii) 'breeder or keeper of horses', or from a medieval German nickname for someone thought to resemble a horse (in either case from Middle High German *ros* 'horse'); (iv) from the medieval male personal name *Roce*, the Norman version of Germanic *Rozzo*, the first element of various compound names beginning with *hrōd* 'fame'; (v) a different form of **Rose** (iv–v) [Alan Ross, 1922–2001, British poet, journalist and editor; Annie Ross (original name Annabelle Short), 1930–, British-born jazz singer; Diana Ross, 1944–, US pop singer; Edmundo Ros, 1910–, Trinidad-born bandleader; Sir James Clark Ross, 1800–62, British Arctic and Antarctic explorer; Jonathan Ross, 1960–, British radio and television broadcaster; Martin Ross, the pen-name of the Irish writer Violet Martin, 1862–1915 (see **Somerville and Ross**); Sir Ronald Ross, 1857–1932, British bacteriologist, who established that mosquitoes transmit malaria]
— **Ross** a British brand of frozen foods, established by the Grimsby fish merchant J. Carl Ross, 1902–86.
— *Ross* a play (1960) by Terence Rattigan based on the life of T.E. Lawrence (Lawrence of Arabia), who adopted the surname Ross when he joined the RAF incognito in 1922
— **Ross Sea** an arm of the South Pacific Ocean, extending into eastern Antarctica between Victoria Land and Marie Byrd Land, and incorporating the **Ross Ice Shelf**. It was discovered by Sir James Clark Ross (see above).

Rosser (i) a Welsh variant of **Roger** (i); (ii) an anglicization of German *Rösser*, literally 'horse dealer', 'groom' or 'carter' (from a derivative of *Ross* 'horse')

Rossetti 'son of *Rossetto*', a pet-form of the Italian male personal name *Rosso*, originally a medieval nickname for someone with red hair or a red complexion (from *rosso* 'red') [Christina Georgina Rossetti, 1830–74, British poet; Dante Gabriel Rossetti (original name Gabriel Charles Dante Rossetti), 1828–82, British painter and poet, brother of Christina]

Rossi 'son of *Rosso*' (see **Rossetti**)

Rossington 'person from Rossington', Yorkshire ('settlement associated with a moor')

Rossiter a different form of **Rochester** [Leonard Rossiter, 1926–84, British actor]

Roth (i) 'person who lives in a woodland clearing' (from both Old English *rod* and Old High German *rod* 'clearing'); (ii) from a medieval German and Jewish nickname for a red-haired person (from Middle High German *rōt* 'red'); (iii) from the first element of various Germanic compound names beginning with *hrōd* 'fame' [Philip Roth, 1933–, US writer; Tim Roth (original name Timothy Smith), 1961–, British actor]

Rothmann, Rothman (i) 'counsellor, person often turned to for advice' (from Middle High German *rāt* 'advice' + *man* 'man'); (ii) a different form of **Roth**
— **Rothman's of Pall Mall** a tobacconist opened in Pall Mall, London in 1890 by Louis Rothman, 1869–1926

Rothschild 'person who lives in a house with a red sign' (from Middle High German *rōt* 'red' + *schilt* 'shield') [Lionel Nathan Rothschild, 1808–79, British financier, son of Nathan, the first practising Jew to become a British MP; Dame Miriam Rothschild, 1908–2005, British entomologist, great-grandniece of Lionel; Nathan Mayer Rothschild, 1777–1836, German-born British financier; Nathaniel Mayer Victor Rothschild (Lord Rothschild), 1910–90, British zoologist, businessman and government advisor, brother of Miriam]
— **N.M. Rothschild & Sons Ltd.** a British investment bank founded in London in 1809 by Nathan Mayer Rothschild (see above)

Rothwell 'person from Rothwell', the name of various places in England ('spring by the glade'). See also **Rowell** (iii)

Round from a medieval nickname for a fat person. See also **Rundle** (ii) [Dorothy Round, 1909–82, British tennis player]

Roundtree, Rountree see **Rowntree**

Rourke, Rorke from the Irish Gaelic personal name *Ruarc*, perhaps based on *ruarc* 'rain squall'. See also **O'Rourke** [Mickey Rourke (original name Philip Andre Rourke, Jr.), 1956–, US actor]
— **Rorke's Drift** a river in Natal, South Africa, named after James Rorke, a ferryman who had drowned in it. It became famous for the defence of the mission station there by British troops against overwhelming odds during the Anglo-Zulu war of 1879.

Rouse, Rous, Rowse from a medieval nickname for a red-haired person (from Old French *rous* 'red'). See also **Rossetti, Rossi, Rousseau, Russell** [A.L. Rowse, 1903–97, British historian

and literary critic; Sir Stanley Rous, 1895–1986, British football referee and administrator]

Rousseau from a French medieval nickname for a red-haired person (literally 'little red one', from Old French *rous* 'red')

Routh 'person from Routh', Humberside (perhaps 'rough ground') [Jonathan Routh, 1927–, British humorist, presenter of the UK version of *Candid Camera* (1960–67)]

Routledge perhaps 'person from Routledge', an unidentified place in England or Scotland. See also **Rutledge** [Patricia Routledge, 1929–, British actress]
— **Routledge** a British publishing firm, founded as George Routledge & Co. in 1851 by George Routledge, 1812–88. It is now part of the Taylor and Francis group.

Row see **Rowe**

Rowan from Gaelic *Ó Ruadháin* 'descendant of *Ruadhán*', a personal name meaning literally 'little red-haired one'. See also **Ruane**
— **Rowan and Martin's Laugh-In** a fast-moving gag-based US television comedy programme (1968–71) fronted by the comedians Dan Rowan, 1922–87, and Dick Martin, 1923–

Rowbottom, Rowbotham, Robotham 'person who lives in a valley overgrown with vegetation' (from Old English *rōh* 'rough, overgrown' + *bothm* 'valley')

Rowden 'person from Rowden', Herefordshire ('overgrown hill')

Rowe, Row (i) 'person who lives in a row of houses or by a hedgerow'; (ii) from the medieval personal name *Row*, either a shortened form of **Rowland** (i) or a different form of *Roul* (see **Rollo**) [Nicholas Rowe, 1674–1718, British dramatist]

Rowell (i) from the medieval personal name *Rowell*, a pet-form of **Rowe** (ii); (ii) 'person from Rowell', Devon ('hill overgrown with vegetation'); (iii) a different form of **Rothwell**

Rowland, Roland (i) from the Norman male personal name *Rolant*, of Germanic origin and meaning literally 'fame-land'; (ii) 'person from Rowland', Derbyshire and Sussex ('wood frequented by roe deer') [Roland ('Tiny') Rowland (original name Roland Walter Fuhrhop), 1917–98, Indian-born (of Anglo-Dutch and German parents) British businessman]

Rowlands 'son of **Rowland** (i)'

Rowlandson 'son of **Rowland** (i)' [Thomas Rowlandson, 1756–1827, British caricaturist]

Rowley 'person from Rowley', the name of various places in England ('rough clearing') [Thomas Rowley, ?1585–?1642, English dramatist]

Rowling 'little **Rollo**' [J.K. Rowling, 1965–, British author; Sir Wallace Edward ('Bill') Rowling, 1927–95, New Zealand politician, prime minister 1974–75]

Rowney (i) 'person from Rowney', Hertfordshire ('overgrown enclosure'); (ii) a different form of **Rooney**

Rowntree, Roundtree, Rountree 'person who lives by a rowan tree' [Benjamin Seebohm Rowntree, 1871–1954, British manufacturer and philanthropist]
— **Rowntree & Co. Ltd.** a British confectionery company founded in 1869 by the York tea dealer and chocolate manufacturer Henry Isaac Rowntree, died 1883, and his brother Joseph Rowntree, 1836–1925. In 1969 it merged with John Mackintosh & Sons Ltd. to become Rowntree Mackintosh.

Rowse see **Rouse**

Roxburgh 'person from Roxburgh', Borders ('Hrōc's fortress')

Roy (i) from a medieval French nickname for someone who behaved in a regal manner, or who played the king in a pageant or festivity (from Old French *roy* 'king'); (ii) from a medieval Scottish nickname for a red-haired person (from Gaelic *ruadh* 'red'); (iii) a different form of **Ray** (i); (iv) a Hindu name, from Sanskrit *rājā* 'king'

Royce (i) from the medieval female personal name *Royse*, of Germanic origin but subsequently associated with *rose*. See also **Rose** (iv); (ii) an anglicization of the German surname *Reuss*, literally either 'shoe-mender' or 'Russian person' [Sir Henry Royce, 1863–1933, British car manufacturer, co-founder of Rolls-Royce (see **Rolls**); Josiah Royce, 1855–1916, US philosopher]

Royle 'person from Royle', Lancashire ('hill frequented by roe deer'). See also **Ryle** (ii)
— **The Royle Family** a British television situation comedy (1998–2000) based on the humdrum life of a working-class Manchester family

Royston (i) 'person from Royston', Hertfordshire ('village by Rohesia's cross'), or 'person from Royston', Yorkshire ('Hrōr's or Róarr's farmstead'); (ii) an anglicization of various similar-sounding Jewish surnames

Rozen, Rozenberg, Rozenfeld see **Rosen, Rosenberg, Rosenfeld**

Ruane a different form of **Rowan**

Rubbra 'person from Rowborough', Isle of Wight, or any of a range of similarly named places in England (all 'overgrown hill') [Edmund Rubbra, 1901–86, British composer]

Rubin, Ruben see **Reuben**

Rubinstein, Rubenstein an invented Jewish name, literally (in German) 'ruby stone' [Artur Rubinstein, 1887–1982, Polish-born US pianist]

Ruck a different form of **Rook**

Rudd (i) from a medieval nickname for a red-haired or ruddy-cheeked person (from Middle English *rudde* 'red'). See also **Rudkin, Rudman**; (ii) an anglicized shortened form of various Jewish names beginning with *Rud-* (e.g. *Rudnitsky*)

Ruddock from a medieval nickname for someone thought to resemble a robin (from Middle English *ruddock* 'robin')

Rudge (i) 'person who lives on a ridge', or 'person from Rudge', Shropshire (in either case from Middle English *rugge* 'ridge'); (ii) from the medieval personal name *Rudge*, a pet-form of **Roger** (i).

See also **Ruggles**; (iii) from a medieval nickname for a red-haired or ruddy-cheeked person (from Old French *ruge* 'red')
— **Barnaby Rudge** a novel (1841) by Charles Dickens, set in the period of the Gordon anti-popery riots of 1780. Barnaby Rudge is the innocent simpleton at the centre of the swirling and often violent action.

Rudkin 'little **Rudd** (i)' [David Rudkin, 1936–, British playwright]

Rudman a different form of **Rudd** (i)

Rudolph, Rudolf from the Germanic male personal name *Rudolf*, literally 'fame-wolf'. See also **Rolf** [Wilma Rudolph, 1940–94, US athlete]

Ruffin from the medieval French male personal name *Ruffin*, from Latin *Rūfīnus*, a derivative of *Rūfus* (literally 'red-haired one') [Jimmy Ruffin, 1939–, US soul singer]

Ruggles 'son of little *Rudge*' (see **Rudge** (ii)) [Carl Ruggles, 1876–1971, US composer]

Ruiz 'son of *Ruy*', a Spanish male personal name that is a shortened form of *Rodrigo* (see **Rodriguez**)

Rule (i) from the medieval male personal name *Rule*, a different form of *Roul* (see **Rollo**); (ii) 'person from Rule', Borders (perhaps 'quick-flowing stream')
— **Rule's** a restaurant established in the West End of London in 1798 by Thomas Rule

Rumbelow, Rumbellow 'person from Rumbelow', the name of various locations in England ('three mounds')

Rumbold from the Norman male personal name *Rumbald*, of Germanic origin and probably meaning literally 'fame-bold'. See also **Rumpole** [Dame Angela Rumbold (*née* Jones), 1932–, British Conservative politician]

Rumford 'person from Romford', Essex ('wide ford') [Kennerley Rumford, 1870–1957, British baritone]

Rumney see **Romney**

Rumpole a different form of **Rumbold** [Horace Rumpole, the eccentric QC created by John Mortimer (originally for a 1975 television play)]

Rumsey 'person from Romsey', Hampshire ('Rūm's island')

Runacres 'person who lives by a rye field' (from Old English *rygen* 'of rye' + *æcer* 'cultivated land'). See also **Runnacles**

Rundle, Rundell (i) 'person from Rundale', Kent ('spacious valley'); (ii) from a medieval nickname for a little fat person (see **Round**)

Runnacles, Runnicles different forms of **Runacres** [Donald Runnicles, 1954–, British conductor]

Runyon, Runyan from Irish Gaelic *Ó Rúnaidhin* 'descendant of *Rúnaidhin*', a personal name meaning literally 'little *Ruanaidh*' (see **Rooney**) [Damon Runyon, 1884–1946, US humorous writer]

Rupert from the Germanic male personal name *Rupert*, which is of the same origin as **Robert**

Rush (i) 'person who lives by an area of rushes'; (ii) from Irish Gaelic *Ó Ruis* 'descendant of *Ros*', a personal name perhaps based on *ros* 'wood' [Geoffrey Rush, 1951–, Australian actor]

Rushforth probably 'person from Ryshworth (earlier Rushford)', Yorkshire ('rushy ford')

Rushmore 'person from Rushmere', Suffolk ('rushy lake')
— **Mount Rushmore** a mountain near Keystone, South Dakota, USA, named after Charles E. Rushmore, a prominent New York lawyer of the latter part of the 19th century. It is the site of the Mount Rushmore National Memorial, figures of four past US presidents carved out of the mountain between 1927 and 1941.

Rushton 'person from Rushton', the name of various places in England ('farmstead where rushes grow') [William Rushton, 1937–96, British satirist and cartoonist]

Rusk probably 'person who lives by a marsh' (from Scottish Gaelic *riasg* 'marsh, bog') [Dean Rusk, 1909–94, US statesman]

Ruskin (i) probably 'little **Rose** (iv)'; (ii) 'tanner' (from Scottish Gaelic *rusgan*, literally 'peelers' (of bark), hence 'tanners') [John Ruskin, 1819–1900, British art and social critic]
— **Ruskin College** a college of Oxford University, set up (as Ruskin Hall) in 1899 to provide residential education for working people, and named in honour of John Ruskin (see above)

Russell, Russel from *Rousel* (literally 'little **Rouse**'), an Anglo-Norman nickname for a red-haired person [Russell, the family name of the dukes of Bedford; Bertrand Russell (3rd Earl Russell), 1872–1970, British philosopher and mathematician, grandson of Lord John; George William Russell (pen-name Æ), 1867–1935, Irish poet and essayist; Lord John Russell (1st Earl Russell), 1792–1878, British Whig (Liberal) politician, prime minister 1846–52, 1865–66; Ken Russell, 1927–, British film director; Rosalind Russell, 1907–76, US actress; Lord William Russell, 1639–83, English Whig politician; Sir William Russell, 1820–1907, British war correspondent; Willy Russell, 1947–, British author and playwright]
— **Jack Russell terrier** a small terrier with short legs and a white coat with patchy black or brown markings. It is named after the Devonshire clergyman John ('Jack') Russell, 1795–1883, who introduced the breed.
— **Russell and Bromley** a British chain of shoe shops, established in Eastbourne, Sussex, in 1880 by Albion Russell and his son-in-law George Frederick Bromley
— **Russell Hobbs** a British manufacturer of electric kettles, coffee pots, etc., established in 1952 by William Russell, 1920–2006, and Peter Hobbs, 1916–
— **Russell lupin** a large perennial lupin developed by the British gardener George Russell, 1857–1951, and introduced by him in 1937
— **Russell's paradox** the contradiction in set theory resulting from assuming that it is possible to form any set whatsoever, contradicted by the set of

all and only things that are not members of themselves. It is named after Bertrand Russell (see above).
— **Russell Square** a square in central London, laid out in 1800 by Humphry Repton and named after the ground landlords, the Russells (dukes of Bedford)
— **Russell's viper** a venomous snake (*Vipera russelli*) common in South Asia. It is named in honour of the Scottish naturalist and physician Patrick Russell, 1727–1805.

Rust (i) from a medieval nickname for a red-haired or ruddy-cheeked person (from Old English *rūst* 'rust'); (ii) 'person who lives by a resting place along a route' (from Middle Low German *ruste* 'rest'); (iii) 'person who lives by an elm tree' (from Swiss German *Rust* 'elm', from Old High German *ruost*)

Ruston 'person from Ruston', the name of several places in England (variously 'farmstead with special roof beams or rafters' and 'Hror's or Róarr's farmstead')

Rutgers 'son of *Rutger*', a Germanic form of **Roger**
— **Rutgers University** a university in New Jersey, USA, founded in 1766 and named subsequently in honour of Colonel Henry Rutgers, 1745–1830, a hero of the Revolutionary War

Ruth from a medieval nickname for a person who took pity on others or who was worthy of pity (from Middle English *reuthe* 'pity') [Babe Ruth (original name George Herman Ruth), 1895–1948, US baseball player]

Rutherford, Rutherfurd 'person from Rutherford', Borders ('cattle ford') [Ernest Rutherford (Lord Rutherford), 1871–1937, New Zealand-born British physicist; Dame Margaret Rutherford, 1892–1972, British actress; Mark Rutherford, pen-name of William Hale White, 1831–1913, British novelist]
— **rutherfordium** a radioactive element (symbol *Rf*). It was named in honour of Lord Rutherford (see above).

Ruthven 'person from Ruthven', the name of various places in Scotland (either 'red marsh' or 'red river'). The name is traditionally pronounced 'riven'.

Rutland 'person from Rutland', English county ('Rota's estate')

Rutledge a different form of **Routledge**

Rutter (i) 'player of the rote (a medieval stringed instrument played by plucking)'. See also **Root** (ii); (ii) from a medieval nickname for a dishonest or untrustworthy person (from Old French *routier* 'robber, mugger') [John Rutter, 1945–, British composer and conductor]

Ryal, Ryall see **Ryle** (i)

Ryan (i) from Irish Gaelic *Ó Ríain* 'descendant of *Rían* or *Ríaghan*'; (ii) a reduced form of *Mulryan*, from Irish Gaelic *Ó Maoilríaghain* 'descendant of the follower of (St) *Ríaghan*', a personal name of uncertain origin and meaning [Meg Ryan (original name Margaret Mary Emily Anne Hyra), 1961–, US actress; Robert Ryan, 1909–73, US actor]

— **Ryanair** an Irish low-cost airline founded in 1985 by Christy Ryan, Tony Ryan and Liam Lonergan

— *Ryan's Daughter* a romantic film melodrama (1970), set in Ireland in 1916, about a village schoolmaster's wife who falls for a British officer. It was directed by David Lean.

— *Saving Private Ryan* a film (1998) about the attempt to find and save a US paratrooper missing in Normandy in the aftermath of D-Day. It was directed by Steven Spielberg.

— *Von Ryan's Express* a film (1965), based on a novel (1964) by Davis Westheimer, about an escape by train from a German prisoner-of-war camp, led by Colonel Joseph L. Ryan (played by Frank Sinatra).

Rycroft 'person who lives by a small rye field', or 'person from Ryecroft', the name of various places in England (in either case from Old English *ryge* 'rye' + *croft* 'small enclosed field')

Ryder see **Rider**

Rye (i) 'person who lives at a place where rye is grown', or 'grower of rye'; (ii) 'person who lives on a small area of raised dry ground surrounded by marsh or fenland' (the initial *r* comes from the misdivision of Middle English *atter ye* 'at the island'); (iii) 'person who lives by a river' (the initial *r* comes from the misdivision of Middle English *atter eye* 'at the river'). See also **Ray** (iii), **Rea** (i), **Ryman**

Ryland 'person who lives on an area of land where rye is grown'

Rylands a different form of **Ryland**

Ryle (i) *also* **Ryal** *or* **Ryall** 'person from Ryle', Northumberland and various other similarly spelt places in England ('hill where rye is grown'); (ii) a different form of **Royle** [Gilbert Ryle,1900–76, British philosopher; Sir Martin Ryle, 1918–84, British astronomer]

Ryman a different form of **Rye** (ii–iii)

S

-s the English possessive ending. Suffixed to a personal name (e.g. *Richard*) it forms a surname (*Richards* – i.e. 'son of Richard'). It is characteristic particularly of southern and western England and Wales (in contrast with the synonymous **-SON**, which predominates in northern England and in Scotland).

Sachs (i) 'person from Saxony', Germany; (ii) *also* **Sacks** *or* **Sax** a Jewish surname perhaps based on an acronym formed from Hebrew *Zera Qodesh SHemo* 'his name is the seed of holiness' [Andrew Sachs, 1930–, German-born British actor; Leonard Sachs, 1909–90, South African actor and music-hall chairman; Oliver Sacks, 1933–, British neurologist and writer]

Sackville 'person from Saqueneville', northern France ('Sachano's settlement') [Sackville, the family name of the earls De La Warr; Thomas Sackville (1st earl of Dorset), 1536–1608, English poet, dramatist and diplomat; Vita Sackville-West, 1892–1962, British writer]

Sadler, Saddler, Sadlier, Sadleir 'saddle-maker' [Michael Sadleir (originally Sadler), 1888–1957, British bibliographer and novelist]
— **Sadler's Wells** a theatre in Finsbury, North London, specializing in ballet and other dance. The original theatre was opened, in 1765, on the site of a medicinal well rediscovered in 1683 by Thomas Sadler.

Sage from a medieval English and French nickname for a wise person

Saggers 'son of **Seagar**'

Sainsbury, Saintsbury 'person from Saintbury', Gloucestershire (probably 'Sæwine's fortified town') [David Sainsbury (Lord Sainsbury), 1940–, British businessman and Labour politician, scion of the Sainsbury grocery family (see below); George Saintsbury, 1845–1933, British literary critic and wine connoisseur]
— **J. Sainsbury** a British supermarket chain, which grew out of a grocer's shop established in Drury Lane, London in 1869 by John James Sainsbury, 1844–1927

Saint from a medieval English and French nickname for a pious person [Eva Marie Saint, 1924–, US actress]

Saint-Clair, Saint-Clare different forms of **Sinclair** [Amber St Clair, the beautiful but promiscuous heroine of Kathleen Winsor's novel *Forever Amber* (1944)]

Saint-John 'person from Saint-Jean', the name of numerous places in France with a church dedicated to St Jean (St John). The name is conventionally pronounced 'sinjən'. [Norman St John-Stevas (Lord St John of Fawesley), 1929–, British Conservative politician]

Salamon see **Salomon**

Salazar 'person from Salazar', Spain (probably 'old hall')

Sales (i) 'person who lives by a group of sallows (a variety of willow)' (from Middle English *salwes* 'sallows'). See also **Sallis**; (ii) from a religious given name adopted in Portugal in honour of the French prelate and devotional writer St Francis de Sales, 1567–1622, who was born in the Château de Sales in Savoy; (iii) 'person from Sales', Portugal (a place-name probably based on an unknown Germanic personal name)

Salinger (i) 'person from Saint-Léger', the name of two places in northern France with a church dedicated to St Leger (see **Ledger**); (ii) a Jewish name, perhaps literally 'person from Solingen', northern Germany. See also **Selinger** [J.D. Salinger, 1919–, US writer; Pierre Salinger, 1925–2004, US politician and journalist]

Salisbury, Salsbury 'person from Salisbury', Wiltshire ('stronghold called Sorvio'), or 'person from Salesbury', Lancashire ('fortified place where willows grow') [Sir Guy Salisbury-Jones, 1896–1985, British general and pioneer of English wine; J.H. Salisbury, 1823–1905, US physician and dietician]
— **Salisbury steak** an upmarket US term for a hamburger, especially as initially promoted by J.H. Salisbury (see above), who recommended that people should eat one three times a day

Sallis a different form of **Sales** (i) [Peter Sallis, 1921–, British actor]

Salmon (i) *also* **Salmond** from the medieval English and French male personal name *Salmon*, a contracted form of **Salomon**; (ii) from the Jewish male personal name *Zalmen*, a derivative (via German) of Hebrew *Shelomo* (see **Solomon**); (iii) a translation of Irish Gaelic *Ó Bradáin* (see **Braden**) [Alex Salmond, 1954–, Scottish National Party politician]
— **salmonella** a rod-shaped bacterium found in the intestine that can cause food poisoning, gastroenteritis and typhoid fever. It was named after the US veterinary surgeon Daniel Elmer Salmon, 1850–1914.

Salmons, Sammons, Sammonds 'son of **Salmon** (i)' [Albert Sammons, 1886–1957, British violinist]

Salomon, Salamon from the Jewish, Danish, Dutch, French, German, Polish and Spanish forms of **Solomon**

Salt (i) 'person from Salt', Staffordshire ('salt pit'); (ii) a different form of **Salter** (i)
— **Saltaire** a town in Yorkshire, founded in 1853 by the local industrialist Sir Titus Salt as a model village for the textile workers in his factory. Its name incorporates that of the River Aire as well as Sir Titus's.

Salter (i) 'person who extracts salt from the ground and/or sells it'. See also **Salt** (ii); (ii) 'player of the psaltery (a medieval stringed instrument)'

Sambrook 'person from Sambrook', Shropshire ('sandy stream')

Samford 'person from Sampford', Devon, Essex and Somerset ('sandy ford'). See also **Sandford**

Sammons, Sammonds see **Salmons**

Samms, Sams 'son of *Sam*', a pet-form of **Samuel**

Sample 'person from Saint-Paul or Saint-Pol', the name of numerous places in northern France with a church dedicated to St Paul. See also **Semple** (i)

Samples a different form of **Sample**

Samson, Sampson from the biblical male personal name *Samson* (from Hebrew *Shimshon*, literally 'little sun'). See also **Sansom** [Anthony Sampson, 1926–2004, British writer and journalist]

Samuel from the biblical male personal name *Samuel* (from Hebrew *Shemuel*, literally 'name of god'). See also **Samms, Samwell** [Herbert Samuel (Viscount Samuel), 1870–1963, British Liberal politician]
— **H. Samuel** a British chain of jeweller's shops founded in Liverpool in 1821 by Moses and Lewis Samuel. It got its name from Moses's widow Harriet Samuel, who took over the firm in 1862.

Samuels 'son of **Samuel**'

Samuelson 'son of **Samuel**'

Samways from a medieval nickname for a fool (from Middle English *samwis* 'foolish', literally 'half-wise')

Samwell a different form of **Samuel**

Sanchez from Spanish *Sánchez*, literally 'son of *Sancho*', a male personal name descended from Latin *Sanctius* or *Sancius* (probably a derivative of *sanctus* 'holy') [Lawrie Sanchez, 1959–, British football manager]

Sand (i) 'person who lives on an area of sandy soil'; (ii) a shortened form of **Alexander**. See also **Sanders**; (iii) an anglicized shortening of Dutch and Flemish *Van den Sande* or *Van den Zande*, 'person from Zande' or other similarly named places in the Low Countries ('sandy place'). See also **Sands**

Sandbach 'person from Sandbach', Cheshire ('sandy valley stream')

Sandberg 'person from Sandberg', the name of various places in Germany and of three farmsteads in Norway ('sand mountain')

Sandburg from an invented Swedish name meaning literally 'sand castle' [Carl Sandburg, 1878–1967, US poet]

Sandell (i) 'person who lives by a sand-hill or by a sandy slope' (from Old English *sand* + *hyll* 'hill' or *hylde* 'slope'); (ii) *also* **Sandel** an invented Swedish name based on *sand* 'sand'

Sandeman 'servant of *Sander*' (see **Sanders**)
— **Sandeman** a British producer of port and sherry, founded in Portugal in 1790 by George Sandeman, 1765–1841

Sanders 'son of *Sander*', a medieval shortened form of **Alexander**. See also **Saunders** [George Sanders, 1906–72, British actor; Harland D. Sanders ('Colonel Sanders'), 1890–1980, US restaurateur who founded the 'Kentucky Fried Chicken' company]
— *Sanders of the River* a collection of stories (1911) by Edgar Wallace, subsequently (1935) filmed, featuring the difficulties faced by the local British colonial commissioner R.G. Sanders in keeping peace among the African tribes

Sanderson 'son of *Sander*' (see **Sanders**) [Joan Sanderson, 1912–92, British actress; Tessa Sanderson, 1956–, British athlete]
— **Sanderson's** a British wallpaper manufacturer, founded in London in 1860 by Arthur Sanderson, 1829–82

Sandford 'person from Sandford', the name of various places in England ('sandy ford'). See also **Samford**

Sandham probably either 'person from Sandham', an unidentified place in England ('homestead on sandy ground'), or 'person from Sandholme', Yorkshire ('sand island') [Andrew Sandham, 1890–1982, English cricketer]

Sandler (i) 'person from Saint-Lô', the name of two places in northern France with a church dedicated to St Lauto, or 'person from Saint-Hilaire-de-Harcouët', a place in northern France with a church dedicated to St Hilary; (ii) 'maker or repairer of shoes' (from Yiddish *sandler* 'shoemaker, cobbler', ultimately from Late Latin *sandelārius*, a derivative of *sandelium* 'shoe') [Adam Sandler, 1966–, US actor and comedian]

Sands, Sandes, Sandys (i) a different form of **Sand** (i); (ii) 'son of **Sand** (ii)' [Duncan Sandys (Lord Duncan-Sandys), 1908–87, British Conservative politician]

Sanger (i) 'singer, choir member', or from a medieval nickname for someone who was always singing (from Old English *sangere* 'singer'); (ii) 'cantor' (from German *Sänger* 'singer') [Frederick Sanger, 1918–, British biochemist; Margaret Sanger (*née* Higgins), 1883–1966, US social reformer]
— **Sanger's Circus** a British touring circus founded in the mid-19th century by John Sanger, 1816–89, and his brother 'Lord' George Sanger, 1827–1911

Sangster a Scottish variant of **Sanger** (i) [Mike Sangster, 1941–85, British tennis player]

Sankey, Sanky (i) 'person from Sankey', Lancashire (from a Celtic river-name perhaps meaning 'sacred'); (ii) from Irish Gaelic *Mac Seanchaidhe* 'son of the chronicler'
— **Moody and Sankey** see **Moody**

Sansom, Sansome different forms of **Samson** [William Sansom, 1926–76, British short-story writer and novelist]

Santiago 'person from Santiago', the name of several places in Spain and Portugal with a church dedicated to St James

Santos (i) from the Spanish and Portuguese personal name *dos Santos*, short for *Todos los Santos* 'all the saints', traditionally given to a child born on All Saints' Day; (ii) 'person from Santos', the name of several places in Portugal and Spain with a church dedicated to all the saints

Sapper probably from a medieval German nickname for someone with a shambling gait (from Middle High German *sappen* 'to walk awkwardly') or for an acquisitive person (from *sappen* 'to acquire')

Sarazen, Sarazin from a medieval French nickname for a swarthy person, or for someone who had gone on a Crusade (from Old French *sarrazin* 'Saracen'). See also **Sarson** (iii) [Gene Sarazen (original name Eugene Saraceni), 1902–99, US golfer]

Sargent, Sargeant, Sergent, Sergeant, Serjeant 'servant' (from Middle English *sergent* 'servant') [John Sergeant, 1944–, British journalist; John Singer Sargent, 1856–1925, US portrait painter; Sir Malcolm Sargent, 1895–1967, British conductor]

Sargentson, Sargeantson, Sergentson, Sergeantson, Serjeantson 'son of **Sargent**'

Sargeson, Sargison different forms of **Sargentson** [Frank Sargeson, pen-name of Norris Frank Davey, 1903–82, New Zealand writer]

Sarson (i) 'son of *Sara*', a Hebrew female personal name meaning literally 'princess'; (ii) 'son of *Saher*' (see **Sayer** (i)); (iii) from a medieval nickname for a swarthy person, or for someone who had gone on a Crusade (from Middle English *sarrazin* 'Saracen'). See also **Sarazen**
— **Sarson's** a British brand of malt vinegar, established in 1794 by Thomas Sarson

Sassoon from the Hebrew male personal name *Sason*, literally 'joy' [Siegfried Sassoon, 1886–1967, British poet and writer; Vidal Sassoon, 1928–, British hairdressing entrepreneur]

Satterthwaite 'person from Satterthwaite', Cumbria ('clearing by a shieling')

Saul, Sawle from the male personal name *Saul* (from Hebrew *Shaul*, literally 'asked-for (child)')

Saunders a different form (originally Scottish) of **Sanders** [Dame Cicely Saunders, 1918–2005, British philanthropist; Jennifer Saunders, 1958–, British comedian, actress and writer]

Savage, Savidge from a medieval nickname for an uncontrollably rude or wild person [Lily Savage, stage-name of Paul **O'Grady** as a drag

performer; Richard Savage, ?1697–1743, British poet]
— **Savage Club** a London gentlemen's club founded in 1857 and named after Richard Savage (see above)

Savary, Savery from the Norman male personal name *Savaric*, of Germanic origin [Thomas Savery, ?1650–1715, English engineer, maker of the first practical steam engine]

Savile, Saville, Savill, Savil probably 'person from Sainville', northern France ('settlement of the Saxons') [Sir Jimmy Savile, 1926–, British disc jockey and television presenter]
— **'Lord Arthur Savile's Crime'** a short story (1887) by Oscar Wilde, satirically examining the predicament of Lord Arthur Savile, who is told by a palmist that he is predestined to commit murder, and feels he should do so before marrying his fiancée
— **Savile Row** a street in the West End of London, laid out in the 1730s and famous latterly for its tailors. It was named after Lady Dorothy Savile, wife of the 3rd earl of Burlington, the local landowner.

Sawyer 'person whose job is sawing wood, woodcutter'. See also **Sayer** (iv)
— **The Adventures of Tom Sawyer** a novel (1876) by Mark Twain recounting the escapades of young Tom Sawyer and his friend Huckleberry Finn on the banks of the Missouri

Sax see **Sachs** (ii)

Saxby (i) 'person from Saxby', Leicestershire and Lincolnshire ('farmstead of the Saxons' or 'Saksi's farmstead'); (ii) from a medieval nickname for a touchy person quick to take offence (from Middle English *sakespey*, literally 'draw-sword', from Old French *sacquespee*)

Saxon (i) from the medieval personal name *Saxon*, literally 'person from Saxony'; (ii) a different form of **Saxton**

Saxton (i) 'person from Saxton', Cambridgeshire and Yorkshire ('farmstead of the Saxons'); (ii) a different form of **Sexton** (i) [Robert Saxton, 1953–, British composer]

Sayer (i) from the medieval male personal name *Saher*, probably from the Germanic personal name *Sigiheri*, literally 'victory-army' (brought into England by the Normans). See also **Sarson** (ii); (ii) 'professional story-teller, reciter of stories and poems'; (iii) 'person who assays metals or tastes food' (from a shortened form of Middle English *assayer* 'tester'); (iv) 'person whose job is sawing wood, woodcutter' (from Middle English *saghier* 'sawyer'). See also **Sawyer**; (v) 'maker or seller of a type of fine-textured medieval cloth known as *say*'; (vi) 'carpenter' (from Welsh *saer* 'carpenter'). See also **Sear** [Leo Sayer (original name Gerard Hugh Sayer), 1948–, British pop singer]

Sayers 'son of **Sayer**' [Dorothy L. Sayers, 1893–1957, British writer]

Saylor 'dancer, acrobat' (from Old French *sailleor*, literally 'jumper'). See also **Seiler** (ii)

Scales a different form of **Scholes** [Prunella Scales (original name Prunella Illingworth), 1932–, British actress]

Scammell perhaps from an unrecorded medieval personal name *Skammel*, derived ultimately from Old Norse *skammr* 'short'

Scanlon, Scanlan from Irish Gaelic *Ó Scannláin* 'descendant of *Scannlánn*', a personal name meaning literally 'little Scannal' (see **Scannell**) [Hugh Scanlon (Lord Scanlon), 1913–2004, British trade-union leader]

Scannell from Irish Gaelic *Ó Scannail* 'descendant of *Scannal*', a nickname meaning literally 'strife' [Vernon Scannell, 1922–, British poet and boxer]

Scarborough 'person from Scarborough', Yorkshire ('Skarthi's stronghold')

Scarfe, Scarff from a nickname for someone thought to look or behave like a cormorant (from Middle English *scarfe* 'cormorant') [Gerald Scarfe, 1936–, British cartoonist]

Scargill 'person from Scargill', Yorkshire ('ravine frequented by diving ducks') [Arthur Scargill, 1941–, British trade-union leader]

Scarisbrick 'person from Scarisbrick', Merseyside ('Skar's hill')

Scarlett, Scarlet 'dyer' or 'maker of richly coloured fabrics' (in either case from Old French *escarlate* 'scarlet cloth')

Scatchard perhaps from a taunting medieval nickname for a long-legged person, based on Anglo-Norman *scache* 'stilt'

Scattergood from a medieval nickname for someone who was generous (or spendthrift) with their money

Schaefer, Schaeffer (i) an anglicization of German *Schäfer*, literally 'shepherd'; (ii) an invented Jewish name based on German *Schäfer* (see i), perhaps in allusion to King David's boyhood career as a shepherd or to the metaphorical notion of God as a shepherd

Schaffer, Shaffer (i) 'steward, bailiff' (from Middle High German *schaffer* 'manager'); (ii) different forms of **Schaefer** (ii) [Anthony Shaffer, 1926–2001, British playwright; Sir Peter Shaffer, 1926–, British playwright, twin brother of Anthony]

Schick (i) from a medieval German nickname for a courteous and well-behaved person (from Middle High German *schic* 'orderly, polite'); (ii) *also* **Shick** an invented Jewish name, perhaps based on (i), or alternatively possibly an acronym based on Hebrew *shem yisrael kodesh* 'the name of Israel is holy'
— **Schick test** an injection of nontoxic diphtheria under the skin, used to determine whether a patient is immune to diphtheria. It is named after the Hungarian-born US paediatrician Bela Schick, 1877–1967.

Schiller (i) from a medieval German nickname for someone with a squint (from a derivative of Middle High German *schilhen* 'to squint'); (ii) *also* **Shiller** a different form of **Schuler** (ii)

Schilling from a medieval German nickname of uncertain significance, based on the name of the coin (Middle High German *schillinc* 'shilling')

Schindler 'maker or layer of shingles (wooden roof-tiles)' (from a derivative of Middle High German *schindel* 'shingle')

Schlegel (i) 'blacksmith' or 'mason' (in either case from Middle High German *slegel* 'sledge-hammer'); (ii) from a medieval German nickname for a vigorous person (from Middle High German *slegel*, as (i)) [the sisters Margaret and Helen Schlegel, and their brother Tibby Schlegel, who represent the life of the mind (as opposed to business and commerce) in E.M. Forster's *Howards End* (1910)]

Schlesinger, Schlessinger 'person from Silesia', east-central Europe. See also **Slazenger, Slessinger** [Arthur Schlesinger, Jr., 1917–2007, US historian and biographer; John Schlesinger, 1926–2003, British film and theatre director]

Schmidt, Schmitt, Schmit 'smith, blacksmith' (from Middle High German *smit*)
— **Schmitt trigger** an electronic circuit that produces an output when the input exceeds a predetermined turn-on or threshold level. It is named after the US electronics engineer Otto H. Schmitt, 1913–.

Schneider 'tailor' (from Middle High German *snīder*, literally 'cutter'). See also **Snider**

Schoenfeld (i) an anglicization of German *Schönfeld* 'person from Schönfeld', the name of various places in Germany ('beautiful area of open country'); (ii) an invented Jewish name based on German *schön* 'beautiful' and *Feld* 'field'. See also **Shonfield**

Schofield, Scofield, Scholefield 'person from Schofield', the name of various places in northern England ('field with a hut') [Paul Scofield, 1922–, British actor]

Scholes, Scoles 'person who lives in a hut', or 'person from Scholes or Scales', the name of various places in northern England (in either case from Old Norse *skáli* 'hut, shed'). See also **Scales** [Paul Scholes, 1974–, English footballer]

Scholl (i) from a medieval German and Dutch nickname for a clodhopping person (from Middle High German and Middle Dutch *scholle* 'lump of earth'); (ii) *also* **Shol** an invented Jewish name, perhaps based on (i), or alternatively possibly an acronym based on Hebrew *shevach leel* 'praise to God'
— **Dr Scholl's** a US-based producer of footwear and footcare products, founded in Chicago in 1906 by the US podiatrist William Mathias Scholl, 1882–1968

Scholtz, Scholz different forms of **Schultz**

Schreiber (i) 'clerk, scribe' (from a derivative of Middle High German *schrīben* 'to write'); (ii) an invented Jewish name based on German *Schreiber* and Yiddish *shrayber* 'writer' as translations of Hebrew *sofer* 'scribe'. See also **Shriver**

Schreiner 'joiner' (from Middle High German *schrīner*, literally 'box-maker') [Olive Schreiner, 1855–1920, South African novelist]

Schroeder, Schroder anglicizations of German *Schröder*, literally 'tailor' (from a derivative of Middle High German *schrōden* 'to cut')

Schubert 'maker or repairer of shoes' (from Middle High German *schuoch* 'shoe' + *würhte* 'maker')

Schuler, Schuller (i) 'scholar, trainee priest' (from German, from *Schule* 'school'); (ii) 'Talmudic scholar', also 'synagogue sexton' (from Yiddish, from *shul* 'synagogue'). See also **Schiller** (ii)

Schulman, Shulman 'Talmudic scholar' or 'sexton of a synagogue' (from Yiddish *shul* 'synagogue' + *man* 'man') [Milton Shulman, 1913–2004, Canadian drama critic]

Schultz, Schulz, Schultze, Schulze, Shultz, Shults (i) 'village headman' (from Old High German *sculdheizo*, literally 'debt-commander'); (ii) an invented Jewish name based on (i), perhaps originally relating to a rabbi as the head of a Jewish community [Charles Schulz, 1922–2000, US cartoonist; George Shultz, 1920–, US academic and businessman, secretary of state 1982–89]

Schumacher 'maker or repairer of shoes' (from Middle High German *schuoch* 'shoe' + *macher* 'maker'). See also **Shoemaker** [E.F. Schumacher, 1911–77, German-born British economist and conservationist]

Schumann, Schuhmann, Schuman 'maker or repairer of shoes' (from Middle High German *schuoch* 'shoe' + *man* 'man') [Elisabeth Schumann, 1885–1952, German-born US soprano; William Schuman, 1910–92, US composer]

Schuster, Shuster 'maker or repairer of shoes' (from Middle High German *schuochsūtære* 'shoe-sewer')

Schutz (i) 'guard, watchman' (from Middle High German *schütze* 'watchman'); (ii) *also* **Schuetz** *or* **Schuetze** 'archer' (also from Middle High German *schütze*, in its later sense 'archer'); (iii) an invented Jewish name, probably based on (ii)

Schwab 'person from Swabia', a region of southern Germany

Schwarz, Schwartz, Schwarze, Schwartze from a medieval German and Jewish nickname for a black-haired or swarthy person (from Middle High German *swarz* and Yiddish *shvarts* 'black'). See also **Swartz**

Schwarzkopf, Schwartzkopf from a medieval German and Jewish nickname for a black-haired person (from Middle High German *swarz* 'black' + *kopf* 'head') [Norman Schwarzkopf, 1934–, US general]

Schweitzer, Schweizer 'Swiss person' (from Middle High German *swīzer* 'Swiss person'). See also **Switser** (ii)

Schweppe 'roof-builder' (from Middle Low German *swepe* 'rafter')

— **Schweppes** a manufacturer of carbonated drinks, founded in Geneva in 1783 by Jean Jacob Schweppe, 1740–1821. He moved his business to London in 1790. In 1969 it merged with the Cadbury Group Ltd. to form Cadbury Schweppes plc.

Sclater see **Slater**

Scobie 'person from Scobie', an unidentified place in Perth and Kinross ('thorny place') [Henry Scobie, the conscience-wracked and ultimately suicidal deputy commissioner of police in Graham Greene's West Africa-set *The Heart of the Matter* (1948)]

Scofield see **Schofield**

Scoles see **Scholes**

Scopes perhaps 'person who lives by a hollow in the ground' (from Middle English *scope* 'scoop, ladle') [John T. Scopes, 1900–70, a Tennessee school-teacher prosecuted in 1925 for teaching Darwinian evolutionary theories]

Scorer, Scorrer (i) 'scout, spy' (from Middle English *scorer*, from Old French); (ii) 'keeper of accounts' (from a derivative of Middle English *scoren* 'to score, record')

Scotland (i) 'person from Scotland'; (ii) 'person from Scotland or Scotlandwell', Perth and Kinross; (iii) from the Norman personal name *Escotland*, literally 'territory of the Scots'

Scott '(Gaelic-speaking) person from Scotland' [C.P. Scott, 1846–1932, British newspaper editor; Doug Scott, 1941–, British mountaineer; Sir George Gilbert Scott, 1811–78, British architect; Sir Giles Gilbert Scott, 1880–1960, British architect, grandson of Sir George; Kristin Scott Thomas, 1960–, British actress; Lt. Cmndr. Montgomery ('Scotty') Scott, chief engineer (played by James Doohan) on the USS *Enterprise* in the US television science-fiction series *Star Trek* (1969–71); Paul Scott, 1920–78, British novelist; Sir Peter Scott, 1909–89, British ornithologist, conservationist and painter, son of Captain Scott; Sir Ridley Scott, 1937–, British film director; Robert Falcon Scott (Captain Scott), 1868–1912, British naval officer and Antarctic explorer; Ronnie Scott (original name Ronald Schatt), 1927–96, British jazz saxophonist and club-owner; Sheila Scott, 1922–88, British aviatrix; Terry Scott, 1927–94, British comic actor; Sir Walter Scott, 1771–1832, Scottish novelist and poet; Zachary Scott, 1914–65, US actor]

— **Beam me up, Scotty!** an order to Lt. Cmndr. 'Scotty' Scott (see above) to return the speaker to the spaceship from a threatening situation on an alien planet below by activating a matter-transfer 'beam'. Though apparently never used in precisely that wording in the programme itself, the expression has become something of a catchphrase, used to mean 'Get me out of here!'.

— **Scott connection** a particular way of connecting two single-phase transformers to convert a three-phase voltage to a two-phase one (or to two single-phase ones), or vice versa, devised in 1894 by the US electrical engineer Charles F. Scott, 1864-1944.

— *Scott-King's Modern Europe* a long short story (1947) by Evelyn Waugh featuring the tribulations of a sheltered English public schoolmaster invited to a conference in a post-World War II one-party European state

— **Scotts Porridge Oats** a proprietary brand of porridge oats first produced in Scotland in 1888 by the A. & R. Scott company. The firm was taken over by the Quaker Oats Company in 1982.

Scovell, Scovel 'person from Escoville', Normandy

Screech perhaps from a medieval nickname for a person with a disagreeably loud or harsh voice

Scribner a different form of **Scrivener**
— **Charles Scribner's Sons** a US publishing company founded in 1846 by Charles Scribner, 1821–71

Scrimgeour, Scrimgeoure, Scrymgeour, Scrimiger 'fencer, fencing-master' (from Old French *eskermisseoure* 'fencer')

Scrimshaw a different form of **Scrimgeour**

Scriven 'clerk, copyist' (from Middle English *scrivein* 'writer', from Old French *escrivein*)

Scrivener, Scrivenor 'clerk, copyist' (from Middle English *scrivein* (see **Scriven**) + the agent suffix *-er*). See also **Scribner**

Scrivens 'son of **Scriven**'

Scrope perhaps from an Old Norse nickname meaning literally 'crab' [Scrope, a family of Norman origin, several of whose members played notable roles in the political life of medieval England, including Richard le Scrope, ?1327–1403, chancellor of England, and his son William le Scrope, ?1350–99, treasurer of England]

Scruggs (i) 'person who lives in an area overgrown with brushwood' (from Middle English *scrogge* 'brushwood'); (ii) 'person from Scrogges', Borders [Earl Scruggs, 1924–, US bluegrass banjoist]

Scruton 'person from Scruton', Yorkshire ('Skurfa's farmstead') [Roger Scruton, 1944–, British philosopher]

Scrutton a different form of **Scruton**

Scrymgeour see **Scrimgeour**

Scudamore perhaps 'person from Scudamore', an unidentified place, probably in the West Country ('shitty marshland'). See also **Skidmore** [Peter Scudamore, 1958–, British National Hunt jockey]

Scudder 'scout, spy' (from Middle English *scut* (from Old French *escoute*, from *escouter* 'to listen') + the agent suffix *-er*)

Scully from Irish Gaelic *Ó Scolaidhe* 'descendant of the scholar'

Seaberg (i) from the Old English female personal name *Sǣburh*, literally 'sea-fortress'; (ii) a partial translation of Swedish *Sjöberg*, literally 'sea-mountain'

Seabrook 'person from Seabrook', Buckinghamshire ('stream called *Sǣge* (literally perhaps 'slow-moving')')

Seagal see **Segal**

Seagar, Seager, Seegar, Seeger from the Middle English male personal name *Segar*, literally 'sea-spear'. See also **Saggers**

Seagrave, Segrave 'person from Seagrave', Leicestershire (probably 'grove near a pit' or 'grove near an animal pen') [Sir Henry Segrave, 1896–1934, British fighter pilot, racing driver and holder of the world land and water speed records]

Seagrove a different form of **Seagrave**

Seal, Seale (i) 'maker of seals or signet rings'; (ii) 'maker of saddles' (from Old French *seele* 'saddle'); (iii) 'person employed at a manor house' (from Middle English *sale* 'hall, manor house'); (iv) 'person who lives by a sallow tree (a variety of willow)' (from Middle English *salwe* 'sallow'); (v) from a medieval nickname for someone thought to resemble a seal (the animal) (e.g. in being plump) [Basil Seal, a rakish character in Evelyn Waugh's *Black Mischief* (1932) and *Put Out More Flags* (1942), who reappears in *Basil Seal Rides Again* (1963); Bobby Seale, 1936–, US civil-rights activist, co-founder of the Black Panthers; Elizabeth Seal, 1933–, British actress and singer]

Sealey, Sealy, Seeley, Seely from a medieval nickname for a cheerful person (from Middle English *seely* 'happy'). See also **Selig**, **Sellick**, **Zealey**

Seaman, Seman (i) from the Old English male personal name *Sǣmann*, literally 'sea-man'; (ii) 'sailor'. See also **Semmence** [David Seaman, 1963–, English footballer]

Sear, Seear different forms of **Sayer**

Search a different form of **Surridge** (ii)

Searle, Searl, Serle from the Norman male personal name *Serlo*, of Germanic origin and perhaps meaning literally 'protector' [Humphrey Searle, 1915–82, British composer; Ronald Searle, 1920–, British cartoonist]

Sears, Seares, Seers (i) 'son of **Sayer**'; (ii) from Irish Gaelic *Mac Saoghair*, perhaps 'son of *Saher*' (see **Sayer** (i)) [Heather Sears, 1935–94, British actress]
— **Sears, Roebuck and Company** a US-based international department-store and mail-order chain, founded in Chicago in 1886 by Richard Sears, 1863–1914, and Alvah Roebuck, 1864–1948

Seaton, Seton 'person from Seaton', the name of various places in England (mainly 'farmstead by the sea') [Ernest Thompson Seton (original name Ernest Seton-Thompson), 1860–1946, British-born US naturalist and writer]

Sebastian from the male personal name *Sebastian* (from Latin *Sebastiānus*, literally 'man from Sebastia', a city on the southern coast of the Black Sea). See also **Best**

Seccombe 'person from Seccombe', Devon ('Secca's valley'). See also **Secombe**

Secker (i) 'maker of sacks or bags' (from a derivative of Old English *sacc* 'sack, bag'); (ii) 'person who lives in a wetland area' (from Middle Low

German *seck* 'wet land'); (iii) a Jewish name based on Middle Low German *sack* 'sack, bag'

Seckerson a different form of **Sexton** (i)

Secombe a different form of **Seccombe** [Sir Harry Secombe, 1921–2001, British comedian and singer]

Seddon perhaps 'person from Seddon', an unidentified place possibly in northwest England [Richard Seddon, 1845–1906, British-born New Zealand politician, prime minister 1893–1906]

Sedgeman, Sedgman 'person who lives in a place where sedges grow', or 'person who uses or works with sedges (e.g. for thatching)' [Frank Sedgman, 1927–, Australian tennis player]

Sedgwick, Sedgewick 'person from Sedgwick', Cumbria ('Sicg's dairy farm') or 'person from Sedgewick', Sussex ('dairy farm where sedges grow'). See also **Sidgwick** [Adam Sedgwick, 1785–1873, British geologist]

Seear see **Sear**

Seed (i) 'grower of plants, gardener'; (ii) from a medieval nickname for a very small person

Seeger (i) from the Germanic male personal name *Sigiheri*, literally 'victory-army'; (ii) see **Seagar** [Pete Seeger, 1919–, US folksinger and songwriter]

Seeley, Seely see **Sealey**

Sefton 'person from Sefton', Lancashire ('farmstead where rushes grow')

Segal, Segall, Seagal (i) 'grower or seller of rye' (from Old French *segal* 'rye'); (ii) *also* **Siegal** an invented Jewish name, based on an acronym formed from Hebrew *segan Levia* 'second-rank Levite' [Erich Segal, 1937–, US academic, author and screenwriter; George Segal, 1934–, US actor; Steven Seagal, 1951–, US actor]

Segrave see **Seagrave**

Seifert, Seiffert, Seyfert from a different form of the German male personal name *Siegfried*, literally 'victory-peace'. See also **Siefert** [Richard Seifert (original name Reuben Seifert), 1910–2001, British architect]

— **Seyfert galaxy** a small spiral galaxy that varies in brightness and emits radio and X rays. The name commemorates the US astronomer C.K. Seyfert, 1911–60, who first described such galaxies.

Seiler (i) *also* **Seyler** 'rope-maker' (from a derivative of Middle High German *seil* 'rope'); (ii) a different form of **Saylor**; (iii) an invented Jewish name, perhaps based on (i), or alternatively a partial anagram of the Hebrew male personal name *Yisrael* (see **Israel**) [Athene Seyler, 1889–1990, British actress]

Seinfeld an invented Jewish name made up of an unidentified first element and German *Feld* 'field'

— **Seinfeld** a US television sitcom, first broadcast in 1993, starring Jerry Seinfeld, 1955–, as himself

Selby 'person from Selby', Yorkshire ('village by a willow copse')

Selden, Seldon 'person from Selden Farm', Sussex (probably 'willow-valley') [John Selden,

1584–1654, English jurist, antiquary and orientalist]

Self, Selfe from the medieval male personal name *Saulf* (from Old English *Sǣwulf*, literally 'sea-wolf') [Will Self, 1961–, British writer]

Selfridge perhaps 'person from Selfridge', an unidentified place in England (possibly 'shelf-ridge')

— **Selfridge's** a British department store, in Oxford Street, London. It was founded in 1909 by the US businessman Gordon Selfridge, 1858–1947.

Selig (i) from a medieval German nickname for a cheerful person (from Middle High German *selig* 'happy'). See also **Sealey**; (ii) *also* **Sellig** from the Yiddish male personal name *Zelik*, literally 'fortunate'. See also **Zelig**

Seligman, Seligmann different forms of **Selig**

Selinger, Sellinger different forms of **Salinger**

— **Sellinger's round** a type of country dance very popular in Elizabethan times. It is said to have been named after Sir Thomas Sellynger, who died around 1470, although another candidate is Sir Anthony Saint-Leger, ?1496–1559, Lord Deputy of Ireland. The traditional tune that accompanies it, also called Sellinger's Round, was memorably set by William Byrd, and a suite of variations called *Divertimento on 'Sellinger's Round'* was composed in 1953–54 by Michael Tippett.

Selkirk 'person from Selkirk', Borders ('church by a hall') [Alexander Selkirk, 1676–1721, Scottish sailor, the original of Daniel Defoe's Robinson Crusoe]

Sell (i) 'person who lives in a rudimentary hut, especially a shepherd or other herdsman' (from Middle English *selle* 'small simple dwelling'). See also **Sells**; (ii) an anglicization of the Hungarian surname *Széll*, literally 'someone who lives in a windswept place' (from Hungarian *szél* 'wind')

Seller, Sellar (i) 'person who works in the cellars of a large house or monastery'; (ii) 'saddler' (from Anglo-Norman *seller* 'saddler', from Old French *sellier*); (iii) 'tradesman, merchant' (from a derivative of Middle English *sellen* 'to sell'); (iv) a different form of **Sell** (i) [W.C. Sellar, 1898–1951, Scottish humorist, co-author (with R.J. Yeatman) of *1066 And All That* (1930)]

Sellers, Sellars 'son of **Seller**' [Elizabeth Sellars, 1923–, British actress; Peter Sellars, 1957–, US opera and theatre director; Peter Sellers, 1925–80, British comic actor]

Sellick, Selleck different forms of **Sealey** [Phyllis Sellick, 1911–, British pianist; Tom Selleck, 1945–, US actor]

Sells a different form of **Sell** (i)

Selman, Sellman (i) from a medieval nickname for a cheerful person (from Middle English *seely* 'happy' + *man*); (ii) 'servant of **Seal** (v) or **Sealey**'

Selvey probably from a variant of *Salewi* (see **Selway**)

Selway from the medieval male personal name *Salewi* (probably from an unrecorded Old English *Sǣlwīg*, literally 'prosperity-war')

Selwood, Sellwood 'person from Selwood', Somerset ('willow-wood')

Selwyn from the medieval male personal names *Seluein* (from Old French, ultimately from Latin *Silvānus*, a derivative of *silva* 'wood'), and *Selewyne* (from Old English *Selewine*, literally 'hall-friend') [John Selwyn Lloyd (Lord Selwyn Lloyd), 1904–78, British Conservative politician]
— **Selwyn College** a college of Cambridge University, founded in 1882 and named in honour of George Augustus Selwyn, 1809–78, first bishop of New Zealand

Semmence 'son of **Seaman** (i)'

Semple (i) *also* **Sempill** different forms of **Sample**; (ii) from a medieval Scottish nickname for a simple, humble person

Sen a Hindu surname derived from Sanskrit *sena* 'army'

Sendall probably 'silk merchant' (from Middle English *sendal* 'thin rich silk')

Senior (i) from a nickname distinguishing the older of two people with the same personal name; (ii) from a medieval nickname for a low-born person who put on airs (from Anglo-Norman *segneur* 'lord')

Sennett a different form of **Sinnott** [Mack Sennett (original name Michael Sinott), 1880–1960, Canadian-born US film producer and director]

Sergent, Sergeant, Serjeant see **Sargent**

Sergentson, Sergeantson, Serjeantson see **Sargentson**

Serle see **Searle**

Serota 'orphan' (from Polish *sierota* 'orphan') [Sir Nicholas Serota, 1946–, British art-gallery administrator]

Serpico perhaps from a derivative of the Italian nickname *Serpe*, applied to a dangerously devious person (from *serpe* 'serpent, reptile')
— **Serpico** a film (1973) starring Al Pacino as New York cop Frank Serpico, who investigated corruption in the force

Service, Servis 'brewer' or 'inn-keeper' (from Anglo-Norman *cerveise* 'ale') [Robert Service, 1874–1958, British-born Canadian poet]

Sessions 'person from Soissons', northern France ('settlement of the Suessiones', a Gaulish tribe). See also **Sissons** (ii) [John Sessions (original name John Marshall), 1953–, British actor and writer; Roger Sessions, 1896–1985, US composer]

Seth (i) a Hindu, Jain and Parsi surname, from Hindi *seth* 'merchant, banker'; (ii) from Gaelic *Mac Sithigh* or *Ó Síthigh* (see **Sheehy**)

Seton see **Seaton**

Setter (i) 'layer of bricks or stones' (from a derivative of Middle English *setten* 'to set, lay'); (ii) 'embroiderer' (from a derivative of Middle English *setten* 'to set, put'); (iii) 'silk weaver' (from Old French *saietier*, a derivative of *sayete*, the name of a sort of silk)

Setters 'son of **Setter**'

Settle 'person from Settle', Yorkshire

Seuss see **Suess**

Severn, Severne (i) 'person who lives by the River Severn'; (ii) from the medieval personal name *Severn*, from Latin *Severīnus*, a derivative of *Severus*, literally 'severe, harsh'. See also **Sorenson** (i)

Sewall see **Sewell**

Seward (i) from the medieval personal names *Seward* (from Old English *Sǣweard*, literally 'sea-guard') and *Siward* (from Old English *Sigeweard*, literally 'victory-guard'); (ii) 'swineherd' (from Old English *sū* 'pig' + *hierde* 'herdsman'); (iii) from Irish Gaelic *Ó Suaird* or *Ó Suairt* 'descendant of *Suart*', from the Old Norse equivalent of Old English *Sǣweard* (see i). See also **Sword** (ii) [Anna Seward (the 'Swan of Lichfield'), 1747–1809, British poet]

Sewell, Sewall (i) 'person from Sewell, Seawell or Showell', Bedfordshire, Northamptonshire and Oxfordshire respectively ('seven springs'); (ii) from the medieval personal names *Sewald* (from Old English *Sǣweald*, literally 'sea-rule') and *Siwald* (from Old English *Sigeweald*, literally 'victory-rule') [Anna Sewell, 1820–78, British author; Brian Sewell, 1936–, British art critic; Rufus Sewell, 1967–, British actor]

Sexton (i) *also* **Sexten** or **Sexston** 'sexton' or 'churchwarden'. See also **Saxton, Seckerson**; (ii) from Irish Gaelic *Ó Seastnáin* 'descendant of *Seastnán*', perhaps a nickname meaning literally 'bodyguard' [Dave Sexton, 1930–, British football manager]

Seyler see **Seiler** (i)

Seymour, Seymore (i) 'person from Saint-Maur-des-Fossées', northern France, where the local church is dedicated to St *Maur* (from Latin *Maurus*; see **Moore** (ii)); (ii) 'person from Seamer', Yorkshire ('place by the pool') [Jane Seymour, ?1509–37, queen of England, third wife of Henry VIII; Jane Seymour (original name Joyce Frankenberg), 1951–, British actress]

Shackelford, Shackleford perhaps 'person from Shackleford Heath', Surrey

Shacklady perhaps from a medieval nickname for a man who had had sexual relations with a woman of higher social class (from *shag* 'to copulate with' (not recorded before the late 17th century) + *lady*)

Shackleton 'person from Shackleton', Yorkshire ('settlement on a tongue of land') [Sir Ernest Shackleton, 1874–1922, Irish-born British explorer]
— **Avro Shackleton** a British long-range patrol bomber, based ultimately on the World War II Avro Lancaster bomber and named in honour of Sir Ernest Shackleton. It was in service with the RAF from 1951 to 1990.

Shacklock 'gaoler' (from late Middle English *shaklock* 'fetter')

Shaddock a different form of **Chadwick**
— **shaddock** an alternative name for the pomelo, a grapefruit-like fruit. It comes from a certain Captain Shaddock, a 16th-century English seaman

who reputedly left seeds of the plant in Barbados on a passage from the East Indies.

Shadwell 'person from Shadwell', London, Norfolk and Yorkshire ('shallow spring') [Thomas Shadwell, ?1642–92, English dramatist]

Shaffer see **Schaffer**

Shaftoe, Shafto 'person from Shaftoe', Northumberland (probably 'ridge with a boundary post')
— **'Bobby Shafto's gone to sea'** an English nursery rhyme, popular since at least the 18th century. At least seven Roberts are on record in the Shafto family of Northeast England, but it is not known which one is referred to in the rhyme. It was used in support of Robert Shafto of Whitworth, County Durham in the parliamentary election of 1761. The first verse runs:
Bobby Shafto's gone to sea,
Silver buckles on his knee;
He'll come back and marry me,
Bonny Bobby Shafto!

Shah (i) a Muslim name, derived from Persian *shāh* 'king'; (ii) a Hindu and Jain name, derived from Gujarati *sah* 'merchant' [Eddy Shah, 1944–, British businessman; Idries Shah (original name Sayyid Idris al-Hashimi), 1924–96, Indian-born British Sufic author]

Shaikh see **Sheikh**

Shakespeare, Shakspeare from a medieval nickname for either a truculent person or possibly a sexually boastful male or even a flasher (literally 'spear-brandisher') [William Shakespeare, 1564–1616, English dramatist and poet]
— **Shakespearean, Shakespearian** of or characteristic of William Shakespeare (see above), or a student of or actor in his plays
— **Shakespeareana, Shakespeariana** things relating to William Shakespeare

Shakoor from a Muslim personal name based on Arabic *shakūr* 'grateful'

Shallcross, Shalcross 'person from Shallcross', Derbyshire ('place by the Shacklecross', an ancient stone cross in the High Peak, its name perhaps denoting a cross to which people could be shackled as a penance). See also **Shawcross**

Shanahan, Shanaghan, Shannahan from Irish Gaelic *Ó Seanacháin* 'descendant of *Seanachán*', literally 'little *Seanach*' (see **Shane** (i)). See also **Shannon**

Shand (i) perhaps a shortened form of **Alexander**; (ii) perhaps 'person from Chandai', Normandy ('Candius's settlement') [Jimmy Shand (Sir James Shand), 1908–2000, Scottish accordionist and bandleader]

Shane (i) from Irish Gaelic *Ó Seanaigh* 'descendant of *Seanach*', a personal name based on *sean* 'old, wise'; (ii) a reduced form of **McShane**

Shankar a Hindu name based on Sanskrit *šankara* 'bringer of happiness or prosperity'

Shanks from a medieval Scottish or northern English nickname for someone with long legs, or for someone who walked in a strange way (from Middle English *schankes* 'legs')

— **Shanks Ltd.** a British manufacturer of water closets and other sanitary ware, established in Barrhead, East Renfrewshire in 1865 by the Scottish plumber John Shanks. In 1969 it merged with Armitage Ware Ltd. to become Armitage Shanks.

Shanley from Irish Gaelic *Mac Seanlaoich* 'son of *Seanlaoch*', a personal name meaning literally 'old hero'

Shannon (i) from Irish Gaelic *Ó Seanáin* 'descendant of *Seanán*', a personal name meaning literally 'little old or wise one'; (ii) a different form of **Shanahan** [Del Shannon (original name Charles Weedon Westover), 1934–90, US rock'n'roll singer]

Shapcott 'person who lives by a sheepcote (an enclosure for sheep)' [Jo Shapcott, 1953–, British poet]

Shapiro (i) 'person from Speyer', Germany; (ii) perhaps an invented Jewish name, based on Hebrew *shapir* 'beautiful' [Helen Shapiro, 1946–, British popular singer]

Shardlow 'person from Shardlow', Derbyshire ('notched hill')

Sharif, Shareef a Muslim name based on Arabic *sharīf* 'illustrious'

Sharkey from Irish Gaelic *Ó Searcaigh* 'descendant of *Searcach*', a nickname meaning literally 'blessed'

Sharma a Hindu name based on Sanskrit *šarmā* 'joy, shelter'

Sharman a different form of **Sherman** (i) [Helen Sharman, 1963–, British astronaut]

Sharp, Sharpe from a medieval nickname for a quick or active person [Becky Sharp, the sharp-witted amoral heroine of W.M. Thackeray's *Vanity Fair* (1848); Cecil Sharp, 1859–1924, British musician and folk-song collector; Lt. Richard Sharpe, a British soldier of Napoleonic times, the invention of the novelist Bernard Cornwell and featuring in the television drama series *Sharpe* (1993–97); Tom Sharpe, 1928–, British novelist]
— **Sharpeville** a township near Vereeniging, South Africa, the scene in 1960 of a riot in which 60 African demonstrators were killed by the police. It was founded in 1942 (as Sharpe Native Township) and named after John Sharpe, at that time mayor of Vereeniging.

Sharples 'person from Sharples Hall', Lancashire (probably 'steep pasture') [Ena Sharples, a gossiping battleaxe (played by Violet Carson) in the early years of the British television soap opera *Coronation Street* (1960–)]

Sharpless a different form of **Sharples** [Sharpless, the US consul in Puccini's opera *Madam Butterfly* (1904)]

Sharratt, Sharrett different forms of **Sherratt**

Sharrock 'person from Shorrock Green', Lancashire (probably 'oak growing on a bank')

Shattock a different form of **Chadwick**

Shaughnessy from Irish Gaelic *Ó Seachnasaigh* 'descendant of *Seachnach*', a personal name perhaps based on *seachnach* 'elusive'. See also **O'Shaughnessy**

Shaw, Shawe (i) 'person who lives by a copse', or 'person from Shaw', the name of various places in England (in either case from Old English *sceaga* 'copse'); (ii) from any of a range of Gaelic surnames based on the personal name *Sithech*, literally 'wolf' [Artie Shaw (original name Arthur Arshawsky), 1910–2004, US jazz clarinettist and bandleader; George Bernard Shaw, 1856–1950, Irish playwright; Norman Shaw, 1831–1912, British architect; Sandie Shaw (original name Sandra Ann Goodrich), 1947–, British pop singer] — **Shavian** of or in the style of George Bernard Shaw (see above) or his plays. First recorded at the beginning of the 20th century, it was based on a mock-Latinization (quite possibly by Shaw himself) of *Shaw* as *Shavius*.

Shawcross a different form of **Shallcross** [Sir Hartley Shawcross (Lord Shawcross), 1902–2003, British barrister and Labour politician]

Shea, Shay from Irish Gaelic *Ó Séaghdha* 'descendant of *Séaghdha*', a nickname meaning literally 'fine' or 'fortunate'. See also **O'Shea**

Sheahan see **Sheehan**

Shealy from Irish Gaelic *Ó Sealbhaigh* 'descendant of *Sealbhach*', a nickname meaning literally 'wealthy'

Shear, Sheer from a medieval nickname for a beautiful person or a fair-haired person (from Middle English *scher* 'bright'). See also **Sher**

Shearer 'sheep-shearer'; also, 'person who trims the surface of newly woven cloth' [Alan Shearer, 1970–, English footballer; Moira Shearer (Lady Kennedy; original name Moira Shearer King), 1926–2006, British ballerina]

Shearman a different form of **Sherman** (i)

Sheedy from Irish Gaelic *Ó Síoda* 'descendant of *Síoda*', a nickname meaning literally 'silk'

Sheehan, Sheahan, Sheean from Irish Gaelic *Ó Síodhacháin* 'descendant of *Síodhachán*', a personal name meaning literally 'little peaceful one'. See also **Sheen, Shine**

Sheehy from the Gaelic personal name *Sítheach*, probably originally a nickname meaning literally 'of the other world, eerie'

Sheekey a different form of **Sheehy**

Sheen, Sheene different forms of **Sheehan** [Barry Sheene (original name Stephen Frank Sheene), 1950–2003, British motorcyclist; Charlie Sheen (original name Carlos Irwin Estévez), 1965–, US actor, son of Martin; Martin Sheen (original name Ramón Gerardo Antonio Estévez), 1940–, US actor; Michael Sheen, 1969–, British actor]

Sheepshanks from a medieval Scottish and northern English nickname for someone with a strange or awkward way of walking (literally 'sheeplegs')

Sheffield 'person from Sheffield', Yorkshire ('open land by the river Sheaf')

Sheikh, Shaikh a Muslim surname, based on Arabic *shaikh* 'political or spiritual leader'

Shelby perhaps a different form of **Selby**, or alternatively 'person from Shelby', an unidentified place in northern England (probably 'settlement with a hut')

Sheldon 'person from Sheldon', Birmingham, Derbyshire and Devon ('hill with a ledge', 'heathy hill with a ledge' and 'valley with a shelf' respectively) — **Sheldonian Theatre** the senate house of Oxford University, designed by Sir Christopher Wren and opened in 1699. It was named after Gilbert Sheldon, 1598–1677, archbishop of Canterbury, who provided the money for it.

Sheldrake from a medieval nickname for a dandyish or vain man (from Middle English *sheldrake* the male of a type of duck with colourful plumage)

Sheldrick a different form of **Sheldrake**

Shelley, Shelly 'person from Shelley', the name of various places in England ('woodland clearing on shelving terrain') [Barbara Shelley, 1933–, British actress; Howard Shelley, 1950–, British pianist; Mary Wollstonecraft Shelley (*née* Godwin), 1797–1851, British writer, wife of Percy; Percy Bysshe Shelley, 1792–1822, British poet]

Shelton 'person from Shelton', the name of various places in England ('farmstead on a shelf of ground'). See also **Shilton, Skelding, Skelton** [Anne Shelton (original name Patricia Sibley), 1928–94, British popular singer]

Shenstone 'person from Shenstone', Staffordshire ('beautiful stone') [William Shenstone, 1714–63, British poet]

Sheppard, Shepperd, Shephard, Shepherd, Shepheard, Shepard, Sheperd 'shepherd' [Allan Shepard, 1923–98, US astronaut, the first American in space (1961); David Shepherd, 1940–, British cricket umpire; David Sheppard (Lord Sheppard), 1929–2005, British churchman and cricketer; E.H. Shepard, 1879–1976, British artist and illustrator; Gillian Shephard (Baroness Shephard), 1940–, British Conservative politician; Jack Sheppard, 1702–24, British thief and highwayman; Sam Shepard (original name Samuel Shepard Rogers, Jr.), 1943–, US playwright and actor] — **Shepheard's Hotel** a hotel in Cairo, founded (as the Hotel des Anglais) in 1841 by Samuel Shepheard, a British farmer's son. It was destroyed during anti-British riots in 1952, but was rebuilt and reopened in 1957. — **Shepherd Market** an area of small narrow streets in Mayfair, London, to the north of Piccadilly, laid out in the mid-1730s by the architect and builder Edward Shepherd. Until comparatively recently it was noted mainly for the prostitutes who operated there.

Sher (i) 'maker of shears or scissors' or 'user of shears (e.g. a barber or sheep-shearer)' (from Yiddish *sher* 'shears, scissors'); (ii) a different form of **Shear** [Sir Anthony Sher, 1949–, South African-born British actor]

Sherard see **Sherrard**

Sheraton 'person from Sheraton', County Durham (probably 'Skurfa's farmstead') [Thomas Sheraton, 1751–1806, British furniture designer]

Sherborne, Sherbourne, Sherborn 'person from Sherborne', the name of various places in England ('bright stream')

Sheridan, Sherridan from Irish Gaelic *Ó Sirideáin* 'descendant of *Sirideán*', a personal name of uncertain origin and meaning [Ann Sheridan (original name Clara Lou Sheridan), 1915–67, US actress; Philip H. Sheridan, 1831–88, Federal general in the US Civil War; Richard Brinsley Sheridan, 1751–1816, Irish-born British playwright]

Sheriff, Sherriff 'sheriff (the representative of the monarch in an English or Welsh county)'. See also **Shreve** [R.C. Sherriff, 1896–1975, British playwright]

Sheringham 'person from Sheringham', Norfolk ('Scīra's people's homestead') [Teddy Sheringham, 1966–, English footballer]

Sherlock from a medieval nickname for a fair-haired person or one with a lock of fair hair (from Middle English *schirloc* 'bright lock')

Sherman (i) *also* **Shurman** 'sheep-shearer' or 'person who trims the surface of newly woven cloth' (from Middle English *shereman*, literally 'shear-man, operator of shears'). See also **Sharman, Shearman**; (ii) 'tailor' (from Yiddish *sher* 'shears, scissors' + *man*) [Sir Alfred Sherman, 1919–, British journalist and political advisor; Cindy Sherman, 1954–, US photographer; William T. Sherman, 1820–91, Federal general in the US Civil War]

— **General Sherman** a name given, in 1879, to a 2200-year-old giant sequoia tree in Giant Forest, in Sequoia National Park, California, in honour of William T. Sherman (see above). With a trunk 1487 cubic metres in volume (as calculated in 2002) it is the world's largest tree, and has been claimed as the world's largest living organism. It is 83.8 metres/274.9 feet high.

— **Sherman tank** the name of what was officially the Medium Tank M4, the main US battle tank of the Second World War. Honouring General Sherman, it was originally bestowed by the British. It has also been used as rhyming slang for *Yank* and *wank*.

Sherrard, Sherard probably from a medieval nickname based on Middle English *shere* 'bright, fair', with the derogatory suffix *-ard*

Sherratt probably a different form of **Sherrard**, or alternatively perhaps of **Sherwood**

Sherriff see **Sheriff**

Sherrin 'person from Sheering', Essex (probably 'Sceara's people's settlement') [Ned Sherrin, 1931–, British producer, director and writer]

Sherrington 'person from Sherington', Buckinghamshire ('settlement associated with Scīra'). See also **Shrimpton** [Sir Charles Scott Sherrington, 1857–1952, British physiologist]

Sherry a reduced form of **McSherry**

Sherwin from a medieval nickname for a quick runner (literally 'shear-wind')

Sherwood 'person from the area of Sherwood Forest', Nottinghamshire ('wood of the shire')

Shick see **Schick** (ii)

Shield (i) 'armourer' (from Middle English *scheld* 'shield'); (ii) 'person who lives by a shallow part of a river' (from Middle English *scheld* 'shallow place'); (iii) a different form of **Shields**

Shields (i) 'person from North or South Shields', North and South Tyneside respectively ('sheds' (referring to temporary fishermen's huts)); (ii) from Irish Gaelic *Ó Siadhail* 'descendant of *Siadhail*', a personal name of unknown origin and meaning [Brooke Shields, 1965–, US model and actress]

Shilling probably from a medieval nickname based on the notion of a shilling (as paid e.g. in rent) (either directly from Middle English *schilling* 'shilling', or as a later anglicization of German *Schilling*)

Shillingford 'person from Shillingford', Devon and Oxfordshire (the latter probably 'ford belonging to Sciella's people')

Shillito a name of unknown derivation and meaning, probably originating in Yorkshire. See also **Sillito**

Shilton 'person from Shilton', the name of various places in English ('farmstead on a shelf of ground'). See also **Shelton, Skelton** [Peter Shilton, 1949–, English footballer]

Shine a different form of **Sheehan**

Shingler 'person whose job is to lay shingles (wooden tiles) on roofs'

Shinn 'person whose job is to strip animal carcases of their hide' (from Middle English *shin* 'skin'). See also **Skinner**

Shipley 'person from Shipley', the name of various places in England ('glade frequented by sheep') [Jenny Shipley, 1952–, New Zealand National Party politician, prime minister 1997–99]

Shipman (i) 'sailor' or 'boatbuilder'; (ii) 'shepherd' (from Middle English *schepman*, literally 'sheepman') [Dr Harold Shipman, 1946–2004, British mass murderer]

Shipp 'sailor' or 'boatbuilder'

Shippam 'person from Shipham', Somerset ('homestead where sheep graze')

— **Shippam's** a British brand of meat and fish paste. The firm was founded in Chichester, Sussex in 1786 by Charles Shippam, a pork butcher, and consolidated by his son, also Charles Shippam, 1828–97. It introduced its potted meat paste in 1892.

Shippen 'person from Shippen' or various other similarly spelled places in England ('cattle shed')

Shippey, Shippy 'person who lives by a sheep enclosure or on an area of raised ground where sheep graze' (from Old English *scēaphæg* 'sheep enclosure' or *scēapēg* 'sheep island')

Shipton 'person from Shipton', the name of various places in England ('sheep enclosure')

[Mother Shipton (original name Ursula Southeil), 1488–?1560, English prophetess and witch]

Shipway 'person who lives by a path along which sheep are driven' (from Middle English *schipway* 'sheep-path')

Shirley 'person from Shirley', the name of various places in England ('bright glade') [James Shirley, 1596–1666, English dramatist; John Shirley-Quirk, 1931–, British baritone]

Shockley (i) perhaps 'person from Shocklach', Cheshire ('boggy stream infested with evil spirits'); (ii) perhaps an anglicization of Swiss German *Schoechli*, literally 'person who lives by the little barn'

Shoe 'maker or repairer of shoes'. See also **Shue**

Shoemaker a translation of **Schumacher**

Shoesmith 'blacksmith who shoes horses, farrier'

Shone from the male personal name *Siôn*, a Welsh form of **John**

Shonfield an anglicization of **Schoenfeld**

Shooter, Shuter 'marksman'. See also **Shutter**

Shore (i) 'person who lives by a river bank or steep slope' (from Old English *scora* 'bank'); (ii) 'person who lives by the seashore'; (iii) an anglicization of the Jewish surname *Schorr* or *Szor*, from German *Schauer*, literally 'inspector' [Jane Shore, died ?1527, mistress of Edward IV; Jemima Shore, the high-flying television reporter and amateur sleuth invented (1977) by Antonia Fraser; Peter Shore (Lord Shore), 1924–2001, British Labour politician]

Shores a different form of **Shore** (i–ii)

Short (i) from a nickname for a short person. See also **Shorter**; (ii) a translation of Irish Gaelic *Mac an Ghirr*, literally 'son of the short man' [Clare Short, 1946–, British Labour politician; Edward Short (Lord Glenamara), 1912–, British Labour politician; Nigel Short, 1965–, British chess player]
— **Short Brothers** a Belfast-based British aerospace company founded in 1908 by the brothers Eustace Short, 1875–1932, Horace Short, 1872–1917, and Oswald Short, 1883–1969
— **Shortstown** a village in Bedfordshire, built in 1917 as a garden village for its employees by Short Brothers (see above)

Shortall, Shorthall, Shortle from the Irish Gaelic surname *Soirtéil*, which was itself a gaelicization of the English surname *Shorthals*, from a medieval nickname meaning literally 'short neck'

Shorter from a nickname for a shorter person

Shorthouse (i) from a medieval nickname for someone who wore short hose (leggings); (ii) a different form of **Shortall**

Shotton 'person from Shotton', the name of various places in Northeast England (variously 'farmstead on a hill', 'farmstead by a steep slope', 'farmstead of the Scots' and 'hill of the Scots')

Shovell 'maker of shovels' or 'person who works with a shovel' [Sir Cloudesley Shovell, 1650–1707, English admiral]

Showalter an anglicization of *Schowalter*, a German surname of unknown origin and meaning

Showell a different form of **Shovell**

Shrapnel a different form of **Carbonell**
— **shrapnel** metal balls or fragments that are scattered when a bomb, shell or bullet explodes. It is named after General Henry Shrapnel, 1761–1842, a British artillery officer who during the Peninsular War invented a shell that produced that effect.

Shreve, Shreeve different forms of **Sheriff**

Shreves, Shreeves 'son of **Shreve**'

Shrimpton a different form of **Sherrington** [Jean Shrimpton, 1942–, British fashion model]

Shriver an anglicization of the Dutch surname *Schriever*, literally 'scribe, clerk' [Lionel Shriver (original name Margaret Ann Shriver), 1957–, US author and journalist; Pam Shriver, 1962–, US tennis player; Sargent Shriver, 1915–, US lawyer, diplomat and academic]

Shue an anglicization of the German surname *Schuh* or *Schue*, literally 'shoe', hence 'maker or repairer of shoes'. See also **Shoe** [Elisabeth Shue, 1963–, US actress]

Shufflebottom, Shufflebotham 'person from Shipperbottom', Lancashire ('valley with a spring where sheep are washed')

Shulman see **Schulman**

Shultz, Shults see **Schultz**

Shurman see **Sherman** (i)

Shuster see **Schuster**

Shute 'person from Shute', Devon ('nook of land') [Nevil Shute (original name Nevil Shute Norway), 1899–1960, British novelist]

Shuter see **Shooter**

Shutt, Shutte 'archer' (from Old English *scytta*, a derivative of *scēotan* 'to shoot')

Shutter a different form of **Shooter**

Shuttleworth 'person from Shuttleworth', the name of various places in northern England ('barred enclosure')
— **Shuttleworth Trust** a trust devoted to education and training in the fields of aeronautics and aviation history. It was founded in 1944 in his memory by the mother of the pilot Richard Shuttleworth, 1909–40, whose collection of early aircraft formed the basis of the **Shuttleworth Collection** now kept at Old Warden airfield, Bedfordshire.

Shutts 'son of **Shutt**'

Sibley from the medieval female personal name *Sibley*, an English form of Latin *Sibilla* (ultimately from Greek *Sibulla*, a name given to a prophetess) [Dame Antoinette Sibley, 1939–, British ballerina]

Sibson 'son of *Sib*', a pet-form of *Sibley* (see **Sibley**)

Siddall, Siddell, Siddle 'person from Siddal', Lancashire and Yorkshire ('wide nook of land')

Siddiqi 'descendant of *Ṭiddīq*', an Arabic personal name meaning literally 'truthful, righteous'

Siddons a name of unknown origin and meaning [Sarah Siddons (*née* Kemble), 1755–1831, English actress]

Sidebottom, Sidebotham 'person from Sidebottom', Cheshire ('wide valley')

Sidgwick, Sidgewick different forms of **Sedgwick** [Henry Sidgwick, 1838–1900, British moral philosopher]
— **Sidgwick and Jackson** a publishing company founded in London in 1908 by Frank Sidgwick, 1879–1939, and Robert Cameron Jackson, 1882–1917

Sidney, Sydney 'person from Sidney', Lincolnshire and Surrey ('wide area of dry land in a fen'); also perhaps 'person from Saint-Denis', the name of a place in Normandy with a church dedicated to St Dennis [Algernon Sidney, 1622–83, English Whig politician; Sir Philip Sidney, 1554–86, English poet, courtier and soldier]
— **Sydney** the capital of New South Wales, Australia. Founded in 1788 by Captain Arthur Phillip, it was named in honour of Thomas Townshend, Lord Sydney, 1732–1800, the then British home secretary (whose title was adopted to mark his descent from Robert Sydney, 2nd earl of Leicester, 1595–1677).
— **Sidney Sussex College** a college of Cambridge University, founded in 1594 under the terms of the will of Lady Frances Sidney, ?1531–88/89, dowager countess of Sussex

Siefert a different form of **Seifert**

Sieff by tradition from the Yiddish male personal name *Zev* (from Hebrew *Zeev*, literally 'wolf')

Siegel (i) *also* **Siegl** from the medieval German personal name *Siegel*, based on a shortened form of any of a range of Germanic names (e.g. *Siegfried*, *Siegmund*) beginning with *Sieg-*, literally 'victory'; (ii) 'maker of seals or signet rings' (from Middle High German *sigel* 'seal'); (iii) see **Segal** (ii)

Sikes see **Sykes**

Sikora from a medieval Polish nickname for a small swarthy person (from Polish *sikora* 'coaltit')

Sikorski, Sikorsky different forms of **Sikora** [Igor Ivan Sikorsky, 1889–1972, Russian-born US aeronautical engineer, inventor of the helicopter]

Silcock from the medieval personal name *Sill* (see **Sill**), with the suffix *-cock* (literally 'cockerel', hence 'jaunty or bumptious young man'), that was often added to create pet-forms of personal names in the Middle Ages

Silcocks, Silcox 'son of **Silcock**'

Silk, Silke (i) 'silk merchant'; (ii) from the medieval personal name *Silk*, a shortened form of **Silkin**; (iii) a translation of Irish Gaelic *Ó Síoda* (see **Sheedy**)

Silkin 'little **Sill**' [John Silkin, 1923–87, British solicitor and Labour politician; Jon Silkin, 1930–97, British poet]

Silkwood probably 'person from Silkwood or Silk Wood', Devon and Gloucestershire [Karen Silkwood, 1946–74, US trade-union activist and campaigner]
— **Silkwood** a film (1983) about the campaign of Karen Silkwood (see above) to expose safety problems in a nuclear processing plant, and her subsequent death. It starred Meryl Streep.

Sill from the medieval male personal name *Sill*, a shortened form of **Silvester**)

Sillett 'little **Sill**'

Sillito, Sillitoe different forms of **Shillito** [Alan Sillitoe, 1928–, British novelist, short-story writer and poet]

Sills 'son of **Sill**' [Beverley Sills (original name Belle Silverman), 1929–, US soprano]

Silva 'person who lives in a wood' (from Old Spanish and Old Portuguese *silva* 'wood')

Silver (i) from a medieval nickname for a wealthy person, or for a person with silver-grey hair; (ii) 'person who lives by the Silver', the name of numerous streams in various parts of England; (iii) a translation of the invented Jewish surname *Silber* (from German *Silber* 'silver') [Long John Silver, the one-legged buccaneer in Robert Louis Stevenson's *Treasure Island* (1883)]
— **Silvertown** a district in London's Docklands, in the borough of Newham. It got its name from S.W. Silver & Co., a local firm producing rubber goods, which built houses for its workforce in the area in the 1850s.

Silverman a translation of the German name *Silbermann* and the Jewish name *Silberman*, both literally 'silver man'

Silvers 'son of **Silver**' [Phil Silvers (original name Philip Silver), 1912–85, US comic actor, portrayer of Sgt. Ernie Bilko in *The Phil Silvers Show* (1955–60)]

Silverstein a partial translation of the German name *Silberstein* 'person from Silberstein', Bavaria ('silver stone'), or of the invented Jewish name *Silberstein*, literally 'silver stone'

Silvester, Sylvester from the male personal name *Silvester*, from Latin, a derivative of *silva* 'wood' [Victor Silvester, 1900–78, British dance-band leader]

Sim, Simm from the medieval male personal name *Sim*, a shortened form of **Simon**. See also **Sime**, **Simkin**, **Simpson**, **Sims** [Alastair Sim, 1900–76, British actor]

Simcock from the medieval personal name *Sim* (see **Sim**), with the suffix *-cock* (literally 'cockerel', hence 'jaunty or bumptious young man'), that was often added to create pet-forms of personal names in the Middle Ages. See also **Sincock**

Simcocks, Simcox, Symcox 'son of **Simcock**'

Sime, Syme different forms of **Sim**

Simeon from the male personal name *Simeon*, a different form of **Simon**

Simes, Symes 'son of **Sime**'

Simkin (i) *also* **Simpkin** 'little **Sim**'; (ii) 'son of *Simke*', a pet-form of the Yiddish female personal name *Sime* (from Hebrew *Simcha*, literally 'joy')

Simkins, Simpkins 'son of **Simkin** (i)'

Simkinson, Simpkinson 'son of **Simkin** (i)'

Simmons, Simmonds, Symmons different forms of **Simons**. See also **Fitzsimmons** [Jean

Simmons, 1929–, British actress; Posy Simmonds, 1945–, British cartoonist]

Simms see **Sims**

Simnel, Simnell 'little **Simon**' [Lambert Simnel, ?1475–1535, English impostor who claimed to be Edward, Earl of Warwick]

Simon, Symon from the male personal name *Simon*, from Hebrew *Shim'on*, probably a derivative of *sham'a* 'to hearken'. See also **Sim**, **Simeon** [Sir John Simon (Viscount Simon), 1873–1954, British lawyer and Conservative politician, lord chancellor 1940–45; Neil Simon, 1927–, US playwright; Paul Simon, 1941–, US singer and songwriter]
— **Simon and Garfunkel** a US folk-rock duo consisting of Paul Simon (see above) and Art Garfunkel (see **Garfunkel**). It was active between 1957 and 1970.

Simone from the male personal name *Simone*, the Italian equivalent of **Simon** [Nina Simone (original name Eunice Kathleen Waymon), 1933–2003, US jazz singer and composer]

Simons, Symons, Symonds 'son of **Simon**'. See also **Simmons** [Arthur Symons, 1865–1945, British poet; John Addington Symonds, 1840–93, British art historian and critic]

Simpson, Simson 'son of **Sim**' [Alan Simpson, 1929–, British comedy scriptwriter; Bobby Simpson, 1936–, Australian cricketer; George Gaylord Simpson, 1902–84, US palaeontologist; Sir James Young Simpson, 1811–70, British obstetrician; John Simpson (original name John Fidler-Simpson), 1944–, British television journalist; N.F. Simpson, 1919–, British surrealist dramatist; O.J. Simpson, 1947–, US American football player, sportscaster and actor; Wallis Simpson ('Mrs Simpson'; Duchess of Windsor; original name Bessie Wallis Warfield), 1896–1986, US divorcee who married Edward VIII after his abdication]
— **Simpson Desert** a large desert in central Australia, approximately 170,000 square kilometres in extent. It was named (in 1939, by the explorer Cecil Madigan) in honour of the Australian geographer and philanthropist Alfred Allen Simpson, 1875–1939.
— **Simpson of Piccadilly** a men's clothing store at 203 Piccadilly, London, opened in 1936 by Alexander Simpson to sell the wares produced by his firm, S. Simpson Ltd. of Stoke Newington. It closed in 1999.
— *The Simpsons* a US television cartoon series (1989–) following the bizarre life of a blue-collar American family, including its slobbish paterfamilias Homer Simpson and his egregious son Bart
— **Simpson's-in-the-Strand** a restaurant at 100 Strand, London, opened (as Simpson's Divan and Tavern) by the caterer John Simpson in 1848. It became famous for its roasts carved at table.

Sims, Simms, Syms 'son of **Sim**' [Joan Sims, 1930–2001, British comedy actress; Sylvia Syms, 1934–, British actress; William Gilmore Simms, 1806–70, US novelist]

Sinatra from a southern Italian personal name derived ultimately from Latin *senātor* 'member of the senate', later 'magistrate' [Frank Sinatra, 1915–98, US singer and actor]
— **Sinatra doctrine** an informal name for the policy pursued by the Soviet Union towards its East European satellites during the period of Mikhail Gorbachev's 'glasnost' at the end of the 1980s, of allowing them to 'go their own way', recalling the 'I did it my way' of the song popularized by Frank Sinatra (see above), 'My Way'

Sinclair 'person from Saint-Clair', the name of numerous places in France with a church dedicated to St Clarus (in the case of the Scottish Sinclair clan, specifically from Saint-Clair-sur-Elle or Saint-Clair-l'Évêque in northern France). See also **Saint-Clair** [Sir Clive Sinclair, 1940–, British engineer and inventor; Upton Sinclair, 1878–1968, US novelist]

Sincock a different form of **Simcock**

Sinden a surname of unknown origin and meaning, associated mainly with Sussex [Sir Donald Sinden, 1923–, British actor]

Singer (i) 'singer, choir member', or from a medieval nickname for someone who was always singing; also, 'cantor in a synagogue' (from Yiddish *zinger* 'singer'); (ii) from a different form of the German surname *Sänger*, literally 'poet' [Isaac Bashevis Singer, 1904–91, Polish-born US novelist and short-story writer; Isaac Merrit Singer, 1811–75, US inventor and entrepreneur, producer of the first commercially successful sewing machine]
— **Abby Singer shot** in US film studio slang, the penultimate shot of the day. The term was inspired by an assistant director of that name at Universal Studios, Hollywood in the 1950s, who was always promising that the next shot would be the last.
— **Singer** a British car manufacturer, which had its beginnings in the Singer Cycle Co., founded in Coventry in 1876 by the engineer George Singer.

Singh from a Sikh and Rajput male personal name derived from Sanskrit *siṁha*, literally 'lion', hence 'great person, hero' [Vijay Singh, 1963–, Fijian golfer]

Singleton 'person from Singleton', Lancashire and Sussex (respectively 'farmstead with a shingled roof' and 'farmstead with tufts of grass') [Valerie Singleton, 1937–, British television broadcaster]

Sinnott, Sinnett, Synnott from the medieval personal name *Sinod* (from Old English *Sigenōth*, literally 'victory-brave'). See also **Sennett**

Sisley from the medieval female personal name *Sisley*, a different form of *Cecilie*, ultimately from Latin *Caecilia* [Alfred Sisley, 1839–99, French-born (of British parents) Impressionist painter]

Sisson 'little **Sisley**' [Rosemary Anne Sisson, 1923–, British author]

Sissons (i) 'son of **Sisson**'; (ii) a different form of **Sessions** [Peter Sissons, 1942–, British television newsreader]

Sitwell perhaps 'person from Sitwell', an unidentified place [Dame Edith Sitwell, 1887–1964, British poet and writer; Sir Osbert Sitwell, 1892–1969, British writer, brother of Edith; Sir Sacheverell Sitwell, 1897–1988, British writer, brother of Edith]

Sixsmith perhaps 'maker of sickles'

Sizer 'member of an assize court'

Skeat, Skeate, Skeet, Skeete from the Old Norse nickname *Skjótr*, literally 'quick' [W.W. Skeat, 1835–1912, British literary scholar and philologist]

Skeen, Skeene see **Skene**

Skeffington 'person from Skeffington', Leicestershire ('settlement associated with Scēaft'). See also **Skevington** [Sir Lumley St George Skeffington, 1771–1850, British playwright and fop]

Skelding 'person from Skelding or Skelden', Yorkshire ('valley of the river Skell') [Alec Skelding, 1886–1960, British cricket umpire]

Skelton 'person from Skelton', Cumbria and Yorkshire ('farmstead on a shelf of ground'). See also **Shelton** [John Skelton, ?1460–1529, English poet; Nick Skelton, 1957–, British showjumper]

Skene, Skeen, Skeene 'person from Skene', Aberdeenshire ('thorn bush')

Skevington a different form of **Skeffington**
— **Skevington's daughter** an instrument of torture that worked by compressing the body forwards from the hips, with the head against the knees, with such force that there was bleeding from the nose and ears. It was invented during Henry VIII's reign by Leonard Skevington or Skeffington, Lieutenant of the Tower of London.

Skewes, Skews see **Skuse**

Skidmore a different form of **Scudamore**

Skinner 'person whose job is to strip animal carcases of their hide'. See also **Shinn** [B.F. Skinner, 1904–90, US behavioural psychologist; Dennis Skinner, 1932–, British Labour politician; Frank Skinner (original name Chris Collins), 1957–, British comedian]
— **Lilley and Skinner** see **Lilly**
— **Lynyrd Skynyrd** a US blues band founded in 1966. Its name was a rewrite of 'Leonard Skinner', the name of a gym teacher at the band members' high school who had had them expelled for having long hair.
— **Skinner box** a sealed box in which an animal is placed with some piece of equipment (e.g. a handle) which it must learn to operate in order to receive a reward or avoid punishment. It is named after B.F. Skinner (see above).
— **Skinnerian** (a supporter) of the behaviourist theories of B.F. Skinner

Skipper (i) 'captain of a ship'; (ii) 'basket-maker' (from a derivative of Middle English *skippe* 'basket'); (iii) 'acrobat', or from a nickname for a bouncy high-spirited person

Skipwith 'person from Skipwith', Yorkshire ('sheep farm')

Skipworth a different form of **Skipwith**

Skuse, Skewes, Skews 'person from Skuse', Cornwall ('place by the elder bush')

Slack, Slacke (i) 'person who lives in a shallow valley', or 'person from Slack', the name of various places in northern England (in either case from Middle English *slack* 'shallow valley'); (ii) from a medieval nickname for a lazy person

Sladden a different form of **Sladen**

Slade 'person who lives in a small valley', or 'person from Slade or Slad', the name of various places in Southwest England (in either case from Old English *slæd* 'small valley') [Felix Slade, 1790–1868, British art collector; Julian Slade, 1930–2006, British author and composer]
— **Slade** a British glam-rock and hard-rock group, formed in 1966 as 'The N'Betweens'. The choice of new name (originally, in 1969, as 'Ambrose Slade', abbreviated to 'Slade' in 1970) was apparently purely random.
— **Slade School of Fine Art** an art school within University College London, opened in 1871 and named in honour of Felix Slade (see above), who had been a generous benefactor of the college
— *The Strange World of Gurney Slade* a British television sitcom (1960) starring Anthony Newley as Gurney Slade, a Walter Mitty-like character (the name was actually taken from Gurney Slade, a village in Somerset)

Sladen probably 'person from Sladen', an unidentified place (probably 'valley with a bog'). See also **Sladden**

Slater, Sclater 'person who lays slates on roofs' [John Slater, 1916–75, British actor; Oscar Slater (original surname Leschziner), 1872–1948, German-born pimp and gambler wrongfully convicted of a notorious 1908 Glasgow murder]

Slattery from Irish Gaelic *Ó Slatarra* or *Ó Slatra* 'descendant of *Slatra*', a nickname meaning literally 'strong' or 'bold' [Tony Slattery, 1959–, British actor and comedian]

Slaughter (i) 'slaughterer (of animals)'; (ii) 'person who lives by a muddy place', or 'person from Upper or Lower Slaughter', Gloucestershire, or various other similarly named places in England (in either case from Middle English *sloghtre* 'muddy place'); (iii) 'person who lives by a sloe tree' (from Old English *slāhtrēow* 'sloe tree') [Karin Slaughter, 1971–, US crime writer; Tod Slaughter (original name Norman Carter Slaughter), 1885–1956, British film actor]

Slavin (i) from Irish Gaelic *Ó Sléibhín* 'descendant of *Sléibhín*', a personal name probably based on *sliabh* 'mountain'; (ii) 'son of *Slave*', a Yiddish female personal name, from Slavic *slava* 'fame, praise'. See also **Slevin**

Slazenger a different form of **Schlesinger**
— **Slazenger** a British sports equipment brand, established in 1881 by the Jewish tailor's son Ralph Slazenger Moss, 1845–1910, and his brother Albert

Sledge 'maker or user of sledgehammers'

Slee a different form of **Sly**

Sleeman a different form of **Slee**

Sleep 'person who lives by a slippery muddy place', or 'person from Sleap or Slape', the name of various places in England (in either case from Old English *slǣp* 'slippery muddy place') [Wayne Sleep, 1948–, British dancer and choreographer]

Slessinger, Slesinger different forms of **Schlesinger**

Slevin a different form of **Slavin** (i)

Sligh see **Sly**

Slim 'person who lives by a muddy place' (from Old English *slīm* 'slime, mud') [William Slim (Viscount Slim), 1891–1970, British field marshal]

Slinger 'person armed with a sling', or from a medieval nickname for someone who was a good shot with a sling

Slingsby 'person from Slingsby', Yorkshire ('Slengr's farmstead')

Sloane, Sloan, Slone from the Gaelic personal name *Sluaghadhán*, literally 'little *Sluaghadh*', from *sluaghadh* 'expedition, raid' [Sir Hans Sloane, 1660–1753, British physician, naturalist and collector; Tod Sloan, 1874–1933, US jockey]
— **on your Tod Sloan** British rhyming slang for *on your own*, based on the name of the US jockey (see above). It now appears almost exclusively in its abbreviated guise as *on your tod*.
— **Sloane Square** a square in Belgravia, southwest London, laid out in the last quarter of the 18th century and named in honour of Sir Hans Sloane (see above), who had owned the land on which it was built

Slocombe, Slocomb, Slocum, Slocumb 'person from Slocum', Devon and Isle of Wight ('valley where sloes grow') [Mrs Slocombe, mature sale-slady with an unfortunate tendency to *double entendre* in the BBC television sitcom *Are You Being Served?* (1973–85)]

Sloman (i) 'person who lives by a swamp or bog', or 'person from Slough', Berkshire, or various other similarly named places in England (in either case from Old English *slōh* 'swamp, bog'); (ii) from a medieval nickname for a slow-moving or slow-witted person; (iii) 'person who lives by a sloe tree' (from Middle English *sloh* 'sloe')

Slone see **Sloane**

Sloper 'maker of overalls' (from a derivative of Middle English *slope* 'overalls') [Ally Sloper, a lazy scheming bulbous-nosed ne'er-do-well, the first true comic-strip character, created in 1867 by Charles Henry Ross in the pages of the British magazine *Judy*]

Sly, Sligh from a medieval nickname for a crafty person. See also **Slee** [Christopher Sly, a drunken Warwickshire tinker who appears in the introductory scene to Shakespeare's *The Taming of the Shrew* (1592)]

Smail (i) see **Smale**; (ii) 'person from Smeghel', a lost place in Sussex ('burrow')

Smails 'son of **Smail** (i)'

Smale, Smail different forms of **Small**

Smales 'son of **Smale**'

Small from a medieval nickname for a short or thin person. See also **Smale, Smiles** [Millie Small, 1942–, Jamaican soul and pop singer]

Smalley 'person from Smalley', Derbyshire and Lancashire ('narrow glade')

Smallman 'subtenant (in the feudal system)'

Smallwood 'person from Smallwood', Cheshire ('narrow wood')

Smart, Smartt from a medieval nickname for a brisk or efficient person [Billy Smart, Jr. (original name Billy Stanley), 1934–2005, British circus performer and proprietor; Christopher Smart, 1722–71, British poet]

Smead, Smeed probably different forms of **Smith**

Smeaton 'person from Smeaton or Smeeton', the name of various places in England and Scotland ('settlement of the smiths')

Smedley 'person from Smedley', an unidentified place probably in Nottinghamshire (perhaps 'smooth glade')

Smee a different form of **Smeed**

Smeed see **Smead**

Smellie, Smelley different forms of **Smillie**

Smethurst 'person from Smethurst', Lancashire ('smooth hill') [Allan Smethurst ('the Singing Postman'), 1927–2000, British postman and singer; Jack Smethurst, 1932–, British actor]

Smiles 'son of **Small**' [Samuel Smiles, 1812–1904, British writer, notably of self-help manuals]

Smiley, Smylie probably different forms of **Smillie** [George Smiley, a British intelligence agent in John Le Carré's espionage novels]

Smillie from a medieval Scottish nickname for an extremely smelly person, or for someone who made extravagant use of perfumes and scents (from a derivative of Middle English *smil* 'odour'). See also **Smellie** [Carol Smillie, 1961–, British television presenter]

Smith, Smyth 'metal worker, smith'. See also **Smythe** [Adam Smith, 1723–90, British philosopher and economist; Bessie Smith, 1894–1937, US blues singer; Sir C. Aubrey Smith, 1863–1948, British actor and cricketer; Chris Smith (Lord Smith), 1951–, British Labour politician; Sir Cyril Smith, 1928–, British Liberal politician; Delia Smith, 1941–, British television cook; Edward J. Smith, 1850–1912, British master mariner, captain of RMS *Titanic*; Dame Ethel Smyth, 1858–1944, British composer and social reformer; F.E. Smith (1st earl of Birkenhead), 1872–1930, British lawyer and Conservative politician, lord chancellor 1919–22; Godfrey Smith, 1926–, British journalist; Harvey Smith, 1938–, British showjumper; Ian Smith, 1919–, Rhodesian politician, prime minister 1964–79; John Smith, 1580–1631, English-born North American colonist; John Smith, 1938–94, British Labour politician; Joseph Smith, 1805–44, US founder of the Church of Jesus Christ of Latter-Day Saints (Mormons); Linda Smith, 1958–2006, British comedian; Liz Smith, 1925–, British actress; Logan Pearsall

Smith, 1865–1946, US man of letters; Madeleine Smith, 1838–1912, Glasgow woman tried for murder and partially exonerated by a verdict of 'not proven'; Dame Maggie Smith, 1934–, British actress; Margaret Smith, see Margaret **Court**; Mel Smith, 1952–, British comedian, actor and director; Mike Smith, 1933–, English cricketer; Patti Smith, 1946–, US punk musician, singer and poet; Sir Paul Smith, 1946–, British fashion designer; Stevie Smith (original name Florence Margaret Smith), 1902–71, British poet and novelist; Sydney Smith, 1771–1845, British clergyman, writer and wit; T. Dan Smith, 1915–93, British Labour local politician, imprisoned for corruption; Wilbur Smith, 1933–, Rhodesian-born author; Will Smith (original name Willard Smith), 1968–, US actor and hip-hop performer]

☆ The commonest surname in Britain, the US, Canada, Australia and New Zealand; 5th commonest in Ireland

● Men with the surname Smith were in the past traditionally given the nickname 'Smudger'

— **Adam Smith Institute** a British political think-tank advocating free-market and other classical liberal policies, founded in 1977 and named in honour of Adam Smith (see above)

— *Alas Smith and Jones* a BBC television comedy sketch programme (1984–92) starring Mel Smith (see above) and Griff Rhys-Jones. Its title mimicked that of *Alias Smith and Jones* (see next).

— *Alias Smith and Jones* a US television western series (1971–74) featuring the exploits of two ex-bank robbers who adopt the aliases Joshua Smith and Thaddeus Jones

— **Granny Smith** a variety of green-skinned eating apple, named after its original cultivator, Maria Ann Smith (known as 'Granny Smith'), ?1801–70, of Eastwood, New South Wales, Australia

— **Harvey Smith** a colloquial British term for a V-sign as a signal of contempt. It originated in an incident in 1971 when the showjumper Harvey Smith (see above) made such a gesture during a televised event.

— **John Smith's Bitter** a brand of bitter, produced at the brewery founded in 1847 in Tadcaster, Yorkshire by John Smith

— **Ladysmith** a small town in eastern South Africa, object of a famous Boer siege in 1899–1900. Established in 1847, it was originally called Windsor, after a local trader. Its name was subsequently changed in honour of Lady Smith (*née* Juana Maria de los Dolores de León), wife of Sir Harry Smith, 1787–1860, governor of Cape Colony.

— *Mr Smith Goes to Washington* a film (1939) directed by Frank Capra and starring James Stewart as a young senator who exposes corruption in high Washington places. It was based on a story by Lewis R. Foster.

— **Psmith** Rupert (in later incarnations Ronald Eustace) Psmith, dandyish Old Etonian (expelled) flaneur and social escapologist in the works of P.G. Wodehouse. Debuting in *Lost Lambs* (1909; later (1935) renamed *Enter Psmith*), he was the first of

the major characters Wodehouse created. The *P* (silent) was his own addition.

— **Smith & Nephew** a British manufacturer of home healthcare products (including Elastoplast), founded in Hull in 1896 by the chemist Thomas James Smith, 1825–96, and his nephew Horatio Nelson Smith, 1874–1960

— **Smith & Wesson** the proprietary name of a make of firearm, especially a type of cartridge revolver, manufactured by the firm of gunsmiths founded in Springfield, Massachusetts by Horace Smith, 1808-93, and Daniel B. Wesson, 1825-1906.

— **smithiantha** a small perennial plant of the genus *Smithiantha*, native to Mexico, which has clusters of red, yellow, or orange bell-shaped flowers. It was named in honour of the botanical artist Matilda Smith, 1854-1926.

— **smithite** a sulpharsenite of silver, $AgAsS_2$, which occurs as red crystals. It was named after the British mineralogist G. F. Herbert Smith, 1872-1953.

— **SmithKline Beecham** a British pharmaceutical company formed in 1989 by the merger of Beecham (see **Beauchamp**) with SmithKline Beckman. The latter originated in a pharmacy opened in Philadelphia, USA in 1830 by John K. Smith. Mahlon Kline joined the firm in 1865. In 2000 the firm combined with Glaxo to become GlaxoSmithKline, but the name Beecham did not disappear altogether: it remains a registered trademark of the combine.

— **the Smith of Smiths** the sobriquet applied by Lord Macaulay to Sydney Smith (see above)

— **Smith Square** a square in Westminster, London, near the Houses of Parliament. It was probably named after Henry Smith, former owner of the land on which it was built in the early 18th century.

— **The Smiths** a British rock group founded in 1982 by Morrissey and Johnny Marr. Many conflicting reasons have been advanced for the choice of name; it may simply have been for its ordinariness.

— **Smith's Crisps** a brand of potato crisps, as originally made in London in 1920 by Frank Smith, a grocer's assistant. The company Smith's Crisps was formed in Australia in 1931 by Smith and a colleague.

— **Smith's Lawn** a polo ground at the southern end of Windsor Great Park. It is first recorded in the 1740s as 'Smith's Lawn Plantation', where trees were grown. The trees were cut down during World War I, and polo was first played there in the 1950s. The identity of Smith is uncertain: perhaps Thomas Smith, a keeper at Manor Lodge, or Bernard Smith, a royal stud groom.

— **W.H. Smith plc** a British firm of stationers, booksellers and newsagents, which originated in a newsagent's shop opened in Mayfair, London in 1792 by Henry Walton Smith, 1738–92. The business was subsequently taken on by his younger son William Henry Smith, 1792–1865, who gave it his name in 1828. His son William Henry Smith, 1825–91, joined the firm in 1846, and it became W.H. Smith and Son (colloquially known simply as 'Smiths').

Smithe see **Smythe**

Smitherman 'servant of a smith' (from Middle English *smither* 'smith' + *man*)

Smithers 'son of *Smither*', a surname meaning literally 'smith' (see **Smitherman**). See also **Smothers**

Smithies a different form of **Smythe** (i)

Smithson, Smythson 'son of **Smith**' [Alison Smithson (*née* Gill), 1928–93, British architect, wife of Peter; Peter Smithson, 1923–2003, British architect, who with his wife (see above) was among the first to introduce the international style of architecture into Britain]
— **Smithsonian Institution** a US research institution in Washington, DC, founded in 1846 under the terms of a bequest by the British mineralogist James Smithson, 1765–1829. It administers many important national collections, including the National Air and Space Museum and the National Collection of Fine Arts.
— **smithsonite** a white or yellow to brown zinc carbonate mineral. It was named after James Smithson (see above).

Smollett from a medieval nickname (literally 'small head') for someone of limited intelligence or with small, delicate features [Captain Smollett, the master of the schooner *Hispaniola* in Robert Louis Stevenson's *Treasure Island* (1883); Tobias Smollett, 1721–71, British novelist]

Smoot an anglicization of Dutch *Smout*, either 'seller of fat or lard' or from a medieval nickname for someone who indulged in rich food (in either case from Dutch *smout* 'fat, lard')

Smothers a different form of **Smithers**
— **The Smothers Brothers** a US music and comedy duo consisting of the brothers Tom Smothers, 1937–, and Dick Smothers, 1939–

Smuts 'son of the smith' (from Low German *smut* 'smith') [Jan Smuts, 1870–1950, South African statesman and general, prime minister 1919–24, 1939–48]

Smyth see **Smith**

Smythe, Smithe (i) 'person who lives by or works at a forge' (from Middle English *smithe* 'forge, smithy'). See also **Smithies**; (ii) a different form of **Smith** [Pat Smythe, 1928–96, British showjumper]

Snaith 'person from Snaith', Yorkshire ('cut off piece of land', from Old Norse *sneith*, a relative of Old English *snǣd* – see **Sneed**)

Snape 'person from Snape', the name of various places in northern England and southern Scotland ('area of poor land used for winter grazing'), or 'person from Snape', the name of various places in southern England ('area of boggy land')

Snead see **Sneed**

Sneath a different form of **Snaith**

Snedden, Sneddon 'person from Sneddon', Dumfries and Galloway ('snow hill')

Sneed, Snead 'person who lives in a cut off piece of land', or 'person from Snead', Worcestershire, or other similarly spelled places elsewhere in England (in either case ultimately from Old English *snǣd* 'cut off piece of land'). See also **Snaith, Snoad** [Sam Snead, 1912–2002, US golfer]

Snell from a medieval nickname for an active or lively person (from Middle English *snell* 'quick') [Peter Snell, 1938–, New Zealand athlete]

Snellgrove, Snelgrove 'person from Snellgrove', an unidentified place (probably 'snail grove')
— **Marshall and Snellgrove** see **Marshall**

Snider, Snyder anglicizations of **Schneider**

Snoad, Snode 'person who lives in a cut off piece of land' (from Old English *snād*, a variant of *snǣd* – see **Sneed**)

Snoddy, Snoddie from a medieval Scottish and Northern Irish nickname meaning literally 'neat little person' (from Middle English *snod* 'neat, trim')

Snodgrass 'person from Snodgrass', North Ayrshire ('smooth grass') [Augustus Snodgrass, a member of the Pickwick Club in Charles Dickens's *Pickwick Papers* (1837)]

Snook, Snooke 'person who lives on a projecting piece of land' (from Middle English *snoke* 'projection')

Snow (i) from a medieval nickname for someone with white hair or a very pale face; (ii) an anglicization of the first element of various invented Jewish names beginning with German *Schnee* or Yiddish *shnee* 'snow' (e.g. *Shneebaum* 'snow-tree') [C.P. Snow (Lord Snow), 1905–80, British novelist and scientist; John Snow, 1813–58, British physician, founder of epidemiology, who established that cholera is caused by contaminated water; John Snow, 1941–, English cricketer; Jon Snow, 1947–, British television journalist, cousin of Peter; Peter Snow, 1938–, British television presenter, cousin of Jon]
— **John Snow College** a college of Durham University, founded in 2001 and named in honour of John Snow the physician (see above)
— **'When I Marry Mr Snow'** a song in Rodgers and Hammerstein's musical *Carousel* (1945). It is sung by the character Carrie Pipperidge, and refers to her intended, the fisherman Enoch Snow.

Snowden 'person from Snowden', Yorkshire ('snow hill') [Philip Snowden (1st Viscount Snowden), 1864–1937, British Labour politician]

Snyder (i) 'tailor' (from a derivative of Middle Dutch *sniden* 'to cut'); (ii) see **Snider**

Soames, Somes 'person from Soham', Cambridgeshire and Suffolk ('homestead by a swampy pool') [Christopher Soames (Lord Soames), 1920–87, British Conservative politician and diplomat; Nicholas Soames, 1948–, British Conservative politician, son of Christopher]

Soane, Soan 'son' (used to distinguish a son from a father with the same given name) [Sir John Soane, 1753–1837, British architect]

Soaper see **Soper**

Soares[1], Soars 'son of *Sore*', from a medieval nickname for a red-haired person (from Anglo-Norman *sor* 'chestnut-coloured')

Soares[2] 'person who looks after pigs' (Portuguese, from Latin *Suerius*, literally 'swineherd'). See also **Suarez**

Sobel, Sobell an invented Jewish name based on Polish *sobol*, the name (related to English *sable*) of a type of marten with highly sought-after fur. It may sometimes have denoted specifically a fur-trader.

Sobers from a medieval nickname for a person who does everything in moderation, especially a teetotaller [Sir Garfield Sobers, 1936–, West Indian cricketer]

Soderberg an anglicization of the Swedish name *Söderberg*, literally 'south mountain'

Solomon, Soloman from the male personal name *Solomon*, the English form of the Hebrew Biblical name *Shelomo* (based on *shalom* 'peace'). See also **Salmon, Salomon**

Solomons 'son of **Solomon**' [Jack Solomons, 1900–79, British boxing promoter]

Somers see **Summers**

Somerscales, Summerscales 'person (an upland shepherd) who in summer lives in a temporary hut' (from Old Norse *sumar* 'summer' + *skáli* 'hut'). See also **Summerskill**

Somerset 'person from Somerset', county in Southwest England ('dwellers at the summer settlement')

Somerville (i) *also* **Sommerville** *or* **Summerville** *or* **Somervell** probably 'person from Sémerville', northern France ('Sigimar's settlement'). See also **Summerfield**; (ii) from Irish Gaelic *Ó Somacháin* (see **Summerly**) [Sir Arthur Somervell, 1863–1937, British composer; Edith Somerville, 1858–1949, Irish author; Mary Somerville, 1780–1872, British scientist]
— **Somerville and Ross** two Irish authors, Edith Somerville (see above) and Martin Ross (see **Ross**), second cousins, who collaborated on many books, notably *Some Experiences of an Irish R.M.* (1899).
— **Somerville College** a college of Oxford University, originally for women only, founded in 1879 and named after Mary Somerville (see above)

Somes see **Soames**

-son suffixed to a personal name (e.g. *Donald*) it forms a surname (*Donaldson* – i.e. 'son of Donald'). As a patronymic formula it dates back to the Old English period, and was subsequently reinforced by Old Norse names ending in *-sune* 'son of'. It is characteristic particularly of northern England and Scotland (in contrast with the synonymous **-S**, which predominates in southern and western England and in Wales).

Sondheim 'person from Sondheim', Bavaria [Stephen Sondheim, 1930–, US composer]

Sonntag, Sontag from a medieval German nickname for a person with a particular connection with Sunday (German *Sonntag*), especially one born on that day; also, an invented Jewish name based on German *Sonntag* [Susan Sontag, 1933–2004, US writer]

Soper, Soaper 'maker of soap' [Donald Soper (Lord Soper), 1903–98, British Methodist minister and pacifist]

Sopwith probably 'person from Sopworth', Wiltshire ('Soppa's farmstead') [Sir Thomas Sopwith, 1888–1989, British aircraft designer and manufacturer and yachtsman]

Sorel, Sorell see **Sorrell**

Sorenson (i) *also* **Sorensen** 'son of *Søren*', a Scandinavian male personal name derived from Latin *Severīnus* (see **Severn** (ii)); (ii) 'son of the son of *Sore*', a Yiddish female personal name (from Hebrew *Sara*, literally 'princess'), with the addition of the Slavic possessive suffix *-in* and German *Sohn* 'son'

Sorrell, Sorel, Sorell from a medieval nickname meaning literally 'little red-haired one' (from a derivative of Anglo-Norman *sorel* 'chestnut')

Sotheby 'person who lives in the southern part of a settlement' (from Old Norse *suthr í bý* 'south in the village'). See also **Suddaby**
— **Sotheby's** a British firm of fine-art auctioneers, founded in London in 1744 by Samuel Baker. It gets its name from John Sotheby, Baker's nephew, who joined the firm in 1776.

Sotheran, Sotheron different forms of **Southern**

Soto 'person from Soto or El Soto', the name of numerous places in Spain ('(the) grove')

Soul, Soule (i) 'person from Soul', the name of various places in France ('sunny place'); (ii) from a medieval nickname for a drunkard (from Old French *soul* 'drunk') [David Soul (original name David Solberg), 1943–, US actor and singer]

Soulsby perhaps 'person from Soulby', Cumbria ('Súla's farmstead')

Souness, Sounness 'person from Souness', Borders ('south promontory' or 'sound promontory') [Graeme Souness, 1953–, Scottish footballer and manager]

Sousa, Souza 'person from Sousa', the name of numerous places in Portugal (perhaps 'salt-marsh'). See also **de Souza** [John Philip Sousa, 1854–1932, US military bandmaster and composer]
— **sousaphone** a large brass instrument with a flaring bell, resembling a tuba. It is named after John Philip Sousa (see above), for whose band it was invented (in 1899).

Souter, Soutar 'shoemaker, cobbler' (from Middle English *soutere* 'shoemaker', ultimately from Latin *suere* 'to sew')

South 'person who lives in the southern part of a settlement, or who has come from a more southerly place'. See also **Southern**

Southall 'person from Southall', the name of various places in England ('southern corner of land')

Southcott 'person from Southcott', the name of various places in Southwest England ('southern cottage') [Joanna Southcott, 1750–1814, British religious fanatic]

Southern a different form of **South**. See also **Sotheran** [Terry Southern, 1924–95, US writer]

Southey 'person from Southey', the name of various places in England ('southern enclosure') [Robert Southey, 1774–1843, British poet and writer]

Southgate (i) 'person from Southgate', Norfolk ('southern gate'); (ii) 'person who lives near the southern gate (e.g. of a walled town)'. See also **Suggett**

Southwell 'person who lives by the southern stream', or 'person from Southwell', Nottinghamshire ('southern stream')

Southwood 'person who lives by the southern wood', or 'person from Southwood', Norfolk ('southern wood')

Souza see **Sousa**

Sowerby 'person from Sowerby', the name of various places in northern England ('farmstead on sour (i.e. swampy) ground')

Sowersby a different form of **Sowerby**

Spackman a different form of **Speakman**

Spain 'person from Épaignes', northern France ('Spanish settlement'), or 'person from Espinay', Brittany ('thorn bushes')

Spalding, **Spaulding** 'person from Spalding', Lincolnshire ('settlement of the Spaldingas', a tribal name perhaps meaning 'people of the area of ditches')

Spark (i) *also* **Sparke** from the Old Norse nickname *Sparkr*, meaning literally 'lively, sprightly'. See also **Spragg**, **Sprague**; (ii) from a medieval German nickname based on Middle High German *spar* 'sparrow' [Dame Muriel Spark (*née* Camberg), 1918–2006, British writer]

Sparks, **Sparkes** 'son of **Spark** (i)'

Sparling 'little **Sparrow**'. See also **Spurling**

Sparrow, **Sparrowe** from a medieval nickname for someone thought to resemble a sparrow (e.g. in perkiness or smallness) [John Sparrow, 1906–92, British academic; Simon Sparrow, the young doctor who is the protagonist of Richard Gordon's *Doctor in the House* (1952) and its sequels]

Speaight see **Speight**

Speak, **Speake**, **Speke**, **Speek** from a medieval nickname for someone thought to resemble a woodpecker (from Middle English *speke* 'woodpecker') [John Hanning Speke, 1827–64, British explorer]

Speakman 'spokesman, advocate' (from Middle English *spekeman*). See also **Spackman**

Spear, **Speare**, **Speir**, **Spier**, **Speer** 'user or maker of spears'; also, from a medieval nickname for a tall thin person, resembling a spear
— **Spear & Jackson** a British manufacturer of saws and garden tools, founded in 1830 by John Spear, died 1851, and Samuel Jackson

Spearman 'soldier armed with a spear'; also, from the medieval personal name *Spereman*, literally 'soldier armed with a spear' [Charles Edward Spearman, 1863–1945, US psychologist]

Spears, **Speares**, **Speirs**, **Spiers** 'son of **Spear**' [Britney Spears, 1981–, US pop singer]
— **Britney Spears** (see above) British rhyming slang for 'beers'
— **Spiers and Pond** a British hotel and restaurant company, founded in Australia in the 1850s by Felix Spiers, 1832–1910, and Christopher Pond, 1826–81. It ceased to exist in 1960.

Spector, **Spektor** 'teacher's assistant in a Jewish school' (from Polish *inspecktor* 'supervisor') [Phil Spector (original name Harvey Phillip Spector), 1940–, US record producer]

Spedding perhaps 'son of **Speed** (i)'

Speed (i) from a medieval nickname for a fortunate or successful person (from Middle English *sped* 'success'), or for a quick runner; (ii) a translation of Irish Gaelic *Ó Fuada* 'descendant of *Fuada*', a personal name based on *fuad* 'haste' [John Speed, ?1552–1629, English historian and cartographer]

Speek see **Speak**

Speer (i) 'user or maker of spears', or from a medieval German nickname for a tall thin person, resembling a spear (from Middle High German *sper* 'spear'); (ii) from a medieval German nickname for someone thought to resemble a sparrow (e.g. in perkiness or smallness) (from Middle High German *spar* 'sparrow'); (iii) a Northern Irish variant of **Spear**; (iv) an invented Jewish name, probably an adoption of (ii) or (iii)

Speight, **Speaight** from a medieval nickname for someone thought to resemble a woodpecker (e.g. in constant chattering) (from Middle English *speght* 'woodpecker') [Johnny Speight, 1921–98, British playwright and scriptwriter]

Speke see **Speak**

Spektor see **Spector**

Speller (i) 'reciter' (from a derivative of Middle English *spellen* 'to discourse'); (ii) a different form of **Spiller**

Spellman, **Spelman** (i) a different form of **Speller**; (ii) 'musician, minstrel' (from Middle High German *spel* 'play' + *man*)

Spence, **Spens** 'servant working in the pantry of a large house or monastery' (from Middle English *spense* 'room where food and drink are stored') [Sir Basil Spence, 1907–76, British architect]

Spencer, **Spenser** different forms of **Spence** [Spencer-Churchill, the family name of the dukes of Marlborough; Lady Diana Spencer, maiden name of Diana, Princess of Wales, 1961–97, former wife of Prince Charles; Edmund Spenser, ?1552–99, English poet; Frank Spencer, hapless hero (played by Michael Crawford) of the BBC television sitcom *Some Mothers Do 'Ave 'Em* (1973–78); Herbert Spencer, 1820–1903, British philosopher; Sir Stanley Spencer, 1891–1959, British painter]
— **spencer** originally, a short double-breasted coat without tails worn by men in the late 18th and early 19th centuries; hence also, a short jacket worn by boys, and a very short jacket worn by women over a high-waisted gown in the same

period. The original usage was inspired by George John Spencer, 2nd Earl Spencer, 1758–1834.

— **Spencer carbine, Spencer rifle** a type of light rifle developed by the US inventor and manufacturer Christopher Miner Spencer, 1833-1922. It was widely used during the US Civil War.

— **Spencer Gulf** a large inlet of the Indian Ocean in South Australia. It was named (in 1802) in honour of George John Spencer (see above).

— **Spencerian** denoting a style of handwriting with perfectly formed letters and ornamentation of capitals. The term commemorates the US calligrapher Platt Rogers Spencer, 1800–64.

— **Spenserian stanza** a stanza devised by Edmund Spenser (see above) that contains eight lines of iambic pentameter and a ninth of iambic hexameter, using the rhyme scheme ababbcbcc

Spender 'steward responsible for the supplies in a large house or monastery' (from a shortened form of Middle English *despendour*, literally 'dispenser') [Dale Spender, 1943–, Australian writer and feminist; Sir Stephen Spender, 1909–95, British poet and editor]

Spendlove from a medieval nickname for someone who spread their amorous affections around freely

Spenlow a different form of **Spendlove** [Dora Spenlow, the eponymous hero's 'child-wife' in Charles Dickens's *David Copperfield* (1849–50)]

Spens, Spenser see **Spence, Spencer**

Spicer 'seller of spices'

Spiegel 'maker or seller of mirrors' (from Middle High German *spiegel* 'mirror') [Sam Spiegel, 1901–85, Austrian-born US film producer]

Spielberg (i) 'person from Spielberg', the name of various places in Germany ('look-out mountain'); (ii) an invented Jewish name, based on German *Spiel* 'play' + *Berg* 'mountain' [Steven Spielberg, 1946–, US film director and producer]

Spier¹ a Scottish variant of **Spear**

Spier² (i) 'look-out, watchman', or from a medieval nickname for an inquisitive person (from a derivative of Middle English *spien* 'to watch'); (ii) perhaps a different form of **Spire** (ii)

Spiers 'son of **Spier²**'

Spillane from Irish Gaelic *Ó Spealáin* 'descendant of *Spealán*', a personal name meaning literally 'little scythe' [Mickey Spillane (original name Frank Morrison Spillane), 1918–2006, US detective-story writer]

Spiller (i) 'acrobat' or 'jester' (from a derivative of Middle English *spillen* 'to play, cavort'); (ii) from a medieval nickname for someone who is squanders things or is always making a mess of things (from a derivative of Middle English *spillen* 'to spoil, waste')

— **Spiller's** a British flour-milling and pet-food company founded in 1829 by the corn dealer Joel Spiller, 1804–53

Spillman from the medieval male personal name *Spileman*, literally 'acrobat' or 'jester' (of the same origin as **Spiller** (i))

Spilsbury 'person from Spelsbury', Oxfordshire ('Spēol's stronghold') [Sir Bernard Spilsbury, 1877–1947, British forensic pathologist; John Spilsbury, ?1739–69, British mapmaker and engraver, inventor of the jigsaw puzzle]

Spindler 'maker or user of spindles'

Spink from a medieval nickname for someone thought to resemble a chaffinch (from Middle English *spink* 'chaffinch')

— **Spink and Son Ltd** a British auction house and fine-art dealer, specializing particularly in coins and medals. It was founded in London in 1666 by John Spink as a goldsmith's and pawnbroker's.

Spinks 'son of **Spink**' [Leon Spinks, 1953–, US boxer; Terry Spinks, 1938–, British boxer]

Spire (i) from a medieval nickname for a tall thin person (from Middle English *spir* 'stalk'); (ii) 'person from Speyer', Germany. See also **Spier²** (ii)

Spires 'son of **Spire** (i)'

Spitz (i) 'person who lives on or by a hill with a pointed summit or by a field with a sharp angle to its edge', or 'person from Spitz', the name of various places in Germany (in either case from German *spitz* 'pointed'); (ii) an invented Jewish name, perhaps based on German *spitz* (see (i)) or on Yiddish *shpitsn* 'lace' [Mark Spitz, 1950–, US swimmer]

Spitzer a different form of **Spitz**

Spivak, Spivack 'singer, cantor' (from Ukrainian *spivak* 'singer')

Spock an anglicization of Dutch *Spaak*, literally 'maker of spokes for wheels' (from Middle Dutch *spaak* 'spoke') [Benjamin Spock, 1903–98, US pediatrician and political activist; Mr Spock, pointy-eared ultra-logical half-Vulcan First Officer (played by Leonard Nimmoy) of the USS *Enterprise* in the US television science-fiction series *Star Trek* (1969–71)]

Spode 'person from Spoad', Shropshire [Josiah Spode I, 1733–97, founder (1770) of the Spode porcelain factory in Staffordshire; Josiah Spode II, 1754–1827, son of Josiah I, who developed the business further]

Spofford a different form of **Spofforth**

Spofforth 'person from Spofforth', Yorkshire ('ford by a small plot of ground') [F.R. Spofforth, 1853–1926, Australian cricketer]

Spong 'person who lives on a narrow strip of land', or 'person from Spong Farm', Kent (in either case from Middle English *spong* 'narrow strip of land')

Spooner 'person whose job was to cover roofs with wooden tiles' (from a derivative of Middle English *spoon* 'chip, wooden tile') [William Spooner, 1844–1930, British clergyman and academic]

— **spoonerism** an accidental transposition of initial consonant sounds or parts of words, especially in an amusing way (e.g. 'half-warmed fish' for 'half-formed wish'), of a type said to have been regularly perpetrated by William Spooner (see above)

Spottiswoode, Spottiswood, Spotswood 'person from Spotswood', Borders (probably 'Spot's wood')
— **Eyre and Spottiswoode** see **Eyre**

Spragg a different form of **Sprague**

Sprague a different form (with transposition of *a* and *r*) of **Spark** (i)

Spratt, Sprat from a medieval nickname for a small person or one of no account [Sir Lancelot Spratt, irascible surgeon in Richard Gordon's *Doctor in the House* (1952) and its sequels]
— '**Jack Sprat could eat no fat**' a popular English nursery rhyme, first recorded in 1639:
Jack Sprat could eat no fat,
His wife could eat no lean,
And so between them both, you see,
They licked the platter clean.
In the 16th and 17th centuries 'Jack Sprat' was a term for a dwarf, which may have been the source of the name in the rhyme.

Sprigg from a medieval nickname for a tall thin person (from Middle English *sprigge* 'twig')

Spriggs 'son of **Sprigg**'

Spring perhaps from a medieval nickname based on Middle English *springen* 'to jump' [Howard Spring, 1889–1968, British journalist and novelist; Tom Spring (original surname Winter), 1795–1851, British prize-fighter]

Springall (i) 'operator of a springald (a type of medieval siege engine)' (from Anglo-Norman *springalde*); (ii) from a medieval nickname for a youthful person (from Middle English *springal* 'youth'). See also **Springle**

Springer (i) from a medieval English, German, Dutch and Jewish nickname for a lively, bouncy person; (ii) 'person who lives by a spring' [Jerry Springer, 1944–, US television talk-show host]

Springett 'little **Spring**'

Springfield 'person from Springfield', Essex ('open land of the dwellers by the spring') [Dusty Springfield (original name Mary Isobel Catherine Bernadette O'Brien), 1939–99, British popular singer (the name *Springfield* was taken from 'The Springfields', the name of the pop/folk trio formed in 1960 of which she was a member along with her brother Dion O'Brien (who renamed himself Tom Springfield) and Tim Feild; that in turn is said to have been inspired by an impromptu rehearsal session in a Somerset field in springtime)]

Springle a different form of **Springall**

Springsteen 'person who lives by stepping stones' (from Dutch *springsteen* 'stepping stone') [Bruce Springsteen, 1949–, US folk and rock singer and songwriter]

Spry from a medieval nickname for a smart and active person [Constance Spry, 1886–1960, British florist and writer on cookery and flower arranging]

Spurling a different form of **Sparling**

Spurrier 'maker of spurs'

Square a Scottish variant of **Squire**

Squire, Squier 'esquire (a young man immediately below the rank of knight in the feudal system)'. See also **Swire** [J.C. Squire, 1884–1958, British literary journalist and essayist]

Squires, Squiers 'son of **Squire**' [Dorothy Squires (original name Edna May Squires), 1915–98, British singer]

Srinivasan a Hindu name, based on Sanskrit *śrīnivāsa* 'abode of good fortune'

Stableford a different form of **Stapleford**
— **Stableford rules** a scoring system in golf in which points are awarded for the results at each hole, adjusted for the player's handicap. It was invented towards the end of the 19th century by Dr Frank Stableford, 1870–1959, of Wallasey and Royal Liverpool Golf Clubs, and first used officially in 1932.

Stacey, Stacy from a pet-form of the medieval male personal name *Stace*, itself a reduced form of **Eustace**

Stack from a medieval nickname for a large, robustly built man (from Middle English *stack* 'haystack') [Robert Stack (original name Charles Langford Modini Stack), 1919–2003, US actor]

Stackpole a different form of **Stackpoole**

Stackpoole, Stackpole 'person from Stackpole', Pembrokeshire ('pool by the rock') (though the place is Welsh, the name is Irish: many Norman settlers made their way to Ireland via Stackpole in the early Middle Ages) [H. de Vere Stacpoole, 1863–1931, British novelist and ship's doctor, of Irish ancestry]

Stacy see **Stacey**

Stadler 'person who lives near a barn or granary' or 'manorial official who receives tithes' (in either case from a derivative of Middle High German *stadel* 'barn, granary') [Craig Stadler, 1953–, US golfer]

Stafford 'person from Stafford', Staffordshire ('ford by a landing place')

Stagg from a medieval nickname for a man thought to resemble a stag

Stahl 'metal worker' or 'armourer' (from Middle High German *stāl* 'steel, armour')

Stainer 'maker of stained glass', also 'dyer' [Sir John Stainer, 1840–1901, British composer and organist]

Staines, Stains 'person from Staines', Surrey ('place at the stone' (probably referring to a milestone))

Stainton 'person from Stainton', the name of various places in northern England ('farmstead on stony ground')

Staley from a medieval nickname for a reliable person (from Middle English *staley*, a reduced form of *stalward* – see **Stallard**)

Stalker (i) 'trapper'; (ii) from a medieval nickname for someone who moves stealthily or furtively [John Stalker, 1945–, British police officer and writer]

Stallard from a medieval nickname for a reliable person (from Middle English *stalward* 'stalwart, reliable'). See also **Staley**, **Stallworthy**

Stallone 'horse-breeder', or from a medieval Italian nickname for someone thought to resemble a stallion (in either case from Italian *stallone* 'stallion') [Sylvester Stallone, 1946–, US actor]

Stallworthy, **Stalworthy** different forms of **Stallard**

Stamford a different form of **Stanford**

Stamp 'person from Étampes', northern France [Gavin Stamp, 1948–, British architectural historian and writer; Terence Stamp, 1938–, British actor]

Stamps a different form of **Stamp**

Stanborough, **Stanbrough** different forms of **Stanbury**

Stanbridge 'person from Stanbridge', the name of various places in England ('stone-built bridge')

Stanbrook, **Stanbrooke** 'person from Stanbrook', Worcestershire ('stony stream')

Stanbury, **Stanberry** 'person from Stanborough', Devon ('stony hill'). See also **Stanborough**

Stancliffe 'person from Stancliffe', Yorkshire ('stony slope')

Standage a different form of **Standish**

Standen 'person from Standen', the name of numerous places in England (variously 'stony valley' and 'stony hill'). See also **Standing**

Standfield a different form of **Stanfield**

Standing a different form of **Standen**

Standish 'person from Standish', Greater Manchester ('stony enclosure'). See also **Standage** [Myles Standish, ?1584–1656, English colonist in America, military leader of the first colony in New England]

Standley a different form of **Stanley**

Stanfield 'person from Stanfield', Norfolk and Staffordshire ('stony field'). See also **Standfield**

Stanford 'person from Stanford', the name of numerous places in England ('stony ford'). See also **Stamford**, **Staniforth** [Sir Charles Villiers Stanford, 1852–1924, Irish composer]

Stanger perhaps 'person armed with a stake' or 'person who lives by a pole or stake' (from a derivative of northern Middle English *stang* 'pole')

Stanhope 'person from Stanhope', County Durham ('stony enclosed valley') [Charles Stanhope (3rd Earl Stanhope), 1753–1816, British politician and scientist, grandson of James; Lady Hester Stanhope, 1776–1839, British political hostess, orientalist and traveller, daughter of Charles; James Stanhope (1st Earl Stanhope), 1673–1721, British soldier and statesman]

— **stanhope** a light open horse-drawn carriage with a single seat and two or four wheels. It was named after the British clergyman Fitzroy Stanhope, 1787–1864, for whom one was first made.

— **stanhopea** a genus of tropical American orchids, named in honour of Philip Henry, 4th Earl Stanhope, 1781–1855

— **Stanhope lens** a cylindrical lens with two convex faces of different radii, enclosed in a metal tube. It was invented by Charles, 3rd Earl Stanhope (see above).

— **Stanhope press** a hand-operated printing-press, the first to be made of iron. It was invented in 1798 by Charles, 3rd Earl Stanhope.

— **Stanhope prize** an annual prize awarded at Oxford University for a historical essay. It was founded in 1855 by the historian Philip Henry, 5th Earl Stanhope, 1805–75.

Stanier 'stonecutter' (from Middle English *stanyer*, a derivative of *stan* 'stone')

Staniforth a different form of **Stanford**

Stanley 'person from Stanley', the name of numerous places in England ('stony glade'). See also **Standley** [Stanley, the family name of the earls of Derby; Sir Henry Morton Stanley (original name John Rowlands), 1841–1904, British journalist and explorer]

— **Stanley** (formerly **Port Stanley**) the capital of the Falkland Islands. It was named in 1843 in honour of Edward Stanley (Lord Stanley; later 14th earl of Derby), 1799–1869, at that time secretary of state for war and the colonies.

— **Stanley Cup** the championship trophy of the National Hockey League of North America, competed for by the professional ice-hockey teams of the USA and Canada. It was named in honour of Frederick Arthur Stanley (Lord Stanley; later 16th earl of Derby), 1841–1908, Governor General of Canada, who presented it in 1892 as a cup for amateur Canadian clubs.

— **Stanley Falls** the former name of Boyoma Falls, a series of seven cataracts on the River Lualuba in Zaïre. It commemorates H.M. Stanley (see above), who explored extensively in the region in 1874–77.

— **Stanley knife** a tradename for a type of knife with a very sharp retractable blade. It is the product of The Stanley Works of New Britain, Connecticut, which was formed in 1920 by a merger of Stanley's Bolt Manufactory, founded in 1843 by Frederick Trent Stanley, 1802–83, and The Stanley Rule and Level Company, founded in 1857 by Frederick's cousin Henry Stanley.

— **Stanley Pool** the former name of Malebo Pool, a broad section of the Zaïre River, on the Congo-Zaïre border. It commemorates H.M. Stanley.

— **Stanleyville** the former name of Kisangani, a river port on the Zaïre River. It was named after H.M. Stanley.

Stannard from the medieval personal name *Stanhard*, literally 'stone-strong' or 'stone-brave'

Stansfield 'person from Stansfield', Yorkshire ('Stān's open land') [Lisa Stansfield, 1966–, British R&B singer]

Stanton 'person from Stanton', the name of various places in England ('farmstead on stony ground' or 'farmstead by prehistoric standing stones'). See also **Stainton**, **Staunton**, **Stenton**

Stanwick, **Stanwyck** 'person from Stanwick', Northamptonshire ('rocking stone') [Barbara Stanwyck (original name Ruby Stevens), 1907–90, US actress]

Stapleford 'person from Stapleford', the name of various places in England ('ford marked by a post'). See also **Stableford**

Staples 'person who lives near a boundary post', or 'person from Staple', the name of various places in England (in either case from Old English *stapol* 'boundary post')

Stapleton, Stapylton 'person from Stapleton', the name of various places in England ('farmstead by a post') [Cyril Stapleton, 1914–74, British conductor and bandleader]

Star (i) from a medieval German and Jewish nickname for someone thought to resemble a starling, especially in constantly chattering (from Middle High German *star* 'starling'); (ii) from a medieval Dutch nickname for a gloomy person or for a person with rigid attitudes (from Middle Dutch *staer* 'gloomy, stiff'); (iii) a translation of **Stern**

Stark from a medieval Scottish and northern English nickname for a strong or resolute person (from Middle English *stark* 'firm') [Dame Freya Stark, 1893–1993, British travel writer; Graham Stark, 1922–, British comic actor]

Starkey, Starkie 'little **Stark**' [David Starkey, 1945–, British historian]

Starling from a medieval nickname for someone thought to resemble a starling, especially in constantly chattering

Starr (i) perhaps from a medieval nickname for someone with a streak of white hair (from Middle English *starre* 'star, white blaze on a horse's head'); (ii) perhaps 'person who lives in a house with the sign of a star' [Freddie Starr (original name Freddie Fowell), 1943–, British comedian; Ringo Starr (original name Richard Starkey), 1940–, British pop drummer, member of The Beatles]

Statham 'person from Statham', Cheshire ('place at the landing stages') [Brian Statham, 1930–2000, English cricketer]

Staunton 'person from Staunton', the name of various places in England ('farmstead on stony ground'). See also **Stainton, Stanton, Stenton** [Imelda Staunton, 1956–, British actress]

Stead (i) 'person from Stead', Yorkshire ('estate, farmstead'); (ii) 'person who looks after stallions', or from a medieval nickname for a sexually voracious man (in either case from Middle English *steed* 'male stud horse, stallion'). See also **Steed** [Christina Stead, 1902–83, Australian novelist; W.T. Stead, 1849–1912, British journalist and newspaper editor]

Steadman, Stedman different forms of **Stead** (ii). See also **Steedman** [Alison Steadman, 1946–, British actress; Ralph Steadman, 1936–, British cartoonist]

Stear see **Steer**

Stearn see **Stern** (i)

Stearns see **Sterns**

Stears see **Steers**

Stebbing (i) 'person from Stebbing', Essex ('Stybba's people's settlement'); (ii) 'person who lives in a woodland clearing' (from Middle English *stebbing* 'clearing')

Stebbings a different form of **Stebbing**

Stebbins a different form of **Stebbings**

Steed, Steede, Stede different forms of **Stead** [John Steed, a British intelligence agent (played by Patrick Macnee) who was the central character of the television drama series *The Avengers* (1961–69) and *The New Avengers* (1976–77)]

Steedman a different form of **Steadman**

Steel, Steele (i) 'worker in a steel foundry'; (ii) from a medieval nickname for someone with steely qualities (e.g. of endurance) [Anthony Steel, 1920–2001, British actor; Barbara Steele, 1937–, British actress; Danielle Steel (original name Danielle Schuelein-Steel), 1947–, US author; David Steel (Lord Steel), 1938–, British Liberal Democrat politician; Sir Richard Steele, 1672–1729, British essayist and dramatist; Tommy Steele (original name Thomas Hicks), 1936–, British pop singer and actor]

Steen (i) see **Stein**[1]; (ii) 'person who lives in an area of stony ground', or 'person who works with stone (e.g. a mason)' (from Low German and Dutch *steen* and Danish, Norwegian and Swedish *sten* 'stone')

Steenson 'son of **Steen** (i)'

Steer, Steere, Stear 'person who tends cattle', or from a medieval nickname for an aggressive person (in either case from Middle English *stēr* 'bullock') [Philip Wilson Steer, 1860–1942, British artist]

Steers, Stears 'son of **Steer**'

Steiger (i) 'person who lives by a steep path' (from a derivative of Middle High German *stīc* 'steep path'); (ii) 'person who lives by a plank bridge' (from a derivative of Middle High German *stec* 'plank bridge') [Rod Steiger, 1925–2002, US actor]

Stein[1], **Steen** from a contracted Scottish form of the personal name **Stephen** [Jock Stein, 1922–85, Scottish football manager]

Stein[2] (i) 'person who lives on stony ground or by a marker stone of some kind', or 'stone-worker (e.g. a mason or quarryman)' (from Middle High German *stein* 'stone'); (ii) an invented Jewish name, based on German *Stein* 'stone' [Gertrude Stein, 1874–1946, US writer; Rick Stein, 1947–, British chef and broadcaster]

Steinbeck 'person from Steinbeck or Steinbach', the name of various places in Germany ('stony stream') [John Steinbeck, 1902–68, US writer]

Steinberg (i) 'person from Steinberg', the name of various places in Germany and Scandinavia ('stone mountain'); (ii) an invented Jewish name, based on German *Stein* 'stone' + *Berg* 'mountain'

Steiner a different form of **Stein**[2] [George Steiner, 1929–, French-born US critic and author]

Steinmetz 'stonemason' (from Middle High German *steinmetze* 'stonemason')

Steinway a partial anglicization of the German surname *Steinweg*, literally 'person who lives by a road or path paved with stone' [Henry Steinway (original name Heinrich Steinweg), 1797–1871, German-born US piano maker, founder of the firm Steinway]

Stenson (i) 'person from Stenson', Derbyshire ('Steinn's farmstead'); (ii) 'son of **Stephen**'. See also **Stinson**

Stenton (i) 'person from Stenton', the name of various places in England ('farmstead on stony ground'). See also **Stainton**, **Stanton**, **Staunton**; (ii) a different form of **Stenson** (i) [Sir Frank Stenton, 1880–1967, British historian]

Stephen, Steven from the male personal name *Stephen*, ultimately from Greek *Stephanos*, literally 'crown'. See also **Stein**[1] [Sir Leslie Stephen, 1832–1904, British critic and man of letters, editor of the *Dictionary of National Biography*]

Stephens, Stevens 'son of **Stephen**' [Cat Stevens (original name Steven Demetre Georgiou; now Yusuf Islam), 1948–, British pop and folk-rock singer/songwriter, teacher and philanthropist; Sir Robert Stephens, 1931–95, British actor; Shakin' Stevens (original name Michael Barrett), 1948–, British rock-and-roll singer; Stella Stevens (*née* Eggleston), 1936–, US actress; Wallace Stevens, 1879–1955, US poet]

— **Stevengraph** the proprietary name of a coloured silk picture woven on a particular type of Jacquard loom developed by the Coventry silk weaver Thomas Stevens, 1828–88

Stephenson, Stevenson 'son of **Stephen**' [Adlai Stevenson, 1900–65, US Democratic politician; George Stephenson, 1781–1848, British railway engineer; Juliet Stevenson, 1956–, British actress; Pamela Stephenson, 1951–, New Zealand-born actress and comedian; Robert Stephenson, 1803–59, British civil engineer and politician, son of George; Robert Louis Stevenson, 1850–94, British novelist]

— **Stevenson screen** a box with louvred sides for containing and protecting a set of meteorological recording instruments. It was invented by the British civil engineer Thomas Stevenson, 1818–87, father of Robert Louis (see above).

— **Stephenson's Rocket** a pioneering railway locomotive designed and built by George Stephenson (see above) in 1829

Steptoe perhaps from a medieval nickname for someone with a light tread

— **Steptoe and Son** a BBC television sitcom (1962–65; 1970–74) about a pair of rag-and-bone men, scrawny old Albert Steptoe (played by Wilfred Brambell) and his would-be upwardly mobile son Harold (Harry H. Corbett). It was written by Alan Simpson and Ray Galton.

Sterling see **Stirling**

Stern (i) *also* **Sterne** *or* **Stearn** *or* **Stearne** from a medieval nickname for a strict or austere person; (ii) 'person who lives in a house with the sign of a star' (from Middle High German *stern* 'star'); (iii) an invented Jewish name, based on German *Stern* 'star' [Isaac Stern, 1920–2001, Russian-born US

violinist; Laurence Sterne, 1713–68, British novelist]

Sternberg (i) 'person from Sternberg', the name of various places in Germany; (ii) an invented Jewish name, based on German *Stern* 'star' + *Berg* 'mountain' [Josef von Sternberg (original name Josef Stern), 1894–1969, Austrian-born US film director]

Sterns, Stearns 'son of **Stern** (i)'

Stetson an English surname of unknown origin and meaning

— **Stetson** a proprietary name for a type of men's hat with a wide brim and high crown, as originally manufactured in the US by the John B. Stetson Company, founded by John Batterson Stetson, 1830-1906.

Steuart see **Stewart**

Steven, Stevens, Stevenson see **Stephen**, **Stephens, Stephenson**

Steventon 'person from Steventon or Stevington', the name of various places in England ('estate associated with Stīfa')

Steward a different form of **Stewart**

Stewart, Stuart, Steuart 'administrative official of an estate' (from Middle English *stiward* 'steward') [Stuart (or Stewart), the ruling dynasty of Scotland from 1371 to 1714 and of England from 1603 to 1714; Alec Stewart, 1963–, English cricketer; Andy Stewart, 1933–93, Scottish singer and entertainer; Charles Edward Stuart ('the Young Pretender'; 'Bonnie Prince Charlie'), 1720–88, pretender to the British throne, son of James Edward; Ed Stewart, 1941–, British radio presenter; J.I.M. Stewart, 1906–94, British novelist, critic and (under the pseudonym Michael Innes) writer of detective fiction; Sir Jackie Stewart, 1939–, British racing driver; James Stewart, 1908–97, US actor and Air Force general; James Edward Stuart ('the Old Pretender'), 1688–1766, son of James II, pretender to the British throne; John McDouall Stuart, 1815–66, British-born Australian explorer; Martha Stewart (*née* Kostyra), 1941–, US domestic guru; Mary Stuart (Mary, Queen of Scots), 1542–87, daughter of James V of Scotland, queen of Scotland, 1542–67, and pretender to the English throne; Michael Stewart (Lord Stewart), 1906–90, British Labour politician; Moira Stuart, 1952–, British television newsreader; Patrick Stewart, 1940–, British actor; Rod Stewart, 1945–, British rock musician]

— **Newton Stewart** a market town in Dumfries and Galloway, founded in the 1670s by William Stewart, third son of the earl of Galloway

— **Newtownstewart** a town in County Tyrone, Northern Ireland, so renamed in about 1628 after its new owner, Sir William Stewart (its original name was Lislas)

— **Portstewart** a seaside resort in County Londonderry, Northern Ireland, named in the 18th century after the Stewart family, local landowners

— **Stewartby** a village in Bedfordshire, built in 1926 by Sir Malcom Stewart, 1872–1951, as a model village for the employees of his brickworks and named in honour of his father Sir Halley Stewart, 1838–1937, vice-chairman of the London Brick Company

— **Stewart Island** the third largest island of New Zealand, to the south of South Island. It was named (in 1809) after William Stewart, a whaling captain who first charted the island. Its Maori name is Rakiura.

— **Stuart Highway** a road in Australia (colloquially known as 'The Track'), linking Port Augusta, South Australia with Darwin, Northern Territories. It is 2834 km/1761 miles long. It was named in honour of John McDouall Stuart (see above), the first European to cross Australia from south to north.

— **Walking Stewart** the sobriquet of John Stewart, 1749–1822, who travelled on foot through large parts of Europe, Asia, North Africa and North America

Stiles see **Styles**

Still, Stille (i) from a medieval English and German nickname for a calm or placid person (from Middle English and Middle High German *stille* 'still, calm'); (ii) 'person who lives by a fish trap in a river' (from Middle English *still* 'fish trap')

Stillingfleet 'person from Stillingfleet', Yorkshire ('stream belonging to Stӯfel's people')

Stillman a different form of **Still**

Stillwell, Stilwell 'person who lives by a quiet stream or spring' [Joseph Stilwell, 1883–1946, US general]

Stimson, Stimpson different forms of **Stinson**

Stinchcombe, Stinchcomb 'person from Stinchcombe', Gloucestershire ('narrow valley frequented by sandpipers')

Stinson a different form of **Stenson** (ii)

Stirling, Sterling 'person from Stirling', Aberdeenshire (perhaps from an ancient river-name) [James Stirling, 1692–1770, Scottish mathematician; Sir James Stirling, 1926–92, British architect]

— **Stirling engine** a type of external-combustion engine invented by the Scottish minister and engineer Robert Stirling, 1790–1878. Heat generated on the outside of the cylinders causes either air or an inert gas inside the cylinders to expand and drive the pistons.

— **Stirling Prize** an annual British award for architecture, inaugurated in 1996 and organized by the Royal Institute of British Architects. It is named in honour of Sir James Stirling (see above).

— **Stirling's formula** a mathematical formula used to calculate the approximate value of the factorial of a very large number. It was devised by James Stirling (see above).

Stobart a different form of **Stobbart**

Stobbart from the medieval personal name *Stubart*, apparently meaning literally 'Stubb-brave' (on the nickname *Stubbe*, see **Stubbs**)

Stobie 'person from Stobo', Borders ('depression in the ground with a tree stump' or 'nook of land with a tree stump')

Stock, Stocke (i) 'person who lives by a tree stump or uprooted tree' (from Middle English *stocke* 'trunk'); (ii) perhaps 'keeper of stocks (the punishment device)'. See also **Stockman, Stocks**; (iii) perhaps from a medieval nickname for a stocky person [Nigel Stock, 1919–86, British actor]

Stockard a different form of **Stoker** (ii)

Stockbridge 'person from Stockbridge', the name of various places in England ('bridge made of logs')

Stockdale 'person from Stockdale', a valley in Cumbria and Yorkshire ('valley with tree stumps')

Stockley, Stockleigh 'person from Stockley or Stockleigh', the name of various places in England ('glade with tree stumps'). See also **Stokeley**

Stockman a different form of **Stock**

Stocks a different form of **Stock**

Stockton 'person from Stockton', the name of several places in England (variously 'farmstead built of logs' and 'farmstead at an outlying hamlet')

Stockwell 'person from Stockwell', Greater London ('spring by a tree stump')

Stoddard a different form of **Stoddart**

Stoddart, Stodart 'horse-breeder' (from Old English *stōt* 'establishment where horses are bred, stud' or *stott* 'horse' + *hierde* 'herdsman'). See also **Stothard**

Stoke 'person from Stoke', the name of numerous places in England (variously 'outlying farmstead' and 'secondary settlement'). See also **Stokes**

Stokeley, Stokely different forms of **Stockley**

Stoker (i) 'stoker' or 'arsonist' (from Middle Dutch *stokere*); (ii) 'trumpeter' (from Gaelic *stocaire*). See also **Stockard**; (iii) a different form of **Stoke** [Bram Stoker (original name Abraham Stoker), 1847–1912, Irish novelist, author of *Dracula* (1897)]

Stokes a different form of **Stoke** [Donald Stokes (Lord Stokes), 1914–, British businessman; Sir George Stokes, 1819–1903, Irish-born British physicist and mathematician]

— **Cheyne-Stokes respiration** see **Cheyne**

— **Stokes-Adams syndrome** episodes of temporary dizziness or fainting, due to disruption or extreme slowing of the heartbeat and consequent brief stoppage of blood flow. The condition was described by the Irish physicians William Stokes, 1804–75, and Robert Adams, 1791–1875.

— **stokesite** a hydrated silicate of calcium and tin, $CaSnSi_3O_9.2H_2O$, found as colourless transparent orthorhombic crystals. It was named in honour of Sir George Stokes (see above).

— **Stokes' law** a law used in the determination of viscosity: the resulting force acting on a sphere, radius r, moving through a fluid with velocity v is $6prgv$, where g is the viscosity of the fluid. It was named after Sir George Stokes.

Stokoe 'person from Stockhow', Cumbria

Stokowski 'person from Stokowo', Poland ('place on a hillside') [Leopold Stokowski, 1882–1977, British-born US conductor]

Stoll (i) 'carpenter', or from a medieval German nickname for someone of rigid or unbending character (in either case from Middle High German *stolle* 'frame, support'); (ii) an invented Jewish name of unknown origin and meaning
— **Stoll-Moss Theatres** see **Moss**

Stolle a different form of **Stoll** [Fred Stolle, 1938–, Australian tennis player]

Stone (i) 'person who lives on stony ground or by a marker stone of some kind', or 'stone-worker (e.g. a mason or quarryman)'; (ii) 'person from Stone', the name of various places in southern and western England ('place at the stone or stones'); (iii) a translation of **Stein**[2] (ii), or of the first element of various compound Jewish surnames beginning with *Stein-* (e.g. **Steinberg**) [Joss Stone (original name Jocelyn Eve Stoker), 1987–, British soul, R&B and blues singer; Oliver Stone, 1946–, US film director; Sharon Stone, 1958–, US actress; Sly Stone (original name Sylvester Stewart), 1943–, US musician and songwriter, founder of the group 'Sly and the Family Stone', which included two of his sisters and a brother]
— *Rodney Stone* a novel (1896) by Arthur Conan Doyle set in the world of Regency prize-fighting and cast in the form of a memoir by the naval officer Rodney Stone
— **Stone's Ginger Wine** a British brand of ginger-flavoured alcoholic drink originally manufactured by the Finsbury Distilling Company (founded 1740). The name came from Joseph Stone, 1809–96, whose grocer's shop in High Holborn, London was one of the company's main outlets.

Stonehouse (i) 'person who lives in a stone-built house', or 'person from Stonehouse', the name of various places in England; (ii) a translation of the Jewish surname *Steinhaus* (from German) [John Stonehouse, 1925–88, British Labour politician who in 1974 attempted to fake his own death]

Stoner (i) 'person who lives in a stone-built house'; (ii) a translation of German **Steiner**

Stones a different form of **Stone** (i–ii)

Stonham 'person from Stonham', Suffolk ('homestead by a stone or on stony ground')

Stonor 'person from Stonor', Oxfordshire ('stony slope')

Stopford 'person from Stockport', Greater Manchester ('market place at an outlying hamlet'; in former times the place-name was pronounced locally as if it were spelled *Stopford*)

Stoppard a different form of **Stopford** [Sir Tom Stoppard (original name Tom Straussler; he took the name Stoppard from his stepfather), 1937–, Czech-born British playwright]

Storer 'official whose job was to distribute provisions in a great household or monastery' (from a derivative of Middle English *stor* 'provisions')

Storey, Story, Storie from the Old Norse nickname *Stóri*, literally 'large man' [David Storey, 1933–, British novelist and playwright]

Storm from a medieval English and northern European nickname for someone with a volatile temperament

Stothard a different form of **Stoddart**

Stott 'cattleman' (from Middle English *stott* 'steer, bullock')

Stoughton 'person from Stoughton', Leicestershire, Surrey and Sussex ('farmstead at an outlying hamlet')
— **Hodder and Stoughton** see **Hodder**

Stourton 'person from Stourton', the name of various places in England ('farmstead on the river Stour')

Stout, Stoute (i) from a medieval nickname for a steadfast or powerful man (from Middle English *stout* 'steadfast'); (ii) perhaps 'person from Stout', an unidentified place, possibly in Devon ('rounded hillock'); (iii) from the Old Norse nickname *Stútr*, literally 'gnat', applied to a small and persistently annoying person [Rex Stout, 1886–1975, US writer]

Stow, Stowe 'person from Stow or Stowe', the name of numerous places in England ('place of assembly' or 'holy place') [Harriet Beecher Stowe (*née* Beecher), 1811–96, US novelist; John Stow, 1525–1605, English chronicler and antiquary]

Stowell 'person from Stowell', Gloucestershire, Somerset and Wiltshire ('stony stream')

Strachan, Strahan, Straughan 'person from Strachan', Aberdeenshire (perhaps 'valley of the foals'). The name is traditionally pronounced 'strawn', but 'stracken' is now more common for the main spelling *Strachan*. [Gordon Strachan, 1957–, Scottish footballer]

Strachey perhaps an alteration of **Tracey** [Lytton Strachey, 1880–1932, British biographer]

Strafford a different form of **Stratford**

Strang a Scottish variant of **Strong**

Strange from a medieval nickname for someone new to an area (from Middle English *strange* 'foreign'). See also **Lestrange**

Strangeways 'person from Strangeways', Greater Manchester ('strong current')

Strangways a different form of **Strangeways**

Stratfield 'person from Stratfield', Berkshire and Hampshire ('open land by a Roman road'). See also **Streatfield**

Stratford 'person from Stratford', the name of several places in England ('ford across a Roman road'). See also **Strafford, Trafford**

Stratton 'person from Stratton', the name of numerous places in England (mainly 'farmstead on a Roman road') [Charles Stratton, 1838–83, US midget (stage-name 'Tom Thumb')]

Strauss, Straus (i) from a medieval German nickname for a quarrelsome person (from Middle High German *strūz* 'quarrel, complaint'); (ii) 'person who lives in a house with the sign of an ostrich', or from a medieval German nickname for someone thought to resemble an ostrich or who wore an ostrich feather in their hat (in either case from

Middle High German *strūze* 'ostrich'); (iii) an invented Jewish name based on German *Strauss* 'ostrich' [Andrew Strauss, 1977–, English cricketer]

Straw 'dealer in straw', or from a medieval nickname for someone with pale yellow hair [Jack Straw, a leader of the London riots during the Peasants' Revolt (1381); Jack Straw, 1946–, British Labour politician (his original first name was John, and he is said to have adopted 'Jack' from the peasants' leader)]

— **Jack Straw's Castle** a former coaching inn on Hampstead Heath, London, named after Jack Straw (see above), who took refuge on the site after the Peasants' Revolt. In the early 21st century it was turned into luxury flats.

Strawson 'son of **Straw**'

Strayhorn perhaps an alteration of **Strachan** [Billy Strayhorn, 1915–67, US jazz pianist and composer]

Streatfield, Streatfeild different forms of **Stratfield** [Noel Streatfeild, 1895–1986, British children's author]

Streek, Streak from a medieval nickname for a stern or stubborn person (from Middle English *streke* 'severe, unbending') [Heath Streak, 1974–, Zimbabwean cricketer]

Streep from a medieval Dutch nickname for someone whose appearance is characterized in some way by streaks or stipes (from Middle Dutch *stīpe* 'stripe') [Meryl Streep (original name Mary Louise Streep), 1949–, US actress]

Street, Streete (i) 'person who lives by the main street of a village or town'; (ii) 'person from Street', the name of various places in southern England ('place by a Roman road') [Janet Street-Porter, 1946–, British journalist and broadcaster]

Streeter a different form of **Street** (i) [Fred Streeter, 1877–1975, British gardener]

Stretton 'person from Stretton', the name of numerous places in England ('farmstead on a Roman road')

Stribling from a medieval nickname for a youthful or inexperienced person (from Middle English *stripling* 'youth')

Strickland 'person from Strickland', Cumbria ('piece of land where bullocks are pastured')

Stride probably from a medieval nickname for someone who walked with long or purposeful strides

Stringer 'maker of string or of bow strings'

Stringfellow from a medieval nickname for a strong man (from Middle English *streng* 'strong' + *felaw* 'fellow') [Peter Stringfellow, 1940–, British nightclub proprietor]

Stronach from a medieval Scottish nickname for an overly inquisitive or interfering person (from Gaelic *sronach* 'nosy')

Strong, Stronge from a medieval nickname for a strong man or (with heavy irony) for a weakling. See also **Strang** [Patience Strong, pen-name of

Winifred Emma May, 1907–90, British versifier; Sir Roy Strong, 1935–, British curator, art historian and writer]

Strother 'person who lives in a marshy overgrown area', or 'person from Strother, Struther or Struthers', the name of various places in Scotland and northern England (in either case from Middle English *strother* 'marshy area overgrown with brushwood'). See also **Struthers**

Stroud 'person from Stroud', Gloucestershire and Middlesex ('marshy area overgrown with brushwood')

Strudwick 'person from Strudgwick', Sussex ('dairy farm in marshy overgrown land')

Struthers a different form of **Strother**

Strutt probably from the Old Norse nickname *Strútr*, denoting someone who wore a particular type of hat

Stuart see **Stewart**

Stubbs 'son of *Stubb*', a medieval nickname for a short fat man (from Old English *stubb* 'tree stump') [George Stubbs, 1724–1806, British animal painter; Imogen Stubbs, 1961–, British actress; Una Stubbs, 1937–, British actress and dancer]

Stuckey 'person from Stiffkey (locally pronounced 'stucky')', Norfolk ('island with tree stumps')

Studd 'person who lives by or is employed on a stud farm' (from Middle English *studde* 'stud')

Studebaker an anglicization of the German name *Studebecker* or *Stutenbecker*, literally 'baker' (from Middle Low German *stute* 'fine white bread' + *becker* 'baker')

— **Studebaker** a US marque of automobiles, founded by the wagon-maker Clement Studebaker, 1831–1901

Studer 'person who lives by a thicket', from a variant of the German surname *Stauder*, a derivative of Middle High German *stūde* 'thicket' [Cheryl Studer, 1955–, US soprano]

Studley 'person from Studley', the name of various places in England ('glade where a herd of horses is kept')

Stukeley, Stukely 'person from Stukeley', Cambridgeshire ('woodland glade with tree stumps')

Sturdy, Sturdee from a medieval nickname for a reckless person (from Middle English *stourdi* 'rash')

Sturgeon 'fishmonger'

Sturgess, Sturges, Sturgis probably from the Old Norse personal name *Thorgils*, literally 'Thor's hostage' [Preston Sturges (original name Edmund Preston Biden), 1898–1959, US screenwriter and director]

Sturman (i) from the Old French name (of Germanic origin) *Esturmin*, literally 'little storm'; (ii) 'steersman, navigator' (from Old Norse *stýrimathr* 'steersman'); (iii) an invented Jewish name, perhaps based on Polish *szturman* 'ship's mate'

Sturt 'person from Sturt', the name of various places in England ('tail-shaped promontory or hill-spur') [Charles Sturt, 1795–1869, British explorer]

Sturtevant, Sturtivant from a medieval nickname for an impulsive or hasty person (from Middle English *sterten* 'to leap' + Anglo-Norman *avaunt* 'forward')

Stuyvesant probably from a medieval Dutch nickname for either a quarrelsome person or an enthusiastic horse rider (from Middle Dutch *stüven* 'to stir up' + *sant* 'sand') [Peter Stuyvesant, 1612–72, Dutch-born American colonist, director-general of the New Netherland colony (later New York)]
— **Peter Stuyvesant** a German brand of cigarette, named after Peter Stuyvesant (see above)

Styles, Stiles (i) 'person who lives by a stile' (from Old English *stigel* 'stile'); (ii) 'person who lives by a steep path' (from Old English *stigol* 'steep path') [Nobby Stiles (official first name 'Norbert'), 1942–, English footballer]

Suarez 'person who looks after pigs' (Spanish *Suárez*, from Latin *Suerius*, literally 'swineherd'). See also **Soares²**

Subramanian a Hindu name, based on Sanskrit *subrahmańya* 'dear to Brahmans'

Such, Sutch (i) perhaps 'person who lives by a tree stump', or from a medieval nickname for a stocky person (in either case from Middle English *suche* 'tree stump', from Old French); (ii) perhaps 'person from La Souche', an unidentified place in northern France ('the tree stump') [David Sutch ('Screaming Lord Sutch'), 1940–99, British pop musician and fringe politician, founder of the Official Monster Raving Loony Party]

Suckling from a medieval nickname for someone of childlike appearance or childish character (from Middle English *suckling* 'infant still feeding on its mother's milk') [Sir John Suckling, 1609–42, English poet and dramatist]

Suddaby a different form of **Sotheby**

Sudworth 'person from Southworth', Cheshire ('southern enclosure')

Suess, Seuss (i) an anglicization of German *Süss*, from a medieval German nickname for a pleasant or agreeable person (from Middle High German *süss* 'sweet, pleasant'). See also **Sussman**; (ii) an invented Jewish name, based on German *süss* 'sweet' [Dr Seuss, the pen-name of the US children's writer and illustrator Theodor Seuss Geisel, 1904–91]

Sugar (i) perhaps from the use of English *sugar* as a term of endearment; (ii) a translation of *Zucker*, as a German name literally either 'sugar dealer' or 'confectioner', or from a medieval nickname for someone with a sweet tooth (in either case from Middle High German *zucker* 'sugar'), as a Jewish name, an invented name based on German *Zucker* 'sugar'; (iii) an anglicization of Hungarian *Sugár*, from a medieval Hungarian nickname for someone with a well-proportioned body (from Hungarian

sugár 'tall and slim') [Sir Alan Sugar, 1947–, British businessman]

Sugarman a translation of **Zuckerman**

Sugden, Sugdon 'person from Sugden', Yorkshire ('valley frequented by sparrows') [Mollie Sugden, 1922–, British actress]

Suggett, Suggitt different forms of **Southgate** (ii)

Sulley 'person from Sulley', an unidentified place probably in the East Midlands ('southern glade')

Sullivan, Sullevan from Irish Gaelic *Ó Súileabháin* 'descendant of *Súileabhán*', a personal name meaning literally 'little dark-eyes'. See also **O'Sullivan** [Sir Arthur Sullivan, 1842–1900, British composer; Ed Sullivan, 1901–74, US television variety-show host; J.L. Sullivan, 1858–1918, US boxer; Louis Sullivan, 1856–1924, US architect]

☆ The third commonest surname in Ireland

Sully (i) 'person from Sully', the name of numerous places in northern France (variously 'Silius's settlement' and 'Solius's settlement'); (ii) perhaps 'person from Sully', Glamorgan (either 'cleft island' or from the Norman family name *de Sully*, as in (iii)); (iii) perhaps a different form of **Sulley**

Summer, Summar (i) from a medieval nickname for someone with a summery disposition, or for someone with a particular connection with the summer; (ii) a translation of Irish Gaelic *Ó Samhraidh* 'descendant of *Samhradh*', a nickname meaning literally 'summer'; (iii) a different form of **Sumner** and of **Sumpter**

Summerfield (i) 'person from Summerfield', Wiltshire; (ii) a Scottish variant of **Somerville** [Eleanor Summerfield, 1921–2001, British actress]

Summerhays, Summerhayes probably 'person living by a summer enclosure (where animals were grazed on upland pastures in the summer)' (from Middle English *sumer* 'summer' + *hay* 'enclosure')

Summerhill 'person from Summerhill', the name of various places in England and Scotland ('hill used for summer grazing')

Summerly from Irish Gaelic *Ó Somacháin* 'descendant of *Somachán*', a nickname meaning literally 'gentle' or 'innocent'

Summers, Somers (i) 'son of **Summer** (i)'; (ii) from Irish Gaelic *Ó Somacháin* (see **Summerly**) [John Somers (Lord Somers), 1651–1716, English statesman under William III, lord chancellor 1697–1700]
— **Ann Summers** a British chain of sex shops, established in 1972. It took its name from that of the firm's founder's secretary.
— **Somers Town** a district of northern Central London, between Euston and St Pancras stations. Laid out at the end of the 18th century, it was named after the Somers family, descendants of Lord Somers (see above), on whose land it was built.

Summerscales see **Somerscales**

Summerskill a different form of **Somerscales** [Edith Summerskill (Baroness Summerskill), 1901–80, British physician, feminist and Labour politician]

Summerson 'son of **Summer** (i)'

Summerton 'person from Somerton', Oxfordshire ('summer farmstead')

Summerville see **Somerville**

Sumner 'summoner (a court official who summoned witnesses)' (from Middle English *sumner* 'summoner'). See also **Summer** (iii) [Gordon Sumner, the real name of the British popular musician known as 'Sting', 1951–]

Sumpter, Sumter 'person who transports goods' (from Middle English *sumter* 'driver of a pack animal')
— **Fort Sumter** a US army post at the entrance to Charleston harbour, South Carolina. It was named in honour of Thomas Sumter, 1734–1832, a leading light of the American Revolution.

Sundberg an invented Swedish name meaning literally 'hill by a strait'

Sunderland 'person from Sunderland', the name of various places in northern England and southern Scotland ('detached estate')

Sundquist an invented Swedish name meaning literally 'twig of the strait'

Sundstrom an anglicization of Swedish *Sundström*, either 'person who lives by a river running into a strait' (from Swedish *sund* 'sound, strait' + *ström* 'river'), or an invented name using those elements

Supple 'person from la Chapelle', northern France ('the chapel')

Surgener, Surgenor a different form of **Surgeon**

Surgeon 'person who carries out surgical operations'

Surridge (i) 'person from Surridge', Devon ('south ridge'); (ii) *also* **Surrage** from the medieval personal name *Seric*, a descendant of both Old English *Sǣrīc*, literally 'sea power', and *Sigerīc*, literally 'victory power'. See also **Search**; (iii) 'person from the south' (from Old French *surreis* 'southerner')

Surtees 'person who lives by the river Tees', in northern England (*Sur-* is from Anglo-Norman *sur* 'on, by') [John Surtees, 1934–, British racing motorcyclist and racing driver; R.S. Surtees, 1803–64, British journalist and novelist]
— **Surtees Society** an organization that publishes original texts relating to the history of the area covered by the ancient kingdom of Northumberland. Its name commemorates the British antiquary and topographer Robert Surtees, 1779–1834.

Susan, Susann (i) from the female personal name *Susan*, ultimately from Hebrew *Shushannah*, literally 'lily'; (ii) from the Jewish male personal name *Susan*, from Arabic *susan* 'lily'; (iii) 'person who lives at the top end of a village or high up the slopes of a valley' (from Old Provençal *susan* 'above') [Jacqueline Susann, 1918–74, US author]

Susskind 'son of *Ziske*', a Yiddish female personal name meaning literally 'little sweet one' [Leonard Susskind, 1940–, US physicist]

Sussman, Susman, Suzman (i) an anglicization of German *Süssmann*, a variant of *Süss* (see **Suess** (i)); (ii) from the Yiddish male personal name *Zusman*, literally 'sweet man' [Helen Suzman (*née* Gavronsky), 1917–, South African politician and human-rights campaigner; Janet Suzman, 1939–, South African-born actress and director]

Sutch see **Such**

Sutcliffe, Sutcliff 'person from Sutcliffe', Yorkshire ('southern cliff or riverbank') [Herbert Sutcliffe, 1894–1978, English cricketer; Peter Sutcliffe, 1946–, British mass murderer ('the Yorkshire Ripper'); Rosemary Sutcliff, 1920–92, British children's author]

Sutherland 'person from Sutherland', former county of northern Scotland ('southern land') [Donald Sutherland, 1935–, Canadian actor; Graham Sutherland, 1903–80, British painter; Dame Joan Sutherland, 1926–, Australian soprano; Kiefer Sutherland, 1966–, US actor, son of Donald]

Sutton 'person from Sutton', the name of numerous places in England ('southern settlement')
— **Sutton's Seeds** a British firm of seed suppliers, founded in Reading in 1806 by John Sutton, 1777–1863

Suzuki a Japanese name, probably based on Japanese *susuki* 'pampas grass'

Svendsen 'son of *Sven*', a Danish and Norwegian male personal name (from Old Norse *Sveinn*, literally 'boy' or 'servant')

Svenson an anglicization of **Svendsen** or of the related Swedish *Svensson*. See also **Swanson** (ii)

Swain, Swaine, Swayn, Swayne (i) 'servant, attendant' (from Middle English *swein*, from Old Norse – see (ii)). See also **Swan** (ii); (ii) from the Old Norse male personal name *Sveinn* (see **Svenson**)

Swainson 'son of **Swain**'

Swallow (i) from a medieval nickname for someone thought to resemble a swallow, especially in swift graceful movement; (ii) 'person from Swallow', Leicestershire ('place on the river Swallow', perhaps literally 'rushing stream')

Swan, Swann (i) from a medieval nickname for someone thought to resemble a swan, especially in being pure or excellent (both attributes associated with the swan in the Middle Ages); also, 'person who lives in a house with the sign of a swan'; (ii) a different form of **Swain** (i) [Donald Swann, 1923–94, British pianist and composer; Sir Joseph Swan, 1828–1914, British physicist]
— **Flanders and Swann** see **Flanders**
— **Swan and Edgar** a drapery department store in Piccadilly Circus, London, founded in the early 19th century by a certain Mr Swan, died 1821, of whom little is known, and William Edgar, 1791–1869. It closed in 1982.

Swannell from the Old Norse female personal name *Svanhildr*, literally 'swan-battle'

Swanson (i) 'son of **Swan** (ii)'; (ii) an angliciza-
tion of the Scandinavian surnames *Svendsen* and
Svensson (see **Svendsen, Svenson**) [Gloria
Swanson, 1897–1983, US actress]

Swanston (i) 'person from Swanston', near Edinburgh (probably 'Swān's settlement'); (ii) a
different form of **Swanton**

Swanton 'person from Swanton', Kent and
Norfolk ('farmstead of the herdsmen') [E.W.
Swanton, 1907–2000, British cricket writer]

Swanwick 'person from Swanwick', Derbyshire
('dairy farm of the herdsmen')

Swarbrick 'person from Swarbrick', Lancashire
('Svartr's slope')

Swartz a different form of **Schwarz**

Swayn, Swayne see **Swain**

Sweatman, Swetman different forms of **Sweet**

Sweeney from Irish Gaelic *Mac Suibhne* 'son of
Suibhne', a nickname meaning literally 'pleasant'.
See also **McQueen**

Sweet from a medieval nickname for a pleasant or
well-liked person (from Middle English *swete*
'sweet, agreeable'). See also **Sweatman** [Henry
Sweet, 1845–1912, British philologist and phone-
tician]

Sweeting (i) from the medieval male personal
name *Sweting*, literally 'son of *Swēta*', an Old
English male personal name meaning literally
'pleasant or well-liked person'; (ii) from a medieval nickname for a pleasant or well-liked person
(from Middle English *sweting* 'darling, sweetheart')

Swetman see **Sweatman**

Swift (i) from a medieval nickname for a quick
runner; (ii) a translation of Irish Gaelic *Ó Fuada*
'descendant of *Fuada*', a personal name based on
fuad 'haste' [Graham Swift, 1949–, British author;
Jonathan Swift, 1667–1745, Irish author and cler-
gyman]

Swinburne, Swinburn 'person from Swinburn',
Northumberland ('stream where pigs drink')
[Algernon Charles Swinburne, 1837–1909, British
poet; Walter Swinburn, 1961–, British jockey]

Swindell a different form of **Swindells**

Swindells perhaps 'person from Swindale', Yorkshire ('valley frequented by pigs')

Swindlehurst probably 'person from Swinglehurst', Yorkshire ('wooded hill ridge frequented by
pigs')

Swingle 'person who works in the production of
linen or hemp' (from Middle English *swingle*, the
name of a type of wooden implement used for
beating flax or hemp)
— **Swingle Singers** a vocal ensemble founded in
Paris in 1962 by the US vocalist and jazz musician
Ward Swingle, 1927–

Swinglehurst a different form of **Swindlehurst**

Swingler 'maker or user of swingles' (see
Swingle)

Swinley 'person from Swinley', Lancashire
('glade where pigs graze')

Swinnerton, Swynnerton 'person from Swynnerton', Staffordshire ('farmstead by the ford used
by pigs')

Swinton 'person from Swinton', the name of
various places in northern England ('pig farm')

Swire a northern English variant of **Squire**

Swithenbank 'person from Swithenbank', an
unidentified place, probably in Yorkshire
('hill-slope cleared by burning')

Switser, Switzer (i) from the medieval nickname
Swetesire (literally 'sweet sir, amiable master'),
applied sarcastically either to someone who used
the expression liberally as a form of address or to
someone with a *de-haut-en-bas* manner; (ii) an
anglicization of **Schweitzer**

Sword (i) 'maker of swords, armourer'; (ii) from
Irish Gaelic *Ó Suaird* (see **Seward** (iii))

Sworder a different form of **Sword** (i)

Swords a different form of **Sword** (ii)

Swynnerton see **Swinnerton**

Sydenham, Syddenham 'person from
Sydenham', the name of various places in England
(mainly 'broad enclosure')
— **Sydenham's chorea** a neurological disease of
children and pregnant women, sometimes
following rheumatic fever, in which those affected
experience involuntary jerking movements of the
body. It is named after the English physician
Thomas Sydenham, 1624–89.

Sydney see **Sidney**

Sykes, Sikes 'person who lives by a marshy
stream' (from Middle English *syke*) [Bill Sikes,
murderous burglar in Charles Dickens's *Oliver
Twist* (1837–8); Eric Sykes, 1923–, British comic
actor and writer]
— **Sykes hydrometer** an instrument used to determine the specific gravity of alcoholic beverages,
invented around 1816 by Bartholomew Sykes
— **Sykes' monkey** a blue-grey guenon (*Cercop-
ithecus albogularis*) native to East Africa. It was
named after the British soldier and naturalist
William Henry Sykes, 1790-1872.
— **Sykes-Picot Agreement** a secret agreement
negotiated in 1916 between Britain and France,
represented by Sir Mark Sykes, 1879–1919, and
Georges Picot, relating to the dismemberment of
the Ottoman Empire after World War I

Sylvester see **Silvester**

Symcox, Syme, Symes see **Simcocks, Sime,
Simes**

Symington 'person from Symington', Ayrshire
and Glasgow ('Simon's settlement')

Symmons see **Simmons**

Symon, Symons see **Simon, Simons**

Syms see **Sims**

Synnott see **Sinnott**

Syrett (i) from the medieval male personal name
Syred (from Old English *Sigerǣd*, literally
'victory-counsel'); (ii) from the medieval female
personal name *Sigerith* (from Old Norse *Sigfrithr*,
literally 'victory-lovely')

T

Taaffe perhaps from an Irish version of the Welsh name *Dafydd* (see **David**), or alternatively 'person who lives by the Taff', the name of two rivers in Wales ('water') [Pat Taafe, 1930–92, Irish jockey]

Tabb perhaps from a medieval personal name *Tabbe*, from an unrecorded Old English *Tæbba*

Tabor (i) *also* **Taber** 'drummer' (from Middle English *tabour* 'drum'); (ii) 'person from Tábor', city in southern Bohemia; (iii) an invented Jewish name based on that of Mount Tabor in Israel [June Tabor, 1947–, British folk singer]

Taft a different form of **Toft** (i) [William Howard Taft, 1857–1930, US lawyer and Republican politician, president 1909–13]
— **Taft-Hartley Act** a US law (1947) placing restrictions on trade unions. It was introduced by Senator Robert Alphonso Taft, 1889–1953, son of William (see above), and Representative Fred A. Hartley, 1902–69.

Taggart, Tagart, Taggert from Gaelic *Mac An tSagairt* 'son of the priest'. See also **McTaggart**
— **Taggart** a British television police drama series (1983–), centring initially on the Scottish detective DCI Jim Taggart (played by Mark McManus; when McManus died in 1994 the series continued without his character)

Tailor, Tailour see **Taylor**

Tait, Taite, Taitt, Teyte from a medieval nickname for a cheerful person (from Old Norse *teitr* 'merry') [Dame Maggie Teyte, 1888–1976, British soprano]

Talbert from the male personal name *Talbert*, brought into England by the Normans but ultimately of Germanic origin, and meaning literally 'bright valley'

Talbot, Talbott probably from a Germanic personal name meaning literally 'messenger of destruction', brought into England by the Normans [Talbot, family name of the earls of Shrewsbury; William Henry Fox Talbot, 1800–77, British photographic pioneer]
— **Château Talbot** a wine-producing château in the St Julien commune of Bordeaux. Its name is said to commemorate John Talbot, 1st earl of Shrewsbury, ?1387–1453, a commander of English forces in France in the latter stages of the Hundred Years War.
— **Port Talbot** an industrial port on Swansea Bay, South Wales. It was developed from the mid-1830s on land owned by the Talbot family of nearby Margam Abbey.
— **Talbot** a British car marque, established in 1903 by Charles Chetwynd-Talbot, 20th earl of Shrews-

bury. In 1935 it became part of the Rootes Group, and in 1938 combined with Sunbeam to become Sunbeam-Talbot. The Talbot name was dropped in 1955; it was briefly revived in 1978, and finally disappeared in 1986.
— **Talbot Village** a village in Dorset founded in the 1860s by the sisters Georgina Charlotte and Mary Anne Talbot as a model village for poor families dispossessed by land enclosures

Talboys, Tallboys (i) 'person from Taillebois', Normandy ('woodland clearing'); (ii) 'woodcutter' (from Old French *tailler* 'to cut' + *bois* 'wood')

Talley, Tally from Irish Gaelic *Ó Taithligh* 'descendant of *Taithleach*', a personal name meaning literally 'peaceable'

Tallis (i) 'person from an unidentified place with a name based on Anglo-Norman *taillis* "woodland clearing"'; (ii) *also* **Talis** an invented Jewish name based on Yiddish *tales* 'prayer shawl' [Thomas Tallis, ?1505–85, English composer]

Tallon (i) from a medieval nickname for a fast runner, or for someone with a deformed or damaged heel (in either case from Old French *talon* 'heel'); (ii) ultimately from an unidentified Germanic personal name beginning with the element *Tal-*, literally 'destroy', brought into England by the Normans

Tally (i) see **Talley**; (ii) a different form of **Tully**

Talmadge, Talmage an anglicization of various similar-sounding Jewish surnames, notably *Tolmach*, literally 'interpreter' (from Russian *tolmach*)

Tambling a different form of **Tamblyn**

Tamblyn, Tamblin from the medieval male personal name *Tamlin*, literally 'little little *Tam*', a different form of *Tom*. See also **Tamplin** [Russ Tamblyn, 1934–, US actor]

Tame (i) 'person from Thame', Oxfordshire ('place on the river Thame'); (ii) from a medieval nickname for a quiet or mild-mannered person (from Middle English *tame* 'not wild')

Tamm (i) 'person from Tamm or Thamm', two places in Germany (perhaps 'place by a dyke', or alternatively from the personal name as in (i)); (ii) from the medieval German personal name *Tamm*, a shortened form of *Tancmar*, literally 'thought-famous'

Tammage a different form of **Tollemache**

Tamplin a different form of **Tamblyn**

Tanaka a Japanese name, meaning literally 'centre of the rice paddy'

Tancock from a shortened variant of the male personal name **Andrew**, with the suffix -*cock* (literally 'cockerel', hence 'jaunty or bumptious young man'), that was often added to create pet-forms of personal names in the Middle Ages

Tancred from the Old French male personal name *Tancred*, brought into England by the Normans but ultimately of Germanic origin, and meaning literally 'thought-counsel'

Tandy from a pet-form of the male personal name **Andrew**

Tangye from the Breton personal name *Tanguy*, a contracted form of *Tanneguy*, literally 'fire-dog'. See also **Tingay** [Derek Tangye, 1912–96, British author]

Tankard (i) 'maker of drinking vessels', or from a medieval nickname for a heavy drinker of alcohol; (ii) from the Norman male personal name *Tancard*, of Germanic origin and meaning literally 'thought-brave'

Tann (i) a different form of **Tanner** (i); (ii) 'forest-dweller' (from Middle High German *tan* 'forest')

Tannahill 'person from Tannahill', Ayrshire

Tanner (i) 'person who tans animal skins'; (ii) 'person from Tanne or Tann', the name of various places in Germany [Elsie Tanner, gossip-worthily promiscuous brunette (played by Pat Phoenix) in the British television soap opera *Coronation Street* (1960–); Roscoe Tanner, 1951–, US tennis player]

Tanqueray a name of unknown origin
— **Tanqueray's Gin** a British brand of gin, founded in 1830 by Charles Tanqueray, 1810–68
— *The Second Mrs Tanqueray* a play (1893) by Sir Arthur Pinero about public and private attitudes towards women with a sexual 'past' in late Victorian Britain

Tansey from Gaelic *Mac an Tánaiste* 'son of the tanist' (a tanist was the heir presumptive to a clan chieftain)

Tansley 'person from Tansley', Derbyshire ('Tãn's glade')

Taplin 'little **Tapp**'

Tapp from the Old English male personal name *Tæppa*, of unknown origin and meaning

Tapper 'inn-keeper' (from Middle English *tapper* 'person who taps barrels, inn-keeper')

Tarbox a different form of **Tarbuck**

Tarbuck 'person from Tarbock Green', Lancashire ('stream with thorn-trees growing beside it') [Jimmy Tarbuck, 1940–, British comedian]

Tarkington 'person from Torkington', Greater Manchester ('settlement associated with Turec'). See also **Turkington** [Booth Tarkington, 1869–1946, US novelist and playwright]

Tarleton, Tarlton 'person from Tarleton', Lancashire ('Thórvaldr's farmstead'), or 'person from Tarlton', Gloucestershire (probably 'farmstead in the forest clearing with thorn-trees') [Richard Tarlton, died 1588, English actor]

Tarr perhaps 'person who caulks ships with tar'

Tarrant (i) 'person who lives by the river Tarrant', Dorset ('trespasser' – i.e. a river that frequently floods the land around it); (ii) from Irish Gaelic *Ó Toráin* 'descendant of *Torán*', a personal name meaning literally 'little hero' [Chris Tarrant, 1946–, British radio and television presenter]

Tasker 'person employed on piecework (especially threshing grain)', from a derivative of Anglo-Norman *tasque* 'task'

Tate from the Old English personal name *Tāta*, of uncertain origin and meaning (perhaps a child's word) [Catherine Tate, 1968–, British comic actress and writer; Harry Tate (original name Ronald Hutchinson), 1874–1940, British music-hall comedian; Maurice Tate, 1895–1956, English cricketer; Nahum Tate, 1652–1715, British poet; Sharon Tate, 1943–69, US actress, murdered by Charles Manson]
— **Tate and Lyle plc** a British-based food manufacturing company, best known as a sugar refiner. It was formed in 1921 by the merger of two firms: Henry Tate and Sons, founded in Liverpool in 1869 by Henry (later Sir Henry) Tate, 1819–99, and Abram Lyle and Sons, founded in Greenock in 1865 by the cooper and shipbuilder Abram Lyle, 1820–91.
— **Tate Gallery** an art gallery on Millbank, London, built in 1897 with the financial support of Sir Henry Tate (see above). It housed British and modern international art. In 2000 its international art was moved to the redesigned Bankside power station, known as **Tate Modern**. The original Tate was renamed **Tate Britain**.

Tatham 'person from Tatham', Lancashire ('Tāta's homestead'). See also **Tatum**

Tatler, Tattler probably from a medieval nickname for someone who limped or stuttered (from a derivative of Middle English *tatelen* 'to falter')

Tatlock probably 'person from Tatlock', an unidentified place, probably in Lancashire or Cheshire [Albert Tatlock, OAP stalwart of the early years of the British television soap opera *Coronation Street* (1960–)]

Tattersall, Tattershall 'person from Tattershall', Lincolnshire ('Tāthere's corner of land')
— **Tattersall's** a British firm of bloodstock auctioneers, founded in London in 1766 by the racehorse owner Richard Tattershall, 1724–95. It moved to Newmarket in 1939.

Tatton 'person from Tatton', Cheshire and Dorset ('Tāta's farm')

Tatum a different form of **Tatham** [Art Tatum, 1910–56, US jazz pianist; Edward Lawrie Tatum, 1909–75, US geneticist]

Tauber (i) 'pigeon breeder' (from a derivative of Middle High German *tūbe* 'pigeon'); (ii) 'horn player' (from Middle High German *toubære*); (iii) from a medieval German and Jewish nickname for a deaf (or stupid) person (from Middle High German *toup* 'deaf')

Taverner, Tavernor, Tavener, Tavenor, Tavner 'innkeeper' [John Taverner, ?1495–1545, English composer; Sir John Tavener, 1944–, British composer]

Tawney 'person from Saint-Aubin-du-Thennay or Saint-Jean-du-Tennay', Normandy [R.H. Tawney, 1880–1962, British economic historian]

Tay (i) perhaps a different form of **Tye**; (ii) 'tea merchant' (from Yiddish *tay* 'tea')
— **Tay-Sachs disease** a genetic disease that principally affects Jewish people of East European ancestry, marked by accumulation of lipids in the brain and nerves and resulting in loss of sight and brain functions. It is named after the British ophthalmologist Warren Tay, 1843–1927, and the US neurologist Bernard Sachs, 1858–1944 who (independently) first described it.

Taylor, Tayler, Tailor, Tailour 'tailor' [A.J.P. Taylor, 1906–90, British historian; Brook Taylor, 1685–1737, English mathematician; Charles Taylor, 1948–, Liberian warlord and political leader, president 1997–2003; Dennis Taylor, 1949–, Northern Irish snooker player; Elizabeth Taylor, 1912–75, British novelist and short-story writer; Dame Elizabeth Taylor, 1932–, British-born US film actress; Frederick Winslow Taylor, 1856–1915, US engineer; Graham Taylor, 1944–, English football manager; Jeremy Taylor, 1613–67, Anglican churchman and theologian; John Taylor, ?1578–1653, English poet (the 'water-poet'); Robert Taylor (original name Spangler Arlington Brough), 1911–69, US film actor; Rod Taylor, 1930–, Australian film actor; Roger Taylor, 1941–, British tennis player; Samantha Taylor-Wood, 1967–, British artist; Shaw Taylor, 1924–, British television presenter; Zachary Taylor, 1784–1850, US general and politician, president 1849–50]
☆ The 4th commonest surname in New Zealand; 5th commonest in Britain; 6th commonest in Australia; 9th commonest in Canada; 10th commonest in the US
— **Taylorian** the usual abbreviated designation of the Taylor Institution, which was established at Oxford University for the teaching of modern languages from money left for that purpose by the English architect Sir Robert Taylor, 1714-88
— **Taylorism** the principles embodied in the Taylor system (see below), or their practical application
— **taylorite** a sulphate of potassium and ammonia discovered in Peruvian guano beds by the US mineral chemist W. J. Taylor, 1833–64.
— **Taylor's** a British firm of port shippers (in full, Taylor, Fladgate and Yeatman). It had its origins in a British trading company established in Portugal in the 1670s by Job Bearsley. The first Taylor (Joseph Taylor) joined the firm in 1816.
— **Taylor's series** a basic theorem of calculus relating an approximation of the value of a continuous function at a point to the successive derivatives of the function evaluated at the point. It is named after Brook Taylor (see above), who developed it.
— **Taylor system** the system of scientific management and work efficiency developed by Frederick W. Taylor (see above).

Teacher 'teacher, instructor', or from a medieval nickname for someone who paraded his knowledge
— **Teachers** a brand of Scotch whisky produced by the firm established by William Teacher, 1811–76. Originally a tailor, he turned to the grocer's trade in 1836 and soon began blending his own whisky.

Teagarden see **Teegarden**

Teague (i) from a Cornish and Welsh nickname for a handsome person (from Cornish *tek* and Welsh *teg* 'beautiful'); (ii) a different form of **Tighe**

Teal, Teale from a medieval nickname for someone thought to resemble a teal (a type of small duck)

Tear, Teare a different form of **McIntyre** [Robert Tear, 1939–, British tenor]

Tearle probably a different form of **Tyrrell**

Tebbit, Tebbitt from the medieval male personal name *Tebald* or *Tibalt*, from the Old French form of **Theobald**. See also **Tibbett** [Norman Tebbit (Lord Tebbit), 1931–, British Conservative politician]

Tedder perhaps from the Old English male personal name *Theodhere*, literally 'people-army' [Arthur Tedder (Lord Tedder), 1890–1967, British air marshal]

Teegarden, Teagarden an anglicization of Dutch and German *Theegarten*, literally 'person who lives by a garden or enclosed plot' (from Low German *te garden* 'the garden or enclosed plot') [Jack Teagarden (original name Weldon Leo Teagarden), 1905–64, US jazz trombonist and vocalist]

Teitelbaum an invented Jewish name based on Yiddish *teytlboym* 'date palm'

Telfer from a medieval Scottish and northern English nickname for a strong man or fearsome warrior (from Old French *tailler* 'to cut' + *fer* 'iron'). See also **Telford, Tulliver**

Telford a different form of **Telfer** (as if from a place-name ending in -*ford*) [Thomas Telford, 1757–1834, British civil engineer]
— **Telford** a new town in Shropshire, to the east of Shrewsbury. Established in 1963, it was named in 1968 after Thomas Telford (see above), who had notable Shropshire connections.

Teller (i) 'weaver' (from Old French *telier* 'weaver, linen-weaver'); (ii) 'person who lives by an area of undergrowth' (from a derivative of Middle Low German *telge* 'twig, undergrowth'); (iii) 'person who lives by a gorge or low-lying area' (from a derivative of Middle High German *telle* 'gorge, depression'); (iv) 'maker of dishes' (from Yiddish *teler* 'plate') [Edward Teller, 1908–2003, Hungarian-born US physicist]

Tempest from a medieval nickname for someone with a volatile or stormy temperament [Lady Annabel Tempest-Vane-Stewart (Lady Goldsmith), 1934–, Anglo-Irish heiress after whom Annabel's nightclub in London was named; Dame Marie Tempest (original name Mary Susan Etherington; Tempest was her mother's maiden name), 1864–1942, British actress]

Templar 'servant of the Knights Templar' [Simon Templar, the modern-day adventurer created by

Leslie Charteris (originally in *Enter the Saint* (1930)), whose sobriquet was 'The Saint']

Temple (i) 'person who worked at or lived near one of the establishments of the Knights Templar (known as 'temples')'; (ii) 'child of unknown parents who had been baptized at the Temple Church, London'; (iii) 'person from Temple', an Edinburgh parish where the local headquarters of the Knights Templar was situated [Paul Temple, a British novelist-detective created by the writer Francis Durbridge, originally for a 1938 radio serial; Shirley Temple (married name Shirley Temple Black), 1928–, US child actress and, later in life, ambassador; Sir William Temple, 1628–99, English diplomat; William Temple, 1881–1944, British churchman, archbishop of Canterbury 1942–44]

Templeton 'person from Templeton', Ayrshire ('settlement with a house of the Knights Templar')

Tenison see **Tennyson**

Tennant, Tennent 'tenant farmer in the feudal system' [David Tennant (original name David McDonald), 1971–, British actor; Emma Tennant, 1937–, British novelist; Margot Tennant (married name Margot Asquith; Countess of Oxford and Asquith), 1864–1945, British socialite, author and wit; Stephen Tennant, 1906–87, British aesthete]

Tenniel perhaps a different form of **Daniel** [Sir John Tenniel, 1820–1914, British cartoonist and book illustrator]

Tennyson, Tennison, Tenison 'son of *Tenney*', a medieval male personal name meaning literally 'little Dennis' [Alfred, Lord Tennyson, 1809–92, British poet; Jane Tennison, police detective played by Helen Mirren in the ITV drama series *Prime Suspect* (1991–2006)]
— **Tennysonian** of or in the style of Alfred, Lord Tennyson (see above)

Terkel see **Turkel**

Ternan a different form of **Tiernan**

Terrell, Terrill, Terrall different forms of **Tyrrell**

Terry (i) *also* **Terrey** from the medieval male person name *Therry* or *Terry*, brought into England by the Normans but ultimately (via Old French *Thierri*) from Germanic *Theodoric*, literally 'people-power'; (ii) 'potter' (from Old French *terrin* 'earthenware vessel'); (iii) from Irish Gaelic *Mac Toirdhealbhaigh* (see **Turley**) [Dame Ellen Terry, 1847–1928, British actress; John Terry, 1980–, English footballer; Quinlan Terry, 1937–, British architect; Terry-Thomas, see **Thomas**]
— **Terrys** a British confectionery firm founded in York in the 1840s by Joseph Terry, 1793–1850. It produced its first chocolates in 1886.

Tesler, Tessler (i) 'person who uses the heads of teasels (a thistle-like plant) to prepare wool for spinning or to brush the surface of newly woven cloth' (from a derivative of Old English *tǣsel* 'teasel'); (ii) 'carpenter' (from Yiddish *tesler* 'carpenter')

Tetley 'person from Tetley', an unidentified place, probably in Yorkshire (perhaps 'Tǣta's or Teitr's

glade') [Glen Tetley, 1926–2007, US-born Canadian dancer and choreographer]
— **Tetley's beer** the brand name of a range of beers brewed by the firm founded in Leeds, Yorkshire in 1822 by Joshua Tetley, 1778–1859
— **Tetley's tea** the brand name of tea produced by the firm founded in Huddersfield, Yorkshire in 1837 by Joseph Tetley, 1811–89, and his brother Edward Tetley, born 1816

Tew (i) 'person from Great, Little or Duns Tew', Oxfordshire ('ridge'); (ii) from a medieval Welsh nickname for a fat person (from Welsh *tew* 'plump')

Tewson, Tuson 'son of *Tuwe* or *Tywe*', a medieval personal name of unknown origin and meaning

Tey a different form of **Tye** [Josephine Tey, pen-name of the British mystery novelist Elizabeth Mackintosh, 1896–1952]

Teyte see **Tait**

Thacker 'thatcher' (from a derivative of northern Middle English *thack* 'thatch')

Thackeray, Thackery, Thackray 'person from Thackray', Yorkshire ('corner of land where reeds for thatching grow') [Jake Thackray, 1938–2002, British poet and singer-songwriter; William Makepeace Thackeray, 1811–63, British novelist]

Thain, Thaine 'low-ranking nobleman or (in Scotland) hereditary tenant of the Crown' (from Middle English *thayn*)

Tharp, Tharpe different forms of **Thorpe** [Twyla Tharp, 1941–, US dancer and choreographer]

Thatcher 'person who lays thatch for roofs, thatcher' [Margaret Thatcher (Baroness Thatcher; *née* Roberts), 1925–, British Conservative politician, prime minister 1979–90]
— **Thatcherism** the political policies and style of government of Margaret Thatcher (see above), typified by privatization, monetarism and hostility to trade unions
— **Thatcherite** (an adherent) of Thatcherism

Thaw (i) perhaps from a variant of the medieval Anglo-Scandinavian personal name *Thor*, itself probably from the first element of any of a range of Old Norse personal names based on *Thórr*, the name of the god of thunder in Norse mythology; (ii) an anglicization of *Thau*, an invented Jewish name based on German *Tau* 'dew' [John Thaw, 1942–2002, British actor]

Thayer an anglicization of French *Taillier*, literally 'tailor' (from Old French *taillere* 'tailor') [Sylvanus Thayer, 1785–1872, US soldier and educator]

Theakston 'person from Theakston', Yorkshire ('Thēodec's farmstead') [Jamie Theakston, 1970–, British television presenter]

Thelwell 'person from Thelwall', Cheshire ('deep pool with a plank bridge') [Norman Thelwell, 1923–2004, British cartoonist]

Theobald, Theobold from the Germanic male personal name *Theobald*, literally 'people-brave' (in the Middle Ages the English form of the personal name was *Tebald* or *Tibalt* (from Old French; see also **Dibble**, **Tebbit**, **Thibault**,

Tibbett, Tibbs, Tippett); the modern form is a learned reconstruction of the original Germanic, adapted from French *Théobald*)

Theodore from the French male personal name *Théodore* (from Greek *Theodōros*, literally 'gift of god')

Theroux an anglicization of French *Théroux*, perhaps 'person who lives by the wells' (from the plural of Old Provençal *théron* 'well') [Paul Theroux, 1941–, US writer]

Thetford 'person from Thetford', Norfolk ('people's ford' (i.e. a public ford))

Thewlis, Thewless from a medieval nickname for a rude person (from Middle English *thewless* 'lacking manners or morals')

Thibault, Thibaut from the Old French male personal name *Teobaud* or *Tibaut*, from Germanic *Theobald* (see **Theobald**)

Thin see **Thynn**

Thirkell, Thirkill from the Old Norse personal name *Thorkell*, literally 'Thor's cauldron'. See also **McCorquodale, Turkel, Turtle** (iii), **Tuttle** [Angela Thirkell, 1890–1961, British novelist]

Thirwell probably 'person from Thirlwall', Northumberland ('gap in the (Roman) wall')

Thistlethwaite 'person from Thistlethwaite', Lancashire ('meadow overgrown with thistles')

Thistlewood 'person from Thistleworth', Sussex ('enclosure overgrown with thistles')

Thom from a shortened form of the personal name **Thomas**. See also **Thoms, Tombs**

Thomas from the male personal name *Thomas*, of biblical origin (from Aramaic *t'ōm'a*, literally 'twin', applied as a nickname to one of Christ's disciples ('doubting Thomas')). See also **McTavish, Tamblyn, Tombs, Tomlin, Tompkins, Tompkiss, Tonkin, Tonks** [D.M. Thomas, 1935–, British novelist and poet; Dylan Thomas, 1914–53, Welsh poet; Edward Thomas, 1878–1917, British poet; George Thomas (Viscount Tonypandy), 1909–97, British Labour politician, speaker of the House of Commons 1976–83; Gerald Thomas, 1920–93, British film director, notably of the *Carry On* films; Sir Keith Thomas, 1933–, British historian; Leslie Thomas, 1931–, British author; R.S. Thomas, 1913–2000, Welsh poet; Ralph Thomas, 1915–2001, British film director, brother of Gerald; Terry-Thomas (original name Thomas Terry Hoar Stevens), 1911–90, British comic actor]

☆ The 10th commonest surname in Britain

— **Thomas Cup** an international badminton trophy, first contested in 1939. It was donated by Sir George Thomas, 1881–1972, president of the International Badminton Federation.

— **Thomas splint** a type of splint for immobilizing the hip, originally developed by the British surgeon H. O. Thomas, 1834–91.

Thomason 'son of **Thomas**'

Thompsett, Thomsett, Tompsett, Tomsett 'little **Thomas**'

Thompson, Thomson 'son of **Thomas**' [Daley Thompson (original name Francis Morgan

Thompson), 1958–, British decathlete; Emma Thompson, 1959–, British actress; E.P. Thompson, 1924–93, British historian; Flora Thompson (*née* Timms), 1876–1947, British author; Francis Thompson, 1859–1907, British poet; Hunter S. Thompson, 1939–2005, US journalist and writer; James Thomson, 1700–48, British poet; James Thomson, 1834–82, British poet; Jeff Thomson, 1950–, Australian cricketer; Sir Joseph John Thomson, 1856–1940, British physicist; Peter Thomson, 1929–, Australian golfer; Roy Thomson (Lord Thomson of Fleet), 1894–1976, Canadian-born British newspaper proprietor; Sadie Thompson, prostitute lusted after by the missionary Davidson in Somerset Maugham's story 'Rain' (1921); Virgil Thomson, 1896–1989, US composer; William Thomson (Lord Kelvin), 1824–1907, British physicist]

— **Major Thompson** a fictional retired English army officer living in France, introduced to the world in Pierre Daninos's *Les carnets du Major Thompson* (1954) and appearing in a series of subsequent novels

— **Thompson** a minor tributary of the Fraser River in southern British Columbia. It was named after the British-Canadian explorer David Thompson, 1770–1857.

— **Thomson effect** the phenomenon of temperature differences within a conductor or semiconductor causing an electric potential gradient. It is named after William Thomson (see above).

— **Thomson Holidays** a British holiday company founded in 1971 by Roy Thomson (see above)

— **Thomson scattering** the scattering of light by free charged particles, especially electrons. It is named after Sir J.J. Thomson (see above).

— **Thomson's gazelle** a small East African gazelle (*Gazella thomsoni*) that has a broad black stripe on its side. It is named after the Scottish explorer Joseph Thomson, 1858–94.

— **Thompson submachine gun** a relatively lightweight submachine gun designed for use as an infantry weapon. It was named in 1919 in honour of US General John T. Thompson, 1860–1940, who had the original idea for it and whose company financed its development.

— **Thompson Twins** a pair of incompetent detectives who provide comic relief in the Tintin stories of Hergé. They first appeared in *Cigars of the Pharaoh* (1932). Their names in the original French were *Dupond* and *Dupont*, the joke being that their names sounded the same but were spelled differently, and in the English version the names of the individual characters are actually *Thomson* and *Thompson*. 'The Thompson Twins' was also the name of a British rock group, active between 1977 and 1993; none of its members were actually called Thompson, nor (like the original Thompson Twins) were any of them real twins.

Thoms 'son of **Thom**'

Thomsen from the Danish, Norwegian, Dutch and North German equivalents of **Thompson**

Thomson see **Thompson**

Thorburn from the medieval Scottish and northern English male personal name *Thorburn*

(from Old Norse *Thórbjörn*, literally 'Thor's bear', 'Thor's warrior' – see **Thorogood**). See also **Thubron** [Archibald Thorburn, 1860–1935, British bird illustrator; Cliff Thorburn, 1948–, Canadian snooker player]

Thoreau (i) from a medieval French nickname for a powerful or violent person (from Old French *thorel* 'bull'); (ii) 'little *Thoré*', a pet-form of the French personal name **Maturin** [Henry David Thoreau, 1817–62, US essayist and philosopher]

Thorley 'person from Thornley', Lancashire ('glade where thorn bushes grow'). See also **Thornley**

Thorn (i) *also* **Thorne** 'person who lives by a thorn bush or thorn hedge', or 'person from Thorne', Kent, Somerset and Yorkshire (in either case from Old English or Old Norse *thorn* 'thorn'); (ii) 'person who lives by a tower' (from Middle Low German *torn* 'tower'); (iii) 'person from Thorn', now Torun, Poland ('tower')
— *Doctor Thorne* a novel (1858) by Anthony Trollope, focussing on the complications of the marriage market among the gentry of Barsetshire
— **Thorn Electrical Industries Ltd.** a British manufacturer of electrical equipment, founded by Jules Thorn in 1928 as The Electric Lamp Service Co. Ltd. In 1977 it merged with EMI to become Thorn-EMI, but it demerged in 1996.

Thornber a different form of **Thornberry**

Thornberry 'person from Thornborough', Yorkshire (probably 'hill where thorn bushes grow'), or 'person from Thornbrough', Northumberland and Yorkshire ('fortified place where thorn bushes grow')

Thornburg, Thornburgh different forms of **Thornberry**

Thorndike, Thorndyke 'person who lives by a ditch growing with thorn bushes' [Dame Sybil Thorndike, 1882–1976, British actress]

Thorne see **Thorn** (i)

Thornhill 'person from Thornhill', the name of various places in England ('hill where thorn bushes grow') [Sir James Thornhill, 1675–1734, English baroque decorative painter; Roger O. Thornhill, the central character (played by Cary Grant) in Alfred Hitchcock's film *North by Northwest* (1959)]

Thornley a different form of **Thorley**

Thornton (i) 'person from Thornton', the name of numerous places in England and Scotland ('farmstead where thorn bushes grow'); (ii) a shortened and adapted translation of Irish Gaelic *Mac Sceacháin* 'son of *Sceachán*', a personal name meaning literally 'little thorn bush'; (iii) from Irish Gaelic *Ó Draighneáin* (see **Drennan**)

Thorogood, Thoroughgood from the medieval personal name *Thurgod* (from Old Norse *Thorgautr*: *Thórr* was the name of the Norse god of thunder, and *Gautr* was the name of a Germanic tribe). See also **Thurgood**

Thorold, Thorrold from the medieval personal name *Turold* (from Old Norse *Thorvaldr*, literally 'Thor's rule' – see **Thorogood**). See also **Torode**

Thorpe, Thorp 'person from Thorpe', the name of various places in England ('outlying village'). See also **Tharp** [Graham Thorpe, 1969–, English cricketer; Ian Thorpe, 1982–, Australian swimmer; Jeremy Thorpe, 1929–, British Liberal politician]

Threadgill a different form of **Threadgold**

Threadgold 'person who embroiders cloth with gold thread'. See also **Treadgold**

Threlfall 'person from Threlfall', Lancashire ('serf's woodland clearing')

Thresher (i) 'person who threshes harvested cereal crops'; (ii) a translation of German *Drescher*, literally 'thresher'
— **Threshers** a British chain of wine shops and off-licenses, founded in 1897 by Samuel Thresher

Thrift (i) from a medieval nickname for a thrifty person; (ii) perhaps an alteration of **Firth**

Thring 'person from Tring', Hertfordshire ('tree-covered hillside')

Throckmorton 'person from Throckmorton', Worcestershire ('farmstead by a pool with a platform') [Sir Nicholas Throckmorton (or Throgmorton), 1515–71, English diplomat]

Throgmorton a different form of **Throckmorton**
— **Throgmorton Street** a street in the City of London, which contains the Stock Exchange. It was named after Sir Nicholas Throckmorton (see **Throckmorton**).

Thrower 'person who makes silk thread from raw silk' (from a derivative of Middle English *throwen* 'to twist') [Percy Thrower, 1913–88, British television gardener]

Thrush from a medieval nickname for someone thought to resemble a thrush, perhaps in cheerfulness

Thubron a different form of **Thorburn**

Thurber a name of unknown origin and meaning [James Thurber, 1894–1961, US humorous writer and cartoonist]

Thurgood a different form of **Thorogood**

Thurlow, Thurloe 'person from Thurlow', Suffolk (probably 'hill where the troop or assembly gathers')

Thurman from the medieval personal name *Thurmond* (from Old Norse *Thormundr*, literally 'Thor-protection' – see **Thorogood**) [Uma Thurman, 1970–, US actress]

Thursby 'person from Thursby', Cumbria ('Thórir's farmstead')

Thursfield 'person from Thursfield', Staffordshire ('Thorvaldr's area of open land')

Thurston (i) 'person from Thurston', Suffolk ('Thori's farmstead'); (ii) from the medieval personal name *Thurston* (from Old Norse *Thorsteinn*, literally 'Thor-stone' (probably alluding to Thor's altar, or conceivably his hammer) – see **Thorogood**). See also **Tutin, Tutton**

Thwaite 'person who lives in a clearing', or 'person from Thwaite', the name of various places in East Anglia and northern England (in either case from Old Norse *thveit* 'clearing') [Anthony Thwaite, 1930–, British poet and critic]

Thwaites, Thwaytes different forms of **Thwaite**

Thynn, Thynne, Thin from a medieval nickname for a thin person [Thynn, family name of the marquesses of Bath]

Tibbett, Tibbitt different forms of **Tebbit**

Tibbetts, Tibbets, Tibbitts, Tibbits 'son of **Tibbett**'

Tibbs 'son of *Tibb*', a shortened form of the medieval personal name *Tibalt* (see **Theobald**)

Tichborne, Tichbourne 'person from Tichborne', Hampshire ('stream where young goats come')

Tickell, Tickel, Tickle 'person from Tickhill', Yorkshire ('Tica's hill' or 'hill where young goats graze')

Ticknell 'person from Ticknall', Derbyshire ('corner of land where young goats are kept')

Tickner, Ticknor probably 'person who lives at a crossroads or fork in a road' (from a derivative of Old English *twicen* 'crossroads, fork in a road')

Tidman (i) from the medieval male personal name *Tideman*, literally 'time-man, season-man'; (ii) 'head of a tithing (a group of originally ten households under the feudal system)' (from Old English *tēothingmann*, literally 'tithing-man'). See also **Tydeman**

Tidmarsh 'person from Tidmarsh', Berkshire ('marsh of the people')

Tidwell 'person from Tideswell', Derbyshire ('Tīdi's spring')

Tidy from a medieval nickname for an excellent or admirable person (from Middle English *tīdi* 'fine, excellent') [Bill Tidy, 1933–, British cartoonist]

Tiernan from Irish Gaelic *Ó Tíghearnáin* 'descendant of *Tíghearnán*', a nickname meaning literally 'little master'. See also **Ternan**

Tierney, Tierny from Irish Gaelic *Ó Tíghearnaigh* 'descendant of *Tíghearnach*', a nickname meaning literally 'lord, master' [Gene Tierney, 1920–91, US actress]

Tiffany, Tiffney from the medieval female personal name *Tiffania* (ultimately, via Old French, from Greek *Theophania*, literally 'vision of god') [Louis Comfort Tiffany, 1848–1933, US artist and designer, most notably of art-nouveau glassware]
— **Breakfast at Tiffany's** a novella (1958) by Truman Capote and a film (1961) rather loosely based on it, featuring the escapades of volatile New York call girl Holly Golightly
— **Tiffany & Co.** a US silver and jewellery firm founded in New York City in 1837 by Charles Lewis Tiffany, 1812–1902, father of Louis (see above)

Tiffin, Tiffen different forms of **Tiffany**
— **Tiffin School** a boys' grammar school in Kingston upon Thames, Greater London, founded in 1880 using funds originally given in the 1630s by two local brewers, the brothers John and Thomas Tiffin, for the education of local children

Tighe from Irish Gaelic *Ó Taidhg* 'descendant of *Tadhg*', a nickname meaning literally 'poet, bard'. See also **Teague** (ii)

Tilbrook 'person from Tilbrook', Cambridgeshire ('Tila's brook')

Tilbury 'person from Tilbury', Essex ('Tila's stronghold')

Tilden probably 'person from Tilden', an unidentified place in England (perhaps 'Tila's valley') [Bill Tilden, 1893–1953, US tennis player]

Tildesley see **Tyldesley**

Tiler see **Tyler**

Till (i) from the Low German male personal name *Till*, literally 'little *Dietrich*' (from Germanic *Theodoric* – see **Terry** (i)); (ii) from the medieval female personal name *Till*, a shortened form of *Matilda*

Tiller 'person who tills the soil, husbandman'. See also **Tillyard**
— **Tiller Girls** a troupe of high-stepping female stage dancers founded in Manchester around 1890 by John Tiller, 1854–1926

Tillett, Tillott 'little **Till** (ii)' [Ben Tillett, 1860–1943, British trade unionist]

Tilley, Tilly, Tillie (i) 'person from Tilley', Shropshire ('woodland clearing overhung by boughs'); (ii) 'person from Tilly', the name of various places in northern France (mainly 'Tilius's settlement'); (iii) 'little **Till** (ii)'; (iv) 'person who tills the soil, husbandman' (from English *tilia*, a derivative of *tilian* 'to till') [Vesta Tilley (original name Matilda Alice Powles), 1864–1952, British music-hall entertainer (as a male impersonator)]
— **Tilley lamp** the proprietary name of a type of portable oil or paraffin lamp in which fuel is supplied to the burner by means of air pressure. It works on the principle of the hydropneumatic blowpipe devised by John Tilley in 1813. W.H. Tilley began manufacturing lamps in 1818.

Tilling from the medieval personal name *Tilling*, literally probably 'son of *Tila*'

Tillinghast 'person from Tillinghurst', Sussex ('Tytta's people's wooded hill')

Tillotson 'son of **Tillett**'

Tillson see **Tilson**

Tilly (i) see **Tilley**; (ii) a different form of **Tully**

Tillyard 'person who tills the earth'

Tilney 'person from Tilney', Norfolk ('area of raised ground suitable (for settlement)') [General Tilney, his sons Henry and Frederick and daughter Eleanor, central characters of Jane Austen's *Northanger Abbey* (1818)]

Tilson, Tillson (i) 'son of **Till** (ii)'; (ii) 'son of *Tile*', a Yiddish female personal name (from Hebrew *Tehila*, literally 'splendour') [Michael Tilson Thomas, 1944–, US conductor]

Tilton 'person from Tilton', Leicestershire ('Tila's farmstead')

Timberlake 'person from Timberlake', a place (now lost) in Worcestershire ('stream where timber is obtained') [Justin Timberlake, 1981–, US pop singer]

Timm, Timme (i) perhaps from an unrecorded Old English male personal name *Timm* (possibly a shortened form of a name related to German *Dietmar* – see (ii)); (ii) from a shortened form of the medieval Dutch and North German male personal name *Dietmar*, literally 'people-famous'

Timmins a different form of **Timmons** (i)

Timmons (i) 'son of little **Timm** (i)'; (ii) from Irish Gaelic *Mac Toimín* 'son of *Toimín*', literally 'little Thomas', *Ó Tiomáin* 'descendant of *Tiomán*', a personal name meaning literally 'little pliant one', or *Ó Tiománaidhe* 'descendant of *Tiománaidhe*', a nickname meaning literally 'driver'

Timms, Tims 'son of **Timm** (i)'

Timothy (i) from the male personal name *Timothy*, of biblical origin (from Greek *Timotheos*, literally 'honour god'); (ii) a name substituted for **Tomelty**

Timpson a different form of **Timson**

Tims see **Timms**

Timson 'son of **Timm** (i)'

Tindall, Tindal, Tindell, Tindle, Tindale, Tyndall, Tyndale 'person from Tynedale', the valley of the river Tyne, northern England, or 'person from Tindale', Cumbria ('Tyne valley') [John Tyndall, 1820–93, Irish physicist; William Tyndale, ?1494–1536, English biblical translator]
— **Tyndall effect** the scattering of light by microscopic particles (e.g. those in dust and colloids), discovered in 1869 by John Tyndall (see above). It accounts for the blueness of the sky.

Tingay a different form of **Tangye**

Tinker 'itinerant mender of pots and pans, tinker'

Tinkler 'itinerant mender of pots and pans, tinker' (from Middle English *tinkler*, a variant of *tinker*)

Tinney from Irish Gaelic *Mac an tSionnaigh*, literally 'son of the fox'

Tinsley 'person from Tinsley', Yorkshire ('Tynni's mound')

Tiplady perhaps from a medieval nickname for a man who had had sexual relations with a woman of higher social class (from *tip*, a different form of *tup* 'to copulate with' + *lady*). See also **Toplady, Topley**

Tipper (i) probably 'maker of arrowheads' (from a derivative of Middle English *tippe* 'tip'); (ii) perhaps from a medieval nickname for a very sexually active man (from a derivative of *tip*, a different form of *tup* – see **Tiplady**)

Tippett a different form of **Tebbit** [Sir Michael Tippett, 1905–98, British composer]

Tipping from the medieval personal name *Tipping*, literally 'son of Tippa'

Tipton 'person from Tipton', West Midlands ('estate associated with Tibba')

Tisdall 'person from Tisdall', an unidentified place (perhaps 'Tissi's valley')

Titchmarsh 'person from Titchmarsh', Northamptonshire ('Tyccea's marsh') [Alan Titchmarsh, 1949–, British television gardener and novelist]

Tite (i) via French from the Germanic personal name *Tito*, a derivative of *theudo* 'people, race'; (ii) from the Old French male personal name *Tite* (from Latin *Titus*)

Titley 'person from Titley', Herefordshire ('Titta's glade')

Titmus, Titmuss from a medieval nickname for someone thought to resemble a titmouse (a bluetit or related bird) [Abi Titmuss, 1976–, British glamour model; Fred Titmus, 1932–, English cricketer; Sir Richard Titmuss, 1907–73, British social scientist]

Titterington 'person from Tytherington', Cheshire ('estate associated with Tydre')

Tobias from *Tobias*, the Greek form of the Hebrew male personal name *Tovya*, literally 'Jehovah is good'

Tobin (i) from Irish Gaelic *Tóibín*, literally 'person from Saint-Aubin', Brittany; (ii) 'little **Tobias**'

Toby, Tobey from the male personal name *Toby*, the English form of **Tobias** [Mark Tobey, 1890–1976, US painter]

Todd, Tod from a medieval nickname for someone thought to resemble a fox (e.g. in cunningness, or in having red hair) (from northern Middle English *tod* 'fox') [Alexander Todd (Lord Todd), 1907–97, British chemist; Ann Todd, 1909–93, British actress; Mike Todd, 1907–58, US stage and film producer; Richard Todd (original name Richard Palethorpe-Todd), 1919–, British actor]
— **Todd-AO** the US proprietary name of a cinematic process developed in the 1950s by Mike Todd (see above) that produces a wide-screen image. *AO* stands for 'American Optical Co'.

Todhunter 'person who hunts foxes' (see **Todd**)

Todman perhaps a different form of **Tuddenham**

Toft (i) 'person from Toft', the name of various places in England ('homestead'). See also **Taft**; (ii) *also* **Tofte** 'person from Toft', the name of various farmsteads and other places in Scandinavia ('homestead')

Tolbert from the medieval personal name *Tolbert*, brought into England by the Normans but ultimately of Germanic origin; its second part means literally 'bright', hence 'famous', but the origin and meaning of *Tol-* are not known

Tolkien probably from the German name *Tollkühn*, literally 'foolish-brave' [J.R.R. Tolkien, 1892–1973, South African-born British scholar and author]

Tollemache probably 'itinerant trader' (from Old French *talemasche* 'knapsack')

Toller (i) 'person from Toller', Dorset ('place by the river *Toller*', a Celtic river-name meaning literally 'hollow stream'); (ii) 'collector of tolls or taxes' (from a derivative of Middle English *toll* 'compulsory payment'). See also **Towler**

Tolley 'little *Toll*' (see **Towle**). See also **Tooley**

Tomalin a different form of **Tomlin**

Tombs, Toombs, Toombes 'son of **Thom**'. See also **Tomes**

Tomelty from Irish Gaelic *Mac Tomhaltaigh* 'son of *Tomaltach*' and *Ó Tomhaltaigh* 'descendant of *Tomaltach*', a nickname probably meaning literally 'glutton'. See also **Tumelty**

Tomes a different form of **Tombs**

Tomkins, Tomkinson see **Tompkins, Tompkinson**

Tomkiss see **Tompkiss**

Tomlin 'little **Thom**'. See also **Tomalin**

Tomlinson 'son of **Tomlin**' [David Tomlinson, 1917–2000, British actor; H.M. Tomlinson, 1873–1958, British novelist and journalist; Sir John Tomlinson, 1946–, British bass; Ray Tomlinson, 1941–, US computer programmer, deviser of e-mail; Ricky Tomlinson, 1939–, British actor]

Tompkins, Tomkins 'son of little **Thom**' [Thomas Tomkins, 1572–1656, Welsh composer and organist]

Tompkinson, Tomkinson 'son of little **Thom**' [Stephen Tompkinson, 1965–, British actor]

Tompkiss, Tomkiss different forms of **Tompkins**

Tompsett, Tomsett see **Thompsett**

Tone a different form of **Town** [Wolfe Tone, 1763–98, Irish nationalist]

Toney from the medieval male personal name *Toney*, a pet-form of **Anthony**

Tong, Tonge, Tongue (i) 'person who makes or uses tongs'; (ii) 'person who lives on a tongue-shaped piece of land', or 'person from Tonge', Leicestershire (in either case from Old English *tunge* 'tongue of land'); also, 'person from Tong', the name of various places in England ('tong-shaped area of land'); (iii) from a medieval nickname for someone who is always talking or nagging, or who has some sort of deformity to their tongue [Pete Tong, 1960–, British disc jockey]
— **Pete Tong** in British rhyming slang, 'wrong' (from the name of the disc jockey – see above). It is generally used in the phrase *go Pete Tong*.

Tonkin 'little **Thom**'

Tonks 'son of **Thom**'

Tooey see **Tuohy**

Toogood from a medieval nickname for an exceptionally excellent person (no doubt sometimes applied ironically) (from Middle English *to* 'very' + *gode* 'good'). See also **Tugwood**

Toohey see **Tuohy**

Tooke, Took from the Old Norse personal name *Tóki*, perhaps a shortened form of *Thorkell* (see **Thirkell**). See also **Tuck, Tuke** [Barry Took, 1928–2002, British comedy writer; John Horne Tooke, 1736–1812, British radical]

Toole (i) from Irish Gaelic *Ó Tuathail* 'descendant of *Tuathal*', a personal name meaning literally 'people-rule'. See also **O'Toole**; (ii) a different form of **Towle**

Tooley a different form of **Tolley** [Sir John Tooley, 1924–, British music administrator]

Toombs, Toombes see **Tombs**

Toomey see **Twomey**

Toon, Toone different forms of **Town**

Tootal, Tootell, Tootill, Tootle 'person who lives on or by a look-out hill', or 'person from Tootle', the name (variously spelled) of several places in England (in either case from Old English *tōt* 'look-out' + *hyll* 'hill'). See also **Tottle**
— **Tootal** a British brand of shirts, which owes its name to Edward Tootal, 1799–1873, who in 1842 became a partner in the Manchester tailoring business founded in 1799 by a Mr Gardner

Tooth (i) from a medieval nickname for someone with a particularly noticeable tooth or teeth; (ii) a partial translation of Irish Gaelic *Mac Confhiaclaigh* 'son of *Cú Fhiaclach*', a personal name meaning literally 'large-toothed hound'

Topham 'person from Topham', Yorkshire (perhaps 'Toppa's homestead')

Toplady a different form of **Tiplady** [Augustus Toplady, 1740–78, British clergyman and hymnist, author of 'Rock of Ages']

Topley a different form of **Tiplady**

Topping 'son of *Toppa*', an Old English male personal name meaning literally 'crest, tuft'

Torode a different form of **Thorold**

Torrence, Torrance, Torrens 'person from Torrance', Dunbartonshire and South Lanarkshire ('hillocks, mounds') [Sam Torrance, 1953–, British golfer]
— **Lake Torrens** a salt lake in South Australia. It was named after the British administrator Sir Robert Torrens, 1814–84.
— **Torrens title** in Australia, a system of registering land ownership in which ownership occurs when the document that transfers the property is lodged at the local land office. It is named after Sir Robert Torrens (see above).

Torres 'person from Torres', the name of numerous places in Spain and Portugal ('towers')

Torvill perhaps 'person from Tourneville', the name of various places in northern France [Jayne Torvill, 1957–, British ice skater]

Tosh a shortened form of **McIntosh**

Toshack from Scottish Gaelic *Mac An Toisich* (see **McIntosh**) [John Toshack, 1949–, Welsh footballer and football manager]

Tottle a different form of **Tootal**

Toulson 'son of *Toll*' (see **Towle**)

Tovey from the Old Norse male personal name *Tófi*, a shortened form of various compound names beginning with *Thorf-* or *Thorv-* (e.g. *Thorvaldr*), based on the name of the thunder god *Thórr* [Sir Donald Tovey, 1875–1940, British musicologist and composer]

Tower (i) 'person who lives near a tower'; (ii) 'maker of white leather (i.e. leather cured with alum rather than tanned)' (from a derivative of Middle English *tawen* 'to prepare')

Towers (i) 'person from Tours', northern France ('settlement of the *Turones*', a Gaulish tribal name); (ii) a different form of **Tower**

Towle, Towell from the medieval male personal name *Toll* (either from Old English *Toll*, of unknown origin, or Old Norse *Tóli*, a shortened form of various compound names beginning with *Thorl-* (e.g. *Thorleifr*), based on the name of the thunder god *Thórr*). See also **Tolley, Toole** (ii), **Toulson**

Towler a different form of **Toller** (ii)

Town, Towne 'person who lives in a main settlement (as opposed to a small hamlet or an outlying farm)' (from Middle English *toun* 'settlement, village'). See also **Toon**

Townend a Yorkshire variant of **Townsend**

Townley, Towneley 'person from Towneley', Lancashire ('woodland clearing containing a settlement')

Towns, Townes different forms of **Town** [Charles Hard Townes, 1915–, US physicist]

Townsend, Townshend 'person who lives at the edge of a village or other settlement'. See also **Townend** [Charles Townshend (2nd Viscount Townshend; 'Turnip Townshend'), 1674–1738, British politician and agricultural reformer; Pete Townshend, 1945–, British rock musician; Peter Townsend, 1914–95, British fighter pilot and royal equerry; Peter Townsend, 1928–, British economist; Sue Townsend, 1946–, British author]
— **Townshend Acts** a series of four acts of parliament passed in Britain in the late 1760s, imposing various revenue duties on the American colonies. Designed to assert British control over the colonies, they in fact provoked great resentment that contributed to the outbreak of the American Revolution. They were named after Charles Townshend, 1725–67, chancellor of the exchequer 1766–67.

Toy, Toye (i) 'maker of sheaths' (from Old French *toie* 'sheath'); (ii) from a medieval nickname for a light-hearted or frivolous person (from Middle English *toy* 'play') [Wendy Toye, 1917–, British actress, dancer and theatre and film director]

Tozer 'person who combs out wool' (from a derivative of Middle English *tosen* 'to tease')

Trace perhaps a different form of **Treece**

Tracey, Tracy (i) 'person from Tracy-Bocage or Tracy-sur-Mer', Normandy ('Thracius's settlement'); (ii) a different form of **Treacy** [Dick Tracy, comic-strip detective created by the US cartoonist Chester Gould in 1931; Jeff Tracy, leader of International Rescue in the ITV puppet science-fiction series *Thunderbirds* (1965–66), created by Gerry and Sylvia Anderson, which also featured his sons Alan, Gordon, John, Scott and Virgil Tracy; Spencer Tracy, 1900–67, US actor; Stan Tracey, 1926–, British jazz pianist and composer]

Trafford 'person from Trafford', Lancashire (originally **Stratford**)

Trager 'person who carries loads (e.g. a porter or pedlar)' (from German *Träger* and Yiddish *treger*, literally 'carrier')

Traherne, Trahern, Trehearne from the Welsh personal name *Trahaearn*, literally 'most iron'. See also **Treharne** [Thomas Traherne, ?1637–74, English poet]

Train (i) 'person who lives by a group of trees', or 'person from Train', the name of several places (variously spelled) in Devon (in either case from Middle English *atte trewen* 'by the trees'); (ii) 'trapper, hunter' (from Middle English *trayne* 'snare, trap')

Trainer, Trainor (i) 'trapper, hunter' (from a derivative of Middle English *trayne* 'snare, trap'); (ii) from Irish Gaelic *Mac Thréinfhir* 'son of *Thréinfhear*', a nickname meaning literally 'champion'. See also **Treanor**

Tranter 'pedlar, hawker' (from Middle English *traunter*)

Trapp, Trappe (i) 'trapper' (from Middle English *trapp* 'trap'); (ii) from a medieval German nickname for a fool (from Middle High German *trappe* 'bustard')

Trask 'person from Thirsk', Yorkshire ('place in a marsh')

Traub 'wine-grower' (from Middle High German *trûbe* 'bunch of grapes')

Travers (i) 'person who lives by a bridge or ford', or 'person who collects tolls at a crossing point' (from Middle English *travers* 'crossing'); (ii) from Irish Gaelic *Ó Treabhair* (see **Trevor** (ii)) [Ben Travers, 1886–1980, British playwright]

Travis, Traviss, Traves different forms of **Travers** (i) [Dave Lee Travis (original name David Patrick Griffin), 1945–, British radio presenter]

Treacher from a medieval nickname for a tricky or deceptive person (from Old French *tricheor* 'trickster, cheat')

Treacy, Treasey from Irish Gaelic *Ó Treasaigh* 'descendant of *Treasach*', a personal name meaning literally 'belligerent'. See also **Tracey** (ii) [Philip Treacy, 1967–, Irish milliner]

Treadgold a different form of **Threadgold**

Treadwell, Tredwell 'person who, as part of the manufacturing process, treads on dampened newly woven cloth to bulk it up; fuller'

Treanor a different form of **Trainer** (ii)

Treasure (i) 'person in charge of finance, treasurer'; (ii) from a medieval nickname for a dearly loved or highly esteemed person

Trebilcock 'person from Trebilcock', Cornwall (apparently 'dear one's farmstead'). The final *-ck* is standardly silent.

Tredinnick 'person from Tredinnick', the name of several places in Cornwall (variously 'fortified farmstead' or 'farmstead overgrown with gorse or bracken')

Tredwell see **Treadwell**

Tree 'person who lives near a (particular noticeable) tree' [Sir Herbert Beerbohm Tree, 1853–1917, British actor and theatre manager, halfbrother of Max Beerbohm]

Treece 'person who lives near a (particular notice-able) group of trees' [Henry Treece, 1911–66, British poet]

Treen 'person from Treen', the name of two places in Cornwall ('farmstead by a fort')

Trefusis 'person from Trefusis', Cornwall ('farm-stead' with an unidentified second element)

Tregear, Tregeare 'person from Tregear', the name of various places in Cornwall ('farmstead surrounded by a hedge')

Tregoning, Tregonning 'person from Tregoning', the name of various places in Cornwall ('Conan's farmstead')

Treharne a different form of **Traherne**

Trehearne see **Traherne**

Trelawney, Trelawny 'person from Trelawny', Cornwall ('farmstead' with an unidentified second element) [Squire Trelawney, leader of the treasure-hunting expedition in Robert Louis Stevenson's *Treasure Island* (1883)]
— *Trelawny of the 'Wells'* a comedy (1898) by Sir Arthur Pinero recording the struggles of the young playwright Tom Wrench to gain recogni-tion. One of his strongest supporters is the young actress Rose Trelawny. The 'Wells' is Sadler's Wells.

Treleaven, Treleven 'person from Treleaven', Cornwall (perhaps 'farmstead on flat ground')

Tremaine, Tremain, Tremayne 'person from Tremaine', the name of various places in Cornwall ('farmstead by a stone') [Rose Tremain, 1943–, British novelist]

Tremblay 'person who lives near a group of aspen trees' (from a derivative of Old French *tremble* 'aspen')

Tremlett 'person from Les Trois Minettes', Normandy ('the three little mines')

Trench 'person from La Tranche', western-central France ('ditch' or 'track through a forest') [Richard Chenevix Trench, 1807–86, British churchman and philologist]

Trenchard 'butcher', or from a medieval French nickname for a violently aggressive person (in either case from a derogatory derivative of Old French *trenchier* 'to cut, hack') [Hugh Trenchard (Viscount Trenchard), 1873–1956, British air force commander, founding father of the RAF]

Trent 'person who lives by the Trent', the name of various rivers in England ('trespasser', i.e. a river liable to flooding)
— *Trent's Last Case* a novel (1913) by E.C. Bentley about the unsuccessful attempt by the amateur sleuth Philip Trent to solve a murder. It is regarded as the first whodunit.

Tresidder 'person from Tresidder', the name of two places in Cornwall ('farmstead' with an unidentified second element)

Tressel, Tressell 'wood turner' (from Old High German *drāsil* 'turner') [Robert Tressell, pen-name of Robert Noonan, ?1870–1911, British house-painter and novelist]

Trethewey 'person from Trethewey', the name of various places in Cornwall ('David's farmstead')

Trethowan 'person from Trethowan', Cornwall (perhaps 'Dewin's farmstead')

Trevarthen 'person from Trevarthen', the name of two places in Cornwall ('Arthen's farmstead')

Trevelyan 'person from Trevelyan', Cornwall ('farmstead by a mill') [G.M. Trevelyan, 1876–1962, British historian]
— **Trevelyan College** a college of Durham University, founded in 1966, originally for women only. It was named in honour of G.M. Trevelyan (see above), chancellor of the university 1950–57.

Treves 'person from Trèves', France (from Latin *Augusta Treverorum* 'city of Augustus among the Treveri', a Celtic tribe)

Trevethan 'person from Trevethan', the name of several places in Cornwall (perhaps 'farmstead by a meadow')

Trevino 'person from Treviño', the name of two places in Spain [Lee Trevino, 1939–, US golfer]

Trevithick 'person from Trevithick', the name of various places in Cornwall ('farmstead' with a range of personal names) [Richard Trevithick, 1771–1833, British engineer, developer of the steam engine]

Trevor (i) 'person from Trevor', the name of various places in Wales ('large farmstead'); (ii) from Irish Gaelic *Ó Treabhair* 'descendant of *Trea-bhar*', a nickname meaning literally 'hard-working, prudent' [Hugh Trevor-Roper (Lord Dacre), 1914–2003, British historian; William Trevor (original name William Trevor Cox), 1928–, Anglo-Irish novelist and short-story writer]

Trew see **True**

Trewin 'person from Trewen', the name of several places in Cornwall (variously 'white farmstead' and 'Gwen's farmstead')

Trezise, Trezize 'person from Trezise or Tresayes', Cornwall ('Englishman's farmstead')

Trick from a medieval nickname for a crafty or tricky person

Tricker a different form of **Trick**

Trickett 'little **Trick**'

Trickey 'person from Trickey', Devon (apparently 'Trick's enclosure')

Trigg, Trigge from the Old Norse nickname *Triggr*, literally 'faithful'

Triggs 'son of **Trigg**'

Trilling from a medieval German nickname based on Middle High German *drīlinc* 'one third', also the name of a coin [Lionel Trilling, 1905–75, US literary critic]

Trim (i) from the Old English male personal name *Trymma*; (ii) from a medieval nickname for a neat tidy person

Trimble a different form of **Trumble** [David Trimble, 1944–, Ulster Unionist politician]

Trimmer 'person who trims cloth'

Trinder 'spinner, braider' (from a derivative of Middle English *trenden* 'to twist, spin, plait') [Tommy Trinder, 1909–89, British comedian]

Tripp (i) 'dancer', or from a medieval nickname for someone who walked oddly (in either case from a derivative of Middle English *trippen* 'to tread lightly, skip'); (ii) 'butcher, tripe dresser' (from Middle English *trippe* 'tripe')

Trobridge see **Trowbridge**

Trollope, Trollop 'person from Troughburn (formerly Trolhop)', Northumberland ('valley where trolls live') [Anthony Trollope, 1815–82, British novelist; Joanna Trollope, 1943–, British novelist]

Troop see **Troup**

Trott a different form of **Trotter** [Albert Trott, 1873–1914, Australian cricketer]

Trotter (i) 'messenger' (from a derivative of Middle English *trotten* 'to walk fast'); (ii) 'grape-treader' (from a derivative of Middle High German *trotte* 'winepress') [Derek 'Del Boy' Trotter, South London wide boy (played by David Jason) in the BBC television sitcom *Only Fools and Horses* (1981–96); Thomas Trotter, 1957–, British organist]

Troubridge, Trubridge different forms of **Trowbridge**

Troughton 'person from Troughton Hall', Lancashire ('settlement by a hollow') [Patrick Troughton, 1920–87, British actor]

Troup, Troupe, Troop 'person from Troup', Aberdeenshire (probably 'outlying village')

Trowbridge, Trobridge 'person from Trowbridge', Wiltshire ('bridge made of logs'). See also **Troubridge**

Trowell 'person from Trowell', Nottinghamshire ('tree stream')

Troy (i) 'person from Troyes', northern France; (ii) from Irish Gaelic *Ó Troighthigh* 'descendant of *Troightheach*', a nickname meaning literally 'foot soldier'; (iii) an anglicization of any of various similar-sounding Jewish names [Sergeant Troy, seducer of Bathsheba Everdene in Thomas Hardy's *Far from the Madding Crowd* (1874)]

Trubridge see **Troubridge**

Trudgill perhaps from an unrecorded Old English personal name meaning literally 'power-battle'

True, Trew from a medieval nickname for a trustworthy person

Trueman, Truman (i) from a medieval nickname for a trustworthy man; (ii) an anglicization of any of various Jewish surnames based on German *treu* 'trustworthy, faithful' (e.g. *Treumann* or *Treuherz*, literally 'true heart') [Christine Truman, 1941–, British tennis player; Fred Trueman, 1931–2006, English cricketer; Harry S. Truman, 1884–1972, US Democratic politician, president 1945–53]

— **Truman Doctrine** a name given to the announcement by Harry S. Truman (see above) on 12 March 1947 that the US would give military and economic aid to Greece and Turkey to help them withstand any possible Soviet takeover, paving the way for the establishment of overseas US bases.

— **Truman's** a British brewing company founded in 1666 by Joseph Truman at the Black Eagle Brewery in Brick Lane, East London, and built into a large and successful concern by his son Sir Benjamin Truman ('Ben Truman'), 1699/1700–80

— *The Truman Show* a film (1998) about a man (played by Jim Carrey) who discovers that (previously unbeknown to him) he is the star of an all-day television soap opera

Trumble, Trumbull from an unrecorded Old English personal name *Trumbeald*, literally 'strong-brave'. See also **Trimble, Turnbull**

Trumper 'trumpeter' (from Old French *trumpeur*) [Victor Trumper, 1877–1915, Australian cricketer]

— **Geo. F. Trumper** a high-class barber's shop in Curzon Street, Mayfair, London, founded in 1875 by George Trumper

Truscott 'person from Truscott', Cornwall ('beyond the wood')

Truslove 'wolf-hunter' (from Old French *trusser* 'to bind up, carry off' + Anglo-Norman *love* 'wolf')

Truss 'pedlar' (from Middle English *truss* 'bundle, package')

Trussell, Trussel perhaps 'pedlar' (from Middle English *trussel* 'little bundle or package')

Truswell a different form of **Trussell**

Tryon a name of Dutch origin but unknown meaning

Tubb probably from the unrecorded Old English male personal name *Tubba* or from the Old Norse personal name *Tubbi*

Tubbs 'son of **Tubb**'

Tubman 'maker of barrels, cooper' [Harriet Tubman, 1830–1913, US abolitionist; William Tubman, 1895–1971, Liberian statesman, president 1943–71]

Tuck a different form of **Tooke** [Friar Tuck, the gormandizing friar who was an associate of Robin Hood]

Tucker (i) 'person who, as part of the manufacturing process, treads on dampened newly woven cloth to bulk it up; fuller' (from a derivative of Middle English *tucken* 'to full cloth'); (ii) perhaps from a medieval nickname for a generous or gallant man (from Old French *tout coeur*, literally 'all heart'); (iii) from Irish Gaelic *Ó Tuachair* 'descendant of *Tuachar*', a personal name meaning literally 'beloved people'; (iv) an anglicization of the Jewish surname *Toker* or *Tocker*, literally 'wood turner' [Sophie Tucker, 1884–1966, US vaudeville singer]

— **'Little Tommy Tucker'** an English nursery rhyme, first recorded around 1744. The first four lines go:

Little Tommy Tucker
Sings for his supper:
What shall we give him?
White bread and butter.

The original of Tommy or Tom Tucker is not known for certain, although a Thomas Tucker was appointed 'Lord of the Revels' at St John's College, Oxford in 1607.

Tuckett perhaps from the Anglo-Scandinavian personal name *Tukka*

Tuckwell probably from an approving medieval nickname for a fuller of cloth (see **Tucker** (i)). See also **Tugwell** [Barry Tuckwell, 1931–, Australian horn player]

Tuddenham 'person from Tuddenham', Norfolk and Suffolk ('Tudda's homestead')

Tudor from the Welsh personal name *Tudur*, of unknown ultimate origin and meaning [Tudor, the ruling dynasty of England from 1485 to 1603; Mary Tudor, 1495–1533, daughter of Henry VII, queen of France 1514–15]

Tuft (i) perhaps 'person who lives by a clump of trees or bushes' (from Middle English *tufte* 'clump of trees or bushes'); (ii) *also* **Tufte** 'person from Tuft', name of several farmsteads in Norway ('site')

Tufts a different form of **Tuft**
— **Tufts University** a university in the suburbs of Boston, Massachusetts, founded in 1852 by the US businessman Charles Tufts, 1781–1876

Tugwell a different form of **Tuckwell**

Tugwood a different form of **Toogood**

Tuhy see **Tuohy**

Tuke a different form of **Tooke**

Tull (i) perhaps from the Old English personal name *Tula*; (ii) an anglicization of German *Tüll*, from a medieval German nickname for a patient person (from Middle High German *dult* 'patience') [Jethro Tull, 1674–1741, English agriculturalist]
— **Jethro Tull** a British progressive-rock group, founded in Blackpool in the 1960s. They adopted the name (somewhat arbitrarily) from the agriculturalist (see above) in 1968.

Tulliver a different form of **Telfer**

Tulloch, Tullock 'person from Tulloch', Highland ('mound, hillock')

Tulloh a different form of **Tulloch** [Bruce Tulloh, 1935–, British athlete]

Tully, Tulley from Irish Gaelic *Ó Taithlagh* 'descendant of *Taithleach*', a nickname meaning literally 'quiet, unaggressive', or *Ó Maol Tuile* 'descendant of the follower of (St) *Tuile*', a personal name derived from *toil* 'will' (i.e. will of God). See also **Tilly** (ii)

Tumelty a different form of **Tomelty**

Tunney from Irish Gaelic *Ó Tonnaigh* 'descendant of *Tonnach*', a personal name meaning literally either 'wavelike' or 'shining' [Gene Tunney (original name James Joseph Tunney), 1898–1978, US boxer]

Tunnicliffe, Tunnicliff 'person from Tonacliffe', Lancashire ('slope or bank where the settlement's water source emerges')

Tunstall 'person from Tunstall', the name of various places in England ('farm site')

Tuohy, Tuhy, Tooey, Toohey, Twohy, Twoohy from Irish Gaelic *Ó Tuathaigh* 'descendant of *Tuathach*', a nickname meaning literally 'ruler, chief'

Tupper (i) 'shepherd in charge of rams' (from a derivative of Middle English *tupe* 'ram'); (ii) an anglicization of German *Tüpper*, literally 'potter' (from a derivative of Middle Low German *duppe* 'pot')
— **Tupperware** the proprietary name (registered in the US in 1956) of a range of plastic containers, vessels, etc. made by the Tupper Corporation, founded in 1938 by Earl S. Tupper, 1907–83 They are sold only at 'parties' held in private homes.

Turk (i) from a medieval nickname for someone thought to resemble a Turk, especially in being bad-tempered, unruly or cruel or in having black hair or a dark complexion; (ii) from the medieval personal name *Turk*, which seems to have been back-formed from **Turkel** on the mistaken belief that it meant 'little Turk'; (iii) a shortened form of **McTurk**; (iv) a Jewish surname denoting a Jew from Turkey or the Ottoman Empire

Turkel, Terkel different forms of **Thirkell**. See also **Turtle** (iii), **Tuttle** [Studs Terkel (original name Louis Terkel), 1912–, US historian and author]

Turkington perhaps a different form of **Tarkington**

Turley from Irish Gaelic *Mac Toirdealbhaigh* 'son of *Toirdealbhach*', a personal name meaning literally 'like Thor (the Norse god of thunder)' or 'like thunder'. See also **Curley** (i)

Turnage (i) a name perhaps of Essex origin, but of unknown derivation and meaning; (ii) probably an anglicization of German *Türnich*, of unknown origin [Mark-Anthony Turnage, 1960–, British composer]

Turnbull a different form of **Trumble** (based on the idea of its being a nickname for a man so strong and brave that he could 'turn' a charging 'bull')

Turner (i) 'turner of wooden (metal, bone, etc.) objects on a lathe'; (ii) 'official in charge of a tournament' (from a derivative of Old French *tornei* 'tournament'); (iii) from a medieval nickname for a swift runner (literally 'turn hare') [Anthea Turner, 1960–, British television presenter; Dame Eva Turner, 1892–1990, British soprano; J.M.W. Turner, 1775–1851, British painter; Lana Turner (original name Julia Jean Mildred Frances Turner), 1920–95, US actress; Nat Turner, 1800–31, US rebel slave; Ted Turner, 1938–, US television executive, creator of CNN; Tina Turner (original name Anna Mae Bullock), 1939–, US rock/pop singer]
— **Turneresque** like or in the style of the paintings of J.M.W. Turner (see above)
— **Turner Prize** a prize awarded annually to an outstanding contemporary British artist under the age of 50. Established in 1984, it is named after J.M.W. Turner.
— **Turner's syndrome** a genetic disorder affecting women in which only one X chromosome per cell is present instead of the usual two, resulting in undeveloped ovaries and underdevelopment of the womb, vagina and breasts. It is named after the US physician Henry Hubert Turner, 1892–1970.

Turney 'person from Tournay, Tournai or Tourny', places in northern France ('Turnus's settlement')

Turpin from an Anglo-Norman form of the Old Norse personal name *Thorfinnr*, based on that of the thunder god *Thórr* and that of the Finnish people. It was probably influenced by the somewhat self-flagellatory early Christian Latin personal name *Turpinus*, based on Latin *turpis* 'ugly, vile'. [Dick Turpin, 1706–39, British highwayman; Randolph Turpin, 1928–66, British boxer]

Turrell a different form of **Tyrrell**

Turtle (i) from a medieval nickname for someone thought to resemble a turtle dove, in being affectionate or sweet-tempered; (ii) from a medieval nickname for a cripple (from Old French *tourtel* 'cripple'); (iii) a different form of **Thirkell** [Amy Turtle, gossipy denizen of the Crossroads Motel in the ITV soap opera *Crossroads* (1964–88)]

Turton 'person from Turton', Lancashire ('Thóri's or Thórr's farmstead')

Turvey 'person from Turvey', Bedfordshire ('island with turf') [Kevin Turvey, boring Brummie teenager created by the British comic actor/writer Rik Mayall]

Tusa (i) 'person from Tusa', Sicily; (ii) 'person from Tusa', Hungary; (iii) from the medieval Hungarian personal name *Tusa*

Tuson see **Tewson**

Tuthill 'person who lives by a hill used as a lookout point', or 'person from Tothill', Lincolnshire or various other similarly named places in England (in either case from Old English *tōt hyll* 'lookout hill')

Tutin a different form of **Thurston** (ii) [Dame Dorothy Tutin, 1930–2001, British actress]

Tutt from the Old English male personal name *Tutta*, of unknown origin and meaning

Tuttle a different form of **Thirkell**

Tutton a different form of **Thurston** (ii)

Twaddle, Twaddell different forms of **Tweddle**

Twain the surname element of a pen-name ('Mark Twain') invented by the US writer Samuel Langhorne Clemens, 1835–1910. It was based on the cry of a Mississippi leadsman calling out the depth of the river at a particular point. [Shania Twain (original name Eileen Regina Edwards; Twain was the surname of her stepfather, an Ojibwa), 1965–, Canadian singer/songwriter]

Tweddle, Tweddell 'person who lives in Tweeddale', the valley of the River Tweed, Scotland. See also **Twaddle, Tweedle**

Tweed 'person who lives by the River Tweed', Scotland (perhaps 'powerful one')

Tweedie, Tweedy 'person from Tweedie', south of Glasgow [Jill Tweedie, 1936–93, British journalist and feminist]

Tweedle a different form of **Tweddle**

Twigg, Twigge from a medieval nickname for a thin person [Stephen Twigg, 1966–, British Labour politician]

Twining 'person from Twyning', Gloucestershire ('settlement of the dwellers between the rivers')
— **Twinings** a British firm of tea merchants founded by Thomas Twining, 1675–1741, who opened his coffee house in London in 1706

Twiss (i) 'person from Twiss', Lancashire ('fork in a river'); (ii) a different form of **Twist** [Peter Twiss, 1921–, British test pilot]

Twist (i) perhaps 'person who twists cotton threads into a cord'; (ii) perhaps 'person from Twist or Twist Wood', Devon and Sussex respectively ('forked place')
— **Oliver Twist** a novel (1837–38) by Charles Dickens which follows the vicissitudes of its eponymous hero, a young orphan, as he falls into and out of the clutches of ill-wishers and criminals

Twohy see **Tuohy**

Twomey, Toomey from Irish Gaelic *Ó Tuama* 'descendant of *Tuama*', a personal name probably derived from *tuaim* 'hill'

Twoohy see **Tuohy**

Twyford 'person from Twyford', the name of various places in England ('double ford')

Tydeman a different form of **Tidman**

Tye (i) 'person who lives by a pasture held in common' (from Middle English *tye* 'common pasture'); (ii) 'person who lives by a river or on an island' (from a misdivision of Middle English *atte eye* 'at the river' and 'at the island'). See also **Tay** (i), **Tey**

Tyldesley, Tildesley 'person from Tyldesley', Lancashire ('Tilweald's glade')

Tyler, Tylor, Tiler 'person who makes or lays tiles' [Anne Tyler, 1941–, US writer; Sir Edward Burnett Tylor, 1832–1917, British anthropologist; John Tyler, 1790–1862, US Whig politician, president 1841–45; Wat Tyler, died 1381, English rebel, leader of the Peasants' Revolt (1381)]

Tynan from Irish Gaelic *Ó Teimhneáin* 'descendant of *Teimhneán*', literally 'little *Teimhean*', a personal name meaning literally 'dark' [Kenneth Tynan, 1927–80, British critic]

Tyndall, Tyndale see **Tindall**

Tyrrell, Tyrel perhaps from a Norman nickname for a stubborn person (from Old French *tirel* 'puller' (i.e. an animal that pulls on its reins)'). See also **Terrell**

Tyrwhitt 'person from Trewhitt', Northumberland ('area covered with dry resinous wood')

Tyson (i) from a medieval nickname for a hot-tempered person (from Old French *tison* 'firebrand'); (ii) a different form of **Dyson** [Frank Tyson, 1930–, English cricketer; Mike Tyson, 1966–, US boxer]

Tyzack 'person from Tizac', southwestern France ('Titius's settlement') [Margaret Tyzack, 1931–, British actress]

U

Udall, Udell 'person from Yewdale', Lancashire ('valley where yew trees grow') [Nicholas Udall, 1505–56, English dramatist]

Ufford 'person from Ufford', Northamptonshire and Suffolk ('Uffa's enclosure')

Ufton 'person from Ufton', Warwickshire ('farmstead with a shed')

Ullett, Ullyet, Ulyet, Ullyett, Ulyett, Ullyatt different forms of **Wolfit** [Roy Ullyett, 1914–2001, British cartoonist]

Ulman, Ullman (i) 'little *Ulrich*', a German male personal name meaning literally 'riches-power'; (ii) 'person from Ulm', Germany [Tracey Ullman, 1959–, British comic actress]

Umfreville, Umfraville, Umphraville 'person from Umfreville', northern France ('Umfroi's settlement')

Umpleby 'person from Anlaby', Yorkshire ('Óláfr's farmstead')

Underdown 'person who lives at the foot of a hill' (from Old English *under* 'below' + *dūn* 'hill')

Underhill 'person who lives at the foot of a hill', or 'person from Underhill', Devon

Underwood 'person who lives at the edge of a wood', or 'person from Underwood', the name of various places in England and Scotland (from Middle English *under* 'below, protected by' + *wude* 'wood') [Derek Underwood, 1945–, English cricketer; Rory Underwood, 1963–, English rugby player]

Ungar, Unger 'Hungarian person', or from a medieval nickname for someone who had some sort of links with Hungary (from German *Ungarn* and Yiddish *Ungern* 'Hungary')

Unsworth 'person from Unsworth', Greater Manchester ('Hund's enclosure') [Barry Unsworth, 1930–, British author]

Unwin from the Old English male personal name *Hūnwine*, literally 'bearcub-friend' (later confused with Old English *unwine* 'enemy') [Sir Stanley Unwin, 1885–1968, British publisher; Stanley Unwin ('Professor' Stanley Unwin), 1911–2002, South African-born British purveyor of comical nonsense language]
— **George Allen & Unwin** see **Allen**

Upchurch 'person from Upchurch', Kent ('church situated high up')

Updike, Updyke an anglicization of Dutch *Opdijk*, literally 'person who lives on a dyke' [John Updike, 1932–, US author]

Upjohn 'son of John' (from Welsh *ap* 'son of' + **John**)

Upshaw probably 'person who lives by a higher copse' (from Old English *upp* 'upper' + *sceaga* 'copse') [Dawn Upshaw, 1960–, US soprano]

Upton 'person from Upton', the name of numerous places in England (mostly 'higher farmstead')

Urban, Urben from the medieval personal name *Urban*, based on Latin *Urbānus*, literally 'town-dweller'

Ure from the medieval Scots male personal name *Ure*, from Old Norse *Ívarr* (see **Iverson**) [Mary Ure, 1933–75, British actress; Midge Ure (original name James Ure), 1953–, British rock-and-roll guitarist and singer/songwriter]

Uren from the Old Celtic personal name *Orbogenos*, probably literally 'of privileged birth'

Urey a different form (produced by Anglo-Norman pronunciation) of the medieval personal name *Wolrich* (see **Wooldridge**) [Harold C. Urey, 1893–1981, US chemist]

Urian a different form of **Uren**

Urquhart 'person from Urquhart', the name of various places in Scotland ('place by the thicket') [Francis Urquhart, wily Conservative politician who is the protagonist of Michael Dobbs's *House of Cards* (1989; televised in 1990 with Ian Richardson as Urquhart) and subsequent novels; Sir Thomas Urquhart, 1611–60, Scottish scholar and translator]

Urwin see **Irwin**

Usborne a different form of **Osborn**

Usher (i) *also* **Ussher** 'door-keeper' or 'official who accompanies someone of high rank'; (ii) from a southern Yiddish pronunciation of the Yiddish male personal name *Osher* (see **Asher** (ii)) [James Ussher, 1581–1656, Irish Protestant churchman who dated the Creation at 4004 bc]
— **'The Fall of the House of Usher'** a Gothic romance (1839) by Edgar Allan Poe describing the extinction of the last of the Usher line, the etiolated Roderick Usher and his equally wan twin Madeline, who is buried alive and returns from the grave to carry off her brother to his death
— **Usher Hall** a concert hall in Edinburgh, opened in 1914. It was built with funds endowed by Andrew Usher, 1826–98, a Scottish whisky distiller.

Ustinov 'son of *Ustin*', the Russian form of the male personal name *Justin* (from Latin *Justīnus*, a derivative of *Justus*, literally 'the just or upright one') [Sir Peter Ustinov, 1921–2004, British writer, director and actor]

Utley, Uttley 'person from Utley', Yorkshire ('Utta's glade') [Alison Uttley, 1884–1976, British children's writer]

Utting from the Old English male personal name *Utting*, literally 'son of Utta'

V

Vail (i) a shortened form of *McVail*, a different form of **McFail**; (ii) *also* **Vale** 'person who lives in a valley'; (iii) see **Veil** (i)

Vaillant from a medieval nickname for a brave person (from Old French *vaillant* 'brave, sturdy')

Vaisey, Vaizey, Vasey from a medieval nickname for a cheerful person (from Anglo-Norman *enveisié* 'merry'). See also **Phasey, Veasey, Voysey**

Vale see **Vail** (ii)

Valentine from the medieval personal name *Valentine* (from Latin *Valentīnus*, a derivative of *Valens*, literally 'brave one') [Alf Valentine, 1930–2004, West Indian cricketer; Dickie Valentine (original name Richard Bryce), 1929–71, British popular singer]

Valentino from the Italian male personal name *Valentino*, literally 'little *Valente*' (from Latin *Valens* – see **Valentine**) [Rudolf Valentino (original name Rodolpho Guglielmi di Valentina d'Antonguolla), 1895–1926, Italian-born US actor]

Valera see **De Valera**

Vallance 'person from Valence', southeastern France (probably 'place of the brave')

Van Allen 'person from Alen or Aalden', Netherlands
— **Van Allen belt** either of two belts surrounding the Earth and containing charged particles held there by the Earth's magnetic field. They were discovered in 1958 by the US physicist James Van Allen, 1914–2006.

Vanbrugh an anglicization of Dutch *Van Bruggen*, literally 'person from Brugge (Bruges)', Belgium ('bridges') [Sir John Vanbrugh, 1664–1726, English playwright and architect]

Van Buren 'person from Buren', Netherlands ('house, shed') [Martin Van Buren, 1782–1862, US Democratic politician, president 1837–41]

Vance a different form of **Fenn** [Cyrus Vance, 1917–2002, US statesman and diplomat]

Vancouver perhaps an altered anglicization of Dutch *Van Coevorden* or *Van Couwen* 'person from Coevorden or Couwen', places in the Netherlands [George Vancouver, 1757–98, British naval officer and explorer]
— **Vancouver** a city and port on the coast of British Columbia, Canada, named after George Vancouver (see above)

Van Dam 'person from Dam or Ten Damme', the name of various places in the Netherlands and Belgium ('dam, dyke, pond')

Vandenberg, Vandenberge, Vandenbergh anglicizations of Dutch *Van den Berg*, literally 'person who lives by or on a mountain'
— **Vandenberg Air Force Base** a US military installation (including a spaceport) in Santa Barbara County, California. It was established in 1941 as an army base called Camp Cooke, and renamed in 1958 in honour of General Hoyt S. Vandenberg, 1899–1954, second chief-of-staff of the US Air Force.

Vandenplas an anglicization of Dutch *Van den Plas*, literally 'person from de Plas', a polder (area of reclaimed land) in South Holland ('the pool')
— **Vanden Plas** a British luxury car marque, established in London in 1910 when the firm of Warwick Wright set up an offshoot of a Belgian firm of car-body makers founded (as carriage-makers) in 1870 by Guillaume van den Plas

Vanderbilt an anglicization of Dutch *Van der Bilt*, literally 'person who lives on or by a low hill' (from Middle Low German *bulte* 'low hill') [Cornelius Vanderbilt, 1794–1877, US financier and railway and shipping magnate and progenitor of a family of powerful US financiers]
— **Vanderbilt University** a university in Nashville, Tennessee endowed by Cornelius Vanderbilt (see above) and founded in 1873

Van der Westhuizen 'person from Westhuizen', the name of various places in the Netherlands ('western house')

Van Dyke, Van Dyck, Van Dyk, Vandyke anglicizations of Dutch *Van Dijk*, literally 'person who lives by a dyke' [Dick Van Dyke, 1925–, US entertainer]

Vane, Vayne different forms of **Fane** [Vane-Tempest-Stewart, family name of the marquesses of Londonderry]

Van Heusen 'person from Hoesen', the name of various places in the Netherlands ('houses') [Jimmy Van Heusen (original name Edward Chester Babcock; he took the name Van Heusen from the shirt manufacturer – see below), 1913–90, US composer of popular songs]
— **Van Heusen** a brand of shirts made by the US firm Phillips Van Heusen. It had its origins in an operation begun in Pennsylvania in 1881 by Moses Phillips. John Van Heusen joined in 1919.

Van Horn, Van Horne 'person from Hoorn', the name of various places in the Netherlands ('nook of land')

Van Houten 'person from Houten', the Netherlands ('forest')

Vann a different form of **Fenn**

Van Sant 'person from Zanten', Belgium [Gus Van Sant, 1952–, US film director]

Van Winkle 'person who lives in a nook of land or on the corner of a street' (from Dutch *winkel* 'corner, nook') [Rip Van Winkle, man who sleeps for twenty years in the eponymous story (1820) by Washington Irving]

Van Zyl, **Van Zijl**, **Van Zile** 'person who lives by a sluice or pump' (from Dutch *zijl* 'sluice, pump')

Varah a different form of **Farrar** [Chad Varah, 1911–, British clergyman, founder of The Samaritans]

Vardon, **Varden** 'person from Verdun', the name of various places in northern France (probably 'hill growing with alder trees') [Dolly Varden, coquettish young woman in Charles Dickens's *Barnaby Rudge* (1841); Harry Vardon, 1870–1937, British golfer]
— **Dolly Varden** an item of 19th-century women's apparel inspired by that of Dickens's Dolly Varden (see above), in particular a print dress patterned with large flowers, with the skirt gathered up in loops, and a large hat bent downwards on one side and decorated profusely with flowers. The name was also given to a type of troutlike fish (*Salvelinus malma*) found in California.

Vargas 'person who lives by a group of huts', 'person who lives by or on steep slopes', 'person who lives by an enclosed pasture that becomes very wet in winter' or 'person from Vargas', Spain (from *vargas*, the plural of Spanish dialect *varga*, which has all the above three meanings)

Varley (i) 'person from Varley', the name of various places in southwestern England ('fern glade'); (ii) 'person from Verly', northern France ('Virilius's settlement')

Varney 'person from Vernay', northern France ('settlement by alder trees'). See also **Verney** [Reg Varney, 1916–, British comic actor]

Vasey see **Vaisey**

Vasquez see **Vazquez**

Vass (i) *also* **Vasse** 'serf' (from Middle English *vasse* 'serf', from Old French); (ii) a different form of **Vaux**; (iii) a different form of **Wass** (ii–iv) [Bailie Vass, the nickname used in *Private Eye* magazine for Sir Alec Douglas-Home (Lord Home; the name was originally that of a Scottish bailie (senior local councillor) with which a photograph of Douglas-Home had been erroneously captioned in a Scottish newspaper)]

Vassall 'servant, retainer' (from Middle English *vassal*, from Old French) [John Vassall, 1924–96, British spy for the Soviet Union]

Vassar an alteration of the French surname *Vasseur*, literally 'vassal, retainer'
— **Vassar College** a liberal-arts college in Poughkeepsie, New York, founded as a women's college in 1861 by the British-born US brewer Matthew Vassar, 1792–1868. It became coeducational in 1969.

Vaughan, **Vaughn** from Welsh *fychan*, literally 'little little one', used to distinguish the younger of two people with the same name, especially son from father [Frankie Vaughan (original name Frank Abelson), 1928–99, British popular singer; Henry Vaughan, 1621–95, English poet; Michael Vaughan, 1974–, English cricketer; Norman Vaughan, 1927–2002, British entertainer; Peter Vaughan (original name Peter Ohm), 1924–, British actor; Robert Vaughn, 1932–, US actor; Sarah Vaughan, 1924–90, US jazz singer; Ralph Vaughan Williams, 1872–1958, British composer]

Vaux 'person from Vaux', northern France ('valleys'). See also **Vass** (ii)
— **Vaux Breweries** a brewery company established in Sunderland in 1837 by Cuthbert Vaux

Vavasour 'tenant ranking below a baron in the feudal system' (from Middle English *vavasour*, from Old French)

Vayne see **Vane**

Vaz a reduced form of **Vazquez**

Vazquez, **Vasquez** anglicizations of Spanish *Vázquez, Vásquez*, literally 'son of *Vasco*', itself a name meaning literally 'Basque person'

Veal, **Veall**, **Veel** (i) used to distinguish the older of two people with the same name, or from a medieval nickname for an old man (in either case from Anglo-Norman *viel* 'old'); (ii) 'herdsman who looks after calves', or from a medieval nickname for a quiet, untroublesome person (in either case from Anglo-Norman *vel* 'calf')

Veasey, **Veazey**, **Vesey**, **Vezey** different forms of **Vaisey**

Veevers, **Veivers** 'dealer in foodstuffs' (from Old French *vivres* 'victuals')

Veil (i) also **Vail** 'watchman' (from Anglo-Norman *veil* 'guard, watchman'); (ii) a Jewish surname of uncertain origin, perhaps an anagram of **Levi**

Velasco a different form of **Belasco**

Vellacott 'person from Vellacott', Devon ('Willa's cottage')

Venables 'person from Venables', northern France (probably 'hunting ground') [Terry Venables, 1943–, English footballer and football manager]

Venn a different form of **Fenn** [Diggory Venn, the humble suitor of Thomasin Yeobright in Thomas Hardy's *The Return of the Native* (1878)]
— **Venn diagram** a mathematical diagram representing sets as circles, with their relationships to each other expressed through their overlapping positions, so that all possible relationships between sets are shown. It is named after the British logician John Venn, 1834–1923.

Ventris, **Ventress** probably from a medieval nickname for a bold or slightly reckless person (from a reduced form of Middle English *aventurous* 'venturesome') [Michael Ventris, 1922–56, British architect and scholar, decipherer of the Mycenaean Greek Linear B script]

Ventura (i) from the medieval Italian, Spanish and Portuguese personal name *Ventura*, a shortened form of *Bonaventura* or *Buenaventura*, literally 'good luck'; (ii) from a medieval Italian nickname for a lucky person (from Italian *ventura* 'fortune, luck') [Vivienne Ventura, 1947–, British film actress]

Venturi 'son of **Ventura**' [Robert Venturi, 1925–, US architect]

Verey see **Very**

Verity from a medieval nickname for a truthful person, or alternatively (and sarcastically) for someone who always made a point of stating that what he was saying was true [Hedley Verity, 1905–43, English cricketer]

Verney, Vernay different forms of **Varney**

Vernon 'person from Vernon', northern France ('settlement by the alder trees') [Edward Vernon, 1684–1757, British admiral whose nickname 'Old Grog' gave rise to the naval slang term *grog* for 'rum and water']
— **Mount Vernon** the home (1759–99) of George Washington, on the Potomac River to the south of Washington. The mansion was named after Edward Vernon (see above), who had been Washington's half-brother Lawrence's commander in the Royal Navy. It is now a national shrine, and many towns and cities in the US have been named after it.
— **Vernon Manuscript** the usual name given to MS Eng.poet.a.1 in the Bodleian Library, a very large late 14th-century manuscript codex containing a miscellany of religious and devotional texts. Its earliest known owner, in the late 16th century, was Walter Vernon of Staffordshire, and it was donated to the Bodleian in 1677 by his descendant Colonel Edward Vernon.

Verran perhaps 'person from Treverran', Cornwall (from Cornish *tre* 'farmstead' with an unknown second element), or 'person from Veryan', Cornwall ('church of St Symphorian')

Very, Verry, Verey, Verrey from a medieval nickname for a truthful or reliable person (from Old French *verai* 'true') [Rosemary Verey, 1919–2001, British garden designer]
— **Very light** a coloured flare fired from a pistol, used as a signal. It is named after its inventor, the US naval officer Edward W. Very, 1847–1910.

Vesey, Vezey see **Veasey**

Vick from a medieval nickname for someone thought to resemble a bishop (e.g. in pious orotundity) (from a misdivision of Anglo-Norman *l'eveske* 'the bishop' as *le vesk*, later *veck* or *vick*) [Graham Vick, 1953–, British opera director]
— **Vicks** the proprietary name of a range of proprietary medicines produced by Procter & Gamble, especially a vapour rub ('VapoRub') originally produced in the 1890s by the pharmacist Lunsford Richardson of Selma, North Carolina, USA. He named it after his brother-in-law, Dr Joshua Vick.
— **Vicksburg** a city in Mississippi, USA, on the Mississippi River. It was founded in 1811 by the Methodist minister Newitt Vick, 1766–1819.

Vickers, Vickars 'son or servant of a vicar'. See also **McVicar** [Jon Vickers, 1926–, Canadian tenor]
— **Vickers** a British engineering company with a variety of interests, including ship-building and the manufacture of aircraft and armaments. It was

founded in Sheffield in 1828 as a steel foundry by Edward Vickers, 1804–97. It was acquired by Rolls-Royce in 1999, and its name finally disappeared in 2004.
— **Vickers gun** any of a range of machine guns produced by the Vickers company in the first half of the 20th century
— **Vickerstown** a district of Barrow-in-Furness, Cumbria, built at the beginning of the 20th century by the Vickers company as a 'marine garden city' for the workers in its shipyards

Vickery, Vickary, Vicary 'parish priest, vicar' (from Middle English *vicarie* 'vicar', from Latin *vicarius*) [Phil Vickery, 1961–, British chef; Phil Vickery, 1976–, English rugby footballer]

Victor from the medieval male personal name *Victor* (from Latin *Victor*, literally 'conqueror')

Vidal from the Spanish male personal name *Vidal* (from Latin *Vitalis* – see **Vitale**) [Gore Vidal, 1925–, US novelist and essayist]

Vidler (i) from a medieval nickname based on Anglo-Norman *vis de leu*, literally 'wolf-face'; (ii) 'violinist, fiddle player'

Vieira from a medieval Portuguese religious nickname based on Portuguese *vieira* 'scallop', denoting someone who had been on a pilgrimage to the shrine of Santiago de Compostella (such pilgrims wore a scallop shell as a badge)

Viggars, Vigars, Viggers, Vigers from a medieval nickname for a strong, well-built person (from Middle English *vigrus* 'vigorous, strong')

Villa (i) 'person from Villa', the name of several places in Spain ('outlying farmstead'); (ii) 'person who lives in a village or town' (Italian, from Latin *villa* 'house, group of houses, settlement')

Villiers, Villers, Villars 'person from Villiers or Villers', the name of numerous places in northern France ('outlying farmstead'). The name is standardly pronounced 'villers'. [Villiers, family name of the earls of Clarendon; George Villiers (1st duke of Buckingham), 1592–1628, English courtier and politician; George Villiers (2nd duke of Buckingham), 1628–87, English courtier, versifier and dramatist]

Vince from a shortened form of the personal name *Vincent* (see **Vincent**)

Vincent from the male personal name *Vincent* (via French from Latin *Vincentius*, based on *vincens* 'conquering'). See also **Vinson** [Gene Vincent (original name Vincent Eugene Craddock), 1935–71, US rockabilly singer]

Vine 'person who lives by or works in a vineyard' [David Vine, 1935–, British television sports presenter]

Viner, Vyner 'wine-grower, vigneron' (from Anglo-Norman *viner*)

Vines a different form of **Vine** [Ellsworth Vines, 1911–94, US tennis player]

Viney probably 'person from Viney', an unidentified place in northern France ('vineyard')

Vining 'person from Fyning', Sussex

Vinson a different form of **Vincent**

Virgin an English vernacular variant of **Virgo**

Virgo, Virgoe presumably from Latin *virgo* 'virgin', used either as a name for someone who had played the part of the Virgin Mary in a medieval mystery play or as a nickname for someone noted for their chastity or (sarcastically) lack of it [John Virgo, 1946–, British snooker player]

Virtue used as a name for someone who had played the part of Virtue in a medieval mystery play, or as a nickname for someone noted for their virtuousness or (sarcastically) for someone who parades their supposed moral superiority

Vitale from the medieval Italian personal name *Vitale* (from Latin *Vitalis*, based on *vita* 'life'). See also **Vidal**

Vivian, Vivien, Vyvyan from the medieval personal name *Vivian* (from Latin *Viviānus*, based on *vivus* 'alive'). See also **Phythian**

Voisey see **Voysey**

Voss a different form of **Fosse**

Vowell a different form of **Fowle**

Vowels, Vowles different forms of **Vowell**

Voyles (i) 'person who lives by or on a bare, treeless hill' (from a different form of Welsh *moel* 'treeless hill'); (ii) from a medieval nickname for a bald man (from a different form of Welsh *moel* 'bald')

Voysey, Voisey different forms of **Vaisey** [C.F.A. Voysey, 1857–1941, British architect and designer] — *The Voysey Inheritance* a play (1905) by Harley Granville-Barker presenting the moral turmoil in the scandal-fearing upper-middle-class Voysey family, which would rather perpetuate the father's illegal speculations with his clients' money than risk public dishonour

Vyner see **Viner**

W

Waddell, **Waddel**, **Waddle** (i) 'person from Wedale (now Stow)', near Edinburgh (perhaps 'pledge valley'). See also **Weddell**; (ii) 'person who lives by a hill where woad grows', or 'person from Woodhill', Wiltshire (in either case from Old English *wād* 'woad' + *hyll* 'hill') [Helen Waddell, 1889–1965, British medieval scholar; Sid Waddell, 1940–, British television darts commentator]

Waddington, **Wadington** 'person from Waddington', the name of various places in northern England ('Wada's settlement') [Conrad Hal Waddington, 1905–75, British embryologist and geneticist]

Wade, **Waide** (i) 'person who lives near a ford', or 'person from Wade', the name of various places in England (in either case from Old English *gewæd* 'ford'); (ii) from the medieval male personal name *Wade*, derived ultimately from Old English *wadan* 'to go' [George Wade, 1673–1748, British field marshal; Virginia Wade, 1945–, British tennis player]
— **Wade Ceramics Ltd.** a British producer of ceramic ware, notably small figurines. It had its origins in the firm of George Wade & Sons Ltd., founded in 1810. Other members of the Wade family formed companies in the later 19th century, and in the 1950s they all joined forces as Wade Potteries.
— **Wade-Giles** a system for writing Chinese in the roman alphabet devised by the British diplomat Sir Thomas Francis Wade, 1818–95, first professor of Chinese at Cambridge University, and later elaborated by Herbert Allen Giles, 1845–1935, Wade's successor in the Cambridge chair

Wadeson, **Waidson** 'son of **Wade** (ii)'

Wadham 'person from Wadham', Devon (perhaps 'Wada's homestead')
— **Wadham College** a college of Oxford University, founded in 1612 under the terms of a bequest by Nicholas Wadham, 1532–1609, a gentleman of North Devon

Wadkins a different form of **Watkins** [Lanny Wadkins, 1949–, US golfer]

Wadley 'person from Wadley', Berkshire ('Wada's glade' or 'glade where woad grows')

Wadsworth 'person from Wadsworth', Yorkshire ('Wæddi's enclosure'). See also **Wordsworth**

Waggoner see **Wagoner**

Waghorn, **Waghorne** (i) perhaps 'hornblower, trumpeter'; (ii) perhaps 'penis-brandisher, flasher'

Wagner 'builder or driver of carts' (from a derivative of Middle High German *wagen* 'cart') [Robert Wagner, 1930–, US actor]

Wagoner, **Waggoner** (i) 'builder or driver of carts'; (ii) an anglicization of **Wagner**

Wagstaff, **Wagstaffe** (i) 'person who carries a staff of office'; (ii) perhaps 'penis-brandisher, flasher'

Wain, **Waine**, **Wayne** 'builder or driver of carts' (from Middle English *wain* 'cart') [John Wain, 1925–94, British novelist and poet; John Wayne (original name Marion Michael Morrison), 1907–79, US actor]
— **John Wayne** in US military slang, a military-issue can opener – so called because it took considerable strength to operate it

Wainwright, **Wainewright**, **Wainright** 'builder of carts' (from Middle English *wain* 'cart' + *wright* 'craftsman, maker') [Alfred Wainwright, 1907–91, British hillwalker and guide author]
— **Wainwrights** a collective terms for all the mountains and hills featured in the guide books written by Alfred Wainwright (see above). There are 214 in his *A Pictorial Guide to the Lakeland Hills* and a further 102 in *The Outlying Fells of Lakeland*.

Waite, **Wait**, **Wayte**, **Wayt**, **Waight** 'watchman' (from Anglo-Norman *waite* 'watchman') [Terry Waite, 1939–, British churchman and hostage]
— **Waitrose** a British supermarket chain, part of the John Lewis Partnership, which originated in a grocery shop opened in London in 1906 by Wallace Wyndham Waite, 1881–1971, and Arthur Rose, 1881–1949

Wake from the Old Norse nickname *Vakr*, literally 'vigilant', or possibly the related Old English personal name *Waca*

Wakefield 'person from Wakefield', Yorkshire ('open land where wakes (a type of festivity) are held') [Edward Gibbon Wakefield, 1796–1862, British colonist in Canada and New Zealand]

Wakeford 'person from Wakeford', an unidentified place in England ('Waca's ford')

Wakeham 'person from Wakeham', Devon and Sussex ('Waca's homestead') [John Wakeham (Lord Wakeham), 1932–, British Conservative politician]

Wakeley, **Wakely**, **Wakley** 'person from Wakeley', Hertfordshire ('Waca's glade')

Wakelin, **Wakeling** from the Anglo-Norman male personal name *Walquelin*, literally 'little *Walho*', a Germanic nickname meaning literally 'foreigner'. See also **Walklin**

Wakeman 'watchman' (from Middle English *wake* 'watch, vigil' + *man*) [Rick Wakeman, 1949–, British progressive-rock keyboardist]

Walcott 'person from Walcott', the name of numerous places (variously spelled) in England ('cottage of the Britons') [Sir Clyde Walcott, 1926–2006, West Indian cricketer; Derek Walcott, 1930–, West Indian poet and playwright]

Waldegrave 'person from Walgrave', Northamptonshire ('grove belonging to Old (a nearby place)') [William Waldegrave (Lord Waldegrave), 1946–, British Conservative politician and banker]

Walden 'person from Walden', the name of various places in England (mainly 'valley of the Britons') [Brian Walden, 1932–, British Labour politician, journalist and broadcaster]

Waldman (i) 'person who lives in a forest' (from Old English *weald* 'forest' + *mann* 'man'); (ii) an anglicization of German *Waldmann*, literally 'person who lives or works in a forest' (from Middle High German *waltman* 'forest-man'); (iii) an invented Jewish name meaning literally 'man of the forest' (from Yiddish *wald* 'forest' + *man*)

Waldorf 'person from Waldorf', the name of various places in Germany (probably 'settlement in a forest')

Waldron (i) 'person from Waldron', Sussex ('house in the forest'); (ii) *also* **Waldren** from the Germanic male personal name *Walahram*, literally 'foreigner-raven'

Wale (i) 'person who lives by an embankment' (from Middle English *wale* 'embankment'); (ii) from a medieval nickname for an amiable or popular person (from Middle English *wale* 'choice, excellent'); (iii) from the Germanic personal name *Walo*, which was either a shortened form of any of various compound names beginning with *walh* 'foreigner' or was itself originally a nickname meaning 'foreigner'

Wales 'son of **Wale** (iii)'

Waley see **Whaley**

Walford 'person from Walford', the name of various places in England (mostly 'ford by a spring')

Walkden 'person from Walkden', Lancashire ('Walca's valley')

Walker (i) 'person who, as part of the manufacturing process, treads on dampened newly woven cloth to bulk it up; fuller'; (ii) 'person from Walker', Northumberland ('marsh by a (Roman) wall') [Alexander Walker, 1930–2003, British film critic; Alice Walker, 1944–, US writer; Annie Walker, original landlady of the Rovers Return in the ITV soap opera *Coronation Street* (1960–); Clint Walker (original name Norman Eugene Walker), 1927–, US actor; Private Joe Walker, amiable spiv in the BBC sitcom *Dad's Army* (1968–77); John Walker, 1952–, New Zealand athlete; Junior Walker (original name Autry DeWalt II), 1942–, US R&B musician; Murray Walker, 1923–, British motor-racing commentator; Peter Walker (Lord Walker), 1932–, British Conservative politician]

— **Johnnie Walker** the trade name of a range of blended whiskies produced in Kilmarnock, East Ayrshire. The original product was put on sale in the 1820s by the Kilmarnock grocer John Walker, 1805–57. His son and grandsons developed it, the latter introducing the name 'Johnnie Walker' in 1909. He is portrayed as a purposefully striding Regency buck.

— **Walker Brothers** a US pop vocalist trio popular in Britain in the 1960s and 1970s. Its members (who were not brothers and whose real names were not Walker) were Scott Walker (original name Noel Scott Engel), 1943–, Gary Walker (original name Gary Leeds), 1942–, and John Walker (original name John Maus), 1943–.

— **Walker's Crisps** a British brand of potato crisps developed in the late 1940s by the firm established in Leicester in the 1880s by the pork butcher Henry Walker

Walkinshaw, Walkingshaw 'person from Walkinshaw', Renfrewshire (probably 'fuller's copse')

Walklin, Walkling different forms of **Wakelin**

Wall (i) *also* **Walle** 'person who lives by a wall (e.g. a city wall)'. See also **Waller** (i); (ii) *also* **Walle** 'person who lives by a spring or stream' (from northern Middle English *walle* 'spring, stream'). See also **Waller** (ii); (iii) a re-anglicization of the Irish Gaelic surname *de Bhál*, itself a gaelicized form of **Vale**. See also **Walls** [Max Wall (original name Maxwell Lorimer), 1908–90, British comedian]

— **Wall's** a British producer of sausages, ice creams and other foodstuffs which had its origins in a pork butcher's opened in London by Richard Wall, 1775–1836. The business was expanded by his son Thomas Wall, born 1817, and in particular by his grandson Thomas Wall, 1846–1930. It produced its first ice cream in 1922.

Wallace, Wallice, Wallis 'Briton, Celt' (from Anglo-Norman *waleis* 'Celtic, Welsh'). See also **Walls** (ii), **Walsh, Waugh** [Alfred Russel Wallace, 1823–1913, British naturalist; Sir Barnes Wallis, 1887–1979, British aeronautical engineer, inventor of the Dambusters' 'bouncing bomb'; Edgar Wallace, 1875–1932, British writer; George Wallace, 1919–98, US Democratic politician; Ian Wallace, 1919–, British singer and broadcaster; John Wallis, 1616–1703, English mathematician, grammarian and founder member of the Royal Society; Lew Wallace, 1827–1905, US soldier, diplomat and writer, author of *Ben Hur* (1880); Nellie Wallace, 1870–1948, British music-hall comedian; Sir William Wallace, ?1270–1305, Scottish patriot]

— **Wallace Collection** an art museum in central London housing a collection formed by the 4th marquess of Hertford and his half-brother Sir Richard Wallace, 1818–90, and donated to the nation in 1897

— **Wallace's line** a hypothetical boundary proposed by Alfred Russel Wallace (see above) in 1858 as separating the Oriental and the Australasian biogeographical regions with distinctive types of wildlife

— **Wallis Islands** a group of islands in the southwestern Pacific Ocean that forms part of the French territory of the Wallis and Futuna Islands. They are named after the Cornish explorer and circumnavigator Samuel Wallis, 1728–95, who discovered them in 1767.

Wallach (i) 'person from Wallach', Germany; (ii) probably from a medieval Jewish nickname for someone from Italy (from Middle High German *walhe* 'foreigner (from a Romance-language-speaking country)')

Walle see **Wall** (i–ii)

Waller (i) 'person who lives by a wall (e.g. a city wall)', or 'person who builds walls'; (ii) 'person who lives by a spring or stream' (see **Wall** (ii)); (iii) 'brine-boiler (someone who boils sea water to extract the salt)' (from a derivative of Middle English *wellen* 'to boil'); (iv) from a medieval nickname for someone of a cheerful disposition (from Anglo-Norman *waller*, a derivative of Old French *galer* 'to make merry') [Edmund Waller, 1606–87, British poet; Fats Waller (original name Thomas Wright Waller), 1904–43, US jazz singer, pianist and composer; Sir William Waller, 1598–1668, English MP and parliamentary general in the Civil War]

Walley see **Whalley**

Wallice see **Wallace**

Wallingford 'person from Wallingford', Oxfordshire ('Wealh's people's ford')

Wallington 'person from Wallington', the name of various places in England (mostly 'farmstead of the Britons')

Wallis see **Wallace**

Walls (i) a different form of **Wall** (i–ii); (ii) probably a different form of **Wallace** [Tom Walls, 1883–1949, British actor]

Walmsley, Walmesley 'person from Walmersley', Greater Manchester (perhaps 'Walhmǣr's glade' or 'Waldmǣr's glade')

Walpole 'person from Walpole', Norfolk and Suffolk (respectively 'pool by the wall' and 'pool of the Britons') [Horace Walpole (4th earl of Orford), 1717–97, British writer, fourth son of Sir Robert; Sir Hugh Walpole, 1884–1941, British novelist; Sir Robert Walpole (1st earl of Orford), 1676–1745, British Whig politician, prime minister 1721–42]

Walsh, Walshe (i) 'Briton, Celt' (from Middle English *walsche* 'foreign, non-Anglo-Saxon, Celtic'). See also **Welch**; (ii) a translation of the Irish Gaelic name *Breathnach*, literally 'British, Welsh' [Courtney Walsh, 1962–, West Indian cricketer; Dermot Walsh, 1924–2002, Irish actor]

☆ The 4th commonest surname in Ireland

Walsingham 'person from Walsingham', Norfolk ('Wæls's people's homestead') [Sir Francis Walsingham, ?1532–90, English statesman and spy-catcher]

Walston 'person from Walsden', Yorkshire (probably 'Walsa's valley')

Walter from the male personal name *Walter*, brought into England by the Normans but ultimately of Germanic origin and meaning literally 'rule-army'. See also **Fitzwalter**, **Water** (ii)

[Harriet Walter, 1950–, British actress; Hubert Walter, died 1205, English churchman and statesman, archbishop of Canterbury from 1193; John Walter, 1739–1812, British newspaper editor, founder of *The Times*]

Walters 'son of **Walter**' [Barbara Walters, 1929–, US television journalist and presenter; Julie Walters, 1950–, British actress]

Walton 'person from Walton', the name of numerous places in England (mostly 'farmstead of the Britons') [Ernest Walton, 1903–95, Irish physicist; Izaak Walton, 1593–1683, English writer, author of *The Compleat Angler* (1653); Kent Walton (original name Kenneth Walton Beckett), 1925–2003, British television wrestling commentator; Sir William Walton, 1902–83, British composer]

— *The Waltons* a US television drama series (1974–82) about the domestic travails of a Virginian family during the 1930s and 1940s

Walwyn (i) from the Old English personal name *Wealdwine*, literally 'power-friend'; (ii) perhaps from the medieval personal name *Walwain*, the Anglo-Norman form of Old French *Gauvain* (see **Gavin**)

Wambaugh an anglicization of German *Wambach*, literally 'person from Wambach', the name of various places in Germany [Joseph Wambaugh, 1937–, US author]

Wanamaker an anglicization of Dutch *Wannamaeker*, literally 'maker of winnowing-baskets' [Sam Wanamaker (original name Samuel Watenmaker), 1919–93, US actor and director; Zoe Wanamaker, 1949–, US-born British actress, daughter of Sam]

Wang (i) from a Chinese clan name meaning literally 'prince'; (ii) 'person from Wang', the name of various states or areas in China. See also **Wong** (i)

Wanless from a medieval nickname for an ineffectual person (from Middle English *wanles* 'hopeless, luckless')

Warbeck 'person from Warbeck', an unidentified place, probably in northern England (the second syllable means 'stream') [Perkin Warbeck, ?1474–99, Flemish pretender to the English throne]

Warboys, Worboys (i) 'person from Warboys', Cambridgeshire ('Wearda's bush'); (ii) 'forester' (from Anglo-Norman *warder* 'to guard' + *bois* 'wood')

Warbrick 'person from Warbreck', Lancashire

Warburton 'person from Warburton', Cheshire ('Wǣrburh's farmstead')

Ward, Warde (i) 'guard, watchman' (from Old English *weard* 'guard'); (ii) from Irish Gaelic *Mac an Bhaird*, literally 'son of the poet'; (iii) an anglicization of the Jewish surname *Warshawsky* (from Polish *Warszawczyk*, literally 'person from Warsaw') [Artemus Ward, pen-name of the US humorous writer Charles Farrar Browne, 1834–67; Barbara Ward, 1914–81, British economist and conservationist; Frederick Ward, 1835–70, Australian bushranger, known as 'Captain Thunderbolt'; Mrs Humphry Ward (Mary Augusta Ward, *née* Arnold), 1851–1920, British novelist; Sir Joseph George Ward, 1856–1930, Australian-born New Zealand Liberal and United Party politician, prime minister 1906–12 and 1928–30; Sir Leslie Ward, 1851–1922, British caricaturist; Simon Ward, 1941–, British actor; Stephen Ward, 1912–63, British osteopath]

— **Wardian case** a close-fitting case with glass sides and top for growing small ferns and other moisture-loving plants indoors, popular in Victorian times. Its name commemorates its inventor, N.B. Ward.

Wardell see **Wardle**

Warden (i) 'person from Warden', the name of various places in England ('lookout hill'); (ii) 'guard, watchman' (from Anglo-Norman *wardein* 'guard')

Wardhaugh 'person from Wardhaugh', an unidentified place in northern England or Scotland (probably 'beacon hill')

Wardlaw 'person from Wardlaw', the name of various places in Scotland ('lookout hill')

Wardle, Wardell 'person from Wardle', Cheshire and Lancashire ('lookout hill'), or 'person from Weardale', the valley of the River Wear, County Durham [Johnnie Wardle, 1923–85, English cricketer]

Wardlow 'person from Wardlow', Derbyshire ('lookout hill')

Wardrop 'person responsible for looking after the garments of a king or nobleman and his household' (from Anglo-Norman *warder* 'to guard' + *robe* 'garment')

Ware (i) 'person from Ware', Hertfordshire ('weir'); (ii) from a medieval nickname for a cautious person (from Middle English *ware* 'wary, cautious'); (iii) 'person who lives by a weir or dam on a river' (from Old English *wær* 'weir'). See also **Weir** (i)

Wareham 'person from Wareham', Dorset ('homestead by a weir')

Wareing see **Waring**

Warfield 'person from Warfield', Berkshire ('open land by a weir')

Warhol an anglicization of Polish *Warchoł*, from a medieval nickname for a contentious person (from Polish *warchoł* 'quarreller') [Andy Warhol (original surname Warhola, from Polish *Warchola*), 1928–87, US pop artist and film producer]

Waring, Wareing, Wearing from the Norman male personal name *Warin*, from the shortened form of any of various Germanic compound names beginning with *warin* 'guard' [Eddie Waring, 1910–86, British television rugby league commentator]

— **Waring and Gillow Ltd.** a London firm of furniture manufacturers formed in 1897 by the merger of two firms founded respectively by S.J. Waring (Lord Waring), 1860–1940, and Robert Gillow, 1704–72

Wark, Warke 'person from Wark', Northumberland ('fortified place') [Kirstie Wark, 1955–, British television journalist]

Warlock perhaps 'incantations' (from Old Norse *varthlokkur*) [Peter Warlock, pseudonym of the British composer Philip Heseltine, 1894–1930]

Warman (i) from the Old English male personal name *Wærmund*, literally 'pledge-protection'; (ii) 'merchant, trader' (from Middle English *ware* 'items for sale, wares' + *man*); (iii) an invented Jewish name probably formed from German *wahr* 'true' or *warm* 'warm' + *Mann* 'man'

Warne, Warn 'person from Warne', Devon (probably 'shaking bog') [Shane Warne, 1969–, Australian cricketer]

— **Frederick Warne & Co.** a British publishing firm, established in 1865 by the bookseller Frederick Warne, 1825–1901

Warner (i) from the medieval personal name *Warnier*, introduced into England by the Normans but ultimately of Germanic origin and meaning literally 'guard-army'; (ii) a different form of **Warrener** [Deborah Warner, 1959–, British theatre director; Jack Warner (original name Horace John Waters), 1895–1981, British actor; Marina Warner, 1946–, British author; Rex Warner, 1905–86, British poet and novelist; Sylvia Townsend Warner, 1893–1978, British novelist]

— **Mary Warner** a punning slang term (first recorded in 1933) for 'marijuana' or a marijuana cigarette

— **Warner Bros.** a US film production company founded in Hollywood in 1918 by the brothers Harry Warner, 1881–1958, Albert Warner, 1883–1967, Sam Warner, 1887–1927, and Jack L. Warner, 1892–1978. They came from a Polish immigrant family whose original name may have been Varna.

Warnock from Scottish Gaelic *Mac Gille Mheànaig* 'son of the followers of (St) *Meàrnag*', a personal name perhaps meaning literally 'little wild one' [Mary Warnock (Baroness Warnock; *née* Wilson), 1924–, British philosopher]

Warr, Warre from a medieval nickname for a soldier or for an aggressive warlike person. See also **De La Warr**

— **Warre & Co** a British firm of port shippers founded in Portugal in 1670. The Warre connection dates from 1729, when William Warre, born 1706, became a partner.

Warrell see **Worrall**

Warren, Warrenne (i) 'person who lives in or is employed in a game park' (from Anglo-Norman *warrene* 'piece of land kept for breeding game'); (ii) 'person from La Varrenne', northern France (probably 'the place of sandy soil') [Earl Warren, 1891–1974, US jurist; Frank Warren, 1952–, British boxing promoter]

• Men with the surname Warren are traditionally given the nickname 'Bunny' (from the notion of a rabbit warren)

— **Warren Commission** a body appointed to investigate the assassination of President John F.

Kennedy in 1963. It was chaired by Earl Warren (see above).
— **Warren Street** a street (and Underground station) in central London. It was named after Sir Peter Warren, father-in-law of Lord Southampton, who owned the land on which it was built.

Warrener, Warriner 'gamekeeper' (from Anglo-Norman *warrennier* 'one who works in a warren' – see **Warren** (i)). See also **Warner** (ii)

Warrington 'person from Warrington', Lancashire ('farmstead by the river dam')

Warton see **Wharton**

Warwick 'person from Warwick', Warwickshire ('premises by the weir'), or 'person from Warwick', Cumbria ('dwelling on the bank') [Dionne Warwick (original name Marie Dionne Warrick), 1940–, US popular singer]

Washbourne, Washbourn 'person from Washbourne', Devon ('stream where washing is done'), or 'person from Washbourne', Gloucestershire ('stream running through alluvial land')

Washbrook 'person from Washbrook', the name of various places in England ('brook where washing is done')

Washburn, Washburne 'person who lives by the Washburn', river in Yorkshire ('Walc's stream')

Washington 'person from Washington', Sussex and Tyne and Wear (respectively 'Wassa's people's estate' and 'estate associated with Wassa') [Booker T. Washington, 1856–1916, US teacher and reformer; Denzel Washington, 1954–, US actor; Dinah Washington (original name Ruth Lee Jones), 1924–63, US blues, jazz and R&B singer; Geno Washington, 1943–, US-born British R&B musician; George Washington, 1732–99, US general and statesman, first president of the US, 1789–97]
— **Washington** one of the Pacific states of the northwestern USA. It was named (in 1889) after George Washington (see above).
— **Washington, DC** the capital city of the USA. Its location, on the Potomac River within the state of Virginia, was chosen by George Washington and it was named after him.
— **washingtonia** either of two species of fan palm of the genus *Washingtonia*, found in California and Mexico and contiguous areas. They were named in honour of George Washington.
— **Washington Square** a square and park in Greenwich Village, New York City, laid out in the late 1820s and early 1830s and named in honour of George Washington

Wass (i) from the Norman personal name *Wazo*, which was probably based on the first element of a Germanic compound name beginning with *wad* 'to go'. See also **Gash, Gass** (ii); (ii) from a medieval German nickname for someone regarded as being 'sharp' in some way (from Middle High German *wasse* 'sharp, cutting'); (iii) from a Swedish nickname for a soldier (from Swedish *vass* 'sharp, cutting'); (iv) an invented Swedish name based on Swedish *vass* 'reed, marsh'. See also **Vass** (iii)

Wassell, Wassall different forms of **Wastell**

Wasserman 'water-carrier' (from Middle High German *wazzer* 'water' + *man* or Yiddish *vaser* 'water' + *man*). See also **Waterman** (iii)

Wastell, Wastall (i) 'person from Wasthills', Worcestershire ('guardhouse'); (ii) 'cake-maker, fancy baker' (from Anglo-Norman *wastel* 'cake'). See also **Wassell**

Watanabe a Japanese surname originally denoting a member of the guild of ferrymen

Water (i) 'person who lives by a stretch of water'; (ii) a different form of **Walter**; (iii) from Irish Gaelic *Ó Fuartháin*, erroneously identified with *Ó Fuaruisce*, literally 'descendant of cold water'

Waterbury perhaps 'person from Waterperry', Oxfordshire ('pear trees near water')

Waterfield 'person from Vatierville', northern France ('Walter's settlement')

Waterhouse 'person who lives in a moated house or in a house by a stretch of water' [Alfred Waterhouse, 1830–1905, British architect; Keith Waterhouse, 1929–, British novelist and journalist]
— **Price Waterhouse** see **Price**

Waterlow 'person from Waterlow', Norfolk
— **Waterlow & Sons Ltd.** a British printing firm specializing in postage stamps, banknotes, etc. It originated in a shop established in 1810 by James Waterlow, to produce copies of legal documents. His five sons expanded the business in the 1850s. In 1960 it was taken over by De La Rue & Co.

Waterman (i) 'person who lives by a stretch of water', 'boatman', or 'water-carrier'; (ii) 'servant of **Walter**'; (iii) an anglicization of **Wasserman** [Dennis Waterman, 1948–, British actor; Dame Fanny Waterman, 1920–, British pianist and teacher, founder of the Leeds International Pianoforte Competition; Lewis Edson Waterman, 1837–1901, US insurance broker, inventor of the modern capillary-feed fountain pen; Pete Waterman, 1947–, British record producer]

Waters (i) 'son of **Walter**'; (ii) a different form of **Water** (ii–iii) [Alice Waters, 1944–, US chef and restaurateur; Elsie Waters, 1895–1990, and her sister Doris Waters, 1904–78, British comedy double act under the name 'Gert and Daisy'; Muddy Waters (original name McKinley Morganfield), 1915–83, US blues musician; Sarah Waters, 1966–, British novelist]

Waterson 'son of **Walter**'

Waterston, Waterstone probably different forms of **Waterson**
— **Waterstone's Booksellers** a British firm of booksellers founded in 1982 by Timothy Waterstone, 1939–

Waterworth 'water-bailiff' (from Middle English *waterward*, literally 'water-guard')

Watford 'person from Watford', Hertfordshire and Northamptonshire ('ford used by hunters')

Watkin 'little **Watt**'

Watkins 'son of **Watkin**'. See also **Wadkins** [Alun Watkins, 1933–, British journalist; Peter Watkins, 1935–, British documentary film-maker; Vernon Watkins, 1906–67, British poet]

Watkinson 'son of **Watkin**'

Watling 'little **Watt**'

Watman (i) from the medieval male personal name *Watman* or *Whatman* (from Old English *Hwæt-mann*, literally 'brave man'); (ii) 'servant of **Watt**'

Watmore, Watmoor see **Whatmore**

Watmough, Whatmough 'person related to **Watt**'. See also **Whatmore**

Watney probably 'person from Watney', an unidentified place in England (the second syllable means 'island, area of dry land in a marsh')
— **Watneys** a British brewery company. It had its origins in the Stag Brewery, established in Westminster in the mid-17th century. It was joined in 1837 by James Watney, 1800–84, who in due course assumed its management. After his death his son James took over, and it became Watney & Co.

Watson 'son of **Watt**' [Chris Watson (original name John Christian Watson), 1867–1941, Chilean-born Australian Labor politician, prime minister 1904; Emily Watson, 1967–, British actress; James Watson, 1928–, US geneticist, propounder (with Francis Crick and others) of the structure of DNA; John Broadus Watson, 1878–1958, US psychologist, founder of behaviourism; Dr John Watson, faithful companion, dogged helper and industrious chronicler of Sherlock Holmes; Sir Robert Watson-Watt, 1892–1973, British physicist, pioneer of radar; Tom Watson, 1949–, US golfer]
— **bet like the Watsons** in Australian slang, to bet large amounts of money. The allusion is said to be to a pair of heavy-wagering brothers of around the turn of the 20th century.
— **George Watson's School** a public school in Edinburgh, founded by George Watson, died 1723, first accountant of the Bank of Scotland
— **watsonia** a South African plant of the iris family which has spikes of red, pink or white flowers like gladioli. It was named after the Scottish naturalist Sir William Watson, 1715–87.

Watt from the medieval male personal name *Watt*, a shortened form of **Walter** [James Watt, 1736–1819, British engineer]
— **watt** the SI unit (symbol **W**) of power equal to the power produced by a current of one ampere acting across a potential difference of one volt. It was named (in 1882) after James Watt (see above).

Watts 'son of **Watt**' [Charlie Watts, 1941–, British rock musician, drummer with the *Rolling Stones*; Dennis ('Dirty Den') Watts, landlord of the Queen Vic pub in the BBC television soap opera *EastEnders* (1985–); G.F. Watts, 1817–1904, British painter and sculptor; Isaac Watts, 1674–1748, English hymnist]

Waugh probably 'foreigner', with specific reference to the Britons who lived in the Strathclyde region of Scotland up until the early Middle Ages (from Old English *walh* 'foreign') [Alec Waugh, 1898–1981, British novelist, brother of Evelyn; Auberon Waugh, 1939–2001, British journalist, son of Evelyn; Evelyn Waugh, 1903–66, British novelist; Harry Waugh, 1904–2001, British wine

merchant and connoisseur; Steve Waugh, 1965–, Australian cricketer]

Wavell 'person from Vauville', northern France ('Walo's settlement') [Archibald Wavell (Earl Wavell), 1883–1950, British field marshal]

Wax (i) 'gatherer or seller of beeswax' (from Middle English *wax*); (ii) an anglicization of the German and Jewish surname *Wachs*, literally 'gatherer or seller of beeswax' (from Middle High German *wahs* 'wax') [Ruby Wax, 1953–, US actress and comedian]

Waxman a different form (either native English or from German *Wachsmann*) of **Wax** [Franz Waxman (original name Franz Wachsmann), 1906–67, Polish-born US composer]

Way, Waye, Wey 'person who lives by a road or path', or 'person from Way or Waye', the name of various places in England (in either case from Old English *wæg* 'path, way')

Wayne see **Wain**

Wayte, Wayt see **Waite**

Wear, Weare (i) 'person who lives near the Wear', a river in northeastern England (perhaps 'winding stream'), or 'person from Weare', Devon and Somerset ('weir'); (ii) see **Weir** (i)

Wearing see **Waring**

Weatherall, Wetherall, Weatherell, Wetherell, Weatherill, Wetherill 'person from Wetheral', Cumbria ('corner of land where rams are kept'). See also **Witherow** [Bernard Weatherill (Lord Weatherill), 1920–2007, British Conservative politician, speaker of the House of Commons 1983–92]
— **Bernard Weatherill Ltd.** a firm of Savile Row tailors founded by Bernard B. Weatherill, father of Bernard Weatherill (see above). After a 1982 merger it became Kilgour Weatherill.

Weatherby see **Wetherby**

Weatherhead, Wetherhead perhaps 'shepherd' (from Middle English *wether* '(castrated) ram' + *herd* 'herdsman'). See also **Wethered**

Weatherill see **Weatherall**

Weatherley, Weatherly 'person from Wetherley or Wedderlie', Cambridgeshire and Berwickshire respectively ('glade frequented by rams')

Weathers 'son of *Weather*', either literally 'shepherd' (from Middle English *wether* '(castrated) ram') or from a medieval nickname for a man thought to resemble a ram

Weathersby a different form of **Wetherby**

Weatherspoon a different form of **Witherspoon**

Weaver (i) 'person who weaves cloth'; (ii) 'person from Weaver Hall', Cheshire (from the river-name *Weaver*, literally 'winding stream'); (iii) a translation of **Weber** [Dennis Weaver, 1924–2006, US actor]

Webb (i) *also* **Webbe** 'person who weaves cloth' (from early Middle English *webbe* 'weaver'); (ii) an anglicization of various Jewish surnames of similar meaning (e.g. **Weber** and *Weberman*) [Sir Aston Webb, 1849–1930, British architect; Beatrice Webb (*née* Potter), 1858–1943, British econo-

mist and socialist, wife of Sidney; Clifton Webb (original name Webb Parmelee Hollenbeck), 1889–1966, US actor; Mary Webb (*née* Meredith), 1881–1927, British novelist; Philip Webb, 1831–1915, British architect; Sidney Webb (Lord Passfield), 1859–1947, British economist and socialist; William Webb Ellis, 1806–72, British clergyman, apocryphal originator of rugby football while a pupil at Rugby School]
— **Webb Ellis Cup, Webb Ellis Trophy** the trophy for which the Rugby World Cup competition has been played since its inception in 1987. It was named in honour of William Webb Ellis (see above).

Webber (i) 'person who weaves cloth' (from early Middle English *webber* 'weaver'); (ii) a different form of **Weber**

Weber 'person who weaves cloth' (from Middle High German *wëber* 'weaver')

Webley probably 'person from Weobley', Herefordshire ('Wiobba's glade')
— **Webley and Scott** a Birmingham firm of small-arms manufacturers founded in 1834 by Philip Webley. Its Webley service revolvers were once standard issue to British army officers.

Webster 'person who weaves cloth' (from early Middle English *webbester* '(female) weaver') [Daniel Webster, 1782–1852, US politician and orator; John Webster, ?1580–?1625, English dramatist; Noah Webster, 1758-1843, US lexicographer]
— **Webster's** the brand name of beer produced by the brewery founded in Halifax, Yorkshire in 1838 by Samuel Webster, 1813–72

Weddell, Weddle different forms of **Waddell**
— **Weddell Sea** an arm of the South Atlantic Ocean, south of Cape Horn and the Falkland Islands. It was named (in 1900) after the British explorer and seal hunter James Weddell, 1787–1834.

Wedderburn 'person from Wedderburn', Berwickshire ('rams' stream')

Wedge from the Old English male personal name *Wegga*. See also **Wegg**

Wedgwood, Wedgewood 'person from Wedgwood', Staffordshire ('wych-elm wood') [Anthony Wedgwood Benn, see Tony **Benn**; Josiah Wedgwood, 1730–95, British potter; Dame Veronica Wedgwood (C.V. Wedgwood), 1910–97, British historian, great-great-great-granddaughter of Josiah]
— **Wedgwood blue** a pale grey-blue associated with the pottery made by Josiah Wedgwood (see above) and his successors at Etruria, Staffordshire
— **Wedgwood ware** high-quality ceramics produced by the firm founded by Josiah Wedgwood. It is known particularly for its classical designs in white relief on a blue or black background.

Weedon, Weeden 'person from Weedon', Buckinghamshire and Northamptonshire ('hill with a temple') [Bert Weedon, 1920–, British guitarist]

Weekley, Weekly 'person from Weekley', Northamptonshire ('wood or clearing by a Romano-British settlement') [Ernest Weekley, 1865–1954, British philologist]

Weeks, Weekes different forms of **Wickes** [Sir Everton Weekes, 1925–, West Indian cricketer]

Weems see **Wemyss**

Wegg a different form of **Wedge**

Weidenfeld 'person who lives in an area of open country used for pasturage or hunting' (from Middle High German *weide* 'pasture, hunting ground' + *feld* 'open land')
— **Weidenfeld & Nicolson** a British publishing company founded in 1948 by the Austrian-born Arthur George Weidenfeld (Lord Weidenfeld), 1919–, and Nigel Nicolson, 1917–2004. It is now part of the Orion Group.

Weightman a different form of **Wightman** (ii)

Weinberg (i) 'person from Weinberg or Weinberge', the name of numerous places in Germany and Austria ('hill where wine-grapes are grown'); (ii) an invented Jewish name based on German *Wein* 'wine' + *Berg* 'hill'

Weinberger a different form of **Weinberg** (i) [Caspar Weinberger, 1917–2006, US lawyer and statesman]

Weiner (i) 'builder or driver of carts' (from a different form of German **Wagner**); (ii) a different form of **Wiener**; (iii) an invented Jewish name based on Yiddish *vayner* 'wine merchant' [Lawrence Weiner, 1942–, US conceptual artist]

Weinreich an invented Jewish name, based on German *Wein* 'wine' + *Reich* 'kingdom' or on German *weinreich* 'abounding in wine or vines' or on an alteration of Yiddish *vayrekh* 'incense'

Weinstein an invented Jewish name based on German *Wein* 'wine' + *Stein* 'stone'. See also **Winston** (iii) [Harvey Weinstein, 1952–, US film producer]

Weinstock (i) 'maker or seller of wine', or 'person who lives in a house with the sign of a grapevine' (in either case from Middle High German *wînstoc* 'grapevine'); (ii) an invented Jewish name based on German *Weinstock* 'grapevine' [Arnold Weinstock (Lord Weinstock), 1924–2002, British businessman]

Weintraub (i) an invented Jewish name based on German *Weintraube* 'grape'; (ii) 'maker or seller of wine' (from Middle High German *wîntrûb* 'grape')

Weir (i) *also* **Wear** *or* **Weare** 'person who lives by a weir or dam on a river'. See also **Ware** (iii); (ii) from Irish Gaelic *Mac An Mhaoir* (see **McNair**), or from any of a range of Irish Gaelic surnames beginning with *Cor-* (e.g. *Ó Corra*) based on the misapprehension that they derive from Irish Gaelic *core* 'weir' [Dame Gillian Weir, 1941–, British organist; Judith Weir, 1954–, British composer; Molly Weir, 1910–2004, British actress; Peter Weir, 1944–, Australian film director]

Weis (i) from a medieval German nickname for a wise person (from Middle High German *wîs* 'wise'); (ii) see **Weiss**

Weisberg 'person from Weisberg', the name of various places in Germany ('white mountain')

Weismann, Weisman (i) from a medieval German nickname for a wise man (from Middle High German *wīs* 'wise' + *man*). See also **Wiseman**; (ii) see **Weissmann**

Weiss, Weis (i) 'person from Weis, Weiss or Weissen', the name of various places in Germany; (ii) from a medieval German and Jewish nickname for someone with white hair or a very pale face (from Middle High German *wīz* 'white'). See also **Wise** (ii)

Weissmann, Weissman from a medieval German nickname or a Jewish nickname for someone with white hair or a very pale face (in the former case from Middle High German *wīz* 'white' + *man*, in the latter from German *weiss* 'white' + *Mann* 'man')

Weissmuller 'miller who produces white flour' (from Middle High German *wīz* 'white' + *müller* 'miller') [Johnny Weissmuller (original name János Weissmüller), 1904–84, Austro-Hungarian-born US swimmer and actor]

Weisz a Hungarian (Jewish) form of **Weiss**

Welborn, Welborne, Welbourn, Wellborn 'person from Welborne or Welbourn', respectively Norfolk and Lincolnshire ('stream fed by a spring')

Welch, Welsh 'Briton, Celt' (from Middle English *welsche* 'foreign, non-Anglo-Saxon, Celtic'). See also **Walsh** (i) [Denton Welch, 1915–48, British writer; Elisabeth Welch, 1908–2003, US-born British singer and actress; Leslie Welch, 1907–80, British memorizer ('the Memory Man'); Raquel Welch (*née* Tejada), 1940–, US actress]

Welcome, Wellcome (i) 'person from Welcombe', Devon and Warwickshire ('valley with a spring'); (ii) from a medieval nickname for a well-liked or very hospitable individual
— **Wellcome Trust** a UK-based medical charity established in 1936 to administer the estate of the US-born British pharmaceutical magnate Sir Henry Wellcome, 1853–1936, inventor of the tablet

Weld 'person who lives in or near a forest (or in a deforested upland area)' (from Middle English *wold* 'forest' or 'cleared upland') [Tuesday Weld (original name Susan Ker Weld), 1943–, US actress]

Weldon 'person from Weldon', Northamptonshire ('hill with a spring') [Fay Weldon (*née* Birkinshaw), 1931–, British writer]

Welford 'person from Welford', the name of various places in England (mainly 'ford by the spring')

Welham, Wellam 'person from Welham', the name of various places in England ('homestead by the spring(s)')

Wellborn see **Welborn**

Wellcome see **Welcome**

Weller 'person who lives by a spring or stream' (from a derivative of Middle English *welle* – see **Wells**) [Paul Weller, 1958–, British singer/songwriter; Sam Weller, Mr Pickwick's irrepressible Cockney servant in Charles Dickens's *Pickwick Papers* (1837)]

Welles see **Wells**

Wellesley 'person from Wellesley', an unidentified place in England ('Wealh's glade') [Wellesley, family name of the dukes of Wellington]

Welling (i) 'person who lives by a spring or stream' (from a derivative of Middle English *welle* – see **Wells**); (ii) 'son of *Wella*', an Old English male personal name

Wellings a different form of **Welling**

Wellington 'person from Wellington', Herefordshire, Shropshire and Somerset ('Wēola's people's settlement')

Wellman, Welman 'person who lives by a spring or stream' (from Middle English *welle* (see **Wells**) + *man*)

Wells, Welles 'person who lives by a spring or stream', or 'person from Wells', the name of various places in England (in either case from the plural of Middle English *welle* 'spring, stream') [Allan Wells, 1952–, Scottish athlete; Billy Wells ('Bombardier' Billy Wells), 1889–1967, British boxer; H.G. Wells, 1866–1946, British writer; John Wells, 1936–98, British actor, writer and satirist; John Wellington Wells, a 'weaver of magic and spells' who is a central character in the Gilbert and Sullivan operetta *The Sorcerer* (1877); Orson Welles, 1915–85, US actor and director; Sumner Welles, 1892–1961, US diplomat]
— **Wells, Fargo and Co.** a US express-delivery business founded in 1852 by Henry Wells, 1805–78, and William Fargo, 1818–81
— **Wellsian** (characteristic) of the writings of H.G. Wells (see above), especially in their exploration of the future

Welsh see **Welch**

Welton 'person from Welton', the name of various places in England ('farmstead by a spring')

Welty from a Swiss German pet-form of the German male personal name *Walther* (see **Walter**) [Eudora Welty, 1909–2001, US writer]

Wemyss, Weems 'person from Wemyss', Fife ('caves'). The name is standardly pronounced 'weemz'.

Wendel, Wendell (i) 'turner of wooden (metal, bone, etc.) objects on a lathe' (from a derivative of Middle High German *wendel* 'turn'); (ii) from a pet-form of the medieval German and Dutch male personal name *Wendo* (from the first element of a Germanic compound name beginning with *wand* 'go, leave'

Wenham 'person from Wenham', Suffolk and Sussex (respectively probably 'homestead by a hill' and 'water meadow with burial mounds')

Wensley 'person from Wensleydale', Yorkshire ('Wændel's glade')

Went 'person who lives by a path' (from Middle English *went* 'way, path')

Wentworth 'person from Wentworth', Cambridgeshire and Yorkshire ('Wintra's enclosure') [A.J. Wentworth, an absent-minded mathe-

matics master created (originally in *Punch* in the 1930s) by H.F. Ellis and subsequently portrayed on television (1982) by Arthur Lowe; Captain Frederick Wentworth, naval officer, the vagaries of whose romantic relationship with Anne Elliot form the main plot of Jane Austen's *Persuasion* (1818); Thomas Wentworth (1st earl of Strafford), 1593–1641, English statesman; William Charles Wentworth, 1793–1872, Australian politician]
— **Wentworth** a residential district in Surrey, famous for its championship golf course. It got its name from Wentworth House, a large house in the area, built on land owned by a Mrs Elizabeth Wentworth, died 1816.

Werner from the German male personal name *Werner* (literally 'guard-army')

Werth (i) 'person who lives on an island (in a river) or on an area of dry ground in a fen' (from Middle High German *wert* 'island'); (ii) see **Worth**

Werther (i) 'person who keeps lookout, guard' (from Middle High German *warte* 'lookout'); (ii) a different form of **Werth**

Wescott, Wescot different forms of **Westcott**

Wesker (i) 'person who lives in a marshy area to the west' (from Middle English *west* + *kerr* 'marshland'); (ii) a different form of **Wishart** [Arnold Wesker, 1912–, British playwright]

Wesley 'person from Westley', Cambridgeshire and Suffolk, or from various other similarly spelled places in England ('western wood or glade'). See also **Westley** [Charles Wesley, 1707–88, British religious leader and hymnist, brother of John; John Wesley, 1703–91, British religious leader, founder of Methodism; Mary Wesley, pen-name of Mary Aline Mynors Farmar, 1912–2002, British novelist; Samuel Wesley, 1766–1837, British composer and organist, son of Charles; Samuel Sebastian Wesley, 1810–76, British organist, son of Samuel]
— **Wesleyan** based on, consisting of or resembling the teachings, practices and beliefs of John and Charles Wesley (see above) or of Methodism

West 'person who lives in the western part of a settlement, or who has come from a more westerly place'. See also **Westerman, Western** [Benjamin West, 1738–1820, American-born British painter; Fred West, 1941–95, and his wife Rosemary (*née* Letts), 1953–, British serial killers; Mae West, 1892–1980, US actress; Nathanael West (original name Nathan Weinstein), 1903–40, US novelist; Peter West, 1920–2003, British journalist and sports commentator; Dame Rebecca West (original name Cicely Isabel Fairfield), 1892–1983, British novelist and journalist; Timothy West, 1934–, British actor]
— **Mae West** an inflatable life jacket, especially one issued to US pilots during World War II (its shape reminded them – if they needed reminding – of Mae West's (see above) large breasts)

Westbrook, Westbrooke 'person from Westbrook', the name of various places in England ('western brook')

Westcott, Westcot 'person from Westcott', Berkshire and Surrey, or from various other similarly spelled places in England ('western cottage'). See also **Wescott**

Westerman a different form of **West**

Western a different form of **West** [Squire Western, bluff fox-hunting character in Henry Fielding's *Tom Jones* (1749)]
— **Western Brothers** a British comedy double act popular in the 1930s and 1940s, consisting of Kenneth Western, 1899–1963, and his second cousin George Western, 1895–1969. Adopting exaggerated upper-class personae, they specialized in comic songs at the piano.

Westgate (i) 'person from Westgate', the name of various places in England ('western gate'); (ii) 'person who lives by the western gate of a city'

Westhead 'person from Westhead', Lancashire (probably 'western headland')

Westlake 'person who lives to the west of a small stream' (from Middle English *west* + *lake* 'small stream')

Westley a different form of **Wesley**

Westmorland, Westmoreland 'person from Westmorland', former county of northwestern England ('district of the people living west of the moors') [William Westmoreland, 1914–2005, US general]

Weston 'person from Weston', the name of numerous places in England ('western farmstead') [Jessie L. Weston, 1850–1928, British medieval scholar and folklorist]

Westrop 'person from Westrop', Wiltshire ('western village')

Westrup (i) a different form of **Westrop**; (ii) 'person from Westrup', the name of various places in Denmark and Germany

Westwood 'person from Westwood', the name of various places in England and Scotland ('western wood') [Lee Westwood, 1973–, British golfer; Vivienne Westwood (*née* Swire), 1941–, British fashion designer]

Wetherall, Wetherell, Wetherill see **Weatherall**

Wetherby, Weatherby 'person from Wetherby', Yorkshire ('farmstead for wethers' (i.e. castrated rams)). See also **Weathersby**

Wethered a different form of **Weatherhead**

Wetherspoon a different form of **Witherspoon**
— **J D Wetherspoon** a British pub chain founded by Tim Martin, 1955–. The name 'Wetherspoon' is that of one of Martin's teachers in a school in New Zealand.

Wetton 'person from Wetton', Staffordshire ('wet hill')

Wey see **Way**

Whale from a medieval nickname for a large overweight person

Whalen a different form of **Whelan**

Whaley, Waley 'person from Whaley or Waley', Derbyshire and Cheshire respectively ('glade by a road') [Arthur Waley, 1889–1966, British sinologist, poet and translator]

Whalley, **Walley** 'person from Whalley', Lancashire ('glade by a round hill')

Wharmby 'person from Quarmby', Yorkshire ('farmstead with a handmill'). See also **Quarmby**

Wharton, **Warton** 'person from Wharton', the name of several places in England (variously 'farmstead by the swaying tree', 'farmstead by the beacon' and 'farmstead by the wharf') [Edith Wharton (née Newbold Jones), 1862–1937, US writer; Harry Wharton, sensible schoolboy in the mayhem of Frank Richards's 'Billy Bunter' stories; Thomas Warton, 1728–90, British poet and critic]

Whateley, **Whately** 'person from Whately', Warwickshire ('clearing where wheat is grown'). See also **Wheatley** [Kevin Whately, 1951–, British actor]

Whatley, **Whatly** 'person from Whatley', Somerset ('clearing where wheat is grown'). See also **Wheatley**

Whatmore, **Whatmoor**, **Watmore**, **Watmoor** (i) 'person from Whatmoor', Shropshire ('wet marsh'); (ii) different forms of **Watmough**

Wheal, **Wheale** see **Wheel**

Wheat, **Wheate** 'grower or seller of wheat'

Wheatcroft 'person from Wheatcroft', Derbyshire ('smallholding where wheat is grown') [Harry Wheatcroft, 1898–1977, British rose grower]

Wheatley, **Wheatly**, **Wheatleigh** 'person from Wheatley', the name of various places in England ('clearing where wheat is grown'). See also **Whateley**, **Whatley** [Alan Wheatley, 1907–91, British actor; Dennis Wheatley, 1897–1977, British novelist of the occult]

Wheaton perhaps 'person from Weeton', Lancashire and Yorkshire (farmstead by willow trees'), or alternatively from an unidentified place called Wheaton ('farmstead where wheat is grown')

Wheatstone probably a different form of **Whetstone** [Sir Charles Wheatstone, 1802–75, British physicist]
— **Wheatstone bridge** a device consisting of an electrical circuit, three known resistances and a galvanometer that is used for measuring an unknown resistance. It is named after Sir Charles Wheatstone (see above), who recognized its potential usefulness (it was invented by Samuel Hunter Christie).

Wheel, **Wheele**, **Wheal**, **Wheale**, **Whewell** 'maker of wheels, wheelwright'; also, 'person who lives by a water-wheel'

Wheelan see **Whelan**

Wheeldon, **Wheelden** 'person from Wheeldon', Derbyshire ('rounded or wheel-shaped hill'). See also **Wheldon**, **Whielden**

Wheeler, **Wheler** 'maker of wheels'. See also **Wyler** (i) [Charles Wheeler, 1923–, British journalist and broadcaster; Jimmy Wheeler (original name Ernest Remnant), 1910–73, British comedian; Sir Mortimer Wheeler, 1890–1976, British archaeologist]

— **Wheeler's** any of a stable of British fish restaurants, the first of which was opened in London in 1929. It was named after a Whitstable shellfish bar known as Wheeler's.

Wheelock 'person from Wheelock', Cheshire ('place by the river *Wheelock*', literally 'winding')

Whelan, **Wheelan** from Irish Gaelic *Ó Faoláin* 'descendant of *Faolán*', a personal name meaning literally 'little wolf'. See also **Phelan**, **Wolf** (iv)

Wheldon a different form of **Wheeldon** [Sir Huw Wheldon, 1916–86, British television producer and executive]

Wheler see **Wheeler**

Whetstone 'person from Whetstone', Greater London and Leicestershire, or 'person from Wheston', Derbyshire (in both cases 'place where whetstones (stones for sharpening knives and other edged tools) can be found'). See also **Wheatstone**

Whewell see **Wheel**

Whicker 'person who lives or works in an outlying settlement' (from a derivative of Old English *wīc* 'outlying settlement' – see **Wick** (i)) [Alan Whicker, 1925–, British broadcaster and writer]
— **Alan Whickers** British rhyming slang for 'knickers'

Whielden 'person from Whielden', Buckinghamshire ('rounded or wheel-shaped valley'). See also **Wheeldon**

Whiffen, **Whiffin**, **Wiffen** perhaps 'person from Whiffen', an unidentified place ('white marsh')

Whineray, **Whinneray** 'person from Whinneray', Cumbria, or 'person who lives in a nook of land growing with gorse' (in either case from Old Norse *hvin* 'whin, gorse' + *vrá* 'nook of land') [Sir Wilson Whineray, 1935–, New Zealand rugby player]

Whinery, **Whinnery** different forms of **Whineray**

Whipp perhaps 'person whose job is administering judicial floggings'

Whipple perhaps 'person who lives by a *whipple* tree (a medieval name for a tree of uncertain identity, perhaps the cornel, a tree of the dogwood family)'
— **Whipple's disease** a disorder of fat metabolism, causing joint pains, excretion of fat in the faeces, wasting, and lymph node enlargement. It is named after the US pathologist George Hoyt Whipple, 1878–1976, who described the disease in 1907.

Whistler 'player of a pipe or flute'; also, from a medieval nickname for someone in the habit of whistling cheerily [James McNeill Whistler, 1834–1903, US painter; Rex Whistler, 1905–44, British artist]

Whiston 'person from Whiston', the name of several places in England (variously 'Witi's farmstead', 'farmstead of the Hwicce (an Anglo-Saxon tribe)' and 'place with the white stone')

Whitaker, **Whittaker** 'person from Whitaker', Lancashire, or from any of a range of similarly spelled places in England (variously 'white field' or 'wheat field'). See also **Whitticase** [Forest

Whitaker, 1961–, US actor; Roger Whittaker, 1936–, Kenyan-born British singer/songwriter]
— **Whitaker's Almanack** an annual compendium of facts relating to the governance, political and social structure, etc. of Britain and other nations of the world and giving an account of events of the previous year. It was founded in 1868 by the publisher and editor Joseph Whitaker, 1820–95.

Whitbread 'baker of fine bread' (from Middle English *whit* 'white' or *whete* 'wheat' + *bred* 'bread')
— **Whitbread Awards** a range of literary prizes, named after their sponsors, Whitbread plc. They were inaugurated in 1971, and continued until 2005 (after which they became the Costa Book Awards).
— **Whitbread plc** a brewing company founded in London in 1742 by Samuel Whitbread, 1720–96

Whitby 'person from Whitby', Cheshire and Yorkshire (respectively 'white manor house' and 'white farmstead')

Whitchurch 'person from Whitchurch', the name of various places in England ('white church (i.e. one built of stone)')

Whitcombe, **Whitcomb** 'person from Whitcombe or Witcombe', the name of several places in England (variously 'wide valley' and 'valley growing with willows')

White, **Whyte** from a medieval nickname for someone with very fair or white hair or with a noticeably pale face [Carol White, 1942–91, British actress; Gilbert White, 1720–93, British naturalist; Marco Pierre White, 1961–, British chef; Patrick White, 1912–90, British-born Australian novelist; T.H. White, 1906–64, British novelist; Sir Willard White, 1946–, Jamaican-born British bass]
● Men with the surname White are traditionally given the nickname 'Chalky' or (especially in the British Army) 'Blanco' (from the proprietary name – based on French *blanc* 'white' – of a substance used to whiten military belts, gaiters, etc.)
— **Dr White's** the proprietary name of a type of sanitary towel produced by the firm of Arthur Berton Ltd. There never was any such person as Dr White.
— **White's** a gentlemen's club in St James's Street, London, founded in 1693 by Francis White, died 1711 (an Italian by birth, his original name was Francesco Bianco)

Whitehead (i) from a medieval nickname for someone with very fair or white hair; (ii) a mistranslation of the Irish Gaelic name *Ó Ceanndubháin* (see **Canavan**), as if it came from *ceann bàn*, literally 'head white'; (iii) a literal translation of the German surnames *Weisshaupt* and *Weisskopf* [A.N. Whitehead, 1861–1947, British philosopher and mathematician]

Whitehorn, **Whitehorne** 'person from Whithorn', Dumfries and Gallowy ('white building') [Katherine Whitehorn, 1926–, British journalist]

Whitehouse 'person who lives in a white house' [Mary Whitehouse (*née* Hutcheson), 1910–2001, British campaigner against permissiveness in the media; Paul Whitehouse, 1959–, British comic actor and writer]

Whitelaw 'person from Whitelaw', the name of various places in northern England and southern Scotland ('white hill') [Billie Whitelaw, 1932–, British actress; William Whitelaw (Viscount Whitelaw), 1918–99, British Conservative politician]

Whiteley, **Whitely** different forms of **Whitley** [Richard Whiteley, 1943–2005, British television presenter]
— **Whiteley's** a department store in Bayswater, London, founded in 1863 by William Whiteley, 1831–1907. It closed in 1981.
— **Whiteley Village** a village in Surrey, laid out in 1911 as a model village with almshouses, in accordance with the provisions of the will of William Whiteley (see above)

Whitelock, **Whitelocke** different forms of **Whitlock** (i)

Whiteman a different form of **Whitman** [Paul Whiteman, 1890–1967, US bandleader]

Whitemore a different form of **Whitmore** (i)

Whiteside probably 'person from Whiteside', the name of various places in England, Scotland and Northern Ireland ('white slope')

Whitfield 'person from Whitfield', the name of various places in England ('area of white (i.e. chalky) land') [David Whitfield, 1925–80, British popular vocalist; June Whitfield, 1925–, British actress]

Whitford 'person from Whitford', Devon ('white ford')

Whitgift 'person from Whitgift', Yorkshire ('Hvítr's dowry') [John Whitgift, ?1530–1604, Anglican churchman, archbishop of Canterbury 1583–1604]
— **Whitgift Centre** a complex of shops and offices in the middle of Croydon, Greater London, on a site previously occupied by Whitgift School
— **Whitgift School** an independent day school for boys in South Croydon, founded in 1595 by John Whitgift (see above)

Whiting 'son of **White**'

Whitlam, **Whitlum** from a medieval nickname for a mild-mannered person (from Middle English *whit* 'white' + *lam* 'lamb') [Gough Whitlam, 1916–, Australian Labor politician, prime minister 1972–75]

Whitley, **Whittley** 'person from Whitley', the name of several places in northern England, variously spelled ('white glade'). See also **Whiteley**
— **Whitley Council** (in Britain) a consultative committee or organization consisting of representatives from the management and staff of a company or industry, set up to discuss industrial relations, working conditions and other work-related issues. They get their name from the British Liberal politician J.H. Whitley, 1866–1935, whose idea they were.

Whitlock (i) from a medieval nickname for someone with very fair or prematurely white hair (from Middle English *whit* 'white' + *lock* 'lock of hair, tress'). See also **Whitelock**; (ii) from the Old English male personal name *Wihtlāc*, literally 'elf-play'

Whitman (i) from a medieval nickname for someone with very fair or prematurely white hair or a noticeably pale face (from Middle English *whit* 'white' + *man*); (ii) 'male servant of someone called "White".' See also **Whiteman** [Slim Whitman (original name Otis Dewey Whitman, Jr.), 1924–, US country-music singer/songwriter; Walt Whitman, 1819–92, US poet]

Whitmarsh 'person from Whitmarsh', Wiltshire ('white marsh')

Whitmore (i) 'person from Whitmore', the name of various places in England ('white moor'). See also **Whitemore**; (ii) perhaps 'person from Whittimere', Shropshire ('pool associated with Hwīta')

Whitney 'person from Whitney', Herefordshire (perhaps 'white island' or 'Hwīta's island') [Eli Whitney, 1765–1825, US inventor of the cotton gin]

Whittaker see **Whitaker**

Whittall see **Whitwell**

Whitticase a different form of **Whitaker**

Whittier 'white-leather tawer (i.e. someone who makes high-quality thin soft pale-coloured leather by a process involving alum and salt)' (from Middle English *whit* 'white' + *tawier* 'tawer') [John Greenleaf Whittier, 1807–92, US poet and anti-slavery campaigner]

Whittington, Whitington 'person from Whittington', the name of various places in England ('estate associated with Hwīta') [Richard Whittington ('Dick' Whittington), died 1423, English merchant, four times Lord Mayor of London, originator of the 'Dick Whittington' legend]
— **Whittington Hospital** a large hospital on Highgate Hill, London, so named after World War II (when it was formed by the amalgamation of other hospitals) in honour of Dick Whittington (see above)
— **Whittington Stone** a commemorative stone near the foot of Highgate Hill, London, where the young Dick Whittington is supposed to have turned round when he heard Bow Bells forecasting that he would be Lord Mayor of London

Whittle (i) 'person from Whittle', the name of various places in England ('white hill'); (ii) see **Whitwell** [Sir Frank Whittle, 1907–96, British aeronautical engineer, developer of the jet engine]

Whitton 'person from Whitton', the name of numerous places in England and Scotland (variously 'Hwīta's farmstead', 'white farmstead' and 'farmstead by a wood')

Whitty, Whittey (i) perhaps 'person from Whitty', an unidentified place in England ('white enclosure'); (ii) perhaps from a medieval nickname for someone with noticeably pale eyes (from Middle English *whit* 'white' + *eye*) [Dame May Whitty, 1865–1948, British actress]

Whitwell, Whittell, Whittle, Whittall 'person from Whitwell', the name of various places in England ('white stream')

Whitworth 'person from Whitworth', the name of various places in England ('Hwīta's enclosure' or 'white enclosure')
— **Armstrong-Whitworth** see **Armstrong**

Whybrow, Wybrow from the medieval female personal name *Wyburgh*, literally 'war-fortress'

Whyte see **White**

Wick, Wicke (i) 'person who lives in an outlying settlement', or person from Wick, the name of various places in England (either case from Old English *wīc* 'outlying settlement'). See also **Whicker**; (ii) from the medieval male personal name *Wikke* (from the first element of any of various Germanic compound personal names beginning with *wīg* 'battle')

Wickens, Wickins 'person who lives in the outlying settlements' (from Old English *wīcum* 'at the outlying settlements' + the Middle English plural ending -*s*)

Wickes, Wicks, Wix, Wykes (i) a different form of **Wick**; (ii) 'son of **Wick**'

Wickham, Wykeham 'person from Wickham', the name of various places in England ('homestead associated with a Romano-British settlement')

Wickliffe see **Wycliffe**

Widdicombe, Widdecombe 'person from Widecombe or Widdicombe', Devon ('valley growing with willows'). See also **Withycombe** [Ann Widdecombe, 1947–, British Conservative politician]

Widdison a different form of **Widdowson**

Widdows 'son of a widow'

Widdowson 'son of a widow'

Widger from the Old English male personal name *Wihtgār*, literally 'elf-spear'

Widmark from an invented Swedish name perhaps meaning literally 'forest land' [Richard Widmark, 1914–, US actor]

Wiener 'person from Vienna', Austria (German *Wien*). See also **Weiner** (ii), **Winner** [Norbert Wiener, 1894–1964, US mathematician, pioneer of cybernetics]

Wiffen see **Whiffen**

Wigder, Wigdor different forms of *Avigdor* (see **D'Avigdor**)

Wigg (i) from a medieval nickname for someone thought to resemble an insect (from Middle English *wigge* 'beetle, bug'); (ii) 'baker of wigs (a sort of small cake or bun, typically cut into wedge-shaped slices)' [George Wigg (Lord Wigg), 1900–83, British Labour politician]

Wiggin (i) from the Germanic male personal name *Wīgant*, literally 'warrior', introduced into England by the Normans; (ii) from the Breton male personal name *Wiucon*, literally 'worthy-noble', introduced into England by the Normans

Wiggins 'son of **Wiggin**'

Wigglesworth 'person from Wigglesworth', Yorkshire ('Wincel's enclosure')

Wiggs 'son of **Wigg**'

Wightman (i) probably from an Old English male personal name *Wihtmann*, literally 'elf-man'; (ii) from a medieval nickname for a strong or brave man (from Middle English *wiht* 'strong, strong-willed, resolute, brave' + *man*). See also **Weightman**
— **Wightman Cup** a tennis trophy presented in 1923 by the US tennis player Hazel Hotchkiss Wightman, 1886–1974, to be contested annually by women's teams from the US and Britain. It was last played for in 1989.

Wigley 'person from Wigley', Derbyshire and Hampshire ('Wicga's glade' or 'glade infested with beetles or similar insects')

Wigmore 'person from Wigmore', Herefordshire ('quaking marsh')

Wignall, **Wignal** 'person from Wignal', Lancashire ('Wicga's nook of land')

Wilber, **Wilbur** from a medieval nickname for someone thought to resemble a wild boar (from Middle English *wild* + *bor* 'boar')

Wilberforce 'person from Wilberfoss', Yorkshire ('Wilburh's ditch') [Mrs Wilberforce, canny little old lady whose house is commandeered by crooks in the film *The Ladykillers* (1955); William Wilberforce, 1759–1833, British philanthropist and anti-slavery campaigner]
— **Wilberforce University** a university in Xenia, Ohio, USA, founded in 1856 and named in honour of William Wilberforce (see above)

Wilbert from a Germanic male personal name meaning literally 'will-bright'

Wilbraham 'person from Wilbraham', Cambridgeshire ('Wilburg's homestead or estate')

Wilbur see **Wilber**

Wilby, **Wilbye** 'person from Wilby', the name of numerous places in England (variously 'farmstead by willow trees', 'place by a circle of willow trees' and 'Willa's farmstead') [James Wilby, 1958–, British actor; John Wilbye, 1574–1638, English composer]

Wilcher a different form of **Wiltshire**

Wilcock, **Willcock** from the male personal name *Will* (see **Will** (i)), with the suffix *-cock* (literally 'cockerel', hence 'jaunty or bumptious young man'), that was often added to create pet-forms of personal names in the Middle Ages

Wilcox, **Willcox**, **Willcocks** 'son of **Wilcock**' [Sir David Willcocks, 1919–, British conductor; Desmond Wilcox, 1931–2000, British television journalist, presenter and producer; Ella Wheeler Wilcox, 1850–1919, US poet]

Wilcoxon, **Willcoxon**, **Wilcoxson** 'son of **Wilcock**'
— **Wilcoxon test** a statistical test of the equality of similar or matched groups of data to determine whether they differ significantly from each other, without any assumptions about the underlying distribution patterns. It is named after the Irish statistician Frank Wilcoxon, 1892–1965.

Wild, **Wilde**, **Wyld**, **Wylde** (i) 'person who lives in an area of wild, uncultivated land', or from a medieval nickname for someone of a violent or uncontrollable disposition; (ii) 'person from Wyld', Berkshire and Dorset ('trap, snare'); (iii) from a medieval German and Jewish nickname for a stranger or an immigrant from another country [Henry Wyld, 1870–1945, British lexicographer; Jonathan Wild, ?1682–1725, English criminal; Marty Wilde (original name Reginald Leonard Smith), 1939–, British rock-and-roll singer; Oscar Wilde (full name Oscar Fingal O'Flahertie Wills Wilde), 1854–1900, Irish-born British dramatist and poet]
— **Wildean** (typical) of (the works of) Oscar Wilde (see above), especially in epigrammatic wit

Wildblood from a medieval nickname for a rakish or hot-headed person

Wilder a different form of **Wild** [Billy Wilder (original name Samuel Wilder), 1906–2002, Austrian-born US film director; Gene Wilder (original name Jerome Silberman), 1933–, US actor; Thornton Wilder, 1897–1975, US novelist and dramatist]

Wilding from the Old English personal name *Wilding*, based on *wilde* 'wild, savage' [Michael Wilding, 1912–79, British actor]

Wildman a different form of **Wild**

Wilds, **Wylds** 'son of **Wild**'

Wildsmith probably 'maker of wheels, wheelwright'

Wilensky 'person from *Wilno*', the Polish name of the Lithuanian city Vilnius

Wiles, **Wyles** (i) from a medieval nickname for a devious or tricky person; (ii) 'hunter, trapper' (from a derivative of Middle English *wile* 'trap, snare')

Wiley (i) see **Wylie** (i); (ii) perhaps a different form of **Willey**
— **John Wiley & Sons, Inc.** a US publishing company, founded in New York in 1807 by Charles Wiley. It took its present name in 1875, after Charles's son John Wiley had joined the firm.

Wilken, **Wilkens** see **Wilkin**, **Wilkins**

Wilkerson 'son of **Wilkin**'

Wilkes, **Wilks** 'son of *Wilk*', a medieval male personal name derived from **Wilkin**, probably on the mistaken belief that it contained the Anglo-Norman diminutive suffix *-in* (rather than the native English *-kin*) [John Wilkes, 1725–97, British journalist and radical politician]
— **Wilkes Land** a large area of land in the Australian Antarctic Territory, named after the explorer Charles Wilkes, 1798–1877, of the US Navy, who discovered the coast in 1838–42

Wilkie, **Willkie** from a medieval Scottish pet-form of **Will** (i) [Sir David Wilkie, 1785–1841, British painter; David Wilkie, 1954–, British swimmer; Wendell Willkie, 1892–1944, US Republican politician]

Wilkin, Wilken from the medieval male personal name *Wilkin*, a pet-form of **Will** (i)

Wilkins, Wilkens 'son of **Wilkin**' [Sir George Wilkins, 1888–1958, Australian-born British explorer; Maurice Wilkins, 1916–2004, New Zealand-born British biophysicist]

Wilkinson 'son of **Wilkin**' [Ellen Wilkinson, 1891–1947, British feminist and Labour politician; Jonny Wilkinson, 1979–, English rugby player; Tom Wilkinson, 1948–, British actor]

— **Wilkinson Sword** a British manufacturer of knives, razors and, originally, swords. The firm was founded in London in 1772 by Henry Nock, and was joined in 1804 by his adopted son James Wilkinson. It became the Wilkinson Sword Company in 1879.

Wilks see **Wilkes**

Will (i) from the male personal name *Will*, a pet-form of **William**. See also **Wilkie, Wilkin, Willett, Willis, Willison, Willman, Wills, Wilson**; (ii) 'person who lives by a spring or stream' (from Middle English *wille* 'well, spring, stream')

Willard from a Germanic personal name meaning literally 'will-brave'

Willcock, Willcox, Willcoxon see **Wilcock, Wilcox, Wilcoxon**

Willett, Willet from a pet-form of **Will** (i) [William Willett, 1856–1915, British builder, originator of daylight-saving time]

Willetts, Willets 'son of **Willett**'

Willey 'person from Willey', the name of various places in England ('glade where willow trees grow'). See also **Wiley** (ii) [Peter Willey, 1949–, English cricketer]

William from the male personal name *William*, introduced into England by the Normans but ultimately of Germanic origin and meaning literally 'will-helmet'. See also **Fitzwilliam, Gilliam, McWilliam, Willmott, Wylie** (ii)

Williams 'son of **William**' [Andy Williams, 1930–, US popular singer; Sir Bernard Williams, 1929–2003, British philosopher, husband of Shirley; Charles Williams, 1886–1945, British poet, novelist and theological writer; Sir Clough Williams-Ellis, 1883–1978, British architect; Dorian Williams, 1914–85, British show-jumping commentator; Emlyn Williams, 1905–87, British playwright, novelist and actor; Esther Williams, 1922–, US swimmer and film actress; Fred Williams, 1927–82, Australian painter; Grace Williams, 1906–77, British composer; Hank Williams (original name Hiram Williams) 1923–53, US country musician; Heathcote Williams, 1941–, British poet and actor; John Williams, 1932–, US composer of film music; John Williams, 1941–, Australian-born British classical guitarist; J.P.R. Williams, 1949–, Welsh rugby player; Kenneth Williams, 1926–88, British comic actor; Nigel Williams, 1948–, British novelist and broadcaster; Raymond Williams, 1921–88, British critic and novelist; Robbie Williams, 1974–, British singer/songwriter; Robin Williams, 1951–, US actor; Roger Williams, ?1604–83, English

colonist, founder of Rhode Island; Rowan Williams, 1950–, British churchman, archbishop of Canterbury 2002–; Serena Williams, 1981–, US tennis player, sister of Venus; Shirley Williams (Baroness Williams; *née* Brittain), 1930–, British Labour and Liberal-Democrat politician; Simon Williams, 1946–, British actor; Ted Williams, 1918–2002, US baseball player; Tennessee Williams (original name Thomas Lanier Williams), 1911–83, US playwright; Venus Williams, 1980–, US tennis player; William Carlos Williams, 1883–1963, US poet]

☆ The third commonest surname in Britain, the US and Australia; 5th commonest in New Zealand

— ***Caleb Williams*** a novel (1794) by William Godwin, following the tribulations of its eponymous hero, an honourable man persecuted by his tyrannical employer

— **Williams** a British Formula 1 motor-racing team, founded in 1969 by Sir Frank Williams, 1942–

— **Williams and Glyn's Bank Ltd** a British bank formed in 1970 by the merger of William Deacon and Co. (founded in 1771 as Raymond, Williams, Vere, Lowe and Fletcher), Glyn, Mills and Co. (founded in 1753 by Richard Glyn and others) and the National Bank. In 1985 it was absorbed into the Royal Bank of Scotland.

— **Williams pear** a variety of pear with juicy white flesh and yellow skin. It is named after the Williams's Nursery of Middlesex, from which it was first commercially distributed in Britain in the early 19th century.

— **Williams tube** a cathode-ray tube used in some early computers to store and display an array of spots representing bits. It is named after the British electrical engineer F.C. Williams, 1911–77, who with others described such a tube in 1948.

Williamson 'son of **William**' [Henry Williamson, 1895–1977, British novelist; Malcolm Williamson, 1931–2003, Australian composer; Nicol Williamson, 1938–, British actor]

Willingham 'person from Willingham', Cambridgeshire and Suffolk ('Wifel's people's homestead')

Willis 'son of **Will** (i)' [Bob Willis, 1949–, English cricketer; Bruce Willis, 1955–, US actor; Henry Willis ('Father' Willis), 1821–1901, British organ builder; Norman Willis, 1933–, British trade-union leader; Ted Willis (Lord Willis), 1918–92, British author and scriptwriter]

Willison 'son of **Will** (i)'

Willman 'servant of **Will** (i)'

Willmore see **Wilmore**

Willmott, Willmot, Wilmot, Wilmott, Wilmut pet-forms of **William** [Ian Wilmut, 1944–, British embryologist, cloner of 'Dolly' the sheep; John Wilmot (2nd earl of Rochester), 1647–80, English lyric poet, satirist and rake]

Willock from the medieval male personal name *Willoc*, a pet-form based on the first syllable of any of a range of Old English compound names beginning with *willa* 'will, desire'

Willoughby 'person from Willoughby', the name of various places in England (mostly 'farmstead by willow trees')

Wills 'son of **Will** (i)' [Helen Wills, see **Moody**; William John Wills, 1834–61, British-born Australian surveyor and explorer]

— **W.D. & H.O. Wills** a British producer of tobacco products, founded in Bristol in 1786 by Henry Overton Wills I, 1761–1826. Control subsequently passed to his sons, William Day Wills, 1797–1865, and Henry Overton Wills II, 1800–71, and the name 'W.D. & H.O. Wills' was adopted in 1830. The firm became part of Imperial Tobacco in 1901, and the brand name 'Wills' was dropped in the UK in 1988 (although it continues in India and elsewhere).

Willshire see **Wilshire**

Willson see **Wilson**

Wilmer from the Old English male personal name *Wilmǣr*, literally 'will-famous'

Wilmore, Willmore 'person from Wildmore or the Weald Moors', Lincolnshire and Shropshire respectively ('uncultivated moorland or marsh')

Wilmot see **Willmott**

Wilshire, Wilsher, Wilshear, Willshire, Willsher, Willshear different forms of **Wiltshire**

— **Wilshire Boulevard** one of the main east-west arterial roads of Los Angeles, California. It was named after H. Gaylord Wilshire, 1861–1927, a real-estate developer from Ohio.

Wilson, Willson 'son of **Will** (i)' [Alexander Wilson, 1766–1813, British-born US ornithologist; A.N. Wilson, 1950–, British author; Sir Angus Wilson, 1913–91, British novelist; Arthur Wilson (Sgt. Wilson), politely bumbling second-in-command (played by John Le Mesurier) to Capt. Mainwaring in the BBC television sitcom *Dad's Army* (1968–77); Bob Wilson, 1941–, British football goalkeeper and television presenter; Brian Wilson, 1942–, US musician, lead singer of 'The Beach Boys'; C.T.R. Wilson, 1869–1959, British physicist; Charles McMoran Wilson (Lord Moran), 1882–1977, British physician, doctor to Winston Churchill; Colin Wilson, 1931–, British novelist and critic; Edmund Wilson, 1895–1972, US literary critic; Edmund Beecher Wilson, 1856–1939, US geneticist, pioneer of chromosome research; Edward Wilson, 1872–1912, British physician, naturalist and polar explorer; Harold Wilson (Lord Wilson), 1916–95, British Labour politician, prime minister 1964–70, 1974–76; Sir Henry Wilson, 1864–1922, British field marshal; Henry Wilson ('Jumbo' Wilson; Lord Wilson), 1881–1964, British field marshal; Jacqueline Wilson, 1945–, British children's author; John Dover Wilson, 1881–1969, British Shakespearian scholar and editor; John Thomas ('Jocky') Wilson, 1951–, Scottish darts player; Mary Wilson (Lady Wilson; *née* Baldwin), 1918–, British poet, wife of Harold; Peter Wilson, 1913–84, British auctioneer; Richard Wilson, 1714–82, British landscape painter; Richard Wilson, 1936–, British actor; Robert Woodrow Wilson, 1936–2002, US astrophysicist; Sandy Wilson, 1924–, British composer, lyricist and playwright; Snoo Wilson, 1948–, British playwright and theatre director; Woodrow Wilson, 1856–1924, US Democratic politician, president 1913–21]

☆ The second commonest surname in New Zealand; 5th commonest in Canada and Australia; 8th commonest in Britain; 9th commonest in the US

● Men with the surname Wilson are traditionally given the nickname 'Tug'

— **Wilson cloud chamber** a device in which the movement of high-energy particles is detected as they pass through a chamber of supersaturated vapour. It was named after its inventor, C.T.R. Wilson (see above).

— **Wilsonian** (characteristic) of (the policies of) Harold Wilson (see above) or of Woodrow Wilson (see above)

— **Wilson's disease** a rare hereditary disease resulting from an inability to metabolize copper and marked by cirrhosis of the liver, damage to other organs and psychiatric disorder. It was named after the British neurologist S.A. Kinnier Wilson, 1878–1937.

— **Wilson's petrel** a small dark seabird (*Oceanites oceanicus*) of southern oceans that breeds in Antarctica but sometimes wanders to the North Atlantic. It was named after Alexander Wilson (see above).

— **Wilson's Promontory** a peninsula in south-eastern Victoria, Australia, the most southerly point on the mainland. It was named after a certain Thomas Wilson of London, a friend of the explorer Matthew Flinders.

Wilton 'person from Wilton', the name of numerous places in England (variously 'farmstead by a spring', 'farmstead where willow trees grow' or (in the case of the Wiltshire town) 'village on the river Wylye') [Penelope Wilton, 1946–, British actress]

— **Wilton's Music Hall** a music hall in Cable Street, in the East End of London, opened in 1853 by John Wilton

— **Wilton's Restaurant** a restaurant in the West End of London, noted especially for its seafood. It originated in a seafood stall opened in 1742 by the London fishmonger George William Wilton.

Wiltshire, Wiltsher, Wiltshear 'person from Wiltshire', county in southern England. See also **Wilcher**, **Wilshire**

Wimbush 'person from Wimbish', Essex (probably 'Wine's copse')

Wimpey, Wimpy perhaps a deliberate alteration of **Impey** [J. Wellington Wimpy, a character in the 'Popeye' cartoons of Elzie C. Segar who is always portrayed eating a hamburger]

— **George Wimpey** a British construction company, founded in Hammersmith, London in 1880 by George Wimpey, 1855–1913

— **Wimpy** an RAF nickname for the Second World War bomber the Vickers Wellington, inspired by J. Wellington Wimpy (see above).

— **Wimpy Bar** any of a chain of hamburger restaurants established in Britain in 1954 by J. Lyons & Co. They got their name from the hamburgerphile J. Wellington Wimpy.

Winch (i) perhaps 'person who lives at a place where boats are winched up out of the water'; (ii) perhaps from a medieval nickname for someone though to resemble a lapwing (from Old English *wince* 'lapwing')

Winchester 'person from Winchester', Hampshire ('Roman town called Venta')

— **Winchester rifle** a type of US breech-loading rifle invented by Oliver F. Winchester, 1810–80. Famed for its use in the Wild West, it had a tubular magazine under the barrel and a horizontal bolt operated by a lever on the underside of the stock.

Winckler see **Winkler**

Wind (i) from a medieval nickname for a fast runner (who runs 'like the wind'); (ii) 'person who lives by a path or road' (from Old English *gewind* 'path')

Winder (i) 'person from Winder', the name of various places in northern England ('shelter against the wind'); (ii) 'person who winds wool'

Windham see **Wyndham**

Windle 'person from Windle or Windhill', Lancashire and Yorkshire respectively ('windy hill')

Windsor 'person from Windsor', Berkshire and Dorset ('slope with a windlass'). See also **Winsor** [Windsor, the (invented) family name of the British royal family since 1917; Barbara Windsor (original name Barbara-Ann Deeks), 1937–, British actress; Frank Windsor, 1927–, British actor]

Winehouse an anglicization of the Jewish surname *Weinhaus*, from German [Amy Winehouse, 1983–, British jazz/soul singer/songwriter]

Winfield a different form of **Wingfield**

Winfrey, Winfree from the Old English personal name *Winfrith*, literally 'friend-peace' [Oprah Winfrey, 1954–, US television talk-show presenter]

Wing 'person from Wing', Buckinghamshire and Rutland (respectively 'settlement of Wiwa's people' and 'place in the field')

Wingard, Wingarde, Wyngarde different forms of **Winyard** [Peter Wyngarde, 1928–, French-born British actor]

Wingate 'person from Wingate', the name of various places in Scotland and northern England ('windswept gap') [Orde Wingate, 1903–44, British general]

Wingett a different form of **Wingate**

Wingfield 'person from Wingfield', the name of several places in England (variously 'Wīga's people's open land', 'open land used for pasturage' and perhaps 'open land frequented by lapwings'). See also **Winfield**

Wingrave 'person from Wingrave', Buckinghamshire ('Wiwa's people's grove')

— *Owen Wingrave* an opera (1970) by Benjamin Britten about a young man, Owen Wingrave, the last of his line, who rebels against the military traditions of his family

Wingrove a different form of **Wingrave**

Winkler, Winckler 'person who lives on a corner or who keeps a corner shop' (from a derivative of Middle High German *winkel* 'corner') [Henry Winkler, 1945–, US actor]

Winn see **Wynn**

Winnard a different form of **Winyard**

Winner a different form of **Wiener** [Michael Winner, 1935–, British film director]

Winnick (i) 'person from Winnick', Cambridgeshire and Northamptonshire ('Wina's outlying farm'); (ii) 'brandy distiller' (from Yiddish *vinik*, derived from words in various Slavic languages containing the elements *vino* 'wine' and *-nik* 'person associated with something')

Winslett, Winslet an English name of unknown origin [Kate Winslet, 1975–, British actress]

Winslow 'person from Winslow', Buckinghamshire ('Wine's mound')

— *The Winslow Boy* a play (1946) by Terence Rattigan about a young naval cadet, Ronnie Winslow, who is expelled from school for stealing a postal order, and his father's efforts to exonerate him

Winsor 'person from Winsor', Devon and Hampshire. See also **Windsor**

Winstanley 'person from Winstanley', Lancashire ('Wynnstān's glade') [Gerrard Winstanley, ?1609–60, English communist, leader of the Diggers]

Winston (i) *also* **Winstone** 'person from Winston or Winstone', the name of numerous places in England (variously 'Wine's farmstead', 'Wynna's stone', etc); (ii) *also* **Winstone** from the Old English male personal name *Wynstān*, literally 'joy-stone'; (iii) an anglicization of **Weinstein** [Howard Winstone, 1939–2000, British boxer; Ray Winstone, 1957–, British actor; Robert Winston (Lord Winston), 1940–, British fertility surgeon]

Winter, Wynter, Wintour (i) from a medieval nickname for someone with a temperament suitable to winter (e.g. cold, gloomy); (ii) from Irish Gaelic *Mac Giolla-Gheimhridh* 'son of the servant of *Geimhreadh*', a nickname meaning literally 'winter'; (iii) an invented or imposed Jewish surname based on German *Winter* 'winter' [Anna Wintour, 1949–, British journalist; Dana Wynter (original name Dagmar Winter), 1931–, German-born British actress; Fred Winter, 1926–2004, British jockey; Mark Wynter (original name Terence Lewis), 1943–, British popular singer]

— **Winter's bark** a tree (*Drimys winteri*) that grows in the mountainous parts of western America from Mexico southwards and has a pungent aromatic bark once used to prevent scurvy. It was named after its discoverer Captain William Winter, who accompanied Francis Drake to the Magellan Straits in 1578.

Winterbottom, Winterbotham 'person who lives in a permanent dwelling in the valley in winter (but in summer lives in the upland pastures)' (from Middle English *winter* + *bottom* 'valley') [Sir Walter Winterbottom, 1913–2002, British football manager]

Winterbourne, Winterbourn, Winterborne 'person from Winterbourne or Winterborne', the name of various places in England ('place by the Winterbourne or Winterborne', a river-name denoting a stream that flowed in the winter but often dried up in the summer)

Winterburn 'person from Winterburn', Yorkshire ('place by the Winterburn' – see **Winterbourne**)

Winters, Wynters 'son of **Winter**' [Bernie Winters (original name Bernie Weinstein), 1932–91, and his brother Mike Winters (original name Michael Weinstein), 1930–, British comedy double-act (as 'Mike and Bernie Winters'); Shelley Winters (original name Shelley Schrift; her mother's maiden name was Winter), 1920–2006, US actress]

Winterson 'son of **Winter**' [Jeanette Winterson, 1959–, British author]

Winterton 'person from Winterton', Lincolnshire and Norfolk (respectively 'Wintra's people's farmstead' and 'winter farmstead')

Winthrop 'person from Winthorpe', Lincolnshire and Nottinghamshire (respectively 'Wina's outlying farmstead' and 'Wīgmund's or Vígmundr's outlying farmstead') [John Winthrop, 1588–1649, English colonizer in North America]

Winton 'person from Winton', the name of numerous places in England and Scotland (variously 'farmstead with pasture' and 'Wine's farmstead') [Dale Winton, 1955–, British television presenter]

Winyard, Wynyard 'person who lives by or works in a vineyard'. See also **Wingard, Winnard**

Wisden perhaps a different form of **Wisdom**
— *Wisden Cricketers' Almanack* an annual publication containing full first-class cricket match scores of the previous season, cricket records and various other material. It was first published in 1864, by the cricketer John Wisden, 1826–84.

Wisdom from a medieval nickname for a wise person [Sir Norman Wisdom, 1915–, British comic actor]

Wise, Wyse (i) from a medieval nickname for a wise person, or for someone believed to be skilled in magic or fortune-telling; (ii) a US anglicization of **Weiss** (ii) [Ernie Wise (original name Ernest Wiseman), 1925–99, British comedian, one half of the double act 'Morecambe and Wise'; Thomas James Wise, 1859–1937, British book collector and forger]

Wiseman (i) from a medieval nickname for a wise person; (ii) a US anglicization of **Weismann** (i) [Nicholas Patrick Stephen Wiseman, 1802–65, British Roman Catholic prelate, first archbishop of Westminster]

Wishart from the Norman personal name *Wischard*, probably formed from Old Norse *viskr* 'wise' + *hard* 'brave'. See also **Wesker** (ii)

[George Wishart, ?1513–46, Scottish Protestant reformer and martyr]

With, Withe see **Wythe**

Witham 'person from Witham', the name of various places in England (mostly 'homestead by a bend (e.g. in a river)')

Wither (i) 'person who lives by a willow tree' (from a derivative of Middle English *wythe* 'willow'); (ii) from the Old Norse male personal name *Vítharr*, literally 'wide messenger'

Witherow perhaps a different form of **Weatherall**

Withers 'son of **Wither** (ii)' [Googie Withers (original name Georgette Withers), 1917–, British actress]

Witherspoon perhaps 'person from Witherspoon', an unidentified place in Scotland ('strip of land where rams are kept'). See also **Weatherspoon, Wetherspoon** [Jimmy Witherspoon, 1920–97, US blues singer; Reese Witherspoon, 1976–, US actress]

Withnell, Withnall 'person from Withnell', Lancashire ('hill with a willow wood')
— *Withnail and I* a film (1987) about a pair of out-of-work actors who settle in a dilapidated country cottage

Withycombe, Withecombe different forms of **Widdicombe**

Witney 'person from Witney', Oxfordshire ('Witta's island')

Witty, Wittey from a medieval nickname for a quick-witted or intelligent person

Wodehouse see **Woodhouse**

Woffenden, Woffendon different forms of **Wolfenden**

Woffit a different form of **Wolfit**

Wogan from the Old Welsh personal name *Gwgan* or *Gwgon*, originally probably a nickname meaning literally 'little scowler' [Terry Wogan, 1938–, Irish radio and television presenter]

Wolcott a different form of **Woolcott**

Wolf, Wolfe (i) *also* **Woolf** *or* **Woolfe** from a shortened form of any of a range of Germanic compound personal names beginning with *wolf* 'wolf' (e.g. **Woolgar**); (ii) *also* **Woolf** *or* **Woolfe** from a medieval nickname for someone thought to have wolflike qualities; (iii) *also* **Wolff** from the Yiddish male personal name *Volf*, literally 'wolf', from German (it is regarded as a Yiddish equivalent to Hebrew *Binyamin*, from Jacob's dying words in Genesis 49:27, 'Benjamin shall ravin as a wolf'); (iv) a translation of Irish Gaelic *Ó Faoláin* (see **Whelan**) [Charles Wolfe, 1791–1823, Irish clergyman and poet; James Wolfe, 1727–59, British general; Leonard Woolf, 1880–1969, British author, publisher and social reformer, husband of Virginia; Thomas Wolfe, 1900–38, US novelist; Tom Wolfe, 1930–, US author and journalist; Virginia Woolf (*née* Stephen), 1882–1941, British author]
— **Wolfe's Own** a nickname given to the 47th Foot, later the Loyal Regiment (North Lancashire), in recognition of their distinguished service under

General James Wolfe (see above) at Quebec in 1759

Wolfenden, **Woolfenden** 'person from Wolfenden', Lancashire ('Wulfhelm's valley'). See also **Woffenden** [John Wolfenden (Lord Wolfenden), 1906–85, British educationalist and government official]
— **Wolfenden Report** a report (1957) recommending that private homosexual acts between consenting adults should be legalized in Britain. The committee that produced it was chaired by John Wolfenden (see above).

Wolfit, **Woolfit**, **Woolfitt** from the medieval male personal name *Wolfet* or *Wolfat* (from Old English *Wulfgēat*, literally 'wolf-Geat' (the name of a Germanic people)). See also **Ullett**, **Woffit**, **Woolett** [Sir Donald Wolfit, 1902–68, British actor and manager]

Wolford a different form of **Woolford**

Wolfram from the Germanic male personal name *Wolfram*, literally 'wolf-raven'

Wolfson 'son of **Wolf**' [Sir Isaac Wolfson, 1897–1991, British businessman and philanthropist]
— **Wolfson College** a graduate college of Cambridge University, previously named University College but renamed in 1973 after receiving a grant from the Wolfson Foundation; also, a graduate college of Oxford University founded in 1966 with grants from the Wolfson and Ford Foundations
— **Wolfson Foundation** a trust for the advancement of health, education and youth in the UK and the Commonwealth, endowed in 1955 by Sir Isaac Wolfson (see above)

Wollaston 'person from Wollaston', the name of several places in England (variously 'Wīglāf's farmstead' and 'Wulflāf's farmstead')

Wollstonecraft see **Wolstonecraft**

Wolpert (i) from the Germanic male personal name *Waldobert*, literally 'power-bright'; (ii) from a Jewish adoption of the German name *Wolpert* (regarded as being a different form of **Wolf** (iii))

Wolseley 'person from Wolseley', Staffordshire [Sir Garnet Wolseley (1st Viscount Wolseley), 1833–1913, British field marshal]
— **Wolseley Cars** a British car manufacturer that had its origins in the Wolseley Sheep-Shearing Machine Co. Ltd., formed in Sydney, Australia in 1887 by Frederick Wolseley, 1837–99. The business moved to Britain in 1889, and produced its first car in 1895. The marque disappeared in 1975.

Wolsey, **Woolsey** from the medieval male personal name *Wulsi* (from Old English *Wulfsige*, literally 'wolf-victory') [Thomas Wolsey (Cardinal Wolsey), ?1475–1530, English churchman and statesman]

Wolstenholme, **Wolstonholme** 'person from Wolstenholme', Lancashire ('Wulfstān's island'). See also **Woosnam** [Kenneth Wolstenholme, 1920–2002, British television football commentator]

Wolston a different form of **Woolston**

Wolstonecraft, **Wollstonecraft**, **Wolstoncraft**, **Wolstencroft**, **Woolstencroft** 'person from Woolstencroft', Cheshire ('Wulfstān's smallholding') [Mary Wollstonecraft, 1759–97, British feminist]

Wolverton 'person from Wolverton, Woolverton or Wolferton', the name of various places in England ('farmstead associated with Wulfhere')

Womack perhaps an alteration of the Dutch surname *Walmack*, from a medieval nickname for a thin person (from Middle Dutch *walmacke* 'twig')

Womble, **Wombell** different forms of **Wombwell**

Wombwell 'person from Wombwell', Yorkshire ('Wamba's stream')

Womersley 'person from Womersley', Yorkshire (probably 'Wilmǣr's glade')

Wong (i) a different form of **Wang**; (ii) a different form of **Huang** [Anna May Wong (original name Wong Liu Tsong), 1905–61, Chinese-American actress]
— **The World of Suzie Wong** a novel (1957) by Richard Mason about an English artist visiting Hong Kong who falls in love with a mysterious Chinese prostitute called Suzie Wong. A film version appeared in 1960.

Wonnacott 'person from Wonnacott', Devon ('Wunna's cottage')

Woo see **Wu**

Wood, **Woode** (i) 'person who lives in or near a wood'; also, 'person who works in a wood; forester or woodcutter'; (ii) from a medieval nickname for an eccentric person or one with a violent temperament (from Middle English *wōd* 'mad') [Charles Wood, 1932–, British playwright; Elijah Wood, 1981–, US actor; Hugh Wood, 1932–, British composer; John Wood the Elder, 1704–54, British architect; John Wood the Younger, 1728–81, British architect, son of John the Elder; Sir Henry Wood, 1869–1944, British conductor; Mrs Henry Wood (Ellen Wood, *née* Price), 1814–87, British novelist; Sir Kingsley Wood, 1881–1943, British Conservative politician; Victoria Wood, 1953–, British comedian and writer]
● Men with the surname Wood are traditionally given the nickname 'Timber' (a notable example was Sir Henry Wood – see above)
— **Jimmy Woodser** in Australian slang, a solitary drinker. The term is first recorded in the 1890s, and its inspiration has been variously identified as James Wood, an 18th-century scion of a British banking family and noted miser, and James Woods, a New South Wales sheep-shearer of the 1880s.
— **Kenwood** a British brand of electric food mixer, launched in 1948 by Kenneth Wood, 1916–97
— **Wood's light** ultraviolet light obtained by using a filter of glass containing nickel oxide to remove visible components. It is named after the US physicist Robert W. Wood, 1868–1955.

Woodall 'person from Woodhall', the name of various places in England ('hall in the wood (perhaps a meeting place for a forest court)') [Trinny Woodall (original name Sarah-Jane

Woodall), 1964–, British fashion adviser and television presenter]

Woodard (i) 'person who pastures pigs in a wood' (from Old English *wudu* 'wood' + *hierda* 'herdsman'); (ii) from the medieval male personal name *Wodard* (from Old English *Wuduheard*, literally 'wood-strong'); (iii) a different form of **Woodward**

Woodbridge 'person from Woodbridge', Suffolk ('wooden bridge' or 'bridge by or in a wood') [Todd Woodbridge, 1971–, Australian tennis player, member (with Mark Woodforde) of the doubles partnership nicknamed 'the Woodies']

Woodburn 'person from Woodburn', the name of various places in Scotland and northern England ('stream flowing through a wood')

Woodbury 'person from Woodbury', the name of various places in England ('fortified place by the wood'), or 'person from Woodborough', Nottinghamshire and Wiltshire (respectively 'fortified place by the wood' and 'wooded hill')

Woodcock (i) 'person from Woodcott, Woodcote, etc'., the name, variously spelled, of several places in England ('cottage in a wood'); (ii) from a medieval nickname for a foolish or gullible person (the woodcock was regarded as an easy bird to catch) [George Woodcock, 1904–79, British trade-union leader]

Wooderson 'son of the woodman' (from Middle English *wooder* 'woodman' + *son*)

Woodfield 'person from Woodfield', Warwickshire (an alteration of earlier *Woodhull*, literally 'wooded hill')

Woodford, Woodforde 'person from Woodford', the name of various places in England and Scotland ('ford by a wood') [James Woodforde, 1740–1803, British clergyman and diarist; Mark Woodforde, 1965–, Australian tennis player, member (with Todd Woodbridge) of the doubles partnership nicknamed 'the Woodies']

Woodfull from the Old English personal name or nickname *Wudufugol*, literally 'wood-bird' [Bill Woodfull, 1897–1965, Australian cricketer]

Woodgate 'person who lives by a gate leading into a wood'

Woodham 'person from Woodham', the name of various places in England (mostly 'homestead by a wood')

Woodhead 'person from Woodhead', the name of various places in England and Scotland ('top end of the wood')

Woodhouse, Wodehouse 'person from Woodhouse', the name of various places in England and Scotland ('house by a wood') [Barbara Woodhouse, 1910–88, British dog trainer; Emma Woodhouse, heroine of Jane Austen's novel *Emma* (1816); P.G. Wodehouse (Sir Pelham Wodehouse), 1881–1975, British comic writer]

Woodley, Woodleigh, Woodlee 'person from Woodley or Woodleigh', the name of various places in England ('woodland glade')

Woodman 'person who lives in or near a wood'; also, 'person who works in a wood; forester or woodcutter'

Woodroof, Woodroofe, Woodrooffe different forms of **Woodruff**

Woodrow 'person who lives in a row of cottages by a wood', or 'person from Woodrow', the name of various places in England (in either case from Old English *wudu* 'wood' + *rāw* 'row')

Woodruff, Woodruffe, Woodrough (i) 'person who lives by a piece of land where the plant woodruff grows'; (ii) perhaps from a medieval nickname for someone who used the aromatic woodruff plant to mask B.O. or (sarcastically) for someone who did not [Maurice Woodruff, 1920–85, British astrologist and medium]

Woods (i) 'person who lives in or near a wood'; (ii) a translation of Irish Gaelic *Ó Cuill* (see **Quill**) or of Scottish Gaelic *Mac Cuill* (see **McColl**) [Tiger Woods (original name Eldrick Woods), 1975–, US golfer]

• Men with the surname Woods are traditionally given the nickname 'Timber'

Woodside 'person from Woodside', the name of various places in Scotland ('wooded hillside')

Woodson 'person from Woodsome', Yorkshire ('houses in the wood')

Woodthorpe 'person from Woodthorpe', the name of various places in England ('outlying farmstead in woodland')

Woodvine 'person who lives by a wood-stack' (from Old English *wudu* 'wood' + *fīn* 'pile') [John Woodvine, 1929–, British actor]

Woodward (i) 'person who looks after the trees and game in a forest; forester' (from Old English *wudu* 'wood' + *weard* 'guard'); (ii) perhaps from the Old English male personal name *Wuduweard* (from as (i)) [Sir Clive Woodward, 1956–, British rugby coach; Edward Woodward, 1930–, British actor; Robert Burns Woodward, 1917–79, US chemist]

Woolard see **Woollard**

Woolcott, Woolcot, Woollcott 'person from Woolcot', Somerset ('cottage by a stream'). See also **Wolcott** [Alexander Woollcott, 1887–1943, US writer and critic]

Wooldridge from the medieval personal name *Wolrich* (from Old English *Wulfrīc*, literally 'wolf-power'). See also **Woolrich, Woolridge** [Ian Wooldridge, 1932–2007, British sports journalist]

Woolett a different form of **Wolfit**

Wooley see **Woolley**

Woolf, Woolfe see **Wolf** (i–ii)

Woolford, Woolforde (i) 'person from Great or Little Wolford', Warwickshire ('place protected against wolves'); (ii) from the medieval male personal name *Wolward* (from Old English *Wulfweard*, literally 'wolf-guard'). See also **Wolford, Woollard**

Woolgar from the medieval male personal name *Wolgar* (from Old English *Wulfgār*, literally 'wolf-spear')

Woollard, Woolard different forms of **Woolford**

Wooller (i) 'wool-worker'; (ii) 'person who lives by a stream or spring' (from a derivative of southwestern Middle English *wall* or *wull* 'stream, spring, well')

Woolley, Wooley 'person from Woolley', the name of various places in England (mostly 'glade where wolves are seen') [Frank Woolley, 1887–1978, English cricketer; Jack Woolley, bluff Midlands businessman (played by Arnold Peters) who has been a fixture since 1962 on the BBC radio soap opera *The Archers*; Sir Leonard Woolley, 1880–1960, British archaeologist; Monty Woolley (original name Edgar Montillion Woolley), 1888–1963, US actor]

Woolner a different form of **Woolnough** [Thomas Woolner, 1825–92, British sculptor and poet]

Woolnough from the medieval male personal name *Wolnoth* or *Wolnaugh* (from Old English *Wulfnōth*, literally 'wolf-daring')

Woolrich a different form of **Wooldridge**

Woolridge a different form of **Wooldridge**

Woolsey see **Wolsey**

Woolstencroft see **Wolstonecraft**

Woolston, Woolstone (i) 'person from Woolston, Woolstone or Wollston', the name of various places in England ('farmstead belonging to Wulf (or to someone with a name beginning with *Wulf-*, e.g. Wulfhere, Wulfsige)'); (ii) from the medieval male personal name *Wolstan* (from Old English *Wulfstān*, literally 'wolf-stone'). See also **Wolston**

Woolworth perhaps 'person from Walworth', County Durham and Greater London ('enclosure of the Britons')
— **Woolworth Building** a skyscraper in New York commissioned by F.W. Woolworth (see below), which from its completion in 1913 until 1926 (when it was overtaken by the Chrysler Building) was the world's tallest building
— **Woolworths** any of a chain of shops, originally specializing in low-priced goods, founded in 1879 by the US businessman Frank Winfield Woolworth, 1852–1919

Woosnam a different form of **Wolstenholme** [Ian Woosnam, 1958–, British golfer; Phil Woosnam, 1932–, Welsh footballer]

Wooster see **Worcester**

Wootton, Wooton, Wootten, Wooten 'person from Wootton', the name of numerous places in England ('farmstead by a wood'). See also **Wotton** [Barbara Wootton (Baroness Wootton; *née* Adam), 1897–1988, British educationalist and economist]

Worboys see **Warboys**

Worcester, Wooster 'person from Worcester', Worcestershire ('Roman town of the Weogora (a Celtic tribal name)') [Bertie Wooster, amiable upper-crust chump in innumerable comic stories (from 1917) by P.G. Wodehouse; Sir Robert Worcester, 1933–, US-born British opinion pollster]

Worden 'person from Worden', Lancashire (probably 'valley with a weir')

Wordsworth a different form of **Wadsworth** [Barry Wordsworth, 1948–, British conductor; Dorothy Wordsworth, 1771–1855, British writer, sister of William; William Wordsworth, 1770–1850, British poet]
— **Wordsworthian** of William Wordsworth (see above) or typical of his style or subject matter, especially in the austerity of his poetic language and his treatment of nature

Workman 'labourer'

Worley (i) perhaps 'person from Warley', Essex and Somerset ('glade with a weir') or 'person from Warley', West Midlands ('cattle pasturage in a glade'); (ii) perhaps a different form of **Wortley**

Wormal a different form of **Wormald**

Wormald 'person from Wormald', Yorkshire ('Wulfrūn's stream or spring'), or 'person from Wormhill', Derbyshire ('serpent hill')

Worrall, Worral, Warrell, Worril 'person from Worrall', Yorkshire ('corner of land where bog myrtle grows') [Anthony Worrall Thompson, 1951–, British chef and restaurateur; Sir Frank Worrell, 1924–67, West Indian cricketer]

Worsley 'person from Worsley', Lancashire and Worcestershire (respectively perhaps 'Weorcgȳth's or Weorchǣth's glade' and 'cattle pasturage in a glade') [Joe Worsley, 1977–, English rugby footballer]

Worsthorne 'person from Worsthorne', Lancashire ('Weorth's thorn bush') [Sir Peregrine Worsthorne (father's original surname Koch de Gooreynd), 1923–, British journalist]

Worth 'person from Worth', the name of various places in England ('enclosure') [Charles Worth, 1826–95, British fashion designer; Harry Worth (original name Harry Illingworth), 1917–89, British comedian and comic actor]
— **Fort Worth** a city in northeastern Texas, founded in 1849 and named in honour of William J. Worth, 1794–1849, a US general who commanded troops in Texas

Worthing 'person from Worthing', Norfolk and Sussex ('Weorth's people's settlement') [Jack Worthing, young man-about-town in Oscar Wilde's *The Importance of Being Earnest* (1895) whose real first name turns out to be Ernest]

Worthington 'person from Worthington', Lancashire and Leicestershire (probably 'estate associated with Weorth') [Frank Worthington, 1948–, English footballer; Stan Worthington, 1905–73, English cricketer]
— **'Don't put your daughter on the stage, Mrs Worthington'** a song (1947) by Noël Coward, vividly delineating the hazards of the theatrical profession
— **Worthington's** a brewery founded in Burton upon Trent in 1744 by William Worthington, 1722–1800

Worthy (i) from a medieval nickname for a upright well-respected citizen; (ii) 'person from Worthy', the name of various places in England ('enclosure')

Wortley 'person from Wortley', the name of two places in Yorkshire (respectively 'glade where vegetables grow' and perhaps 'Wyrca's glade')

Wortman (i) 'grower or seller of vegetables or herbs' (from Middle English *wort* 'plant, vegetable' + *man*); (ii) from a medieval Jewish nickname for a trustworthy or truthful person (from Yiddish *vort* 'word' + *man*)

Worton 'person from Worton', the name of various places in England (mostly 'vegetable garden')

Wotton a different form of **Wootton** [Sir Henry Wotton, 1568–1639, English poet]

Wragg, Wragge from the Old Norse personal name *Wraghi* [Harry Wragg, 1902–85, British jockey]

Wray, Wrey 'person from Wray', the name, variously spelled, of several places in northern England ('corner of land, nook') [Fay Wray, 1907–2004, Canadian-born US actress]

Wren, Wrenn (i) from a medieval nickname for someone thought to resemble a wren, especially in small size; (ii) from Irish Gaelic *Ó Rinn* 'descendant of *Rinn*', a personal name perhaps based on *reann* 'spear'. See also **Wrinn** [Sir Christopher Wren, 1632–1723, English architect and scientist; P.C. Wren, 1885–1941, British novelist]

Wrey see **Wray**

Wrigglesworth a different form of the earlier *Wrigglesford* 'person from Woodlesford', Yorkshire (originally *Wridelsford*, perhaps 'ford among bushes')

Wright 'maker of machinery, tools, etc'. (from Old English *wryhta* 'craftsman') [Billy Wright, 1924–94, English footballer; Frank Lloyd Wright, 1867–1959, US architect; Ian Wright, 1963–, English footballer; Joseph Wright of Derby, 1734–97, British painter; Joseph Wright, 1855–1930, British philologist; Judith Wright, 1915–2002, Australian poet; Peter Wright, 1916–95, British intelligence officer; Richard Wright, 1908–60, US novelist and critic]

● Men with the surname Wright are traditionally given the nickname 'Lefty' (punning on *right*)

— **Wright Brothers** Orville Wright, 1871–1958, and his brother Wilbur Wright, 1867–1912, US aviators who made the first flight in a powered and controlled aeroplane on 17 December 1903

Wrightson 'son of **Wright**'

Wrigley 'person from Wrigley Head', Lancashire
— **Wm. Wrigley Jr. Company** a US manufacturer of chewing gum, founded in Chicago in 1891 by William Wrigley, Jr., 1861–1932.
— **Wrigley Building** a skyscraper built in Chicago in the 1920s as the headquarters of the Wrigley Company

Wrinn a different form of **Wren** (ii)

Wu, Woo 'person from Wu', an ancient Chinese province

Wyatt from the medieval male personal name *Wyot* (from Old English *Wīgheard*, literally 'war-brave') [James Wyatt, 1746–1813, British architect; Sir Thomas Wyatt, 1503–42, English poet]

Wycliffe, Wyclif 'person from Wycliffe', County Durham ('white cliff') [John Wycliffe (or Wyclif), ?1330–84, English philosopher and religious reformer]
— **Wycliffe** an ITV police drama series (1993–98), starring Jack Shepherd as Det. Supt. Charles Wycliffe of the Devon and Cornwall Constabulary.
— **Wycliffite** a follower of John Wycliffe (see above)

Wyld, Wylde see **Wild**

Wyler (i) a different form of **Wheeler**; (ii) an anglicization of the German-Jewish surname *Weiler* or *Weiller*, literally 'person from Weiler', the name of various places in southern Germany [William Wyler (original name Wilhelm Weiller), 1902–81, German-born US film director]

Wylie (i) *also* **Wiley** 'person from Wylye', Wiltshire ('place on the (river) Wylye', a pre-English river-name perhaps meaning literally 'tricky stream'); (ii) from a Scottish pet-form of **William**

Wyllie a different form of **Wylie** (ii)

Wyman, Wymann from the medieval male personal name *Wymund* (from Old English *Wīgmund*, literally 'war-protection') [Bill Wyman (original name William Perks), 1936–, British pop musician, bassist of 'The Rolling Stones'; Jane Wyman (original name Sarah Jane Mayfield), 1914–, US actress]

Wymark a different form of **Wymer** (ii) [Patrick Wymark (original name Patrick Cheeseman), 1926–70, British actor]

Wymer (i) from the medieval male personal name *Wymer* (from Old English *Wīgmǣr*, literally 'war-famous'); (ii) from the Old Breton male personal name *Wiumarch*, literally 'worthy-horse'

Wyndham, Windham (i) 'person from Wyndham', Sussex ('Winda's water meadow'), or 'person from Wymondham', Leicestershire and Norfolk ('Wīgmund's homestead'); (ii) from Irish Gaelic *Ó Gaoithín* 'descendant of *Gaoithín*', a personal name meaning literally 'little wind' [John Wyndham, pen-name of John Wyndham Parkes Lucas Beynon Harris, 1903–69, British science-fiction writer]
— **Wyndham's Theatre** a theatre in Charing Cross Road, London, founded in 1899 by Charles Wyndham, 1837–1919, manager of the Criterion Theatre

Wyngarde see **Wingard**

Wynn, Wynne, Winn from the Old English personal name *Wine*, literally 'friend', or from the first element of any of various compound names beginning with *Wine* [Godfrey Winn, 1906–71, British journalist and novelist; Greville Wynn, 1919–90, British businessman and part-time spy]

Wynter, Wynters see **Winter, Winters**

Wynyard see **Winyard**

Wyse see **Wise**

Wythe, Wyth, Withe, With 'person who lives by a willow tree' (from Middle English *wythe* 'willow') [Peter Withe, 1951–, English footballer]

XYZ

X used as a substitute surname for someone whose true name is unknown or who wishes to remain incognito or mysterious [Malcom X (original name Malcolm Little), 1925–65, US political activist]

Yale 'person from Iâl', northeastern Wales (from Welsh *iâl* 'fertile or arable upland')
— **Yale** the proprietary name of a range of locks, especially a type of cylinder lock using a flat serrated key, invented around 1848 by the US locksmith Linus Yale, Jr., 1821-68.
— **Yale University** a university in New Haven, Connecticut, US, founded in 1701. It is named after Elihu Yale, 1648–1721, who donated his books to the college.

Yallop perhaps from the Old Norse personal name *Hjálpr*, literally 'help', or alternatively 'person who lives in a yellow valley' (from Middle English *yelow* 'yellow' + *hop* 'enclosed valley')

Yamamoto a Japanese surname meaning literally 'person who lives among or at the foot of the mountains'

Yang (i) from a Korean clan name; (ii) 'person from Yang', an ancient Chinese state. See also **Yeung**

Yapp, Yap from a medieval nickname for a sly or devious person (from Middle English *yap* 'bent, devious')

Yarbrough, Yarborough 'person from Yarborough or Yarburgh', places in Lincolnshire ('place by the earthwork')

Yardley 'person from Yardley', the name of various places in England ('wood or glade where rods are obtained'). See also **Yeardley**

Yarham 'person from Yarham', an unidentified place in England (perhaps 'homestead or water meadow by the Yare', a river in Norfolk)

Yarnell, Yarnall different forms of **Arnold** (i)

Yarnold a different form of **Arnold** (i)

Yarrow (i) 'person who lives in a place where yarrow grows abundantly'; (ii) 'person who lives by the Yarrow', either of two rivers in Lancashire and the Scottish Borders ('rough one')

Yarwood (i) 'person from Yarwood', Cheshire ('wood frequented by eagles'); (ii) from the Welsh personal name *Iorwerth*, literally 'handsome lord' [Mike Yarwood, 1941–, British impressionist]

Yates, Yeats, Yeates 'person who lives by the town gates' (from Middle English *yates* 'gates'); also, 'gatekeeper'. See also **Yeatman** [Dornford Yates, pen-name of Cecil William Mercer, 1885–1960, British thriller writer; Jack Butler Yeats, 1871–1957, Irish painter, brother of William; Paula Yates, 1960–2000, British model

and television presenter; William Butler Yeats, 1865–1939, Irish poet and dramatist]
— **Yeatsian** (characteristic) of W.B. Yeats or his writing

Yaxley 'person from Yaxley', Cambridgeshire and Suffolk ('glade where cuckoos are heard')

Yeadon 'person from Yeadon', Yorkshire ('steep hill')

Yeager an anglicization of **Jaeger** [Chuck Yeager (original name Charles Elwood Yeager), 1923–, US aviator]

Yeaman a different form of **Yeoman** (ii)

Yeardley a different form of **Yardley**

Yeatman a different form of **Yates** [R.J. Yeatman, 1897–1968, Scottish humorist, co-author (with W.C. Sellar) of *1066 And All That* (1930)]

Yeats, Yeates see **Yates**

Yelland 'person from Yelland', the name of various places in England ('old land') [David Yelland, 1963–, British journalist]

Yeo, Yeoh 'person who lives by a stream' (from southwestern Middle English *yo* 'stream, river') [Tim Yeo, 1945–, British Conservative politician]

Yeoman (i) 'servant of middle rank in a medieval noble household' or, later in the Middle Ages, 'small landholder'. See also **Youngman**; (ii) a different form of **Yeo**. See also **Yeaman**

Yeomans 'son of **Yeoman** (i)'. See also **Youmans**

Yerkes an anglicization of the Dutch and German surname *Jerkes*, literally 'son of *Jerke*' (a variant of *Georg* '**George**')

Yeung a different form of **Yang** (ii)

Yonge, Yong see **Young**

York, Yorke 'person from York', Yorkshire [Michael York (original name Michael Johnson), 1942–, British actor; Susannah York (original name Susannah Fletcher), 1942–, British actress]
— **Yorke Peninsula** a peninsula in southeastern South Australia, between the Gulf of St Vincent and the Spencer Gulf. It was named, in 1802, in honour of the British politician Charles Philip Yorke, 1764–1834, at that time Secretary at War.

Yoshida 'person from Yoshida', the name of numerous places in Japan ('lucky rice paddy')

Youens 'son of **Ewan**'

Youle, Youell see **Yule**

Youmans a different form of **Yeomans**

Young, Younge, Yonge, Yong (i) from a distinguishing name used to denote the younger of two people with the same personal name, especially a son from a father; (ii) an anglicization of any of a range of semantically parallel surnames in other languages (e.g. French *Lejeune*, German *Jung* and Dutch *de Jong*); (iii) a different form of **Yang** (ii) [Arthur Young, 1741–1820, British agricultural and travel writer; Brigham Young, 1801–77, US Mormon leader; Charlotte M. Yonge, 1823–1901, British novelist; Cy Young (original name Denton True Young), 1867–1955, US baseball player; Francis Brett Young, 1884–1954, British novelist; Gig Young (original name Byron Elsworth Barr), 1913–78, US actor; Sir Jimmy Young (original name Leslie Ronald Young), 1921–, British popular singer and radio presenter; Kirsty Young, 1968–, British television presenter and newsreader; Lester Young, 1909–59, US jazz saxophonist; Muriel Young, 1928–2001, British television presenter; Nat Young, 1947–, Australian surfer; Robert Young, 1907–98, US actor; Thomas Young, 1773–1829, British physician, physicist and Egyptologist]

— **Young & Co.** a brewing company founded in Wandsworth, South London in 1831 by Charles Young and Anthony Bainbridge. Its Wandsworth brewery closed in 2006.

— **Young's modulus** in the science of elasticity of materials, the ratio of stress to strain. It is named after Thomas Young (see above).

— **Youngstown** a city in Ohio, USA, founded in 1796 by John Young

Younger (i) from a distinguishing name used to denote the younger of two people with the same personal name, especially a son from a father; (ii) an anglicization of Middle Dutch *jongheer* 'young nobleman'

Youngman a different form of **Yeoman** (i)

Younis from the Arabic male personal name *Yūnus*, the name of a prophet (the Biblical *Jonah*)

Youssef, Yousef, Yousuf, Yusuf from the Arabic male personal name *Yūsuf*, the name of a prophet (the Biblical **Joseph**)

Yule, Yuill, Yuille, Yuile, Yuell, Youle, Youell from a medieval nickname for someone who was born at (or had some other significant connection with) Christmas

Zachary from the male personal name *Zachary* (via the Biblical name *Zacharias* from Hebrew *Zecharya*, literally 'remember god')

Zander (i) 'person who lives on sandy soil' (from a derivative of German *Sand* 'sand'); (ii) 'tooth-puller' (a role of barber-surgeons in the Middle Ages) (from a derivative of Middle High German *zant* 'tooth'); (iii) an invented Jewish name based on German *Sander* or *Zander* 'pike-perch'

Zangwill an invented Jewish name based on Hebrew *zangvil* 'ginger'

Zappa 'agricultural labourer' (from Italian *zappa* 'mattock') [Frank Zappa, 1940–93, US musician-composer]

Zealey, Zealley different forms of **Sealey**

Zeldin 'son of *Zelde*', a Yiddish female personal name based on Middle High German *sælde* 'fortunate, blessed'

Zelig a different form of **Selig** (ii)

— **Zelig** a film (1983) by Woody Allen about a protean nebbich, Leonard Zelig (played by Allen), who unaccountably pops up at various key points of 20th-century history

Zeller 'person who lives by a hermit's cell or by a wayside shrine', or 'person from Zelle or Celle', the name of various places in Germany, in either case from a derivative of Middle High German *zelle* (from Latin *cella* 'small room')

Zhang (i) 'stretch open a bow', by tradition a surname given to Hui, grandson of the legendary Chinese emperor Huang Di (2697–2595 BC), who is said to have invented bows and arrows; (ii) 'person from Zhang', an area in the present-day province of Shandong

Zhou 'person of the Zhou clan', which ultimately got its name from the city of Zhouyuan in the present-day Shaanxi province of China

Ziegler 'person who lays tiles (on a roof)' (from a derivative of Middle High German *ziegel* 'roof tile') [Philip Ziegler, 1929–, British author]

Zielinski from a medieval Polish nickname for someone whose face had a sickly greenish palor, or who usually wore green clothes, or who was immature or inexperienced (from a derivative of Polish *zielony* 'green')

Zimbalist 'player of the cymbals' (from a derivative of Middle High German *zymbele* 'cymbal') [Efrem Zimbalist, Jr., 1918–, US actor; Stephanie Zimbalist, 1956–, US actress, daughter of Efrem]

Zimmermann, Zimmerman 'carpenter' (from Middle High German *zimbermann*, literally 'timber-man') [Robert Zimmerman, original name of Bob **Dylan**]

Zink, Zinke (i) 'person who lives on a headland or in craggy country' (from Middle High German *zinke* 'point, tip, peak'); (ii) from a medieval German nickname for someone with a long pointed nose (likewise from Middle High German *zinke*)

Zinman 'person who makes things out of pewter' (from Yiddish *tsin* 'pewter' + *man*)

Zinn 'person who makes things out of pewter' (from Middle High German *zin* 'pewter')

Zito from the medieval Italian male personal name *Zito*, from a southern Italian nickname for a young bachelor

Zoller 'customs officer' (from Middle High German *zoller*)

Zorn from a medieval German and Jewish nickname for a bad-tempered person (from Middle High German *zorn* 'anger')

Zuber (i) 'person from Zuber', Switzerland ('mountain stream'); (ii) 'maker of barrels', or 'person who lives in a house with the sign of a barrel' (from Middle High German *zuber* 'small barrel (typically with two handles)')

Zucker (i) 'sugar-dealer' or 'confectioner', or from a medieval German nickname for someone with a sweet tooth (in either case from Middle High German *zucker* 'sugar'); (ii) an invented Jewish name based on German *Zucker* 'sugar'; (iii) from a medieval German nickname for someone thought to be a thief (from Middle High German *zücker* 'thief')

Zuckerman, **Zukerman** different forms of **Zucker** (i; iii) [Pinchas Zukerman, 1948–, Israeli-born US violinist; Solly Zuckerman (Lord Zuckerman), 1904–93, South African-born British zoologist and government adviser]